FML

NFL

Withdraw.

Bloomsbury Anthology of Quotations

Anthology of QUOTATIONS

OVER 12,000 QUOTATIONS

ARRANGED BY THEME

BLOOMSBURY

A BLOOMSBURY REFERENCE BOOK
Created from the Bloomsbury Database of Quotations

Bloomsbury Publishing Plc 2002

First published in 2002 by
Bloomsbury Publishing Plc
38 Soho Square
London W1D 3HB

www.bloomsburymagazine.com

A CIP record for this book is available from the British Library.

ISBN 0 7475 5454 4

10 9 8 7 6 5 4 3 2 1

Typeset by Hewer Text Ltd, Edinburgh
Printed and bound in Great Britain by Clays Ltd, St Ives plc

Contents

Bloomsbury Anthology of Quotations is drawn from
the Bloomsbury Database of Quotations, originally edited by
Bill Swainson with Sarah Waldram as Managing Editor.

Editor
James Randall

Database Manager
Edmund Wright

Project Manager
Katy McAdam

Production Editor
Nicky Thompson

EDITORIAL CONSULTANTS

Vastiana Belfon
Researcher in African,
Afro-Caribbean, and
Afro-American culture

Douglas Houston
Poet and author

Neil Powell
Author and critic

David Bellos
Princeton University

Michael Hulse
Translator and poet

Ramesh Rajballie
Historian

John Caley
Han Shang Tang Books,
London

John Wyse Jackson
Editor, author, and
bookseller

Dr Joseph Rhymer
Writer and theologian

Katherine Darton
MIND, London

Dr Catriona Kelly
New College, Oxford

Dr R. M. Youngson
Consultant
ophthalmologist and
medical writer

John Durant
Science Museum,
London

Alberto Manguel
Author

Susan North
Victoria and Albert
Museum, London

Zhou Xun
School of Oriental and
African Studies, London

EDITORIAL CONTRIBUTORS

Paul Binding
Edward Butcher
Robert Clarke
Julia Cresswell

Steve Eddy
Laura Lawrie
Tina Persaud

Jeffrey Petts
Peter Porter
Eva Salzman

Jo Shapcott
Snezana Vujovic
Heather Wardle

Contributing Editors

Stephen Adamson
Mark Crean
Sheila Dallas
Claire Ellerton
Dominique Enright
Kathy Fahey

Hannah Griffiths
Stan Kurzban
Andrew McAllister
Molly McGrann
David Milsted
Vanessa Mitchell

Lisa Nave
Jenny Parrott
Sandra Scott
Pauline Sidey
Eleanor Stanley
Susan Turner

Richard Tyrrel
Pamela White
Kamala Wickramasinghe
Sarah Yates
Emily Young

Proofreaders

David Barnett

Ruth Hillmore

Irene Lakhani

BLOOMSBURY REFERENCE

Publisher
Nigel Newton

Publishing Director
Dr Kathy Rooney

Production Director
Penny Edwards

Introduction

When a thing has been said and said well, have no scruple. Take it and copy it.
Anatole France

An anthology of quotations is a collection of fragments of the past, of things said or written by a diversity of people. Sometimes the quotations are an individual's only surviving words, and sometimes they are hidden in obscure texts or buried in a distant archive, living in the hinterland of the popular imagination. The *Blooms-bury Anthology of Quotations* aims to retrieve the best sayings from the past, as well as record those of the recent present, yielding sublimely cast words that stand out from the linguistic morass of contemporary culture.

The Italian writer Italo Calvino wrote, 'We are bombarded today by such a quantity of images that we can no longer distinguish direct experience from what we have seen for a few seconds on television. The memory is littered with bits and pieces of images, like a rubbish dump.' This book attempts to sift out the empty words, false signs, and mixed messages of our shared culture to find the phrases that are original and vital and speak eloquently about our world.

With this in mind, we have selected over 12,000 quotations of a pioneering international scope and historical depth, ranging from classical Greece to the twenty-first century, and from cultures as far apart as ancient China, Renaissance Europe, and contemporary South Africa. The quotations are divided into over 700 themes, representing the best and most striking things said on every topic from Human Rights to Freedom, from the Middle East to Women, and from Philosophy to the Weather.

The quotations anthology, while following an old tradition, is a twentieth-century invention. H. L. Mencken was the first to collect sayings structured by themes rather than authors in his 1942 *Dictionary of Quotations on Historical Principles from Ancient and Modern Sources.* The *Bloomsbury Anthology of Quotations* has firm roots in the traditions of the past, absorbing ancient proverbs and well-known sayings, but it goes further, embracing all aspects of popular and literary culture from pop music and the Internet to political soundbites and modern literary aphorisms.

There are many ways to look at everything, and the quotations here represent a great variety of opinions and styles from around the world. Each quotation may not be equally true, but each one has its place, reflecting the wealth of ways in which people have used language to describe new things and to express ideas, feelings, moral dilemmas, theoretical questions, and desires.

'A word is not the same with one writer as with another,' the French writer and poet Charles Péguy wrote. 'One tears it from his guts. The other pulls it out of his overcoat pocket.' Quoting over 3,400 authors, this book demonstrates how people through the ages have spoken and written memorable things in their individual styles on subjects that are part of all of our lives. From William Shakespeare and Julian Barnes on Love to Samuel Johnson and Lennon & McCartney on Friendship, you will find all kinds of quotations that are both informative and inspirational.

There is a great range of attitudes to the past, the present, and the future represented in this book. The British priest and writer Ronald Knox comments that 'It is so stupid of modern civilization to have given up believing in the devil when he is the only explanation of it', while the Canadian-born US writer Saul Bellow writes 'The past is no good to us. The future is full of anxiety. Only the present is real—the here-and-now. Seize the day.' But the connections between quotations from different people, places, and cultures are stronger than their differences. All involve an author capturing something about a subject, exemplifying an event or an emotion, or offering a summary of a point of view.

Ambitious in scope, the book delves deeply into key subjects such as Art, Society, Travel, Politics, Psychology, Nature, Science, and History, and has a particularly strong focus on areas such as Language and Literature (related themes range from Reading, Storytelling, and World Literature to Literary Insults, Poetry, and Wordplay). Included also are the more general themes of Inspiration, Talent, Creativity, Originality, and Ideas. There are many novel themes you may choose to look up, from European Cities and Computers to Artistic Styles and Globalization.

The *Bloomsbury Anthology of Quotations* presents a dynamic linguistic culture in progress, neither moribund nor lost for words but in hot pursuit of truth through language, engaging with both the traditional and the modern. Ours is a time of great changes in the way we experience language and ideas, changes driven by technological and global forces. So while we continue to celebrate the words of writers such as Confucius, William Shakespeare, and John Milton, we must also salute the words of modern authors from Derek Walcott to James Joyce, Ted Hughes to Nelson Mandela, Seamus Heaney to Michael Ondaatje, and Maya Angelou to James Kelman.

The book bridges all kinds of traditions, ways of thinking, areas of knowledge, and literary styles. We may not know what Aristotle would have had to say about genetics or how Thomas Paine would have pronounced on the Internet, but there is reasonable evidence in their existing ideas to suggest that both authors would have insights into these and many other aspects of the modern condition. In this anthology we have tried to capture something of the global spirit of modern culture, including quotations that reflect humankind's engagement with the world. We hope that you, the reader, enjoy exploring this world through these quotations, whether you are idly browsing or looking for specific inspiration.

A note on navigation

This anthology is a kaleidoscope of impressions, statements, thoughts, feelings, and expressions. To help with navigation through these quotations, we have included two indexes: a **keyword index** and an **author index**. These are both simple to use, are arranged alphabetically, and have references to the number of the quotation and the name of the theme under which the respective quotation will be found. The keyword index helps you to track down a half-remembered quotation or a quotation that uses a specific word, while the author index allows you to find all the quotations by a particular author under different themes. In addition to the indexes, there are cross-references that connect related themes together. These are listed under each theme.

A

Ability

see also **Genius, Talent**

1 When you can do the common things of life in an uncommon way you'll command the attention of the world.
George Washington Carver (1864–1943) US inventor and horticulturist. Quoted in *World's Great Men of Color* (Joel Augustus Rogers; 1947), vol. 2

2 The most perfect technique is that which is not noticed at all.
Pablo Casals (1876–1973) Catalan cellist, conductor, and composer. Quoted in *The Song of the Birds* (Julian Lloyd Webber, ed.; 1985)

3 I'm worst at what I do best and for this gift I feel blest.
Kurt Cobain (1967–94) US rock musician. Song lyric. 'Nevermind' (1991)

4 The superior man is distressed by his want of ability.
Confucius (551–479 BC) Chinese philosopher, administrator, and moralist. *Analects* (5th century BC)

5 If you think you can or think you can't you're probably right.
Henry Ford (1863–1947) US car manufacturer. Quoted in *Survival of the Smartest* (Haim Mendelson and Johannes Ziegler; 1999)

6 We never do anything well till we cease to think about the manner of doing it.
William Hazlitt (1778–1830) British essayist and critic. 'On Prejudice', *Sketches and Essays* (William Carew Hazlitt, ed.; 1839)

7 A gentleman of thirty-two who could calculate an eclipse, survey an estate, tie an artery, plan an edifice, try a cause, break a horse, dance a minuet, and play the violin.
James Parton (1822–91) US writer. Referring to Thomas Jefferson. *Life of Thomas Jefferson: Third President of the United States* (1874), ch. 19

8 It is always pleasant to be urged to do something on the ground that one can do it well.
George Santayana (1863–1952) Spanish-born US philosopher, poet, and novelist. Quoted in *The Letters of George Santayana* (Daniel Cory, ed.; 1956)

9 It is all about technique. The great mistake of this century is to put inspiration and creativity first.
Vivienne Westwood (b. 1941) British fashion designer. *Observer* (May 15, 1994), 'Sayings of the Week'

Abortion

see also **Babies, Birth, Pregnancy**

1 Until that day when women, and only women, shall determine which American males must, by law, have vasectomies, then—and only then—will you or any man have the right to determine which American women can have abortions.
Betty Beale, US journalist. *Ms* (March 1982)

2 The 'immorality' of women, favourite theme of misogynists, is not to be wondered at; how could they fail to feel an inner mistrust of the presumptuous principles that men publicly proclaim and secretly disregard? . . . The one thing they are sure of is this rifled and bleeding womb, the shreds of crimson life, this child that is not there. It is at her first abortion that woman begins to 'know'.
Simone de Beauvoir (1908–86) French writer and feminist theorist. *The Second Sex* (1949)

3 This right of privacy . . . is broad enough to encompass a woman's decision whether or not to terminate her pregnancy.
Harry A. Blackmun (1908–99) US associate justice of the US Supreme Court. Said during a Supreme Court decision in the *Roe v. Wade* case concerning the right to abortion, ruling that a woman's right to abortion was constitutionally protected. Majority opinion of the Supreme Court (1973)

4 Abortions will not let you forget. You remember the children you got that you did not get.
Gwendolyn Brooks (1917–2000) US poet and novelist. 'The Mother', *A Street in Bronzeville* (1945), st. 1

5 If men could get pregnant, abortion would be a sacrament.
Florynce R. Kennedy (1916–2000) US lawyer and activist. Quoted in 'The Verbal Karate of Florynce R. Kennedy, Esq.', *Ms* (Gloria Steinem; March 1973)

6 It serves me right for putting all my eggs in one bastard.
Dorothy Parker (1893–1967) US writer and wit. Said on going into hospital for an abortion. Quoted in *You Might As Well Live* (John Keats; 1970), pt. 2, ch. 3

7 Most women decide to have abortions reluctantly, and with trepidation, as the lesser of two evils. No woman has an abortion for *fun*.
Joan Smith (b. 1953) British writer and journalist. *Misogynies* (1989)

8 To hinder a birth is merely speedier man-killing; nor does it matter whether you take away a life that is born, or destroy one that is coming to the birth. That is a man which is going to be one; you have the fruit already in its seed.
Tertullian (160?–220?) Carthaginian theological writer. *Apologeticus* (197?)

9 Abortion, for many women, is more than an experience of suffering beyond anything most men will ever know, it is an act of mercy, and an act of self-defence.
Alice Walker (b. 1944) US novelist and poet. April 8, 1989. Speech at Pro-Choice/Keep Abortion Legal Rally, Washington, DC, *Her Blue Body Everything We Know* (1991)

Absence

see also **Nihilism, Nothingness**

1 I thought I told you to wait in the car.
Tallulah Bankhead (1903–68) US actor. When greeted by a former admirer after many years. Attrib.

2 Absence is to love what wind is to fire; it extinguishes the small, it inflames the great.
Bussy-Rabutin (1618–93) French soldier and writer. *Histoire Amoureuse des Gaules* (1665)

3 The absent are always in the wrong.
Philippe Destouches (1680–1754) French playwright. *L'Obstacle Imprévu* (1717), Act 1, Scene 6

4 The absence which you glory,
Is that which makes you sorry,
And burn in vain:
For thought is not the weapon,
Wherewith thought's ease men cheapen,
Absence is pain.
Fulke Greville (1554–1628) English courtier and poet. 1590? 'Caelica', *Caelica* (1633), quoted in *Selected Poems of Fulke Greville* (Neil Powell, ed.; 1990)

5 A house can be haunted by those who were never there
If there was where they were missed.
Louis MacNeice (1907–63) Irish-born British poet. 1957–60. 'Selva Oscura', *Selected Poems of Louis MacNeice* (1964), ll. 1–2

6 Why should I go? She won't be there.
Arthur Miller (b. 1915) US playwright. 1962. Said when asked if he would attend Marilyn Monroe's funeral. Attrib.

7 It's when the thing itself is missing that you have to supply the word.
Henri de Montherlant (1896–1972) French novelist and playwright. *La Reine Morte* (1942), Act 2, Scene 1

8 Most of what matters in your life takes place in your absence.
Salman Rushdie (b. 1947) Indian-born British novelist. *Midnight's Children* (1981)

9 The hour is come, but not the man.
Sir Walter Scott (1771–1832) Scottish novelist. *The Heart of Midlothian* (1818), ch. 4

10 QUINCE All for your delight
We are not here.
William Shakespeare (1564–1616) English poet and playwright. *A Midsummer Night's Dream* (1595–96), Act 5, Scene 1

11 I've been trying for some time now to develop a lifestyle that doesn't require my presence.
Garry Trudeau (b. 1948) US cartoonist. Referring to avoiding parties in Washington, DC. Quoted in *Ear on Washington* (Diana McLellan; 1982)

12 A vacuum is a hell of a lot better than some of the stuff that nature replaces it with.
Tennessee Williams (1911–83) US playwright. *Cat on a Hot Tin Roof* (1955)

Academics

see also **Education, Research, Teachers, University**

1 A professor is one who talks in someone else's sleep.
W. H. Auden (1907–73) British poet. Attrib.

2 It is not in the power of professors of demonstrative sciences to change their opinions at pleasure, and adopt first one side and then the other.
Galileo (1564–1642) Italian scientist. Letter to Cristina di Lorena, Granduchess of Tuscany (1615)

3 As I was saying the other day.
Luis Ponce de León (1527–91) Spanish monk, poet, and scholar. Remark on resuming a lecture interrupted by five years of imprisonment. Attrib.

4 The surprising thing about this paper is that a man who could write it would.
John Littlewood (1885–1977) British mathematician. *A Mathematician's Miscellany* (1953)

5 A *raznochinetz* needs no memory—it is enough for him to tell the books he has read, and his biography is done.
Osip Mandelstam (1891–1938) Russian poet, writer, and translator. *Raznochinetz* is a Russian word meaning a classless scholar. *The Noise of Time* (Clarence Brown, tr.; 1923), ch. 13

Accidents

see also **Fate, Mistakes**

1 We have to recognise *accident*, i.e., the fact that there is no formula, no 'principle', which covers all things; that there is no totality or system of things.
John Anderson (1893–1962) British-born Australian philosopher. *Studies in Empirical Philosophy* (1962)

2 Whenever you fall, pick up something.
Oswald Theodore Avery (1877–1955) Canadian-born US physician and bacteriologist. Attrib.

3 ACCIDENT, n. An inevitable occurrence due to the action of immutable natural laws.
Ambrose Bierce (1842–1914?) US writer and journalist. *The Devil's Dictionary* (1911)

4 I was very drunk. I suddenly said, 'It's time for our William Tell act. Put a glass on your head'.
William S. Burroughs (1914–97) US writer. Before accidentally killing his wife, by shooting a bullet through her head in a drunken party game. Quoted in *The Life and Legacy of William Burroughs: The Priest They Called Him* (Graham Caveney; 1998)

5 Accidents will occur in the best-regulated families; and in families not regulated by that pervading influence which sanctifies while it enhances them I would say, in short, by the influence of Woman, in the lofty character of Wife, they may be expected with confidence, and must be borne with philosophy.
Charles Dickens (1812–70) British novelist. Said by Mr. Micawber. *David Copperfield* (1850), ch. 28

6 My good man, I'm not a strawberry.
Edward VII (1841–1910) British monarch. Rebuking a footman who had spilt cream on him. Quoted in *The Last Country Houses* (C. Aslat; 1982)

7 For once reality and his brain came into contact, and the result was fatal.
T. H. Huxley (1825–95) British biologist. Referring to Bishop Samuel Wilberforce's death after falling from his horse. Quoted in *The Faber Book of Science* (John Carey, ed.; 1995)

8 And those who have undergone life in Alaska claim that in the making of the world God grew tired, and when He came to the last barrowload, 'just dumped it anyhow', and that was how Alaska happened to be.
Jack London (1876–1916) US writer. 'Gold Hunters of the North', *Revolution and other Essays* (1910)

9   now and then
     there is a person born
     who is so unlucky
     that he runs into accidents
     which started out to happen
     to somebody else.

     Don Marquis (1878–1937) US journalist and writer. 'archy says',
     archy's life of mehitabel (1933)

10   Don't go into Mr McGregor's garden: your
     Father had an accident there; he was put in a pie
     by Mrs McGregor.

     Beatrix Potter (1866–1943) British children's writer and illustrator. 1900.
     The Tale of Peter Rabbit (1900 edition)

11   There are no small accidents on this circuit.

     Ayrton Senna (1960–94) Brazilian motor-racing driver. Remark made
     before the 1994 San Marino Grand Prix, during which he
     was killed. *Independent* (December 22, 1994)

12   HAMLET I have shot my arrow o'er the house
     And hurt my brother.

     William Shakespeare (1564–1616) English poet and playwright. *Hamlet*
     (1601), Act 5, Scene 2

13   The chapter of accidents is the longest chapter in
     the book.

     John Wilkes (1725–97) British politician and reformer. Quoted in *The
     Doctor* (Robert Southey; 1847), ch. 18

Achievement

see also **Progress, Success**

1   How can one catch tiger cubs without entering
     the tiger's lair?

     Banchao (32–102) Chinese diplomat and military leader. Quoted in
     History of the Later Han (Fan Ye; 398–445?)

2   Who cares about great marks left behind? We
     have one life, rigidly defined. Just one. One life.
     We have nothing else.

     Ugo Betti (1892–1953) Italian playwright and poet. *The Inquiry* (Gino
     Rizzo, tr.; 1944–45)

3   The great law of culture is: Let each become all
     that he was created capable of becoming.

     Thomas Carlyle (1795–1881) Scottish historian and essayist. 'Jean Paul
     Friedrich Richter', *Critical and Miscellaneous Essays* (1838)

4   Now, gentlemen, let us do something today
     which the world may talk of hereafter.

     Cuthbert Collingwood (1748–1810) British admiral. October 21, 1805.
     Said before the Battle of Trafalgar. Quoted in *A Selection
     from the Correspondence of Lord Collingwood* (G. L.
     Newnham Collingwood, ed.; 1828), vol. 1

5   Year by year we are becoming better equipped to
     accomplish the things we are striving for. But
     what are we actually striving for?

     Bertrand de Jouvenel (1903–87) French political scientist, economist, and
     journalist. 1970. Quoted in *The Jingle Bell Principle* (Miroslav
     Holub; 1992)

6   Almost everything that is great has been done by
     youth.

     Benjamin Disraeli (1804–81) British prime minister and writer.
     Coningsby (1844), bk. 3, ch. 1

7   Yes, I have climbed to the top of the greasy pole.

     Benjamin Disraeli (1804–81) British prime minister and writer. 1869.
     Said after being appointed prime minister. Quoted in *Life of
     Benjamin Disraeli* (W. Monypenny and G. Buckle; 1916),
     vol. 4, ch. 16

8   Anything worth doing is worth doing poorly at
     first.

     Robert Downey, Jr. (b. 1965) US actor. *The Charlie Rose Show*
     (December 21, 1995)

9   The reward of a thing well done is to have done it.

     Ralph Waldo Emerson (1803–82) US poet and essayist. 'New England
     Reformers', *Essays, Second Series* (1844)

10   Never let success hide its emptiness from you,
     achievement its nothingness, toil its desolation.
     And so . . . keep alive the incentive to push on
     further, that pain in the soul which drives us
     beyond ourselves.

     Dag Hammarskjöld (1905–61) Swedish statesman and diplomat.
     Markings (Leif Sjöberg and W. H. Auden, trs.; 1964)

11   Never measure the height of a mountain, until
     you have reached the top. Then you will see how
     low it was.

     Dag Hammarskjöld (1905–61) Swedish statesman and diplomat.
     Markings (Leif Sjöberg and W. H. Auden, trs.; 1964)

12   It is not by spectacular achievements that man
     can be transformed, but by will.

     Henrik Ibsen (1828–1906) Norwegian playwright. *Brand* (1865), Act 2

13   Anybody can be Pope; the proof of this is that I
     have become one.

     John XXIII (1881–1963) Italian pope. Quoted in *Wit and Wisdom of
     Good Pope John* (Henri Fresquet; 1964)

14   The ultimate measure of a man is not where he
     stands in moments of comfort and convenience,
     but where he stands at times of challenge and
     controversy.

     Martin Luther King, Jr. (1929–68) US civil rights leader. *Strength To
     Love* (1963)

15   The heights by great men reached and kept
     Were not attained by sudden flight,
     But they, while their companions slept,
     Were toiling upward in the night.

     Henry Wadsworth Longfellow (1807–82) US poet. 'The Ladder of Saint
     Augustine' (1850)

16   I have discovered the secret that after climbing a
     great hill, one only finds that there are many
     more hills to climb.

     Nelson Mandela (b. 1918) South African president and lawyer. *Long
     Walk to Freedom* (1994)

17   You can do anything in this world if you are
     prepared to take the consequences.

     Somerset Maugham (1874–1965) British writer. *The Circle* (1921)

18   The world is divided into people who do things
     and people who get the credit. Try, if you can, to
     belong to the first class. There's far less
     competition.

     Dwight Whitney Morrow (1873–1931) US diplomat and politician. Letter
     to his son, quoted in *Dwight Morrow* (Harold Nicolson;
     1935), ch. 3

19   Nothing great is achieved without chimeras.

     Ernest Renan (1823–92) French philosopher, philologist, and historian.
     1848. *L'Avenir de la Science: Pensées de 1848* (1890), ch. 19

20   Think nothing done while aught remains to do.

     Samuel Rogers (1763–1855) British poet and art collector. *Human Life*
     (1819)

21   Is there anything in life so disenchanting as
     attainment?

     Robert Louis Stevenson (1850–94) Scottish novelist, essayist, and poet.
     'The Adventure of a Hansom Cab', *The New Arabian Nights*
     (1882)

22   In the end, you're measured not by how much
     you undertake but by what you finally
     accomplish.

     Donald Trump (b. 1946) US real estate developer. *Trump: the Art of
     the Deal* (co-written with Tony Schwartz; 1987)

23 People at the top of the tree are those without qualifications to detain them at the bottom.
Peter Ustinov (b. 1921) British actor, director, and writer. Attrib.

24 To achieve great things we must live as though we were never going to die.
Marquis de Vauvenargues (1715–47) French soldier and moralist. *Réflexions et Maximes* (1746)

25 The secret I learned early on from my father was to run scared and never think I had made it.
Thomas Watson, Jr. (1914–93) US business executive. Quoted in *Key Management Ideas* (Stuart Crainer; 1996)

Acting and Actors

see also Films, Performance, Theatre

1 For an actress to be a success she must have the face of Venus, the brains of Minerva, the grace of Terpsichore, the memory of Macaulay, the figure of Juno, and the hide of a rhinoceros.
Ethel Barrymore (1879–1959) US actor. Quoted in *The Theater in the Fifties* (George Jean Nathan; 1953)

2 An actor's a guy who, if you ain't talking about him, ain't listening.
Marlon Brando (b. 1924) US actor. 1955. *Observer* (January 1956), 'Sayings of the Year'

3 The secret of acting is sincerity. If you can fake that, you've got it made.
George Burns (1896–1996) US comedian and actor. 1986. Attrib.

4 An actor is something less than a man while an actress is something more than a woman.
Richard Burton (1925–84) British actor. Quoted in *Halliwell's Filmgoer's and Video Viewer's Companion (8th ed.)* (Leslie Halliwell; 1990)

5 I made mistakes in drama. I thought drama was when actors cried. But drama is when the audience cries.
Frank Capra (1897–1991) Italian-born US film director. *Cinemas No. 12, Antenne 2* (French television; February 1983), quoted in *Chambers Film Quotes* (Tony Crawley, ed.; 1991)

6 Just say your lines and don't trip over the furniture.
Noël Coward (1899–1973) British playwright, actor, and songwriter. Advice for actors. Speech at the Gallery First-Nighters' Club (1962)

7 Don't Put Your Daughter on the Stage, Mrs Worthington
Noël Coward (1899–1973) British playwright, actor, and songwriter. 1935. Song title.

8 Show me a great actor and I'll show you a lousy husband. Show me a great actress, and you've seen the devil.
W. C. Fields (1879–1946) US entertainer. Attrib.

9 It is easier to get an actor to be a cowboy than to get a cowboy to be an actor.
John Ford (1895–1973) US filmmaker. Attrib.

10 Actresses will happen in the best regulated families.
Oliver Herford (1863–1935) British-born US poet, illustrator, and wit. Attrib.

11 Actors should be treated like cattle.
Alfred Hitchcock (1899–1980) British-born US film director. Said in clarification of a remark attributed to him, 'Actors are like cattle'. Quoted in *Star Speak* (Doug McClelland; 1987)

12 You can't direct a Laughton picture. The best you can hope for is to referee.
Alfred Hitchcock (1899–1980) British-born US film director. Referring to the actor Charles Laughton. Attrib.

13 If I'd made a hit as a *human being* then perhaps I'd be sailing in films now.
Bert Lahr (1895–1967) US actor. Referring to his Cowardly Lion performance in *The Wizard of Oz* (1939). Quoted in *Notes on a Cowardly Lion* (John Lahr; 1969)

14 It is the strength to resist the extraneous that renders acting powerful and beautiful.
David Mamet (b. 1947) US writer and film director. 'Some Lessons from Television', *A Whore's Profession: Notes and Essays* (1994)

15 The less you do, the better you do it.
Marcello Mastroianni (1924–96) Italian film actor. Advice on being a successful actor. Interview, *Il Corriere della Sera* (August 3, 1985), quoted in *Chambers Film Quotes* (Tony Crawley, ed.; 1991)

16 Much better to play a maid than to be one.
Hattie McDaniel (1898–1952) US actor. Quoted in *Black Hollywood: The Black Performer in Motion Pictures* (Gary Null; 1990)

17 Never work with animals or children.
Mottos and Slogans. Show business maxim.

18 You must have—besides intuition and sensitivity—a cutting edge that allows you to reach what you need. Also, you have to know life—bastards included—and it takes a bit of one to know one, don't you think?
Laurence Olivier (1907–89) British actor and director. Advice on being a successful actor. Interview, *Daily Mail* (March 28, 1986), quoted in *Chambers Film Quotes* (Tony Crawley, ed.; 1991)

19 The art of acting consists in keeping people from coughing.
Ralph Richardson (1902–83) British actor. *Observer* (1947)

20 There used to be a me behind the mask, but I had it surgically removed.
Peter Sellers (1925–80) British comic actor. Attrib.

21 A character actor is one who cannot act and therefore makes an elaborate study of disguise and stage tricks by which acting can be grotesquely simulated.
George Bernard Shaw (1856–1950) Irish playwright. Attrib.

22 The art of an actor is the knowledge of the logic of actions in a play and the ability to put them all on one thread in a consecutive order.
Constantin Stanislavsky (1863–1938) Russian actor and theatre director. Quoted in *The Stanislavski Method* (Sonia Moore; 1960)

23 When you play a nasty man, search for what is good in him.
Constantin Stanislavsky (1863–1938) Russian actor and theatre director. Quoted in *The Stanislavski Method* (Sonia Moore; 1960)

24 It sounds pompous, but it's the nearest thing I can do to being God. I'm trying to create human beings and so does He.
Rod Steiger (b. 1925) US film actor. October 10, 1970. Attrib.

25 There's no such thing as The Method. The term method-acting is so much nonsense. There are many methods . . . My father merely used a method of teaching based on the ideas of Stanislavsky—self-discipline, how to think out a role and use imagination.
Susan Strasberg (b. 1938) US actor. 1961. Referring to her father, Lee Strasberg, who was the leading teacher of so-called method-acting, in a publicity release for *Scream of Fear* (1961). Attrib.

26 When you're working for a good director, you become subjective and submissive. You become his concubine. All that you seek is his pleasure.

Donald Sutherland (b. 1934) Canadian-born US film actor. Quoted in *Film Yearbook 1986* (1986)

27 Days off.

Spencer Tracy (1900–67) US film actor. Explaining what he looked for in a script. Attrib.

28 The actor must have no personality at all . . . You must give the impression that the scenario was never written. That you're inventing it at the precise moment you act it—an elaborate kind of improvisation.

Jean-Louis Trintignant (b. 1931) French actor. Interview, *Films Illustrated* (July 1979), quoted in *Chambers Film Quotes* (Tony Crawley, ed.; 1991)

29 An actor is never so great as when he reminds you of an animal—falling like a cat, lying like a dog, moving like a fox.

François Truffaut (1932–84) French film director and screenwriter. Attrib.

30 Every actor in his heart believes everything bad that's printed about him.

Orson Welles (1915–85) US actor, director, producer, and writer. Attrib.

Action

see also **Achievement, Effort, Work**

1 The origin of action—its efficient, not its final cause—is choice, and that of choice is desire and reasoning with a view to an end.

Aristotle (384–322 BC) Greek philosopher. *Nicomachean Ethics* (4th century BC), 1139a

2 This is the urgency: Live! and have your blooming in the noise of the whirlwind.

Gwendolyn Brooks (1917–2000) US poet and novelist. 'The Second Sermon on the Warpland', *The Mecca* (1968)

3 Deliberation is the work of many men. Action, of one alone.

Charles de Gaulle (1890–1970) French president. *Mémoires de Guerre* (1954–59), vol. 2

4 We must beat the iron while it is hot, but we may polish it at leisure.

John Dryden (1631–1700) English poet, playwright, and literary critic. *Aeneis* (1697), Dedication

5 Our acts our angels are, or good or ill, Our fatal shadows that walk by us still.

John Fletcher (1579–1625) English playwright. *An Honest Man's Fortune* (1647), Epilogue

6 The deed is all, and not the glory.

Johann Wolfgang von Goethe (1749–1832) German poet, playwright, and scientist. 'Hochgebirg', *Faust* (1832), pt. 2

7 That action is best, which procures the greatest happiness for the greatest numbers.

Francis Hutcheson (1694–1746) Irish-born English philosopher. *Inquiry into the Original of our Ideas of Beauty and Virtue* (1725), pt. 2, sect. 3

8 A strictly voluntary act has to be guided by idea, perception, and volition, throughout its entire course.

William James (1842–1910) US psychologist and philosopher. *The Principles of Psychology* (1890), vol. 1

9 I have it here in black and white It must be done like lightning.

Ben Jonson (1572–1637) English playwright and poet. *Every Man in His Humour* (1598), Act 4, Scene 5

10 No action is in itself good or bad, but only such according to convention.

Somerset Maugham (1874–1965) British writer. *A Writer's Notebook* (1949)

11 If you say . . . 'I am unable to do it', when the task is one of striding over the North Sea . . . a genuine case of inability to act. But if you say, 'I am unable to do it', when it is one of massaging an elder's joints for him . . . a case of refusal to act, not of inability.

Mencius (371?–288? BC) Chinese philosopher. 4th century BC. Quoted in *Mencius* (D. C. Lau, tr.; 1970), bk. 1

12 I don't know everything, I just do everything.

Toni Morrison (b. 1931) US novelist. *Sula* (1973)

13 Few men of action have been able to make a graceful exit at the appropriate time.

Malcolm Muggeridge (1903–90) British journalist. *Chronicles of Wasted Time* (1972)

14 Activity is the only reality.

Novalis (1772–1801) German poet and novelist. *The Disciples at Sais* (1801)

15 The end must justify the means.

Matthew Prior (1664–1721) English diplomat and poet. 'Hans Carvel' (1701)

16 Only the actions of the just Smell sweet, and blossom in their dust.

James Shirley (1596–1666) English playwright. *The Contention of Ajax and Ulysses* (1659), Act 1, Scene 3

17 We know what a person thinks not when he tells us what he thinks, but by his actions.

Isaac Bashevis Singer (1904–91) Polish-born US writer. Interview, *New York Times Magazine* (November 28, 1978)

18 You must take the will for the deed.

Jonathan Swift (1667–1745) Irish writer and clergyman. *Polite Conversation* (1738), Dialogue 2

19 We can't all do everything.

Virgil (70–19 BC) Roman poet. *Eclogues* (37 BC), no. 8, l. 63

20 Any serious attempt to try and do something worthwhile is ritualistic.

Derek Walcott (b. 1930) St. Lucian poet and playwright. Interview, *Writers at Work* (George Plimpton, ed.; 1988)

Addiction

see also **Alcohol, Drugs, Obsessions**

1 Cocaine isn't habit-forming—I should know—I've been using it for years.

Tallulah Bankhead (1903–68) US actor. *Tallulah* (1952), ch. 4

2 The Chief Defect of Henry King Was chewing little bits of String.

Hilaire Belloc (1870–1953) French-born British writer. 'Henry King', *Cautionary Tales* (1907)

3 Just as the human body can crave more and more of a drug that is actually poisoning it, so a society can crave lethal weapons, cadavers, or human organs which if freely traded, would inflict social damage.

Warren Bennis (b. 1925) US educationalist and writer. *Beyond Leadership: Balancing Economics, Ethics and Ecology* (co-written with Jagdish Parikh and Ronnie Lessem; 1994)

4 I'll die young, but it's like kissing God.

Lenny Bruce (1925–66) US comedian. Referring to his drug addiction. Attrib.

5 Every form of addiction is bad, no matter whether the narcotic be alcohol or morphine or idealism.

Carl Gustav Jung (1875–1961) Swiss psychoanalyst. *Memories, Dreams, Reflections* (1962), ch. 12

Admiration

see **Praise, Respect**

Adolescence

see **Childhood, Youth**

Adultery

see also **Infidelity, Marriage**

1 You must have noticed that the main idea of that great work is this: if a woman leaves her lawful husband to live with another man, this inevitably makes her a prostitute. Don't argue! That's exactly what it is.

Anna Akhmatova (1888–1966) Russian poet. May 18, 1939. Referring to Leo Tolstoy's novel *Anna Karenina* (1875–77). Quoted in *The Akhmatova Journals: 1938–41* (Lydia Chukovskaya, ed.; 1989)

2 When you've been married a few years—you can't help window shopping.

Alan Ayckbourn (b. 1939) British playwright and director. *Round and Round the Garden* (1973), Act 1, Scene 1

3 One cubic foot less of space and it would have constituted adultery.

Robert Benchley (1889–1945) US humorist, writer, editor, and critic. Describing an office shared with the writer Dorothy Parker. Attrib.

4 Splendid couple—slept with both of them.

Maurice Bowra (1898–1971) British scholar and classicist. Referring to a well-known literary couple. Attrib.

5 Do you seriously expect me to be the first Prince of Wales in history not to have a mistress?

Prince Charles (b. 1948) British prince. *Daily Mail* (December 1994)

6 Do not adultery commit;
Advantage rarely comes of it.

Arthur Hugh Clough (1819–61) British poet. 'The Latest Decalogue' (1862)

7 There were three of us in this marriage, so it was a bit crowded.

Princess Diana (1961–97) British princess. Referring to the relationship between her husband and Camilla Parker-Bowles. *Panorama* (1995)

8 No, I shall have mistresses.

George II (1683–1760) German-born British monarch. Reply to Queen Caroline's suggestion, as she lay on her deathbed, that he should marry again after her death. Quoted in *Memoirs of the Reign of George the Second* (John Hervey; 1848), vol. 2

9 When you marry your mistress, you create a job vacancy.

James Goldsmith (1933–97) French-born British businessman and politician. Attrib.

10 There are few who would not rather be taken in adultery than in provincialism.

Aldous Huxley (1894–1963) British novelist and essayist. *Antic Hay* (1923), ch. 10

11 Who would not shudder to think of the misery that may be caused by a single dangerous intimacy? And how much suffering could be avoided if it were more often thought of!

Pierre Choderlos de Laclos (1741–1803) French novelist and politician. *Les Liaisons Dangereuses* (1782), Letter 175

12 You know, of course, that the Tasmanians, who never committed adultery, are now extinct.

Somerset Maugham (1874–1965) British writer. *The Bread-Winner* (1930)

13 Adultery is the application of democracy to love.

H. L. Mencken (1880–1956) US journalist, critic, and editor. 1920. 'Sententiæ', *The Vintage Mencken* (Alistair Cooke, ed.; 1955)

14 In his heart, he knows your wife.

Mottos and Slogans. 1976. Car bumper sticker. Following President Jimmy Carter's admission in a *Playboy* interview that he had 'committed adultery in his heart many times'. Adapted from Barry Goldwater's 1964 presidential election slogan: 'In your heart you know he's right'.

15 A father will have compassion on his son. A mother will never forget her child. A brother will cover the sin of his sister. But what husband ever forgave the faithlessness of his wife?

Margaret of Navarre (1492–1549) French writer and patron of literature. *Mirror of the Sinful Soul* (1531)

16 Lady, lady, should you meet,
One whose ways are all discreet,
One who murmurs that his wife
Is the lodestar of his life,
One who keeps assuring you
That he never was untrue,
Never loved another one . . .
Lady, lady, better run!

Dorothy Parker (1893–1967) US writer and wit. 'Social Note', *Enough Rope* (1926)

17 One man's folly is another man's wife.

Helen Rowland (1876–1950) US writer, journalist, and humorist. *A Guide to Men* (1922)

18 With all my heart. Whose wife shall it be?

Horne Tooke (1736–1812) British lawyer, clergyman, and politician. Replying to the suggestion that he take a wife. Attrib.

19 The first breath of adultery is the freest; after it, constraints aping marriage develop.

John Updike (b. 1932) US writer. *Couples* (1968), ch. 5

20 No, my dear, it is *I* who am surprised; you are merely astonished.

Noah Webster (1758–1843) US lexicographer and writer. Responding to his wife's comment that she had been surprised to find him embracing their maid. Attrib.

Adulthood

see also **Experience, Middle Age, Parents**

1 If this was adulthood the only improvement she could detect in her situation was that she could now eat dessert without eating her vegetables.

Lisa Alther (b. 1944) US writer. *Kinflicks* (1976)

2 What is an adult? A child blown up by age.

Simone de Beauvoir (1908–86) French writer and feminist theorist. 1967. *The Woman Destroyed* (Patrick O'Brien, tr.; 1971)

3 How many roads must a man walk down
Before you call him a man?

Bob Dylan (b. 1941) US singer and songwriter. Song lyric. 'Blowin' in the Wind' (1962)

4 One of the most obvious facts about grown-ups to a child is that they have forgotten what it is like to be a child.

Randall Jarrell (1914–65) US author and poet. Quoted in *The Man Who Loved Children* (Christina Stead; 1965), Introduction

5 An adult is one who has ceased to grow vertically but not horizontally.

Proverb.

6 Adults are obsolete children.

Dr. Seuss (1904–91) US writer and illustrator. Attrib.

7 Men come of age at sixty, women at fifteen.

James Stephens (1882–1950) Irish novelist and poet. *Observer* (October 1, 1944), 'Sayings of the Week'

Advertising

see also **Business, Marketing, Materialism**

1 The advertisement . . . abolishes the space where contemplation moved and all but hits us between the eyes with things as a car, growing to gigantic proportions, careens at us out of a film screen.

Walter Benjamin (1892–1940) German writer and critic. 'One-Way Street', *Reflections* (Peter Demetz, ed.; 1986)

2 Advertising isn't a science. It's persuasion. And persuasion is an art.

William Bernbach (1911–82) US advertising executive. Quoted in *Speaking Freely* (Stuart Berg Flexner and Anne H. Soukhanov; 1997)

3 The most important element of success in ad writing is the product itself.

William Bernbach (1911–82) US advertising executive. Quoted in 'William Bernbach', *The Art of Writing Advertising* (Denis Higgins; 1965)

4 When a man throws an empty cigarette package from an automobile, he is liable to a fine of $50. When a man throws a billboard across a view, he is richly rewarded.

Pat Brown (1905–96) US politician. Quoted in *Ogilvy on Advertising* (David Ogilvy; 1983)

5 How beautiful it would be for someone who could not read.

G. K. Chesterton (1874–1936) British writer and poet. Referring to the lights on Broadway. Attrib.

6 Advertising is the most fun you can have with your clothes on.

Jerry Della Femina (b. 1936) US advertising executive. *From Those Wonderful Folks Who Gave You Pearl Harbor* (Charles Sopkin, ed.; 1970)

7 We don't know how to sell products based on performance. Everything we sell, we sell on image.

Roberto Goizueta (b. 1931) US business executive. *Wall Street Journal* (February 3, 1997)

8 Advertising . . . legitimizes the idealized, stereotyped roles of women as temptress, wife, mother, and sex object.

Lucy Komisar (b. 1942) US writer. *Women in Sexist Society* (1971)

9 The advertising industry thus encourages the pseudo-emancipation of women, flattering them with its insinuating reminder, You've come a long way, baby, and disguising the freedom to consume as genuine autonomy.

Christopher Lasch (1932–94) US historian and social critic. *The Culture of Narcissism* (1979)

10 Advertising may be described as the science of arresting human intelligence long enough to get money from it.

Stephen Leacock (1869–1944) British-born Canadian writer and economist. *Garden of Folly* (1924)

11 Half the money I spend on advertising is wasted, and the trouble is I don't know which half.

William Hesketh Lever Leverhulme (1851–1925) British industrialist and philanthropist. Quoted in *Confessions of an Advertising Man* (David Ogilvy; 1964)

12 Advertising is an environmental striptease for a world of abundance.

Marshall McLuhan (1911–80) Canadian sociologist. Quoted in *Subliminal Seduction* (Wilson Key; 1973)

13 I think that I shall never see
A billboard lovely as a tree.
Perhaps unless the billboards fall,
I'll never see a tree at all.

Ogden Nash (1902–71) US humorist. 'Song of the Open Road' (1933)

14 When you have nothing to say, sing it.

David Ogilvy (1911–99) US advertising executive. *Ogilvy on Advertising* (1983)

15 Modernity desacralized the human body, and advertising has used it as a marketing tool.

Octavio Paz (1914–98) Mexican author and poet. *The Double Flame* (1993)

16 The Marlboro Man has nothing to do with Russia. Why should we respond to it?

Viktor Pelevin (b. 1962) Russian novelist. *Business Week* (January 27, 1997)

Aesthetics

see also **Art, The Arts, Beauty**

1 The mystery of æsthetic like that of material creation is accomplished. The artist, like the God of the creation, remains within or behind or beyond or above his handiwork, invisible, refined out of existence, indifferent, paring his fingernails.

James Joyce (1882–1941) Irish writer. *A Portrait of the Artist as a Young Man* (1916), ch. 5

2 one loves form only
and form only comes
into existence when
the thing is born.

Charles Olson (1910–70) US poet. 'I, Maximus of Gloucester, to You', *The Maximus Poems 1–10* (1953)

3 I hate that aesthetic game of the eye and the mind, played by these connoisseurs, these mandarins who 'appreciate' beauty. What *is* beauty anyway? There's no such thing. I never 'appreciate', any more than I 'like'. I love or hate.

Pablo Picasso (1881–1973) Spanish painter and sculptor. Quoted in *Life with Picasso* (Françoise Gilot and Carlton Lake; 1964), ch. 2

4 What is ugly in Art is only that which is without character, that is, that which offers no truth at all, either exterior or interior.

Auguste Rodin (1840–1917) French sculptor. Attrib.

5 You shouldn't say it is not good. You should say you do not like it; and then, you know, you're perfectly safe.

James Abbott McNeill Whistler (1834–1903) US painter and etcher. Quoted in *Whistler Stories* (D. C. Seitz; 1913)

Africa

see also African Countries, World Literature

1   I see several Africas and one
    vertical in the tumultous event
    with its screens and nodules,
    a little separated, but within
    the century, like a heart in reserve.
    Aimé Césaire (b. 1913) Martiniquan poet, teacher, and political leader.
    Ferrements (1960)

2   The final interpretation of African history is the
    responsibility of scholars of African descent.
    John Henrik Clarke (1915–98) US historian and educator. Address to the
    Regional Conference on Afro-American History, University of
    Detroit (May 11–13, 1967), 'A New Approach to African
    History'

3   What is Africa to me: Copper sun or scarlet sea
    Jungle star or jungle track
    Strong bronzed men, or regal black
    Women from whose loins I sprang
    When the birds of Eden sang?
    One three centuries removed
    From the scenes his fathers loved
    Spicy grove, cinnamon tree, What is Africa to
    me?
    Countee Cullen (1903–46) US poet, novelist, and playwright. 'Heritage',
    Color (1925)

4   The 'scramble for Africa' took place on the
    assumption that the land and the peoples were
    there for the taking.
    Norman Davies (b. 1939) British historian and writer. Referring to the
    efforts by European nations to colonize all of Africa's land
    and people during the 19th and 20th centuries. As well as
    involving the genocide of African peoples, the struggle
    increased antagonisms between the European powers. Europe:
    A History (1996), ch. 10

5   No one knows when the hour of Africa's
    Redemption cometh. It is in the wind. It is
    coming. One day like a storm, it will be here.
    When that day comes all Africa will stand
    together.
    Marcus Garvey (1887–1940) Jamaican-born black nationalist leader and
    publisher. Quoted in The Philosophy and Opinions of Marcus
    Garvey (Amy Jacques Garvey, ed.; 1923)

6   The only thing Africa has left is the future.
    Marita Golden (b. 1950) US writer and teacher. A Woman's Place
    (1986)

7   The African is conditioned, by the cultural and
    social institutions of centuries, to a freedom of
    which Europe has little conception, and it is not
    in his nature to accept serfdom for ever.
    Jomo Kenyatta (1897?–1978) Kenyan president. Facing Mount Kenya
    (1938)

8   When a white man in Africa by accident looks
    into the eyes of a native and sees the human
    being (which it is his chief preoccupation to
    avoid), his sense of guilt, which he denies, fumes
    up in resentment and he brings down the whip.
    Doris Lessing (b. 1919) British novelist and short-story writer. The Grass
    is Singing (1950), ch. 8

9   Africa must refuse to be humiliated, exploited,
    and pushed around. And with the same
    determination we must refuse to humiliate,
    exploit or push others around.
    Julius Kambarage Nyerere (1922–99) Tanzanian president. February 29,
    1968. Freedom and Development (1973)

10 Africans have lived so long on promises. What
    they want to see are a few concrete deeds. They
    are tired of listening to pious sermons about
    'democracy' and 'freedom' while the chains of
    servitude still hang around their necks.
    George Padmore (1902–59) Trinidadian campaigner. Pan-Africanism
    (1956)

11 There is always something new out of Africa.
    Pliny the Elder (23?–79) Roman scholar. Natural History (77), bk. 8

12 Negritude is the sum total of the values of the
    civilization of the African world. It is not
    racialism, it is culture.
    Léopold Senghor (1906–2001) Senegalese president, poet, and intellectual.
    1962. 'Pierre Teilhard de Chardin et la Politique Africaine',
    Léopold Sédar Senghor: Prose and Poetry (John Reed and
    Clive Wake, eds.; 1965)

13 On the liberation of the African depends the
    liberation of the whole world. The future of the
    world lies with the oppressed and the Africans
    are the most oppressed people on earth.
    Robert Mangaliso Sobukwe (1924–78) South African nationalist leader.
    Speech at Fort Hare University (October 21, 1949), quoted in
    How Can Man Die Better . . . Sobukwe and Apartheid
    (Benjamin Pogrund; 1990)

14 Your bounty threatens me, Mandela,
    that taut Drumskin of your heart on which our
    millions
    Dance. I fear we latch, fat leeches
    On your veins.
    Wole Soyinka (b. 1934) Nigerian novelist, playwright, poet, and lecturer.
    'Your Logic Frightens Me Mandela', Mandela's Earth and
    Other Poems (1988)

15 How can I turn from Africa and live?
    Derek Walcott (b. 1930) St. Lucian poet and playwright. 1984. 'In a
    Green Night', Collected Poems: 1948–84 (1986)

African Countries

see also Africa

1   I've a bad case of the Buthelezi Blues, or is it
    post-Natal depression?
    Anonymous. 1990s. Graffiti.

2   We have set out on a quest for true humanity,
    and somewhere on the distant horizon we can see
    the glittering prize . . . In time we shall be in a
    position to bestow upon South Africa the greatest
    gift possible—a more human face.
    Stephen Biko (1946–77) South African political leader. 1973. 'Black
    Consciousness and the Quest for a True Humanity', Steve
    Biko: I Write What I Like (Aelred Stubbs, ed.; 1978)

3   My feelings are that for the first time we are
    participating in an election that will have
    legitimacy. Now we can go to the polling booth
    without a bad conscience.
    P. W. Botha (b. 1916) South African prime minister. Referring to the
    first free elections to be held in South Africa after the collapse
    of apartheid. Independent (April 28, 1994)

4   South Africa, renowned both far and wide
    For politics and little else beside.
    Roy Campbell (1901–57) South African-born poet, translator, and
    journalist. 1928. 'The Wayzgoose', Collected Poems of Roy
    Campbell (1949), pt. 1, ll. 3–4

5   Christ in this country would quite likely have
    been arrested under the Suppression of
    Communism Act.
    Joost de Blank (1908–68) Dutch-born British churchman. Referring to
    South Africa. Observer (October 27, 1963), 'Sayings of the
    Week'

6 Mr Mandela has walked a long road and now stands at the top of the hill. A traveller would sit down and admire the view. But a man of destiny knows that beyond this hill lies another and another. The journey is never complete.

F. W. de Klerk (b. 1936) South African president. May 2, 1994. *Observer* (May 8, 1994), 'Sayings of the Week'

7 There is no such thing as a nonracial society in a multiracial country.

F. W. de Klerk (b. 1936) South African president. *Time* (1994)

8 Years of imprisonment could not stamp out our determination to be free. Years of intimidation and violence could not stop us. And we will not be stopped now.

Nelson Mandela (b. 1918) South African president and lawyer. Press conference (April 26, 1994)

9 The task at hand will not be easy, but you have mandated us to change South Africa from a land in which the majority lived with little hope, to one in which they can live and work with dignity, with a sense of self-esteem and confidence in the future.

Nelson Mandela (b. 1918) South African president and lawyer. At his inauguration as president. Speech (May 10, 1994)

10 My fellow South Africans, today we are entering a new era for our country and its people. Today we celebrate not the victory of a party, but a victory for all the people of South Africa.

Nelson Mandela (b. 1918) South African president and lawyer. Following his election to the presidency. Speech, Cape Town (May 9, 1994)

11 It indicates the deadly weight of the terrible tradition of a dialogue between master and servant which we have to overcome.

Nelson Mandela (b. 1918) South African president and lawyer. Referring to the first meeting between the government and the African National Congress. *Independent* (May 5, 1990), 'Quote Unquote'

12 The hardest lesson of my life has come to me late. It is that a nation can win freedom without its people becoming free.

Joshua Nkomo (1917–99) Zimbabwean nationalist leader. *The Story of My Life* (1984)

13 We prefer self-government with danger to servitude in tranquility.

Kwame Nkrumah (1909–72) Ghanaian president. 1948. *I Speak of Freedom* (1961)

14 From no quarter shall we accept direction, or neo-colonialism, and at no time shall we lower our guard against the subversion of our Government or our people. Neither our principles, our country, nor our freedom to determine our own future are for sale.

Julius Kambarage Nyerere (1922–99) Tanzanian president. June 4, 1965. Said in a speech at a state banquet for Chou en Lai, the first leader of the People's Republic of China. *Freedom and Socialism* (1968)

15 The South African Police would leave no stone unturned to see that nothing disturbed the even terror of their lives.

Tom Sharpe (b. 1928) British novelist. *Indecent Exposure* (1973), ch. 1

16 For many years I was ashamed of being South African. Now I allow myself to feel nostalgic.

Anthony Sher (b. 1949) South African-born British actor. *Sunday Times* (July 8, 1990)

17 The history of the Christian church in South Africa is the history of a faith betrayed.

Oliver Tambo (1917–93) South African nationalist leader. Address to World Consultation of the World Council of Churches (June 1980), quoted in *Oliver Tambo Speaks* (Adelaide Tambo, ed.; 1987)

18 Improbable as it is, unlikely as it is, we are being set up as a beacon of hope for the world.

Desmond Tutu (b. 1931) South African clergyman and civil rights activist. *Times* (October 11, 1994)

Afterlife

see also **Death and Dying, Eternity, Immortality**

1 I don't believe in an afterlife, although I am bringing a change of underwear.

Woody Allen (b. 1935) US film actor and director. *Without Feathers* (1976)

2 Be happy with what you have and make provision for the day of your return to God . . . The journey is long, the appointment is on the day of the Resurrection, the destiny is Heaven or the fire of Hell.

Abu Abdullah Muhammad al-Harithi al-Baghdadi al-Mufid (*fl.* 10th century) Iraqi scholar and jurist. 10th century. 'The Life of the Commander of the Faithful', *The Book of Guidance into the Lives of the Twelve Imams* (I. K. A. Howard, tr.; 1981)

3 Were the happiness of the next world as closely apprehended as the felicities of this, it were a martyrdom to live.

Thomas Browne (1605–82) English physician and writer. *Urn Burial* (1658), ch. 4

4 If I must be reborn, I prefer not to be aware, to be always divided against myself, to be a monster; I have no doubt cursed myself through my actions, but have I done enough so that I will be reborn as an animal?

Vikram Chandra (b. 1961) Indian-born US writer. 'The Book of Return', *Red Earth and Pouring Rain* (1995)

5 A thousand tymes have I herd men telle
That ther ys joy in hevene and peyne in helle,
And I acorde wel that it ys so;
But, natheless, yet wot I wel also
That ther nis noon dwellyng in this contree,
That eyther hath in hevene or helle ybe.

Geoffrey Chaucer (1343?–1400) English poet. 'The Prologue', *The Legend of Good Women* (1380–86), quoted in *The Works of Geoffrey Chaucer* (F. N. Robinson, ed.; 1957)

6 We have no reliable guarantee that the afterlife will be any less exasperating than this one, have we?

Noël Coward (1899–1973) British playwright, actor, and songwriter. *Blithe Spirit* (1941), Act 1

7 My defence at the Last Judgement would be 'I was trying to connect up and use all the fragments I was born with'.

E. M. Forster (1879–1970) British novelist. Letter to Forest Reid (1915), quoted in *A Queer Reader* (Patrick Higgins, ed.; 1993)

8 With magnificent inflexibility he resisted every temptation to magical thought, and he rejected the illusion, so dear to Egyptians in particular, of a life after death.

Sigmund Freud (1856–1939) Austrian psychoanalyst. Referring to the Pharaoh Akhenaton, 'the heretic king' of the 18th dynasty. 'Moses and Monotheism', *The Origins of Religion* (Albert Dickson, ed., Ken Jones, tr.; 1939)

9 We sometimes congratulate ourselves at the
   moment of waking from a troubled dream; it
   may be so the moment after death.

   Nathaniel Hawthorne (1804–64) US novelist and short-story writer. *The
   American Notebooks* (1836?), ch. 1

10 Work and pray, live on hay,
   You'll get pie in the sky when you die.

   Joe Hill (1879–1915) Swedish-born US trade union leader and songwriter.
   'The Preacher and the Slave', *Songs of the Workers* (1911)

11 Silently, in a dream she had come to him after
   her death, her wasted body within its loose
   brown graveclothes giving off an odour of wax
   and rosewood.

   James Joyce (1882–1941) Irish writer. *Ulysses* (1922)

12 The knowledge of the other world can be
   obtained here only by losing some of that
   intelligence which is necessary for this present
   world.

   Immanuel Kant (1724–1804) German philosopher. 'Dream of a Spirit-
   Seer' (E. F. Goerwicz, tr.; 1766)

13 Is there another life? Shall I awake and find all
   this a dream? There must be, we cannot be
   created for this sort of suffering.

   John Keats (1795–1821) English poet. Letter to Charles Brown
   (September 30, 1820), quoted in *Letters of John Keats*
   (Robert Gittings, ed.; 1970)

14 Verily the life to come shall be better for thee
   than this present life: and thy Lord shall give thee
   a reward wherewith thou shalt be well pleased.
   Did he not find thee an orphan, and hath he not
   taken care of thee? And did he not find thee
   wandering in error, and hath he not guided thee
   into the truth?

   The Koran (7th century), Sura 93

15 I am going in search of a great perhaps.

   François Rabelais (1494?–1553?) French humanist and satirist. 1553?
   Last words. A number of different quotations are attributed
   to Rabelais as his last words. Quoted in *Rabelais et ses
   Oeuvres* (Jean Fleury; 1877), vol. 1, ch. 3, pt. 15

16 To emphasize the afterlife is to deny life. To
   concentrate on Heaven is to create hell.

   Tom Robbins (b. 1936) US writer. *Skinny Legs and All* (1990)

17 After your death you will be what you were
   before your birth.

   Arthur Schopenhauer (1788–1860) German philosopher. *Parerga and
   Paralipomena* (1851)

18 HAMLET The dread of something after death—
   The undiscover'd country, from whose bourn
   No traveller returns.

   William Shakespeare (1564–1616) English poet and playwright. *Hamlet*
   (1601), Act 3, Scene 1

19 ARTHUR Heaven take my soul, and England my
   bones.

   William Shakespeare (1564–1616) English poet and playwright. *King
   John* (1591–98), Act 4, Scene 3

20 Here, where the world is quiet;
   Here, where all trouble seems
   Dead winds' and spent waves' riot
   In doubtful dreams of dreams.

   Algernon Charles Swinburne (1837–1909) British poet. 'The Garden of
   Proserpine', *Poems and Ballads: First Series* (1866), st. 1

21 I am going a long way
   With these thou seest—if indeed I go
   (For all my mind is clouded with a doubt)—
   To the island-valley of Avilion;

   Where falls not hail, or rain, or any snow,
   Nor ever wind blows loudly; but it lies
   Deep-meadow'd, happy, fair with orchard lawns
   And bowery hollows crown'd with summer sea,
   Where I will heal me of my grievous wound.

   Alfred Tennyson (1809–92) British poet. 'The Passing of Arthur',
   Idylls of the King (1869), ll. 424–432

22 One world at a time.

   Henry David Thoreau (1817–62) US writer. May 1862. Said on being
   asked his opinion of the hereafter a few days before his death.
   Attrib.

Age

see also **Childhood, Middle Age, Old Age, Youth**

1 Alonso of Aragon was wont to say in
   commendation of age, that age appears to be best
   in four things—old wood best to burn, old wine
   to drink, old friends to trust, and old authors to
   read.

   Francis Bacon (1561–1626) English philosopher, statesman, and lawyer.
   Apothegms (1624)

2 Age will not be defied.

   Francis Bacon (1561–1626) English philosopher, statesman, and lawyer.
   'Of Regiment of Health', *Essays* (1625)

3 What Youth deemed crystal, Age finds out was
   dew.

   Robert Browning (1812–89) British poet. 'Jochanan Hakkadosh', st.
   101, l. 302, quoted in *The Poetical Works of Robert
   Browning* (1888–94)

4 Man arrives as a novice at each age of his life.

   Nicolas Chamfort (1741–94) French writer. *Caractères et Anecdotes*
   (1795)

5 Young men think old men are fools; but old men
   know young men are fools.

   George Chapman (1559?–1634) English poet and playwright. *All Fools*
   (1605), Act 5, Scene 1

6 The Master said, 'At fifteen I set my heart on
   learning; at thirty I took my stand; at forty I
   came to be free from doubts; at fifty I
   understood the Decree of Heaven; at sixty my ear
   was attuned; at seventy I followed my heart's
   desire without overstepping the line'.

   Confucius (551–479 BC) Chinese philosopher, administrator, and moralist.
   5th century BC. Quoted in *The Analects* (D. C. Lau, tr.;
   1979), bk. 2, no. 4

7 Youth is a blunder; Manhood a struggle; Old
   Age a regret.

   Benjamin Disraeli (1804–81) British prime minister and writer.
   Coningsby (1844), bk. 3, ch. 1

8 If only youth knew, if only age could.

   Henri Estienne (1528–98) French scholar and printer. *Les Prémices*
   (1594), epigram 191

9 At sixteen I was stupid, confused, insecure, and
   indecisive. At twenty-five I was wise, self-
   confident, prepossessing, and assertive. At forty-
   five I am stupid, confused, insecure, and
   indecisive. Who would have supposed that
   maturity is only a short break in adolescence?

   Jules Feiffer (b. 1929) US writer, cartoonist, and humorist. *Observer*
   (February 3, 1974)

10 At twenty years of age, the will reigns; at thirty,
   the wit; and at forty, the judgement.

   Benjamin Franklin (1706–90) US statesman and scientist. *Poor
   Richard's Almanack* (1741), June

11 We do not necessarily improve with age: for better or worse we become more like ourselves.

Peter Hall (b. 1930) British theatre director. *Observer* (January 24, 1988), 'Sayings of the Week'

12 Whenever a man's friends begin to compliment him about looking young, he may be sure that they think he is growing old.

Washington Irving (1783–1859) US writer. 'Bachelors', *Bracebridge Hall* (1822)

13 It is sobering to consider that when Mozart was my age he had already been dead for a year.

Tom Lehrer (b. 1928) US mathematician and songwriter. Quoted in *An Encyclopedia of Quotations about Music* (Nat Shapiro; 1978)

14 The four stages of man are infancy, childhood, adolescence, and obsolescence.

Art Linkletter (b. 1912) Canadian-born US radio and television broadcaster. *A Child's Garden of Misinformation* (1965), ch. 8

15 Age is our reconciliation with dullness.

Robert Lowell (1917–77) US poet. 'Last Summer at Milgate', *The Dolphin* (1973)

16 Age is other things too. It is wisdom, if one has lived one's life properly. It is experience and knowledge. And it is getting to know all the ways the world turns, so that if you cannot turn the world the way you want, you can at least get out of the way so you won't get run over.

Miriam Makeba (b. 1932) South African singer and political activist. *My Story* (1988)

17 A man is only as old as the woman he feels.

Groucho Marx (1895–1977) US comedian and film actor. Remark (1950?), attrib.

18 Self-parody is the first portent of age.

Larry McMurtry (b. 1936) US writer. *Some Can Whistle* (1989), pt. 1, ch. 14

19 Age will bring all things, and everyone knows, Madame, that twenty is no age to be a prude.

Molière (1622–73) French playwright. *Le Misanthrope* (1666), Act 3, Scene 4

20 Let us take care that age does not make more wrinkles on our spirit than on our face.

Michel de Montaigne (1533–92) French essayist. Quoted in *The Jingle Bell Principle* (Miroslav Holub; 1992)

21 Age doesn't protect you from love. But love, to some extent, protects you from age.

Jeanne Moreau (b. 1928) French actor. Attrib.

22 Each generation imagines itself to be more intelligent than the one that went before it, and wiser than the one that comes after it.

George Orwell (1903–50) British writer. Attrib. Book review (1945)

23 The young have aspirations that never come to pass, the old have reminiscences of what never happened. It's only the middle-aged who are really conscious of their limitations.

Saki (1870–1916) British short-story writer. 'Reginald at the Carlton', *Reginald* (1904)

24 When I was young, I was told: 'You'll see, when you're fifty'. I am fifty and I haven't seen a thing.

Erik Satie (1866–1925) French composer. Letter to his brother, quoted in *Erik Satie* (Pierre-Daniel Templier; 1932), ch. 1

25 She was once cool but Mr. Gravity's been very unkind to that woman.

Jennifer Saunders (b. 1958) British comedian. Said as Edina. *Absolutely Fabulous* (BBC television; 1990s)

26 Crabbed age and youth cannot live together: Youth is full of pleasure, age is full of care; Youth like summer morn, age like winter weather; Youth like summer brave, age like winter bare.

William Shakespeare (1564–1616) English poet and playwright. *The Passionate Pilgrim* (1599), st. 12

27 One's prime is elusive. You little girls, when you grow up, must be on the alert to recognize your prime at whatever time of your life it may occur. You must then live it to the full.

Muriel Spark (b. 1918) British novelist. *The Prime of Miss Jean Brodie* (1961), ch. 1

28 The mark of the immature man is that he wants to die nobly for a cause, while the mark of the mature man is that he wants to live humbly for one.

Wilhelm Stekel (1868–1940) Austrian psychiatrist. Quoted in *The Catcher in the Rye* (J. D. Salinger; 1951), ch. 24

29 No wise man ever wished to be younger.

Jonathan Swift (1667–1745) Irish writer and clergyman. *Moral and Diverting* (1711)

30 A man is as old as his arteries.

Thomas Sydenham (1624–89) English physician. Quoted in *Bulletin of the New York Academy of Medicine* (F. H. Garrison; 1928)

31 It is charming to totter into vogue.

Horace Walpole (1717–97) British writer. Letter to George Selwyn (December 2, 1765), quoted in *Correspondence* (Yale edition), vol. 30

32 We are all American at puberty; we die French.

Evelyn Waugh (1903–66) British novelist. July 18, 1961. 'Irregular Notes', *Diaries of Evelyn Waugh* (Michael Davie, ed.; 1976)

33 The older one grows the more one likes indecency.

Virginia Woolf (1882–1941) British novelist and critic. 'Monday or Tuesday' (1921)

34 My heart leaps up when I behold
A rainbow in the sky:
So was it when my life began;
So is it now I am a man;
So be it when I shall grow old,
Or let me die!
The Child is Father of the Man;
And I could wish my days to be
Bound each to each by natural piety.

William Wordsworth (1770–1850) English poet. March 26, 1802. 'My Heart Leaps Up When I Behold', *Poems in Two Volumes* (1807), vol. 2

35 I am thirty, the same as our People's Republic. For a republic thirty is still young. But a girl of thirty is virtually on the shelf.

Zhang Jie (b. 1937) Chinese writer. *Love Must Not be Forgotten* (1982)

Aggression

see also **Anger, Hate, Violence**

1 Oh, the shark has pretty teeth, dear,
And he shows them pearly white.
Just a jack-knife has Macheath, dear
And he keeps it out of sight.

Bertolt Brecht (1898–1956) German playwright and poet. 'The Ballad of Mack the Knife', *The Threepenny Opera* (1929), prologue

2 So soon as the man overtook me, he was but a word and a blow.

John Bunyan (1628–88) English preacher and writer. *The Pilgrim's Progress* (1678), pt. 1

3 Who overcomes
By force hath overcome but half his foe.
John Milton (1608–74) English writer. Said by Satan. *Paradise Lost* (1667), bk. 1, ll. 648–649

4 The strongest and the fiercest spirit
That fought in heaven; now fiercer by despair:
His trust was with the eternal to be deemed
Equal in strength, and rather than be less
Cared not to be at all.
John Milton (1608–74) English writer. Referring to Satan. *Paradise Lost* (1667), bk. 2, l. 44

5 Let dogs delight to bark and bite,
For God hath made them so;
Let bears and lions growl and fight,
For 'tis their nature too.
Isaac Watts (1674–1748) English theologian and hymnwriter. 'Against Quarrelling', *Divine Songs for Children* (1715)

Agreement

see also **Arguments, Compromise, Understanding**

1 All colours will agree in the dark.
Francis Bacon (1561–1626) English philosopher, statesman, and lawyer. 'Of Unity in Religion', *Essays* (1625)

2 When you say that you agree to a thing in principle you mean that you have not the slightest intention of carrying it out in practice.
Prince Otto von Bismarck (1815–98) German chancellor. Attrib.

3 I could never divide my self from any man upon the difference of an opinion, or be angry with his judgment for not agreeing with me in that, from which perhaps within a few days I should dissent my self.
Thomas Browne (1605–82) English physician and writer. *Religio Medici* (1642), pt. 1, sect. 6

4 'My idea of an agreeable person', said Hugo Bohun, 'is a person who agrees with me'.
Benjamin Disraeli (1804–81) British prime minister and writer. *Lothair* (1870), ch. 35

5 Unanimity of opinion may be fitting for a church, for the frightened or greedy victims of some (ancient or modern) myth, or for the weak and willing followers of some tyrant. Variety of opinion is necessary for objective knowledge.
Paul K. Feyerabend (1924–94) German philosopher. *Against Method* (1975)

6 You cannot shake hands with a clenched fist.
Indira Gandhi (1917–84) Indian prime minister. Remark, press conference, New Delhi (October 19, 1971)

7 To me it is a strangely appealing and even elevating thought that the age-old covenant between man and dog was 'signed' voluntarily and without obligation by each of the contracting parties.
Konrad Lorenz (1903–89) Austrian zoologist. *King Solomon's Ring* (Marjorie Kerr Wilson, tr.; 1949)

8 Love-quarrels oft in pleasing concord end.
John Milton (1608–74) English writer. 'Samson Agonistes', *Paradise Regain'd . . . To Which is added Samson Agonistes* (1671), l. 1008

9 Our agenda is now exhausted. The secretary general is exhausted. All of you are exhausted. I find it comforting that, beginning with our very first day, we find ourselves in such complete unanimity.
Paul Henri Spaak (1899–1972) Belgian prime minister. Concluding the first General Assembly meeting of the United Nations, in San Francisco. Speech (1946)

10 Ah! don't say you agree with me. When people agree with me I always feel that I must be wrong.
Oscar Wilde (1854–1900) Irish poet, playwright, and wit. 'The Critic as Artist', *Intentions* (1891), pt. 2

AIDS

see also **Illness, Medicine**

1 AIDS is a perfect illness because it is so alien to human nature and has as its function to destroy life in the most cruel and systematic way.
Reinaldo Arenas (1943–90) Cuban writer. *Before Night Falls* (Dolores M. Koch, tr.; 2001)

2 The vicious circle of fear, prejudice and ignorance has increased the spread of AIDS to an alarming level. Due to fear and prejudice, many still do not want to listen. After all, AIDS is a killer.
Princess Diana (1961–97) British princess. February 1993. *Independent* (February 17, 1993)

3 When you have AIDS, you're judged on how much sex you've had and what kind. There's nothing wrong with putting your arms around someone, holding them, feeling great.
Harvey Fierstein (b. 1954) US actor and playwright. *Playboy* (August 1988)

4 Now as I watch the progress of the plague,
The friends surrounding me fall sick, grow thin,
And drop away.
Thom Gunn (b. 1929) British poet. Referring to AIDS. 'The Missing', *The Man with Night Sweats* (1992)

5 I stare at death in a mirror behind the bar
And wonder when I sacrificed my blood,
And how I could not recognise the face
That smiled with the mouth, the eyes, of death—
In Manchester, London or Amsterdam.
I do not hate that face, only the bell.
Adam Johnson (1975–93) British poet. 'The Playground Bell' (1992)

6 If you turn your back on these people, you yourself are an animal. You may be a well-dressed animal, but you are nevertheless an animal.
Ed Koch (b. 1924) US lawyer and politician. Referring to people with AIDS. State of the City Address, New York City (March 16, 1987)

7 We're all going to go crazy, living this epidemic every minute, while the rest of the world goes on out there, all around us, as if nothing is happening . . . We're living through war, but where they're living it's peacetime, and we're all in the same country.
Larry Kramer (b. 1935) US playwright. *The Normal Heart* (1985)

8 The way to stop the spread of HIV is not to make sex illegal, but to make it safe.
Ian McKellen (b. 1939) British actor. *Times* (December 5, 1991)

9 Every time you sleep with a boy you sleep with all his old girlfriends.
Mottos and Slogans. 1987. AIDS education slogan.

10 AIDS obliges people to think of sex as having, possibly the direst of consequences: suicide. Or murder.
Susan Sontag (b. 1933) US writer. *AIDS and its Metaphors* (1989), ch. 7

11 If art is to confront AIDS more honestly than the media have done, it must begin in tact, avoid humour and end in anger.
Edmund White (b. 1940) US writer. 1987. Quoted in *A Queer Reader* (Patrick Higgins, ed.; 1993)

Alcohol

see also **Drinks and Drinking, Drugs**

1 I'm so holy that when I touch wine, it turns into water.
Sir Aga Khan III (1877–1957) Indian religious leader and statesman. Remark in defence of drinking alcohol. Quoted in *Who's Really Who* (Compton Miller; 1983)

2 So who's in a hurry?
Robert Benchley (1889–1945) US humorist, writer, editor, and critic. When asked whether he knew that drinking was a slow death. Attrib.

3 Freedom and Whisky gang tegither!
Robert Burns (1759–96) Scottish poet and songwriter. 'The Author's Earnest Cry and Prayer' (1786), l. 185

4 Alcohol is like love: the first kiss is magic, the second is intimate, the third is routine. After that you just take the girl's clothes off.
Raymond Chandler (1888–1959) US novelist. *The Long Goodbye* (1953)

5 He knew the tavernes wel in every toun.
Geoffrey Chaucer (1343?–1400) English poet. Referring to the friar. 'The General Prologue', *The Canterbury Tales* (1390?), l. 240, quoted in *The Works of Geoffrey Chaucer* (F. N. Robinson, ed.; 1957)

6 Apart from cheese and tulips, the main product of the country is advocaat, a drink made from lawyers.
Alan Coren (b. 1938) British writer and humorist. Referring to Holland. 'All You Need to Know about Europe', *The Sanity Inspector* (1974)

7 First you take a drink, then the drink takes a drink, then the drink takes you.
F. Scott Fitzgerald (1896–1940) US writer. 1964. Quoted in *Ackroyd* (Jules Feiffer; 1977)

8 Oh many a peer of England brews
Livelier liquor than the Muse
And malt does more than Milton can
To justify God's ways to man.
A. E. Housman (1859–1936) British poet and classicist. Referring to beer, of which malt is one of the ingredients. 'The Welsh Marches', *A Shropshire Lad* (1896), no. 62, st. 2, quoted in *The Collected Poems of A. E. Housman* (John Carter, ed.; 1967)

9 The sway of alcohol over mankind is unquestionably due to its power to stimulate the mystical faculties of human nature.
William James (1842–1910) US psychologist and philosopher. *The Varieties of Religious Experience* (1902)

10 We drink one another's health and spoil our own.
Jerome K. Jerome (1859–1927) British novelist and playwright. 'On Eating and Drinking', *Idle Thoughts of an Idle Fellow* (1886)

11 A tavern chair is the throne of human felicity.
Samuel Johnson (1709–84) British lexicographer and writer. 1755. Quoted in 'Extracts from Hawkin's Life of Samuel Johnson', *Johnsonian Miscellanies* (G. B. Hill, ed.; 1897), vol. 2

12 Claret is the liquor for boys; port for men; but he who aspires to be a hero must drink brandy.
Samuel Johnson (1709–84) British lexicographer and writer. April 7, 1779. Quoted in *Life of Samuel Johnson* (James Boswell; 1791)

13 I've made it a rule never to drink by daylight and never to refuse a drink after dark.
H. L. Mencken (1880–1956) US journalist, critic, and editor. *New York Post* (September 18, 1945)

14 Candy
Is dandy
But liquor
Is quicker.
Ogden Nash (1902–71) US humorist. 'Reflection on Ice-Breaking', *Hard Lines* (1931)

15 When money's tight and it's hard to get
And your horse has also ran,
When all you have is a heap of debt—
A PINT OF PLAIN IS YOUR ONLY MAN.
Flann O'Brien (1911–66) Irish novelist and journalist. *At Swim-Two-Birds* (1939)

16 A torchlight procession marching down your throat.
John L. O'Sullivan (1813–95) US writer. Referring to whisky. Quoted in *Collections and Recollections* (G. W. E. Russell; 1898), ch. 19

17 MACDUFF What three things does drink especially provoke?
PORTER Marry, sir, nose-painting, sleep, and urine.
William Shakespeare (1564–1616) English poet and playwright. *Macbeth* (1606), Act 2, Scene 3

18 PORTER It provokes the desire, but it takes away the performance. Therefore much drink may be said to be an equivocator with lecher.
William Shakespeare (1564–1616) English poet and playwright. *Macbeth* (1606), Act 2, Scene 3

19 I am only a beer teetotaller, not a champagne teetotaller.
George Bernard Shaw (1856–1950) Irish playwright. *Candida* (1904), Act 3

20 Alcohol is a very necessary article . . . It enables Parliament to do things at eleven at night that no sane person would do at eleven in the morning.
George Bernard Shaw (1856–1950) Irish playwright. *Major Barbara* (1907), Act 2

21 Gin was mother's milk to her.
George Bernard Shaw (1856–1950) Irish playwright. *Pygmalion* (1914)

22 Well, then, my stomach must just digest in its waistcoat.
Richard Brinsley Sheridan (1751–1816) Irish-born British playwright and politician. On being warned that his drinking would destroy the coat of his stomach. Quoted in *The Fine Art of Political Wit* (L. Harris; 1965)

23 If I had all the money I've spent on drink, I'd go out and spend it on drink.
Vivian Stanshall (1943–95) British rock musician and humorist. Attrib.

24 We were to do more business after dinner; but after dinner is after dinner—an old saying and a true, 'much drinking, little thinking'.
Jonathan Swift (1667–1745) Irish writer and clergyman. *Journal to Stella* (February 26, 1712)

25 There are two things that will be believed of any man whatsoever, and one of them is that he has taken to drink.
Booth Tarkington (1869–1946) US novelist. *Penrod* (1914), ch. 10

26 An alcoholic is someone you don't like who drinks as much as you do.
Dylan Thomas (1914–53) Welsh poet, playwright, and short-story writer. Quoted in *Life of Dylan Thomas* (Constantine Fitzgibbon; 1965), ch. 6

27 It was my Uncle George who discovered that alcohol was a food well in advance of modern medical thought.
P. G. Wodehouse (1881–1975) British-born US humorous writer. *The Inimitable Jeeves* (1923), ch. 16

Alibis and Excuses

see also **Apologies**, **Mistakes**

1   He said true things, but called them by wrong
    names.
    Robert Browning (1812–89) British poet. 'Bishop Blougram's
    Apology', *Men and Women* (1855), l. 996

2   Macavity, Macavity, there's no one like
    Macavity,
    There never was a Cat of such deceitfulness and
    suavity.
    He always has an alibi, and one or two to spare:
    At whatever time the deed took place—
    MACAVITY WASN'T THERE!
    T. S. Eliot (1888–1965) US-born British poet and playwright. 'Macavity:
    The Mystery Cat', *Old Possum's Book of Practical Cats*
    (1939)

3   A man always has two reasons for what he
    does—a good one and the real one.
    John Pierpont Morgan (1837–1913) US financier, art collector, and
    philanthropist. Quoted in *Roosevelt: The Story of a Friendship*
    (Owen Wister; 1930)

4   I have two huge lions tearing at my flanks, the
    so-called Emperor Otto and John, King of
    England. Both try with all their might to upset
    the Kingdom of France. I cannot leave the
    country myself or do without my son here.
    Philip II (1165–1223) French monarch. Explaining his refusal to
    crusade against the Albigensian heretics. Remark to Pope
    Innocent III (13th century), attrib.

5   One of man's greatest failings is that he looks
    almost always for an excuse in the misfortune
    that befalls him through his own fault, before
    looking for a remedy—which means he often
    finds the remedy too late.
    Cardinal de Retz (1613–79) French ecclesiastic and politician. *Mémoires*
    (1717)

6   I have invented an invaluable permanent invalid
    called Bunbury, in order that I may be able to go
    down into the country whenever I choose.
    Oscar Wilde (1854–1900) Irish poet, playwright, and wit. *The
    Importance of Being Earnest* (1895), Act 1

Ambition

see also **Achievement**, **Hope**, **Success**

1   He does not wish to appear the best, but to be it.
    Aeschylus (525?–456 BC) Greek tragedian and dramatist. *Seven Against
    Thebes* (467 BC), l. 592

2   Ah, but a man's reach should exceed his grasp,
    Or what's a heaven for?
    Robert Browning (1812–89) British poet. 'Andrea del Sarto', *Men
    and Women* (1855), ll. 97–8

3   Well it is known that ambition can creep as well
    as soar.
    Edmund Burke (1729–97) Irish-born British statesman and political
    philosopher. *Letters on a Regicide Peace* (1796), letter 1

4   What millions died—that Caesar might be great!
    Thomas Campbell (1777–1844) Scottish poet. 'Pleasures of Hope'
    (1799), pt. 2

5   It is important what you still have planned at the
    end. It shows the extent of injustice in your
    death.
    Elias Canetti (1905–94) Bulgarian-born writer. *The Human Province*
    (1973)

6   She had, I kid you not, left lipstick on every pair
    of underpants further up the hierarchy than
    assistant director on her way to the top.
    Angela Carter (1940–92) British novelist, essayist, and short-story writer.
    Wise Children (1991)

7   No man is sure he does not need to climb.
    It is not human to feel safely placed.
    William Empson (1906–84) British poet and literary critic. 'Reflection
    from Anita Loos', *Collected Poems* (Robin Skelton, ed.; 1955)

8   I've got a great ambition to die of exhaustion
    rather than boredom.
    Angus Grossart (b. 1937) Scottish banker. *Sunday Telegraph*
    (September 16, 1984)

9   With a suitcase full of clothes and underwear in
    my hand and an indomitable will in my heart, I
    set out for Vienna . . . I too hoped to become
    'something'.
    Adolf Hitler (1889–1945) Austrian-born German dictator. *Mein Kampf*
    (1933)

10 Mama exhorted her children at every opportunity
    to 'jump at de sun'. We might not land on the
    sun, but at least we would get off the ground.
    Zora Neale Hurston (1891?–1960) US writer and folklorist. *Dust Tracks
    on a Road* (1942)

11 Your legacy should be that you made it better
    than it was when you got it.
    Lee Iacocca (b. 1924) US business executive. *Talking Straight* (1988)

12 If I can conceive it and believe it, I can achieve it.
    It's not my *ap*titude but my *att*itude that will
    determine my *alt*itude—*with a little intestinal
    fortitude!*
    Jesse Jackson (b. 1941) US clergyman, civil rights leader, and politician.
    Ebony (August 1988)

13 Every man has a lurking wish to appear
    considerable in his native place.
    Samuel Johnson (1709–84) British lexicographer and writer. July 17,
    1771. Quoted in Letter to Sir Joshua Reynolds, *Life of
    Samuel Johnson* (James Boswell; 1791)

14 I would sooner fail than not be among the
    greatest.
    John Keats (1795–1821) English poet. Letter to James Hessey
    (October 8, 1818), quoted in *Letters of John Keats* (H. E.
    Rollins, ed.; 1958), vol. 1

15 I believe that this nation should commit itself to
    achieving the goal, before this decade is out, of
    landing a man on the Moon and returning him
    safely to earth.
    John Fitzgerald Kennedy (1917–63) US president. Address to joint
    session of Congress (May 25, 1961)

16 A slave has but one master; an ambitious man
    has as many masters as there are people who
    may be useful in bettering his position.
    Jean de La Bruyère (1645–96) French essayist and moralist. *Characters,
    or the Manners of the Age* (1688)

17 If you would hit the mark, you must aim a little
    above it;
    Every arrow that flies feels the attraction of
    earth.
    Henry Wadsworth Longfellow (1807–82) US poet. *Elegiac Verse* (1880)

18 Because it is there.
    George Mallory (1886–1924) British mountaineer. In reply to the
    question 'Why do you want to climb Mount Everest?' *New
    York Times* (March 18, 1923)

19 For the resounding glory of eras to come,
For the lofty tribe of people then,
I've relinquished the cup at the elder's feast
And my happiness and my honour.

Osip Mandelstam (1891–1938) Russian poet, writer, and translator.
'Wolf' (1931), ll. 1–4, quoted in *The Eyesight of Wasps*
(James Greene, tr.; 1989)

20 Be ashamed to die until you have won some
victory for humanity.

Horace Mann (1796–1859) US educator. Commencement Address,
Antioch College, Yellow Springs, Ohio (1859)

21 Ambition, in a private man a vice,
Is in a prince the virtue.

Philip Massinger (1583–1640) English playwright. *The Bashful Lover*
(1636), Act 1, Scene 2

22 A woman who pulled herself up by her bra
straps.

Bette Midler (b. 1945) US singer and actor. Introducing the singer
Madonna at a concert in New York. Comment (1985)

23 He who does not hope to win has already lost.

José Juaquín Olmedo (1780–1847) Ecuadorian poet and statesman.
Attrib.

24 If you do not raise your eyes you will think that
you are at the highest point.

Antonio Porchia (1886–1968) Italian-born Argentinian writer. *Voces*
(W. S. Merwin, tr.; 1968)

25 Ambition is the grand enemy of all peace.

John Cowper Powys (1872–1963) British novelist, essayist, and poet. *The
Meaning of Culture* (1929)

26 The ripest peach is highest on the tree.

James Whitcomb Riley (1849–1916) US poet. 'The Ripest Peach', st. 1

27 GUILDENSTERN Dreams indeed are ambition.
For the very substance of the ambitious is merely
the shadow of a dream.

William Shakespeare (1564–1616) English poet and playwright. *Hamlet*
(1601), Act 2, Scene 2

28 BRUTUS 'Tis a common proof,
That lowliness is young ambition's ladder,
Whereto the climber-upward turns his face;
But when he once attains the upmost round,
He then unto the ladder turns his back,
Looks in the clouds, scorning the base degrees
By which he did ascend.

William Shakespeare (1564–1616) English poet and playwright. Brutus
persuading himself of Caesar's ambition. *Julius Caesar* (1599),
Act 2, Scene 1

29 O sacred hunger of ambitious minds.

Edmund Spenser (1552?–99) English poet. *The Faerie Queene*
(1596), bk. 5, can. 12, st. 1

30 And he that strives to touch the stars,
Oft stumbles at a straw.

Edmund Spenser (1552?–99) English poet. 'July', *The Shepherd's
Calendar* (1579)

31 Wealth I seek not; hope nor love,
Nor a friend to know me;
All I seek, the heaven above
And the road below me.

Robert Louis Stevenson (1850–94) Scottish novelist, essayist, and poet.
'The Vagabond', *Songs of Travel* (1895), st. 4

32 Ambition often puts Men upon doing the
meanest offices; so climbing is performed in the
same position with creeping.

Jonathan Swift (1667–1745) Irish writer and clergyman. Attrib.

33 There is always room at the top.

Daniel Webster (1782–1852) US lawyer, politician, and orator. When
advised not to become a lawyer because the profession was
overcrowded. John Braine (1922–86) borrowed the phrase for
his novel *Room at the Top* (1957). Attrib.

34 Ambition, madam, is a great man's madness.

John Webster (1578?–1632?) English playwright. *The Duchess of Malfi*
(1623), Act 1, Scene 1

American Cities

see also **Cities**, **United States**

1 It is a joint where the bulls and the foxes live
well and the lambs wind up head-down from the
hook.

Nelson Algren (1909–81) US novelist and short-story writer. Referring to
Chicago, Illinois. *Chicago: City on the Make* (1951)

2 San Francisco is perhaps the most European of
all American cities.

Cecil Beaton (1904–80) British photographer and theatrical designer. *It
Gives Me Great Pleasure* (1955)

3 I knew that what you needed in a big American
city was a deep no-affect belt, a critical mass of
indifference . . . But now the moronic inferno
had caught up with me.

Saul Bellow (b. 1915) Canadian-born US writer. Source of the title of
Martin Amis's book on contemporary America, *Moronic
Inferno* (1986). *Humboldt's Gift* (1975)

4 New York makes one think of the collapse of
civilization, about Sodom and Gomorrah, the end
of the world. The end wouldn't come as a
surprise here. Many people already bank on it.

Saul Bellow (b. 1915) Canadian-born US writer. *Mr. Sammler's Planet*
(1970), pt. 1

5 What is barely hinted at in other American cities
is condensed and enlarged in New York.

Saul Bellow (b. 1915) Canadian-born US writer. Quoted in *New York*
(Mike Marquese and Bill Harris; 1985)

6 I had read so much for so long about murders
and street crime that I felt a personal gratitude to
anyone who left me alone. I wanted to hand out
cards that said, 'Thank you for not killing me'.

Bill Bryson (b. 1951) US writer. *The Lost Continent* (1989), ch. 14

7 To qualify for a Los Angelean, you need three
things: (a) a driver's licence; (b) your own tennis
court; (c) a preference for snorting cocaine.

Michael Caine (b. 1933) British actor. *Photoplay* (February 1984)

8 The reason there's so much smog in L.A. is so
God can't see what they're doing down there.

Glen Campbell (b. 1934) US singer. Quoted in *The Wit and
Wisdom of Rock and Roll* (Maxim Jabukowski, ed.; 1983)

9 The present in New York is so powerful that the
past is lost.

John Jay Chapman (1862–1933) US writer. Letter (1909)

10 New York, New York—a helluva town,
The Bronx is up but the Battery's down.

Betty Comden (b. 1915) US librettist and lyricist. 'New York, New
York', *New York, New York* (co-written with Adolph Green;
1945)

11 I Left My Heart in San Francisco

Douglas Cross, US songwriter. 1954. Song title. Popularized by
Tony Bennett.

12 It is sometimes called the City of Magnificent Distances but it might with greater propriety be termed the City of Magnificent Intentions.
Charles Dickens (1812–70) British novelist. Referring to Washington, DC. *American Notes* (1842)

13 A good part of any day in Los Angeles is spent driving alone, through streets devoid of meaning to the driver, which is one reason the place exhilarates some people, and floods others with an amorphous unease.
Joan Didion (b. 1934) US journalist and writer. 1991. 'Pacific Distances', *Sentimental Journeys* (1992)

14 We say the cows laid out Boston. Well there are worse surveyors.
Ralph Waldo Emerson (1803–82) US poet and essayist. 'Wealth', *The Conduct of Life* (1860)

15 Los Angeles is where you've got to be an actor. You have no choice. You go there or New York. I flipped a coin . . . It came up New York. So I flipped it again.
Harrison Ford (b. 1942) US film actor. *Cinema* (1981)

16 New York . . . that unnatural city where every one is an exile, none more so than the American.
Charlotte Perkins Gilman (1860–1935) US feminist writer. *The Living of Charlotte Perkins Gilman: An Autobiography* (1935), ch. 20

17 A city where everyone mutinies but no one deserts.
Harry Hershfield, US cartoonist. Referring to New York. *New York Post* (1974)

18 This city has been an act of real estate rather than an act of God or man.
Ada Louise Huxtable (b. 1921?) US architecture critic. Referring to Texas City, Texas. *New York Times* (1977)

19 To live sanely in Los Angeles . . . you have to cultivate the art of staying awake.
Christopher Isherwood (1904–86) British-born US writer. 1947. 'Los Angeles', *Exhumations* (1966)

20 That Indian swamp in the wilderness.
Thomas Jefferson (1743–1826) US president. Referring to Washington, DC. Attrib.

21 New York is the most fatally fascinating thing in America.
James Weldon Johnson (1871–1938) US writer, lawyer, and diplomat. *The Autobiography of an Ex-Colored Man* (1912)

22 Now I could see Denver looming ahead of me like the Promised Land, way out there beneath the stars, across the prairies of Iowa and the plains of Nebraska.
Jack Kerouac (1922–69) US writer. *On the Road* (1957), pt. 1, ch. 3

23 I wandered out like a haggard ghost, and there she was, Frisco—long, bleak streets with trolley wires all shrouded in fog and whiteness.
Jack Kerouac (1922–69) US writer. Said by Sal Paradise on first arriving, by bus, in San Francisco. *On the Road* (1957), pt. 1, ch. 11

24 LA is the loneliest and most brutal of American cities; New York gets god-awful cold in the winter but there's a feeling of wacky comradeship . . . LA is a jungle.
Jack Kerouac (1922–69) US writer. *On the Road* (1957), pt. 1, ch. 13

25 New York with its millions and millions hustling forever for a buck among themselves, the mad dream—grabbing, taking, giving, sighing, dying, just so they could be buried in those awful cemetery cities beyond Long Island City.
Jack Kerouac (1922–69) US writer. Said by Sal Paradise on first returning to New York after his trip to the West Coast. *On the Road* (1957), pt. 1, ch. 14

26 New York now leads the world's great cities in the number of people around whom you shouldn't make a sudden move.
David Letterman (b. 1947) US entertainer. *Late Night with David Letterman* (February 9, 1984)

27 Not by the earthquake daunted
Nor by new fears made tame,
Painting her face and laughing
Plays her a new-found game.
Vachel Lindsay (1879–1931) US poet. Referring to San Francisco. 'The Lily that will not Repent', *Collected Poems* (1923)

28 New York was Heaven to me. And Harlem was Seventh Heaven.
Malcolm X (1925–65) US Black activist. *The Autobiography of Malcolm X* (1965), ch. 5

29 Nineteen suburbs in search of a metropolis.
H. L. Mencken (1880–1956) US journalist, critic, and editor. Referring to Los Angeles. *Americana* (1925)

30 Savannah is a living tomb about which there still clings a sensuous aura as in old Corinth.
Henry Miller (1891–1980) US novelist. Referring to Savannah, Georgia, and the ancient city of Corinth in Greece. *The Air-Conditioned Nightmare* (1945)

31 This embryo capital, where Fancy sees
Squares in morasses, obelisks in trees;
Which second-sighted seers, ev'n now, adorn
With shrines unbuilt and heroes yet unborn.
Thomas Moore (1779–1852) Irish poet. Referring to Washington, DC. 'To Thomas Hume, Esq., M.D., from the City of Washington', *Poems Relating to America* (1806)

32 'This is a city of water', said Mr. Garner. 'Everything travels by water and what the rivers can't carry the canals take. A queen of a city . . . If you have to live in a city—this is it'.
Toni Morrison (b. 1931) US novelist. Referring to Cincinnati, Ohio. *Beloved* (1987)

33 Washington *en petit*, seen through a reversed glass.
Frederick Law Olmsted (1822–1903) US landscape architect. Referring to Austin, Texas. *A Journey through Texas* (1857)

34 Philadelphia, a metropolis sometimes known as the City of Brotherly Love, but more accurately as the City of Bleak November Afternoons.
S. J. Perelman (1904–79) US humorist. 'Westward Ho!' (1948)

35 San Narciso lay further south, near L.A. Like many named places in California it was less an identifiable city than a group of concepts.
Thomas Pynchon (b. 1937) US novelist. *The Crying of Lot 49* (1966), ch. 2

36 It's a mass of irony for all the world to see It's the nation's capital, it's Washington, D.C.
Gil Scott-Heron (b. 1949) US musician, writer, and poet. Song lyric. 'Washington D.C.' (1982)

37 There are two million interesting people in New York and only seventy-eight in Los Angeles.
Neil Simon (b. 1927) US playwright. Interview, *Playboy* (February 1979)

38 By Grand Central Station I Sat Down and Wept
Elizabeth Smart (1913–86) US poet and novelist. 1945. Book title. Paraphrasing Psalm 137:1.

39 American cities are like badger holes, ringed with trash—all of them—surrounded by piles of wrecked and rusting automobiles, and almost smothered with rubbish.
John Steinbeck (1902–68) US novelist. *Travels with Charley: In Search of America* (1962), pt. 2

40 A week in Vegas is like stumbling into a Time Warp, a regression to the late fifties. Which is wholly understandable when you see the people who come here, the Big Spenders from places like Denver and Dallas.

Hunter S. Thompson (b. 1939) US writer and journalist. November 1971. *Fear and Loathing in Las Vegas* (1972), ch. 8

41 In Boston they ask, How much does he know? In New York, How much is he worth? In Philadelphia, Who were his parents?

Mark Twain (1835–1910) US writer and humorist. *What Paul Bourger Thinks of Us* (1897)

42 City of orgies, walks, and joys.

Walt Whitman (1819–92) US poet. Referring to Manhattan. 'City of Orgies', *Calamus* (1860), no. 18

43 I too lived, Brooklyn of ample hills was mine, I too walked the streets of Manhattan island, and bathed in the waters around it.

Walt Whitman (1819–92) US poet. 'Crossing Brooklyn Ferry', *Leaves of Grass* (1856), can. 5, ll. 4–6

44 New York is a small place when it comes to the part of it that wakes up just as the rest is going to bed.

P. G. Wodehouse (1881–1975) British-born US humorous writer. 'The Aunt and the Sluggard', *My Man Jeeves* (1919)

45 One belongs to New York instantly. One belongs to it as much in five minutes as in five years.

Thomas Wolfe (1900–38) US novelist. *The Web and the Rock* (1939)

46 The Rome, the Paris, the London of the 20th century, the dense magnetic rock, the irresistible destination of all those who insist on being where things are happening.

Tom Wolfe (b. 1930) US journalist and novelist. Referring to Manhattan, New York. *The Bonfire of the Vanities* (1987)

American Imperialism

see also Imperialism, United States

1 It is worse than immoral, it's a mistake.

Dean Acheson (1893–1971) US lawyer and statesman. Describing the Vietnam war. Attrib.

2 The way to get out of Vietnam is to declare victory and leave.

George Aiken (1892–1984) US politician. Referring to the Vietnam War (1959–75). Quoted in *Time* (December 31, 1984)

3 Our goal is not the conquest of Iraq. It is the liberation of Kuwait.

George Bush (b. 1924) US president. Referring to the Gulf War (1991). *Times* (January 16, 1991)

4 I hope to see the day when the American flag will gloat over every square foot of the British North American possessions clear to the North Pole.

Kenneth Clark (1850–1921) US politician. Speech to the House of Representatives (June 1911)

5 Americans think of themselves collectively as a huge rescue squad on a twenty-four-hour call to any spot on the globe where dispute and conflict may erupt.

Eldridge Cleaver (b. 1935) US writer and civil rights activist. 'Rallying Round the Flag', *Soul on Ice* (1968)

6 As long as Donald Duck strolls with his smiling countenance so *innocently* about the streets of our country, as long as Donald is power and our collective representative, then imperialism and the bourgeoisie can sleep peacefully.

Ariel Dorfman (b. 1942) Chilean playwright and novelist. *How to Read Donald Duck* (with Armand Mattelart; 1971)

7 Unless Americans come to realize that they are not stronger in the world because they have the bomb but weaker because of their vulnerability to atomic attack, they are not likely to conduct their policy at Lake Success or in their relations with Russia in a spirit that furthers the arrival at an understanding.

Albert Einstein (1879–1955) German-born US physicist. Following its establishment in 1945 the United Nations General Assembly met temporarily in Lake Success, New York State, pending the setting up of a permanent headquarters. Open letter (1947)

8 The American war in Vietnam destroyed three ancient civilizations. They had survived through millennia everything history can do, which is always plenty, but they could not survive us, who understood nothing about them, nor valued them, and do not grieve for them.

Martha Gellhorn (1908–98) US journalist and author. 'Last Words on Vietnam, 1987', *The Face of War* (1988)

9 If World War I enabled American cinema to ruin French cinema, World War II, together with the advent of television, enabled it to finance, that is to say ruin, all the cinemas of Europe.

Jean-Luc Godard (b. 1930) French film director. *Histoires du Cinéma* (1989)

10 You've got to forget about this civilian. Whenever you drop bombs, you're going to hit civilians.

Barry Goldwater (1909–98) US politician. Speech, New York (January 23, 1967)

11 The contemporary American faith that it is a universal nation implies that all humans are born American, and become anything else by accident—or error.

John Gray (b. 1948) British academic. *False Dawn* (1998)

12 The security we profess to seek in foreign adventures we will lose in our decaying cities.

Martin Luther King, Jr. (1929–68) US civil rights leader. 1967. Referring to US Vietnam policy. Address, Riverside Church, New York, *History Today* (April 1998), vol. 48

13 US foreign policy at bottom is to bring Canada into as many situations affecting themselves as possible with a view to leading ultimately to the annexation of our two countries.

W. L. Mackenzie King (1874–1950) Canadian prime minister. Diary (June 30, 1950)

14 My solution to the problem would be to tell them . . . they've got to draw in their horns or we're going to bomb them into the Stone Age.

Curtis Emerson LeMay (1906–90) US air-force chief. Referring to the North Vietnamese. *Mission with LeMay* (1965)

15 If the Devil was devoted to destroying all belief in conservative values among the intelligent and prosperous, he could not have picked a finer instrument to his purpose than the war in Vietnam.

Norman Mailer (b. 1923) US novelist and journalist. *St. George and the Godfather* (1972)

16 The average good Christian American secretly loved the war in Vietnam ... America needed the war. It would need a war so long as technology expanded on every road of communication, and the cities and corporations spread like cancer.

Norman Mailer (b. 1923) US novelist and journalist. 'History as Novel: The Steps of the Pentagon', *The Armies of the Night* (1968), bk. 1, pt. 4, ch. 7

17 In every other great war of this century, we have had the support of what is generally accepted as the decent opinion of mankind. We do not have that today.

Eugene J. McCarthy (b. 1916) US politician and writer. Referring to the Vietnam War (1959–75). *The Limits of Power* (1967)

18 Although we sought to do the right thing—and believed we were doing the right thing—in my judgment, hindsight proves us wrong.

Robert McNamara (b. 1916) US politician and business executive. *In Retrospect: The Tragedy and Lessons of Vietnam* (co-written with Brian Van de Mark; 1995)

19 A mighty nation moving west,
With all its steely sinews set
Against the living forest.
Hear the shouts, the shots of pioneers,
The rended forests, rolling wheels.

Joaquin Miller (1839–1913) US poet. 'Westward Ho!', *Songs of the Sierra* (1871), ll. 3–7

20 The US has broken the second rule of war. That is, don't go fighting with your land army on the mainland of Asia. Rule One is don't march on Moscow. I developed these two rules myself.

Sir Bernard Law Montgomery of Alamein (1887–1976) British field marshal. Referring to American policy in Vietnam. Speech to the House of Lords, quoted in *Hansard* (May 30, 1962)

21 Hey, hey, LBJ, How many kids did you kill today?

Mottos and Slogans. 1960s. Anti-Vietnam War slogan. 'LBJ' refers to President Lyndon Baines Johnson.

22 It became necessary to destroy the town of Ben Tre to save it.

Newspapers. Said by a US major in Vietnam. *Observer* (February 11, 1968), 'Sayings of the Week'

23 We must never forget that if the war in Vietnam is lost ... the right of free speech will be extinguished throughout the world.

Richard Nixon (1913–94) US president. *New York Times* (October 27, 1965)

24 If Kuwait and Saudi Arabia sold bananas or oranges, the Americans would not go there. They are there because Kuwait is an oil monarchy.

Julius Kambarage Nyerere (1922–99) Tanzanian president. September 27, 1990. Referring to the international response to the Iraqi invasion of Kuwait (August 1990). *Independent* (September 28, 1990)

25 The Americans don't really understand what's going on in Bosnia. To them it's the unspellables killing the unpronounceables.

P. J. O'Rourke (b. 1947) US writer and humorist. *Sun* (1993)

26 A spirit of hostile interference against us ... checking the fulfilment of our manifest destiny to overspread the continent allotted by Providence for the free development of our yearly multiplying millions.

John L. O'Sullivan (1813–95) US writer. Referring to opposition to the annexation of Texas by the United States. *United States Magazine and Democratic Review* (1845), vol. 17

27 I believe the US is a truly monstrous force in the world, now off the leash for obvious reasons.

Harold Pinter (b. 1930) British playwright, theatre director, and screenwriter. *Independent* (September 20, 1993)

28 A stirring victory for the forces of aggression against lawlessness.

Dan Quayle (b. 1947) US politician. Referring to the Gulf War. Attrib.

29 It's silly talking about how many years we will have to spend in Vietnam when we could pave the whole country and put parking stripes on it and still be home for Christmas.

Ronald Reagan (b. 1911) US president and actor. Interview, *Fresno Bee* (October 10, 1965)

30 To win in Vietnam, we will have to exterminate a nation.

Benjamin Spock (1903–98) US pediatrician. *Dr. Spock on Vietnam* (1968), ch. 7

31 We're Americans, we're a simple people, but if you piss us off we'll bomb your cities.

Robin Williams (b. 1951) US actor and comedian. Attrib.

32 I want to take this occasion to say that the United States will never again seek one additional foot of territory by conquest.

Woodrow Wilson (1856–1924) US president. Speech, Mobile, Alabama (October 27, 1913)

American Literature

see also Literature, United States

1 Novelist, essayist, dramatist, epigrammist, television polemicist, controversialist, pansexualist, socialist and socialite: if there is a key to Gore Vidal's public character it has something to do with his towering immodesty, the enjoyable superbity of his self love.

Martin Amis (b. 1949) British writer. *The Moronic Inferno* (1986)

2 The United States was nothing but a vast prison house for Poe, within which he moved in a state of feverish imagination, like someone born to breathe a sweeter air.

Charles Baudelaire (1821–67) French poet. Referring to Edgar Allan Poe. *Edgar Allan Poe, his Life and Works* (1856)

3 By his feeling of guilt and his preoccupation with ethics, Hawthorne is grounded in Puritanism; by his love of beauty and his fantastic invention he is related to ... Edgar Allan Poe.

Jorge Luis Borges (1899–1986) Argentinian writer and poet. Referring to Nathaniel Hawthorne. *An Introduction to American Literature* (1967), ch. 3

4 Faulkner's hallucinatory tendencies are not unworthy of Shakespeare.

Jorge Luis Borges (1899–1986) Argentinian writer and poet. Referring to William Faulkner. *An Introduction to American Literature* (1967), ch. 4

5 Gertrude Stein ... is perhaps less important for her work, unreadable at times and intentionally obscure, than for her personal influence and her curious literary theories.

Jorge Luis Borges (1899–1986) Argentinian writer and poet. *An Introduction to American Literature* (1967), ch. 9

6 Salinger was the perfect *New Yorker* writer, whose promise and celebrity delivered less and less.

Leo Brandy, US academic. Referring to J. D. Salinger. Quoted in 'Naturalists, and Novelists of Manners', *Harvard Guide to Contemporary American Writing* (Daniel Hoffman, ed.; 1979)

7 Fitzgerald was an alcoholic, a spendthrift and a superstar playboy possessed of a beauty and a glamour that only a Byron could support without artistic ruination.
Anthony Burgess (1917–93) British writer and critic. Referring to F. Scott Fitzgerald. *Observer* (February 7, 1982)

8 If it is true that talent recreates life while genius has the additional gift of crowning it with myths, Melville is first and foremost a creator of myths.
Albert Camus (1913–60) Algerian-born French novelist, essayist, and playwright. Referring to Herman Melville. 'Herman Melville' (1952), quoted in *Albert Camus: Selected Essays and Notebooks* (P. Thody, ed., tr.; 1970)

9 Melville's . . . books . . . are at one and the same time both obvious and obscure, as dark as the noonday sun and yet as clear as deep water.
Albert Camus (1913–60) Algerian-born French novelist, essayist, and playwright. Referring to Herman Melville. 'Herman Melville' (1952), quoted in *Albert Camus: Selected Essays and Notebooks* (P. Thody, ed., tr.; 1970)

10 He is the bully on the Left Bank, always ready to twist the milksop's arm.
Cyril Connolly (1903–74) British writer and journalist. Referring to Ernest Hemingway. *Observer* (May 24, 1964)

11 The average American loves his family. If he has any love left over for some other person, he generally selects Mark Twain.
Thomas Alva Edison (1847–1931) US inventor. Attrib.

12 Sometimes I don't know whether Zelda and I are real or whether we are characters in one of my novels.
F. Scott Fitzgerald (1896–1940) US writer. Said of himself and his wife. Quoted in *A Second Flowering* (Malcolm Cowley; 1973)

13 In a life so retired it was inevitable that the main events should be the death of friends, and Emily Dickinson became a prolific writer of notes of condolence.
Northrop Frye (1912–91) Canadian academic. Quoted in *Major Writers of America* (Perry Miller, ed.; 1962)

14 Jack Kerouac sat beside me on a busted rusty iron pole, companion,
we thought the same thoughts of the sun, bleak and blue and sad-eyed, surrounded
by the gnarled steel roots of trees of machinery.
Allen Ginsberg (1926–97) US poet. 'Sunflower Sutra', *Howl and Other Poems* (1956)

15 The work of Henry James always seemed divisible by a simple dynastic arrangement into three reigns: James I, James II, and the Old Pretender.
Philip Guedalla (1889–1944) British writer. 'Some Critics', *Supers and Supermen* (1920)

16 All modern American literature comes from one book by Mark Twain called *Huckleberry Finn*.
Ernest Hemingway (1899–1961) US writer. *The Adventures of Huckleberry Finn* was published in 1884. *Green Hills of Africa* (1935), ch. 1

17 It is not my fault that certain so-called Bohemian elements have found in my writings something to hang their peculiar beatnik theories on.
Jack Kerouac (1922–69) US writer. *New York Journal-American* (December 8, 1960)

18 We are beat, man. Beat means beatific, it means you get the beat.
Jack Kerouac (1922–69) US writer. Quoted in *Playboy* (1988)

19 Our American professors like their literature clear and cold and pure and very dead.
Sinclair Lewis (1885–1951) US novelist. On receiving a Nobel Prize in literature. (December 12, 1930)

20 It is very consistent and well-assimilated Darwinism, adorned, unfortunately, by a cheap and poorly comprehended Nietzscheanism. However, it poses as the wisdom of nature itself and as the permanent law of life.
Osip Mandelstam (1891–1938) Russian poet, writer, and translator. Referring to the anti-intellectual philosophy of Jack London's writing as a response to technological progress. 'Jack London' (1912), quoted in *The Collected Critical Prose and Letters of Osip Mandelstam* (J. G. Harris, ed., tr., C. Link, tr.; 1991)

21 America . . . initiated her own particular philology from which Whitman emerged; and he, like a new Adam, began giving things names, began behaving like Homer himself, offering a model for a primitive American poetry of nomenclature.
Osip Mandelstam (1891–1938) Russian poet, writer, and translator. 'On the Nature of the Word' (1925), quoted in *The Collected Critical Prose and Letters of Osip Mandelstam* (J. G. Harris, ed., tr., C. Link, tr.; 1991)

22 My home is not in this world, nor in the next. I am a man without a home, without a friend, without a wife. I am a monster who belongs to a reality that does not exist yet.
Henry Miller (1891–1980) US novelist. *Tropic of Capricorn* (1939)

23 We have to acknowledge that the thing we call 'literature' is more pluralistic now, just as society ought to be. The melting pot never worked. We ought to be able to accept on equal terms everybody from the Hasidim to Walter Lippmann, from the Rastafarians to Ralph Bunche.
Toni Morrison (b. 1931) US novelist. Walter Lippmann was a political journalist and writer, and Ralph Bunche a scholar and diplomat. *Newsweek* (March 30, 1981)

24 Mr. Miller is a discerning though hardboiled person giving his opinions about life. I find his prose difficult to quote, because of the unprintable words which are scattered all over it.
George Orwell (1903–50) British writer. 1935. Reviewing Henry Miller's *Tropic of Cancer* (1934). Quoted in *Collected Essays, Journalism and Letters of George Orwell* (Sonia Orwell and Ian Angus, eds.; 1968), vol. 1

25 That quality of sensitive innocence which Holden Caulfield retained beneath his rebellious mannerisms has developed into a note of religious mysticism.
Ian Ousby, British critic. Holden Caulfield is the hero of J. D. Salinger's novel, *The Catcher in the Rye* (1951). *50 American Novels* (1979)

26 Here is the difference between Dante, Milton, and me. They wrote about hell and never saw the place. I wrote about Chicago after looking the town over for years and years.
Carl Sandburg (1878–1967) US poet and biographer. Quoted in *Carl Sandburg* (Harry Golden; 1961)

27 The Fitzgeralds never got round to seeing the sights because, as Jazz Age celebrities, they were the sights. They wanted to have a good time and a good time was had by all for a short time.
Gore Vidal (b. 1925) US novelist and essayist. 1980. Referring to F. Scott and Zelda Fitzgerald's stay in Europe. 'F. Scott Fitzgerald's Case', *The Second American Revolution* (1982)

28 American writers want to be not good but great; and so are neither.
Gore Vidal (b. 1925) US novelist and essayist. *Two Sisters* (1970)

29 Think of the United States today—the facts of these . . . fifty or sixty nations of equals . . . Think, in comparison, of the petty environage and limited area of the poets of past and present Europe.
Walt Whitman (1819–92) US poet. *Democratic Vistas* (1871)

30 I am the opposite of a stage magician. He gives you illusion that has the appearance of truth. I give you truth in the pleasant disguise of illusion.
Tennessee Williams (1911–83) US playwright. *The Glass Menagerie* (1945), Scene 1

31 Poe gave the sense for the first time in America that literature is *serious*, not a matter of courtesy but of truth.
William Carlos Williams (1883–1963) US poet, novelist, and physician. Referring to Edgar Allan Poe. 'Edgar Allan Poe', *In the American Grain* (1925)

32 Writing a novel about this astonishing metropolis . . . cramming as much of New York City between the covers as you could, was the most tempting, the most challenging, and the most obvious idea that an American writer could possibly have.
Tom Wolfe (b. 1930) US journalist and novelist. *Harper's* (November 1989)

Americans

see also **United States**

1 Americans would rather live next to a pervert heroin addict Communist pornographer than a person with an unkempt lawn.
Dave Barry (b. 1947) US humorist. *The Taming of the Screw* (1983)

2 Americans have a perfect right to exist. But he did often find himself wishing Mr. Rhodes had not enabled them to exercise that right at Oxford.
Max Beerbohm (1872–1956) British essayist, critic, and caricaturist. *Zuleika Dobson* (1911)

3 Most of the people on long-distance buses are one of the following: actively schizoid, armed and dangerous, in a drugged stupor, just released from prison, or nuns.
Bill Bryson (b. 1951) US writer. *The Lost Continent* (1989), ch. 14

4 We become not a melting pot but a beautiful mosaic. Different people, different beliefs, different yearnings, different hopes, different dreams.
Jimmy Carter (b. 1924) US president. Speech, Pittsburgh, Pennsylvania (October 27, 1976)

5 There is nothing the matter with Americans except their ideals. The real American is all right; it is the ideal American who is all wrong.
G. K. Chesterton (1874–1936) British writer and poet. *New York Times* (February 1, 1931)

6 Sure enough at Oxford, I was another Yank half a step behind.
Bill Clinton (b. 1946) US president. Bill Clinton was a Rhodes Scholar at Oxford. *Observer* (June 12, 1994), 'Sayings of the Week'

7 What then is the American, this new man?
Jean de Crèvecoeur (1735–1813) French-born US writer and farmer. *Letters from an American Farmer* (1782)

8 Long Island represents the American's idea of what God would have done with Nature if he'd had the money.
Peter Fleming (1907–71) British travel writer. Letter (September 29, 1929)

9 There are three species: first, the servile American . . . Then there is the conceited American . . . 3rd. The thinking American.
Margaret Fuller (1810–50) US writer and reformer. Referring to the types of 'the American in Europe'. 'Things and Thoughts in Europe', *New York Daily Tribune* (November 27, 1847), quoted in *The Heath Anthology of American Literature* (Paul Lauter, ed.; 1998), vol. 1

10 In the modern world, we Americans are the old inhabitants. We first had political freedom, high industrial production, an economy of abundance.
Paul Goodman (1911–72) US writer, teacher, and psychotherapist. *Growing Up Absurd* (1960)

11 Scratch an American and you get a Seventh Day Adventist every time.
Lord Hailsham (1907–2001) British statesman. *Observer* (June 1, 1969), 'Sayings of the Week'

12 To Americans English manners are far more frightening than none at all.
Randall Jarrell (1914–65) US author and poet. *Pictures from an Institution* (1954), pt. I, ch. 5

13 I am willing to love all mankind, *except an American*.
Samuel Johnson (1709–84) British lexicographer and writer. April 15, 1778. Quoted in *Life of Samuel Johnson* (James Boswell; 1791)

14 Americans have plenty of everything and the best of nothing.
John Keats (b. 1920) US writer. *You Might As Well Live* (1970)

15 There won't be any revolution in America . . . The people are too clean. They spend all their time changing their shirts and washing themselves. You can't feel fierce and revolutionary in a bathroom.
Eric Linklater (1899–1974) British writer. *Juan in America* (1931), pt. 5, ch. 3

16 American women expect to find in their husbands a perfection that English women only hope to find in their butlers.
Somerset Maugham (1874–1965) British writer. *A Writer's Notebook* (1949)

17 When you become used to never being alone you may consider yourself Americanized.
André Maurois (1885–1967) French writer. Attrib.

18 She remembered drifters she had listened to, Americans speaking their own language carefully, scholarly, as if they were in exile from somewhere else invisible yet congruent with the cheered land she lived in.
Thomas Pynchon (b. 1937) US novelist. *The Crying of Lot 49* (1966), ch. 6

19 Americans love being conned if you can do it in a style that is both grand and entertaining.
Ishmael Reed (b. 1938) US writer. *Yellow Back Radio Broke-Down* (1969)

20 In America everybody is of the opinion that he has no social superiors, since all men are equal, but he does not admit that he has no social inferiors.
Bertrand Russell (1872–1970) British philosopher and mathematician. *Unpopular Essays* (1950)

21 Americans tend to identify with foreign societies or cultures projecting a pioneering spirit . . . On the other hand Americans often mistrust or do not have much interest in traditional cultures, even those in the throes of revolutionary renewal.
Edward W. Said (b. 1935) Palestinian-born US writer and educator. 'The Formation of American Public Opinion on the Question of Palestine' (1980)

22 An American is either a Jew, or an anti-Semite, unless he is both at the same time.
Jean-Paul Sartre (1905–80) French philosopher, playwright, and novelist. *The Condemned of Altona* (1960)

23 Americans expect to be loved.
Wole Soyinka (b. 1934) Nigerian novelist, playwright, poet, and lecturer. *The Interpreters* (1965)

24 Born in the USA
Bruce Springsteen (b. 1949) US rock singer and songwriter. 1984. Song title.

25 That strange blend of the commercial traveller, the missionary, and the barbarian conqueror, which was the American abroad.
Olaf Stapledon (1886–1950) British philosopher and science-fiction writer. *Last and First Men* (1930), ch. 3

26 Two generations of Americans know more about the Ford coil than the clitoris, about the planetary system of gears than about the solar system of stars.
John Steinbeck (1902–68) US novelist. *Cannery Row* (1945), ch. 11

27 Any American who is prepared to run for President should automatically, by definition, be disqualified from ever doing so.
Gore Vidal (b. 1925) US novelist and essayist. Attrib.

28 Everybody in America was supposed to grab whatever he could and hold onto it. Some Americans were very good at grabbing and holding, were fabulously well-to-do. Others couldn't get their hands on doodley-squat.
Kurt Vonnegut (b. 1922) US novelist. *Breakfast of Champions* (1973), ch. 1

29 No white American ever thinks that any other race is wholly civilized until he wears the white man's clothes, eats the white man's food, speaks the white man's language and professes the white man's religion.
Booker T. Washington (1856–1915) US educator and political activist. *Up from Slavery* (1901)

30 MRS ALLONBY They say, Lady Hunstanton, that when good Americans die they go to Paris.
LADY HUNSTANTON Indeed? And when bad Americans die, where do they go to?
LORD ILLINGWORTH Oh, they go to America.
Oscar Wilde (1854–1900) Irish poet, playwright, and wit. *A Woman of No Importance* (1893), Act 1

American War of Independence

see also **United States**

1 The history of our revolution will be one continued lie from one end to the other.
John Adams (1735–1826) US president. Letter to Dr. Benjamin Rush (April 4, 1790)

2 We set out to oppose Tyranny in all its Strides, and I hope we shall persevere.
Abraham Clark (1726–94) US politician. Letter to John Hart (February 8, 1777)

3 We must indeed all hang together, or most assuredly, we shall all hang separately.
Benjamin Franklin (1706–90) US statesman and scientist. On signing the Declaration of Independence. Remark (July 4, 1776)

4 I can never suppose this country so far lost to all ideas of self-importance as to be willing to grant America independence; if that could ever be adopted I shall despair of this country being ever preserved from a state of inferiority and consequently falling into a very low class among the European States.
George III (1738–1820) British monarch. Letter to Lord North (March 7, 1780)

5 I know not what course others may take; but as for me, give me liberty or give me death!
Patrick Henry (1736–99) American statesman and orator. Speech to the Virginia Convention (March 23, 1775)

6 We hold these truths to be self-evident: that all men are created equal; that they are endowed by their Creator with certain unalienable rights; that among these are life, liberty, and the pursuit of happiness.
Thomas Jefferson (1743–1826) US president. *Declaration of Independence* (July 4, 1776)

7 When in the course of human events, it becomes necessary for one people to dissolve the political bonds which have connected them with another, and to assume among the powers of the earth the separate and equal station to which the laws of nature's God entitle them, a decent respect to the opinions of mankind requires that they should declare the causes which impel them to the separation.
Thomas Jefferson (1743–1826) US president. *Declaration of Independence* (July 4, 1776), Preamble

8 We fight not to enslave, but to set a country free, and to make room upon the earth for honest men to live in.
Thomas Paine (1737–1809) English writer and political philosopher. *The American Crisis* (September 12, 1777), no. 4

9 I can answer but for three things: a firm belief in the justice of our cause, close attention in the prosecution of it, and the strictest integrity.
George Washington (1732–99) US president. June 19, 1775. Said on being elected to command the army. Quoted in *Quotations in History* (Alan and Veronica Palmer; 1976)

Anarchy

see also **Chaos, Freedom, Politics**

1 The urge for destruction is also a creative urge!
Mikhail Bakunin (1814–76) Russian-born anarchist. Under pseudonym 'Jules Elysard'. 'Die Reaktion in Deutschland', *Jahrbuch für Wissenschaft und Kunst* (1842)

2 Let us therefore trust the eternal Spirit which destroys and annihilates only because it is the unfathomable and eternal source of all life. The passion for destruction is a creative passion too.
Mikhail Bakunin (1814–76) Russian-born anarchist. Quoted in *Bakunin on Anarchy* (Sam Dolgoff, ed.; 1973)

3 I am a Tory Anarchist, I should like everyone to go about doing just as he pleased—short of altering any of the things to which I have grown accustomed.
Max Beerbohm (1872–1956) British essayist, critic, and caricaturist. Attrib.

4 Any training in art is at least a partial training in anarchy.

John Cage (1912–92) US composer. International Dance Course for Professional Choreographers and Composers, Surrey University, Guildford (August 1981)

5 In the culture that secretly subscribes to the piratical ethic of 'every man for himself' . . . the logical culmination of this ethic, on a person-to-person level, is that the weak are seen as the natural and just prey of the strong.

Eldridge Cleaver (b. 1935) US writer and civil rights activist. *Soul on Ice* (1968)

6 No one can go on being a rebel too long without turning into an autocrat.

Lawrence Durrell (1912–90) British novelist and poet. *Balthazar* (1958), pt. 2

7 The artist, and particularly the poet, is always an anarchist, and can only listen to the voices that rise up from within his own being, three imperious voices: the voice of Death, with all its presentiments; the voice of Love and the voice of Art.

Federico García Lorca (1899–1936) Spanish poet and playwright. 1933. Quoted in *Federico García Lorca* (Ian Gibson; 1989), pt. 2, ch. 6

8 It will surely be one of history's darkest ironies if the Enlightenment project of a world civilization ends in a chaos of sovereign states and stateless peoples struggling for the necessities of survival.

John Gray (b. 1948) British academic. *False Dawn* (1998)

9 To this war of every man, against every man, this also is consequent; that nothing can be unjust. The notions of right and wrong, justice and injustice have there no place. Where there is no common power, there is no law; where no law, no injustice.

Thomas Hobbes (1588–1679) English philosopher and political thinker. *Leviathan* (1651)

10 There is nothing stable in the world; uproar's your only music.

John Keats (1795–1821) English poet. Letter to Georgiana and Thomas Keats (January 13, 1818), quoted in *Letters of John Keats* (H. E. Rollins, ed.; 1958), vol. 1

11 Enter and sack the decadent civilization of this unhappy country; destroy its temples, finish off its gods, tear the veil from its novices and raise them up to be mothers to civilize the species . . . do not be stopped by altars nor by tombs . . . fight, kill, die.

Alejandro Lerroux (1864–1949) Spanish political leader. Referring to Spain. Quoted in *Success and Failure of Picasso* (John Berger; 1965)

12 We will destroy museums and libraries, and fight against moralism, feminism, and all utilitarian cowardice.

Filippo Tommaso Marinetti (1876–1944) Italian writer, poet, and political activist. 'Founding and First Manifesto of Futurism' (1909), quoted in *Cubism, Futurism and Constructivism* (J. M. Nash; 1974)

13 We will glorify war—the world's only hygiene—militarism, patriotism, the destructive gesture of the Anarchist, the beautiful ideas that kill, contempt for women.

Filippo Tommaso Marinetti (1876–1944) Italian writer, poet, and political activist. 'Founding and First Manifesto of Futurism' (1909), quoted in *Cubism, Futurism and Constructivism* (J. M. Nash; 1974)

14 Anarchism is deeply rooted in Spain and is likely to outlive Communism when the Russian influence is withdrawn.

George Orwell (1903–50) British writer. *Homage to Catalonia* (1938)

15 Altogether, they are a people unique upon the face of the earth. A friend of mine well calls them the philosophic anarchists of the North.

Robert Edwin Peary (1856–1920) US explorer. Referring to the Inuit. *The North Pole* (1910), ch. 5

16 Anarchism is founded on the observation that since few men are wise enough to rule themselves, even fewer are wise enough to rule others.

Ayn Rand (1905–82) Russian-born US writer and philosopher. *The Fountainhead* (1943)

17 Walk on the Wild Side

Lou Reed (b. 1942) US rock singer and songwriter. 1972. Song title. Taken from Nelson Algren's novel *A Walk on the Wild Side* (1956, film 1962).

18 Things fall apart; the centre cannot hold;
Mere anarchy is loosed upon the world,
The blood-dimmed tide is loosed, and everywhere
The ceremony of innocence is drowned;
The best lack all conviction, while the worst
Are full of passionate intensity.

W. B. Yeats (1865–1939) Irish poet and playwright. 1919. 'The Second Coming', *Michael Robartes and the Dancer* (1921), st. 1

Angels

1 Her shadow never wrote
The semblance of a man.

Rafael Alberti (1902–99) Spanish poet. 'The Angelic Angel', *Concerning the Angels* (1929)

2 And the angel of the Lord appeared unto him in a flame of fire out of the midst of a bush: and he looked, and, behold, the bush burned with fire, and the bush was not consumed.

Bible. Exodus, *King James Bible* (1611), 3:2

3 An angel, are you?
Mister, let me tell you
The magistrates
Want no comic-singers in town this winter.

George Mackay Brown (1921–96) Scottish poet and novelist. The poem is an ironic treatment of the Christmas story. 'The Keeper of the Midnight Gate', *Winterfold* (1976)

4 Angels can fly because they take themselves lightly.

G. K. Chesterton (1874–1936) British writer and poet. *Orthodoxy* (1909), ch. 7

5 We are ne'er like angels till our passion dies.

Thomas Dekker (1572?–1632?) English playwright. *The Honest Whore* (1630), pt.2, Act 1, Scene 2

6 Now walk the angels on the walls of heaven,
As sentinels to warn th' immortal souls
To entertain divine Zenocrate.

Christopher Marlowe (1564–93) English playwright and poet. Referring to the death of Zenocrate, Tamburlaine's wife. *Tamburlaine the Great* (1587?), pt. 2, Act 2, Scene 4

7 Fallen cherub, to be weak is miserable,
Doing or suffering: but of this be sure,
To do aught good never will be our task,
But ever to do ill our sole delight.

John Milton (1608–74) English writer. Satan addressing the cherubim. *Paradise Lost* (1667), bk. 1, ll. 157–160

8 For Spirits when they please
Can either sex assume, or both, so soft
And uncompounded is their essence pure,
Not tied or manacled with joint or limb,
Nor founded on the brittle strength of bones,
Like cumbrous flesh, but in what shape they choose.

John Milton (1608–74) English writer. Referring to the nature of angels. *Paradise Lost* (1667), bk. 1, ll. 423–428

9 In heaven an angel is nobody in particular.

George Bernard Shaw (1856–1950) Irish playwright. 'Maxims for Revolutionists', *Man and Superman* (1903)

10 I am the necessary angel of earth,
Since, in my sight, you see the earth again.

Wallace Stevens (1879–1955) US poet. 'Angel Surrounded by Paysans', *Selected Poems* (1955)

11 The angel in his cloud
Serenely gazing at the violent abyss,
Plucks on his strings to pluck abysmal glory.

Wallace Stevens (1879–1955) US poet. 'It Must Give Pleasure', *Selected Poems* (1955)

12 The mules that angels ride come slowly down
The blazing passes, from beyond the sun.

Wallace Stevens (1879–1955) US poet. 'Le Monocle de Mon Oncle', *Selected Poems* (1955)

Anger

see also **Aggression**, **Hate**

1 An angry man is always a stupid man.

Chinua Achebe (b. 1930) Nigerian novelist, poet, and essayist. *Anthills of the Savannah* (1987)

2 Bitterness is like cancer. It eats upon the host. But anger is like fire. It burns all clean.

Maya Angelou (b. 1928) US writer. Quoted in *Writing Lives: Conversations Between Women Writers* (Mary Chamberlain, ed.; 1988)

3 The man who gets angry at the right things and with the right people, and in the right way and at the right time and for the right length of time, is commended.

Aristotle (384–322 BC) Greek philosopher. *Nicomachean Ethics* (4th century BC), bk. 4

4 Rage can only with difficulty, and never entirely, be brought under the domination of the intelligence and is therefore not susceptible to any arguments whatever.

James Baldwin (1924–87) US writer and civil rights activist. 'Stranger in the Village', *Notes of a Native Son* (1955)

5 He that is slow to anger is better than the mighty; and he that ruleth his spirit than he that taketh a city.

Bible. Proverbs, *King James Bible* (1611), 16:32

6 Black tulips in my heart,
flames on my lips:
from which forest did you come to me,
all you crosses of anger?

Mahmoud Darwish (b. 1942) Palestinian poet. 'To the Reader', *When the Words Burn* (John Mikhail Asfour, ed., tr.; 1988), ll. 1–4

7 We boil at different degrees.

Ralph Waldo Emerson (1803–82) US poet and essayist. 'Eloquence', *Society and Solitude* (1870)

8 Anger is one of the sinews of the soul.

Thomas Fuller (1608–61) English historian. *The Holy State and the Profane State* (1642)

9 Spleen can subsist on any kind of food.

William Hazlitt (1778–1830) British essayist and critic. 'On Wit and Humour', *Essays on the English Comic Writers* (1819)

10 Anger is a momentary madness, so control your passion or it will control you.

Horace (65–8 BC) Roman poet. *Epistles* (20? BC), bk. 1, no. 2, l. 62

11 A tart temper never mellows with age, and a sharp tongue is the only edged tool that grows keener with constant use.

Washington Irving (1783–1859) US writer. 'Rip Van Winkle', *The Sketch Book* (1819–20)

12 I'm part of a righteous people who anger slowly but rage undammed.

George Jackson (1941–71) US political activist and writer. March 24, 1970. Letter, *Soledad Brother* (1970)

13 Even if nature says no, indignation makes me write verse.

Juvenal (65?–128?) Roman poet. *Satires* (98?–128?), no. 1, l. 79

14 Anger is an emotion that has some hope in it.

Charles Mingus (1922–79) US jazz musician. *Beneath the Underdog* (1971)

15 There is a sense of being in anger. A reality and presence. An awareness of worth. It is a lovely surging.

Toni Morrison (b. 1931) US novelist. *The Bluest Eye* (1970)

16 Anger is never without an argument, but seldom with a good one.

Sir George Savile (1633–95) English politician and pamphleteer. 'Of Anger', *Political, Moral, and Miscellaneous Thoughts and Reflections* (1750)

17 When angry, count four; when very angry, swear.

Mark Twain (1835–1910) US writer and humorist. *Pudd'nhead Wilson* (1894), ch. 10

18 The anger that breaks the soul into bodies;
the body into dissimilar organs
and the organ, into octave thoughts;
the anger of the poor
has one central fire against two craters.

César Vallejo (1892–1938) Peruvian poet. 'The Anger that Breaks the Man', *Sermon on Barbarism* (1936–38), st. 4

19 Why such great anger in those heavenly minds?

Virgil (70–19 BC) Roman poet. Referring to the gods. *Aeneid* (29–19 BC), bk. 1, l. 11

Animals

see also **Birds**, **Nature**

1 The donkey has been to Jerusalem forty times, but he is still a donkey.

Anonymous. Armenian proverb.

2 I gave my beauty and my youth to men. I am going to give my wisdom and experience to animals.

Brigitte Bardot (b. 1934) French film actor and animal rights activist. Referring to her animal-rights campaign. *Guardian* (1987)

3 Mothers of large families (who claim to common sense)
Will find a Tiger well repays the trouble and expense.

Hilaire Belloc (1870–1953) French-born British writer. 1896. 'The Tiger', *The Bad Child's Book of Beasts*, quoted in *Complete Verse* (1991)

4 It's the one species I wouldn't mind seeing vanish from the face of the earth. I wish they were like the White Rhino—six of them left in the Serengeti National Park, and all males.

Alan Bennett (b. 1934) British playwright, actor, and director. Referring to dogs. *Getting On* (1971), Act 1

5 A full-grown horse or dog is beyond comparison a more rational, as well as a more conversable animal, than an infant of a day, or a week, or even a month, old. But suppose that the case were otherwise, what would it avail? The question is not, Can they *reason*? nor, Can they *talk*? but, Can they *suffer*?

Jeremy Bentham (1748–1832) British philosopher, economist, jurist, and social reformer. *An Introduction to the Principles of Morals and Legislation* (1789)

6 And the Lord God said, It is not good that the man should be alone; I will make him an helpmeet for him.
And out of the ground the Lord God formed every beast of the field, and every fowl of the air; and brought them unto Adam to see what he would call them.

Bible. Genesis, *King James Bible* (1611), 2:18–19

7 Tyger! Tyger! burning bright
In the forests of the night,
What immortal hand or eye
Could frame thy fearful symmetry?

William Blake (1757–1827) British poet, painter, engraver, and mystic. 'The Tyger', *Songs of Experience* (1789–94), ll. 1–4

8 Rats!
They fought the dogs and killed the cats,
And bit the babies in the cradles.

Robert Browning (1812–89) British poet. 'The Pied Piper of Hamelin', *Dramatic Lyrics* (1842), st. 2

9 The third member of the company was a cat the size of a pig, black as soot and with luxuriant cavalry officer's whiskers.

Mikhail Bulgakov (1891–1940) Russian novelist and playwright. 1929–40. Description of Behemoth, the Devil's cat. *The Master and Margarita* (Michael Glenny, tr.; 1966), ch. 4

10 Wee, sleekit, cow'rin', tim'rous beastie,
O what a panic's in thy breastie!

Robert Burns (1759–96) Scottish poet and songwriter. 'To a Mouse' (1786)

11 The great pleasure of a dog is that you may make a fool of yourself with him and not only will he not scold you, he will make a fool of himself too.

Samuel Butler (1835–1902) British writer and composer. Quoted in *Note Books* (H. Festing Jones, ed.; 1912)

12 Whenever you observe an animal closely, you feel as if a human being sitting inside were making fun of you.

Elias Canetti (1905–94) Bulgarian-born writer. *The Human Province* (1973)

13 How doth the little crocodile
Improve his shining tail,
And pour the waters of the Nile
On every golden scale!

Lewis Carroll (1832–98) British writer and mathematician. *Alice's Adventures in Wonderland* (1865), ch. 2

14 This time it vanished quite slowly, beginning with the end of the tail, and ending with the grin, which remained some time after the rest of it had gone.

Lewis Carroll (1832–98) British writer and mathematician. Describing the Cheshire Cat. *Alice's Adventures in Wonderland* (1865), ch. 6

15 The devil's walking parody
On all four-footed things.

G. K. Chesterton (1874–1936) British writer and poet. 'The Donkey', *The Wild Knight and Other Poems* (1900)

16 Animals are such agreeable friends—they ask no questions, they pass no criticisms.

George Eliot (1819–80) British novelist. 'Mr Gilfil's Love Story', *Scenes of Clerical Life* (1858), ch. 7

17 Dogs show us their tongues as if they thought we were doctors.

Ramón Gómez de la Serna (1888–1963) Spanish novelist. Quoted in *The Spanish Avant Garde* (Derek Harris, ed.; 1995)

18 Laboratory guinea pigs say to themselves: I bet they would not do that to polar bears.

Ramón Gómez de la Serna (1888–1963) Spanish novelist. Quoted in *The Spanish Avant Garde* (Derek Harris, ed.; 1995)

19 Underwater eyes, an eel's
Oil of water body, neither fish nor beast is the otter:
Four-legged yet water-gifted, to outfish fish;
With webbed feet and long ruddering tail
And a round head like an old tomcat.

Ted Hughes (1930–98) British writer and poet. 'An Otter', *Lupercal* (1960)

20 He spins from the bars, but there's no cage to him
More than to the visionary his cell:
His stride is wildernesses of freedom:
The world rolls under the long thrust of his heel.
Over the cage floor the horizons come.

Ted Hughes (1930–98) British writer and poet. 'The Jaguar', *The Hawk in the Rain* (1957)

21 Now Chil the Kite brings home the night
That Mang the Bat sets free—
The herds are shut in byre and hut
For loosed till dawn are we.

Rudyard Kipling (1865–1936) Indian-born British writer and poet. 'Night-Song in the Jungle'—chapter-heading quotation. The song of the wolf pack. 'Mowgli's Brothers', *The Jungle Book* (1894)

22 I've always reckoned a camel is a horse designed by a committee.

Freddie Laker (b. 1922) British airline entrepreneur. Quoted in *Sunday Times* (July 16, 1972)

23 Her sensitive, long, pure-bred face
Her full antipodal eyes, so dark,
So big and quiet and remote, having watched so many empty
dawns in silent Australia.

D. H. Lawrence (1885–1930) British writer. 'Kangaroo', *Birds, Beasts and Flowers* (1923)

24 And I think in this empty world there was room for me and a mountain lion.
And I think, in the world beyond, how easily we might spare a million or two of humans
And never miss them,
Yet what a gap in the world, the missing white frost-face
of that slim yellow mountain-lion!

D. H. Lawrence (1885–1930) British writer. 'Mountain-Lion', *Birds, Beasts and Flowers* (1923)

25 If a fish is the movement of water embodied, given shape, then cat is a diagram and pattern of subtle air.

Doris Lessing (b. 1919) British novelist and short-story writer. *Particularly Cats* (1967), ch. 2

26 The bliss of animals lies in this, that, on their lower level, they shadow the bliss of those—few at any moment on the earth—who do not 'look before and after, and pine for what is not' but live in the holy carelessness of the eternal now.

George MacDonald (1824–1905) Scottish novelist and poet. 'Sir Gibbie', *George MacDonald, an Anthology* (C. S. Lewis, ed.; 1946)

27 I am a Bear of Very Little Brain, and long words Bother me.

A. A. Milne (1882–1956) British writer. *Winnie the Pooh* (1926), ch. 4

28 The serpent subtlest beast of all the field.

John Milton (1608–74) English writer. *Paradise Lost* (1667), bk. 9, l. 86

29 When I play with my cat, who knows whether she is not amusing herself with me more than I with her?

Michel de Montaigne (1533–92) French essayist. *Essays* (1580–88), bk. 2

30 For myself, I have not been able without distress to see pursued and killed an innocent animal which is defenceless and which does us no harm.

Michel de Montaigne (1533–92) French essayist. 'On Cruelty', *Essays* (1580–88)

31 The trouble with a kitten is THAT When it grows up, it's always a CAT.

Ogden Nash (1902–71) US humorist. 'The Kitten', *The Face Is Familiar* (1942)

32 After his long fast, the toad has a very spiritual look, like a strict Anglo-Catholic towards the end of Lent.

George Orwell (1903–50) British writer. 'As I Please', *Tribune* (April 1946), quoted in *The Collected Essays, Journalism and Letters of George Orwell* (Sonia Orwell and Ian Angus, eds.; 1968), vol. 4

33 Cats are autocrats of naked self-interest. They are both amoral and immoral, consciously breaking rules . . . the cat may be the only animal who savors the perverse or reflects upon it.

Camille Paglia (b. 1947) US academic and author. *Sexual Personae* (1990)

34 Learn from the beasts the physic of the field.

Alexander Pope (1688–1744) English poet. *An Essay on Man* (1733), Epistle 3, l. 172

35 Eye, gazelle, delicate wanderer, Drinker of horizon's fluid line.

Stephen Spender (1909–95) British poet and critic. 'Preludes', *Collected Poems* (1955), ll. 35–36

36 The bear, the ponderous cinnamon, snarls in his mountain At summer thunder and sleeps through winter snow.

Wallace Stevens (1879–1955) US poet. 'Notes Toward a Supreme Fiction', *Selected Poems* (1955)

37 There are two things for which animals are to be envied: they know nothing of future evils, or of what people say about them.

Voltaire (1694–1778) French writer and philosopher. Letter (1739)

38 The animals of the planet are in desperate peril . . . Without free animal life I believe we will lose the spiritual equivalent of oxygen.

Alice Walker (b. 1944) US novelist and poet. 'The Universe Responds: Or, How I Learned We Can Have Peace on Earth', *Living By the Word* (1988)

39 The shape of an African elephant's ear Is the shape of Africa. The shape of an Indian elephant's ear Is the shape of India.

Heathcote Williams (b. 1941) British poet and dramatist. *Sacred Elephant* (1989)

40 His coat resembles the snow deep snow the male snow which attacks and kills.

William Carlos Williams (1883–1963) US poet, novelist, and physician. 'The Polar Bear', *Pictures from Brueghel and Other Poems* (1962), quoted in *The Selected Poems of William Carlos Williams* (Charles Tomlinson, ed.; 1976)

Answers

see also **Questions, Reason**

1 'Forty-two', said Deep Thought, with infinite majesty and calm.

Douglas Adams (1952–2001) British writer. Answering the question: 'What is the meaning of Life, the Universe and Everything?' *The Hitch Hiker's Guide to the Galaxy* (1979), ch. 27

2 But answer came there none— And this was scarcely odd because They'd eaten every one.

Lewis Carroll (1832–98) British writer and mathematician. *Through the Looking-Glass and What Alice Found There* (1871), ch. 4

3 If we find the answer to that, it would be the ultimate triumph of human reason—for then we would know the mind of God.

Stephen Hawking (b. 1942) British physicist. The answer to the question: Why do we and the universe exist? *A Brief History of Time* (1988), ch. 11

4 I refute it *thus*.

Samuel Johnson (1709–84) British lexicographer and writer. August 6, 1763. Replying to James Boswell's contention that they were unable to refute Bishop Berkeley's theory that matter cannot be conceived to exist independent of the mind, by kicking a large stone with his foot. Quoted in *Life of Samuel Johnson* (James Boswell; 1791)

5 There ain't no answer. There ain't going to be any answer. There never has been an answer. That's the answer.

Gertrude Stein (1874–1946) US writer. *Brewsie and Willie* (1946), ch. 7

6 The riddle does not exist. If a question can be framed at all, it is also possible to answer it.

Ludwig Wittgenstein (1889–1951) Austrian philosopher. *Tractatus Logico-Philosophicus* (1921)

Anticipation

see also **The Future, Hope**

1 We can't always cross a bridge until we come to it; but I always like to lay down a pontoon ahead of time.

Bernard Mannes Baruch (1870–1965) US financier, statesman, and philanthropist. Quoted in *The Home Book of Humorous Quotations* (A. K. Adams, ed.; 1969)

2 What we anticipate seldom occurs; what we least expected generally happens.

Benjamin Disraeli (1804–81) British prime minister and writer. *Henrietta Temple* (1837), bk. 2, ch. 4

3 Nothing is so good as it seems beforehand.

George Eliot (1819–80) British novelist. *Silas Marner* (1861), ch. 18

4 Once we find the fruits of success, the taste is nothing like we had anticipated.
William Inge (1913–73) US playwright. Attrib.

5 IAGO This is the night
That either makes me or fordoes me quite.
William Shakespeare (1564–1616) English poet and playwright. *Othello* (1602–04), Act 5, Scene 1

6 MARIA Here comes the trout that must be caught with tickling.
William Shakespeare (1564–1616) English poet and playwright. *Twelfth Night* (1601), Act 2, Scene 5

Anxiety

see Fear, Paranoia, Worry

Apartheid

see also Inequality, Prejudice, Racism

1 All my life had been dominated by a sign, often invisible but no less real for that, which said: RESERVED FOR EUROPEANS ONLY.
Peter Abrahams (b. 1919) South African-born novelist, journalist, and political commentator. *Tell Freedom* (1954)

2 The biggest mistake the black world ever made was to assume that whoever opposed apartheid was an ally.
Stephen Biko (1946–77) South African political leader. January 1971. 'White Racism and Black Consciousness', *Steve Biko: I Write What I Like* (Aeelred Stubbs, ed.; 1978)

3 People think we do not understand our black and coloured countrymen. But there is a special relationship between us.
Elize Botha (d. 1997) South African wife of P. W. Botha. Remark (1987)

4 Today we have closed the book on apartheid.
F. W. de Klerk (b. 1936) South African president. After a referendum of white South Africans had endorsed his government's reform programme. *Independent* (March 19, 1992)

5 Any discrimination based simply on race or color is barbarous, we care not how hallowed it be by custom, expedience, or prejudice.
W. E. B. Du Bois (1868–1963) US sociologist, poet, and novelist. The Niagara Movement was founded in 1905 to protest against racial segregation in the United States. The Niagara Movement Declaration of Principles (1905)

6 I know a Southerner who owned an amusement park and almost went out of his mind over where to put us on the merry-go-round.
Dick Gregory (b. 1932) US comedian and civil rights activist. *From the Back of the Bus* (1962)

7 There are no 'white' or 'colored' signs on the foxholes or graveyards of battle.
John Fitzgerald Kennedy (1917–63) US president. Message to the US Congress (June 19, 1963)

8 Sanctions are now the only feasible, non-violent way of ending apartheid. The other road to change is covered with blood.
Neil Kinnock (b. 1942) British politician. Speech (1988)

9 Between the anvil of united mass action and the hammer of the armed struggle we shall crush apartheid and white minority racist rule.
Nelson Mandela (b. 1918) South African president and lawyer. June 1980. *The Struggle is My Life* (1990)

10 There is the racial policy of the Union of South Africa, which is in no sense different from the racial policy of Hitler, except that they have not gone to those extremes that Hitler went to.
Jawaharlal Nehru (1889–1964) Indian prime minister. Referring to South Africa's policy of Apartheid (1948–89) and to Adolf Hitler. Speech to the Lok-Sabha (the lower house of the Indian parliament; September 30, 1956)

11 NEGROES ALLOWED IN.
St. Louis, May 4 (AP)—The St. Louis major league baseball teams, the Cardinals and Browns, have discontinued their old policy of restricting Negroes to the bleachers and pavilion at Sportsman's Park. Negroes now may purchase seats in the grandstand.
Newspapers. *New York Times Book of Baseball History* (1944)

12 My only concern was to get home after a hard day's work.
Rosa Parks (b. 1913) US civil rights activist. Commenting on her refusal to leave a 'whites only' seat in a bus. *Time* (December 15, 1975)

13 We don't want apartheid liberalized. We want it dismantled. You can't improve something that is intrinsically evil.
Desmond Tutu (b. 1931) South African clergyman and civil rights activist. *Observer* (March 10, 1985), 'Sayings of the Week'

14 I draw the line in the dust and toss the gauntlet before the feet of tyranny, and I say segregation now, segregation tomorrow, segregation forever.
George Wallace (1919–98) US politician. Inaugural address as governor of Alabama (1963)

Apologies

see also Alibis and Excuses, Regret

1 Never make a defence or apology before you be accused.
Charles I (1600–49) Scottish-born monarch. Letter to Lord Wentworth (September 3, 1636), quoted in *Letters to King Charles I* (Charles Petrie, ed.; 1935)

2 I should never be allowed out in private.
Randolph Churchill (1911–68) British journalist. Apologizing to a hostess whose dinner party he had ruined. Quoted in *Randolph: A Study of Churchill's Son* (B. Roberts; 1984)

3 Apologies only account for that which they do not alter.
Benjamin Disraeli (1804–81) British prime minister and writer. Speech (July 28, 1871)

4 I have eaten
the plums
that were in
the icebox
and which
you were probably
saving
for breakfast.
William Carlos Williams (1883–1963) US poet, novelist, and physician. 'This is Just to Say', *Poems* (1934), quoted in *The Penguin Book of American Verse* (Geoffrey Moore, ed.; 1977)

5 It is a good rule in life never to apologize. The right sort of people do not want apologies, and the wrong sort take a mean advantage of them.
P. G. Wodehouse (1881–1975) British-born US humorous writer. *The Man Upstairs* (1914)

Appearance

see also **Aesthetics, Beauty, The Face**

1   I am not at all the sort of person you and I took me for.

Jane Carlyle (1801–66) Scottish diarist. Letter to Thomas Carlyle (May 7, 1822), quoted in *Collected Letters of Thomas and Jane Welsh Carlyle* (C. R. Sanders et al., eds.; 1970), vol. 2

2   She never had the looks to lose so she never lost them.

Angela Carter (1940–92) British novelist, essayist, and short-story writer. *Wise Children* (1991)

3   Keep up appearances; there lies the test
The world will give thee credit for the rest.

Charles Churchill (1731–64) British poet. *Night* (1761), ll. 311–312

4   Appearances are not held to be a clue to the truth. But we seem to have no other.

Ivy Compton-Burnett (1884–1969) British novelist. *Manservant and Maidservant* (1947)

5   Sunburn is very becoming—but only when it is even—one must be careful not to look like a mixed grill.

Noël Coward (1899–1973) British playwright, actor, and songwriter. *The Lido Beach* (1928)

6   Any man may be in good spirits and good temper when he's well dressed. There ain't much credit in that.

Charles Dickens (1812–70) British novelist. Said by Mark Tapley. *Martin Chuzzlewit* (1844), ch. 5

7   A Being, erect upon two legs, and bearing all the outward semblance of a man, and not of a monster.

Charles Dickens (1812–70) British novelist. Said by Buzfuz. *Pickwick Papers* (1837), ch. 34

8   Outside, among your fellows, among strangers, you must preserve appearances, a hundred things you cannot do, but inside, the terrible freedom!

Ralph Waldo Emerson (1803–82) US poet and essayist. Attrib.

9   Things are seldom what they seem,
Skim milk masquerades as cream.

W. S. Gilbert (1836–1911) British librettist and playwright. *HMS Pinafore* (1878), Act 2

10 We tolerate shapes in human beings that would horrify us if we saw them in a horse.

William Ralph Inge (1860–1954) British churchman. Attrib.

11 A luminous body will appear more brilliant in proportion as it is surrounded by deep shadow.

Leonardo da Vinci (1452–1519) Italian artist, engineer, and inventor. *Notebooks* (1508–18)

12 All is not golde that outward shewith bright.

John Lydgate (1370?–1451?) English poet. 'As a Mydsomer Rose', no. 63, l. 12, quoted in *The Minor Poems of John Lydgate* (Henry Noble MacCrauken, ed.; 1910–34)

13 A man who looks a part has the soul of that part.

Guy de Maupassant (1850–93) French writer. *Mont-Oriol* (1887)

14 Always present your front to the world.

Molière (1622–73) French playwright. *L'Avare* (1669), Act 3, Scene 1

15 The image is one thing and a human being is another.

Elvis Presley (1935–77) US pop singer. 1972. Attrib.

16 Things are entirely what they appear to be and *behind them . . .* there is nothing.

Jean-Paul Sartre (1905–80) French philosopher, playwright, and novelist. *Nausea* (1938)

17 AUFIDIUS Thou hast a grim appearance, and thy face
Bears a command in't; though thy tackle's torn,
Thou show'st a noble vessel. What's thy name?

William Shakespeare (1564–1616) English poet and playwright. Said on seeing Coriolanus 'in mean apparel, disguis'd and muffled'. *Coriolanus* (1608), Act 4, Scene 5

18 Examine the contents, not the bottle.

The Talmud (4th century? BC)

19 It is only shallow people who do not judge by appearances.

Oscar Wilde (1854–1900) Irish poet, playwright, and wit. *The Picture of Dorian Gray* (1891), ch. 2

Appetite

see also **Desire, Eating, Food, Hunger**

1   Subdue your appetites my dears, and you've conquered human nature.

Charles Dickens (1812–70) British novelist. Said by Mr. Squeers. *Nicholas Nickleby* (1839), ch. 5

2   I have a Catholic soul, but a Lutheran stomach.

Desiderius Erasmus (1466?–1536) Dutch humanist, scholar, and writer. Replying to criticism of his failure to fast during Lent. Attrib.

3   I eat like a vulture. Unfortunately the resemblance doesn't end there.

Groucho Marx (1895–1977) US comedian and film actor. Attrib.

4   Appetite comes with eating.

François Rabelais (1494?–1553?) French humanist and satirist. *Gargantua* (1534), bk. 1, ch. 5

5   BENEDICK Doth not the appetite alter? A man loves the meat in his youth that he cannot endure in his age.

William Shakespeare (1564–1616) English poet and playwright. *Much Ado About Nothing* (1598–99), Act 2, Scene 3

Architecture

see also **Cities, Design, Houses**

1   A structure becomes architecture and not sculpture when its elements no longer have their justification in nature.

Guillaume Apollinaire (1880–1918) Italian-born French poet. 1913. *The Cubist Painters* (L. Abel, tr.; 1944)

2   In my experience, if you have to keep the lavatory door shut by extending your left leg, it's modern architecture.

Nancy Banks-Smith, British journalist. *Guardian* (February 20, 1979)

3   Architecture is inhabited sculpture.

Constantin Brancusi (1876–1957) Romanian-born French sculptor. Quoted in *Themes and Episodes* (Igor Stravinsky; 1966)

4   Like a carbuncle on the face of an old and valued friend.

Prince Charles (b. 1948) British prince. May 10, 1984. Referring to a proposed modern extension to the National Gallery. *Times* (May 31, 1984)

5   Architecture completes nature.

Giorgio de Chirico (1888–1978) Italian painter. *The Sense of Architecture* (1920)

6   The Gothic cathedral is a blossoming in stone subdued by the insatiable demand of harmony in man. The mountain of granite blooms into eternal flower.

Ralph Waldo Emerson (1803–82) US poet and essayist. 'History', *Essays* (1841)

7 Light (God's eldest daughter) is a principal beauty in building.
Thomas Fuller (1608–61) English historian. 'Of Building', *The Holy State and the Profane State* (1642)

8 A monument to air-conditioned anality, executive culture and social control.
Jonathan Glancey, British journalist. Referring to Canary Wharf, London. *Guardian* (April 20, 1998)

9 Architecture begins where engineering ends.
Walter Gropius (1883–1969) German-born US architect. Speech, Harvard Department of Architecture, *Architects on Architecture* (Paul Heyer, ed.; 1978)

10 A modern, harmonic and lively architecture is the visible sign of an authentic democracy.
Walter Gropius (1883–1969) German-born US architect. *Observer* (December 8, 1968), 'Sayings of the Week'

11 For construction, do not the branches of the trees, the stems, by turn rigid and undulating, furnish us with models?
Hector Germain Guimard (1867–1942) French architect. 1899. Quoted in *The Anti-Rationalists* (Nikolaus Pevsner; 1973)

12 Good architects nurture the psychological, mental, and spiritual needs of the people who will inhabit their structures.
Craig R. Hickman, US author. *The Future 500* (co-written with Michael A. Silva; 1987)

13 Architecture is the art of how to waste space.
Philip Johnson (b. 1906) US architect. *New York Times* (December 27, 1964)

14 Architecture is a thing of art, a phenomenon of the emotions, lying outside questions of construction and beyond them.
Le Corbusier (1887–1965) Swiss-born French architect. 1923. *Towards a New Architecture* (Frederick Etchells, tr.; 1927)

15 Architecture is the masterly, correct, and magnificent play of masses brought together in light.
Le Corbusier (1887–1965) Swiss-born French architect. 1923. *Towards a New Architecture* (Frederick Etchells, tr.; 1927)

16 Architecture only exists when there is a poetic emotion.
Le Corbusier (1887–1965) Swiss-born French architect. 1923. *Towards a New Architecture* (Frederick Etchells, tr.; 1927)

17 Less is more.
Ludwig Mies van der Rohe (1886–1969) German-born US architect. Also said by Robert Browning in 'Andrea del Sarto', l. 78. *New York Herald Tribune* (1959)

18 Architecture is not in the empty building, but in the vital interchange between building and participant.
Cesar Pelli (b. 1926) Argentine-born US architect. Quoted in *Contemporary Architects* (Muriel Emmanuel, ed.; 1994)

19 Architecture is the most inescapable of the higher arts.
Anthony Quinton (b. 1925) British philosopher and broadcaster. *Times* (1982)

20 We may, without offending any laws of good taste, require of an architect, as we do of a novelist, that he should be not only correct, but entertaining.
John Ruskin (1819–1900) British art critic, writer, and reformer. *Stones of Venice* (1851–53)

21 An architect should live as little in cities as a painter. Send him to our hills, and let him study there what nature understands by a buttress, and what by a dome.
John Ruskin (1819–1900) British art critic, writer, and reformer. *The Seven Lamps of Architecture* (1849)

22 When we build let us think that we build for ever.
John Ruskin (1819–1900) British art critic, writer, and reformer. 'The Lamp of Memory', *The Seven Lamps of Architecture* (1849)

23 Architecture in general is frozen music.
Friedrich Wilhelm Joseph von Schelling (1775–1854) German philosopher. *Philosophie der Kunst* (1809)

24 Orthodox modern architecture is progressive, if not revolutionary, utopian, and puristic; it is dissatisfied with *existing* conditions.
Robert Venturi (b. 1925) US architect and writer. 'A Significance for A and P Parking Lots', *Learning from Las Vegas* (co-written with Denise Scott Brown and Stephen Izenour; 1972), pt. 1

25 In iconographic terms, the cathedral is a decorated shed.
Robert Venturi (b. 1925) US architect and writer. 'Historical and Other Precedents', *Learning from Las Vegas* (co-written with Denise Scott Brown and Stephen Izenour; 1972), pt. 2

26 The series of triumphal arches in Rome is a prototype of the billboard . . . The triumphal arches in the Roman Forum were spatial markers channeling processional paths within a complex urban landscape. On Route 66 the billboards . . . perform a similar formal-spatial function.
Robert Venturi (b. 1925) US architect and writer. 'Silent-White Majority Architecture', *Learning from Las Vegas* (co-written with Denise Scott Brown and Stephen Izenour; 1972), pt. 2

27 Less is a bore.
Robert Venturi (b. 1925) US architect and writer. Criticizing the minimalist style of architecture, and a riposte to Ludwig Mies van der Rohe's maxim, 'Less is more'. Quoted in *Icons* (James Park, ed.; 1991)

28 The ancient Romans built their greatest masterpieces of architecture, the amphitheatres, for wild beasts to fight in.
Voltaire (1694–1778) French writer and philosopher. Letter to the Commissioner of the Paris Police (1733), quoted in *Dictionary of Art Quotations* (Ian Crofton; 1988)

29 Architecture has its political use; public buildings being the ornament of a country; it establishes a nation, draws people and commerce; makes the people love their native country.
Christopher Wren (1632–1723) English architect, scientist, and mathematician. *Parentalia* (1750)

30 No house should ever be built *on* a hill or *on* anything. It should be *of* the hill. Belonging to it. Hill and house should live together each the happier for the other.
Frank Lloyd Wright (1867–1959) US architect. *An Autobiography* (1932)

31 Architecture is life, or at least it is life itself taking form and therefore it is the truest record of life as it was lived in the world yesterday, as it is lived today or ever will be lived.
Frank Lloyd Wright (1867–1959) US architect. *An Organic Architecture* (1907)

32 An architect's most useful tools are an eraser at the drafting board, and a wrecking bar at the site.
Frank Lloyd Wright (1867–1959) US architect. Attrib.

33   The tall modern office building is the machine
      pure and simple . . . the engine, the motor, and
      the battleship are the works of art of the century.
      Frank Lloyd Wright (1867–1959) US architect. Attrib.

Arguments

see also **Compromise, Reason, Truth**

1   Hear the other side.
      Saint Augustine of Hippo (354–430) Numidian Christian theologian and
      Doctor of the Church. *De Duabus Animabus contra Manicheos*
      (400?), bk. 14, ch. 2

2   Let's contend no more, Love,
      Strive nor weep:
      All be as before, Love,
      – Only sleep!
      Robert Browning (1812–89) British poet. 'A Woman's Last Word',
      Men and Women (1855)

3   There is only one way under high heaven to get
      the best of an argument—and that is to avoid it.
      Dale Carnegie (1888–1955) US writer and speaker. *Dale Carnegie's
      Scrapbook* (Dorothy Carnegie, ed.; 1959)

4   A noisy man is always in the right.
      William Cowper (1731–1800) British poet. 'Conversation' (1782),
      l. 114, quoted in *The Works of William Cowper* (Robert
      Southey, ed.; 1835–37)

5   Never go to bed mad. Stay up and fight.
      Phyllis Diller (b. 1917) US writer, comedian, and pianist. *Phyllis Diller's
      Housekeeping Hints* (1966)

6   A knock-down argument: 'tis but a word and a
      blow.
      John Dryden (1631–1700) English poet, playwright, and literary critic.
      Amphitryon (1690), Act 1, Scene 1

7   Many a long dispute among divines may be thus
      abridged: It is so. It is not so. It is so. It is not
      so.
      Benjamin Franklin (1706–90) US statesman and scientist. *Poor
      Richard's Almanack* (1743)

8   In every age and clime we see,
      Two of a trade can ne'er agree.
      John Gay (1685–1732) English poet and playwright. 'The Rat-Catcher
      and the Cats', *Fables* (1727), st. 1, ll. 21–22

9   There is no arguing with Johnson; for when his
      pistol misses fire, he knocks you down with the
      butt end of it.
      Oliver Goldsmith (1730–74) Irish-born British novelist, playwright, and
      poet. October 26, 1769. Referring to his friend, Samuel
      Johnson. Quoted in *The Life of Samuel Johnson* (James
      Boswell; 1791)

10   It takes in reality only one to make a quarrel. It
      is useless for the sheep to pass resolutions in
      favour of vegetarianism while the wolf remains of
      a different opinion.
      William Ralph Inge (1860–1954) British churchman. 'Patriotism',
      Outspoken Essays (1919), First series

11   Quarrels would not last so long if the fault were
      on only one side.
      François La Rochefoucauld (1613–80) French epigrammatist and moralist.
      Reflections, or Sentences and Moral Maxims (1665), no. 496

12   I'm arm'd with more than complete steel—
      The justice of my quarrel.
      Christopher Marlowe (1564–93) English playwright and poet. This play is
      also attributed to others. *Lust's Dominion*, Act 4, Scene 3

13   Sir, you have the advantage of me.
      —Not yet I haven't, but wait till I get you outside.
      Groucho Marx (1895–1977) US comedian and film actor. *Monkey
      Business* (S. J. Perelman, Will B. Johnstone, and Arthur
      Sheekman; 1931)

14   One often contradicts an opinion when what is
      uncongenial is really the tone in which it was
      conveyed.
      Friedrich Wilhelm Nietzsche (1844–1900) German philosopher and poet.
      Human, All Too Human (1878–80)

15   The argument of the broken window pane is the
      most valuable argument in modern politics.
      Emmeline Pankhurst (1858–1928) British suffragette. Quoted in *The
      Strange Death of Liberal England* (George Dangerfield; 1936), pt. 2, ch. 3, sect. 4

16   Who overrefines his argument brings himself to
      grief.
      Petrarch (1304–74) Italian poet and scholar. 'To Laura in Life' (14th
      century), Canzoniere 11

17   A man who criticizes the length of an argument
      must be required to support his grumble with a
      proof that a briefer statement would have left
      him more able to demonstrate real truth by
      reasoned argument.
      Plato (428?–347? BC) Greek philosopher. *Sophist* (370? BC)

18   The most savage controversies are those about
      matters as to which there is no good evidence
      either way.
      Bertrand Russell (1872–1970) British philosopher and mathematician.
      Unpopular Essays (1950)

19   BENEDICK In a false quarrel there is no true
      valour.
      William Shakespeare (1564–1616) English poet and playwright. *Much
      Ado About Nothing* (1598–99), Act 5, Scene 1

20   A man never tells you anything until you
      contradict him.
      George Bernard Shaw (1856–1950) Irish playwright. Attrib.

21   The quarrel is a very pretty quarrel as it stands;
      we should only spoil it by trying to explain it.
      Richard Brinsley Sheridan (1751–1816) Irish-born British playwright and
      politician. *The Rivals* (1775), Act 4, Scene 3

22   I love argument, I love debate. I don't expect
      anyone just to sit there and agree with me, that's
      not their job.
      Margaret Thatcher (b. 1925) British prime minister. *Times* (1980)

23   Arguments are to be avoided: they are always
      vulgar and often unconvincing.
      Oscar Wilde (1854–1900) Irish poet, playwright, and wit. Attrib.

24   Reading the Socratic dialogues one has the
      feeling: what a frightful waste of time! What's
      the point of these arguments that prove nothing
      and clarify nothing?
      Ludwig Wittgenstein (1889–1951) Austrian philosopher. 1931. Quoted
      in *Culture and Value* (G. H. von Wright and Heikki Nyman,
      eds.; 1980)

Arrogance

see also **Boasts, Pride, Self-Confidence, Vanity**

1   With their arrogant manner, they fill up the road;
      The horses they ride glisten in the dust.
      Bai Juyi (772–846) Chinese poet. Expressing a Confucian concern
      that the ruling class conduct themselves responsibly. 'The
      Frivolous Rich' (8th–9th century), quoted in *China's Imperial
      Past* (Charles O. Hucker; 1975)

2 Sometimes I look back on my life and wonder just how one man could achieve all I've done.
   James Brown (b. 1928) US singer, songwriter, and producer. Quoted in *The Wit and Wisdom of Rock and Roll* (Maxim Jabukowski, ed.; 1983)

3 If I could explain it to the average person, I wouldn't have been worth the Nobel Prize.
   Richard Phillips Feynman (1918–88) US physicist. He was awarded a Nobel Prize for his work on quantum electrodynamics. *People* (July 22, 1985)

4 Sir, I have found you an argument but I am not obliged to find you an understanding.
   Samuel Johnson (1709–84) British lexicographer and writer. June, 1784. Said to an opponent in a drawn-out argument, who had said to Johnson, 'I don't understand you, Sir'. Quoted in *Life of Samuel Johnson* (James Boswell; 1791)

5 I could readily see in Emerson a gaping flaw. It was the insinuation that had he lived in those days when the world was made, he might have offered some valuable suggestions.
   Herman Melville (1819–91) US novelist. Referring to Ralph Waldo Emerson. Attrib.

6 God tells me how he wants this music played— and you get in his way.
   Arturo Toscanini (1867–1957) Italian conductor. Said to players in his orchestra. Remark (1930)

7 Arrogance functions on the oxygen of its own modesty. The self-confidence that is part of being young is sensibly flexible.
   Jerome Weidman (1913–98) US writer. *Praying for Rain* (1986), ch. 2

8 Nature is usually wrong.
   James Abbott McNeill Whistler (1834–1903) US painter and etcher. *The Gentle Art of Making Enemies* (1890)

Art

see also **Aesthetics, Artistic Styles, Artists, Painting, Photography, Sculpture**

1 Art will remain the most astonishing activity of mankind born out of struggle between wisdom and madness, between dream and reality in our mind.
   Magdalena Abakanowicz (b. 1930) Polish sculptor and graphic artist. Quoted in *Magdalena Abakanowicz* (Barbara Rose, ed.; 1993)

2 The object of art is to give life a shape.
   Jean Anouilh (1910–87) French playwright. *The Rehearsal* (1950)

3 The important thing about Dada, it seems to me, is that Dadaists despised what is commonly regarded as art, but put the whole universe on the lofty throne of art.
   Jean Arp (1887–1966) German-born French sculptor. 'Looking', *Arp* (James Thrall Soby, ed.; 1958)

4 Art is the spiritual life, made possible by science.
   W. H. Auden (1907–73) British poet. 1959. Quoted in *The Jingle Bell Principle* (Miroslav Holub; 1992)

5 All art is a kind of confession, more or less oblique. All artists, if they are to survive are forced, at last, to tell the whole story, to vomit the anguish up.
   James Baldwin (1924–87) US writer and civil rights activist. 'The Northern Protestant', *Nobody Knows My Name* (1961)

6 In art there is liberation. The essential in artistic creativity is victory over the burden of necessity.
   Nikolai Berdyaev (1874–1948) Ukrainian philosopher. *The Meaning of the Creative Act* (Donald A. Lowrie, tr.; 1916)

7 Art is a way of recognizing oneself, which is why it will always be modern.
   Louise Bourgeois (b. 1911) French-born US sculptor. Quoted in *Bourgeois* (Donald Kuspit; 1988)

8 Art is the only thing that can go on mattering once it has stopped hurting.
   Elizabeth Bowen (1899–1973) Irish novelist and short-story writer. *The Heat of the Day* (1949)

9 Art is meant to disturb, science reassures.
   Georges Braque (1882–1963) French painter and sculptor. *Le Jour et la Nuit: Cahiers 1917–52* (1952)

10 The difference between art and life is that art is more bearable.
   Charles Bukowski (1920–94) German-born US writer. *Notes of a Dirty Old Man* (1969)

11 Art seems to me above all a state of soul.
   Marc Chagall (1887–1985) Russian-born French painter and designer. Quoted in *My Life* (Elizabeth Abbott, tr.; 1922)

12 Art is the community's medicine for the worst disease of mind, the corruption of consciousness.
   R. G. Collingwood (1889–1943) British philosopher, historian, and archaeologist. *The Principles of Art* (1938)

13 Art for art's sake.
   Victor Cousin (1792–1867) French philosopher. 1818. Lecture at the Sorbonne, Paris. 'Cours de Philosophie', *Du Vrai, du beau et du bien* (1853), pt. 2

14 Art is ruled uniquely by the imagination.
   Benedetto Croce (1866–1952) Italian philosopher, historian, and politician. *Esthetic* (1902), ch. 1

15 Art is the terms of an armistice signed with fate.
   Bernard DeVoto (1897–1955) US writer and historian. *Mark Twain at Work* (1942)

16 A sketch is generally more spirited than a picture. It is the artist's work when he is full of inspiration and ardour, when reflection has toned down nothing; it is the artist's soul expressing itself freely on canvas.
   Denis Diderot (1713–84) French encyclopedist and philosopher. 1765. Quoted in *Diderot on Art* (John Goodman, tr.; 1995)

17 Art is the stored honey of the human soul, gathered on wings of misery and travail.
   Theodore Dreiser (1871–1945) US novelist. *Life, Art and America* (1917)

18 Art may be bad, good or indifferent, but, whatever adjective is used, we must call it art, and bad art is still art in the same way as a bad emotion is still an emotion.
   Marcel Duchamp (1887–1968) French-born US artist. 'The Creative Act', *Art News* (Summer 1957), 56, no. 4

19 The conscious utterance of thought, by speech or action, to any end, is Art . . . Art is the spirit's voluntary use and combination of things to serve its end.
   Ralph Waldo Emerson (1803–82) US poet and essayist. 'Thoughts on Art', *The Dial* (January 1841), vol. 1, no. 3

20 Art is like theater. If you want to whisper, you have to whisper loudly enough so that the audience hears you, and . . . has to know it's a whisper. So the artist has to be able to blow the subtleties up proportionally, and at the same time have them be recognized as subtle. It's what makes a good artist, even if he is painting badly.
   Eric Fischl (b. 1948) US painter. Quoted in 'Expressionism Today: An Artist's Symposium', *Art in America* (Carter Ratcliff; December 1982), 70, no. 2

21 For me art is a continuous discovery into reality, an exploration of visual data which has been going on for centuries, each artist contributing to the next generation's advancement. I wanted to go a step further and extend the boundaries.
Audrey Flack (b. 1931) US painter and sculptor. 1970. Quoted in *Art Talk: Conversations with 15 Women Artists* (Cindy Nemser; 1975)

22 Art is long, life short; judgment difficult, opportunity transient.
Johann Wolfgang von Goethe (1749–1832) German poet, playwright, and scientist. *Wilhelm Meisters Lehrjahre* (1795–96), bk. 7, ch. 9

23 Art lives through the imaginations of people who are seeing it. Without that contact there is no art.
Keith Haring (1958–90) US painter. Quoted in *Flash Art* (March 1984)

24 Art cannot be separated from life. It is the expression of the greatest need of which life is capable, and we value art not because of the skilled product, but because of its revelation of a life's experience.
Robert Henri (1865–1929) US painter and teacher. 'The New York Exhibition of Independent Artists', *The Craftsman* (1910)

25 I rarely draw what I see. I draw what I feel in my body.
Barbara Hepworth (1903–75) British sculptor. Quoted in *Barbara Hepworth* (A. M. Hammacher; 1968)

26 I've always been interested in the insanities of people rather than nature; it would never occur to me to do the Grand Canyon.
Al Hirschfeld (b. 1903) US caricaturist. Referring to his caricatures. Remark (November 9, 1991)

27 Drawing is the true test of art.
Jean-Auguste Dominique Ingres (1780–1867) French artist. *Pensées d'Ingres* (1922)

28 A great work of art bears its meaning on its face.
C. L. R. James (1901–89) Trinidadian writer, political theorist, and educator. Quoted in *The C.L.R. James Reader* (Anna Grimshaw, ed.; 1992)

29 Art is the objectification of feeling, and the subjectification of nature.
Susanne K. Langer (1895–1985) US philosopher. *Mind* (1967), vol. 1, pt. 2, ch. 4

30 Organized perception is what art is all about . . . It is a process. It has nothing to do with any external form the painting takes, it has to do with a way of building a unified pattern of seeing.
Roy Lichtenstein (1923–97) US painter. 1963. Quoted in 'What is Pop Art? Interviews with Eight Painters', *Art News* (G. R. Swenson; February 1964), 62, no. 10

31 The whole of art is an appeal to a reality which is not without us but in our minds.
Desmond MacCarthy (1878–1952) British poet and writer. 'Modern Drama', *Theatre* (1954)

32 The final purpose of art is to intensify, even, if necessary, to exacerbate, the moral consciousness of people.
Norman Mailer (b. 1923) US novelist and journalist. 'Hip, Hell, and the Navigator', *Western Review* (Winter 1959)

33 The only domain where the divine is visible is that of art, whatever name we choose to call it.
André Malraux (1901–76) French writer and statesman. *La Métamorphose des Dieux* (1957), pt. 2, ch. 1

34 Art is a revolt against fate.
André Malraux (1901–76) French writer and statesman. *Les Voix du Silence* (1951), pt. 4, ch. 7

35 No plastic expression can ever be more than a residue of an experience.
Man Ray (1890–1976) US painter and photographer. 'The Age of Light', *Photographs by Man Ray* (1934), introduction

36 What I dream of is an art of balance, of purity and serenity . . . a soothing, calming influence on the mind, rather like a good armchair which provides relaxation from physical fatigue.
Henri Matisse (1869–1954) French painter and sculptor. *Notes d'un peintre* (1908), quoted in *Écrits et propos sur l'art* (Dominique Fourcade; 1972)

37 Art is not a mirror to reflect the world, but a hammer with which to shape it.
Vladimir Mayakovsky (1893–1930) Russian poet and playwright. 1925? Quoted in *Guardian* (December 11, 1974)

38 You don't gain even a centimetre of freedom from art that's governed by cold formulas. You only get your freedom by sweating for it, by an inner struggle.
Joan Miró (1893–1983) Catalan painter. Interview, *Correo Literario* (Barcelona; March 15, 1951)

39 All art deals with the absurd and aims at the simple. Good art speaks truth, indeed *is* truth, perhaps the only truth.
Iris Murdoch (1919–99) Irish-born British novelist and philosopher. 'Bradley Pearson's Foreword', *The Black Prince* (1974)

40 Art is not an end in itself, but a means of addressing humanity.
Modest Mussorgsky (1839–81) Russian composer. Attrib.

41 To speak of morals in art is to speak of legislature in sex. Art is the sex of the imagination.
G. J. Nathan (1882–1958) US drama critic. *American Mercury* (July 1926)

42 The arts then act like a reflecting mirror. The artist is like the hand that holds and moves the mirror, this way and that way, to explore all corners of the universe. But what is reflected in the mirror depends on where the holder stands in relation to the object.
Ngugi wa Thiongo (b. 1938) Kenyan writer. 'Freedom of the Artist: People's Artists Versus People's Rulers', *Barrel of a Pen* (1983)

43 All art constantly aspires towards the condition of music.
Walter Pater (1839–94) British critic. 'The School of Giorgione', *Studies on the History of the Renaissance* (1873)

44 I refuse to give the title of art to anything irrational, and if you want to raise objection on this point I am ready to justify my position.
Plato (428?–347? BC) Greek philosopher. Referring to cookery. *Gorgias* (4th century BC)

45 If the art, then, makes an object in conformity with what it is and what it has . . . it itself is more, and more truly, beautiful in that it possesses the beauty of art, a thing greater and fairer than whatever may exist in the external object.
Plotinus (205–270) Egyptian-born Roman philosopher. Quoted in *Enneads* (Stephen MacKenna, tr.; 1930), vol. 5

46 It is extremely important that art be unjustifiable.
Robert Rauschenberg (b. 1925) US painter. 1963. Quoted in 'Note on Painting', *Pop Art Redefined* (John Russell and Suzi Gablik; 1969)

47 Art cannot be described. It proves itself only in its performance.
Gerhard Richter (b. 1932) German painter. 1970. Quoted in *Gerhard Richter* (Rolf Günter Dienst; 1972)

48 The function of art is not to illustrate a truth—or even a question—that is known in advance—but to put to the world questions (and perhaps also, eventually, answers) that themselves cannot yet be conceived.

Alain Robbe-Grillet (b. 1922) French novelist and screenwriter. 'À quoi servent les théories', *Pour un nouveau roman* (1963)

49 Art must take reality by surprise.

Françoise Sagan (b. 1935) French writer. Interview, *Writers at Work* (1958)

50 Art is a daughter of Freedom, and takes her orders from the necessity inherent in minds, not from the exigencies of matter.

Friedrich von Schiller (1759–1805) German poet, playwright, and historian. Tenth letter (1793), quoted in *On the Aesthetic Education of Man* (E. M. Wilkinson and C. A. Willoughby, eds., trs.; 1967)

51 All art is but imitation of nature.

Seneca, 'the Elder' (55?–AD 40?) Roman rhetorician. Quoted by his son, Lucius Annaeus Seneca, in *Epistulae Morales. Epistulae Morales* (63?), quoted in *Seneca. Epistulae Morales* (Richard M. Gummere; 1925)

52 Size determines an object, but scale determines art.

Robert Smithson (1938–73) US artist and art theorist. 1972. 'The Spiral Jetty', *Robert Smithson: Collected Writings* (Jack Flam, ed.; 1996)

53 Real art has the capacity to make us nervous. By reducing the work of art to its content and then interpreting *that*, one tames the work of art.

Susan Sontag (b. 1933) US writer. 'Against Interpretation', *Against Interpretation* (1966)

54 I have never believed in the intrinsic value of art. In itself it seems to me to be nothing. What is important is its role as a spur, a springboard, which helps us attain knowledge.

Antoni Tàpies (b. 1923) Spanish painter. 'Declaracions', *La pràtica de l'art* (1971)

55 The goal of all art is . . . to explain to people the reason for their appearance on this planet; or, if not to explain, at least to pose the question.

Andrey Tarkovsky (1932–86) Russian filmmaker. *Sculpting in Time: Reflections on the Cinema* (1989)

56 Art is not a handicraft, it is the transmission of feeling the artist has experienced.

Leo Tolstoy (1828–1910) Russian writer. *What is Art?* (1898), ch. 19

57 Art is History's nostalgia, it prefers a thatched roof to a concrete factory, and the huge church above a bleached village.

Derek Walcott (b. 1930) St. Lucian poet and playwright. *Omeros* (1990), bk. 6, ch. 45, sect. 2

58 A work of art has an author and yet, when it is perfect, it has something which is anonymous about it.

Simone Weil (1909–43) French philosopher, mystic, and political activist. 'Gravity and Grace' (1947)

59 Any authentic work of art must start an argument between the artist and his audience.

Rebecca West (1892–1983) Irish-born British novelist, critic, and journalist. *The Court and the Castle* (1957), pt. 1, ch. 1

60 Art is the imposing of a pattern on experience, and our aesthetic enjoyment is recognition of the pattern.

A. N. Whitehead (1861–1947) British philosopher and mathematician. *Dialogues with Alfred North Whitehead* (Lucien Price, ed.; 1954), ch. 228

61 Art is the most intense mode of individualism that the world has known.

Oscar Wilde (1854–1900) Irish poet, playwright, and wit. *The Soul of Man Under Socialism* (1891)

Artifice

see also **Delusion, Fantasy, Reality**

1 All things are artificial, for nature is the art of God.

Thomas Browne (1605–82) English physician and writer. *Religio Medici* (1642), pt. 1, sect. 16

2 She's genuinely bogus.

Christopher Hassall (1912–63) British writer, poet, and librettist. Referring to Dame Edith Sitwell, the British writer and critic known for her eccentric behaviour and dress. Attrib.

3 Strip the phoney tinsel off Hollywood and you'll find the real tinsel underneath.

Oscar Levant (1906–72) US pianist and actor. Attrib.

4 BASSANIO Ornament is but the guiled shore
To a most dangerous sea; the beauteous scarf
Veiling an Indian beauty; in a word,
The seeming truth which cunning times put on
To entrap the wisest.

William Shakespeare (1564–1616) English poet and playwright. *The Merchant of Venice* (1596–98), Act 3, Scene 2

Artistic Styles

see also **Art, Artists, Painting, Photography, Sculpture**

1 One can't carry one's father's corpse about everywhere.

Guillaume Apollinaire (1880–1918) Italian-born French poet. Referring to the need for a clean break between the old (the impressionists) and the new (the cubists). 'Sur la Peinture', *Méditations Esthétiques: Les Peintres Cubistes* (1913), pt. 1

2 I love nature but not its substitutes. Naturalistic, illusionistic art is a substitute.

Jean Arp (1887–1966) German-born French sculptor. Quoted in *On My Way, Poetry and Essays. 1912 . . . 1947* (Ralph Manheim, tr.; 1948)

3 What modern art means is that you have to keep finding new ways to express yourself, to express the problems, that there are no settled ways, no fixed approach.

Louise Bourgeois (b. 1911) French-born US sculptor. Quoted in *Bourgeois* (Donald Kuspit; 1988)

4 I am far more concerned about being in tune with nature than copying it.

Georges Braque (1882–1963) French painter and sculptor. Quoted in 'Late Lyrics: Braque', *Art in America* (Jed Perl; February 1983), vol. 71

5 Each artist has a tendency to reproduce or imitate his own likeness . . . And so you will see that if a painter is choleric he will show anger in his works; if phlegmatic, mildness; if devout, religion; if lustful, sensuality.

Vicente Carducho (1576?–1638) Italian-born Spanish painter and theorist. 1633. Quoted in *Dialogues on Painting* (D. G. Cruzada Villaamil, ed.; 1865)

6 The necessity of realism in art; not a realism which transcribes the vain appearances that we think real, with no other end, but an artistic realism, which tears these appearances from the false reality of interest where we perceive them, in order to transport them into the higher reality of a disinterested life.

Téodor de Wyzewa (1862–1914) Polish-born French critic and theorist. 1886. 'L'Art wagnérien: la peinture', Nos Maîtres (1897)

7 There are only two styles of portrait painting; the serious and the smirk.

Charles Dickens (1812–70) British novelist. Said by Miss La Creevy. Nicholas Nickleby (1839), ch. 10

8 There is no neutral naturalism. The artist, no less than the writer, needs a vocabulary before he can embark on a 'copy' of reality.

E. H. Gombrich (b. 1909) Austrian-born British art historian. Art and Illusion (1960)

9 The visible world, I think, is abstract and mysterious enough, I don't think one needs to depart from it in order to make art.

Philip Guston (1913–80) Canadian-born US painter. 1978. Quoted in 'Philip Guston Talking', Philip Guston (Renee McKee, ed.; 1982)

10 In terms of conceptual art, the sheep had already made its statement.

Damien Hirst (b. 1965) British artist. Referring to the vandalizing of one of his works, which featured a preserved dead sheep. Observer (August 21, 1994), 'Sayings of the Week'

11 Modern art can only be born where signs become symbols.

Wassily Kandinsky (1866–1944) Russian-born French painter. 1926. Quoted in Point and Line to Plane (H. Rebay, ed.; 1947)

12 Conceptual art is another kind of artistic style. And style blocks any attempt at revolutionary thinking and activity.

Jannis Kounellis (b. 1936) Greek-born Italian artist. Quoted in 'Structure and Sensibility: An interview with Jannis Kounellis', Avalanche (Willoughby Sharp; Summer 1972), no. 5

13 In Conceptual art the idea or concept is the most important aspect of the work . . . all planning and decisions are made beforehand and the execution is a perfunctory affair. The idea becomes the machine that makes the art.

Sol LeWitt (b. 1928) US artist. 'Paragraphs on Conceptual Art', Artforum (Summer, 1967)

14 In England, pop art and fine art stand resolutely back to back.

Colin MacInnes (1914–76) British novelist and journalist. 'Pop Songs and Teenagers', England, Half English (1961)

15 Exactitude is not truth.

Henri Matisse (1869–1954) French painter and sculptor. Quoted in Matisse on Art (Jack D. Flam; 1973)

16 We cannot use Impressionism when we paint a huge street in New York, nor can we use Futurism when we paint a beautiful woman who is before us. May our brush keep time with our vibrations.

Joan Miró (1893–1983) Catalan painter. Letter to J. F. Ràfols (September 13, 1917)

17 Abstract is not a style . . . This is just a use of space and form: it's an ambivalence of forms and space.

Joan Mitchell (1926–92) US painter. Quoted in 'Conversations with Joan Mitchell', Joan Mitchell: New Paintings (Yves Michaud; 1986)

18 We declare that the elements of art are all based on a dynamic rhythm.

Antoine Pevsner (1886–1962) Russian-born French sculptor and painter. Realist Manifesto (co-written with Naum Gabo; 1920)

19 When I was their age, I could draw like Raphael, but it took me a lifetime to learn to draw like them.

Pablo Picasso (1881–1973) Spanish painter and sculptor. Visiting an exhibition of drawings by children. Quoted in Picasso: His Life and Work (Sir Roland Penrose; 1958)

20 Fine art can only be defined as exclusive, negative, absolute and timeless. It is not practical, useful, related, applicable, or subservient to anything else.

Ad Reinhardt (1913–67) US painter, multimedia artist, and photographer. Twelve Rules for a New Academy (1953), quoted in Art-As-Art: The Selected Writings of Ad Reinhardt (Barbara Rose, ed.; 1975)

21 Fine art has its own thought, its own history and tradition, its own reason, its own discipline. It has its own 'integrity' and not someone else's 'integration' with something else.

Ad Reinhardt (1913–67) US painter, multimedia artist, and photographer. Twelve Rules for a New Academy (1953), quoted in Art-As-Art: The Selected Writings of Ad Reinhardt (Barbara Rose, ed.; 1975)

22 A mere copier of nature can never produce anything great.

Sir Joshua Reynolds (1723–92) British painter and writer. Discourse to the students of the Royal Academy (December 14, 1770), quoted in Discourses on Art (R. Wark, ed.; 1975), no. 3

23 Fine art is that in which the hand, the head, and the heart of man go together.

John Ruskin (1819–1900) British art critic, writer, and reformer. The Two Paths (1859), lecture 2

24 Art cannot imitate nature entirely, even if the artist is perfect, because, even if a painter makes something similar to man in everything, yet it will not have life.

Girolamo Savonarola (1452–98) Italian preacher and reformer. Sermon on the Psalm Quam Bonus (1493)

25 How can you say one style is better than another? You ought to be able to be an Abstract-Expressionist next week, or a Pop artist, or a realist, without feeling you've given up something.

Andy Warhol (1928?–87) US artist and filmmaker. Quoted in Modern Arts Criticism (G. R. Swenson; 1963)

26 Suddenly we all felt like insiders because even though Pop was everywhere . . . to us, it was the new Art. Once you 'got' Pop, you could never see a sign the same way again. And once you thought Pop, you could never see America the same way again.

Andy Warhol (1928?–87) US artist and filmmaker. The moment described occurred while Warhol and others drove to California in 1963. Quoted in POPism: The Warhol '60s (Andy Warhol and Pat Hackett; 1980)

27 All art forms and techniques of foreign origin when transplanted to China must be remodelled and assimilated so they possess national features and become our own.

Zhou Yang (1908–89) Chinese politician. The Path of Socialist Literature and Art in China (1960)

Artists

see also Art, Artistic Styles, The Arts

1 God created the world—so they say—
and on the seventh day,
when he was quietly resting,
He jumped up suddenly and said:
I've forgotten something:
The eyes and the hand of Picasso.

Rafael Alberti (1902–99) Spanish poet. Untitled, The Eight Names of Picasso (1992)

2 The artist who makes himself accessible is self-destructive.

Howard Barker (b. 1946) British playwright. *Times* (January 3, 1990)

3 Noble Painters and Sculptors, imitating that first maker, also form in their minds an example of superior beauty, and in beholding it they emend nature with faultless colour or line.

Giovanni Pietro Bellori (1615–96) Italian art theorist and antiquarian. Quoted in Bellori's 'Idea', *Idea, A Concept in Art Theory* (Erwin Panofsky, ed., J. S. Peake, tr.; 1968)

4 A Catalan wizard who fools with shapes.

Bernard Berenson (1865–1959) Lithuanian-born US art historian. Referring to Pablo Picasso. Quoted in *Berenson: A Biography* (Sylvia Sprigge; 1960)

5 I wanted to become a work of art myself, and not an artist.

Bernard Berenson (1865–1959) Lithuanian-born US art historian. Quoted in *Sunset and Twilight: Diaries 1947–58* (N. Mariano, ed.; 1964)

6 It is comparatively easy to achieve a certain unity in a picture by allowing one colour to dominate, or by muting all the colours. Matisse did neither. He clashed his colours together like cymbals and the effect was like a lullaby.

John Berger (b. 1926) British novelist, essayist, and art critic. *Toward Reality: Essays in Seeing* (1962)

7 When Sir Joshua Reynolds died
All Nature was degraded;
The King dropped a tear in the Queen's ear,
And all his pictures faded.

William Blake (1757–1827) British poet, painter, engraver, and mystic. 1808? *Annotations to Reynolds' Discourses* (1808)

8 Debussy, Cézanne, Mallarmé: What do they teach us? Perhaps this—that one must dream one's revolution, not only construct it.

Pierre Boulez (b. 1925) French composer and conductor. 'La Corruption dans les Encensoirs', *Relevés d'Apprenti* (1966)

9 Remember I'm an artist. And you know what that means in a court of law. Next worst to an actress.

Joyce Cary (1888–1957) Irish-born British novelist. *The Horse's Mouth* (1944), ch. 14

10 The artist must scorn all judgement that is not based on an intelligent observation of character.

Paul Cézanne (1839–1906) French painter. Letter to Emile Bernard (1904), quoted in *Letters of Paul Cézanne* (John Rewald, ed.; 1976)

11 The artist must prophesy not in the sense that he foretells things to come, but in the sense that he tells his audience, at the risk of their displeasure, the secrets of their own hearts.

R. G. Collingwood (1889–1943) British philosopher, historian, and archaeologist. *The Principles of Art* (1938)

12 To give a body and a perfect form to your thought, this alone is what it is to be an artist.

Jacques-Louis David (1748–1825) French painter. 1796. Statement to his pupils, *Le Peintre Louis David 1748–1825: Souvenirs et Documents Inédits* (1880)

13 An artist is a creature driven by demons.

William Faulkner (1897–1962) US novelist. Interview, *Paris Review* (Spring 1956)

14 The aim of every artist is to arrest motion, which is life, by artificial means and hold it fixed so that a hundred years later, when a stranger looks at it, it moves again since it is life.

William Faulkner (1897–1962) US novelist. Interview, *Paris Review* (Spring 1956)

15 I do not believe any artist works in a state of fever. Even the mystics begin working only after the ineffable dove of the Holy Spirit has already abandoned their cells.

Federico García Lorca (1899–1936) Spanish poet and playwright. 1926. 'The Poetic Imagination of Luis de Góngora', *Deep Song* (Christopher Maurer, tr.; 1980)

16 No artist is ahead of his time. He *is* his time; it is just that others are behind the times.

Martha Graham (1893–1991) US dancer and choreographer. *Observer Magazine* (July 8, 1979)

17 We live in an age where the artist is forgotten. He is a researcher. I see myself that way.

David Hockney (b. 1937) British artist. *Observer* (June 9, 1991)

18 It is very good advice to believe only what an artist does, rather than what he says about his work.

David Hockney (b. 1937) British artist. Attrib.

19 His sickness has created atrocities that are repellent. Every one of his paintings deforms man, his body and his face.

Vladimir Semyonovich Kemenov, Russian art critic. Referring to Pablo Picasso. Attrib.

20 Being an artist now means to question the nature of art.

Joseph Kosuth (b. 1945) US conceptual artist. Quoted in *Arte Povera* (Germano Celant; 1968)

21 Everybody is an artist until he begins to learn: everybody becomes an artist after he has stopped learning.

Taban Lo Liyong (b. 1939) Sudanese poet, novelist, and short-story writer. *The Uniformed Man* (1971)

22 The product of the artist has become less important than the *fact* of the artist . . . In our society this person is much more important than anything he might create.

David Mamet (b. 1947) US writer and film director. 'Exuvial Magic', *Writing in Restaurants* (1986)

23 A common vice among artists—or rather bad artists—is a certain kind of mental cowardice because of which they refuse to take up any position whatsoever, invoking a misunderstood notion of the freedom of art, or other equally crass commonplaces.

Piero Manzoni (1933–63) Italian painter and multimedia artist. 'For the Discovery of Zone of Images' (1957), quoted in *Piero Manzoni* (Tate Gallery, London; 1974)

24 The great artist is one who conquers the romantic in himself.

Henry Miller (1891–1980) US novelist. *Black Spring* (1936)

25 We Catalans believe you must always plant your feet firmly on the ground if you want to be able to jump up in the air. The fact that I come down to earth from time to time makes it possible for me to jump all the higher.

Joan Miró (1893–1983) Catalan painter. Interview, *Partisan Review* (New York; February 1948)

26 The observation of nature is part of an artist's life, it enlarges his form and knowledge, keeps him fresh and from working only by formula, and feeds inspiration.

Henry Moore (1898–1986) British sculptor. Attrib.

27 I don't believe any real artists have ever been nonpolitical. They may have been insensitive to this particular plight or insensitive to that, but they were political because that's what an artist is—a politician.

Toni Morrison (b. 1931) US novelist. Interview, *Black Creation Annual* (1974–75)

28 Like any artist with no art form she became dangerous.

Toni Morrison (b. 1931) US novelist. *Sula* (1973)

29 All artists dream of a silence which they must enter, as some creatures return to the sea to spawn.

Iris Murdoch (1919–99) Irish-born British novelist and philosopher. Attrib.

30 Great artists have no country.

Alfred de Musset (1810–57) French poet and playwright. *Lorenzaccio* (1834), Act 1, Scene 5

31 Being an artist means ceasing to take seriously that very serious person we are when we are not an artist.

José Ortega y Gasset (1883–1955) Spanish writer and philosopher. *The Dehumanization of Art* (1925)

32 The artist's hand is more powerful still.
It washes all the dust and dirt away
So life, reality, the simple truth
Come freshly coloured from his dye works.

Boris Pasternak (1890–1960) Russian poet and novelist. 'After the Storm' (1956), quoted in *Boris Pasternak: The Tragic Years 1930–60* (Ann Pasternak Slater and Craig Raine, eds., trs.; 1990)

33 Artists are the monks of the bourgeois state.

Cesare Pavese (1908–50) Italian novelist and poet. July 25, 1940. *The Burning Brand: Diaries 1935–50* (1952)

34 Artists, as a rule, do not live in the purple; they live mainly in the red.

Lord Pearce (1901–85) British judge. Attrib.

35 It is better to be an artist, and delight in the contemplation of beauty, though this be only represented by nude nymphs, than to be indifferent and incredulous in everything.

Benito Pérez Galdós (1843–1920) Spanish novelist and playwright. *Doña Perfecta* (1876)

36 An artist must know how to convince others of the truth of his lies.

Pablo Picasso (1881–1973) Spanish painter and sculptor. Attrib.

37 In a few generations you can breed a racehorse. The recipe for making a man like Delacroix is less well known.

Pierre Auguste Renoir (1841–1919) French painter. Attrib.

38 He who resolves never to ransack any mind but his own, will be soon reduced, from mere barrenness, to the poorest of all imitations; he will be obliged to imitate himself, and to repeat what he has before often repeated.

Sir Joshua Reynolds (1723–92) British painter and writer. Discourse to the students of the Royal Academy (December 10, 1774), quoted in *Discourses on Art* (R. Wark, ed.; 1975), no. 15

39 An artist is a person who has invented an artist.

Harold Rosenberg (1906–78) US art historian. *Discovering the Present: Three Decades in Art, Culture and Politics* (1973)

40 I have seen, and heard, much of Cockney impudence before now; but never expected to hear a coxcomb ask two hundred guineas for flinging a pot of paint in the public's face.

John Ruskin (1819–1900) British art critic, writer, and reformer. June 18, 1877. Referring to Whistler's painting 'Nocturne in Black and Gold'. *Fors Clavigera* (1871–84), letter 79

41 Nobody cares much at heart about Titian, only there is a strange undercurrent of everlasting murmur about his name, which means the deep consent of all great men that he is greater than they.

John Ruskin (1819–1900) British art critic, writer, and reformer. *The Two Paths* (1859), lecture 2

42 Where artists can give to others . . . is in their discovery of a point of convergence where a physical fact denotes a state of consciousness. This is how art is generative.

Julian Schnabel (b. 1951) US painter and conceptual artist. 1983. Quoted in *Julian Schnabel: Paintings 1975–87* (Whitechapel Gallery, London; 1986)

43 Artists often depend on the manipulation of symbols to present ideas and associations not always apparent in such symbols. If all ideas and associations were evident there would be little need for artists to give expression to them . . . no need to make art.

Andres Serrano (b. 1950) US artist. The letter was written in defence of a photograph by Andres Serrano that was criticized by Jesse Helms in Congress. The addressee, Hugh Southern, was acting chairman of the National Endowment for the Arts. Letter to Hugh Southern (May 18, 1989), quoted in *Theories and Documents of Contemporary Art: A Sourcebook of Artists' Writings* (Kristine Stiles and Peter Selz, eds.; 1996)

44 The artist who always paints the same scene pleases the public for the sole reason that it recognises him with ease and thinks itself a connoisseur.

Alfred Stevens (1818–75) British artist. Attrib.

45 What is an artist? For every thousand people there's nine hundred doing the work, ninety doing well, nine doing good, and one lucky bastard who's the artist.

Tom Stoppard (b. 1937) Czech-born British playwright and screenwriter. Also used with slightly differing words in *Artist Descending a Staircase* (1972). *Travesties* (1974), Act 1

46 Artists go through periodic crises in which they feel an urge to destroy themselves. This is important, because if we succeed in mastering the crisis we rise again, as if reborn, from our own ashes.

Antoni Tàpies (b. 1923) Spanish painter. Quoted in *Conversations with Antoni Tàpies* (Barbara Catoir; 1991)

47 A genius with the IQ of a moron.

Gore Vidal (b. 1925) US novelist and essayist. Referring to Andy Warhol. Interview, *Observer* (June 18, 1989)

The Arts

see also **Art**, **Films**, **Literature**, **Music**, **Opera**, **Painting**, **Photography**, **Theatre**

1 Music, Beauty, are within us . . . great works are those that awaken our spirit, great men are those who give them form.

Louis-Ferdinand Céline (1894–1961) French novelist and physician. *Semmelweis* (1936)

2 The excellence of every art is its intensity, capable of making all disagreeables evaporate, from their being in close relationship with beauty and truth.

John Keats (1795–1821) English poet. Letter to George and Thomas Keats (December 21, 1817)

3 Art raises its head when religions relax their hold.

Friedrich Wilhelm Nietzsche (1844–1900) German philosopher and poet. *Human, All Too Human* (1878–80)

4 The arts cannot thrive except where men are free
   to be themselves and to be in charge of the
   discipline of their own energies and ardors. The
   conditions for democracy and art are one.
   Franklin D. Roosevelt (1882–1945) US president. Speech on the
   occasion of the dedication of the Museum of Modern Art,
   New York City (May 10, 1939)

5 The two pioneering forces of modern sensibility
   are Jewish seriousness and homosexual
   aestheticism and irony.
   Susan Sontag (b. 1933) US writer. 'Notes on Camp', *Against
   Interpretation* (1966)

6 The secret of the arts is to correct nature.
   Voltaire (1694–1778) French writer and philosopher. 'À M. de
   Verrière', *Épîtres* (1769)

Asia

see also Asian Cities, Asian Countries

1 The Archipelago has lasting fascination. It is not
   easy to shake off the spell of island life.
   Joseph Conrad (1857–1924) Polish-born British novelist. Referring to
   the Malay Archipelago, extending from Indonesia, through
   the Philippines, to New Guinea. *Victory* (1915), pt. 2, ch. 1

2 Asia is not going to be civilized after the methods
   of the West. There is too much Asia and she is
   too old.
   Rudyard Kipling (1865–1936) Indian-born British writer and poet. 'The
   Man Who Was', *Life's Handicap* (1891)

3 The wind from the East prevails over the West.
   Mao Zedong (1893–1976) Chinese statesman. September 5, 1958.
   Quoted in *Maoism: Slogans and Practice* (Vladimir Glebov;
   1978)

4 The orient . . . vacillates between the West's
   contempt for what is familiar and its shivers of
   delight in—or fear of—novelty.
   Edward W. Said (b. 1935) Palestinian-born US writer and educator.
   Orientalism (1978)

5 It was easier to conquer it than to know what to
   do with it.
   Horace Walpole (1717–97) British writer. Referring to the East. Letter
   to Sir Horace Mann (March 27, 1772), quoted in
   Correspondence (Yale, ed.), vol. 23

6 There is every likelihood that the centre of world
   economy will shift to the Asia-Pacific in the next
   century. This economic growth will be
   accompanied by a cultural renaissance of
   historical importance.
   George Yeo (b. 1954) Singaporean politician. Quoted in *Singapore:
   Global City for the Arts* (Singapore Economic Development
   Board; 1994)

Asian Cities

see also Asia, Cities

1 A city of teeming millions and multi-millionaires.
   of beggars, lepers, haves and have-nots
   of dug-up trenches pavements and roads;
   oh, is the pattern of developing Calcutta—
   . . . a city battered, shattered and shivering,
   maimed, mauled and man handled.
   Sudhansu Mohan Banerjee, Indian civil servant and academic. 'Long
   Live Calcutta', *The Voice of the Indian Poets* (Pranab
   Bandyopadhyay, ed.; 1975)

2 To write about Peking's food and cooking one
   has to write about Peking itself, for they are such
   an integral part of the city's life.
   Kenneth H. Lo (1913–95) British cookery writer. *Peking Cooking* (1970)

3 Stay too long in a room filled with orchids and
   you no longer notice their fragrance. I must have
   lived in Beijing too long, for I no longer notice its
   quiet. To me, it was a very lively place indeed.
   Lu Xun (1881–1936) Chinese writer. 1922. 'A Comedy of Ducks',
   Diary of a Madman and Other Stories (William A. Lyell, tr.;
   1990)

4 The whole city is arrayed in squares just like a
   chess-board, and disposed in a manner so perfect
   and masterly that it is impossible to give a
   description that should do it justice.
   Marco Polo (1254–1324) Venetian merchant and traveller. Referring to
   Kublai Khan's capital, Cambaluc (later Beijing). *The Travels
   of Marco Polo* (1298–99)

Asian Countries

see also Asia, Asian Cities

1 On the Chinese mainland, the Anti-Rightist
   campaign was followed by the Cultural
   Revolution, an earthshaking disaster without
   precedent in the history of human civilization.
   Bo Yang (b. 1920) Taiwanese writer. Speech, Iowa University
   (September 24, 1984)

2 We should not reward China with improved
   trade status when it has . . . failed to make
   sufficient progress on human rights since the
   Tiananmen Square massacre.
   Bill Clinton (b. 1946) US president. The Tiananmen Square Protest
   took place in 1989. *Putting People First: How We Can All
   Change America* (co-written with Al Gore; 1992)

3 Over time, the more we bring China into the
   world, the more the world will bring freedom to
   China.
   Bill Clinton (b. 1946) US president. *Time* (1998)

4 Any relationship between Tibet and China will
   have to be based on the principles of equality,
   respect, trust, and mutual benefit.
   Dalai Lama (b. 1935) Tibetan spiritual leader. Speech on acceptance
   of a Nobel Prize in peace, Stockholm, Sweden (December 10,
   1989)

5 We know our cause is just. Because violence can
   only breed more violence and suffering, our
   struggle must remain nonviolent and free of
   hatred. We are trying to end the suffering of our
   people, not to inflict suffering on others.
   Dalai Lama (b. 1935) Tibetan spiritual leader. Referring to Tibet.
   Speech on acceptance of a Nobel Prize in peace, Stockholm,
   Sweden (December 10, 1989)

6 It is my dream that the entire Tibetan plateau
   should become a free refuge where humanity and
   nature can live in peace and in harmonious
   balance. It would be a place where people from
   all over the world could come to seek the true
   meaning of peace within themselves, away from
   the tensions and pressures of much of the rest of
   the world.
   Dalai Lama (b. 1935) Tibetan spiritual leader. Speech, Oslo
   (December 11, 1989)

7 All six million Tibetans should be on the list of
   endangered peoples. This struggle is thus my first
   responsibility.
   Dalai Lama (b. 1935) Tibetan spiritual leader. *My Tibet* (co-written
   with Galen Rowell; 1990)

8 By Marxism we mean Marxism that is integrated
with Chinese conditions, and by socialism we
mean socialism that is tailored to Chinese
conditions and has Chinese characteristics.
Deng Xiaoping (1904–97) Chinese statesman. 'Build Socialism with
Chinese Characteristics' (June 30, 1984), quoted in *Deng
Xiaoping: Speeches and Writings* (Robert Maxwell, ed.;
1987)

9 No foreign country can expect China to be its
vassal nor can it expect China to accept anything
harmful to China's interests.
Deng Xiaoping (1904–97) Chinese statesman. Opening Speech to the
12th National Congress of the Communist Party of China
(September 1, 1982), quoted in *Deng Xiaoping: Speeches and
Writings* (Robert Maxwell, ed.; 1987)

10 The modern image of China was not created by
the government of the Qing Dynasty, nor by the
northern warlords, nor by Chiang Kai-shek and
his son. It is the People's Republic of China that
has transformed China's image.
Deng Xiaoping (1904–97) Chinese statesman. *One Country, Two
Systems* (1984), quoted in *Deng Xiaoping: Speeches and
Writings* (Robert Maxwell, ed.; 1987)

11 If India won her freedom through truth and non-
violence, India would not only point the way to
all the exploited Asiatic nations, she would
become a torch-bearer for the Negro races.
Mahatma Gandhi (1869–1948) Indian national leader. Quoted in
Questions in the Philosophy of Restraint (Indira Rothermund;
1963)

12 Almost one out of every four people in the world
is Chinese, you know, even though many of them
might not look it.
Joseph Heller (1923–99) US novelist. *Good as Gold* (1979)

13 A relay race, run with a Ming vase instead of a
baton.
Geoffrey Howe (b. 1926) British politician. Describing the handover of
Hong Kong to China in 1997. *Sunday Times* (July 20, 1997)

14 There is nothing Japan really wants to buy from
foreign countries except, possibly, neckties with
unusual designs.
Yoshihiro Inayama, Japanese business executive. *Sydney Morning
Herald* (August 3, 1984), 'Sayings of the Week'

15 History shows that anything conducive to our
national stability is good.
Jiang Zemin (b. 1926) Chinese president. Referring to the massacre
in Tiananmen Square (1989). *Times* (May 14, 1994)

16 We got one little island—600 square kilometres.
You unwind this, you will not drop on soft
paddy fields, it is hard, hard concrete, your bones
are broken and it's kaput.
Kuan Yew Lee (b. 1923) Singaporean statesman. Referring to the
consequences of Singapore's embracing Western values.
Speech, National Day, *Independent* (November 24, 1995)

17 I had one simple guiding principle of survival
from the very start, that Singapore had to be
better organised than the countries of the region.
Kuan Yew Lee (b. 1923) Singaporean statesman. Explaining that to
survive as a city state, Singapore had to leap-frog its
neighbours economically. *Straits Times* (Singapore; June 8,
1996)

18 People of the Philippines, I have returned.
Douglas MacArthur (1880–1964) US general. Referring to his return
to lead the reconquest of the Philippines from Japan (1944–
45). Under orders, he had left the Philippines for Australia
before the Japanese invasion in 1942. Radio broadcast, Leyte,
Philippines (October 20, 1944)

19 Letting a hundred flowers blossom and a
hundred schools of thought contend is the policy
for promoting the progress of the arts and the
sciences and a flourishing socialist culture in our
land.
Mao Zedong (1893–1976) Chinese statesman. February 27, 1957.
Speech, *Quotations of Chairman Mao* (1966)

20 Many dare not openly admit that contradictions
still exist among the people of our country,
although it is these very contradictions that are
pushing our society forward.
Mao Zedong (1893–1976) Chinese statesman. Quoted in
'Continuation of the Revolution under the Dictatorship of the
Proletariat', *Maoism: Slogans and Practice* (Vladimir Glebov;
1978)

21 Contemporary China has grown out of the China
of the past; we are Marxist in our historical
approach and must not lop off our history. We
should sum up our history from Confucius to
Sun Yat-sen and take over this valuable legacy.
Mao Zedong (1893–1976) Chinese statesman. 1938. Quoted in *The
Chinese* (Alain Peyrefitte, Graham Webb, tr.; 1977)

22 We must tell the people and tell our comrades
that there will be twists and turns in our road.
There are still many obstacles and difficulties
along the road of revolution. We must be
prepared to follow the road which exists and
turns.
Mao Zedong (1893–1976) Chinese statesman. 1945. Quoted in *The
Chinese* (Alain Peyrefitte, Graham Webb, tr.; 1977)

23 Their major commodity was . . . people. They
exported people—domestic servants to Kuwait,
prostitutes to Japan and Lagos, nurses to Dubai,
tailors to Jeddah, construction workers to Iraq.
Timothy Mo (b. 1950) Hong Kong-born British novelist. Referring to the
economy of the Philippines. *Brownout on Breadfruit
Boulevard* (1995), ch. 1

24 The country was on the slide, in the mire, had
teetered on the brink of the crater so long no one
suffered from vertigo any more. They were a
nation as blasé as steeplejacks and as
irresponsible as crows.
Timothy Mo (b. 1950) Hong Kong-born British novelist. Referring to the
Philippines. *Brownout on Breadfruit Boulevard* (1995), ch. 1

25 At the stroke of the midnight hour, India will
awake to life and freedom. A moment comes,
which comes but rarely in history, when we step
out from the old to the new, when an age ends,
and when the sound of a nation, long suppressed,
finds utterance.
Jawaharlal Nehru (1889–1964) Indian prime minister. Referring to
Indian independence. Speech to the Lok Sabha, the lower
house of the Indian parliament (August 14, 1947)

26 Even the Hooligan was probably invented in
China centuries before we thought of him.
Saki (1870–1916) British short-story writer. 'Reginald on House-
Parties', *Reginald* (1904)

27 To the Chinese we have given
kerosene, bullets, Bibles
and they have given us radishes, soy beans, silk,
poems, paintings, proverbs,
porcelain, egg foo yong,
gunpowder, Fourth of July firecrackers, fireworks
and labor gangs for the first Pacific railways.
Carl Sandburg (1878–1967) US poet and biographer. 'The Copperfaces,
the Red Men', *The People, Yes* (1936)

28 The more recent flood of pop culture and the secularization of literature have raised the alarm that serious culture is being engulfed.

Wang Meng (b. 1934) Chinese writer and politician. 'Literary Debates in China Today' (Taotao Liu, tr.; 1997)

29 It is impossible to modernize the country unless you let the intelligence of a thousand million individuals unfold.

Xu Wenli (b. 1944) Chinese dissident. February 1980. Referring to China. Attrib.

30 From time immemorial, China has had people who obey, and people who are thugs, but China has never had citizens.

Yu Jie (b. 1973) Chinese writer. 1990s. Quoted in 'Fire and Ice', Far Eastern Economic Review (Matty Forney; April 1998)

Assassination

see also Killing, Murder

1 I have too great a soul to die like a criminal.

John Wilkes Booth (1839–65) US actor and assassin. John Wilkes Booth assassinated President Abraham Lincoln on April 14, 1865. He died resisting arrest 12 days later. Attrib.

2 I am sure no man in England will take away my life to make you King.

Charles II (1630–85) English monarch. 1678. Said to his brother James following revelation of the Popish Plot fabricated by Titus Oates. Quoted in Political and Literary Anecdotes (William King; 1818)

3 They really are bad shots.

Charles de Gaulle (1890–1970) French president. Remark after narrowly escaping death in an assassination attempt. Quoted in Ten First Ladies of the World (Pauline Frederick; 1962)

4 You may assassinate us but you won't intimidate us.

Arthur Griffith (1872–1922) Irish nationalist. 1922. Referring to Eamon de Valera's threats to kill Free State supporters. Quoted in Michael Collins: A Biography (Tim Pat Coogan; 1990)

5 What would be the first thing I'd do if I were president? Buy a bullet proof vest!

Eddy Murphy (b. 1961) US comedian, actor, and director. Ebony (July 1988)

6 I thought of assassinating many whom I regarded as obstacles between our country and its future. I began to expose their crimes and set myself as a judge of their actions and of the harm that these brought upon the country.

Gamal Abdel Nasser (1918–70) Egyptian statesman. The Philosophy of the Revolution (1952)

7 Friends and comrades, I do not quite know what to tell you and how to say it. Our beloved leader, Bapu as we called him, the father of our nation, is no more. The light has gone out . . .

Jawaharlal Nehru (1889–1964) Indian prime minister. Referring to the assassination of Mahatma Gandhi. Broadcast on All India Radio (January 30, 1948)

8 Honey, I forgot to duck.

Ronald Reagan (b. 1911) US president and actor. March 30, 1981. Said to his wife, Nancy, after an assassination attempt by John Hinckley III. Sunday Times (December 3, 1989)

9 Assassination is the extreme form of censorship.

George Bernard Shaw (1856–1950) Irish playwright. 'Limits to Toleration', The Shewing-Up of Blanco Posnet (1911)

10 Robert Kennedy . . . died last night . . . Martin Luther King was shot a month ago . . . And every day my Government gives me a count of corpses created by military science in Vietnam. So it goes.

Kurt Vonnegut (b. 1922) US novelist. Slaughterhouse-Five (1969), ch. 10

Astronomy

see also Science, The Universe

1 Those who first invented and then named the constellations were storytellers.

John Berger (b. 1926) British novelist, essayist, and art critic. And Our Faces, My Heart, Brief as Photos (1984)

2 If we relate the life of a star to the life of a man . . . the Sun is but a week old . . . Life has existed on this planet for two or three days of the week that has passed; the whole of human history lies within the last second, and there are eighty years to come.

Arthur C. Clarke (b. 1917) British writer and scientist. By Space Possessed (1993)

3 The wonder is, not that the field of the stars is so vast, but that man has measured it.

Anatole France (1844–1924) French novelist, poet, and critic. The Garden of Epicurus (1894)

4 In my studies of astronomy and philosophy I hold this opinion about the universe, that the Sun remains fixed in the centre of the circle of heavenly bodies, without changing its place; and the Earth, turning upon itself, moves round the Sun.

Galileo (1564–1642) Italian scientist. Letter to Cristina di Lorena, Grandduchess of Tuscany (1615)

5 It is the Holy Spirit's intention to teach us how to go to heaven, not how the heavens go.

Galileo (1564–1642) Italian scientist. Letter to Cristina di Lorena, Grandduchess of Tuscany (1615)

6 Yet it moves.

Galileo (1564–1642) Italian scientist. Referring to the earth, and supposedly said after his recantation before the Inquisition of belief in the Copernican system, which proposed that the earth revolved round the sun. Remark (1632), attrib.

7 I therefore concluded, and decided unhesitatingly, that there are three stars in the heavens moving about Jupiter, as Venus and Mercury round the Sun; which at length was established as clear as daylight by numerous other subsequent observations.

Galileo (1564–1642) Italian scientist. Referring to his observations with a telescope he had made. The Starry Messenger (March 1610)

8 A black hole has no hair.

John Archibald Wheeler (b. 1911) US theoretical physicist. Referring to the No-Hair Theorem, which states that black holes are characterized by only a limited number of quantities. Gravitation (co-written with Charles W. Misner and Kip S. Thorne; 1973)

9 There is nothing in the world except empty curved space. Matter, charge, electromagnetism, and other fields are only manifestations of the curvature of space.

John Archibald Wheeler (b. 1911) US theoretical physicist. 1957. Quoted in New Scientist (September 26, 1974)

Atheism

see also Belief, God, Nihilism

1   I cannot be angry at God, in whom I do not believe.
Simone de Beauvoir (1908–86) French writer and feminist theorist. *Observer* (January 7, 1979)

2   That is the rock of atheism. The tiniest spasm of pain, be it in a single atom, and divine creation is utterly torn asunder.
Georg Büchner (1813–37) German dramatist. *Danton's Death* (1835), Act 3, Scene 1, quoted in *Complete Plays, Lenz and Other Writings* (John Reddick, tr.; 1993)

3   I am an atheist still, thank God.
Luis Buñuel (1900–83) Spanish film director. *Le Monde* (December 16, 1959)

4   I don't know that atheists should be considered citizens, nor should they be considered patriots. This is one nation under God.
George Bush (b. 1924) US president. *Free Inquiry* magazine (1988)

5   The church and the rumshop! . . . They're one and the same, you know. Both a damn conspiracy to keep us pacified and in ignorance.
Paule Marshall (b. 1929) US novelist, teacher, and journalist. *The Chosen Place, The Timeless People* (1969)

6   It has been said that the highest praise of God consists in the denial of Him by the atheist, who finds creation so perfect that he can dispense with a creator.
Marcel Proust (1871–1922) French novelist. 1921. Le Côté de Guermantes, *À la Recherche du Temps Perdu* (1913–27)

7   God, Satan, Paradise and Hell all vanished one day in my fifteenth year, when I quite abruptly lost my faith.
Salman Rushdie (b. 1947) Indian-born British novelist. *Imaginary Homelands* (1991), pt. 12, ch. 2

8   I was told that the Chinese said they would bury me by the Western Lake and build a shrine to my memory. I have some slight regret that this did not happen, as I might have become a god, which would have been very *chic* for an atheist.
Bertrand Russell (1872–1970) British philosopher and mathematician. *The Autobiography of Bertrand Russell* (1967–69), vol. 2, ch. 3

9   By night an atheist half believes a God.
Edward Young (1683–1765) English poet. *The Complaint, or Night Thoughts on Life, Death, and Immortality* (1742–45), bk. 5, l. 176

Athens

see European Cities

Audiences

see also Films, Performance, Theatre

1   Long experience has taught me that in England nobody goes to the theatre unless he or she has bronchitis.
James Agate (1877–1947) British theatre critic. *Ego* (June 9, 1943)

2   Audiences? No, the plural is impossible. Whether it be in Butte, Montana, or Broadway, it's an audience. The same great hulking monster with four thousand eyes and forty thousand teeth.
John Barrymore (1882–1942) US actor. Letter to playwright Ashton Stevens (April 1906), quoted in *Good Night, Sweet Prince* (Gene Fowler; 1943)

3   In the theatre the audience want to be surprised—but by things that they expect.
Tristan Bernard (1866–1947) French novelist and dramatist. *Contes, Répliques et Bon Mots* (Patrice Boussel, ed.; 1964)

4   Convicts are the best audience I ever played for.
Johnny Cash (b. 1932) US country music singer-songwriter and guitarist. Attrib.

5   Always make the audience suffer as much as possible.
Alfred Hitchcock (1899–1980) British-born US film director. Quoted in *Filmgoer's Book of Quotes* (Leslie Halliwell; 1973)

6   On stage I have to make love to 25,000 different people, then I go home alone.
Janis Joplin (1943–70) US rock singer. Quoted in *The Wit and Wisdom of Rock and Roll* (Maxim Jabukowski, ed.; 1983)

7   There are performances where the public is quite without talent.
Louis Jouvet (1887–1951) French actor, director, and writer. Quoted in *The Jingle Bell Principle* (Miroslav Holub; 1992)

8   Would the people in the cheaper seats clap your hands? And the rest of you, if you'll just rattle your jewellery.
John Lennon (1940–80) British rock musician. Remark, Royal Variety performance (November 4, 1963)

9   I know it's like a Nuremberg Rally, but our fans are sensible people.
Brian May (b. 1947) British rock guitarist and songwriter. Referring to a concert by Queen. Quoted in *The Wit and Wisdom of Rock and Roll* (Maxim Jabukowski, ed.; 1983)

10   Don't clap too hard—it's a very old building.
John Osborne (1929–94) British playwright and screenwriter. *The Entertainer* (1957), Scene 7

11   Those people on the stage are making such a noise I can't hear a word you're saying.
Henry Taylor Parker (1867–1934) US music critic. Rebuking some talkative members of an audience, near whom he was sitting. Quoted in *The Humor of Music* (L. Humphrey; 1971)

12   I know two kinds of audience only—one coughing and one not coughing.
Artur Schnabel (1882–1951) Austrian pianist and composer. *My Life and Music* (Edward Crankshaw, ed.; 1961), pt. 2, ch. 10

13   Applause is a receipt, not a note of demand.
Artur Schnabel (1882–1951) Austrian pianist and composer. *Saturday Review of Literature* (September 29, 1951)

14   I quite agree with you, sir, but what can two do against so many?
George Bernard Shaw (1856–1950) Irish playwright. Responding to a solitary hiss heard amid the applause at the first performance of *Arms and the Man* in 1894. Quoted in *Oxford Book of Literary Anecdotes* (James Sutherland, ed.; 1975)

15   I always think of the audience when I'm directing—because I am the audience.
Steven Spielberg (b. 1947) US film director. 1987. Quoted in *Film Yearbook 1988* (1988)

16   The audience is a huge mirror reflecting the actor's creativity. We must learn to look into this mirror and see what we create. An actor must act as the character and listen as an actor.
Constantin Stanislavsky (1863–1938) Russian actor and theatre director. Quoted in *The Stanislavski Method* (Sonia Moore; 1960)

17   The play was a great success, but the audience was a disaster.
Oscar Wilde (1854–1900) Irish poet, playwright, and wit. Referring to a play that had recently failed. Attrib.

18 An audience is never wrong. An individual
    member of it may be an imbecile, but a thousand
    imbeciles together in the dark—that's critical
    genius.
    Billy Wilder (1906–2002) Austrian-born US film director and screenwriter.
    Arena (BBC Television; January 24, 1992)

Australia

1 Being lost in Australia gives you a lovely feeling
   of security.
   Bruce Chatwin (1940–89) British writer and traveller. *The Songlines* (1987)

2 For Australian culture . . . the world of the
   Aboriginal has become the 'cursed and precious'
   part of the subconscious . . . the unknown Other
   who keeps the longing for identity in a constant
   crisis and inflames it.
   Stefan Hertmans (b. 1951) Belgian writer and academic. *Intercities* (2001)

3 Never had a colony been founded so far from its
   parent state, or in such ignorance of the land it
   occupied.
   Robert Hughes (b. 1938) Australian writer and critic. *The Fatal Shore*
   (1987)

4 The jail of infinite space.
   Robert Hughes (b. 1938) Australian writer and critic. Referring to
   Australia. *The Fatal Shore* (1987)

5 Earth is here so kind, that just tickle her with a
   hoe and she laughs with a harvest.
   Douglas Jerrold (1803–57) British playwright. 'A Land of Plenty', *Wit
   and Opinions* (Blanchard Jerrold, ed.; 1859)

6 And all lying mysteriously within the Australian
   underdark, that peculiar, lost weary aloofness of
   Australia. There was the vast town of Sydney.
   And it didn't seem to be real, it seemed to be
   sprinkled on the surface of a darkness into which
   it never penetrated.
   D. H. Lawrence (1885–1930) British writer. *Kangaroo* (1923), ch. 1

7 The indifference—the fern-dark indifference of
   this remote golden Australia. Not to care—from
   the bottom of one's soul, not to care.
   D. H. Lawrence (1885–1930) British writer. *Kangaroo* (1923), ch. 10

8 Waiting for the Australian republic is like waiting
   for the other shoe to drop. We all know it is
   coming; according to one's convictions it is
   therefore either a sour and uncreative delaying
   operation or a sort of null interregnum in which
   all energies are frustrated.
   Les Murray (b. 1938) Australian poet. 'The Australian Republic', *The
   Paperbark Tree* (1992)

Austria

see **Europe, European Countries**

Authoritarianism

see also **Dictators, Fascism, Totalitarianism, Tyranny**

1 The intention of autocracy is the glory of the
   citizen, the state, and the sovereign.
   Catherine the Great (1729–96) German-born Russian empress. 1767.
   Quoted in *The Nakaz: the draft instructions for a legal code*
   (Nikolai Chechulin, ed.; 1907)

2 I shall be an autocrat: that's my trade. And the
   good Lord will forgive me: that's his.
   Catherine the Great (1729–96) German-born Russian empress. Attrib.

3 To live by one man's will became the cause of all
   men's misery.
   Richard Hooker (1554?–1600) English theologian. *Of the Laws of
   Ecclesiastical Polity* (1594), bk. 1

4 Illiterates have to dictate.
   Stanislaw Lec (1909–66) Polish writer. 1964. Quoted in *The Jingle
   Bell Principle* (Miroslav Holub; 1992)

5 I am painted as the greatest little dictator, which
   is ridiculous—you always take some
   consultations.
   Margaret Thatcher (b. 1925) British prime minister. *Times* (1983)

Authors

see **Writers**

Autobiography

see also **Biography, Books, Diaries, Literature, The Self**

1 Autobiography is the poor man's history.
   Raymond Carver (1938–88) US poet, short-story writer, and essayist.
   'Blackbird Pie', *Where I'm Calling From* (1988)

2 An autobiography is an obituary in serial form
   with the last instalment missing.
   Quentin Crisp (1908–99) British writer. *The Naked Civil Servant*
   (1968)

3 Every artist writes his own autobiography.
   Havelock Ellis (1859–1939) British psychologist. 'Tolstoy', *The New
   Spirit* (1890)

4 To write one's memoirs is to speak ill of
   everybody except oneself.
   Henri Philippe Pétain (1856–1951) French political and military leader.
   Observer (May 26, 1946)

5 These are not memoirs about myself. These are
   memoirs about other people. Others will write
   about us. And naturally they'll lie through their
   teeth—but that's their business.
   Dmitri Shostakovich (1906–75) Russian composer. 1971–75. The
   opening paragraph of the composer's posthumously published
   memoirs. *Testimony: The Memoirs of Shostakovich* (Solomon
   Volkov, ed., Antonina W. Bouis, tr.; 1979), ch. 1

Autumn

see also **Seasons**

1 How well I know what I mean to do
   When the long dark autumn-evenings come.
   Robert Browning (1812–89) British poet. 'By the Fire-Side', *Men and
   Women* (1855), st. 1

2 The melancholy days are come, the saddest of the
   year,
   Of wailing winds and naked woods and
   meadows brown and sear.
   William Cullen Bryant (1794–1878) US poet and journalist. 'The Death
   of the Flowers' (1832), st. 1

3 I saw old Autumn in the misty morn
   Stand shadowless like Silence, listening
   To silence.
   Thomas Hood (1799–1845) British poet and humorist. 'Ode: Autumn'
   (1827), st. 1

4 Season of mists and mellow fruitfulness,
Close bosom-friend of the maturing sun;
Conspiring with him how to load and bless
With fruit the vines that round the thatch-eaves
run.

John Keats (1795–1821) English poet. 'To Autumn' (1820), st. 1, ll.
1–4

5 Yet once more, O ye laurels, and once more
Ye myrtles brown, with ivy never sere,
I come to pluck your berries harsh and crude,
And with forced fingers rude,
Shatter your leaves before the mellowing year.

John Milton (1608–74) English writer. 1638. 'Lycidas', *Poems of Mr.
John Milton* (1645), ll. 1–5

6 When lofty trees I see barren of leaves,
Which erst from heat did canopy the herd,
And summer's green all girded up in sheaves,
Borne on the bier with white and bristly beard.

William Shakespeare (1564–1616) English poet and playwright. Sonnet
12 (1609)

7 O wild West Wind, thou breath of Autumn's
being,
Thou, from whose unseen presence the leaves
dead
Are driven, like ghosts from an enchanter fleeing,
Yellow, and black, and pale, and hectic red,
Pestilence-stricken multitudes.

Percy Bysshe Shelley (1792–1822) English poet. 'Ode to the West
Wind' (1819), ll. 1–5

8 The last red leaf is whirl'd away,
The rooks are blown about the skies.

Alfred Tennyson (1809–92) British poet. 1833–49. 'A. H. H.' (Arthur
Henry Hallam) was the fiancé of Tennyson's sister Emily and
died suddenly in September 1833. *In Memoriam A. H. H.*
(1850), can. 15, st. 1

9 The drawn-out sobs of the violins of autumn
wound my heart with a monotonous languor.

Paul Verlaine (1844–96) French poet. 'Chanson d'Automne', *Poèmes
Saturniens* (1866)

Awards

see also **Achievement, Success, Victory**

1 I don't deserve this, but I have arthritis, and I
don't deserve that either.

Jack Benny (1894–1974) US actor and comedian. Said when accepting
an award. Attrib.

2 Nothing would disgust me more morally than
winning an Oscar.

Luis Buñuel (1900–83) Spanish film director. *Variety* (1971), quoted
in *Chambers Film Quotes* (Tony Crawley, ed.; 1991)

3 My mother polishes them to an inch of their lives
until the metal shows. That sums up the
Academy Awards—all glitter on the outside and
base metal coming through. Nice presents for a
day. But they don't make you any better.

Glenda Jackson (b. 1936) British actor and politician. Referring to her
two Oscars: *Women in Love* (1969) and *A Touch of Class*
(1973). *People* (March 18, 1985), quoted in *Chambers Film
Quotes* (Tony Crawley, ed.; 1991)

4 I am not going to thank anybody—because I did
it all myself.

Spike Milligan (1918–2002) Indian-born British humorist, writer, and actor.
On receiving the British Comedy Award for Lifetime
Achievement. Speech (1994)

5 I brought a lot of tranquillisers and my mother.

Emma Thompson (b. 1959) British actor. 1992. Remark on receiving
the Oscar for Best Actress for her performance in *Howards
End* (1991). Attrib.

B

Babies

see also **Birth, Children, Parents, Pregnancy**

1 The eyes will see no evil colours, the ears will hear no evil sounds, the mouth will speak no evil words: this is the meaning of the foetal education.
Anonymous. 'Biographies of Virtuous Women', *Song Encyclopedia* (9th century), quoted in *Imperfect Conceptions: Medical Knowledge, Birth Defects, and Eugenics in China* (Frank Dikotter; 1998)

2 Madam, all babies look like me.
Winston Churchill (1874–1965) British prime minister and writer. When a woman said her baby looked like him. Attrib.

3 There is no more sombre enemy of good art than the pram in the hall.
Cyril Connolly (1903–74) British writer and journalist. *Enemies of Promise* (1938), ch. 14

4 If men had to have babies they would only ever have one each.
Princess Diana (1961–97) British princess. *Observer* (July 29, 1984), 'Sayings of the Week'

5 Every baby born into the world is a finer one than the last.
Charles Dickens (1812–70) British novelist. *Nicholas Nickleby* (1839), ch. 36

6 I often think it's comical
How Nature always does contrive
That every boy and every gal
That's born into the world alive
Is either a little Liberal
Or else a little Conservative!
W. S. Gilbert (1836–1911) British librettist and playwright. *Iolanthe* (1882), Act 1, 'Private Willis' Song'

7 A loud noise at one end and no sense of responsibility at the other.
Ronald Knox (1888–1957) British priest and writer. Definition of a baby. Attrib.

8 The new-born child does not realize that his body is more a part of himself than surrounding objects . . . and it is only by degrees, through pain, that he understands the fact of the body.
Somerset Maugham (1874–1965) British writer. *Of Human Bondage* (1915), ch. 13

9 All these are yours, baby born of woman, if you'll only go to sleep.
Gabriela Mistral (1889–1957) Spanish poet, diplomat, and educator. 'If You'll Only Go to Sleep', *Tenura* (1924)

10 Babies are, then, obviously narcissistic but not in the way adults are, not even Spinoza's God, and I am a little afraid that Freud sometimes forgets that the narcissistic baby has no sense of self.
Jean Piaget (1896–1980) Swiss psychologist. Referring to Baruch Spinoza and Sigmund Freud. 'The First Year of Life of the Child' (1927), quoted in *The Essential Piaget* (H. E. Gruber and J. Jacques Vonèche, eds.; 1977)

11 Nothing grows in our garden, only washing. And babies.
Dylan Thomas (1914–53) Welsh poet, playwright, and short-story writer. Thomas's 'play for voices', written for the BBC and first broadcast on January 25, 1954. *Under Milk Wood* (1954)

12 Begin, baby boy: if you haven't had a smile for your parent, then neither will a god think you worth inviting to dinner, nor a goddess to bed.
Virgil (70–19 BC) Roman poet. *Eclogues* (37 BC), no. 4, l. 62

Ballet

see **Dancing**

Barcelona

see **European Cities**

Beauty

see also **Aesthetics, Appearance**

1 Beauty can be as isolating as genius, or deformity. I have always been aware of a relationship between madness and beauty.
Richard Avedon (b. 1923) US fashion and portrait photographer. Quoted in *Model: The Ugly Business of Beautiful Women* (Michael Gross; 1995)

2 There is no excellent beauty that hath not some strangeness in the proportion.
Francis Bacon (1561–1626) English philosopher, statesman, and lawyer. 'Of Beauty', *Essays* (1625)

3 What do I care that you are good? Be beautiful! and be sad!
Charles Baudelaire (1821–67) French poet. 'Madrigal Triste', *Nouvelles Fleurs du Mal* (1868), st.1

4 Exuberance is Beauty.
William Blake (1757–1827) British poet, painter, engraver, and mystic. 'Proverbs of Hell', *The Marriage of Heaven and Hell* (1790–93), plate 10, l. 4

5 For beauty being the best of all we know
Sums up the unsearchable and secret aims
Of nature.
Robert Bridges (1844–1930) British poet. 'The Growth of Love' (1876), st. 8, ll. 1–3

6 Incredibly, inordinately, devastatingly, immortally, calamitously, hearteningly, adorably beautiful.
Rupert Brooke (1887–1915) British poet. Referring to the actor Cathleen Nesbitt. Quoted in 'Rupert Brooke', *Rupert Brooke* (C. Hassall; 1972)

7 That's it, baby, if you've got it, flaunt it.
Mel Brooks (b. 1926) US film actor and director. *The Producers* (1968)

8 Beauty in distress is much the most affecting
beauty.
Edmund Burke (1729–97) Irish-born British statesman and political
philosopher. *A Philosophical Inquiry into the Origin of Our
Ideas of the Sublime and Beautiful* (1757), pt. 3

9 She walks in beauty, like the night
Of cloudless climes and starry skies;
And all that's best of dark and bright
Meet in her aspect and her eyes.
Lord Byron (1788–1824) British poet. 'She Walks in Beauty' (1815)

10 Everything has beauty, but not everyone sees it.
Confucius (551–479 BC) Chinese philosopher, administrator, and moralist.
Analects (5th century BC)

11 Beauty is the lover's gift.
William Congreve (1670–1729) English playwright and poet. *The Way of
the World* (1700), Act 2, Scene 4

12 Beauty will be edible or will not exist.
Salvador Dali (1904–89) Spanish surrealist painter. Quoted in
Surrealist Art (Sarane Alexandrian; 1970)

13 You can't order the masses to love beauty any
more than you can reasonably insist that they
must walk on their hands.
Claude Debussy (1862–1918) French composer. *Monsieur Croche,
Antidilettante* (1921)

14 Her beauty was like silence in a cup of water.
Denis Devlin (1908–59) Irish poet. 'Little Elegy', *Collected Poems*
(1964)

15 It is proportion that beautifies everything, this
whole Universe consists of it, and Musicke is
measured by it.
Orlando Gibbons (1583–1625) English composer and organist. *First Set
of Madrigals* (1612)

16 Beauty in things exists in the mind which
contemplates them.
David Hume (1711–76) Scottish philosopher and historian. 'Of
Tragedy', *Essays, Moral and Political* (1741)

17 Beauty is altogether in the eye of the beholder.
Margaret Wolfe Hungerford (1855?–97) Irish novelist. *Molly Bawn* (1878)

18 The *beautiful* is that which pleases universally
without a concept.
Immanuel Kant (1724–1804) German philosopher. *Critique of
Judgment* (1790)

19 'Beauty is truth, truth beauty',—that is all
Ye know on earth, and all ye need to know.
John Keats (1795–1821) English poet. 'Ode on a Grecian Urn'
(1820), st. 5, ll. 9–10

20 A thing of beauty is a joy for ever:
Its loveliness increases; it will never
Pass into nothingness; but still will keep
A bower quiet for us, and a sleep
Full of sweet dreams, and health, and quiet
breathing.
John Keats (1795–1821) English poet. The opening lines of the
poem. *Endymion* (1818), bk. 1, ll. 1–5

21 There can be no fullness or complete realization
of utility without beauty, refinement and charm,
for the simple reason that their absence must . . .
be intolerable to both maker and consumer.
Bernard Leach (1887–1979) British potter. *The Potter's Book* (1940)

22 What we find beautiful in a work of art is not
found beautiful by the eye, but by our
imagination through the eye.
Gotthold Ephraim Lessing (1729–81) German playwright and critic.
Laokoon (1766), ch. 6, quoted in *Laocoon, Nathan the Wise
& Minna von Barnhelm* (W. A. Steel, ed.; 1930)

23 Yet beauty, though injurious, hath strange power,
After offence returning, to regain
Love once possessed.
John Milton (1608–74) English writer. 'Samson Agonistes', *Paradise
Regain'd . . . To Which is Added Samson Agonistes* (1671), ll.
1003–04

24 At some point in life the world's beauty becomes
enough. You don't need to photograph, paint or
even remember it. It is enough.
Toni Morrison (b. 1931) US novelist. *Tar Baby* (1981)

25 Beauty is our weapon against nature; by it we
make objects, giving them limit, symmetry,
proportion. Beauty halts and freezes the melting
flux of nature.
Camille Paglia (b. 1947) US academic and author. *Sexual Personae* (1990)

26 I would define, in brief, the poetry of words as
the rhythmical creation of Beauty.
Edgar Allan Poe (1809–49) US poet and writer. *The Poetic Principle*
(1850)

27 Fair tresses man's imperial race insnare,
And beauty draws us with a single hair.
Alexander Pope (1688–1744) English poet. *The Rape of the Lock*
(1712), can. 2, ll. 27–28

28 The idea of beauty does not descend into matter
unless this is prepared as carefully as possible.
Nicolas Poussin (1594–1665) French painter. Quoted in *Lives of the
Modern Painters, Sculptors and Architects* (Giovanni Pietro
Bellori; 1672)

29 Really, there is no beautiful style, no beautiful
design, and no beautiful colour: there is just one
beauty, that of the truth that is revealed.
Auguste Rodin (1840–1917) French sculptor. Attrib.

30 Remember that the most beautiful things in the
world are the most useless; peacocks and lilies
for instance.
John Ruskin (1819–1900) British art critic, writer, and reformer. *Stones
of Venice* (1851)

31 All other forms of perception divide a man,
because they are exclusively based either on the
sensuous or on the intellectual part of his being;
only the perception of the Beautiful makes
something whole of him, because both his
natures must accord with it.
Friedrich von Schiller (1759–1805) German poet, playwright, and historian.
On the Aesthetic Education of Man (1795)

32 Beauty alone makes all the world happy, and
every being forgets its limitations as long as it
experiences her enchantment.
Friedrich von Schiller (1759–1805) German poet, playwright, and historian.
On the Aesthetic Education of Man (1795)

33 From fairest creatures we desire increase,
That thereby beauty's rose might never die.
William Shakespeare (1564–1616) English poet and playwright. Sonnet 1
(1609)

34 If I could write the beauty of your eyes
And in fresh numbers number all your graces,
The age to come would say, 'This poet lies;
Such heavenly touches ne'er touched earthly faces'.
William Shakespeare (1564–1616) English poet and playwright. Sonnet
17 (1609)

35 ROMEO O! she doth teach the torches to burn bright
It seems she hangs upon the cheek of night
Like a rich jewel in an Ethiop's ear;
Beauty too rich for use, for earth too dear.
William Shakespeare (1564–1616) English poet and playwright. *Romeo
and Juliet* (1595), Act 1, Scene 5

36 Beauty itself doth of itself persuade
The eyes of men without an orator.
William Shakespeare (1564–1616) English poet and playwright. *The Rape of Lucrece* (1594)

37 For she was beautiful—her beauty made
The bright world dim, and everything beside
Seemed like the fleeting image of a shade.
Percy Bysshe Shelley (1792–1822) English poet. 1820. *The Witch of Atlas*, st. 12, quoted in *Posthumous Poems* (Mrs. Shelley, ed.; 1824)

38 What is most beautiful in virile men is something feminine; what is most beautiful in feminine women is something masculine.
Susan Sontag (b. 1933) US writer. 'Notes on Camp', *Against Interpretation* (1966)

39 Beauty is momentary in the mind—
The fitful tracing of a portal;
But in the flesh it is immortal.
The body dies; the body's beauty lives.
Wallace Stevens (1879–1955) US poet. 'Peter Quince at the Clavier', *Harmonium* (1923)

40 People don't want to like you. You're young and beautiful and successful.
Christie Turlington (b. 1969) US fashion model. Referring to being a model. Quoted in *Model: The Ugly Business of Beautiful Women* (Michael Gross; 1995)

41 All the beauty of the world, 't is but skin deep.
Ralph Venning (1621?–74) English writer. 1647. 'The Triumph of Assurance', *Orthodoxe Paradoxes* (1650)

42 It is better to be beautiful than to be good. But . . . it is better to be good than to be ugly.
Oscar Wilde (1854–1900) Irish poet, playwright, and wit. *The Picture of Dorian Gray* (1891), ch. 17

43 Beauty is a shell
from the sea
where she rules triumphant
till love has had its way with her.
William Carlos Williams (1883–1963) US poet, novelist, and physician. 'Song', *Pictures from Brueghel and Other Poems* (1962), quoted in *The Selected Poems of William Carlos Williams* (Charles Tomlinson, ed.; 1976)

44 The most marvelous is not
the beauty, deep as that is,
but the classic attempt
at beauty, at the swamp's center.
William Carlos Williams (1883–1963) US poet, novelist, and physician. 'The Hard Core of Beauty', *The Collected Later Poems* (1950), quoted in *The Selected Poems of William Carlos Williams* (Charles Tomlinson, ed.; 1976)

45 The beauty myth of the present is more insidious than any mystique of femininity yet: A century ago, Nora slammed the door of the doll's house . . . where women are trapped today, there is no door to slam.
Naomi Wolf (b. 1962) US writer. *The Beauty Myth: How Images of Beauty are Used Against Women* (1990)

Beginning

see also **Creation, First Lines**

1 Endings are elusive, middles are nowhere to be found, but worst of all is to begin, to begin, to begin.
Donald Barthelme (1931–89) US novelist and short-story writer. 'The Dolt', *Unspeakable Practices, Unnatural Acts* (1968)

2 'Where shall I begin, please your Majesty?' he asked.
'Begin at the beginning' the King said, gravely, 'and go on till you come to the end: then stop'.
Lewis Carroll (1832–98) British writer and mathematician. *Alice's Adventures in Wonderland* (1865), ch. 11

3 The distance doesn't matter; it is only the first step that is the most difficult.
Marie du Deffand (1697–1780) French literary hostess. Referring to the legend of Saint Denis, who is traditionally believed to have carried his severed head for six miles after his execution. Letter to d'Alembert (July 7, 1763)

4 Turn over a new leaf.
Thomas Dekker (1572?–1632?) English playwright. *The Honest Whore* (1630), pt. 2, Act 2, Scene 1

5 What we call the beginning is often the end
And to make an end is to make a beginning.
The end is where we start from.
T. S. Eliot (1888–1965) US-born British poet and playwright. 'Little Gidding', *Four Quartets* (1942)

6 A bad beginning makes a bad ending.
Euripides (480?–406? BC) Greek playwright. *Aeolus* (5th century BC), fragment 32

7 With the possible exception of the equator, everything begins somewhere.
Peter Fleming (1907–71) British travel writer. *One's Company* (1934)

8 Everything from an egg.
William Harvey (1578–1657) English physician. *On the Generation of Animals* (1651), Dedication

9 To have begun is half the job: be bold and be sensible.
Horace (65–8 BC) Roman poet. *Epistles* (20? BC), bk. 1, no. 2, l. 40

10 A journey of a thousand miles must begin with a single step.
Laozi (570?–490? BC) Chinese philosopher. The *Daode Jing* is an early Chinese Taoist text. While attributed to Laozi, it probably dates from the 3rd century BC *Daode Jing* (Unknown), 1

11 Beginning to tell a story is like making a pass at a total stranger in a restaurant.
Amos Oz (b. 1939) Israeli writer. 1996. *The Story Begins* (Maggie Bar-Tura, tr.; 2000)

Being

see also **Existence, Life**

1 I think, therefore I am.
René Descartes (1596–1650) French philosopher and mathematician. *Discourse on Method* (1637), pt. 4

2 Nothing, as thus immediate and equal to itself, is also conversely the same as Being is. The truth of Being and of Nothing is accordingly the unity of the two: and this unity is *Becoming*.
G. W. F. Hegel (1770–1831) German philosopher. *Encyclopaedia of the Philosophical Sciences* (1817)

3 Man is not the lord of beings. Man is the shepherd of Being.
Martin Heidegger (1889–1976) German philosopher. *Letter on Humanism* (1947)

4 We are too late for the gods
and too early for Being. Being's poem,
just begun, is man.
Martin Heidegger (1889–1976) German philosopher. *Poetry, Language, Thought* (1971)

5 I must *search for being* if I want to find my real self. But it is not till I fail in this search for intrinsic being that I begin to philosophize.
Karl Jaspers (1883–1969) German philosopher. *Philosophy* (1932), vol. 1

6 The background reveals the true being and state of being of the man or thing. If I do not possess the background, I make the man transparent, the thing transparent.
Juan Ramón Jiménez (1881–1958) Spanish poet. 'José Marti', *Selected Writings* (1957)

7 What one ought to say is: I am not wherever I am the plaything of my thought; I think of what I am where I do not think to think.
Jacques Lacan (1901–81) French philosopher and psychologist. 'Agency of the Letter in the Unconscious', *Ecrits* (1966)

8 Whatever this is that I am, it is a little flesh and breath, and the ruling part.
Marcus Aurelius (121–180) Roman emperor and philosopher. *Meditations* (170–180), bk. 2, sect. 2

9 A curious thing about the ontological problem is its simplicity. It can be put in three Anglo-Saxon monosyllables: 'What is there?' It can be answered, moreover, in a word—'Everything'.
Willard V. Quine (1908–2000) US philosopher. *From a Logical Point of View* (1953)

10 Never Being, But Always at the Edge of Being
Stephen Spender (1909–95) British poet and critic. Title of poem. (1933)

Belief

see also **Faith, Fanaticism, Philosophy, Religion**

1 How can I believe in God when just last week I got my tongue caught in the roller of an electric typewriter?
Woody Allen (b. 1935) US film actor and director. 1975. 'Selections from the Allen Notebooks', *Without Feathers* (1976)

2 I would as soon believe
in paradise as in
nothing.
A. R. Ammons (b. 1926) US poet. 'The Dwelling' (1987), quoted in *The Norton Anthology of American Literature* (Nina Baym, ed.; 1998), vol. 2

3 I'm a Communist by day and a Catholic as soon as it gets dark.
Brendan Behan (1923–64) Irish playwright and author. Attrib.

4 Then saith he to Thomas, Reach hither thy finger, and behold my hands; and reach hither thy hand, and thrust it into my side: and be not faithless, but believing.
And Thomas answered and said unto him, My Lord and my God.
Bible. John, *King James Bible* (1611), 20:27–28

5 If thou canst believe, all things are possible to him that believeth. And straightway the father of the child cried out, and said with tears, Lord, I believe; help thou mine unbelief.
Bible. Mark, *King James Bible* (1611), 9:23–24

6 To believe only possibilities, is not faith, but mere Philosophy.
Thomas Browne (1605–82) English physician and writer. *Religio Medici* (1642), pt. 1, sect. 48

7 Ten men love what I hate,
Shun what I follow, slight what I receive;
Ten, who in ears and eyes
Match me: we all surmise,
They this thing, and I that: whom shall my soul believe?
Robert Browning (1812–89) British poet. 'Rabbi Ben Ezra', *Dramatis Personae* (1864), st. 22, ll. 209–212

8 One miracle is just as easy to believe as another.
William Jennings Bryan (1860–1925) US politician and lawyer. Said during the trial of John Scopes for teaching evolution in Tennessee. Remark (July 21, 1925)

9 Why, sometimes I've believed as many as six impossible things before breakfast.
Lewis Carroll (1832–98) British writer and mathematician. *Through the Looking-Glass and What Alice Found There* (1871), ch. 5

10 If you'll believe in me, I'll believe in you.
Lewis Carroll (1832–98) British writer and mathematician. *Through the Looking-Glass and What Alice Found There* (1871), ch. 7

11 *Action will furnish belief,*—but will that belief be the true one?
This is the point, you know.
Arthur Hugh Clough (1819–61) British poet. *Amours de voyage* (1858)

12 To believe and to understand are not diverse things, but the same things in different periods of growth.
Samuel Taylor Coleridge (1772–1834) British poet. *Aids to Reflection* (1825)

13 The true believer is in a high degree protected against the danger of certain neurotic afflictions; by accepting the universal neurosis he is spared the task of forming a personal neurosis.
Sigmund Freud (1856–1939) Austrian psychoanalyst. *The Future of an Illusion* (1927), ch. 8

14 I don't believe in God, but I'm afraid of Him.
Gabriel García Márquez (b. 1928) Colombian novelist. *Love in the Time of Cholera* (1985)

15 I believe in God, family, and McDonald's and in the office, that order is reversed.
Ray Kroc (1902–84) US restaurateur. Ray Kroc was the founder and president of the McDonald's chain. Quoted in *McDonald's: Behind the Arches* (John F. Love; 1986)

16 There seems to be a terrible misunderstanding on the part of a great many people to the effect that when you cease to believe you may cease to behave.
Louis Kronenberger (1904–80) US writer and critic. *Company Manners* (1954)

17 A pious man is one who would be an atheist if the king were.
Jean de La Bruyère (1645–96) French essayist and moralist. *Characters, or the Manners of the Age* (1688)

18 Credulity is the man's weakness, but the child's strength.
Charles Lamb (1775–1834) British essayist. 'Witches and other Night Fears', *Essays of Elia* (1823)

19 To arrive at the truth in all things, we ought always to be ready to believe that what seems to us white is black if the hierarchical Church so defines it.
Ignatius of Loyola (1491–1556) Spanish theologian. *Spiritual Exercises* (1548)

20 Believe in yourself, but do not always refuse to believe in others.

Joaquim Maria Machado de Assis (1839–1908) Brazilian novelist and short-story writer. *Epitaph of a Small Winner* (1880)

21 An idea isn't responsible for the people who believe in it.

Don Marquis (1878–1937) US journalist and writer. *New York Sun* (1918?)

22 Dogma thinks it knows. Belief knows it does not. Dogma is credulous. Belief is sceptical, but for ever open-minded.

Graham Dunstan Martin (b. 1932) British writer and academic. *Shadows in the Cave: Mapping the Conscious Universe* (1990)

23 *Doublethink* means the power of holding two contradictory beliefs in one's mind simultaneously, and accepting both of them.

George Orwell (1903–50) British writer. *Nineteen Eighty-Four* (1949), pt. 2, ch. 9

24 It is necessary to the happiness of man that he be mentally faithful to himself. Infidelity does not consist in believing, or in disbelieving, it consists in professing to believe what one does not believe.

Thomas Paine (1737–1809) English writer and political philosopher. *The Age of Reason* (1794), pt. 1

25 Let us say, 'Either God is or he is not' . . . Let us weigh up the gain and loss involved in calling heads that God exists . . . Let us assess the two cases: if you win you win everything, if you lose you lose nothing. Do not hesitate then: wager that he does exist.

Blaise Pascal (1623–62) French philosopher, mathematician, and physicist. *Pensées* (1669), no. 418

26 Our belief in any particular natural law cannot have a safer basis than our unsuccessful critical attempts to refute it.

Karl Popper (1902–94) Austrian-born British philosopher. *Conjectures and Refutations* (1963)

27 Man makes holy what he believes as he makes beautiful what he loves.

Ernest Renan (1823–92) French philosopher, philologist, and historian. 'La Tentation du Christ', *Études d'Histoire Religieuse* (1857)

28 My relationship with formal religious belief has been somewhat chequered.

Salman Rushdie (b. 1947) Indian-born British novelist. *Imaginary Homelands* (1991), pt. 12, ch. 2

29 Of course not. After all, I may be wrong.

Bertrand Russell (1872–1970) British philosopher and mathematician. On being asked whether he would be prepared to die for his beliefs. Attrib.

30 I believe because it is impossible.

Tertullian (160?–220?) Carthaginian theological writer. The usual misquotation of 'It is certain because it is impossible'. *De Carne Christi* (2nd–3rd century), ch. 5

31 The equation of religion with belief is rather recent.

Arnold Toynbee (1889–1975) British historian. 'What are the Criteria for Comparisons Between Religions?', *Christianity Among the Religions of the World* (1958), pt. 1

32 The temerity to believe in nothing.

Ivan Turgenev (1818–83) Russian novelist. *Fathers and Sons* (1862), ch. 14

33 If there were a verb meaning 'to believe falsely', it would not have any significant first person, present indicative.

Ludwig Wittgenstein (1889–1951) Austrian philosopher. Quoted in *A Certain World* (W. H. Auden; 1970)

Bereavement

see also **Death and Dying, Sorrow**

1 What we mourn for the dead is the loss of their hopes.

John Berger (b. 1926) British novelist, essayist, and art critic. *And Our Faces, My Heart, Brief as Photos* (1984)

2 Ah! surely nothing dies but something mourns!

Lord Byron (1788–1824) British poet. *Don Juan* (1819–24), can. 3, st. 108

3 Some hang above the tombs,
Some weep in empty rooms,
I, when the iris blooms,
Remember.

Mary Coleridge (1861–1907) British poet. *Poems* (1907), no. 146

4 One often calms one's grief by recounting it.

Corneille (1606–84) French playwright. *Polyeucte* (1643), Act 1, Scene 3

5 In normal mourning early psychotic anxieties are reactivated; the mourner is in fact ill, but, because this state of mind is so common and seems so natural to us, we do not call mourning an illness.

Melanie Klein (1882–1960) Austrian psychoanalyst. 'Mourning and Manic-Depressive States' (1940), quoted in *The Selected Melanie Klein* (Juliet Mitchell, ed.; 1986)

6 Why are you weeping? Did you imagine that I was immortal?

Louis XIV (1638–1715) French monarch. 1715. Noticing as he lay on his deathbed that his attendants were crying. Quoted in *Louis XIV* (Vincent Cronin; 1964)

7 Thee Shepherd, thee the woods, and desert caves,
With wild thyme and the gadding vine o'ergrown,
And all their echoes mourn.

John Milton (1608–74) English writer. 1638. 'Lycidas', *Poems of Mr. John Milton* (1645), ll. 39–41

8 Then I remembered that I had never cried for my father's death . . . I laid my face to the smooth face of the marble and howled my loss into the cold salt rain.

Sylvia Plath (1932–63) US poet and novelist. *The Bell Jar* (1963), ch. 13

9 Grief tears his heart, and drives him to and fro
In all the raging impotence of woe.

Alexander Pope (1688–1744) English poet. *The Iliad of Homer* (1715–20), bk. 22, ll. 526–527

10 A lady asked me why, on most occasions, I wore black. 'Are you in mourning?'
'Yes'.
'For whom are you in mourning?'
'For the world'.

Edith Sitwell (1887–1964) British poet, critic, and writer. *Taken Care Of* (1965), ch. 1

11 Come not, when I am dead
To drop thy foolish tears upon my grave,
To trample round my fallen head,
And vex the unhappy dust thou wouldst not save.

Alfred Tennyson (1809–92) British poet. 1850. 'Come Not When I Am Dead', *Poems* (1851), st. 1

12 Grief has turned her fair.

Oscar Wilde (1854–1900) Irish poet, playwright, and wit. Referring to the fact that a recently bereaved lady friend had dyed her hair blond. Attrib.

Berlin

see European Cities

Betrayal

see also Faith, Loyalty

1   We have seen today a gallant, civilised and democratic people betrayed and handed over to a ruthless despotism.

Clement Attlee (1883–1967) British politician. Said during a debate on the Munich Pact (September 29, 1938), under which Britain and France recognized Nazi Germany's claim to the Sudetenland, Czechoslovakia. Speech to Parliament (October 3, 1938)

2   By the glare of false science betray'd,
That leads to bewilder, and dazzles to blind.

James Beattie (1735–1803) Scottish poet and philosopher. *The Hermit* (1797)

3   No man can serve two masters: for either he will hate the one, and love the other; or else he will hold to the one, and despise the other. Ye cannot serve God and mammon.

Bible. Matthew, *King James Bible* (1611), 6:24

4   What will ye give me, and I will deliver him unto you? And they covenanted with him for thirty pieces of silver.

Bible. Judas Iscariot's agreement with the chief priests for the betrayal of Jesus. Judas returned the money after the condemnation of Jesus (Matthew 27:3–5). Matthew, *King James Bible* (1611), 26:15

5   You too, Brutus?

Julius Caesar (100–44 BC) Roman general and statesman. 44 BC. Last words, on seeing that Brutus is one of his murderers. Quoted in *The Twelve Caesars* (Suetonius; AD 121?)

6   You dirty double-crossing rat!

James Cagney (1899–1986) US actor. Usually misquoted by impressionists as 'You dirty rat'. *Blonde Crazy* (1931)

7   They say you can rat, but you can't re-rat.

Winston Churchill (1874–1965) British prime minister and writer. Referring to changing political parties more than once. Remark (January 26, 1941), quoted in *The Fringes of Power* (John Colville; 1985), vol. 1

8   We never are but by ourselves betrayed.

William Congreve (1670–1729) English playwright and poet. *The Old Bachelor* (1693), Act 3, Scene 1

9   To save a man's life against his will is the same as killing him.

Horace (65–8 BC) Roman poet. *Ars Poetica* (19–8 BC), l. 466

10   It is rather like sending your opening batsmen to the crease, only for them to find that their bats have been broken before the game by the team captain.

Geoffrey Howe (b. 1926) British politician. On his resignation from the government and referring to his differences with Margaret Thatcher over European policy. Speech to Parliament, *Hansard* (November 13, 1990)

11   I'm waiting for the cock to crow.

William Morris Hughes (1864–1952) British-born Australian prime minister. Said in the Australian Parliament, after being viciously criticized by a member of his own party. Quoted in *The Fine Art of Political Wit* (Leon A. Harris; 1964)

12   I let down my friends, I let down my country. I let down our system of government.

Richard Nixon (1913–94) US president. *Observer* (May 8, 1977), 'Sayings of the Week'

13   Wherever man would not be on our side and would not spend his efforts for the right, we take it that that man is a man against us.

Hugh O'Neill (1540?–1616) Irish patriot. Letter to Sir John McCoughleyn (February 6, 1600), quoted in *A Celtic Miscellany* (Kenneth Hurlstone Jackson; 1951)

14   To betray, you must first belong. I never belonged.

Kim Philby (1912–88) British intelligence officer and spy. *Sunday Times* (December 17, 1967)

15   In a civil war, a general must know—and I'm afraid it's a thing rather of instinct than of practice—he must know exactly when to move over to the other side.

Henry Reed (1914–86) British poet and radio playwright. Unpublished radio play. *Not a Drum was Heard: The War Memoirs of General Gland* (1959)

16   Widowed wife, and married maid,
Betrothed, betrayer, and betrayed!

Sir Walter Scott (1771–1832) Scottish novelist. *The Betrothed* (1825), ch. 15

17   ANTONY The hearts
That spaniel'd me at heels, to whom I gave
Their wishes, do discandy, melt their sweets
On blossoming Caesar.

William Shakespeare (1564–1616) English poet and playwright. *Antony and Cleopatra* (1606–07), Act 4, Scene 12

18   APEMANTUS Men shut their doors against a setting sun.

William Shakespeare (1564–1616) English poet and playwright. *Timon of Athens* (1607?), Act 1, Scene 2

Bigotry

see also Prejudice, Racism, Xenophobia

1   What about it? Do you want to crucify the boy?

Lew Grade (1906–98) Ukrainian-born British film and television producer and impresario. Referring to the revelation that an actor portraying Christ on television was living with a woman to whom he was not married. Attrib.

2   We hear about constitutional rights, free speech, and the free press. Every time I hear those words I say to myself, 'That man is a Red, that man is a Communist'. You never heard a real American talk in that manner.

Frank Hague (1876–1956) US politician. Speech, Jersey City Chamber of Commerce (January 12, 1938)

3   You can't teach an old dogma new tricks.

Dorothy Parker (1893–1967) US writer and wit. Quoted in *Wit's End: Days and Nights of the Algonquin Round Table* (James R. Gaines; 1977)

4   The resort to stereotype is the first refuge and chief strategy of the bigot.

Bayard Rustin (1910–87) US civil rights leader. 1967. 'The Premise of the Stereotype', *Down The Line* (1971)

5   We have just enough religion to make us hate, but not enough to make us love one another.

Jonathan Swift (1667–1745) Irish writer and clergyman. *Thoughts on Various Subjects* (1711)

Biography

see also Autobiography, Books

1   A shilling life will give you all the facts.

W. H. Auden (1907–73) British poet. *Look, Stranger* (1936), no. 13, quoted in *Collected Poems* (Edward Mendelson, ed.; 1976)

2 Anyone who attempts to relate his life loses himself in the immediate.

Augusto Roa Bastos (b. 1917) Paraguayan writer. *I the Supreme* (1974)

3 I imagine, sometimes, that if a film could be made of one's life, every other frame would be death. It goes so fast we're not aware of it.

Saul Bellow (b. 1915) Canadian-born US writer. *The Dean's December* (1982)

4 Does it really matter whose story this is? Every creature on earth deserves to have its story told.

Ivan Bunin (1870–1953) Russian novelist and poet. 'Chang's Dreams' (Sophie Lund, tr.; 1916)

5 History is the essence of innumerable biographies.

Thomas Carlyle (1795–1881) Scottish historian and essayist. 'History', *Critical and Miscellaneous Essays* (1838)

6 A well-written Life is almost as rare as a well-spent one.

Thomas Carlyle (1795–1881) Scottish historian and essayist. 'Richter', *Critical and Miscellaneous Essays* (1838)

7 Read no history: nothing but biography, for that is life without theory.

Benjamin Disraeli (1804–81) British prime minister and writer. *Contarini Fleming* (1832), pt. 1, ch. 23

8 There is properly no history; only biography.

Ralph Waldo Emerson (1803–82) US poet and essayist. 'History', *Essays* (1841)

9 It is not a Life at all. It is a Reticence in three volumes.

William Ewart Gladstone (1809–98) British statesman. Referring to J. W. Cross's *George Eliot's Life* (1885). Quoted in *As We Were* (E. F. Benson; 1930), ch. 6

10 A biography of this type should start off something like this: 'So-and-so, whose other name was so-and-so, was a native of such-and-such a place'; but I don't really know what Ah Q's surname was.

Lu Xun (1881–1936) Chinese writer. 'The True Story of Ah Q' (December 1921)

11 Campbell has added another terror to death.

John Singleton Copley Lyndhurst (1772–1863) US-born British politician. Referring to Lord Campbell's controversial *Lives of the Lord Chancellors* (1845–47), from which Lyndhurst was excluded because he was still alive. Quoted in *Seventy-Two Years at the Bar* (E. Bowen-Rowlands; 1924), ch. 10

12 There is no life that can be recaptured wholly; as it was. Which is to say that all biography is ultimately fiction.

Bernard Malamud (1914–86) US writer. *Dublin's Lives* (1979)

13 Every life is, more or less, a ruin among whose debris we have to discover what the person ought to have been.

José Ortega y Gasset (1883–1955) Spanish writer and philosopher. 'In Search of Goethe from Within', *Partisan Review* (December 1949)

14 Had I been brighter, the ladies been gentler, the Scotch been weaker, had the gods been kinder, had the dice been hotter, this could have been a one-sentence story: Once upon a time I lived happily ever after.

Mickey Rooney (b. 1920) US film actor. Attrib.

15 There is no such thing as psychological. Let us say that one can improve the biography of the person.

Jean-Paul Sartre (1905–80) French philosopher, playwright, and novelist. Quoted in *The Divided Self* (R. D. Laing; 1960), ch. 8

16 To tell the story of Coleridge without the opium is to tell the story of Hamlet without mentioning the Ghost.

Leslie Stephen (1832–1904) British biographer, critic, and philosopher. Referring to Samuel Taylor Coleridge. 'Coleridge', *Hours in a Library* (1874–79)

17 There is no psychology; there is only biography and autobiography.

Thomas Szasz (b. 1920) Hungarian-born US psychiatrist. 'Psychology', *The Second Sin* (1973)

18 In these days a man is nobody unless his biography is kept so far posted up that it may be ready for the national breakfast-table on the morning after his demise.

Anthony Trollope (1815–82) British novelist. *Doctor Thorne* (1858), ch. 25

19 Just how difficult it is to write biography can be reckoned by anybody who sits down and considers just how many people know the real truth about his or her love affairs.

Rebecca West (1892–1983) Irish-born British novelist, critic, and journalist. *Vogue* (1952)

Biology

see **The Body, Evolution, Genetics, Nature, Science**

Birds

see also **Animals, Nature**

1 Even in a golden cage, the nightingale is homesick.

Anonymous. Armenian proverb.

2 The bird seeks the tree, not the tree the bird.

Anonymous. Mexican proverb.

3 Here are instructions for being a pigeon: 1. Walk around aimlessly for a while, pecking at cigarette butts and other inappropriate items. 2. Take fright at someone walking along the platform and fly off to a girder. 3. Have a shit. 4. Repeat.

Bill Bryson (b. 1951) US writer. *Notes From a Small Island* (1995), ch. 10

4 The bisy larke, messager of day.

Geoffrey Chaucer (1343?–1400) English poet. 'The Knight's Tale', *The Canterbury Tales* (1390), l. 1491, quoted in *The Works of Geoffrey Chaucer* (F.N. Robinson, ed.; 1987)

5 I caught this morning morning's minion, king-dom of daylight's dauphin, dapple-dawn-drawn Falcon.

Gerard Manley Hopkins (1844–89) British poet, priest, and classicist. 'The Windhover' (1877), quoted in *Poems* (Robert Bridges, ed.; 1918)

6 I can imagine, in some otherworld
Primeval-dumb, far back
In that most awful stillness, that only gasped and hummed,
Humming-birds raced down the avenues . . .
Probably he was a jabbing, terrifying monster.
We look at him through the wrong end of the long telescope of Time,
Luckily for us.

D. H. Lawrence (1885–1930) British writer. 'Humming-Bird', *Birds, Beasts and Flowers* (1923)

7 A bird is an instrument working according to a
   mathematical law, which instrument it is within
   the capacity of man to reproduce, with all its
   movements.
   Leonardo da Vinci (1452–1519) Italian artist, engineer, and inventor.
   Quoted in *The Notebooks of Leonardo da Vinci* (Edward
   McCurdy, tr.; 1928)

8 Oh, sometimes people annoy me dreadfully—
   such airs they put on—talking about the 'dumb
   animals'. Dumb! Huh! Why, I knew a macaw
   once who could say 'Good morning!' in seven
   different ways without once opening his mouth.
   Hugh Lofting (1886–1947) British-born US children's writer and illustrator.
   Said by Polynesia the parrot. *The Story of Dr. Doolittle*
   (1922)

9 Sweet bird, that shunn'st the noise of folly,
   Most musical, most melancholy!
   John Milton (1608–74) English writer. Referring to the nightingale. 'Il
   Penseroso', *Poems of Mr. John Milton* (1645), ll. 61–62

10 Caged birds accept each other but flight is what
   they long for.
   Tennessee Williams (1911–83) US playwright. *Camino Real* (1953),
   block 7

Birth

see also **Babies, Fathers, Mothers, Pregnancy**

1 My mother groan'd, my father wept,
   Into the dangerous world I leapt;
   Helpless, naked, piping loud,
   Like a fiend hid in a cloud.
   William Blake (1757–1827) British poet, painter, engraver, and mystic.
   'Infant Sorrow', *Songs of Experience* (1789–94), ll. 1–4

2 With what shift and pains we come into the
   World we remember not; but 'tis commonly
   found no easy matter to get out of it.
   Thomas Browne (1605–82) English physician and writer. This essay was
   published posthumously. *Christian Morals* (1716), pt. 2

3 For man's greatest crime is to have been born.
   Pedro Calderón de la Barca (1600–81) Spanish playwright and poet. *Life
   is a Dream* (1635), Act 1

4 The history of man for the nine months
   preceding his birth would, probably, be far more
   interesting and contain events of greater moment
   than all the three-score and ten years that follow
   it.
   Samuel Taylor Coleridge (1772–1834) British poet. Quoted in *Aesthetic
   and Literary Miscellanies* (T. Ashe, ed.; 1885)

5 I came upstairs into the world; for I was born in
   a cellar.
   William Congreve (1670–1729) English playwright and poet. *Love for
   Love* (1695), Act 2, Scene 7

6 Men tell us our lives are free of danger.
   We stay at home. They go to war. Rubbish. I'd
   rather face three assaults
   In line of battle, than bear one child.
   Euripides (480?–406? BC) Greek playwright. *Medea* (Leo Aylen, tr.;
   431 BC), ll. 248–51

7 Man always dies before he is fully born.
   Erich Fromm (1900–80) German-born US psychoanalyst and philosopher.
   Man for Himself (1947), ch. 3

8 Man's main task in life is to give *birth* to himself.
   Erich Fromm (1900–80) German-born US psychoanalyst and philosopher.
   Man for Himself (1947), ch. 4

9 A mountain in labour shouted so loud that
   everyone, summoned by the noise, ran up
   expecting that she would be delivered of a city
   bigger than Paris; she brought forth a mouse.
   Jean de La Fontaine (1621–95) French writer and poet. 'La Montagne
   qui accouche', *Fables* (1668), bk. 5

10 I am not yet born; O fill me
   With strength against those who would freeze my
   humanity, would dragoon me into a lethal
   automaton,
   would make me a cog in a machine, a thing with
   one face, a thing.
   Louis MacNeice (1907–63) Irish-born British poet. 1944. 'Prayer Before
   Birth', *Holes in the Sky* (1948)

11 I was born in Belfast between the mountain and
   the gantries
   To the hooting of lost sirens and the clang of trams.
   Louis MacNeice (1907–63) Irish-born British poet. 'Carrickfergus', *The
   Earth Compels* (1938), ll. 1–2

12 In the dark womb where I began
   My mother's life made me a man.
   Through all the months of human birth
   Her beauty fed my common earth.
   I cannot see, nor breathe, nor stir,
   But through the death of some of her.
   John Masefield (1878–1967) British poet and playwright. 1910. 'C. L. M.',
   The Collected Poems of John Masefield (1923), st. 1, ll. 1–6

13 Dear Mary, We all knew you had it in you.
   Dorothy Parker (1893–1967) US writer and wit. Referring to the
   successful outcome of a much-publicized pregnancy. Telegram
   sent to a friend, quoted in 'Our Mrs. Parker', *While Rome
   Burns* (Alexander Woollcott; 1934)

14 They came out of their mothers' bellies
   to find themselves on sidewalks or in prehistoric
   fields,
   inscribed in birth registers
   which want all history to forget them.
   Pier Paolo Pasolini (1922–75) Italian filmmaker. 'The Desire for
   Wealth of the Roman Lumpenproletariat' (1961)

15 At the moment of childbirth, every woman has
   the same aura of isolation, as though she were
   abandoned, alone.
   Boris Pasternak (1890–1960) Russian poet and novelist. *Doctor
   Zhivago* (Max Hayward and Manya Harari, trs.; 1958), ch.
   9, sect. 3

16 Man alone at the very moment of his birth, cast
   naked upon the naked earth, does she abandon
   to cries and lamentations.
   Pliny the Elder (23?–79) Roman scholar. Referring to nature. *Natural
   History* (77), bk. 7, sect. 2

17 LEAR When we are born, we cry that we are come
   To this great stage of fools.
   William Shakespeare (1564–1616) English poet and playwright. *King
   Lear* (1605–06), Act 4, Scene 6

18 I was born on a day
   God was sick.
   César Vallejo (1892–1938) Peruvian poet. 'Espergesia', *The Black
   Heralds* (1918)

19 Our birth is but a sleep and a forgetting:
   The Soul that rises with us, our life's Star,
   Hath had elsewhere its setting,
   And cometh from afar:
   Not in entire forgetfulness,
   And not in utter nakedness,
   But trailing clouds of glory do we come
   From God, who is our home.
   William Wordsworth (1770–1850) English poet. 1802?–06. 'Ode: Intimations
   of Immortality from Recollections of Early Childhood', *Poems in
   Two Volumes* (1807), vol. 2, st. 5, ll. 58–65

Bitterness

see **Anger, Hate**

Blasphemy

see also **Belief, Censorship, Heresy**

1 To what extent would people tolerate blasphemies if they gave them amusement?
Paul Auster (b. 1947) US writer. 'City of Glass', *New York Trilogy* (1987)

2 If hybridity is heresy, to blaspheme is to dream.
Homi Bhabha (b. 1949) British writer and academic. *The Location of Culture* (1994)

3 Beware of the community in which blasphemy does not exist: underneath, atheism runs rampant.
Antonio Machado (1875–1939) Spanish poet and playwright. *Juan de Mairena* (1936)

4 Where it is a duty to worship the sun it is pretty sure to be a crime to examine the laws of heat.
John Morley (1838–1923) British statesman and writer. *Voltaire* (1872)

5 Mahound shakes his head, 'Your blasphemy, Salman, can't be forgiven. Did you think I wouldn't work it out? To set your words against the Words of God'.
Salman Rushdie (b. 1947) Indian-born British novelist. *The Satanic Verses* (1988), pt. 6

6 ISABELLA That in the captain's but a choleric word Which in the soldier is flat blasphemy.
William Shakespeare (1564–1616) English poet and playwright. *Measure for Measure* (1604), Act 2, Scene 2

7 All great truths begin as blasphemies.
George Bernard Shaw (1856–1950) Irish playwright. *Annajanska* (1919)

Boasts

see also **Arrogance, Pride**

1 If I were not Alexander, I would be Diogenes.
Alexander the Great (356–323 BC) Macedonian monarch. Quoted in 'Alexander', *Parallel Lives* (Plutarch; 120?), ch. 14, section 3

2 I'm so fast I could hit you before God gets the news.
Muhammad Ali (b. 1942) US boxer. *New York Times* (June 29, 1975)

3 Boast not thyself of tomorrow; for thou knowest not what a day may bring forth.
Bible. Proverbs, *King James Bible* (1611), 27:1

4 I have done almost every human activity inside a taxi which does not require main drainage.
Alan Brien (b. 1925) British critic and journalist. *Punch* (July 5, 1972)

5 Brag, sweet tenor bull,
descant on Rawthey's madrigal,
each pebble its part
for the fells' late spring.
Basil Bunting (1900–85) British poet. *Briggflatts* (1966), ll. 1–4

6 I came, I saw, I conquered.
Julius Caesar (100–44 BC) Roman general and statesman. Inscription used in Caesar's triumph of 48 BC to celebrate his victory over Pompey at Pharsalia, and referring to his characteristically swift and ruthless tactics. Quoted in *The Twelve Caesars* (Suetonius; AD 121?)

7 I met a traveler from Arkansas
Who boasted of his state as beautiful
for diamonds and apples.
Robert Frost (1874–1963) US poet. 'New Hampshire', *New Hampshire* (1923), ll. 9–11, quoted in *The Poetry of Robert Frost* (Edward Connery Lathem, ed.; 1971)

8 I am the very model of a modern Major-General,
I've information vegetable, animal and mineral,
I know the kings of England, and I quote the fights historical,
From Marathon to Waterloo, in order categorical.
W. S. Gilbert (1836–1911) British librettist and playwright. *The Pirates of Penzance* (1879), Act 1, 'The Major General's Song'

9 The clever men at Oxford
Know all that there is to be knowed.
But they none of them know one half as much
As intelligent Mr Toad.
Kenneth Grahame (1859–1932) British banker and children's writer. *The Wind in the Willows* (1908), ch. 10

10 The mother of battles will be our battle of victory and martyrdom.
Saddam Hussein (b. 1937) Iraqi president. January 6, 1991. Referring to the imminent Gulf War. Speech, Baghdad, *Times* (January 7, 1991)

11 You ain't heard nothin' yet, folks.
Al Jolson (1886–1950) Russian-born US actor and singer. July 1927. The first speech in a 'talkie' film, *The Jazz Singer*; later adopted as a catch phrase by President Ronald Reagan. *The Jazz Singer* (1927)

12 I can piss the old boy in the snow.
Max Liebermann (1847–1935) German painter and etcher. Remark to an artist who said he could not draw General Paul von Hindenburg's face. Quoted in *Conversations with Stravinsky* (Igor Stravinsky and Robert Craft; 1959)

13 France has more need of me than I have need of France.
Napoleon I (1769–1821) French emperor. Speech (December 31, 1813)

14 The Jews have produced only three originative geniuses: Christ, Spinoza, and myself.
Gertrude Stein (1874–1946) US writer. Quoted in *Charmed Circle* (J. Mellow; 1974)

15 And when we open our dikes, the waters are ten feet deep.
Wilhelmina (1880–1962) Dutch monarch. Replying to a boast by Wilhelm II that his guardsmen were all seven feet tall. Attrib.

Boats

see also **The Sea, Travel**

1 A wise captain carries more ballast than sail.
Anonymous. Jamaican proverb.

2 My experience of ships is that on them one makes an interesting discovery about the world. One finds one can do without it completely.
Malcolm Bradbury (1932–2000) British academic, novelist, and critic. *Stepping Westward* (1965), bk. 1, ch. 2

3 She walks the waters like a thing of life,
And seems to dare the elements to strife.
Lord Byron (1788–1824) British poet. *The Corsair* (1814), can. 1, st. 3

4 I entertained on a cruising trip that was so much fun that I had to sink my yacht to make my guests go home.
F. Scott Fitzgerald (1896–1940) US writer. 'Notebooks K', *The Crack-Up: with Other Uncollected Pieces, Note-Books and Unpublished Letters* (Edmund Wilson, ed.; 1945)

5   With my own hands I had done my trick at the
     wheel and guided a hundred tons of wood and iron
     through a few million tons of wind and waves.
     Jack London (1876–1916) US writer. *The Cruise of the Snark* (1911)

6   Ships that pass in the night, and speak each other
     in passing . . .
     Only a look and a voice; then darkness again
     and a silence.
     Henry Wadsworth Longfellow (1807–82) US poet. 'The Theologian's
     Tale: Elizabeth', *Tales of a Wayside Inn* (1874)

7   Quinquireme of Nineveh from distant Ophir
     Rowing home to haven in sunny Palestine,
     With a cargo of ivory,
     And apes and peacocks,
     Sandalwood, cedarwood, and sweet white wine.
     John Masefield (1878–1967) British poet and playwright. 'Cargoes'
     (1903), st. 1

8   Lighter than a cork I danced on the waves.
     Arthur Rimbaud (1854–91) French poet. *Le Bateau Ivre* (1871)

The Body

see also **The Face**, **The Heart**, **The Self**

1   The people of knowledge said that 'The body is
     the kingdom of the self and its city'.
     Muhyid-Din Abu Zakariyya ibn Sharaf al-Nawawi (1233–77) Syrian Islamic
     scholar. 13th century. *The Complete Forty Hadith*
     (Abdassamad Clarke, tr.; 1988), 6th Hadith

2   A healthy body is the guest-chamber of the soul,
     a sick, its prison.
     Francis Bacon (1561–1626) English philosopher, statesman, and lawyer.
     'Valetudo', *De Augmentis Scientiarum* (1623)

3   BODY-SNATCHER, n. A robber of grave-worms.
     One who supplies the young physicians with that
     with which the old physicians have supplied the
     undertaker.
     Ambrose Bierce (1842–1914?) US writer and journalist. *The Devil's
     Dictionary* (1911)

4   DIAPHRAGM, n. A muscular partition separating
     disorders of the chest from disorders of the
     bowels.
     Ambrose Bierce (1842–1914?) US writer and journalist. *The Devil's
     Dictionary* (1911)

5   I have finally come to the conclusion that a good
     reliable set of bowels is worth more to a man
     than any quantity of brains.
     Josh Billings (1818–85) US humorist. Quoted in *Bartlett's
     Unfamiliar Quotations* (Leonard Louis Levinson, ed.; 1972)

6   Man has no Body distinct from his Soul; for that
     call'd Body is a portion of Soul discern'd by the
     five Senses, the chief inlets of Soul in this age.
     William Blake (1757–1827) British poet, painter, engraver, and mystic.
     'The Voice of the Devil', *The Marriage of Heaven and Hell*
     (1790–93), plate 4

7   My anatomy is only part of an infinitely complex
     organisation, my self.
     Angela Carter (1940–92) British novelist, essayist, and short-story writer.
     'Polemical Preface', *The Sadeian Woman* (1979)

8   Eating disorders, whether it be anorexia or
     bulimia, show how individuals can turn the
     nourishment of the body into a painful attack on
     themselves and they have at the core a far deeper
     problem than mere vanity.
     Princess Diana (1961–97) British princess. April, 1993. *Times* (April
     28, 1993)

9   The body is truly the garment of the soul, which
     has a living voice; for that reason it is fitting that
     the body simultaneously with the soul repeatedly
     sing praises to God through the voice.
     Hildegarde of Bingen (1098–1179) German abbess, composer, and mystic.
     1178? Attrib.

10   Some physiologists will have it that the stomach
     is a mill;—others, that it is fermenting vat;—
     others again that it is a stew-pan;—but in my
     view of the matter, it is neither a mill, a
     fermenting vat, nor a stew-pan—but a stomach,
     gentlemen, a stomach.
     William Hunter (1718–83) Scottish anatomist and obstetrician.
     Manuscript notes from his lectures. Quoted in *A Treatise on
     Diet* (J. A. Paris; 1824), Epigraph

11   The human body is a machine which winds its
     own springs: the living image of perpetual
     movement.
     Julien Offroy de La Mettrie (1709–51) French philosopher and physician.
     The Man-Machine (1747)

12   Skin is like wax paper that holds everything in
     without dripping.
     Art Linkletter (b. 1912) Canadian-born US radio and television broadcaster.
     From a collection of statements by unidentified children. *A
     Child's Garden of Misinformation* (1965), ch. 5

13   The human body . . . indeed is like a ship; its
     bones being the stiff standing-rigging, and the
     sinews the small running ropes, that manage all
     the motions.
     Herman Melville (1819–91) US novelist. *Redburn* (1849), ch. 13

14   The human body is private property. We have to
     have a search warrant to look inside, and even
     then an investigator is confined to a few
     experimental tappings here and there, some
     gropings on the party wall, a torch flashed rather
     hesitantly into some of the dark corners.
     Jonathan Miller (b. 1934) British psychologist, director, and writer.
     'Perishable Goods', *The Body in Question* (February 15,
     1979)

15   I say that it touches a man that his blood is sea
     water and his tears are salt, that the seed of his
     loins is scarcely different from the same cells in a
     seaweed, and that stuff like his bones are coral
     made.
     Donald Culross Peattie (1898–1964) US naturalist. 'April First', *An
     Almanac for Moderns* (1935)

16   The part of Quoyle that was wonderful was,
     unfortunately, attached to the rest of him.
     E. Annie Proulx (b. 1935) US writer. Referring to his penis. 'Love
     Knot', *The Shipping News* (1993), ch. 2

17   Our body is a machine for living. It is organized
     for that, it is its nature. Let life go on in it
     unhindered and let it defend itself, it will do
     more than if you paralyze it by encumbering it
     with remedies.
     Leo Tolstoy (1828–1910) Russian writer. *War and Peace* (1865–69),
     bk. 10, ch. 29

18   If anything is sacred the human body is sacred.
     Walt Whitman (1819–92) US poet. 1855. 'I Sing the Body Electric',
     Leaves of Grass (1881), pt. 8

19   The women say that they perceive their bodies in
     their entirety. They say they do not favour any of
     its parts on the grounds that it was formerly a
     forbidden object.
     Monique Wittig (b. 1935) French writer. *Les Guérillères* (1969)

Boldness

see Certainty, Courage, Self-Confidence

Books

see also Fiction, Libraries, Literature, Reading, Writing

1   The sky opens,
    the soil turns into books
    and in every book is God. Awakened,
    the sleep of stone is gone from my face,
    and no mirage is now in my eye.

    Adonis (b. 1929) Syrian poet. 'The Days of the Hawk', *When the Words Burn* (John Mikhail Asfour, ed., tr.; 1988)

2   Books create eras and nations, just as eras and
    nations create books.

    Jean-Jaques Ampère (1800–64) French writer and historian. 'De l'histoire de la littérature Française', *Mélanges d'Histoire Littéraire et de Littérature* (1876)

3   Some books are undeservedly forgotten; none are
    undeservedly remembered.

    W. H. Auden (1907–73) British poet. 'Reading', *The Dyer's Hand* (1963)

4   Some books are to be tasted, others to be
    swallowed, and some few to be chewed and
    digested.

    Francis Bacon (1561–1626) English philosopher, statesman, and lawyer. 'Of Studies', *Essays* (1625)

5   My next work shall be on rice paper wound
    about a spool, with a perforated line every six
    inches and on sale in Boots. The length of each
    chapter will be carefully calculated to suit with
    the average free motion . . . The Beckett Bowel
    Books.

    Samuel Beckett (1906–89) Irish playwright, novelist, and poet. Written in irritation and dismay at the early rejection of his novel *Murphy* by publisher after publisher in the United States and Britain. The novel was eventually published by Routledge & Sons, London, in 1938. Letter to Mary Manning Howe (November 14, 1936), quoted in *Damned to Fame: the Life of Samuel Beckett* (James Knowlson; 1996), ch. 10

6   The work is the death mask of its conception.

    Walter Benjamin (1892–1940) German writer and critic. 'One-Way Street', *Reflections* (Peter Demetz, ed.; 1986)

7   Your first book is the only one that matters.
    Perhaps a writer should write only that one. That
    is the one moment when you make the big leap;
    the opportunity to express yourself is offered that
    once, and you untie the knot within you then or
    never again.

    Italo Calvino (1923–85) Cuban-born Italian novelist and short-story writer. 1947. *The Path to the Nest of Spiders* (William Weaver, tr.; 1964), preface

8   A good book is the purest essence of a human
    soul.

    Thomas Carlyle (1795–1881) Scottish historian and essayist. Speech made in support of the London Library. *Carlyle and the London Library* (F. Harrison; 1840)

9   'What is the use of a book', thought Alice,
    'without pictures or conversations?'

    Lewis Carroll (1832–98) British writer and mathematician. *Alice's Adventures in Wonderland* (1865), ch. 1

10 A book by a great man is a compromise between
    the reader and himself.

    Eugène Delacroix (1798–1863) French painter. Letter to Honoré de Balzac, *Correspondances* (1832)

11 All that is literature seeks to communicate power;
    all that is not literature, to communicate
    knowledge.

    Thomas De Quincey (1785–1859) British essayist and critic. 'Letters to a Young Man Whose Education has been Neglected', *London Magazine* (1823), no. 3

12 The good of a book lies in being read. A book is
    made up of signs that speak of other signs, which
    in their turn speak of things. Without an eye to
    read them, a book contains signs that produce no
    concepts; therefore it is dumb.

    Umberto Eco (b. 1932) Italian writer and literary scholar. *The Name of the Rose* (William Weaver, tr.; 1980), Fifth Day: Vespers

13 A book is not harmless merely because no one is
    consciously offended by it.

    T. S. Eliot (1888–1965) US-born British poet and playwright. 1935. 'Religion and Literature', *T.S. Eliot Selected Essays* (1966)

14 The book written against fame and learning has
    the author's name on the title page.

    Ralph Waldo Emerson (1803–82) US poet and essayist. *Journals* (1860–66)

15 Books are made not like children but like
    pyramids . . . and they're just as useless! and they
    stay in the desert! . . . Jackals piss at their foot
    and the bourgeois climb up on them.

    Gustave Flaubert (1821–80) French novelist. Letter to Ernest Feydeau (November/December 1857), quoted in *Correspondence, 1857–64* (M. Nadeau, ed.; 1965)

16 Only two classes of books are of universal
    appeal. The very best and the very worst.

    Ford Madox Ford (1873–1939) British novelist. *Joseph Conrad* (1924)

17 A well chosen anthology is a complete dispensary
    of medicine for the more common mental
    disorders, and may be used as much for
    prevention as cure.

    Robert Graves (1895–1985) British poet and novelist. *On English Poetry* (1922), ch. 29

18 For a true writer each book should be a new
    beginning where he tries again for something that
    is beyond attainment.

    Ernest Hemingway (1899–1961) US writer. Acceptance speech, Nobel Prize in literature (1954)

19 All good books are alike in that they are truer
    than if they had really happened and after you
    are finished reading one you will feel that all that
    happened to you and afterwards it all belongs to
    you: the good and the bad, the ecstasy, the
    remorse and sorrow, the people and the places
    and how the weather was.

    Ernest Hemingway (1899–1961) US writer. 'Old Newsman Writes', *Esquire* (December 1934)

20 The proper study of mankind is books.

    Aldous Huxley (1894–1963) British novelist and essayist. A reference to Alexander Pope's famous line 'The proper study of mankind is man', in *An Essay on Man*, Epistle 2, ll.1–2. *Crome Yellow* (1921), ch. 28

21 A bad book is as much a labour to write as a
    good one; it comes as sincerely from the author's
    soul.

    Aldous Huxley (1894–1963) British novelist and essayist. *Point Counter Point* (1928)

22 A classic book is a book that survives the
    circumstances that made it possible yet alone
    keeps those circumstances alive.

    Alfred Kazin (1915–98) US writer and critic. Quoted in *The New Republic* (August 29, 1988)

23 To every man who struggles with his own soul in mystery, a book that is a book flowers once, and seeds, and is gone.

D. H. Lawrence (1885–1930) British writer. 'A Bibliography of D. H. L.', *Phoenix* (1929)

24 Never judge a cover by its book.

Fran Lebowitz (b. 1951?) US writer and columnist. *Metropolitan Life* (1978)

25 There can hardly be a stranger commodity in the world than books. Printed by people who don't understand them; sold by people who don't understand them; bound, criticized and read by people who don't understand them; and now even written by people who don't understand them.

Georg Christoph Lichtenberg (1742–99) German physicist and writer. *Aphorisms* (1764–99)

26 Only that which brings something quite new is really worthy of the name of a book.

Georg Christoph Lichtenberg (1742–99) German physicist and writer. Quoted in *The Jingle Bell Principle* (Miroslav Holub; 1992)

27 He felt about books as doctors feel about medicines, or managers about plays—cynical but hopeful.

Rose Macaulay (1881–1958) British poet, novelist, and essayist. *Crewe Train* (1926), pt. 2, ch. 8

28 It was a book to kill time for those who like it better dead.

Rose Macaulay (1881–1958) British poet, novelist, and essayist. Attrib.

29 The difference between writing a book and being on television is the difference between conceiving a child and having a baby made in a test tube.

Norman Mailer (b. 1923) US novelist and journalist. Quoted in *Conversations with Norman Mailer* (J. Michael Lennon; 1988)

30 Casting my mind's eye over the whole of fiction, the only absolutely original creation that I can think of is Don Quixote.

Somerset Maugham (1874–1965) British writer. *Ten Novels and their Authors* (1954), ch. 1

31 There is an impression abroad that everyone has it in him to write one book; but if by this is implied a good book the impression is false.

Somerset Maugham (1874–1965) British writer. *The Summing Up* (1938)

32 In recommending a book to a friend the less said the better. The moment you praise a book too highly you awaken resistance in your listener.

Henry Miller (1891–1980) US novelist. *The Books In My Life* (1957)

33 A good book is the precious life-blood of a master spirit, embalmed and treasured up on purpose to a life beyond life.

John Milton (1608–74) English writer. *Areopagitica* (1644)

34 Who kills a man kills a reasonable creature, God's image; but he who destroys a good book, kills reason itself, kills the image of God, as it were in the eye.

John Milton (1608–74) English writer. *Areopagitica* (1644)

35 It has been said that a careful reading of *Anna Karenina*, if it teaches you nothing else, will teach you how to make strawberry jam.

Julian Mitchell (b. 1935) British writer and playwright. *Radio Times* (October 30, 1976)

36 An encomium in Greek has a marvellous effect on the title page of a book.

Molière (1622–73) French playwright. *Les Précieuses Ridicules* (1659), preface

37 It could be said of me that in this book I have only made up a bunch of other men's flowers, providing of my own only the string that ties them together.

Michel de Montaigne (1533–92) French essayist. *Essays* (1580–88), bk. 3, ch. 7

38 I had to do the books I did because there were no books about those subjects to give me what I wanted. I had to clear up my world, elucidate it, for myself.

V. S. Naipaul (b. 1932) Trinidadian-born British novelist. Nobel lecture (December 7, 2001)

39 The books one reads in childhood, and perhaps most of all the bad and good bad books, create in one's mind a sort of false map of the world, a series of fabulous countries into which one can retreat at odd moments throughout the rest of life, and which in some cases can even survive a visit to the real countries which they are supposed to represent.

George Orwell (1903–50) British writer. 'Riding Down from Bangor' (1946)

40 *Ulysses* . . . I rather wish I had never read it. It gives me an inferiority complex . . . I feel like a eunuch who has taken a course in voice production and can pass himself off fairly well as a bass or a baritone, but if you listen closely you can hear the good old squeak.

George Orwell (1903–50) British writer. Referring to *Ulysses* (1922) by James Joyce. Letter (September 1934)

41 A good book is a piece of writing that implies that things don't exist, a kind of absence, or death . . . it is futile to look outside the book for a realm that is located beyond the words.

Orhan Pamuk (b. 1952) Turkish novelist. *The New Life* (Guneli Gun, tr.; 1994)

42 At last, an unprintable book that is readable.

Ezra Pound (1885–1972) US poet, translator, and critic. Referring to *Tropic of Cancer* by Henry Miller; also quoted as 'A dirty book worth reading'. Remark (1934)

43 An anthology is like all the plums and orange peel picked out of a cake.

Walter Alexander Raleigh (1861–1922) British critic and essayist. Letter to Mrs. Robert Bridges (January 15, 1915)

44 No one says a novel has to be one thing. It can be anything it wants to be, a vaudeville show, the six o'clock news, the mumblings of wild men saddled by demons.

Ishmael Reed (b. 1938) US writer. *Yellow Back Radio Broke-Down* (1969)

45 Everybody writes a book too many.

Mordecai Richler (b. 1931) Canadian novelist. *Observer* (January 9, 1985), 'Sayings of the Week'

46 When a new book is published, read an old one.

Samuel Rogers (1763–1855) British poet and art collector. Attrib.

47 We all know that books burn—yet we have the greater knowledge that books cannot be killed by fire. People die, but books never die. No man and no force can abolish memory . . . In this war, we know, books are weapons.

Franklin D. Roosevelt (1882–1945) US president. Message to the American Booksellers Association (May 6, 1942)

48 All books are divisible into two classes, the books of the hour, and the books of all time.

John Ruskin (1819–1900) British art critic, writer, and reformer. 'Of Kings' Treasuries', *Sesame and Lilies* (1865)

49 What really knocks me out is a book that, when you're all done reading it, you wish the author that wrote it was a terrific friend of yours and you could call him up on the phone whenever you felt like it.

J. D. Salinger (b. 1919) US novelist. *The Catcher in the Rye* (1951)

50 A best-seller is the gilded tomb of a mediocre talent.

Logan Pearsall Smith (1865–1946) US-born British writer. 'Arts and Letters', *Afterthoughts* (1931)

51 No furniture so charming as books.

Sydney Smith (1771–1845) British clergyman, essayist, and wit. Quoted in *A Memoir of the Rev. Sydney Smith* (Lady Holland; 1855), vol. 1, ch. 9

52 What you don't know would make a great book.

Sydney Smith (1771–1845) British clergyman, essayist, and wit. Quoted in 'Recipe for Salad', *A Memoir of the Rev. Sydney Smith* (Lady Holland; 1855), vol. 1, ch. 11

53 A book is like a man—clever and dull, brave and cowardly, beautiful and ugly. For every flowering thought there will be a page like a wet and mangy mongrel, and for every looping flight a tap on the wing and a reminder that wax cannot hold the feathers firm too near the sun.

John Steinbeck (1902–68) US novelist. Quoted in 'On Publishing', *Writers at Work* (George Plimpton, ed.; 1977), 4th series

54 The portability, the tactile presence, the secrets of companionship inherent in books as we have grown accustomed to them, still look to be irreplaceable.

George Steiner (b. 1929) US scholar and critic. *Grammars of Creation* (2001)

55 Digressions, incontestably, are the sunshine; they are the life, the soul of reading; take them out of this book for instance, you might as well take the book along with them.

Laurence Sterne (1713–68) Irish-born British writer and clergyman. *Tristram Shandy* (1759–67), bk. 1, ch. 22

56 My brother-in-law wrote an unusual murder story. The victim got killed by a man from another book.

Robert Sylvester (1907–75) US writer. Attrib.

57 A travel book . . . is the simplest sort of narrative, an explanation which is its own excuse for the gathering up and the going.

Paul Theroux (b. 1941) US writer. *The Old Patagonian Express: By Train Through the Americas* (1979), ch. 1

58 Of all the needs a book has the chief need is that it be readable.

Anthony Trollope (1815–82) British novelist. *Autobiography* (1883), ch. 19

59 The lies of novels are never gratuitous: they compensate for the inadequacies of life.

Mario Vargas Llosa (b. 1936) Peruvian writer. 'The Truth of Lies' (1989)

60 If it is true that it is what we run from that chases us, then *The Color Purple* . . . is the book that ran me down while I sat with my back to it in a field.

Alice Walker (b. 1944) US novelist and poet. 1992. *The Color Purple* (1992, 10th anniversary edition), Preface

61 There is no such thing as a moral or an immoral book. Books are well written, or badly written.

Oscar Wilde (1854–1900) Irish poet, playwright, and wit. *The Picture of Dorian Gray* (1891), Preface

62 I am embalmed in a book of Henry James; the American Scene: like a fly in amber. I don't expect to get out; but it is very quiet and luminous.

Virginia Woolf (1882–1941) British novelist and critic. Letter to Lady Robert Cecil (August 16, 1907), quoted in *The Letters of Virginia Woolf* (Nigel Nicolson, ed.; 1975), vol. 1

63 Books are what the world values as representing Tao. But books are only words, and the valuable part of words is the thought therein contained.

Zhuangzi (369?–286 BC) Chinese philosopher and teacher. 'The Tao of God', quoted in *Chuang Tzu* (Herbert A. Giles, tr.; 1980), ch. 13

Bores and Boredom

see also **World-Weariness**

1 The old repeat themselves and the young have nothing to say. The boredom is mutual.

Jacques Bainville (1879–1936) French journalist and historian. Lecture, 'Le Charme de la conversation' (1937)

2 Nothing happens, nobody comes, nobody goes, it's awful!

Samuel Beckett (1906–89) Irish playwright, novelist, and poet. *Waiting for Godot* (1954), Act 1

3 BORE, n. A person who talks when you wish him to listen.

Ambrose Bierce (1842–1914?) US writer and journalist. *The Devil's Dictionary* (1911)

4 Society is now one polish'd horde,
Form'd of two mighty tribes, the *Bores* and *Bored*.

Lord Byron (1788–1824) British poet. *Don Juan* (1819–24), can. 13, st. 95

5 I'm so bored with it all.

Winston Churchill (1874–1965) British prime minister and writer. Said to be his last words. Quoted in *Clementine* (M. Soames; 1965)

6 I wanted to be bored to death, as good a way to go as any.

Peter De Vries (1910–93) US novelist. *Comfort Me With Apples* (1956), ch. 17

7 We were as nearly bored as enthusiasm would permit.

Edmund Gosse (1849–1928) British writer and critic. Referring to a play by Algernon Swinburne. Quoted in *Edward Marsh, Patron of the Arts* (Christopher Hassall; 1959), ch.6

8 The effect of boredom on a large scale in history is underestimated. It is a main cause of revolutions, and would soon bring to an end all the static Utopias and the farmyard civilization of the Fabians.

William Ralph Inge (1860–1954) British churchman. *The End of an Age* (1948), ch. 6

9 We live in stirring times—tea-stirring times.

Christopher Isherwood (1904–86) British-born US writer. *Mr Norris Changes Trains* (1935)

10 This is a day that yawns like a caesura:
Quiet since dawn, and wearily drawn out.

Osip Mandelstam (1891–1938) Russian poet, writer, and translator. 1914. 'Orioles in the Woods . . . ', *Stone* (Robert Tracy, tr.; 1915), ll. 5–6

11 Is not life a hundred times too short for us to bore ourselves?

Friedrich Wilhelm Nietzsche (1844–1900) German philosopher and poet. *Beyond Good and Evil* (1886)

12 Another lion gave a grievous roar;
And the first lion thought the last a bore.
William Barnes Rhodes (1772–1826) British playwright. *Bombastes Furioso* (1810), Act 1, Scene 4

13 Boredom is . . . a vital problem for the moralist, since half the sins of mankind are caused by the fear of it.
Bertrand Russell (1872–1970) British philosopher and mathematician. *The Conquest of Happiness* (1930), ch. 4

14 Dear World, I am leaving you because I am bored. I am leaving you with your worries. Good luck.
George Sanders (1906–72) British film actor. Suicide note. (1972)

15 LEWIS Life is as tedious as a twice-told tale Vexing the dull ear of a drowsy man.
William Shakespeare (1564–1616) English poet and playwright. *King John* (1591–98), Act 3, Scene 4

16 Neither principalities nor powers should force me into the drawing-room, where sat the three unhappy women of my party, being entertained within an inch of their lives by Mrs McRory.
Edith Somerville (1858–1949) Irish writer. 'Sharper Than a Ferret's Tooth', *Further Experiences of an Irish R.M.* (1899)

17 Any event is welcome in prison, even the threat of cerebro-spinal meningitis and unpleasant needle jabs.
Wole Soyinka (b. 1934) Nigerian novelist, playwright, poet, and lecturer. *The Man Died* (1975)

18 Somebody's boring me, I think it's me.
Dylan Thomas (1914–53) Welsh poet, playwright, and short-story writer. Remark made after he had been talking continuously for some time. Quoted in *Four Absentees* (Rayner Heppenstall; 1960)

Boston

see American Cities

Brevity

see also Clarity, Simplicity

1 !
1862. The entire contents of a telegram sent to Hugo by his publishers, in response to his telegram '?', asking how *Les Misérables* was selling. Quoted in *The Literary Life* (R. Hendrickson; 1981)

2 You lose.
Calvin Coolidge (1872–1933) US president. When a woman at a dinner told him that someone had bet her that she would not get more than two words out of him. Attrib.

3 Good things, when short, are twice as good.
Baltasar Gracián (1601–58) Spanish writer and Jesuit. *The Art of Worldly Wisdom* (1647)

4 I strive to be brief, and I become obscure.
Horace (65–8 BC) Roman poet. *Ars Poetica* (19–8 BC), l. 25

5 In art economy is always beauty.
Henry James (1843–1916) US-born British writer and critic. 'The Altar of the Dead', *Prefaces* (1909)

6 There are writers who can express in as little as twenty pages what I occasionally need as many as two for.
Karl Kraus (1874–1936) Austrian writer. 1909. Quoted in 'Sprüche und Widersprüche', *Karl Kraus* (Harry Zohn; 1971)

7 But the shortest works are always the best.
Jean de La Fontaine (1621–95) French writer and poet. 'Les Lapins', *Fables* (1668), bk. 10

8 POLONIUS Brevity is the soul of wit.
William Shakespeare (1564–1616) English poet and playwright. *Hamlet* (1601), Act 2, Scene 2

Bribery

see also Corruption, Crime, Money

1 What makes all doctrines plain and clear?
About two hundred pounds a year.
And that which was prov'd true before
Prove false again? Two hundred more.
Samuel Butler (1612–80) English satirist. *Hudibras* (1678), pt. 3, can. 1, ll. 1277–80

2 To a shower of gold most things are penetrable.
Thomas Carlyle (1795–1881) Scottish historian and essayist. *The French Revolution* (1837), pt. 1, bk. 3, ch. 7

3 The Democrats only come here when they want votes. They brought sweets to bribe us.
The Communists used to bring vodka. It was more successful.
Galina Denisova, Russian shopkeeper. August, 1993. Speaking to her neighbour. *Times* (August 11, 1993)

4 Usually it is the accumulation of small gratuities rather than any direct bribe that gradually obligates the people in power.
Harrison W. Fox, Jr., US author. *Doing Business in Washington* (co-written with Martin Schnitzer; 1981)

5 I have often noticed that a bribe . . . has that effect—it changes a relation. The man who offers a bribe gives away a little of his own importance; the bribe once accepted, he becomes the inferior, like a man who has paid for a woman.
Graham Greene (1904–91) British novelist. *The Comedians* (1966), pt. 1, ch. 4

6 You need to rent an MP just like you rent a London taxi.
Ian Greer, British political lobbyist. *Observer* (October 23, 1994), 'Sayings of the Week'

7 If a man does things for you which seem to be a miracle, you pay him. Why grumble?
Adnan Khasoggi (b. 1935) Saudi Arabian entrepreneur. Referring to bribery. *News of the World* (May 24, 1986)

8 The taking of a Bribe or Gratuity, should be punished with as severe penalties as the defrauding of the State.
William Penn (1644–1718) English preacher and colonialist. *Some Fruits of Solitude* (1693), pt. 1, no. 384

9 I'll make him an offer he can't refuse.
Mario Puzo (b. 1920) US novelist. *The Godfather* (1969)

10 If a minister just twists my arm I'll just stand there and have it twisted, but it'll be a long time before it falls off.
Sir Denis Rooke (b. 1924) British business executive. *Daily Express* (November 12, 1981)

11 CLOWN Though authority be a stubborn bear, yet he is oft led by the nose with gold.
William Shakespeare (1564–1616) English poet and playwright. *The Winter's Tale* (1610–11), Act 4, Scene 4

Britain

see also British Cities, British Imperialism, England, Europe, Northern Ireland, Scotland, Wales

1 A nation of shop-keepers are very seldom so disinterested.

Samuel Adams (1722–1803) American revolutionary leader. Referring to Britain, following the Declaration of Independence, July 4, 1776. Speech, Philadelphia (August 1, 1776)

2 I cannot believe that the great British people, in order to protect their identity, would now be cowering on the very island from which they set sail to travel the world.

Édouard Balladur (b. 1929) Turkish-born French prime minister. May 1994. On British suspicion of the European Union. *Observer* (May 8, 1994), 'Sayings of the Week'

3 Think of what our Nation stands for,
Books from Boots' and country lanes,
Free speech, free passes, class distinction,
Democracy and proper drains.

John Betjeman (1906–84) British poet and broadcaster. 'In Westminster Abbey', *John Betjeman's Collected Poems* (1958)

4 A perfect model for a kingdom, for an aristocracy, or for a democracy.

Simón Bolívar (1783–1830) Venezuelan soldier and statesman. Quoted in *Simón Bolívar and the Age of Revolution* (John Lynch; 1983)

5 Yes, it is wonderful to be British—until one comes to Britain.

Edward R. Braithwaite (b. 1920) Guyanese novelist and educator. *To Sir, With Love* (1959)

6 It sometimes occurs to me that the British have more heritage than is good for them.

Bill Bryson (b. 1951) US writer. *Notes From a Small Island* (1995)

7 The people Hitler never understood, and whose actions continued to exasperate him to the end of his life, were the British.

Alan Bullock (b. 1914) British academic and historian. *Hitler, A Study in Tyranny* (1952), ch. 8

8 Britain has lived for too long on borrowed time, borrowed money and even borrowed ideas.

Jim Callaghan (b. 1912) British prime minister. *Observer* (October 3, 1976), 'Sayings of the Week'

9 The British love permanence more than they love beauty.

Hugh Casson (1910–99) British architect. *Observer* (June 14, 1964), 'Sayings of the Week'

10 It must be owned, that the Graces do not seem to be natives of Great Britain; and I doubt, the best of us here have more of rough than polished diamond.

Lord Chesterfield (1694–1773) English statesman and writer. November 18, 1748. *Letters to his Son* (1774)

11 The maxim of the British people is 'Business as usual'.

Winston Churchill (1874–1965) British prime minister and writer. Speech at the Guildhall, London (November 9, 1914)

12 They are the only people who like to be told how bad things are—who like to be told the worst.

Winston Churchill (1874–1965) British prime minister and writer. 1921. Speech referring to the British.

13 The imbecility of her military leaders abroad, and the fatal want of energy in her councils at home, had lowered the character of Great Britain from the proud elevation on which it had been placed.

James Fenimore Cooper (1789–1851) US novelist. *The Last of the Mohicans* (1826), quoted in *The Leatherstocking Saga* (Allan Nevins, ed.; 1955)

14 In Dundee and Penzance and Ealing
We're imbued with appropriate feeling:
We're British and loyal
And love every royal
And tonight we shall drink till we're reeling.

Wendy Cope (b. 1945) British poet. 'All-Purpose Poem for State Occasions', *Making Cocoa for Kingsley Amis* (1986)

15 Regions Caesar never knew
Thy posterity shall sway,
Where his eagles never flew,
None invincible as they.

William Cowper (1731–1800) British poet. 'Boadicea: An Ode' (1782), ll. 29–32, quoted in *Cowper: Poetical Works* (H.S. Milford, ed.; 1934)

16 Oh! what a snug little Island,
A right little, tight little Island!

Charles Dibdin (1745–1814) British actor, composer, and playwright. 'The Snug Little Island', *The British Raft* (1797)

17 Britain is not a country that is easily rocked by revolution . . . In Britain our institutions evolve. We are a Fabian Society writ large.

William Hamilton (b. 1917) Scottish politician. *My Queen and I* (1975), ch. 9

18 We may be a small island, but we are not a small people.

Edward Heath (b. 1916) British prime minister. *Observer* (June 21, 1970), 'Sayings of the Week'

19 His home! the Western giant smiles,
And twirls the spotty globe to find it;
This little speck, the British Isles?
'T is but a freckle,—never mind it.

Oliver Wendell Holmes (1841–1935) US judge. 'A Good Time Going!', *The Complete Poetical Works of Oliver Wendell Holmes* (1912)

20 This is a very fine country to be acutely ill or injured in, but take my advice and do not be old and frail or mentally ill here—at least not for a few years. This is definitely not a good country to be deaf or blind in either.

Keith Joseph (1918–94) British politician. *Observer* (July 1, 1973), 'Sayings of the Week'

21 The British, he thought, must be gluttons for satire: even the weather forecast seemed to be some kind of spoof, predicting every possible combination of weather for the next twenty-four hours without actually committing itself to anything specific.

David Lodge (b. 1935) British novelist and critic. A visiting US academic's first experience of Britain and the British. *Changing Places* (1975), ch. 2

22 We know no spectacle so ridiculous as the British public in one of its periodical fits of morality.

Thomas Babington Macaulay (1800–59) British politician, historian, and writer. 'Moore's *Life of Lord Byron*', *Essays Contributed to the Edinburgh Review* (1843)

23 We have a Calvinistic creed, a Popish liturgy, and an Arminian clergy.

William Pitt the Elder (1708–78) British prime minister. Speech to the House of Lords (May 19, 1772)

British Cities

see also Britain, Cities, European Cities

1 Home of lost causes, and forsaken beliefs, and unpopular names, and impossible loyalties!
   Matthew Arnold (1822–88) British poet and critic. Referring to Oxford. *Essays in Criticism, First Series* (1865), Preface

2 Wiv a ladder and some glasses,
   You could see to 'Ackney Marshes,
   If it wasn't for the 'ouses in between.
   Edgar Bateman (*fl.* 1894) British songwriter. 'If it wasn't for the 'ouses in between' (co-written with George Le Brunn; 1894)

3 The fields from Islington to Marybone,
   To Primrose Hill and Saint John's Wood,
   Were builded over with pillars of gold,
   And there Jerusalems pillars stood.
   William Blake (1757–1827) British poet, painter, engraver, and mystic. 'To The Jews', *Jerusalem* (1804–20), pl. 27, ll. 1–4, quoted in *The Poetry and Prose of William Blake* (David V. Erdman, ed.; 1965)

4 But what is to be the fate of the great wen of all? The monster, called . . . 'the metropolis of the empire'?
   William Cobbett (1763–1835) British writer, journalist, and reformer. January 5, 1822. Referring to London. *Rural Rides* (1830)

5 Oh, London is a fine town,
   A very famous city,
   Where all the streets are paved with gold,
   And all the maidens pretty.
   George Colman (1762–1836) British playwright and theatre owner. *The Heir at Law* (1797), Act 1, Scene 2

6 London: a nation, not a city.
   Benjamin Disraeli (1804–81) British prime minister and writer. *Lothair* (1870), ch. 27

7 London is a modern Babylon.
   Benjamin Disraeli (1804–81) British prime minister and writer. *Tancred* (1847), bk. 5, ch. 5

8 Unreal City,
   Under the brown fog of a winter dawn,
   A crowd flowed over London bridge, so many,
   I had not thought death had undone so many.
   T. S. Eliot (1888–1965) US-born British poet and playwright. 'The Burial of the Dead', *The Waste Land* (1922)

9 Any time you're Lambeth way,
   Any evening, any day,
   You'll find us all doin' the Lambeth walk.
   Douglas Furber (1885–1961) British songwriter. Song lyric. 'Doin' the Lambeth Walk' (1937)

10 Crowds without company, and dissipation without pleasure.
   Edward Gibbon (1737–94) British historian. Referring to London. *Memoirs of My Life* (1796), ch. 5

11 Cuckoo-echoing, bell-swarmèd, lark-charmèd, rook-racked, river-rounded.
   Gerard Manley Hopkins (1844–89) British poet, priest, and classicist. 'Duns Scotus' Oxford' (1879), quoted in *Poems* (Robert Bridges, ed.; 1918)

12 London doesn't love the latent or the lurking, has neither time, nor taste, nor sense for anything less discernible than the red flag in front of the steam-roller. It wants cash over the counter and letters ten feet high.
   Henry James (1843–1916) US-born British writer and critic. *The Awkward Age* (1899)

13 London was a city not to be visited, but to be captured.
   James Weldon Johnson (1871–1938) US writer, lawyer, and diplomat. *Along This Way* (1933)

14 When a man is tired of London, he is tired of life; for there is in London all that life can afford.
   Samuel Johnson (1709–84) British lexicographer and writer. September 20, 1777. Quoted in *Life of Samuel Johnson* (James Boswell; 1791)

15 The flushpots of Euston and the hanging garments of Marylebone.
   James Joyce (1882–1941) Irish writer. *Finnegans Wake* (1939)

16 Forget six counties overhung with smoke,
   Forget the snorting steam and piston stroke
   Forget the spreading of the hideous town;
   Think rather of the pack-horse on the down,
   And dream of London, small and white and clean,
   The clear Thames bordered by its gardens green.
   William Morris (1834–96) British designer, socialist reformer, and poet. 'The Wanderers', *The Earthly Paradise* (1868–70), Prologue, ll. 1–6

17 The parks are the lungs of London.
   William Pitt the Elder (1708–78) British prime minister. Quoted by William Windham in Parliament (June 30, 1808)

18 This is the city of perspiring dreams.
   Frederic Raphael (b. 1931) British writer. Referring to Cambridge, playing on the expression 'dreaming spires', used to describe Oxford. 'An Early Life', *The Glittering Prizes* (1976), pt. 3

19 I would sell London, if I could find a suitable purchaser.
   Richard I (1157–99) English monarch. 1189? Comment while raising money for the third Crusade. Quoted in *Historia Rerum Anglicarum* (William of Newburgh; 1196–98?), bk. 4, ch. 5

20 London, that great sea, whose ebb and flow
   At once is deaf and loud, and on the shore
   Vomits its wrecks, and still howls on for more.
   Percy Bysshe Shelley (1792–1822) English poet. Written from the Leghorn home of Maria Gisborne, who was in London. 'Letter to Maria Gisborne' (July 1, 1820), l. 193, quoted in *Posthumous Poems* (Mrs. Shelley, ed.; 1824)

21 Here it is that humanity achieves for itself both perfection and brutalization, that civilization produces its wonders, and that civilized man becomes again almost a savage.
   Alexis de Tocqueville (1805–59) French writer and politician. July 2, 1835. Referring to Manchester. *Voyage en Angleterre et en Irlande de 1835* (1835)

22 That old monkish place which I have a horror of.
   Victoria (1819–1901) British monarch. Referring to Oxford. (October 31, 1859)

23 Earth has not anything to show more fair:
   Dull would he be of soul who could pass by
   A sight so touching in its majesty:
   The City now doth, like a garment, wear
   The beauty of the morning; silent, bare,
   Ships, towers, domes, theatres, and temples lie
   Open unto the fields, and to the sky;
   All bright and glittering in the smokeless air.
   William Wordsworth (1770–1850) English poet. September 3, 1802. 'Composed Upon Westminster Bridge', *Poems in Two Volumes* (1807), vol. 1, ll. 1–8

British Imperialism

see also **Britain**, **Imperialism**

1 Great Britain has lost an Empire and has not yet found a role.

Dean Acheson (1893–1971) US lawyer and statesman. Speech, West Point Military Academy (December 5, 1962)

2 Establish such a politie of civil and military power and create and secure such a large revenue . . . as may be the foundation of a large, well-grounded sure English dominion in India for all time to come.

Anonymous. *Dispatch from the East India Company to its Chief Executive in Surat* (mid-18th century)

3 The Falklands thing was a fight between two bald men over a comb.

Jorge Luis Borges (1899–1986) Argentinian writer and poet. Referring to the war between Argentina and the United Kingdom over the Falkland Islands, 1982. *Time* (February 14, 1983)

4 Individuals pass like shadows; but the commonwealth is fixed and stable.

Edmund Burke (1729–97) Irish-born British statesman and political philosopher. Remark (February 11, 1780)

5 I impeach him in the name of the people of India, whose rights he has ridden under foot, and whose country he has turned into a desert. Lastly, in the name of human nature itself, in the name of both sexes, in the name of every age, in the name of every rank, I impeach the common enemy and oppressor of all!

Edmund Burke (1729–97) Irish-born British statesman and political philosopher. Speech for the prosecution at the impeachment of Warren Hastings, former governor-general of India. Quoted in *Essay on Warren Hastings* (Thomas Macaulay; 1852)

6 Ten thousand schemes of petulance and pride Despatch her scheming children far and wide: Some east, some west, some everywhere but north, In quest of lawless gain, they issue forth. And thus—accursed be the day and year! She sent a Pict to play the felon here.

Lord Byron (1788–1824) British poet. 1811. Referring in general to Britain and in particular to Lord Elgin (the 'Pict'), who removed the marble sculptures from the Parthenon and shipped them to London, where they have been kept (since 1816) in the British Museum. *The Curse of Minerva* (1812)

7 England may as well dam up the waters from the Nile with bulrushes as to fetter the step of Freedom, more proud and firm in this youthful land.

Lydia Maria Child (1802–80) US abolitionist, suffrage campaigner, and writer. *The Rebels* (1825), ch. 4

8 I have not become the King's First Minister in order to preside over the liquidation of the British Empire.

Winston Churchill (1874–1965) British prime minister and writer. Speech at Mansion House, London (November 10, 1942)

9 India is a geographical term. It is no more a united nation than the Equator.

Winston Churchill (1874–1965) British prime minister and writer. Speech at the Royal Albert Hall (March 18, 1931)

10 The loss of India would mark and consummate the downfall of the British Empire. That great organism would pass at a stroke out of life into history. From such a catastrophe there could be no recovery.

Winston Churchill (1874–1965) British prime minister and writer. Speech, London (December 12, 1930)

11 It is only when you get to see and realize what India is—that she is the strength and the greatness of England—it is only then that you feel that every nerve a man may strain, every energy he may put forward, cannot be devoted to a nobler purpose than keeping tight the cords that hold India to ourselves.

George Nathaniel Curzon (1859–1925) British statesman. Speech, Southport (March 15, 1893)

12 The British flag has never flown over a more powerful or a more united empire . . . Never did our voice count for more in the councils of nations; or in determining the future destinies of mankind.

George Nathaniel Curzon (1859–1925) British statesman. Speech to the House of Lords (November 18, 1918)

13 The East is a career.

Benjamin Disraeli (1804–81) British prime minister and writer. *Tancred* (1847), bk. 2, ch. 14

14 My mission is to pacify Ireland.

William Ewart Gladstone (1809–98) British statesman. December 1, 1868. Referring to forming his first Cabinet. Quoted in *Gladstone 1809–74* (H. C. G. Matthew; 1986), ch. 5

15 We don't want to fight, but, by jingo if we do, We've got the ships, we've got the men, we've got the money too. We've fought the Bear before, and while Britons shall be true, The Russians shall not have Constantinople.

George William Hunt (1829?–1904) British writer. Song lyric, which gave rise to the use of the word 'jingoism', meaning bombastic and xenophobic patriotism. 'We Don't Want to Fight' (1878)

16 They gave us six fishhooks and two blankets embroidered with smallpox.

Paul Muldoon (b. 1951) Irish poet. Narrated in the voice of a Native American, defeated by the British. 'Meeting the British', *Meeting the British* (1987), ll. 17–18

17 His Majesty's dominions, on which the sun never sets.

Christopher North (1785–1854) Scottish poet, essayist, and critic. 'Noctes Ambrosianae', *Blackwood's Magazine* (April 20, 1829), no. 42

18 The Empire is a Commonwealth of Nations.

Lord Rosebery (1847–1929) British prime minister and biographer. Speech, Adelaide (January 18, 1884)

19 We the English seem, as it were, to have conquered and peopled half the world in a fit of absence of mind.

Sir John Robert Seeley (1834–95) British historian. *The Expansion of England* (1883), Lecture 1

20 The national anthem belongs to the eighteenth century. In it you find us ordering God about to do our political work.

George Bernard Shaw (1856–1950) Irish playwright. Attrib.

21 Don't ever ask where the Empire's gone. It's hush-hush.

Julian Slade (b. 1930) British author and composer. Song lyric. 'Hush-Hush', *Salad Days* (1954)

22 To found a great empire for the sole purpose of raising up a people of customers, may at first sight appear a project fit only for a nation of shopkeepers. It is, however, a project altogether unfit for a nation of shopkeepers; but extremely fit for a nation whose government is influenced by shopkeepers.

Adam Smith (1723–90) Scottish economist and philosopher. *Wealth of Nations* (1776), vol. 2, bk. 4, ch. 8

23 On this question of principle . . . they raised their flag against a power . . . which has dotted over the surface of the whole globe with her possessions and military posts, whose morning drumbeat, following the sun, and keeping company with the hours, circles the earth with one continuous and unbroken strain of the martial airs of England.
Daniel Webster (1782–1852) US lawyer, politician, and orator. Referring to the American colonies' fight for independence from British rule. Speech, US Senate (May 7, 1834)

Buddhism

see also **Religion**

1 What does it mean that I am in this endless universe, thinking that I'm a man sitting under the stars on this terrace of earth, but actually empty and awake through the emptiness and awakedness of everything?
Jack Kerouac (1922–69) US writer. *The Dharma Bums* (1958)

2 Zen . . . does not confuse spirituality with thinking about God while one is peeling the potatoes. Zen spirituality is just to peel the potatoes.
Alan Watts (1915–73) British-born US mystic and writer. *The Way of Zen* (1957), pt. 2, ch. 2

Bureaucracy

see also **Business**

1 A committee is a cul-de-sac down which ideas are lured and then quietly strangled.
Hilaire Belloc (1870–1953) French-born British writer. 1973. Attrib.

2 My discovery was this: I had become the victim of a vast, amorphous, unwitting, unconscious conspiracy to prevent me from doing anything whatever to change the university's status quo.
Warren Bennis (b. 1925) US educationalist and writer. Referring to university bureaucracy. Quoted in *How to Get Ahead in Business* (Tom Cannon, ed.; 1993)

3 Remove the document—and you remove the man.
Mikhail Bulgakov (1891–1940) Russian novelist and playwright. 1929–40. *The Master and Margarita* (Michael Glenny, tr.; 1966), ch. 24

4 I'm surprised that a government organization could do it that quickly.
Jimmy Carter (b. 1924) US president. During a visit to Egypt, after being told that it took twenty years to build the Great Pyramid. Remark, *Time* (March 1979)

5 Whatever was required to be done, the Circumlocution Office was beforehand with all the public departments in the art of perceiving—HOW NOT TO DO IT.
Charles Dickens (1812–70) British novelist. *Little Dorrit* (1857), bk. 1, ch. 10

6 A Royal Commission is a broody hen sitting on a china egg.
Michael Foot (b. 1913) British politician and writer. Speech to Parliament (1964)

7 A committee is an animal with four back legs.
John Le Carré (b. 1931) British novelist. *Tinker, Tailor, Soldier, Spy* (1974)

8 A committee should consist of three men, two of whom are absent.
Herbert Beerbohm Tree (1853–1917) British actor and theatrical impresario. Quoted in *Beerbohm Tree* (Hesketh Pearson; 1956)

9 The British civil service . . . is a beautifully designed and effective braking mechanism.
Shirley Williams (b. 1930) British politician. Speech, Royal Institute of Public Administration (February 11, 1980)

Business

see also **Bureaucracy, Capitalism, Economics**

1 CORPORATION, n. An ingenious device for securing individual profit without individual responsibility.
Ambrose Bierce (1842–1914?) US writer and journalist. *The Cynic's Word Book* (1906)

2 What good is the moon if you cannot buy it or sell it?
Ivan Boesky (b. 1937) US financier. Said to his wife. Quoted in *Times* (1986)

3 How come when I want a pair of hands I get a human being as well?
Henry Ford (1863–1947) US car manufacturer. Quoted in *The Witch Doctors* (John Micklethwait and Adrian Wooldridge; 1996)

4 A business that makes nothing but money is a poor kind of business.
Henry Ford (1863–1947) US car manufacturer. Attrib.

5 Man does not only sell commodities, he sells himself and feels himself to be a commodity.
Erich Fromm (1900–80) German-born US psychoanalyst and philosopher. *The Fear of Freedom* (1942)

6 He that resolves to deal with none but honest men must leave off dealing.
Thomas Fuller (1654–1734) English physician and writer. *Gnomologia* (1732)

7 The truly successful businessman is essentially a dissenter, a rebel who is seldom if ever satisfied with the status quo.
J. Paul Getty (1892–1976) US oil magnate. *How to be Rich* (1966)

8 The secret isn't counting the beans, it's growing more beans.
Roberto Goizueta (b. 1931) US business executive. *Fortune* (November 13, 1995)

9 Commerce is the art of exploiting the need or desire someone has for something.
Edmond de Goncourt (1822–96) French novelist and diarist. July 1864. *Le Journal des Goncourts* (co-written with Jules de Goncourt; 1887–96)

10 Columbus didn't have a business plan when he discovered America.
Andrew S. Grove (b. 1936) Hungarian-born US business executive. *New Yorker* (April 11, 1994)

11 Industry is a bit like the human body. The cells are continuously dying and unless new cells are created, sooner or later the whole thing will collapse and disappear.
John Harvey-Jones (b. 1924) British business executive and author. *Making It Happen: Reflections on Leadership* (1987)

12 Business is often about killing your favourite children to allow others to succeed.
John Harvey-Jones (b. 1924) British business executive and author. Referring to the need to close part of a business to help the rest. *Troubleshooter* (1990)

13 Big business is only small business with an extra nought on the end.

Robert Holmes à Court (1937–90) Australian entrepreneur. *Sydney Morning Herald* (August 25, 1985), 'Sayings of the Week'

14 When you are skinning your customers, you should leave some skin on to grow so that you can skin them again.

Nikita Khrushchev (1894–1971) Soviet statesman. Addressed to British business executives. *Observer* (May 28, 1961), 'Sayings of the Week'

15 The businessman has the same fundamental psychology as the artist, inventor, or statesman. He has set himself at a certain work and the work absorbs and becomes himself. It is the expression of his personality; he lives in its growth and perfection according to his plans.

Frank Hyneman Knight (1885–1972) US economist. *Risk, Uncertainty and Profit* (1971)

16 If Thomas Edison had gone to business school, we would all be reading by larger candles.

Mark McCormack (b. 1930) US sports agent, promoter, and lawyer. *What They Don't Teach You at Harvard Business School* (1984)

17 Most large US corporations are run like the Soviet economy.

Kenichi Ohmae (b. 1943) Japanese business strategist. *The Mind of the Strategist* (1982)

18 It is nonsense to refer to business as 'the private sector'—does anything have as much public impact as businesses?

Sir Peter Parker (b. 1924) British business executive. 'Most Quoted, Least Heeded: the 5 Senses of Follett', *Mary Parker Follett: Prophet of Management* (1995)

19 Business is the most important engine for social change in this country.

Lawrence Perlman (b. 1938) US business executive. *Twin Cities Business Monthly* (November 1994)

20 You're not going to transform society until you transform business. But you're not going to transform business by pretending it's not a business.

Lawrence Perlman (b. 1938) US business executive. *Twin Cities Business Monthly* (November 1994)

21 All business, from potato chips to washing machines to jet engines, is about people selling to people.

Tom Peters (b. 1942) US management consultant and author. *A Passion for Excellence* (co-written with Nancy Austin; 1985)

22 Today's sales should be better than yesterday's— and worse than tomorrow's.

Proverb.

23 In the factory we make cosmetics. In the store we sell hope.

Charles Revson (1906–75) US business executive. Quoted in *Fire and Ice* (A. Tobias; 1976), ch. 8

24 Being good is good business.

Anita Roddick (b. 1942) British business executive. *Sunday Express* (November 2, 1986), magazine

25 It might be said that it is the ideal of the employer to have production without employees and the ideal of the employee is to have income without work.

E. F. Schumacher (1911–77) German-born British economist. *Observer* (May 4, 1975), 'Sayings of the Week'

26 Either the business community recognizes values other than its own bottom line and supports interests other than its own or it will be . . . like the feudal lords of the eleventh century.

Robert C. Solomon (b. 1942) US author. *The New World of Business* (1994)

27 Every one lives by selling something.

Robert Louis Stevenson (1850–94) Scottish novelist, essayist, and poet. 'Beggars', *Across the Plains* (1892), pt. 3

28 If there was a market in mass-produced portable nuclear weapons, we'd market them too.

Alan Sugar (b. 1947) British entrepreneur. *Observer* (September 14, 1986), 'Quotes of the Week'

29 I have heard of a man who had a mind to sell his house, and therefore carried a piece of brick in his pocket, which he shewed as a pattern to encourage purchasers.

Jonathan Swift (1667–1745) Irish writer and clergyman. *The Drapier's Letters* (August 4, 1724), no. 2

30 All business sagacity reduces itself in the last analysis to a judicious use of sabotage.

Thorstein Bunde Veblen (1857–1929) US social scientist and economist. *The Nature of Peace* (1917)

31 There is a commodity in human experience. If it's happened to one person, it has happened to thousands of others.

Oprah Winfrey (b. 1954) US chat show host, actor, and businesswoman. Quoted in *Time* (August 8, 1988)

32 When two men in business always agree, one of them is unnecessary.

William Wrigley, Jr. (1861–1932) US business executive. Attrib.

C

Capitalism

see also Business, Economics, Globalization, Money

1   Under capitalism power and money have become commensurable qualities. Any given amount of money may be converted into a specific power, and the market value of all power can be calculated.
Walter Benjamin (1892–1940) German writer and critic. 'Moscow', *Reflections* (Peter Demetz, ed.; 1986)

2   The historic role of capitalism . . . to destroy history, to sever every link with the past and to orientate all effort and imagination to that which is about to occur.
John Berger (b. 1926) British novelist, essayist, and art critic. 1999. *Pig Earth* (1999 edition), Introduction

3   To speak of limits to growth under a capitalistic market economy is as meaningless as to speak of limits to warfare under a warrior society.
Murray Bookchin (b. 1921) US historian and social ecologist. *Remaking Society* (1990)

4   Capitalism without bankruptcy is like Christianity without hell.
Frank Borman (b. 1928) US astronaut and business executive. *Observer* (1986)

5   While the oppressive conditions of feudalism led to a quest for freedom and individuality, the conditions of capitalism have led to a quest for community and social justice.
Severyn Bruyn (b. 1927) US author. Quoted in 'A New Direction for Community Development in the United States', *Real-Life Economics* (Paul Ekins and Manfred Max-Neef, eds.; 1992)

6   History suggests that capitalism is a necessary condition for political freedom. Clearly it is not a sufficient condition.
Milton Friedman (b. 1912) US economist. *Capitalism and Freedom* (1962)

7   Capital as such is not evil; it is its wrong use that is evil. Capital in some form or other will always be needed.
Mahatma Gandhi (1869–1948) Indian national leader. *Harijan* (1940)

8   The market came with the dawn of civilization and it is not capitalism's invention.
Mikhail Gorbachev (b. 1931) Russian statesman. *Guardian* (June 20, 1990)

9   Global democratic capitalism is as unrealizable a condition as worldwide communism.
John Gray (b. 1948) British academic. *False Dawn* (1998)

10   The late-twentieth-century free market experiment is an attempt to legitimate through democratic institutions severe limits on the scope and content of democratic control over economic life.
John Gray (b. 1948) British academic. *False Dawn* (1998)

11   If I had to give a definition of capitalism I would say: the process whereby American girls turn into American women.
Christopher Hampton (b. 1946) British playwright. *Savages* (1973), Scene 16

12   We change the rules of football or cricket to improve the quality of the game; we can change the rules by which capitalism is played too. If we can't, what kind of democracy is it?
Will Hutton (b. 1950) British author and newspaper editor. *Stakeholding and its Critics* (1997)

13   Co-operative capitalism does not spontaneously emerge from free markets—it needs to be designed.
Will Hutton (b. 1950) British author and newspaper editor. *The State We're In* (1995)

14   Successful capitalism demands a fusion of co-operation and competition and a means of grafting such a hybrid into the soil of the economic, political and social system.
Will Hutton (b. 1950) British author and newspaper editor. *The State We're In* (1995)

15   Capitalism tends to produce a multiplicity of petty dictators each in command of his own little business kingdom. State Socialism tends to produce a single, centralised, totalitarian dictatorship, wielding absolute authority . . . through a hierarchy of bureaucratic agents.
Aldous Huxley (1894–1963) British novelist and essayist. *Ends and Means* (1937)

16   The American model is a form of state capitalism in which the great corporations of the military-industrial complex fatten on the largess of the state, while the poor and disadvantaged get a firm dose of *laissez-faire*.
Michael Ignatieff (b. 1947) Canadian-born British writer and broadcaster. *Observer* (September 15, 1991)

17   In a consumer society there are inevitably two kinds of slaves: the prisoners of addiction and the prisoners of envy.
Ivan Illich (b. 1926) Austrian-born US educator and researcher. *Tools for Conviviality* (1973), ch. 3

18   The decoration on the front of the Mercedes has almost become our national emblem instead of the pick and hoe displayed on our coat of arms.
Kenneth David Kaunda (b. 1924) Zambian president. June 1975. Quoted in *Kenneth Kaunda* (Philip Brownrigg; 1989)

19   'Primitive capitalism' is capitalism in a state of nature, red in tooth and claw—a state where those employers whose ideal would be mastery over slaves, find they can rub along by . . . displaying scant regard for the labour force.
William Keegan (b. 1938) British author and journalist. *The Spectre of Capitalism* (1992)

20 The spectre of capitalism haunts not only the former USSR and Eastern Europe, but the whole world.

William Keegan (b. 1938) British author and journalist. *The Spectre of Capitalism* (1992)

21 Capital is built in the past, owned in the present, and deployed to create future value.

Peter Keen, US business executive. 'Transforming Intellectual Property into Intellectual Capital: Competing in the Trust Economy', *Capital for Our Time* (Nicholas Imparato, ed.; 1999)

22 Militarism . . . is one of the chief bulwarks of capitalism, and the day that militarism is undermined, capitalism will fail.

Helen Keller (1880–1968) US writer and lecturer. *The Story of My Life* (1903)

23 Modern capitalism is absolutely irreligious, without internal union, without much public spirit, often, though not always, a mere congeries of possessors and pursuers.

John Maynard Keynes (1883–1946) British economist. *Essays in Persuasion* (1925)

24 The capitalist leaders of the City and in parliament are incapable of distinguishing novel measures for safeguarding capitalism from what they call Bolshevism.

John Maynard Keynes (1883–1946) British economist. *Essays in Persuasion* (1925)

25 I think that Capitalism, wisely managed, can probably be made more efficient for attaining economic ends than any alternative system yet in sight, but that in itself it is in many ways extremely objectionable.

John Maynard Keynes (1883–1946) British economist. *The End of Laissez-Faire* (1925), ch. 5

26 Capitalists are a self-nominating group. To join them is a matter of seizing an opportunity, mobilizing one's savings, borrowing from relatives, friends, and banks, working hard and intelligently, and testing one's acumen and luck.

Robert Lekachman, US author. *Capitalism for Beginners* (1981)

27 Under capitalism we have a state in the proper sense of the word, that is, a special machine for the suppression of one class by another.

Vladimir Ilyich Lenin (1870–1924) Russian revolutionary leader. *The State and Revolution* (1919), ch. 5

28 We know more about the motives, habits, and most intimate arcana of the primitive peoples of New Guinea or elsewhere, than we do of the denizens of the executive suites in Unilever House.

Roy Lewis, US writer. Referring to the international industrial company Unilever and its headquarters in London. *The Boss* (co-written with Rosemary Stewart; 1958)

29 The early bird who catches the worm works for someone who comes in late and owns the worm farm.

John D. MacDonald (1916–86) US writer. *McGee* (1975)

30 You show me a capitalist, I'll show you a bloodsucker.

Malcolm X (1925–65) US Black activist. Speech at the Audubon ballroom (December 20, 1964), quoted in *Malcolm X Speaks* (George Breitman, ed.; 1965)

31 Not every problem someone has with his girlfriend is necessarily due to the capitalist mode of production.

Herbert Marcuse (1898–1979) German-born US philosopher. *Listener* (1978)

32 Capitalist production begets, with the inexorability of a law of nature, its own negation.

Karl Marx (1818–83) German philosopher. *Das Kapital* (1867), ch. 15

33 It is not this or that tangible steel or brass machine which we want to get rid of, but the great intangible machine of commercial tyranny which oppresses the lives of us all.

William Morris (1834–96) British designer, socialist reformer, and poet. Quoted in *The Arts and Crafts Movement* (Thomas Sanderson; 1905)

34 Capitalism was born out of an ethos, an ethos of work and sacrifice, but today it lacks even the means to think about what it is for.

Geoff Mulgan (b. 1961) British author and political analyst. *Connexity* (1997)

35 Man is the only creature that consumes without producing.

George Orwell (1903–50) British writer. *Animal Farm* (1945), ch. 1

36 Capitalism is an art form, an Apollonian fabrication to rival nature. It is hypocritical for feminists and intellectuals to enjoy the pleasures and conveniences of capitalism while sneering at it.

Camille Paglia (b. 1947) US academic and author. *Sexual Personae* (1990)

37 I have gone to war too . . . I am going to fight capitalism even if it kills me. It is wrong that people like you should be comfortable and well fed while all around you people are starving.

Sylvia Pankhurst (1882–1960) British suffragette. Quoted in *The Fighting Pankhursts* (David Mitchell; 1967)

38 Our democratic capitalist society has converted Eros into an employee of Mammon.

Octavio Paz (1914–98) Mexican author and poet. *Observer* (June 19, 1994), 'Sayings of the Week'

39 Buy up the sunset! Buy it up! Buy it up! Buy . . . buy . . . buy. A copper for a seat, sirs. A copper for the view.

Mervyn Peake (1911–68) British novelist, poet, and artist. *Titus Alone* (1959), ch. 66

40 Capitalism is the exploitation of man by man. Communism is the complete opposite.

Proverb.

41 The capitalist achievement does not typically consist in providing more silk stockings for queens but in bringing them within the reach of factory girls in return for steadily decreasing amounts of effort.

Joseph Alois Schumpeter (1883–1950) Austrian-born US economist. *Capitalism, Socialism, and Democracy* (1942)

42 Capital accounting in its formally most rational shape . . . presupposes the battle of man with man.

Max Weber (1864–1920) German economist and social historian. Quoted in *Economy and Society* (Guenther Roth and Claus Wittich, eds.; 1978), ch. 1

43 As long as capital—both human and money— can move toward opportunity, trade will not balance.

Walter B. Wriston (1919–98) US banker. Speech (January 25, 1993)

The Caribbean

see also **Central America**

1 I long for the nights that fall blackly, suddenly, without warning. I long for a violent shower of rain at night. I long to hear the tinny tattoo of heavy raindrops on a roof, or the drops of rain on the broad leaves of that wonderful plant, the wild tannia.
V. S. Naipaul (b. 1932) Trinidadian-born British novelist. Letter to his father (1952)

2 The region has long been victim of that first great book of magical realism, the Diary of Christopher Columbus—a transformative text in which the very geography of the region was fused with that of the Asian world in the misnomer West Indies.
Caryl Phillips (b. 1958) British writer. 'Reluctant Hero', *Guardian* (October 12, 2001)

3 The West Indian mind historically hungover, exhausted, prefers to take its revenge in nostalgia, to narrow its eyelids in a schizophrenic daydream of an Eden that existed before its exile.
Derek Walcott (b. 1930) St. Lucian poet and playwright. *What the Twilight Says* (1998)

4 Who in the New World does not have a horror of the past, whether his ancestor was torturer or victim? Who in the depth of conscience, is not silently screaming for pardon or revenge?
Derek Walcott (b. 1930) St. Lucian poet and playwright. *What the Twilight Says* (1998)

5 I see these islands and I feel to bawl, 'area of darkness' with V.S. Nightfall.
Derek Walcott (b. 1930) St. Lucian poet and playwright. Referring to V.S. Naipaul. *What the Twilight Says* (1998)

6 I came from a place that likes grandeur; it likes large gestures; it is not inhibited by flourish; it is a rhetorical society; it is a society of physical performance; it is a society of style.
Derek Walcott (b. 1930) St. Lucian poet and playwright. Interview, *Writers at Work* (George Plimpton, ed.; 1988)

Cars

see also **Travel**

1 I think that cars today are almost the exact equivalent of the great Gothic cathedrals . . . the supreme creation of an era, conceived with passion by unknown artists.
Roland Barthes (1915–80) French philosopher and writer. 'La Nouvelle Citroën', *Mythologies* (1957)

2 AUTOMOBILE, n. A four-wheeled vehicle that runs up hills and down pedestrians.
Ambrose Bierce (1842–1914?) US writer and journalist. *The Devil's Dictionary* (1911)

3 Motorists (as they used to be called) were utterly irresponsible in their dealings with each other and with the pedestrian public; for their benefit homicide was legalised.
L. P. Hartley (1895–1972) British novelist. *Facial Justice* (1960), ch. 5

4 Everywhere,
giant finned cars nose forward like fish; a savage servility
slides by on grease.
Robert Lowell (1917–77) US poet. 'For the Union Dead', *For the Union Dead* (1964)

5 The car has become the carapace, the protective and aggressive shell, of urban and suburban man.
Marshall McLuhan (1911–80) Canadian sociologist. *Understanding Media* (1964), ch. 22

6 *Rush hour*: that hour when traffic is almost at a standstill.
J. C. Morton (1893–1979) British journalist and writer. *Morton's Folly* (1933)

7 It is the overtakers who keep the undertakers busy.
William Ewart Pitts (b. 1900) British policeman. *Observer* (December 22, 1963), 'Sayings of the Week'

Celebrity

see also **Fame, Marketing, Popularity**

1 A celebrity is a person who works hard all his life to become known, then wears dark glasses to avoid being recognized.
Fred Allen (1894–1956) US comedian. *Treadmill to Oblivion* (1954)

2 Do not let that trouble Your Excellency; perhaps the greetings are intended for me.
Ludwig van Beethoven (1770–1827) German composer. Said when walking with Goethe, when Goethe complained about greetings from passers-by. Quoted in *Thayer's Life of Beethoven* (Elliot Forbes, ed.; 1967)

3 He had a genius for backing into the limelight.
Lord Berners (1883–1950) British composer and painter. Referring to T. E. Lawrence. Attrib.

4 The gas was on in the Institute,
The flare was up in the gym,
A man was running a mineral line,
A lass was singing a hymn,
When Captain Webb the Dawley man,
Captain Webb from Dawley,
Came swimming along the old canal
That carried the bricks to Lawley.
John Betjeman (1906–84) British poet and broadcaster. 1940. Captain Matthew Webb (1848–83), the first man to swim the English channel (1875), was born in the Midlands town of Dawley. 'A Shropshire Lad', *John Betjeman's Collected Poems* (1958)

5 The celebrity is a person who is known for his well-knownness.
Daniel J. Boorstin (b. 1914) US historian and librarian. 'From Hero to Celebrity: The Human Pseudo-event', *The Image* (1961)

6 Celebrity: I picture myself as a marble bust with legs to run everywhere.
Jean Cocteau (1889–1963) French film director, novelist, and playwright. 'Des Beaux-arts Considérés comme un Assassinat', *Essai de Critique Indirecte* (1932)

7 I'm just a lucky slob from Ohio who happened to be in the right place at the right time.
Clark Gable (1901–60) US film actor. Attrib.

8 I'm afraid of losing my obscurity. Genuineness only thrives in the dark. Like celery.
Aldous Huxley (1894–1963) British novelist and essayist. *Those Barren Leaves* (1925), pt. 1, ch. 1

9 The nice thing about being a celebrity is that when you bore people, they think it's their fault.
Henry Kissinger (b. 1923) German-born US politician and diplomat. *Reader's Digest* (April 1985)

10 When I meet those remarkable people whose company is coveted, I often wish they would show off a little more.
Desmond MacCarthy (1878–1952) British poet and writer. 'Good Talk', *Theatre* (1954)

11 You're not a star until they can spell your name in Karachi.

Roger Moore (b. 1927) British film actor. *Film Yearbook* (1987), quoted in *Chambers Film Quotes* (Tony Crawley, ed.; 1991)

12 If you have to tell them who you are, you aren't anybody.

Gregory Peck (b. 1916) US film actor. Remarking upon the failure of anyone in a crowded restaurant to recognize him. Quoted in *Pieces of Eight* (Sydney J. Harris; 1982)

13 I have no use for bodyguards, but I have very specific use for two highly trained certified public accountants.

Elvis Presley (1935–77) US pop singer. Quoted in 'Don't Play Golf with Richard Branson', *Expensive Habits: the Dark Side of the Music Industry* (Simon Garfield; 1986)

14 They didn't act like people and they didn't act like actors. It's hard to explain. They acted more like they knew they were celebrities and all. I mean they were good, but they were *too* good.

J. D. Salinger (b. 1919) US novelist. Holden Caulfield's response to the Lunts' acting style. Alfred Lunt (1893–1977) and Lynn Fontanne (1887?–1983) were a husband and wife acting team and frequently worked together. *The Catcher in the Rye* (1951), ch. 17

15 Getting stardom and, once you've got it, keeping it, is like fighting a war. You plan your campaign, recruit your troops, equip them properly, and then fight until you've stormed the cities you want. Then you dig in and defend your position.

Nina Simone (b. 1933) US jazz singer, pianist, and songwriter. *I Put a Spell On You: The Autobiography* (1991)

16 This is a movie, not a lifeboat.

Spencer Tracy (1900–67) US film actor. Defending his demand for equal billing with Katharine Hepburn. Attrib.

Censorship

see also **Blasphemy, Books, Free Speech**

1 More to the point, would you allow your gamekeeper to read it?

Anonymous. 1960. Referring to Mervyn Griffiths-Jones' remark, 'Is it a book you would . . . wish your wife or your servants to read?', during the *Lady Chatterley's Lover* obscenity trial. Lady Chatterley's lover is her husband's gamekeeper.

2 Everyone knows that there is no fineness or accuracy of suppression. If you hold down one thing you hold down the adjoining.

Saul Bellow (b. 1915) Canadian-born US writer. *The Adventures of Augie March* (1953), ch. 1

3 I acknowledge Shakespeare to be the world's greatest dramatic poet, but regret that no parent could place the uncorrected book in the hands of his daughter, and therefore I have prepared *The Family Shakespeare*.

Thomas Bowdler (1754–1825) British editor. Referring to his censored edition of the works of William Shakespeare, which gave rise to the term 'bowdlerize'. *The Family Shakespeare* (1818), preface

4 To defend society from sex is no one's business. To defend it from officiousness is the duty of everyone who values freedom—or sex.

Brigid Brophy (1929–95) British novelist and critic. *Observer* (August 9, 1970), 'Sayings of the Week'

5 Manuscripts don't burn.

Mikhail Bulgakov (1891–1940) Russian novelist and playwright. 1929–40. *The Master and Margarita* (Michael Glenny, tr.; 1966), ch. 24

6 Every sentence . . . that appears in the public press is perused and revised and deleted in the interests of advertisers and bondholders. The fountain of national life is poisoned at the source.

John Dos Passos (1896–1970) US novelist. *Manhattan Transfer* (1925), pt. 2

7 Oh, I get it. It's simple. PG means the hero gets the girl, 15 means that the villain gets the girl and 18 means that everybody gets the girl.

Michael Douglas (b. 1944) US film actor. Referring to British censor ratings. *Film Yearbook 1989*, quoted in *Chambers Film Quotes* (Tony Crawley, ed.; 1991)

8 The only censor is the audience, which will decide whether it wants it and how soon it gets fed up with it.

David McAdam Eccles (1904–99) British politician. Attrib.

9 Don't join the book burners. Don't think you are going to conceal faults by concealing evidence that they ever existed.

Dwight D. Eisenhower (1890–1969) US general and president. Speech, Dartmouth College (June 14, 1953)

10 What progress we are making. In the Middle Ages they would have burned me. Now they are content with burning my books.

Sigmund Freud (1856–1939) Austrian psychoanalyst. Referring to the public burning of his books in Berlin. Letter to Ernest Jones (1933)

11 Where there is official censorship it is a sign that speech is serious. Where there is none, it is pretty certain that the official spokesmen have all the loud-speakers.

Paul Goodman (1911–72) US writer, teacher, and psychotherapist. *Growing Up Absurd* (1960)

12 Let's find out what everyone is doing, And then stop everyone from doing it.

A. P. Herbert (1890–1971) British writer and politician. 'Let's Stop Somebody', *Ballads for Broadbrows* (1930)

13 Half of his bed was piled a foot high with books, so he could just roll over and pick one up. Books were specially printed for him. Sometimes the print run was two copies—one for the record, one for Mao.

Jung Chang (b. 1952) Chinese-born British writer and lecturer. Referring to Mao Zedong and banned books in China. Interview, *Straits Times* (Singapore; May 5, 1997)

14 The author of the Satanic Verses book, which is against Islam, the Prophet and the Koran, and all those involved in its publication who were aware of its content, are sentenced to death. I ask all Muslims to execute them wherever they find them.

Ruhollah Khomeini (1900–89) Iranian religious and political leader. Statement announcing a death sentence against Salman Rushdie, following the publication of his novel *The Satanic Verses* (1988). Fatwa (February 14, 1989)

15 We live in oppressive times. We have, as a nation, become our own thought police; but instead of calling the process by which we limit our expression of dissent and wonder 'censorship', we call it 'concern for commercial viability'.

David Mamet (b. 1947) US writer and film director. 'Radio Drama', *Writing in Restaurants* (1986)

16 What then, from the point of view of the broad masses of the people, should be the criteria today for distinguishing fragrant flowers from poisonous weeds?

Mao Zedong (1893–1976) Chinese statesman. 'On the Correct Handling of Contradictions among the People' (1957), quoted in *Selected Readings from Mao Zedong* (1967)

17 Ugly hell, gape not! come not, Lucifer!
I'll burn my books!
Christopher Marlowe (1564–93) English playwright and poet. *Doctor Faustus* (1592?), Act 5, Scene 2, ll. 199–200

18 Censors are necessary, increasingly necessary, if America is to avoid having a vital literature.
Don Marquis (1878–1937) US journalist and writer. *Prefaces: Foreword to a Literary Censor's Autobiography* (1919)

19 PBS are engaging in a very serious game of self-censorship. Because they are publicly funded, they're desperately afraid their life's blood will be taken from them for making homosexuals look like regular human beings . . . I'm making personal pleas to everyone I know who can write a cheque.
Armistead Maupin (b. 1944) US novelist. Referring to the banning of the television adaptation of *Tales of the City* by the US television network Public Broadcasting Service (PBS). *Times* (June 15, 1994)

20 I'm fed up to the teeth with agit-prop, too, I'd like to scribble love ballads for you—they're profitable, charming and halcyon.
But I mastered myself, and crushed under foot the throat of my very own songs.
Vladimir Mayakovsky (1893–1930) Russian poet and playwright. 'At the Top of My Voice' (1930), quoted in *Mayakovsky* (Herbert Marshall, ed., tr.; 1965)

21 No, don't suppress. What shall we get by suppression? That such literature will be distributed around the corner and read with such satisfaction, as I have a couple of hundred times read in manuscript form poems by Yesenin.
Vladimir Mayakovsky (1893–1930) Russian poet and playwright. Referring to the proposed suppression of Mikhail Bulgakov's play based on his novel, *The White Guard* (1925), and also Sergey Yesenin. Speech at discussion on 'Theatre Politics of the Soviet Government' (October 2, 1926), quoted in *Mayakovsky* (H. Marshall, ed., tr.; 1965), introduction

22 The trouble with censors is that they worry if a girl has cleavage. They ought to worry if she hasn't any.
Marilyn Monroe (1926–62) US film actor. Attrib.

23 There is in our hands as citizens an instrument to mould the minds of the young and to create great and good and noble citizens for the future.
Edward Shortt (1862–1935) British politician. Referring to the British Board of Film Censors. Remark (1929)

24 Censorship is more depraving and corrupting than anything pornography can produce.
Tony Smythe (b. 1938) British civil rights activist. *Observer* (September 18, 1972), 'Sayings of the Week'

25 No regime has ever loved great writers, only minor ones.
Alexander Solzhenitsyn (b. 1918) Russian novelist. *The First Circle* (1968), ch. 57

26 God forbid that any book should be banned. The practice is as indefensible as infanticide.
Rebecca West (1892–1983) Irish-born British novelist, critic, and journalist. 'The Tosh Horse', *The Strange Necessity* (1928)

27 Vietnam was the first war ever fought without any censorship. Without censorship, things can get terribly confused in the public mind.
William C. Westmoreland (b. 1914) US military commander. Referring to the Vietnam War (1959–75). *Time* (April 5, 1982)

28 I am beginning to feel a little more like an author now that I have had a book banned. The literary life in this country begins in jail.
E. B. White (1899–1985) US writer and humorist. Referring to the banning by the US military of *One Man's Meat* (1942). Letter to Stanley Hart White (June 1944)

29 No matter if the film is banned, the most important thing is believing in it.
Wong Kar Wai, Hong Kong-born Chinese film director. Quoted in 'Taking Risks', *China in Focus* (Tam Ly; 1998)

30 I cannot continue my work, because no creative activity is possible in an atmosphere of systematic persecution that increases in intensity from year to year.
Yevgeny Zamyatin (1884–1937) Russian writer. 'Letter to Stalin' (June 1931), quoted in *The Dragon and Other Stories* (Mirra Ginsburg, ed., tr.; 1966)

Central America

see also **The Caribbean, South America**

1 I was a man who was lucky enough to have discovered a political theory, a man who was caught up in the whirlpool of Cuba's political crisis long before becoming a fully fledged Communist . . . Discovering Marxism . . . was like finding a map in the forest.
Fidel Castro (b. 1927) Cuban leader. *Chile* (November 18, 1971)

2 Poor Mexico, so far from God and so near to the United States.
Porfirio Díaz (1830–1915) Mexican president. Referring to the beginning of the Mexican War (1846–48). Attrib.

3 All the government gives us is charity at election time. Afterwards, death returns to our homes.
Subcomandante Marcos (b. 1958) Mexican revolutionary leader. Leader of the Zapatistas, a rebel movement in the Chiapas region of Mexico. *Independent* (January 12, 1994)

Certainty

see also **Knowledge, Truth**

1 The mind longs for certainty, and perhaps it longs most for a certainty which clubs it down. What the mind can understand, what it can ploddingly prove and approve, might be what it most despises.
Julian Barnes (b. 1946) British writer. *Staring at the Sun* (1988)

2 POSITIVE, adj. Mistaken at the top of one's voice.
Ambrose Bierce (1842–1914?) US writer and journalist. *The Devil's Dictionary* (1911)

3 Two things are certain: 1) people no longer care what happens to other people; and 2) nothing makes any real difference any longer.
Raymond Carver (1938–88) US poet, short-story writer, and essayist. 'So Much Water, So Close to Home', *Fires: Essays, Stories and Poems* (1983)

4 When nothing is sure, everything is possible.
Margaret Drabble (b. 1939) British novelist and writer. *The Middle Ground* (1980)

5 Ther can no great smoke arise, but there must be some fire.
John Lyly (1554?–1606) English writer. *Euphues: An Anatomy of Wit* (1578)

6 It is easy to be certain. One has only to be sufficiently vague.
C. S. Peirce (1839–1914) US physicist and philosopher. Quoted in *Collected Papers* (Charles Hartshore and Paul Weiss, eds.; 1931–58), vol. 2

7 We possess nothing certainly except the past.
Evelyn Waugh (1903–66) British novelist. *Brideshead Revisited* (1945)

Chance

see also **Destiny, Fate, Misfortune**

1   Art is in love with chance, and chance with art.
Agathon (446?–401 BC) Greek tragic poet. Attrib.

2   We cannot bear to regard ourselves simply as
playthings of blind chance; we cannot admit to
feeling ourselves abandoned.
Ugo Betti (1892–1953) Italian playwright and poet. Struggle Till Dawn
(G. H. McWilliam, tr.; 1949)

3   If chance is defined as an event produced by
random motion without any causal nexus, I
would say there is no such thing as chance.
Boethius (480?–524?) Roman philosopher and statesman. The
Consolation of Philosophy (523?)

4   Many things happen between the cup and the lip.
Robert Burton (1577–1640) English scholar and churchman. The
Anatomy of Melancholy (1621), pt. 2, sect. 2

5   I shall never believe that God plays dice with the
world.
Albert Einstein (1879–1955) German-born US physicist. Einstein's
objection to the quantum theory, in which physical events can
only be known in terms of probabilities. It is sometimes
quoted as 'God does not play dice with the Universe'. Letter
to Max Born (December 4, 1926), quoted in Einstein und
Born Briefwechsel (1969)

6   well archy the world is full of ups and downs but
toujours gai is my motto.
Don Marquis (1878–1937) US journalist and writer. mehitabel the cat
to archy the cockroach. 'the song of mehitabel', archy and
mehitabel (1927)

7   More is owing to what we call chance, that is,
philosophically speaking, to the observation of
events arising from unknown causes, than to any
proper design, or pre-conceived theory of the
business.
Joseph Priestley (1733–1804) British theologian and scientist. Experiments
and Observations of Different Types of Air (1775)

8   When you take the bull by the horns . . . what
happens is a toss up.
William Pett Ridge (1857–1930) British writer. Love at Paddington
Green, ch. 4

9   KING RICHARD III I have set my life upon a cast,
And I will stand the hazard of the die.
William Shakespeare (1564–1616) English poet and playwright. Richard
III (1591), Act 5, Scene 4

10   FALSTAFF They say there is divinity in odd
numbers, either in nativity, chance, or death.
William Shakespeare (1564–1616) English poet and playwright. The
Merry Wives of Windsor (1597), Act 5, Scene 1

11   Times go by turns, and chances change by course,
From foul to fair, from better hap to worse.
Robert Southwell (1561–95) English poet and martyr. 'Times go by
Turn' (1595?), st. 1

Change

see also **Metamorphosis, Revolution**

1   When you're through changing, you're through.
Bruce Barton (1886–1967) US business executive, author, and politician.
Attrib.

2   Reform never comes to a class or a people unless
and until those concerned have worked out their
own salvation.
Joseph Ephraim Casely-Hayford (1865–1930) Ghanaian journalist, lawyer,
and nationalist. Ethiopia Unbound: Studies in Race
Emancipation (1911)

3   Never look for birds of this year in the nests of
the last.
Miguel de Cervantes (1547–1616) Spanish novelist and playwright. Don
Quixote (1605–15), pt. 2, ch. 74

4   Well, the principle seems the same. The water
still keeps falling over.
Winston Churchill (1874–1965) British prime minister and writer. When
asked whether the Niagara Falls looked the same as when he
first saw them. Closing the Ring (1951), ch. 5

5   It is only the wisest and the stupidest that cannot
change.
Confucius (551–479 BC) Chinese philosopher, administrator, and moralist.
Analects (5th century BC)

6   They must often change, who would be constant
in happiness or wisdom.
Confucius (551–479 BC) Chinese philosopher, administrator, and moralist.
Analects (5th century BC)

7   The Times They Are A-Changin'
Bob Dylan (b. 1941) US singer and songwriter. Song title. 'The Times
They Are A-Changin' ' (1964)

8   One must never lose time in vainly regretting the
past nor in complaining about the changes which
cause us discomfort, for change is the very
essence of life.
Anatole France (1844–1924) French novelist, poet, and critic. Attrib.

9   He who fears change
More than disasters,
What can he do to forestall
The threatening disaster?
Max Frisch (1911–91) Swiss playwright and novelist. 1958. The Fire
Raisers (Michael Bullock, tr.; 1962), Scene 3

10   Variety's the source of joy below,
From whence still fresh revolving pleasures flow.
In books and love, the mind one end pursues,
And only change th'expiring flame renews.
John Gay (1685–1732) English poet and playwright. 'Lesser Epistles On
a Miscellany To Bernard Linott', ll. 41–44, quoted in The
Poetical Works of John Gay (G. C. Faber, ed.; 1926)

11   The displacement of a little sand can change
occasionally the course of big rivers.
Manuel González Prada (1844–1918) Peruvian politician and writer. Horas
de Lucha (1908)

12   Very often we support change, and then are
swept away by the change. I think that . . . you
just make your own response to your own
generation. A response adequate to your time.
Nadine Gordimer (b. 1923) South African novelist. Times (June 1,
1990)

13   Change is the one constant in life.
Rosa Guy (b. 1928) Trinidadian-born US writer. 'The Human Spirit',
Caribbean Women Writers (Selwyn R. Cudjoe, ed.; 1990)

14   Continuous change is comfortable change. The
past is then the guide to the future.
Charles Handy (b. 1932) Irish-born British management educator and
writer. Referring to the need for radical or 'discontinuous'
change in business. The Age of Unreason (1989)

15   Ah! stirring times we live in—stirring times.
Thomas Hardy (1840–1928) British novelist and poet. Far From the
Madding Crowd (1874), ch. 15

16   Everything flows and nothing stays.
Heraclitus (fl. 500 BC) Greek philosopher. 5th century? BC. Quoted in
Cratylus (Plato; 4th century? BC)

17   You can't step twice into the same river.
Heraclitus (fl. 500 BC) Greek philosopher. 5th century? BC. Quoted in
Cratylus (Plato; 4th century? BC)

18 Thus times do shift, each thing his turn does hold;
New things succeed, as former things grow old.

Robert Herrick (1591–1674) English poet. 'Ceremonies for Candlemas Eve', *Hesperides* (1648), ll. 21–22

19 A permanent state of transition is man's most noble condition.

Juan Ramón Jiménez (1881–1958) Spanish poet. 'Heroic Reason', *Selected Writings* (1957)

20 We cannot change anything unless we accept it. Condemnation does not liberate, it oppresses.

Carl Gustav Jung (1875–1961) Swiss psychoanalyst. Quoted in *Psychological Reflections: an Anthology of the Writings of C. G. Jung* (Jolande Jacobi, ed.; 1953)

21 God changes not what is in a people, until they change what is in themselves.

The Koran (7th century), Sura 13, v. 11

22 A single breaker may recede; but the tide is eventually coming in.

Thomas Babington Macaulay (1800–59) British politician, historian, and writer. 1830. 'On Southey's *Colloquies of Society*', *Essays Contributed to the Edinburgh Review* (1843)

23 It should be borne in mind that there is nothing more difficult to arrange, more doubtful of success and more dangerous to carry through than initiating changes in a state's constitution.

Niccolò Machiavelli (1469–1527) Italian historian, statesman, and political philosopher. Quoted in *Key Management Ideas* (Stuart Crainer; 1996)

24 The philosophers have only interpreted the world in various ways; the point is to change it.

Karl Marx (1818–83) German philosopher. *Theses on Feuerbach* (1845)

25 Feel by turns the bitter change
Of fierce extremes, extremes by change more fierce.

John Milton (1608–74) English writer. *Paradise Lost* (1667), bk. 2, ll. 598–599

26 In the most primitive societies . . . the principal function of ritual, religion, of culture as it is practised is, in fact, almost to stop change . . . The principal function of the most vital and living traditions today is precisely to provide the instruments of rapid change.

J. Robert Oppenheimer (1904–67) US nuclear physicist. 1959. Quoted in *The Jingle Bell Principle* (Miroslav Holub; 1992)

27 We meant to change a nation, and instead, we changed a world.

Ronald Reagan (b. 1911) US president and actor. Communication to the publisher of the *Presidential Biblical Scorecard* (January 11, 1989)

28 Forward, forward let us range,
Let the great world spin forever down the ringing grooves of change.

Alfred Tennyson (1809–92) British poet. 1837–38. 'Locksley Hall', *Poems* (1842), ll. 181–182

29 Man has a limited biological capacity for change. When this capacity is overwhelmed, it is in 'future shock'.

Alvin Toffler (b. 1928) US writer. *Future Shock* (1970)

30 Customs and convictions change; respectable people are the last to know, or to admit, the change, and the ones most offended by fresh reflections of the facts in the mirror of art.

John Updike (b. 1932) US writer. *New Yorker* (July 30, 1990)

31 Using forced language we speak of a cosmic-historical process of Change. When such a process is at work, even sages have no power over it . . . The sage's role is merely to know its origins and foresee its movements.

Yan Fu (1853–1921) Chinese reformer and translator. 1895. 'On the Speed of World Change' (Charlotte Furth, tr.; 1916)

Chaos

see also **Anarchy, Confusion**

1 I have great belief in the fact that whenever there is chaos, it creates wonderful thinking. I consider chaos a gift.

Septima Poinsette Clark (1898–1987) US educator. *Ready From Within* (1986)

2 The irregular side of nature, the discontinuous and erratic side—these have been puzzles to science, or worse, monstrosities.

James Gleick (b. 1954) US science writer. *Chaos* (1987)

3 Predictability: Does the Flap of a Butterfly's Wings in Brazil Set Off a Tornado in Texas?

Edward Lorenz (b. 1917) US meteorologist and educator. 1979. Paper title. The best known illustration of 'chaos theory', a term first used by mathematician James Yorke in 1972.

4 Where eldest Night
And Chaos, ancestors of Nature, hold
Eternal anarchy, amidst the noise
Of endless wars, and by confusion stand.
For Hot, Cold, Moist, and Dry, four champions fierce
Strive here for mastery.

John Milton (1608–74) English writer. *Paradise Lost* (1667), bk. 2, ll. 894–899

5 ULYSSES Take but degree away, untune that string,
And hark what discord follows! Each thing meets
In mere oppugnancy.

William Shakespeare (1564–1616) English poet and playwright. *Troilus and Cressida* (1602), Act 1, Scene 3

Character

see also **Acting and Actors, Human Nature, Identity, The Self, The Soul**

1 It is not only fine feathers that make fine birds.

Aesop (620?–560 BC) Greek writer. 'The Jay and the Peacock', *Aesop's Fables* (6th century BC)

2 Nature made him, and then broke the mould.

Ludovico Ariosto (1474–1533) Italian poet. Referring to Charlemagne's paladin, Roland. *Orlando Furioso* (1532), can. 10, st. 84

3 I had certain disagreeable qualities and a shameful audacity very much needed.

Nancy Astor (1879–1964) US-born British politician. Attrib.

4 She was nothing more than a mere good-tempered, civil, and obliging young woman; as such we could scarcely dislike her—she was only an object of contempt.

Jane Austen (1775–1817) British novelist. 'Letter the 13th', *Love and Friendship* (1790)

5 She was a woman of mean understanding, little information, and uncertain temper.

Jane Austen (1775–1817) British novelist. *Pride and Prejudice* (1813), ch. 1

6 I have always found that the man whose second thoughts are good is worth watching.

J. M. Barrie (1860–1937) British playwright and novelist. *What Every Woman Knows* (1908), Act 3

7 You are no better than you should be.

Beaumont & Fletcher, English playwrights. *The Coxcomb* (1610), Act 4, Scene 3

8 His letters, say they, are weighty and powerful; but his bodily presence is weak, and his speech contemptible.

Bible. II Corinthians, *King James Bible* (1611), 10:10

9 If you are not yourself, if you surrender your personality, you have nothing left to give the world. You have no pleasure, no use, nothing which will attract and charm me, for by the suppression of your individuality, you lose your distinctive character.

Edward Wilmot Blyden (1832–1912) Liberian educator, statesman, and diplomat. *Sierra Leone Times* (May 27, 1893)

10 Of good natural parts and of a liberal education.

Miguel de Cervantes (1547–1616) Spanish novelist and playwright. *Don Quixote* (1605–15), pt. 1, bk. 3, ch. 8

11 Tell me what company thou keepest, and I'll tell thee what thou art.

Miguel de Cervantes (1547–1616) Spanish novelist and playwright. *Don Quixote* (1605–15), pt. 2, ch. 23

12 Our great poet-teacher, has given us 126 clearly-drawn and thoroughly individual female characters, who has depicted women with full appreciation of their highest qualities, yet with accurate perception of their defects and foibles.

Mary Cowden Clarke (1809–98) British writer and critic. Referring to William Shakespeare. *Shakespeare as the Girl's Friend* (1887), vol. 4

13 Men are like plants; the goodness and flavour of the fruit proceeds from the peculiar soil and exposition in which they grow.

Jean de Crèvecoeur (1735–1813) French-born US writer and farmer. *Letters from an American Farmer* (1782)

14 Character is the interpretation of habits.

John Dewey (1859–1952) US philosopher and educator. *Human Nature and Conduct* (1922)

15 In came Mrs. Fezziwig, one vast substantial smile.

Charles Dickens (1812–70) British novelist. *A Christmas Carol* (1843)

16 He'd be sharper than a serpent's tooth, if he wasn't as dull as ditch water.

Charles Dickens (1812–70) British novelist. A reference to *King Lear* by William Shakespeare. *Our Mutual Friend* (1865), bk. 3, ch. 10

17 From a timid, shy girl I had become a woman of resolute character, who could not longer be frightened by the struggle with troubles.

Anna Dostoyevsky (1846–1918) Russian diarist and writer. *Dostoyevsky Portrayed by His Wife* (1887)

18 He of a temper was so absolute
As that it seem'd when Nature him began,
She meant to shew all, that might be in man.

Michael Drayton (1563–1631) English poet. *The Barons' Wars* (1603), can. 2, st. 40

19 Our deeds still travel with us from afar,
And what we have been makes us what we are.

George Eliot (1819–80) British novelist. *Middlemarch* (1871–72), ch. 70, heading

20 A foolish consistency is the hobgoblin of little minds, adored by little statesmen and philosophers and divines. With consistency a great soul has simply nothing to do.

Ralph Waldo Emerson (1803–82) US poet and essayist. 'Self-Reliance', *Essays* (1841)

21 The three grades of character are superior, medium and inferior: the superior is just good, the medium is capable of development either in an upward or a downward direction, and the inferior is just evil.

Han Yu (768–824) Chinese writer and poet. 'The Truth About One's Underlying Character' (8th–9th century), quoted in *Essays by Han Yu* (A. C. Barnes, tr.; 1979)

22 I often feel, and ever more deeply I realize, that fate and character are the same conception.

Friedrich Leopold von Hardenberg (1772–1801) German poet. Often quoted as 'Character is Destiny'. *Heinrich von Ofterdingen* (1802), bk. 2

23 A nice unparticular man.

Thomas Hardy (1840–1928) British novelist and poet. *Far From the Madding Crowd* (1874), ch. 8

24 Strong enough to answer back to desires, to despise distinctions, and a whole man in himself, polished and well-rounded.

Horace (65–8 BC) Roman poet. *Satires* (30 BC), bk. 2, no. 7, l. 85

25 He was only the Mild and Melancholy one foolishly disguised as a complete Man.

Aldous Huxley (1894–1963) British novelist and essayist. *Antic Hay* (1923), ch. 9

26 What is character but the determination of incident? What is incident but the illustration of character?

Henry James (1843–1916) US-born British writer and critic. 'The Art of Fiction', *Partial Portraits* (1888)

27 The second you step out of the confines of the personality the public has set up for you, they get incensed. Public reaction tends to keep actors as personalities instead of allowing them to act. It's a very corrupting influence.

Paul Newman (b. 1925) US film actor. *Photoplay* (1977), quoted in *Chambers Film Quotes* (Tony Crawley, ed.; 1991)

28 Whoever has the luck to be born a character can laugh even at death. Because a character will never die! A man will die, a writer, the instrument of creation: but what he has created will never die!

Luigi Pirandello (1867–1936) Italian dramatist, novelist, and short-story writer. *Six Characters in Search of an Author* (1921), Act 1

29 You can tell a lot about a fellow's character by the way he eats jelly beans.

Ronald Reagan (b. 1911) US president and actor. *New York Times* (January 15, 1981)

30 Where the character is not great, there is no great man . . . Never mind success. It is a question of being great, not seeming it.

Romain Rolland (1866–1944) French writer. *The Life of Beethoven* (1903), Preface

31 If you ask me to play myself, I will not know what to do. I do not know who or what I am.

Peter Sellers (1925–80) British comic actor. Attrib.

32 FALSTAFF Care I for the limb, the thews, the stature, bulk, and big assemblance of a man! Give me the spirit.

William Shakespeare (1564–1616) English poet and playwright. *Henry IV, Part 2* (1597), Act 3, Scene 2

33 The only thing that endures is character. Fame and wealth—all that is illusion.

O. J. Simpson (b. 1947) US American football player, broadcaster, and actor. Said on his acquittal of murder charges. *Guardian* (December 30, 1995)

34 Education has for its object the formation of character.

Herbert Spencer (1820–1903) British philosopher. *Social Statics* (1850), pt. 2, ch. 17, sect. 4

35 I've met a lot of hardboiled eggs in my time, but you're twenty minutes.

Billy Wilder (1906–2002) Austrian-born US film director and screenwriter. *Ace in the Hole* (co-written with Lesser Samuels and Walter Newman; 1951)

36 In or about December, 1910, human *character* changed.

Virginia Woolf (1882–1941) British novelist and critic. 'Mr Bennett and Mrs Brown', *The Common Reader: First Series* (1925)

Charm

see also **Appearance, Deception, Self-Confidence**

1 Fine words and an insinuating appearance are seldom associated with true virtue.

Confucius (551–479 BC) Chinese philosopher, administrator, and moralist. *Analects* (5th century BC)

2 All charming people have something to conceal, usually their total dependence on the appreciation of others.

Cyril Connolly (1903–74) British writer and journalist. *Enemies of Promise* (1938), ch. 16

3 Do not all charms fly
At the mere touch of cold philosophy?

John Keats (1795–1821) English poet. 'Lamia' (1820), pt. 2, ll. 229–230

4 Oozing charm from every pore,
He oiled his way around the floor.

Alan Jay Lerner (1918–86) US lyricist and librettist. Song lyric. *My Fair Lady* (1956), Act 2, Scene 1

5 Charm is a product of the unexpected.

José Martí (1853–95) Cuban writer and patriot. Attrib.

6 It is absurd to divide people into good and bad. People are either charming or tedious.

Oscar Wilde (1854–1900) Irish poet, playwright, and wit. *Lady Windermere's Fan* (1892), Act 1

Chicago

see **American Cities**

Childhood

see also **Children, Growing Up, Youth**

1 Our common origins
brought us together
and we separated
a forest written by the earth
and told by the seasons
Child that I once was, advance,
What now brings us together?
And what have we to say to each other?

Adonis (b. 1929) Syrian poet. 'Beginning Speech', *Modern Arabic Poetry* (Salma Khadra Jayyusi, ed.; 1987), ll. 9–16

2 Political history is far too criminal and pathological to be a fit subject of study for the young. Children should acquire their heroes and villains from fiction.

W. H. Auden (1907–73) British poet. *A Certain World: A Commonplace Book* (1970)

3 Were we closer to the ground as children, or is the grass emptier now?

Alan Bennett (b. 1934) British playwright, actor, and director. *Forty Years On* (1969)

4 CHILDHOOD, n. The period of human life intermediate between the idiocy of infancy and the folly of youth—two removes from the sin of manhood and three from the remorse of age.

Ambrose Bierce (1842–1914?) US writer and journalist. *The Devil's Dictionary* (1911)

5 Childhood is a treasure whose geography you never clearly reveal. In it you mix up eras and ages, laughter and the illusion of having laughed, places and sensations that weren't even born there.

Patrick Chamoiseau (b. 1953) Martiniquan writer. *Childhood* (1993)

6 All the joy, all the uncertainties, and all the solitude of childhood suddenly came back to me with that, the unmistakable flavour of the hams my grandmother made.

Gabriel García Márquez (b. 1928) Colombian novelist. 'Watching the Rain in Galicia', *Granta Book of Travel* (Bill Buford, ed.; 1991)

7 Once upon a time and a very good time it was there was a moocow coming down along the road and this moocow that was coming down along the road met a nicens little boy named baby tuckoo.

James Joyce (1882–1941) Irish writer. Opening sentence. *A Portrait of the Artist as a Young Man* (1916)

8 At every step the child should be allowed to meet the real experiences of life; the thorns should never be plucked from his roses.

Ellen Key (1849–1926) Swedish reformer and educationalist. *The Century of the Child* (1900), ch. 3

9 The childhood shows the man,
As morning shows the day. Be famous then
By wisdom; as thy empire must extend,
So let extend thy mind o'er all the world.

John Milton (1608–74) English writer. Satan to Christ. *Paradise Regained* (1671), bk. 4, ll. 220–223

10 I have all that I lost
and I go carrying my childhood
like a favorite flower
that perfumes my hand.

Gabriela Mistral (1889–1957) Spanish poet, diplomat, and educator. 'We Were All to be Queens', *Tala* (1938)

11 I'd the upbringing a nun would envy and that's the truth. Until I was fifteen I was more familiar with Africa than with my own body.

Joe Orton (1933–67) British playwright. *Entertaining Mr Sloane* (1964)

12 Is childhood a necessary evil, or have characteristics of the childish mentality a functional significance that defines a genuine activity?

Jean Piaget (1896–1980) Swiss psychologist. 'Science of Education and the Psychology of the Child' (1935), quoted in *The Essential Piaget* (H. E. Gruber and J. Jacques Vonèche, eds.; 1977)

13 The child's first year of life is unfortunately still an abyss of mysteries for the psychologist.

Jean Piaget (1896–1980) Swiss psychologist. 'The First Year of Life of the Child' (1927), quoted in *The Essential Piaget* (H. E. Gruber and J. Jacques Vonèche, eds.; 1977)

14 I remember, I remember
How my childhood fleeted by,—
The mirth of its December
And the warmth of its July.

Winthrop Praed (1802–39) British poet. 'I remember, I remember' (1840?)

15 We live in our own world,
A world that is too small
For you to stoop and enter
Even on hands and knees,
The adult subterfuge.

R. S. Thomas (1913–2000) Welsh poet and clergyman. 'Children's Song', *Song at the Year's Turning: Poems 1942–54* (1955)

16 As for being a General, well, at the age of four with paper hats and wooden swords we're all Generals. Only some of us never grow out of it.

Peter Ustinov (b. 1921) British actor, director, and writer. *Romanoff and Juliet* (1956), Act 1

Children

see also **Childhood, Family, Growing Up**

1 It was no wonder that people were so horrible when they started life as children.

Kingsley Amis (1922–95) British novelist. *One Fat Englishman* (1963), ch. 14

2 Children's talent to endure stems from their ignorance of alternatives.

Maya Angelou (b. 1928) US writer. *I Know Why The Caged Bird Sings* (1970)

3 Children have never been very good at listening to their elders, but they have never failed to imitate them.

James Baldwin (1924–87) US writer and civil rights activist. *Esquire* (1960)

4 The distinction between children and adults . . . is at bottom a specious one, I feel. There are only individual egos, crazy for love.

Donald Barthelme (1931–89) US novelist and short-story writer. 'Me and Mrs. Mandible', *Come Back, Dr. Caligari* (1964)

5 They never lynch children, babies, no matter what they do they are whitewashed in advance.

Samuel Beckett (1906–89) Irish playwright, novelist, and poet. 1946. 'The Expelled', *The Expelled and Other Novellas* (1980)

6 You can do anything with children if you only play with them.

Prince Otto von Bismarck (1815–98) German chancellor. Attrib.

7 'If the child is father of the man', she asked, 'then who is the mother of the woman?'

Angela Carter (1940–92) British novelist, essayist, and short-story writer. *Wise Children* (1991)

8 The thing that best defines a child is the total inability to receive information from anything not plugged in.

Bill Cosby (b. 1937) US actor, author, and comedian. *Childhood* (1991)

9 The value of marriage is not that adults produce children but that children produce adults.

Peter De Vries (1910–93) US novelist. *The Tunnel of Love* (1954), ch. 8

10 It is only rarely that one can see in a little boy the promise of a man, but one can almost always see in a little girl the threat of a woman.

Alexandre Dumas (1802–70) French novelist and playwright. 1865. Attrib.

11 We are willing to spend the least amount of money to keep a kid at home, more to put him in a foster home, and the most to institutionalize him.

Marian Wright Edelman (b. 1939) US lawyer. *Psychology Today* (June 1975)

12 Problem children tend to grow up into problem adults and problem adults tend to produce more problem children.

David Farrington (b. 1944) British criminal psychologist. *Times* (May 19, 1994)

13 She discovered with great delight that one doesn't love one's children just because they are one's children but because of the friendship formed when raising them.

Gabriel García Márquez (b. 1928) Colombian novelist. Referring to Fermina Daza. *Love in the Time of Cholera* (1985)

14 You may give them your love but not your thoughts.
For they have their own thoughts.
You may house their bodies but not their souls,
For their souls dwell in the house of tomorrow, which
you cannot visit, not even in your dreams.

Kahlil Gibran (1883–1931) Lebanese-born US mystic, painter, and poet. 'On Children', *The Prophet* (1923)

15 Sculpture museums are places where parents hear their children say surprising things: Daddy my fig leaf hasn't grown yet!

Ramón Gómez de la Serna (1888–1963) Spanish novelist. Quoted in *The Spanish Avant Garde* (Derek Harris, ed.; 1995)

16 Anything to me is sweeter
Than to see Shock-headed Peter.

Heinrich Hoffman (1809–94) German physician and poet. 'Shock-headed Peter', *Struwwelpeter* (1845)

17 The door flew open, in he ran,
The great, long, red-legged scissor-man
'Ah!' said Mamma, 'I knew he'd come
To naughty little Suck-a-Thumb'.

Heinrich Hoffman (1809–94) German physician and poet. 'The Little Suck-a-Thumb', *Struwwelpeter* (1845)

18 My theory is, children should be born without parents—if born they must be.

Langston Hughes (1902–67) US novelist, playwright, and short-story writer. Quoted in *The Life of Langston Hughes: Vol. 1, 1902–41* (Arnold Rampersad; 1966)

19 The proper time to influence the character of a child is about a hundred years before he is born.

William Ralph Inge (1860–1954) British churchman. *Observer* (June 21, 1929)

20 Madame, I would have given you another!

Alfred Jarry (1873–1907) French playwright and poet. Said on being reprimanded by a woman for firing his pistol in the vicinity of her child, who might have been killed. Quoted in *Recollections of a Picture Dealer* (Ambroise Vollard; 1936)

21 Children do not give up their innate imagination, curiosity, dreaminess easily. You have to love them to get them to do that.

R. D. Laing (1927–89) Scottish psychiatrist. *The Politics of Experience* (1967), ch. 3

22 A child's a plaything for an hour.

Mary Ann Lamb (1764–1847) British writer. Sometimes attributed to
Charles Lamb, with whom she sometimes collaborated.
'Parental Recollections', *Poetry for Children* (1809)

23 A child of five would understand this.
Send somebody to fetch a child of five.

Groucho Marx (1895–1977) US comedian and film actor. *Duck Soup*
(Bert Kalmar, Harry Ruby, Arthur Sheekman, and Nat Perrin;
1933)

24 James James
Morrison Morrison
Weatherby George Dupree
Took great
Care of his Mother,
Though he was only three.

A. A. Milne (1882–1956) British writer. 'Disobedience', *When We
Were Very Young* (1924)

25 Children aren't happy with nothing to ignore,
And that's what parents were created for.

Ogden Nash (1902–71) US humorist. 'The Parent', *Happy Days*
(1933)

26 One stops being a child when one realizes that
telling one's trouble does not make it better.

Cesare Pavese (1908–50) Italian novelist and poet. *This Business of
Living: A Diary 1935–50* (1952)

27 At all ages children are driven to figure out what
it takes to succeed among their peers and to give
these strategies precedence over anything their
parents foist on them.

Steven Pinker (b. 1954) US cognitive scientist and author. 'How the
Mind Works', *Guardian* (January 17, 1998)

28 The biggest influence that parents have on their
children is at the moment of conception.

Steven Pinker (b. 1954) US cognitive scientist and author. *How the
Mind Works* (1997)

29 A child is a guest in the house, to be loved and
respected—never possessed, since he belongs to
God.

J. D. Salinger (b. 1919) US novelist. *Raise High the Roofbeams,
Carpenters* (1963)

30 There's a time when you have to explain to your
children why they're born, and it's a marvelous
thing if you know the reason by then.

Hazel Scott (1920–81) US jazz musician, actor, and feminist. *Ms* (1974)

31 LEAR How sharper than a serpent's tooth it is
To have a thankless child!

William Shakespeare (1564–1616) English poet and playwright. *King
Lear* (1605–06), Act 1, Scene 4

32 Children . . . have no use for psychology. They
detest sociology. They still believe in God, the
family, angels, devils, witches, goblins, logic,
clarity, punctuation, and other such obsolete
stuff . . . When a book is boring, they yawn
openly. They don't expect their writer to redeem
humanity, but leave to adults such childish
illusions.

Isaac Bashevis Singer (1904–91) Polish-born US writer. Nobel Prize
address, Stockholm (December 10, 1978)

33 There are only two things a child will share
willingly—communicable diseases and his
mother's age.

Benjamin Spock (1903–98) US pediatrician. Attrib.

34 Never have children, only grandchildren.

Gore Vidal (b. 1925) US novelist and essayist. *Two Sisters* (1970)

35 In psychology it must be said that the infant falls
to pieces unless held together, and physical care
is psychological care at these stages.

Donald W. Winnicott (1896–1971) British psychoanalyst and child
psychiatrist. Attrib.

36 Three years she grew in sun and shower,
Then Nature said, 'A lovelier flower
On earth was never sown;
This child I to myself will take;
She shall be mine, and I will make
A Lady of my own'.

William Wordsworth (1770–1850) English poet. 1799. One of the
'Lucy poems'. The identity of Lucy, the subject of the
poems, is a matter of speculation. 'Three Years She Grew
in Sun and Shower', *Lyrical Ballads* (2nd ed.; 1800), st. 1,
ll. 1–6

37 There are no illegitimate children—only
illegitimate parents.

Léon R. Yankwich, US lawyer and judge. Quoting columnist O. O.
McIntyre. Decision of the State District Court, Southern
District of California (June 1978)

China

see Asian Countries

Choice

see also Decision, Freedom

1 The rose that all are praising
Is not the rose for me.

Thomas Haynes Bayly (1797–1839) British writer. 'The Rose That All
Are Praising', *Songs, Ballads, and Other Poems* (1844)

2 Beggars can't be choosers.

Beaumont & Fletcher, English playwrights. *The Scornful Lady* (1616),
Act 5, Scene 3

3 It's man who decides, not heaven.

Chen Yi (1901–72) Chinese military leader and statesman. *To My
Children* (1961), quoted in *Literature of the People's Republic
of China* (Kai-yu Hsu, ed.; 1980)

4 Any colour, so long as it's black.

Henry Ford (1863–1947) US car manufacturer. Referring to the colour
options offered for the Model-T Ford car. Quoted in *Ford*
(Allan Nevins; 1957), vol. 2, ch. 15

5 Two roads diverged in a wood, and I—
I took the one less traveled by,
And that has made all the difference.

Robert Frost (1874–1963) US poet. 'The Road Not Taken',
Mountain Interval (1916), st. 4

6 The intellect of man is forced to choose
Perfection of the life, or of the work.

W. B. Yeats (1865–1939) Irish poet and playwright. 1932. 'The
Choice', *The Winding Stair and Other Poems* (1933),
ll. 1–2

7 I have heard that in Chu there is a sacred
tortoise which has been dead some three
thousand years . . . Now would this tortoise
rather be dead and have its remains venerated, or
be alive and wagging its tail in the mud?

Zhuangzi (369?–286 BC) Chinese philosopher and teacher. Said in
response to an invitation to take up public office. 'Autumn
Floods', quoted in *Chuang Tzu* (Herbert A. Giles, tr.; 1980),
ch. 17

Christianity

see also Faith, God, Religion

1 'Christianity, of course, but why journalism?'

Arthur Balfour (1848–1930) British prime minister. 1920. In reply to Frank Harris's remark, ' . . . all the faults of the age come from Christianity and journalism'. Quoted in *The Autobiography of Margot Asquith* (Margot Asquith; 1962), ch. 10

2 And Jesus said unto them, I am the bread of life: he that cometh to me shall never hunger; and he that believeth on me shall never thirst.

Bible. John, *King James Bible* (1611), 6:35

3 Then spake Jesus again unto them, saying, I am the light of the world: he that followeth me shall not walk in darkness, but shall have the light of life.

Bible. John, *King James Bible* (1611), 8:12

4 CHRISTIAN, n. One who believes that the New Testament is a divinely inspired book admirably suited to the spiritual needs of his neighbor. One who follows the teachings of Christ in so far as they are not inconsistent with a life of sin.

Ambrose Bierce (1842–1914?) US writer and journalist. *The Devil's Dictionary* (1911)

5 If 'Christianity' is to mean the taking the Gospels as our rule of life, then we none of us are Christians and, no matter what we say, we all know we ought not to be.

F. H. Bradley (1846–1924) British philosopher. Unpublished essay on Christian morality (undated), quoted in *A Dictionary of Philosophical Quotations* (A. J. Ayer and Jane O'Grady, eds.; 1992)

6 The Christian ideal has not been tried and found wanting; it has been found difficult and left untried.

G. K. Chesterton (1874–1936) British writer and poet. 'The Unfinished Temple', *What's Wrong with the World* (1910), pt. 1

7 He who begins by loving Christianity better than Truth will proceed by loving his own sect or church better than Christianity, and end by loving himself better than all.

Samuel Taylor Coleridge (1772–1834) British poet. 'Moral and Religious Aphorisms', *Aids to Reflection* (1825), no. 25

8 Believe me now, my Christian friends, Believe your friend call'd Hammon: 'You cannot to your God attend, And serve the God of Mammon'.

Jupiter Hammon (1711–1800?) US writer. *A Dialogue Intitled the Kind Master and the Dutiful Servant* (1783)

9 The *Christian Religion* not only was at first attended with miracles, but even at this day cannot be believed by any reasonable person without one.

David Hume (1711–76) Scottish philosopher and historian. *A Treatise of Human Nature* (1739–40)

10 The central symbol of Christianity must have, above all else, a psychological meaning, for without this it . . . would have been relegated long ago to the dusty cabinet of spiritual monstrosities.

Carl Gustav Jung (1875–1961) Swiss psychoanalyst. 1958. 'A Psychological Approach to the Dogma of the Trinity', *Collected Works* (1969), vol. 2

11 The gospel is meant to comfort the afflicted and afflict the comfortable.

Garrison Keillor (b. 1942) US writer and broadcaster. 'Winter', *Lake Wobegon Days* (1985)

12 There has been said much that is strange, much that is deplorable, much that is revolting about Christianity; but the most stupid thing ever said about it is that it is to a certain degree true.

Søren Kierkegaard (1813–55) Danish philosopher. *Concluding Unscientific Postscript* (1846)

13 Either this is not the gospel or we are not Christians.

Thomas Linacre (1460?–1524) English physician and humanist. Referring to reading the Christian gospels for the first time, late in his life. Attrib.

14 No kingdom has ever had as many civil wars as the kingdom of Christ.

Montesquieu (1689–1755) French writer and jurist. *Lettres Persanes* (1721), no. 29

15 I call Christianity the one great curse, the one enormous and innermost perversion, the one great instinct of revenge, for which no means are too venomous, too underhand, too underground and too petty—I call it the one immortal blemish of mankind.

Friedrich Wilhelm Nietzsche (1844–1900) German philosopher and poet. *The Antichrist* (1888), Aphorism 62

16 The real context of a living faith today is the history of oppression and of the struggle for liberation from this oppression.

Pablo Richard (b. 1939) Chilean theologian. Pablo Richard was one of the founders of the 'Christians for Socialism' movement, who fought for the principled struggle of Catholic ethics against modern capitalism. *Christians for Socialism* (co-written with Gonzalo Arroyo and Sergio Mendez Arceo; 1975)

17 I say quite deliberately that the Christian religion, as organized in its Churches, has been and still is the principal enemy of moral progress in the world.

Bertrand Russell (1872–1970) British philosopher and mathematician. *Why I Am Not a Christian* (1927)

18 Whether you think Jesus was God or not, you must admit that he was a first-rate political economist.

George Bernard Shaw (1856–1950) Irish playwright. 'Jesus as Economist', *Androcles and the Lion* (1912), Preface

19 Christianity is the most materialistic of all great religions.

William Temple (1881–1944) British clergyman. Introduction, *Readings in St John's Gospel* (1939), vol. 1

20 Platonism provided Christianity with its unique Gospel of Redemption, with a universal theoretical foundation of mysticism: in the great process by which the world comes forth from God and returns to God, through the Logos or knowledge of God.

Ernst Troeltsch (1865–1923) German theologian and scholar. *The Social Teaching of the Christian Church* (O. Wyon, tr.; 1912)

21 You remind me that the Apostle Paul told women to be silent in church. I would remind you of the word of this same apostle that in Christ there is no longer male nor female.

Katharina Zell (1497–1562) German church worker and hymnwriter. *Entschuldigung Katherina Schultzinn* (1524)

Christmas

see also **Christianity, Festivals, Religion**

1 I have often thought, says Sir Roger, it happens very well that Christmas should fall out in the Middle of Winter.

Joseph Addison (1672–1719) English essayist, poet, and statesman. Sir Roger de Coverley was a fictional archetype of the old-fashioned and eccentric English country squire. *Spectator* (January 8, 1712), no. 269

2 I'm dreaming of a white Christmas.

Irving Berlin (1888–1989) Russian-born US composer and lyricist. 'White Christmas', *Holiday Inn* (1942)

3 And she brought forth her firstborn son, and wrapped him in swaddling clothes, and laid him in a manger; because there was no room for them in the inn.

Bible. Luke, *King James Bible* (1611), 2:7

4 O little town of Bethlehem,
How still we see thee lie;
Above thy deep and dreamless sleep
The silent stars go by.

Phillips Brooks (1835–93) US Episcopal bishop and evangelist. Christmas carol. 'O Little Town of Bethlehem' (1868), verse 1

5 The twelfth day of Christmas,
My true love sent to me
Twelve lords a-leaping,
Eleven ladies dancing,
Ten pipers piping,
Nine drummers drumming,
Eight maids a-milking,
Seven swans a-swimming,
Six geese a-laying,
Five gold rings,
Four colly birds,
Three French hens,
Two turtle doves,
And a partridge in a pear tree.

Children's Verse. Nursery rhyme. *Mirth without Mischief* (1780)

6 As I sat on a sunny bank,
On Christmas Day in the morning,
I spied three ships come sailing by.

Folk Verse. 'As I Sat on a Sunny Bank' (Traditional)

7 The holly and the ivy,
When they are both full grown,
Of all the trees that are in the wood,
The holly bears the crown.
O, the rising of the sun
And the running of the deer,
The playing of the merry organ,
Sweet singing in the choir.

Folk Verse. 'The Holly and the Ivy'

8 Good King Wenceslas looked out,
On the Feast of Stephen;
When the snow lay round about,
Deep and crisp and even.

John Mason Neale (1818–66) English clergyman and hymnwriter. 'Good King Wenceslas' (1912?)

9 O come all ye faithful,
Joyful and triumphant,
O come ye, O come ye to Bethlehem.

Frederick Oakeley (1802–80) British churchman. Translated from the Latin hymn, 'Adeste Fideles'. 'O Come All Ye Faithful' (1841)

10 It came upon the midnight clear,
That glorious song of old,
From Angels bending near the earth
To touch their harps of gold;
'Peace on the earth; good will to man
From Heaven's all gracious King'.
The world in solemn stillness lay
To hear the angels sing.

E. H. Sears (1810–76) US clergyman and hymnwriter. Song lyric. 'The Angel's Song' (1850), st. 1

11 While shepherds watch'd their flocks by night,
All seated on the ground,
The Angel of the Lord came down,
And Glory shone around.

Nahum Tate (1652–1715) Irish-born English poet and playwright. *Supplement to the New Version of the Psalms* (1700)

12 At Christmas play and make good cheer,
For Christmas comes but once a year.

Thomas Tusser (1524–80) English farmer and writer. 'The Farmer's Daily Diet', *Hundredth Good Pointes of Husbandrie* (1557)

Cities

see also **American Cities, Architecture, Asian Cities, European Cities**

1 The first Care in building of Cities, is to make them airy and well perflated; infectious Distempers must necessarily be propagated amongst Mankind living close together.

John Arbuthnot (1667–1735) Scottish writer and physician. 'An Essay Concerning the Effects of Air on Human Bodies' (1732)

2 The Babelization of great capitals and their cultural relativism are to me the unmistakeable sign of modernity.

Juan Goytisolo (b. 1931) Spanish novelist and essayist. 1985. 'Mudejarism Today', *Saracen Chronicles* (1992)

3 The only credential the city asked was the boldness to dream. For those who did, it unlocked its gates and its treasures, not caring who they were or where they came from.

Moss Hart (1904–61) US playwright and stage director. *Act One* (1959)

4 If cities were built by the sound of music, then some edifices would appear to be constructed by grave, solemn tones; others to have danced forth to light, fantastic airs.

Nathaniel Hawthorne (1804–64) US novelist and short-story writer. *Notebooks* (1839)

5 There is hardly one in three of us who live in the cities who is not sick with unused self.

Ben Hecht (1894–1964) US writer. *Child of the Century* (1954)

6 If God-given and man-made are an unnecessary, even false, opposition, then the city made by human hands is also natural in its own right . . . Cities belong to human nature; nature does not begin outside the city walls.

James Hillman (b. 1926) US author. 'Natural Beauty Without Nature', *Spring* (1985)

7 The urban man is an uprooted tree, he can put out leaves, flowers and grow fruit but what a nostalgia his leaf, flower, and fruit will always have for mother earth.

Juan Ramón Jiménez (1881–1958) Spanish poet. 'Aristocracy and Democracy', *Selected Writings* (1957)

8 The materials of city planning are: sky, space, trees, steel, and cement; in that order and that hierarchy.

Le Corbusier (1887–1965) Swiss-born French architect. Attrib.

9 Of two fs,
as I see it,
is this city composed: one fraud, the other
fornication.
Gregório Mattos e Guerra (1636?–96) Brazilian poet. Referring to
Salvador, Brazil. 'He Defines His City', *Crônica do Viver
Bahiano* (1882)

10 A city must be a place where groups of women
and men are seeking and developing the highest
things they know.
Margaret Mead (1901–78) US anthropologist. *Redbook* (August 1978)

11 A city is a place where there is no need to wait
for next week to get the answer to a question, to
taste the food of any country, to find new voices
to listen to and familiar ones to listen to again.
Margaret Mead (1901–78) US anthropologist. *World Enough* (1975)

12 Clearly, then, the city is not a concrete jungle, it
is a human zoo.
Desmond Morris (b. 1928) British ethnologist and writer. *The Human
Zoo* (1969), Introduction

13 How soon country people forget. When they fall
in love with a city it is forever, and it is like
forever . . . There, in a city, they are not so much
new as themselves: their stronger, riskier selves.
Toni Morrison (b. 1931) US novelist. *Jazz* (1991)

14 SICINIUS What is the city but the people?
William Shakespeare (1564–1616) English poet and playwright.
Coriolanus (1608), Act 3, Scene 1

15 Divine nature gave the fields, human art built the
cities.
Marcus Terentius Varro (116–27 BC) Roman scholar. *De Re Rustica*,
bk. 3, sect. 1

16 'I wonder what they teach them in the city'.
'That's easy', announced Chonkin. 'To live off
the fat of the countryside'.
Vladimir Voinovich (b. 1932) Russian novelist. *The Life and
Extraordinary Adventures of Private Ivan Chonkin* (Richard
Lourie, tr.; 1969), pt. 1, ch. 6

17 A great city is that which has the greatest men
and women.
Walt Whitman (1819–92) US poet. 1856. 'Song of the Broad Axe',
Leaves of Grass (1881), pt. 5

Civilization

see also **Culture, Modernity, Society**

1 Civilization is a method of living, an attitude of
equal respect for all men.
Jane Addams (1860–1935) US social reformer and feminist. Speech,
Honolulu (1933)

2 The crimes of extreme civilization are certainly
worse than those of extreme barbarism.
Jules-Amédée Barbey d'Aurevilly (1808–89) French novelist and critic. 'La
vengeance d'une femme', *Les Diaboliques* (1874)

3 A civilization that proves incapable of solving the
problems it creates is a decadent civilization.
Aimé Césaire (b. 1913) Martiniquan poet, teacher, and political leader.
Discourse on Colonialism (1955)

4 They talk to me about civilization, I talk about
proletarianization and mystification.
Aimé Césaire (b. 1913) Martiniquan poet, teacher, and political leader.
Discourse on Colonialism (1955)

5 Our boasted civilization is but a thin veneer,
which cracks and scales off at the first impact of
primal passions.
Charles W. Chesnutt (1858–1932) US writer and educator. *The Marrow
of Tradition* (1901)

6 All great civilisations, in their early stages, are
based on success in war.
Kenneth Clark (1903–83) British art historian. *Civilisation* (1969)

7 Civilization: if it is not in man's heart—well,
then, it is nowhere.
Georges Duhamel (1884–1966) French writer and physician. *Civilization*
(1918)

8 History assures us that civilizations decay quite
leisurely.
Will Durant (1885–1981) US historian. *The Lessons of History* (co-
written with Ariel Durant; 1968)

9 In essence the Renaissance was simply the green
end of one of civilization's hardest winters.
John Fowles (b. 1926) British novelist. *The French Lieutenant's
Woman* (1969), ch. 10

10 I think it would be a good idea.
Mahatma Gandhi (1869–1948) Indian national leader. On being asked
for his view on Western civilization. Attrib.

11 You gotta say this for the white race—its self
confidence knows no bounds. Who else could go
to a small island in the Pacific where there's no
poverty, no crime, no unemployment, no war,
and no worry—and call it a 'primitive society'?
Dick Gregory (b. 1932) US comedian and civil rights activist. *From the
Back of the Bus* (1962)

12 Keys to the Void of civilization are realized not
by escapism from dire inheritances, not by
political glosses upon endemic tragedy, but by
immersion in the terrifying legacies of the past
and the wholly unexpected insights into shared
fates and freedoms such insights may offer.
Wilson Harris (b. 1921) Guyanese-born writer. *Jonestown* (1996)

13 So does civilization question itself, in dread at its
foundations, through composite epic survivors of
feud, or conflict, or genocide, or death-dealing
regimes.
Wilson Harris (b. 1921) Guyanese-born writer. *Jonestown* (1996)

14 There is precious little in civilization to appeal to
a Yeti.
Edmund Hillary (b. 1919) New Zealand mountaineer. June 1960.
Observer (June 3, 1960), 'Sayings of the Week'

15 Our civilization is founded on the shambles, and
every individual existence goes out in a lonely
spasm of helpless agony.
William James (1842–1910) US psychologist and philosopher. *The
Varieties of Religious Experience* (1902)

16 Civilization is an architecture of responses. Its
perfection, like that of any dwelling house, is
measured by the comfort man feels in it, by the
added portion of liberty it procures for him.
Cheikh Hamidou Kane (b. 1928) Senegalese writer, lawyer, and politician.
Ambiguous Adventure (1961)

17 If people dug up the remains of this civilization a
thousand years hence, and found Epstein's statues
and that man Ellis, they would think we were
just savages.
Doris Lessing (b. 1919) British novelist and short-story writer. Referring
to the sculptor Jacob Epstein and the essayist and
psychologist of sex Henry Havelock Ellis. *Martha Quest*
(1952), pt. 1, ch. 1

18 A study of history shows that civilizations that abandon the quest for knowledge are doomed to disintegration.

Bernard Lovell (b. 1913) British astronomer. *Observer* (May 14, 1972), 'Sayings of the Week'

19 Spokesmen for Western civilisation reach for the word 'primitive' whenever they encounter a music with strong rhythmic foundations.

Humphrey Lyttelton (b. 1921) British jazz trumpeter. *The Best of Jazz* (1978), ch. 14

20 what man calls civilization
always results in deserts.

Don Marquis (1878–1937) US journalist and writer. A warning letter, typed by archy the cockroach, who is too small and light to use the shift key. 'what the ants are saying', *archy does his part* (1935)

21 The degree of a nation's civilization is marked by its disregard for the necessities of existence.

Somerset Maugham (1874–1965) British writer. *Our Betters* (1917), Act 1

22 I have precious little sympathy for the selfish propriety of civilized man, and if a war of races should occur between the beasts and Lord Man, I would be tempted to sympathize with the bears.

John Muir (1838–1914) US naturalist and explorer. *A Thousand Mile Walk to the Gulf* (1916), quoted in *John Muir: The Eight Wilderness Discovery Books* (1992)

23 Civilization is the progress toward a society of privacy. The savage's whole existence is public, ruled by the laws of his tribe. Civilization is the process of setting man free from men.

Ayn Rand (1905–82) Russian-born US writer and philosopher. *The Fountainhead* (1943)

24 You can't say civilization don't advance, however, for in every war they kill you a new way.

Will Rogers (1879–1935) US actor, writer, and humorist. *New York Times* (December 23, 1929)

25 No people is wholly civilized where a distinction is drawn between stealing an office and stealing a purse.

Theodore Roosevelt (1858–1919) US president. Speech, Chicago, Illinois (June 22, 1912)

26 The passing from the state of nature to the civil society produces a remarkable change in man; it puts justice as a rule of conduct in place of instinct, and gives his actions the moral quality they previously lacked.

Jean-Jacques Rousseau (1712–78) French philosopher and writer. *The Social Contract* (1762)

27 One of the most remarkable intuitions in Western thought was Rousseau's noble Savage: the idea that perhaps civilization has something to learn from the primitive.

Gary Snyder (b. 1930) US poet, essayist, and translator. 1967. Referring to Jean-Jacques Rousseau. 'Poetry and the Primitive', *Earth House Hold* (1969)

28 An Aristotle was but the rubbish of an Adam, and Athens but the rudiments of Paradise.

Robert South (1634–1716) English theologian. *Twelve Sermons* (1692), vol. 1, sermon 2

29 Civilization is a movement, not a condition; it is a voyage, not a harbour.

Arnold Toynbee (1889–1975) British historian. *Reader's Digest* (October 1958)

30 But I reckon I got to light out for the Territory ahead of the rest, because Aunt Sally she's going to adopt me and sivilize me and I can't stand it. I been there before.

Mark Twain (1835–1910) US writer and humorist. Huckleberry Finn's closing words. *The Adventures of Huckleberry Finn* (1884), ch. 43

Civil Rights

see also **Equality, Human Rights, Liberty, Slavery, Women's Rights**

1 If we do not now dare everything, the fulfillment of that prophecy, re-created from the Bible in song by a slave, is upon us: God gave Noah the rainbow sign, No more water, the fire next time!

James Baldwin (1924–87) US writer and civil rights activist. *The Fire Next Time* (1963)

2 The right of citizens of the United States to vote shall not be denied or abridged by the United States or by any State on account of sex.

Constitution of the United States, US system of fundamental laws. *Amendments to the Constitution* (1920), Article 19

3 The law regards man as man and takes no account of his surroundings or of his colour when his civil rights as guaranteed by the supreme law of the land are involved.

John Marshall Harlan (1833–1911) US jurist. Sole dissenting opinion in a legal case. *Plessy v. Ferguson* (1896), 163 US, 537

4 Negroes, like all other Americans, are being asked at the moment to prepare to defend democracy. But Negroes would very much like to have a little more democracy to defend.

Langston Hughes (1902–67) US novelist, playwright, and short-story writer. Speech to Fourth American Writers' Congress (June 6–8, 1941), quoted in *Good Morning Revolution: Uncollected Writings of Langston Hughes* (Faith Berry, ed.; 1992)

5 There are those who say to you—we are rushing this issue of civil rights. I say we are 172 years late.

Hubert H. Humphrey (1911–78) US vice president. Speech, Democrat National Convention (July 14, 1948)

6 Nonviolent direct action seeks to create such a crisis and foster such a tension that a community which has constantly refused to negotiate is forced to confront the issue.

Martin Luther King, Jr. (1929–68) US civil rights leader. Letter from Birmingham Jail, Alabama (April 16, 1963)

7 It may be true that the law cannot make a man love me, but it can keep him from lynching me, and I think that's pretty important.

Martin Luther King, Jr. (1929–68) US civil rights leader. *Wall Street Journal* (November 13, 1962)

8 Rights that depend on the sufferance of the state are of uncertain tenure.

Suzanne La Follette (1893–1983) US writer and politician. *Concerning Women* (1926)

9 The struggle is my life. I will continue fighting for freedom until the end of my days.

Nelson Mandela (b. 1918) South African president and lawyer. June 26, 1961. Press statement, *The Struggle is My Life* (1990)

10 I'm the world's original gradualist. I just think ninety-odd years is gradual enough.

Thurgood Marshall (1908–93) US civil rights lawyer and jurist. Referring to President Dwight D. Eisenhower's call for patience regarding the progress of civil rights. Quoted in *I. F. Stone's Weekly* (May 19, 1958)

11 Power to the People.
Bobby Seale (b. 1936) US civil rights activist. Attrib.

12 Black power . . . is a call for a black people in this country to unite, to recognize their heritage, to build a sense of community . . . It is a call to reject the racist institutions and values of this society.
Kwame Touré (b. 1941) Trinidadian-born US civil rights activist. Kwame Touré is usually credited with creating the phrase 'black power'. *Black Power: The Politics of Liberation in America* (1967)

13 It is by the goodness of God that in our country we have those three unspeakably precious things: freedom of speech, freedom of conscience, and the prudence never to practise either of them.
Mark Twain (1835–1910) US writer and humorist. *Following the Equator* (1897), ch. 20

14 No man should be a serf, nor do homage or any manner of service to any lord, but should give fourpence rent for an acre of land, and that no one should work for any man but as his own will, and on terms of a regular covenant.
Wat Tyler (d. 1381) English rebel leader. Attrib. *Anonimalle Chronicle* (14th century)

15 Just give us a little time and one of these days we'll emancipate *you!*
Roy Wilkins (1901–81) US civil rights activist, newspaper editor, and writer. Address to white people, quoted in *Contemporary Black Leaders* (Elton Fax; 1970)

16 Black is beautiful when it is a slum kid studying to enter college . . . or a slum mother battling to give her kids a chance for a better life. But white is beautiful, too, when it helps to change society to make our system work for black people.
Whitney M. Young, Jr. (1921–71) US social worker and civil rights leader. *Beyond Racism: Building an Open Society* (1969)

Clarity

see also **Brevity, Certainty, Simplicity**

1 As clear and as manifest as the nose in a man's face.
Robert Burton (1577–1640) English scholar and churchman. *The Anatomy of Melancholy* (1621), pt. 3, sect. 3

2 I know what I've told you I'm going to say, I'm going to say. And what else I say, well, I'll take some time to figure out—figure that out.
George Bush (b. 1924) US president. Remark at a press conference (December 4, 1990)

3 Hit the nail on the head.
John Fletcher (1579–1625) English playwright. 'Love's Cure', *The Lover's Progress* (1623), Act 2, Scene 1

4 I guess I should warn you. If I turn out to be particularly clear, you've probably misunderstood what I've said.
Alan Greenspan (b. 1926) US economist. *Financial Times* (December 24, 1988), 'Quotes of the Year'

5 Unless one is a genius, it is best to aim at being intelligible.
Anthony Hope (1863–1933) British novelist and playwright. *The Dolly Dialogues* (1894), no. 15

6 Clarity is the politeness of the man of letters.
Jules Renard (1864–1910) French writer. October 7, 1892. *Journal* (1877–1910)

Class

see also **Equality, Society, Wealth**

1 You can measure the social caste of a person by the distance between the husband's and wife's apartments.
Alfonso XIII (1886–1941) Spanish monarch. Attrib.

2 It doesn't matter about being born in a duckyard, as long as you're hatched from a swan's egg.
Hans Christian Andersen (1805–75) Danish writer. 'The Ugly Duckling', *Fairy Tales* (L. W. Kingsland, tr.; 1959–61)

3 I often, therefore, when I want to distinguish clearly the aristocratic class from the Philistines proper, or middle class, name the former, in my own mind *the Barbarians*.
Matthew Arnold (1822–88) British poet and critic. *Culture and Anarchy* (1869), ch. 3

4 Equal wealth and opportunities of culture . . . have simply made us all members of one class.
Edward Bellamy (1850–98) US essayist and journalist. *Looking Backward, 2000–1887* (1888), ch. 14

5 Outer space is no place for a person of breeding.
Lady Violet Bonham-Carter (1887–1969) British politician and publicist. Attrib.

6 The great Unwashed.
Henry Peter Brougham (1778–1868) British lawyer and politician. Attrib.

7 Without class differences, England would cease to be the living theatre it is.
Anthony Burgess (1917–93) British writer and critic. *Observer* (May 26, 1985), 'Sayings of the Week'

8 Welcome to the wrong side of the tracks.
Angela Carter (1940–92) British novelist, essayist, and short-story writer. *Wise Children* (1991)

9 Of course they have, or I wouldn't be sitting here talking to someone like you.
Barbara Cartland (1901–2000) British novelist. When asked in a radio interview whether she thought that British class barriers had broken down. Quoted in *Class* (J. Cooper; 1978)

10 One of those refined people who go out to sew for the rich because they cannot bear contact with the poor.
Colette (1873–1954) French novelist. *The Other One* (1929)

11 Two nations; between whom there is no intercourse and no sympathy; who are as ignorant of each other's habits, thoughts, and feelings, as if they were dwellers in different zones, or inhabitants of different planets; who are formed by a different breeding, are fed by a different food, are ordered by different manners, and are not governed by the same laws.
Benjamin Disraeli (1804–81) British prime minister and writer. Referring to the rich and the poor. The inspiration for the 'One Nation' Conservatism of Stanley Baldwin. *Sybil* (1845), bk. 2, ch. 5

12 He is used to dealing with estate workers. I cannot see how anyone can say he is out of touch.
Caroline Douglas-Home (b. 1937) British aristocrat. October, 1963. Referring to her father's suitability for his new role as prime minister. *Daily Herald* (October 21, 1963)

13 It was seen that all past history, with the exception of its primitive stages, was the history of class struggles.
Friedrich Engels (1820–95) German socialist. *Socialism: Utopian and Scientific* (1892)

14 He differed from the healthy type that was essentially middle-class—he never seemed to perspire.
F. Scott Fitzgerald (1896–1940) US writer. *This Side of Paradise* (1920), bk. 1, ch. 2

15 The bourgeois prefers comfort to pleasure, convenience to liberty, and a pleasant temperature to the deathly inner consuming fire.
Hermann Hesse (1877–1962) German-born Swiss novelist and poet. 'Treatise of the Steppenwolf', *Steppenwolf* (1927)

16 '*Bourgeois*', I observed, 'is an epithet which the riff-raff apply to what is respectable, and the aristocracy to what is decent'.
Anthony Hope (1863–1933) British novelist and playwright. *The Dolly Dialogues* (1894), no. 17

17 The cruelties of property and privilege are always more ferocious than the revenges of poverty and oppression. For the one aims at perpetuating resented injustice, the other is merely a momentary passion soon appeased.
C. L. R. James (1901–89) Trinidadian writer, political theorist, and educator. *The Black Jacobins* (1938)

18 You may be the most liberal Liberal Englishman, and yet you cannot fail to see the categorical difference between the responsible and the irresponsible classes.
D. H. Lawrence (1885–1930) British writer. *Kangaroo* (1923), ch. 1

19 A working class hero is something to be.
John Lennon (1940–80) British rock musician. Song lyric. 'Working Class Hero' (1970)

20 The working classes are never embarrassed by money—only the absence of it.
Ken Livingstone (b. 1945) British politician. September 1987

21 The extremes of life differ but in this:—Above, Vice smiles and revels—below, Crime frowns and starves.
Bulwer Lytton (1803–73) British novelist and politician. *Money* (1840), Act 3, Scene 1

22 Never descend to the ways of those above you.
George Mallaby (1902–78) British diplomat and writer. *From My Level: Unwritten Minutes* (1965)

23 As to the so-called 'love of mankind', there has been no such all-embracing love since humanity was divided into classes.
Mao Zedong (1893–1976) Chinese statesman. *Talks at the Yan'an Forum on Art and Literature* (1942), quoted in *Mao Tsetung: An Anthology of His Writings* (Anne Fremantle, ed.; 1962)

24 The history of all hitherto existing society is the history of class struggles.
Karl Marx (1818–83) German philosopher. *The Communist Manifesto* (co-written with Friedrich Engels; 1848)

25 Britain is the society where the ruling class does not rule, the working class does not work, and the middle class is not in the middle.
George Mikes (1912–87) Hungarian-born British writer and humorist. *English Humour for Beginners* (1980)

26 Only on the third class tourist class passengers' deck was it a sultry overcast morning, but then if you do things on the cheap you must expect these things.
Spike Milligan (1918–2002) Indian-born British humorist, writer, and actor. *A Dustbin of Milligan* (1963)

27 Who is it that exercises social power today? Who imposes the forms of his own mind on the period? Without a doubt, the man of the middle class.
José Ortega y Gasset (1883–1955) Spanish writer and philosopher. *The Revolt of the Masses* (1930)

28 We have nothing to lose but our aitches.
George Orwell (1903–50) British writer. Referring to the middle classes; a parody of Karl Marx. *The Road to Wigan Pier* (1937), ch. 13

29 I acquired a certain pedantic presumption and the slightest touch of ostentation, which subsequently, thank goodness, I've completely cured myself of.
Benito Pérez Galdós (1843–1920) Spanish novelist and playwright. *El Amigo Manso* (1882), ch. 2

30 Prison will not work until we start sending a better class of people there.
Laurence J. Peter (1919–90) Canadian writer. Attrib.

31 In an unconscious gesture of television-enforced democracy, mistress and servant both scrabbled unseeingly in the same bowl of nuts.
Arundhati Roy (b. 1960) Indian writer. *The God of Small Things* (1997), 'Big Man the Laltain, Small Man the Mombatti'

32 There are two classes in good society in England. The equestrian classes and the neurotic classes.
George Bernard Shaw (1856–1950) Irish playwright. *Heartbreak House* (1919)

33 It is impossible for an Englishman to open his mouth, without making some other Englishman despise him.
George Bernard Shaw (1856–1950) Irish playwright. *Pygmalion* (1914), Preface

34 It is impossible for one class to appreciate the wrongs of another.
Elizabeth Cady Stanton (1815–1902) US suffragette. *History of Woman Suffrage* (co-written with Susan B. Anthony and Matilda Gage; 1881), vol. 1

35 The ship follows Soviet custom: it is riddled with class distinctions so subtle, it takes a trained Marxist to appreciate them.
Paul Theroux (b. 1941) US writer. *The Great Railway Bazaar* (1975), ch. 30

36 I have often observed in women of her type a tendency to regard all athletics as inferior forms of fox-hunting.
Evelyn Waugh (1903–66) British novelist. *Decline and Fall* (1928), pt. 1, ch. 10

37 You never find an Englishman among the underdogs—except in England of course.
Evelyn Waugh (1903–66) British novelist. *The Loved One* (1948), ch. 1

38 Really, if the lower orders don't set us a good example, what on earth is the use of them?
Oscar Wilde (1854–1900) Irish poet, playwright, and wit. *The Importance of Being Earnest* (1895), Act 1

Classical Music

see Music, Musicians

Cleverness

see Intellect, Intelligence, Knowledge

Clothes

see also **Fashion, Style**

1 A dress that is not worn wears itself out.
Anonymous. Armenian proverb.

2 She just wore
Enough for modesty—no more.
Robert Williams Buchanan (1841–1901) British poet, novelist, and playwright. 'White Rose and Red' (1873), pt. 1, sect. 5, ll. 60–61

3 A Dandy is a Clothes-wearing Man, a Man whose trade, office, and existence consists in the wearing of Clothes. Every faculty of his soul, spirit, purse, and person is heroically consecrated to this one object, the wearing of Clothes wisely and well: so that as others dress to live, he lives to dress.
Thomas Carlyle (1795–1881) Scottish historian and essayist. Sartor Resartus (1833–34)

4 I go to a better tailor than any of you and pay more for my clothes. The only difference is that you probably don't sleep in yours.
Clarence Darrow (1857–1938) US lawyer. Reply when teased by reporters about his appearance. Quoted in 2500 Anecdotes (Edmund Fuller; 1943)

5 The Englishman's dress is like a traitor's body that hath been hanged, drawn, and quartered, and is set up in various places; his cod-piece is in Denmark, the collar of his doublet and the belly in France; the wing and narrow sleeve in Italy; the short waist hangs over a Dutch butcher's stall in Utrecht; his huge slops speak Spanishly . . . And thus we that mock every nation for keeping of one fashion, yet steal patches from every one of them to piece out our pride.
Thomas Dekker (1572?–1632?) English playwright. Seven Deadly Sins of London (1606)

6 The proper design of cloathing is to be a covering for shame, a fence from the injuries of the weather, and a distinction of sexes and degrees.
Samuel Fawconer (fl. 1765) British sermonizer. An Essay on Modern Luxury (1765)

7 The sense of being well-dressed gives a feeling of inward tranquillity which religion is powerless to bestow.
Miss C. F. Forbes (1817–1911) British writer. Quoted in Letters and Social Aims (R. W. Emerson; 1876)

8 Those who make their dress a principal part of themselves, will, in general, become of no more value than their dress.
William Hazlitt (1778–1830) British essayist and critic. 'On the Clerical Character', Table Talk (1821–22)

9 A sensational event was changing from the brown suit to the gray the contents of his pockets. He was earnest about these objects. They were of eternal importance, like baseball or the Republican party.
Sinclair Lewis (1885–1951) US novelist. Babbitt (1922)

10 Our buttons operate in synchronization with ourselves; they form a sort of cheap and comfortable senate, which always votes in favour of our motions.
Joaquim Maria Machado de Assis (1839–1908) Brazilian novelist and short-story writer. Referring to buttons on clothing. Philosopher or Dog? (Clotilde Wilson, tr.; 1892)

11 It is not everyone who has the right to be plainly dressed.
Napoleon I (1769–1821) French emperor. 1802. Quoted in Memoirs of Madame de Rémusat (Mrs. Cashel Howey and John Lillie, trs.; 1880), vol. 1, ch. 2

12 Brevity is the soul of lingerie.
Dorothy Parker (1893–1967) US writer and wit. 1916. Caption written for Vogue. Quoted in You Might As Well Live (John Keats; 1970)

13 You will not learn how to be beautiful from fashion magazines. What have you to do with fashion? Take no notice of it; just wear what suits you.
Paul Poiret (1879–1944) French fashion designer. 1927. Quoted in Poiret (Yvonne Deslandres; 1987)

14 I have often said that I wish I had invented blue jeans, the most spectacular, the most practical, the most relaxed and nonchalant. They have expression, modesty, sex appeal, simplicity— all I hope for in my clothes.
Yves Saint Laurent (b. 1936) Algerian-born French couturier. Quoted in Yves Saint Laurent (Costume Institute Exhibition catalogue, Metropolitan Museum, New York City; 1984), ch. 2

15 His socks compelled one's attention without losing one's respect.
Saki (1870–1916) British short-story writer. 'Ministers of Grace', The Chronicles of Clovis (1911)

16 A dress has no life of its own unless it is worn, and as soon as this happens another personality takes over from you and animates it, or tries to, glorifies or destroys it, or makes it into a song of beauty.
Elsa Schiaparelli (1890–1973) Italian fashion designer. A Shocking Life (1954)

17 LEAR Through tatter'd clothes small vices do appear;
Robes and furr'd gowns hide all.
William Shakespeare (1564–1616) English poet and playwright. King Lear (1605–06), Act 4, Scene 6

18 She wears her clothes, as if they were thrown on her with a pitchfork.
Jonathan Swift (1667–1745) Irish writer and clergyman. Polite Conversation (1738), Dialogue 1

19 What I do is restricted by the cloth and the human body. My job is to make that cloth give expression to the body.
Vivienne Westwood (b. 1941) British fashion designer. Times (November 16, 1992)

20 Hats divide generally into three classes: offensive hats, defensive hats, and shrapnel.
Katharine Whitehorn (b. 1926) British journalist and writer. 'Hats', Shouts and Murmurs (1963)

Cold War

see also **Communism, United States**

1 We all know the Iron Curtain has been demolished, but in its place an economic and social curtain might come down.
Jozsef Antall (1932–93) Hungarian prime minister. Independent (October 29, 1992)

2 What we ought to do is to send up a flight of a thousand B-29s and drop a million Sears Roebuck catalogs all over Russia.
Bruce Barton (1886–1967) US business executive, author, and politician. Remark (1940s), quoted in America (Alistair Cooke; 1973)

3   Let us not be deceived—we are today in the
    midst of a cold war.
    Bernard Mannes Baruch (1870–1965) US financier, statesman, and
    philanthropist. Speech to the South Carolina legislature (April
    16, 1947)

4   Russia is no longer our enemy and therefore we
    shouldn't be locked into a Cold War mentality
    that says we keep the peace by blowing each
    other up. In my attitude, that's old, that's tired,
    that's stale.
    George W. Bush (b. 1948) US president. Speech, Des Moines, Iowa
    (June 8, 2001)

5   Detente is like the race in *Alice in Wonderland*
    where everyone had to have a prize.
    Lord Carrington (b. 1919) British politician. Speech (March, 1980)

6   Surely the right course is to test the Russians, not
    the bombs.
    Hugh Gaitskell (1906–63) British politician. *Observer* (June 23,
    1957), 'Sayings of the Week'

7   Freedom has many flaws and our democracy is
    imperfect, but we have never had to put up a
    wall to keep our people in.
    John Fitzgerald Kennedy (1917–63) US president. Referring to the
    Berlin Wall, the fortified wall that was erected in 1961 by the
    communist GDR (German Democratic Republic) to divide
    East Berlin from West Berlin. Speech, City Hall, West Berlin,
    Germany (June 26, 1963)

8   Khruschev reminds me of the tiger hunter who
    had picked a place on the wall to hang the tiger's
    skin long before he has caught the tiger. This
    tiger has other ideas.
    John Fitzgerald Kennedy (1917–63) US president. Referring to Nikita
    Khrushchev. *New York Times* (December 24, 1961)

9   Revolutions are not made for export.
    Nikita Khrushchev (1894–1971) Soviet statesman. Speech to the 21st
    Congress of the Communist Party of the Soviet Union,
    Moscow (January 27, 1959)

10 Now we are in a period which I can characterize
    as a period of cold peace.
    Trygve Lie (1896–1968) Norwegian statesman. *Observer* (August 21,
    1949), 'Sayings of the Week'

11 There is an iron curtain across Europe.
    T. St Vincent Troubridge (1895–1963) British army officer. Also said by
    Winston Churchill and Joseph Goebbels. *Sunday Empire
    News* (October 21, 1945)

Colonialism

see also **Decolonization, Imperialism**

1   The fault of a colonial economy is that it is
    dishonest: it misrepresents reality. In practice it is
    simply a way of keeping costs off the books of
    an exploitative interest.
    Wendell Berry (b. 1934) US poet, novelist, and essayist. 1986. Referring
    to his view that the US economy 'preys on its internal
    colonies'. 'Does Community Have a Value?', *The Landscape
    of Harmony* (1987)

2   I should be judged as a captain who went from
    Spain to the Indies to conquer a people numerous
    and warlike, whose manners and religion are
    very different from ours, who live in sierras and
    mountains, without fixed settlements.
    Christopher Columbus (1451–1506) Italian explorer and colonialist. Letter
    to Doña Juana de Torres (October 1500)

3   Colonialism forces the people it dominates to ask
    themselves the question constantly: 'In reality,
    who am I?'
    Frantz Fanon (1925–61) Martiniquan social scientist, physician, and
    psychiatrist. 'Colonial War and Mental Disorders', *The
    Wretched of the Earth* (1961)

4   Colonialism is not satisfied merely with holding a
    people in its grip and emptying the native's brain
    of all form and content. By a kind of peverted
    logic, it turns to the past of the oppressed people,
    and distorts, disfigures and destroys it.
    Frantz Fanon (1925–61) Martiniquan social scientist, physician, and psychiatrist.
    'On National Culture', *The Wretched of the Earth* (1961)

5   To remain a great nation or to become one, you
    must colonise.
    Léon Gambetta (1838–82) French statesman. Quoted in *Europe Since
    1870* (James Joll; 1973), ch. 4

6   On a day in September 1802 a small group of
    Greeks, Turks and Englishmen assembled on the
    Acropolis. They had come to witness the removal
    of a metope from the structure of the Parthenon.
    Christopher Hitchens (b. 1949) British author and journalist. Referring
    to the so-called Elgin Marbles, later brought to Britain by
    Lord Elgin and now in the British Museum. *The Elgin
    Marbles* (1997)

7   When old settlers say 'One has to understand the
    country', what they mean is, 'You have to get
    used to our ideas about the native'. They are
    saying, in effect, 'Learn our ideas, or otherwise
    get out; we don't want you'.
    Doris Lessing (b. 1919) British novelist and short-story writer. Referring
    specifically to South Africa. *The Grass is Singing* (1950), ch. 1

8   As long as we are ruled by others we shall lay
    our mistakes at their door, and our sense of
    responsibility will remain dulled. Freedom brings
    responsibilities, and our experience can be
    enriched only by the acceptance of these
    responsibilities.
    Kwame Nkrumah (1909–72) Ghanaian president. *The Autobiography
    of Kwame Nkrumah* (1959)

Colour

see also **Appearance, Art, Painting**

1   All colours are a mixture of three things, the
    light, the medium through which the light is seen
    such as water and air, and the colours forming
    the ground from which the light happens to be
    reflected.
    Aristotle (384–322 BC) Greek philosopher. *On Colour*

2   When what is black is mixed with the light of the
    sun and fire, the result is always red.
    Aristotle (384–322 BC) Greek philosopher. *On Colour*

3   It was the Rainbow gave thee birth,
    And left thee all her lovely hues.
    W. H. Davies (1871–1940) British poet. 'The Kingfisher' (1910)

4   I suffer from an incurable disease—colour
    blindness.
    Joost de Blank (1908–68) Dutch-born British churchman. Attrib.

5   In dress we associate the character of the colour
    with the character of the person. We may thus
    observe the relation of colours singly, and in
    combination, to the colour of the complexion,
    age and station.
    Johann Wolfgang von Goethe (1749–1832) German poet, playwright, and
    scientist. *Theory of Colour* (1810)

6 There is a black which is old and a black which is fresh.
Hokusai (1760–1849) Japanese painter and engraver. Attrib.

7 Blue is the universal love in which man bathes— it is the terrestrial paradise . . . Blue transcends the solemn geography of human limits.
Derek Jarman (1942–94) British artist, film director, and writer. *Chroma* (1994)

8 Violet is red withdrawn from humanity by blue.
Wassily Kandinsky (1866–1944) Russian-born French painter. Attrib.

9 Color is sensibility turned into matter, matter in its primordial state.
Yves Klein (1928–62) French painter. 'My Position in the Battle Between Line and Color' (1958)

10 Colours in painting are like allurements for persuading the eyes, as the sweetness of metre functions in poetry.
Nicolas Poussin (1594–1665) French painter. Attrib.

11 A colour shines in its surroundings. Just as eyes only smile in a face.
Ludwig Wittgenstein (1889–1951) Austrian philosopher. *Remarks on Colour*

Comedy

see also **Humour, Laughter, Theatre**

1 Comedy is tragedy that happens to other people.
Angela Carter (1940–92) British novelist, essayist, and short-story writer. *Wise Children* (1991)

2 All I need to make a comedy is a park, a policeman and a pretty girl.
Charlie Chaplin (1889–1977) British actor and director. *My Autobiography* (1964), ch. 10

3 What a fine comedy this world would be if one did not play a part in it!
Denis Diderot (1713–84) French encyclopedist and philosopher. Quoted in *Diderot's Letters to Sophie Volland* (Peter France, tr.; 1974)

4 Comedy is medicine.
Trevor Griffiths (b. 1935) British playwright. *Comedians* (1976), Act 1

5 One always writes comedy at the moment of deepest hysteria.
V. S. Naipaul (b. 1932) Trinidadian-born British novelist. Attrib.

6 Comedy, we may say, is society protecting itself—with a smile.
J. B. Priestley (1894–1984) British writer. *George Meredith* (1926)

7 A comedian can only last till he either takes himself serious or his audience takes him serious.
Will Rogers (1879–1935) US actor, writer, and humorist. Newspaper article (1931)

8 If tragedy is an experience of hyperinvolvement, comedy is an experience of underinvolvement, of detachment.
Susan Sontag (b. 1933) US writer. 'Notes on Camp', *Against Interpretation* (1966)

9 In the best comedy, there is clearly something wrong, but it is secret and understated—not even implied—comedy is the public version of a private darkness.
Paul Theroux (b. 1941) US writer. *My Secret History* (1996)

10 This world is a comedy to those who think, a tragedy to those who feel.
Horace Walpole (1717–97) British writer. Letter to Anne, Countess of Upper Ossory (August 16, 1776)

11 My comedy is like emotional hang-gliding.
Robin Williams (b. 1951) US actor and comedian. *Playboy* (October 1982)

Comfort

see also **Happiness**

1 Minds like bodies, will often fall into a pimpled, ill-conditioned state from mere excess of comfort.
Charles Dickens (1812–70) British novelist. *Barnaby Rudge* (1841), ch. 7

2 A minimum of comfort is necessary for the practice of virtue.
Patrice Lumumba (1925–61) Congolese prime minister. *Congo, My Country* (1962)

3 Every man, wherever he goes, is encompassed by a cloud of comforting convictions, which move with him like flies on a summer day.
Bertrand Russell (1872–1970) British philosopher and mathematician. 'Dreams and Facts', *Sceptical Essays* (1928)

4 KING JOHN I beg cold comfort.
William Shakespeare (1564–1616) English poet and playwright. *King John* (1591–98), Act 5, Scene 7

Commercialism

see **Capitalism, Materialism**

Commitment

see also **Faith, Loyalty**

1 If you'll be my voice today, I'll be yours for the next four years.
Bill Clinton (b. 1946) US president. Election day, while suffering from laryngitis. Speech (November 3, 1992)

2 There are men who would even be afraid to commit themselves to the doctrine that castor oil is a laxative.
Camille Flammarion (1842–1925) French astronomer. Attrib.

3 Catholics and Communists have committed great crimes, but at least they have not stood aside, like an established society, and been indifferent. I would rather have blood on my hands than water like Pilate.
Graham Greene (1904–91) British novelist. *The Comedians* (1966), pt. 3, ch. 4

4 It isn't until you begin to fight in your own cause that you (a) become really committed to winning, and (b) become a genuine ally of other people struggling for their freedom.
Robin Morgan (b. 1941) US writer. *Sisterhood Is Powerful: an Anthology of Writings from the Women's Liberation Movement* (1970), Introduction

5 Miss Brodie said: 'Pavlova contemplates her swans in order to perfect her swan dance, she studies them. This is true dedication. You must all grow up to be dedicated women as I have dedicated myself to you'.
Muriel Spark (b. 1918) British novelist. *The Prime of Miss Jean Brodie* (1961), ch. 3

6 Behold, I do not give lectures or a little charity, When I give I give myself.
Walt Whitman (1819–92) US poet. 1855. 'Song of Myself', *Leaves of Grass* (1881), pt. 40

Commitment in Love

see also **Faithfulness, Trust**

1   Whilst I loved much, I never loved long, but was inconstant to them all for the sake of all.
Henry St. John Bolingbroke (1678–1751) English statesman. Letter to Charles Wyndham (December 26, 1735)

2   It is my will to go with the man I love. I do not wish to count the cost. I do not wish to consider whether it is good. I do not wish to know whether he loves me. It is my will to go with him whom I love.
Bertolt Brecht (1898–1956) German playwright and poet. *The Good Person of Szechwan* (1943)

3   Oh that the desert were my dwelling-place,
With one fair spirit for my minister,
That I might all forget the human race,
And hating no one, love but only her!
Lord Byron (1788–1824) British poet. *Childe Harold's Pilgrimage* (1812–18), can. 4, st. 177

4   Then talk not of inconstancy,
False hearts and broken vows;
If I, by miracle, can be
This livelong minute true to thee,
'Tis all that heaven allows.
2nd Earl of Rochester (1647–80) English courtier and poet. 'Love and Life', *The New Oxford Book of English Verse* (Helen Gardner, ed.; 1972)

5   Miss Madeleine Philips was making it very manifest to Captain Douglas that she herself was a career; that a lover with any other career in view need not—as the advertisements say—apply.
H. G. Wells (1866–1946) British writer. *Bealby* (1915), pt. 5, ch. 5

Communication

see also **Conversation, Media, Speech**

1   A habit the pleasure of which increases with practice, but becomes more irksome with neglect.
Abigail Adams (1744–1818) US feminist. Referring to writing letters. Letter to her daughter (May 8, 1808)

2   I knew one that when he wrote a letter, he would put that which was most material in the postscript, as if it had been a by-matter.
Francis Bacon (1561–1626) English philosopher, statesman, and lawyer. 'Of Cunning', *Essays* (1625)

3   It is generally better to deal by speech than by letter.
Francis Bacon (1561–1626) English philosopher, statesman, and lawyer. 'Of Negotiating', *Essays* (1625)

4   In communications, familiarity breeds apathy.
William Bernbach (1911–82) US advertising executive. *Bill Bernbach Said . . .* (1989)

5   The new technology is as important to modern man as the discovery of fire was to early man. We are going to turn in the distant future into a race of people who possess extraordinary communication with one another—and the language of communication will be art.
Francis Ford Coppola (b. 1939) US film director, producer, and screenwriter. Quoted in *Francis Ford Coppola: A Film-Maker's Life* (Michael Schumacher; 1999)

6   Sir, more than kisses, letters mingle souls.
John Donne (1572?–1631) English metaphysical poet and divine. 'Verse Letter to Sir Henry Wotton' (1597–98), l. 1

7   E. T. phone home.
E. T., US film character. Said by the alien E.T., who had been stranded on earth, and referring to his desire to contact his own planet. *E. T. The Extra-Terrestrial* (Melissa Mathison; 1982)

8   If there is one general law of communication it is that we never communicate as effectively as we think we do.
Charles Handy (b. 1932) Irish-born British management educator and writer. *Understanding Organisations* (1976)

9   Don't you like writing letters? I do because it's such a swell way to keep from working and yet feel you've done something.
Ernest Hemingway (1899–1961) US writer. Letter to F. Scott Fitzgerald (July 1, 1925)

10 It is better not to express what one means than to express what one does not mean.
Karl Kraus (1874–1936) Austrian writer. 1909. Quoted in 'Sprüche und Widersprüche', *Karl Kraus* (Harry Zohn; 1971)

11 The medium is the message. This is merely to say that the personal and social consequences of any medium . . . result from the new scale that is introduced into our affairs by each extension of ourselves or by any new technology.
Marshall McLuhan (1911–80) Canadian sociologist. *Understanding Media* (1964), ch. 1

12 And this certainly has to be the most historic phone call ever made.
Richard Nixon (1913–94) US president. Telephone call to astronauts on the moon (July 20, 1969)

13 In saying what is obvious, never choose cunning. Yelling works better.
Cynthia Ozick (b. 1928) US novelist and short-story writer. Quoted in 'We Are the Crazy Lady and Other Feisty Feminist Fables', *The First Ms. Reader* (Francine Klagsbrun, ed.; 1972)

14 I have made this letter longer than usual, only because I have not had the time to make it shorter.
Blaise Pascal (1623–62) French philosopher, mathematician, and physicist. *Lettres Provinciales* (1657), no. 16

15 The phone call, when it comes, rips easily across the room . . . like a rude metal double-fart.
Thomas Pynchon (b. 1937) US novelist. *Gravity's Rainbow* (1973)

16 It's easy to get people's attention, what counts is getting their *interest*.
A. Philip Randolph (1889–1979) US trade union leader and civil rights activist. Quoted in *Contemporary Black Leaders* (Elton Fax; 1970)

17 Addresses are given to us to conceal our whereabouts.
Saki (1870–1916) British short-story writer. *Reginald in Russia* (1910)

18 Dialogue cannot create the need to change, but it certainly facilitates the process of change.
Edgar H. Schein (b. 1928) US educator and author. *Process Consultation Revisited: Building the Helping Relationship* (1999)

19 We are in great haste to construct a magnetic telegraph from Maine to Texas; but Maine and Texas, it may be, have nothing important to communicate.
Henry David Thoreau (1817–62) US writer. Quoted in *Intellectual Capital* (Thomas A. Stewart; 1997)

20 The present century, in proclaiming the advent of a new age of communication and information . . . forgot to deal with the great problem of talk, which is how to find someone to listen.

Theodore Zeldin (b. 1933) British historian. *An Intimate History of Humanity* (1994)

Communism

see also **Cold War**, **Russia**, **Socialism**

1 Communism will not come terrible like an army with banners, but like a Corporation dustman carting off the rubbish of the ages.

Brendan Behan (1923–64) Irish playwright and author. 1950. Quoted in *Dead As Doornails* (Anthony Cronin; 1976), ch. 3

2 Its relationship to democratic institutions is that of the death watch beetle—it is not a Party, it is a conspiracy.

Aneurin Bevan (1897–1960) Welsh-born British politician. Referring to the Communist Party. Attrib. *Tribune* (1950s)

3 The psychological impact of anti-communism on ordinary people in this country runs very deep. There is something about the word 'communism' that, for the unenlightened, evokes not only the enemy, but also something immoral, something dirty.

Angela Davis (b. 1944) US civil rights activist, educator, and writer. *Angela Davis: An Autobiography* (1974)

4 The state is not 'abolished', it withers away.

Friedrich Engels (1820–95) German socialist. *Anti-Dühring* (1878), pt. 3, ch. 2

5 The proletariat seizes the public power, and by means of this transforms the socialized means of production, slipping from the hands of the bourgeoisie, into public property.

Friedrich Engels (1820–95) German socialist. *Socialism: Utopian and Scientific* (1892)

6 The members of our secret service have apparently spent so much time looking under the beds for Communists, they haven't had time to look in the bed.

Michael Foot (b. 1913) British politician and writer. 1963. Referring to the Profumo affair. Attrib.

7 Only socialism would put up with it for so long. Capitalism would have gone bankrupt years ago.

Mikhail Gorbachev (b. 1931) Russian statesman. Talking of sub-standard manufacturing practises in the Soviet Union. TV documentary (March 23, 1987)

8 I think there is a certain basis of truth in the fear which the Russian government is beginning to have of communism: for communism is Tsarist autocracy turned upside down.

Aleksandr Ivanovich Herzen (1812–70) Russian writer and political thinker. *My Past and Thoughts* (1854)

9 The failure of communism as an economic system is made all the more ironic by the arrogance of the original conception, which was no less than to export the 'revolution' to the entire world.

William Keegan (b. 1938) British author and journalist. *The Spectre of Capitalism* (1992)

10 At the same time a persecuting and missionary religion and an experimental economic technique.

John Maynard Keynes (1883–1946) British economist. Referring to Leninism. *Essays in Persuasion* (1925)

11 Every year humanity takes a step towards Communism. Maybe not you, but at all events your grandson will surely be a Communist.

Nikita Khrushchev (1894–1971) Soviet statesman. Remark to Sir William Hayter (June 1956)

12 Those who wait for that must wait until a shrimp learns to whistle.

Nikita Khrushchev (1894–1971) Soviet statesman. Referring to the chances of the Soviet Union rejecting communism. Attrib.

13 Communism will never be defeated by atomic bombs . . . Our greatest defense against Communism is to take offensive action on behalf of justice and righteousness . . . We must . . . seek to remove . . . conditions of poverty, injustice, and racial discrimination.

Martin Luther King, Jr. (1929–68) US civil rights leader. Quoted in *Rebels Against War* (Lawrence Wittner; 1969)

14 When the whole of mankind consciously remoulds itself and changes the world, the era of world communism will dawn.

Mao Zedong (1893–1976) Chinese statesman. *On Practice* (1937)

15 Every Communist must grasp the truth, 'Political power grows out of the barrel of a gun'.

Mao Zedong (1893–1976) Chinese statesman. November 6, 1938. Speech, *Selected Works* (1961), vol. 2

16 A spectre is haunting Europe—the specter of communism.

Karl Marx (1818–83) German philosopher. Opening words. *The Communist Manifesto* (co-written with Friedrich Engels; 1848)

17 In communist society . . . society regulates the general production and thus makes it possible for me to do one thing today and another tomorrow, to hunt in the morning, fish in the afternoon, rear cattle in the evening, criticize after dinner, just as I have a mind.

Karl Marx (1818–83) German philosopher. *The German Ideology* (1846)

18 It looks like a duck, walks like a duck, and quacks like a duck.

Joseph McCarthy (1909–57) US politician. Suggested method of identifying a communist. McCarthy gave his name to the anticommunist movement in the 1940s and 1950s, which was institutionalized as the House Un-American Activities Committee. Attrib.

19 Between complete Socialism and Communism there is no difference whatever in my mind. Communism is in fact the completion of Socialism; when that ceases to be militant and becomes triumphant, it will be Communism.

William Morris (1834–96) British designer, socialist reformer, and poet. Speech to Hammersmith Socialist Society, London (1893)

20 All right then, make the whole republic into a collective farm—but it'll still end up the property of one man!

Andrei Platonov (1899–1951) Russian writer. December 1929-April 1930. A peasant's prophetic response to collectivization. *The Foundation Pit* (Robert Chandler and Geoffrey Smith, trs.; December 1929–April 1930)

21 Communism is like prohibition, it's a good idea but it won't work.

Will Rogers (1879–1935) US actor, writer, and humorist. 1927. *Weekly Articles* (1981), vol. 3

22 For us in Russia communism is a dead dog, while, for many people in the West, it is still a living lion.

Alexander Solzhenitsyn (b. 1918) Russian novelist. *Listener* (February 15, 1979)

23 Communism fits Germany as a saddle does a cow.

Joseph Stalin (1879–1953) Soviet dictator. August 1944. Quoted in *Quotations in History* (A. Palmer and V. Palmer; 1976)

24 I have seen the future and it works.

Lincoln Steffens (1866–1936) US journalist. Said originally to US economist and financier Bernard Baruch, after visiting the Soviet Union in 1919. *Letters* (1938), vol. 1

25 Communism is the corruption of a dream of justice.

Adlai Stevenson (1900–65) US statesman. Speech, Urbana (1951)

26 Communism continued to haunt Europe as a spectre—a name men gave to their own fears and blunders. But the crusade against Communism was even more imaginary than the spectre of Communism.

A. J. P. Taylor (1906–90) British historian. *The Origins of the Second World War* (1961), ch. 2

27 Lenin's method leads to this: the party organization at first substitutes itself for the party as a whole. Then the central committee substitutes itself for the party organization, and finally a single dictator substitutes himself for the central committee.

Leon Trotsky (1879–1940) Russian revolutionary leader. Attrib.

Competition

see also **Failure, Loss, Success, Victory**

1 It ain't over 'til it's over.

Yogi Berra (b. 1925) US baseball player, manager, and coach. Said at the time of the 1973 pennant race, when Berra's team the Mets were being notoriously inconsistent. Remark (1973)

2 Keeping up with the Joneses was a full-time job with my mother and father. It was not until many years later when I lived alone that I realized how much cheaper it was to drag the Joneses down to my level.

Quentin Crisp (1908–99) British writer. *The Naked Civil Servant* (1968)

3 It's hard for me to deal with other prima donnas.

Marvin Gaye (1939–84) US singer and songwriter. Referring to Diana Ross. Quoted in *Divided Soul: The Life of Marvin Gaye* (David Ritz; 1985)

4 Competition is a performance stimulant.

Rosabeth Moss Kanter (b. 1943) US management educator, consultant, and writer. *When Giants Learn to Dance* (1989)

5 Intellectual capital is the sum of everything everybody in a company knows that gives it a competitive edge.

Thomas A. Stewart (b. 1948) US journalist. *Intellectual Capital* (1997)

Complaints

see also **Alibis and Excuses, Apologies, Insults**

1 Here I am, brain the size of a planet and they ask me to take you down the bridge.

Douglas Adams (1952–2001) British writer. A typical complaint from Marvin the computer. *The Hitch Hiker's Guide to the Galaxy* (1979), ch. 11

2 To complain of the age we live in, to murmur at the present possessors of power, to lament the past, to conceive extravagant hopes of the future, are the common dispositions of the greatest part of mankind.

Edmund Burke (1729–97) Irish-born British statesman and political philosopher. *Thoughts on the Cause of the Present Discontents* (1770)

3 The world is disgracefully managed, one hardly knows to whom to complain.

Ronald Firbank (1886–1926) British novelist. *Vainglory* (1915)

4 Nobody ever tells me anything.

John Galsworthy (1867–1933) British novelist and playwright. Repeatedly said by James Forsyte in *The Man of Property* (1906) and *In Chancery* (1920). *The Man of Property* (1906), pt. 1, ch. 1

5 I can't get no satisfaction.

Mick Jagger (b. 1943) British rock musician and songwriter. Song lyric. 'Satisfaction' (co-written with Keith Richards; 1965)

6 Nay, Madam, when you are declaiming, declaim; and when you are calculating, calculate.

Samuel Johnson (1709–84) British lexicographer and writer. April 29, 1776. Commenting on Mrs. Thrale's discourse on the price of children's clothes. Quoted in *Life of Samuel Johnson* (James Boswell; 1791)

7 I want to register a complaint. Do you know who sneaked into my room at three o'clock this morning? . . .
—Who? . . .
Nobody, and that's my complaint.

Groucho Marx (1895–1977) US comedian and film actor. *Monkey Business* (S. J. Perelman, Will B. Johnstone, and Arthur Sheekman; 1931)

8 I have always been a grumbler. I am designed for the part—sagging face, weighty underlip, rumbling, resonant voice. Money couldn't buy a better grumbling outfit.

J. B. Priestley (1894–1984) British writer. *Guardian* (August 15, 1984)

9 There are so many things to complain of in this household that it would never have occurred to me to complain of rheumatism.

Saki (1870–1916) British short-story writer. 'The Quest', *The Chronicles of Clovis* (1911)

10 QUEEN The lady doth protest too much, methinks.

William Shakespeare (1564–1616) English poet and playwright. *Hamlet* (1601), Act 3, Scene 2

Compliments

see also **Flattery, Praise, Sycophancy**

1 SONYA I'm not beautiful.
HELEN You have lovely hair.
SONYA No, when a woman isn't beautiful, people always say, 'You have lovely eyes, you have lovely hair'.

Anton Chekhov (1860–1904) Russian playwright and short-story writer. *Uncle Vanya* (1897), Act 3

2 Most people are such fools that it is really no great compliment to say that a man is above the average.

Somerset Maugham (1874–1965) British writer. *A Writer's Notebook* (1949)

3 I get no kick from champagne.
Mere alcohol doesn't thrill me at all,
So tell me why should it be true
That I get a kick out of you?

Cole Porter (1893–1964) US songwriter and composer. Song lyric. 'I Get a Kick Out of You', *Anything Goes* (1934)

4 She would rather light candles than curse the darkness, and her glow has warmed the world.

Adlai Stevenson (1900–65) US statesman. 1962. On learning of the death of Eleanor Roosevelt. *New York Times* (November 8, 1962)

5 As time requireth, a man of marvellous mirth and pastimes, and sometimes of as sad gravity, as who say: a man for all seasons.

Robert Whittington (b. 16th century) English writer. Referring to Sir Thomas More. After Erasmus. 'De Constructione Nominum', *Vulgaria* (1521), pt. 2

Compromise

see also **Decision, Diplomacy**

1 When manufacturers compromise, they change our dreams. When creators do not compromise, they change reality.

Edward Bond (b. 1934) British playwright. *The Hidden Plot* (2000)

2 A cockroach world of compromise.

Angela Carter (1940–92) British novelist, essayist, and short-story writer. *Wise Children* (1991)

3 Compromise used to mean that half a loaf was better than no bread. Among modern statesmen it really seems to mean that half a loaf is better than a whole loaf.

G. K. Chesterton (1874–1936) British writer and poet. *What's Wrong with the World* (1910)

4 Compromise is . . . on the same plane as fighting. War will continue—between capital and labor, between nation and nation—until we relinquish the ideas of concession and compromise.

Mary Parker Follett (1868–1933) US social worker and management theorist. *The New State* (1920)

5 It is quite unnecessary for me to bend and bow my reason, for that my knees will suffice.

Michel de Montaigne (1533–92) French essayist. Quoted in *The Jingle Bell Principle* (Miroslav Holub; 1992)

6 TOUCHSTONE Your 'If' is the only peace-maker; much virtue in 'If'.

William Shakespeare (1564–1616) English poet and playwright. *As You Like It* (1599), Act 5, Scene 4

Computers

see also **Internet, Machines, Technology**

1 Computer networks have a tremendous capacity . . . to bring people together by extending the already diverse and complex ties that people have among themselves.

Philip A. Agre, US author. 'Building Community Networks', *Reinventing Technology, Rediscovering Community: Critical Explorations of Computing as a Social Practice* (Philip A. Agre and Douglas Schuler, eds.; 1997)

2 In these days of computer viruses, asking if you may put your disk into someone's computer is the technological equivalent of unsafe sex.

Ruth Dudley Edwards (b. 1944) Irish historian and journalist. *Independent* (January 9, 1995)

3 The world is divided between users of the Macintosh computer and users of MS-DOS compatible computers. I am firmly of the opinion that the Macintosh is Catholic and that DOS is Protestant.

Umberto Eco (b. 1932) Italian writer and literary scholar. 'La bustina di Minerva', *Espresso* (September 30, 1994)

4 I've heard that myth quite seriously expressed in my church—that the beast in the Book of Revelation will be a monster computer.

Bill Ellis, British specialist in modern folklore. *Independent* (December 13, 1994)

5 Digital tools magnify the abilities that make us unique in the world: the ability to think, the ability to articulate our thoughts, the ability to work together to act on those thoughts.

Bill Gates (b. 1955) US business executive. *Business@the Speed of Thought: Using a Digital Nervous System* (co-written with Collins Hemingway; 1999)

6 It's like a light bulb. When it's broken, unplug it, throw it away and plug in another.

Ted Hoff (b. 1937) US electronics engineer. Explaining how he would repair a computer. Attrib.

7 From then on, when anything went wrong with a computer, we said it had bugs in it.

Grace Murray Hopper (1906–92) US navy officer and mathematician. 1945. Referring to the extraction of a 2-inch-long moth from an experimental computer. Quoted in *Speaking Freely* (Stuart Berg Flexner and Anne H. Soukhanov; 1997)

8 To err is human, but to really foul things up requires a computer.

Philip Howard (b. 1933) British journalist and author. *Times* (February 25, 1987)

9 Computers and art can bring out the worst in each other when they first meet . . . Technology can be a jalapeno pepper in a French sauce.

Nicholas Negroponte, US business executive and writer. *Being Digital* (1995)

10 Like a force of nature, the digital age cannot be denied or stopped. It has four very powerful qualities that will result in its ultimate triumph: decentralizing, globalizing, harmonizing, and empowering.

Nicholas Negroponte, US business executive and writer. *Being Digital* (1995)

11 It is almost genetic in its nature, in that each generation will become more digital than the preceding one.

Nicholas Negroponte, US business executive and writer. Referring to the impact of computer technologies on society. *Being Digital* (1995)

12 The democratization of computer power would alter the balance between the individual and the institution.

Frank Rose, US author. *West of Eden* (1989)

13 Macintosh was an artificial arrangement of silicon and metal designed to manipulate electrons according to the strict rules of logic; but its appeal transcended logic . . . this was no mere 'productivity tool' but a machine to free the human spirit.

Frank Rose, US author. Referring to a computer made by Apple Computer Inc. *West of Eden* (1989)

14 Computers seemed destined to be nodes on the network, not bastions of individual creativity.

Frank Rose, US author. Referring to the rise of the Internet. *West of Eden* (1989)

15 If computerized information services have any natural place in a democratic society, it is in the public library.

Theodore Roszak (b. 1933) US writer and editor. *The Cult of Information* (1986)

16 Computer technology . . . could play a role in rebuilding community by improving communication, economic opportunity, civic participation, and education.

Douglas Schuler, US author. *Reinventing Technology* (co-edited with Philip E. Agre; 1997)

17 Computers today are superhuman in their ability to handle numbers, but still infantile in their ability to handle ideas and concepts.

Clive Sinclair (b. 1940) British inventor and entrepreneur. Quoted in 'Creativity and Inventiveness', *The Roots of Excellence* (Ronnie Lessem; 1985), ch. 5

18 What I'd like to see, in due course, is a computer which has some sort of personality so that you can go round to it in the morning and talk to it.

Clive Sinclair (b. 1940) British inventor and entrepreneur. Quoted in 'Creativity and Inventiveness', *The Roots of Excellence* (Ronnie Lessem; 1985), ch. 5

19 The rise of computers . . . is forcing machinery to adapt to our idiosyncratic humanity.

Thomas A. Stewart (b. 1948) US journalist. *Intellectual Capital* (1997)

20 Footprints across an artificial reality are as evanescent as data on the Ethernet.

Clifford Stoll, US astronomer and author. Ethernet is a trademark for a system for exchanging messages between computers on a local area network. *Silicon Snake Oil* (1995)

21 Our networks aren't simple connections of cables and computers; they're cooperative communities.

Clifford Stoll, US astronomer and author. Referring to use of the Internet among groups of people. *Silicon Snake Oil* (1995)

22 First get it through your head that computers are big, expensive, fast, dumb adding-machine-typewriters. Then realize that most of the computer technicians that you're likely to meet or hire are complicators, not simplifiers.

Robert Townsend (b. 1920) US business executive. *Further Up the Organization* (1984)

23 No crash-proof system can be built unless it is made for an idiot.

Ellen Ullman, US author. Referring to the design of computer software. 'Out of Time: Reflections on the Programming Life', *Harper's* (June 1995)

24 I think there is a world market for about five computers.

Thomas J. Watson (1874–1956) US industrialist. 1943. Attrib.

Conceit

see also **Arrogance**, **Pride**, **Vanity**

1 It was prettily devised of Aesop, 'The fly sat upon the axletree of the chariot-wheel and said, what a dust do I raise'.

Francis Bacon (1561–1626) English philosopher, statesman, and lawyer. 'Of Vain-Glory', *Essays* (1625)

2 Only the insane take themselves quite seriously.

Max Beerbohm (1872–1956) British essayist, critic, and caricaturist. Quoted in *Max: A Biography* (D. Cecil; 1964)

3 He was like a cock who thought the sun had risen to hear him crow.

George Eliot (1819–80) British novelist. *Adam Bede* (1854)

4 Conceit is the finest armour a man can wear.

Jerome K. Jerome (1859–1927) British novelist and playwright. *Idle Thoughts of an Idle Fellow* (1886)

5 You must not think me necessarily foolish because I am facetious, nor will I consider you necessarily wise because you are grave.

Sydney Smith (1771–1845) British clergyman, essayist, and wit. Letter to Bishop Blomfield (1840)

6 Isn't it? I know in my case I would grow intolerably conceited.

James Abbott McNeill Whistler (1834–1903) US painter and etcher. Replying to the pointed observation that it was as well that we do not see ourselves as others see us. Quoted in *The Man Whistler* (H. Pearson; 1978)

Conflict

see also **Fighting**, **War**

1 We should look in society not for consensus, but for ineliminable and acceptable conflicts, and for rationally controlled hostilities, as the normal condition of mankind . . . Harmony and inner consensus come with death.

Stuart Hampshire (1914–83) British philosopher. *Innocence and Experience* (1989)

2 Antagonism is a form of struggle within a contradiction, but not the universal form.

Mao Zedong (1893–1976) Chinese statesman. *On Contradiction* (1937), quoted in *Mao Tsetung: An Anthology of His Writings* (Anne Fremantle, ed.; 1962)

3 Arms on armour clashing brayed
Horrible discord, and the madding wheels
Of brazen chariots raged; dire was the noise
Of conflict.

John Milton (1608–74) English writer. The war in Heaven. *Paradise Lost* (1667), bk. 6, ll. 209–212

Conformity

see also **Normality**, **Orthodoxy**

1 When in Rome, live as the Romans do: when elsewhere, live as they live elsewhere.

Saint Ambrose (339?–397) German-born Roman Doctor of the Church. Advice given to Saint Augustine. Attrib.

2 Our researchers into Public Opinion are content
That he held the proper opinions for the time of year;
When there was peace, he was for peace; when there was war, he went.

W. H. Auden (1907–73) British poet. 'The Unknown Citizen' (1940)

3 You cannot make a man by standing a sheep on its hind legs. But by standing a flock of sheep in that position you can make a crowd of men.

Max Beerbohm (1872–1956) British essayist, critic, and caricaturist. *Zuleika Dobson* (1911), ch. 9

4 He that complies against his will,
Is of his own opinion still.

Samuel Butler (1612–80) English satirist. *Hudibras* (1678), pt. 3, can. 2

5 It's a burden to us even to be human beings—men with our own real body and blood; we are ashamed of it, we think it a disgrace and try to contrive to be some sort of impossible generalized man.

Fyodor Dostoyevsky (1821–81) Russian novelist. *Notes from the Underground* (1864)

6 The conformist is not born. He is made . . .
Many teachers and professors seem hell-bent on
imbuing their students with a desire to achieve
'security' above all.

J. Paul Getty (1892–1976) US oil magnate. *How to be Rich* (1966)

7 When people are free to do as they please, they
usually imitate each other.

Eric Hoffer (1902–83) US philosopher and longshoreman. *The
Passionate State of Mind* (1954)

8 Homogeneity is a form of denial . . . because
diversity, the differences between groups, is still the
excuse for discrimination, disempowerment and
even genocide. We have been taught to hate or
deny our differences rather than to welcome them.

Nancy Kline, US author. *Time to Think* (1999)

Confusion

see also **Chaos**

1 Anyone who isn't confused here doesn't really
understand what's going on.

Anonymous. Referring to the sectarian problems in Northern
Ireland.

2 If confusion is the sign of the times, I see at the
root of this confusion a rupture between things
and words, between things and the ideas and
signs that are their representation.

Antonin Artaud (1896–1948) French actor, playwright, and writer. *The
Theatre and its Double* (1938)

3 I've not got a first in philosophy without being
able to muddy things pretty satisfactorily.

John Banham (b. 1940) British business executive. 1986. Referring to
his vagueness in interviews. *Guardian* (May 1, 1986)

4 Misunderstandings pile up, as if autumn's fallen
leaves were to be confused with an indication of
spring.

Ariel Dorfman (b. 1942) Chilean playwright and novelist. *Hard Rain*
(1973)

5 I had nothing to offer anybody except my own
confusion.

Jack Kerouac (1922–69) US writer. *On the Road* (1957), pt. 2

6 Confusion is a word we have invented for an
order which is not understood.

Henry Miller (1891–1980) US novelist. 'On the Ovarian Trolley: An
Interlude', *Tropic of Capricorn* (1939)

7 CASCA For mine own part, it was Greek to me.

William Shakespeare (1564–1616) English poet and playwright. *Julius
Caesar* (1599), Act 1, Scene 2

Conscience

see also **Honesty, Morality**

1 There is another man within me, that's angry
with me, rebukes, commands, and dastards me.

Thomas Browne (1605–82) English physician and writer. *Religio Medici*
(1642)

2 Conscience and self-love, if we understand our
true happiness, always lead us the same way.

Joseph Butler (1692–1752) English philosopher and theologian. *Fifteen
Sermons* (1726), no. 3

3 Why should not *Conscience* have *Vacation*
As well as other Courts o' th' Nation?

Samuel Butler (1612–80) English satirist. *Hudibras* (1664), pt. 2,
can. 2, ll. 323–324

4 All a man can betray is his conscience.

Joseph Conrad (1857–1924) Polish-born British novelist. *Under Western
Eyes* (1911)

5 Never do anything against conscience, even if the
state demands it.

Albert Einstein (1879–1955) German-born US physicist. Quoted in
Albert Einstein, Philosopher-Scientist (Paul A. Schilpp, ed.;
1949)

6 Evil societies always kill their consciences.

James Farmer (b. 1920) US civil rights leader. *Lay Bare The Heart:
An Autobiography of the Civil Rights Movement* (1985)

7 Conscience is the internal perception of the
rejection of a particular wish operating within us.

Sigmund Freud (1856–1939) Austrian psychoanalyst. *Totem and Taboo*
(1913)

8 The paradoxical—and tragic—situation of a man
is that his conscience is weakest when he needs it
most.

Erich Fromm (1900–80) German-born US psychoanalyst and philosopher.
Man for Himself (1947)

9 The disease of an evil conscience is beyond the
practice of all the physicians of all the countries
in the world.

William Ewart Gladstone (1809–98) British statesman. Speech at
Plumstead, London (1887)

10 Conscience is a coward, and those faults it has
not strength enough to prevent it seldom has
justice enough to accuse.

Oliver Goldsmith (1730–74) Irish-born British novelist, playwright, and
poet. *The Vicar of Wakefield* (1766), ch. 13

11 I cannot and will not cut my conscience to fit
this year's fashions, even though I long ago came
to the conclusion that I was not a political
person and could have no comfortable place in
any political group.

Lillian Hellman (1905–84) US playwright. Hellman was called before
the House (of Representatives) Committee on Un-American
Activities in 1952. She testified about her own activities, but
refused to discuss those of anybody else. Letter to John S.
Wood, *US Congress Committee Hearing on Un-American
Activities* (May 19, 1952), pt. 8

12 The one thing that doesn't abide by majority rule
is a person's conscience.

Harper Lee (b. 1926) US writer. *To Kill a Mockingbird* (1960),
ch. 11

13 Conscience is the inner voice that warns us
somebody may be looking.

H. L. Mencken (1880–1956) US journalist, critic, and editor. *A Little
Book in C Major* (1916)

14 We cannot appeal to the conscience of the world
when our own conscience is asleep.

Carl von Ossietzky (1889–1938) German pacifist and journalist.
'Defeated Germany' (1920), quoted in *The Stolen Republic.
Selected Writings of Carl von Ossietzky* (Bruno Frei, ed.;
1971)

15 Don't you see that that blessed conscience of
yours is nothing but other people inside you?

Luigi Pirandello (1867–1936) Italian dramatist, novelist, and short-
story writer. *Each in His Own Way* (Arthur Livingstone, tr.;
1924)

16 A bad conscience creates malignant behaviour.
You make somebody else bad in order to free
yourself from responsibility. We call that the
Emotional Plague.

Wilhelm Reich (1897–1957) Austrian psychoanalyst. 1952. Quoted in
Reich Speaks of Freud (M. Higgins, ed.; 1967)

17 A man has less conscience when in love than in any other condition.

Arthur Schopenhauer (1788–1860) German philosopher. 'The World as Will and Ideas' (1819), quoted in *The Metaphysics of Love and the Sexes* (R. B. Haldane and J. Kemp, eds.; 1886)

18 HAMLET The play's the thing
Wherein I'll catch the conscience of the King.

William Shakespeare (1564–1616) English poet and playwright. *Hamlet* (1601), Act 2, Scene 2

19 HAMLET Thus conscience does make cowards of us all;
And thus the native hue of resolution
Is sicklied o'er with the pale cast of thought.

William Shakespeare (1564–1616) English poet and playwright. *Hamlet* (1601), Act 3, Scene 1

20 WOLSEY A peace above all earthly dignities,
A still and quiet conscience.

William Shakespeare (1564–1616) English poet and playwright. *Henry VIII* (1613), Act 3, Scene 2

21 KING RICHARD III My conscience hath a thousand several tongues,
And every tongue brings in several tale,
And every tale condemns me for a villain.

William Shakespeare (1564–1616) English poet and playwright. *Richard III* (1591), Act 5, Scene 3

22 Labor to keep alive in your breast that little spark of celestial fire, called conscience.

George Washington (1732–99) US president. Washington's copybook when a schoolboy. 'Rules of Civility and Decent Behavior' (1740?), quoted in *The Writings of George Washington* (Jared Sparks; 1834–37), vol. 2

23 He was greatly pained at how little he was pained by the events of the afternoon.

Evelyn Waugh (1903–66) British novelist. *Decline and Fall* (1928), pt. 3, ch. 4

Consciousness

see also **Being, Mind, Philosophy**

1 Every mental act is conscious; it includes within it a consciousness of itself.

Franz Brentano (1838–1917) German philosopher. *Psychology from an Empirical Standpoint* (1874)

2 Consciousness can neither be described nor defined.

John Dewey (1859–1952) US philosopher and educator. *Psychology* (1887)

3 The act of bringing anything into consciousness consists in separating it out from other elements through this distinguishing activity of attention.

John Dewey (1859–1952) US philosopher and educator. *Psychology* (1887)

4 The conscious mind may be compared to a fountain playing in the sun and falling back into the great subterranean pool of subconscious from which it rises.

Sigmund Freud (1856–1939) Austrian psychoanalyst. Quoted in *Bartlett's Unfamiliar Quotations* (Leonard Louis Levinson, ed.; 1972)

5 The poets and philosophers before me have discovered the unconscious; I have discovered the scientific method with which the unconscious can be studied.

Sigmund Freud (1856–1939) Austrian psychoanalyst. 1926. Remark on his 70th birthday. Quoted in *The Liberal Imagination* (Lionel Trilling; 1957)

6 One reason for the importance of the Freudian concept of the Unconscious is that it seems to provide a realm within which the dark gods can communicate with the baroque complexities of our semantic structures.

Ernest Gellner (1925–95) British anthropologist and philosopher. *The Psychoanalytic Movement* (1985)

7 Consciousness is thoroughgoing dialectical restlessness, this melee of presentations derived from sense and thought, whose differences collapse into oneness.

G. W. F. Hegel (1770–1831) German philosopher. 1807. *The Phenomenology of Mind* (J. B. Baillie, tr.; 1910)

8 For consciousness is, on the one hand, consciousness of the object, on the other, consciousness of itself.

G. W. F. Hegel (1770–1831) German philosopher. 1807. *The Phenomenology of Mind* (J. B. Baillie, tr.; 1910)

9 In work consciousness becomes aware of itself as it in truth is, and its empty notion of itself disappears.

G. W. F. Hegel (1770–1831) German philosopher. 1807. *The Phenomenology of Mind* (J. B. Baillie, tr.; 1910)

10 Consciousness . . . is nothing jointed; it flows. A 'river' or a 'stream' are the metaphors by which it is most naturally described.

William James (1842–1910) US psychologist and philosopher. *The Principles of Psychology* (1890), vol. 1

11 Consciousness, from our natal day, is of a teeming multiplicity of objects and relations, and what we call simple sensations are results of discriminative attention, pushed often to a very high degree.

William James (1842–1910) US psychologist and philosopher. *The Principles of Psychology* (1890), vol. 1

12 A consciousness constructs . . . that linguistic mechanism which will provide another consciousness with the chance of having the same thoughts, but nothing really passes between them.

Maurice Merleau-Ponty (1908–61) French existentialist philosopher. Quoted in *The Essential Writings of Merleau-Ponty* (A. L. Fisher, ed.; 1969)

13 We know what it is like to be conscious, but not how to put it in satisfactory scientific terms. Whatever it may precisely be, consciousness is a state of the body, a state of nerves.

Willard V. Quine (1908–2000) US philosopher. *Quiddities: An Intermittently Philosophical Dictionary* (1987)

14 All consciousness is consciousness *of* something.

Jean-Paul Sartre (1905–80) French philosopher, playwright, and novelist. *The Psychology of Imagination* (1948)

Consequences

see also **Choice, Destiny, Influence**

1 In nature one thing just happens after another. Cause and effect have their place only in our imaginative arrangements and extensions of these primary facts.

A. J. Ayer (1910–89) British philosopher. *The Central Questions of Philosophy* (1973)

2 Be not deceived: God is not mocked: for whatsoever a man soweth, that shall he also reap.

Bible. Galatians, *King James Bible* (1611), 6:7

3 We have no other notion of cause and effect, but
that of certain objects, which have *always
conjoin'd* together, and which in all past
instances have always been found inseparable.
David Hume (1711–76) Scottish philosopher and historian. *A Treatise of
Human Nature* (1739–40)

4 Logical consequences are the scarecrows of fools
and the beacons of wise men.
T. H. Huxley (1825–95) British biologist. 'On the Hypothesis that
Animals are Automata', *Science and Culture and Other
Essays* (1881)

5 The saws are sawing wood, But wood is also
sawing the saws . . . The wood sawn into boards
is fashioned into furniture. Saws just break and
are discarded.
Liu Shahe (b. 1931) Chinese writer and editor. 1972. Quoted in *The
Red Azalea* (Edward Morin, ed.; 1990)

6 MACBETH That but this blow
Might be the be-all and the end-all here—
But here upon this bank and shoal of time—
We'd jump the life to come.
William Shakespeare (1564–1616) English poet and playwright. *Macbeth*
(1606), Act 1, Scene 7

7 DROMIO Returned so soon! rather approach'd
too late.
The capon burns, the pig falls from the spit;
The clock hath strucken twelve upon the bell
My mistress made it one upon my cheek;
She is so hot because the meat is cold,
The meat is cold because you have not come
home,
You come not home because you have no
stomach,
You have no stomach, having broke your fast;
But we, that know what 'tis to fast and pray,
Are penitent for your default to-day.
William Shakespeare (1564–1616) English poet and playwright. *The
Comedy of Errors* (1594), Act 1, Scene 2

8 All organisms, including humans, are greatly
influenced by the consequences produced by their
own behaviour.
B. F. Skinner (1904–90) US psychologist. 'The Behavior of
Organisms' (1938)

Conservation

see **The Environment, Nature**

Conservatism

see also **Politics**

1 CONSERVATIVE, n. A statesman who is enamored
of existing evils, as distinguished from the
Liberal, who wishes to replace them with others.
Ambrose Bierce (1842–1914?) US writer and journalist. *The Devil's
Dictionary* (1911)

2 Considering the circumstances in which the
country finds itself, the most conservative thing is
to be a revolutionary.
Francisco Cambó (1876–1947) Spanish banker, industrialist, and political
leader. As the leader of the Catalan Conservatives, Francisco
Cambó supported Catalonian independence. Many so-called
revolutionaries were in favour of a united Spanish republic,
which he thought posed a threat to the independence of
Catalonia. Quoted in *The Spanish Labyrinth* (Gerald Brenan;
1943)

3 All conservatism is based upon the idea that if
you leave things alone you leave them as they
are. But you do not. If you leave a thing alone
you leave it to a torrent of change.
G. K. Chesterton (1874–1936) British writer and poet. *Orthodoxy*
(1909), ch. 7

4 A Conservative government is an organized
hypocrisy.
Benjamin Disraeli (1804–81) British prime minister and writer. Speech in
Parliament, *Hansard* (March 17, 1845), col. 1028

5 These are the days when men of all social
disciplines and all political faiths seek the
comfortable and the accepted; when the man of
controversy is looked upon as a disturbing
influence; when originality is taken to be a mark
of instability; and when, in minor modification of
the scriptural parable, the bland lead the bland.
J. K. Galbraith (b. 1908) Canadian-born US economist. *The Affluent
Society* (1958), ch. 1, sect. 3

6 Their Europeanism is nothing but imperialism
with an inferiority complex.
Denis Healey (b. 1917) British statesman. October 1962. Referring
to the policies of the Conservative Party. *Observer* (October
7, 1962), 'Sayings of the Week'

7 I do not know which makes a man more
conservative—to know nothing but the present,
or nothing but the past.
John Maynard Keynes (1883–1946) British economist. *The End of
Laissez-Faire* (1925), bk. 1

8 What is conservatism? Is it not adherence to the
old and tried, against the new and untried?
Abraham Lincoln (1809–65) US president. Speech (February 27,
1860)

9 It is time to get back to basics: to self-discipline
and respect for the law, to consideration for
others, to accepting responsibility for yourself
and your family, and not shuffling it off on the
state.
John Major (b. 1943) British prime minister. Speech, Conservative
party conference (October 8, 1993)

10 All reactionaries are paper tigers.
Mao Zedong (1893–1976) Chinese statesman. November 1957.
Speech to Communist International Congress, Moscow,
Selected Works (1961), vol. 4

11 The idea of the sacred is quite simply one of the
most conservative notions in any culture, because
it seeks to turn other ideas—Uncertainty,
Progress, Change—into crimes.
Salman Rushdie (b. 1947) Indian-born British novelist. *Imaginary
Homelands* (1991), pt. 12, ch. 4

Contempt

see also **Anger, Hate**

1 That whisky priest, I wish we had never had him
in the house.
Graham Greene (1904–91) British novelist. *The Power and the Glory*
(1940), pt. 1

2 Contempt mates well with pity.
Gloria Naylor (b. 1950) US novelist, producer, and playwright. *Linden
Hills* (1985)

3 HERO Disdain and scorn ride sparkling in her
eyes.
William Shakespeare (1564–1616) English poet and playwright. *Much
Ado About Nothing* (1598–99), Act 3, Scene 1

4 GLOUCESTER Teach not thy lip such scorn, for it was made
For kissing, lady, not for such contempt.
William Shakespeare (1564–1616) English poet and playwright. *Richard III* (1591), Act 1, Scene 2

Conversation

see also **Communication**, **Speech**

1 I have but ninepence in ready money, but I can draw for a thousand pounds.
Joseph Addison (1672–1719) English essayist, poet, and statesman. Comparing his ability to make conversation with his ability to write. Reply to a woman who complained 'of his having talked little in company'. Quoted in *Life of Samuel Johnson* (James Boswell; 1791), May 7, 1773

2 Unrhymed, unrhythmical, the chatter goes: Yet no one hears his own remarks as prose.
W. H. Auden (1907–73) British poet. 1963? 'At the Party', *Collected Poems* (Edward Mendelson, ed.; 1991), st. 1, ll. 1–2

3 'My idea of good company, Mr. Elliot, is the company of clever, well-informed people, who have a great deal of conversation; that is what I call good company'.
'You are mistaken', said he gently, 'that is not good company, that is the best'.
Jane Austen (1775–1817) British novelist. *Persuasion* (1818), ch. 16

4 Take away the miseries and you take away some folks' reason for living. Their conversation piece anyway.
Toni Cade Bambara (1939–95) US novelist, short-story writer, and educator. *The Salt Eaters* (1980)

5 I went to the Village at night and listened to the finest talkers in New York . . . But Humboldt was the best of them all. He was simply the Mozart of conversation.
Saul Bellow (b. 1915) Canadian-born US writer. *Humboldt's Gift* (1975)

6 JOHNSON Well, we had a good talk.
BOSWELL Yes, Sir; you tossed and gored several persons.
James Boswell (1740–95) Scottish lawyer and biographer. 1768. *The Life of Samuel Johnson* (1791), Summer 1768

7 Although there exist many thousand subjects for elegant conversation, there are persons who cannot meet a cripple without talking about feet.
Ernest Bramah (1868–1942) British writer. *The Wallet of Kai Lung* (1900)

8 So much they talk'd, so very little said.
Charles Churchill (1731–64) British poet. *The Rosciad* (1761), l. 550

9 It is his reasonable conversation which mostly frightens us in a madman.
Anatole France (1844–1924) French novelist, poet, and critic. Attrib.

10 Never speak of yourself to others; make them talk about themselves instead: therein lies the whole art of pleasing. Everyone knows it and everyone forgets it.
Edmond de Goncourt (1822–96) French novelist and diarist. *Idées et Sensations* (co-written with Jules de Goncourt; 1866)

11 Talking's something you can't do judiciously unless you keep in practice.
Dashiell Hammett (1894–1961) US detective-story writer. *The Maltese Falcon* (1930)

12 An indigestion is an excellent common-place for two people that never met before.
William Hazlitt (1778–1830) British essayist and critic. 'The Fight', *Literary Remains of W. Hazlitt* (1836)

13 When two Englishmen meet, their first talk is of the weather.
Samuel Johnson (1709–84) British lexicographer and writer. *The Idler* (June 24, 1758), no. 11

14 That is the happiest conversation where there is no competition, no vanity, but a calm quiet interchange of sentiments.
Samuel Johnson (1709–84) British lexicographer and writer. April 14, 1775. Quoted in *Life of Samuel Johnson* (James Boswell; 1791)

15 And the talk slid north, and the talk slid south With the sliding puffs from the hookah-mouth
Four things greater than all things are,
Women and Horses and Power and War.
Rudyard Kipling (1865–1936) Indian-born British writer and poet. 1890. 'Ballad of the King's Jest', *Barrack-Room Ballads and Other Verses* (1892)

16 The most incomprehensible talk comes from people who have no other use for language than to make themselves understood.
Karl Kraus (1874–1936) Austrian writer. 1909. Quoted in 'Sprüche und Widersprüche', *Karl Kraus* (Harry Zohn; 1971)

17 There is only one rule for being a good talker— learn to listen.
Christopher Darlington Morley (1890–1957) US writer and journalist. Attrib.

18 Beware of the conversationalist who adds 'in other words'. He is merely starting afresh.
Robert Morley (1908–92) British actor and playwright. *Observer* (December 6, 1964), 'Sayings of the Week'

19 Ideal conversation must be an exchange of thought, and not, as many of those who worry most about their shortcomings believe, an eloquent exhibition of wit or oratory.
Emily Post (1872–1960) US writer and columnist. *Etiquette* (1922), ch. 6

20 Conversation has a kind of charm about it, an insinuating and insidious something that elicits secrets from us just like love or liquor.
Seneca, 'the Younger' (4? BC–AD 65) Roman writer, philosopher, and statesman. *Epistulae Morales* (63?)

21 There is no such thing as conversation. It is an illusion. There are intersecting monologues, that is all.
Rebecca West (1892–1983) Irish-born British novelist, critic, and journalist. *There is No Conversation* (1935), ch. 1

22 No, no, Oscar, you forget. When you and I are together we never talk about anything except me.
James Abbott McNeill Whistler (1834–1903) US painter and etcher. Cable replying to Oscar Wilde's message: 'When you and I are together we never talk about anything except ourselves'. *The Gentle Art of Making Enemies* (1890)

23 A good listener is not someone who has nothing to say. A good listener is a good talker with a sore throat.
Katharine Whitehorn (b. 1926) British journalist and writer. Attrib.

24 'What ho!' I said, 'What ho!' said Motty. 'What ho! What ho!' 'What ho! What ho! What ho!' After that it seemed rather difficult to go on with the conversation.
P. G. Wodehouse (1881–1975) British-born US humorous writer. *Carry On, Jeeves!* (1925)

Cooking

see also **Eating, Food**

1 Too many cooks spoil the broth, but it only takes one to burn it.
Julia Child (b. 1912) US chef, writer, and television personality. Referring to the Woman Suffrage movement. *Julia Child's Kitchen* (1975), Introduction

2 Life is too short to stuff a mushroom.
Shirley Conran (b. 1932) British designer, novelist, and journalist. *Superwoman* (1975), Epigraph

3 Many excellent cooks are spoiled by going into the arts.
Paul Gauguin (1848–1903) French painter. Quoted in *Modern Plutarch* (John Cournos; 1928)

4 Take your hare when it is cased.
Hannah Glasse (1708–70) British cookery writer. The saying 'First catch your hare' has often been attributed incorrectly to Mrs. Beaton. It is proverbial and dates from the 14th century. The word 'cased' means 'skinned'. *The Art of Cookery Made Plain and Easy* (1747), ch. 1

5 Serve up in a clean dish, and throw the whole out of the window as fast as possible.
Edward Lear (1812–88) British writer and artist. 'To make an Amblongus Pie', *Nonsense Songs* (1871), quoted in *The Complete Nonsense of Edward Lear* (Holbrook Jackson, ed.; 1947)

6 You've been beating this steak too much, cook; it's too tender. Don't I always say that to be good, a whale-steak must be tough?
Herman Melville (1819–91) US novelist. *Moby Dick* (1851)

7 Cookery . . . a form of pandering which corresponds to medicine, and in the same way physical training has its counterfeit in beauty-culture.
Plato (428?–347? BC) Greek philosopher. *Gorgias* (4th century BC)

8 The vulgar boil, the learned roast an egg.
Alexander Pope (1688–1744) English poet. *Satires and Epistles of Horace Imitated* (1734), bk. 2, Epistle 2, l. 85

9 A good cook is like a sorceress who dispenses happiness.
Elsa Schiaparelli (1890–1973) Italian fashion designer. *A Shocking Life* (1954)

10 SECOND SERVANT 'Tis an ill cook that cannot lick his own fingers.
William Shakespeare (1564–1616) English poet and playwright. *Romeo and Juliet* (1595), Act 4, Scene 2

11 Broth is the foundation of Cookery.
Louis Eustache Ude (*fl.* 1810?) French chef. *The French Cook* (1813)

Corruption

see also **Bribery, Crime**

1 We have a cancer within, close to the Presidency, that is growing. It is growing daily.
John Dean (b. 1938) US presidential counsel. 1973. From a taped conversation with the president, Richard Nixon. Referring to the Watergate scandal. *The White House Transcripts* (1974)

2 We become like all mankind
Decent without Indecent within.
Mbella Sonne Dipoko (b. 1936) Cameroon novelist and poet. 'Our Destiny', *Black & White in Love* (1972)

3 It is no accident that the symbol of a bishop is a crook, and the sign of an archbishop is a double-cross.
Gregory Dix (1901–52) British monk. Attrib. Letter to *Times* (December 3, 1977)

4 Whatever is old corrupts, and the past turns to snakes.
Ralph Waldo Emerson (1803–82) US poet and essayist. 'Works and Days', *Society and Solitude* (1870)

5 Corruption, the most infallible symptom of constitutional liberty.
Edward Gibbon (1737–94) British historian. *The Decline and Fall of the Roman Empire* (1776–88), ch. 21

6 They had been corrupted by money, and he had been corrupted by sentiment. Sentiment was the more dangerous, because you couldn't name its price. A man open to bribes was to be relied upon below a certain figure, but sentiment might uncoil in the heart at a name, a photograph, even a smell remembered.
Graham Greene (1904–91) British novelist. *The Heart of the Matter* (1948), bk. 1, pt. 1, ch. 2

7 I don't give a shit what happens. I want you all to stonewall it, let them plead the Fifth Amendment, cover-up or anything else, if it'll save it, save the plan.
Richard Nixon (1913–94) US president. In a taped conversation referring to the Watergate cover-up. Remark (March 22, 1973)

8 When the President does it, that means it is not illegal.
Richard Nixon (1913–94) US president. Television interview (May 19, 1977), quoted in *I Gave Them a Sword* (David Frost; 1978), ch.8

9 When I want a peerage, I shall buy one like an honest man.
Lord Northcliffe (1865–1922) Irish-born British publisher. Quoted in *Swaff* (Tom Driberg; 1974), ch. 2

10 All things can corrupt perverted minds.
Ovid (43 BC–AD 17?) Roman poet. *Tristia* (AD 9)

11 Everything is perfect coming from the hands of the Creator; everything degenerates in the hands of man.
Jean-Jacques Rousseau (1712–78) French philosopher and writer. *Émile* (1762)

12 For sweetest things turn sourest by their deeds: Lilies that fester smell far worse than weeds.
William Shakespeare (1564–1616) English poet and playwright. Sonnet 94 (1609)

13 MARCELLUS Something is rotten in the state of Denmark.
William Shakespeare (1564–1616) English poet and playwright. *Hamlet* (1601), Act 1, Scene 4

14 KING In the corrupted currents of this world Offence's gilded hand may shove by justice.
William Shakespeare (1564–1616) English poet and playwright. *Hamlet* (1601), Act 3, Scene 3

15 You won the elections, but I won the count.
Anastasio Somoza Debayle (1925–80) Nicaraguan dictator. Replying to allegations of ballot-rigging. *Guardian* (June 17, 1977)

16 As long as I count the votes, what are you going to do about it?
Boss Tweed (1823–78) US politician. Referring to a ballot. Boss Tweed was notoriously corrupt. Remark, New York City (November 1871)

Countryside

see also **The Environment, Landscapes, Nature**

1   For the moors, for the moors where the short grass
    Like velvet beneath us should lie!
    For the moors, for the moors where each high pass
    Rose sunny against the clear sky!
    Emily Brontë (1818–48) British poet and novelist. 'Stanzas from
    November 1838' (November 1838)

2   It is my belief, Watson, founded upon my
    experience, that the lowest and vilest alleys of
    London do not present a more dreadful record of
    sin than does the smiling and beautiful
    countryside.
    Arthur Conan Doyle (1859–1930) Scottish-born British writer and physician.
    'Copper Beeches', *The Adventures of Sherlock Holmes* (1892)

3   DUKE SENIOR Hath not old custom made this life
    more sweet
    Than that of painted pomp? Are not these woods
    More free from peril than the envious court?
    Here feel we but the penalty of Adam,
    The seasons' difference; as, the icy fang
    And churlish chiding of the winter's wind,
    Which, when it bites and blows upon my body,
    Even till I shrink with cold, I smile and say,
    'This is no flattery'.
    William Shakespeare (1564–1616) English poet and playwright. *As You
    Like It* (1599), Act 2, Scene 1

4   Fortunate too is the man who has come to know
    the gods of the countryside.
    Virgil (70–19 BC) Roman poet. *Georgics* (29 BC), no. 2, l. 493

Courage

see also **Heroism, Self-Confidence**

1   The Red Badge of Courage
    Stephen Crane (1871–1900) US writer and journalist. Title of novel.
    (1895)

2   Courage is the price that Life exacts for granting
    peace.
    Amelia Earhart (1897–1937) US aviator. *Courage* (1927)

3   Nothing gives a fearful man more courage than
    another's fear.
    Umberto Eco (b. 1932) Italian writer and literary scholar. *The Name of
    the Rose* (William Weaver, tr.; 1980), Third Day: After
    Compline

4   Many will call me an adventurer—and that I am,
    only one of a different sort: one of those who
    risks his skin to prove his platitudes.
    Che Guevara (1928–67) Argentinian-born revolutionary. Written on
    leaving Cuba to resume an active role as a guerrilla leader,
    initially in the Congo and then Bolivia. Last letter to his
    parents (1965)

5   Grace under pressure.
    Ernest Hemingway (1899–1961) US writer. Said on being asked for
    his definition of 'guts' in an interview with Dorothy Parker.
    Quoted in 'The Artist's Reward', *New Yorker* (Dorothy
    Parker; November 30, 1929)

6   Tender-handed stroke a nettle,
    And it stings you for your pains;
    Grasp it like a man of mettle,
    And it soft as silk remains.
    Aaron Hill (1685–1750) English poet and playwright. 'Tender Handed
    Stroke of a Nettle', *The Works of the Late Aaron Hill* (1753),
    st. 1

7   If the world should break and fall on him, its
    ruins would strike him unafraid.
    Horace (65–8 BC) Roman poet. Referring to the 'just and tenacious
    man'. *Odes* (23? BC), bk. 3, no. 3, l. 7

8   Let your courage rise with danger.
    Albert Luthuli (1898–1967) Rhodesian-born South African nationalist
    leader. Quoted in *Long Walk to Freedom* (Nelson Mandela;
    1994)

9   'It is hard to be brave', said Piglet, sniffing
    slightly, 'when you're only a Very Small Animal'.
    A. A. Milne (1882–1956) British writer. 'Kanga and Baby Roo',
    Winnie the Pooh (1926)

10 Courage consists of staying at home, close to
    nature, which could not care less about our
    disasters.
    Joan Miró (1893–1983) Catalan painter. Interview, *Cahiers D'Art*
    (Paris; 1936)

11 Any fool can be brave on a battle field when it's
    be brave or else be killed.
    Margaret Mitchell (1900–49) US novelist. *Gone with the Wind*
    (1936), ch. 31

12 As to moral courage, I have very rarely met with
    two o'clock in the morning courage: I mean
    instantaneous courage.
    Napoleon I (1769–1821) French emperor. *Les Cases, Mémorial de
    Ste-Hélène* (1815)

13 These are the times that try men's souls. The
    summer soldier and the sunshine patriot will, in
    this crisis, shrink from the service of their
    country; but he that stands it now, deserves the
    love and thanks of man and woman.
    Thomas Paine (1737–1809) English writer and political philosopher.
    Referring to the American War of Independence (1775–83).
    The American Crisis (December 23, 1776), no. 1

14 The brave man thinks of himself the last of all.
    Friedrich von Schiller (1759–1805) German poet, playwright, and historian.
    Wilhelm Tell (Patrick Maxwell, tr.; 1804), Act 1, Scene 1

15 AUSTRIA Courage mounteth with occasion.
    William Shakespeare (1564–1616) English poet and playwright. *King
    John* (1591–98), Act 2, Scene 1

16 Those who have courage to love should have
    courage to suffer.
    Anthony Trollope (1815–82) British novelist. *The Bertrams* (1859),
    ch. 27

17 Blessings on your young courage, boy; that's the
    way to the stars.
    Virgil (70–19 BC) Roman poet. *Aeneid* (29–19 BC), bk. 9, l. 641

18 Fortune favours the bold.
    Virgil (70–19 BC) Roman poet. *Aeneid* (29–19 BC), bk. 10, l. 284

Cowardice

see also **Fear, Weakness**

1   'I'm very brave generally', he went on in a low
    voice: 'only to-day I happen to have a headache'.
    Lewis Carroll (1832–98) British writer and mathematician. The White
    Knight. *Through the Looking-Glass and What Alice Found
    There* (1871), ch. 4

2   To know what is right and not to do it is the
    worst cowardice.
    Confucius (551–479 BC) Chinese philosopher, administrator, and moralist.
    Analects (5th century BC)

3   None but a coward dares to boast that he has
    never known fear.
    Ferdinand Foch (1851–1929) French general. Attrib.

4 Cowards in scarlet pass for men of war.

George Granville (1666–1735) British poet and playwright. *The She Gallants* (1696), Act 5

5 I hate a fellow whom pride, or cowardice, or laziness drives into a corner, and who does nothing when he is there but sit and *growl*; let him come out as I do, and *bark*.

Samuel Johnson (1709–84) British lexicographer and writer. October 10, 1782. Quoted in *Life of Samuel Johnson* (James Boswell; 1791)

6 I'm a hero with coward's legs. I'm a hero from the waist up.

Spike Milligan (1918–2002) Indian-born British humorist, writer, and actor. *Puckoon* (1963)

7 Some kids are cissies by nature, but I was a cissy by conviction.

Frank O'Connor (1903–66) Irish writer. 'The Genius', *My Oedipus Complex and Other Stories* (1953)

8 HAMLET What, frighted with false fire?

William Shakespeare (1564–1616) English poet and playwright. *Hamlet* (1601), Act 3, Scene 2

9 NYM I dare not fight; but I will wink and hold out mine iron.

William Shakespeare (1564–1616) English poet and playwright. *Henry V* (1599), Act 2, Scene 1

10 CAESAR Cowards die many times before their deaths:
The valiant never taste of death but once.

William Shakespeare (1564–1616) English poet and playwright. Dismissing his wife's fears for his life. *Julius Caesar* (1599), Act 2, Scene 2

11 I loathe people who keep dogs. They are cowards who haven't got the guts to bite people themselves.

August Strindberg (1849–1912) Swedish dramatist. *A Madman's Diary* (1895), pt. 3

Creation

see also **Beginning, Creativity, Evolution**

1 Had I been present at the Creation, I would have given some useful hints for the better ordering of the universe.

Alfonso X (1221–84) Spanish monarch. Referring to the complicated Ptolemaic model of the universe. Often quoted as, 'Had I been consulted I would have recommended something simpler'. Attrib.

2 In a sense human flesh is made of stardust. Every atom in the human body, excluding only the primordial hydrogen atoms, was fashioned in stars that formed, grew old and exploded most violently before the Sun and Earth came into being.

Nigel Calder (b. 1931) British science writer and broadcaster. January 27, 1977. Originally broadcast. *The Key to the Universe: a Report on the New Physics* (1977)

3 The mass starts into a million suns;
Earths round each sun with quick explosions burst,
And second planets issue from the first.

Erasmus Darwin (1731–1802) British physician, biologist, and poet. The first proposal of a 'big bang' theory of the universe. *The Botanic Garden* (1789–91)

4 Look, in short, at practically anything—the coot's feet, the mantis's face, a banana, the human ear—and see that not only did the creator create everything, but that he is apt to create *anything*. He'll stop at nothing.

Annie Dillard (b. 1945) US writer. *Pilgrim at Tinker's Creek* (1974), ch. 8

5 Everything has been written, everything has been said, everything has been made: that's what God heard before creating the world, when there was nothing yet. I have also heard that one, he may have answered from the old, split Nothingness. And then he began.

Macedonio Fernández (1874–1952) Argentinian philosopher, poet, and novelist. *The Museum of Eternity's Novel* (1967)

6 It took the whole of Creation
To produce my foot, my each feather:
Now I hold Creation in my foot.

Ted Hughes (1930–98) British writer and poet. 'Hawk Roosting', *Lupercal* (1960)

7 God comforted the gods.
If everything were left to him, he promised,
He could produce a new humanity -
Different from the first model and far
More prudently fashioned.

Ted Hughes (1930–98) British writer and poet. *Tales from Ovid* (1997)

8 God, or some other artist as resourceful,
Began to sort it out.
Land here, sky there.
And sea there.

Ted Hughes (1930–98) British writer and poet. *Tales from Ovid* (1997)

9 How could things have been as they are, were there not an original, inherent principle or order somewhere?

David Hume (1711–76) Scottish philosopher and historian. *Dialogues Concerning Natural Religion* (1779)

10 Do you not see that Allah has created the heavens and the earth with truth? He can destroy you if He wills and bring into being a new creation: that is no difficult thing for Him.

The Koran (7th century), Sura 14, ll. 19–20

11 We created man from dry clay, from black moulded loam, and before him Satan from smokeless fire.

The Koran (7th century), Sura 15, ll. 26–27

12 Our planet . . . consists largely of lumps of fall-out from a star-sized hydrogen bomb . . . Within our bodies, no less than three million atoms rendered unstable in that event still erupt every minute, releasing a tiny fraction of the energy stored from that fierce fire of long ago.

James Lovelock (b. 1919) British scientist. *Gaia: A New Look at Life on Earth* (1979)

13 If one can call the Creator to account, then I think he ought to be faulted for being too prodigal in the creation of life and too prodigal in its destruction.

Lu Xun (1881–1936) Chinese writer. 'Some Rabbits and a Cat' (1922)

14 Although, on this account, God could not have known what Adam and Eve, or Satan, would do if he created them, he could surely know what they *might* do . . . If so, he was taking, literally, a hell of a risk.

J. L. Mackie (1917–81) British philosopher. *The Miracle of Theism* (1982)

15 The planets in their station listening stood,
While the bright pomp ascended jubilant.
Open, ye everlasting gates, they sung,
Open, ye heavens, your living doors; let in
The great creator from his work returned
Magnificent, his six days' work, a world.

John Milton (1608–74) English writer. The Creation. *Paradise Lost* (1667), bk. 7, ll. 563–568

16 Occasionally someone remarks on what a lucky coincidence it is that the Earth is perfectly suitable for life . . . But this is, at least in part, a confusion of cause and effect.

Carl Sagan (1934–96) US astronomer and writer. *Cosmos* (1980)

17 We now have direct evidence of the birth of the Universe and its evolution . . . ripples in space-time laid down earlier than the first billionth of a second. If you're religious, it's like seeing God.

George Smoot (b. 1945) US astrophysicist. *Wrinkles in Time* (co-written with Keay Davidson; 1993)

18 The uniformity of earth's life, more astonishing than its diversity, is accountable by the high probability that we derived, originally, from some single cell, fertilized in a bolt of lightning as the earth cooled.

Lewis Thomas (1913–93) US physician and writer. *The Lives of a Cell* (1974)

19 The standard view in biology that all life emerged from a primordial soup on the Earth is far less likely than a tornado blowing through a junk yard and assembling a Boeing 747.

Chandra Wickramasinghe (b. 1939) Sri-Lankan born British scientist. 'Is Life an Astronomical Phenomenon?' (1980)

Creativity

see also **Creation, Imagination, Inventions, Writing**

1 Contradictions if well understood and managed can spark off the fires of invention. Orthodoxy whether of the right or of the left is the graveyard of creativity.

Chinua Achebe (b. 1930) Nigerian novelist, poet, and essayist. *Anthills of the Savannah* (1987)

2 Originality is the essence of true scholarship. Creativity is the soul of the true scholar.

Nnamdi Azikiwe (1904–96) Nigerian president, newspaper editor, and financier. Speech to Methodist Boy's High School, Lagos (November 11, 1934), quoted in *Zik: A Selection from the Speeches of Nnamdi Azikiwe* (1961)

3 Every animal leaves traces of what it was; man alone leaves traces of what he created.

Jacob Bronowski (1908–74) Polish-born British mathematician, poet, and humanist. *The Ascent of Man* (1973), ch. 1

4 Creative imagination awakens early. As children we are all 'makers'. Later, as a rule, we're broken of the habit; so the art of being a creative writer consists, among other things, in not allowing life or people or money to turn us aside from it.

Stig Dagerman (1923–54) Swedish writer. 'A Child's Memories', *Our Need of Faith* (Naomi Walford, tr.; 1955)

5 The artistic impulse seems not to wish to produce finished work. It certainly deserts us halfway, after the idea is born; and if we go on, art is labor.

Clarence Shepard Day (1874–1935) US writer. *This Simian World* (1920)

6 Man owes his success to his creativity. No one doubts the need for it. It is most useful in good times and essential in bad.

Edward de Bono (b. 1933) Maltese-born British psychologist and writer. *Lateral Thinking for Management* (1971)

7 It's like driving a car at night. You never see further than your headlights, but you can make the whole trip that way.

E. L. Doctorow (b. 1931) US novelist. Referring to his own creative technique. Quoted in *Writers at Work* (George Plimpton, ed.; 1988)

8 All in all the creative act is not performed by the artist alone; the spectator brings the work in contact with the external world by deciphering and interpreting its inner qualifications and thus adds his contribution to the creative act.

Marcel Duchamp (1887–1968) French-born US artist. Quoted in 'The Creative Act', *Marcel Duchamp* (Robert Lebel, ed., George Heard Hamilton, tr.; 1959)

9 'Who *is* the Potter, pray, and who the Pot?'

Edward FitzGerald (1809–83) British poet and translator. *The Rubáiyát of Omar Khayyám* (1859), st. 60

10 Creativeness often consists in turning up what is already there. Did you know that left and right shoes were thought up only a little more than a century ago?

Bernice Fitz-Gibbon (1895?–1982) US advertising executive. Attrib.

11 Yes, creation comes out more beautiful from a form rebellious to work, verse, marble, onyx, or enamel.

Théophile Gautier (1811–72) French poet and critic. 'L'Art', *Emaux et Camées* (1852)

12 All men are creative but few are artists.

Paul Goodman (1911–72) US writer, teacher, and psychotherapist. *Growing Up Absurd* (1960)

13 'Painters and poets alike have always had licence to dare anything'. We know that, and we both claim and allow to others in their turn this indulgence.

Horace (65–8 BC) Roman poet. The origin of 'artistic licence'. *Ars Poetica* (19–8 BC), l. 9

14 April 26 Welcome, O life! I go to encounter for the millionth time the reality of experience and to forge in the smithy of my soul the uncreated conscience of my race.

James Joyce (1882–1941) Irish writer. *A Portrait of the Artist as a Young Man* (1916), ch. 5

15 Creativity is a highfalutin word for the work I have to do between now and Tuesday.

Ray Kroc (1902–84) US restaurateur. Attrib.

16 I work like a gardener or a wine grower. Everything takes time. My vocabulary of forms, for example, did not come to me all at once. It formulated itself almost in spite of me.

Joan Miró (1893–1983) Catalan painter. Interview, *XXe Siècle* (Paris; February 15, 1959)

17 Man cannot produce a single work without the assistance of the slow, assiduous, corrosive worm of thought.

Eugenio Montale (1896–1981) Italian poet. *Poet in Our Time* (1972)

18 Those first songs I wrote, I was just taking notes at a fantastic rock concert that was going on inside my head.

Jim Morrison (1943–71) US rock singer and songwriter. Attrib.

19 I do not believe in the kind of art which has not forced its way out through man's need to open his heart—all art, literature as well as music, must be created with one's heart's blood.

Edvard Munch (1863–1944) Norwegian artist. Attrib.

20 We live at a time when man believes himself fabulously capable of creation, but he does not know what to create.

José Ortega y Gasset (1883–1955) Spanish writer and philosopher. *The Revolt of the Masses* (1930)

21 The more constraints one imposes, the more one frees one's self of the chains that shackle the spirit . . . the arbitrariness of the constraint only serves to obtain precision of execution.

Igor Stravinsky (1882–1971) Russian-born US composer. Quoted in *The Jingle Bell Principle* (Miroslav Holub; 1992)

22 The worst crime is to leave a man's hands empty. Men are born makers, with that primal simplicity in every maker since Adam. This is pre-history.

Derek Walcott (b. 1930) St. Lucian poet and playwright. *Omeros* (1990)

23 Technical skill is mastery of complexity while creativity is mastery of simplicity.

E. C. Zeeman (b. 1923) British mathematician. *Catastrophe Theory* (1977)

Cricket

see **Sports and Games**

Crime

see also **Corruption, Law, Society, Theft, Vice**

1 I think crime pays. The hours are good, you travel a lot.

Woody Allen (b. 1935) US film actor and director. *Take the Money and Run* (1969)

2 No punishment has ever possessed enough power of deterrence to prevent the commission of crimes. On the contrary, whatever the punishment, once a specific crime has appeared for the first time, its reappearance is more likely than its initial emergence could ever have been.

Hannah Arendt (1906–75) German-born US philosopher and historian. *Eichmann in Jerusalem* (1963), epilogue

3 Only crime and the criminal, it is true, confront us with the perplexity of radical evil; but only the hypocrite is really rotten to the core.

Hannah Arendt (1906–75) German-born US philosopher and historian. *On Revolution* (1963), ch. 2

4 How many crimes committed merely because their authors could not endure being wrong!

Albert Camus (1913–60) Algerian-born French novelist, essayist, and playwright. *The Fall* (1956)

5 When a doctor does go wrong he is the first of criminals. He has nerve and he has knowledge.

Arthur Conan Doyle (1859–1930) Scottish-born British writer and physician. 'The Speckled Band', *The Adventures of Sherlock Holmes* (1892)

6 He is the Napoleon of crime.

Arthur Conan Doyle (1859–1930) Scottish-born British writer and physician. Referring to Professor Moriarty. 'The Final Problem', *The Memoirs of Sherlock Holmes* (1894)

7 The reason of idleness and crime is the deferring of our hopes. Whilst we are waiting we beguile the time with jokes, with sleep, with eating, and with crimes.

Ralph Waldo Emerson (1803–82) US poet and essayist. 'Nominalist and Realist', *Essays, Second Series* (1844)

8 There are more criminals out of jail than in jail, the only difference is that the majority of those who are out, are such skillful criminals that they know how to keep themselves out.

Marcus Garvey (1887–1940) Jamaican-born black nationalist leader and publisher. Speech, Carnegie Hall, New York (August 1, 1924)

9 Crimes of which a people is ashamed constitute its real history. The same is true of man.

Jean Genet (1910–86) French writer. *The Screens* (1973), preparatory notes

10 Every crime destroys more Edens than our own.

Nathaniel Hawthorne (1804–64) US novelist and short-story writer. *The Marble Faun* (1860), vol. 1, ch. 23

11 Street crime begins psychologically in a walkless world; it begins on the drawing board of that planner who sees cities as collections of highrise buildings and convenience malls, with streets as mere efficient modes of access.

James Hillman (b. 1926) US author. 'Walking', *The City as Dwelling* (1980)

12 He who secretly meditates crime is as guilty as if he had committed the offence.

Juvenal (65?–128?) Roman poet. *Satires* (98?–128?), 13, l. 209

13 What man have you ever seen who was content with one crime only?

Juvenal (65?–128?) Roman poet. *Satires* (98?–128?), 13, l. 243

14 He had broken the law. How he had come to do so, it passed his imagination to recall. Crime always seems impossible in retrospect.

Stephen Leacock (1869–1944) British-born Canadian writer and economist. 'The Hostelry of Mr. Smith', *Sunshine Sketches of a Little Town* (1912)

15 Sometimes virtual crimes lie dormant, and operas are stored away in a maestro's head, only to await the creative influence of genius to inspire their opening bars.

Joaquim Maria Machado de Assis (1839–1908) Brazilian novelist and short-story writer. *Philosopher or Dog?* (Clotilde Wilson, tr.; 1892)

16 The study of crime begins with the knowledge of oneself.

Henry Miller (1891–1980) US novelist. 'The Soul of Anæsthesia', *The Air-Conditioned Nightmare* (1945)

17 We are more sensible of what is done against custom than against Nature.

Plutarch (46?–120?) Greek biographer and philosopher. 'Of Eating of Flesh' (1st–2nd century), Tract 1

18 Society . . . prepares crimes; criminals are only the instruments necessary for executing them.

Lambert Adolphe Jacques Quételet (1796–1874) Belgian astronomer and statistician. *On Man* (1835)

19 Crime, like virtue, has its degrees.

Racine (1639–99) French playwright. *Phèdre* (1677), Act 4, Scene 2

20 Crime which is prosperous and lucky is called virtue.

Seneca, 'the Younger' (4? BC–AD 65) Roman writer, philosopher, and statesman. 1st century AD. *Hercules Furens* (1st century), l. 251

21 From the one crime recognize them all as culprits.

Virgil (70–19 BC) Roman poet. *Aeneid* (29–19 BC), bk. 2, l. 65

22 I came to the conclusion many years ago that
almost all crime is due to the repressed desire for
aesthetic expression.
Evelyn Waugh (1903–66) British novelist. *Decline and Fall* (1928),
pt. 3. ch. 1

23 The crime is not to avoid failure. The crime is
not to give triumph a chance.
Huw Wheldon (1916–86) Welsh broadcaster and television executive.
Advice given to television producers. Attrib.

Criticism

see also **The Arts, Critics, Literary Insults, Reading**

1 I am bound by my own definition of criticism: a
disinterested endeavour to learn and propagate
the best that is known and thought in the world.
Matthew Arnold (1822–88) British poet and critic. 'Functions of
Criticism at the Present Time', *Essays in Criticism, First Series*
(1865)

2 A criticism of life under the conditions fixed for
such a criticism by the laws of poetic truth and
poetic beauty.
Matthew Arnold (1822–88) British poet and critic. 'The Study of
Poetry', *Essays in Criticism, Second Series* (1888)

3 There is less in this than meets the eye.
Tallulah Bankhead (1903–68) US actor. Referring to the play
Aglavaine and Selysette (1896) by Maurice Maeterlinck, said
to Alexander Woollcott. 'Capsule Criticism', *Shouts and
Murmurs* (A. Woollcott; 1922)

4 The pot calls the kettle black.
Miguel de Cervantes (1547–1616) Spanish novelist and playwright. *Don
Quixote* (1605–15), pt. 2, ch. 43

5 A great deal of contemporary criticism reads to
me like a man saying: 'Of course I do not like
green cheese: I am very fond of brown sherry'.
G. K. Chesterton (1874–1936) British writer and poet. 'On Jonathan
Swift', *All I Survey* (1933)

6 It was very close to the real thing—but it seemed
to last twice as long and be just as noisy.
Noël Coward (1899–1973) British playwright, actor, and songwriter. 1962.
Referring to the opening of Lionel Bart's musical *Blitz*. Attrib.

7 Come mothers and fathers
Throughout the land
And don't criticize
What you can't understand.
Bob Dylan (b. 1941) US singer and songwriter. Song lyric. 'The Times
They Are A-Changin' ' (1964)

8 Value judgments are founded on the study of
literature; the study of literature can never be
founded on value judgments.
Northrop Frye (1912–91) Canadian academic. *Anatomy of Criticism*
(1957)

9 Abuse is often of service. There is nothing so
dangerous to an author as silence.
Samuel Johnson (1709–84) British lexicographer and writer. Attrib.

10 The pleasure of criticizing robs us of the pleasure
of being moved by some very fine things.
Jean de La Bruyère (1645–96) French essayist and moralist. *Characters,
or the Manners of the Age* (1688)

11 When the reviews are bad I tell my staff that they
can join me as I cry all the way to the bank.
Liberace (1919–87) US pianist and entertainer. Said when asked
whether he minded being criticized. *Liberace: An
Autobiography* (1973), ch. 2

12 Talking about music is like dancing about
architecture.
Steve Martin (b. 1945) US comedian, actor, and writer. Attrib.

13 I was so long writing my review that I never got
around to reading the book.
Groucho Marx (1895–1977) US comedian and film actor. 1950? Attrib.

14 People ask you for criticism, but they only want
praise.
Somerset Maugham (1874–1965) British writer. *Of Human Bondage*
(1915), ch. 50

15 All of us, readers and writers, are bereft when
criticism remains too polite or too fearful to
notice a disrupting darkness before its eyes.
Toni Morrison (b. 1931) US novelist. *Playing in the Dark: Whiteness
and the Literary Imagination* (1992)

16 Prolonged, indiscriminate reviewing of books
involves constantly inventing reactions towards
books about which one has no spontaneous
feelings whatsoever.
George Orwell (1903–50) British writer. 'Confessions of a Book
Reviewer' (1946)

17 And make each day a critic on the last.
Alexander Pope (1688–1744) English poet. *An Essay on Criticism*
(1711), l. 571

18 Re-vision—the act of looking back, of seeing
with fresh eyes, of entering an old text from a
new critical direction—is for women more than a
chapter in cultural history: it is an act of survival.
Adrienne Rich (b. 1929) US poet and educator. 'When We Dead
Awaken', *On Lies, Secrets, and Silence* (1979)

19 I never read anything concerning my work. I feel
that criticism is a letter to the public which the
author, since it is not directed to him, does not
have to open and read.
Rainer Maria Rilke (1875–1926) Austrian poet and novelist. *Letters of
Rainer Maria Rilke* (Jane Bannard Greene and M. D. Norton,
trs.; 1945)

20 But whether thus submissively or not, at least be
sure that you go to the author to get at his
meaning, not to find yours.
John Ruskin (1819–1900) British art critic, writer, and reformer. 'Of
Kings' Treasuries', *Sesame and Lilies* (1865)

21 It does not follow . . . that the right to criticize
Shakespeare involves the power of writing better
plays. And in fact . . . I do not profess to write
better plays.
George Bernard Shaw (1856–1950) Irish playwright. *Three Plays for
Puritans* (1901), Preface

22 I never read a book before reviewing it; it
prejudices a man so.
Sydney Smith (1771–1845) British clergyman, essayist, and wit. Quoted
in *The Smith of Smiths* (H. Pearson; 1934), ch. 3

23 Interpretation is the revenge of the intellect upon art.
Susan Sontag (b. 1933) US writer. *Against Interpretation* (1966)

24 Your book has much in common with your
dress. As an arrangement of words it is graceless
without being random . . . as an experience it is
like sharing a cell with a fanatic in search of a
mania.
Tom Stoppard (b. 1937) Czech-born British playwright and screenwriter.
Travesties (1974), Act 2

25 You do not get a man's most effective criticism
until you provoke him. Severe truth is expressed
with some bitterness.
Henry David Thoreau (1817–62) US writer. *Journal* (March 15, 1854),
quoted in *The Writings of Henry David Thoreau* (1906)

26 Writing criticism is to writing fiction and poetry as hugging the shore is to sailing the open sea.
John Updike (b. 1932) US writer. *Hugging the Shore* (1983), Foreword

27 A strange, horrible business, but I suppose good enough for Shakespeare's day.
Victoria (1819–1901) British monarch. Giving her opinion of *King Lear*. Attrib.

28 I do not think this poem will reach its destination.
Voltaire (1694–1778) French writer and philosopher. Reviewing Rousseau's poem 'Ode to Posterity'. Attrib.

29 I saw it at a disadvantage—the curtain was up.
Walter Winchell (1879–1972) US journalist and broadcaster. Referring to a show starring Earl Carroll. Quoted in *Come to Judgment* (Alden Whiteman; 1980)

30 Praise and blame are much the same for the writer. One is better for your vanity, but neither gets you much further with your work.
Jeanette Winterson (b. 1959) British novelist. *Guardian* (June 18, 1994)

Critics

see also The Arts, Criticism, Media

1 The dog barks but the caravan passes on.
Mohamed al-Fayed (b. 1933) Egyptian businessman. Referring to his critics. Interview, *Daily Express* (March 14, 1990)

2 A critic is a bunch of biases held loosely together by a sense of taste.
Whitney Balliett (b. 1926) US jazz critic. *Dinosaurs in the Morning* (1962), introductory note

3 I will try to account for the degree of my aesthetic emotion. That, I conceive, is the function of the critic.
Clive Bell (1881–1964) British art critic. *Art* (1914), pt. 3, ch. 3

4 Intellectual currents can generate a sufficient head of water for the critic to install his power station on them.
Walter Benjamin (1892–1940) German writer and critic. 'Moscow', *Reflections* (Peter Demetz, ed.; 1986)

5 He who discommendeth others obliquely commendeth himself.
Thomas Browne (1605–82) English physician and writer. This essay was published posthumously. *Christian Morals* (1716), pt. 1

6 There spoke up a brisk little somebody, Critic and whippersnapper, in a rage To set things right.
Robert Browning (1812–89) British poet. 'Balaustion's Adventure' (1871), ll. 306–308

7 Critics! . . . Those cut-throat bandits in the paths of fame.
Robert Burns (1759–96) Scottish poet and songwriter. Attrib.

8 A man must serve his time to every trade Save censure—critics all are ready made Take hackney'd jokes from Miller, got by rote, With just enough of learning to misquote.
Lord Byron (1788–1824) British poet. *English Bards and Scotch Reviewers* (1809), ll. 63–6

9 I can explain all the poems that ever were invented—and a good many that haven't been invented just yet.
Lewis Carroll (1832–98) British writer and mathematician. *Through the Looking-Glass and What Alice Found There* (1871), ch. 6

10 If I had listened to the critics I'd have died drunk in the gutter.
Anton Chekhov (1860–1904) Russian playwright and short-story writer. Quoted in *Timebends* (Arthur Miller; 1987)

11 A good critic is one who narrates the adventures of his mind among masterpieces.
Anatole France (1844–1924) French novelist, poet, and critic. *The Literary Life* (1888), Preface

12 I sometimes think His critical judgement is so exquisite It leaves us nothing to admire except his opinion.
Christopher Fry (b. 1907) British playwright. *The Dark is Light Enough* (1954), Act 2

13 The critic is the historian who records the order of creation. In vain for the maker, who knows without learning it, but not in vain for the mind of his race.
Margaret Fuller (1810–50) US writer and reformer. *A Short Essay on Critics in Art, Literature and the Drama* (19th century)

14 The critic is . . . the younger brother of genius. Next to invention is the power of interpreting invention; next to beauty the power of appreciating beauty . . . The critic, then, should be not merely a poet, not merely a philosopher, not merely an observer, but tempered of all three.
Margaret Fuller (1810–50) US writer and reformer. 'A Short Essay on Critics', *The Dial* (1840), quoted in *The Heath Anthology of American Literature* (Paul Lauter, ed.; 1998), vol. 1

15 Asking a working writer what he thinks about critics is like asking a lamp-post how it feels about dogs.
Christopher Hampton (b. 1946) British playwright. *Sunday Times Magazine* (October 16, 1977)

16 A gifted glassblower of language.
John Hersey (1914–93) US writer. 1988. Referring to the literary critic I. A. Richards. *New Yorker* (July 18, 1988)

17 There is a certain race of men that either imagine it their duty, or make it their amusement, to hinder the reception of every work of learning or genius, who stand as sentinels in the avenues of fame, and value themselves upon giving Ignorance and Envy the first notice of a prey.
Samuel Johnson (1709–84) British lexicographer and writer. *The Rambler* (1750–52)

18 A fly, Sir, may sting a stately horse and make him wince; but one is but an insect, and the other is a horse still.
Samuel Johnson (1709–84) British lexicographer and writer. 1754. Referring to critics. Quoted in *Life of Samuel Johnson* (James Boswell; 1791)

19 He is your only good damner, and if I am ever damned I should like to be damned by him.
John Keats (1795–1821) English poet. Referring to William Hazlitt. Attrib.

20 Never trust the artist. Trust the tale. The proper function of a critic is to save the tale from the artist who created it.
D. H. Lawrence (1885–1930) British writer. *Studies in Classic American Literature* (1923), ch. 1

21 A drama critic is a person who surprises the playwright by informing him what he meant.
Wilson Mizner (1876–1933) US playwright. Attrib.

22 A critic should be a conduit, a bridge, but not a law.
Toni Morrison (b. 1931) US novelist. Interview, *Black Creation Annual* (1974–75)

23 Insects sting, not from malice, but because they want to live. It is the same with critics—they desire our blood, not our pain.

Friedrich Wilhelm Nietzsche (1844–1900) German philosopher and poet. *Miscellaneous Maxims and Reflections* (1880)

24 A critic is a legless man who teaches running.

Jackson Pollock (1912–56) US artist. Attrib.

25 Nor in the critic let the man be lost.

Alexander Pope (1688–1744) English poet. *An Essay on Criticism* (1711), l. 523

26 The greater part of critics are parasites, who, if nothing had been written, would find nothing to write.

J. B. Priestley (1894–1984) British writer. *Outcries and Asides* (1974)

27 And better had they ne'er been born,
Who read to doubt, or read to scorn.

Sir Walter Scott (1771–1832) Scottish novelist. *The Monastery* (1820), ch. 12

28 Pay no attention to what the critics say. No statue has ever been put up to a critic.

Jean Sibelius (1865–1957) Finnish composer. Attrib.

29 Unless a reviewer has the courage to give you unqualified praise, I say ignore the bastard.

John Steinbeck (1902–68) US novelist. 1958. Remark made during a chance meeting with J. K. Galbraith; both men were reading a hostile review of Galbraith's book. Quoted in *The Affluent Society* (John Kenneth Galbraith; 1977), Introduction

30 Time is the only critic without ambition.

John Steinbeck (1902–68) US novelist. Quoted in 'On Critics', *Writers at Work* (George Plimpton, ed.; 1977)

31 I doubt that art needed Ruskin any more than a moving train needs one of its passengers to shove it.

Tom Stoppard (b. 1937) Czech-born British playwright and screenwriter. Referring to John Ruskin. *Times Literary Supplement* (June 3, 1977)

32 I had another dream the other day about music critics. They were small and rodent-like with padlocked ears, as if they had stepped out of a painting by Goya.

Igor Stravinsky (1882–1971) Russian-born US composer. *Evening Standard* (October 29, 1969)

33 A critic is a man who knows the way but can't drive the car.

Kenneth Tynan (1927–80) British theatre critic. *New York Times Magazine* (January 9, 1966)

34 A good drama critic is one who perceives what is happening in the theatre of his time. A great drama critic also perceives what is not happening.

Kenneth Tynan (1927–80) British theatre critic. *Tynan Right and Left* (1967), Foreword

35 Has anybody ever seen a dramatic critic in the daytime? Of course not. They come out after dark, up to no good.

P. G. Wodehouse (1881–1975) British-born US humorous writer. Attrib.

Cruelty

see also **Hate, Pain, Suffering, Torture**

1 Fear is the parent of cruelty.

J. A. Froude (1818–94) British historian. 'Party Politics', *Short Studies on Great Subjects* (1877)

2 The idea that if you inflict cruelty on the living animal immediately before slaughter the result will be greater flavour and tenderness in the carcass still exists today.

Andrew Higgins (b. 1958) British journalist. *Independent on Sunday* (August 25, 1991)

3 At this, good Tray grew very red,
And growled, and bit him till he bled.

Heinrich Hoffman (1809–94) German physician and poet. 'Cruel Frederick', *Struwelpeter* (1845)

4 Cruelty is contagious in uncivilized communities.

Harriet Ann Jacobs (1813–97) US writer. *Incidents in the Life of a Slave Girl* (1861)

5 I cannot see how to refute the arguments for the subjectivity of ethical values, but I find myself incapable of believing that all that is wrong with wanton cruelty is that I don't like it.

Bertrand Russell (1872–1970) British philosopher and mathematician. 'Notes on Philosophy', *Philosophy* (1960), vol. 35

6 The infliction of cruelty with a good conscience is a delight to moralists. That is why they invented Hell.

Bertrand Russell (1872–1970) British philosopher and mathematician. 'On the Value of Scepticism', *Sceptical Essays* (1928)

7 HAMLET Let me be cruel, not unnatural;
I will speak daggers to her, but use none.

William Shakespeare (1564–1616) English poet and playwright. *Hamlet* (1601), Act 3, Scene 2

8 HAMLET I must be cruel only to be kind.

William Shakespeare (1564–1616) English poet and playwright. *Hamlet* (1601), Act 3, Scene 4

9 The cruelty of most people is lack of imagination, their brutality is ignorance.

Kurt Tucholsky (1890–1935) German philosopher. Quoted in 'Selected Aphorisms', *Kurt Tucholsky. The Ironic Sentimentalist* (Bryan P. Grenville; 1981)

Culture

see also **The Arts, Society**

1 Culture is the passion for sweetness and light, and (what is more) the passion for making them prevail.

Matthew Arnold (1822–88) British poet and critic. *Literature and Dogma* (1873), Preface

2 'Culture' is simply how one lives, and is connected to history by habit.

Imamu Amiri Baraka (b. 1934) US author, editor, playwright, and political activist. *Blues People: Negro Music in White America* (1963)

3 In the transmission of human culture, people always attempt to replicate, to pass on to the next generation the skills and values of the parents, but the attempt always fails because cultural transmission is geared to learning, not DNA.

Gregory Bateson (1904–80) British-born US anthropologist. *Mind and Nature* (1978)

4 Culture has never the translucidity of custom; it abhors all simplification.

Frantz Fanon (1925–61) Martiniquan social scientist, physician, and psychiatrist. 'On National Culture', *The Wretched of the Earth* (1961)

5 Looked at . . . from the side of universal mind *qua* general spiritual substance, culture means nothing else than that this substance gives itself its own self-consciousness, brings about its own inherent process and its own reflection into self.

G. W. F. Hegel (1770–1831) German philosopher. 1807. *The Phenomenology of Mind* (J. B. Baillie, tr.; 1910)

6 Whenever I hear the word 'culture' . . . I reach for my gun.

Hanns Johst (1890–1978) German novelist and playwright. Popularly attributed to Hermann Goering. The actual line Johst wrote was: 'Whenever I hear the word culture . . . I release the safety-catch of my Browning'. *Schlageter* (1933), Act 1, Scene 1

7 A people needs legends, heroes, myths. Deny them these and you have won half the battle against them.

John Oliver Killens (1916–87) US novelist, film scriptwriter, and educator. 'The Black Writer Vis-à-Vis His Country', *Black Man's Burden* (1965)

8 Culture is perishing in overproduction, in an avalanche of words, in the madness of quantity.

Milan Kundera (b. 1929) Czech novelist. *Immortality* (1991)

9 Culture is an instrument wielded by professors to manufacture professors, who when their turn comes will manufacture professors.

Simone Weil (1909–43) French philosopher, mystic, and political activist. *The Need for Roots* (A. F. Wills, tr.; 1952)

Curiosity

see also **Questions, Research**

1 Where now? Who now? When now? Unquestioning. I, say I. Unbelieving. Questions, hypotheses, call them that. Keep going, going on, call that going, call that on.

Samuel Beckett (1906–89) Irish playwright, novelist, and poet. *The Unnamable* (1958)

2 'Curiouser and curiouser!' cried Alice.

Lewis Carroll (1832–98) British writer and mathematician. *Alice's Adventures in Wonderland* (1865), ch. 2

3 There is no such thing on earth as an uninteresting subject; the only thing that can exist is an uninterested person.

G. K. Chesterton (1874–1936) British writer and poet. *Heretics* (1905), ch. 1

4 He was the most relentlessly curious man in history. Everything he saw made him ask how and why. Why does one find sea-shells in the mountains? How do they build locks in Flanders? . . . Find out; write it down; if you can see it, draw it.

Kenneth Clark (1903–83) British art historian. 1970. Referring to Leonardo da Vinci. *Civilisation* (1969)

5 I've always been interested in people, but I've never liked them.

Somerset Maugham (1874–1965) British writer. *Observer* (August 28, 1949), 'Sayings of the Week'

6 Curiosity will conquer fear even more than bravery will.

James Stephens (1882–1950) Irish novelist and poet. *The Crock of Gold* (1912)

7 My curiosity was aroused to fever-pitch, and my uncle tried in vain to restrain me. When he saw that my impatience was likely to do me more harm than the satisfaction of my curiosity, he gave way.

Jules Verne (1828–1905) French writer. *Journey to the Centre of the Earth* (1864)

Cynicism

see also **Insults, Nihilism, Truth**

1 Youthful cynicism is sad to observe, because it indicates not so much knowledge learned from bitter experiences as insufficient trust even to attempt the future.

Maya Angelou (b. 1928) US writer. *The Heart of a Woman* (1981)

2 One is not superior merely because one sees the world in an odious light.

René Chateaubriand (1768–1848) French writer and statesman. Attrib.

3 Diogenes lighted a candle in the daytime, and went round saying, 'I am looking for an honest man'.

Diogenes Laërtius (*fl.* 3rd century) Greek historian and biographer. Referring to Diogenes of Sinope, 'the Cynic'. 'Diogenes', *Lives of the Philosophers* (3rd century?)

4 Cynicism is an unpleasant way of saying the truth.

Lillian Hellman (1905–84) US playwright. *The Little Foxes* (1939), Act 1

5 One fifth of the people are against everything all the time.

Robert Kennedy (1925–68) US statesman. *Observer* (May 10, 1964), 'Sayings of the Week'

6 A cynic is a man who, when he smells flowers, looks around for a coffin.

H. L. Mencken (1880–1956) US journalist, critic, and editor. Attrib.

7 The worst cynicism: a belief in luck.

Joyce Carol Oates (b. 1938) US writer. *Do What You Will* (1970), pt. 2, ch. 15

8 All seems infected that th' infected spy,
As all looks yellow to the jaundiced eye.

Alexander Pope (1688–1744) English poet. *An Essay on Criticism* (1711), ll. 558–559

9 Cynicism is humour in ill-health.

H. G. Wells (1866–1946) British writer. 'The Last Trump', *Short Stories* (1927)

10 A man who knows the price of everything and the value of nothing.

Oscar Wilde (1854–1900) Irish poet, playwright, and wit. Referring to a cynic. *Lady Windermere's Fan* (1892), Act 3

D

Damnation

see also **The Devil**, **Hell**

1 Observing the doctrine of Particular Election, and those who preached it up to make the Bible clash and contradict itself, by preaching somewhat like this: You can and you can't—You shall and you shan't—You will and you won't—And you will be damned if you do—And you will be damned if you don't.

Lorenzo Dow (1777–1834) US churchman. *Reflections on the Love of God* (1836), ch. 6, 'The Doctrine of Particular Election'

2 FAUSTUS And what are you that live with Lucifer?
MEPHISTOPHELES Unhappy spirits that fell with Lucifer,
Conspired against our God with Lucifer,
And are for ever damned with Lucifer.

Christopher Marlowe (1564–93) English playwright and poet. *Doctor Faustus* (1592?), Act 1, Scene 3

3 *O lente, lente currite noctis equi.*
The stars move still, time runs, the clock will strike,
The devil will come, and Faustus must be damned.

Christopher Marlowe (1564–93) English playwright and poet. *Doctor Faustus* (1592?), Act 5, Scene 2, ll. 152–154

4 Him the almighty power
Hurled headlong flaming from the ethereal sky
With hideous ruin and combustion down
To bottomless perdition, there to dwell
In adamantine chains and penal fire,
Who durst defy the omnipotent to arms.

John Milton (1608–74) English writer. Satan's descent to hell. *Paradise Lost* (1667), bk. 1, ll. 44–49

5 Headlong themselves they threw
Down from the verge of heaven, eternal wrath
Burnt after them to the bottomless pit.

John Milton (1608–74) English writer. Christ drives the fallen angels out of Heaven. *Paradise Lost* (1667), bk. 6, ll. 864–866

Dancing

see also **The Arts**, **The Body**, **Music**

1 You might almost call me a wallflower. At parties I never dance unless I have to.

Fred Astaire (1899–1987) US dancer and actor. 1946. Quoted in *Fred Astaire* (Michael Freedland; 1976)

2 All the dancer's gestures are signs of things, and the dance is called rational, because it aptly signifies and displays something over and above the pleasure of the senses.

Saint Augustine of Hippo (354–430) Numidian Christian theologian and Doctor of the Church. 412–427? Quoted in *Dancing on My Grave* (Gelsey Kirkland co-written with Greg Lawrence; 1986), Preliminaries

3 A dance is a measured pace, as a verse is a measured speech.

Francis Bacon (1561–1626) English philosopher, statesman, and lawyer. *The Advancement of Learning* (1605), bk. 2

4 No sober man dances, unless he happens to be mad.

Cicero (106–43 BC) Roman orator and statesman. Quoted in *World History of Dance* (Curt Sachs; 1937)

5 Before I go out on the stage, I must place a motor in my soul . . . if I do not get time to put that motor in my soul, I cannot dance.

Isadora Duncan (1877–1927) US dancer. *My Life* (1927)

6 I'm sure if everyone knew how physically cruel dancing really is, nobody would watch—only those people who enjoy bullfights!

Margot Fonteyn (1919–91) British ballet dancer. Quoted in *The Art of Margot Fonteyn* (Keith Money; 1965)

7 Shall We Dance?

Oscar Hammerstein II (1895–1960) US lyricist and librettist. Song title. *The King and I* (music by Richard Rodgers; 1951)

8 The trouble with nude dancing is that not everything stops when the music stops.

Robert Helpmann (1909–86) Australian dancer and choreographer. After the opening night of *Oh, Calcutta!*. Remark (1969), quoted in *The Frank Muir Book: An Irreverent Companion to Social History* (Frank Muir; 1976)

9 I could dance with you till the cows come home. Better still, I'll dance with the cows till *you* come home.

Groucho Marx (1895–1977) US comedian and film actor. *Duck Soup* (Bert Kalmar, Harry Ruby, Arthur Sheekman, and Nat Perrin; 1933)

10 Come, and trip it as you go
On the light fantastic toe.

John Milton (1608–74) English writer. 'L'Allegro', *Poems of Mr. John Milton* (1645), ll. 33–34

11 All the disasters of mankind, all the fatal misfortunes that histories are so full of, the blunders of politicians, the miscarriages of great commanders, all this comes from want of skill in dancing.

Molière (1622–73) French playwright. *Le Bourgeois Gentilhomme* (1670), Act 1, Scene 2

12 Well it's one for the money,
Two for the show,
Three to get ready,
now go, cat, go.
But don't you
Step on my blue suede shoes.

Carl Perkins (b. 1932) US rock singer and songwriter. Song lyric. 'Blue Suede Shoes' (1956)

13 Hence it is from the representation of things spoken by means of posture and gesture that the whole of the art of dance has been elaborated.

Plato (428?–347? BC) Greek philosopher. Quoted in *Dancing on my Grave* (Gelsey Kirkland with Greg Lawrence; 1986), Preliminaries

14 Whosoever knoweth the power of the dance, dwelleth in God.

Jalal al-Din Muhammad Rumi (1207–73) Persian mystic and poet. Quoted in *Portrait of Mr. Balanchine* (Lincoln Kirstein; 1984)

15 A perpendicular expression of a horizontal desire.

George Bernard Shaw (1856–1950) Irish playwright. Referring to dancing. Quoted in *Revolt into Style* (George Melly; 1970)

Danger

see also **Fear, Threats, Tragedy, Warning**

1 The most dangerous creation of any society is that man who has nothing to lose, for his purity, by definition, is unassailable.

James Baldwin (1924–87) US writer and civil rights activist. *Nobody Knows My Name* (1961)

2 Dangers by being despised grow great.

Edmund Burke (1729–97) Irish-born British statesman and political philosopher. Speech to the British Parliament (May 11, 1792)

3 There is no trap so deadly as the trap you set for yourself.

Raymond Chandler (1888–1959) US novelist. Said by Philip Marlowe. *The Long Goodbye* (1953)

4 Danger, the spur of all great minds.

George Chapman (1559?–1634) English poet and playwright. Co-written with Ben Jonson and John Marston. *The Revenge of Bussy D'Ambois* (1613), Act 5, Scene 1

5 The danger chiefly lies in acting well,
No crime's so great as daring to excel.

Charles Churchill (1731–64) British poet. 'An Epistle to William Hogarth' (1763), l. 51

6 There are always great dangers in letting the best be the enemy of the good.

Roy Jenkins (b. 1920) British statesman. Speech to Parliament (1975)

7 I give you bitter pills in sugar coating. The pills are harmless, the poison is in the sugar.

Stanislaw Lec (1909–66) Polish writer. *Unkempt Thoughts* (1962)

8 Believe me! The secret of reaping the greatest fruitfulness and the greatest enjoyment from life is to live dangerously!

Friedrich Wilhelm Nietzsche (1844–1900) German philosopher and poet. *The Gay Science* (1882), bk. 4

9 Whoever has not felt the danger of our times palpitating under his hand, has not really penetrated to the vitals of destiny, he has merely pricked its surface.

José Ortega y Gasset (1883–1955) Spanish writer and philosopher. *The Revolt of the Masses* (1930)

10 Look back, and smile at perils past.

Sir Walter Scott (1771–1832) Scottish novelist. *The Bridal of Triermain* (1813), Introduction

11 HOTSPUR Out of this nettle, danger, we pluck this flower, safety.

William Shakespeare (1564–1616) English poet and playwright. *Henry IV, Part 1* (1597), Act 2, Scene 3

12 There's a snake hidden in the grass.

Virgil (70–19 BC) Roman poet. *Eclogues* (37 BC), no. 3, l. 93

Darkness

see also **Evening, Night**

1 There is radiance in the darkness, if we could but see. To be able to see this radiance, all you need do is to cultivate the courage to look.

Obafemi Awolowo (1909–87) Nigerian lawyer and politician. June 30, 1967. *Voice of Courage: Selected Speeches of Chief Obafemi Awolowo* (1981), vol. 2

2 Dark as pitch.

John Bunyan (1628–88) English preacher and writer. *The Pilgrim's Progress* (1678), pt. 1

3 I'm not frightened of the darkness outside. It's the darkness inside houses I don't like.

Shelagh Delaney (b. 1939) British playwright. *A Taste of Honey* (1958), Act 1, Scene 1

4 All I know is a door into the dark.

Seamus Heaney (b. 1939) Irish poet. 'The Forge', *Door into the Dark* (1969), l. 1

5 By this glass filled with darkness to the brim
and this heart that's never full,
let us praise the Lord, matter of Nothingness,
who carved our reason out of faith.

Antonio Machado (1875–1939) Spanish poet and playwright. 'Siesta, In Memory of Abel Martin', *Selected Poems* (Alan S. Trueblood, tr.; 1982), ll. 13–16

6 O dark, dark, dark, amid the blaze of noon,
Irrecoverably dark, total eclipse
Without all hope of day!

John Milton (1608–74) English writer. 'Samson Agonistes', *Paradise Regain'd . . . To Which is added Samson Agonistes* (1671), l. 80

7 Those who look from their darkness into the tribal fire must be bold enough to cross it.

Derek Walcott (b. 1930) St. Lucian poet and playwright. *What the Twilight Says* (1998)

Death and Dying

see also **Afterlife, Bereavement, Last Words, Mortality, Obituaries**

1 It's not that I'm afraid to die. I just don't want to be there when it happens.

Woody Allen (b. 1935) US film actor and director. 'Death (A Play)', *Without Feathers* (1976)

2 When a man dies, the angels ask about what he brought while the people ask about what he has left behind.

Abu Abdullah Muhammad al-Harithi al-Baghdadi al-Mufid (fl. 10th century) Iraqi scholar and jurist. 10th century. 'The Life of the Commander of the Faithful', *The Book of Guidance Into the Lives of the Twelve Imams* (I. K. A. Howard, tr.; 1981)

3 Death not merely ends life, it also bestows upon it a silent completeness, snatched from the hazardous flux to which all things human are subject.

Hannah Arendt (1906–75) German-born US philosopher and historian. 'Thinking', *The Life of the Mind* (1975), pt. 3, ch. 16

4 To die will be an awfully big adventure.

J. M. Barrie (1860–1937) British playwright and novelist. *Peter Pan* (1904), Act 3

5 I don't know when I died. It always seemed to me I died old, about ninety years old, and what years.

Samuel Beckett (1906–89) Irish playwright, novelist, and poet. 1946. 'The Calmative', *The Expelled and Other Novellas* (1980)

6   GRAVE, n. A place in which the dead are laid to await the coming of the medical student.
Ambrose Bierce (1842–1914?) US writer and journalist. *The Devil's Dictionary* (1911)

7   Death is the supreme festival on the road to freedom.
Dietrich Bonhoeffer (1906–45) German theologian. 1943–44. *Letters and Papers from Prison* (Eberhard Bethge, ed.; 1981)

8   In the midst of life we are in death.
Book of Common Prayer. Burial of the Dead (1662), First anthem

9   We all labour against our own cure, for death is the cure of all diseases.
Thomas Browne (1605–82) English physician and writer. *Religio Medici* (1642)

10 Death comes along like a gas bill one can't pay.
Anthony Burgess (1917–93) British writer and critic. Interview, *Playboy Magazine* (September 1974)

11 When one has no imagination, dying doesn't mean much, when one has, dying means too much.
Louis-Ferdinand Céline (1894–1961) French novelist and physician. *Voyage au Bout de la Nuit* (1932)

12 To look upon a life ready to die petrifies all life.
Patrick Chamoiseau (b. 1953) Martiniquan writer. *Texaco* (1992)

13 'Now, sires', quoth he, 'if that you be so leef
To fynde Death, turn up this croked way,
For in that grove I lafte hym, by my fey,
Under a tree, and there he wole abyde'.
Geoffrey Chaucer (1343?–1400) English poet. The old man's advice to the three youths who set out from a tavern to conquer death. 'The Pardoner's Tale', *The Canterbury Tales* (1390?), ll. 760–764, quoted in *The Works of Geoffrey Chaucer* (F. N. Robinson, ed.; 1957)

14 The debt which cancels all others.
Charles Colton (1780–1832) British cleric and writer. *Lacon* (1820), vol. 2

15 Mistah Kurtz—he dead.
Joseph Conrad (1857–1924) Polish-born British novelist. *Heart of Darkness* (1902), ch. 3

16 He'd make a lovely corpse.
Charles Dickens (1812–70) British novelist. Said by Mrs. Gamp. *Martin Chuzzlewit* (1844), ch. 25

17 Death is no more than an obituary. Anyone's death, including our own, is yesterday's news.
E. L. Doctorow (b. 1931) US novelist. *The Waterworks* (1994)

18 At the round earth's imagin'd corners, blow
Your trumpets, Angels, and arise, arise
From death you numberless infinities
Of souls, and to your scattered bodies go.
John Donne (1572?–1631) English metaphysical poet and divine. *Holy Sonnets* (1618), no. 7

19 Like pilgrims to th'appointed place we tend;
The world's an inn, and death the journey's end.
John Dryden (1631–1700) English poet, playwright, and literary critic. *Palamon and Arcite* (1700), bk. 3, ll. 883–884

20 He not busy being born is a-busy dying.
Bob Dylan (b. 1941) US singer and songwriter. Song lyric. 'It's Alright Ma (I'm Only Bleeding)', *Bringing It All Back Home* (1965)

21 Pain and death are a part of life. To reject them is to reject life itself.
Havelock Ellis (1859–1939) British psychologist. *On Life and Sex: Essays of Love and Virtue* (1922), vol. 2

22 So death, the most terrifying of ills, is nothing to us, since so long as we exist, death is not with us; but when death comes, then we do not exist.
Epicurus (341–270 BC) Greek philosopher. Letter to Menoeceus (3rd century BC)

23 O Death, thou comest when I had thee least in mind!
Everyman. *Everyman* (1509?–19?), l. 119

24 The nihilists say it is the end; the fundamentalists, the beginning; when in reality it is no more than a single tenant or family moving out of a tenement or a town.
William Faulkner (1897–1962) US novelist. Referring to death. *As I Lay Dying* (1930)

25 Anyone's death always releases something like an aura of stupefaction, so difficult is it to grasp this irruption of nothingness and to believe that it has actually taken place.
Gustave Flaubert (1821–80) French novelist. *Madame Bovary* (1857), pt. 3, ch. 9

26 He hath shook hands with time.
John Ford (1586–1640?) English playwright. *The Broken Heart* (1633), Act 5, Scene 2

27 Death destroys a man, the idea of Death saves him.
E. M. Forster (1879–1970) British novelist. *Howards End* (1910), ch. 27

28 In this world nothing can be said to be certain but death and taxes.
Benjamin Franklin (1706–90) US statesman and scientist. Letter to Jean-Baptiste Le Roy (November 13, 1789), quoted in *Works of Benjamin Franklin* (1817), ch. 6

29 A person doesn't die when he should but when he can.
Gabriel García Márquez (b. 1928) Colombian novelist. *One Hundred Years of Solitude* (1967)

30 Do not seek death. Death will find you. But seek the road which makes death a fulfillment.
Dag Hammarskjöld (1905–61) Swedish statesman and diplomat. *Markings* (Leif Sjöberg and W. H. Auden, trs.; 1964)

31 Once you're dead, you're made for life.
Jimi Hendrix (1942–70) US rock musician. Attrib.

32 Death is a delightful hiding-place for weary men.
Herodotus (484?–425 BC) Greek historian. *The Histories* (450? BC), bk. 7, ch. 46

33 I believe that the struggle against death, the unconditional and self-willed determination to life, is the motive power behind the lives and activities of all outstanding men.
Hermann Hesse (1877–1962) German-born Swiss novelist and poet. 'Treatise of the Steppenwolf', *Steppenwolf* (1927)

34 I die because I do not die.
Saint John of the Cross (1542–91) Spanish poet, mystic, and Doctor of the Church. 'Coplas del alma que pena por ver a dios' (1578)

35 A—sudden—at—the—moment—though—not—from—lingering—illness—often—previously—expectorated—demise, Lenehan said. And with a great future behind him.
James Joyce (1882–1941) Irish writer. *Ulysses* (1922)

36 The more we are making advancements in science, the more we seem to fear and deny the reality of death.
Elisabeth Kübler-Ross (b. 1926) Swiss-born US psychiatrist and author. *On Death and Dying* (1969), ch. 1

37 Death never takes the wise man by surprise; he is always ready to go.

Jean de La Fontaine (1621–95) French writer and poet. *Fables* (1668), bk. 8

38 The living are just the dead on holiday.

Maurice Maeterlinck (1862–1949) Belgian playwright and poet. Attrib.

39 A man's dying is more the survivors' affair than his own.

Thomas Mann (1875–1955) German writer. *The Magic Mountain* (1924), ch. 6

40 Death is psychosomatic.

Charles Manson (b. 1934) US cult leader and murderer. *Esquire* (1971)

41 Either he's dead or my watch has stopped.

Groucho Marx (1895–1977) US comedian and film actor. On taking a man's pulse. *A Day at the Races* (R. Pirosh, G. Seaton, and G. Oppenheimer; 1937)

42 Dying is a very dull, dreary affair. And my advice to you is to have nothing whatever to do with it.

Somerset Maugham (1874–1965) British writer. Quoted in *Escape from the Shadows* (Robin Maugham; 1972)

43 Whom the gods love dies young.

Menander (342?–291? BC) Greek playwright and poet. *Dis Exapaton* (327?–320? BC)

44 One dies only once, and it's for such a long time.

Molière (1622–73) French playwright. *Le Dépit Amoureux* (1656), Act 5, Scene 3

45 He who would teach men to die would at the same time teach them to live.

Michel de Montaigne (1533–92) French essayist. *Essays* (1580–88), bk. 1, ch. 20

46 There is only one way to be prepared for death: to be sated. In the soul, in the heart, in the spirit, in the flesh. To the brim.

Henri de Montherlant (1896–1972) French novelist and playwright. *Mors et Vita* (1932)

47 It's not pining, it's passed on. This parrot is no more. It's ceased to be. It's expired. It's gone to meet its maker. This is a late parrot. It's a stiff. Bereft of life it rests in peace. It would be pushing up the daisies if you hadn't nailed it to the perch. It's rung down the curtain and joined the choir invisible. It's an ex-parrot.

Monty Python's Flying Circus, British television series. 'Dead Parrot' sketch, *Monty Python's Flying Circus* (December 14, 1969), Episode 8

48 Life is a great surprise. I do not see why death should not be an even greater one.

Vladimir Nabokov (1899–1977) Russian-born US novelist, poet, and critic. 'Commentary', *Pale Fire* (1962)

49 We die containing a richness of lovers and tribes, tastes we have swallowed, bodies we have plunged into and swum up as if rivers of wisdom, characters we have climbed into as if trees, fears we have hidden as if in caves.

Michael Ondaatje (b. 1943) Sri Lankan-born Canadian novelist and poet. *The English Patient* (1992)

50 Death . . .
You isolate me, you give me the certainty of life.

Pier Paolo Pasolini (1922–75) Italian filmmaker. 'Fragment: To Death' (1961)

51 Many men on the point of an edifying death would be furious if they were suddenly restored to life.

Cesare Pavese (1908–50) Italian novelist and poet. Attrib.

52 When a man lies dying, he does not die from the disease alone. He dies from his whole life.

Charles Pierre Péguy (1873–1914) French writer and poet. Quoted in 'The Search for Truth', *Basic Verities* (Ann and Julian Green, trs.; 1943)

53 Dying
is an art, like everything else.
I do it exceptionally well.

Sylvia Plath (1932–63) US poet and novelist. October 1962. 'Lady Lazarus', *Ariel* (1965)

54 Someone told us that Jim Morrison had just died in a bathtub in Paris. And the immediate reaction was, 'How fabulous, in a bathtub, in Paris, how *faaaantastic*'.

Lou Reed (b. 1942) US rock singer and songwriter. Jim Morrison was the lead singer and songwriter for The Doors, the 1960s rock group. Quoted in *Lou Reed: Between the Lines* (Michael Wrenn; 1993)

55 Death is the greatest kick of all, that's why they save it for last.

Robert Reisner (1921–74) US writer and humorist. 'Death', *Graffiti: Two Thousand Years of Wall Writing* (1974)

56 KING RICHARD II The worst is death, and death will have his day.

William Shakespeare (1564–1616) English poet and playwright. *Richard II* (1595), Act 3, Scene 2

57 Death is the veil which those who live call life: They sleep, and it is lifted.

Percy Bysshe Shelley (1792–1822) English poet. *Prometheus Unbound* (1820), Act 3, Scene. 3, ll. 113–114

58 Nobody heard him, the dead man,
But still he lay moaning:
I was much further out than you thought
And not waving but drowning.

Stevie Smith (1902–71) British poet and novelist. 'Not Waving But Drowning' (1957)

59 Death is not the greatest of ills; it is worse to want to die, and not be able to.

Sophocles (496?–406? BC) Greek playwright. *Electra* (418–410? BC), l. 1007

60 My name is death; the last best friend am I.

Robert Southey (1774–1843) English poet and writer. 'The Dream', *Carmen Nuptiale: The Lay of the Laureate* (1816)

61 A single death is a tragedy; a million is a statistic.

Joseph Stalin (1879–1953) Soviet dictator. Attrib.

62 Death is the mother of beauty:
hence from her,
Alone, shall come fulfillment to our dreams
And our desires.

Wallace Stevens (1879–1955) US poet. 'Sunday Morning', *Selected Poems* (1955)

63 It is impossible that anything so natural, so necessary, and so universal as death, should ever have been designed by Providence as an evil to mankind.

Jonathan Swift (1667–1745) Irish writer and clergyman. Published posthumously. *Thoughts on Religion* (1765)

64 Do not go gentle into that good night,
Old age should burn and rave at close of day;
Rage, rage, against the dying of the light.

Dylan Thomas (1914–53) Welsh poet, playwright, and short-story writer. 1951. Written when his father became seriously ill. 'Do Not Go Gentle into that Good Night', *In Country Sleep* (1952), ll. 1–3

65 Death is the price paid by life for an enhancement of the complexity of a live organism's structure.

Arnold Toynbee (1889–1975) British historian. *Life After Death* (co-written with Arthur Koestler and others; 1975)

66 The human race is the only one that knows it must die, and it knows this only through its experience. A child brought up alone and transported to a desert island would have no more idea of death than a cat or a plant.

Voltaire (1694–1778) French writer and philosopher. Quoted in *The Oxford Book of Death* (D. J. Enright; 1987)

67 I know death hath ten thousand several doors For men to take their exits.

John Webster (1578?–1632?) English playwright. *The Duchess of Malfi* (1623), Act 4, Scene 2

68 For he who lives more lives than one More deaths than one must die.

Oscar Wilde (1854–1900) Irish poet, playwright, and wit. *The Ballad of Reading Gaol* (1898), pt. 3, st. 37

69 Begin the preparation for your death And from the fortieth winter by that thought Test every work of intellect or faith, And everything that your own hands have wrought.

W. B. Yeats (1865–1939) Irish poet and playwright. 'Vacillation' (1933), sect. 3, ll. 10–13

Debt

see also **Economics**, **Money**, **Poverty**

1 A debt may get mouldy, but it never decays.

Chinua Achebe (b. 1930) Nigerian novelist, poet, and essayist. *No Longer At Ease* (1960)

2 If you borrow $2000 dollars from a bank and can't pay it back, you have a problem, but if you borrow a million and can't repay, they have a problem.

Anonymous. Quoted in *The Art of Getting Your Own Sweet Way* (Philip B. Crosby; 1981)

3 Dreading that climax of all human ills, The inflammation of his weekly bills.

Lord Byron (1788–1824) British poet. *Don Juan* (1819–24), can. 3, st. 35

4 When debts are not paid because they cannot be paid, the best thing to do is not to talk about them, and shuffle the cards again.

Camilo José Cela (1916–2002) Spanish writer. *Journey to the Alcarria* (1948)

5 If there's anyone listening to whom I owe money, I'm prepared to forget it if you are.

Errol Flynn (1909–59) Australian-born US actor. Attrib.

6 I owe you everything, Sire, but I believe I can pay some of my debt with this gift.

Jules Mazarin (1602–61) Italian-born French statesman and cardinal. Remark to Louis XIV shortly before his death. Referring to Jean-Baptiste Colbert. Attrib.

7 Be still indebted to somebody or other, that there may be somebody always to pray for you.

François Rabelais (1494?–1553?) French humanist and satirist. *Gargantua and Pantagruel* (1546), bk. 3

8 I owe much; I have nothing; the rest I leave to the poor.

François Rabelais (1494?–1553?) French humanist and satirist. 1553? Last words. A number of different quotations are attributed to Rabelais as his last words. Attrib.

9 The deficit is big enough to take care of itself.

Ronald Reagan (b. 1911) US president and actor. *Newsweek* (November 21, 1988)

10 All decent people live beyond their incomes; those who aren't respectable live beyond other people's; a few gifted individuals manage to do both.

Saki (1870–1916) British short-story writer. 'The Match-Maker', *The Chronicles of Clovis* (1911)

11 No, this right hand shall work it all off.

Sir Walter Scott (1771–1832) Scottish novelist. 1826. Refusing offers of help following his bankruptcy (1826), and referring to his intention to write his way out of debt. Quoted in *Century of Anecdote* (J. Timbs; 1864)

12 A small debt makes a man your debtor, a large one makes him your enemy.

Seneca, 'the Elder' (55? BC–AD 40?) Roman rhetorician. *Epistulae Ad Lucilium*

13 A promise made is a debt unpaid.

Robert W. Service (1874–1958) Canadian poet. McGee, a 'fictitious' person, was the name of an accountholder at the bank where he worked. 'The Cremation of Sam McGee', *Songs of a Sourdough* (1907)

14 FALSTAFF I can get no remedy against this consumption of the purse; borrowing only lingers and lingers it out, but the disease is incurable.

William Shakespeare (1564–1616) English poet and playwright. *Henry IV, Part 2* (1597), Act 1, Scene 2

15 STEPHANO He that dies pays all debts.

William Shakespeare (1564–1616) English poet and playwright. *The Tempest* (1611), Act 3, Scene 2

16 Thank God, that's settled.

Richard Brinsley Sheridan (1751–1816) Irish-born British playwright and politician. Handing one of his creditors an IOU. Quoted in *Wit, Wisdom, and Foibles of the Great* (C. Shriner; 1918)

17 It is not my interest to pay the principal, nor my principle to pay the interest.

Richard Brinsley Sheridan (1751–1816) Irish-born British playwright and politician. Said to his tailor who had requested he pay a debt, or at least the interest on it. Attrib.

18 Crito, we owe a cock to Aesculapius; please pay it and don't let it pass.

Socrates (470?–399? BC) Greek philosopher. 399 BC. Last words before his execution by drinking hemlock. Quoted in *Phaedo* (Plato)

19 Live Now, Pay Later

Jack Trevor Story (1917–91) British novelist. 1963. Novel title.

20 Bankruptcy is a sacred state, a condition beyond conditions, as theologians might say, and attempts to investigate it are necessarily obscene, like spiritualism.

John Updike (b. 1932) US writer. 'The Bankrupt Man', *Hugging the Shore* (1983)

Deception

see also **Delusion**, **Gullibility**, **Lying**

1 The lamb that belonged to the sheep whose skin the wolf was wearing began to follow the wolf in the sheep's clothing.

Aesop (620?–560 BC) Greek writer. 'The Wolf in Sheep's Clothing', *Aesop's Fables* (6th century BC)

2 Like strawberry wives, that laid two or three great strawberries at the mouth of their pot, and all the rest were little ones.

Francis Bacon (1561–1626) English philosopher, statesman, and lawyer. Describing the tactics of the Commission of Sales in their dealings with Elizabeth I. *Apothegms New and Old* (1625)

3 If you dissemble sometimes your knowledge of that you are thought to know, you shall be thought, another time, to know that you know not.

Francis Bacon (1561–1626) English philosopher, statesman, and lawyer. 'Of Discourse', *Essays* (1625)

4 The heart is deceitful above all things, and desperately wicked: who can know it?

Bible. Jeremiah, *King James Bible* (1611), 17:9

5 This Life's dim Windows of the Soul
Distorts the Heavens from Pole to Pole
And leads you to Believe a Lie
When you see with, not thro' the Eye.

William Blake (1757–1827) British poet, painter, engraver, and mystic. 'The Everlasting Gospel', *The Everlasting Gospel* (1818?), ll. 103–106, quoted in *The Poetry and Prose of William Blake* (David V. Erdman, ed.; 1965)

6 All the deceits of the world, the flesh, and the devil.

Book of Common Prayer. The Litany (1662)

7 The smylere with the knyf under the cloke.

Geoffrey Chaucer (1343?–1400) English poet. 'The Knight's Tale', *The Canterbury Tales* (1390?), l. 1999, quoted in *The Works of Geoffrey Chaucer* (F. N. Robinson, ed.; 1957)

8 The worst crime is faking it.

Kurt Cobain (1967–94) US rock musician. *Observer* (April 17, 1994), 'Sayings of the Week'

9 Much truth is spoken, that more may be concealed.

Charles John Darling (1849–1936) British judge and writer. *Scintillae Juris* (1877)

10 What a world of gammon and spinnage it is, though, ain't it!

Charles Dickens (1812–70) British novelist. Said by Miss Mowcher, using a euphemism for humbug and deception. *David Copperfield* (1850), ch. 22

11 Frank and explicit—that is the right line to take when you wish to conceal your own mind and confuse the minds of others.

Benjamin Disraeli (1804–81) British prime minister and writer. *Sybil* (1845), bk. 6, ch. 1

12 We are only undeceived
Of that which, deceiving, could no longer harm.

T. S. Eliot (1888–1965) US-born British poet and playwright. 'East Coker', *Four Quartets* (1940)

13 Ah, colonel, all's fair in love and war, you know.

Nathan Bedford Forrest (1821–77) US general. Remark to a captured enemy officer who had been tricked into surrendering. *A Civil War Treasury of Tales, Legends and Folklore* (Benjamin Albert Botkin, ed.; 1960)

14 The world wants to be deceived.

Sebastian Franck (1499?–1542?) German theologian. 'Paradoxa Ducenta Octoginta', *Paradoxa* (1534), no. 238

15 It is a political error to practice deceit, if deceit is carried too far.

Frederick II (1712–86) Prussian monarch. *Antimachiavell* (1740)

16 Joking is the third best method of hoodwinking people. The second best is sentimentality . . . But the best and safest method . . . is to tell the plain unvarnished truth.

Max Frisch (1911–91) Swiss playwright and novelist. 1958. *The Fire Raisers* (Michael Bullock, tr.; 1962), Scene 4

17 Not all that tempts your wand'ring eyes
And heedless hearts, is lawful prize;
Nor all that glisters, gold.

Thomas Gray (1716–71) British poet. 'On a Favourite Cat, Drowned in a Tub of Gold Fishes' (1748), st. 7, ll. 4–6, quoted in *The Poems of Thomas Gray: William Collins: Oliver Goldsmith* (Roger Lonsdale, ed.; 1969)

18 When is a man not a man? when he is a—yours till the rending of the rocks—Sham

James Joyce (1882–1941) Irish writer. *Finnegans Wake* (1939)

19 How can we be sure that we are not impostors?

Jacques Lacan (1901–81) French philosopher and psychologist. *The Four Fundamental Concepts of Psycho-Analysis* (Jacques-Alain Miller, ed., Alan Sheridan, tr.; 1977)

20 You can fool some of the people all the time and all the people some of the time; but you can't fool all the people all the time.

Abraham Lincoln (1809–65) US president. Attrib.

21 Deceive boys with toys, but men with oaths.

Lysander (d. 395 BC) Spartan naval commander. Quoted in *Lives* (Plutarch; 1st century?), 8

22 Cunning and deceit will every time serve a man better than force.

Niccolò Machiavelli (1469–1527) Italian historian, statesman, and political philosopher. *The Prince* (1513)

23 Men are apt to deceive themselves in big things, but they rarely do so in particulars.

Niccolò Machiavelli (1469–1527) Italian historian, statesman, and political philosopher. *The Prince* (1513)

24 Beware, for I have found no trade more profitable than the selling of dreams.

Naguib Mahfouz (b. 1911) Egyptian writer. Said by Sheikh Abd-Rabbih al-Ta-ih. *Echoes of an Autobiography* (1994)

25 Woe to him who doesn't know how to wear his mask, be he king or pope!

Luigi Pirandello (1867–1936) Italian dramatist, novelist, and short-story writer. *Henry IV* (Edward Storer, tr.; 1922)

26 O what a tangled web we weave,
When first we practise to deceive!

Sir Walter Scott (1771–1832) Scottish novelist. *Marmion* (1808), can. 6, st. 17

27 For I have sworn thee fair, and thought thee bright,
Who art as black as hell, as dark as night.

William Shakespeare (1564–1616) English poet and playwright. Sonnet 147 (1609)

28 MACBETH False face must hide what the false heart doth know.

William Shakespeare (1564–1616) English poet and playwright. *Macbeth* (1606), Act 1, Scene 7

29 IAGO But I will wear my heart upon my sleeve For daws to peck at: I am not what I am.

William Shakespeare (1564–1616) English poet and playwright. *Othello* (1602–04), Act 1, Scene 1

30 GLOUCESTER And thus I clothe my naked villany
With odd old ends stol'n forth of holy writ,
And seem a saint when most I play the devil.

William Shakespeare (1564–1616) English poet and playwright. *Richard III* (1591), Act 1, Scene 3

31 BASSANIO So may the outward shows be least themselves:
The world is still deceived with ornament.
In law, what plea so tainted and corrupt
But, being season'd with a gracious voice,
Obscures the show of evil? In religion,
What damned error, but some sober brow
Will bless it and approve it with a text,
Hiding the grossness with fair ornament?
There is no vice so simple but assumes
Some mark of virtue on his outward parts.

William Shakespeare (1564–1616) English poet and playwright. *The Merchant of Venice* (1596–98), Act 3, Scene 2

32 You can fool too many of the people too much of the time.
James Thurber (1894–1961) US writer, cartoonist, and humorist. 'The Owl Who Was God', *Fables for Our Time* (1940)

33 Do not trust the horse, Trojans. Whatever it is, I fear the Greeks even when they bring gifts.
Virgil (70–19 BC) Roman poet. *Aeneid* (29–19 BC), bk. 2, l. 48

Decision

see also **Choice, Judgment, Leadership**

1 Get me inside any boardroom and I'll get any decision.
Alan Bond (b. 1938) Australian business executive. *Daily Telegraph* (June 27, 1989)

2 Columbus did not seek a new route to the Indies in response to a majority directive.
Milton Friedman (b. 1912) US economist. Referring to Christopher Columbus. *The Reader's Digest* (June 1, 1978)

3 Persuade the decision makers that the decision you want is their idea.
Michael Shea (b. 1938) Scottish author and broadcaster. *Influence* (1988)

4 All decisions should be made as low as possible in the organization. The Charge of the Light Brigade was ordered by an officer who wasn't there looking at the territory.
Robert Townsend (b. 1920) US business executive. *Up the Organization* (1970)

5 But there comes a moment in everybody's life when he must decide whether he'll live among human beings or not—a fool among fools or a fool alone.
Thornton Wilder (1897–1975) US novelist and playwright. *The Matchmaker* (1954), Act 4

Declarations of Love

see also **Love, Seduction**

1 I've Got a Crush on You
Ira Gershwin (1896–1983) US lyricist. 1920s. Song title.

2 The surest way to hit a woman's heart is to take aim kneeling.
Douglas Jerrold (1803–57) British playwright. *Wit and Opinions* (Blanchard Jerrold, ed.; 1859)

3 Send two dozen roses to Room 424 and put 'Emily, I love you' on the back of the bill.
Groucho Marx (1895–1977) US comedian and film actor. *A Night in Casablanca* (Joseph Fields, Roland Kibbee, and Frank Tashlin; 1946)

4 I loved Kirk so much, I would have skied down Mount Everest in the nude with a carnation up my nose.
Joyce McKinney (b. 1950) US beauty queen. Ms. McKinney was accused of kidnapping an ex-lover who had rejected her. Evidence to British court (1977)

5 You're the Nile,
You're the Tower of Pisa,
You're the smile
On the Mona Lisa . . .
But if, Baby, I'm the bottom you're the top!
Cole Porter (1893–1964) US songwriter and composer. Song lyric. 'You're the Top', *Anything Goes* (1936)

6 I've Got You Under My Skin
Cole Porter (1893–1964) US songwriter and composer. Song title. *Born to Dance* (1936)

7 Night and day, you are the one,
Only you beneath the moon and under the sun.
Cole Porter (1893–1964) US songwriter and composer. Song lyric. 'Night and Day', *The Gay Divorce* (1932)

8 When a man is in love
how can he use old words?
Should a woman
desiring her lover
lie down with grammarians and linguists?
Nizar Qabbani (b. 1923) Syrian poet. 'Language', *Modern Arabic Poetry* (Salma Khadra Jayyusi, ed.; 1987), ll. 1–6

9 The day I met you I tore up
all my maps
all my prophecies
like an Arab stallion I smelled the rain.
Nizar Qabbani (b. 1923) Syrian poet. 'Poems', *Modern Arabic Poetry* (Salma Khadra Jayyusi, ed.; 1987), no. 2, ll. 1–4

10 When God gave you to me
I felt that he had loaded
everything my way
and unsaid all his sacred books.
Nizar Qabbani (b. 1923) Syrian poet. 'Poems', *Modern Arabic Poetry* (Salma Khadra Jayyusi, ed.; 1987), no. 8, ll. 2–4

11 I'll Be Your Mirror
Lou Reed (b. 1942) US rock singer and songwriter. 1967. Song title. Sung by Nico.

12 Anyway I just got your beautiful letter and I love you to pieces, distraction, etc.
J. D. Salinger (b. 1919) US novelist. Written by Franny in a letter to Lane. 'Franny', *Franny and Zooey* (1961)

13 KING She is so conjunctive to my life and soul
That, as the star moves not but in his sphere,
I could not but by her.
William Shakespeare (1564–1616) English poet and playwright. *Hamlet* (1601), Act 4, Scene 7

14 BENEDICK I do love nothing in the world so well as you; is not that strange?
William Shakespeare (1564–1616) English poet and playwright. *Much Ado About Nothing* (1598–99), Act 4, Scene 1

15 OTHELLO Excellent wretch! Perdition catch my soul
But I do love thee! and when I love thee not,
Chaos is come again.
William Shakespeare (1564–1616) English poet and playwright. Referring to Desdemona. *Othello* (1602–04), Act 3, Scene 3

16 JULIET My bounty is as boundless as the sea,
My love as deep; the more I give to thee,
The more I have, for both are infinite.
William Shakespeare (1564–1616) English poet and playwright. *Romeo and Juliet* (1595), Act 2, Scene 2

Decolonization

see also **Freedom, Imperialism, Independence**

1 What I desire is that Marxism and communism should serve the black people, not that the black people should serve Marxism and communism. Doctrines and movements must be for men, and not men for doctrines and movements.
Aimé Césaire (b. 1913) Martiniquan poet, teacher, and political leader. *Communism and the French Intellectuals, 1914–60* (David Caute; 1964)

2 Peace to our neighbours, but anathema to the name of France.

Jean Jacques Dessalines (1758–1806) West African-born Haitian revolutionary and monarch. Dessalines was the self-proclaimed emperor of Haiti (1804–06). *From Dessalines to Duvalier* (David Nicholls; 1988)

3 You may, if you like, cut us to pieces. You may shatter us at the canon's mouth. If you act contrary to our will we shall not help you and without our help, we know that you cannot move one step forward. It is likely that you will laugh at all this in the intoxication of your power.

Mahatma Gandhi (1869–1948) Indian national leader. Addressing the British. Quoted in *Questions in the Philosophy of Restraint* (Indira Rothermund; 1963)

4 We believe in the freedom of Africa for the Negro people of the world, and by the principle of Europe for the Europeans, and Asia for the Asiatics, we also demand Africa for the Africans at home and abroad.

Marcus Garvey (1887–1940) Jamaican-born black nationalist leader and publisher. Bill of Rights adopted by the first International Convention of the Negro People of the World (August 1920)

5 Australia and New Zealand are perhaps the clearest exemplars of the transformation of former European colonies into post-western multicultural states.

John Gray (b. 1948) British academic. *False Dawn* (1998)

6 The great battleground for the defense and expansion of freedom today is the whole southern half of the globe . . . Their revolution is the greatest in human history. They seek an end to injustice, tyranny, and exploitation. More than an end, they seek a beginning.

John Fitzgerald Kennedy (1917–63) US president. Supplementary State of the Union Address (May 25, 1961)

7 Colonies are made to be lost.

Henri de Montherlant (1896–1972) French novelist and playwright. *Le Maître de Santiago* (1947), Act 1, Scene 4

Defeat

see also **Failure, Loss**

1 As always, victory finds a hundred fathers, but defeat is an orphan.

Galeazzo Ciano (1903–44) Italian politician. Speech (September 9, 1942)

2 Of all I had, only honour and life have been spared.

Francis I (1494–1547) French monarch. Referring to his defeat at the Battle of Pavia; usually misquoted as 'All is lost save honour'. Letter to his mother, Louise of Savoy (February 24, 1525)

3 We wuz robbed—We should have stood in bed.

Joe Jacobs (1896–1940) US boxing manager. Referring to Max Schmeling's defeat by Jack Sharkey in the heavyweight title fight, June 21, 1932. Quoted in *Strong Cigars and Lovely Women* (J. Lardner; 1932)

4 Of the two lights of Christendom, one has been extinguished.

Pius II (1405–64) Italian pope. Referring to the fall of Constantinople to the Turks (May 29, 1453). Attrib.

5 Please understand that there is no one depressed in *this* house; we are not interested in the possibilities of defeat; they do not exist.

Victoria (1819–1901) British monarch. Remark to British prime minister Arthur Balfour, referring to the Boer War (1899–1902). Quoted in *Life of Robert, Marquis of Salisbury* (Gwendolen Cecil; 1931)

Delusion

see also **Delusions of Love, Fantasy, Self-Delusion**

1 But yet the light that led astray
Was light from Heaven.

Robert Burns (1759–96) Scottish poet and songwriter. 'The Vision' (1785)

2 Things and actions are what they are, and the consequences of them will be what they will be: why then should we desire to be deceived?

Joseph Butler (1692–1752) English philosopher and theologian. *Fifteen Sermons* (1726), no. 7

3 Take care, your worship, those things over there are not giants but windmills.

Miguel de Cervantes (1547–1616) Spanish novelist and playwright. *Don Quixote* (1605–15), pt. 1, ch. 8

4 Didn't I tell you, Don Quixote, sir, to turn back, for they were not armies you were going to attack, but flocks of sheep?

Miguel de Cervantes (1547–1616) Spanish novelist and playwright. *Don Quixote* (1605–15), pt. 1, ch. 18

5 The world projected in the fantasy of delusion imprisons the consciousness that projects it.

Michel Foucault (1926–84) French philosopher. *Mental Illness and Psychology* (1976)

6 A poor girl may have an illusion that a prince will come and fetch her home. It is possible; some such cases have occurred. That the Messiah will come and found a golden age is much less probable.

Sigmund Freud (1856–1939) Austrian psychoanalyst. 1928. *The Future of an Illusion* (1927), ch. 6

7 Man is fed with fables through life, and leaves it in the belief he knows something of what has been passing, when in truth he has known nothing but what has passed under his own eye.

Thomas Jefferson (1743–1826) US president. Letter to Thomas Cooper (1823)

8 Alas, all the castles I have, are built with air, thou know'st.

Ben Jonson (1572–1637) English playwright and poet. *Eastward Ho* (1604), Act 2, Scene 2

9 How could God do this to me after all I have done for him?

Louis XIV (1638–1715) French monarch. On receiving news of the French army's defeat at the Battle of Blenheim (August 13, 1704). Remark (1704)

10 Hence, vain deluding Joys,
The brood of Folly without father bred.

John Milton (1608–74) English writer. 'Il Penseroso' (1645), l. 1

11 Delusions may be the only things which render life tolerable and, as such, are jealously defended against all the assaults of reason.

Anthony Storr (b. 1920) British writer and psychiatrist. *The Integrated Personality* (1960)

12 It is amazing how complete is the delusion that beauty is goodness.

Leo Tolstoy (1828–1910) Russian writer. *The Kreutzer Sonata* (1889)

Delusions of Love

see also **Love, Lovers, Relationships**

1 The eyes of a lover tell lies.

Peter Abrahams (b. 1919) South African-born novelist, journalist, and political commentator. *Mine Boy* (1946)

2 If all else perished, and he remained, I should still continue to be; and if all else remained, and he were annihilated, the universe would turn to a mighty stranger: I should not seem a part of it.

Emily Brontë (1818–48) British poet and novelist. *Wuthering Heights* (1847), ch. 9

3 Who told you there was no such thing as real, true, eternal love? Cut out his lying tongue!

Mikhail Bulgakov (1891–1940) Russian novelist and playwright. 1929–40. *The Master and Margarita* (Michael Glenny, tr.; 1966), ch. 19

4 It's only make believe that I love you.

Oscar Hammerstein II (1895–1960) US lyricist and librettist. Song lyric. 'Only Make Believe', *Show Boat* (music by Jerome Kern; 1927)

5 Many a man in love with a dimple makes the mistake of marrying the whole girl.

Stephen Leacock (1869–1944) British-born Canadian writer and economist. *Literary Lapses* (1910)

6 Love is the delusion that one woman differs from another.

H. L. Mencken (1880–1956) US journalist, critic, and editor. *A Mencken Chrestomathy* (1949), ch. 30

7 For love deceives the best of womankind.

Alexander Pope (1688–1744) English poet. *The Odyssey of Homer* (1725), bk. 15, l. 463

8 So true a fool is love that in your will, Though you do anything, he thinks no ill.

William Shakespeare (1564–1616) English poet and playwright. Sonnet 57 (1609)

9 When my love swears that she is made of truth, I do believe her, though I know she lies.

William Shakespeare (1564–1616) English poet and playwright. Sonnet 138 (1609)

10 TITANIA My Oberon! what visions have I seen! Methought I was enamour'd of an ass.

William Shakespeare (1564–1616) English poet and playwright. *A Midsummer Night's Dream* (1595–96), Act 4, Scene 1

11 DESDEMONA I am not merry, but I do beguile The thing I am by seeming otherwise.

William Shakespeare (1564–1616) English poet and playwright. *Othello* (1602–04), Act 2, Scene 1

12 MERCUTIO O! then, I see Queen Mab hath been with you.
She is the fairies' midwife . . .
And in this state she gallops night by night
Through lovers' brains, and then they dream of love.

William Shakespeare (1564–1616) English poet and playwright. *Romeo and Juliet* (1595), Act 1, Scene 4

13 JESSICA But love is blind, and lovers cannot see The pretty follies that themselves commit.

William Shakespeare (1564–1616) English poet and playwright. *The Merchant of Venice* (1596–98), Act 2, Scene 6

Democracy

see also **Freedom, Free Speech, Government, Politics**

1 The one pervading evil of democracy is the tyranny of the majority.

Lord Acton (1834–1902) British historian. *The History of Freedom* (John Figgis and Reginald Laurence, eds.; 1907)

2 The voice of the people is the voice of God.

Alcuin (735–804) English cleric, theologian, and scholar. Letter to Charlemagne (800), quoted in *Works* (1863), vol. 1

3 No community can be said to possess local self-government if the executive can, at his pleasure, send military forces to patrol its streets under pretense of enforcing some law.

John Peter Altgeld (1847–1902) German-born US lawyer and politician. Protesting at the use of federal troops to break a strike by employees of the Pullman railway carriage company. Letter to US President Grover Cleveland (July 6, 1894)

4 Democracy means government by discussion but it is only effective if you can stop people talking.

Clement Attlee (1883–1967) British politician. Speech at Oxford (June 14, 1957), quoted in *Times* (June 15, 1957)

5 There is no greater farce than to talk of democracy. To begin with, it is a lie; it has never existed in any great country.

Henri Bourassa (1868–1952) Canadian politician and journalist. *Le Devoir* (February 11, 1943)

6 The people are the masters.

Edmund Burke (1729–97) Irish-born British statesman and political philosopher. Speech to the British Parliament, 'On the Economical Reform' (February 11, 1780)

7 Man is by his constitution a religious animal. A perfect democracy is therefore the most shameless thing in the world.

Edmund Burke (1729–97) Irish-born British statesman and political philosopher. *Reflections on the Revolution in France* (1790)

8 I am not one of those who think that the people are never in the wrong. They have been so, frequently and outrageously, both in other countries and in this. But I do say, that in all disputes between them and their rulers, the presumption is at least upon a par in favour of the people.

Edmund Burke (1729–97) Irish-born British statesman and political philosopher. *Thoughts on the Cause of the Present Discontents* (1770)

9 One man shall have one vote.

John Cartwright (1740–1824) British politician and reformer. *People's Barrier Against Undue Influence* (1780), ch. 1

10 Democracy means choosing your dictators, after they've told you what it is you want to hear.

Alan Coren (b. 1938) British writer and humorist. Attrib.

11 Democracy has to be institutionalized and written into law, so as to make sure that institutions and laws do not change whenever the leadership changes, or whenever the leaders change their views or shift the focus of their attention.

Deng Xiaoping (1904–97) Chinese statesman. 'Emancipate the Mind, Seek Truth from Facts and Unite as One in Looking to the Future' (December 13, 1978), quoted in *Deng Xiaoping: Speeches and Writings* (Robert Maxwell, ed.; 1987)

12 Nor is the People's Judgment always true: The Most may err as grossly as the Few.

John Dryden (1631–1700) English poet, playwright, and literary critic. *Absalom and Achitophel* (1681), pt. 1

13 What concerns everyone can only be resolved by everyone.

Friedrich Dürrenmatt (1921–90) Swiss writer. *The Physicists* (1962)

14 We cannot safely leave politics to politicians, or political economy to college professors. The people themselves must think, because the people alone can act.

Henry George (1839–97) US economist. *Social Problems* (1883)

15 All the world over, I will back the masses against the classes.

William Ewart Gladstone (1809–98) British statesman. Speech at Liverpool (June 28, 1886)

16 Some comrades apparently find it hard to
understand that democracy is just a slogan.
Mikhail Gorbachev (b. 1931) Russian statesman. *Observer* (February
1, 1987), 'Sayings of the Week'

17 Democracy is the wholesome and pure air
without which a socialist public organisation
cannot live a full-blooded life.
Mikhail Gorbachev (b. 1931) Russian statesman. *Report to the 27th
Party Congress of the Communist Party of the USSR*
(February 25, 1986)

18 Something may falter in the game of democracy
when we elect others to rule us who are oblivious
of the blood on their hands, the red blood, the
pagan blood, and thus may unwittingly lead us
into hell.
Wilson Harris (b. 1921) Guyanese-born writer. Said by Masters.
Carnival (1985)

19 I swear to the Lord
I still can't see
Why Democracy means
Everybody but me.
Langston Hughes (1902–67) US novelist, playwright, and short-story writer.
'The Black Man Speaks', *Jim Crow's Last Stand* (1943)

20 You are the heroic example of democracy's
solidarity and universality, in face of the
shameful 'accommodating' spirit of those who
interpret democratic principles with their eyes on
hoards of wealth or the industrial shares which
they want to preserve from any risk.
Dolores Ibárruri (1895–1989) Spanish politician and journalist. Farewell
speech to the International Brigades, after their defeat in the
Spanish Civil War. 'Goodbye, Brothers, Till Our Speedy
Reunion', speech, Barcelona (September 1938)

21 Public participation in the process of government
is the essence of democracy.
Lyndon Baines Johnson (1908–73) US president. Message to the US
Congress (May 25, 1967)

22 The vote is the most powerful instrument ever
devised by man for breaking down injustice and
destroying the terrible walls which imprison men
because they are different from other men.
Lyndon Baines Johnson (1908–73) US president. Speech, Washington,
D.C. (August 6, 1965)

23 A democratic nation of persons, of individuals, is
an impossibility, and a fratricidal goal. Each
American one of us must consciously choose to
become a willing and outspoken part of the
people who, together, will determine our
individual chances for happiness, and justice.
June Jordan (b. 1936) US journalist, writer, and activist. *Waking Up In
The Middle Of Some American Dreams* (1986)

24 Democracy is a difficult kind of government. It
requires the highest qualities of self-discipline,
restraint, a willingness to make commitments and
sacrifices for the general interest, and it also
requires knowledge.
John Fitzgerald Kennedy (1917–63) US president. Speech, Dublin
Castle, Republic of Ireland (June 28, 1963)

25 Democracy is the superior form of government,
because it is based on a respect for man as a
reasonable being.
John Fitzgerald Kennedy (1917–63) US president. *Why England Slept*
(1940)

26 A democracy is a state which recognizes the
subjecting of the minority to the majority.
Vladimir Ilyich Lenin (1870–1924) Russian revolutionary leader. *The State
and Revolution* (1919), ch. 4

27 The ballot is stronger than the bullet.
Abraham Lincoln (1809–65) US president. Speech at Bloomington,
Illinois (May 19, 1856)

28 No man is good enough to govern another man
without that other's consent.
Abraham Lincoln (1809–65) US president. Speech at Peoria, Illinois
(October 16, 1854)

29 Democracy gives every man a right to be his own
oppressor.
James Russell Lowell (1819–91) US poet, editor, essayist, and diplomat.
The Bigelow Papers (1867), vol. 2

30 Democracies . . . have in general been as short in
their lives as they have been violent in their
deaths.
James Madison (1751–1836) US president. *Independent Journal*
(November 23, 1787), quoted in *The Federalist* (Alexander
Hamilton, ed.; 1788), no. 10

31 A modern democracy is a tyranny whose borders
are undefined; one discovers how far one can go
only by traveling in a straight line until one is
stopped.
Norman Mailer (b. 1923) US novelist and journalist. *The Presidential
Papers* (1963), Preface

32 Since my release, I have become more convinced
than ever that the real makers of history are the
ordinary men and women of our country; their
participation in every decision about the future is
the only guarantee of true democracy and
freedom.
Nelson Mandela (b. 1918) South African president and lawyer. *The
Struggle is My Life* (1990)

33 Democracy sometimes seems to be an end, but it
is in fact only a means.
Mao Zedong (1893–1976) Chinese statesman. *On the Correct
Handling of Contradiction* (1957), quoted in *Mao Tsetung:
An Anthology of His Writings* (Anne Fremantle, ed.; 1962)

34 Democracy is the theory that the common people
know what they want, and deserve to get it good
and hard.
H. L. Mencken (1880–1956) US journalist, critic, and editor. *A Little
Book in C Major* (1916)

35 Democracy is . . . a form of religion; it is the
worship of jackals by jackasses.
H. L. Mencken (1880–1956) US journalist, critic, and editor. 1920.
'Sententiæ', *The Vintage Mencken* (Alistair Cooke, ed.; 1955)

36 The disease which must be cured, the volcano
which must be extinguished, the gangrene which
must be burned out with a hot iron, the hydra
with jaws open to swallow up the social order.
Metternich (1773–1859) Austrian diplomat and statesman. Referring to
French-style democracy. Quoted in *Europe: A History*
(Norman Davies; 1996), ch. 10

37 Man's capacity for justice makes democracy
possible, but man's inclination to injustice makes
democracy necessary.
Reinhold Niebuhr (1892–1971) US theologian. *Children of Light and
Children of Darkness* (1944), Foreword

38 A democracy—that is a government of all the
people, by all the people, for all the people; of
course, a government of the principles of eternal
justice, the unchanging law of God; for shortness'
sake I will call it the idea of Freedom.
Theodore Parker (1810–60) US clergyman. Speech, 'The American
Idea', at the New England Anti-Slavery Convention, Boston
(May 29, 1850)

39 Democracy is a charming form of government, full of variety and disorder, and dispensing a sort of equality to equals and unequals alike.
Plato (428?–347? BC) Greek philosopher. *The Republic* (370? BC), bk. 8

40 Democracy passes into despotism.
Plato (428?–347? BC) Greek philosopher. *The Republic* (370? BC), bk. 8

41 There are two truths in this world that should never be separated: 1. that sovereignty rests with the people; 2. that the people should never exercise it.
Antoine de Rivarol (1753–1801) French journalist. *Journal Politique National* (1790), vol. 1, no. 13

42 In the strict sense of the term, there has never been a true democracy, and there never will be. It is contrary to the natural order that the greater number should govern and the smaller number be governed.
Jean-Jacques Rousseau (1712–78) French philosopher and writer. *The Social Contract* (1762)

43 'Electronic democracy' can open new doors for participation but it is no panacea . . . democracy without democratic processes is just a word.
Douglas Schuler, US author. *Reinventing Technology* (Co-edited with Philip E. Agre; 1997)

44 We must be thoroughly democratic and patronise everybody without distinction of class.
George Bernard Shaw (1856–1950) Irish playwright. *John Bull's Other Island* (1907)

45 All the ills of democracy can be cured by more democracy.
Al Smith (1873–1944) US politician. Speech, Albany, New York (June 27, 1933), quoted in *New York Times* (July 28, 1933)

46 It's not the voting that's democracy; it's the counting.
Tom Stoppard (b. 1937) Czech-born British playwright and screenwriter. *Jumpers* (1972), Act 1

47 People are not willing to be governed by those who do not speak their language.
Norman Tebbit (b. 1931) British politician. *Observer* (November 24, 1991)

48 The people's government, made for the people, made by the people, and answerable to the people.
Daniel Webster (1782–1852) US lawyer, politician, and orator. January 26, 1830. Referring to Foote's resolution. Speech to the US Senate, quoted in *The Writings and Speeches of Daniel Webster* (J. W. McIntyre, ed.; 1903), vol. 6

49 Democracy means simply the bludgeoning of the people by the people for the people.
Oscar Wilde (1854–1900) Irish poet, playwright, and wit. *The Soul of Man Under Socialism* (1891)

Depression

see also **Illness, Mind, Therapy**

1 Can there be misery—(*he yawns*)—loftier than mine?
Samuel Beckett (1906–89) Irish playwright, novelist, and poet. *Endgame* (1958)

2 After great pain, a formal feeling comes—
The Nerves sit ceremonious like tombs.
Emily Dickinson (1830–86) US poet. 1862? 'After Great Pain, a Formal Feeling Comes', *Further Poems* (1929), quoted in *The Penguin Book of American Verse* (Geoffrey Moore, ed.; 1977)

3 In the real dark night of the soul it is always three o'clock in the morning.
F. Scott Fitzgerald (1896–1940) US writer. Referring to Saint John of the Cross's: 'The dark night of the soul'. *Esquire* (March 1936)

4 By simply radiating gloom he acts as a depressant.
Karen Horney (1885–1952) German-born US psychoanalyst. Referring to the sadist's impulse to frustrate joy in others. *Our Inner Conflicts* (1945)

5 I am in that temper that if I were under water I would scarcely kick to come to the top.
John Keats (1795–1821) English poet. Letter to Benjamin Bailey (May 21, 1818), quoted in *Letters of John Keats* (H. E. Rollins, ed.; 1958), vol. 1

6 Some days called for the blues.
Paule Marshall (b. 1929) US novelist, teacher, and journalist. *Praisesong for the Widow* (1983)

7 Have you any idea
How long a night can last, spent
Lying alone and sobbing?
Michitsuna no Haha (935?–995) Japanese diarist. 974? Quoted in *Hundred Poets, A Poem Apiece* (13th century)

8 'Good morning, Little Piglet', said Eeyore. 'If it *is* a good morning', he said. 'Which I doubt', said he. 'Not that it matters', he said.
A. A. Milne (1882–1956) British writer. Typical of Eeyore's negative outlook. 'Eeyore Has a Birthday', *Winnie the Pooh* (1926)

9 TITUS If there were reason for these miseries,
Then into limits could I bind my woes.
When heaven doth weep, doth not the earth o'erflow?
If the winds rage, doth not the sea wax mad,
Threat'ning the welkin with his big-swol'n face?
William Shakespeare (1564–1616) English poet and playwright. *Titus Andronicus* (1590), Act 3, Scene 1

10 Noble deeds and hot baths are the best cures for depression.
Dodie Smith (1896–1990) British playwright, novelist, and theatrical producer. *I Capture the Castle* (1948), pt. 1, ch. 3

11 Mysteriously and in ways that are totally remote from normal experience, the gray drizzle of horror induced by depression takes on the quality of physical pain . . . it is entirely natural that the victim begins to think ceaselessly of oblivion.
William Styron (b. 1925) US novelist. *Darkness Visible* (1990), quoted in *Depression* (Constance Hammen; 1997), ch. 1

12 I wonder whether for a person like myself whose most intense moments were those of depression a cure that destroys the depression may not destroy the intensity—a desperate remedy.
Edward Thomas (1878–1917) British poet, biographer, and critic. Quoted in *Edward Thomas* (R. George Thomas; 1985)

13 There are many pathways to a depressive illness. Unfortunately one of these pathways often leads on to suicide.
Lewis Wolpert (b. 1929) British biologist and writer. *Malignant Sadness* (1999)

Design

see also **Architecture, Art, Beauty**

1 Design occupies a unique space between art and science. Designers must be sensitive to what is technically possible and what is humanly desirable.
Terence Conran (b. 1931) British designer and entrepreneur. *Terence Conran on Design* (1996)

2 Design is the tribute art pays to industry.

Paul Finch, British architectural journalist. *Definitions of Design* (1995)

3 Maximum meaning—minimum means.

Abram Games (1914–96) British graphic designer. Quoted in
Contemporary Designers (Colin Naylor, ed.; 1990)

4 Art has to move you and design does not, unless
it's a good design for a bus.

David Hockney (b. 1937) British artist. *Guardian* (October 26, 1988)

5 Demand bare walls in your bedroom, your living
room, and your dining room . . . Buy only
practical furniture and never buy 'decorative'
pieces. If you want to see bad taste, go into the
houses of the rich. Put only a few pictures on
your walls and none but good ones.

Le Corbusier (1887–1965) Swiss-born French architect. Attrib.

6 If you design something too well, you don't get
another job for 30 years.

Raymond Loewy (1893–1986) US industrial designer. 1934. Quoted in
*Royal Designers on Design: a Selection of Addresses by Royal
Designers for Industry* (The Design Council, London; 1986)

7 The design of a pepper pot is as important as the
conception of a cathedral.

Margaret Macdonald Mackintosh (1865–1933) Scottish designer. Quoted
in *Terence Conran on Design* (Terence Conran; 1996)

8 Design is the conscious effort to impose
meaningful order.

Victor Papanek (b. 1925) Austrian-born US designer, teacher, and writer.
*Design for the Real World: Human Ecology and Social
Change* (1984)

9 I can't think how many times I've wanted to
leave a dinner table after spending too long in a
designer chair.

Paul Smith (b. 1946) British fashion designer. *Observer* (December
12, 1995)

Desire

see also **Appetite, Lust, Passion, Vitality**

1 You don't want no pie in the sky when you die.
You want something here on the ground while
you're still around.

Muhammad Ali (b. 1942) US boxer. Attrib.

2 It is a miserable state of mind to have few things
to desire and many things to fear.

Francis Bacon (1561–1626) English philosopher, statesman, and lawyer.
'Of Empire', *Essays* (1625)

3 Sooner murder an infant in its cradle than nurse
unacted desires.

William Blake (1757–1827) British poet, painter, engraver, and mystic.
'Proverbs of Hell', *The Marriage of Heaven and Hell* (1790–
93), plate 10, l. 7

4 Those who restrain desire, do so because theirs is
weak enough to be restrained.

William Blake (1757–1827) British poet, painter, engraver, and mystic.
'The Voice of the Devil', *The Marriage of Heaven and Hell*
(1790–93), plates 5–6

5 The Desire of Man being Infinite, the possession
is Infinite, and himself Infinite.

William Blake (1757–1827) British poet, painter, engraver, and mystic.
There is No Natural Religion (1788)

6 O'er her warm cheek and rising bosom move
The bloom of young Desire and purple light of Love.

Thomas Gray (1716–71) British poet. 'A Pindaric Ode', *The Progress
of Poesy* (1754), st. 3, ll. 12–13

7 The desire of the moth for the star.

James Joyce (1882–1941) Irish writer. Commenting on the interruption
of a music recital when a moth flew into the singer's mouth.
Quoted in *James Joyce* (Richard Ellmann; 1959)

8 He who is eternally without desire
Perceives the spiritual side of it;
He who is permanently with desire
Perceives the limit of it.

Laozi (570?–490? BC) Chinese philosopher. The *Daode Jing* is an
early Chinese Taoist text. While attributed to Laozi, it
probably dates from the 3rd century BC *Daode Jing*, quoted
in *Sacred Texts of the World* (Ninian Smart and Richard D.
Hecht, eds.; 1982)

9 Life is a petty thing unless there is pounding
within it an enormous desire to extend its
boundaries. We live in proportion to the extent
to which we yearn to live more.

José Ortega y Gasset (1883–1955) Spanish writer and philosopher. *The
Dehumanization of Art* (1925)

10 There is nothing like desire for preventing the
thing one says from bearing any resemblance to
what one has in mind.

Marcel Proust (1871–1922) French novelist. 1921. Le Côté de
Guermantes, *À la Recherche du Temps Perdu* (1913–27)

11 A desire is in fact never satisfied to the letter
precisely because of the abyss that separates the
real from the imaginary.

Jean-Paul Sartre (1905–80) French philosopher, playwright, and novelist.
The Psychology of Imagination (1948)

12 POINS Is it not strange that desire should so
many years outlive performance?

William Shakespeare (1564–1616) English poet and playwright. *Henry
IV, Part 2* (1597), Act 2, Scene 4

13 BEROWNE At Christmas I no more desire a rose
Than wish a snow in May's newfangled shows.

William Shakespeare (1564–1616) English poet and playwright. *Love's
Labour's Lost* (1595), Act 1, Scene 1

14 Desire is the very essence of man.

Baruch Spinoza (1632–77) Dutch philosopher and theologian. *Ethics*
(1677), pt. 3, prop. 59, def. 1

15 Adam was but human—this explains it all. He
did not want the apple for the apple's sake, he
wanted it only because it was forbidden.

Mark Twain (1835–1910) US writer and humorist. 'Pudd'nhead
Wilson's Calendar', *Pudd'nhead Wilson* (1894), ch. 2

Despair

see also **Fear, Horror**

1 The glacier knocks in the cupboard,
The desert sighs in the bed,
And the crack in the tea-cup opens
A lane to the land of the dead.

W. H. Auden (1907–73) British poet. 1937. 'As I Walked Out One
Evening', *W. H. Auden: Collected Poems* (Edward
Mendelson, ed.; 1976)

2 One morning
his face fell out of the mirror
into his hands:
he let it fall.

Hans W. Cohn (b. 1916) German psychotherapist and poet. 'Fall' (1970–
72), quoted in *German Poetry 1910–75* (Michael Hamburger,
ed., tr.; 1977)

3 'God save thee, ancient Mariner!
From the fiends that plague thee thus!—
Why look'st thou so?'—With my cross-bow
I shot the Albatross.

Samuel Taylor Coleridge (1772–1834) British poet. 'The Rime of the
Ancient Mariner', *Lyrical Ballads* (1798), pt. 1

4 Where does one go from a world of insanity?
Somewhere on the other side of despair.
T. S. Eliot (1888–1965) US-born British poet and playwright. *The Family Reunion* (1939), Act 2, Scene 2

5 What are the roots that clutch, what branches grow
Out of this stony rubbish? Son of man,
You cannot say, or guess, for you know only
A heap of broken images.
T. S. Eliot (1888–1965) US-born British poet and playwright. 'The Burial of the Dead', *The Waste Land* (1922)

6 The person who sings only the blues is like someone in a deep pit yelling for help.
Mahalia Jackson (1911–72) US gospel singer. *Movin' On Up* (Mahalia Jackson and Evan McLeod Wylie; 1966)

7 Utter despair, impossible to pull myself together; only when I have become satisfied with my sufferings can I stop.
Franz Kafka (1883–1924) Czech writer. *The Diaries of Franz Kafka* (Max Brod, ed.; 1948)

8 Where can you scream? It's a serious question: where can you go in society and scream?
R. D. Laing (1927–89) Scottish psychiatrist. Quoted in *Mad to be Normal: Conversations with R. D. Laing* (Bob Mullan, ed.; 1995), Introduction

9 The sadness was at her center, the desolated center where the self that was no self made its home.
Toni Morrison (b. 1931) US novelist. *Beloved* (1987)

10 The sky was suddenly blood-red—I stopped and leaned against the fence, dead tired. I saw the flaming clouds like blood and a sword—the bluish-black fjord and town—my friends walked on—I stood there, trembling with anxiety—and I felt as though Nature were convulsed by a great unending scream.
Edvard Munch (1863–1944) Norwegian artist. Letter (1892)

11 My only hope lies in my despair.
Racine (1639–99) French playwright. *Bajazet* (1672), Act 1, Scene 4

12 When in disgrace with fortune and men's eyes
I all alone beweep my outcast state,
And trouble deaf heaven with my bootless cries,
And look upon myself, and curse my fate,
Wishing me like to one more rich in hope
Featur'd like him, like him with friends possess'd,
Desiring this man's art, and that man's scope,
With what I most enjoy contented least.
William Shakespeare (1564–1616) English poet and playwright. Sonnet 29 (1609)

13 KING RICHARD III I shall despair. There is no creature loves me;
And if I die, no soul will pity me:
Nay, wherefore should they, since that I myself
Find in myself no pity to myself?
William Shakespeare (1564–1616) English poet and playwright. *Richard III* (1591), Act 5, Scene 3

14 I could lie down like a tired child,
And weep away the life of care
Which I have borne and yet must bear,
Till death like sleep might steal on me.
Percy Bysshe Shelley (1792–1822) English poet. 'Stanzas Written in Dejection, Near Naples' (1818), st. 4, quoted in *Posthumous Poems* (Mrs. Shelley, ed.; 1824)

15 And now that the purgatory is over
I invent phrases, thoughts, days,
a short story where blindness
may be lived as nakedness.
Converted into words
desperation is impossible.
Jenaro Talens (b. 1946) Spanish educator and poet. 'Effects of Light on the Plants', *A Bilingual Anthology of Contemporary Spanish Poetry* (Luis A. Ramos-García, ed.; 1997), ll. 1–6

16 A still small voice spake unto me,
'Thou art so full of misery,
Were it not better not to be?'
Alfred Tennyson (1809–92) British poet. 'The Two Voices', *Poems* (1832), st. 1

17 The mass of men lead lives of quiet desperation.
Henry David Thoreau (1817–62) US writer. 'Economy', *Walden, or, Life in the Woods* (1854)

Destiny

see also **Fate**

1 I felt as if I were walking with destiny, and that all my past life had been but a preparation for this hour and this trial.
Winston Churchill (1874–1965) British prime minister and writer. Referring to the outbreak of World War II. *The Gathering Storm* (1948), ch. 38

2 Every people should be the originators of their own designs, the projector of their own schemes, and creators of the events that lead to their destiny—the consummation of their desires.
Martin Robinson Delany (1812–85) US physician, abolitionist, and newspaper editor. *The Condition, Elevation, Emigration and Destiny of the Colored People of the United States, Politically Considered* (1852)

3 'Tis all a Chequer-board of Nights and Days
Where Destiny with Men for Pieces plays:
Hither and thither moves, and mates, and slays,
And one by one back in the Closet lays.
Edward FitzGerald (1809–83) British poet and translator. 1868. *The Rubáiyát of Omar Khayyám* (1868 edn.), st. 50

4 The whole secret of a successful life is to find out what it is one's destiny to do, and then do it.
Henry Ford (1863–1947) US car manufacturer. 'Success', *Forum* (October 1928)

5 Anatomy is destiny.
Sigmund Freud (1856–1939) Austrian psychoanalyst. *Collected Writings* (1924), vol. 5

6 Everyman has his own destiny: The only imperative is to follow it, to accept it, no matter where it leads him.
Henry Miller (1891–1980) US novelist. *The Wisdom of the Heart* (1941)

7 There is a mysterious cycle in human events. To some generations much is given. Of other generations much is expected. This generation has a rendezvous with destiny.
Franklin D. Roosevelt (1882–1945) US president. Speech accepting the Democratic Party presidential nomination (June 26, 1936)

8 PROLOGUE From forth the fatal loins of these two foes
A pair of star-cross'd lovers take their life.
William Shakespeare (1564–1616) English poet and playwright. *Romeo and Juliet* (1595), Prologue

Determination

see also **Courage**, **Desire**, **Effort**

1 There is no such thing as a great talent without great will-power.

Honoré de Balzac (1799–1850) French writer. *La Muse du Département* (1843)

2 Let's meet, and either do, or die.

Beaumont & Fletcher, English playwrights. *The Island Princess* (1621), Act 2, Scene 2

3 We must just KBO ('Keep Buggering On').

Winston Churchill (1874–1965) British prime minister and writer. 1941. Remark (December 1941), quoted in *Finest Hour* (Martin Gilbert; 1983)

4 Attempt the end, and never stand to doubt; Nothing's so hard but search will find it out.

Robert Herrick (1591–1674) English poet. 'Seek and Find', *Hesperides* (1648), ll. 1–2

5 I will have this done, so I order it done; let my will replace reasoned judgement.

Juvenal (65?–128?) Roman poet. *Satires* (98?–128?), no. 6, l. 223

6 What though the field be lost?
All is not lost; the unconquerable will,
And study of revenge, immortal hate,
And courage never to submit or yield:
And what is else not to be overcome?

John Milton (1608–74) English writer. Said by Satan. *Paradise Lost* (1667), bk. 1, ll. 105–109

7 CLEOPATRA My resolution's plac'd, and I have nothing
Of woman in me; now from head to foot
I am marble-constant; now the fleeting moon
No planet is of mine.

William Shakespeare (1564–1616) English poet and playwright. *Antony and Cleopatra* (1606–07), Act 5, Scene 2

8 PHILIP THE BASTARD Bell, book, and candle, shall not drive me back,
When gold and silver becks me to come on.

William Shakespeare (1564–1616) English poet and playwright. *King John* (1591–98), Act 3, Scene 3

9 He gave a deep sigh—I saw the iron enter into his soul!

Laurence Sterne (1713–68) Irish-born British writer and clergyman. 'The Captive, Paris', *A Sentimental Journey Through France and Italy* (1768)

10 I will . . . let appear these burning fires that were threatening to consume me,
I will lift what has too long kept down these smoldering fires—I will now expose them and use them.

Walt Whitman (1819–92) US poet. 'Premonition' (1856–60)

The Devil

see also **Damnation**, **Evil**, **Morality**, **Temptation**

1 There are in every man, at every hour, two simultaneous postulations, one towards God, the other towards Satan.

Charles Baudelaire (1821–67) French poet. 'Mon Coeur Mis à Nu', *Journaux Intimes* (1887)

2 Thus the devil played at chess with me, and yielding a pawn, thought to gain a queen of me, taking advantage of my honest endeavours.

Thomas Browne (1605–82) English physician and writer. *Religio Medici* (1635?), pt. 2

3 'And the devil doesn't exist either, I suppose?'

Mikhail Bulgakov (1891–1940) Russian novelist and playwright. 1929–40. Said by the Devil to one who has denied the historical existence of Jesus. *The Master and Margarita* (Michael Glenny, tr.; 1966), ch. 3

4 The Devil himself, which is the author of confusion and lies.

Robert Burton (1577–1640) English scholar and churchman. *The Anatomy of Melancholy* (1621), pt. 3, sect. 4

5 Good intentions can be evil,
Both hands can be full of grease.
You know that sometimes Satan comes as a man of peace.

Bob Dylan (b. 1941) US singer and songwriter. Song lyric. 'Man of Peace' (1983)

6 Omniscient am I not, but well-informed.

Johann Wolfgang von Goethe (1749–1832) German poet, playwright, and scientist. Said by Mephistopheles. *Faust* (1808), pt. 1

7 The Lucifer legend is in no sense an absurd fairytale; like the story of the serpent in the Garden of Eden, it is a 'therapeutic' myth.

Carl Gustav Jung (1875–1961) Swiss psychoanalyst. 1958. 'A Psychological Approach to the Dogma of the Trinity', *Collected Works* (1969), vol. 2

8 Men are possessed by the devil in two ways; corporally or spiritually. Those whom he possesses corporally . . . he has permission from God to vex and agitate, but he has no power over their souls.

Martin Luther (1483–1546) German theologian and religious reformer. *Colloquia Mensalia* (1652)

9 For where God built a church, there the Devil would also build a chapel.

Martin Luther (1483–1546) German theologian and religious reformer. 1540? *Table Talk* (1566), no. 67

10 His form had yet not lost
All her original brightness, nor appeared
Less than archangel ruined, and the excess
Of glory obscured.

John Milton (1608–74) English writer. Referring to Satan. *Paradise Lost* (1667), bk. 1, ll. 591–594

11 Incensed with indignatio Satan stood
Unterrified, and like a comet burned,
That fires the length of Ophiucus huge
In the Arctic sky, and from his horrid hair
Shakes pestilence and war.

John Milton (1608–74) English writer. *Paradise Lost* (1667), bk. 2, ll. 707–711

12 EMILIA O! the more angel she,
And you the blacker devil.

William Shakespeare (1564–1616) English poet and playwright. *Othello* (1602–04), Act 5, Scene 2

13 DROMIO Marry, he must have a long spoon that must eat with the devil.

William Shakespeare (1564–1616) English poet and playwright. *The Comedy of Errors* (1594), Act 4, Scene 3

14 ANTONIO The devil can cite Scripture for his purpose.

William Shakespeare (1564–1616) English poet and playwright. *The Merchant of Venice* (1596–98), Act 1, Scene 3

15 The prince of darkness is a gentleman.

John Suckling (1609–42) English poet. *The Goblins* (1638)

Diaries

see also **Autobiography**, **Books**

1 Only good girls keep diaries. Bad girls don't have the time.
Tallulah Bankhead (1903–68) US actor. Attrib.

2 I soothe my conscience now with the thought that it is better for hard words to be on paper than that Mummy should carry them in her heart.
Anne Frank (1929–45) German diarist. January 2, 1944. *Anne Frank: The Diary of a Young Girl* (1947)

3 What is a diary as a rule? A document useful to the person who keeps it, dull to the contemporary who reads it, invaluable to the student, centuries afterwards, who treasures it!
Ellen Terry (1847–1928) British actor. *The Story of My Life* (1908), ch. 14

4 He would like to destroy his old diaries and to appear before his children and the public only in his patriarchal robes. His vanity is immense!
Sofya Tolstoy (1844–1919) Russian writer. 1890. Referring to Leo Tolstoy. *A Diary of Tolstoy's Wife* (1860–91)

5 I always say, keep a diary and some day it'll keep you.
Mae West (1892–1980) US actor and comedian. *Every Day's A Holiday* (1937)

6 I never travel without my diary. One should always have something sensational to read in the train.
Oscar Wilde (1854–1900) Irish poet, playwright, and wit. *The Importance of Being Earnest* (1895), Act 2

Dictators

see also **Authoritarianism**, **Fascism**, **Tyranny**

1 I picked Franco out when he was a nobody. He has double-crossed and deceived me at every turn.
Alfonso XIII (1886–1941) Spanish monarch. Referring to Francisco Franco. Quoted in *Franco* (Paul Preston; 1993)

2 I believe in benevolent dictatorship provided I am the dictator.
Richard Branson (b. 1950) British entrepreneur and publicist. Remark (1984)

3 There sunk the greatest, nor the worst of men,
Whose spirit, antithetically mixt,
One moment of the mightiest, and again
On little objects with like firmness fixt.
Extreme in all things!
Lord Byron (1788–1824) British poet. Referring to Napoleon. *Childe Harold's Pilgrimage* (1812–18), can. 3, st. 36

4 Dictators ride to and fro upon tigers which they dare not dismount. And the tigers are getting hungry.
Winston Churchill (1874–1965) British prime minister and writer. *While England Slept* (1938)

5 I often think how much easier the world would have been to manage if Herr Hitler and Signor Mussolini had been at Oxford.
Lord Halifax (1881–1959) British statesman. Speech, York (November 4, 1937)

6 With us the Leader and the Idea are one, and every party member has to do what the Leader orders.
Adolf Hitler (1889–1945) Austrian-born German dictator. Conversation with Otto Strasser (as recounted by Strasser; May 21, 1930), quoted in *Hitler and Stalin: Parallel Lives* (Alan Bullock; 1991), ch. 5

7 In every age the vilest specimens of human nature are to be found among demagogues.
Thomas Babington Macaulay (1800–59) British politician, historian, and writer. 1848. *History of England from the Accession of James II* (1848–61), vol. 1, ch. 5

8 The Italians will laugh at me; every time Hitler occupies a country he sends me a message.
Benito Mussolini (1883–1945) Italian dictator. Quoted in *Hitler* (Alan Bullock; 1952), ch. 8

9 That garrulous monk.
Benito Mussolini (1883–1945) Italian dictator. Referring to Adolf Hitler. Quoted in *The Second World War* (Winston Churchill; 1948–53)

10 Executive power is exercised by the President of the Governing Junta, who, with the title of President of the Republic of Chile, administers the State and is the Supreme Chief of the Nation.
Augusto Pinochet (b. 1915) Chilean dictator. Legal decree no.1 (September 11, 1973), quoted in *Pinochet: The Politics of Power* (Genaro Arriagada; 1988)

11 Neither my moral nor spiritual formation permits me to be a dictator . . . If I were a dictator, you can be certain many things would have happened.
Augusto Pinochet (b. 1915) Chilean dictator. Quoted in *A Nation of Enemies* (Pamela Constable and Arturo Valenzuela; 1991)

12 Tired of making himself loved, he wants to make himself feared.
Racine (1639–99) French playwright. *Brittanicus* (1669), Act 1, Scene 1

13 Germany was the cause of Hitler just as much as Chicago is responsible for the Chicago Tribune.
Alexander Woollcott (1887–1943) US writer and critic. Radio interview (1943)

Digestion

see also **Eating**, **Food**, **Health and Healthy Living**

1 INDIGESTION, n. A disease which the patient and his friends frequently mistake for deep religious conviction and concern for the salvation of mankind.
Ambrose Bierce (1842–1914?) US writer and journalist. *The Devil's Dictionary* (1911)

2 The healthy stomach is nothing if not conservative. Few radicals have good digestions.
Samuel Butler (1835–1902) British writer and composer. Quoted in *Note Books* (H. Festing Jones, ed.; 1912)

3 It's a very odd thing—
As odd as can be—
That whatever Miss T eats
Turns into Miss T.
Walter de la Mare (1873–1956) British poet and novelist. 'Miss T', *Peacock Pie* (1913)

4 A good eater must be a good man; for a good eater must have a good digestion, and a good digestion depends upon a good conscience.
Benjamin Disraeli (1804–81) British prime minister and writer. *The Young Duke* (1831)

5   Indigestion is charged by God with enforcing morality on the stomach.
Victor Hugo (1802–85) French poet, novelist, and playwright. *Les Misérables* (1862), bk. 3, ch. 7

6   Confirmed dispepsia is the apparatus of illusions.
George Meredith (1828–1909) British novelist and poet. *The Ordeal of Richard Feverel* (1859)

7   The abdomen is the reason why man does not easily take himself for a god.
Friedrich Wilhelm Nietzsche (1844–1900) German philosopher and poet. *Beyond Good and Evil* (1886)

8   My wife hath something in her gizzard, that only waits an opportunity of being provoked to bring up.
Samuel Pepys (1633–1703) English diarist and civil servant. *Diary* (June 17, 1668)

9   GAUNT Things sweet to taste prove in digestion sour.
William Shakespeare (1564–1616) English poet and playwright. *Richard II* (1595), Act 1, Scene 3

10   I am convinced digestion is the great secret of life.
Sydney Smith (1771–1845) British clergyman, essayist, and wit. Letter to Arthur Kinglake (1837)

11   The fate of a nation has often depended upon the good or bad digestion of a prime minister.
Voltaire (1694–1778) French writer and philosopher. Attrib.

Diplomacy

see also **Conflict, Politics**

1   We believe in a League system in which the whole world should be ranged against an aggressor.
Clement Attlee (1883–1967) British politician. Speech to Parliament, *Hansard* (March 11, 1935)

2   It is better for aged diplomats to be bored than for young men to die.
Warren Robinson Austin (1877–1962) US diplomat. Response when asked if he got tired during long debates at the UN. Attrib.

3   Nations touch at their summits.
Walter Bagehot (1826–77) British economist and journalist. 'The House of Lords', *The English Constitution* (1867)

4   To rattle the sabre at every diplomatic entanglement . . . is not only blind but criminal.
Theobald von Bethmann Hollweg (1856–1921) German chancellor. Remark to Crown Prince Wilhelm of Germany (November 15, 1913), quoted in *Europe: A History* (Norman Davies; 1996), ch. 10

5   ALLIANCE, n. In international politics, the union of two thieves who have their hands so deeply inserted in each other's pockets that they cannot separately plunder a third.
Ambrose Bierce (1842–1914?) US writer and journalist. *The Devil's Dictionary* (1911)

6   Going as if he trod upon eggs.
Robert Burton (1577–1640) English scholar and churchman. *The Anatomy of Melancholy* (1621), pt. 3, sect. 2

7   You saw the president yesterday. I thought he was very forward-leaning, as they say in diplomatic nuanced circles.
George W. Bush (b. 1948) US president. Referring to his meeting with Russian President Vladimir Putin in Rome. Remark (July 23, 2001)

8   It is nought good a slepyng hound to wake.
Geoffrey Chaucer (1343?–1400) English poet. *Troilus and Criseyde* (1380–86), bk. 3, l. 764, quoted in *The Works of Geoffrey Chaucer* (F. N. Robinson, ed.; 1957)

9   To jaw-jaw is better than to war-war.
Winston Churchill (1874–1965) British prime minister and writer. Speech, Washington (June 26, 1954)

10   An appeaser is one who feeds a crocodile—hoping that it will eat him last.
Winston Churchill (1874–1965) British prime minister and writer. 1954. Attrib.

11   Treaties are like roses and young girls—they last while they last.
Charles de Gaulle (1890–1970) French president. Speech at the Élysée Palace, Paris (July 2, 1963)

12   When a diplomat says yes, he means perhaps. When he says perhaps he means no. When he says no, he is not a diplomat. When a lady says no, she means perhaps. When she says perhaps, she means yes. But when she says yes, she is no lady.
Lord Denning (1899–1999) British judge. Speech to the Magistrates Association (October 14, 1982)

13   The ability to get to the verge without getting into the war is the necessary art. If you cannot master it, you inevitably get into war. If you try to run away from it, if you are scared to go to the brink, you are lost.
John Foster Dulles (1888–1959) US statesman and diplomat. Dulles's use of the word 'brink' in this context led to the invention of the word 'brinkmanship'. *Life* (January 16, 1956)

14   We must face the fact that the United Nations is not yet the international equivalent of our own legal system and the rule of law.
Anthony Eden (1897–1977) British prime minister. Speech to Parliament, *Hansard* (November 1, 1956)

15   REPORTER If Mr Stalin dies, what will be the effect on international affairs?
EDEN That is a good question for you to ask, not a wise question for me to answer.
Anthony Eden (1897–1977) British prime minister. March 4, 1953. *Times* (March 5, 1953)

16   During the last few weeks I have felt that the Suez Canal was flowing through my drawing room.
Clarissa Eden (1920–85) British aristocrat. Said during the Suez crisis. Speech, Gateshead (November 1956)

17   There can be no law if we were to invoke one code of international conduct for those who oppose us and another for our friends.
Dwight D. Eisenhower (1890–1969) US general and president. Said at the time of the Suez Crisis. Radio broadcast (October 31, 1956)

18   A diplomat is a man who always remembers a woman's birthday but never remembers her age.
Robert Frost (1874–1963) US poet. Attrib.

19   We must look for ways to improve the international situation and build a new world—and we must do it together.
Mikhail Gorbachev (b. 1931) Russian statesman. Speech to the United Nations (December 7, 1988)

20   Megaphone diplomacy leads to a dialogue of the deaf.
Geoffrey Howe (b. 1926) British politician. *Observer* (September 29, 1985), 'Sayings of the Week'

21 Let us never negotiate out of fear, but let us never fear to negotiate.

John Fitzgerald Kennedy (1917–63) US president. Inaugural address as president of the United States (January 20, 1961)

22 Diplomacy is a game of chess in which the nations are checkmated.

Karl Kraus (1874–1936) Austrian writer. 1918. Quoted in *Karl Kraus* (Harry Zohn; 1971)

23 A real diplomat is one who can cut his neighbour's throat without having his neighbour notice it.

Trygve Lie (1896–1968) Norwegian statesman. Attrib.

24 The friendly understanding that exists between my government and hers.

Louis-Philippe (1773–1850) French monarch. Referring to an informal understanding reached between Britain and France on December 27, 1843. The more familiar phrase, 'entente cordiale', was first used in 1844. Remark (December 27, 1843)

25 Forever poised between a cliché and an indiscretion.

Harold Macmillan (1894–1986) British prime minister. Referring to a foreign secretary's life. *Newsweek* (April 30, 1956)

26 The expression 'positive neutrality' is a contradiction in terms. There can be no more positive neutrality than there can be a vegetarian tiger.

V. K. Krishna Menon (1896–1974) Indian politician and diplomat. *New York Times* (October 18, 1960)

27 We have no eternal allies and we have no perpetual enemies. Our interests are eternal and perpetual, and those interests it is our duty to follow.

Lord Palmerston (1784–1865) British prime minister. Speech to Parliament (March 1, 1848)

28 I am like a doctor . . . If the patient doesn't want all the pills I've recommended that's up to him. But I must warn that next time I will have to come as a surgeon with a knife.

Javier Pérez de Cuéllar (b. 1920) Peruvian diplomat. Referring to his decision, as secretary-general of the United Nations, to introduce cost-cutting measures. *Guardian* (May 10, 1986)

29 There is a homely adage which runs 'Speak softly and carry a big stick, you will go far'.

Theodore Roosevelt (1858–1919) US president. Speech at Minnesota State Fair (September 2, 1901)

30 We're eyeball to eyeball and I think the other fellow just blinked.

Dean Rusk (1909–94) US educator and politician. Referring to the Cuban Missile Crisis. Quoted in *Political Dictionary* (William Safire; 1968)

31 ORLANDO I do desire we may be better strangers.

William Shakespeare (1564–1616) English poet and playwright. *As You Like It* (1599), Act 3, Scene 2

32 A diplomat these days is nothing but a head-waiter who's allowed to sit down occasionally.

Peter Ustinov (b. 1921) British actor, director, and writer. *Romanoff and Juliet* (1956), Act 1

33 An ambassador is an honest man sent to lie abroad for the good of his country.

Henry Wotton (1568–1639) English poet and diplomat. Written in Christopher Fleckmore's album (1604), quoted in *Reliquiae Wottonianae* (Izaak Walton; 1651)

Disappointment

see also **Depression, Disillusionment, Sorrow, Unhappiness**

1 Many count their chickens before they are hatched; and where they expect bacon, meet with broken bones.

Miguel de Cervantes (1547–1616) Spanish novelist and playwright. *Don Quixote* (1605–15), pt. 2, ch. 55

2 Blessed is he who expects nothing, for he shall not be disappointed.

Benjamin Franklin (1706–90) US statesman and scientist. *Poor Richard's Almanack* (1787)

3 You can't always get what you want,
But, if you try sometimes, you just might find,
You get what you need.

Mick Jagger (b. 1943) British rock musician and songwriter. Song lyric. 'You Can't Always Get What You Want' (co-written with Keith Richards; 1969)

4 Levin wanted friendship and got friendliness; he wanted steak and they offered spam.

Bernard Malamud (1914–86) US writer. *A New Life* (1961), pt. 6

5 The hills step off into whiteness.
People or stars
Regard me sadly, I disappoint them.

Sylvia Plath (1932–63) US poet and novelist. 1962–63. 'Sheep in Fog', *Ariel* (1965)

6 Oh, I wish that God had not given me what I prayed for! It was not so good as I thought.

Johanna Spyri (1827–1901) Swiss writer. *Heidi* (1880–81), ch. 11

Disaster

see also **Accidents, Misfortune, Tragedy**

1 The crash of the whole solar and stellar systems could only kill you once.

Thomas Carlyle (1795–1881) Scottish historian and essayist. Letter to John Carlyle (1831)

2 Well: while was fashioning
This creature of cleaving wing,
The Immanent Will that stirs and urges everything
Prepared a sinister mate
For her—so gaily great—
A Shape of Ice, for the time far and dissociate.
And as the smart ship grew
In stature, grace, and hue,
In shadowy silent distance grew the Iceberg too.

Thomas Hardy (1840–1928) British novelist and poet. Referring to the sinking of the *Titanic*, April 14, 1912. 'The Convergence of the Twain', *Satires of Circumstance* (1914), sts. 6, 7, and 8

3 When disasters come at the same time, they compete with each other.

Naguib Mahfouz (b. 1911) Egyptian writer. *Palace of Desire* (1957)

Discontent

see **Unhappiness**

Discovery

see also **Innovation, Inventions**

1 *Eureka!*
I have found it!

Archimedes (287?–212 BC) Sicilian-born Greek mathematician and inventor. An exclamation of joy supposedly uttered as, stepping into a bath and noticing the water overflowing, he saw the answer to a problem and began the train of thought that led to his principle of buoyancy. *De Architectura* (220? BC), bk. 8, Preface, sect. 10

2 Look, stranger, at this island now
   The leaping light for your delight discovers.
   W. H. Auden (1907–73) British poet. 1935. 'On This Island' (1936),
   st. 1, ll. 1–2, quoted in *Collected Poems* (Edward Mendelson,
   ed.; 1991)

3 I believe that the earthly Paradise lies here, which
   no one can enter except by God's leave. I believe
   that this land which your Highnesses have
   commanded me to discover is very great, and
   that there are many other lands in the south of
   which there have never been reports.
   Christopher Columbus (1451–1506) Italian explorer and colonialist. On
   his third voyage, Christopher Columbus sighted South
   America from Trinidad on July 31, 1498. Narrative of his
   third voyage (1498)

4 The Italian navigator has reached the New
   World.
   Arthur Holly Compton (1892–1962) US physicist. Reporting the fact
   that Italian scientist Enrico Fermi had produced the first self-
   sustaining atomic chain reaction. Coded telephone message to
   James B. Conant (December 2, 1942)

5 We have discovered the secret of life!
   Francis Crick (b. 1916) British biophysicist. 1953. On entering a
   Cambridge pub with James Watson to announce the fact that
   they had unravelled the structure of DNA. *The Double Helix*
   (James D. Watson; 1968)

6 One does not discover new lands without
   consenting to lose sight of the shore for a very
   long time.
   André Gide (1869–1951) French novelist and critic. *The Counterfeiters*
   (1925)

7 Christopher Columbus, as everyone knows, is
   honoured by posterity because he was the last
   one to discover America.
   James Joyce (1882–1941) Irish writer. September 5, 1912. 'The
   Mirage of the Fisherman of Aran', *Critical Writings*
   (Ellsworth Mason and Richard Ellmann, eds.; 1959)

8 Pigmies placed on the shoulders of giants see
   more than the giants themselves.
   Lucan (39–65) Roman poet. *Didacus Stella* (65?), 10

9 The people—could you patent the sun?
   Jonas E. Salk (1914–95) US physician and virologist. On being asked
   who owned the patent on his antipolio vaccine. Attrib.

10 POLONIUS And thus do we of wisdom and of
   reach,
   With windlasses and with assays of bias,
   By indirections find directions out.
   William Shakespeare (1564–1616) English poet and playwright. *Hamlet*
   (1601), Act 2, Scene 1

11 We often discover what *will* do, by finding out
   what will not do; and probably he who never
   made a mistake never made a discovery.
   Samuel Smiles (1812–1904) Scottish writer. *Self-Help* (1859), ch. 11

Disease

see also **Illness, Medicine**

Disillusionment

see also **Pessimism, Sorrow, Unhappiness**

1 How can a man who has once strayed into
   Heaven ever hope to make terms with the earth?
   Alain-Fournier (1886–1914) French writer and journalist. *Le Grand
   Meaulnes* (1913), pt. 3, ch. 4

2 If you live long enough, you'll see that every
   victory turns into a defeat.
   Simone de Beauvoir (1908–86) French writer and feminist theorist. *All
   Men Are Mortal* (1946)

3 The glory dropped from their youth and love,
   And both perceived they had dreamed a dream.
   Robert Browning (1812–89) British poet. 'The Statue and the Bust',
   Men and Women (1855), l. 152

4 Lovely day: sun—zephyr—view—window open—
   liver—pills—proofs—bills—weed-killer—yah!
   Edward Elgar (1857–1934) British composer, conductor, and violinist.
   Remark (May 20, 1900)

5 A new generation grown to find all Gods dead,
   all wars fought, all faiths in man shaken.
   F. Scott Fitzgerald (1896–1940) US writer. *Tales of the Jazz Age*
   (1922)

6 Goodbye Yellow Brick Road
   Bernie Taupin (b. 1950) British songwriter. 1973. Song title. The
   music was by Elton John.

Disorder

see also **Anarchy, Chaos**

1 Chaos umpire sits,
   And by decision more embroils the fray
   By which he reigns: next him high arbiter
   Chance governs all.
   John Milton (1608–74) English writer. *Paradise Lost* (1667), bk. 2,
   ll. 907–1000

2 Wherefore with thee
   Came not all hell broke loose.
   John Milton (1608–74) English writer. Gabriel questions Satan who
   has been discovered in Eden. *Paradise Lost* (1667), bk. 4,
   ll. 918–919

3 OLIVIA Why, this is very midsummer madness.
   William Shakespeare (1564–1616) English poet and playwright. *Twelfth
   Night* (1601), Act 3, Scene 4

4 I was struck all of a heap.
   Richard Brinsley Sheridan (1751–1816) Irish-born British playwright and
   politician. *The Duenna* (1775), Act 2, Scene 2

Divorce

see also **Marriage, Parting, Separation**

1 I came not into this realm as merchandise, nor
   yet to be married to any merchant.
   Catherine of Aragón (1485–1536) Spanish-born English queen consort.
   Replying to the request that she acquiesce to the marriage of
   Henry VIII and Anne Boleyn. Letter (1533)

2 So that ends my first experience with matrimony,
   which I always thought a highly overrated
   performance.
   Isadora Duncan (1877–1927) US dancer. Said on her separation from
   Sergey Yesenin. *New York Times* (1923)

3 At the funeral of the marriage
   My wife and I paced
   On either side of the hearse,
   Our children racing behind it.
   Paul Durcan (b. 1944) Irish poet. 'At the Funeral of the Marriage',
   The Berlin Wall Café (1985)

4 If divorce has increased one thousand percent,
   don't blame the woman's movement. Blame our
   obsolete sex roles on which our marriages were
   based.
   Betty Friedan (b. 1921) US writer. Remark (January 20, 1974)

5 Suffer the women whom ye divorce to dwell in some part of the houses wherein ye dwell; according to the room and conveniences of the habitations which ye possess; and make them not uneasy, that ye may reduce them to straits.
The Koran (7th century), Sura 65

6 When married people don't get on they can separate, but if they're not married it's impossible. It's a tie that only death can sever.
Somerset Maugham (1874–1965) British writer. *The Circle* (1921), Act 3

7 A Roman divorced from his wife, being highly blamed by his friends, who demanded, 'Was she not chaste? Was she not fair? Was she not fruitful?' holding out his shoe, asked them whether it was not new and well made. 'Yet', added he, 'none of you can tell where it pinches me'.
Plutarch (46?–120?) Greek biographer and philosopher. 'Life of Aemilius Paulus', *Parallel Lives* (1st–2nd century)

8 Everyone should have a divorce once, I can recommend it.
Lou Reed (b. 1942) US rock singer and songwriter. Quoted in *Lou Reed: Between the Lines* (Michael Wrenn; 1993)

9 Divorce? Never. But murder often!
Sybil Thorndike (1882–1976) British actor. Replying to a query as to whether she had considered divorce from Sir Lewis Casson. Attrib.

Doctors

see also **Health and Healthy Living, Illness, Medicine**

1 I am dying with the help of too many physicians.
Alexander the Great (356–323 BC) Macedonian monarch. 323 BC. Attrib.

2 Give me a doctor partridge-plump,
Short in the leg and broad in the rump,
An endomorph with gentle hands,
Who'll never make absurd demands
That I abandon all my vices
Nor pull a long face in a crisis,
But with a twinkle in his eye
Will tell me that I have to die.
W. H. Auden (1907–73) British poet. 1927–32. Also published under the title 'Footnotes to Doctor Shelton' (1951). 'Shorts', *W. H. Auden: Collected Poems* (Edward Mendelson, ed.; 1991), no. 10

3 Doctors are just the same as lawyers; the only difference is that lawyers merely rob you, whereas doctors rob you and kill you, too.
Anton Chekhov (1860–1904) Russian playwright and short-story writer. *Ivanov* (1887), Act 1

4 Physicians, when the cause of disease is discovered, consider that the cure is discovered.
Cicero (106–43 BC) Roman orator and statesman. Attrib.

5 Physicians must discover the weaknesses of the human mind, and even condescend to humour them, or they will never be called in to cure the infirmities of the body.
Charles Colton (1780–1832) British cleric and writer. *Lacon* (1820), vol. 1

6 He had surrendered all reality, all dread and fear, to the doctor beside him, as people do.
William Faulkner (1897–1962) US novelist. *Light in August* (1932), ch. 17

7 Every physician almost hath his favourite disease.
Henry Fielding (1707–54) British novelist and playwright. *Tom Jones* (1749), bk. 2, ch. 9

8 Medicine absorbs the physician's whole being because it is concerned with the entire human organism.
Johann Wolfgang von Goethe (1749–1832) German poet, playwright, and scientist. Attrib.

9 It is the duty of a doctor to prolong life. It is not his duty to prolong the act of dying.
Thomas Horder (1871–1955) British physician. Speech to the House of Lords (December 1936)

10 The common people say, that physicians are the class of people who kill other men in the most polite and courteous manner.
John of Salisbury (1115?–80) English philosopher and humanist. *Policraticus* (1159?), bk. 2, ch. 29

11 Life in itself is short enough, but the physicians with their art, know to their amusement, how to make it still shorter.
Petrarch (1304–74) Italian poet and scholar. Letter to Pope Clement VI, *Invectives* (14th century), Preface

12 In illness the physician is a father; in convalescence a friend; when health is restored, he is a guardian.
Indian proverb.

13 The physician cannot prescribe by letter the proper time for eating or bathing; he must feel the pulse.
Seneca, 'the Younger' (4? BC–AD 65) Roman writer, philosopher, and statesman. *Epistulae Morales* (63?), no. 12

14 Apollo was held the god of physic and sender of disease. Both were originally the same trade, and still continue.
Jonathan Swift (1667–1745) Irish writer and clergyman. *Moral and Diverting* (1711)

15 This is where the strength of the physician lies, be he a quack, a homeopath, or an allopath. He supplies the perennial demand for comfort, the craving for sympathy that every human sufferer feels.
Leo Tolstoy (1828–1910) Russian writer. *War and Peace* (1865–69), pt. 9, ch. 16

16 A physician is one who pours drugs of which he knows little into a body of which he knows less.
Voltaire (1694–1778) French writer and philosopher. Attrib.

Dogs

see **Animals**

Doomsday

see also **Damnation, Ending, Hell**

1 On that day We shall roll up the heaven like a scroll of parchment. As we first created man, so will We bring him back to life.
Referring to the resurrection of human life after the world has been brought to an end. *The Koran* (7th century), Sura 21, l. 104

2 When all the world dissolves,
And every creature shall be purified,
All place shall be hell that is not heaven.
Christopher Marlowe (1564–93) English playwright and poet. *Doctor Faustus* (1592?), Act 2, Scene 1

Doubt

see also **Indecision**, **Scepticism**

1 Everyone who observes himself doubting observes a truth, and about that which he observes he is certain; therefore he is certain about a truth . . . Hence one who can doubt at all ought not to doubt about the existence of truth.

Saint Augustine of Hippo (354–430) Numidian Christian theologian and Doctor of the Church. *De Vera Religione* (390?), ch. 39, no. 73

2 If a man will begin with certainties, he shall end in doubts; but if he will be content to begin with doubts, he shall end in certainties.

Francis Bacon (1561–1626) English philosopher, statesman, and lawyer. *The Advancement of Learning* (1605), bk. 1

3 Doubt is a necessary precondition to meaningful action. Fear is the great mover in the end.

Donald Barthelme (1931–89) US novelist and short-story writer. 'The Rise of Capitalism', *Sadness* (1972)

4 Oh! let us never, never doubt
What nobody is sure about!

Hilaire Belloc (1870–1953) French-born British writer. 'The Microbe', *More Beasts for Worse Children* (1897)

5 It's not useless to tell you that, at this stage,
I don't believe in preachers or generals
or in Miss Universe's buttocks
or in the executioner's repentance
or in the catechism of comfort
or in God's slim forgiving.

Mario Benedetti (b. 1920) Uruguayan writer and poet. 'Creed', *Poemas de Otros* (1974)

6 'Yes', I answered you last night;
'No', this morning, sir, I say
Colours seen by candle-light
Will not look the same by day.

Elizabeth Barrett Browning (1806–61) British poet. 'The Lady's Yes' (1844)

7 It ain't necessarily so—
The things that you're liable
To read in the Bible—
It ain't necessarily so.

George Gershwin (1898–1937) US composer. Song lyric. 'It Ain't Necessarily So', *Porgy and Bess* (1935)

8 *Negative Capability*, that is, when a man is capable of being in uncertainties, mysteries, doubts, without any irritable reaching after fact and reason.

John Keats (1795–1821) English poet. Letter to George and Thomas Keats (December 21, 1817), quoted in *Letters of John Keats* (H. E. Rollins, ed.; 1958), vol. 1

9 The method which begins by doubting in order to philosophize is just as suited to its purpose as making a soldier lie down in a heap in order to teach him to stand up straight.

Søren Kierkegaard (1813–55) Danish philosopher. *The Journals of Søren Kierkegaard* (Alexander Dru, tr.; 1938)

10 The pragmatist knows that doubt is an art which has to be acquired with difficulty.

C. S. Peirce (1839–1914) US physicist and philosopher. *Collected Papers* (Undated)

11 To doubt everything or to believe everything are two equally convenient solutions; both dispense with the necessity of reflection.

Jules Henri Poincaré (1854–1912) French mathematician and scientist. *La Science et l'Hypothèse* (1903), Introduction

12 To teach how to live without certainty and yet without being paralysed by hesitation is perhaps the chief thing that philosophy, in our age, can do for those who study it.

Bertrand Russell (1872–1970) British philosopher and mathematician. *A History of Western Philosophy* (1945)

13 MACBETH I had else been perfect,
Whole as the marble, founded as the rock,
As broad and general as the casing air,
But now I am cabin'd, cribb'd, confin'd, bound in
To saucy doubts and fears.

William Shakespeare (1564–1616) English poet and playwright. *Macbeth* (1606), Act 3, Scene 4

14 Life is doubt,
and faith without doubt is nothing but death.

Miguel de Unamuno y Jugo (1864–1936) Spanish writer and philosopher. 'Salmo II', *Poesías* (1907)

15 If you tried to doubt everything you would not get as far as doubting anything. The game of doubting itself presupposes certainty.

Ludwig Wittgenstein (1889–1951) Austrian philosopher. 1950. Quoted in *On Certainty* (G. E. E. Anscombe, ed.; 1969)

Dreams

see also **Delusion**, **Fantasy**, **Hope**

1 The dream is real, my friends. The failure to make it work is the unreality.

Toni Cade Bambara (1939–95) US novelist, short-story writer, and educator. *The Salt Eaters* (1980)

2 For I see now that I am asleep that I dream when I am awake.

Pedro Calderón de la Barca (1600–81) Spanish playwright and poet. *Life is a Dream* (1635), Act 2

3 What is life? A frenzy. What is life? An illusion, a shadow, a fiction, and the greatest good is worth little; since all of life is a dream, and dreams are dreams.

Pedro Calderón de la Barca (1600–81) Spanish playwright and poet. *Life is a Dream* (1635), Act 2

4 The power of dreams . . . is tied to the multiformity of animals: with their disappearance one may soon expect the dreams to dry up as well.

Elias Canetti (1905–94) Bulgarian-born writer. *The Agony of Flies* (1992)

5 Dreams release the soul's love urge.

Annette Elisabeth von Droste-Hülshoff (1797–1848) German poet. 'Sleepless Night', *An Anthology of German Poetry from Hölderlin to Rilke* (Angel Flores, ed., Herman Salinger, tr.; 1960)

6 A dream is a scripture, and many scriptures are nothing but dreams.

Umberto Eco (b. 1932) Italian writer and literary scholar. *The Name of the Rose* (William Weaver, tr.; 1980), Sixth Day: After Terce

7 Our dreams are our real life.

Federico Fellini (1920–93) Italian film director. Quoted in *Halliwell's Filmgoer's Companion* (Leslie Halliwell; 1993)

8 God pity a one-dream man.

Robert Goddard (1882–1945) US physicist. Quoted in *Broca's Brain* (Carl Sagan; 1980)

9 If his dream lasts, he'll turn the age to gold.

Ben Jonson (1572–1637) English playwright and poet. *The Alchemist* (1610), Act 1, Scene 1

10 Was it a vision, or a waking dream?
    Fled is that music:—Do I wake or sleep?
    John Keats (1795–1821) English poet. 'Ode to a Nightingale' (1820),
    st. 8, ll. 5–6

11 Spirit is dreaming in man.
    Søren Kierkegaard (1813–55) Danish philosopher. 1844. *The Concept
    of Dread* (W. Lowrie, tr.; 1957)

12 I have a dream that one day on the red hills of
    Georgia the sons of former slaves and sons of
    former slaveowners will be able to sit down
    together at the table of brotherhood . . . I have a
    dream that my four little children will one day
    live in a nation where they will be not judged by
    the color of their skin but by the content of their
    character.
    Martin Luther King, Jr. (1929–68) US civil rights leader. August 28,
    1963. Speech at civil rights march in Washington, DC, *New
    York Times* (August 29, 1963)

13 All men dream: but not equally. Those who
    dream by night . . . wake in the day to find that
    it was vanity: but the dreamers of the day are
    dangerous men, for they may act their dream
    with open eyes, to make it possible.
    T. E. Lawrence (1888–1935) British adventurer, soldier and writer. *Seven
    Pillars of Wisdom* (1926), ch. 1

14 Those who have likened our life to a dream were
    more right, by chance, than they realized. We are
    awake while sleeping, and waking sleep.
    Michel de Montaigne (1533–92) French essayist. *Essays* (1580–88),
    bk. 2, ch. 12

15 Dreams are necessary to life.
    Anaïs Nin (1903–77) French writer. June 1936. Letter to her mother,
    The Diary of Anaïs Nin (1967), vol. 2

16 A dream can be the highest point of a life.
    Ben Okri (b. 1959) Nigerian novelist, short-story writer, and poet. *The
    Famished Road* (1991)

17 All that we see or seem
    Is but a dream within a dream.
    Edgar Allan Poe (1809–49) US poet and writer. *A Dream within a
    Dream* (1827), l. 10

18 The hope I dreamed of was a dream,
    Was but a dream; and now I wake,
    Exceeding comfortless, and worn, and old,
    For a dream's sake.
    Christina Rossetti (1830–94) British poet. 'Mirage' (1862)

19 Only dreaming is of interest,
    What is life without dreams?
    Edmond Rostand (1868–1918) French playwright. *La Princesse
    Lointaine* (1895)

20 What constitutes the nature of the dream is that
    reality eludes altogether the consciousness which
    desires to recapture it.
    Jean-Paul Sartre (1905–80) French philosopher, playwright, and novelist.
    The Psychology of Imagination (1948)

21 For as a looking glass sheweth the image or
    figure thereunto opposite, so in dreams the
    phantasy and imagination informs the
    understanding of such things as haunt the
    outward sense.
    Reginald Scot (1538–99) English author. *The Discoverie of
    Witchcraft* (16th century)

22 BOTTOM I have had a dream, past the wit of man
    to say what dream it was.
    William Shakespeare (1564–1616) English poet and playwright. *A
    Midsummer Night's Dream* (1595–96), Act 4, Scene 1

23 PUCK If we shadows have offended,
    Think but this, and all is mended,
    That you have but slumber'd here
    While these visions did appear.
    William Shakespeare (1564–1616) English poet and playwright. *A
    Midsummer Night's Dream* (1595–96), Act 5, Scene 1

24 PROSPERO We are such stuff
    As dreams are made on; and our little life
    Is rounded with a sleep.
    William Shakespeare (1564–1616) English poet and playwright. *The
    Tempest* (1611), Act 4, Scene 1

25 My dreams were all my own; I accounted for
    them to nobody; they were my refuge when
    annoyed—my dearest pleasure when free.
    Mary Wollstonecraft Shelley (1797–1851) British novelist. *Frankenstein*
    (1818), Preface

26 I arise from dreams of thee
    In the first sweet sleep of night.
    When the winds are breathing low,
    And the stars are shining bright.
    Percy Bysshe Shelley (1792–1822) English poet. 1822. First published
    in *The Liberal* as 'Song Written for an Indian Air' (1822).
    Now known as 'The Indian Serenade'. *Posthumous Poems*
    (Mrs. Shelley, ed.; 1824)

27 Many's the long night I've dreamed of cheese—
    toasted, mostly.
    Robert Louis Stevenson (1850–94) Scottish novelist, essayist, and poet.
    Treasure Island (1883), ch. 15

28 Dreams are true while they last, and do we not
    live in dreams?
    Alfred Tennyson (1809–92) British poet. 'The Higher Pantheism', *The
    Holy Grail and Other Poems* (1869), st. 2

29 For life is but a dream whose shapes return,
    Some frequently, some seldom, some by night
    And some by day.
    James Thomson (1834–82) British poet. 'The City of Dreadful Night'
    (1874), can. 1

30 Since the individual's desire to dominate his
    environment is not a desirable trait in a society
    which every day grows more and more confining,
    the average man must take to daydreaming.
    Gore Vidal (b. 1925) US novelist and essayist. 'Tarzan Revisited',
    Esquire (December 1963)

31 Dreams
    are cages
    within which we
    observe the cages
    without.
    William Wantling (1933–74) US poet and novelist. 'Dreams Are Cages',
    The Awakening (1969)

32 What is a dream?
    What is reality? Just a demarcation in human
    memory.
    Xu Yunuo (1893–1958) Chinese writer and editor. *Little Poems* (1922),
    quoted in *Anthology of Modern Chinese Poetry* (Michelle
    Yeh, ed., tr.; 1992)

33 But I, being poor, have only my dreams;
    I have spread my dreams under your feet;
    Tread softly because you tread on my dreams.
    W. B. Yeats (1865–1939) Irish poet and playwright. 'He Wishes for
    the Cloths of Heaven', *The Wind Among the Reeds* (1899),
    ll. 6–8

34 I do not know whether I was then a man
    dreaming I was a butterfly, or whether I am now
    a butterfly dreaming I am a man.
    Zhuangzi (369?–286 BC) Chinese philosopher and teacher. Quoted in
    Chuang Tzu (Herbert A. Giles, tr.; 1980), ch. 2

Drinks and Drinking

see also Alcohol, Wine

1 The infusion of a China plant sweetened with the pith of an Indian cane.
Joseph Addison (1672–1719) English essayist, poet, and statesman. Referring to tea with sugar. *Spectator* (1711), no. 69

2 If I had known there was no Latin word for tea I would have let the vulgar stuff alone.
Hilaire Belloc (1870–1953) French-born British writer. Attrib.

3 I am willing to taste any drink once.
James Branch Cabell (1879–1958) US novelist and journalist. *Jurgen* (1919)

4 Drink to-day, and drown all sorrow;
You shall perhaps not do 't to-morrow.
John Fletcher (1579–1625) English playwright. Also known as *Rollo, Duke of Normandy*, in collaboration with Jonson and others. *The Bloody Brother* (1616), Act 2, Scene 2

5 The apéritif is the evensong of the French.
Paul Morand (1888–1976) French writer and diplomat. 'La nuit des six-jours', *Ouvert la Nuit* (1922)

6 There are two reasons for drinking; one is, when you are thirsty, to cure it; the other, when you are not thirsty, to prevent it . . . Prevention is better than cure.
Thomas Love Peacock (1785–1866) British novelist and poet. *Melincourt* (1817)

7 I drink for the thirst to come.
François Rabelais (1494?–1553?) French humanist and satirist. *Gargantua* (1534), bk. 1, ch. 5

8 I drink no more than a sponge.
François Rabelais (1494?–1553?) French humanist and satirist. *Gargantua* (1534), bk. 1, ch. 5

9 What will you drink if you stop drinking? I shall drink water. It's a mixer, Patsy.
Jennifer Saunders (b. 1958) British comedian. Patsy to Edina. *Absolutely Fabulous* (BBC television; 1990s)

10 Instant coffee is just old beans that have been cremated.
Jennifer Saunders (b. 1958) British comedian. Said as Edina. *Absolutely Fabulous* (BBC television; 1990s)

11 We are told, and very plainly too, that hot drinks—tea, coffee, chocolate, cocoa and all drinks of this kind are not good for man.
Joseph Smith (1805–44) US founder of Mormon church. *The Word of Wisdom* (February 27, 1823)

12 Water is the only drink for a wise man.
Henry David Thoreau (1817–62) US writer. *Walden, or, Life in the Woods* (1854)

13 I think it must be so, for I have been drinking it for sixty-five years and I am not dead yet.
Voltaire (1694–1778) French writer and philosopher. On learning that coffee was considered a slow poison. Attrib.

Drugs

see also Addiction, Alcohol, Smoking

1 OPIATE, n. An unlocked door in the prison of Identity. It leads into the jail yard.
Ambrose Bierce (1842–1914?) US writer and journalist. *The Devil's Dictionary* (1911)

2 Kick is seeing things from a special angle. Kick is momentary freedom from the claims of the ageing, cautious, nagging, frightened flesh.
William S. Burroughs (1914–97) US writer. Originally published under the pseudonym William Lee. *Junkie* (1953), ch. 15

3 Junk is the ideal product . . . the ultimate merchandise. No sales talk necessary. The client will crawl through a sewer and beg to buy.
William S. Burroughs (1914–97) US writer. *The Naked Lunch* (1959), Introduction

4 When I was in England, I experimented with marijuana a time or two and I didn't like it. I didn't inhale.
Bill Clinton (b. 1946) US president. Remark made during the US presidential election campaign replying to Republican accusations that he had taken drugs and had played a leading role in the movement against the Vietnam War. *Washington Post* (March 30, 1992)

5 Opium gives and takes away. It defeats the steady habit of exertion; but it creates spasms of irregular exertion! It ruins the natural power of life; but it develops preternatural paroxysms of intermitting power.
Thomas De Quincey (1785–1859) British essayist and critic. *Confessions of an English Opium Eater* (1821), pt. 2

6 Thou hast the keys of Paradise, oh, just, subtle, and mighty opium!
Thomas De Quincey (1785–1859) British essayist and critic. *Confessions of an English Opium Eater* (1821), pt. 2

7 Drug misuse is not a disease, it's a decision, like the decision to step out in front of a moving car. You would call that not a disease but an error of judgement.
Philip K. Dick (1928–82) US science-fiction writer. 'Author's Note', *A Scanner Darkly* (1977)

8 'For me', said Sherlock Holmes, 'there still remains the cocaine bottle'.
Arthur Conan Doyle (1859–1930) Scottish-born British writer and physician. 'The Strange Story of Jonathan Small', *The Sign of Four* (1889)

9 Hey! Mr Tambourine Man, play a song for me. I'm not sleepy and there is no place I'm going to.
Bob Dylan (b. 1941) US singer and songwriter. Song lyric. A 'Tambourine Man' is a drug dealer. 'Mr Tambourine Man' (1965)

10 Acid has changed consciousness entirely. The US has changed in the last few years and it's because that whole first psychedelic thing meant: Here's this new consciousness, this new freedom, and it's here in yourself.
Jerry Garcia (1942–95) US rock band leader, guitarist, and songwriter. 1970. Quoted in *Rock 'n' Roll Babylon* (Gary Herman; 1994)

11 Medicines are nothing in themselves, if not properly used, but the very hands of the gods, if employed with reason and prudence.
Herophilus (335?–280? BC) Greek anatomist. Attrib.

12 A miracle drug is any drug that will do what the label says it will do.
Eric Hodgins (1899–1971) US writer and editor. *Episode* (1964)

13 There can be no doubt that if tranquillizers could be bought as easily and cheaply as aspirin they would be consumed, not by the billions, as they are at present, but by the scores and hundreds of billions.
Aldous Huxley (1894–1963) British novelist and essayist. *Brave New World Revisited* (1958), ch. 8

14 Along with many scientists he considered the discovery of psychedelics one of the three major scientific break-throughs of the twentieth century, the other two being the splitting of the atom and the manipulation of genetic structures.

Laura Huxley (b. 1911) Italian-born US musician and writer. Referring to Aldous Huxley. *This Timeless Moment* (1968)

15 Drugs are the greatest threat to our national security.

Jesse Jackson (b. 1941) US clergyman, civil rights leader, and politician. *The Koppel Report* (ABC Television; September 13, 1988)

16 The most deadly thing about cocaine is that it separates you from your soul.

Quincy Jones (b. 1933) US record producer and musician. Quoted in *Divided Soul* (David Ritz; 1985)

17 Pursuing the religious life today without using psychedelic drugs is like studying astronomy with the naked eye because that's how they did it in the first century AD

Timothy Leary (1920–96) US psychologist and guru. *The Politics of Ecstasy* (1968)

18 Turn on, tune in, drop out.

Timothy Leary (1920–96) US psychologist and guru. June 1966. Lecture, *The Politics of Ecstasy* (1968)

19 I will lift up mine eyes unto the pills. Almost everyone takes them, from the humble aspirin to the multi-coloured, king-sized three deckers, which put you to sleep, wake you up, stimulate and soothe you all in one. It is an age of pills.

Malcolm Muggeridge (1903–90) British journalist. *New Statesman* (August 3, 1962)

20 No drug, not even alcohol, causes the fundamental ills of society. If we're looking for sources of our troubles, we shouldn't test people for drugs, we should test them for stupidity, ignorance, greed, and love of power.

P. J. O'Rourke (b. 1947) US writer and humorist. 'Studying For Our Drug Test', *Give War a Chance* (1992)

21 A drug is that substance which, when injected into a rat, will produce a scientific report.

Proverb.

22 I'm going to try for the the kingdom if I can,
'Cause it makes me feel like I'm a man,
When I put a spike into my vein,
And I tell you things aren't quite the same,
When I'm rushing on my run,
And I feel just like Jesus' son.

Lou Reed (b. 1942) US rock singer and songwriter. Song lyric. 'Heroin' (1967)

23 If you're gonna get wasted, get wasted elegantly.

Keith Richards (b. 1943) British rock musician. Quoted in *The Wit and Wisdom of Rock and Roll* (Maxim Jabukowski, ed.; 1983)

24 Cocaine—such a perfunctory, unintelligent drug. Ideal for those who seek euphoria and refuse to look inward.

Luisa Valenzuela (b. 1938) Argentinian writer. *The Lizard's Tail* (Gregory Rabassa, tr.; 1983)

25 Cocaine is God's way of saying you're making too much money.

Robin Williams (b. 1951) US actor and comedian. *Screen International* (December 15, 1990)

Drunkenness

see also **Alcohol, Drinks and Drinking**

1 No, thank you, I was born intoxicated.

Æ (George William Russell; 1867–1935) Irish poet. Refusing a drink that was offered him. Quoted in *10,000 Jokes, Toasts, and Stories* (L. Copeland)

2 His mouth has been used as a latrine by some small animal of the night.

Kingsley Amis (1922–95) British novelist. Describing a hangover. *Lucky Jim* (1954)

3 Drunkenness, the ruin of reason, the destruction of strength, premature old age, momentary death.

Saint Basil the Great (329?–379?) Greek father of the Church. *Homilies* (4th century), no. 14, ch. 7

4 For when the wine is in, the wit is out.

Thomas Becon (1512–67) English cleric. *Catechism* (1560), no. 375

5 If you want to know where God is, ask a drunk.

Charles Bukowski (1920–94) German-born US writer. *Notes of a Dirty Old Man* (1969)

6 There's some are fou o' love divine,
There's some are fou o' brandy.

Robert Burns (1759–96) Scottish poet and songwriter. 'Fou' is dialect for 'drunk'. 'The Holy Fair' (1786), st. 27

7 Man, being reasonable, must get drunk;
The best of life is but intoxication.

Lord Byron (1788–1824) British poet. *Don Juan* (1819–24), can. 2, st. 179

8 Drunk in charge of a narrative.

Angela Carter (1940–92) British novelist, essayist, and short-story writer. *Wise Children* (1991)

9 He calls drunkenness an expression identical with ruin.

Diogenes Läertius (*fl.* 3rd century) Greek historian and biographer. Referring to Pythagoras. 'Pythagoras', *Lives of the Philosophers* (200?)

10 I am as sober as a Judge.

Henry Fielding (1707–54) British novelist and playwright. *Don Quixote in England* (1734), Act 3, Scene 14

11 What shall we do with the drunken sailor
Early in the morning?
Hoo-ray and up she rises
Early in the morning.

Folk Verse. Traditional English song lyric. 'What shall we do with the drunken sailor?'

12 Drunkenness is never anything but a substitute for happiness. It amounts to buying the dream of a thing when you haven't money enough to buy the dreamed-of thing materially.

André Gide (1869–1951) French novelist and critic. *Journal* (1939–51)

13 If merely 'feeling good' could decide, drunkenness would be the supremely valid human experience.

William James (1842–1910) US psychologist and philosopher. *The Varieties of Religious Experience* (1902)

14 No, Sir; there were people who died of dropsies, which they contracted in trying to get drunk.

Samuel Johnson (1709–84) British lexicographer and writer. 1773. Scornfully criticizing the strength of the wine in Scotland before the Act of Union (1707) in response to James Boswell's claim that there had been a lot of drunkenness. Quoted in *Journal of a Tour to the Hebrides* (James Boswell; 1785)

15 A man who exposes himself when he is intoxicated, has not the art of getting drunk.

Samuel Johnson (1709–84) British lexicographer and writer. April 24, 1779. Quoted in *Life of Samuel Johnson* (James Boswell; 1791)

16 First the man takes a drink, then the drink takes
    a drink, then the drink takes the man.
    Mottos and Slogans. Temperance slogan.

17 One more drink and I'd be under the host.
    Dorothy Parker (1893–1967) US writer and wit. Quoted in *You Might
    As Well Live* (John Keats; 1970)

18 Drunkenness . . . spoils health, dismounts the
    mind, and unmans men.
    William Penn (1644–1718) English preacher and colonialist. *Some Fruits
    of Solitude* (1693), no. 72

19 Drunkenness is temporary suicide; the happiness
    that it brings is merely negative, a momentary
    cessation of unhappiness.
    Bertrand Russell (1872–1970) British philosopher and mathematician. *The
    Conquest of Happiness* (1930)

20 Drunkenness is simply voluntary insanity.
    Seneca, 'the Younger' (4? BC–AD 65) Roman writer, philosopher, and
    statesman. *Epistulae Morales* (63?), no. 83

21 But I'm not so think as you drunk I am.
    J. C. Squire (1884–1958) British writer. 'Ballade of Soporific
    Absorption' (1931)

22 Fifteen men on the dead man's chest
    Yo-ho-ho, and a bottle of rum!
    Drink and the devil had done for the rest—
    Yo-ho-ho, and a bottle of rum!
    Robert Louis Stevenson (1850–94) Scottish novelist, essayist, and poet.
    Treasure Island (1883), ch. 1

Dublin

see **European Cities, Ireland**

E

The Earth

see also **The Environment, The World**

1 Mostly harmless.

Douglas Adams (1952–2001) British writer. Description of planet
Earth. *The Hitch Hiker's Guide to the Galaxy* (1979), ch. 6

2 Far out in the uncharted backwaters of the
unfashionable end of the Western Spiral arm of
the Galaxy lies a small unregarded yellow sun.
Orbiting this at a distance of roughly ninety-two
million miles is an utterly insignificant little blue
green planet whose ape-descended life forms are
so amazingly primitive that they still think digital
watches are a pretty neat idea.

Douglas Adams (1952–2001) British writer. *The Hitch Hiker's Guide
to the Galaxy* (1979), Introduction

3 To man the earth seems altogether
No more a mother, but a step-dame rather.

Guillaume du Bartas (1544–90) French poet. 'First Week, Third Day',
Divine Weekes and Workes (1578)

4 The earth is blue like an orange.

Paul Éluard (1895–1952) French surrealist poet. *L'Amour, la Poésie*
(1929)

5 I am a passenger on the spaceship, Earth.

R. Buckminster Fuller (1895–1983) US architect, designer, and inventor.
Operating Manual for Spaceship Earth (1969), ch. 1

6 The most important thing about Spaceship
Earth—an instruction book didn't come with it.

R. Buckminster Fuller (1895–1983) US architect, designer, and inventor.
Operating Manual for Spaceship Earth (1969), ch. 4

7 The Earth is just too small and fragile a basket
for the human race to keep all its eggs in.

Robert Heinlein (1907–88) US writer. Speech (Undated)

8 The axis of the earth sticks out visibly through
the centre of each and every town or city.

Oliver Wendell Holmes (1841–1935) US judge. *The Autocrat of the
Breakfast-Table* (1858), ch. 6

9 One would think
that the earth was the road
Of the body,
that the sea was the road
Of the soul.

Juan Ramón Jiménez (1881–1958) Spanish poet. 'Dream Nocturne',
Roots and Wings: Poetry from Spain, 1900–75 (Hardie St.
Martin, ed.; 1976), ll. 6–10

10 We have since defined Gaia as a complex entity
involving the Earth's biosphere, atmosphere,
oceans, and soil; the totality constituting a
feedback or cybernetic system which seeks an
optimal physical and chemical environment for
life on this planet.

James Lovelock (b. 1919) British scientist. *Gaia: a New Look at Life
on Earth* (1979)

11 Pity the planet, all joy gone
from this sweet volcanic cone.

Robert Lowell (1917–77) US poet. 'Waking Early Sunday Morning',
Near the Ocean (1967), st. 14

Eating

see also **Digestion, Food, Hunger**

1 A picnic is the Englishman's grand gesture, his
final defiance flung in the face of fate. No climate
in the world is less propitious to picnics than the
climate of England, yet with a recklessness which
is almost sublime the English rush out of doors
to eat a meal on every possible and impossible
occasion.

Georgina Battiscombe (b. 1905) British author. *English Picnics* (1951)

2 EAT, v.i. To perform successively (and
successfully) the functions of mastication,
humectation, and deglutition.

Ambrose Bierce (1842–1914?) US writer and journalist. *The Devil's
Dictionary* (1911)

3 I'm a man
More dined against than dining.

Maurice Bowra (1898–1971) British scholar and classicist. Quoted in
Summoned by Bells (John Betjeman; 1960)

4 The most repulsive thing you could ever imagine
is the inside of a camel's mouth. That and
watching a girl eat octopus or squid.

Marlon Brando (b. 1924) US actor. *Playboy Magazine* (January
1979)

5 So munch on, crunch on, take your nuncheon,
Breakfast, supper, dinner, luncheon.

Robert Browning (1812–89) British poet. 'The Pied Piper of
Hamelin', *Dramatic Lyrics* (1842), st. 7

6 All human history attests
That happiness for man,—the hungry sinner!—
Since Eve ate apples, much depends on dinner.

Lord Byron (1788–1824) British poet. *Don Juan* (1819–24), can. 13,
st. 99

7 He used to say that other men lived to eat, but
that he ate to live.

Diogenes Laërtius (*fl.* 3rd century) Greek historian and biographer.
Referring to Socrates. 'Socrates', *Lives of the Philosophers*
(3rd century?)

8 I eat my peas with honey
I've done it all my life,
They do taste kind of funny,
But it keeps them on the knife.

Folk Verse. Traditional nonsense rhyme. 'Peas'

9 The best number for a dinner party is two—
myself and a dam' good head waiter.

Nubar Sarkis Gulbenkian (1896–1972) Turkish-born British philanthropist.
Daily Telegraph (January 14, 1965)

10 Tea for two, and two for tea
Otto Harbach (1873–1963) US playwright and librettist. Song lyric. 'Tea for Two, and Two for Tea', *No! No! Nanette* (1924)

11 I do wish we could chat longer, but I'm having an old friend for dinner.
Anthony Hopkins (b. 1937) Welsh stage and film actor. 1991. Said as Hannibal Lecter, a cannibalistic psychopath, speaking by telephone to FBI agent Clarice Starling (Jodie Foster) in the final line from the film, based on Thomas Harris's bestseller *The Silence of the Lambs* (1988). *The Silence of the Lambs* (Ted Tally; 1990)

12 The act of putting into your mouth what the earth has grown is perhaps the most direct interaction with the earth.
Frances Moore Lappé (b. 1944) US ecologist and author. *Diet for a Small Planet* (1971), pt. 1

13 Eating cannot be a solitary affair, but must be shared with the people you love or are doing business with; it increases the pleasure.
Vivienne Lo (b. 1958) British historian and writer. *150 Recipes from the Teahouse* (1997)

14 To eat well in England you should have breakfast three times a day.
Somerset Maugham (1874–1965) British writer. Attrib.

15 No man is lonely while eating spaghetti.
Robert Morley (1908–92) British actor and playwright. Attrib.

16 Strange to see how a good dinner and feasting reconciles everybody.
Samuel Pepys (1633–1703) English diarist and civil servant. *Diary* (November 9, 1665)

17 The man who can dominate a London dinner-table can dominate the world.
Oscar Wilde (1854–1900) Irish poet, playwright, and wit. Attrib. *Oscar Wilde* (R. Aldington; 1946)

Ecology

see also **The Environment, Nature**

1 When you destroy a blade of grass
You poison England at her roots:
Remember no man's foot can pass
Where evermore no green life shoots.
Gordon Bottomley (1874–1948) British poet and playwright. 'To Ironfounders and Others' (1912)

2 The 'control of nature' is a phrase conceived in arrogance, born of the Neanderthal age of biology and the convenience of man.
Rachel Carson (1907–64) US ecologist. *Silent Spring* (1962)

3 We cannot hope either to understand or to manage the carbon in the atmosphere unless we understand and manage the trees and the soil too.
Freeman Dyson (b. 1923) British-born US physicist. *From Eros to Gaia* (1993)

4 Both biological and cultural diversity are now severely threatened and working for their preservation is a critical task.
Murray Gell-Mann (b. 1929) US particle physicist. *The Quark and the Jaguar* (1994)

5 That land is a community is the basic concept of ecology, but that land is to be loved and respected is an extension of ethics.
Aldo Leopold (1886–1948) US naturalist, conservationist, and philosopher. Quoted in *National Geographic Magazine* (November 1981)

6 dear boss it wont be long now it wont be long . . .
till the earth is barren as the moon . . .
i relay this information without any fear
that humanity will take warning and reform
signed archy.
Don Marquis (1878–1937) US journalist and writer. A warning letter, typed by archy the cockroach, who is too small and light to use the shift key. 'what the ants are saying', *archy does his part* (1935)

7 I became an ecologist long before I heard the word.
Chico Mendes (1944–88) Brazilian rubber tapper and ecological campaigner. Attrib.

8 Objective knowing is alienated knowing; and alienated knowing is sooner or later, ecologically disastrous knowing. Before the earth could become an industrial garbage can it had first to become a research laboratory.
Theodore Roszak (b. 1933) US writer and editor. *Where the Wasteland Ends* (1972), ch. 7

9 Ecology . . . ought to be a compulsory subject for all economists.
E. F. Schumacher (1911–77) German-born British economist. Lecture, Blackpool, 'Clean Air and Future Energy' (October 19, 1967)

10 Sometime in the last ten years the best brains of the Occident discovered to their amazement that we live in an Environment. This discovery has been forced on us by the realization that we are approaching the limits of something.
Gary Snyder (b. 1930) US poet, essayist, and translator. 1976. Referring to the increasing prominence of ecological matters in Western thought. 'Re-Inhabitation', *The Old Ways* (1977)

11 Over the long haul of life on the planet, it is the ecologists, and not the bookkeepers of business, who are the ultimate accountants.
Stewart L. Udall (b. 1920) US politician and conservationist. Address, Congress of Optimum Population and Environment (June 9, 1970)

12 A land ethic for tomorrow should . . . stress the oneness of our resources and the live-and-help-live logic of the great chain of life.
Stewart L. Udall (b. 1920) US politician and conservationist. *The Quiet Crisis* (1963), ch. 14

Economics

see also **Business, Capitalism, Globalization, Marxism, Money**

1 Economic activity should not only be efficient in its use of resources but should also be socially just, and environmentally and ecologically sustainable.
Warren Bennis (b. 1925) US educationalist and writer. *Beyond Leadership: Balancing Economics, Ethics and Ecology* (co-written with Jagdish Parikh and Ronnie Lessem; 1994)

2 Sustainable development challenges the entire industrial and commercial system to restructure itself.
Warren Bennis (b. 1925) US educationalist and writer. *Beyond Leadership: Balancing Economics, Ethics and Ecology* (co-written with Jagdish Parikh and Ronnie Lessem; 1994)

3 Our present economy . . . does not account for affection at all, which is to say that it does not account for value. It is simply a description of the career of money as it preys upon both nature and human society.
Wendell Berry (b. 1934) US poet, novelist, and essayist. 1985. 'Preserving Wildness', *The Landscape of Harmony* (1987)

4   ECONOMY, n. Purchasing the barrel of whiskey that you do not need for the price of the cow that you cannot afford.
Ambrose Bierce (1842–1914?) US writer and journalist. *The Devil's Dictionary* (1911)

5   The successful economies of the future will excel at generating and disseminating knowledge, and commercially exploiting it.
Tony Blair (b. 1953) British prime minister. Lecture to the Fabian Society, London (1998)

6   An economist is a man who knows 100 ways of making love but doesn't know any women.
Art Buchwald (b. 1925) US humorist. Attrib.

7   Respectable Professors of the Dismal Science.
Thomas Carlyle (1795–1881) Scottish historian and essayist. Referring to economists. *Latter-Day Pamphlets* (1850), 1

8   There are two problems in my life. The political ones are insoluble and the economic ones are incomprehensible.
Alec Douglas-Home (1903–95) British prime minister. Speech (January 1964)

9   Everybody is always in favour of general economy and particular expenditure.
Anthony Eden (1897–1977) British prime minister. *Observer* (June 17, 1956), 'Sayings of the Week'

10 If freedom were not so economically efficient it certainly wouldn't stand a chance.
Milton Friedman (b. 1912) US economist. Remark (March 1987)

11 Perhaps it is a sense of history that divides good economics from bad.
J. K. Galbraith (b. 1908) Canadian-born US economist. *The Age of Uncertainty* (television series; 1977)

12 The natural counterpart of a free market economy is a politics of insecurity.
John Gray (b. 1948) British academic. *False Dawn* (1998)

13 Much of what we took for granted in our free-market system was not nature at all, but culture. The dismantling of the central planning function does not, as some had supposed, automatically establish market capitalism.
Alan Greenspan (b. 1926) US economist. Quoted in 'Genuflecting at the Altar of Market Economics', *International Herald Tribune* (William Pfaff; July 14, 1997)

14 Classical economic theory . . . makes no mention of one vital ingredient—the time that it takes to build an economic force.
John Harvey-Jones (b. 1924) British business executive and author. Quoted in *The Spectre of Capitalism* (William Keegan; 1992)

15 A mature economic system would appreciate an ancient forest or undisturbed grassland as the ideal for qualitative growth—fecund, abundant, and dynamic, mature but highly evolved.
Paul Hawken, US author. *The Ecology of Commerce* (1993)

16 The attempt to isolate economics from other disciplines—notably politics, history, philosophy, finance, constitutional theory and sociology—has fatally disabled its power to explain what is happening in the world.
Will Hutton (b. 1950) British author and newspaper editor. *The State We're In* (1995)

17 There is . . . no surer means of overturning the existing basis of society than to debauch the currency.
John Maynard Keynes (1883–1946) British economist. *Economic Consequences of the Peace* (1919)

18 One nanny said, 'Feed a cold'; she was a neo-Keynesian. Another nanny said, 'Starve a cold'; she was a monetarist.
Harold Macmillan (1894–1986) British prime minister. Maiden speech to the House of Lords. Quoted in *Hansard* (1984)

19 The harsh truth is that if the policy isn't hurting, it isn't working.
John Major (b. 1943) British prime minister. Referring to his government's determination to counter inflation with high interest rates. Speech, Northampton (October 27, 1989)

20 The sum total of these relations of production constitutes the economic structure of society—the real foundation, on which rise legal and political superstructures and to which correspond definite forms of social consciousness.
Karl Marx (1818–83) German philosopher. *Critique of Political Economy* (1859)

21 The weather forecast has no effect on the weather but the economics forecast may well affect the economy.
John Mason (b. 1940) British politician and solicitor. Presidential address to the British Association (1983)

22 The policy challenge of sustainable development consists of finding a path towards a positive social and ecological coevolution.
Richard Norgaard (b. 1943) US author. Quoted in 'Coevolution of Economy, Society and Environment', *Real-Life Economics* (Paul Ekins and Manfred Max-Neef, eds.; 1992)

23 Expenditure rises to meet income.
Cyril Northcote Parkinson (1909–93) British political scientist, historian, and writer. *The Law and the Profits* (1960), ch. 1

24 An economist is an expert who will know tomorrow why the things he predicted yesterday didn't happen today.
Laurence J. Peter (1919–90) Canadian writer. Quoted in *The Financial Times Guide to Using the Financial Pages* (Romesh Vaitilingam; 1996)

25 A man can be forgiven a lot if he can quote Shakespeare in an economic crisis.
Prince Philip (b. 1921) Greek-born British consort of Queen Elizabeth II. Attrib.

26 Any economy in which more individuals escape entrapment in sterile, bureaucratic corporate slots or menial roles and expand their potential can be argued to be morally superior.
George Poste (b. 1944) British-born US business executive. Speech (June 14, 1997)

27 A budget is a method of worrying before you spend instead of afterwards.
Proverb.

28 The purpose of studying economics is not to acquire a set of ready-made answers to economic questions, but to learn how to avoid being deceived by economists.
Joan Robinson (1903–83) British economist. *Marx, Marshall and Keynes* (1955)

29 Economics is as much a study in fantasy and aspiration as in hard numbers—maybe more so.
Theodore Roszak (b. 1933) US writer and editor. *The Making of a Counter Culture* (1995), Introduction

30 A nobler economics . . . is not afraid to discuss spirit and conscience, moral purpose and the meaning of life, an economics that aims to educate and elevate people, not merely to measure their low-grade behaviour.
Theodore Roszak (b. 1933) US writer and editor. Defining a humanistic economics. Quoted in *Small is Beautiful: Economics as if People Mattered* (Ernst F. Schumacher; 1973)

31 Man does not live by GNP alone.

P. A. Samuelson (b. 1915) US economist. 1948. GNP means gross national product. *Economics: an Introductory Analysis* (1964)

32 I have yet to meet the famous Rational Economic Man theorists describe. Real people have always done inexplicable things from time to time, and they show no sign of stopping.

Charles Sanford, Jr. (b. 1936) US business executive. Speech (October 1994)

33 Call a thing immoral or ugly, soul destroying or a degradation of man, a peril to the peace of our world or to the well-being of future generations; as long as you have not shown it to be 'uneconomic' you have not really questioned its right to exist, grow and prosper.

E. F. Schumacher (1911–77) German-born British economist. Lecture, Blackpool, 'Clean Air and Future Energy' (October 19, 1967)

34 Modern economic thinking . . . is peculiarly unable to consider the long term and to appreciate man's dependence on the natural world.

E. F. Schumacher (1911–77) German-born British economist. Lecture, Blackpool, 'Clean Air and Future Energy' (October 19, 1967)

35 If all economists were laid end to end, they would not reach a conclusion.

George Bernard Shaw (1856–1950) Irish playwright. Attrib.

36 To try to understand the workings of the economy by means of macroeconomics is rather like trying to understand how a clock works by observing the movements of the hands on its face.

David Simpson (b. 1936) Scottish economist. 'What Economists Need to Know', *Royal Bank of Scotland Review* (December 1988)

37 Economics without ethics is a discipline without substance.

Robert C. Solomon (b. 1942) US author. *The New World of Business* (1994)

Editors

see Journalism, Publishing

Education

see also Learning, Literacy, Teachers, University

1 'Reeling and Writhing, of course, to begin with', the Mock Turtle replied; 'and then the different branches of Arithmetic—Ambition, Distraction, Uglification, and Derision'.

Lewis Carroll (1832–98) British writer and mathematician. *Alice's Adventures in Wonderland* (1865), ch. 9

2 Education is simply the soul of a society as it passes from one generation to another.

G. K. Chesterton (1874–1936) British writer and poet. *Observer* (July 6, 1924), 'Sayings of the Week'

3 The educational process has no end beyond itself; it is its own end.

John Dewey (1859–1952) US philosopher and educator. *Democracy and Education* (1916)

4 It was a saying of his that education was an ornament in prosperity and a refuge in adversity.

Diogenes Laërtius (*fl.* 3rd century) Greek historian and biographer. 'Aristotle', quoted in *Lives and Opinions of the Eminent Philosophers* (C. D. Yonge, tr.; 1853)

5 Upon the education of the people of this country the fate of this country depends.

Benjamin Disraeli (1804–81) British prime minister and writer. Speech in Parliament (June 15, 1874)

6 Education is that which remains, if one has forgotten everything one learned in school.

Albert Einstein (1879–1955) German-born US physicist. *Out of My Later Years* (1950)

7 I pay the schoolmaster, but 'tis the schoolboys that educate my son.

Ralph Waldo Emerson (1803–82) US poet and essayist. *Journals* (1860–66)

8 When a man's education is finished, he is finished.

E. A. Filene (1860–1937) US financier. Attrib.

9 Spoon feeding in the long run teaches us nothing but the shape of the spoon.

E. M. Forster (1879–1970) British novelist. *Observer* (October 7, 1951), 'Sayings of the Week'

10 The philosophic aim of education must be to get each one out of his isolated class and into the one humanity.

Paul Goodman (1911–72) US writer, teacher, and psychotherapist. *Compulsory Mis-education* (1964)

11 Education made us what we are.

Claude Adrien Helvétius (1715–71) French philosopher. 'Discours 3', *De l'Esprit* (1758), ch. 30

12 Discussion in class, which means letting twenty young blockheads and two cocky neurotics discuss something that neither their teacher nor they know.

Vladimir Nabokov (1899–1977) Russian-born US novelist, poet, and critic. *Pnin* (1957), ch. 6

13 He was sent, as usual, to a public school, where a little learning was painfully beaten into him, and from thence to the university where it was carefully taken out of him.

Thomas Love Peacock (1785–1866) British novelist and poet. *Nightmare Abbey* (1818), ch. 1

14 Not art, not books, but life itself is the true basis of teaching and education.

Johann Heinrich Pestalozzi (1746–1827) Swiss educational reformer. Quoted in *The Education of Man: Aphorisms* (Heinz and Ruth Norden, trs.; 1951)

15 What else is education but the reverent joining of the past to the gloom of the future by making wise use of the present?

Johann Heinrich Pestalozzi (1746–1827) Swiss educational reformer. Quoted in *The Education of Man: Aphorisms* (Heinz and Ruth Norden, trs.; 1951)

16 Real education must ultimately be limited to one who INSISTS on knowing, the rest is mere sheep-herding.

Ezra Pound (1885–1972) US poet, translator, and critic. *ABC of Reading* (1934), ch. 8

17 A man who has never gone to school may steal from a freight car, but if he has a university education he may steal the whole railroad.

Franklin D. Roosevelt (1882–1945) US president. Attrib.

18 A learned man is an idler who kills time by study.

George Bernard Shaw (1856–1950) Irish playwright. *Man and Superman* (1903)

19 To me education is a leading out of what is already there in the pupil's soul. To Miss Mackay it is a putting in of something that is not there, and that is not what I call education, I call it intrusion.

Muriel Spark (b. 1918) British novelist. *The Prime of Miss Jean Brodie* (1961), ch. 2

20 What does education often do? It makes a straight cut ditch of a free meandering brook.

Henry David Thoreau (1817–62) US writer. *Journal* (October/November 1850), quoted in *The Writings of Henry David Thoreau* (1906)

21 Soap and education are not as sudden as a massacre, but they are more deadly in the long run.

Mark Twain (1835–1910) US writer and humorist. 'Facts Concerning the Recent Resignation', *A Curious Dream* (1872)

22 I have never let my schooling interfere with my education.

Mark Twain (1835–1910) US writer and humorist. Attrib.

23 The Founding Fathers in their wisdom decided that children were an unnatural strain on parents. So they provided jails called schools, equipped with tortures called an education.

John Updike (b. 1932) US writer. *The Centaur* (1963), ch. 4

24 Teaching has ruined more American novelists than drink.

Gore Vidal (b. 1925) US novelist and essayist. Quoted in 'Conversations with Gore Vidal', *Oui* (Beverly Kempton; April 1975)

25 Education is an admirable thing, but it is well to remember from time to time that nothing that is worth knowing can be taught.

Oscar Wilde (1854–1900) Irish poet, playwright, and wit. Attrib.

Effort

see also **Action, Work**

1 If you want to know where the apathy is, you're probably sitting on it.

Florynce R. Kennedy (1916–2000) US lawyer and activist. *Color Me Flo: My Hard Life and Good Times* (1976)

2 Always strive to excel, but only on weekends.

Richard Rorty (b. 1931) US philosopher. *New York Times Magazine* (February 12, 1990)

Egotism

see also **The Self, Selfishness**

1 Against whom?

Alfred Adler (1870–1937) Austrian psychiatrist. Said when he heard that an egocentric had fallen in love. 'Exponent of the Soul', *Some of My Best Friends* (J. Bishop; 1920)

2 She wanted to be the reason for everything and so was the cause of nothing.

Djuna Barnes (1892–1982) US writer and illustrator. *Nightwood* (1936)

3 EGOIST, n. A person of low taste, more interested in himself than in me.

Ambrose Bierce (1842–1914?) US writer and journalist. *The Devil's Dictionary* (1911)

4 Someone said of a very great egotist: 'He would burn your house down to cook himself a couple of eggs'.

Nicolas Chamfort (1741–94) French writer. *Caractères et Anecdotes* (1795)

5 An aggregate of egos is a mob.

Northrop Frye (1912–91) Canadian academic. *The Well-Tempered Critic* (1963)

6 If the Almighty himself played the violin, the credits would still read 'Rubinstein, God, and Piatigorsky', in that order.

Jascha Heifetz (1901–87) Russian-born US violinist. Whenever he played with Artur Rubinstein (piano) and Gregor Piatigorsky (cello), Rubinstein always got top billing. *Los Angeles Times* (August 29, 1982)

7 For the sake of a few fine imaginative or domestic passages, are we to be bullied into a certain Philosophy engendered in the whims of an Egotist.

John Keats (1795–1821) English poet. Criticizing poetry such as Wordsworth's 'that has a palpable design on us'. Letter to John Hamilton Reynolds (February 3, 1818), quoted in *Selected Letters of John Keats* (Robert Gittings, ed.; 1970)

8 A man gets so little recognition he might turn into a megalomaniac.

Karl Kraus (1874–1936) Austrian writer. 1909. Quoted in 'Sprüche und Widersprüche', *Karl Kraus* (Harry Zohn; 1971)

9 Egotism is the anesthetic that dulls the pains of stupidity.

Frank Leahy (1908–73) US American football coach. *Look* (January 10, 1955)

10 The human ego is like an insatiable tick. If it is not killed, it can burrow under the layers of the soul and feed upon the man within, gorging itself until there is no man left.

Julius Lester (b. 1939) US writer, educator, and political activist. November 23, 1968. *Revolutionary Notes* (1970)

11 To love oneself is the beginning of a lifelong romance.

Oscar Wilde (1854–1900) Irish poet, playwright, and wit. *An Ideal Husband* (1895), Act 3

Elitism

see also **Class, Equality, Privilege**

1 Democracy! Bah! When I hear that word I reach for my feather boa!

Allen Ginsberg (1926–97) US poet. *Journals: Early Fifties Early Sixties* (October 1960)

2 If it is art, it is not for the masses.

Arnold Schoenberg (1874–1951) Austrian-born US composer. Letter to W. S. Schlamm (July 1, 1945), quoted in *Arnold Schoenberg Letters* (Erwin Stein, ed.; 1964)

3 All my pupils are the crème de la crème.

Muriel Spark (b. 1918) British novelist. *The Prime of Miss Jean Brodie* (1961)

Emigration

see also **Exile, Globalization, Xenophobia**

1 Being thus arrived in a good harbor, and brought safe to land, they fell upon their knees and blessed the God of Heaven who had brought them over the vast and furious ocean.

William Bradford (1590–1657) English-born American religious leader and colonist. *History of Plymouth Plantation, 1620–47* (Charles Deane, ed.; 1856), ch. 7

2 Can you take your country with you on the soles of your shoes?

Georg Büchner (1813–37) German dramatist. *Danton's Death* (1835), Act 3, Scene 1, quoted in *Complete Plays, Lenz and Other Writings* (John Reddick, tr.; 1993)

3 To western woods, and lonely plains,
Palemon from the crowd departs,
Where Nature's wildest genius reigns,
To tame the soil, and plant the arts—
What wonders there shall freedom show,
What mighty states successive grow!

Philip Freneau (1752–1832) US poet. Traditionally any young man
who sets out on a journey, 'Palamon' appeared in Chaucer's
The Knight's Tale (1390?). 'On the Emigration to America
and Peopling the Western Country' (1785), st. 1

4 The ocean and hunger and some other urge made
the Cantonese people explorers and Americans.

Maxine Hong Kingston (b. 1940) US writer. *China Men* (1980)

5 Stella, an ordinary American, indistinguishable!
No one could guess what hell she had crawled
out of until she opened her mouth and up coiled
the smoke of accent.

Cynthia Ozick (b. 1928) US novelist and short-story writer. The thoughts
of Rosa. Stella is a Jew who has migrated from Europe. *The
Shawl* (1980)

6 The real fact is that I could no longer stand their
eternal cold mutton.

Cecil Rhodes (1853–1902) British colonial statesman and financier.
Referring to why he had left his friends in England and come
to South Africa. Quoted in *Cecil Rhodes* (G. le Sueur; 1913)

7 'When I was your age', my mother said, 'I ate
herring and black bread for thirty-six days in the
bottom of a ship to get from Antwerp to New
York. Outside of New York there's nothing.
Only a great big garbage pail they call Europe'.

Jerome Weidman (1913–98) US writer. *Praying for Rain* (1986),
ch. 1

8 As far as we can see, both in front and near the
horizon is dotted with white wagon covers of
emigrants, like a string of beads.

James Wilkins, US pioneer. 1850. Referring to the stream of
wagons on the Oregon Trail. In 1850, 52,500 people
emigrated to the West. Quoted in *The Oregon Trail* (W. E.
Hill; 1987), Introduction

Emotion

see also Anger, Euphoria, Fear, Happiness, The Heart, Hope,
Love

1 There are some feelings time cannot benumb,
Nor torture shake, or mine would now be cold
and dumb.

Lord Byron (1788–1824) British poet. *Childe Harold's Pilgrimage*
(1812–18), can. 4, st. 19

2 There is a road from the eye to the heart that
does not go through the intellect.

G. K. Chesterton (1874–1936) British writer and poet. *The Defendant*
(1901)

3 'There are strings', said Mr Tappertit, 'in the
human heart that had better not be wibrated'.

Charles Dickens (1812–70) British novelist. *Barnaby Rudge* (1841),
ch. 22

4 I'm a nymphomaniac of the heart.

Gabriel García Márquez (b. 1928) Colombian novelist. 1983. Interview,
Playboy Magazine (February, 1983)

5 As you pass from the tender years of youth into
harsh and embittered manhood, make sure you
take with you on your journey all the human
emotions! Don't leave them on the road, for you
will not pick them up afterwards!

Nikolay Gogol (1809–52) Russian novelist and playwright. *Dead Souls*
(1842), pt. 1, ch. 6

6 The seven constituents of emotional make-up are:
joy, anger, sorrow, fear, love, hatred, and desire.
A man of superior emotional make-up will
display these emotions in a balanced manner.

Han Yu (768–824) Chinese writer and poet. 'The Truth About One's
Underlying Character' (8th–9th century), quoted in *Essays by
Han Yu* (A. C. Barnes, tr.; 1979)

7 Grief and disappointment give rise to anger,
anger to envy, envy to malice, and malice to grief
again, till the whole circle be completed.

David Hume (1711–76) Scottish philosopher and historian. *A Treatise of
Human Nature* (1739–40)

8 A man who has not passed through the inferno
of his passions has never overcome them.

Carl Gustav Jung (1875–1961) Swiss psychoanalyst. *Memories,
Dreams, Reflections* (1962), ch. 9

9 Emotions are the lowest form of consciousness.
Emotional actions are the most contracted,
narrowing, dangerous form of behavior.

Timothy Leary (1920–96) US psychologist and guru. *The Politics of
Ecstasy* (1968)

10 The young man who has not wept is a savage,
and the old man who will not laugh is a fool.

George Santayana (1863–1952) Spanish-born US philosopher, poet, and
novelist. *Dialogues in Limbo* (1926)

11 If you want to know how you really feel about
someone take note of the impression an
unexpected letter from him makes on you when
you first see it on the doormat.

Arthur Schopenhauer (1788–1860) German philosopher. *Parerga and
Paralipomena* (1851)

12 My heart sings, full of sadness—the shadows
lengthen.

Jean Sibelius (1865–1957) Finnish composer. Written when trying to
compose his Fifth Symphony against a background of
troubling war news. Diary entry (October 1914)

13 A man gets tired of feeling too much.

Wole Soyinka (b. 1934) Nigerian novelist, playwright, poet, and lecturer.
The Road (1965)

14 Strong emotions and passions are the causes not
only of mental but also of physical illness.

Susruta (*fl.* 4th century) Hindu physician. Attrib.

Ending

see also Doomsday

1 It all comes to the same thing at the end.

Robert Browning (1812–89) British poet. 'Any Wife to Any
Husband', *Men and Women* (1855), st. 16

2 It is closing time in the gardens of the West.

Cyril Connolly (1903–74) British writer and journalist. *The Condemned
Playground* (1945)

3 Where should we go after the last frontiers,
where should the birds fly after the last sky?

Mahmoud Darwish (b. 1942) Palestinian poet. 'Earth Scrapes Us',
Modern Arabic Poetry (Salma Khadra Jayyusi, ed.; 1987),
no. 1

4 The last sound on the worthless earth will be two
human beings trying to launch a homemade
spaceship and already quarrelling about where
they are going next.

William Faulkner (1897–1962) US novelist. Speech to UNESCO
Commission, New York (1959)

5 Every epoch bears its own ending within itself.
Fields of rape, canola fields, the white-eyed,
walking dead.

Carolyn Forché, US poet. *The Angel of History* (1991)

6 'Tis the last rose of summer
Left blooming alone;
All her lovely companions
Are faded and gone.

Thomas Moore (1779–1852) Irish poet. "'Tis the Last Rose', *Irish Melodies* (1807)

7 The Last Hurrah

Edwin O'Connor (1918–68) US writer. 1956. Title of novel based on the political career of James M. Curley.

8 HECTOR The end crowns all,
And that old common arbitrator, Time,
Will one day end it.

William Shakespeare (1564–1616) English poet and playwright. *Troilus and Cressida* (1602), Act 4, Scene 5

9 We have reached an important point when the end begins to come into view.

William C. Westmoreland (b. 1914) US military commander. Referring to the Vietnam War (1959–75). Speech, National Press Club (November 21, 1967)

10 The crowd are on the pitch. They think it's all over. It is now.

Kenneth Wolstenholme (d. 2002) British sports commentator. Said at the end of his football commentary on the World Cup final between England and Germany when Geoff Hurst of England scored a goal in the final seconds of the match. *1966 World Cup Final* (BBC Television; 1966)

Endurance

see also **Determination, Persistence, Survival**

1 You may write me down in history
With your bitter, twisted lies,
You may trod me in the very dirt
But still, like dust, I'll rise.

Maya Angelou (b. 1928) US writer. 'Still I Rise', *And Still I Rise* (1976)

2 Come night, strike hour
Days go, I endure.

Guillaume Apollinaire (1880–1918) Italian-born French poet. 'Le Pont Mirabeau', *Alcools* (1913)

3 The first Day's Night had come—
And grateful that a thing
So terrible—had been endured—
I told my Soul to sing.

Emily Dickinson (1830–86) US poet. 1862? 'The First Day's Night Had Come' (1947), ll. 1–4, quoted in *Beyond Bedlam: Poems Written out of Mental Distress* (Ken Smith and Matthew Sweeney, eds.; 1997)

4 Sorrow and silence are strong, and patient endurance is godlike.

Henry Wadsworth Longfellow (1807–82) US poet. *Evangeline* (1847), pt. 2, l. 60

5 TOUCHSTONE I had rather bear with you than bear you.

William Shakespeare (1564–1616) English poet and playwright. *As You Like It* (1599), Act 2, Scene 4

6 GLOUCESTER I am tied to the stake, and I must stand the course.

William Shakespeare (1564–1616) English poet and playwright. *King Lear* (1605–06), Act 3, Scene 7

7 EDGAR Men must endure
Their going hence, even as their coming hither:
Ripeness is all.

William Shakespeare (1564–1616) English poet and playwright. *King Lear* (1605–06), Act 5, Scene 2

8 LEONATO For there was never yet philosopher
That could endure the toothache patiently.

William Shakespeare (1564–1616) English poet and playwright. *Much Ado About Nothing* (1598–99), Act 5, Scene 1

9 SHYLOCK Still have I borne it with a patient shrug,
For sufferance is the badge of all our tribe.

William Shakespeare (1564–1616) English poet and playwright. *The Merchant of Venice* (1596–98), Act 1, Scene 3

10 Maybe one day we shall be glad to remember even these hardships.

Virgil (70–19 BC) Roman poet. *Aeneid* (29–19 BC), bk. 1, l. 203

11 This suspense is terrible. I hope it will last.

Oscar Wilde (1854–1900) Irish poet, playwright, and wit. *The Importance of Being Earnest* (1895), Act 3

Enemies

see also **Conflict, Contempt, Hate**

1 Not while I'm alive, he ain't.

Ernest Bevin (1881–1951) British trade union leader and statesman. Remark on being told that Aneurin Bevan was 'his own worst enemy'. Also attributed to others. Quoted in *Aneurin Bevan* (Michael Foot; 1973)

2 My cousin Francis and I are in perfect accord—
he wants Milan, and so do I.

Charles V (1500–58) Belgian-born Spanish monarch. Referring to his dispute with Francis I of France over Italian territory. *The Story of Civilization* (William Durant; 1950–67), vol. 5

3 It is the enemy who can truly teach us to practice the virtues of compassion and tolerance.

Dalai Lama (b. 1935) Tibetan spiritual leader. *Ocean of Wisdom: Guidelines for Living* (1989)

4 I respect only those who resist me; but I cannot tolerate them.

Charles de Gaulle (1890–1970) French president. *New York Times Magazine* (May 12, 1966)

5 He who is reluctant to recognize me opposes me.

Frantz Fanon (1925–61) Martiniquan social scientist, physician, and psychiatrist. *Black Skin, White Masks* (1952)

6 You are honored by your friends . . .
distinguished by your enemies. I have been very distinguished.

J. Edgar Hoover (1895–1972) US criminologist and government official. Quoted in *J. Edgar Hoover* (Curt Gentry; 1991)

7 Eminence engenders enemies.

C. L. R. James (1901–89) Trinidadian writer, political theorist, and educator. *The Black Jacobins* (1938)

8 Always forgive your enemies—but never forget their names.

Robert Kennedy (1925–68) US statesman. Attrib.

9 I don't have a warm personal enemy left. They've all died off. I miss them terribly because they helped define me.

Clare Boothe Luce (1903–87) US playwright, journalist, and public official. Remark on *The Dick Cavett Show*, ABC television (July 21, 1981)

10 You must despise your enemy strategically, but respect him tactically.

Mao Zedong (1893–1976) Chinese statesman. Attrib.

11 Of the enemies of the soul—
the world, the devil, the flesh—
the *world* is the most serious and most dangerous.

Gabriela Mistral (1889–1957) Spanish poet, diplomat, and educator. 'We Were All to be Queens', *Tala* (1938)

12 We have met the enemy, and they are ours.

Oliver Hazard Perry (1785–1819) US naval commander. Reporting his victory in a naval battle on Lake Erie. Remark (1813), quoted in *Familiar Quotations* (John Bartlett; 1863)

13 I hate admitting that my enemies have a point.

Salman Rushdie (b. 1947) Indian-born British novelist. Said by Hamza in the 'Mahound' section of the novel. 'Mahound', *The Satanic Verses* (1988)

14 It takes your enemy and your friend, working together, to hurt you to the heart; the one to slander you and the other to get the news to you.

Mark Twain (1835–1910) US writer and humorist. *Following the Equator* (1897), ch. 45

15 The best is the enemy of the good.

Voltaire (1694–1778) French writer and philosopher. Originally from an Italian proverb quoted in Voltaire's *Dictionnaire philosophique*. 'Art Dramatique': 'Le meglio è l'inimico del bene'. 'La Béguele', *Contes* (1772), l. 2

Energy

see **Passion**, **Vitality**

England

see also **Britain**, **British Cities**

1 They came from three very powerful nations of the Germans; that is, from the *Saxones*, *Angli*, and *Iutae*.

Bede (673?–735) English monk and scholar. Referring to the Anglo-Saxon invaders of England. *Ecclesiastical History* (731)

2 And did those feet in ancient time
Walk upon England's mountains green?
And was the holy Lamb of God
On England's pleasant pastures seen?

William Blake (1757–1827) British poet, painter, engraver, and mystic. Better known as the hymn 'Jerusalem', with music by Sir Hubert Parry; not to be confused with Blake's longer poem *Jerusalem*. *Milton: A Poem in Two Books* (1804–08), no. 1, Preface, ll. 1–4

3 I will not cease from Mental Fight,
Nor shall my Sword sleep in my hand,
Till we have built Jerusalem
In England's green and pleasant Land.

William Blake (1757–1827) British poet, painter, engraver, and mystic. Better known as the hymn 'Jerusalem', with music by Sir Hubert Parry; not to be confused with Blake's longer poem *Jerusalem*. *Milton: A Poem in Two Books* (1804–08), no. 1, Preface, ll. 13–16

4 I like the English. They have the most rigid code of immorality in the world.

Malcolm Bradbury (1932–2000) British academic, novelist, and critic. *Eating People is Wrong* (1959), ch. 5

5 The English winter—ending in July,
To recommence in August.

Lord Byron (1788–1824) British poet. *Don Juan* (1819–24), can. 13, st. 42

6 Before the Roman came to Rye or out to Severn strode,
The rolling English drunkard made the rolling English road.

G. K. Chesterton (1874–1936) British writer and poet. 'The Rolling English Road' (1914)

7 England—a happy land we know,
Where follies naturally grow.

Charles Churchill (1731–64) British poet. *The Ghost* (1763), bk. 1, l. 111

8 From this amphibious ill-born mob began
That vain, ill-natured thing, an Englishman.

Daniel Defoe (1660–1731) English novelist and journalist. *The True-Born Englishman* (1701), pt. 1, l. 132

9 But 'tis the talent of our English nation,
Still to be plotting some new reformation.

John Dryden (1631–1700) English poet, playwright, and literary critic. 'The Prologue at Oxford' (1680), ll. 9–10, quoted in *The Poems and Fables of John Dryden* (James Kinsley, ed.; 1962)

10 The English character has the iron force of the Latins, but not the frankness and expansion. Like their fruits, they need a summer sky to give them more sweetness and a richer flavor.

Margaret Fuller (1810–50) US writer and reformer. 'American Literature', *Papers on Literature and Art* (1846), quoted in *The Heath Anthology of American Literature* (Paul Lauter, ed.; 1998), vol. 1

11 Never judge a country by its politics. After all, we English are quite honest by nature, aren't we?

Alfred Hitchcock (1899–1980) British-born US film director. A line from the film directed by Alfred Hitchcock. *The Lady Vanishes* (Screenplay by Sidney Gilliat and Frank Launder; 1938)

12 An Englishman is never so natural as when he is holding his tongue.

Henry James (1843–1916) US-born British writer and critic. *The Portrait of a Lady* (1881), ch. 10

13 If an earthquake were to engulf England to-morrow, the English would manage to meet and dine somewhere among the rubbish, just to celebrate the event.

Douglas Jerrold (1803–57) British playwright. *The Life and Remains of Douglas Jerrold* (Blanchard Jerrold; 1859), ch. 14

14 Happy is England! I could be content
To see no other verdure than its own;
To feel no other breezes than are blown
Through its tall woods with high romances blent.

John Keats (1795–1821) English poet. 'Happy is England!', *Keats's Poems* (1817)

15 England has become a squalid, uncomfortable, ugly place . . . an intolerant, racist, homophobic, narrow-minded, authoritarian rat-hole run by vicious suburban-minded, materialistic philistines.

Hanif Kureishi (b. 1954) British writer and filmmaker. 1988. Quoted in *A Queer Reader* (Patrick Higgins, ed.; 1993)

16 The only England he had known was a kind of corpse in future argument with itself, a dead voice bearing witness to its own achievement, passionate in incest with its past.

George Lamming (b. 1927) Barbadian writer. *Season of Adventure* (1960)

17 An Englishman's way of speaking absolutely classifies him
The moment he talks he makes some other Englishman despise him.

Alan Jay Lerner (1918–86) US lyricist and librettist. *My Fair Lady* (1956), Act 1, Scene 1

18 A ready means of being cherished by the English is to adopt the simple expedient of living a long time. I have little doubt that if, say, Oscar Wilde had lived into his nineties, instead of dying in his forties, he would have been considered a benign, distinguished figure suitable to preside at a school

prize-giving or to instruct and exhort scoutmasters at their jamborees. He might even have been knighted.

Malcolm Muggeridge (1903–90) British journalist. *Tread Softly For You Tread on My Jokes* (1966)

19 It is not for nothing that, in the English language alone, to accuse someone of trying to be funny is highly abusive.

Malcolm Muggeridge (1903–90) British journalist. *Tread Softly For You Tread on My Jokes* (1966)

20 England is a nation of shopkeepers.

Napoleon I (1769–1821) French emperor. Quoted in *Napoleon in Exile* (Barry O'Meara; 1822), vol. 2

21 Not only England, but also every Englishman is an island.

Novalis (1772–1801) German poet and novelist. 1799. Quoted in *Fragments* (R. Martin, ed.; 1988)

22 A family with the wrong members in control— that, perhaps, is as near as one can come to describing England in a phrase.

George Orwell (1903–50) British writer. 'England Your England', *The Lion and the Unicorn* (1941)

23 But Lord! to see the absurd nature of Englishmen, that cannot forbear laughing and jeering at everything that looks strange.

Samuel Pepys (1633–1703) English diarist and civil servant. *Diary* (November 27, 1662)

24 The English expect that everything should be the same, even in Central Asia, as it is in England, and grumble when it is not.

Vita Sackville-West (1892–1962) British poet and novelist. 'Passenger to Teheran', *Virago Book of Women Travellers* (Mary Morris, ed.; 1996)

25 England is the paradise of individuality, eccentricity, heresy, anomalies, hobbies, and humors.

George Santayana (1863–1952) Spanish-born US philosopher, poet, and novelist. 'The British Character', *Soliloquies in England* (1922)

26 GAUNT This royal throne of kings, this sceptred isle,
This earth of majesty, this seat of Mars,
This other Eden, demi-paradise,
This fortress built by Nature for herself
Against infection and the hand of war.

William Shakespeare (1564–1616) English poet and playwright. *Richard II* (1595), Act 2, Scene 1

27 An Englishman thinks he is moral when he is only uncomfortable.

George Bernard Shaw (1856–1950) Irish playwright. *Man and Superman* (1903), Act 3

28 What a pity it is that we have no amusements in England but vice and religion!

Sydney Smith (1771–1845) British clergyman, essayist, and wit. Quoted in *The Smith of Smiths* (H. Pearson; 1934), ch. 10

29 The national sport of England is obstacle-racing. People fill their rooms with useless and cumbersome furniture, and spend the rest of their lives in trying to dodge it.

Herbert Beerbohm Tree (1853–1917) British actor and theatrical impresario. Attrib. *Beerbohm Tree* (Hesketh Pearson; 1956)

30 An Englishman does not joke about such an important matter as a bet.

Jules Verne (1828–1905) French writer. *Around the World in Eighty Days* (1873)

31 The English nation is the only one on earth which has successfully regulated the power of its kings by resisting them, and which . . . has established that beneficial government under which the Prince, all powerful for good, is restrained from doing ill.

Voltaire (1694–1778) French writer and philosopher. *Lettres Anglaises ou Philosophiques* (1734)

32 We must be free or die, who speak the tongue
That Shakespeare spake; the faith and morals hold
Which Milton held.

William Wordsworth (1770–1850) English poet. 1802. 'It Is Not To Be Thought Of', *Poems in Two Volumes* (1807), vol. 1, ll. 11–13

33 Let us attack in her own waters perfidious Albion!

Augustin Ximénèz (1726–1817) French poet. October 1793. 'L'Ère des Français', *Poésies Révolutionnaires et Contre-révolutionnaires* (1821)

Entertainment

see also **The Arts, Films, Television, Theatre**

1 There's No Business Like Show Business

Irving Berlin (1888–1989) Russian-born US composer and lyricist. Song title. 'Annie Get Your Gun' (1946)

2 You know, I go to the theatre to be entertained . . . I don't want to see plays about rape, sodomy and drug addiction . . . I can get all that at home.

Peter Cook (1937–95) British writer, actor, and comedian. Caption to cartoon. *Observer* (July 8, 1962)

3 Show business offers more solid promises than Catholicism.

John Guare (b. 1938) US playwright. *Independent* (April 25, 1992)

4 Life would be tolerable, were it not for its amusements.

George Cornewall Lewis (1806–63) British statesman and writer. *Times* (September 18, 1872)

5 Most people think that entertainers see the world. But after the twenty-sixth city . . . your hotel room is your world.

Stevie Wonder (b. 1950) US singer, songwriter, and activist. Quoted in *The Wit and Wisdom of Rock and Roll* (Maxim Jabukowski, ed.; 1983)

The Environment

see also **Ecology, Landscapes, Nature, The World**

1 Man has been endowed with reason, with the power to create, so that he can add to what he's been given. But up to now he hasn't been a creator, only a destroyer. Forests keep disappearing, rivers dry up, wild life's become extinct, the climate's ruined and the land grows poorer and uglier every day.

Anton Chekhov (1860–1904) Russian playwright and short-story writer. *Uncle Vanya* (1897), Act 1

2 Inner harmony is attained only when, by some means, terms are made with the environment.

John Dewey (1859–1952) US philosopher and educator. *Art as Experience* (1934)

3 Industrialization is something which is happening to the biosphere.

Edward Goldsmith (b. 1928) British business executive and ecologist. 'De-Industrializing Society', *The Great U-Turn* (1988)

4   The supreme reality of our time is . . . our common vulnerability on this planet.
John Fitzgerald Kennedy (1917–63) US president. Address to the Irish Parliament, Dublin (June 28, 1963)

5   The impulse to mar and to destroy is as ancient and almost as nearly universal as the impulse to create. The one is an easier way than the other of demonstrating power.
Joseph Wood Krutch (1893–1970) US essayist and naturalist. *The Best of Two Worlds* (1950)

6   Conservation is a state of harmony between men and land.
Aldo Leopold (1886–1948) US naturalist, conservationist, and philosopher. 'The Land Ethic', *A Sand County Almanac* (1949), pt. 3

7   Wild things were taken for granted until progress began to do away with them . . . we face the question whether a still higher 'standard of living' is worth its cost in things natural, wild, and free.
Aldo Leopold (1886–1948) US naturalist, conservationist, and philosopher. Quoted in *National Geographic Magazine* (November 1981)

8   We won't have a society if we destroy the environment.
Margaret Mead (1901–78) US anthropologist. Attrib.

9   They paved Paradise,
Put up a parking lot.
Joni Mitchell (b. 1943) Canadian singer and songwriter. Song lyric. 'Big Yellow Taxi' (1970)

10   Woodman, spare that tree!
Touch not a single bough!
In youth it sheltered me,
And I'll protect it now.
George Pope Morris (1802–64) US journalist and poet. 'Spare That Tree' (1830)

11   What have they done to the earth? . . .
Ravaged and plundered and ripped her and did her,
Struck her with knives in the side of the dawn
And tied her with fences and dragged her down.
Jim Morrison (1943–71) US rock singer and songwriter. Song lyric. 'When the Music's Over' (1967)

12   The early exhaustion of our fossil fuels will require the use of such other sources of power as water, wind, and sun.
Newspapers. *Scientific American* (May 14, 1921)

13   In remaking the world in the likeness of a steam-heated, air-conditioned metropolis of apartment buildings we have violated . . . our kinship with nature.
Ross Parmenter (b. 1912) Canadian-born US music critic and writer. 'Inward Sign', *The Plant in My Window* (1949)

14   Every luxury must be paid for, and everything is a luxury, starting with the world.
Cesare Pavese (1908–50) Italian novelist and poet. Attrib.

15   Many people, politicians and the public alike, believe that global warming is a rock-solid certainty.
Lee R. Raymond (b. 1938) US business executive. *New York Times* (December 12, 1997)

16   The work is going well, but it looks like the end of the world.
Sherwood Rowland (b. 1927) US chemist. Referring to his research into the destruction of the ozone layer. Attrib.

17   The environment is man's first right. Without a safe environment, man cannot exist to claim other rights, be they political, social, or economic.
Ken Saro-Wiwa (1941–95) Nigerian writer and political and human rights activist. 1995. Message sent from prison upon winning the 1995 Goldman Environmental prize for campaigning against oil companies' environmental destruction in his native Ogoniland. He was hanged in November 1995 on politically motivated charges of incitement to murder. Quoted in *National Geographic Magazine* (April 1996)

18   The emergence of intelligence, I am convinced, tends to unbalance the ecology. In other words, intelligence is the great polluter. It is not until a creature begins to manage its environment that nature is thrown into disorder.
Clifford D. Simak (1904–88) US writer. *Shakespeare's Planet* (1976)

19   A citizen of an advanced industrialized nation consumes in six months the energy and raw materials that have to last the citizen of a developing country his entire lifetime.
Maurice F. Strong (b. 1929) Canadian environmentalist and business executive. Attrib.

20   Any fine morning a power saw can fell a tree that took a thousand years to grow.
Edwin Way Teale (1899–1980) US naturalist, writer, and photographer. *Autumn Across America* (1956)

21   In wildness is the preservation of the world.
Henry David Thoreau (1817–62) US writer. Adopted as the motto of the Wilderness Society. 'Walking', *Excursions* (1863)

22   Talk of mysteries! Think of our life in nature . . . rocks, trees, wind on our cheeks! the *solid* earth! the *actual* world! the *common sense! Contact! Contact! Who* are we? *where* are we?
Henry David Thoreau (1817–62) US writer. 'Ktaadn', *The Maine Woods* (1848)

23   By avarice and selfishness, and a groveling habit, from which none of us is free, of regarding the soil as property . . . the landscape is deformed.
Henry David Thoreau (1817–62) US writer. 'The Bean Field', *Walden, or, Life in the Woods* (1854)

24   The most common trait of all primitive peoples is a reverence for lifegiving earth, and the native American shared this elemental ethic: the land was alive to his loving touch, and he, its son, was brother to all creatures.
Stewart L. Udall (b. 1920) US politician and conservationist. *The Quiet Crisis* (1963), ch. 1

25   We live in a land of vanishing beauty, of increasing ugliness, of shrinking open space, and of an overall environment that is diminished daily by pollution and noise and blight.
Stewart L. Udall (b. 1920) US politician and conservationist. Referring to the United States. *The Quiet Crisis* (1963), Foreword

26   The more we get out of the world the less we leave, and in the long run we shall have to pay our debts at a time that may be very inconvenient for our own survival.
Norbert Wiener (1894–1964) US mathematician. *The Human Use of Human Beings* (1950)

Envy

see also **Desire, Jealousy**

1   I am sure the grapes are sour.
Aesop (620?–560 BC) Greek writer. 'The Fox and the Grapes', *Aesop's Fables* (6th century BC)

2 The dullard's envy of brilliant men is always
   assuaged by the suspicion that they will come to
   a bad end.
   Max Beerbohm (1872–1956) British essayist, critic, and caricaturist.
   Zuleika Dobson (1911)

3 He who ascends to mountain-tops shall find
   The loftiest peaks most wrapt in clouds and
   snow;
   He who surpasses or subdues mankind
   Must look down on the hate of those below.
   Lord Byron (1788–1824) British poet. *Childe Harold's Pilgrimage*
   (1812–18), can. 3, st. 45

4 Fools may our scorn, not envy raise,
   For envy is a kind of praise.
   John Gay (1685–1732) English poet and playwright. 'The Hound and
   the Huntsman', *Fables* (1727), st. 1, l. 44

5 An envious heart makes a treacherous ear.
   Zora Neale Hurston (1891?–1960) US writer and folklorist. *Their Eyes
   Were Watching God* (1937)

6 Frankly, I don't mind not being President. I just
   mind that someone else is.
   Edward M. Kennedy (b. 1932) US politician. Speech, Gridiron Club,
   Washington, DC. (March 22, 1986)

7 Envy will merit as its shade pursue,
   But like a shadow proves the substance true.
   Alexander Pope (1688–1744) English poet. *An Essay on Criticism*
   (1711), l. 466–467

8 May the eyes in your face
   Survive the green ice
   Of envy's mean gaze.
   Theodore Roethke (1908–63) US poet. 'To a Young Wife', *The Far
   Field* (1964)

9 The man with toothache thinks everyone happy
   whose teeth are sound.
   George Bernard Shaw (1856–1950) Irish playwright. *Man and
   Superman* (1903)

10 I envy not in any moods
   The captive void of noble rage,
   The linnet born within the cage,
   That never knew the summer woods.
   Alfred Tennyson (1809–92) British poet. 1833–49. 'A. H. H.' (Arthur
   Henry Hallam) was the fiancé of Tennyson's sister Emily and
   died suddenly in September 1833. *In Memoriam A. H. H.*
   (1850), can. 27, st. 1

11 Whenever a friend succeeds, a little something in
   me dies.
   Gore Vidal (b. 1925) US novelist and essayist. *Sunday Times
   Magazine* (September 16, 1973)

Equality

see also **Civil Rights, Class, Human Rights, Women's Rights**

1 Anyone who pushes for equality, or criticises the
   male Anglo-Saxon world, is declared 'PC' and
   thereby discredited and silenced. McCarthyism to
   counteract imagined totalitarianism. Where have
   we seen that before?
   Yasmin Alibhai-Brown, British writer and broadcaster. *Independent*
   (August 11, 1993)

2 The true republic: men their rights and nothing
   more; women their rights and nothing less.
   Susan B. Anthony (1820–1906) US social reformer. Motto printed on
   the front of her newspaper, *The Revolution* (1868–70).

3 From the point of view of sexual morality the
   aeroplane is valuable in war in that it destroys
   men and women in equal numbers.
   Ernest William Barnes (1874–1953) British prelate and mathematician.
   Rise of Christianity (1947)

4 What makes equality such a difficult business is
   that we only want it with our superiors.
   Henry Becque (1837–99) French playwright. *Querelles Littéraires*
   (1890)

5 'Every man to count for one and no one to count
   for more than one' . . . appears, more than any
   other formula, to constitute the irreducible
   minimum of the ideal of equality.
   Isaiah Berlin (1909–97) Latvian-born British philosopher and historian of
   ideas. *Concepts and Categories* (1978)

6 Equality, Child, like freedom, exists only where
   you are now. Only as an egg in the womb are
   we all equal.
   Oriana Fallaci (b. 1930) Italian writer. *Letter to a Child Never Born*
   (1975)

7 All men are equal—all men, that is to say, who
   possess umbrellas.
   E. M. Forster (1879–1970) British novelist. *Howards End* (1910),
   ch. 6

8 The majestic egalitarianism of the law, which
   forbids rich and poor alike to sleep under
   bridges, to beg in the streets, and to steal bread.
   Anatole France (1844–1924) French novelist, poet, and critic. *The Red
   Lily* (1894), ch. 7

9 That all men are equal is a proposition to which,
   at ordinary times, no sane individual has ever
   given his assent.
   Aldous Huxley (1894–1963) British novelist and essayist. *Proper Studies*
   (1927)

10 It is better that some should be unhappy than
   that none should be happy, which would be the
   case in a general state of equality.
   Samuel Johnson (1709–84) British lexicographer and writer. April 7,
   1776. Quoted in *Life of Samuel Johnson* (James Boswell;
   1791)

11 The earth is the mother of all people, and all
   people should have equal rights upon it. You
   might as well expect the rivers to run backward
   as that any man who was born a free man
   should be contented when penned up and denied
   liberty.
   Chief Joseph (1840?–1904) Native American Nez Percé leader. 'An
   Indian's View of Indian Affairs', *North American Review*
   (1879)

12 There are very few jobs that actually require a
   penis or vagina. All other jobs should be open to
   everybody.
   Florynce R. Kennedy (1916–2000) US lawyer and activist. 1974.
   'Freelancer with No Time to Write', *Writer's Digest* (February
   1974)

13 We are confronted primarily with a moral
   issue . . . whether all Americans are to be
   afforded equal rights and equal opportunities,
   whether we are going to treat our fellow
   Americans as we want to be treated.
   John Fitzgerald Kennedy (1917–63) US president. Referring to race
   riots in Alabama. Radio broadcast (June 11, 1963)

14 I want to be the white man's brother, not his
   brother-in-law.
   Martin Luther King, Jr. (1929–68) US civil rights leader. *New York
   Journal-American* (September 10, 1962)

15 I have a dream that one day this nation will rise
up, live out the true meaning of its creed: we
hold these truths to be self-evident, that all men
are created equal.

Martin Luther King, Jr. (1929–68) US civil rights leader. August 28,
1963. Referring to the Declaration of Independence (1776).
Speech at civil rights march in Washington, DC, *New York
Times* (August 29, 1963)

16 A good many observers have remarked that if
equality could come at once the Negro would not
be ready for it. I submit that the white American
is even more unprepared.

Martin Luther King, Jr. (1929–68) US civil rights leader. *Where Do We
Go From Here: Chaos or Community?* (1967)

17 Above the titles of wife and mother, which,
although dear, are transitory and accidental,
there is the title human being, which precedes
and out-ranks every other.

Mary Ashton Livermore (1820–1905) US social reformer and writer. *What
Shall We Do with Our Daughters?* (1883), ch. 7

18 Equality of opportunity means equal opportunity
to be unequal.

Iain Macleod (1913–70) British politician. Quoted in *Way Of Life*
(John Boyd-Carpenter; 1980)

19 The cry of equality pulls everyone down.

Iris Murdoch (1919–99) Irish-born British novelist and philosopher.
Observer (September 1987), 'Sayings of the Week'

20 This isn't going to be a good country for any of
us to live in until it's a good country for all of us
to live in.

Richard Nixon (1913–94) US president. *Observer* (September 29,
1968), 'Sayings of the Week'

21 All animals are equal, but some animals are more
equal than others.

George Orwell (1903–50) British writer. *Animal Farm* (1945), ch. 10

22 Given the natural differences between human
beings, equality is an ethical aspiration that
cannot be realized without recourse either to
despotism or to an act of fraternity.

Octavio Paz (1914–98) Mexican author and poet. *New York Times*
(December 8, 1991)

23 EQUALITY . . . is the thing. It is the only true and
central premise from which constructive ideas can
radiate freely and be operated without prejudice.

Mervyn Peake (1911–68) British novelist, poet, and artist. 'The Sun
Goes Down Again', *Titus Groan* (1946)

24 All social primary goods are to be distributed
equally unless an unequal distribution is to the
advantage of everyone.

John Rawls (b. 1921) US philosopher. *A Theory of Justice* (1971)

25 Who ever walked behind anyone to freedom? If
we can't go hand in hand, I don't want to go.

Hazel Scott (1920–81) US jazz musician, actor, and feminist. *Ms* (1974)

26 Life levels all men: death reveals the eminent.

George Bernard Shaw (1856–1950) Irish playwright. 'Maxims for
Revolutionists', *Man and Superman* (1903)

27 We hold these truths to be self-evident: that all
men and women are created equal.

Elizabeth Cady Stanton (1815–1902) US suffragette. July 19–20, 1848.
'Declaration of Sentiments' at the First Women's Rights
Convention, Seneca Falls, New York, *History of Woman
Suffrage* (co-written with Susan B. Anthony and Matilda
Gage; 1881), vol. 1

28 Let us exert every ounce of man's energy and
everything produced by him to ensure that
everywhere the common people of the world get
their due from life.

Madame Sun (1890–1981) Chinese writer and revolutionary. Address,
The Chinese Women's Fight for Freedom (July–August 1956)

29 Everybody should have an equal chance—but
they shouldn't have a flying start.

Harold Wilson (1916–95) British prime minister. *Observer* (1963),
'Sayings of the Year'

Errors

see Failure, Mistakes

Eternity

see also Immortality, Infinity, Time

1 Motion being eternal, the first mover, if there is
but one, will be eternal also.

Aristotle (384–322 BC) Greek philosopher. *Physics* (4th century BC), 259a

2 A circular eternity may seem atrocious to the
spectator, but it is satisfactory to individuals
inside. Free from bad news and disease, they
always live as if it were the first time, and do not
remember previous times.

Adolfo Bioy Casares (1914–99) Argentinian writer. *The Invention of
Morel* (1964)

3 Who can speak of eternity without a solecism, or
think thereof without an ecstasy? Time we may
comprehend, 'tis but five days elder than ourselves.

Thomas Browne (1605–82) English physician and writer. *Religio Medici*
(1642), pt. 1, sect. 11

4 The stars will still remain when the shadows of
our presence and our deeds have vanished from
the earth. There is no man who does not know
that. Why, then, will we not turn our eyes
towards the stars? Why?

Mikhail Bulgakov (1891–1940) Russian novelist and playwright. The last
words of the novel. *The White Guard* (Michael Glenny, tr.;
1925)

5 Eternity was in that moment.

William Congreve (1670–1729) English playwright and poet. *The Old
Bachelor* (1693), Act 4, Scene 7

6 One can take eternity and time to be predicates
of God since, being the Ancient of Days, he is the
cause of all time and eternity. Yet he is before
time and beyond time and is the source of the
variety of time and of seasons.

Dionysius the Areopagite (fl. 1st century) Greek church leader and martyr.
1st century AD. Some modern scholars now identify the work
attributed to Dionysius to a 6th-century Neoplatonist known
as Pseudo-Dionysius. Quoted in 'The Divine Names', *Pseudo-
Dionysius, The Complete Works* (C. Luibheid, tr.; 1987)

7 Even forever comes to an end.

Rosa Guy (b. 1928) Trinidadian-born US writer. *A Measure of Time*
(1983)

8 All things from eternity are of like forms and
come round in a circle.

Marcus Aurelius (121–180) Roman emperor and philosopher. *Meditations*
(170–180), bk. 2, sect. 14

9 Eternity's a terrible thought. I mean, where's it
going to end?

Tom Stoppard (b. 1937) Czech-born British playwright and screenwriter.
Rosencrantz and Guildenstern Are Dead (1966), Act 2

10 I saw Eternity the other night
Like a great Ring of pure and endless light.
Henry Vaughan (1622–95) English poet and mystic. 'The World', *Silex Scintillans* (1650–55), quoted in *The Metaphysical Poets* (Helen Gardner, ed.; 1957)

11 I will concentrate on the beauty of one blue hill in the distance, and for me, that moment will be eternity.
Alice Walker (b. 1944) US novelist and poet. *Possessing the Secret of Joy* (1992)

Ethics

see Evil, Good, Morality

Euphoria

see also Happiness

1 He who binds to himself a joy
Doth the winged life destroy;
But he who kisses the joy as it flies
Lives in Eternity's sunrise.
William Blake (1757–1827) British poet, painter, engraver, and mystic. *Manuscript Notebooks* (1811), no. 59

2 'Scuse me while I kiss the sky.
Jimi Hendrix (1942–70) US rock musician. Song lyric. 'Purple Haze' (1967)

3 You made my life a cause for singing. Bless you, for coming back at last!
Henrik Ibsen (1828–1906) Norwegian playwright. Said by Solveig about Peer Gynt on the latter's return. *Peer Gynt* (1867)

4 And then spring came like a shout of joy to the woods . . . 'I have to scream a spring scream or I'll burst'. Ronia explained.
Astrid Lindgren (1907–2002) Swedish writer. *Ronia, the Robber's Daughter* (Patricia Crampton, tr.; 1981)

5 When I have done some such thing, I am exalted. I glow all over . . . Every fiber of me is thrilling with it. It is very natural. It is a mere matter of satisfaction at adjustment to environment. It is success.
Jack London (1876–1916) US writer. *The Cruise of the Snark* (1911)

6 While on the shop and street I gazed
My body of a sudden blazed;
And twenty minutes more or less
It seemed, so great my happiness,
That I was blessèd and could bless.
W. B. Yeats (1865–1939) Irish poet and playwright. 1931. 'Vacillation', *The Winding Stair and Other Poems* (1933), pt. 4, st. 2

Europe

see also Britain, European Cities, European Countries, European Languages, European Literature

1 The whole world is covered over with the hell of Europe.
Ayi Kwei Armah (b. 1939) Ghanaian writer and educator. Referring to European imperialism. *Why Are We So Blest?* (1972)

2 You cannot divide peace in Europe. You must have one peace running right through.
Clement Attlee (1883–1967) British politician. Speech to Parliament (March 26, 1936)

3 You cannot settle the problems of Europe by long-distance telephone calls and telegrams. Round the table we must get, but do not present us with faits accomplis when we get there.
Ernest Bevin (1881–1951) British trade union leader and statesman. Speech, Labour Party Conference, Blackpool (May 19, 1945)

4 If you open that Pandora's Box you never know what Trojan 'orses will jump out.
Ernest Bevin (1881–1951) British trade union leader and statesman. Referring to the Council of Europe. *Ernest Bevin and the Foreign Office* (Sir Roderick Barclay; 1975), ch. 3

5 Any war that breaks out must place the survival of the European order in jeopardy.
Prince Otto von Bismarck (1815–98) German chancellor. Letter to the German ambassador in Vienna (November 1883), quoted in *Germany, 1866–1945* (Gordon A. Craig; 1978)

6 I always hear the word 'Europe' on the lips of politicians who seek from other posers what they dare not demand in their own name.
Prince Otto von Bismarck (1815–98) German chancellor. Remark (January 9, 1871)

7 Your map of Africa is very fine, but my map of Africa is here in Europe. Here is Russia and here is France and here we are in the middle. That is my map of Africa.
Prince Otto von Bismarck (1815–98) German chancellor. Attrib. *Germany, 1866–1945* (Gordon A. Craig; 1978), ch. 4

8 A Europe living in peace calls for its members to be willing to listen to the arguments of the others, for the struggle of convictions and interests will continue. Europe needs tolerance. It needs freedom of thought, not moral indifference.
Willy Brandt (1913–92) German statesman. Address given on the presentation of a Nobel Prize in peace (December 11, 1971), quoted in *Willy Brandt, Peace* (Klaus Reiff, ed.; 1971)

9 Europe should not unite against something, but for something, namely for the betterment of the European nations and for their constructive role in the world.
Willy Brandt (1913–92) German statesman. Lecture, Düsseldorf (November 30, 1967), 'Permanent Peace in Europe as the Goal', quoted in *Willy Brandt, Peace* (Klaus Reiff, ed.; 1971)

10 Not a future. At least not in Europe. America's different, of course, but America's really only a kind of Russia. You've no idea how pleasant it is not to have any future. It's like having a totally efficient contraceptive.
Anthony Burgess (1917–93) British writer and critic. *Honey for the Bears* (1963), pt. 2, ch. 6

11 But the age of chivalry is gone. That of sophisters, economists, and calculators, has succeeded; and the glory of Europe is extinguished for ever.
Edmund Burke (1729–97) Irish-born British statesman and political philosopher. *Reflections on the Revolution in France* (1790)

12 We must build a kind of United States of Europe.
Winston Churchill (1874–1965) British prime minister and writer. Speech, Zurich (September 19, 1946)

13 I have never read it. You should not waste your time.
Kenneth Clarke (b. 1940) British politician. Referring to the Maastricht Treaty (1992). *Independent* (March 17, 1995)

14 At the present time there cannot be any other Europe than a Europe of states, apart of course from myths, stories, and parades.
Charles de Gaulle (1890–1970) French president. Press conference, Paris (May 15, 1962)

15 I've come to think of Europe as a hardcover book, America as the paperback version.
Don DeLillo (b. 1936) US novelist. Said by Owen Brademas. *The Names* (1982)

16 Europe is not just about material results, it is about spirit. Europe is a state of mind.
Jacques Delors (b. 1925) French statesman. *Independent* (May 19, 1994)

17 The construction of Europe is not a boxing match.
Jacques Delors (b. 1925) French statesman. *Independent* (May 19, 1994)

18 The hardest thing is to convince European citizens that even the most powerful nation is no longer able to act alone.
Jacques Delors (b. 1925) French statesman. As president of the European Union (1985–95), Jacques Delors was responsible for the Maastricht Treaty (1992) which reflected the intention of member states to broaden their political and economic cooperation. *Independent* (May 19, 1994)

19 What else is Europe but a conglomeration of mistakes? Mistakes that are so diverse that they complement each other and balance one another. Taken separately, we're each unbearable in our own way.
Hans Enzensberger (b. 1929) German poet. 1987. 'Polish Incidents', *Europe, Europe* (Martin Chambers, tr.; 1989)

20 It means the end of a thousand years of history.
Hugh Gaitskell (1906–63) British politician. Referring to the prospect of Britain joining a European federation. Speech, Labour Party Conference (October 3, 1962)

21 No one of sound mind and memory can ever again permit such a concentration of power in the heart of Europe.
Günter Grass (b. 1927) German writer. Referring to plans to reunify Germany. Germany was divided after its defeat in World War II. The reunification of Germany took place on October 3, 1990. 'Don't Reunify Germany', *New York Times* (January 27, 1990)

22 In 1914 Europe had arrived at a point in which every country except Germany was afraid of the present, and Germany was afraid of the future.
Edward Grey (1862–1933) British statesman. Speech (July 24, 1924), quoted in *Quotations in History* (A. Palmer and V. Palmer; 1976)

23 Only through resolute commitment to the realization of European unification can we obviate a relapse into the destructive nationalism of the past.
Helmut Kohl (b. 1930) German statesman. Speech to the Bundestag, Bonn (June 17, 1992)

24 The only lasting solution is that Europe itself should gradually find its way to an internal equilibrium and a limitation of armaments by political appeasement.
Lord Lothian (1882–1940) British journalist and statesman. *Times* (May 4, 1934)

25 Our policy is directed not against any country or doctrine but against hunger, poverty, desperation, and chaos. Its purpose should be the revival of a working economy in the world so as to permit the emergence of political and social conditions in which free institutions can exist.
George Marshall (1880–1959) US military commander and politician. Announcing the European Recovery Plan (the Marshall Plan). Address, Harvard University (June 5, 1947)

26 When Paris sneezes, Europe catches cold.
Metternich (1773–1859) Austrian diplomat and statesman. Reflecting his anxiety preceding the July Revolution in France (1830), which caused the abdication of King Charles X. Letter, *Liberalism* (January 26, 1830)

27 Whatever it is I read about Europe is war. Them white men is always fightin'. War'a the Roses, the Crew-sades, the Revolution, the Kaiser, Hitler, the com'unists. Shit! All they care 'bout, war an' money, money an' land.
Walter Mosley (b. 1952) US novelist. *A Red Death* (1991), ch. 30

28 This Berlin-Rome connection is not so much a diaphragm as an axis, around which can revolve all those states of Europe with a will towards collaboration and peace.
Benito Mussolini (1883–1945) Italian dictator. Speech, Milan (November 1, 1936)

29 The European who is beginning to predominate . . . must then be, in relation to the complex civilization into which he had been born, a primitive man, a barbarian appearing on the stage through the trap-door, a vertical invader.
José Ortega y Gasset (1883–1955) Spanish writer and philosopher. *The Revolt of the Masses* (1930)

30 Unquestionably there never was a time in the history of this country when, from the situation of Europe, we might more reasonably expect fifteen years of peace, than we may at this present moment.
William Pitt the Younger (1759–1806) British prime minister. Revolutionary France declared war on Britain on February 1, 1793. Speech to Parliament (February 17, 1792)

31 This going into Europe will not turn out to be the thrilling mutual exchange supposed. It is more like nine middle-aged couples with failing marriages meeting in a darkened bedroom in a Brussels hotel for a Group Grope.
E. P. Thompson (b. 1924) British historian. *Sunday Times* (April 27, 1975)

32 That Europe's nothin' on earth but a great big auction, that's all it is.
Tennessee Williams (1911–83) US playwright. *Cat on a Hot Tin Roof* (1955), Act 1

33 Europe has not yet freed itself from the heritage of the Cold War and is in danger of plunging into a Cold Peace.
Boris Yeltsin (b. 1931) Russian president. *Independent* (December 6, 1994)

European Cities

see also **British Cities, Cities, Europe, European Countries**

1 Things felt oddly bigger to me in Paris. The sky was more present than in New York, its whims more fragile . . . The Paris sky has its own laws, and they function independently of the city below.
Paul Auster (b. 1947) US writer. *New York Trilogy* (1987), pt. 3

2 Streets full of water. Please advise.
Robert Benchley (1889–1945) US humorist, writer, editor, and critic. Telegram sent to his editor on arriving in Venice. Quoted in 'Robert Benchley', *Wits End* (R. E. Drennan; 1973)

3 London is a teenager, an urchin . . . Paris, I believe, is a man in his twenties in love with an older woman.
John Berger (b. 1926) British novelist, essayist, and art critic. 'Imagine Paris', *Keeping a Rendezvous* (1991)

4 Your first day in Dublin is always your worst.
John Berryman (1914–72) US poet. 'The Dream Songs', *His Toy, His Dream, His Rest* (1968), l. 299

5 Rome's just a city like anywhere else. A vastly overrated city, I'd say. It trades on belief just as Stratford trades on Shakespeare.

Anthony Burgess (1917–93) British writer and critic. *Mr. Enderby* (1963), pt. 2, ch. 2

6 While stands the Coliseum, Rome shall stand; When falls the Coliseum, Rome shall fall; And when Rome falls—the World.

Lord Byron (1788–1824) British poet. *Childe Harold's Pilgrimage* (1812–18), can. 4, st. 145

7 Venice is like eating an entire box of chocolate liqueurs at one go.

Truman Capote (1924–84) US novelist. *Observer* (November 26, 1961), 'Sayings of the Week'

8 When thou art at Rome, do as they do at Rome.

Miguel de Cervantes (1547–1616) Spanish novelist and playwright. *Don Quixote* (1605–15), pt. 2, ch. 54

9 Do let's go to Moscow. We must go. Please! There's nowhere in the world like Moscow.

Anton Chekhov (1860–1904) Russian playwright and short-story writer. *The Three Sisters* (1901), Act 3

10 I wished to be a citizen of the world, not of a single city.

Desiderius Erasmus (1466?–1536) Dutch humanist, scholar, and writer. Referring to his refusal of a suggestion that he be made a citizen of Zurich. Letter to Laurimus (February 1, 1523)

11 If you are lucky enough to have lived in Paris as a young man, then wherever you go for the rest of your life, it stays with you, for Paris is a moveable feast.

Ernest Hemingway (1899–1961) US writer. *A Moveable Feast* (1964), Epigraph

12 Paris is worth a Mass.

Henry IV (1553–1610) French monarch. Said on entering Paris, having secured its submission to his authority by becoming a Roman Catholic. Remark (March 1594)

13 Is Paris burning?

Adolf Hitler (1889–1945) Austrian-born German dictator. Referring to the liberation of Paris by the Allies. Remark (August 25, 1944), quoted in *Is Paris Burning?* (Larry Collins and Dominique Lapierre; 1965), ch. 5

14 In Rome you long for the country; in the country—oh inconstant!—you praise the distant city to the stars.

Horace (65–8 BC) Roman poet. *Satires* (35? BC), bk. 2, satire 7, l. 28

15 Paris practices its sins as lightly as it does its religion, while London practices both very seriously.

James Weldon Johnson (1871–1938) US writer, lawyer, and diplomat. *The Autobiography of an Ex-Colored Man* (1912)

16 Dublin, though a place much worse than London, is not so bad as Iceland.

Samuel Johnson (1709–84) British lexicographer and writer. Letter to Mrs. Christopher Smart, *Life of Samuel Johnson* (James Boswell; 1791)

17 When I die, Dublin will be written on my heart.

James Joyce (1882–1941) Irish writer. 1939. Quoted in *Oliver St John Gogarty* (Ulick O'Connor; 1964), ch. 6

18 To live in Petersburg is to sleep in a grave.

Osip Mandelstam (1891–1938) Russian poet, writer, and translator. 'O Lord, Help Me to Live Through This Night . . . ', *Osip Mandelstam: Selected Poems* (Clarence Brown and W. S. Merwin, tr.; 1973), l. 3

19 Hagia Sophia—here the Lord ordained That nations and emperors must halt!

Osip Mandelstam (1891–1938) Russian poet, writer, and translator. 1912. Referring to the church built in Istanbul (532–537) under the auspices of Justinian I, and which became a mosque following the Ottoman conquest (1453). 'Hagia Sophia', *Stone* (Robert Tracy, tr.; 1915), ll. 1–2

20 Then to the Cistern of 1001 columns . . . Terrible place to be robbed or murdered in. At whatever point you look, you see lines of pillars, like trees in an orchard arranged in the quincus style.

Herman Melville (1819–91) US novelist. December 13, 1856. Referring to the Cistern of Philoxenus in Istanbul. Quoted in *Journal of a Visit to Europe and the Levant* (H. C. Horsford, ed.; 1955)

21 Lunch kills half of Paris, supper the other half.

Montesquieu (1689–1755) French writer and jurist. Attrib.

22 It is a city where you can see a sparrow fall to the ground, and God watching it.

Conor Cruise O'Brien (b. 1917) Irish historian, critic, and politician. Referring to Dublin. Attrib.

23 I love Paris in the springtime.

Cole Porter (1893–1964) US songwriter and composer. Song lyric. 'I Love Paris', *Can-Can* (1953)

24 Paris loves lovers.

Cole Porter (1893–1964) US songwriter and composer. Song lyric, from the film version of the play *Ninotchka* by Melchior Lengyel. 'Silk Stockings', *Ninotchka* (1955)

25 Let there be light! said Liberty, And like sunrise from the sea, Athens arose!

Percy Bysshe Shelley (1792–1822) English poet. Inspired by the Greeks' revolt against Ottoman rule in 1821. *Hellas* (1822), ll. 682–684

26 He so improved the city that he justly boasted that he found it brick and left it marble.

Suetonius (69?–140?) Roman historian and biographer. Referring to the improvements Roman Emperor Augustus had made to Rome. 'Augustus', *Lives of the Caesars* (121?)

27 Leningrad is like no other city in Russia or on earth. It seems to reject the half-Asiatic hinterland on whose rim it hangs, and to have exchanged this troubled parentage for the grace of eighteenth century Europe.

Colin Thubron (b. 1939) British travel writer and novelist. Under Communism, the city of Saint Petersburg was known as Leningrad. *Among the Russians* (1983), ch. 4

28 Venice, the eldest Child of Liberty. She was a maiden City, bright and free.

William Wordsworth (1770–1850) English poet. 1802. Venice, a republic since the Middle Ages, was conquered by Napoleon in 1797. 'On the Extinction of the Venetian Republic', *Poems in Two Volumes* (1807), vol. 1, ll. 4–5

29 Gripped with bitter cold, Petersburg burned in delirium.

Yevgeny Zamyatin (1884–1937) Russian writer. 'The Dragon' (1918)

European Countries

see also Britain, European Cities, European Languages, European Literature, Ireland, Nations

1 I do not know what will become of Germany when I am no longer on hand unless we can still manage to create Europe in time.

Konrad Adenauer (1876–1967) West German chancellor. Remark to Paul Henri Spaak (September 1954)

2 The Austrian government . . . is a system of despotism tempered by casualness.
Viktor Adler (1852–1918) Austrian politician. Speech, International Socialist Congress, Paris (July 17, 1889)

3 A German is someone who cannot tell a lie without believing it himself.
Theodor Adorno (1903–69) German philosopher, sociologist, and musicologist. *Minima Moralia* (E. F. N. Jephcott, tr.; 1951)

4 The French took three years of struggle and shed oceans of blood to win their liberty. All we have needed in Spain have been two days of explanation and one of rejoicing.
Juan Valera Alcala Galiano (1824–1905) Spanish writer. 1870. Commenting on the revolution of 1868, that restored the constitution after a period of absolutist rule. Quoted in *The Spanish Labyrinth* (Gerald Brenan; 1943)

5 A constitution or national army is totally out of the question. I will allow neither one nor the other in any form.
Alexander II (1818–81) Russian monarch. Referring to Poland, during a period of demonstrations and uprisings demanding independence from Russia. Letter to Grand Duke Constantine, Viceroy of Poland (June 10, 1862)

6 We now have different foundations and different principles governing the state . . . these great changes effected by our nation in the space of only six years represent grandiose movements, more sublime and intense than what is commonly meant by the word revolution.
Kemal Ataturk (1881–1938) Turkish statesman. 1928. Referring to the establishment of Turkey as a modern and secular state after the abolition of the Sultanate in 1922. Quoted in *Le Kémalisme* (Tekin Alp; 1937)

7 I am bored with France, particularly as everybody here resembles Voltaire.
Charles Baudelaire (1821–67) French poet. 'Mon Coeur Mis à Nu', *Journaux Intimes* (1887)

8 We do not live alone in Europe but with three other Powers that hate and envy us.
Prince Otto von Bismarck (1815–98) German chancellor. Referring to Prussia's victory over Austria-Hungary at Königgrätz. Letter to his wife (July 9, 1866), quoted in *Germany, 1866–1945* (Gordon A. Craig; 1978)

9 In Prussia it is only the kings who make revolution.
Prince Otto von Bismarck (1815–98) German chancellor. Remark to Napoleon III (1862)

10 A good German cannot be a nationalist. A good German knows that he cannot refuse a European calling. Through Europe, Germany returns to itself and to the constructive forces of its history.
Willy Brandt (1913–92) German statesman. Address given on the presentation of a Nobel Prize in peace (December 11, 1971), quoted in *Willy Brandt, Peace* (Klaus Reiff, ed.; 1971)

11 Spain, since the loss of its Catholic faith, has been above everything else a country in search of an ideology.
Gerald Brenan (1894–1987) Maltese-born British writer and novelist. *The Spanish Labyrinth* (1943)

12 Fair Greece! sad relic of departed worth! Immortal, though no more! though fallen, great!
Lord Byron (1788–1824) British poet. *Childe Harold's Pilgrimage* (1812–18), can. 2, st. 73

13 Land of lost gods and godlike men.
Lord Byron (1788–1824) British poet. Referring to Greece. *Childe Harold's Pilgrimage* (1812–18), can. 2, st. 85

14 The isles of Greece, the isles of Greece! Where burning Sappho loved and sung, Where grew the arts of war and peace, Where Delos rose, and Phoebus sprung! Eternal summer gilds them yet, But all, except their sun, is set.
Lord Byron (1788–1824) British poet. *Don Juan* (1819–24), can. 3, st. 86

15 France was a long despotism tempered by epigrams.
Thomas Carlyle (1795–1881) Scottish historian and essayist. *The French Revolution* (1837), pt. 1, bk. 1, ch. 1

16 O free, strong people, O noble, brave race, clearly worthy of the Roman Empire; the Pole and the Dane hold our famous harbour and the gateway to the sea! On the east our most powerful peoples are enslaved, Bohemians, Moravians, Slovaks, and Silesians; they live like limbs cut from the body of our Germany.
Conrad Celtis (1459–1508) German humanist and poet. Inaugural address, University of Ingolstadt, Bavaria (1492)

17 There are few virtues which the Poles do not possess and there are few errors they have ever avoided.
Winston Churchill (1874–1965) British prime minister and writer. 1945. Speech to Parliament (August 1945)

18 Since both its national products, snow and chocolate, melt, the cuckoo clock was invented solely in order to give tourists something solid to remember it by.
Alan Coren (b. 1938) British writer and humorist. Referring to Switzerland. 'And Though They Do Their Best', *The Sanity Inspector* (1974)

19 The Greeks do not appear either licentious or puritanical so much as practical and open-minded. Their world was full of explicit erotica, about which they were sublimely unembarrassed.
Norman Davies (b. 1939) British historian and writer. *Europe: A History* (1996), ch. 2

20 The French will only be united under the threat of danger. Nobody can simply bring together a country that has 265 kinds of cheese.
Charles de Gaulle (1890–1970) French president. Election speech (1951)

21 France, mother of arts, of warfare, and of laws.
Joachim du Bellay (1522?–60) French poet. Sonnet 9, *Les Regrets* (1558)

22 The Swiss who are not a people so much as a neat clean quite solvent business.
William Faulkner (1897–1962) US novelist. *Intruder in the Dust* (1948), ch. 7

23 We have shed the blood of our dead to make a nation and to create an empire . . . we want the hard, the difficult life, the life of virile peoples . . . we offered five hundred thousand dead for the salvation and unity of Spain in the first European battle of the new order.
Francisco Franco (1892–1975) Spanish general and dictator. Referring to the Spanish Civil War (1936–39). Speech, Madrid (July 17, 1940), quoted in *Franco* (Paul Preston; 1993)

24 Will you know where the ancient glory of your Rome, the gravity of your senate . . . the stainless and invincible courage in the conflict have gone? . . . All these things are with us Germans.
Frederick I (1123?–90) German-born emperor and monarch. Referring to an antipapal revolt. Remark to envoys from the Senate of Rome (1155), quoted in *Quotations in History* (Alan and Veronica Palmer; 1976)

25 The highlights and shadows of our history give
us cause to reflect in these days, to reflect on that
which was done in the name of Germany. That
will not repeat itself.

Hans-Dietrich Genscher (b. 1927) German politician. *Independent*
(October 5, 1990)

26 This is a day of jubilation, a day of remembrance
and gratitude. Our common task now is to
establish a new European order.

Hans-Dietrich Genscher (b. 1927) German politician. Referring to the
conclusion of the agreement to reunite East and West
Germany. *Independent* (September 10, 1990)

27 Our leader said in Nuremberg, 'We have made
human beings once more of millions of people
who were in misery'. Anyone who will not deny
himself a pound of butter for that is not worthy
to be a German.

Hermann Goering (1893–1946) German Nazi leader. Referring to Adolf
Hitler. Speech, Sportpalast, Berlin (October 28, 1936)

28 A reunited Germany would be a colossus,
bedevilled by complexes and blocking its own
path and the path of European unity.

Günter Grass (b. 1927) German writer. 'Don't Reunify Germany',
New York Times (January 27, 1990)

29 One of the mistakes the Germans made, in this
century and also in the time before, was that they
were not brave enough to be afraid.

Günter Grass (b. 1927) German writer. Comment, *Voices* (Channel 4
television; June 27, 1985)

30 Sweden should be *Folkhemmet*, the people's
home, the good society which functions like a
good home . . . where equality, consideration,
cooperation, and helpfulness prevail.

Per Albin Hansson (1885–1946) Swedish statesman. Speech, Stockholm
(1928)

31 The relationship of Germany to the family of
European peoples and the relationship of that
family to Germany by tradition—simply
because of its size, power and central position—
the most important element in European stability.

Vaclav Havel (b. 1936) Czech statesman and playwright. Said on the
occasion of the visit of the German president to Prague.
Speech (February 15, 1990), quoted in *When the Wall Came
Down* (Harold James and Marla Stone, eds.; 1992)

32 All our agreements with Poland have a purely
temporary significance. I have no intention of
maintaining a serious relationship with Poland.

Adolf Hitler (1889–1945) Austrian-born German dictator. Referring to
the German-Polish nonaggression treaty that was effective
from 1924 and terminated in 1934. Poland tried to continue
diplomatic relations, but German demands became
increasingly aggressive and Germany eventually invaded
Poland on September 1, 1939. Remark (October 18, 1934),
quoted in *Germany, 1866–1945* (Gordon A. Craig; 1978),
ch. 19

33 Now Poland is in the position in which I wanted
her . . . I am only afraid that at the last moment
some swine or other will submit to me a plan for
mediation.

Adolf Hitler (1889–1945) Austrian-born German dictator. Said ten days
before the German army invaded Poland. Remark (August 22,
1939), quoted in *Germany, 1866–1945* (Gordon A. Craig;
1978), ch. 19

34 Holland . . . lies so low they're only saved by
being dammed.

Thomas Hood (1799–1845) British poet and humorist. 'Letter from
Martha Penny to Rebecca Page', *Up the Rhine* (1840)

35 To the Greeks the Muse gave native wit, to the
Greeks the gift of graceful eloquence.

Horace (65–8 BC) Roman poet. *Ars Poetica* (19–8 BC), l. 323

36 The history of the German nation-state is at an
end. What we . . . can achieve as a great nation
is insight into the world's situation: that today
the idea of the nation-state is a calamity for
Europe and all the continents.

Karl Jaspers (1883–1969) German philosopher. *Freedom and
Reconciliation* (1960)

37 Ankara might be able to drain the sea, but it will
not be able to catch the fish.

Yasar Kemal (b. 1923) Turkish novelist. Referring to the limits to
freedom of expression in Turkey. Ankara is the capital of
Turkey. Quoted in *Kurdistan* (Jonathan C. Randal; 1998)

38 Switzerland only seems small because it's all
folded up. If you opened it out it would be
bigger than the US.

Neil Kinnock (b. 1942) British politician. *Time* (April 7, 1997)

39 Germany is our fatherland, the united Europe
our future.

Helmut Kohl (b. 1930) German statesman. On the unification of
Germany. *Times* (October 1990)

40 The Germans, who are now coming together in
the spirit of freedom, will never pose a threat.
Rather will they, I am convinced, be an asset to a
Europe which is growing more and more
together.

Helmut Kohl (b. 1930) German statesman. 1989. Quoted in *When
the Wall Came Down* (Harold James and Marla Stone, eds.;
1992)

41 Prussia: freedom of movement with a muzzle.
Austria: an isolation cell in which screaming is
allowed.

Karl Kraus (1874–1936) Austrian writer. 1909. Referring to the
political cultures of Prussia and Austria. Quoted in 'Sprüche
und Widersprüche', *Karl Kraus* (Harry Zohn; 1971)

42 France is revolutionary or she is nothing at all.
The Revolution of 1789 is her political religion.

Alphonse de Lamartine (1790–1869) French poet and politician. *Histoire
des Girondins* (1847)

43 I have chased the English out of France . . . with
venison pies and good wine.

Louis XI (1423–83) French monarch. Remark at a banquet after the
Treaty of Pecquigny (August 29, 1475)

44 National Socialism was not imposed on the
German people from outside but has century-old
roots in German life itself.

Thomas Mann (1875–1955) German writer. Letter (March 30, 1945),
quoted in *Letters of Thomas Mann 1889–1955* (Richard
Winston and Clara Winston, trs.; 1975)

45 The German is the eternal student, the eternal
searcher, among the peoples of the earth.

Thomas Mann (1875–1955) German writer. 1947. *Doctor Faustus*
(H. T. Lowe-Porter, tr.; 1949), ch. 14

46 England is an empire, Germany is a nation, a
race, France is a person.

Jules Michelet (1798–1874) French historian. 1867. 'Tableau de la
France', *History of France* (1833–67)

47 That bastard of the Versailles treaty.

Vyacheslav Mikhailovich Molotov (1890–1986) Soviet statesman.
Referring to Poland. Attrib.

48 Austria is Switzerland speaking pure German and
with history added.

J. E. Morpurgo (1918–2000) British writer and academic. *The Road to
Athens* (1963)

49 Coffee for all.

Mottos and Slogans. The phrase gained political currency during the regime of Felipe González (1982–96), and referred to the policy of degrees of regional autonomy throughout Spain, with more regional power for Catalonia and the Basque Country in particular. Quoted in *The Spaniards* (John Hooper; 1986)

50 Germany has been wrecked by the exaggerations of the idea of power, by the blind confidence that force and naked steel are the sole measure of all things, and that justice and truth are just phrases, possibly useful as a way of swindling the stupid.

Carl von Ossietzky (1889–1938) German pacifist and journalist. 'The Coming Germany' (1918), quoted in *The Stolen Republic. Selected Writings of Carl von Ossietzky* (Bruno Frei, ed.; 1971)

51 No reasonable person today can doubt that Germany can only be linked with the democratic world in the sign of pacifism.

Carl von Ossietzky (1889–1938) German pacifist and journalist. 'The Pacifists' (1924), quoted in *The Stolen Republic. Selected Writings of Carl von Ossietzky* (Bruno Frei, ed.; 1971)

52 England's detached position from the Continent gives certain politicians like those of the Beaverbrook school the illusion that Britain can pursue a policy of 'splendid isolation'. But the fact remains that, thanks to the aeroplane, England has become as much a part of Europe as any continental State.

George Padmore (1902–59) Trinidadian campaigner. *Africa and World Peace* (1937)

53 Moor and Spaniard are more brothers than it appears. Take away a bit of religion, and another bit of language, and the relationship and family resemblance are obvious . . . how many Spaniards do we see who are Moors disguised as Christians?

Benito Pérez Galdós (1843–1920) Spanish novelist and playwright. Quoted in *Saracen Chronicles* (Juan Goytisolo; 1992)

54 France, the eternal resort of Germany in disorder.

Romain Rolland (1866–1944) French writer. 'La révolte', *Jean-Christophe* (1903–12), vol. 4

55 Thou Paradise of exiles, Italy!

Percy Bysshe Shelley (1792–1822) English poet. *Julian and Maddalo* (1818), l. 57, quoted in *Posthumous Poems* (Mrs. Shelley, ed.; 1824)

56 It is my policy to keep all the nationalities in the monarchy in a balanced state of well-modulated dissatisfaction.

Eduard von Taaffe (1833–95) Austrian statesman. *Letters* (1881), quoted in *Europe: A History* (Norman Davies; 1996), ch. 10

57 People in England want something to read, the French something to taste, the Germans something to think.

Kurt Tucholsky (1890–1935) German philosopher. Quoted in 'Selected Aphorisms', *Kurt Tucholsky. The Ironic Sentimentalist* (Bryan P. Grenville; 1981)

58 France has neither winter nor summer nor morals—apart from these drawbacks it is a fine country.

Mark Twain (1835–1910) US writer and humorist. Quoted in *Notebooks* (1935)

59 Since World War II, Italy has managed, with characteristic artistry, to create a society that combines a number of the least appealing aspects of socialism with practically all the vices of capitalism.

Gore Vidal (b. 1925) US novelist and essayist. 1979. 'Sciasci's Italy', *The Second American Revolution* (1982)

60 In Italy for thirty years under the Borgias they had warfare, terror, murder, bloodshed—they produced Michelangelo, Leonardo da Vinci and the Renaissance. In Switzerland they had brotherly love, five hundred years of democracy and peace, and what did they produce . . . ? The cuckoo clock.

Orson Welles (1915–85) US actor, director, producer, and writer. As Harry Lime in Carol Reed's celebrated film, *The Third Man* (co-written with Graham Greene and Carol Reed; 1949)

61 The French, for all their slogans, are becoming modern. Liberty, yes; equality, yes, of a sort; fraternity—with their women—highly questionable.

John A. Williams (b. 1925) US writer. *The Man Who Cried I Am* (1968)

62 Food isolates the French almost as much as their language. That would not be serious if France were at least certain of remaining a refuge for good food.

Theodore Zeldin (b. 1933) British historian. *The French* (1983)

European Languages

1 Speak in French when you can't think of the English for a thing.

Lewis Carroll (1832–98) British writer and mathematician. *Through the Looking-Glass and What Alice Found There* (1871), ch. 2

2 I speak Spanish to God, Italian to women, French to men, and German to my horse.

Charles V (1500–58) Belgian-born Spanish monarch. Attrib.

3 What is not clear is not French; what is not clear is, moreover, English, Italian, Greek, or Latin.

Antoine de Rivarol (1753–1801) French journalist. *Discours sur l'Universalité de la Langue Française* (1784)

4 Whenever the literary German dives into a sentence, that is the last you are going to see of him till he emerges on the other side of his Atlantic with his verb in his mouth.

Mark Twain (1835–1910) US writer and humorist. *A Connecticut Yankee at King Arthur's Court* (1889)

5 I can understand German as well as the maniac that invented it, but I talk it best through an interpreter.

Mark Twain (1835–1910) US writer and humorist. 'The Awful German Language', *A Tramp Abroad* (1880)

6 My philological studies have satisfied me that a gifted person should learn English (barring spelling and pronouncing) in thirty hours, French in thirty days, and German in thirty years.

Mark Twain (1835–1910) US writer and humorist. 'The Awful German Language', *A Tramp Abroad* (1880)

7 English is the language of the fox; Castilian, the language of the hedgehog.

Claudio Véliz (b. 1930) Chilean writer. Referring to the saying of Archilochus, the early Greek lyric poet, 'The fox knows many things but the hedgehog one big one'. *The New World of the Gothic Fox* (1994)

European Literature

1 In Victor Hugo we have the average sensual man impassioned and grandiloquent; in Zola we have the average sensual man going near the ground.

Matthew Arnold (1822–88) British poet and critic. *Discourses in America* (1885)

2   My work as a writer has from the beginning
    aimed at tracing the lightning flashes of the
    mental circuits that capture and link points
    distant from each other in time and space.

    Italo Calvino (1923–85) Cuban-born Italian novelist and short-story writer.
    1985. 'Quickness', *Six Memos for the Next Millennium*
    (Patrick Creagh, tr.; 1992)

3   I have done but very little but read Voltaire since
    I saw you. He is an exquisite fellow. One thing
    in him is particularly striking—his clear
    knowledge of the limits of human understanding.

    James Currie (1756–1805) Scottish physician and writer. Letter to
    Thomas Creevey (December 17, 1798)

4   Thou art my master and my author, thou art he
    from whom alone I took the style whose beauty
    has done me honour.

    Dante Alighieri (1265–1321) Italian poet. Referring to Virgil.
    'Inferno', *Divine Comedy* (1307?–21?), pt. 1

5   One does not arrest Voltaire.

    Charles de Gaulle (1890–1970) French president. Explaining why he
    had not arrested Jean-Paul Sartre for urging French soldiers in
    Algeria to desert. *Encounter* (June 1975)

6   Tolstoy, Turgenev, Chekov, Maupassant,
    Flaubert, France—knew that great truth, they
    only use the body, and that sparingly, to reveal
    the soul.

    John Galsworthy (1867–1933) British novelist and playwright. Letter to
    Edward Garnett (April 3, 1914), quoted in *The Life and
    Letters of John Galsworthy* (Harold Vincent Marrot; 1935)

7   Gide was a critic of colonialism, but his Algeria
    is simply an erotic fantasy.

    Ernest Gellner (1925–95) British anthropologist and philosopher.
    Referring to André Gide. *Encounters with Nationalism* (1994)

8   Jean Cocteau thinks me a bad thief. That's
    because, after him, I am first and foremost a
    writer. Thieves think me a bad writer.

    Jean Genet (1910–86) French writer. *The Thief's Journal* (1949)

9   Politically speaking, he might as well have been
    living on the moon as in Imperial Russia.

    Ronald Hingley (b. 1920) British biographer and critic. Referring to
    Anton Chekhov. *A New Life of Anton Chekhov* (1976)

10 Rabelais is the wondrous mask of ancient
    comedy . . . henceforth a human living face,
    remaining enormous and coming among us to
    laugh at us and with us.

    Victor Hugo (1802–85) French poet, novelist, and playwright. Attrib.

11 I was travelling post from Tiflis. The only
    luggage I had on my cart was one small
    portmanteau half-filled with travel notes on
    Georgia. Luckily for you most of them have been
    lost.

    Mikhail Lermontov (1814–41) Russian poet and novelist. Opening
    words. *A Hero of Our Time* (Paul Foote, tr.; 1840)

12 No, I was no one's contemporary—ever.
    That would have been above my station.
    How I loathe that other with my name.
    He certainly never was me.

    Osip Mandelstam (1891–1938) Russian poet, writer, and translator. 1923.
    'No, I was no one's contemporary . . . ', *Poems* (1928), ll. 1–
    4, quoted in *Osip Mandelstam: Selected Poems* (Clarence
    Brown and W. S. Merwin, tr.; 1973)

13 Official Germany celebrated Goethe, not as a
    poet and prophet, but above all as opium.

    Carl von Ossietzky (1889–1938) German pacifist and journalist. 1932.
    Referring to Johann Wolfgang von Goethe. Quoted in
    Weimar Culture (Peter Gay; 1969)

14 This newfangled plaything called the novel,
    which is the greatest invention of Western
    culture, is none of our culture's business.

    Orhan Pamuk (b. 1952) Turkish novelist. *The New Life* (Guneli Gun,
    tr.; 1994)

15 Cervantes laughed chivalry out of fashion.

    Horace Walpole (1717–97) British writer. Referring to Miguel de
    Cervantes. Letter to Sir Horace Mann (July 19, 1774)

16 I know that while I have been proclaimed a
    Right winger here because of my habit of writing
    to my conscience rather than according to
    command, I shall sooner or later probably be
    declared a Bolshevik for the same reason abroad.

    Yevgeny Zamyatin (1884–1937) Russian writer. 'Letter to Stalin' (June
    1931), quoted in *The Dragon and Other Stories* (Mirra
    Ginsburg, ed., tr.; 1966)

Evening

see also **Darkness**, **Night**

1   Here is the charming evening, the criminal's
    friend;
    It comes like an accomplice, with stealthy tread.

    Charles Baudelaire (1821–67) French poet. 'Tableaux Parisiens', *Les
    Fleurs du Mal* (1857), no. 95, 'Le Crépuscule du soir'

2   The Curfew tolls the knell of parting day,
    The lowing herd winds slowly o'er the lea,
    The plowman homeward plods his weary way,
    And leaves the world to darkness and to me.

    Thomas Gray (1716–71) British poet. 'Elegy Written in a Country
    Churchyard' (1751), st. 1

3   Now came still evening on, and twilight grey
    Had in her sober livery all things clad.

    John Milton (1608–74) English writer. *Paradise Lost* (1667), bk. 4,
    l. 598

4   The evening star,
    Love's harbinger.

    John Milton (1608–74) English writer. *Paradise Lost* (1667), bk. 11,
    ll. 588–589

5   It is a beauteous evening, calm and free,
    The holy time is quiet as a nun,
    Breathless with adoration; the broad sun
    Is sinking down in its tranquillity;
    The gentleness of heaven broods o'er the Sea.

    William Wordsworth (1770–1850) English poet. August, 1802. Also
    known as 'Evening on Calais Beach' and 'Calais Sands'. 'It Is
    a Beauteous Evening, Calm and Free', *Poems in Two Volumes*
    (1807), vol. 1, ll. 1–5

Evil

see also **The Devil**, **Morality**

1   Evil denotes the absence of Good. But it is not
    every absence of good that is called evil.

    Thomas Aquinas (1225–74) Italian theologian and philosopher. *Summa
    Theologica* (1266–73), I, pt. 1a

2   The fearsome word-and-thought-defying banality
    of evil.

    Hannah Arendt (1906–75) German-born US philosopher and historian.
    Eichmann in Jerusalem (1963)

3   Good can imagine Evil; but Evil cannot imagine
    Good.

    W. H. Auden (1907–73) British poet. 'Footnotes to Dr. Sheldon'
    (1970)

4 Often the fear of one evil leads us into a worse.
Nicolas Boileau (1636–1711) French poet and critic. *L'Art Poétique* (1674), pt. 1

5 The wickedness of the world is so great you have to run your legs off to avoid having them stolen from under you.
Bertolt Brecht (1898–1956) German playwright and poet. *The Threepenny Opera* (1929)

6 When bad men combine, the good must associate; else they will fall one by one, an unpitied sacrifice in a contemptible struggle.
Edmund Burke (1729–97) Irish-born British statesman and political philosopher. *Thoughts on the Cause of the Present Discontents* (1770)

7 It is necessary only for the good man to do nothing for evil to triumph.
Edmund Burke (1729–97) Irish-born British statesman and political philosopher. Attrib.

8 The face of 'evil' is always the face of total need.
William S. Burroughs (1914–97) US writer. *The Naked Lunch* (1959), Introduction

9 An Axis of Evil.
George W. Bush (b. 1948) US president. In May 2002, US Undersecretary of State John Bolton added Cuba, Libya, and Syria. State of the Union Address (January 29, 2002). Referring to Iraq, Iran, and North Korea.

10 Evil comes at leisure like the disease; good comes in a hurry like the doctor.
G. K. Chesterton (1874–1936) British writer and poet. *The Man who was Orthodox* (1963)

11 A belief in a supernatural source of evil is not necessary; men alone are quite capable of every wickedness.
Joseph Conrad (1857–1924) Polish-born British novelist. *Under Western Eyes* (1911), pt. 2

12 All evils are equal when they are extreme.
Corneille (1606–84) French playwright. *Horace* (1640), Act 2, Scene 8

13 The real problem is in the hearts and minds of men. It is easier to denature plutonium than to denature the evil spirit of man.
Albert Einstein (1879–1955) German-born US physicist. Quoted in *Disturbing the Universe* (Freeman Dyson; 1979), ch. 5

14 LEONTINE Don't let us make imaginary evils, when you know we have so many real ones to encounter.
Oliver Goldsmith (1730–74) Irish-born British novelist, playwright, and poet. *The Good-Natur'd Man* (1768), Act 1

15 Is he willing to prevent evil, but not able? then is he impotent. Is he able, but not willing? then is he malevolent. Is he both able and willing? whence then is evil?
David Hume (1711–76) Scottish philosopher and historian. *Dialogues Concerning Natural Religion* (1779)

16 Will someone tell me where I am least likely to meet these necessary evils?
James Joyce (1882–1941) Irish writer. *Ulysses* (1922)

17 God does nothing to stop this nefarious activity and leaves it all to man (who is notoriously stupid, unconscious, and easily led astray).
Carl Gustav Jung (1875–1961) Swiss psychoanalyst. 1958. Referring to the problem of evil. 'A Psychological Approach to the Dogma of the Trinity', *Collected Works* (1969), vol. 2

18 Of two evils, the lesser is always to be chosen.
Thomas à Kempis (1379?–1471) German monk and religious writer. *The Imitation of Christ* (1415–24?), bk. 3, ch. 12

19 He who passively accepts evil is as much involved in it as he who helps to perpetrate it.
Martin Luther King, Jr. (1929–68) US civil rights leader. *Stride Toward Freedom* (1964)

20 In order to be true to one's conscience and true to God, a righteous man has no alternative but to refuse to cooperate with an evil system.
Martin Luther King, Jr. (1929–68) US civil rights leader. *Stride Toward Freedom* (1964)

21 There exist some evils so terrible and some misfortunes so horrible that we dare not think of them . . . but if they happen to fall on us, we find ourselves stronger than we imagined, we grapple with our ill luck, and behave better than we expected we should.
Jean de La Bruyère (1645–96) French essayist and moralist. *Characters, or the Manners of the Age* (1688)

22 There is scarcely a single man sufficiently aware to know all the evil he does.
François La Rochefoucauld (1613–80) French epigrammatist and moralist. *Reflections, or Sentences and Moral Maxims* (1665), no. 269

23 Evil has encircled man from all sides, so man has devised good in all courses of action.
Naguib Mahfouz (b. 1911) Egyptian writer. Said by Sheikh Abd-Rabbih al-Ta-ih. *Echoes of an Autobiography* (1994)

24 So farewell hope, and with hope farewell fear,
Farewell remorse: all good to me is lost;
Evil be thou my good.
John Milton (1608–74) English writer. Said by Satan. *Paradise Lost* (1667), bk. 4, ll. 108–110

25 The oldest and best known evil was ever more supportable than one that was new and untried.
Michel de Montaigne (1533–92) French essayist. *Essays* (1580–88), bk. 3, ch. 9

26 The purpose of evil was to survive it.
Toni Morrison (b. 1931) US novelist. *Sula* (1973)

27 It is sufficient evil for a man that he should despise his brother.
Muhammad (570?–632?) Arab religious leader and prophet. Reported as spoken by Muhammad by Abu Dharr al-Ghifari. Quoted in *The Complete Forty Hadith* (Muhyid-Din al-Nawawi; 13th century), 36th Hadith

28 Of two evils I have chose the least.
Matthew Prior (1664–1721) English diplomat and poet. *Ode in Imitation of Horace* (1692)

29 He who approves evil is guilty of it.
Tamil proverb.

30 That is the curse of every evil deed,
That, propagating still, it brings forth evil.
Friedrich von Schiller (1759–1805) German poet, playwright, and historian. 1797–98. *Piccolomini* (1800), Act 5, Scene 1

31 ANTONY The evil that men do lives after them;
The good is oft interred with their bones.
William Shakespeare (1564–1616) English poet and playwright. *Julius Caesar* (1599), Act 3, Scene 2

32 BANQUO Oftentimes, to win us to our harm,
The instruments of darkness tell us truths;
Win us with honest trifles, to betray's
In deepest consequence.
William Shakespeare (1564–1616) English poet and playwright. *Macbeth* (1606), Act 1, Scene 3

33 All spirits are enslaved which serve things evil.
Percy Bysshe Shelley (1792–1822) English poet. *Prometheus Unbound* (1820), Act 2, Scene 4, l. 110

34 A bold bad man, that dar'd to call by name
Great Gorgon, Prince of darkness and dead night.

Edmund Spenser (1552?–99) English poet. *The Faerie Queene*
(1596), bk. 1, can. 1, st. 37

35 Evil visited us yesterday.

Ron Taylor, British teacher. Referring to the killing of
schoolchildren and their teacher by Thomas Hamilton at
Dunblane, Scotland. Remark (March 14, 1996)

36 Whenever I'm caught between two evils, I take
the one I've never tried.

Mae West (1892–1980) US actor and comedian. *Klondike Annie* (1936)

Evolution

see also **Change, Creation, Extinction, Metamorphosis, Nature,
Survival**

1 Descended from the apes? My dear, we will hope
it is not true. But if it is, let us pray that it may
not become generally known.

Anonymous. Remark by the wife of a canon of Worcester
Cathedral. *Man's Most Dangerous Myth: The Fallacy of Race*
(F. Ashley Montagu; 1942)

2 The whole history of life until man has been that
of the effort of consciousness to raise matter, and
of the more or less complete overwhelming of
consciousness by the matter which has fallen
back on it.

Henri-Louis Bergson (1859–1941) French philosopher. *Creative
Evolution* (Arthur Mitchell, tr.; 1907)

3 A hen is only an egg's way of making another egg.

Samuel Butler (1835–1902) British writer and composer. *Life and Habit*
(1878)

4 I have no patience whatever with these gorilla
damnifications of humanity.

Thomas Carlyle (1795–1881) Scottish historian and essayist. Referring
to Charles Darwin. Quoted in *Famous Sayings and Their
Authors* (Edward Latham, ed.; 1904)

5 It may be said that natural selection is daily and
hourly scrutinizing, throughout the world, every
variation, even the slightest; rejecting that which
is bad, preserving and adding up all that is good;
silently and insensibly working, wherever and
whenever opportunity offers, at the improvement
of each organic being in relation to its organic
and inorganic conditions of life.

Charles Darwin (1809–82) British naturalist. *On the Origin of Species
by Means of Natural Selection* (1859)

6 I have called this principle, by which each slight
variation, if useful, is preserved, by the term of
Natural Selection.

Charles Darwin (1809–82) British naturalist. *On the Origin of the
Species* (1859), ch. 3

7 The main conclusion arrived at in this work,
namely, that man is descended from some lowly
organized form, will, I regret to think, be highly
distasteful to many. But there can hardly be a
doubt that we are descended from barbarians.

Charles Darwin (1809–82) British naturalist. *The Descent of Man* (1871)

8 Any animal whatever, endowed with well-marked
social instincts, the parental and filial affections
being here included, would inevitably acquire a
moral sense or conscience, as soon as its
intellectual powers had become as well, or nearly
as well developed, as in man.

Charles Darwin (1809–82) British naturalist. His reply to those who
maintained that human conscience was implanted by God at
the Creation. *The Descent of Man* (1871)

9 The evolution of the human race will not be
accomplished in the ten thousand years of tame
animals, but in the million years of wild animals,
because man is and will always be a wild animal.

Charles Galton Darwin (1887–1962) British physicist. *The Next Ten
Million Years* (1952), ch. 4

10 Five per cent vision is better than no vision at all.
Five per cent hearing is better than no hearing at
all. Five per cent flight efficiency is better than no
flight at all. It is thoroughly believable that every
organ or apparatus that we actually see is the
product of a smooth trajectory through animal
space, a trajectory in which every intermediate
stage assisted survival and reproduction.

Richard Dawkins (b. 1941) British ethologist. Rebutting the
Creationist assertion that fully developed organs could not
have arisen 'by chance'. *The Blind Watchmaker* (1986)

11 The question is this: Is man an ape or an angel?
I, my lord, am on the side of the angels.

Benjamin Disraeli (1804–81) British prime minister and writer.
November 25, 1864. Speech at the Diocesan Conference,
Times (November 26, 1864)

12 How like us is that ugly brute, the ape!

Quintus Ennius (239–169? BC) Roman poet. 3rd–2nd century BC. *De
Divinatione* (Cicero; H. Rackham, tr.; 1942), bk. 50

13 Philip is a living example of natural selection. He
was as fitted to survive in this modern world as a
tapeworm in an intestine.

William Golding (1911–93) British novelist. *Free Fall* (1959), ch. 2

14 Evolution is an inference from thousands of
independent sources, the only conceptual
structure that can make unified sense of all this
disparate information.

Stephen Jay Gould (1941–2002) US geologist and writer. *Leonardo's
Mountain of Clams and the Diet of Worms: Essays on
Natural History* (1998)

15 Humans arose, rather, as a fortuitous and
contingent outcome of thousands of linked events,
any one of which could have occurred differently
and sent history on an alternative pathway that
would not have led to consciousness.

Stephen Jay Gould (1941–2002) US geologist and writer. 'The Evolution
of Life on Earth', *Scientific American* (October 1994)

16 History employs evolution to structure biological
events in time.

Stephen Jay Gould (1941–2002) US geologist and writer. *The
Flamingo's Smile* (1985)

17 Evolution has been a matter of days well-lived,
chameleon strength, energy, zappy sex, sunshine
stored up, inventiveness, competitiveness, and the
whole fun of busy brain cells.

Edward Hoagland (b. 1932) US novelist, naturalist, and essayist. 1972.
'Thoughts on Returning to the City', *Heart's Desire* (1988)

18 A man has no reason to be ashamed of having an
ape for his grandfather. If there were an ancestor
whom I should feel shame in recalling it would
rather be a *man*—a man of restless and versatile
intellect—who . . . plunges into scientific
questions with which he has no real acquaintance,
only to obscure them by an aimless rhetoric, and
distract the attention of his hearers from the real
point at issue by eloquent digressions and skilled
appeals to religious prejudice.

T. H. Huxley (1825–95) British biologist. Replying to Bishop Samuel
Wilberforce in the debate on Darwin's theory of evolution at
the meeting of the British Association at Oxford, June 30,
1860. The version above is commonly quoted. After hearing
Wilberforce's speech, and before rising himself, Huxley is said

to have remarked, 'The Lord has delivered him into my hands!' Speech (June 30, 1860), quoted in *Life and Letters of Thomas Henry Huxley* (Leonard Huxley, ed.; 1900)

19 Man as we know him is a poor creature; but he is halfway between an ape and a god and he is travelling in the right direction.
William Ralph Inge (1860–1954) British churchman. 'Confessio Fidei', *Outspoken Essays* (1922), Second series

20 Man appears to be the missing link between anthropoid apes and human beings.
Konrad Lorenz (1903–89) Austrian zoologist. *New York Times Magazine* (John Pfeiffer; April 11, 1965)

21 The generations of living things pass in a short time, and like runners hand on the torch of life.
Lucretius (99?–55? BC) Roman philosopher and poet. *De Rerum Natura* (1st century BC), pt. 2, l. 75

22 Species do not evolve toward perfection, but quite the contrary. The weak, in fact, always prevail over the strong, not only because they are in the majority, but also because they are the more crafty.
Friedrich Wilhelm Nietzsche (1844–1900) German philosopher and poet. *The Twilight of the Idols* (1888)

23 The monkey, without effort, the monkey became man
who not much later split the atom.
Raymond Queneau (1903–76) French writer. *Petite Cosmogonie Portative* (1950), song 6

24 The secrets of evolution are death and time—the deaths of enormous numbers of life forms that were imperfectly adapted to the environment; and time for a long succession of small mutations.
Carl Sagan (1934–96) US astronomer and writer. *Cosmos* (1980)

25 The tide of evolution carries everything before it, thoughts no less than bodies, and persons no less than nations.
George Santayana (1863–1952) Spanish-born US philosopher, poet, and novelist. *Little Essays* (1920), 44

26 Survival of the fittest.
Herbert Spencer (1820–1903) British philosopher. A phrase often misattributed to Charles Darwin. *Principles of Biology* (1865), pt. 3, ch. 12

27 And, in conclusion, I would like to ask the gentleman . . . whether the ape from which he is descended was on his grandmother's or his grandfather's side of the family.
Samuel Wilberforce (1805–73) British churchman. Speech (June 30, 1860)

28 If history and science have taught us anything, it is that passion and desire are not the same as truth. The human mind evolved to believe in the gods. It did not evolve to believe in biology.
Edward O. Wilson (b. 1929) US evolutionary biologist. *Consilience: The Unity of Knowledge* (1998)

Excellence

see also **Genius, Perfection**

1 By different methods different men excel; But where is he who can do all things well?
Charles Churchill (1731–64) British poet. 'An Epistle to William Hogarth' (1763), ll. 573–574

2 One of those men who reach such an acute limited excellence at twenty-one that everything afterward savours of anti-climax.
F. Scott Fitzgerald (1896–1940) US writer. *The Great Gatsby* (1925), ch. 1

3 HAMLET So excellent a king, that was to this Hyperion to a satyr.
William Shakespeare (1564–1616) English poet and playwright. *Hamlet* (1601), Act 1, Scene 2

Excess

see also **Extravagance, Luxury**

1 A Superfluity of Good Things
Abbé d' Allainval (1700–53) French playwright. Play title, also translated as *An Embarrassment of Riches. A Superfluity of Good Things* (1726)

2 The road of excess leads to the palace of wisdom.
William Blake (1757–1827) British poet, painter, engraver, and mystic. 'Proverbs of Hell', *The Marriage of Heaven and Hell* (1790–93), l. 3

3 There is moderation even in excess.
Benjamin Disraeli (1804–81) British prime minister and writer. *Vivian Grey* (1826), bk. 6, ch. 1

4 Anything worth doing is worth doing to excess.
Edwin Herbert Land (1909–91) US scientist and inventor. Attrib.

5 CELIA Well said; that was laid on with a trowel.
William Shakespeare (1564–1616) English poet and playwright. *As You Like It* (1599), Act 1, Scene 2

6 SALISBURY To gild refined gold, to paint the lily, To throw a perfume on the violet, To smooth the ice, or add another hue Unto the rainbow, or with taper-light To seek the beauteous eye of heaven to garnish, Is wasteful and ridiculous excess.
William Shakespeare (1564–1616) English poet and playwright. *King John* (1591–98), Act 4, Scene 2

7 If they can take it for ten minutes, then play it for fifteen. That's our policy. Always leave them wanting less.
Andy Warhol (1928?–87) US artist and filmmaker. Quoted in *Lou Reed: Between the Lines* (Michael Wrenn; 1993)

8 Moderation is a fatal thing, Lady Hunstanton. Nothing succeeds like excess.
Oscar Wilde (1854–1900) Irish poet, playwright, and wit. *A Woman of No Importance* (1893), Act 3

Excuses

see **Alibis and Excuses**

Execution

see also **Death and Dying, Martyrdom, Punishment**

1 And when they were come to the place, which is called Calvary, there they crucified him, and the malefactors, one on the right hand, and the other on the left.
Bible. Luke, *King James Bible* (1611), 23:33

2 It is a strange, strange fate, and now, as I stand face to face with death, I feel just as if they were going to kill a boy. For I feel like a boy—and my hands are so free from blood and my heart always so compassionate and pitiful that I cannot comprehend that anyone wants to hang me.
Roger Casement (1864–1916) Irish nationalist. Sir Roger Casement, knighted for his exposés of inhumane treatment of native

peoples in Congo Free State and Brazil, was convicted of high treason and executed (1916) for aiding the Irish independence movement. He helped secure Germany's agreement to send 20,000 rifles to Ireland in support of the Easter Rebellion, an uprising of Irish patriots. 'Ms. found in Casement's condemned cell' (1916)

3 Hanging men in our country jails does not prevent murder. It makes murderers.

Clarence Darrow (1857–1938) US lawyer. Speech to prisoners, Cook County Jail (1902)

4 Does capital punishment tend to the security of the people? By no means. It hardens the hearts of men, and makes the loss of life appear light to them; and it renders life insecure, inasmuch as the law holds out that property is of greater value than life.

Elizabeth Fry (1780–1845) British prison reformer. Quoted in *Women's Record: Sketches of All Distinguished Women* (Sarah Josepha Hale; 1853)

5 In the slaughterhouses of human flesh the hangmen hummed patriotic songs.

Eduardo Galeano (b. 1940) Uruguayan writer. 'Fascism in Latin America: A Letter to a Mexican Editor', *We Say No* (1992)

6 Awaiting the sensation of a short, sharp shock, From a cheap and chippy chopper on a big black block.

W. S. Gilbert (1836–1911) British librettist and playwright. *The Mikado* (1885), Act 2, 'Trio'

7 Depend upon it, Sir, when a man knows he is to be hanged in a fortnight, it concentrates his mind wonderfully.

Samuel Johnson (1709–84) British lexicographer and writer. September 19, 1777. Referring to the forthcoming execution of Dr. William Dodd. Quoted in *Life of Samuel Johnson* (James Boswell; 1791)

8 Youth, youth, thou had'st better been starv'd by thy nurse, Than to live to be hanged for cutting a purse.

Ben Jonson (1572–1637) English playwright and poet. *Batholomew Fair* (1614), Act 3, Scene 1

9 If we are to abolish the death penalty, I should like to see the first step taken by our friends the murderers.

Alphonse Karr (1808–90) French writer. *The Wasps, (6th Series)* (1849)

10 I could not look on Death, which being known, Men led me to him, blindfold and alone.

Rudyard Kipling (1865–1936) Indian-born British writer and poet. 'Epitaphs—The Coward', *The Years Between* (1919)

11 Many men would take the death-sentence without a whimper to escape the life-sentence which fate carries in her other hand.

T. E. Lawrence (1888–1935) British adventurer, soldier and writer. *The Mint* (1955), pt. 1, ch. 4

12 Most people were dissatisfied, because a shooting was not such a fine spectacle as a decapitation; and what a ridiculous culprit he had been too, to pass through so many streets without singing a single line from an opera.

Lu Xun (1881–1936) Chinese writer. Referring to the execution of Ah Q, the illiterate peasant protagonist. 'The True Story of Ah Q' (December 1921), ch. 9

13 Here they hang a man first and then they try him.

Molière (1622–73) French playwright. *Monsieur de Pourceaugnac* (1670), Act 3, Scene 2

14 Pluck up thy spirits, man, and be not afraid to do thine office; my neck is very short; take heed therefore thou strike not awry, for saving of thine honesty.

Thomas More (1478–1535) English statesman and writer. July 7, 1535. Said to the headsman at his execution. Quoted in *Life of Sir Thomas More* (William Roper; 1626)

15 The world itself is but a large prison, out of which some are daily led to execution.

Walter Raleigh (1554–1618) British explorer, courtier, and writer. 1603. Said when returning to prison after his trial for treason. Attrib.

16 Oh liberty! Oh liberty! What crimes are committed in thy name!

Madame Roland (1754–93) French revolutionary. 1793. Said as she mounted the steps of the guillotine at her execution. Attrib. *Histoire des Girondins* (A. de Lamartine; 1847), bk. 51, ch. 8

17 FIRST CLOWN What is he that builds stronger than either the mason, the shipwright, or the carpenter?
SECOND CLOWN The gallows-maker; for that frame outlives a thousand tenants.

William Shakespeare (1564–1616) English poet and playwright. *Hamlet* (1601), Act 5, Scene 1

18 Between the possibility of being hanged in all innocence, and the certainty of a public and merited disgrace, no gentleman of spirit could long hesitate.

Robert Louis Stevenson (1850–94) Scottish novelist, essayist, and poet. *The Wrong Box* (co-written with Lloyd Osbourne; 1889), ch. 10

19 In this country it is good to kill an admiral from time to time, to encourage the others.

Voltaire (1694–1778) French writer and philosopher. Referring to the execution of the British admiral Byng for failing to defeat the French at Minorca (1757). *Candide* (1759), ch. 23

20 There is only one cure for grey hair. It was invented by a Frenchman. It is called the guillotine.

P. G. Wodehouse (1881–1975) British-born US humorous writer. *The Old Reliable* (1951)

Exercise

see also **Health and Healthy Living, Sports and Games**

1 If you walk hard enough, you probably don't need any other God.

Bruce Chatwin (1940–89) British writer and traveller. *In Patagonia* (1977)

2 I get my exercise acting as a pallbearer to my friends who exercise.

Chauncey Depew (1834–1928) US lawyer and public official. Attrib.

3 Whenever I feel like exercise, I lie down until the feeling passes.

Robert M. Hutchins (1899–1977) US educator. Attrib.

Exile

see also **Emigration, Strangers**

1 An exile has no place anywhere, because there is no place because the place where we started to dream, where we discovered the natural world around us, read our first book, loved for the first time, is always the world of our dreams.

Reinaldo Arenas (1943–90) Cuban writer. *Before Night Falls* (Dolores M. Koch, tr.; 2001)

2 Wandering between two worlds, one dead,
The other powerless to be born.

Matthew Arnold (1822–88) British poet and critic. 'Stanzas from the Grande Chartreuse' (1855)

3 Over all the world
Men move unhoming, and eternally
Concerned: a swarm of bees who have lost their queen.

Christopher Fry (b. 1907) British playwright. *Venus Observed* (1950), Act 2, Scene 1

4 Exile has turned you into a completely different being, who has nothing to do with the one your countrymen once knew: their law is no longer your law: their justice is no longer your justice . . . as anonymous as the passing stranger, you will visit your own dwelling and dogs will bark at your heels.

Juan Goytisolo (b. 1931) Spanish novelist and essayist. Referring to Juan Sin Tierra ('Juan the Landless'), the novel's hero. *Juan the Landless* (1975)

5 An exile in my circumstances is a branch cut from its tree; it is dead but it has an affectation of life.

John Mitchell (1815–75) Irish writer and nationalist. *Jail Journal* (1854)

6 The whole peninsula of Florida was weighted down with regret. Everyone had left behind a real life.

Cynthia Ozick (b. 1928) US novelist and short-story writer. *Rosa* (1984)

7 BOLINGBROKE Eating the bitter bread of banishment.

William Shakespeare (1564–1616) English poet and playwright. *Richard II* (1595), Act 3, Scene 1

Existence

see also Being, Experience, Life

1 Something than which nothing greater can be thought so truly exists that it is not possible to think of it as not existing.

Saint Anselm (1033–1109) Italian-born philosopher and prelate. *Proslogion* (1078)

2 We always find something, eh, Didi, to give us the impression that we exist?

Samuel Beckett (1906–89) Irish playwright, novelist, and poet. *Waiting for Godot* (1954), Act 2

3 The table I write on, I say, exists, that is, I see and feel it; and if I were out of my study I should say it existed, meaning thereby that if I was in my study I might perceive it, or that some other spirit actually does perceive it.

Bishop Berkeley (1685–1753) Irish prelate and philosopher. *A Treatise Concerning the Principles of Human Knowledge* (1710)

4 At a given moment I open my eyes and exist. And before that, during all eternity, what was there? Nothing.

Ugo Betti (1892–1953) Italian playwright and poet. *The Inquiry* (Gino Rizzo, tr.; 1944–45)

5 But when the days of golden dreams had perished, And even Despair was powerless to destroy, Then did I learn how existence could be cherished, Strengthened, and fed without the aid of joy.

Emily Brontë (1818–48) British poet and novelist. 'Remembrance' (1846)

6 Observing that this truth 'I am thinking, therefore I exist' was so firm and sure . . . the sceptics were incapable of shaking it, I decided that I could accept it . . . as the first principle of the philosophy I was seeking.

René Descartes (1596–1650) French philosopher and mathematician. *Discourse on Method* (1637)

7 While I could pretend that I had no body and that there was no world and no place for me to be in, I could not for all that pretend that I did not exist . . . Accordingly this 'I' . . . is entirely distinct from the body.

René Descartes (1596–1650) French philosopher and mathematician. The original statement of 'Cartesian Dualism'. *Discourse on Method* (1637)

8 But what then am I? A thing that thinks. What is that? A thing that doubts, understands, affirms, denies, is willing, is unwilling, and also imagines and has sensory perceptions.

René Descartes (1596–1650) French philosopher and mathematician. *Meditations on First Philosophy* (1641), Second Meditation

9 What has been understood no longer exists.

Paul Éluard (1895–1952) French surrealist poet. 'Le Miroir d'un Moment', *Capitale de la Douleur* (1926)

10 Everything that has been will be, everything that will be is, everything that will be has been.

Eugène Ionesco (1909–94) Romanian-born French playwright. *Exit the King* (1962)

11 As far as we can discern, the sole purpose of human existence is to kindle a light in the darkness of mere being.

Carl Gustav Jung (1875–1961) Swiss psychoanalyst. *Memories, Dreams, Reflections* (1962), ch. 11

12 Since all possible things have a claim to existence in God's understanding in proportion to their perfections, the result of all these claims must be the most perfect actual world which is possible.

Gottfried Wilhelm Leibniz (1646–1716) German philosopher and mathematician. 'The Principles of Nature and Grace, based on Reason' (1714), quoted in *G. W. Leibniz: Philosophical Essays and Letters* (L. E. Loemker, ed.; 1969)

13 The proper function of man is to live, not to exist. I shall not waste my days in trying to prolong them. I shall use my time.

Jack London (1876–1916) US writer. *Bulletin* (December 2, 1916)

14 Out of all possible universes, the only one which can exist, in the sense that it can be known, is simply the one which satisfies the narrow conditions necessary for the development of intelligent life.

Bernard Lovell (b. 1913) British astronomer. *In the Centre of Immensities* (1979)

15 Every moment of one's existence one is growing into more or retreating into less. One is always living a little more or dying a little bit.

Norman Mailer (b. 1923) US novelist and journalist. 'Hip, Hell, and the Navigator', *Western Review* (Winter 1959)

16 The world is not what I think, but what I live through.

Maurice Merleau-Ponty (1908–61) French existentialist philosopher. *Phenomenology of Perception* (1945)

17 There are two senses, and two only, of the word 'exist': one exists as a thing or else one exists as a consciousness.

Maurice Merleau-Ponty (1908–61) French existentialist philosopher. Quoted in *The Essential Writings of Merleau-Ponty* (A. L. Fisher, ed.; 1969)

18 But the Universe exists, things must happen in it, all equally improbable, and man is one of these things.

Jacques Lucien Monod (1910–76) French biochemist. Inaugural lecture on taking the chair of molecular biology, Collège de France (November 3, 1967)

19 I know perfectly well that I don't want to do anything; to do something is to create existence— and there's quite enough existence as it is.

Jean-Paul Sartre (1905–80) French philosopher, playwright, and novelist. *Nausea* (1938)

20 But what do I get from existence? If it is full I have only distress, if empty only boredom. How can you offer me so poor a reward for so much labour and so much suffering?

Arthur Schopenhauer (1788–1860) German philosopher. *Parerga and Paralipomena* (1851)

21 Our existence has no foundation on which to rest except the transient present. Thus its form is essentially unceasing motion, without any possibility of that repose which we continually strive after.

Arthur Schopenhauer (1788–1860) German philosopher. *Parerga and Paralipomena* (1851)

22 Existence itself does not feel horrible; it feels like an ecstasy, rather, which we only have to be still to experience.

John Updike (b. 1932) US writer. *Self-Consciousness: Memoirs* (1989), ch. 6

Experience

see also **Existence, Knowledge, Life**

1 Experience is a good teacher, but she sends in terrific bills.

Minna Antrim (1856–1950) US writer. *Naked Truth and Veiled Allusions* (1902)

2 To a great experience one thing is essential, an experiencing nature.

Walter Bagehot (1826–77) British economist and journalist. Referring to William Shakespeare. 'Shakespeare—the Individual', *Estimates of Some Englishmen and Scotchmen* (1858)

3 One should try everything once, except incest and folk-dancing.

Arnold Bax (1883–1953) British composer. *Farewell to My Youth* (1943)

4 You will think me lamentably crude: my experience of life has been drawn from life itself.

Max Beerbohm (1872–1956) British essayist, critic, and caricaturist. *Zuleika Dobson* (1911), ch. 7

5 Experience isn't interesting till it begins to repeat itself—in fact, till it does that, it hardly *is* experience.

Elizabeth Bowen (1899–1973) Irish novelist and short-story writer. *The Death of the Heart* (1938)

6 Experience consists of experiencing that which one does not wish to experience.

Sigmund Freud (1856–1939) Austrian psychoanalyst. *Jokes and Their Relation to the Unconscious* (1905)

7 Experience teaches slowly, and at the cost of mistakes.

J. A. Froude (1818–94) British historian. 'Party Politics', *Short Studies on Great Subjects* (1877)

8 It's taken me all my life to learn what not to play.

Dizzy Gillespie (1917–93) US jazz trumpeter and bandleader. Quoted in *Jazz Is* (Nat Hentoff; 1976)

9 A moment's insight is sometimes worth a life's experience.

Oliver Wendell Holmes (1841–1935) US judge. *The Professor at the Breakfast-Table* (1860), ch. 10

10 Experience is never limited, and it is never complete; it is an immense sensibility, a kind of huge spider-web of the finest silken threads suspended in the chamber of consciousness, and catching every air-borne particle in its tissue.

Henry James (1843–1916) US-born British writer and critic. 'The Art of Fiction', *Partial Portraits* (1888)

11 Nothing ever becomes real till it is experienced— even a proverb is no proverb to you till your life has illustrated it.

John Keats (1795–1821) English poet. Letter to George and Georgiana Keats (March 19, 1818), quoted in *Letters of John Keats* (H. E. Rollins, ed.; 1958), vol. 2

12 Axioms in philosophy are not axioms until they are proved upon our pulses; we read fine things but never feel them to the full until we have gone the same steps as the author.

John Keats (1795–1821) English poet. May 3, 1818. Quoted in *Letters of John Keats* (Robert Gittings, ed.; 1970)

13 Any scientist who has ever been in love knows that he may understand everything about sex hormones but the actual experience is something quite different.

Kathleen Lonsdale (1903–71) Irish-born British crystallographer. *Universities Quarterly* (1963), no. 17

14 Experience is the mother of science.

Proverb.

15 The felt unreliability of human experience brought about by the inhuman acceleration of historical change has led every sensitive modern mind to the recording of some kind of nausea, of intellectual vertigo.

Susan Sontag (b. 1933) US writer. 'The Anthropologist as Hero', *Against Interpretation* (1966)

16 When the torrent sweeps a man against a boulder, you must expect him to scream, and you need not be surprised if the scream is sometimes a theory.

Robert Louis Stevenson (1850–94) Scottish novelist, essayist, and poet. *Virginibus Puerisque* (1881)

17 Yet all experience is an arch wherethro'
Gleams that untravelled world, whose margin fades
For ever and for ever when I move.

Alfred Tennyson (1809–92) British poet. 1833. 'Ulysses', *Poems* (1842), ll. 19–21

18 Trust one who has gone through it.

Virgil (70–19 BC) Roman poet. *Aeneid* (29–19 BC), bk. 11, l. 283

19 Experience is the name everyone gives to their mistakes.

Oscar Wilde (1854–1900) Irish poet, playwright, and wit. *Lady Windermere's Fan* (1892), Act 3

Experiments

see also **Discovery, Research, Science**

1 Experimental science is the mistress of the speculative sciences, it alone is able to give us important truths within the confines of the other sciences, which those sciences can learn in no other way.

Roger Bacon (1220?–92) English monk, philosopher, and scientist. *Opus Majus* (1266–67)

2 I think that only daring speculation can lead us further and not accumulation of facts.

Albert Einstein (1879–1955) German-born US physicist. *Albert Einstein, Michele Besso: Correspondence 1903–55* (1972)

3 No amount of experimentation can ever prove me right; a single experiment can prove me wrong.

Albert Einstein (1879–1955) German-born US physicist. Attrib.

4 All the world is a laboratory to the inquiring mind.

Martin H. Fischer (1879–1962) German-born US physician and author. *Fischerisms* (Howard Fabing and Ray Marr, eds.; 1944)

5 I'm really an experimentalist. I used to say 'I think with my hands'. I just like manipulation.

Dorothy Hodgkin (1910–94) Egyptian-born British crystallographer and chemist. Quoted in *A Passion for Science* (Lewis Wolpert and Alison Richards; 1988)

6 Laboratorium est oratorium. The place where we do our scientific work is a place of prayer.

Joseph Needham (1900–95) British biochemist and Sinologist. Quoted in *The Harvest of a Quiet Eye* (A. L. Mackay; 1977)

7 Where observation is concerned, chance favours only the prepared mind.

Louis Pasteur (1822–95) French scientist. Inauguration lecture, Faculty of Science, University of Lille (December 7, 1854), quoted in *La Vie de Pasteur* (R. Vallery-Radot; 1900), ch. 4

8 Experiment alone crowns the efforts of medicine, experiment limited only by the natural range of the powers of the human mind. Observation discloses in the animal organism numerous phenomena existing side by side, and interconnected now profoundly, now indirectly, or accidentally. Confronted with a multitude of different assumptions the mind must *guess* the real nature of this connection.

Ivan Petrovich Pavlov (1849–1936) Russian physiologist. *Experimental Psychology and Other Essays* (1958), pt. 10

9 He had been eight years upon a project for extracting sun-beams out of cucumbers, which were to be put into vials hermetically sealed, and let out to warm the air in raw inclement summers.

Jonathan Swift (1667–1745) Irish writer and clergyman. 'A Voyage to Laputa', *Gulliver's Travels* (1726), ch. 5

Exploitation

see also Colonialism, Manipulation, Oppression, Slavery

1 You can only help one of your luckless brothers by trampling down a dozen others.

Bertolt Brecht (1898–1956) German playwright and poet. *The Good Person of Szechwan* (1943)

2 The ass will carry his load, but not a double load; ride not a free horse to death.

Miguel de Cervantes (1547–1616) Spanish novelist and playwright. *Don Quixote* (1605–15), pt. 2, ch. 71

3 You don't have to be good with figures to know you've been had.

Bo Diddley (b. 1928) US singer, guitarist, and songwriter. Referring to his first album, *Bo Diddley* (1955), not making him any money despite its popularity. Quoted in 'Bo Diddley', *Off the Record: An Oral History of Popular Music* (Joe Smith; 1988)

4 Exploitation and manipulation produce boredom and triviality; they cripple man, and all factors that make man into a psychic cripple turn him also into a sadist or a destroyer.

Erich Fromm (1900–80) German-born US psychoanalyst and philosopher. *The Anatomy of Human Destructiveness* (1973)

5 For the sadist, exploitation becomes a kind of passion in its own right . . . The need to feed, vampirelike, on the emotional vitality of another person is as a rule completely unconscious.

Karen Horney (1885–1952) German-born US psychoanalyst. *Our Inner Conflicts* (1945)

6 Ever get the feeling you've been cheated?

Johnny Rotten (b. 1957) British rock musician. January 1978. Addressing the audience at the end of the last Sex Pistols' concert in San Francisco. Probably alluding to punk rock's unconventional use of the music industry to achieve success, as well as to their apparent lack of musical talent. Quoted in 'Blank Generation', *Dancing in the Street* (Robert Palmer; 1996)

7 I have climbed highest mountains,
I have run through the fields,
Only to be with you . . .
But I still haven't found what I'm looking for.

U2, Irish rock group. Song lyric. 'I Still Haven't Found What I'm Looking For', *The Joshua Tree* (Larry Mullen, Adam Clayton, Paul Hewson, and David Evans; 1986)

8 If we thus ask, 'Why should money be made out of men?' Benjamin Franklin himself, although he was a colourless deist, answers in his autobiography with a quotation from the Bible.

Max Weber (1864–1920) German economist and social historian. 1904–05. *The Protestant Ethic and the Spirit of Capitalism* (Talcott Parsons, tr.; 1930)

Exploration

see also Discovery, Space, Travel

1 They are ill discoverers that think there is no land, when they can see nothing but sea.

Francis Bacon (1561–1626) English philosopher, statesman, and lawyer. *The Advancement of Learning* (1605), bk. 2

2 I can't say I was ever lost, but I was bewildered once for three days.

Daniel Boone (1734–1820) American pioneer. Reply when asked if he had ever been lost. Attrib.

3 Exploring is delightful to look forward to and back upon, but it is not comfortable at the time, unless it be of such an easy nature as not to deserve the name.

Samuel Butler (1835–1902) British writer and composer. *Erewhon* (1872)

4 Here the people could stand it no longer and complained of the long voyage; but the Admiral cheered them as best he could, holding out good hope of the advantages they would have. He added that it was useless to complain, he had come to go to the Indies, and so had to continue it until he found them, with the help of Our Lord.

Christopher Columbus (1451–1506) Italian explorer and colonialist. *Journal of the First Voyage to America, 1492–93* (October 10, 1492)

5 The known world was too small for Alexander; the eaves of a roof are infinity for a swallow.

Joaquim Maria Machado de Assis (1839–1908) Brazilian novelist and short-story writer. Referring to Alexander the Great. *Epitaph of a Small Winner* (1880)

6 Nothing easier. One step beyond the pole, you see, and the north wind becomes a south one.

Robert Edwin Peary (1856–1920) US explorer. Explaining how he knew he had reached the North Pole. Attrib.

7 Had we lived, I should have had a tale to tell of the hardihood, endurance, and courage of my companions which would have stirred the heart of every Englishman. These rough notes and our dead bodies must tell the tale.

Captain Scott (1868–1912) British explorer. Message to the public (1912)

8 Great God! this is an awful place.

Captain Scott (1868–1912) British explorer. Referring to the South Pole. *Journal* (January 17, 1912)

9 Crossing Piccadilly Circus.

Joseph Thomson (1858–95) Scottish geologist and explorer. Replying to J. M. Barrie, who asked what was the most hazardous part of his expedition to Africa. Quoted in *J. M. Barrie* (Janet Dunbar; 1970)

10 These new regions of America which we found and explored with the fleet . . . we may rightly call a New World . . . a continent more densely peopled and abounding in animals than our Europe or Asia or Africa.

Amerigo Vespucci (1454–1512) Italian navigator and explorer. Letter to Lorenzo di Pierfrancesco de' Medici (1503)

Extinction

see also **Death and Dying, Evolution, Survival**

1 In the end, it is the threat of universal extinction hanging over all the world today that changes, totally and forever, the nature of reality and brings into devastating question the true meaning of man's history.

James Baldwin (1924–87) US writer and civil rights activist. *The Fire Next Time* (1963)

2 The Dodo never had a chance. He seems to have been invented for the sole purpose of becoming extinct and that was all he was good for.

Will Cuppy (1884–1949) US humorist and critic. 'The Dodo', *How to Become Extinct* (1941)

3 Hiroshima, the flower, petalled off into extinction. How can it be? Where did I gather these multiples of death?
My mind becomes a fire-bird and erupts into dark, dark flights.

Fazil Hüsnü Dag larca (b. 1914) Turkish poet. 'Guilt Driven Madness', *Modern Turkish Poetry* (Feyyaz Kayacan Fergar, ed.; 1992)

4 I am sorry to say that there is too much point to the wisecrack that life is extinct on other planets because their scientists were more advanced than ours.

John Fitzgerald Kennedy (1917–63) US president. Speech (December 11, 1959)

5 God seems to have left the receiver off the hook, and time is running out.

Arthur Koestler (1905–83) Hungarian-born British writer and journalist. *The Ghost in the Machine* (1967), ch. 18

6 Hitherto man had to live with the idea of death as an individual; from now onward mankind will have to live with the idea of its death as a species.

Arthur Koestler (1905–83) Hungarian-born British writer and journalist. Referring to the development of the atomic bomb. Attrib.

7 Amidst the vicissitudes of the earth's surface, species cannot be immortal, but must perish, one after another, like the individuals which compose them. There is no possibility of escaping from this conclusion.

Charles Lyell (1797–1875) British geologist. *Principles of Geology* (1830–33)

8 The dinosaur didn't know it was extinct either. Dinosaurs never had it so good, as just before they vanished.

Marshall McLuhan (1911–80) Canadian sociologist. *Weekend Magazine* (March 18, 1967), no. 11

9 The human race may well become extinct before the end of the century.

Bertrand Russell (1872–1970) British philosopher and mathematician. Interview, *Playboy* (March 1963)

Extravagance

see also **Excess, Luxury**

1 We owe something to extravagance, for thrift and adventure seldom go hand in hand.

Jennie Churchill (1854–1921) US-born British hostess and writer. 'Extravagance', *Pearson's* (1915)

2 It would have been cheaper to lower the Atlantic.

Lew Grade (1906–98) Ukrainian-born British film and television producer and impresario. Referring to the cost of his film, *Raise the Titanic* (1980). *The Sun* (December 22, 1987)

3 He sometimes forgets that he is Caesar, but I always remember that I am Caesar's daughter.

Julia (39 BC–AD 14) Roman daughter of Emperor Augustus. Replying to suggestions that she should live in the simple style of her father, which contrasted with her own extravagance. Quoted in *Saturnalia* (Macrobius; AD 400?)

4 If you can't be elegant, at least be extravagant.

Franco Moschino (1950–95) Italian fashion designer. Quoted in *Elle* (April 1998)

5 The walls of the halls and chambers are all covered with gold and silver and decorated with pictures of dragons and birds and horsemen and various breeds of beasts and scenes of battle. The ceiling is similarly adorned . . . nothing to be seen anywhere but gold and pictures.

Marco Polo (1254–1324) Venetian merchant and traveller. Referring to Kublai Khan's palace, the inspiration for Samuel Taylor Coleridge's description of Kubla Khan's 'stately pleasure-dome'. 'Kubilai Khan', *The Travels of Marco Polo* (1298–99)

Extremes

see also **Fanaticism**

1 Each one of us, in his timidity, has a limit beyond which he is outraged.

Man Ray (1890–1976) US painter and photographer. 'The Age of Light', *Photographs by Man Ray* (1934), Introduction

2 I am driven
Into a desperate strait and cannot steer
A middle course

Philip Massinger (1583–1640) English playwright. *The Great Duke of Florence* (1627), Act 3, Scene 1

3 Extreme trends are breeding grounds for equally powerful countertrends.

Stephen S. Roach, US economist. Referring to the workings of the free-market system. 'A New Competitive Dilemma', *Wall Street Journal* (June 20, 1996)

4 The freakish is no longer a private zone, difficult of access. People who are bizarre, in sexual disgrace, emotionally violent are seen daily on the newsstands, on TV, in the subways. Hobbesian man roams the streets, quite visible, with glitter in his hair.

Susan Sontag (b. 1933) US writer. 'America, Seen Through Photographs, Darkly', *On Photography* (1977)

5 Every communist has a fascist frown, every fascist a communist smile.

Muriel Spark (b. 1918) British novelist. *The Girls of Slender Means* (1963), ch. 4

6 Extreme justice is extreme injury.

Voltaire (1694–1778) French writer and philosopher. *Oedipe* (1718), Act 3, Scene 3

F

The Face

see also **Appearance**, **The Body**, **Identity**

1 Your cameraman might enjoy himself, because my face looks like a wedding cake left out in the rain.
W. H. Auden (1907–73) British poet. *W. H. Auden: A Biography* (Humphrey Carpenter; 1981)

2 I think your whole life shows in your face and you should be proud of that.
Lauren Bacall (b. 1924) US stage and film actor. Remark (1988)

3 The face of Garbo is an Idea, that of Hepburn, an Event.
Roland Barthes (1915–80) French philosopher and writer. Referring to Greta Garbo and Audrey Hepburn. *Mythologies* (1957)

4 Alas, after a certain age every man is responsible for his face.
Albert Camus (1913–60) Algerian-born French novelist, essayist, and playwright. *The Fall* (1956)

5 He had a face like a benediction.
Miguel de Cervantes (1547–1616) Spanish novelist and playwright. *Don Quixote* (1605–15), pt. 1, bk. 4

6 The face the index of a feeling mind.
George Crabbe (1754–1832) British poet and clergyman. *Tales of the Hall* (1819), bk. 16, 'Lady Barbara', l. 124

7 He had but one eye, and the popular prejudice runs in favour of two.
Charles Dickens (1812–70) British novelist. Description of Mr. Squeers. *Nicholas Nickleby* (1839), ch. 4

8 Mirrors are the windows of the devil, overlooking nothing but a landscape of lies!
Leon Garfield (1921–96) British writer. *The Prisoners of September* (1975), ch. 2

9 A smile that snapped back after using, like a stretched rubber band.
Sinclair Lewis (1885–1951) US novelist. Attrib.

10 There is no one so bound to his own face that he does not cherish the hope of presenting another to the world.
Antonio Machado (1875–1939) Spanish poet and playwright. *Juan de Mairena* (1943)

11 There's a man outside with a big black mustache. —Tell him I've got one.
Groucho Marx (1895–1977) US comedian and film actor. *Horse Feathers* (Bert Kalmar, Harry Ruby, S. J. Perelman, and Will B. Johnstone; 1932)

12 Had Cleopatra's nose been shorter, the whole face of the world would have changed.
Blaise Pascal (1623–62) French philosopher, mathematician, and physicist. *Pensées* (1669), sect. 2, no. 162

13 It is bad enough to be condemned to drag around this image in which nature has imprisoned me. Why should I consent to the perpetuation of the image of this image?
Plotinus (205–270) Egyptian-born Roman philosopher. Refusing to have his portrait painted. Attrib.

14 A smile that floated without support in the air.
Marcel Proust (1871–1922) French novelist. *À la Recherche du Temps Perdu* (1913–27)

15 The human face is indeed, like the face of the God of some Oriental theogony, a whole cluster of faces, crowded together but on different surfaces so that one does not see them all at once.
Marcel Proust (1871–1922) French novelist. 1918. À l'ombre des jeunes filles en fleurs, *À la Recherche du Temps Perdu* (1913–27)

16 SMITH The reflection in my shaving mirror tells me things nobody else would.
Gabriela Roepke Bahamonde (b. 1920) Chilean playwright. *A White Butterfly* (1960)

17 My nose is huge! Vile snub-nose, flat-nosed ass, flat-head, let me inform you that I am proud of such an appendage, since a big nose is the proper sign of a friendly, good, courteous, witty, liberal, and brave man, such as I am.
Edmond Rostand (1868–1918) French playwright. *Cyrano de Bergerac* (1898), Act 1, Scene 1

18 LADY MACBETH Your face, my thane, is as a book where men
May read strange matters. To beguile the time,
Look like the time; bear welcome in your eye,
Your hand, your tongue: look like the innocent flower,
But be the serpent under't.
William Shakespeare (1564–1616) English poet and playwright. *Macbeth* (1606), Act 1, Scene 5

19 Big chap with a small moustache and the sort of eye that can open an oyster at sixty paces.
P. G. Wodehouse (1881–1975) British-born US humorous writer. *The Code of the Woosters* (1938), ch. 2

20 The stationmaster's whiskers are of a Victorian bushiness and give the impression of having been grown under glass.
P. G. Wodehouse (1881–1975) British-born US humorous writer. Quoted in *Wodehouse at Work to the End* (Richard Usborne; 1961), ch. 2

Facts

see also **Information**, **Knowledge**, **Truth**

1   Facts do not make history; facts do not
even make events . . . a fact is an isolated
particle of experience, is reflected light
without a source, planet with no sun, star
without constellation, constellation beyond
galaxy, galaxy outside the universe—fact is
nothing.
Russell Banks (b. 1940) US novelist. *Affliction* (1989)

2   Facts can't be recounted; much less twice over,
and far less still by different persons. I've already
drummed that thoroughly into your head. What
happens is that your wretched memory
remembers the words and forgets what's behind
them.
Augusto Roa Bastos (b. 1917) Paraguayan writer. *I the Supreme*
(1974)

3   To treat your facts with imagination is one thing,
to imagine your facts is another.
John Burroughs (1837–1921) US naturalist and writer. *The Heart of
Burroughs Journals* (C. Barrus, ed.; 1967)

4   I must begin with a good body of facts and not
from a principle (in which I always suspect some
fallacy) and then as much deduction as you
please.
Charles Darwin (1809–82) British naturalist. Letter to J. Fiske
(December 8, 1874)

5   Now, what I want is Facts . . . Facts alone are
wanted in life.
Charles Dickens (1812–70) British novelist. Said by Mrs. Gradgrind.
Hard Times (1854), bk. 1, ch. 1

6   Facts are not science—as the dictionary is not
literature.
Martin H. Fischer (1879–1962) German-born US physician and
author. *Fischerisms* (Howard Fabing and Ray Marr, eds.;
1944)

7   Facts do not cease to exist because they are
ignored.
Aldous Huxley (1894–1963) British novelist and essayist. *Proper Studies*
(1927)

8   Facts are ventriloquists' dummies. Sitting on a
wise man's knee they may be made to utter
words of wisdom; elsewhere they say nothing or
talk nonsense.
Aldous Huxley (1894–1963) British novelist and essayist. *Time Must
Have a Stop* (1944)

9   Once a newspaper touches a story, the facts are
lost forever, even to the protagonists.
Norman Mailer (b. 1923) US novelist and journalist. *The Presidential
Papers* (1963)

10 Facts to be dealt with, as the sea is, the demand
that they be played by . . . the ear!
Charles Olson (1910–70) US poet. 'I, Maximus of Gloucester, to
You', *The Maximus Poems 1–10* (1953)

11 People who mistake facts for ideas are incomplete
thinkers; they are gossips.
Cynthia Ozick (b. 1928) US novelist and short-story writer. Quoted
in 'We Are the Crazy Lady and Other Feisty Feminist
Fables', *The First Ms. Reader* (Francine Klagsbrun, ed.;
1972)

12 A fact is like a sack which won't stand up when
it is empty. In order that it may stand up, one
has to put into it the reason and sentiment which
have caused it to exist.
Luigi Pirandello (1867–1936) Italian dramatist, novelist, and short-story
writer. *Six Characters in Search of an Author* (Edward Storer,
tr.; 1921)

13 The facts are to blame, my friend. We are all
imprisoned by facts: I was born, I exist.
Luigi Pirandello (1867–1936) Italian dramatist, novelist, and short-story
writer. *The Rules of the Game* (William Murray, tr.; 1918)

14 Facts speak louder than statistics.
Geoffrey Streatfield (1897–1978) British lawyer. *Observer* (March 19,
1950), 'Sayings of the Week'

15 The modern delusion that if only we know
enough facts we shall arrive at the answer.
A. J. P. Taylor (1906–90) British historian. *Times Literary Supplement*
(April 27, 1951)

16 Some circumstantial evidence is very strong, as
when you find a trout in the milk.
Henry David Thoreau (1817–62) US writer. *Journal* (1850), quoted in
The Writings of Henry David Thoreau (1906)

Failure

see also **Mistakes**

1   Well, back to the old drawing board.
Peter Arno (1904–68) US cartoonist. Caption to a cartoon of people
leaving a crashed plane. *New Yorker*

2   All men that are ruined are ruined on the side of
their natural propensities.
Edmund Burke (1729–97) Irish-born British statesman and political
philosopher. *Letters on a Regicide Peace* (1796), no. 1

3   Many go out for wool, and come home shorn
themselves.
Miguel de Cervantes (1547–1616) Spanish novelist and playwright. *Don
Quixote* (1605–15), pt. 2, ch. 37

4   She knows there's no success like failure
And that failure's no success at all.
Bob Dylan (b. 1941) US singer and songwriter. Song lyric. 'Love
Minus Zero No Limit' (1965)

5   Failing is good as long as it doesn't become a
habit.
Michael Eisner (b. 1942) US entertainment executive. Speech (April 19,
1996)

6   If at first you don't succeed, try, try again. Then
quit. No use being a damn fool about it.
W. C. Fields (1879–1946) US entertainer. Attrib.

7   He was a self-made man who owed his lack of
success to nobody.
Joseph Heller (1923–99) US novelist. *Catch-22* (1961), ch. 3

8   In the long run, failure was the only thing that
worked predictably.
Joseph Heller (1923–99) US novelist. *Good as Gold* (1979)

9   Teach a highly educated person that it is not a
disgrace to fail and he must analyze every failure
to find its cause. He must learn how to fail
intelligently, for failing is one of the greatest arts
in the world.
Charles Kettering (1876–1958) US inventor and business executive.
Strategy and Business (1997)

10 Pursue failure. Failure is success's only launching pad.
Tom Peters (b. 1942) US management consultant and author. *Liberation Management* (1992)

11 The father saw other failures multiply like an explosion of virulent cells—failure to speak clearly; failure to sit up straight; failure to get up in the morning; failure in attitude; failure in ambition and ability; indeed in everything.
E. Annie Proulx (b. 1935) US writer. 'Quoyle', *The Shipping News* (1993), ch. 1

12 CORIOLANUS Like a dull actor now
I have forgot my part and I am out,
Even to a full disgrace.
William Shakespeare (1564–1616) English poet and playwright. *Coriolanus* (1608), Act 5, Scene 3

13 Failure is inevitable. Success is elusive.
Steven Spielberg (b. 1947) US film director. *OM* (December 1984)

14 Never having been able to succeed in the world, he took his revenge by speaking ill of it.
Voltaire (1694–1778) French writer and philosopher. *Zadig* (1747), ch. 4

Fairies

see also **The Supernatural**

1 Every time a child says 'I don't believe in fairies' there is a little fairy somewhere that falls down dead.
J. M. Barrie (1860–1937) British playwright and novelist. *Peter Pan* (1904), Act 1

2 There are fairies at the bottom of our garden.
Rose Fyleman (1877–1957) British writer of children's books. 'The Fairies', *Fairies and Chimneys* (1918)

3 She was a gordian shape of dazzling hue,
Vermilion-spotted, golden, green, and blue;
Striped like a zebra, freckled like a pard,
Eyed like a peacock, and all crimson barr'd.
John Keats (1795–1821) English poet. 'Lamia' (1820), pt. 1, l. 47

Faith

see also **Belief, Faithfulness, Trust**

1 One cathedral is worth a hundred theologians capable of proving the existence of God by logic.
Julian Barnes (b. 1946) British writer. *Staring at the Sun* (1988)

2 Without faith nothing is possible. With it, nothing is impossible.
Mary McLeod Bethune (1875–1955) US educator and human-rights activist. 'My Last Will and Testament' (1975)

3 Now faith is the substance of things hoped for, the evidence of things not seen.
Bible. Hebrews, *King James Bible* (1611), 11:1

4 Ask, and it shall be given you; seek, and ye shall find; knock, and it shall be opened unto you: For every one that asketh receiveth; and he that seeketh findeth; and to him that knocketh it shall be opened.
Bible. Matthew, *King James Bible* (1611), 7:7–8

5 If ye have faith as a grain of mustard seed, ye shall say unto this mountain, Remove hence to yonder place; and it shall remove; and nothing shall be impossible unto you.
Bible. Matthew, *King James Bible* (1611), 17:20

6 That willing suspension of disbelief for the moment, which constitutes poetic faith.
Samuel Taylor Coleridge (1772–1834) British poet. *Biographia Literaria* (1817), ch. 14

7 If you think you can win, you can win. Faith is necessary to victory.
William Hazlitt (1778–1830) British essayist and critic. 'On Great and Little Things' (1836)

8 Faith is a charisma not granted to all; instead man has the gift of thought, which can strive after the highest things.
Carl Gustav Jung (1875–1961) Swiss psychoanalyst. 1958. 'A Psychological Approach to the Dogma of the Trinity', *Collected Works* (1969), vol. 2

9 There can be no progress if people have no faith in tomorrow.
John Fitzgerald Kennedy (1917–63) US president. Speech to the Inter-American Press Association, Miami Beach, Florida (November 18, 1963)

10 There is no faith which has never yet been broken, except that of a truly faithful dog.
Konrad Lorenz (1903–89) Austrian zoologist. *King Solomon's Ring* (Marjorie Kerr Wilson, tr.; 1949)

11 Faith may be defined briefly as an illogical belief in the occurrence of the improbable.
H. L. Mencken (1880–1956) US journalist, critic, and editor. 'Types of Men', *Prejudices* (1922)

12 But Faith, fanatic Faith, once wedded fast
To some dear falsehood, hugs it to the last.
Thomas Moore (1779–1852) Irish poet. 'Lalla Rookh' (1817), can. 3, l. 356

13 Nothing in life is more wonderful than faith—the one great moving force which we can neither weigh in the balance nor test in the crucible.
William Osler (1849–1919) Canadian physician. 1910. Quoted in *The Life of Sir William Osler* (Harvey Cushing; 1925), vol. 2, ch. 30

14 Faith is a risk and a gamble. Absolute certainty can never be faith.
Adam Clayton Powell, Jr. (1908–72) US clergyman and civil rights leader. 'Palm Sunday', *Keep the Faith, Baby* (1967)

15 POSTHUMUS Hang there like fruit, my soul,
Till the tree die!
William Shakespeare (1564–1616) English poet and playwright. Said on recognizing his wife Imogen, whom he thought lost. *Cymbeline* (1609–10), Act 5, Scene 5

16 'Tis not the dying for a faith that's so hard, Master Harry—every man of every nation has done that—'tis the living up to it that is difficult.
William Makepeace Thackeray (1811–63) British novelist. *The History of Henry Esmond* (1852), ch. 6

17 Faith consists in believing when it is beyond the power of reason to believe. It is not enough that a thing be possible for it to be believed.
Voltaire (1694–1778) French writer and philosopher. *Questions sur l'Encyclopédie* (1770–72)

Faithfulness

see also **Commitment, Commitment in Love, Faith, Loyalty**

1   We only part to meet again.
Change, as ye list, ye winds; my heart shall be
The faithful compass that still points to thee.
John Gay (1685–1732) English poet and playwright. 'Sweet William's Farewell to Black-Eyed Susan' (1720)

2   But I'm always true to you, darlin', in my fashion,
Yes, I'm always true to you, darlin', in my way.
Cole Porter (1893–1964) US songwriter and composer. Song lyric. 'Always True to You in My Fashion', Kiss Me Kate (1948)

3   I loved you when you were inconstant. What should I have done if you had been faithful?
Racine (1639–99) French playwright. Andromaque (1667), Act 4, Scene 5

4   TROILUS I am as true as truth's simplicity,
And simpler than the infancy of truth.
William Shakespeare (1564–1616) English poet and playwright. Troilus and Cressida (1602), Act 3, Scene 2

Fame

see also **Celebrity, Popularity**

1   Fame is like a river, that beareth up things light and swollen, and drowns things weighty and solid.
Francis Bacon (1561–1626) English philosopher, statesman, and lawyer. 'Of Praise', Essays (1625)

2   I should like one of these days to be so well known, so popular, so celebrated, so famous, that it would permit me . . . to break wind in society, and society would think it a most natural thing.
Honoré de Balzac (1799–1850) French writer. Attrib.

3   The glory and the nothing of a name.
Lord Byron (1788–1824) British poet. 'Churchill's Grave' (1816), l. 43

4   What is the end of fame? 'Tis but to fill
A certain portion of uncertain paper.
Lord Byron (1788–1824) British poet. Don Juan (1819–24), can. 1, st. 218

5   I awoke one morning and found myself famous.
Lord Byron (1788–1824) British poet. Remark made after the publication of the first canto of Childe Harold's Pilgrimage (1812). Entry in Memoranda (1812)

6   The Zulus know Chaplin better than Arkansas knows Garbo.
Charlie Chaplin (1889–1977) British actor and director. Atlantic Monthly (August 1939)

7   I owe my fame only to myself.
Corneille (1606–84) French playwright. 'Excuse à Ariste', Poésies (1660)

8   Fame creates its own standard. A guy who twitches his lip is just another guy with a lip twitch—unless he's Humphrey Bogart.
Sammy Davis, Jr. (1925–90) US singer and entertainer. Yes I Can (1965)

9   Fame is a food that dead men eat,
I have no stomach for such meat.
Austin Dobson (1840–1921) British poet. 1906. 'Fame Is a Food that Dead Men Eat', Collected Poems: By Austin Dobson: Ninth Edition (1913), ll. 1–2

10 Fame is sometimes like unto a kind of mushroom, which Pliny recounts to be the greatest miracle in nature, because growing and having no root.
Thomas Fuller (1608–61) English historian. The Holy State and the Profane State (1642)

11 Fame is a powerful aphrodisiac.
Graham Greene (1904–91) British novelist. Radio Times (September 10, 1964)

12 Who would not rather have the fame of Archimedes than that of his conqueror Marcellus?
William Rowan Hamilton (1805–65) Irish mathematician. Quoted in Mathematical Circles Revisited (H. Eves; 1971)

13 It is a mark of many famous people that they cannot part with their brightest hour: what worked once must always work.
Lillian Hellman (1905–84) US playwright. 'Theater', Pentimento (1973)

14 I handle fame by not being famous . . . I'm not famous to me.
Bob Marley (1945–81) Jamaican musician, singer, and songwriter. December 1974. Quoted in Bob Marley in His Own Words (Ian McCann; 1993)

15 Fame is the spur that the clear spirit doth raise
(That last infirmity of noble mind)
To scorn delights, and live laborious days.
John Milton (1608–74) English writer. 1638. 'Lycidas', Poems of Mr. John Milton (1645), ll. 70–72

16 Fame and tranquility can never be bedfellows.
Michel de Montaigne (1533–92) French essayist. Essays (1580–88), bk. 1, ch. 39

17 I don't care what you say about me, as long as you say something.
James Gregory Mumford (1863–1914) US surgeon. Quoted in George M. Cohan (John McCabe; 1973)

18 'What are you famous for?'
'For nothing. I am just famous'.
Iris Murdoch (1919–99) Irish-born British novelist and philosopher. The Flight from the Enchanter (1955)

19 My time has not yet come either; some are born posthumously.
Friedrich Wilhelm Nietzsche (1844–1900) German philosopher and poet. Ecce Homo (1888)

20 It's vulgar to be famous,
That isn't what makes you great . . .
You must work at your work
not dream of your destiny.
Boris Pasternak (1890–1960) Russian poet and novelist. 'It's vulgar to be famous . . . ' (May 5, 1956), quoted in Boris Pasternak: The Tragic Years 1930–60 (Ann Pasternak Slater and Craig Raine, eds., trs.; 1990)

21 For famous men have the whole earth as their memorial.
Pericles (495?–429? BC) Greek statesman. 430 BC. Histories (Rex Warner, tr.; 1961), bk. 2, ch. 43, sect. 3

22 Fame is a constant effort.
Jules Renard (1864–1910) French writer. 1887. Journal (1877–1910)

23 Fame, after all, is no more than the quintessence of all the misunderstandings collecting round a new name.
Rainer Maria Rilke (1875–1926) Austrian poet and novelist. Auguste Rodin (1903)

24 Born of the sun, they travelled a short while
towards the sun
And left the vivid air signed with their honour.

Stephen Spender (1909–95) British poet and critic. 'I Think
Continually of Those Who Were Truly Great' (1933)

25 Why am I so famous? What am I doing right?
What are the others doing so wrong?

Barbra Streisand (b. 1942) US singer, film actor, director, and producer.
Playboy (October 1977), quoted in *Chambers Film Quotes*
(Tony Crawley, ed.; 1991)

26 Censure is the tax a man pays to the public for
being eminent.

Jonathan Swift (1667–1745) Irish writer and clergyman. *Thoughts on
Various Subjects* (1711)

27 Love of fame is the last thing even learned men
can bear to be parted from.

Tacitus (55?–117?) Roman historian. *Histories* (104?–109?), bk. 4,
ch. 6

28 To famous men all the earth is a sepulchre.

Thucydides (460?–400? BC) Athenian historian and general. *History of
the Peloponnesian War* (431–400? BC), bk. 2, ch. 43

29 The only man who wasn't spoilt by being
lionized was Daniel.

Herbert Beerbohm Tree (1853–1917) British actor and theatrical
impresario. Attrib. *Beerbohm Tree* (Hesketh Pearson; 1956)

30 In the future, everyone will be famous for 15
minutes.

Andy Warhol (1928?–87) US artist and filmmaker. Catalogue of his
photo exhibition in Stockholm (1968)

31 There is only one thing in the world worse than
being talked about, and that is not being talked
about.

Oscar Wilde (1854–1900) Irish poet, playwright, and wit. *The Picture of
Dorian Gray* (1891), ch. 1

Family

see also **Children, Home, Parents**

1 My own family were split down the middle,
politically, as in every other way.

Beryl Bainbridge (b. 1934) British author and journalist. *Forever
England North and South* (1987)

2 The sink is the great symbol of the bloodiness of
family life. All life is bad, but family life is worse.

Dave Barry (b. 1947) US humorist. *As Far as You Can Go* (1963),
pt. I, ch. 1

3 If my aunt had bollocks she'd be me uncle.

Brendan Behan (1923–64) Irish playwright and author. *Richard's Cork
Leg* (1972), Act 1

4 I think the family is the place where the most
ridiculous and least respectable things in the
world go on.

Ugo Betti (1892–1953) Italian playwright and poet. *The Inquiry* (Gino
Rizzo, tr.; 1944–45)

5 The family is strongest where objective reality is
most likely to be misinterpreted.

Don DeLillo (b. 1936) US novelist. *White Noise* (1985)

6 I am the family face;
Flesh perishes, I live on.

Thomas Hardy (1840–1928) British novelist and poet. 'Heredity',
Moments of Vision (1917)

7 A person may be indebted for a nose or an eye,
for a graceful carriage or a voluble discourse, to
a great-aunt or uncle, whose existence he has
scarcely heard of.

William Hazlitt (1778–1830) British essayist and critic. 'On Personal
Character', *London Magazine* (1821)

8 Good families are generally worse than any
others.

Anthony Hope (1863–1933) British novelist and playwright. *The Prisoner
of Zenda* (1894), ch. 1

9 If Nature had arranged that husbands and wives
should have children alternately, there would
never be more than *three* in a family.

Laurence Housman (1865–1959) British writer and illustrator. Attrib.

10 Families ain't just born, you got to work at 'em,
even when there ain't much to work with.

Marsha Hunt (b. 1946) US singer, actor, and writer. *Joy* (1990)

11 There is not enough magic in a bloodline to forge
an instant, irrevocable bond.

James Earl Jones (b. 1931) US actor. *James Earl Jones: Voices and
Silences* (Jones & Niven; 1993)

12 Far from being the basis of the good society, the
family, with its narrow privacy and tawdry
secrets, is the source of all our discontents.

Edmund Leach (1910–89) British social anthropologist. BBC Reith
Lecture, *Listener* (November 30, 1967)

13 Murder, like talent, seems occasionally to run in
families.

George Henry Lewes (1817–78) British philosopher and writer. *The
Physiology of Common Life* (1859), ch. 12

14 A group of closely related persons living under
one roof; it is a convenience, often a necessity,
sometimes a pleasure, sometimes the reverse; but
who first exalted it as admirable, an almost
religious ideal?

Rose Macaulay (1881–1958) British poet, novelist, and essayist. On the
family. *The World My Wilderness* (1950), ch. 20

15 My feeling about in-laws was that they were
outlaws.

Malcolm X (1925–65) US Black activist. *The Autobiography of
Malcolm X* (1965)

16 Nobody has ever before asked the nuclear family
to live all by itself in a box the way we do. With
no relatives, no support, we've put it in an
impossible situation.

Margaret Mead (1901–78) US anthropologist. Quoted in *New Realities*
(June 1978)

17 No matter how many communes anybody
invents, the family always creeps back.

Margaret Mead (1901–78) US anthropologist. Attrib.

18 Blood really is thicker than water, and no aspect
of human existence is untouched by that part of
our psychology.

Steven Pinker (b. 1954) US cognitive scientist and author. *How the
Mind Works* (1997)

19 Family is a mixed blessing. You're glad to have
one, but it's also like receiving a life sentence for
a crime you didn't commit.

Richard Pryor (b. 1940) US comedian and actor. *Pryor Convictions
and other Life Sentences* (1995)

20 HAMLET A little more than kin, and less than
kind.

William Shakespeare (1564–1616) English poet and playwright. *Hamlet*
(1601), Act 1, Scene 2

21 I'm sorry to hear that, sir, you don't happen to
have the shilling about you now, do you?

Tom Sheridan (1775–1817) British administrator. To his father, on
learning that he was to be cut off in his will with a shilling.
The Fine Art of Political Wit (L. Harris; 1965)

22 The family, that dear octopus from whose
tentacles we never quite escape, nor in our
innermost hearts never quite wish to.

Dodie Smith (1896–1990) British playwright, novelist, and theatrical
producer. *Dear Octopus* (1938)

23 It is hazardous to shake a family tree. One never
knows what will fall out. Undesirable birds have
an impish way of roosting among the finest
genealogical branches.

Melvin Tolson (1900–66) US poet and teacher. 'I am an Unprejudiced
Negro' (August 26, 1939)

24 All happy families resemble one another, each
unhappy family is unhappy in its own way.

Leo Tolstoy (1828–1910) Russian writer. *Anna Karenina* (1875–77),
pt. 1, ch. 1

Famine

see **Hunger**

Fanaticism

see also **Belief, Bigotry, Extremes, Obsessions**

1 Christians have burnt each other, quite persuaded
That all the Apostles would have done as they
did.

Lord Byron (1788–1824) British poet. *Don Juan* (1819–24), can. 1,
st. 83

2 A fanatic is a man who does what he thinks th'
Lord wud do if He knew th' facts iv the case.

Finley Peter Dunne (1867–1936) US humorist and journalist. 'Casual
Observations', *Mr. Dooley's Opinions* (1900)

3 Fear prophets . . . and those prepared to die for
the truth, for as a rule they make many others
die with them, often before them, at times instead
of them.

Umberto Eco (b. 1932) Italian writer and literary scholar. *The Name of
the Rose* (William Weaver, tr.; 1980), Seventh Day: Night (2)

4 Fervor is the weapon of choice of the impotent.

Frantz Fanon (1925–61) Martiniquan social scientist, physician, and
psychiatrist. *Black Skin, White Masks* (1952)

5 Defined in psychological terms, a fanatic is a
man who consciously over-compensates a secret
doubt.

Aldous Huxley (1894–1963) British novelist and essayist. 'Vulgarity in
Literature', *Music At Night And Other Essays* (1949)

6 Irrationally held truths may be more harmful
than reasoned errors.

T. H. Huxley (1825–95) British biologist. 'The Coming of Age of the
Origin of Species', *Science and Culture and Other Essays*
(1881)

7 Fundamentalism is a spectre that is stalking the
globe, but Islam is not its synonym.

Rana Kabbani (b. 1958) Syrian cultural historian. *Imperial Fictions:
Europe's Myths of the Orient* (1994)

8 Fanatics have their dreams, wherewith they weave
A paradise for a sect.

John Keats (1795–1821) English poet. *The Fall of Hyperion: A
Dream* (1819), can. 1, ll. 1–2

9 The American Nazis were all fanatics, yes, poor
mad tormented fanatics . . . but this man's
conviction stood in his eyes as if his soul had
been focused to a single point of light.

Norman Mailer (b. 1923) US novelist and journalist. 'History as Novel:
The Steps of the Pentagon', *The Armies of the Night* (1968),
bk. 1, pt. 4, ch. 2

10 There is apt to be a lunatic fringe among the
votaries of any forward movement.

Theodore Roosevelt (1858–1919) US president. Quoted in *Speaking
Freely* (Stuart Berg Flexner and Anne H. Soukhanov; 1997)

11 The ability to understand a question from all sides
meant one was totally unfit for action. Fanatical
enthusiasm was the mark of the real man.

Thucydides (460?–400? BC) Athenian historian and general. On the
Athenian mood during Peloponnesian War (431–400? BC)
History of the Peloponnesian War (431–400? BC)

12 Those who can't find anything to live for,
always invent something to die for.
Then they want the rest of us to die
for it too.

Lew Welch (1926–71) US poet. 'The Basic Con', *Ring of Bone:
Collected Poems 1950–71* (Donald M. Allen, ed.; 1973)

13 They charge me with fanaticism. If to be feelingly
alive to the sufferings of my fellow-creatures is to
be a fanatic, I am one of the most incurable
fanatics ever permitted to be at large.

William Wilberforce (1759–1833) British abolitionist and politician. Speech
in Parliament (June 19, 1816)

Fantasy

see also **Dreams, Fiction, Imagination**

1 If one is lucky, a solitary fantasy can totally
transform one million realities.

Maya Angelou (b. 1928) US writer. *The Heart of a Woman* (1981)

2 One may be quixotic in an anomalous case, but
to be so as a general rule is absurd.

Pío Baroja (1872–1956) Basque writer. *The Tree of Knowledge* (1911)

3 The road to the City of Emeralds is paved with
yellow brick.

L. Frank Baum (1856–1919) US writer. The sentence in the original
novel that led to the song 'Follow the Yellow Brick Road' in
the film, *The Wizard of Oz* (1939). *The Wonderful Wizard of
Oz* (1900), ch. 2

4 Sheer animated fantasy is still my first and
deepest production impulse. The fable is the best
storytelling device ever conceived, and the screen
is its best medium.

Walt Disney (1901–66) US film producer and animator. Quoted in *The
Disney Touch* (Ron Grover; 1996)

5 Somewhere over the rainbow,
Way up high:
There's a land that I heard of
Once in a lullaby.

E. Y. Harburg (1896–1981) US librettist and lyricist. Song lyric. 'Over
the Rainbow', *The Wizard of Oz* (1939)

6 Castles in the air—they're so easy to take refuge
in. So easy to build, too.

Henrik Ibsen (1828–1906) Norwegian playwright. *The Master Builder*
(1892), Act 3

7 A fantasy can be equivalent to a paradise and if
the fantasy passes, better yet, because eternal
paradise would be very boring.

Juan Ramón Jiménez (1881–1958) Spanish poet. 'To Burn
Completely', *Selected Writings* (1957)

8 Picture yourself in a boat on a river with
   tangerine trees and marmalade skies.
   Somebody calls you, you answer quite slowly a
   girl with kaleidoscope eyes.
   Lennon & McCartney, British rock musicians. 'Lucy in the Sky with
   Diamonds', *Sergeant Pepper's Lonely Hearts Club Band*
   (1967)

9 How beautiful it would be to see man wrestle
   with his illusions and vanquish them.
   Naguib Mahfouz (b. 1911) Egyptian writer. Said by Kamal. *Palace of
   Desire* (1957)

10 The human mind invents its Puss-in-Boots and its
   coaches that turn into pumpkins at midnight
   because neither the believer nor the atheist is
   completely satisfied with appearances.
   André Malraux (1901–76) French writer and statesman. *Antimémoires*
   (1967), Preface

11 A thousand fantasies
   Begin to throng into my memory
   Of calling shapes, and beckoning shadows dire,
   And airy tongues, that syllable men's names
   On sands, and shores, and desert wildernesses.
   John Milton (1608–74) English writer. *Comus* (1637), ll. 205–209

12 I don't think there is any difference between
   fantasy and reality in the way these should be
   approached in a film. Of course if you live that
   way you are clinically insane.
   Martin Scorsese (b. 1942) US filmmaker. 'Mean Streets—Alice
   Doesn't Live Here Anymore—Taxi Driver', *Scorsese on
   Scorsese* (Ian Christie and David Thompson, eds.; 1989),
   ch. 3

13 We had fed the heart on fantasies,
   The heart's grown brutal from the fare;
   More substance in our enmities
   Than in our love.
   W. B. Yeats (1865–1939) Irish poet and playwright. 'Meditations In
   Time of Civil War', *The Tower* (1928), 'The Stare's Nest by
   My Window', ll. 16–19

Fascism

see also **Authoritarianism, Dictators, The Holocaust,
Totalitarianism, World War II**

1 Fascism is the open, terrorist dictatorship of the
   most reactionary, most chauvinist, and most
   imperialist elements of finance capital.
   Anonymous. *Theses and Decisions of the Third Plenum of the
   Executive Committee of the Communist International* (1934)

2 One people, one empire, one leader.
   Anonymous. 1930s. Slogan of the German National Socialist
   (Nazi) Party, referring to Adolf Hitler.

3 Fascism is not itself a new order of society. It is
   the future refusing to be born.
   Aneurin Bevan (1897–1960) Welsh-born British politician. Attrib.

4 I deny Hitler's right, I deny any state's right, to
   put a limitation on the progress of the human
   mind.
   Ernest Bevin (1881–1951) British trade union leader and statesman.
   Speech, Swansea (November 1, 1941)

5 One Fatherland, One State, One Leader.
   Francisco Franco (1892–1975) Spanish general and dictator. 1936.
   Slogan. This deliberately echoed Hitler's *Ein Volk, ein Reich,
   ein Führer*. All newspapers in the Nationalist regions of Spain
   had to carry these words under the masthead. Quoted in
   Franco (Paul Preston; 1993)

6 It was no secret that this time the revolution
   would have to be bloody . . . When we spoke of
   it, we called it 'The Night of the Long Knives'.
   Adolf Hitler (1889–1945) Austrian-born German dictator. Referring
   to the murder of Hitler's opponents within the Nazi Party
   on June 29–30, 1934. 'Night of the Long Knives' was
   taken by Hitler from an early Nazi marching song.
   Quoted in *The House Hitler Built* (S. H. Roberts; 1937),
   pt. 2, ch. 3

7 Fascism is not an article for export.
   Benito Mussolini (1883–1945) Italian dictator. Reported in the
   German press. Remark (1932)

8 We have buried the putrid corpse of liberty.
   Benito Mussolini (1883–1945) Italian dictator. Speech (1934), quoted
   in *Bolshevism, Fascism and the Liberal-Democratic State*
   (Maurice Farr Parmelee; 1935)

9 The keystone of the Fascist doctrine is its
   conception of the State, of its essence, its
   functions, and its aims. For Fascism the State is
   absolute, individuals and groups relative.
   Benito Mussolini (1883–1945) Italian dictator. *Fascism: Doctrine and
   Institutions* (1935)

10 I should be pleased, I suppose, that Hitler has
   carried out a revolution on our lines. But they are
   Germans. So they will end by ruining our idea.
   Benito Mussolini (1883–1945) Italian dictator. 1935. Referring to
   fascism, which he regarded as a uniquely Italian philosophy.
   Quoted in *Benito Mussolini* (C. Hibbert; 1975), pt. 2, ch. 1

11 Fascism is a religion; the twentieth century will
   be known in history as the century of Fascism.
   Benito Mussolini (1883–1945) Italian dictator. 1933. On Hitler's
   seizing power. Quoted in *Sawdust Caesar: the Untold History
   of Mussolini and Fascism* (George Seldes; 1935), ch. 24

12 Fascism means war.
   John St. Loe Strachey (1901–63) British politician. The phrase became
   a slogan of the political left. *The Menace of Fascism* (1933)

13 One of the radicalized and demoniacal quasi-
   religions—Nazism.
   Paul Tillich (1886–1965) German-born US theologian and philosopher.
   Christianity and the Encounter of the World Religions (1961),
   ch. 2

14 Fascism was a fairly popular political philosophy
   which made sacred whatever nation and race the
   philosopher happened to belong to.
   Kurt Vonnegut (b. 1922) US novelist. *Breakfast of Champions*
   (1973), ch. 17

Fashion

see also **Clothes, Design**

1 Fashion is made to become unfashionable.
   Coco Chanel (1883–1971) French fashion designer. *Life* (1957)

2 Fashion—a word which knaves and fools may
   use,
   Their knavery and folly to excuse.
   Charles Churchill (1731–64) British poet. *The Rosciad* (1761),
   ll. 455–456

3 One had as good be out of the world, as out of
   the fashion.
   Colley Cibber (1671–1757) British actor and playwright. *Love's Last
   Shift* (1696), Act 2

4 One week he's in polka dots, the next week he's
   in stripes.
   'Cos he's a dedicated follower of fashion.
   Ray Davies (b. 1944) British pop musician. Song lyric. 'Dedicated
   Follower of Fashion' (1966)

5 Fashion's job is to combat the tedium of routine existence.

Carrie Donovan, US fashion journalist. *New York Times* (May 4, 1986)

6 Fashion is a sub-art and is not intellectual. Fashion is a business and operates best when it is born out of instincts. Fashion appeals to the senses and comes from gut feeling . . . True fashion comes straight out of the jungle.

John B. Fairchild (b. 1927) US publisher. *Chic Savages* (1989)

7 In fashion, you're always creating authority through provocation. The worst thing is to be overlooked because you're not provocative. You have to be on the edge of changing sensibilities.

Milton Glaser (b. 1929) US graphic designer and illustrator. Referring to the use of blatant sexuality in fashion advertising. *New York Times* (April 19, 1986)

8 Fashion is the image of an age and can tell its story better than a speech.

Karl Lagerfeld (b. 1938) German-born French fashion designer. *Daily Telegraph* (October 20, 1994)

9 Models are the apex of consumer society. Pure image . . . Modeling is the purest kind of performance, uncomplicated by content.

Jay McInerney, US writer. *Model Behaviour* (1998)

10 God, fashion moves fast.

Alexander McQueen (b. 1969) British fashion designer. *Daily Telegraph* (October 14, 1996)

11 Design is not a philosophy—it's for life.

Issey Miyake (b. 1938) Japanese fashion designer. Attrib.

12 In olden days, a glimpse of stocking
Was looked on as something shocking,
But now, Heaven knows,
Anything goes.

Cole Porter (1893–1964) US songwriter and composer. Song lyric. 'Anything Goes', *Anything Goes* (1934)

13 Her frocks are built in Paris but she wears them with a strong English accent.

Saki (1870–1916) British short-story writer. 'Reginald on Women', *Reginald* (1904)

14 For an idea ever to be fashionable is ominous, since it must afterwards be always old-fashioned.

George Santayana (1863–1952) Spanish-born US philosopher, poet, and novelist. 'Modernism and Christianity', *Winds of Doctrine* (1913)

15 The only label she wears is 'drip dry'.

Jennifer Saunders (b. 1958) British comedian. Said as Edina. *Absolutely Fabulous* (BBC television; 1990s)

16 Fashions, after all, are only induced epidemics.

George Bernard Shaw (1856–1950) Irish playwright. *The Doctor's Dilemma* (1911), Preface

17 Fashion is about profit and expansion, and trends reduced to the level of soundbites—Long is the new short! Brown is the new black! . . . Whatever happened to character and honesty and individuality?

Paul Smith (b. 1946) British fashion designer. *Vogue* (London; May 1998)

18 A love of fashion makes the economy go round.

Liz Tilberis (1947–?) US editor. *Vogue* (August 1987)

19 Bangs manes bouffants beehives Beatle caps butter faces brush-on lashes decal eyes puffy sweaters French thrust bras flailing leather blue jeans stretch pants stretch jeans honeydew bottoms.

Tom Wolfe (b. 1930) US journalist and novelist. *The Kandy-Kolored Tangerine-Flake Streamline Baby* (1965)

Fate

see also **Chance, Destiny**

1 Anything that, in happening, causes itself to happen, happens again.

Douglas Adams (1952–2001) British writer. *Mostly Harmless* (1992)

2 I returned, and saw under the sun, that the race is not to the swift, nor the battle to the strong, neither yet bread to the wise, nor yet riches to men of understanding, nor yet favour to men of skill; but time and chance happeneth to them all.

Bible. Ecclesiastes, *King James Bible* (1611), 9:11

3 If it is fated for you to recover from this illness, you will recover whether or not you call a doctor; similarly if it is fated for you not to recover from this illness, you will not recover whether or not you call a doctor . . . there is no point in calling a doctor.

Cicero (106–43 BC) Roman orator and statesman. 43? BC. An example of the 'Idle Argument'. *De Fato* (D. Charles, tr.), ll. 12, 28–29

4 Each man the architect of his own fate.

Appius Claudius Caecus (fl. 300 BC) Roman statesman. *De Civitate* (300? BC), bk. 1

5 The best of men cannot suspend their fate:
The good die early, and the bad die late.

Daniel Defoe (1660–1731) English novelist and journalist. *Character of the late Dr. S. Annesley* (1697)

6 Let us hope . . . that a kind of Providence will put a speedy end to the acts of God under which we have been laboring.

Peter De Vries (1910–93) US novelist. *The Mackerel Plaza* (1958), ch. 3

7 For those whom God to ruin has designed,
He fits for fate, and first destroys their mind.

John Dryden (1631–1700) English poet, playwright, and literary critic. *The Hind and the Panther* (1687), pt. 3, l. 1093

8 Tempt not the stars, young man, thou canst not play
With the severity of fate.

John Ford (1586–1640?) English playwright. *The Broken Heart* (1633), Act 1, Scene 3

9 The man who once cursed his fate, now, curses himself—and pays his psychoanalyst.

John W. Gardner (1912–77) US writer and public official. *No Easy Victories* (1968)

10 It is Fate that draws the plan; as the story issues from a deed of terror, and the hero is continually driven forward to a deed of terror, the work is tragic in the highest sense, and admits of no other than a tragic end.

Johann Wolfgang von Goethe (1749–1832) German poet, playwright, and scientist. 1795. Referring to William Shakespeare's *Hamlet*. Quoted in *The Great Critics* (James Harry Smith and Edd Winfield Parks, eds.; 1951)

11 Though men determine, the gods doo dispose; and oft times many things fall out betweene the cup and the lip.

Robert Greene (1560?–92) English poet and pamphleteer. *Perimedes the Blacke-Smith* (1588)

12 No man gets away from his reckoning, but with luck he may learn how to face it.

Neil Gunn (1891–1973) Scottish writer. *Blood Hunt* (1952)

13 'Justice' was done, and the President of the Immortals (in Aeschylean phrase) had ended his sport with Tess.

Thomas Hardy (1840–1928) British novelist and poet. *Tess of the D'Urbervilles* (1891), ch. 59

14 I go the way that Providence dictates with the assurance of a sleepwalker.

Adolf Hitler (1889–1945) Austrian-born German dictator. Referring to his successful reoccupation of the Rhineland, in violation of the Versailles Treaty and despite being advised against the attempt. Speech, Munich (March 15, 1936), quoted in *Hitler: Reden und Proklamationen 1932–45* (Max Domarus, ed.; 1962)

15 Do not try to find out—we're forbidden to know—what end the gods have in store for me, or for you.

Horace (65–8 BC) Roman poet. *Odes* (23? BC), bk. 1, no. 11, l. 1

16 Truly there is a tide in the affairs of men; but there is no gulf-stream setting forever in one direction.

James Russell Lowell (1819–91) US poet, editor, essayist, and diplomat. 'New England Two Centuries Ago', *Literary Essays* (1899), vol. 2

17 What doctrine call you this? Che sera, sera: What will be, shall be?

Christopher Marlowe (1564–93) English playwright and poet. *Doctor Faustus* (1592?), Act 1, Scene 1

18 It lies not in our power to love or hate For will in us is overrul'd by fate.

Christopher Marlowe (1564–93) English playwright and poet. *Hero and Leander* (1593)

19 We may become the makers of our fate when we have ceased to pose as its prophets.

Karl Popper (1902–94) Austrian-born British philosopher. *The Open Society and Its Enemies* (1945)

20 Man never found the deities so kindly As to assure him that he'd live tomorrow.

François Rabelais (1494?–1553?) French humanist and satirist. *Gargantua and Pantagruel* (1546), bk. 3, ch. 2

21 I wake to sleep, and take my waking slow. I feel my fate in what I cannot fear. I learn by going where I have to go.

Theodore Roethke (1908–63) US poet. *The Waking* (1953)

22 Not from the stars do I my judgment pluck, And yet methinks I have astronomy.

William Shakespeare (1564–1616) English poet and playwright. Sonnet 14 (1609)

23 HAMLET The time is out of joint; O cursed spite, That ever I was born to set it right!

William Shakespeare (1564–1616) English poet and playwright. *Hamlet* (1601), Act 1, Scene 5

24 HAMLET Let Hercules himself do what he may, The cat will mew, and dog will have his day.

William Shakespeare (1564–1616) English poet and playwright. *Hamlet* (1601), Act 5, Scene 1

25 HAMLET There's a divinity that shapes our ends, Rough-hew them how we will.

William Shakespeare (1564–1616) English poet and playwright. *Hamlet* (1601), Act 5, Scene 2

26 GLOUCESTER As flies to wanton boys are we to th' gods— They kill us for their sport.

William Shakespeare (1564–1616) English poet and playwright. *King Lear* (1605–06), Act 4, Scene 1

27 EDMUND The wheel is come full circle.

William Shakespeare (1564–1616) English poet and playwright. *King Lear* (1605–06), Act 5, Scene 3

28 Nothing is inevitable until it happens.

A. J. P. Taylor (1906–90) British historian. *Daily Telegraph* (January 7, 1980)

29 For man is man and master of his fate.

Alfred Tennyson (1809–92) British poet. 'The Marriage of Geraint', *Idylls of the King* (1859), l. 355

30 We are merely the stars' tennis-balls, struck and bandied Which way please them.

John Webster (1578?–1632?) English playwright. *The Duchess of Malfi* (1623), Act 5, Scene 4

Fathers

see also **Children, Family, Parents**

1 Okonkwo's fear ... was not external but lay deep within himself. It was the fear of himself, lest he should be found to resemble his father.

Chinua Achebe (b. 1930) Nigerian novelist, poet, and essayist. *Things Fall Apart* (1958)

2 my father moved through dooms of love through sames of am through haves of give, singing each morning out of each night my father moved through depths of height.

e. e. cummings (1894–1962) US poet and painter. 'my father moved through dooms of love', *50 Poems* (1940), quoted in *The Penguin Book of American Verse* (Geoffrey Moore, ed.; 1977)

3 My father was frightened of his mother. I was frightened of my father, and I'm damned well going to make sure that my children are frightened of me.

George V (1865–1936) British monarch. Quoted in *Lord Derby, 'King of Lancashire'* (Randolph Churchill; 1959)

4 The worst misfortune that can happen to an ordinary man is to have an extraordinary father.

Austin O'Malley (1858–1932) US writer. Attrib.

5 It's all any reasonable child can expect if the dad is present at the conception.

Joe Orton (1933–67) British playwright. *Entertaining Mr Sloane* (1964)

6 Any father whose son raises a hand against him is guilty: of having produced a son who raised his hand against him.

Charles Pierre Péguy (1873–1914) French writer and poet. *Cahiers de la Quinzaine* (December 2, 1906)

7 You do not do, you do not do Anymore, black shoe In which I have lived like a foot For thirty years.

Sylvia Plath (1932–63) US poet and novelist. 'Daddy', *Ariel* (1965), quoted in *The Penguin Book of American Verse* (Geoffrey Moore, ed.; 1977)

8 LAUNCELOT It is a wise father that knows his own child.

William Shakespeare (1564–1616) English poet and playwright. *The Merchant of Venice* (1596–98), Act 2, Scene 2

9 He that loves not his wife and children, feeds a lioness at home and broods a nest of sorrows.

Jeremy Taylor (1613–67) English theologian. 'Sermon 18', *Twenty-seven Sermons* (1651)

10 No man is responsible for his father. That is entirely his mother's affair.

Margaret Turnbull (d. 1942) Scottish-born US writer and playwright. *Alabaster Lamps* (1925)

11 When I was a boy of 14 my father was so ignorant I could hardly stand to have the old man around. But when I got to be 21, I was astonished at how much he had learnt in 7 years.

Mark Twain (1835–1910) US writer and humorist. Quoted in *The Jingle Bell Principle* (Miroslav Holub; 1992)

12 Come, Robert, you shall drink twice while I drink once, for I cannot permit the son in his sober senses to witness the intoxication of his father.

Horace Walpole (1717–97) British writer. Explaining why he filled his son's glass twice for every glass he drank himself. Attrib.

Fear

see also **Despair, Horror, Paranoia**

1 Of the world as it exists, one cannot be enough afraid.

Theodor Adorno (1903–69) German philosopher, sociologist, and musicologist. Attrib.

2 Men fear death, as children fear to go in the dark; and as that natural fear in children is increased with tales, so is the other.

Francis Bacon (1561–1626) English philosopher, statesman, and lawyer. 'Of Death', *Essays* (1625)

3 I do not believe that any man fears to be dead, but only the stroke of death.

Francis Bacon (1561–1626) English philosopher, statesman, and lawyer. 'An Essay on Death', *The Remaines of the Right Honourable Francis Lord Verulam* (1648)

4 I have three phobias which, could I mute them, would make my life as slick as a sonnet, but as dull as ditch water: I hate to go to bed, I hate to get up, and I hate to be alone.

Tallulah Bankhead (1903–68) US actor. *Tallulah* (1952), ch. 1

5 It is more comfortable to fear God than to fear nothingness.

Edward Bond (b. 1934) British playwright. *The Hidden Plot* (2000)

6 We confess our bad qualities to others out of fear of appearing naive or ridiculous by not being aware of them.

Gerald Brenan (1894–1987) Maltese-born British writer and novelist. *Thoughts in a Dry Season* (1978)

7 I am almost frighted out of my seven senses.

Miguel de Cervantes (1547–1616) Spanish novelist and playwright. *Don Quixote* (1605–15), pt. 1, bk. 3, ch. 9

8 Fear has many eyes and can see things underground.

Miguel de Cervantes (1547–1616) Spanish novelist and playwright. *Don Quixote* (1605–15), pt. 1, ch. 20

9 You may take the most gallant sailor, the most intrepid airman, or the most audacious soldier, put them at a table together—what do you get? *The sum of their fears.*

Winston Churchill (1874–1965) British prime minister and writer. November 16, 1943. Talking about the Chiefs of Staffs system. *The Blast of War* (H. Macmillan; 1967), ch. 16

10 I wants to make your flesh creep.

Charles Dickens (1812–70) British novelist. Said by the Fat Boy. *Pickwick Papers* (1837), ch. 8

11 In every hedge and ditch both day and night We fear our death, of every leafe affright.

Guillaume du Bartas (1544–90) French poet. 'Second Week, First Day', *Divine Weekes and Workes* (1578)

12 And I will show you something different from either
Your shadow at morning striding behind you,
Or your shadow at evening rising to meet you
I will show you fear in a handful of dust.

T. S. Eliot (1888–1965) US-born British poet and playwright. 'The Burial of the Dead', *The Waste Land* (1922)

13 I felt nothing, nothing but fear; I could neither eat nor sleep—fear clawed at my mind and body and shook me.

Anne Frank (1929–45) German diarist. March 25, 1944. 'Fear', *Anne Frank: The Diary of a Young Girl* (1947)

14 Today the Grand Inquisitor came into the room, but as soon as I heard his footsteps I hid under the table.

Nikolay Gogol (1809–52) Russian novelist and playwright. Said by the 'madman'. The Grand Inquisitor is the head of a religious inquisition. 'Diary of a Madman' (1835), quoted in *Diary of a Madman and Other Stories* (Ronald Wilks, tr.; 1972)

15 When you suffer an attack of nerves you're being attacked by the nervous system. What chance has a man got against a system?

Russell Hoban (b. 1925) US-born British novelist, children's writer, and illustrator. *The Lion of Boaz-Jachin and Jachin-Boaz* (1973), ch. 13

16 You can discover what your enemy fears most by observing the means he uses to frighten you.

Eric Hoffer (1902–83) US philosopher and longshoreman. Quoted in *The Faber Book of Aphorisms* (1964)

17 A sound of cornered-animal fear and hate and surrender and defiance . . . like the last sound the treed and shot and falling animal makes as the dogs get him, when he finally doesn't care any more about anything but himself and his dying.

Ken Kesey (b. 1935) US writer. *One Flew Over the Cuckoo's Nest* (1962), pt. 4

18 Few men who have liberated themselves from the fear of God and the fear of death are yet able to liberate themselves from the fear of man.

Lin Yutang (1895–1976) Chinese-born writer and philologist. *The Importance of Living* (1937)

19 In a world we find terrifying, we ratify that which doesn't threaten us.

David Mamet (b. 1947) US writer and film director. 'Notes for a Catalog for Raymond Saunders', *Writing in Restaurants* (1986)

20 I am a living symbol of the white man's fear.

Winnie Mandela (b. 1934) South African social worker and political activist. *Part of My Soul Went With Him* (1985)

21 For where no hope is left, is left no fear.

John Milton (1608–74) English writer. *Paradise Regained* (1671), bk. 3, l. 206

22 Fear is very exciting. People like to get scared. It's exactly like the moment before you have an orgasm.

Jim Morrison (1943–71) US rock singer and songwriter. Quoted in *No One Here Gets out Alive* (Jerry Hopkins and Danny Sugerman; 1980)

23 What difference do it make if the thing you scared of is real or not?

Toni Morrison (b. 1931) US novelist. *Song of Solomon* (1977)

24 I fear God, dear Abner, and I have no other fear.

Racine (1639–99) French playwright. *Athalie* (1691), Act 1, Scene 1

25 Of all the passions fear weakens judgment most.

Cardinal de Retz (1613–79) French ecclesiastic and politician. *Mémoires* (1717)

26 Let me assert my firm belief that the only thing we have to fear is fear itself.

Franklin D. Roosevelt (1882–1945) US president. March 4, 1933. First inaugural address, *Public Papers* (1938), vol. 2

27 He who pretends to look on death without fear lies. All men are afraid of dying, this is the great law of sentient beings, without which the entire human species would soon be destroyed.

Jean-Jacques Rousseau (1712–78) French philosopher and writer. *Julie ou la Nouvelle Héloïse* (1760)

28 Fear is of being in the world whereas anguish is anguish before myself.

Jean-Paul Sartre (1905–80) French philosopher, playwright, and novelist. *Being and Nothingness* (1943)

29 CHARMIAN In time we hate that which we often fear.

William Shakespeare (1564–1616) English poet and playwright. *Antony and Cleopatra* (1606–07), Act 1, Scene 3

30 LADY MACBETH Yet do I fear thy nature;
It is too full o' th' milk of human kindness
To catch the nearest way.

William Shakespeare (1564–1616) English poet and playwright. *Macbeth* (1606), Act 1, Scene 5

31 MACBETH The devil damn thee black, thou cream-faced loon!
Where gott'st thou that goose look?

William Shakespeare (1564–1616) English poet and playwright. *Macbeth* (1606), Act 5, Scene 3

32 KING RICHARD III By the apostle Paul, shadows to-night
Have struck more terror to the soul of Richard
Than can the substance of ten thousand soldiers.

William Shakespeare (1564–1616) English poet and playwright. *Richard III* (1591), Act 5, Scene 3

33 Her own mother lived the latter years of her life in the horrible suspicion that electricity was dripping invisibly all over the house.

James Thurber (1894–1961) US writer, cartoonist, and humorist. *My Life and Hard Times* (1933), ch. 2

34 Fear lent wings to his feet.

Virgil (70–19 BC) Roman poet. *Aeneid* (29–19 BC), bk. 8

35 Awe is composed of reverence and dread. I often think that people today have nothing left but the dread.

Christa Wolf (b. 1929) German writer. 1983. *Cassandra. A Novel and Four Essays* (Jan van Heurck, tr.; 1984)

36 The fear which we get from reading ghost stories of the supernatural is a refined and spiritualized essence of fear.

Virginia Woolf (1882–1941) British novelist and critic. Referring to Dorothy Scarborough's *The Supernatural in Modern English Fiction* (1917). Review, *The Supernatural in Fiction* (1918)

Femininity

see **Sexuality**, **Women**

Feminism

see **Women's Rights**

Festivals

see also **The Arts**, **Music**, **Parties**

1 The drunkards they are wading,
The punks and chapmen trading;
Who'd see the Fair without his lading?

Ben Jonson (1572–1637) English playwright and poet. *Batholomew Fair* (1614), Act 2, Scene 1

2 You must wake and call me early, call me early, mother dear;
To-morrow 'ill be the happiest time of all the glad New-year,

Of all the glad New-year, mother, the maddest merriest day;
For I'm to be Queen o' the May, mother, I'm to be Queen o' the May.

Alfred Tennyson (1809–92) British poet. 'The May Queen', *Poems* (1832), st. 1

Fiction

see also **Books**, **Fantasy**, **Literature**, **Storytelling**

1 We live in a world ruled by fictions of every kind—mass-merchandizing, advertising, the pre-empting of any original response to experience by the television screen. We live inside an enormous novel. It is now less and less necessary for the writer to invent the fictional content of his novel . . . the writer's task is to invent reality.

J. G. Ballard (b. 1930) Chinese-born British writer. 1995. *Crash* (1995 edition), Introduction

2 There is no longer any such thing as fiction or non-fiction; there's only narrative.

E. L. Doctorow (b. 1931) US novelist. Quoted in *New York Times Book Review* (1988)

3 Good fiction is made of that which is real, and reality is difficult to come by.

Ralph Ellison (1914–94) US writer, jazz musician, and photographer. *Shadow and Act* (1964), Introduction

4 There is no more beautiful mission than to create the free novel, than to fabricate a world that we will never reach, regardless of how long we live!

Ramón Gómez de la Serna (1888–1963) Spanish novelist. *Ismos* (1931)

5 If fiction is the suprareal spirit of the imagination, then poetry is the ultimate fiction.

Nadine Gordimer (b. 1923) South African novelist. *Living in Hope and History* (1999)

6 If we change the stories we live by, quite possibly we change our lives.

Ben Okri (b. 1959) Nigerian novelist, short-story writer, and poet. *A Way of Being Free* (1997)

7 Contentment and fulfilment don't make for very good fiction.

Anthony Trollope (1815–82) British novelist. Attrib. *Times* (June 25, 1994)

8 Religious cultures produce poetry and theatre but only rarely great novels. Fiction is an art of societies where faith is experiencing a certain crisis, *where one needs to believe something*.

Mario Vargas Llosa (b. 1936) Peruvian writer. 'The Truth of Lies' (1989)

9 Fiction is indispensable for mankind . . . everyone needs to incorporate into his real life a fictional life, some kind of lie that by some mechanism or other he transforms the truth.

Mario Vargas Llosa (b. 1936) Peruvian writer. *A Writer's Reality* (1990)

Fighting

see also **Aggression**, **Conflict**, **Violence**, **War**

1 'You know', he said very gravely, 'it's one of the most serious things that can possibly happen to one in a battle—to get one's head cut off'.

Lewis Carroll (1832–98) British writer and mathematician. The White Knight. *Through the Looking-Glass and What Alice Found There* (1871), ch. 4

2   'Tis better to have fought and lost,
    Than never to have fought at all.
    Arthur Hugh Clough (1819–61) British poet. A parody of Tennyson's
    ''Tis better to have loved and lost'. 'Peschiera' (1854)

3   Everywhere I hear the sound of marching,
    charging feet, boy.
    'Cause summer's here and the time is right for
    fighting in the street.
    Mick Jagger (b. 1943) British rock musician and songwriter. Song lyric.
    'Street Fighting Man' (co-written with Keith Richards; 1968)

4   Punches did not often hurt in a fight, but there
    came a point in following hours when you
    descended into your punishment. Pain would
    begin; a slow exploration of the damage done.
    Norman Mailer (b. 1923) US novelist and journalist. 'The Siege of
    Chicago', Miami and the Siege of Chicago (1968)

5   There are not fifty ways of fighting, there's only
    one, and that's to win. Neither revolution nor
    war consists in doing what one pleases.
    André Malraux (1901–76) French writer and statesman. L'Espoir (1938)

6   Our swords shall play the orators for us.
    Christopher Marlowe (1564–93) English playwright and poet.
    Tamburlaine the Great (1587?), Act 1, Scene 2, l. 132

7   Fighting is like champagne. It goes to the heads
    of cowards as quickly as of heroes.
    Margaret Mitchell (1900–49) US novelist. Said by Ashley Wilkes.
    Gone with the Wind (1936), ch. 31

8   OTHELLO Keep up your bright swords, for the
    dew will rust them.
    William Shakespeare (1564–1616) English poet and playwright. Othello
    (1602–04), Act 1, Scene 2

Films

see also **Acting and Actors, The Arts, Hollywood, Television**

1   The minute frames of celluloid coined by its
    machines are currency of excellent circulation
    among the children of every corner of the Earth;
    the only currency universally accepted.
    Francisco Ayala (b. 1906) Spanish writer. Referring to cinema.
    Investigation into the Cinema (1929)

2   Movies are the repository of myth.Therein lies
    their power. An alternative history, that of
    human psyche, is contained and unfolded in the
    old stories and tales. Film carries on this
    tradition.
    John Boorman (b. 1933) British film director. Money into Light: The
    Emerald Forest—a Diary (1985)

3   Movie-making is the process of turning money
    into light. All they have at the end of the day is
    images flickering on a wall.
    John Boorman (b. 1933) British film director. Quoted in The Oxford
    Book of Money (Kevin Jackson, ed.; 1995)

4   A film is a petrified fountain of thought.
    Jean Cocteau (1889–1963) French film director, novelist, and playwright.
    Esquire (February 1961)

5   It's like I'm at a poker table with five guys. And
    they're all betting two or three thousand dollars
    a hand, and I've got about eighty-seven cents in
    front of me. So I'm always having to take off my
    shirt and bet my pants. Because I want to be in
    the game. I want to play.
    Francis Ford Coppola (b. 1939) US film director, producer, and
    screenwriter. Quoted in Francis Ford Coppola: A Film-Maker's
    Life (Michael Schumacher; 1999)

6   When you start you want to make the greatest
    film in the world, but when you get into it, you
    just want to get it done, let it be passable and
    not embarrassing.
    Francis Ford Coppola (b. 1939) US film director, producer, and
    screenwriter. Quoted in Francis Ford Coppola: A Film-Maker's
    Life (Michael Schumacher; 1999)

7   All films are subversive.
    David Cronenberg (b. 1943) Canadian filmmaker. Interview, French
    television (1989), quoted in Chambers Film Quotes (Tony
    Crawley, ed.; 1991)

8   Every time I make a picture the critics' estimate
    of American public taste goes down ten percent.
    Cecil B. De Mille (1881–1959) US film producer and director. Halliwell's
    Filmgoer's and Video Viewer's Companion (Leslie Halliwell;
    1984)

9   I always direct the same film. I can't distinguish
    one from the other.
    Federico Fellini (1920–93) Italian film director. Quoted in Halliwell's
    Filmgoer's Companion (Leslie Halliwell; 1993)

10 I don't care for modern films. Cars crashing over
    cliffs and close-ups of people's feet.
    Lillian Gish (1893–1993) US actor. Attrib.

11 The dream of the Nouvelle Vague is to make
    Spartacus in Hollywood on a ten million dollar
    budget.
    Jean-Luc Godard (b. 1930) French film director. Cahiers du Cinéma
    (December 1962)

12 Photography is truth. And cinema is truth
    twenty-four times a second.
    Jean-Luc Godard (b. 1930) French film director. Le Petit Soldat (1960)

13 I like a film to have a beginning, a middle, and
    an end, but not necessarily in that order.
    Jean-Luc Godard (b. 1930) French film director. Attrib. Time
    (September 14, 1981)

14 A wide screen just makes a bad film twice as
    bad.
    Samuel Goldwyn (1882–1974) Polish-born US film producer. Remark
    (1956)

15 The cinema is not a slice of life but a piece of
    cake.
    Alfred Hitchcock (1899–1980) British-born US film director. Sunday
    Times (March 6, 1977)

16 There are two kinds of directors—allies and
    judges.
    John Hurt (b. 1940) British actor. Radio Times (1971), quoted in
    Chambers Film Quotes (Tony Crawley, ed.; 1991)

17 The directing of a picture involves coming out of
    your individual loneliness and taking a
    controlling part in putting together a small
    world.
    John Huston (1906–87) US film director and actor. New York Journal
    (March 31, 1960)

18 A work of art doesn't dare you to realize it. It
    germinates and gestates by itself.
    John Huston (1906–87) US film director and actor. Reply to a tribute
    from the Directors' Guild of America. Variety (April 26,
    1982)

19 The cinema, like the detective story, makes it
    possible to experience without danger all the
    excitement, passion and desirousness which must
    be suppressed in a humanitarian ordering of
    society.
    Carl Gustav Jung (1875–1961) Swiss psychoanalyst. Attrib.

20 Good movies make you care, make you believe in possibilities again.

Pauline Kael (1919–2001) US film critic. *Going Steady* (1970)

21 I can understand Fellini and most of the others who build streets, houses and even artificial seas in the studio: in this way not so many people get to see the shameful and insignificant job of directing.

Krzysztof Kieslowski (1941–96) Polish film director. Referring to Federico Fellini. *Kieslowski on Kieslowski* (1993), Epigraph

22 The very meaninglessness of life forces man to create his own meaning. If it can be written or thought, it can be filmed.

Stanley Kubrick (1928–99) US film director. *Halliwell's Filmgoer's and Video Viewer's Companion* (1999)

23 For me film has to be close to music. If you're not close to music, it's very difficult to believe you could structure a whole film. I don't know any good director who does not have a good ear.

Emir Kusturica (b. 1955) Bosnian filmmaker. Interview, *Sight and Sound* (December 1997)

24 The producer must be a prophet and a general, a diplomat and a peacemaker, a miser and a spendthrift. He must have vision tempered by hindsight, daring governed by caution, the patience of a saint, and the iron of a Cromwell.

Jesse L. Lasky (1880–1958) US film producer. Attrib.

25 Traditionally British Cinema hasn't developed the expectation that there will be ideas in films. If you're interested in ideas, you don't have to go to the cinema here—British Cinema is modelled on American movies and West End Theatre.

Ken Loach (b. 1936) British film and television director. *Stills* (June 1986), quoted in *Take Ten Contemporary British Film Makers* (Jonathon Hacker and David Price; 1991)

26 A novelist sits over his work like a god, but he knows he's a particularly minor god. Whereas a director making a small movie is a bona fide general of a small army.

Norman Mailer (b. 1923) US novelist and journalist. *Tough Guys Don't Dance* publicity release (1987), quoted in *Chambers Film Quotes* (Tony Crawley, ed.; 1991)

27 A good film script should be able to do completely without dialogue.

David Mamet (b. 1947) US writer and film director. *Independent* (November 11, 1988)

28 The immense popularity of American movies abroad demonstrates that Europe is the unfinished negative of which America is the proof.

Mary McCarthy (1912–89) US writer. 'America the Beautiful', *On the Contrary* (1961)

29 Film throws up an enormous amount of dust and heat and noise, urgent meetings and so on, which have nothing to do with making a film, but to do with people who are not creatively involved guarding their investments. I suppose it's what you should expect when people are spending the GNP of small countries to make other people less bored for 100 minutes.

Ian McEwan (b. 1948) British writer. *Independent* (August 19, 1993)

30 What's history going to say about the movies? All those rows of seats facing a blank screen? Crazy!

Robert Mitchum (1917–97) US film actor. Attrib.

31 Of course all films are surrealist. They are making something that looks like the real world but isn't.

Michael Powell (1905–90) British filmmaker. Quoted in *Halliwell's Filmgoer's Companion* (Leslie Halliwell; 1993)

32 The medium is too powerful and important an influence on the way we live—the way we see ourselves—to be left solely to the tyranny of the box-office or reduced to the sum of the lowest common denominator of public taste.

David Puttnam (b. 1941) British film producer. 1989. Attrib.

33 Movies are an inherently stupid art form that often relies on scams, tricks, stunts, gambits, ploys, ruses, or gags that are logically or physically impossible, and often both.

Joe Queenan, US journalist and writer. 'Don't Try This at Home', *If You're Talking to Me Your Career Must Be in Trouble* (1994)

34 A film must be alive. When this happens it smashes, devours, pulverizes any synopsis, plot, story. It speaks, talks and explains itself. It constantly changes itself, its characters weave in and out of the screen. Their performance is different at each screening.

Francisco Regueiro (b. 1934) Spanish filmmaker. Remark, Cannes Film Festival (May 1985), quoted in *Chambers Film Quotes* (Tony Crawley, ed.; 1991)

35 A director makes only one film in his life. Then he breaks it into pieces and makes it again.

Jean Renoir (1894–1979) French film director. Quoted in *Halliwell's Filmgoer's Companion* (Leslie Halliwell; 1993)

36 Making a movie is like going down a mine— once you've started you bid a metaphorical goodbye to the daylight and the outside world for the duration.

John Schlesinger (b. 1926) British film director. Attrib.

37 Screenplays are not works of art. They are invitations to others to collaborate on a work of art.

Paul Schrader (b. 1946) US film director, screenwriter, and actor. Quoted in *Writers in Hollywood 1915–51* (Ian Hamilton; 1990), Preface

38 I compare the great film with a horse race in which every one of the horses finishes at the wire in a dead heat . . . writer, director, cinematographer, and all the crew . . . Too often the victory is accorded to the director.

Budd Schulberg (b. 1914) US novelist, screenwriter, and journalist. Interview, *Cineaste* (1981)

39 I always tell the younger film-makers and students: Do it like the painters used to . . . Study the old masters. Enrich your palette. Expand the canvas. There's always so much more to learn.

Martin Scorsese (b. 1942) US filmmaker. *Scorsese: A Personal Journey Through American Movies* (1997)

40 I don't really see a conflict between the church and the movies, the sacred and the profane . . . there are major differences, but I could also see great similarities . . . Both are places for people to come together and share.

Martin Scorsese (b. 1942) US filmmaker. *Scorsese: A Personal Journey Through American Movies* (1997)

41 Cinema's a matter of what's in the frame and what's out.

Martin Scorsese (b. 1942) US filmmaker. Attrib.

42 The trouble, Mr. Goldwyn, is that you are only interested in art and I am only interested in money.

George Bernard Shaw (1856–1950) Irish playwright. Turning down Samuel Goldwyn's offer to buy the screen rights of his plays. Quoted in *The Great Goldwyn* (Alva Johnson; 1937), ch. 3

43 Collaboration—that's the word producers use. That means, don't forget to kiss ass from beginning to end.

Sam Shepard (b. 1943) US playwright and film actor. *Newsweek* (November 11, 1985), quoted in *Chambers Film Quotes* (Tony Crawley, ed.; 1991)

44 The most expensive habit in the world is celluloid, not heroin, and I need a fix every two years.

Steven Spielberg (b. 1947) US film director. *OM* (December 1984)

45 Movies for me are a heightened reality. Making reality fun to live with, as opposed to something you run from and protect yourself from.

Steven Spielberg (b. 1947) US film director. 1978. Attrib.

46 Not a historical document, but a metaphorical truth that represents a decade of aggression, a culture that worships aggression and makes money from it.

Oliver Stone (b. 1946) US film director and screenwriter. Referring to his film *Natural Born Killers* (1994). *Independent* (February 21, 1995)

47 All along I've been trying to express what I really am through light.

Vittorio Storaro (b. 1940) Italian cinematographer. Interview, *Projections 6* (John Boorman and Walter Donohue, eds.; 1996)

48 Take that black box away. I can't act in front of it.

Herbert Beerbohm Tree (1853–1917) British actor and theatrical impresario. Referring to the presence of the camera while performing in a silent film. Remark (1916), quoted in *Hollywood: The Pioneers* (Kevin Brownlow; 1979)

49 To make a film is to improve on life, to arrange it to suit oneself . . . to construct something which is at once a new toy and a vase in which one can arrange in a permanent way the ideas one feels in the morning.

François Truffaut (1932–84) French film director and screenwriter. Quoted in *Halliwell's Filmgoer's Companion* (Leslie Halliwell; 1993)

50 It's the biggest electric train set a boy ever had.

Orson Welles (1915–85) US actor, director, producer, and writer. Referring to the Radio-Keith-Orpheum (RKO) studios. Quoted in *The Fabulous Orson Welles* (Peter Noble; 1956), ch. 7

51 It is my conviction that a film has to be preceded by a dream, either a real dream of the sort that you wake up and remember, or a daydream.

Wim Wenders (b. 1945) German filmmaker. *The Act of Seeing* (1988)

52 There have always been . . . two kinds of cinema: the purely industrial kind, no different than say the car industry, and the other sort with the blank sheet of paper, or the blank screen in the morning.

Wim Wenders (b. 1945) German filmmaker. *The Act of Seeing* (1988)

53 I have ten commandments. The first nine are, thou shalt not bore. The tenth is, thou shalt have right of final cut.

Billy Wilder (1906–2002) Austrian-born US film director and screenwriter. Attrib.

Fire

see also **Danger**

1 Every spark adds to the fire.

Anonymous. US proverb.

2 All things, oh priests, are on fire . . . The eye is on fire; forms are on fire; eye-consciousness on fire; impressions received by the eye are on fire.

Buddha (563?–483? BC) Nepalese-born founder of Buddhism. *The Fire Sermon* (528? BC)

3 I am ashes where once I was fire.

Lord Byron (1788–1824) British poet. 'To the Countess of Blessington' (1823)

4 This fatal night about ten, began that deplorable fire near Fish Street in London . . . all the sky were of a fiery aspect, like the top of a burning Oven, and the light seen above 40 miles round about for many nights.

John Evelyn (1620–1706) English diarist. The Fire of London (September 2–5, 1666) began in a bakehouse in Pudding Lane and spread to two thirds of the city. *Diary* (September 2–3, 1666)

5 Big fires flare up in a wind, but little ones are blown out unless they are carried in under cover.

Saint Francis de Sales (1567–1622) French churchman and writer. *Introduction to The Devout Life* (1609), pt. 3, ch. 34

6 O delicate walker, babbler, dialectician Fire, O enemy and image of ourselves.

Louis MacNeice (1907–63) Irish-born British poet. November 1942. Referring to the London Blitz. 'Brother Fire', *The Collected Poems of Louis MacNeice* (E. R. Dodds, ed.; 1966)

7 A man may surely be allowed to take a glass of wine by his own fireside.

Richard Brinsley Sheridan (1751–1816) Irish-born British playwright and politician. February 24, 1809. As he sat in a coffeehouse watching his Drury Lane Theatre burn down. Quoted in *Memoirs of the Life of the Rt. Hon. Richard Brinsley Sheridan* (T. Moore; 1825), vol. 2

First Lines

see also **Books**

1 If I'm out of my mind, it's all right with me, thought Moses Herzog.

Saul Bellow (b. 1915) Canadian-born US writer. Opening words. *Herzog* (1964)

2 Everything has already begun before, the first line of the first page of every novel refers to something that has already happened outside the book.

Italo Calvino (1923–85) Cuban-born Italian novelist and short-story writer. *If on a Winter's Night a Traveller* (William Weaver, tr.; 1979)

3 It was the best of times, it was the worst of times, it was the age of wisdom, it was the age of foolishness, it was the epoch of belief, it was the epoch of incredulity, it was the season of Light, it was the season of Darkness, it was the spring of hope, it was the winter of despair, we had everything before us, we had nothing before us, we were all going direct to Heaven, we were all going direct the other way.

Charles Dickens (1812–70) British novelist. Opening words. *A Tale of Two Cities* (1859), bk.1, ch.1

4 Last night I dreamt I went to Manderley again.

Daphne du Maurier (1907–89) British writer. Opening words. *Rebecca* (1938), ch. 1

5   Many years later, as he faced the firing squad, Colonel Aureliano Buendía was to remember that distant afternoon when his father took him to discover ice.

Gabriel García Márquez (b. 1928) Colombian novelist. Opening words. *One Hundred Years of Solitude* (1967)

6   Lolita, light of my life, fire of my loins. My sin, my Soul.

Vladimir Nabokov (1899–1977) Russian-born US novelist, poet, and critic. Opening words. *Lolita* (1955), ch. 1

7   It was a bright cold day in April and the clocks were striking thirteen.

George Orwell (1903–50) British writer. Opening words. *Nineteen Eighty-Four* (1949), pt. 1, ch. 1

8   I shall tell you a tale of four little rabbits whose names were Flopsy, Mopsy, Cottontail and Peter.

Beatrix Potter (1866–1943) British children's writer and illustrator. 1900. Opening words. *The Tale of Peter Rabbit* (1900 edition)

9   If you really want to hear about it, the first thing you'll probably want to know is where I was born and what my lousy childhood was like, and how my parents were occupied and all before they had me, and all that David Copperfield kind of crap.

J. D. Salinger (b. 1919) US novelist. Opening words. *The Catcher in the Rye* (1951), ch. 1

10 A long time ago in a galaxy far, far away.

Star Wars, US film series. Opening words. *Star Wars* (George Lucas; 1977)

11 'They order', said I, 'this matter better in France'.

Laurence Sterne (1713–68) Irish-born British writer and clergyman. Opening words. *A Sentimental Journey Through France and Italy* (1768)

12 In a hole in the ground there lived a hobbit.

J. R. R. Tolkien (1892–1973) South African-born British scholar, philologist, and writer. Opening words. *The Hobbit* (1937), ch. 1

Flattery

see also **Compliments, Praise, Sycophancy**

1   It is happy for you that you possess the talent of flattering with delicacy. May I ask whether these pleasing attentions proceed from the impulse of the moment, or are the result of previous study?

Jane Austen (1775–1817) British novelist. *Pride and Prejudice* (1813), ch. 14

2   The flattery of posterity is not worth much more than contemporary flattery, which is worth nothing.

Jorge Luis Borges (1899–1986) Argentinian writer and poet. *Dreamtigers* (Mildred Boyer, ed.; 1964)

3   Remember Mary Archer in the witness box. Your vision of her will probably never disappear. Has she elegance? Has she fragrance? Would she have—without the strain of this trial—a radiance?

Bernard Caulfield (1914–94) British judge. Summing up the court case between Jeffrey Archer and the *News of the World*, July 1987. *Times* (July 24, 1987)

4   Every woman is infallibly to be gained by every sort of flattery, and every man by one sort or other.

Lord Chesterfield (1694–1773) English statesman and writer. March 16, 1752. *Letters to his Son* (1774)

5   It is flattering some men to endure them.

George Savile Halifax (1633–95) English statesman. 'Of Company', *Political, Moral and Miscellaneous Thoughts and Reflections* (1750)

6   Madam, before you flatter a man so grossly to his face, you should consider whether or not your flattery is worth his having.

Samuel Johnson (1709–84) British lexicographer and writer. August 1778. Said to Hannah More. Quoted in *Diary and Letters of Madame d'Arblay* (Charlotte Barrett, ed.; 1842–46), vol. 1, ch. 2

7   Be advised that all flatterers live at the expense of those who listen to them.

Jean de La Fontaine (1621–95) French writer and poet. 'Le Corbeau et le Renard', *Fables* (1668), bk. 1

8   Your eyes shine like the pants of my blue serge suit.

Groucho Marx (1895–1977) US comedian and film actor. *The Cocoanuts* (George S. Kaufman and Morrie Ryskind; 1929)

9   A little flattery will support a man through great fatigue.

James Monroe (1758–1831) US president. Attrib.

10 APEMANTUS He that loves to be flattered is worthy o' the flatterer.

William Shakespeare (1564–1616) English poet and playwright. *Timon of Athens* (1607?), Act 1, Scene 1

11 None are more taken in with flattery than the proud, who wish to be the first and are not.

Baruch Spinoza (1632–77) Dutch philosopher and theologian. *Ethics* (1677), pt. 4, Appendix, no. 21

12 I suppose flattery hurts no one, that is, if he doesn't inhale.

Adlai Stevenson (1900–65) US statesman. Television broadcast (March 30, 1952), quoted in *Adlai E. Stevenson* (N. F. Busch; 1952), ch. 5

13 'Tis an old maxim in the schools,
That flattery's the food of fools;
Yet now and then your men of wit
Will condescend to take a bit.

Jonathan Swift (1667–1745) Irish writer and clergyman. 'Cadenus and Vanessa' (1713)

Flirtation

see also **Seduction, Sex**

1   So, I gave her eyes my own eyes to take,
My hand sought hers as in earnest need,
And round she turned for my noble sake,
And gave me herself indeed.

Robert Browning (1812–89) British poet. 'A Light Woman', *Men and Women* (1855)

2   Merely innocent flirtation,
Not quite adultery, but adulteration.

Lord Byron (1788–1824) British poet. *Don Juan* (1819–24), can. 12, st. 63

3   How, like a moth, the simple maid
Still plays about the flame!

John Gay (1685–1732) English poet and playwright. *The Beggar's Opera* (1728), Act 1, Scene 4

4   Flirting is a promise of sexual intercourse without the guarantee.

Milan Kundera (b. 1929) Czech novelist. *The Unbearable Lightness of Being* (1984)

5 I know your feet must be tired 'cuz you been running through my mind *all* day!

Will Smith (b. 1968) US singer and actor. As Will, the Fresh Prince of Bel-Air. 'That's No Lady, That's My Cousin', *The Fresh Prince of Bel-Air* (1995)

6 I always did like a man in uniform. And that one fits you grand. Why don't you come up sometime and see me?

Mae West (1892–1980) US actor and comedian. Often misquoted as 'Come up and see me some time'. *She Done Him Wrong* (1933)

7 The amount of women in London who flirt with their own husbands is perfectly scandalous. It looks so bad. It is simply washing one's clean linen in public.

Oscar Wilde (1854–1900) Irish poet, playwright, and wit. *The Importance of Being Earnest* (1895), Act 1

8 A woman will flirt with anyone in the world as long as other people are looking on.

Oscar Wilde (1854–1900) Irish poet, playwright, and wit. *The Picture of Dorian Gray* (1891)

Flowers

see also **Beauty**, **Gardens**, **Nature**

1 Alas, Alack
Oh, no man knows
Through what wild centuries
Roves back the rose.

Walter de la Mare (1873–1956) British poet and novelist. 'All That's Past', *The Listeners* (1912)

2 Roses at first were white,
Till they co'd not agree,
Whether my Sappho's breast,
Or they more white sho'd be.

Robert Herrick (1591–1674) English poet. 'How Roses Came Red', *Hesperides* (1648), st. 1

3 Sudden a thought came like a full-blown rose,
Flushing his brow, and in his pained heart
Made purple riot.

John Keats (1795–1821) English poet. 'The Eve of Saint Agnes' (1820), st. 16

4 Their smiles,
Wan as primroses gather'd at midnight
By chilly finger'd spring.

John Keats (1795–1821) English poet. *Endymion* (1818), bk. 4, ll. 969–971

5 Good God, I forgot the violets!

Walter Savage Landor (1775–1864) British poet and writer. Having thrown his cook out of an open window on to the flowerbed below. Quoted in *The Frank Muir Book: An Irreverent Companion to Social History* (Frank Muir; 1976)

6 When roses are fresh, they are concerned little or not at all with man's anger; but if they are dying they will vex the human soul at the slightest provocation.

Joaquim Maria Machado de Assis (1839–1908) Brazilian novelist and short-story writer. *Philosopher or Dog?* (Clotilde Wilson, tr.; 1892)

7 And I will make thee beds of roses
And a thousand fragrant posies.

Christopher Marlowe (1564–93) English playwright and poet. 'The Passionate Shepherd to his Love' (1599), st. 3, ll. 1–2

8 The flowers anew, returning seasons bring!
But beauty faded has no second spring.

Ambrose Philips (1674?–1749) English poet, playwright, and politician. 'Lobbin', *The First Pastoral* (1708), l. 47

9 I once thought that orchid could be steadfast:
it bore me no fruit, it was all show.
Forsaking its beauty, it followed the common;
it wrongly is ranked in the hosts of sweet scent.

Qu Yuan (343?–289 BC) Chinese poet. 'The Li Sao' (4th–3rd century BC), quoted in *An Anthology of Chinese Literature* (Stephen Owen, tr.; 1996)

10 The rose is fairest when 'tis budding new,
And hope is brightest when it dawns from fears.
The rose is sweetest wash'd with morning dew,
And love is loveliest when embalm'd in tears.

Sir Walter Scott (1771–1832) Scottish novelist. *Lady of the Lake* (1810), can. 3, st. 1

11 Rose is a rose is a rose is a rose.

Gertrude Stein (1874–1946) US writer. *Sacred Emily* (1913)

12 STUDENT (*speaking of the hyacinth*). The bulb is . . . an image of the Cosmos. This is why Buddha sits holding the earth-bulb, his eyes brooding as he watches it grow, outward and upward, transforming itself into a heaven.

August Strindberg (1849–1912) Swedish dramatist. 1907. *The Ghost Sonata* (Elizabeth Sprigge, tr.; 1955)

13 They are for prima donnas or corpses—I am neither.

Arturo Toscanini (1867–1957) Italian conductor. Refusing a floral wreath at the end of a performance. Attrib.

14 Thou unassuming common-place
Of Nature.

William Wordsworth (1770–1850) English poet. 1802. Companion piece to 'To the Daisy' ('In Youth from Rock to Rock I Went'). 'To the Daisy', *Poems in Two Volumes* (1807), vol. 2, ll. 5–6

Flying

see also **Travel**

1 When it comes to flying, I am a nervous passenger but a confident drinker and Valium-swallower.

Martin Amis (b. 1949) British writer. 'Emergency Landing', *Worst Journeys* (Keath Fraser, ed.; 1991)

2 The butterfly, a cabbage-white,
(His honest idiocy of flight)
Will never now, it is too late,
Master the art of flying straight.

Robert Graves (1895–1985) British poet and novelist. 'Flying Crooked', *Robert Graves: Collected Poems* (1975)

3 At a thousand feet we make quick decisions about our loyalties, the other engine might fail.

Paulette Jiles (b. 1943) US-born Canadian poet and writer. 'Night Flight to Attiwapiskat', *Worst Journeys* (Keath Fraser, ed.; 1991)

4 A man with wings large enough and duly attached might learn to overcome the resistance of the air, and conquering it succeed in subjugating it and raise himself upon it.

Leonardo da Vinci (1452–1519) Italian artist, engineer, and inventor. *Notebooks* (1508–18)

5 Oh, I have slipped the surly bonds of earth,
And danced the skies on laughter silvered wings;
Sunward I've climbed and joined the tumbling mirth
Of sun-split clouds and done a hundred things
You have not dreamed of.

John Gillespie Magee (1922–41) British-born US wartime pilot. Quoted by President Ronald Reagan after the 'Challenger' space shuttle disaster, January 28, 1986. 'High Flight' (1941)

6 Thank God men cannot as yet fly and lay waste the sky as well as the earth.

Henry David Thoreau (1817–62) US writer. *Journal* (January 3, 1861), quoted in *The Writings of Henry David Thoreau* (1906)

7 There are only two emotions in a plane: boredom and terror.

Orson Welles (1915–85) US actor, director, producer, and writer. *Observer* (May 12, 1985), 'Sayings of the Week'

8 After these years of experience, I look with amazement on our audacity in attempting flights with a new and untried machine under such circumstances.

Orville Wright (1871–1948) US aviator. Referring to the first successful flight at Kitty Hawk, North Carolina (December 4, 1902). *Flying* (December 1913)

9 Success. Four flights Thursday morning. All against twenty-one-mile wind. Started from level with engine power alone. Average speed through air thirty-one miles. Longest fifty-nine seconds. Inform press. Home Christmas.

Wilbur Wright (1867–1912) US engineer and inventor. Sent from Kitty Hawk, North Carolina, after having successfully completed the world's first powered flights. Telegram to the Reverend Milton Wright (co-written with Orville Wright; December 17, 1903)

Food

see also Cooking, Digestion, Eating, Hunger

1 Food is our common ground, a universal experience.

James Beard (1903–85) US chef and author. *Beard on Food* (1974)

2 Filling her compact & delicious body with chicken paprika, she glanced at me twice.

John Berryman (1914–72) US poet. *The Dream Songs* (1968)

3 Tell me what you eat and I will tell you what you are.

Anthelme Brillat-Savarin (1755–1826) French politician, gastronome, and writer. 'Aphorismes, pour servir de prolégomènes', *Physiologie du Goût* (1825), no. 4

4 In England there are sixty different religions, and only one sauce.

Francesco Caracciolo (1752–99) Neapolitan diplomat and admiral. 18th century. *Notes and Queries* (December 1968)

5 The right diet directs sexual energy into the parts that matter.

Barbara Cartland (1901–2000) British novelist. Remark (January 1981)

6 A couple of flitches of bacon are worth fifty thousand Methodist sermons and religious tracts. They are great softeners of temper and promoters of domestic harmony.

William Cobbett (1763–1835) British writer, journalist, and reformer. *Cottage Economy* (1821)

7 A highly geological home-made cake.

Charles Dickens (1812–70) British novelist. *Martin Chuzzlewit* (1844), ch.5

8 Bouillabaisse is only good because cooked by the French, who, if they cared to try, could produce an excellent and nutritious substitute out of cigar stumps and empty matchboxes.

Norman Douglas (1868–1952) British writer. 'Rain on the Hills', *Siren Land* (1911)

9 Grasshoppers and other members of the locust family, for example, are exceptionally nutritious food. Merely a handful provides the daily allowance of vitamin A, as well as protein, carbohydrate, and fat.

Peter Farb (1929–80) US anthropologist and writer. *Consuming Passions: the Anthropology of Eating* (co-written with George Armelagos; 1980)

10 The way to a man's heart is through his stomach.

Fanny Fern (1811–72) US writer. *Fern Leaves* (1853)

11 Food is the beginning of wisdom. The first condition of putting anything into your head and heart, is to put something into your stomach.

Ludwig Andreas Feuerbach (1804–72) German philosopher. Quoted in *From Hegel to Marx* (Sidney Hook; 1936)

12 A census taker once tried to test me. I ate his liver with some fava beans and a nice Chianti.

Anthony Hopkins (b. 1937) Welsh stage and film actor. As the cannibalistic serial killer Hannibal Lecter in the film, based on Thomas Harris's bestseller *The Silence of the Lambs* (1988). *The Silence of the Lambs* (Ted Tally; 1990)

13 If there's one thing above all a vulture can't stand, it's a glass eye.

Frank McKinney Hubbard (1868–1930) US caricaturist. Attrib.

14 I verily believe that the earth in one year produces enough food to last for thirty. Why, then, have we not enough?

Richard Jefferies (1848–87) British naturalist and writer. *The Story of My Heart* (1883)

15 A cucumber should be well sliced, and dressed with pepper and vinegar, and then thrown out, as good for nothing.

Samuel Johnson (1709–84) British lexicographer and writer. October 5, 1773. Quoted in *Journal of a Tour to the Hebrides* (James Boswell; 1785)

16 Mr Leopold Bloom ate with relish the inner organs of beasts and fowls.

James Joyce (1882–1941) Irish writer. *Ulysses* (1922)

17 Sweet corn was our family's weakness. We were prepared to resist atheistic Communism, immoral Hollywood, hard liquor, gambling and dancing, smoking, fornication, but if Satan had come around with sweet corn, we at least would have listened to what he had to say.

Garrison Keillor (b. 1942) US writer and broadcaster. 1988. *Leaving Home* (1988 edition), Foreword

18 I hate a man who swallows it, affecting not to know what he is eating. I suspect his taste in higher matters.

Charles Lamb (1775–1834) British essayist. Referring to food. 'Grace before Meat', *Essays of Elia* (1823)

19 Food is an important part of a balanced diet.

Fran Lebowitz (b. 1951?) US writer and columnist. *Metropolitan Life* (1978)

20 Thou canst not serve both cod and salmon.

Ada Leverson (1862–1933) British writer and journalist. Reply when offered a choice of fish at dinner. Quoted in *Times* (November 7, 1970)

21 The southern Chinese . . . will eat almost anything . . . Southerners themselves tell the story about the Indian and the Cantonese confronted by a creature from outer space: the Indian falls to his knees and begins to worship it, while the Chinese searches his memory for a suitable recipe.

Paul Levy (b. 1941) British author and broadcaster. *Out to Lunch* (1986)

22 The Chinese do not draw any distinction between food and medicine.

Lin Yutang (1895–1976) Chinese-born writer and philologist. *The Importance of Living* (1937)

23 This piece of cod passes all understanding.

Edwin Landseer Lutyens (1869–1944) British architect. Comment made in a restaurant. Attrib.

24 The King asked
The Queen, and
The Queen asked
The Dairymaid:
'Could we have some butter for
The Royal slice of bread?'

A. A. Milne (1882–1956) British writer. 'The King's Breakfast', *When We Were Very Young* (1924)

25 I live on good soup, not fine words.

Molière (1622–73) French playwright. *Les Femmes Savantes* (1672), Act 2, Scene 7

26 The average pound of food in America travels 1,200 miles before it reaches the kitchen table, and the total transport distances of the ingredients in a pot of German yoghurt totals over 6,000 miles.

Helena Norberg-Hodge, British ecologist and author. 'Globalisation Versus Community', *The Future of Progress* (Helena Norberg-Hodge, Peter Goering, and Steven Gorelick, eds.; 1992)

27 Many times . . . during my twenty-three years of Arctic exploration, I have thanked God for even a bite of raw dog.

Robert Edwin Peary (1856–1920) US explorer. *The North Pole* (1910), ch. 9

28 Every cuisine tells a story. Jewish food tells the story of an uprooted, migrating people and their vanished worlds.

Claudia Roden (b. 1937) Egyptian-born British cookery writer. *The Book of Jewish Food* (1997)

29 A man of my spiritual intensity does not eat corpses.

George Bernard Shaw (1856–1950) Irish playwright. Attrib.

30 I have been assured by a very knowing American of my acquaintance in London, that a young healthy child well nursed is at a year old a most delicious, nourishing, and wholesome food, whether stewed, roasted, baked, or boiled, and I make no doubt that it will equally serve in a fricassee, or a ragout.

Jonathan Swift (1667–1745) Irish writer and clergyman. 'A Modest Proposal for Preventing the Children of Ireland from being a Burden to their Parents or Country' (1729)

31 He was a bold man that first ate an oyster.

Jonathan Swift (1667–1745) Irish writer and clergyman. *Polite Conversation* (1738), Dialogue 2

32 Cauliflower is nothing but cabbage with a college education.

Mark Twain (1835–1910) US writer and humorist. 'Pudd'nhead Wilson's Calendar', *Pudd'nhead Wilson* (1894), ch. 5

Foolishness

see also **Gullibility, Ignorance, Nonsense, Stupidity**

1 Why should we Always imagine Others to be Fools, Just because they love us?

Ama Ata Aidoo (b. 1942) Ghanaian writer. *Our Sister Killjoy, or Reflections from a Black-eyed Squint* (1977)

2 A fool bolts pleasure, then complains of moral indigestion.

Minna Antrim (1856–1950) US writer. *Naked Truth and Veiled Allusions* (1902)

3 For ye suffer fools gladly, seeing ye yourselves are wise.

Bible. II Corinthians, *King James Bible* (1611), 11:19

4 Answer a fool according to his folly, lest he be wise in his own conceit.

Bible. Proverbs, *King James Bible* (1611), 26:5

5 MAUSOLEUM, n. The final and funniest folly of the rich.

Ambrose Bierce (1842–1914?) US writer and journalist. *The Devil's Dictionary* (1911)

6 A fool always finds a greater fool to admire him.

Nicolas Boileau (1636–1711) French poet and critic. *L'Art Poétique* (1674), pt. 1

7 The world is made up for the most part of fools and knaves, both irreconcilable foes to truth.

Duke of Buckingham (1628–87) English statesman. 'To Mr Clifford On His Humane Reason', quoted in (Dramatic Works; 1715), vol. 2

8 He's a muddle-headed fool, with frequent lucid intervals.

Miguel de Cervantes (1547–1616) Spanish novelist and playwright. Sancho Panza describing Don Quixote. *Don Quixote* (1605–15), pt. 2, ch. 18

9 Who are a little wise the best fools be.

John Donne (1572?–1631) English metaphysical poet and divine. 'The Triple Fool', *Songs and Sonnets* (1635), l. 22

10 I am two fools, I know,
For loving, and for saying so
In whining Poetry.

John Donne (1572?–1631) English metaphysical poet and divine. 'The Triple Fool', *Songs and Sonnets* (1635), ll. 1–3

11 Mix a little foolishness with your serious plans: it's lovely to be silly at the right moment.

Horace (65–8 BC) Roman poet. 23? BC. *Odes* (13? BC), bk. 4, no. 12, l. 27

12 You cannot fashion a wit out of two half-wits.

Neil Kinnock (b. 1942) British politician. *Times* (1983)

13 A knowledgeable fool is a greater fool than an ignorant fool.

Molière (1622–73) French playwright. *Les Femmes Savantes* (1672), Act 4, Scene 3

14 A learned fool is more foolish than an ignorant one.

Molière (1622–73) French playwright. *Les Femmes Savantes* (1672), Act 4, Scene 3

15 There are two kinds of folly, the one madness and the other ignorance.

Plato (428?–347? BC) Greek philosopher. *Timaeus* (4th century BC)

16 The best plan is, as the common proverb has it, to profit by the folly of others.

Pliny the Elder (23?–79) Roman scholar. *Natural History* (77), bk. 28, sect. 31

17 He is a fool who lets slip a bird in the hand for a bird in the bush.

Plutarch (46?–120?) Greek biographer and philosopher. 'Of Garrulity' (1st–2nd century)

18 For fools rush in where angels fear to tread.

Alexander Pope (1688–1744) English poet. *An Essay on Criticism* (1711), l. 625

19 No creature smarts so little as a fool.

Alexander Pope (1688–1744) English poet. *Epistle to Dr. Arbuthnot* (1735), l. 84

20 The follies which a man regrets most in his life are those which he didn't commit when he had the opportunity.

Helen Rowland (1876–1950) US writer, journalist, and humorist. *A Guide to Men* (1922)

21 It takes a woman twenty years to make a man of her son, and another woman twenty minutes to make a fool of him.

Helen Rowland (1876–1950) US writer, journalist, and humorist. *Reflections of a Bachelor Girl* (1909)

22 Thou little thinkest what a little foolery governs the world.

John Selden (1584–1654) English historian, jurist, and politician. 'Pope', *Table Talk* (1689)

23 PUCK Lord, what fools these mortals be!

William Shakespeare (1564–1616) English poet and playwright. *A Midsummer Night's Dream* (1595–96), Act 3, Scene 2

24 SILVIUS If thou rememb'rest not the slightest folly
That ever love did make thee run into,
Thou hast not lov'd.

William Shakespeare (1564–1616) English poet and playwright. Song lyric. *As You Like It* (1599), Act 2, Scene 4

25 HAMLET A knavish speech sleeps in a foolish ear.

William Shakespeare (1564–1616) English poet and playwright. *Hamlet* (1601), Act 4, Scene 2

26 A Fool and his words are soon parted.

William Shenstone (1714–63) British poet. 'On Reserve' (1764)

27 The ultimate result of shielding men from the effects of folly, is to fill the world with fools.

Herbert Spencer (1820–1903) British philosopher. 'State Tamperings with Money and Banks', *Essays* (1891), vol. 3

28 Looking foolish does the spirit good. The need not to look foolish is one of youth's many burdens; as we get older we are exempted from more and more.

John Updike (b. 1932) US writer. *Self-Consciousness: Memoirs* (1989)

Football

see Sports and Games

Forgetting

see also Memory

1 What is not recorded is not remembered.

Benazir Bhutto (b. 1953) Pakistani stateswoman. *Daughter of Destiny* (1989)

2 It's a good deed to forget a poor joke.

Brendan Bracken (1901–58) British newspaper publisher and politician. *Observer* (October 17, 1943), 'Sayings of the Week'

3 We live in a world where amnesia is the most wished-for state. When did history become a bad word?

John Guare (b. 1938) US playwright. *International Herald Tribune* (June 13, 1990)

4 Forgetfulness is an indispensable condition of the memory.

Alfred Jarry (1873–1907) French playwright and poet. 'Toomai et les Éléphants', *Le Périple de la Littérature et de l'Art* (1903)

5 The struggle of man against power is the struggle of memory against forgetting.

Milan Kundera (b. 1929) Czech novelist. *The Book of Laughter and Forgetting* (1982)

6 To endeavour to forget anyone is a certain way of thinking of nothing else.

Jean de La Bruyère (1645–96) French essayist and moralist. *Characters, or the Manners of the Age* (1688)

7 If the first way of evading responsibility is not to recollect at all, the second and most widespread way of silencing the voice of memory is to embellish and streamline one's recollections . . . The operation can be performed on an individual life history, or on the past of a whole nation.

Nadezhda Mandelstam (1899–1980) Russian writer. 1970. *Hope Abandoned* (Max Hayward, tr.; 1972), ch. 18, 'Memory'

8 The richness of life lies in the memories we have forgotten.

Cesare Pavese (1908–50) Italian novelist and poet. February 13, 1940. *This Business of Living: A Diary 1935–50* (1952)

9 I've a grand memory for forgetting, David.

Robert Louis Stevenson (1850–94) Scottish novelist, essayist, and poet. *Kidnapped* (1886), ch. 18

10 There are three things I always forget. Names, faces and—the third I can't remember.

Italo Svevo (1861–1928) Italian writer. Attrib.

11 I can never remember whether it snowed for six days and six nights when I was twelve or whether it snowed for twelve days and twelve nights when I was six.

Dylan Thomas (1914–53) Welsh poet, playwright, and short-story writer. Originally written as a radio script. *A Child's Christmas in Wales* (1945)

Forgiveness

see also Love, Revenge

1 The act of forgiving can never be predicted: it is the only reaction that acts in an unexpected way and thus retains, though being a reaction, something of the original character of action.

Hannah Arendt (1906–75) German-born US philosopher and historian. 'Action', *The Human Condition* (1958), ch. 33

2 Let me say before I go any further that I forgive nobody. I wish them all an atrocious life and then the fires and ice of hell and in the execrable generations to come an honoured name.

Samuel Beckett (1906–89) Irish playwright, novelist, and poet. *Malone Dies* (1951)

3 Then said Jesus, Father, forgive them; for they know not what they do. And they parted his raiment, and cast lots.

Bible. Luke, *King James Bible* (1611), 23:34

4 Reason to rule, but mercy to forgive:
The first is law, the last prerogative.

John Dryden (1631–1700) English poet, playwright, and literary critic. *The Hind and the Panther* (1687), pt. 1, ll. 261–262

5 A worthy man is not mindful of past injuries.

Euripides (480?–406? BC) Greek playwright. *Andromache* (5th century BC), l. 1164

6 I don't hold no grudges more'n five years.

William Kennedy (b. 1928) US screenwriter and novelist. Said by the character Francis Phelan. *Ironweed* (1983)

7   He fainted on his vengefulness, and strove
    To ape the magnanimity of love.
    George Meredith (1828–1909) British novelist and poet. 'Modern Love'
    (1862)

8   If a man should rob me of my money, I can
    forgive him; if a man should shoot at me, I can
    forgive him; if a man should sell me and all my
    family to a slave ship, so that we should pass all
    the rest of our lives in slavery in the West Indies,
    I can forgive him; but if a man takes away the
    character of the people of my country, I never
    can forgive him.
    John Henry Naimbanna (1767–93) Sierra Leonean son of King Naimbanna.
    Quoted in Black Writers in Britain 1760–1890 (Paul Edwards
    and David Dabydeen; 1991)

9   I do not have to forgive my enemies, I have had
    them all shot.
    Ramón María Narváez (1800–68) Spanish general and politician. 1868.
    Said on his deathbed, when asked by a priest if he forgave his
    enemies. Attrib.

10 To err is human; to forgive, divine.
    Alexander Pope (1688–1744) English poet. An Essay on Criticism
    (1711), l. 525

11 DUKE OF VENICE The robb'd that smiles steals
    something from the thief.
    William Shakespeare (1564–1616) English poet and playwright. Othello
    (1602–04), Act 1, Scene 3

12 Beware of the man who does not return your
    blow: he neither forgives you nor allows you to
    forgive yourself.
    George Bernard Shaw (1856–1950) Irish playwright. 'Maxims for
    Revolutionists', Man and Superman (1903)

13 The stupid neither forgive nor forget; the naïve
    forgive and forget; the wise forgive but do not forget.
    Thomas Szasz (b. 1920) Hungarian-born US psychiatrist. 'Personal
    Conduct', The Second Sin (1973)

14 O God, if there is a God, forgive him his sins, if
    there is such a thing as sin.
    Evelyn Waugh (1903–66) British novelist. Brideshead Revisited
    (1945)

Fortune

see Chance, Destiny, Fate

France

see Europe, European Countries

Frankness

see also Honesty, Sincerity, Truth

1   Ramp up my genius, be not retrograde;
    But boldly nominate a spade a spade.
    Ben Jonson (1572–1637) English playwright and poet. The Poetaster
    (1601), Act 5, Scene 1

2   'When I makes tea I makes tea', as old mother
    Grogan said. 'And when I makes water I makes
    water'.
    James Joyce (1882–1941) Irish writer. Ulysses (1922)

3   We only confess our little faults to persuade
    people that we have no large ones.
    François La Rochefoucauld (1613–80) French epigrammatist and moralist.
    Reflections, or Sentences and Moral Maxims (1665), no. 327

4   I maintain that, if everyone knew what others
    said about him, there would not be four friends
    in the world.
    Blaise Pascal (1623–62) French philosopher, mathematician, and physicist.
    Pensées (1669), no. 101

5   A pair of gold earrings for the price of a prawn
    sandwich. The sandwich will last longer.
    Gerald Ratner (b. 1949) British business executive. One of the remarks
    that forced Gerald Ratner to quit as chief executive (1986–92)
    of the Ratner's Group of high street jewellers. Marketing
    (April 27, 1990)

6   The great consolation in life is to say what one
    thinks.
    Voltaire (1694–1778) French writer and philosopher. Letter (1765)

7   On an occasion of this kind it becomes more
    than a moral duty to speak one's mind. It
    becomes a pleasure.
    Oscar Wilde (1854–1900) Irish poet, playwright, and wit. The
    Importance of Being Earnest (1895), Act 2

Freedom

see also Democracy, Free Speech, Liberalism, Liberty

1   Freedom is always somewhere else. It is always
    the freedom one would like to have and never
    the freedom that one has.
    Martin Ahrends (b. 1951) German writer. 'The Great Waiting, or The
    Freedom of the East', New German Critique (Winter 1991)

2   No cause is left but the most ancient of all, the
    one, in fact, that from the beginning of our
    history has determined the very existence of
    politics, the cause of freedom versus tyranny.
    Hannah Arendt (1906–75) German-born US philosopher and historian. On
    Revolution (1963), Introduction

3   Freedom is not something that anybody can be
    given; freedom is something people take and
    people are as free as they want to be.
    James Baldwin (1924–87) US writer and civil rights activist. 'Notes for
    a Hypothetical Novel', Nobody Knows My Name (1961)

4   A man is either free or he is not. There cannot be
    any apprenticeship for freedom.
    Imamu Amiri Baraka (b. 1934) US author, editor, playwright, and political
    activist. 'Tokenism: 300 Years for Five Cents', Home: Social
    Essays (1966)

5   So free we seem, so fettered fast we are!
    Robert Browning (1812–89) British poet. 'Andrea del Sarto', Men
    and Women (1855)

6   For freedom's battle once begun,
    Bequeath'd by bleeding Sire to Son,
    Though baffled oft is ever won.
    Lord Byron (1788–1824) British poet. The Giaour (1813), l. 123

7   I call that mind free which jealously guards its
    intellectual rights and powers, which calls no
    man master, which does not content itself with a
    passive or hereditary faith, which opens itself to
    light whensoever it may come, which receives
    new truth as an angel from heaven.
    William Ellery Channing (1780–1842) US clergyman. Sermon. 'Spiritual
    Freedom' (1830)

8   O God . . . I am free, deliver me from freedom!
    Paul Claudel (1868–1955) French writer and diplomat. 'L'esprit et
    l'eau', Cinq Grandes Odes (1910)

9 The progress of freedom depends more upon the maintenance of peace, the spread of commerce, and the diffusion of education, than upon the labours of cabinets and foreign offices.

Richard Cobden (1804–65) British economist and politician. Speech to Parliament (June 26, 1850)

10 But what is Freedom? Rightly understood, A universal licence to be good.

Hartley Coleridge (1796–1849) British poet. 'Liberty' (1833)

11 Freedom has a thousand charms to show, That slaves, howe'er contented, never know.

William Cowper (1731–1800) British poet. 'Table Talk' (1782), ll. 260–261

12 I only ask to be free. The butterflies are free. Mankind will surely not deny to Harold Skimpole what it concedes to the butterflies!

Charles Dickens (1812–70) British novelist. Said by Harold Skimpole. *Bleak House* (1853), ch. 6

13 The word *freedom* has no meaning; there are and there can be no free beings.

Denis Diderot (1713–84) French encyclopedist and philosopher. Letter to Landois (1756)

14 Freedom is the right to be wrong, not the right to do wrong.

John Diefenbaker (1895–1979) Canadian statesman. Quoted in *Reader's Digest* (September 1979)

15 The right to be let alone is indeed the beginning of all freedom.

William Orville Douglas (1898–1980) US jurist. *An Almanac of Liberty* (1954)

16 He who believes in freedom of the will has never loved and never hated.

Marie von Ebner-Eschenbach (1830–1916) Austrian novelist and poet. Quoted in *The New Quotable Woman* (Elaine Partnow; 1993)

17 By academic freedom I understand the right to search for truth and to publish and teach what one holds to be true. This right implies also a duty: one must not conceal any part of what one has recognized to be true.

Albert Einstein (1879–1955) German-born US physicist. Letter (March 13, 1954)

18 History does not long entrust the care of freedom to the weak or the timid.

Dwight D. Eisenhower (1890–1969) US general and president. Inaugural address, Washington, DC (January 20, 1953)

19 Freedom does not consist in the dream of independence from natural laws, but in the knowledge of these laws, and in the possibility this gives of systematically making them work towards definite ends.

Friedrich Engels (1820–95) German socialist. *Anti-Dühring* (1878)

20 Freedom has never been free.

Medgar Evers (1925–63) US civil rights leader. Speech (June 7, 1963)

21 As with all forms of liberation, of which the liberation of women is only one example, it is easy to suppose in a time of freedom that the darker days of repression can never come again.

Antonia Fraser (b. 1932) British historian. *The Weaker Vessel* (1984), Epilogue

22 Freedom in economic arrangements is itself a component of freedom broadly understood, so economic freedom is an end in itself.

Milton Friedman (b. 1912) US economist. *Capitalism and Freedom* (1962), ch. 1

23 All emancipation is from within. That is to say, real emancipation. As a man thinketh so is he.

Marcus Garvey (1887–1940) Jamaican-born black nationalist leader and publisher. *The Black Man* (June–December 1935)

24 O Freedom, what liberties are taken in thy name!

Daniel George (1890–1967) British writer. A parody of the reputed last words of Madame Roland, a French revolutionary who was guillotined (1793). Remark (1963)

25 Man's innate yearning for freedom can be suppressed but never destroyed.

Vasily Grossman (1905–64) Russian writer. 1960. *Life and Fate* (Robert Chandler, tr.; 1980), pt. 1, ch. 50

26 This freedom, this liberty, this beautiful and terrible thing, needful to man as air, usable as earth.

Robert E. Hayden (1913–80) US poet. 1962. 'Frederick Douglass, a Ballad of Remembrance', *Collected Poems* (1996)

27 The final cause of the World at large, we allege to be the consciousness of its own freedom on the part of Spirit, and ipso facto, the reality of that freedom.

G. W. F. Hegel (1770–1831) German philosopher. *The Philosophy of History* (1832)

28 Freedom is the most-used word of our time. What it is seems obvious to all . . . Yet there is nothing more obscure, more ambiguous, more abused.

Karl Jaspers (1883–1969) German philosopher. *Future of Mankind* (1958)

29 Freedom of religion; freedom of the press, and freedom of person under the protection of the *habeas corpus*, and trial by juries impartially selected. These principles form the bright constellation which has gone before us, and guided our steps through an age of revolution and reformation.

Thomas Jefferson (1743–1826) US president. Inaugural address, Washington, DC (March 4, 1801)

30 Freedom is never voluntarily given up by the oppressor.

Martin Luther King, Jr. (1929–68) US civil rights leader. 1963. He was briefly in prison on civil disorder charges in Birmingham, Alabama. Letter from Birmingham Jail, *History Today* (April 1998), vol. 48

31 Give me your tired, your poor, Your huddled masses yearning to breathe free.

Emma Lazarus (1849–87) US poet. Used as an inscription on the Statue of Liberty, New York City (1886). 'The New Colossus' (1883)

32 Freedom is always and exclusively the freedom for the one who thinks differently.

Rosa Luxemburg (1871–1919) Russian-born German socialist leader and revolutionary. *The Russian Revolution* (1918), sect. 4

33 Many politicians . . . are in the habit of laying it down . . . that no people ought to be free till they are fit to use their freedom. The maxim is worthy of the fool in the old story, who resolved not to go into the water till he had learnt to swim. If men are to wait for liberty till they become wise and good in slavery, they may indeed wait for ever.

Thomas Babington Macaulay (1800–59) British politician, historian, and writer. 1825. 'On Milton', *Essays Contributed to the Edinburgh Review* (1843)

34 There is no easy walk to freedom anywhere and many of us will have to pass through the valley of the shadow of death again and again before we reach the mountain tops of our desires.

Nelson Mandela (b. 1918) South African president and lawyer. September 21, 1953. Adapted from a statement by Nehru. Presidential address to ANC Conference, *The Struggle is My Life* (1990)

35 The freedom flame can never be put down by anybody.

Nelson Mandela (b. 1918) South African president and lawyer. December 31, 1999. Said whilst passing a memorial candle to Thabo Mbeki, his successor as South Africa's president, in a New Year's Eve visit to the prison cell on Robben Island where he had been imprisoned for over 20 years. *Time* (January 1, 2000)

36 I cannot and will not give any undertaking at a time when I, and you, the people, are not free. Your freedom and mine cannot be separated.

Nelson Mandela (b. 1918) South African president and lawyer. Message from prison, read by his daughter to a rally in Soweto. (February 10, 1985)

37 Freedom is a more complex and delicate thing than force. It is not as simple to live under as force is.

Thomas Mann (1875–1955) German writer. Letter (December 1938), quoted in *Letters of Thomas Mann 1889–1955* (Richard Winston and Clara Winston, trs.; 1975)

38 The dagger plunged in the name of Freedom is plunged into the breast of Freedom.

José Martí (1853–95) Cuban writer and patriot. Attrib.

39 None can love freedom heartily, but good men; the rest love not freedom, but licence.

John Milton (1608–74) English writer. *The Tenure of Kings and Magistrates* (1649)

40 Freedom . . . is not an inconsequential chucking of one's weight about, it is the disciplined overcoming of self.

Iris Murdoch (1919–99) Irish-born British novelist and philosopher. *The Sovereignty of Good* (1970)

41 We cannot defend freedom abroad by deserting it at home.

Ed Murrow (1908–65) US journalist and broadcaster. Attrib.

42 The price of freedom can never be too high.

Joshua Nkomo (1917–99) Zimbabwean nationalist leader. *The Story of My Life* (1984)

43 Without discipline true freedom cannot survive.

Kwame Nkrumah (1909–72) Ghanaian president. *The Autobiography of Kwame Nkrumah* (1959)

44 If we are to live our lives in peace and harmony, and if we are to achieve our ambitions of improving the conditions under which we live, we must have both freedom and discipline. For freedom without discipline is anarchy; discipline without freedom is tyranny.

Julius Kambarage Nyerere (1922–99) Tanzanian president. TANU policy paper, October 16, 1968. *Freedom and Development* (1973)

45 Those who expect to reap the blessings of freedom must, like men, undergo the fatigue of supporting it.

Thomas Paine (1737–1809) English writer and political philosopher. *The American Crisis* (September 12, 1777), no. 4

46 We look forward to a world founded upon four essential human freedoms. The first is freedom of speech and expression—everywhere in the world. The second is freedom of every person to worship God in his own way—everywhere in the world. The third is freedom from want—everywhere in the world. The fourth is freedom from fear—anywhere in the world.

Franklin D. Roosevelt (1882–1945) US president. Speech to Congress, *Public Papers* (January 6, 1941), vol. 10

47 Man was born free and everywhere he is in chains.

Jean-Jacques Rousseau (1712–78) French philosopher and writer. *The Social Contract* (1762)

48 Man is condemned to be free.

Jean-Paul Sartre (1905–80) French philosopher, playwright, and novelist. *Existentialism is a Humanism* (1947)

49 Freedom lives only in the realm of dreams,
And in song only blooms the beautiful.

Friedrich von Schiller (1759–1805) German poet, playwright, and historian. *Der Antritt des neuen Jahrhunderts* (1801)

50 We have to believe in free will. We've got no choice.

Isaac Bashevis Singer (1904–91) Polish-born US writer. *Times* (June 21, 1982)

51 If only enlightenment is granted, freedom is almost sure to follow; where enlightenment is little more than three or four years of the three Rs and freedom is freedom from poverty.

Gayatri Spivak (b. 1942) Indian-born US educator and writer. Reversing Immanuel Kant's concept that enlightenment follows freedom, to comment on the situation in rural Bangladesh. 'Thinking Academic Freedom in Gendered Post-Coloniality' (August 11, 1992)

52 We, for our part, have a first and indispensable need, that of our dignity. Now, there is no dignity without freedom . . . . We prefer freedom in poverty to riches in slavery.

Sékou Touré (1922–84) Guinean president. 1958. *Sékou Touré's Guinea: An Experiment in Nation Building* (Ladipo Adamolekun; 1976)

53 Freedom is an indivisible word. If we want to enjoy it, and fight for it, we must be prepared to extend it to everyone, whether they are rich or poor, whether they agree with us or not, no matter what their race or the color of their skin.

Wendell Lewis Willkie (1892–1944) US politician and lawyer. *One World* (1943), ch. 13

54 Every people should be left free to determine its own policy, its own way of development, unhindered, unthreatened, unafraid, the little along with the great and powerful . . . These are American principles.

Woodrow Wilson (1856–1924) US president. Address to Congress (January 22, 1917)

55 The focal point of all reforms should be human liberation, and the respect for human value and human rights. The free development of each individual is the basis for all social progress.

Xu Wenli (b. 1944) Chinese dissident. 1980. Attrib.

Free Speech

see also **Censorship, Civil Rights, Freedom, Liberty**

1 Go out and speak for the inarticulate and the submerged.

Max Aitken Beaverbrook, Lord (1879–1964) Canadian-born British newspaper owner and politician. Said to Godfrey Winn. Quoted in *Somerset Maugham* (E. Morgan; 1980)

2 What should be said is that Salman has the right to blaspheme, but it is the same citizen's right as anyone at Speakers' Corner.

David Hare (b. 1947) British playwright. Referring to the author Salman Rushdie, whose novel *The Satanic Verses* (1988) was the subject of a *fatwa* (1988) issued by the Ayatollah Khomenei calling for the author's death. *Sunday Times* (February 11, 1990)

3 The most stringent protection of free speech would not protect a man in falsely shouting 'Fire!' in a theater and causing a panic.

Oliver Wendell Holmes, Jr. (1841–1935) US judge. Supreme Court opinion, *Schenck vs. United States* (1919)

4 American freedom consists largely in talking nonsense.

Edgar Watson Howe (1853–1937) US novelist. *Preaching from the Audience* (1926)

5 I have got no further than this: Every man has a right to utter what he thinks truth, and every other man has a right to knock him down for it. Martyrdom is the test.

Samuel Johnson (1709–84) British lexicographer and writer. 1780. Quoted in *Life of Samuel Johnson* (James Boswell; 1791)

6 One of the few remaining freedoms we have is the blank page. No one can prescribe how we should fill it.

James Kelman (b. 1946) Scottish writer. *Guardian* (October 12, 1994)

7 The freedom of the press is one of the greatest bulwarks of liberty, and can never be restrained but by despotic governments.

George Mason (1725–92) US statesman. *Virginia Bill of Rights* (June 12, 1776), Article 1

8 Freedom is the right to tell people what they do not want to hear.

George Orwell (1903–50) British writer. *The Road to Wigan Pier* (1937)

9 I call upon the intellectual community in this country and abroad to stand up for freedom of the imagination, an issue much larger than my book or indeed my life.

Salman Rushdie (b. 1947) Indian-born British novelist. Referring to the *fatwa* issued against his life by Iranian Orthodox Muslims because of the purported blasphemy against Islam contained in his book *The Satanic Verses*. Public statement (February 14, 1989)

10 MILNE No matter how imperfect things are, if you've got a free press everything is correctable, and without it everything is conceivable.
RUTH I'm with you on the free press. It's the newspapers I can't stand.

Tom Stoppard (b. 1937) Czech-born British playwright and screenwriter. *Night and Day* (1978), Act 1

11 We must no longer be afraid of the multifarious views and opinions expressed by the people.

Suharto (b. 1921) Indonesian statesman. Referring to the day his information minister insisted that press controls remain in place. *Straits Times* (September 1, 1990)

12 Freedom of the press in Britain is freedom to print such of the proprietor's prejudices as the advertisers don't object to.

Hannen Swaffer (1879–1962) British journalist. 1928? Quoted in *Swaff* (Tom Driberg; 1974), ch. 2

13 I never approved either the errors of his book, or the trivial truths he so vigorously laid down. I have, however, stoutly taken his side when absurd men have condemned him for these same truths.

Voltaire (1694–1778) French writer and philosopher. Referring to Helvetius's *De L'Esprit*, which was publicly burned in 1758; usually misquoted as 'I disapprove of what you say, but I will defend to the death your right to say it'. 'Man', *Dictionnaire Philosophique* (1764)

14 If you want to find out how much freedom you have, make some kind of explicit sexual statement and wait for it all to crash down around you.

Vivienne Westwood (b. 1941) British fashion designer. Quoted in *Rock 'n' Roll Babylon* (Gary Herman; 1994)

French Revolution

see also **Equality, Liberty, Revolution**

1 The French Revolution is merely the herald of a far greater and much more solemn revolution, which will be the last . . . The hour has come for founding the Republic of Equals, that great refuge open to every man.

François Noël Babeuf (1760–97) French revolutionary. *Conjuration des Égaux* (1796)

2 We didn't make the revolution, the revolution made us.

Georg Büchner (1813–37) German dramatist. Referring to the French Revolution (1789–99). *Danton's Death* (1835), Act 2, Scene 1, quoted in *Complete Plays, Lenz and Other Writings* (John Reddick, tr.; 1993)

3 Make the Revolution a parent of settlement, and not a nursery of future revolutions.

Edmund Burke (1729–97) Irish-born British statesman and political philosopher. *Reflections on the Revolution in France* (1790)

4 Be my brother or I kill you.

Nicolas Chamfort (1741–94) French writer. His interpretation of the revolutionary rallying cry: 'Fraternité ou la mort!' ('Fraternity or death!') 'Notice Historique sur la Vie et les Écrits de Chamfort', *Oeuvres Complètes* (P. R. Anguis, ed.; 1824)

5 From today and from this place there begins a new epoch in the history of the world.

Johann Wolfgang von Goethe (1749–1832) German poet, playwright, and scientist. 1792. On witnessing the victory of the French revolutionary army over invading Prussian forces at the Battle of Valmy (September 1792). Quoted in *The Story of Civilization* (William Durant; 1950–67), vol. 2

6 Nothing.

Louis XVI (1754–93) French monarch. Diary entry on the day the Bastille fell. Diary (July 14, 1789)

7 It is through violence that one must achieve liberty, and the moment has come for us to organize a temporary despotism of liberty to crush the despotism of kings.

Jean Paul Marat (1743–93) French revolutionary politician and journalist. Referring to the French Revolution (1789–99). Jean Paul Marat was one of the chief advocates of violence and dictatorial measures to defend the Revolution. He was assassinated by a young aristocrat, Charlotte Corday, on July 13, 1793. *L'Ami du Peuple* (April 1793)

8 It seems to be the inevitable outcome for man never to be entirely free: everywhere princes head towards despotism, and the people towards servitude.

Jean Paul Marat (1743–93) French revolutionary politician and journalist. *Les Chaînes de l'Esclavage* (1793)

9 No National Assembly ever threatened to be so stormy as that which will decide the fate of the monarchy, and which is gathering in such haste, and with so much distrust on both sides.

Comte de Mirabeau (1749–91) French revolutionary statesman. Remark (December 6, 1788)

10 Freedom! Equality! Brotherhood!

Mottos and Slogans. Motto of the French Revolutionaries, but known to be of earlier origin. (18th century)

11 Maybe it would have been better if neither of us had been born.

Napoleon I (1769–1821) French emperor. Said while looking at the tomb of the philosopher Jean-Jacques Rousseau, whose theories had influenced the French Revolution. Quoted in *The Story of Civilization* (William Durant; 1935), vol. 2

12 What is the will of the people? It is the power of the French.

William Pitt the Younger (1759–1806) British prime minister. Referring to the French Revolution (from 1789), popularly considered to have been effected by the will of the people, which temporarily transformed the country from an absolute monarchy into a republic of theoretically free and equal citizens. Under William Pitt, Britain declared war on France in 1793. Speech to Parliament (February 1, 1793)

13 Citizens, we are talking of a republic, and yet Louis lives! We are talking of a republic, and the person of the King still stands between us and liberty.

Maximilien Robespierre (1758–94) French lawyer and revolutionary. Referring to Louis XVI. Convention (December 3, 1792)

14 Any law which violates the indefeasible rights of man is essentially unjust and tyrannical; it is not a law at all.

Maximilien Robespierre (1758–94) French lawyer and revolutionary. Part of a declaration, this figured in Robespierre's 'Projet' of April 21, 1793. *Declaration of the Rights of Man* (April 24, 1793), Article 6

15 If one had to look for one indisputable story of transformation in the French Revolution, it would be the creation of the juridical entity of the citizen.

Simon Schama (b. 1945) British-born US historian. *Citizens: A Chronicle of the French Revolution* (1989), Epilogue

16 Who will dare deny that the Third Estate contains within itself all that is needed to constitute a nation?

Abbé Sieyès (1748–1836) French clergyman and political theorist. The 'Third Estate' comprised all the French people except the nobility (the First Estate) and the clergy (the Second Estate). *Qu'est-ce que le Tiers État?* (January 1789)

17 It is still too early to form a final judgement on the French Revolution.

G. M. Trevelyan (1876–1962) British historian. Speech, National Book League (May 30, 1945)

18 There has been reason to fear that the Revolution may, like Saturn, devour each of her children one by one.

Pierre-Victurnien Vergniaud (1753–93) French revolutionary politician. November 1793. Said at his trial. Attrib.

19 Bliss was it in that dawn to be alive,
But to be young was very heaven!

William Wordsworth (1770–1850) English poet. 1804–05. Referring to the French Revolution. 'France (Concluded)', *The Prelude* (1850), bk. 11, ll. 108–109

Friendship

see also Love, Relationships, Society

1 The good person is related to his friend as to himself (for his friend is another self).

Aristotle (384–322 BC) Greek philosopher. *Nicomachean Ethics* (4th century BC), 1166a

2 Friendship has splendours that love knows not. It grows stronger when crossed, whereas obstacles kill love. Friendship resists time, which wearies and severs couples. It has heights unknown to love.

Mariama Bâ (1929–81) Senegalese novelist and campaigner for women's rights. *So Long a Letter* (1979)

3 It redoubleth joys, and cutteth griefs in halves.

Francis Bacon (1561–1626) English philosopher, statesman, and lawyer. 'Of Friendship', *Essays* (1625)

4 If a man have not a friend he may quit the stage.

Francis Bacon (1561–1626) English philosopher, statesman, and lawyer. Quoted in *Homosexuality: A History* (Colin Spencer; 1995)

5 Owe no man anything, but to love one another: for he that loveth another hath fulfilled the law.

Bible. Romans, *King James Bible* (1611), 13:8

6 Louis, I think this is the beginning of a beautiful friendship.

Humphrey Bogart (1899–1957) US actor. Said as Rick to the policeman, Louis. The last words of the film. *Casablanca* (Julius J. Epstein, Philip G. Epstein, Howard Koch; 1942)

7 I don't trust him. We're friends.

Bertolt Brecht (1898–1956) German playwright and poet. *Mother Courage and Her Children* (1941), Scene 3

8 Should auld acquaintance be forgot,
And never brought to min'?

Robert Burns (1759–96) Scottish poet and songwriter. 'Auld Lang Syne' (1796)

9 Friendship is Love without his wings!

Lord Byron (1788–1824) British poet. 'L'Amitié est l'Amour sans Ailes' (1831)

10 Only solitary men know the full joys of friendship. Others have their family—but to a solitary and an exile his friends are everything.

Willa Cather (1873–1947) US novelist, poet, and journalist. *Shadows on the Rock* (1931), bk. 3, ch. 5

11 Two may talk together under the same roof for many years, yet never really meet; and two others at first speech are old friends.

Mary Catherwood (1847–1902) US writer. 'Marianson', *Mackinac and Lake Stories* (1899)

12 Have no friends not equal to yourself.

Confucius (551–479 BC) Chinese philosopher, administrator, and moralist. *Analects* (5th century BC)

13 Fate chooses your relations, you choose your friends.

Jacques Delille (1738–1813) French poet and abbot. *Malheur et Pitié* (1803)

14 A Friend may well be reckoned the masterpiece of Nature.

Ralph Waldo Emerson (1803–82) US poet and essayist. 'Friendship', *Essays* (1841)

15 It is not so much our friends' help that helps us as the confident knowledge that they will help us.

Epicurus (341–270 BC) Greek philosopher. (3rd century BC)

16 In prosperity men friends may find,
Which in adversity be full unkind.

Everyman. *Everyman* (1509?–19?), ll. 309–310

17 Friendship is a disinterested commerce between equals; love, an abject intercourse between tyrants and slaves.

Oliver Goldsmith (1730–74) Irish-born British novelist, playwright, and poet. *The Good-Natur'd Man* (1768), Act 1

18 Of all the heavenly gifts that mortal men commend,
    What trusty treasure in the world can countervail a friend?

    Nicholas Grimald (1519–62) English poet. 'Of Friendship' (1557)

19 Distance sometimes endears friendship, and absence sweeteneth it.

    James Howell (1594?–1666) English writer. 1645–55. *Familiar Letters of James Howell* (W. H. Bennett, ed.; 1890), bk. 1, pt. 1, no. 6

20 I know nothing about platonic love except that it is not to be found in the works of Plato.

    Edgar Jepson (1863–1938) British novelist. Quoted in *Ego 5* (James Agate, ed.; August 24, 1940)

21 If a man does not make new acquaintance as he advances through life, he will soon find himself left alone. A man, Sir, should keep his friendship in *constant repair*.

    Samuel Johnson (1709–84) British lexicographer and writer. 1755. Quoted in *Life of Samuel Johnson* (James Boswell; 1791)

22 Sir, I look upon every day to be lost, in which I do not make a new acquaintance.

    Samuel Johnson (1709–84) British lexicographer and writer. November 1784. Quoted in *Life of Samuel Johnson* (James Boswell; 1791)

23 Friends are God's apology for relations.

    Hugh Kingsmill (1889–1949) British writer, critic, and anthologist. Quoted in *The Best of Hugh Kingsmill* (Michael Holroyd; 1970), Introduction

24 I get by with a little help from my friends.

    Lennon & McCartney, British rock musicians. Song lyric. 'With a Little Help from My Friends' (1967)

25 Friendship is unnecessary, like philosophy, like art . . . . It has no survival value; rather it is one of those things that give value to survival.

    C. S. Lewis (1898–1963) Irish-born British novelist. 'Friendship', *The Four Loves* (1960)

26 Men seem to kick friendship around like a football, but it doesn't seem to crack. Women treat it as glass and it goes to pieces.

    Anne Morrow Lindbergh (1906–2001) US writer. Attrib.

27 Friendships made o'er wine are slight;
    Like it, they only act one night.

    Friedrich von Logau (1604–55) German poet and writer. 1654? Quoted in *A German Treasury* (Stanley Mason, tr.; 1993)

28 There is no man so friendless but what he can find a friend sincere enough to tell him disagreeable truths.

    Bulwer Lytton (1803–73) British novelist and politician. *What Will He Do With It?* (1858), vol. 1, bk. 3, ch. 15

29 A true bond of friendship is usually only possible between people of roughly equal status. This equality is demonstrated in many indirect ways, but it is reinforced in face-to-face encounters by a matching of the posture of relaxation or alertness.

    Desmond Morris (b. 1928) British ethnologist and writer. 'Postural Echo', *Manwatching* (1977)

30 Sometimes being a friend means mastering the art of timing. There is a time for silence. A time to let go and allow people to hurl themselves into their own destiny. And a time to prepare to pick up the pieces when it's all over.

    Gloria Naylor (b. 1950) US novelist, producer, and playwright. *The Women of Brewster Place* (1982)

31 Each friend represents a world in us, a world possibly not born until they arrive, and it is only by this meeting that a new world is born.

    Anaïs Nin (1903–77) French writer. March 1937. *The Diary of Anaïs Nin* (1967), vol. 2

32 Love is rarer than genius itself. And friendship is rarer than love.

    Charles Pierre Péguy (1873–1914) French writer and poet. 'The Search for Truth', *Basic Verities* (A. and J. Green, trs.; 1943)

33 Nothing is there more friendly to a man than a friend in need.

    Plautus (254?–184 BC) Roman comic playwright. *Epidicus* (3rd–2nd century BC), Act 3, Scene 3

34 A friendship from which the everyday disappears becomes an allegory.

    Jules Romains (1885–1972) French writer. *Les Hommes de Bonne Volonté* (1932–46), vol. 2

35 To like and dislike the same things, that is indeed true friendship.

    Sallust (86?–35? BC) Roman historian and politician. *Bellum Catilinae* (43 BC)

36 HELENA So we grew together,
    Like to a double cherry, seeming parted,
    But yet an union in partition,
    Two lovely berries moulded on one stem;
    So, with two seeming bodies, but one heart.

    William Shakespeare (1564–1616) English poet and playwright. *A Midsummer Night's Dream* (1595–96), Act 3, Scene 2

37 CASSIUS A friend should bear his friend's infirmities,
    But Brutus makes mine greater than they are.

    William Shakespeare (1564–1616) English poet and playwright. Answering Brutus' accusation of corruption. *Julius Caesar* (1599), Act 4, Scene 3

38 CLAUDIO Friendship is constant in all other things
    Save in the office and affairs of love.

    William Shakespeare (1564–1616) English poet and playwright. *Much Ado About Nothing* (1598–99), Act 2, Scene 1

39 Have you not heard
    When a man marries, dies, or turns Hindoo,
    His best friends hear no more of him?

    Percy Bysshe Shelley (1792–1822) English poet. July 21, 1820. Referring to Thomas Love Peacock, who worked for the East India Company and who had recently married. 'Letter to Maria Gisborne' (1820), l. 235, quoted in *Posthumous Poems* (Mrs. Shelley, ed.; 1824)

40 Don't tell your friends their social faults, they will cure the fault and never forgive you.

    Logan Pearsall Smith (1865–1946) US-born British writer. *Afterthoughts* (1931)

41 I might give my life for my friend, but he had better not ask me to do up a parcel.

    Logan Pearsall Smith (1865–1946) US-born British writer. *Trivia* (1902)

42 So long as we are loved by others I should say that we are almost indispensable; and no man is useless while he has a friend.

    Robert Louis Stevenson (1850–94) Scottish novelist, essayist, and poet. 'Lay Morals', *Across the Plains* (1892)

43 He showed me his bill of fare to tempt me to dine with him; Poh, said I, I value not your bill of fare, give me your bill of company.

    Jonathan Swift (1667–1745) Irish writer and clergyman. *Journal to Stella* (September 2, 1711)

44 Such a good friend that she will throw all her acquaintances into the water for the pleasure of fishing them out again.

Charles Maurice de Talleyrand (1754–1838) French statesman and diplomat. Said to Napoleon of Madame de Staël. Quoted in *Talleyrand* (A. Duff Cooper; 1932), ch.3

45 He makes no friend who never made a foe.

Alfred Tennyson (1809–92) British poet. 'Lancelot and Elaine', *Idylls of the King* (1859), l. 1081

46 The wicked can have only accomplices, the voluptuous have companions in debauchery, self-seekers have associates, the politic assemble the factions, the typical idler has connections, princes have courtiers. Only the virtuous have friends.

Voltaire (1694–1778) French writer and philosopher. 'Friendship', *Dictionnaire Philosophique* (1764)

47 Learn to reject friendship, or rather the dream of friendship. To want friendship is a great fault. Friendship ought to be a gratuitous joy, like the joys afforded by art, or life (like aesthetic joys).

Simone Weil (1909–43) French philosopher, mystic, and political activist. 'The Pre-War Notebook', *First and Last Notebooks* (Richard Rees, ed.; 1970)

48 I will make divine magnetic lands,
With the love of comrades,
With the life-long love of comrades.

Walt Whitman (1819–92) US poet. 1860. 'For You O Democracy', *Leaves of Grass* (1892), Calamus, no. 5

49 Think where man's glory most begins and ends,
And say my glory was I had such friends.

W. B. Yeats (1865–1939) Irish poet and playwright. 1937. 'The Municipal Gallery Re-visited', *New Poems* (1938), pt. 7, ll. 7–8

Fundamentalism

see **Belief, Fanaticism, Religion**

Funerals

see also **Bereavement, Death and Dying**

1 Stop all the clocks, cut off the telephone,
Prevent the dog from barking with a juicy bone,
Silence the pianos and with muffled drum
Bring out the coffin, let the mourners come.

W. H. Auden (1907–73) British poet. 1936. Made famous by the film *Four Weddings and a Funeral* (1994). 'Twelve Songs', *Collected Poems* (Edward Mendelson, ed.; 1991), No. 9, st. 1

2 When we attend the funerals of our friends we grieve for them, but when we go to those of other people it is chiefly our own deaths that we mourn for.

Gerald Brenan (1894–1987) Maltese-born British writer and novelist. 'Death', *Thoughts in a Dry Season* (1978)

3 For myself, I wish to be driven to the cemetery in a removals van.

André Breton (1896–1966) French writer. *Premier Manifeste du Surréalisme: Contre la Mort* (1924)

4 I bet you a hundred bucks he ain't in here.

Charles Bancroft Dillingham (1868–1934) US theatrical manager and producer. Referring to the escapologist Harry Houdini; said at his funeral, while carrying his coffin. Attrib.

5 Rained-on, flower-laden
Coffin after coffin
Seemed to float from the door
Of the packed cathedral
Like blossoms on slow water.

Seamus Heaney (b. 1939) Irish poet. 'Casualty', *Field Work* (1979), ll. 50–54

6 They say such nice things about people at their funerals that it makes me sad to realize I'm going to miss mine by just a few days.

Garrison Keillor (b. 1942) US writer and broadcaster. December 13, 1984. 'Lecture in San Francisco', *Lake Wobegon Days* (1985)

7 Memorial services are the cocktail parties of the geriatric set.

Harold Macmillan (1894–1986) British prime minister. Quoted in *Macmillan 1957–86* (Alistair Horne; 1991), vol. 2

8 Petty intrigues and dramatic scenes among the relatives as they prepare for the funeral are innumerable. Without them, a funeral doesn't look like one.

Es'kia Mphahlele (b. 1919) South African novelist, teacher, and political activist. 'In Corner B', *Stories from Central and Southern Africa* (Paul A. Scanlon, ed.; 1983)

Futility

see also **Nihilism, Nothingness**

1 We know life is futile. A man who considers that his life is of very wonderful importance is awfully close to a padded cell.

Clarence Darrow (1857–1938) US lawyer. Lecture, University of Chicago (1929)

2 It's but little good you'll do a-watering the last year's crop.

George Eliot (1819–80) British novelist. *Adam Bede* (1854)

3 However, one cannot put a quart in a pint cup.

Charlotte Perkins Gilman (1860–1935) US feminist writer. *The Living of Charlotte Perkins Gilman: An Autobiography* (1935), ch. 4

4 A useless life is an early death.

Johann Wolfgang von Goethe (1749–1832) German poet, playwright, and scientist. *Iphigenie auf Tauris* (1787), Act 1, Scene 2

5 All my life I had been looking forward to something happening, some extrinsic event that would alter my life, and now suddenly, inspired by the abusive hopelessness of everything, I felt relieved.

Henry Miller (1891–1980) US novelist. *Tropic of Cancer* (1934)

6 I'm not going to re-arrange the furniture on the deck of the Titanic.

Rogers Morton (1914–79) US businessman and politician. Refusing attempts to rescue President Gerald Ford's re-election campaign, 1976. *The Washington Post* (May 16, 1976)

7 Worse, to have lived without even attempting to lay claim to one's portion of the earth; to have lived and died as one had been born, unnecessary and unaccommodated.

V. S. Naipaul (b. 1932) Trinidadian-born British novelist. *A House for Mr. Biswas* (1961), Prologue

8 It is no use trying to tug the glacier backwards.

Tibetan proverb.

9 Such another victory and we are ruined.

Pyrrhus (318?–272 BC) Epirian monarch. 279 BC. Referring to the costliness of his victory at the Battle of Asculum, which gave rise to the phrase, a Pyrrhic victory. Quoted in 'Pyrrhus', *Parallel Lives* (Plutarch), ch. 21, sect. 9

The Future

see also Prophecy, Time, Twenty-first Century

1 The future, gentlemen, is the faith of our age: it is the torch of the past, the guiding star of the present.
Jean-Jaques Ampère (1800–64) French writer and historian. 'Les Renaissances', *Mélanges d'Histoire Littéraire et de Littérature* (1876)

2 The future is like heaven—everyone exalts it but no one wants to go there now.
James Baldwin (1924–87) US writer and civil rights activist. 'A Fly in Buttermilk', *Nobody Knows My Name* (1961)

3 There is never a time in the future in which we will work out our salvation. The challenge is in the moment, the time is always now.
James Baldwin (1924–87) US writer and civil rights activist. 'Faulkner and Desegregation', *Nobody Knows My Name* (1961)

4 FUTURE, n. That period of time in which our affairs prosper, our friends are true and our happiness is assured.
Ambrose Bierce (1842–1914?) US writer and journalist. *The Devil's Dictionary* (1911)

5 The future is the only kind of property that the masters willingly concede to slaves.
Albert Camus (1913–60) Algerian-born French novelist, essayist, and playwright. *The Rebel* (1951)

6 Those who talk about the future are scoundrels. It is the present that matters. To evoke one's posterity is to make a speech to maggots.
Louis-Ferdinand Céline (1894–1961) French novelist and physician. *Voyage au Bout de la Nuit* (1932)

7 I have learned to live each day as it comes, and not to borrow trouble by dreading tomorrow. It is the dark menace of the future that makes cowards of us.
Dorothy Dix (1861–1951) US journalist and writer. *Dorothy Dix, Her Book* (1926), Introduction

8 I never think of the future. It comes soon enough.
Albert Einstein (1879–1955) German-born US physicist. Comment during an interview. *Belgenland* (December 1930)

9 It is everlastingly true that on the whole the best guide to the future is to be found in a proper understanding of the lessons of the past.
Warren G. Harding (1865–1923) US president. Quoted in *The Meaning of History* (N. Gordon and Joyce Carper; 1991)

10 I know of no way of judging the future but by the past.
Patrick Henry (1736–99) American statesman and orator. Speech to the Virginia Convention (March 23, 1775)

11 I like the dreams of the future better than the history of the past.
Thomas Jefferson (1743–1826) US president. Quoted in *Time* (January 9, 1978)

12 Yesterday is not ours to recover, but tomorrow is ours to win or lose.
Lyndon Baines Johnson (1908–73) US president. Address to the nation (November 28, 1963)

13 Chasing after the future is the worst conformism of all, a craven flattery of the mighty. For the future is always mightier than the present.
Milan Kundera (b. 1929) Czech novelist. *The Art of the Novel* (1986)

14 The architecture of our future is not only unfinished; the scaffolding has hardly gone up.
George Lamming (b. 1927) Barbadian writer. 'The West Indian People' (1966), quoted in *Caribbean Essays* (Andrew Salkey, ed.; 1973)

15 The future of humanity is uncertain, even in the most prosperous of countries, and the quality of life deteriorates; and yet I believe what is being discovered about the infinitely large and infinitely small is sufficient to absolve the end of the century and millennium.
Primo Levi (1919–87) Italian writer and chemist. *Other People's Trade* (1985)

16 The Future is something which everyone reaches at the rate of sixty minutes an hour, whatever he does, whoever he is.
C. S. Lewis (1898–1963) Irish-born British novelist. *The Screwtape Letters* (1942), no. 25

17 The future will one day be the present and will seem as unimportant as the present does now.
Somerset Maugham (1874–1965) British writer. *The Summing Up* (1938)

18 All I know about the future is that it is what you make of it.
Walter Mosley (b. 1952) US novelist. Lecture, Royal Festival Hall, London (January 28, 1998)

19 If you want a picture of the future, imagine a boot stamping on a human face—for ever . . . And remember that it is for ever.
George Orwell (1903–50) British writer. *Nineteen Eighty-Four* (1949), pt. 3, ch. 3

20 It may not be until the human future has been restored to us that desire can again find a natural place.
Jonathan Schell (b. 1943) US author. Referring to the threat posed by nuclear weapons. *The Fate of the Earth* (1982)

21 The future is made of the same stuff as the present.
Simone Weil (1909–43) French philosopher, mystic, and political activist. 1940–42. 'Some Thoughts on the Love of God', *On Science, Necessity and the Love of God* (Richard Rees, ed.; 1968)

22 The world of the future will be an ever more demanding struggle against the limits of our intelligence, not a comfortable hammock in which we can lie down to be waited upon by our robot slaves.
Norbert Wiener (1894–1964) US mathematician. *God and Golem, Inc.* (1964)

G

Gambling

see also **Chance**

1 Gwine to run all night!
Gwine to run all day!
I bet my money on the bob-tail nag.
Somebody bet on the bay.

Stephen Foster (1826–64) US composer of popular songs. Song. 'Camptown Races' (1850)

2 OSCAR I'm eight hundred dollars behind in alimony, so let's up the stakes.

Neil Simon (b. 1927) US playwright. Referring to a poker game. *The Odd Couple* (1965)

3 Poker shouldn't be played in a house with women.

Tennessee Williams (1911–83) US playwright. *A Streetcar Named Desire* (1947)

Gardens

see also **Flowers**, **Trees**

1 God Almighty first planted a garden. And indeed it is the purest of human pleasures.

Francis Bacon (1561–1626) English philosopher, statesman, and lawyer. 'Of Gardens', *Essays* (1625)

2 God the first garden made, and the first city Cain.

Abraham Cowley (1618–67) English poet. *The Garden* (1664), essay 5

3 Annihilating all that's made
To a green thought in a green shade.

Andrew Marvell (1621–78) English poet and government official. 'The Garden' (1650?), st. 6, ll. 7–8

4 I have a garden of my own,
But so with roses overgrown,
And lilies, that you would it guess
To be a little wilderness.

Andrew Marvell (1621–78) English poet and government official. 'The Nymph Complaining for the Death of her Fawn' (1681), ll. 71–74.

5 My heart shall be thy garden.

Alice Meynell (1847–1922) British poet and literary critic. 'The Garden' (1875)

6 The fountains are dry and the roses over.
Incense of death. Your day approaches.
The pears fatten like little buddhas.
A blue mist is dragging the lake.

Sylvia Plath (1932–63) US poet and novelist. 1959. 'The Manor Garden', *The Colossus* (1960)

7 That evening
my garden awoke
The fingers of the wind
unhinged its fences
Grasses swayed, flowers bursting,
fruits ripening
in the blissful dance of wind and rain.

Fadwa Tuqan (b. 1917) Palestinian poet. 'In the Flux', *Modern Arabic Poetry* (Salma Khadra Jayyusi, ed.; 1987), ll. 22–28

8 'That is well said', replied Candide, 'but we must cultivate our garden'.

Voltaire (1694–1778) French writer and philosopher. *Candide* (1759), ch. 30

Generosity

see also **Gifts**, **Help**, **Kindness**

1 I've made shoes for everyone, even you, while I still go barefoot.

Bob Dylan (b. 1941) US singer and songwriter. Song lyric. 'I and I' (1983)

2 Liberality lies less in giving liberally than in the timeliness of the gift.

Jean de La Bruyère (1645–96) French essayist and moralist. *Characters, or the Manners of the Age* (1688)

3 If there's anything that you want,
If there's anything I can do,
Just call on me,
And I'll send it along with love from me to you.

Lennon & McCartney, British rock musicians. 'From Me to You', *Please Please Me* (1963)

4 A gen'rous heart repairs a sland'rous tongue.

Alexander Pope (1688–1744) English poet. *The Odyssey of Homer* (1725), bk. 8, l. 432

5 There is nothing more praiseworthy than generosity, but nothing less to be carried to excess.

Cardinal de Retz (1613–79) French ecclesiastic and politician. *Mémoires* (1717)

6 Thy need is yet greater than mine.

Philip Sidney (1554–86) English poet, courtier, and soldier. September 22, 1586. Giving his own water bottle to a dying soldier after he had himself been wounded at the Battle of Zutphen. Quoted in *Life of the Renowned Sir Philip Sidney* (Sir Fulke Greville; 1652)

7 He gave what little wealth he had
To build a house for fools and mad;
And showed, by one satiric touch,
No nation wanted it so much.

Jonathan Swift (1667–1745) Irish writer and clergyman. Referring to his founding of St. Patrick's mental hospital in Dublin (1757). 'Verses on the Death of Dr. Swift' (1731), ll. 479–482

Genetics

see also **Evolution, Science**

1 It would be a mistake for the United States Senate to allow any kind of human cloning to come out of that chamber.

George W. Bush (b. 1948) US president. Remark, Washington, DC (April 10, 2002)

2 We are survival machines—robot vehicles blindly programmed to preserve the selfish molecules known as genes. This is a truth which still fills me with astonishment.

Richard Dawkins (b. 1941) British ethologist. *The Selfish Gene* (1976)

3 God creates man, man destroys God, man creates dinosaurs.

Jeff Goldblum (b. 1952) US film actor. As Ian Malcolm. *Jurassic Park* (Michael Crichton and David Koepp; 1993)

4 A million million spermatozoa,
All of them alive:
Out of their cataclysm but one poor Noah
Dare hope to survive.

Aldous Huxley (1894–1963) British novelist and essayist. *Fifth Philosopher's Song* (1920)

5 If all the DNA in all the cells in a single human being were stretched out it would reach the moon and back eight thousand times.

Steve Jones (b. 1944) British geneticist. *The Language of the Genes* (1991)

6 There have been claims that we may soon find the gene that makes us human. The ancestral message will then at last allow us to understand what we really are. The idea seems to me ridiculous.

Steve Jones (b. 1944) British geneticist. *The Language of the Genes* (1991)

7 I like people. I like animals, too—whales and quail, dinosaurs and dodos. But I like human beings especially, and I am unhappy that the pool of human germ plasm, which determines the nature of the human race, is deteriorating.

Linus Pauling (1901–94) US scientist. Said on winning the Nobel Prize for peace. Referring to radioactive fallout. *New York Times* (October 13, 1962)

8 The law of heredity is that all undesirable traits come from the other parent.

Proverb.

9 While our behavior is still significantly controlled by our genetic inheritance, we have, through our brains, a much richer opportunity to blaze new behavioral and cultural pathways on short timescales.

Carl Sagan (1934–96) US astronomer and writer. *The Dragons of Eden* (1977), Introduction

10 It is from the progeny of this parent cell that we all take our looks; we still share genes around, and the resemblance of the enzymes of grasses to those of whales is in fact a family resemblance.

Lewis Thomas (1913–93) US physician and writer. *The Lives of a Cell* (1974)

11 Biology has at least 50 more interesting years.

James Dewey Watson (b. 1928) US biochemist. Remark (December 31, 1984)

12 I can splice a gene or two, can make you walk with a monkey's head or run on bitch's legs or see through the eyes of a newt: or smell like a rose.

Fay Weldon (b. 1933) British writer. Said by Carl May, a geneticist. *The Cloning of Joanna May* (1989)

13 I see a world of accident and not design, never perfectable left to itself. So I intervene. I can make a thousand thousand of you if I choose, fragment all living things and recreate them.

Fay Weldon (b. 1933) British writer. Said by Carl May, a geneticist. *The Cloning of Joanna May* (1989)

14 No species . . . possesses a purpose beyond the imperatives created by genetic history.

Edward O. Wilson (b. 1929) US evolutionary biologist. 'Dilemma', *On Human Nature* (1978)

15 We are compelled to drive toward total knowledge, right down to the levels of the neuron and the gene. When we have progressed enough to explain ourselves in these mechanistic terms . . . the result might be hard to accept.

Edward O. Wilson (b. 1929) US evolutionary biologist. 'Man: From Sociobiology to Sociology', *Sociobiology: The New Synthesis* (1975)

16 In the process of natural selection, then, any device that can insert a higher proportion of certain genes into subsequent generations will come to characterize the species.

Edward O. Wilson (b. 1929) US evolutionary biologist. 'The Morality of the Gene', *Sociobiology: The New Synthesis* (1975)

17 Genetic control will be the weapon of the future.

Jeanette Winterson (b. 1959) British novelist. *Art and Lies* (1994)

Genius

see also **Ability, Talent**

1 The function of genius is to furnish cretins with ideas twenty years later.

Louis Aragon (1897–1982) French writer. 'La Porte-plume', *Traité du Style* (1928)

2 I'm a genius and there's nothing I can do about it.

Captain Beefheart (b. 1941) US singer and songwriter. Quoted in *The Wit and Wisdom of Rock and Roll* (Maxim Jabukowski, ed.; 1983)

3 Genius is only a greater aptitude for patience.

Comte de Buffon (1707–88) French naturalist. Quoted in *Voyage à Montbar* (Herault de Sechelles; 1803)

4 Almost everyone is born a genius and buried an idiot.

Charles Bukowski (1920–94) German-born US writer. *Notes of a Dirty Old Man* (1969)

5 Genius (which means transcendent capacity of taking trouble, first of all).

Thomas Carlyle (1795–1881) Scottish historian and essayist. *Frederick the Great* (1858), vol. 4, ch. 3

6 Genius hath electric power
Which earth can never tame.

Lydia Maria Child (1802–80) US abolitionist, suffrage campaigner, and writer. Attrib.

7 Genius is of no country.

Charles Churchill (1731–64) British poet. *The Rosciad* (1761), l. 207

8 Genius is one per cent inspiration and ninety-nine per cent perspiration.

Thomas Alva Edison (1847–1931) US inventor. Quoted in *Harper's Magazine* (September 1932)

9 True genius walks along a line, and, perhaps, our greatest pleasure is in seeing it so often near falling, without being ever actually down.

Oliver Goldsmith (1730–74) Irish-born British novelist, playwright, and poet. 'The Characteristics of Greatness', *The Bee* (1759), no. 4

10 The true genius is a mind of large general powers, accidentally determined to some particular direction.
Samuel Johnson (1709–84) British lexicographer and writer. 'Cowley', *Lives of the English Poets* (1779–81)

11 A genius is somebody a computer cannot programme.
Taban Lo Liyong (b. 1939) Sudanese poet, novelist, and short-story writer. *Meditations of Taban Lo Liyong* (1975)

12 Genius does what it must, and Talent does what it can.
Meredith Owen (1831–91) British statesman and poet. 'Last Words of a Sensitive Second-rate Poet' (1868)

13 The genius of Einstein leads to Hiroshima.
Pablo Picasso (1881–1973) Spanish painter and sculptor. Remark to Françoise Gilot (1964), quoted in *Life with Picasso* (Françoise Gilot and Carlton Lake; 1964), pt. 2

14 Geniuses are wonks. The typical genius pays dues for at least ten years before contributing anything of lasting value. (Mozart composed symphonies at eight, but they weren't very good.)
Steven Pinker (b. 1954) US cognitive scientist and author. *How the Mind Works* (1997)

15 One science only will one genius fit:
So vast is art, so narrow human wit.
Alexander Pope (1688–1744) English poet. *An Essay on Criticism* (1711), ll. 60–61

16 It is genius, and not the want of it, that adulterates philosophy, and fills it with error and false theory.
Thomas Reid (1710–96) Scottish philosopher. *Inquiry into the Human Mind on the Principles of Common Sense* (1764)

17 A genius! For thirty-seven years I've practiced fourteen hours a day, and now they call me a genius!
Pablo de Sarasate (1844–1908) Spanish violinist and composer. On being hailed as a genius by a critic. Attrib.

18 There is no great genius without a tincture of madness.
Seneca, 'the Younger' (4? BC–AD 65) Roman writer, philosopher, and statesman. *De Tranquillitate Animi* (63?), no. 17, sect. 10

19 It takes a lot of time to be a genius, you have to sit around so much doing nothing, really doing nothing.
Gertrude Stein (1874–1946) US writer. *Everybody's Autobiography* (1937)

20 When a true genius appears in the world, you may know him by this sign, that the dunces are all in confederacy against him.
Jonathan Swift (1667–1745) Irish writer and clergyman. *Thoughts on Various Subjects* (1711)

21 Everyone denies I am a genius—but nobody ever called me one!
Orson Welles (1915–85) US actor, director, producer, and writer. Attrib.

22 Nothing, except my genius.
Oscar Wilde (1854–1900) Irish poet, playwright, and wit. 1882. Replying to a US customs official on being asked if he had anything to declare. Attrib.

Germany

see Europe, European Countries

Gifts

see also Generosity

1 If one receives a plum one must return a peach.
Anonymous. Vietnamese proverb.

2 The manner of giving is worth more than the gift.
Corneille (1606–84) French playwright. *Le Menteur* (1644), Act 1, Scene 1

3 It is said that gifts persuade even the gods.
Euripides (480?–406? BC) Greek playwright. *Medea* (431 BC), l. 964

4 The first great gift we can bestow on others is a good example.
Thomas Morell (1703–84) British classicist. Attrib.

5 Why is it no one ever sent me yet
One perfect limousine, do you suppose?
Ah no, it's always just my luck to get
One perfect rose.
Dorothy Parker (1893–1967) US writer and wit. 'One Perfect Rose', *Enough Rope* (1926)

6 I know what I have given you. I do not know what you have received.
Antonio Porchia (1886–1968) Italian-born Argentinian writer. *Voces* (W. S. Merwin, tr.; 1968)

7 OPHELIA For to the noble mind
Rich gifts wax poor when givers prove unkind.
William Shakespeare (1564–1616) English poet and playwright. *Hamlet* (1601), Act 3, Scene 1

8 The Gods themselves cannot recall their gifts.
Alfred Tennyson (1809–92) British poet. February 1860. 'Tithonus', *Enoch Arden* (1864), l. 49

Globalization

see also Capitalism, Economics, Imperialism, Media, Twenty-first Century

1 The economic and military unification of the world has not brought peace but genocide.
John Berger (b. 1926) British novelist, essayist, and art critic. 1999. *Pig Earth* (1999 edition), Introduction

2 I realise why people protest against globalisation. We watch aspects of it with trepidation. We feel powerless, as if we were now pushed to and fro by forces far beyond our control.
Tony Blair (b. 1953) British prime minister. Speech, Labour Party Conference (October 2, 2001)

3 In the emerging global economy, everything is mobile: capital, factories, even entire industries. The only resource that's really rooted in a nation—and the ultimate source of all its wealth—is its people.
Bill Clinton (b. 1946) US president. *Putting People First: How We Can All Change America* (co-written with Al Gore; 1992)

4 We desperately need . . . a national and global economy in which people act not only as consumers but as citizens, in which workers reassert their responsibility for themselves and the success of their companies.
Hillary Clinton (b. 1947) US lawyer and first lady. *It Takes a Village* (1996)

5 The daily agony of Third World peoples is served up as a spectacle for permanent enjoyment in the utopia of bourgeois liberty . . . the misery of the Third World is packaged and canned to liberate the masters who produce it and consume it.
Ariel Dorfman (b. 1942) Chilean playwright and novelist. *How to Read Donald Duck* (with Armand Mattelart; 1971)

6 No two countries that both have a McDonald's have ever fought a war against each other.
Thomas L. Friedman, US journalist and author. *New York Times* (December 8, 1996)

7 Modern liberal political and economic institutions not only coexist with religion and other traditional elements of culture, but many actually work better in conjunction with them.
Francis Fukuyama (b. 1952) US economist and historian. *Trust* (1995)

8 The growing technical prowess of nations such as India unnerves some people in developed countries who fear a loss of jobs and opportunities. I think these fears are misplaced. Economics is not a zero-sum game.
Bill Gates (b. 1955) US business executive. *New York Times* (April 8, 1997)

9 Global problems respond to local initiatives but they also demand global solutions.
Anthony Giddens (b. 1938) British economist. *The Third Way: The Renewal of Social Democracy* (1998)

10 A truly global economy is being created by the worldwide spread of new technologies, not by the spread of free markets . . . the result is not a universal free market but an anarchy of sovereign states, rival capitalisms and stateless zones.
John Gray (b. 1948) British academic. *False Dawn* (1998)

11 The global market as it is presently organized does not allow the world's peoples to coexist harmoniously. It impels them to become rivals for resources while instituting no methods for conserving.
John Gray (b. 1948) British academic. *False Dawn* (1998)

12 Nothing disrupts global markets quite as well as submarines.
Paul Krugman (b. 1953) US economist. Referring to the effect of world wars on economics. Interview, *Strategy and Business* (1998)

13 I believe world civilization can be built only upon the common basis of international living . . . The ideal life . . . to live in an English cottage, with American heating, and have a Japanese wife, a French mistress, and a Chinese cook.
Lin Yutang (1895–1976) Chinese-born writer and philologist. Quoted in *Lin Yutang: The Best of An Old Friend* (A. J. Anderson, ed.; 1975)

14 The new electronic interdependence recreates the world in the image of a global village.
Marshall McLuhan (1911–80) Canadian sociologist. *The Gutenberg Galaxy* (1962)

15 Can the West realize its ideal of one world where all can flourish together while continuing to base much of its economy on the military?
Fatima Mernissi (b. 1941) Moroccan writer. *Islam and Democracy* (1992)

16 There is no such thing as a global village. Most media are rooted in their national and local cultures.
Rupert Murdoch (b. 1931) Australian-born US media entrepreneur. *Business Review Weekly* (November 17, 1989)

17 The mobility of capital today means that the comparative advantage once enjoyed by states or regions has been usurped by transnational corporations.
Helena Norberg-Hodge, British ecologist and author. 'Globalisation Versus Community', *The Future of Progress* (Helena Norberg-Hodge, Peter Goering, and Steven Gorelick, eds.; 1992)

18 Today's global economy is genuinely borderless. Information, capital, and innovation flow all over the world at top speed, enabled by technology and fuelled by the consumers' desires for access to the best and least expensive products.
Kenichi Ohmae (b. 1943) Japanese business strategist. *The End of the Nation State* (1995), Epigraph

19 No nation can be competitive in (and can be a net exporter of) everything.
Michael E. Porter (b. 1947) US author. *The Competitive Advantage of Nations* (1990)

20 In the last decade of the 20th century . . . Walls of enmity have fallen, borders have disappeared, powers have crumbled and ideologies collapsed, states have been born, states have died and the gates of emigration have been flung open.
Yitzhak Rabin (1922–95) Israeli statesman. Speech to the Israeli parliament, Tel Aviv (July 13, 1992), quoted in *Murder in the Name of God* (Michael Karpin and Ina Friedman; 1999)

21 We are living through a transformation that will rearrange the politics and economics of the coming century. There will be no *national* products or technologies, no national corporations, no national industries. There will no longer be national economies.
Robert B. Reich (b. 1946) US economist. *The Work of Nations* (1991)

22 How do you react to the prospects of the world population doubling over the next few decades? First you may say, Great, 5 billion more customers.
Robert B. Shapiro (b. 1938) US business executive. January-February 1997. *Harvard Business Review* (January–February 1997)

23 We can't expect the rest of the world to abandon their aspirations just so we can continue to enjoy clean air and water.
Robert B. Shapiro (b. 1938) US business executive. Referring to the threat of global pollution and global warming. *Harvard Business Review* (January–February 1997)

24 When a system of national currencies run by central banks is transformed into a global electronic marketplace driven by currency traders, power changes hands.
Walter B. Wriston (1919–98) US banker. Speech (January 25, 1993)

Glory

see also **Success**, **Victory**

1 What price Glory?
Maxwell Anderson (1888–1959) US playwright. Play title. *What Price Glory?* (co-written with Laurence Stallings; 1924)

2 Let us not scorn glory too much: nothing, other than virtue, is more beautiful.
René Chateaubriand (1768–1848) French writer and statesman. *Itinéraire de Paris à Jérusalem* (1811), pt. 1

3 Myn be the travaille, and thyn be the glorie!
Geoffrey Chaucer (1343?–1400) English poet. 'The Knight's Tale', *The Canterbury Tales* (1390?), l. 2406, quoted in *The Works of Geoffrey Chaucer* (F. N. Robinson, ed.; 1957)

4 Our greatest glory is not in never falling, but in rising every time we fall.

Confucius (551–479 BC) Chinese philosopher, administrator, and moralist. *Analects* (5th century BC)

5 How vainly men themselves amaze
To win the palm, the oak, or bays.

Andrew Marvell (1621–78) English poet and government official. 'Palm', 'oak', and 'bays' describe the wreaths awarded for athletic, civic, and poetic achievements. 'The Garden' (1650?), st. 1

6 A livelier emerald twinkles in the grass,
A purer sapphire melts into the sea.

Alfred Tennyson (1809–92) British poet. *Maud: A Monodrama* (1855), pt. 1, sect. 8, st. 6, ll. 649–650

7 May God deny you peace but give you glory!

Miguel de Unamuno y Jugo (1864–1936) Spanish writer and philosopher. Closing words of the book. *The Tragic Sense of Life in Men and Peoples* (1913)

God

see also **Belief, Fanaticism, Religion**

1 To know God's nature one would have to be God Himself.

Joseph Albo (1380?–1444?) Spanish philosopher of Judaism. 1485. *Sefer ha-Ikkarim* (Louis Jacobs, tr.)

2 If the Prophet was Allah's hearing and vision and tongue, then Allah and He alone is the Hearer, the Seer, the Speaker.

al-Ghazali (1058–1111) Islamic philosopher and theologian. *The Niche for Lights* (11th–12th century), quoted in *Four Sufi Classics* (Idris Shah, ed.; 1980)

3 His approach is foretold only by his own preparations. Thunder is the cracking of his joints, as a warrior limbering up for action.

Anonymous. Referring to Ngai, the high-god of the Gikuyu people of Kenya. Quoted in 'Ngai, the High-God of the Gikuyu', *Sacred Texts of the World* (Ninian Smart and Richard D. Hecht, eds.; 1982)

4 The sacred land is the land of the godhead. It was not only created and maintained by the godhead, it is the godhead itself and represents the totality of Upperworld and Underworld.

Anonymous. From the tradition of the Nagaju Dayak of southern Borneo. Quoted in 'The Hornbill, the Watersnake and the Institutions of the Ngaju Dayak', *Sacred Texts of the World* (Ninian Smart and Richard D. Hecht, eds.; 1982)

5 Every man thinks God is on his side. The rich and powerful know that he is.

Jean Anouilh (1910–87) French playwright. *The Lark* (1953)

6 Whatever is in motion must be moved by something else. Moreover, this something else . . . must itself be moved by something else, and that in turn by yet another thing . . . So we reach a first mover which is not moved by anything. And this all men think of as God.

Thomas Aquinas (1225–74) Italian theologian and philosopher. *Summa Theologica* (1266–73), I, pt. 1

7 Ours is the one God, uncreated and eternal, invisible, immutable, incomprehensible, inconceivable, to be grasped only by the mind and by reason.

Athenagoras (*fl.* 2nd century) Greek philosopher and spiritual leader. 177? Addressed to the Roman emperor Marcus Aurelius. Quoted in 'A Plea Regarding Christians', *The Early Christians* (E. Arnold; 1970)

8 All proofs or disproofs that we tender
Of His existence are returned
Unopened to the sender.

W. H. Auden (1907–73) British poet. 1958. 'Friday's Child', *W. H. Auden: Collected Poems* (Edward Mendelson, ed.; 1991)

9 God, or rather the fiction of God, is the consecration and the intellectual and moral source of all slavery . . . and the freedom of mankind will never be complete until the disastrous and insidious fiction of a heavenly master is annihilated.

Mikhail Bakunin (1814–76) Russian-born anarchist. Quoted in *Bakunin on Anarchy* (Sam Dolgoff, ed.; 1973)

10 If the concept of God has any validity or use, it can only be to make us larger, freer, and more loving. If God cannot do this, then it is time we got rid of Him.

James Baldwin (1924–87) US writer and civil rights activist. *The Fire Next Time* (1963)

11 God is man idealized.

Imamu Amiri Baraka (b. 1934) US author, editor, playwright, and political activist. 'The Legacy of Malcolm X, and the Coming of the Black Nation', *Home: Social Essays* (1966)

12 God has been replaced, as he has all over the West, with respectability and air conditioning.

Imamu Amiri Baraka (b. 1934) US author, editor, playwright, and political activist. 'What does Nonviolence Mean?', *Home: Social Essays* (1966)

13 I know I am God because when I pray to him I find I'm talking to myself.

Peter Barnes (b. 1931) British playwright and director. *The Ruling Class* (1968)

14 God is the only being who, to rule, doesn't even need to exist.

Charles Baudelaire (1821–67) French poet. 'Fusées', *Journaux Intimes* (1887)

15 The Lord is a man of war: the Lord is his name.

Bible. Exodus, *King James Bible* (1611), 15:3

16 A God who let us prove his existence would be an idol.

Dietrich Bonhoeffer (1906–45) German theologian. An attempt at a Lutheran catechism. *'If you believe it, you have it'* (1931), quoted in *No Rusty Swords* (E. Robinson and J. Bowden, eds.; 1965)

17 Man has learned to cope with all questions of importance without recourse to God as a working hypothesis.

Dietrich Bonhoeffer (1906–45) German theologian. June 8, 1944. *Letters and Papers from Prison* (Eberhard Bethge, ed.; 1981)

18 God is the perfect poet,
Who in his person acts his own creations.

Robert Browning (1812–89) British poet. *Paracelsus* (1835), pt. 2, ll. 648–5

19 God does not want to be believed in, to be debated and defended by us, but simply to be realized through us.

Martin Buber (1878–1965) Austrian-born Israeli philosopher of religion and Zionist. 1923. Quoted in *On Judaism* (N. Glazer, ed., Eva Jose et al., trs.; 1967)

20 God is Love—I dare say. But what a mischievous devil Love is!

Samuel Butler (1835–1902) British writer and composer. Quoted in *Note Books* (H. Festing Jones, ed.; 1912)

21 If God exists, all depends on him and we can do nothing against his will. If he does not exist, everything depends on us.

Albert Camus (1913–60) Algerian-born French novelist, essayist, and playwright. *The Myth of Sisyphus* (1942)

22 Thou shalt have one God only; who
Would be at the expense of two?

Arthur Hugh Clough (1819–61) British poet. 'The Latest Decalogue' (1862), ll. 1–2

23 Imagine the Lord talking French! Aside from a few odd words in Hebrew, I took it completely for granted that God had never spoken anything but the most dignified English.
Clarence Shepard Day (1874–1935) US writer. 'Father Interferes', *Life with Father* (1935)

24 It is the final proof of God's omnipotence that he need not exist in order to save us.
Peter De Vries (1910–93) US novelist. *The Mackerel Plaza* (1958), ch. 1

25 God is a mathematician of a very high order, and He used very advanced mathematics in constructing the universe.
Paul Dirac (1902–84) British physicist and Nobel laureate. *Scientific American* (May 1963)

26 It is what man does not know of God Composes the visible poem of the world.
Richard Eberhart (b. 1904) US poet. 'On a Squirrel Crossing the Road in Autumn in New England', *Collected Poems 1930–76* (1976)

27 It seems hard to sneak a look at God's cards. But that he plays dice and uses 'telepathic' methods (as the present quantum theory requires of him) is something that I cannot believe for a single moment.
Albert Einstein (1879–1955) German-born US physicist. Letter to Cornelius Lanczos (February 14, 1938), quoted in *Albert Einstein, The Human Side* (Helen Dukas and Banesh Hoffman; 1979)

28 It would indeed be very nice if there were a God, who was both creator of the world and a benevolent providence, if there were a moral world order and a future life . . . It is very odd that this is all just as we should wish it ourselves.
Sigmund Freud (1856–1939) Austrian psychoanalyst. 1928. *The Future of an Illusion* (1927), ch. 6

29 Forgive, O Lord, my little jokes on Thee And I'll forgive Thy great big one on me.
Robert Frost (1874–1963) US poet. 'Cluster of Faith', *In the Clearing* (1962)

30 The god of the Christians, God of my childhood, does not make love. He is perhaps the only god that has never made love out of all the gods of all the religions in the history of the world.
Eduardo Galeano (b. 1940) Uruguayan writer. *The Book of Embraces* (1989)

31 God has no religion.
Mahatma Gandhi (1869–1948) Indian national leader. Attrib.

32 If God hadn't rested on Sunday, He would have had time to finish the world.
Gabriel García Márquez (b. 1928) Colombian novelist. *The Funerals of Mama Grande* (1974)

33 An inordinate fondness for beetles.
J. B. S. Haldane (1892–1964) British geneticist. Reply when asked what inferences could be drawn about the nature of God from a study of his works. Quoted in *Reader's Digest* (February 1979)

34 God not only plays dice. He also sometimes throws the dice where they cannot be seen.
Stephen Hawking (b. 1942) British physicist. Referring to Albert Einstein's objection to quantum theory, 'I shall never believe that God plays dice with the world'. Quoted in *Nature* (1975), no. 257

35 An Act of God was defined as 'something which no reasonable man could have expected'.
A. P. Herbert (1890–1971) British writer and politician. 'Act of God', *Uncommon Law* (1935)

36 Nothing that God ever made is the same thing to more than one person.
Zora Neale Hurston (1891?–1960) US writer and folklorist. *Dust Tracks on a Road* (1942)

37 Operationally, God is beginning to resemble not a ruler but the last fading smile of a cosmic Cheshire cat.
Julian Huxley (1887–1975) British biologist. Referring to the Cheshire Cat in Lewis Carroll's children's classic, *Alice's Adventures in Wonderland* (1865). *Religion Without Revelation* (1957), ch. 3

38 Man proposes but God disposes.
Thomas à Kempis (1379?–1471) German monk and religious writer. *The Imitation of Christ* (1415–24?), bk. 1, ch. 19, sect. 2

39 The whole world is a name of God, for a name is a sign, and all the creatures that exist in the world are signs of the Sacred Essence of God.
Ruhollah Khomeini (1900–89) Iranian religious and political leader. 1979. 'Everything is a Name of God', *Islam and Revolution* (H. Algar, tr.; 1985)

40 God is but a word invented to explain the world.
Alphonse de Lamartine (1790–1869) French poet and politician. 'Le Tombeau d'une Mère', *Nouvelles Harmonies Poétiques et Religieuses* (1832)

41 I have no need of that hypothesis.
Pierre Simon Laplace (1749–1827) French mathematician and astronomer. On being asked by Napoleon why he had made no mention of God in his book about the universe, *Mécanique céleste*. Quoted in *Men of Mathematics* (E. T. Bell; 1937)

42 God is love, but get it in writing.
Gypsy Rose Lee (1914–70) US entertainer. Attrib.

43 As there is an infinite number of possible universes in the ideas of God, and as only one can exist, there must be a sufficient reason for God's choice, to determine him to one rather than to another.
Gottfried Wilhelm Leibniz (1646–1716) German philosopher and mathematician. *Monadology* (1714)

44 He's vulgar. Wormwood. He has a bourgeois mind.
C. S. Lewis (1898–1963) Irish-born British novelist. *The Screwtape Letters*, no. 22

45 After all, is our idea of God anything more than personified incomprehensibility?
Georg Christoph Lichtenberg (1742–99) German physicist and writer. Quoted in *The Reflections of Lichtenberg* (Norman Alliston, tr.; 1908)

46 Who has seen the face of the God of Spain? My heart is waiting
for that man of Iberia with rough hands
who will know how to carve from the ilex of Castile
the austere God of that brown earth.
Antonio Machado (1875–1939) Spanish poet and playwright. 'The Iberian God' (1913), ll. 63–67

47 The God of distance and of absence, of the anchor in the sea, the open sea . . . He frees us from the world in its omnipresence, and opens up a way where we can walk.
Antonio Machado (1875–1939) Spanish poet and playwright. 'Siesta, In Memory of Abel Martin', *Selected Poems* (Alan S. Trueblood, tr.; 1982), ll. 9–12

48 There, but for the Grace of God, goes God.
Herman J. Mankiewicz (1897–1953) US screenwriter and film producer. 1941. Said of Orson Welles during the making of *Citizen Kane* (1941). Also attributed to others. Quoted in *The Citizen Kane Book* (Pauline Kael; 1971)

49 Petitions pour into the Big House.
Haven't the people learned yet that God
is an absentee landlord?
Norman McCaig (1910–96) Scottish poet. 'The Kirk' (1980)

50 I have found God, but he is insufficient. I am
only spiritually dead. Physically I am alive.
Morally I am free.
Henry Miller (1891–1980) US novelist. *Tropic of Cancer* (1934)

51 There is a very good saying that if triangles
invented a god, they would make him three-
sided.
Montesquieu (1689–1755) French writer and jurist. *Lettres Persanes*
(1721)

52 Every man fashions and stays with the gods he
thinks support him in his need.
Es'kia Mphahlele (b. 1919) South African novelist, teacher, and political
activist. *The African Image* (1974)

53 God is dead: but considering the state the species
Man is in, there will perhaps be caves, for ages
yet, in which his shadow will be shown.
Friedrich Wilhelm Nietzsche (1844–1900) German philosopher and poet.
The Gay Science (1882), bk. 3

54 God is really only another artist. He invented the
giraffe, the elephant, and the cat. He has no real
style, He just goes on trying other things.
Pablo Picasso (1881–1973) Spanish painter and sculptor. Quoted in *Life
with Picasso* (Françoise Gilot and Carlton Lake; 1964), pt. 1

55 God can stand being told by Professor Ayer and
Marghanita Laski that He doesn't exist.
J. B. Priestley (1894–1984) British writer. Referring to A. J. Ayer.
'The BBC's Duty to Society', *Listener* (July 1, 1965)

56 God is not a word or a concept but a
consciousness we can realize here and now in the
flesh. Religion is more than worship of a
personal god.
Sarvepalli Radhakrishnan (1888–1975) Indian philosopher and statesman.
Eastern Religions and Western Thought (1939), ch. 4

57 God, he whom everyone knows, by name.
Jules Renard (1864–1910) French writer. April 1894. *Journal* (1877–
1910)

58 I fled Him, down the nights and down the days;
I fled Him, down the arches of the years;
I fled Him, down the labyrinthine ways
Of my own mind; and in the mist of tears
I hid from Him, and under running laughter.
Francis Thompson (1859–1907) British poet and critic. 'The Hound of
Heaven', *Poems* (1893)

59 God made everything out of nothing. But the
nothingness shows through.
Paul Valéry (1871–1945) French poet and philosopher. *Mauvaises
Pensées et Autres* (1942)

60 If God did not exist, it would be necessary to
invent Him.
Voltaire (1694–1778) French writer and philosopher. 'À l'auteur du
livre des trois Imposteurs', *Épîtres* (1769)

61 If God made us in His image, we have certainly
returned the compliment.
Voltaire (1694–1778) French writer and philosopher. *Le Sottisier*
(1778?), ch. 32

62 Any God I ever felt in church I brought in with me.
Alice Walker (b. 1944) US novelist and poet. *The Color Purple* (1982)

63 When I found out I thought that God was white,
and a man, I lost interest.
Alice Walker (b. 1944) US novelist and poet. *The Color Purple* (1982)

Good

see also **Morality, Virtue**

1 We call the intention good which is right in itself,
but the action is good, not because it contains
within it some good, but because it issued from a
good intention.
Peter Abelard (1079–1142?) French theologian and philosopher.
Abailard's Ethics (J. Ramsey McCallum, tr.; 1935)

2 Men are good in one way, but bad in many.
Aristotle (384–322 BC) Greek philosopher. *Nicomachean Ethics* (4th
century BC), 1106b

3 Goodness does not consist in greatness, but
greatness in goodness.
Athenaeus (*fl.* 2nd century) Egyptian-born Greek writer. *The
Deipnosophists* (2nd century), xiv, 6

4 Men have never been good, they are not good,
they never will be good.
Karl Barth (1886–1968) Swiss theologian. *Time* (April 12, 1954)

5 Prove all things; hold fast that which is good.
Bible. I Thessalonians, *King James Bible* (1611), 5:21

6 He who would do good to another, must do it in
Minute Particulars:
General Good is the plea of the scoundrel,
hypocrite & flatterer:
For Art & Science cannot exist but in minutely
organized Particulars.
William Blake (1757–1827) British poet, painter, engraver, and mystic.
Jerusalem (1804–20), ch. 3, pl. 55, ll. 60–62, quoted in *The
Poetry and Prose of William Blake* (David V. Erdman, ed.;
1965)

7 The greatest good.
Cicero (106–43 BC) Roman orator and statesman. *De Officiis* (44 BC),
bk. 1, ch. 5

8 He tried the luxury of doing good.
George Crabbe (1754–1832) British poet and clergyman. *Tales of the
Hall* (1819), bk. 3, 'Boys at School', l. 139

9 No people do so much harm as those who go
about doing good.
Mandell Creighton (1843–1901) British churchman and historian. *The
Life and Letters of Mandell Creighton* (Louise Creighton, ed.;
1904)

10 What, after all,
Is a halo? It's only one more thing to keep clean.
Christopher Fry (b. 1907) British playwright. *The Lady's Not for
Burning* (1949), Act 1

11 Thus to relieve the wretched was his pride,
And even his failings leaned to virtue's side.
Oliver Goldsmith (1730–74) Irish-born British novelist, playwright, and
poet. Referring to the village preacher. *The Deserted Village*
(1770)

12 A good man can be stupid and still be good. But
a bad man must have brains.
Maksim Gorky (1868–1936) Russian novelist, playwright, and short-story
writer. *The Lower Depths* (1903)

13 You was a good man, and did good things.
Thomas Hardy (1840–1928) British novelist and poet. *The
Woodlanders* (1887), ch. 48

14 Good, but not religious-good.
Thomas Hardy (1840–1928) British novelist and poet. *Under the
Greenwood Tree* (1872), ch. 2

15 All men are good when free from passion,
interest, or error.
Eugenio María de Hostos (1839–1903) Puerto Rican educator, social
reformer, and journalist. 'Hombres e Ideas', *Obras* (1939–54)

16 A good will is good not because of what it effects
or accomplishes, nor because of its fitness to
attain some proposed end; it is good only
through its willing, i.e. it is good in itself.
Immanuel Kant (1724–1804) German philosopher. *Grounding for the
Metaphysics of Morals* (1785)

17 There is no possibility of thinking of anything at
all in the world, or even out of it, which can be
regarded as good without qualification, except a
good will.
Immanuel Kant (1724–1804) German philosopher. *Grounding for the
Metaphysics of Morals* (1785)

18 Goodness does not more certainly make men
happy than happiness makes them good.
Walter Savage Landor (1775–1864) British poet and writer. 'Lord
Brooke and Sir Philip Sidney', *Imaginary Conversations of
Literary Men and Statesmen* (1824)

19 Man's goodness is a flame that can be hidden
but never extinguished.
Nelson Mandela (b. 1918) South African president and lawyer. *Long
Walk to Freedom* (1994)

20 There is no man so good, who, were he to
submit all his thoughts and actions to the laws,
would not deserve hanging ten times in his life.
Michel de Montaigne (1533–92) French essayist. *Essays* (1580–88),
bk. 3, ch. 9

21 Let him who finds good praise Allah and let him
who finds other than that blame no one but himself.
Muhammad (570?–632?) Arab religious leader and prophet. 610?–632?
Reported as spoken by Muhammad by Abu Dharr al-Ghifari.
Quoted in *Forty Hadith Qudsi* (E. Ibrahim and D. Johnson-
Davies, eds., trs.; 1988), 17th Hadith

22 The good is, like nature, an immense landscape
in which man advances through centuries of
exploration.
José Ortega y Gasset (1883–1955) Spanish writer and philosopher.
Meditations on Quixote (1914)

23 If we could see all the evil that may spring from
good, what should we do?
Luigi Pirandello (1867–1936) Italian dramatist, novelist, and short-story writer.
Six Characters in Search of an Author (Edward Storer, tr.; 1921)

24 The good is the beautiful.
Plato (428?–347? BC) Greek philosopher. *Lysias* (370? BC)

25 The good are better made by ill,
As odours crushed are sweeter still.
Samuel Rogers (1763–1855) British poet and art collector. 'Jacqueline'
(1814), st. 3

26 ALBANY Wisdom and goodness to the vile seem vile;
Filths savour but themselves.
William Shakespeare (1564–1616) English poet and playwright. *King
Lear* (1605–06), Act 4, Scene 2

27 PORTIA How far that little candle throws his beams!
So shines a good deed in a naughty world.
William Shakespeare (1564–1616) English poet and playwright. *The
Merchant of Venice* (1596–98), Act 5, Scene 1

28 Oh yet we trust that somehow good
Will be the final goal of ill.
Alfred Tennyson (1809–92) British poet. 1833–49. 'A. H. H.',
(Arthur Henry Hallam) was the fiancé of Tennyson's sister
Emily and died suddenly in September 1833. *In Memoriam
A. H. H.* (1850), can. 54, st. 1

29 On that best portion of a good man's life,
His little, nameless, unremembered, acts
Of kindness and of love.
William Wordsworth (1770–1850) English poet. July 13, 1798.
Subtitled: 'On Revisiting the Banks of the Wye During a
Tour, July 13, 1798'. 'Lines Composed a Few Miles Above
Tintern Abbey', *Lyrical Ballads* (1798), ll. 33–35

30 Oh, Sir! the good die first,
And they whose hearts are dry as summer dust
Burn to the socket.
William Wordsworth (1770–1850) English poet. 'The Wanderer', *The
Excursion* (1814), bk. 1, ll. 500–503

31 Understanding the good is fundamental, and if
we hold this firm we shall have begun. If we
enlarge it, we can become great; but if we regard
it lightly, we shall shrivel. The potentiality of its
flourishing rests with man and no other.
Zhu Xi (1130–1200) Chinese philosopher. *Jinsi lu* (1175–76), quoted
in *China's Imperial Past* (Charles O. Hucker; 1975)

Gossip

see also **Conversation, Rumour**

1 At last the secret is out, as it always must come
in the end,
The delicious story is ripe to tell to the intimate
friend;
Over the tea-cups and in the square the tongue
has its desire;
Still waters run deep, my dear, there's never
smoke without fire.
W. H. Auden (1907–73) British poet. 'Twelve Songs' (1936), No. 8,
st. 1, quoted in *Collected Poems* (Edward Mendelson, ed.;
1991)

2 That alchemy of quiet malice, by which women
can concoct a subtle poison from ordinary
trifles.
Nathaniel Hawthorne (1804–64) US novelist and short-story writer.
Referring to gossip. *The Scarlet Letter* (1850), ch. 5

3 Blood sport is brought to its ultimate refinement
in the gossip columns.
Bernard Ingham (b. 1932) British journalist. *Observer* (December 28,
1986), 'Sayings of the Week'

4 Men have always detested women's gossip
because they suspect the truth: their
measurements are being taken and compared.
Erica Jong (b. 1942) US writer. *Fear of Flying* (1973)

5 He's gone, and who knows how he may report
Thy words by adding fuel to the flame?
John Milton (1608–74) English writer. The chorus to Samson.
'Samson Agonistes', *Paradise Regain'd . . . To Which is added
Samson Agonistes* (1671), ll. 1350–51

6 It is a public scandal that gives offence, and it is
no sin to sin in secret.
Molière (1622–73) French playwright. *Tartuffe* (1664), Act 4, Scene 5

7 A cruel story runs on wheels, and every hand oils
the wheels as they run.
Ouida (1839–1908) British novelist. 'Moths', *Wisdom, Wit and
Pathos* (1877)

8 No one gossips about other people's secret
virtues.
Bertrand Russell (1872–1970) British philosopher and mathematician. *On
Education* (1926)

9 It is folly of too many to mistake the echo of a
London coffee-house for the voice of the
kingdom.
Jonathan Swift (1667–1745) Irish writer and clergyman. *The Conduct
of the Allies* (1711)

10 Talk had feet and could walk and gossip had
wings and could fly.
Margaret Walker (b. 1915) US poet, novelist, and journalist. *Jubilee*
(1966)

Government

see also Law, Politics, Power

1　The great object of the institution of civil government is the improvement of those who are parties to the social compact.
John Quincy Adams (1767–1848) US president. First Message to the US Congress (1825)

2　That form of government is best in which every man, whoever he is, can act best and live happily.
Aristotle (384–322 BC) Greek philosopher. *Politics* (335–322? BC), 1324a

3　The government must always be in advance of the public opinion.
Adolf Heinrich von Arnim-Boytzenburg (1803–68) German statesman. Speech (April 2, 1848)

4　The four pillars of government . . . (which are religion, justice, counsel, and treasure).
Francis Bacon (1561–1626) English philosopher, statesman, and lawyer. 'Of Seditions and Troubles', *Essays* (1625)

5　It has been said that England invented the phrase, 'Her Majesty's Opposition'; that it was the first government which made a criticism of administration as much a part of the policy as administration itself. This critical opposition is the consequence of cabinet government.
Walter Bagehot (1826–77) British economist and journalist. 'The Cabinet', *The English Constitution* (1867)

6　Government is the common enemy. All weapons are justifiable in the noble struggle against this terrible curse.
Alexander Berkman (1870–1936) Lithuanian-born US writer and anarchist. *Prison Memoirs of an Anarchist* (1912)

7　The object of government in peace and in war is not the glory of rulers or of races, but the happiness of the common man.
William Henry Beveridge (1879–1963) British economist and social reformer. *Social Insurance and Allied Services* (1942), pt. 7

8　Government intervention is necessary to protect the weak and ensure that all gain some of the benefit of economic progress.
Tony Blair (b. 1953) British prime minister. Lecture to the Fabian Society, London (1998)

9　Do not adopt the best system of government, but the one that is most likely to succeed.
Simón Bolívar (1783–1830) Venezuelan soldier and statesman. Letter to Jamaica (September 6, 1815)

10　Those who seek to change an established government by force of arms assume a fearful responsibility—a responsibility which nothing but the clearest and most intolerable injustice will acquit them for assuming.
George Brown (1818–80) Scottish-born Canadian journalist and politician. Speech, Toronto (1863)

11　Government is a contrivance of human wisdom to provide for human wants. Men have a right that these wants should be provided for by this wisdom.
Edmund Burke (1729–97) Irish-born British statesman and political philosopher. *Reflections on the Revolution in France* (1790)

12　Too bad all the people who know how to run the country are busy driving cabs and cutting hair.
George Burns (1896–1996) US comedian and actor. Attrib.

13　The government of the absolute majority instead of the government of the people is but the government of the strongest interests; and when not efficiently checked, it is the most tyrannical and oppressive that can be devised.
John C. Calhoun (1782–1850) US statesman. Speech to the Senate (February 15, 1833)

14　A simple and proper function of government is just to make it easy for us to do good and difficult for us to do wrong.
Jimmy Carter (b. 1924) US president. Acceptance speech, Democrat National Convention, New York City (July 15, 1976)

15　No Government can be long secure without a formidable Opposition.
Benjamin Disraeli (1804–81) British prime minister and writer. *Coningsby* (1844), bk. 2, ch. 1

16　That fatal drollery called a representative government.
Benjamin Disraeli (1804–81) British prime minister and writer. *Tancred* (1847), bk. 2, ch. 13

17　No one before 1929 . . . expected governments to be able to manage the economic weather. Since then every government in every country promises to be able to cure recessions.
Peter Drucker (b. 1909) Austrian-born US management consultant. *Post-capitalist Society* (1993)

18　No one's more touchy than people in government departments.
Nikolay Gogol (1809–52) Russian novelist and playwright. 'The Overcoat' (1842), quoted in *Diary of a Madman and Other Stories* (Ronald Wilks, tr.; 1972).

19　A government that is big enough to give you all you want is big enough to take it all away.
Barry Goldwater (1909–98) US politician. Quoted in *Bachman's Book of Freedom Quotations* (M. Ivens and R. Dunstan; 1978)

20　To model our political systems upon speculations of lasting tranquillity is to calculate on the weaker springs of the human character.
Alexander Hamilton (1757–1804) US statesman. *The Federalist* (co-written with James Madison and John Jay; 1787–88)

21　Governments and revolutionaries would compel society to take on the shape of their imagining, whereas poets are typically more concerned to conjure with their own and their readers' sense of what is possible or desirable or, indeed, imaginable.
Seamus Heaney (b. 1939) Irish poet. 'The Redress of Poetry', *The Redress of Poetry* (1995)

22　They that are discontented under *monarchy*, call it *tyranny*; and they that are displeased with *aristocracy*, call it *oligarchy*; so also, they which find themselves grieved under a *democracy*, call it *anarchy*, which signifies the want of government; and yet I think no man believes, that want of government, is any new kind of government.
Thomas Hobbes (1588–1679) English philosopher and political thinker. *Leviathan* (1651), pt. 2, ch. 19

23　To rule by fettering the mind through fear of punishment in another world, is just as base as to use force.
Hypatia (370?–415) Greek philosopher, mathematician, and astronomer. Quoted in 'Hypatia', *Little Journeys to the Homes of Great Teachers* (Elbert Hubbard; 1908)

24　There are no necessary evils in government. Its evils exist only in its abuses.
Andrew Jackson (1767–1845) US president. Veto of the Bank Bill (July 10, 1832)

25 I will govern according to the common weal, but not according to the common will.

James I (1566–1625) English monarch. 1621. Quoted in *History of the English People* (J. R. Green; 1879), pt. 7, ch. 4

26 Every government degenerates when trusted to the rulers of the people alone. The people themselves therefore are its only safe depositories.

Thomas Jefferson (1743–1826) US president. *Notes on the State of Virginia* (1785)

27 We reject a blue-print of the Western model of a two-party system of government because we do not subscribe to the notion of the government and the governed in opposition to one another. One clamouring for duties and the other crying for rights.

Jomo Kenyatta (1897?–1978) Kenyan president. Quoted in *Nationalism and New States in Africa* (Ali Al'Amin Mazrui and Michael Tidy; 1984)

28 The important thing for Government is not to do things which individuals are doing already, and to do them a little better or a little worse; but to do those things which at present are not done at all.

John Maynard Keynes (1883–1946) British economist. *The End of Laissez-Faire* (1925), ch. 4

29 The art of government is to deal with threats before they become overwhelming.

Henry Kissinger (b. 1923) German-born US politician and diplomat. *Meet the Press* (NBC television; July 31, 1988)

30 We give the impression of being in office but not in power.

Norman Lamont (b. 1942) British politician. *Observer* (June 13, 1993)

31 While the state exists there can be no freedom. When there is freedom there will be no state.

Vladimir Ilyich Lenin (1870–1924) Russian revolutionary leader. *The State and Revolution* (1919), ch. 5

32 In a free society the state does not administer the affairs of men. It administers justice among men who conduct their own affairs.

Walter Lippmann (1889–1974) US writer and editor. *The Good Society* (1937)

33 What is our task? To make Britain a fit country for heroes to live in.

David Lloyd George (1863–1945) British prime minister. Following the armistice that marked the end of World War I. Speech, Wolverhampton (November 24, 1918)

34 Give me better wood and I will make you a better cabinet.

John A. Macdonald (1815–91) Scottish-born Canadian statesman. Referring to criticism of his choice of cabinet ministers. Attrib.

35 The nanny state.

Iain Macleod (1913–70) British politician. Referring to overprotective government. *Spectator* (1960s)

36 To have good government, you often need less, not more, democracy.

Kishore Mahbubani (b. 1948) Singaporean diplomat. *Observer* (April 17, 1994), 'Sayings of the Week'

37 Every country has the government it deserves.

Joseph Marie de Maistre (1753–1821) French political philosopher and diplomat. Letter (August 15, 1811), quoted in *Lettres et Opuscules Inédits* (1851), vol. 1, no. 53

38 Government is, or ought to be, instituted for the common benefit, protection and security of the people, nation, or community; of all the various modes and forms of government, that is best which is capable of producing the greatest degree of happiness and safety, and is most effectively secured against the danger of maladministration.

George Mason (1725–92) US statesman. *Virginia Bill of Rights* (June 12, 1776), Article 1

39 The worst government is the most moral. One composed of cynics is often very tolerant and human. But when fanatics are on top there is no limit to oppression.

H. L. Mencken (1880–1956) US journalist, critic, and editor. 'Minority Report', *Notebooks* (1956)

40 Government obliges it: absolute power has its reasons that the Republic does not know of.

François Mitterrand (1916–96) French president. *Le Coup d'État Permanent* (1964), pt. 3

41 It's no use if we win the applause but lose the fight.

Mahathir bin Mohamad (b. 1925) Malaysian prime minister. Referring to concentrating on economic growth over other political concerns. *Straits Times* (September 1, 1990)

42 Increasingly it is possible for governments to choose only *between* evils.

Julius Kambarage Nyerere (1922–99) Tanzanian president. Lecture at the Africa Education Trust, London, quoted in *Guardian* (June 10, 1997)

43 Government, even in its best state, is but a necessary evil; in its worst state, an intolerable one.

Thomas Paine (1737–1809) English writer and political philosopher. *Common Sense* (1776), ch. 1

44 The function of a government is to calm, rather than to excite agitation.

Lord Palmerston (1784–1865) British prime minister. Quoted in *Gladstone and Palmerston* (P. Guedela; 1928)

45 Let the people think they govern and they will be governed.

William Penn (1644–1718) English preacher and colonialist. *Some Fruits of Solitude* (1693), no. 337

46 We live under a government of men and morning newspapers.

Wendell Phillips (1811–84) US reformer. Speech (January 28, 1852)

47 Government is not the solution to the problem— government is the problem.

Ronald Reagan (b. 1911) US president and actor. Attrib.

48 Any institution which does not suppose the people good, and the magistrate corruptible, is evil.

Maximilien Robespierre (1758–94) French lawyer and revolutionary. *Declaration of the Rights of Man* (April 24, 1793)

49 I don't make jokes—I just watch the government and report the facts.

Will Rogers (1879–1935) US actor, writer, and humorist. 'A Rogers Thesaurus', *Saturday Review* (August 25, 1962)

50 Better the occasional faults of a government that lives in a spirit of charity than the consistent omissions of a government frozen in the ice of its own indifference.

Franklin D. Roosevelt (1882–1945) US president. Speech, Philadelphia, Pennsylvania (June 27, 1936)

51 The foundation of the government of a nation must be built upon the rights of the people, but the administration must be entrusted to experts.

Sun Yat-sen (1866–1925) Chinese revolutionary and nationalist leader. *The Three Principles of the People* (Frank W. Price; 1953)

52 In place of the conception of the Power-State we are led to that of the Welfare-State.

William Temple (1881–1944) British clergyman. *Citizen and Churchman* (1941), ch. 2

53 I heartily accept the motto, 'That government is best which governs least'; and I should like to see it acted up to more rapidly and systematically. Carried out, it finally amounts to this, which I also believe, 'That government is best which governs not at all'.

Henry David Thoreau (1817–62) US writer. *On the Duty of Civil Disobedience* (1849)

54 Government is either organized benevolence or organized madness; its peculiar magnitude permits no shading.

John Updike (b. 1932) US writer. *Buchanan Dying* (1974), Act 1

55 Governments need to have both shepherds and butchers.

Voltaire (1694–1778) French writer and philosopher. *The Piccini Notebooks* (1735–50?)

56 When his horse is uneasy harnessed to a carriage, a gentleman is not comfortable in the carriage; just so, when the common people are uneasy under an administration, a gentleman is not comfortable in his post.

Xunzi (300?–235? BC) Chinese philosopher. 3rd century BC. Quoted in *China's Imperial Past* (Charles O. Hucker; 1975)

Grammar

see also **Language, Rules, Words**

1 I dare not alter these things; they come to me from above.

Alfred Austin (1835–1913) British poet. 1900? When accused of writing ungrammatical verse. *A Number of People: A Book of Reminiscences* (Edward Marsh; 1939)

2 A great error to waste young gentlemen's years so long in learning Latin by so tedious a grammar.

Gilbert Burnet (1643–1715) Scottish bishop and historian. Quoted in *The Later Stuarts* (Sir George Clark; 1934)

3 When I split an infinitive, god damn it, I split it so it stays split.

Raymond Chandler (1888–1959) US novelist. Letter to Edward Weeks, his English publisher (January 18, 1947)

4 Colorless green ideas sleep furiously.

Noam Chomsky (b. 1928) US linguist and political activist. Used by Chomsky to demonstrate that an utterance can be grammatical without having meaning. *Syntactic Structures* (1957), ch. 2

5 This is the sort of English up with which I will not put.

Winston Churchill (1874–1965) British prime minister and writer. Said to be a comment written in the margin of a report by a civil servant, referring to the person's use of a preposition at the end of a sentence. An alternative version of the remark substitutes 'bloody nonsense' for 'English'. Attrib. *Plain Words* (E. Gowers; 1948), ch. 9

6 The only man woman or child who wrote a simple declarative sentence with seven grammatical errors 'is dead'.

e. e. cummings (1894–1962) US poet and painter. Referring to Warren G. Harding. *ViVa* (1931)

7 I will not go down to posterity talking bad grammar.

Benjamin Disraeli (1804–81) British prime minister and writer. March 31, 1881. Remark made when correcting proofs of his last parliamentary speech. *Disraeli* (Robert Blake; 1966), ch. 32

8 Correct English is the slang of prigs who write history and essays. And the strongest slang of all is the slang of poets.

George Eliot (1819–80) British novelist. *Middlemarch* (1871–72), ch. 11

9 I have laboured to refine our language to grammatical purity, and to clear it from colloquial barbarisms, licentious idioms, and irregular combinations.

Samuel Johnson (1709–84) British lexicographer and writer. *The Rambler* (1750–52)

10 Grammere, that grounde is of al.

William Langland (1330?–1400?) English poet. *The Vision of Piers Plowman* (1365–86), Passus 18, l. 107

11 Grammar, which can govern even kings.

Molière (1622–73) French playwright. *Les Femmes Savantes* (1672), Act 2, Scene 6

12 I don't want to talk grammar, I want to talk like a lady.

George Bernard Shaw (1856–1950) Irish playwright. *Pygmalion* (1914)

13 I am the Roman Emperor, and am above grammar.

Sigismund (1368–1437) German-born emperor. Responding to criticism of his Latin. Attrib.

Gratitude

see also **Generosity, Praise**

1 Gratitude, like love, is never a dependable international emotion.

Joseph Alsop (1910–89) US journalist. November, 1952. *Observer* (November 1952)

2 A man's indebtedness . . . is not virtue; his repayment is. Virtue begins when he dedicates himself actively to the job of gratitude.

Ruth Benedict (1887–1948) US anthropologist. *The Chrysanthemum and the Sword* (1946), ch. 6

3 He ne'er consider'd it, as loth
To look a gift-horse in the mouth.

Samuel Butler (1612–80) English satirist. *Hudibras* (1663), pt. 1, can. 1, ll. 483–4

4 Our gratitude to most benefactors is the same as our feeling for dentists who have pulled our teeth. We acknowledge the good they have done and the evil from which they have delivered us, but we remember the pain they occasioned and do not love them very much.

Nicolas Chamfort (1741–94) French writer. *Maximes et Pensées* (1795)

5 Maybe the only thing worse than having to give gratitude constantly all the time, is having to receive it.

William Faulkner (1897–1962) US novelist. *Requiem for a Nun* (1951), Act 2, Scene 1

6 The still small voice of gratitude.

Thomas Gray (1716–71) British poet. 'Quartetto', *Ode for Music* (1769), st. 6, l. 8

7 In most of mankind gratitude is merely a secret hope for greater favours.

François La Rochefoucauld (1613–80) French epigrammatist and moralist. *Reflections, or Sentences and Moral Maxims* (1665), no. 298

8 CAPULET Thank me no thankings, nor proud me no prouds.

William Shakespeare (1564–1616) English poet and playwright. *Romeo and Juliet* (1595), Act 3, Scene 5

Greatness

see also **Genius, Heroism**

1 Great men are but life-sized. Most of them, indeed, are rather short.

Max Beerbohm (1872–1956) British essayist, critic, and caricaturist. *And Even Now* (1921)

2 Great things are done when Men & Mountains meet;
This is not done by Jostling in the Street.

William Blake (1757–1827) British poet, painter, engraver, and mystic. *Manuscript Notebooks* (1811), no. 64

3 Great actions are not always true sons
Of great and mighty resolutions.

Samuel Butler (1612–80) English satirist. *Hudibras* (1663), pt. 1, can. 1, ll. 885–886

4 They never fail who die
In a great cause.

Lord Byron (1788–1824) British poet. *Marino Faliero*, Act 2, Scene 2, ll. 93–94, quoted in *The Works of Lord Byron* (13 vols.) (Ernest Hartley Coleridge and R. E. Prothero, eds.; 1898–1904)

5 No great man lives in vain. The history of the world is but the biography of great men.

Thomas Carlyle (1795–1881) Scottish historian and essayist. 'The Hero as a Divinity', *On Heroes, Hero-Worship, and the Heroic in History* (1841)

6 Man is only truly great when he acts from the passions.

Benjamin Disraeli (1804–81) British prime minister and writer. *Coningsby* (1844), bk. 4, ch. 13

7 For he was great, ere fortune made him so.

John Dryden (1631–1700) English poet, playwright, and literary critic. Remark on the death of Oliver Cromwell. *Heroic Stanzas* (1659)

8 To be great is to be misunderstood.

Ralph Waldo Emerson (1803–82) US poet and essayist. 'Self-Reliance', *Essays* (1841)

9 World-historical men—the heroes of an epoch—must be recognized as its clear-sighted ones; their deeds and their words are the best of their time.

G. W. F. Hegel (1770–1831) German philosopher. *The Philosophy of History* (1832)

10 We must not measure greatness from the mansion down, but from the manger up.

Jesse Jackson (b. 1941) US clergyman, civil rights leader, and politician. Speech to the Democratic National Convention, San Francisco (July 17, 1984)

11 The grandeur of the dooms
We have imagined for the mighty dead.

John Keats (1795–1821) English poet. *Endymion* (1818), bk. 1, ll. 20–21

12 The great man . . . walks across his century and leaves the marks of his feet all over it, ripping out the dates on his galoshes as he passes.

Stephen Leacock (1869–1944) British-born Canadian writer and economist. 'The Life of John Smith', *Literary Lapses* (1910)

13 The lives of small men are like spiders' webs; they are studded with minute skeletons of greatness.

Dambudzo Marechera (1952–87) Zimbabwean writer and poet. 'The House of Hunger', *The House of Hunger* (1978)

14 If we stand tall it is because we stand on the shoulders of many ancestors.

Yoruba proverb.

15 Great men can't be ruled.

Ayn Rand (1905–82) Russian-born US writer and philosopher. *The Fountainhead* (1943)

16 MALVOLIO *reads* 'Some are born great, some achieve greatness, and some have greatness thrust upon 'em'.

William Shakespeare (1564–1616) English poet and playwright. *Twelfth Night* (1601), Act 2, Scene 5

17 'My name is Ozymandias, king of kings:
Look on my works, ye Mighty, and despair!'

Percy Bysshe Shelley (1792–1822) English poet. 'Ozymandias' (January 1818), quoted in *The Poetical Works* (Mrs. Shelley, ed.; 1839)

18 I think continually of those who were truly great—
The names of those who in their lives fought for life,
Who wore at their hearts the fire's centre.

Stephen Spender (1909–95) British poet and critic. 'I Think Continually of Those Who Were Truly Great' (1933)

19 There is
One great society alone on earth:
The noble living and the noble dead.

William Wordsworth (1770–1850) English poet. 1804–05. 'France (Concluded)', *The Prelude* (1850), bk. 11, ll. 393–395

Greece

see **Europe, European Countries**

Greed

see also **Desire, Excess, Hunger**

1 Thinking to get at once all the gold that the goose could give, he killed it, and opened it only to find—nothing.

Aesop (620?–560 BC) Greek writer. 'The Goose with the Golden Eggs', *Aesop's Fables* (6th century BC)

2 GLUTTON, n. A person who escapes the evils of moderation by committing dyspepsia.

Ambrose Bierce (1842–1914?) US writer and journalist. *The Devil's Dictionary* (1911)

3 He has an oar in every man's boat, and a finger in every pie.

Miguel de Cervantes (1547–1616) Spanish novelist and playwright. *Don Quixote* (1605–15), pt. 2, ch. 22

4 Gluttony is an emotional escape, a sign something is eating us.

Peter De Vries (1910–93) US novelist. *Comfort Me with Apples* (1956), ch. 7

5 Greed is essential to the proper functioning of our economic system . . . On the supply side we call it hustle or ambition or push and shove. On the demand side, we call it consumerism or, playfully, 'shop till you drop'.

William Dimma, US business executive. *Time* (November 15, 1989)

6 Greed is a bottomless pit which exhausts the person in an endless effort to satisfy the need without ever reaching satisfaction.

Erich Fromm (1900–80) German-born US psychoanalyst and philosopher. *Escape from Freedom* (1941)

7 Excess of wealth is cause of covetousness.

Christopher Marlowe (1564–93) English playwright and poet. *The Jew of Malta* (1590?), Act 1, Scene 2

8 People will swim through shit if you put a few bob in it.

Peter Sellers (1925–80) British comic actor. Quoted in *Halliwell's Filmgoer's Companion* (John Walker, ed.; 1999)

9 HOSTESS He hath eaten me out of house and home.

William Shakespeare (1564–1616) English poet and playwright. *Henry IV, Part 2* (1597), Act 2, Scene 1

10 PHILIP THE BASTARD That smooth-fac'd gentleman, tickling Commodity,
Commodity, the bias of the world.

William Shakespeare (1564–1616) English poet and playwright. *King John* (1591–98), Act 2, Scene 1

11 The impulse to acquisition, pursuit of gain, of
    money . . . has in itself nothing to do with
    capitalism . . . One may say that it has been
    common to all sorts and conditions of men at all
    times and in all cultures of the earth.
    Max Weber (1864–1920) German economist and social historian. 1904–
    05. *The Protestant Ethic and the Spirit of Capitalism* (Talcott
    Parsons, tr.; 1930)

Greetings

see also Friendship, Introductions

1 Take me to your leader.
    Anonymous. Customary line spoken by fictional alien invaders
    and imperialists.

2 What's up, Doc?
    Bugs Bunny, US cartoon character. Used in 'Bugs Bunny' cartoons
    (1937–63).

3 Wery glad to see you indeed, and hope our
    acquaintance may be a long 'un, as the gen'l'm'n
    said to the fi' pun' note.
    Charles Dickens (1812–70) British novelist. *The Pickwick Papers*
    (1837), ch. 25

4 In what other land save this one is the
    commonest form of greeting not 'Good day', nor
    'How d'ye do', but 'Love'? That greeting is
    Aloha–love, I love you, my love to you . . . It is a
    positive affirmation of the warmth of one's own
    heart-giving.
    Jack London (1876–1916) US writer. Referring to Hawaii. *My
    Hawaiian Aloha* (1916)

5 Dr. Livingstone, I presume?
    Henry Morton Stanley (1841–1904) British-born US explorer and journalist.
    October 28, 1871. Said on finding the missionary David
    Livingstone at Ujiji on Lake Tanganyika. *How I Found
    Livingstone* (1872), ch. 11

6 Hail fellow, well met,
    All dirty and wet:
    Find out, if you can,
    Who's master, who's man.
    Jonathan Swift (1667–1745) Irish writer and clergyman. 'My Lady's
    Lamentation' (1728)

Growing Up

see also Adulthood, Childhood, Youth

1 What they don't understand about birthdays and
    what they never tell you is that when you're
    eleven, you're also ten, and nine, and eight, and
    seven, and six, and five, and four, and three, and
    two, and one.
    Sandra Cisneros (b. 1954) US poet and writer. 'Eleven', *Women
    Hollering Creek* (1991)

2 *Arms and the man I sing*, and sing for joy,
    Who was last year all elbows and a boy.
    J. V. Cunningham (1911–85) US poet. 'Arms and the man I sing'
    quotes the opening to the *Aeneid* (19 BC) by Virgil. 'A
    Century of Epigrams', *The Collected Poems and Epigrams of
    J. V. Cunningham* (1971), no. 68

3 Too many people grow up. That's the real
    trouble with the world, too many people grow
    up. They forget. They don't remember what it's
    like to be 12 years old. They patronise, they treat
    children as inferiors. Well I won't do that.
    Walt Disney (1901–66) US film producer and animator. Attrib.

4 Perhaps the surest way to tell when a female goes
    over the boundary from childhood into
    meaningful adolescence is to watch how long it
    takes her to get to bed at night.
    Hildegarde Dolson (1908–81) US fiction writer. 'How Beautiful with
    Mud', *We Shook the Family Tree* (1946)

5 I wasn't good
    At growing up. Never learned
    The natives' art of life.
    U. A. Fanthorpe (b. 1929) British poet. 'Growing Up' (1984)

6 The psychic development of the individual is a
    short repetition of the course of development of
    the race.
    Sigmund Freud (1856–1939) Austrian psychoanalyst. 1910. *Leonardo
    da Vinci* (A. A. Brill, tr.; 1916)

7 Growth is a greater mystery than death. All of us
    can understand failure, we all contain failure and
    death within us, but not even the successful man
    can begin to describe the impalpable elations and
    apprehensions of growth.
    Norman Mailer (b. 1923) US novelist and journalist. *Advertisements for
    Myself* (1959)

8 Even though the appearance of formal thought is
    not a direct consequence of puberty, could we
    not say that it is a manifestation of cerebral
    transformations due to the maturation of the
    nervous system?
    Jean Piaget (1896–1980) Swiss psychologist. 'The Growth of Logical
    Thinking from Childhood to Adolescence' (1927), quoted in
    The Essential Piaget (H. E. Gruber and J. Jacques Vonèche,
    eds.; 1977)

9 So much of growing up is an unbearable waiting.
    A constant longing for another time. Another
    season.
    Sonia Sanchez (b. 1934) US poet and writer. 'Graduation Notes',
    Under a Soprano Sky (1987)

10 Just at the age 'twixt boy and youth,
    When thought is speech, and speech is truth.
    Sir Walter Scott (1771–1832) Scottish novelist. *Marmion* (1808),
    Introduction, can. 2

11 A child becomes an adult when he realizes that
    he has a right not only to be right but also to be
    wrong.
    Thomas Szasz (b. 1920) Hungarian-born US psychiatrist. 'Childhood',
    The Second Sin (1973)

Guilt

see also Conscience, Emotion

1 It is quite gratifying to feel guilty if you haven't
    done anything wrong: how noble! Whereas it is
    rather hard and certainly depressing to admit
    guilt and to repent.
    Hannah Arendt (1906–75) German-born US philosopher and historian.
    Eichmann in Jerusalem (1963), ch. 15

2 Dread remorse when you are tempted to err,
    Miss Eyre: remorse is the poison of life.
    Charlotte Brontë (1816–55) British novelist. *Jane Eyre* (1847), ch. 14

3 Now I am ashamed of confessing that I have
    nothing to confess.
    Fanny Burney (1752–1840) British novelist and diarist. *Evelina* (1778),
    Letter 59

4 Let this be your wall of brass, to have nothing on
    your conscience, no guilt to make you turn pale.
    Horace (65–8 BC) Roman poet. *Epistles* (20? BC), bk. 1, no. 1, l. 60

5 There is nothing to be said in mitigation.
International Military Tribunal of the Nuremberg Trials, international legal agreement. 1946. Concluding passage of the Judgment on Hermann Goering, the German Nazi leader. He was found guilty on all counts by the International Military Tribunal and was sentenced to death by hanging on October 15, 1946. 'Judgment: Law, Crime, and Punishment', *The Anatomy of the Nuremberg Trials* (T. Taylor; 1993), ch. 21

6 The sentence is that the individual shall throughout his life be dragged to the place of execution. In other words, remorse has become insane.
Søren Kierkegaard (1813–55) Danish philosopher. 1844. Referring to the fear of death. *The Concept of Dread* (W. Lowrie, tr.; 1957)

7 Remorse is nothing but the wry face that a conscience makes when it sees itself hideous.
Joaquim Maria Machado de Assis (1839–1908) Brazilian novelist and short-story writer. *Epitaph of a Small Winner* (1880)

8 Why, are you not as guilty, in (I'm sure)
As deep as I? And we should stick together.
Thomas Middleton (1580?–1627) English playwright. *The Changeling* (co-written with William Rowley; 1622), Act 3, Scene 4

9 Christ, can you imagine what a guilty skunk she made me feel. If she'd only admitted once she didn't believe any more in her pipe dream that some day I'd behave!
Eugene O'Neill (1888–1953) US playwright. *The Iceman Cometh* (1946)

10 In the Freudian system, the guilt is very complicated. In Gestalt therapy, the guilt thing is much simpler. We see guilt as projected *resentment* . . . find out what you resent, and the guilt will vanish and you will try to make the other person feel guilty.
Fritz Perls (1893–1970) German-born US psychiatrist. 'Gestalt Therapy Verbatim', quoted in *A Complete Guide to Therapy* (Joel Kovel, ed.; 1976)

11 If you give me six lines written by the most honest man, I will find something in them to hang him.
Cardinal Richelieu (1585–1642) French churchman and statesman. Attrib.

12 It is not the criminal things which are hardest to confess, but the ridiculous and shameful.
Jean-Jacques Rousseau (1712–78) French philosopher and writer. 1765–70. *Confessions* (1782)

13 ENOBARBUS I am alone the villain of the earth,
And feel I am so most.
William Shakespeare (1564–1616) English poet and playwright. *Antony and Cleopatra* (1606–07), Act 4, Scene 6

14 HAMLET I have heard,
That guilty creatures sitting at a play
Have by the very cunning of the scene
Been struck so to the soul that presently
They have proclaim'd their malefactions;
For murder, though it have no tongue, will speak
With most miraculous organ.
William Shakespeare (1564–1616) English poet and playwright. *Hamlet* (1601), Act 2, Scene 2

15 KING O! my offence is rank, it smells to heaven.
William Shakespeare (1564–1616) English poet and playwright. *Hamlet* (1601), Act 3, Scene 3

16 GLOUCESTER Suspicion always haunts the guilty mind;
The thief doth fear each bush an officer.
William Shakespeare (1564–1616) English poet and playwright. To Henry VI, who senses his impending murder. *Henry VI, Part 3* (1592), Act 5, Scene 6

17 LADY MACBETH Here's the smell of the blood still. All the perfumes of Arabia will not sweeten this little hand.
William Shakespeare (1564–1616) English poet and playwright. *Macbeth* (1606), Act 5, Scene 1

18 LADY MACBETH Out, damned spot! out, I say!
William Shakespeare (1564–1616) English poet and playwright. Referring to the blood on her hands. *Macbeth* (1606), Act 5, Scene 1

19 MACBETH Canst thou not minister to a mind diseas'd,
Pluck from the memory a rooted sorrow,
Raze out the written troubles of the brain,
And with some sweet oblivious antidote
Cleanse the stuff'd bosom of that perilous stuff
Which weighs upon the heart?
DOCTOR Therein the patient
Must minister to himself.
MACBETH Throw physic to the dogs; I'll none of it.
William Shakespeare (1564–1616) English poet and playwright. *Macbeth* (1606), Act 5, Scene 3

20 Father, I cannot tell a lie. I did it with my little hatchet.
George Washington (1732–99) US president. Referring to cutting a cherry tree. Attrib. *Life of George Washington* (M. L. Weems; 1810, 10th edition), ch. 2

21 Let guilty men remember their black deeds
Do lean on crutches, made of slender reeds.
John Webster (1578?–1632?) English playwright. *The White Devil* (1612), Act 5, Scene 6

Gullibility

see also Deception, Foolishness

1 There's a sucker born every minute.
P. T. Barnum (1810–91) US impresario. Attrib.

2 A game which a sharper once played with a dupe, entitled 'Heads I win, tails you lose'.
John Wilson Croker (1780–1857) Irish-born British politician and essayist. A 'sharper' is one who cheats or swindles. *Croker Papers* (1884)

3 I hold that the characteristic of the present age is craving credulity.
Benjamin Disraeli (1804–81) British prime minister and writer. November 25, 1864. Said to the Society for Increasing Endowments of Small Livings in the Diocese of Oxford. *Times* (November 26, 1864)

4 Never give a sucker an even break.
W. C. Fields (1879–1946) US entertainer. 1941. Attrib.

5 The most positive men are the most credulous.
Alexander Pope (1688–1744) English poet. 'Thoughts on Various Subjects', *Miscellanies* (1727)

6 IAGO He hath a person and a smooth dispose
Fram'd to make a woman false.
The Moor is of a free and open nature,
That thinks men honest that but seem to be so.
William Shakespeare (1564–1616) English poet and playwright. *Othello* (1602–04), Act 1, Scene 3

7 IAGO Work on,
My medicine, work! Thus credulous fools are caught.
William Shakespeare (1564–1616) English poet and playwright. *Othello* (1602–04), Act 4, Scene 1

8 Man is a dupable animal. Quacks in medicine, quacks in religion, and quacks in politics know this, and act upon that knowledge.
Robert Southey (1774–1843) English poet and writer. *The Doctor* (1812), ch. 87

H

Happiness

see also Emotion, Euphoria

1   One imagines the birth of happiness to be accompanied by some great spectacular upheaval. One can imagine it flowering in the most luxurious setting. Yet happiness is born of a trifle, feeds on nothing.
    Mariama Bâ (1929–81) Senegalese novelist and campaigner for women's rights. *Scarlet Song* (1981)

2   She supposed that basically she was an unhappy person who was happy.
    Beryl Bainbridge (b. 1934) British author and journalist. *Forever England North and South* (1987)

3   Happy beings are grave. They carry their happiness cautiously, as they would a glass filled to the brim which the slightest movement could cause to spill over, or break.
    Jules-Amédée Barbey d'Aurevilly (1808–89) French novelist and critic. 'Le Bonheur dans le crime', *Les Diaboliques* (1874)

4   I wonder why happiness is despised nowadays: dismissively confused with comfort or complacency, judged an enemy of social—even technological—progress.
    Julian Barnes (b. 1946) British writer. *Metroland* (1980)

5   WINNIE Oh, this *is* a happy day, this will have been another happy day! (*Pause.*) After all. (*Pause.*) So far.
    Samuel Beckett (1906–89) Irish playwright, novelist, and poet. *Happy Days* (1961), Act 2

6   Happiness occurs when people can give the whole of themselves to the moment being lived, when Being and Becoming are the same thing.
    John Berger (b. 1926) British novelist, essayist, and art critic. 'The Soul and the Operator', *Keeping a Rendezvous* (1991)

7   It was roses, roses, all the way.
    Robert Browning (1812–89) British poet. 'The Patriot', *Men and Women* (1855), st. 1

8   One cannot divine nor forecast the conditions that will make happiness; one only stumbles upon them by chance, in a lucky hour, at the world's end somewhere.
    Willa Cather (1873–1947) US novelist, poet, and journalist. 'Le Lavandou', *Virago Book of Women Travellers* (Mary Morris, ed.; 1996)

9   Happiness is a mystery like religion, and should never be rationalized.
    G. K. Chesterton (1874–1936) British writer and poet. *Heretics* (1905), ch. 7

10 'Alas!' said she, 'we ne'er can be
    Made happy by compulsion!'
    Samuel Taylor Coleridge (1772–1834) British poet. 'The Three Graves' (1798), pt. 4, st. 12

11 Domestic happiness, thou only bliss
    Of Paradise that has surviv'd the fall!
    William Cowper (1731–1800) British poet. 'The Garden', *The Task* (1785), bk. 3, ll. 41–42

12 I cherish mental images I have of three perfectly happy people. One collects stones. Another—an Englishman, say—watches clouds. The third lives on a coast and collects drops of seawater which he examines microscopically and mounts.
    Annie Dillard (b. 1945) US writer. *Pilgrim at Tinker's Creek* (1974), ch. 2

13 Happy the Man, and happy he alone,
    He who can call today his own:
    He who, secure within, can say,
    Tomorrow do thy worst, for I have liv'd today.
    John Dryden (1631–1700) English poet, playwright, and literary critic. *Translation of Horace's Odes* (1685), bk. 3, ode 29

14 I remember riding in a taxi one afternoon between very tall buildings under a mauve and rosy sky; I began to bawl because I had everything I wanted and knew I would never be so happy again.
    F. Scott Fitzgerald (1896–1940) US writer. 1932. 'The Crack-Up', *The Crack-Up: with Other Uncollected Pieces, Note-Books and Unpublished Letters* (Edmund Wilson, ed.; 1945)

15 Happiness is the deferred fulfilment of a prehistoric wish. That is why wealth brings so little happiness; money is not an infantile wish.
    Sigmund Freud (1856–1939) Austrian psychoanalyst. January 18, 1898. Said to Wilhelm Fliess. Quoted in *The Oxford Book of Money* (Kevin Jackson, ed.; 1995)

16 In order to be utterly happy the only thing necessary is to refrain from comparing this moment with other moments in the past, which I often did not fully enjoy because I was comparing them with other moments of the future.
    André Gide (1869–1951) French novelist and critic. *Journal* (1939–51)

17 To marvel at nothing is just about the one and only thing, Numicius, that can make a man happy and keep him that way.
    Horace (65–8 BC) Roman poet. *Epistles* (20? BC), bk. 1, no. 6, l. 1

18 Not the owner of many possessions will you be right to call happy: he more rightly deserves the name of happy who knows how to use the gods' gifts wisely and to put up with rough poverty, and who fears dishonour more than death.
    Horace (65–8 BC) Roman poet. 23? BC. *Odes* (13? BC), bk. 4, no. 9, l. 45

19 The supreme happiness of life is the conviction that we are loved.
    Victor Hugo (1802–85) French poet, novelist, and playwright. 'Fantine', *Les Misérables* (1862), bk. 5, ch. 4

20 When intention, ability, success, and correctness come together, there happiness is perfected.
Husain (626–680) Islamic religious leader. Quoted in 'The Lives of the Other Imams: Imam Ali ben al-Husayn', *The Book of Guidance into the Lives of the Twelve Imams* (Abu al-Mufid; 10th century)

21 Happiness is like coke—something you get as a by-product in the process of making something else.
Aldous Huxley (1894–1963) British novelist and essayist. Coke is a by-product of coal that has been distilled to get rid of its volatile components. *Point Counter Point* (1928)

22 He is happiest of whom the world says least, good or bad.
Thomas Jefferson (1743–1826) US president. Letter to John Adams (1786)

23 If you are foolish enough to be contented, don't show it, but grumble with the rest.
Jerome K. Jerome (1859–1927) British novelist and playwright. *Idle Thoughts of an Idle Fellow* (1886)

24 There is nothing which has yet been contrived by man, by which so much happiness is produced as by a good tavern or inn.
Samuel Johnson (1709–84) British lexicographer and writer. March 21, 1776. Quoted in *Life of Samuel Johnson* (James Boswell; 1791)

25 The Gracehoper was always jigging ajog, hoppy on akkant of his joycity.
James Joyce (1882–1941) Irish writer. *Finnegans Wake* (1939)

26 Happiness is not an ideal of reason but of imagination.
Immanuel Kant (1724–1804) German philosopher. *Fundamental Principles of the Metaphysics of Ethics* (1785)

27 As the maker of images
Carves the human shape
Out of granite,
So, out of the rock
Of thine experience,
Hew thine eternal happiness.
Jiddu Krishnamurti (1895–1986) Indian theosophist. *The Song of Life* (1931), pt. 28, st. 4

28 We are never so happy nor so unhappy as we imagine.
François La Rochefoucauld (1613–80) French epigrammatist and moralist. *Reflections, or Sentences and Moral Maxims* (1665), no. 49

29 Well, I find that a change of nuisances is as good as a vacation.
David Lloyd George (1863–1945) British prime minister. On being asked how he maintained his cheerfulness when beset by numerous political obstacles. Attrib.

30 Let no one trust the happiness of the moment; there is in it a drop of gall. When time has gone by and the spasm has ended, then, if ever, one can truly enjoy the event.
Joaquim Maria Machado de Assis (1839–1908) Brazilian novelist and short-story writer. *Epitaph of a Small Winner* (1880)

31 Great joys, like griefs, are silent.
Shackerley Marmion (1603–39) English playwright. *Holland's Leaguer* (1632), Act 5, Scene 1

32 Ask yourself whether you are happy, and you cease to be so.
John Stuart Mill (1806–73) British philosopher and social reformer. *Autobiography* (1873), ch. 5

33 I have no money, no resources, no hopes. I am the happiest man alive.
Henry Miller (1891–1980) US novelist. *Tropic of Cancer* (1934)

34 If one only wished to be happy, this could be easily accomplished; but we wish to be happier than other people, and this is always difficult, for we believe others to be happier than they are.
Montesquieu (1689–1755) French writer and jurist. Attrib.

35 The form most contradictory to human life that can appear among the human species is the 'self-satisfied man'.
José Ortega y Gasset (1883–1955) Spanish writer and philosopher. *The Revolt of the Masses* (1930)

36 When a small child . . . I thought that success spelled happiness. I was wrong. Happiness is like a butterfly which appears and delights us for one brief moment, but soon flits away.
Anna Pavlova (1882–1931) Russian ballet dancer. Quoted in 'Pages of My Life', *Pavlova: A Biography* (A. H. Franks, ed.; 1956)

37 Smile if it kills you. The physiology of smiling diffuses a lot of anger and angst. It makes your body and soul feel better.
Tom Peters (b. 1942) US management consultant and author. *The Pursuit of WOW!* (1994)

38 Anacharsis said a man's felicity consists not in the outward and visible favours and blessings of Fortune, but in the inward and unseen perfections and riches of the mind.
Plutarch (46?–120?) Greek biographer and philosopher. 'The Banquet of the Seven Wise Men' (1st–2nd century)

39 Happiness is beneficial for the body, but it is grief that develops the powers of the mind.
Marcel Proust (1871–1922) French novelist. 1927. Le Temps Retrouvé, *À la Recherche du Temps Perdu* (1913–27)

40 No man is happy who does not think himself so.
Publilius Syrus (*fl.* 1st century BC) Roman writer. 1st century BC. *Maxims* (Darius Lyman, tr.), 584

41 One inch of joy surmounts of grief a span,
Because to laugh is proper to the man.
François Rabelais (1494?–1553?) French humanist and satirist. 'Rabelais to the Reader', *Gargantua and Pantagruel* (1546), bk. 1

42 The happiness of the wicked runs away like a raging stream.
Racine (1639–99) French playwright. *Athalie* (1691), Act 2, Scene 7

43 Happiness: a good bank account, a good cook, a good digestion.
Jean-Jacques Rousseau (1712–78) French philosopher and writer. Attrib.

44 Happiness is not best achieved by those who seek it directly.
Bertrand Russell (1872–1970) British philosopher and mathematician. *Mysticism and Logic* (1918)

45 Every time I talk to a savant I feel quite sure that happiness is no longer a possibility. Yet when I talk with my gardener, I'm convinced of the opposite.
Bertrand Russell (1872–1970) British philosopher and mathematician. Attrib.

46 There is only one happiness in life, to love and be loved.
George Sand (1804–76) French novelist. Letter to Lina Calamatta (March 31, 1862)

47 Happiness is the only sanction of life; where happiness fails, existence remains a mad and lamentable experiment.
George Santayana (1863–1952) Spanish-born US philosopher, poet, and novelist. *The Life of Reason* (1905–06)

48 Joy, beautiful radiance of the gods, daughter of Elysium, we set foot in your heavenly shrine dazzled by your brilliance. Your charms reunite what common use has harshly divided: all men become brothers under your tender wing.
Friedrich von Schiller (1759–1805) German poet, playwright, and historian. 'Ode to Joy' (1785), st. 1

49 ORLANDO Oh! how bitter a thing it is to look into happiness through another man's eyes.
William Shakespeare (1564–1616) English poet and playwright. *As You Like It* (1599), Act 5, Scene 2

50 A lifetime of happiness: no man alive could bear it: it would be hell on earth.
George Bernard Shaw (1856–1950) Irish playwright. *Man and Superman* (1903), Act 1

51 Mankind are always happy for having been happy, so that if you make them happy now, you make them happy twenty years hence by the memory of it.
Sydney Smith (1771–1845) British clergyman, essayist, and wit. 1804–06. *Sketches of Moral Philosophy* (1849)

52 A man is happy so long as he chooses to be happy and nothing can stop him.
Alexander Solzhenitsyn (b. 1918) Russian novelist. *Cancer Ward* (1968)

53 There is no duty we so much underrate as the duty of being happy.
Robert Louis Stevenson (1850–94) Scottish novelist, essayist, and poet. 'An Apology for Idlers', *Virginibus Puerisque* (1881)

54 Happiness is an imaginary condition, formerly often attributed by the living to the dead, now usually attributed by adults to children, and by children to adults.
Thomas Szasz (b. 1920) Hungarian-born US psychiatrist. 'Emotions', *The Second Sin* (1973)

55 What concerns me is not the happiness of all men, but that of each.
Boris Vian (1920–59) French writer. *L'Écume des Jours* (1947)

56 Happiness is no laughing matter.
Richard Whately (1787–1863) British theologian and logician. *Apophthegms* (1854)

Haste

see also **Procrastination**

1 Make haste slowly.
Augustus (63 BC–AD 14) Roman emperor. 'Augustus', *Lives of the Caesars* (121?)

2 Desire to have things done quickly prevents their being done thoroughly.
Confucius (551–479 BC) Chinese philosopher, administrator, and moralist. *Analects* (5th century BC)

3 I found that all through the years you never appreciate anything if you get it in a hurry.
Ella Fitzgerald (1918–96) US jazz singer. *Ella: The Life and Times of Ella Fitzgerald* (Sid Colin; 1986)

4 The greatest assassin of life is haste, the desire to reach things before the right time which means overreaching them.
Juan Ramón Jiménez (1881–1958) Spanish poet. 'Heroic Reason', *Selected Writings* (1957)

5 The haste of a fool is the slowest thing in the world.
Thomas Shadwell (1642?–92) English playwright and poet. *A True Widow* (1679), Act 3, Scene 1

6 CLEOPATRA Celerity is never more admir'd Than by the negligent.
William Shakespeare (1564–1616) English poet and playwright. *Antony and Cleopatra* (1606–07), Act 3, Scene 7

7 IMOGEN O, for a horse with wings!
William Shakespeare (1564–1616) English poet and playwright. *Cymbeline* (1609–10), Act 3, Scene 2

8 MACBETH If it were done when 'tis done, then 'twere well It were done quickly.
William Shakespeare (1564–1616) English poet and playwright. *Macbeth* (1606), Act 1, Scene 7

9 He sows hurry and reaps indigestion.
Robert Louis Stevenson (1850–94) Scottish novelist, essayist, and poet. 'An Apology for Idlers', *Virginibus Puerisque* (1881)

10 Though I am always in haste, I am never in a hurry.
John Wesley (1703–91) English religious leader. Letter to Miss March (December 10, 1777), quoted in *Letters* (J. Telford, ed.; 1931), vol. 6

Hate

see also **Anger**, **Contempt**, **Misanthropy**, **Misogyny**

1 To be loved is to be fortunate, but to be hated is to achieve distinction.
Minna Antrim (1856–1950) US writer. *Naked Truth and Veiled Allusions* (1902)

2 It does not matter much what a man hates, provided he hates something.
Samuel Butler (1835–1902) British writer and composer. Quoted in *Note Books* (H. Festing Jones, ed.; 1912)

3 Now hatred is by far the longest pleasure; Men love in haste, but they detest at leisure.
Lord Byron (1788–1824) British poet. *Don Juan* (1819–24), can. 13, st. 4

4 The price of hating other human beings is loving oneself less.
Eldridge Cleaver (b. 1935) US writer and civil rights activist. 'On Becoming', *Soul on Ice* (1968)

5 Heaven has no rage like love to hatred turned, Nor hell a fury like a woman scorned.
William Congreve (1670–1729) English playwright and poet. *The Mourning Bride* (1697), Act 3, Scene 8

6 Hate is also creative: it creates more hate.
Henry Dumas (1934–68) US writer and poet. 'Thought', *Knees of A Natural Man: The Selected Poetry of Henry Dumas* (Eugene B. Redmond, ed.; 1989)

7 I hate all that don't love me, and slight all that do.
George Farquhar (1678–1707) Irish playwright. *The Constant Couple* (1699), Act 1, Scene 2

8 I never hated a man enough to give him diamonds back.
Zsa Zsa Gabor (b. 1918) Hungarian-born US film actor. *Observer* (August 28, 1957), 'Sayings of the Week'

9 The dupe of friendship, and the fool of love; have I not reason to hate and to despise myself? Indeed I do; and chiefly for not having hated and despised the world enough.
William Hazlitt (1778–1830) British essayist and critic. 'On the Pleasure of Hating', *The Plain Speaker* (1826)

10 If you hate a person, you hate something in him that is part of yourself. What isn't part of ourselves doesn't disturb us.
Hermann Hesse (1877–1962) German-born Swiss novelist and poet. *Demian* (1919)

11   The world is like a map of antipathies, almost of hates, in which everyone picks the symbolic colour of his difference.
Juan Ramón Jiménez (1881–1958) Spanish poet. 'Heroic Reason', *Selected Writings* (1957)

12   If one judges love by its visible effects, it looks more like hatred than like friendship.
François La Rochefoucauld (1613–80) French epigrammatist and moralist. *Reflections, or Sentences and Moral Maxims* (1665), no. 72

13   Let me look at the foulness and ugliness of my body. Let me see myself as an ulcerous sore running with every horrible and disgusting poison.
Ignatius of Loyola (1491–1556) Spanish theologian. *Spiritual Exercises* (1548), no. 58

14   The worst of the present day is that men hate one another so damnably. For my part I love them all.
Lord Melbourne (1779–1848) British prime minister. Attrib.

15   My loathings are simple: stupidity, oppression, crime, cruelty, soft music.
Vladimir Nabokov (1899–1977) Russian-born US novelist, poet, and critic. Attrib.

16   Hatred is a feeling which leads to the extinction of values.
José Ortega y Gasset (1883–1955) Spanish writer and philosopher. *Meditations on Quixote* (1914)

17   Oh, I have loved him too much to feel no hate for him.
Racine (1639–99) French playwright. *Andromaque* (1667), Act 2, Scene 1

18   Few people can be happy unless they hate some other person, nation or creed.
Bertrand Russell (1872–1970) British philosopher and mathematician. Attrib.

19   Malice is of a low stature, but it hath very long arms.
Sir George Savile (1633–95) English politician and pamphleteer. 'Of Malice and Envy', *Political, Moral, and Miscellaneous Thoughts and Reflections* (1750)

20   Disgust is cheap. I asked for self-disgust.
Wole Soyinka (b. 1934) Nigerian novelist, playwright, poet, and lecturer. *Madmen and Specialists* (1971)

21   A woman despises a man for loving her, unless she returns his love.
Elizabeth Stoddard (1823–1902) US novelist and poet. *Two Men* (1865), ch. 32

22   I've found, in my own writing, that a little hatred, keenly directed, is a useful thing.
Alice Walker (b. 1944) US novelist and poet. 'The Unglamorous but Worthwhile Duties of the Black Revolutionary Artist, or of the Black Writer Who Simply Works and Writes', *In Search of Our Mothers' Gardens* (1983)

Health and Healthy Living

see also Digestion, Exercise, Food, Medicine

1   Health is the first of all liberties, and happiness gives us the energy which is the basis of health.
Henri Frédéric Amiel (1821–81) Swiss writer and philosopher. 1865. *Journal intime* (1883–84)

2   In sickness, respect health principally; and in health, action. For those that put their bodies to endure in health, may in most sicknesses, which are not very sharp, be cured only with diet and tendering.
Francis Bacon (1561–1626) English philosopher, statesman, and lawyer. 'Of Regiment of Health', *Essays* (1625)

3   Health indeed is a precious thing, to recover and preserve which, we undergo any misery, drink bitter potions, freely give our goods: restore a man to his health, his purse lies open to thee.
Robert Burton (1577–1640) English scholar and churchman. *The Anatomy of Melancholy* (1621), pt. 3, sect. 1

4   A person often falls very ill in order to become someone else and then returns to health much disappointed.
Elias Canetti (1905–94) Bulgarian-born writer. *The Agony of Flies* (1992)

5   The health of the people is really the foundation upon which all their happiness and all their powers as a State depend.
Benjamin Disraeli (1804–81) British prime minister and writer. Speech (June 24, 1877)

6   The multitude of the sick shall not make us deny the existence of health.
Ralph Waldo Emerson (1803–82) US poet and essayist. 'Worship', *The Conduct of Life* (1860)

7   HEALTHY Too much health, the cause of illness.
Gustave Flaubert (1821–80) French novelist. *Le Dictionnaire des Idées Reçues* (1911)

8   I have the body of a man half my age. Unfortunately, he's in terrible shape.
George Foreman (b. 1949) US boxer. *Guardian* (December 28, 1996), Weekend

9   The scientific truth may be put quite briefly: eat moderately, having an ordinary mixed diet, and don't worry.
Robert Hutchison (1871–1960) British doctor. *Newcastle Medical Journal* (1932), vol. 12

10   If I had my way I'd make health catching instead of disease.
Robert G. Ingersoll (1833–99) US lawyer. Attrib.

11   O health! health! the blessing of the rich! the riches of the poor! who can buy thee at too deare a rate, since there is no enjoying this world, without thee?
Ben Jonson (1572–1637) English playwright and poet. *Volpone* (1606), Act 2, Scene 2

12   To preserve one's health by too strict a regime is in itself a tedious malady.
François La Rochefoucauld (1613–80) French epigrammatist and moralist. *Reflections, or Sentences and Moral Maxims* (1665), no. 208

13   Health is a precious thing, and the only one, in truth, which deserves that we employ in its pursuit not only time, sweat, trouble, and worldly goods, but even life . . . As far as I am concerned, no road that would lead us to health is either arduous or expensive.
Michel de Montaigne (1533–92) French essayist. *Essays* (1580–88), bk. 2

14   Attention to health is the greatest hindrance to life.
Plato (428?–347? BC) Greek philosopher. 4th century? BC. Attrib.

15   A man ought to handle his body like the sail of a ship, and neither lower and reduce it much when no cloud is in sight, nor be slack and careless in managing it when he comes to suspect something is wrong.
Plutarch (46?–120?) Greek biographer and philosopher. 'Advice About Keeping Well', *Moralia* (1st–2nd century)

16   Half of the secret of resistance to disease is cleanliness; the other half is dirtiness.
Proverb.

17 Without health life is not life; it is unlivable . . .
    Without health, life spells but languor and an
    image of death.
    François Rabelais (1494?–1553?) French humanist and satirist.
    Gargantua and Pantagruel (1546), bk. 4, Prologue

18 Use your health even to the point of wearing it
    out. That is what it is for. Spend all you have
    before you die, and do not outlive yourself.
    George Bernard Shaw (1856–1950) Irish playwright. 'Preface on
    Doctors', *The Doctor's Dilemma* (1911)

19 The preservation of health is a duty. Few seem
    conscious that there is such a thing as physical
    morality.
    Herbert Spencer (1820–1903) British philosopher. Attrib.

20 A substance that makes you ill if you don't
    eat it.
    Albert Szent-Györgyi (1898–1986) Hungarian-born US biochemist. His
    definition of a vitamin. Attrib.

21 'Tis healthy to be sick sometimes.
    Henry David Thoreau (1817–62) US writer. Attrib.

22 He destroys his health by labouring to preserve it.
    Virgil (70–19 BC) Roman poet. *Aeneid* (29–19 BC), bk. 12

23 Regimen is superior to medicine.
    Voltaire (1694–1778) French writer and philosopher. 'Physicians',
    Dictionnaire Philosophique (1764)

Hearing

see Senses

The Heart

see also The Body, Emotion

1 The precious porcelain of human clay.
   Lord Byron (1788–1824) British poet. *Don Juan* (1819–24), can. 4,
   st. 11

2 What comes from the heart, goes to the heart.
   Samuel Taylor Coleridge (1772–1834) British poet. 1833. *Table Talk*
   (1835)

3 When I first gave my mind to vivisection, as a
   means of discovering the motions and uses of the
   heart . . . I found the task so truly arduous, so
   full of difficulties, that I was almost tempted to
   think with Fracastorius, that the motion of the
   heart was only to be comprehended by God.
   William Harvey (1578–1657) English physician. *Anatomical Essay on
   the Motion of the Heart and Blood in Animals* (1628), ch. 1

4 What other dungeon is so dark as one's own
   heart! What jailer so inexorable as one's self.
   Nathaniel Hawthorne (1804–64) US novelist and short-story writer. *The
   House of Seven Gables* (1851)

5 The thing that eats the heart is mostly heart.
   Stanley Kunitz (b. 1905) US poet. Final line. 'The Thing That Eats
   the Heart' (1958)

6 The heart is an organ of fire.
   Michael Ondaatje (b. 1943) Sri Lankan-born Canadian novelist and poet.
   The English Patient (1992)

7 In a full heart there is room for everything, and
   in an empty heart there is room for nothing.
   Antonio Porchia (1886–1968) Italian-born Argentinian writer. *Voces* (W.
   S. Merwin, tr.; 1968)

8 Thanks to the human heart by which we live,
   Thanks to its tenderness, its joys and fears,
   To me the meanest flower that blows can give
   Thoughts that do often lie too deep for tears.
   William Wordsworth (1770–1850) English poet. 1802?–06. 'Ode:
   Intimations of Immortality from Recollections of Early
   Childhood', *Poems in Two Volumes* (1807), vol. 2, st. 11,
   ll. 204–207

9 Out-worn heart, in a time out-worn,
   Come clear of the nets of wrong and right;
   Laugh, heart, again in the grey twilight,
   Sigh, heart, again in the dew of the morn.
   W. B. Yeats (1865–1939) Irish poet and playwright. 1893? 'Into the
   Twilight', *The Wind Among the Reeds* (1899), st. 1

Heaven

see also Afterlife, Hell

1 In hope to merit Heaven by making earth a
   Hell.
   Lord Byron (1788–1824) British poet. *Childe Harold's Pilgrimage*
   (1812–18), can. 1, l. 305

2 When man tries to imagine Paradise on earth, the
   immediate result is a very respectable Hell.
   Paul Claudel (1868–1955) French writer and diplomat. *Conversations
   dans le Loir-et-Cher* (1929)

3 Knock, knock, knockin' on Heaven's door.
   Bob Dylan (b. 1941) US singer and songwriter. Song lyric. 'Knockin'
   on Heaven's Door' (1973)

4 Heav'n but the Vision of fulfill'd Desire,
   And Hell the Shadow of a Soul on fire.
   Edward FitzGerald (1809–83) British poet and translator. 1859. *The
   Rubáiyát of Omar Khayyám* (1868 edn.), st. 72

5 The immortals will send you to the Elysian plain
   at the ends of the earth, where fair-haired
   Rhadamanthys is. There life is supremely easy for
   men. No snow is there, nor ever heavy winter
   storm, nor rain, and Ocean is ever sending gusts
   of the clear-blowing west wind to bring coolness
   to men.
   Homer (*fl.* 8th century BC) Greek poet. The Elysian plains or fields
   (also known as Elysium) were the mythical land at the
   farthest corner of the earth where distinguished heroes were
   carried after they died and immortalized. They were
   considered to be a paradisal utopia. *Iliad* (8th century BC),
   bk. 4, ll. 563–569

6 Even the paradise of fools is not an unpleasant
   abode while it is inhabitable.
   William Ralph Inge (1860–1954) British churchman. Attrib.

7 If we opened for the unbelievers a gate in heaven
   and they ascended through it higher and higher,
   still they would say: 'Our eyes were dazzled:
   truly, we must have been bewitched'.
   The Koran (7th century), Sura 15, ll. 14

8 Heaven and hell
   Are words
   To frighten thee to right action.
   Jiddu Krishnamurti (1895–1986) Indian theosophist. *The Song of Life*
   (1931), pt. 28, st. 3

9 Probably no invention came more easily to man
   than Heaven.
   Georg Christoph Lichtenberg (1742–99) German physicist and writer.
   Aphorisms (1764–99)

10 Priests at Jerusalem sell . . . tickets for heaven. Printed paper with Dove in middle & Father & Son each side. Divided into seats like plan of theatre on benefit night.

Herman Melville (1819–91) US novelist. February 5, 1857. Quoted in *Journal of a Visit to Europe and the Levant* (H. C. Horsford, ed.; 1955)

11 A heaven on earth.

John Milton (1608–74) English writer. Referring to the Garden of Eden. *Paradise Lost* (1667), bk. 4, l. 208

12 The gates of Paradise will be opened on Mondays and on Thursdays.

Muhammad (570?–632?) Arab religious leader and prophet. 610?–632? Reported as spoken by Muhammad by Abu Hurairah, one of his companions. Quoted in *Forty Hadith Qudsi* (E. Ibrahim and D. Johnson-Davies, eds., trs.; 1988), 20th Hadith

13 It may be only glory that we seek here, but I persuade myself that, as long as we remain here, that is right. Another glory awaits us in heaven and he who reaches there will not wish even to think of earthly fame.

Petrarch (1304–74) Italian poet and scholar. *Secretum* (14th century)

14 The true paradises are the paradises that we have lost.

Marcel Proust (1871–1922) French novelist. Le Temps Retrouvé, À la Recherche du Temps Perdu (1913–27)

15 The Hindu ideal thus affirms that . . . the Kingdom of God is within us and we need not wait for its attainment till some undated future or look for an apocalyptic display in the sky.

Sarvepalli Radhakrishnan (1888–1975) Indian philosopher and statesman. *Eastern Religions and Western Thought* (1939), ch. 2

16 For observe, that to hope for Paradise is to live in Paradise, a very different thing from actually getting there.

Vita Sackville-West (1892–1962) British poet and novelist. *Passenger to Tehran* (1926), ch. 1

17 THE STATUE If you go to Heaven without being naturally qualified for it you will not enjoy yourself there.

George Bernard Shaw (1856–1950) Irish playwright. Said by the Statue of the Commander, who is visiting Don Juan in Hell, to his daughter Donna Aña, who thinks she wants to go to Heaven. *Man and Superman* (1903)

18 Heaven, as conventionally conceived, is a place so inane, so dull, so useless, so miserable, that nobody has ever ventured to describe a whole day in heaven, though plenty of people have described a day at the seaside.

George Bernard Shaw (1856–1950) Irish playwright. *Misalliance* (1914), Preface

19 Is there no change of death in paradise? Does ripe fruit never fall?

Wallace Stevens (1879–1955) US poet. 'Sunday Morning', *Selected Poems* (1955), st. 6

20 Heaven affords
unlimited accommodation
to the simple-minded.

R. S. Thomas (1913–2000) Welsh poet and clergyman. 1986. 'Revision', *Collected Poems* (1993)

21 Grant me paradise in this world; I'm not so sure I'll reach it in the next.

Tintoretto (1518?–94) Italian painter. 1581. Arguing that he be allowed to paint the *Paradiso* at the Doge's palace in Venice, despite his advanced age. Attrib.

22 That's the main charm of heaven—there's all kinds here—which wouldn't be the case if you let the preachers tell it.

Mark Twain (1835–1910) US writer and humorist. *Captain Stormfield's Visit to Heaven* (1909)

Hell

see also **Afterlife, The Devil, Heaven**

1 That's what hell will be like, small chat to the babbling of Lethe about the good old days when we wished we were dead.

Samuel Beckett (1906–89) Irish playwright, novelist, and poet. *Embers* (1959)

2 Hell, madame, is to love no more.

Georges Bernanos (1888–1948) French novelist and essayist. *Journal d'un Curé de Campagne* (1936), ch. 2

3 Hell has three gates: lust, anger, and greed.

The Bhagavad-Gita

4 The heart of man is the place the Devil's in: I feel sometimes a hell within myself.

Thomas Browne (1605–82) English physician and writer. *Religio Medici* (1642), pt. 1, sect. 51

5 Ah, Tam! ah, Tam! thou'll get thy fairin'!
In hell they'll roast thee like a herrin'!

Robert Burns (1759–96) Scottish poet and songwriter. 'Tam o' Shanter' (1791), ll. 201–202

6 Hell is oneself;
Hell is alone, the other figures in it
Merely projections. There is nothing to escape from
And nothing to escape to. One is always alone.

T. S. Eliot (1888–1965) US-born British poet and playwright. *The Cocktail Party* (1950), Act 1, Scene 3

7 Look not for fire in Hell, each man brings his own fire . . . Yes, Mahmut murmured, from this earth each takes his own fire.

Yasar Kemal (b. 1923) Turkish novelist. Mahmut, the hero of the novel, is reflecting on an inscription he has seen written on the side of a cart in Istanbul. *The Birds Have Also Gone* (1987)

8 There is wishful thinking in Hell as well as on earth.

C. S. Lewis (1898–1963) Irish-born British novelist. *The Screwtape Letters* (1942), Preface

9 I'm draggin' the audience to hell with me.

Jerry Lee Lewis (b. 1935) US rock-and-roll singer and pianist. Referring to his stage performances. Quoted in *Hellfire: The Jerry Lee Lewis Story* (Nick Tosches; 1982)

10 I myself am hell,
nobody's here.

Robert Lowell (1917–77) US poet. 'Skunk Hour', *Life Studies* (1956), quoted in *The Penguin Book of American Verse* (Geoffrey Moore, ed.; 1977)

11 The attempt to force human beings to despise themselves . . . is what I call hell.

André Malraux (1901–76) French writer and statesman. 'La Condition humaine', *Antimémoires* (1967), pt. 2

12 Why this is hell, nor am I out of it.

Christopher Marlowe (1564–93) English playwright and poet. *Doctor Faustus* (1592?), Act 1, Scene 3

13 Me miserable! which way shall I fly
Infinite wrath, and infinite despair?
Which way I fly is hell; myself am hell;
And in the lowest deep a lower deep
Still threatening to devour me opens wide,
To which the hell I suffer seems a heaven.
John Milton (1608–74) English writer. Said by Satan. *Paradise Lost* (1667), bk. 4, ll. 73–78

14 Hell was right now. Daddy always said that folks misread the Bible. Couldn't be no punishment worse than having to live here on earth, he said.
Gloria Naylor (b. 1950) US novelist, producer, and playwright. *Mama Day* (1988)

15 I fancy that the Hell of Too Many People would occupy a respectable place in the hierarchy of infernal regions.
J. B. Priestley (1894–1984) British writer. 'Too Many People', *Self-Selected Essays* (1932)

16 I believe I am in hell, therefore I am.
Arthur Rimbaud (1854–91) French poet. 'Nuit de l'Enfer', *Une Saison en Enfer* (1873)

17 There is no other hell for man than the stupidity and wickedness of his own kind.
Marquis de Sade (1740–1814) French philosopher and novelist. *Histoire de Juliette* (1797)

18 Hell is full of musical amateurs, music is the brandy of the damned.
George Bernard Shaw (1856–1950) Irish playwright. *Man and Superman* (1903)

19 Hell is a city much like London—
A populous and smoky city.
Percy Bysshe Shelley (1792–1822) English poet. A humorous follow up to two earlier works on the Peter Bell theme, *A Tale* by William Wordsworth and *A Lyrical Ballad* by John Hamilton Reynolds. 'Peter Bell the Third' (1819), pt. 3, st. 1, quoted in *The Poetical Works* (Mrs. Shelley, ed.; 1839)

20 Easy is the way down to the Underworld: by night and by day dark Dis's door stands open; but to withdraw one's steps and to make a way out to the upper air, that's the task, that is the labour.
Virgil (70–19 BC) Roman poet. *Aeneid* (29–19 BC), bk. 6, l. 126

21 If I am unable to make the gods above relent, I shall move Hell.
Virgil (70–19 BC) Roman poet. *Aeneid* (29–19 BC), bk. 7, l. 312

22 Mortals rub their skeptical eyes
that hell is a beach-fire at night where embers dance,
with temporal fireflies like thoughts of Paradise.
Derek Walcott (b. 1930) St. Lucian poet and playwright. *The Bounty* (1997)

Help

see also **Friendship, Generosity**

1 But what is past my help is past my care.
Beaumont & Fletcher, English playwrights. *The Double Marriage* (1621), Act 1, Scene 2

2 Bind up their wounds—but look the other way.
W. S. Gilbert (1836–1911) British librettist and playwright. *Princess Ida* (1884), Act 3

3 The golden rule is, to help those we love to escape from us; and never try to begin to help people, or influence them till they ask, but wait for them.
Friedrich Hügel (1852–1925) Italian-born British theologian and philosopher. Advice to his niece. *Letters to a Niece* (1928), Introduction

4 People must help one another; it is nature's law.
Jean de La Fontaine (1621–95) French writer and poet. 'L'Âne et le Chien', *Fables* (1668), bk. 8

5 You may help a lame dog over a stile but he is still a lame dog on the other side.
Ernest Newman (1868–1959) English music critic. Quoted in *Berlioz, Romantic and Classic* (Peter Heyworth, ed.; 1972)

Heresy

see also **Blasphemy, Treason**

1 IMPIETY, n. Your irreverence toward my deity.
Ambrose Bierce (1842–1914?) US writer and journalist. *The Devil's Dictionary* (1911)

2 A single friar who goes counter to all Christianity for a thousand years must be wrong.
Charles V (1500–58) Belgian-born Spanish monarch. Referring to Martin Luther. Speech at the Diet of Worms (April 19, 1521)

3 They that approve a private opinion, call it opinion; but they that mislike it, heresy: and yet heresy signifies no more than private opinion.
Thomas Hobbes (1588–1679) English philosopher and political thinker. *Leviathan* (1651), pt. 1, ch. 11

4 Sacred cows make the tastiest hamburger.
Abbie Hoffman (1936–89) US political activist. Attrib.

5 It is the customary fate of new truths to begin as heresies and to end as superstitions.
T. H. Huxley (1825–95) British biologist. 'The Coming of Age of the Origin of Species', *Science and Culture and Other Essays* (1881)

6 The heresy of one age becomes the orthodoxy of the next.
Helen Keller (1880–1968) US writer and lecturer. *Optimism* (1903)

7 Modern heretics are not burned at the stake. They are relegated to backwaters or pressured to resign.
Art Kleiner, US editor and journalist. *The Age of Heretics* (1996)

8 I shall never be a heretic, I may err in dispute; but I do not wish to decide anything finally; on the other hand, I am not bound by the opinions of men.
Martin Luther (1483–1546) German theologian and religious reformer. Letter (August 28, 1518)

9 Where it is a duty to worship the sun it is pretty sure to be a crime to examine the laws of heat.
John Morley (1838–1923) British statesman and writer. *Voltaire* (1872)

10 I was fired from there, finally, for a lot of things, among them my insistence that the Immaculate Conception was spontaneous combustion.
Dorothy Parker (1893–1967) US writer and wit. Quoted in *Writers at Work* (Malcolm Cowley; 1958)

11 PAULINA It is an heretic that makes the fire, Not she which burns in 't.
William Shakespeare (1564–1616) English poet and playwright. *The Winter's Tale* (1610–11), Act 2, Scene 3

Heroism

see also **Courage, Greatness**

1 Superman, disguised as Clark Kent, mild-mannered reporter for a great metropolitan newspaper, fights a never-ending battle for truth, justice, and the American way.
Anonymous. Hence the catch phrase 'Mild-mannered Clark Kent'. Introduction to US radio series (1950s)

2 The hero appears only when the tiger is dead.
Anonymous. Burmese proverb.

3 ANDREA Unhappy the land that has no heroes.
GALILEO No, unhappy the land that needs heroes.
Bertolt Brecht (1898–1956) German playwright and poet. *The Life of Galileo* (1938–39), Scene 13

4 In short, he was a perfect cavaliero,
And to his very valet seem'd a hero.
Lord Byron (1788–1824) British poet. *Beppo* (1818)

5 The Hero can be Poet, Prophet, King, Priest or what you will, according to the kind of world he finds himself born into.
Thomas Carlyle (1795–1881) Scottish historian and essayist. 'The Hero as Poet', *On Heroes, Hero-Worship, and the Heroic in History* (1841)

6 Where would the merit be if heroes were never afraid?
Alphonse Daudet (1840–97) French writer. *Tartarin de Tarascon* (1872), episode 3, ch. 5

7 Show me a hero and I will write you a tragedy.
F. Scott Fitzgerald (1896–1940) US writer. 1936. 'Notebooks E', *The Crack-Up: with Other Uncollected Pieces, Note-Books and Unpublished Letters* (Edmund Wilson, ed.; 1945)

8 Today's hero, the urban animal . . . can no longer be exclusively national, or even European, but instead must be turned . . . inside out, scrambled, bastardized, fertilized by the contributions of any number of different civilizations and geographical regions.
Juan Goytisolo (b. 1931) Spanish novelist and essayist. 1985. 'Mudejarism Today', *Saracen Chronicles* (1992)

9 Shakespeare has no heroes.
Samuel Johnson (1709–84) British lexicographer and writer. Attrib.

10 Ultimately a hero is a man who would argue with Gods, and awakens devils to contest his vision.
Norman Mailer (b. 1923) US novelist and journalist. *The Presidential Papers* (1963)

11 Superman comics are a fable, not of strength, but of disintegration. They appeal to the preadolescent mind not because they reiterate grandiose delusions, but because they reiterate a very deep cry for help.
David Mamet (b. 1947) US writer and film director. 'Kryptonite', *A Whore's Profession: Notes and Essays* (1994)

12 The chief business of the nation, as a nation, is the setting up of heroes, mainly bogus.
H. L. Mencken (1880–1956) US journalist, critic, and editor. *Prejudices* (1923)

13 The epic disappeared along with the age of personal heroism; there can be no epic with artillery.
Ernest Renan (1823–92) French philosopher, philologist, and historian. *Dialogues et Fragments Philosophiques* (1876)

14 Being a hero is about the shortest-lived profession on earth.
Will Rogers (1879–1935) US actor, writer, and humorist. 'A Rogers Thesaurus', *Saturday Review* (August 25, 1962)

15 A hero is the one who does what he can. The others do not.
Romain Rolland (1866–1944) French writer. 1912. 'L'Adolescent', *Jean-Christophe* (1903–12), vol. 3

16 The only absolutely and unapproachably heroic element in the soldier's work seems to be—that he is paid little for it—and regularly.
John Ruskin (1819–1900) British art critic, writer, and reformer. *The Crown of Wild Olive* (1866)

17 There are few heroes or villains. Most people are average, neither black nor white, but grey . . . And it's in that grey middle ground that the fundamental conflicts of our age take place.
Dmitri Shostakovich (1906–75) Russian composer. 1971–75. *Testimony: The Memoirs of Shostakovich* (Solomon Volkov, ed., Antonina W. Bouis, tr.; 1979), ch. 1

18 Faster than a speeding bullet, more powerful than a locomotive, able to leap tall buildings at a single bound—look, up there in the sky, it's a bird, it's a plane, it's Superman!
Jerry Siegel (1914–96) US comic-strip writer. Comic strip. *Superman* (co-written with Joe Shuster; June 1938)

19 Thou hast great allies:
Thy friends are exultations, agonies,
And love, and man's unconquerable mind.
William Wordsworth (1770–1850) English poet. August 1802. Toussaint L'Ouverture, the son of a slave, led the rebellion that ended slavery in Haiti in 1794 and drove out the French. He resisted Napoleon's efforts to reestablish French control, was captured, and died in prison in 1803. 'To Toussaint L'Ouverture', *Poems in Two Volumes* (1807), vol. 1, ll. 12–14

Historians

see also **Academics**, **History**

1 The historian must not try to know what is truth, if he values his honesty; for if he cares for his truths, he is certain to falsify his facts.
Henry Adams (1838–1918) US historian. *The Education of Henry Adams* (1907)

2 The historian who attempts to interpret the past in terms of present-day values often undertakes the almost impossible task of serving two masters—of trying to be both a chronicler and a chameleon.
Thomas A. Bailey (1902–83) US historian. 'The Mythmakers of American History', *Journal of American History* (June 1968)

3 History does not repeat itself. Historians repeat each other.
Arthur Balfour (1848–1930) British prime minister. Attrib.

4 The historian who writes history . . . performs an act of faith . . . His faith is at bottom a conviction that something true can be known about the movement of history and his conviction is a subjective decision, not a purely objective discovery.
Charles Beard (1874–1948) US historian. Quoted in *The Law of Civilization and Decay* (Brooks Adams; 1895), Introduction

5 No one can really *know* the life of his own day, let alone that of times long past. Always the historian sees as in a mirror darkly, the reds and golds rendered drab by the shadows of time.
Earl R. Beck (b. 1916) US historian. Attrib.

6 The 'facts' of history do not exist for any historian until he creates them, and into every fact he creates some part of his individual experience must enter.
Carl Becker (1873–1945) US historian. 'Detachment and the Writing of History', *Atlantic Monthly* (October 1910)

7 The historian is merely trying to do in time what the anthropologist does in space.
Robert Frederick Berkhofer, Jr. (b. 1931) US historian. *A Behavioral Approach to Historical Analysis* (1969)

8 The historians of facts who omit the most interesting thing about history—namely, its invention.

Elias Canetti (1905–94) Bulgarian-born writer. *The Agony of Flies* (1992)

9 The historian is after all, the skilled detective who asks questions, locates and follows clues, and must not reveal the solution until the tale is told.

John Clive (1924–90) British historian. *Not by Fact Alone: Essays on the Writing and Reading of History* (1989)

10 Behind the oft-repeated statement that each generation must write its own history lies a tragic situation . . . the historian is doomed to be forever writing in the sand.

Avery O. Craven (1885–1980) US historian. 'An Historical Adventure', *Journal of American History* (June 1964)

11 All historians must tell their tale convincingly, or be ignored.

Norman Davies (b. 1939) British historian and writer. *Europe: A History* (1996), Introduction

12 When historians and social critics have exhausted their resources in a vain attempt to find a thread of consistency in a body of data, they invariably take refuge in the discovery of paradox.

Carl N. Degler (b. 1921) US historian. 'Understanding the South', *Journal of Southern History* (November 1964)

13 We find but few historians of all ages, who have been diligent enough in their search for truth: it is their common method to take on trust what they distribute to the public; by which means a falsehood once received from a famed writer becomes traditional to posterity.

John Dryden (1631–1700) English poet, playwright, and literary critic. *Life of Plutarch* (1683–86)

14 The day is past when historians glory in war. Rather, with all thoughtful men, they deplore the barbarism of mankind which has made war so large a part of human history.

W. E. B. Du Bois (1868–1963) US sociologist, poet, and novelist. *The Gift of Black Folk* (1924)

15 The historian must have . . . some conception of how men who are not historians behave. Otherwise he will move in a world of the dead.

E. M. Forster (1879–1970) British novelist. 'Captain Edward Gibbon', *Abinger Harvest* (1936)

16 Historians relate, not so much what is done, as what they would have believed.

Benjamin Franklin (1706–90) US statesman and scientist. *Poor Richard's Almanack* (1732)

17 Historians tell the story of the past, novelists the story of the present.

Edmond de Goncourt (1822–96) French novelist and diarist. *Le Journal des Goncourts* (1851–96)

18 History is too serious to be left to historians.

Iain Macleod (1913–70) British politician. *Observer* (July 16, 1961), 'Sayings of the Week'

19 The talent of historians lies in their creating a true ensemble out of facts which are but half-true.

Ernest Renan (1823–92) French philosopher, philologist, and historian. *The Life of Jesus* (1863), Preface to 13th edn.

20 A historian is a prophet in reverse.

Friedrich von Schlegel (1772–1829) German critic and philosopher. *Das Athenäum* (1798–1800)

21 The real task of the historian is to throw overboard all facts but the essential.

A. J. P. Taylor (1906–90) British historian. *Manchester Guardian* (October 18, 1944)

22 Historians seek to be detached, impartial. In fact no historian starts out with his mind a blank, gradually to be filled by the evidence.

A. J. P. Taylor (1906–90) British historian. 'The Rise and Fall of 'Pure'. Diplomatic History', *Times Literary Supplement* (January 6, 1956)

23 Historians are like deaf people who go on answering questions that no one has asked them.

Leo Tolstoy (1828–1910) Russian writer. Quoted in 'Being an Historian', *A Discovery of Australia* (Manning Clark; 1976)

History

see also **Historians, Myths, The Past**

1 History, despite its
wrenching pain,
Cannot be unlived, but if
faced with courage, need not be
lived again.

Maya Angelou (b. 1928) US writer. Read at the inauguration of President Bill Clinton. 'On the Pulse of Morning' (January 20, 1993)

2 It is what the masses endure, how they resist, how they struggle that forms the body of true history. It is the coming into being, the bringing forth of the new . . . that is the heart of true history.

Herbert Aptheker (b. 1915) US historian. *A Documentary History of the Negro People in the United States* (1951)

3 In the modern age history emerged as something it never had been before . . . a man-made process, the only all comprehending process which owed its existence exclusively to the human race.

Hannah Arendt (1906–75) German-born US philosopher and historian. *Between Past and Future: Six Exercises in Political Thought* (1961)

4 History does repeat itself, with variations, and the price seems to go up each time.

Thomas A. Bailey (1902–83) US historian. 'The Mythmakers of American History', *Journal of American History* (June 1968)

5 The drama of people struggling with the conditions that confine them through the cycles of limited life spans is the heart of all living history, and the development of that drama itself, not a metahistorical scheme of classifying events, must provide the framework for any effective interpretation of history.

Bernard Bailyn (b. 1922) US historian. 'The Challenge of Modern Historiography', *American Historical Review* (February 1982)

6 People are trapped in history and history is trapped in them.

James Baldwin (1924–87) US writer and civil rights activist. 'Stranger in the Village', *Notes of a Native Son* (1955)

7 History, I contend, is the present.

James Baldwin (1924–87) US writer and civil rights activist. Quoted in *Emerge* (January 1990)

8 That is the triumph of history—truth absolute is not at hand; the original with which to match the copy does not exist.

Jacques Barzun (b. 1907) French-born US writer, cultural critic, and educator. *Clio and the Doctors* (1974)

9 If an historian were to relate truthfully all the crimes, weaknesses, and disorders of mankind, his readers would take his work for satire rather than for history.

Pierre Bayle (1647–1706) French philosopher and critic. *Historical and Critical Dictionary* (1697)

10 It is by becoming unmoral that history serves the highest morality.

Charles Beard (1874–1948) US historian. 'The Historian and Society', *Canadian Historical Review* (March 1933)

11 Let us admit that there are two histories, the actual series of events that once occurred; and the ideal series that we affirm and hold in memory.

Carl Becker (1873–1945) US historian. 'Everyman His Own Historian', *American Historical Review* (January 1932)

12 HISTORY, n. An account, mostly false, of events, mostly unimportant, which are brought about by rulers, mostly knaves, and soldiers, mostly fools.

Ambrose Bierce (1842–1914?) US writer and journalist. *The Devil's Dictionary* (1911)

13 That great dust-heap called 'history'.

Augustine Birrell (1850–1933) British statesman and writer. 'Carlyle', *Obiter Dicta* (1884)

14 If history cannot give us panaceas, it is the best possible cure of the yen for panaceas. And the only proven antidote for utopianism.

Daniel J. Boorstin (b. 1914) US historian and librarian. Quoted in *Newsweek* (July 6, 1970)

15 Those who mill around at the crossroads of history do so at their own peril.

David L. Boren (b. 1941) US politician. *Chicago Tribune* (January 5, 1990)

16 The riddle of history is not in Reason but in Desire; not in labor, but in love.

Norman O. Brown (b. 1913) US writer and educator. *Life Against Death* (1959)

17 In the Romantic age, history, like art and poetry, was more real than reality, more trustworthy than science. It was a noble definition of history; but then history was a noble subject.

George H. Callcott (b. 1929) US historian. *History in the United States 1800–60* (1970)

18 History, in illuminating the past, illuminates the present, and in illuminating the present, illuminates the future.

Benjamin Cardozo (1870–1938) US Supreme Court justice. *The Nature of the Judicial Process* (1921)

19 The hour of their crime does not strike simultaneously for all nations. This explains the permanence of history.

E. M. Cioran (1911–95) Romanian-born French philosopher and writer. Quoted in *The Faber Book of Aphorisms* (W. H. Auden and L. Kronenberger, eds.; 1964)

20 History is a clock that people use to tell their political and cultural time of day. It is also a compass that people use to find themselves on the map of human geography.

John Henrik Clarke (1915–98) US historian and educator. *African People in World History* (1993)

21 For a people to be without History, or to be ignorant of its history, is as for a man to be without memory—condemned forever to make the same discoveries that have been made in the past, invent the same techniques, wrestle with the same

problems, commit the same errors; and condemned, too, to forfeit the rich pleasures of recollection.

Henry Steele Commager (1902–98) US historian. *The Study of History* (1966)

22 History is a vast early warning system.

Norman Cousins (1915–90) US newspaper editor. Attrib. *Saturday Review* (April 15, 1978)

23 All history is the history of thought.

Benedetto Croce (1866–1952) Italian philosopher, historian, and politician. Referring to the role of imaginative re-creation in historical writing. Attrib.

24 The history of the past is a record of man's cruel inhumanity to man—of one imperfect vessel accusing and shattering another for the faults of both . . . There might be some excuse if man could turn from the frail, cracked vessels, and bring to trial the great potter for the imperfect work of his hand.

Clarence Darrow (1857–1938) US lawyer. Quoted in *The Meaning of History* (N. Gordon and Joyce Carper; 1991)

25 Our historic imagination is at best slightly developed. We generalize and idealize the past egregiously. We set up little toys to stand as symbols for centuries and the complicated lives of countless individuals.

John Dewey (1859–1952) US philosopher and educator. *Characters and Events* (1929)

26 Examine the history of all nations and all centuries and you will always find men subject to three codes: the code of nature, the code of society, and the code of religion . . . these codes were never in harmony.

Denis Diderot (1713–84) French encyclopedist and philosopher. *Supplément au Voyage de Bougainville* (1935)

27 A history without moral dimension is a history without human causation and hence what is natural is what occurs and what occurs is natural.

John P. Diggins (b. 1935) US historian. 'Consciousness and Ideology in American History', *American Historical Review* (February 1971)

28 History is philosophy teaching by examples.

Dionysius of Halicarnassus (fl. 30 BC) Greek historian and critic. *Ars Rhetorica* (1st century BC), ch. 11, sect. 2

29 History is a post-mortem examination. It tells ye what a country died iv. But I'd like to know what it lived iv.

Finley Peter Dunne (1867–1936) US humorist and journalist. Said by Mr. Dooley, an Irish saloonkeeper, whose opinions formed a well-known series of sketches written by Finley Peter Dunne. Quoted in *Mr. Dooley Remembers: the Informal Memoirs of Finley Peter Dunne* (Philip Dunne, ed.; 1963)

30 History is a fragment of biology: the life of man is a portion of the vicissitudes of organisms on land and sea.

Will Durant (1885–1981) US historian. *The Lessons of History* (co-written with Ariel Durant; 1968)

31 History smiles at all attempts to force its flow into theoretical patterns or logical grooves; it plays havoc with our generalizations, breaks all our rules; history is baroque.

Will Durant (1885–1981) US historian. *The Lessons of History* (co-written with Ariel Durant; 1968)

32 History teaches us that men and nations behave wisely once they have exhausted all other alternatives.

Abba Eban (b. 1915) South African-born Israeli statesman. December 16, 1970. Speech, *Times* (December 17, 1970)

33   Neither a wise man nor a brave man lies down on the tracks of history to wait for the train of the future to run over him.
Dwight D. Eisenhower (1890–1969) US general and president. Quoted in *Time* (October 6, 1952)

34   History is vanishing allegory.
Ralph Waldo Emerson (1803–82) US poet and essayist. *Journals* (1909–14)

35   According to the materialist conception of history, the ultimate determining element in history is the production and reproduction of real life.
Friedrich Engels (1820–95) German socialist. Letter to J. Bloch (1895)

36   History is more or less bunk. It's tradition. We don't want tradition. We want to live in the present and the only history that is worth a tinker's damn is the history we make today.
Henry Ford (1863–1947) US car manufacturer. *Chicago Tribune* (May 25, 1916)

37   The history which bears and determines us has the form of a war rather than that of a language: relations of power, not relations of meaning. History has no 'meaning', though this is not to say that it is absurd or incoherent.
Michel Foucault (1926–84) French philosopher. Quoted in *Power/Knowledge* (C. Gordon, ed., tr., L. Marshall, J. Mepham, and K. Soper, trs.; 1980)

38   Happy that Nation, fortunate that age, whose history is not diverting.
Benjamin Franklin (1706–90) US statesman and scientist. *Poor Richard's Almanack* (1732)

39   It is not the literal past, the 'facts' of history, that shape us, but images of the past embodied in language.
Brian Friel (b. 1929) Irish dramatist. *Translations* (1980), Act 3

40   History never looks like history when you are living through it. It always looks confusing and messy, and it always feels uncomfortable.
John W. Gardner (1912–77) US writer and public official. *No Easy Victories* (1968)

41   The world's history is a divine poem, of which the history of every nation is a canto, and every man a word.
James A. Garfield (1831–81) US statesman. Attrib. *The Meaning of History* (N. Gordon and Joyce Carper; 1991)

42   History subverts the stereotype of science as a precise, heartless enterprise that strips the uniqueness from any complexity and reduces everything to timeless, repeatable and controlled experiments in a laboratory.
Stephen Jay Gould (1941–2002) US geologist and writer. *The Flamingo's Smile* (1985)

43   History offers no comfort. It hands out hard lessons. It makes absurd reading, mostly. Admittedly, it moves on, but progress is not the result of history. History is never-ending. We are always inside history, never outside it.
Günter Grass (b. 1927) German writer. *Documents on the Workings of Politics* (1971)

44   History is written by the winners.
Alex Haley (1921–92) US writer. Interview, *The David Frost Television Show* (April 20, 1972)

45   A people not prepared to face its own history cannot manage to face its own future.
Karl-Heinz Hansen, German politician. 1978. Attrib.

46   What experience and history teach is this—that people and governments have never learned anything from history, or acted upon any lessons they might have drawn from it.
G. W. F. Hegel (1770–1831) German philosopher. 1830. *Lectures on the Philosophy of History* (1837), Introduction

47   History was a trash-bag of coincidences torn open in a wind. Surely, Watt with his steam engine, Faraday with his electric motor, and Edison with his incandescent light bulb did not have it as their goal to contribute to a fuel shortage some day that would place their countries at the mercy of Arab oil.
Joseph Heller (1923–99) US novelist. *Good as Gold* (1979)

48   A page of history is worth a volume of logic.
Oliver Wendell Holmes, Jr. (1841–1935) US judge. *New York Trust Co. vs. Eisner* (1921)

49   The charm of history and its enigmatic lesson consist in the fact that, from age to age, nothing changes and yet everything is completely different.
Aldous Huxley (1894–1963) British novelist and essayist. *The Devils of Loudon* (1952)

50   For what is history, but . . . huge libel on human nature, to which we industriously add page after page, volume after volume, as if we were holding up a monument to the honor, rather than the infamy of our species.
Washington Irving (1783–1859) US writer. *A History of New York* (1809)

51   History is a bath of blood.
William James (1842–1910) US psychologist and philosopher. *Memories and Studies* (1911)

52   'History', Stephen said, 'is a nightmare from which I am trying to awake'.
James Joyce (1882–1941) Irish writer. *Ulysses* (1922)

53   I like history because my reading of it is accompanied by the comforting certainty that all the people I meet in its pages are dead.
Cecil Francis Lloyd (1884–1938) English-born Canadian poet. *Sunlight and Shadow* (1928)

54   Hegel says somewhere that all great events and personalities in world history reappear in one fashion or another. He forgot to add: the first time as tragedy, the second as farce.
Karl Marx (1818–83) German philosopher. *The Eighteenth Brumaire of Louis Napoleon* (1852), sect. 1

55   With the world a war began, which will end with the world, and not before: that of man against nature, of the spiritual against the material, of freedom against fate. History is nothing more than the account of this unending struggle.
Jules Michelet (1798–1874) French historian. *L'Histoire Universelle* (1831), Introduction

56   History never stops. It progresses ceaselessly day and night. Trying to stop it is like trying to stop Geography.
Augusto Monterroso (b. 1921) Guatemalan-born Mexican writer. 'Aforismos, dichos, etc.', *The Rest is Silence* (1978)

57   And history? What use is history? Is history not the opium of the imagination?
Edwin Morgan (b. 1920) Scottish poet. 1972. 'The Resources of Scotland', *Crossing the Border* (1990)

58   We have need of history in its entirety, not to fall back into it, but to see if we can escape it.
José Ortega y Gasset (1883–1955) Spanish writer and philosopher. *The Revolt of the Masses* (1930)

59 There is no history of mankind, there are only many histories of all kinds of aspects of human life. And one of these is the history of political power. This is elevated into the history of the world.
Karl Popper (1902–94) Austrian-born British philosopher. *The Open Society and Its Enemies* (1945)

60 Hitler's rule does not spell the end of the historical process. If ever the historical *raison d'être* of psychoanalysis and its sociological function was needed, the current phase of historical development must prove it.
Wilhelm Reich (1897–1957) Austrian psychoanalyst. 1933. Quoted in *Reich Speaks of Freud* (M. Higgins, ed.; 1967)

61 The whole of contemporary history, the World Wars, the War of Dreams, the Man on the Moon, science, literature, philosophy, the pursuit of knowledge—was no more than a blink of the Earth Woman's eye.
Arundhati Roy (b. 1960) Indian writer. *The God of Small Things* (1997), 'Pappachi's Mouth'

62 The twins were too young to know that these were only history's henchmen . . . civilization's fear of nature, men's fear of women, power's fear of powerlessness. Man's subliminal urge to destroy what he could neither subdue or deify.
Arundhati Roy (b. 1960) Indian writer. *The God of Small Things* (1997), 'The History House'

63 The history of the World is the World's court of justice.
Friedrich von Schiller (1759–1805) German poet, playwright, and historian. *Jena* (May 26, 1789)

64 Well, some people say I'm pessimistic because I recognize the eternal cycle of evil. All I say is, look at the history of mankind *right up to this moment* and what do you find?
Wole Soyinka (b. 1934) Nigerian novelist, playwright, poet, and lecturer. Quoted in *Talking with African Writers* (Jane Wilkinson; 1992)

65 All our ancient history, as one of our wits remarked, is no more than accepted fiction.
Voltaire (1694–1778) French writer and philosopher. *Jeannot et Colin* (1764)

66 History is a cage, a conundrum we must escape or resolve before our art can go freely about its business.
John Edgar Wideman (b. 1941) US writer. *Breaking Ice: An Anthology of Contemporary African-American Fiction* (Terry McMillan, ed.; 1992)

67 History is the vast and complex tale of the working of the spirit of man.
George M. Wrong (1860–1948) Canadian historian. *Canadian Historical Review* (1936)

Holland

see **Europe, European Countries**

Hollywood

see also **Acting and Actors, Films**

1 Hollywood is the place where people from Iowa mistake each other for stars.
Fred Allen (1894–1956) US comedian. Quoted in *Filmgoer's Book of Quotes* (Leslie Halliwell; 1973)

2 The people are unreal. The flowers are unreal, they don't smell. The fruit is unreal, it doesn't taste of anything. The whole place is a glaring, gaudy, nightmarish set, built up in the desert.
Ethel Barrymore (1879–1959) US actor. 1923. Referring to Hollywood. Quoted in *Filmgoer's Book of Quotes* (Leslie Halliwell; 1973)

3 To survive there, you need the ambition of a Latin-American revolutionary, the ego of a grand opera tenor, and the physical stamina of a cow pony.
Billie Burke (1886–1970) US actor. Referring to Hollywood. Quoted in *Filmgoer's Book of Quotes* (Leslie Halliwell; 1973)

4 If my books had been any worse I should not have been invited to Hollywood, and if they had been any better I should not have come.
Raymond Chandler (1888–1959) US novelist. December 12, 1945. Letter to Charles W. Morton, *Raymond Chandler Speaking* (Dorothy Gardner and Katherine S. Walker; 1962)

5 Hollywood is a world with all the personality of a paper cup.
Raymond Chandler (1888–1959) US novelist. Attrib.

6 There's a big trend in Hollywood of taking very good European films and turning them into very bad American films. I've been offered a few of those, but it's really a perverse activity. I'd rather go on the dole.
Roddy Doyle (b. 1958) Irish novelist and playwright. *Independent* (April 25, 1994)

7 Hollywood will rot on the windmills of Eternity
Hollywood whose movies stick in the throat of God
Yes Hollywood will get what it deserves.
Allen Ginsberg (1926–97) US poet. 'America' (1956)

8 Lionel Barrymore first played my grandfather, later my father, and finally, he played my husband. If he'd lived, I'm sure I'd have played his mother. That's the way it is in Hollywood. The men get younger and the women get older.
Lillian Gish (1893–1993) US actor. Quoted in *Film Yearbook 1984* (1984)

9 All the cops in LA looked like handsome gigolos; obviously they'd come to LA to make the movies. Everybody had come to make the movies, even me.
Jack Kerouac (1922–69) US writer. Said by Sal Paradise on trying to find work in Los Angeles and Hollywood. *On the Road* (1957), pt. 1, ch. 13

10 Hollywood is a corporate mentality—like Socialist mentality. All the people are paid to say no. Very few to say yes. Because if you say yes and you're wrong—you're fired.
Andrei Konchalovsky (b. 1937) Russian-born film director. *Knave* (October 1986), quoted in *Chambers Film Quotes* (Tony Crawley, ed.; 1991)

11 Believe me, it was a tonic for my inferiority complex which is so readily developed in Hollywood.
Bert Lahr (1895–1967) US actor. Referring to his success in *The Wizard of Oz*. Quoted in *Notes on a Cowardly Lion* (John Lahr; 1969)

12 Tits and sand—that's what we used to call sex and violence in Hollywood.
Burt Lancaster (1913–94) US actor. *Photoplay* (April 1983), quoted in *Chambers Film Quotes* (Tony Crawley, ed.; 1991)

13 We Americans have always considered
    Hollywood, at best, a sinkhole of depraved
    venality. And, of course, it is. It is not a
    Protective Monastery of Aesthetic Truth. It
    is a place where everything is incredibly
    expensive.
    David Mamet (b. 1947) US writer and film director. 'A Playwright in
    Hollywood', *Writing in Restaurants* (1986)

14 A trip through a sewer in a glass-bottomed boat.
    Wilson Mizner (1876–1933) US playwright. Referring to Hollywood.
    Quoted in *The Incredible Mizners* (Rupert Hart-Davis; 1953)

15 Hollywood is a place where they'll pay you a
    thousand dollars for a kiss and fifty cents for
    your soul.
    Marilyn Monroe (1926–62) US film actor. Quoted in 'Acting', *Marilyn
    Monroe* (Guus Luijters; 1990)

16 The Communist plan for Hollywood was
    remarkably simple. It was merely to take over the
    motion picture business. Not only for its profits,
    as the hoodlums had tried—but also for a grand
    worldwide propaganda base.
    Ronald Reagan (b. 1911) US president and actor. *Where's the Rest of
    Me?* (1965)

17 In Hollywood, if you don't have happiness you
    send out for it.
    Rex Reed (b. 1938) US columnist and actor. Quoted in *Colombo's
    Hollywood* (J. R. Colombo; 1979)

18 Everyone in Hollywood is looking for the
    blockbuster. They tell you their last movie 'only
    grossed $70 million', as if that were some kind of
    crime.
    Neil Simon (b. 1927) US playwright. *Times* (August 4, 1990)

19 You can seduce a man's wife there, attack his
    daughter and wipe your hands on his canary, but
    if you don't like his movie, you're dead.
    Josef Von Sternberg (1894–1969) Austrian-born US film director.
    Referring to Hollywood. Quoted in *20th Century Quotations*
    (Frank S. Pepper; 1984)

20 My own start in movies was a lucky one, thanks
    to a contract that for almost 30 years remained
    unique in Hollywood history. That contract . . .
    challenged for a brief moment the basic premise
    of the whole studio system. Quite simply, I was
    left alone.
    Orson Welles (1915–85) US actor, director, producer, and writer.
    Referring to *Citizen Kane* (1941). *Look* (March 11, 1970),
    quoted in *Chambers Film Quotes* (Tony Crawley, ed.; 1991)

21 All Hollywood corrupts; absolute Hollywood
    corrupts absolutely.
    Edmund Wilson (1895–1972) US critic and writer. May 1938. Alluding
    to Lord Acton's famous saying: 'Power tends to corrupt, and
    absolute power corrupts absolutely'. 'Old Antichrist's
    Sayings', *Letters on Literature and Politics 1912–72* (1977)

The Holocaust

see also Fascism, World War II

1   The concentration camps, by making death itself
    anonymous (making it impossible to tell whether
    a prisoner is dead or alive), robbed death of its
    meaning as the end of a fulfilled life.
    Hannah Arendt (1906–75) German-born US philosopher and historian. *The
    Origins of Totalitarianism* (1951), ch. 12, sect. 3

2   I herewith commission you to carry out all
    preparations with regard to . . . a *total solution*
    of the Jewish question, in those territories of
    Europe which are under German influence.
    Hermann Goering (1893–1946) German Nazi leader. July 31, 1941.
    Written order sent to Reinhard Heydrich, deputy chief of the
    SS. Quoted in *The Rise and Fall of the Third Reich* (W. L.
    Shirer; 1962)

3   The final solution of the Jewish problem.
    Adolf Hitler (1889–1945) Austrian-born German dictator. Referring to
    the proposed extermination of the Jews in the concentration
    camps. Quoted in *The Final Solution* (Gerald Reitlinger;
    1968)

4   Auschwitz was the modern industrial application
    of a policy of extermination on which European
    world domination had long since rested.
    Sven Lindqvist (b. 1932) Swedish writer. 1992. *Exterminate All the
    Brutes* (Joan Tate, tr.; 1997)

5   The murder of the European Jews was no *shoah*.
    It was the ultimate logical outcome of the ancient
    status of the Jews in Western Civilization.
    Amos Oz (b. 1939) Israeli writer. 1967. *Shoah* is a Hebrew word
    meaning 'catastrophe'. 'The Meaning of Homeland', *Under
    This Blazing Light* (1979)

6   We know that a man can read Goethe or Rilke
    in the evening, that he can play Bach or
    Schubert, and go to his day's work at Auschwitz
    in the morning.
    George Steiner (b. 1929) US scholar and critic. Referring to Johann
    Sebastian Bach, Johann Wolfgang von Goethe, Rainer Maria
    Rilke, and Franz Peter Schubert. Auschwitz was a Nazi-run
    concentration camp in Poland during World War II (1939–
    45). *Language and Silence* (1967), preface

7   I was the accuser, God the accused. My eyes
    were open and I was alone—terribly alone in a
    world without God and without man.
    Elie Wiesel (b. 1928) Romanian-born US writer. Referring to the
    Holocaust. *Night* (Stella Rodway, tr.; 1958)

Home

see also Exile, Family, Houses

1   Ah, what is more blessed than to put cares away,
    when the mind lays by its burden, and tired with
    labour of far travel we have come to our own
    home and rest on the couch we have longed for?
    Catullus (84?–54? BC) Roman poet. *Carmina* (60? BC), 31

2   Many a man who thinks to found a home
    discovers that he has merely opened a tavern for
    his friends.
    Norman Douglas (1868–1952) British writer. *South Wind* (1917), ch. 24

3   Homes, as well as being made of bricks and
    mortar, melamine and foam rubber, are also
    made of ideas.
    Adrian Forty (b. 1948) British architectural historian. *Objects of Desire*
    (1974)

4   Home is the place where, when you have to go
    there,
    They have to take you in.
    Robert Frost (1874–1963) US poet. 'The Death of the Hired Man',
    North of Boston (1914)

5   What's the good of a home, if you are never in it?
    George Grossmith (1847–1912) British entertainer, singer, and writer. *The
    Diary of a Nobody* (1892), ch. 1

6 It takes a heap o' livin' in a house t' make it home.

Edgar A. Guest (1881–1959) British-born US poet and journalist. 'Home', *The Collected Works of Edgar A. Guest* (1934)

7 If you want to know how to value home, you should go abroad for a while among strangers.

Thomas Chandler Haliburton (1796–1865) Canadian writer and jurist. 'Sam Slick', *Nova Scotian* (1838)

8 I am breathing the air of home again!
My cheeks glow and understand.
And all this dirt on the road, it is
the filth of my fatherland.

Heinrich Heine (1797–1856) German poet. 1844. *Deutschland. A Winter's Tale* (T. J. Reed, tr.; 1986)

9 A home is not dead but living, and like all living things must obey the laws of nature by constantly changing. At least it can have a long life before finally coming to an end. I would like to think of my home passing through the generations.

Carl Larsson (1853–1919) Swedish painter and illustrator. 1919. About his home, Lilla Hyttnäs, in Sundborn, Sweden. *On the Sunny Side* (Michael Snodin, tr.; 1997)

10 In fact there was but one thing wrong with the Babbitt house; it was not a home.

Sinclair Lewis (1885–1951) US novelist. *Babbitt* (1922), ch. 2

11 A person can run for years but sooner or later he has to take a stand in the place which, for better or worse, he calls home, do what he can to change there.

Paule Marshall (b. 1929) US novelist, teacher, and journalist. *The Chosen Place, the Timeless People* (1969)

12 Home, the spot of earth supremely blest,
A dearer, sweeter spot than all the rest.

Robert Montgomery (1807–55) British clergyman and poet. Attrib.

13 Home is not where you live, but where they understand you.

Christian Morgenstern (1871–1914) German poet. Attrib.

14 Home. You can move away from it, but you never leave it. Not as long as it holds something to be missed.

Gloria Naylor (b. 1950) US novelist, producer, and playwright. *Mama Day* (1988)

15 Mid pleasures and palaces though we may roam,
Be it ever so humble, there's no place like home.

John Howard Payne (1791–1852) US actor and playwright. 'Home, Sweet Home', *Clari, the Maid of Milan* (1823)

16 Home is where I was safe. Home is what I fled from.

Mervyn Peake (1911–68) British novelist, poet, and artist. *Titus Alone* (1959), ch. 50

Homosexuality

see also Men, Sexuality, Women

1 Love I did the fairest boy,
That these fields did ere enjoy.

Richard Barnfield (1574–1627) English poet. 'Sonnet 12', *A History of Gay Literature* (Gregory Woods; 1998)

2 In addition to the normal sexual urge in men and women, Nature in her sovereign mood had endowed at birth certain male and female individuals with the homosexual urge.

Karoly Maria Benkert (1824–82) Hungarian physician. 1869. One of the first uses of the term 'homosexual'. Quoted in *Homosexuality: A History* (Colin Spencer; 1995)

3 I became one of the stately homos of England.

Quentin Crisp (1908–99) British writer. *The Naked Civil Servant* (1968)

4 America I'm putting my queer shoulder to the wheel.

Allen Ginsberg (1926–97) US poet. 'America' (1956)

5 It was the year of Trouble for Men, a talc and aftershave lotion of peculiar suggestiveness that, without any noticeable advertising, had permeated the gay world in a matter of weeks.

Alan Hollinghurst (b. 1954) British novelist. *The Swimming-Pool Library* (1988)

6 Once you've arranged the entire seating of Lancing College Chapel to sit next to the boy you fancy, anything is possible.

Kit Lambert (1935–81) British pop group manager. Quoted in *The Lamberts* (Andrew Motion; 1986)

7 What I particularly admired about the debate was the way that every speaker managed to give the impression that he personally had never met a homosexual in his life.

Osbert Lancaster (1908–86) English cartoonist and writer. July 1960. Caption to a cartoon of two women talking at a party. *A Queer Reader* (Patrick Higgins, ed.; 1993)

8 The 'homo' is the legitimate child of the 'suffragette'.

Wyndham Lewis (1882–1957) British novelist and painter. *The Art of Being Ruled* (1926), pt. 8, ch. 4

9 When I was in the military, they gave me a medal for killing two men, and a discharge for loving one.

Leonard Matlovich (d. 1991) US soldier in the Air Force. Quoted in *Homosexuality: A History* (Colin Spencer; 1995)

10 Outing is a nasty word for telling the truth.

Armistead Maupin (b. 1944) US novelist. Outing is the practice of making public the fact that somebody is homosexual when that person wants the information kept private. Remark (June 1991), quoted in *A Queer Reader* (Patrick Higgins, ed.; 1993)

11 Terry and I are both from the South and we're subjected to the most heterosexual propaganda of all. If propaganda worked we'd be straight.

Armistead Maupin (b. 1944) US novelist. *Sunday Times* (February 4, 1990)

12 Cruising, he had long ago decided, was a lot like hitchhiking. It was best to dress like the person you wanted to pick up.

Armistead Maupin (b. 1944) US novelist. *Tales of the City* (1978), quoted in *A Queer Reader* (Patrick Higgins, ed.; 1993)

13 Constant conditioning in my youth and social pressure in every department of my life all failed to convert me to heterosexuality.

Ian McKellen (b. 1939) British actor. *Times* (December 5, 1991)

14 Those lesbians and gay men who do have difficulties with their sexuality suffer them because of the prejudice and discrimination they face.

Ian McKellen (b. 1939) British actor. *Times* (December 5, 1991)

15 This sort of thing may be tolerated by the French, but we are British—thank God.

Sir Bernard Law Montgomery of Alamein (1887–1976) British field marshal. Comment on a bill to relax the laws against homosexuals. Speech, *Daily Mail* (May 27, 1965)

16 I will resist the efforts of some to obtain government endorsement of homosexuality.

Ronald Reagan (b. 1911) US president and actor. Remark (August 18, 1984)

17 If Michelangelo had been straight, the Sistine Chapel would have been wallpapered.

Robin Tyler, US comedian. Speech to a Gay Rights Rally, Washington (January 9, 1988)

18 It's fun to stay at the YMCA
They have everything there for young men to enjoy
You can hang out with all the boys.

Village People, US pop group. Song lyric. 'YMCA' (1979)

19 The 'Love that dare not speak its name' in this century is such a great affection of an elder for a younger man as there was between David and Jonathan . . . and such as you find in the sonnets of Michelangelo and Shakespeare.

Oscar Wilde (1854–1900) Irish poet, playwright, and wit. Referring to homosexuality. Quoting a poem by Lord Alfred Douglas. Speech at his first trial for sodomy (1895), quoted in *A Queer Reader* (Patrick Higgins, ed.; 1993)

20 It seems to me a most extraordinary thing that one may not feel regard and affection for a young man without it being criminal.

William III (1650–1702) English monarch. Quoted in *Homosexuality: A History* (Colin Spencer; 1995)

21 I don't want to be involved in some sort of scandal, but I've covered the waterfront.

Tennessee Williams (1911–83) US playwright. 1970. Quoted in *A Queer Reader* (Patrick Higgins, ed.; 1993)

Honesty

see also **Frankness, Truth**

1 A man may say, 'From now on I'm going to speak the truth'. But the truth hears him and hides before he's done speaking.

Saul Bellow (b. 1915) Canadian-born US writer. *Herzog* (1964)

2 I have tried if I could reach that great resolution of his to be honest without a thought of heaven or hell.

Thomas Browne (1605–82) English physician and writer. Referring to Seneca. *Religio Medici* (1642), pt. 1, sect. 47

3 Hide nothing from the masses of our people. Tell no lies. Expose lies whenever they are told. Mask no difficulties, mistakes, failures. Claim no easy victories.

Amilcar Cabral (1921–73) Guinean revolutionary leader and freedom fighter. Party directive (1965), quoted in *Revolution in Guinea: An African People's Struggle, Selected Texts by Amilcar Cabral* (Richard Handyside, ed.; 1969)

4 Fealty to party has no claims against fidelity to truth.

Frederick Douglass (1817–95) US abolitionist, writer, and orator. *Frederick Douglass' Paper* (September 10, 1852)

5 To live outside the law, you must be honest.

Bob Dylan (b. 1941) US singer and songwriter. Song lyric. 'Absolutely Sweet Marie', *Blonde on Blonde* (1966)

6 The life of an honest man must be an apostasy and a perpetual desertion . . . For the man who wishes to remain faithful to truth must make himself continually unfaithful to all the continual, successive, indefatigable renascent errors.

Charles Pierre Péguy (1873–1914) French writer and poet. 'The Search for Truth', *Basic Verities* (Ann and Julian Green, trs.; 1943), quoted in

7 A wit 's a feather, and a chief a rod;
An honest man 's the noblest work of God.

Alexander Pope (1688–1744) English poet. *An Essay on Man* (1733), Epistle 4, ll. 247–248

8 Intellectual honesty is more than what's legislated; it is inherent in the best people, those who take a broader view of their action than simply 'What's in it for me?'

Charles Sanford, Jr. (b. 1936) US business executive. Speech (1995)

9 HAMLET To be honest, as this world goes, is to be one man pick'd out of ten thousand.

William Shakespeare (1564–1616) English poet and playwright. *Hamlet* (1601), Act 2, Scene 2

10 VERGES I thank God I am as honest as any man living that is an old man and no honester than I.

William Shakespeare (1564–1616) English poet and playwright. *Much Ado About Nothing* (1598–99), Act 3, Scene 5

11 IAGO O wretched fool!
That liv'st to make thine honesty a vice.
O monstrous world! Take note, take note, O world!
To be direct and honest is not safe.

William Shakespeare (1564–1616) English poet and playwright. *Othello* (1602–04), Act 3, Scene 3

12 AUTOLYCUS Ha, ha! what a fool Honesty is! and Trust, his sworn brother, a very simple gentleman!

William Shakespeare (1564–1616) English poet and playwright. *The Winter's Tale* (1610–11), Act 4, Scene 4

13 AUTOLYCUS Though I am not naturally honest, I am so sometimes by chance.

William Shakespeare (1564–1616) English poet and playwright. *The Winter's Tale* (1610–11), Act 4, Scene 4

14 Old proverbe says,
That byrd ys not honest
That fyleth hys owne nest.

John Skelton (1460?–1529) English poet and satirist. Quoted in *The Poetical Works of John Skelton* (Rev. Alexander Dyce; 1856), Poems Against Garnesche

15 Honesty is the best policy; but he who is governed by that maxim is not an honest man.

Richard Whately (1787–1863) British theologian and logician. *Apophthegms* (1854)

Hope

see also **Anticipation, Optimism**

1 When hope dies, what else lives?

Ama Ata Aidoo (b. 1942) Ghanaian writer. *Our Sister Killjoy, or Reflections from a Black-Eyed Squint* (1977)

2 Hope . . . Go after her—she'll fly away
Ignore her—she'll chase you
She'll always keep you company
Until your breathing stops.

Ai Qing (1910–96) Chinese poet. 'Hope' (1950s), quoted in *The Red Azalea* (Edward Morin, ed.; 1990)

3 Hope is a good breakfast, but it is a bad supper.

Francis Bacon (1561–1626) English philosopher, statesman, and lawyer. *Apothegms* (1624)

4 Hope is the power of being cheerful in circumstances which we know to be desperate.

G. K. Chesterton (1874–1936) British writer and poet. *Heretics* (1905), ch. 12

5 He has no hope who never had a fear.

William Cowper (1731–1800) British poet. 'Truth' (1782), l. 298, quoted in *The Works of William Cowper* (Robert Southey, ed.; 1835–37)

6 'Hope' is the thing with feathers—
That perches in the soul—
And sings the tune without the words—
And never stops—at all.

Emily Dickinson (1830–86) US poet. No. 254 (1861), st. 1, quoted in *The Complete Poems of Emily Dickinson* (Thomas H. Johnson, ed.; 1970)

7 Hope raises no dust.

Paul Éluard (1895–1952) French surrealist poet. 'Ailleurs, Ici, Partout', *Poésie ininterrompue* (1946)

8 Swing low sweet chariot,
Comin' for to carry me home,
I looked over Jordan an' what did I see?
A band of Angels coming after me,
Comin' for to carry me home.

Folk Verse. Spiritual. Also sung by English Rugby Union supporters. 'Sweet Chariot'

9 He that lives upon hope will die fasting.

Benjamin Franklin (1706–90) US statesman and scientist. *Poor Richard's Almanack* (1758), Preface

10 And yet, hope pursues me, encircles me, bites me; like a dying wolf tightening its grip for the last time.

Federico García Lorca (1899–1936) Spanish poet and playwright. *Doña Rosita the Spinster* (1935), Act 3

11 'While there is life, there's hope', he cried;
'Then why such haste?' so groaned and died.

John Gay (1685–1732) English poet and playwright. 'The Sick Man and the Angel', *Fables* (1727), st. 1, l. 27

12 So little cause for carolings
Of such ecstatic sound
Was written on terrestrial things
Afar or nigh around,
That I could think there trembled through
His happy good-night air
Some blessed Hope, whereof he knew
And I was unaware.

Thomas Hardy (1840–1928) British novelist and poet. Referring to the song of a thrush on a winter's day. 'The Darkling Thrush', *Poems of the Past and Present* (1901)

13 Hope is necessary in every condition. The miseries of poverty, sickness, of captivity, would, without this comfort, be insupportable.

Samuel Johnson (1709–84) British lexicographer and writer. *The Rambler* (1750–52)

14 'Hope isn't the kind of thing that you can say either exists or doesn't exist', I thought to myself. 'It's like a path across the land—it's not there to begin with, but when lots of people go the same way, it comes into being'.

Lu Xun (1881–1936) Chinese writer. 'Hair' (1921)

15 Hope is our only hope.

Jack Mapanje (b. 1945) Malawian poet, theoretical linguist, and educator. 'If Chiuta Were Man', *Of Chameleons and Gods* (1991)

16 Hope elevates, and joy
Brightens his crest.

John Milton (1608–74) English writer. Satan of Adam. *Paradise Lost* (1667), bk. 9, ll. 633–634

17 Hope against hope, and ask till ye receive.

James Montgomery (1771–1854) Scottish poet and hymnwriter. 'The World Before the Flood', *The Poetical Works of James Montgomery* (1840–41), can. 5

18 One shouldn't offer hope cheaply.

Ben Okri (b. 1959) Nigerian novelist, short-story writer, and poet. Quoted in *Talking with African Writers* (Jane Wilkinson; 1992)

19 Things which you do not hope happen more frequently than things which you do hope.

Plautus (254?–184 BC) Roman comic playwright. *Mostellaria* (3rd–2nd century BC), Act 1, Scene 3

20 Hope springs eternal in the human breast;
Man never Is, but always To be blest.
The soul, uneasy, and confin'd from home,
Rests and expatiates in a life to come.

Alexander Pope (1688–1744) English poet. *An Essay on Man* (1733), Epistle 1, ll. 95–96

21 Our hopes, like towering falcons, aim
At objects in an airy height;
The little pleasure of the game
Is from afar to view the flight.

Matthew Prior (1664–1721) English diplomat and poet. 'To the Hon. Charles Montague' (1692)

22 For hope is but the dream of those that wake.

Matthew Prior (1664–1721) English diplomat and poet. *Solomon* (1718), bk. 2

23 CLAUDIO The miserable have no other medicine
But only hope.

William Shakespeare (1564–1616) English poet and playwright. *Measure for Measure* (1604), Act 3, Scene 1

24 The morning of hope wipes out the darkness of despair, now is the long-awaited daybreak.

Ahmad Shawqi (1868–1932) Egyptian poet. Quoted in *A History of the Arab Peoples* (Albert Hourani; 1991)

25 It is hope that maintains most of mankind.

Sophocles (496?–406? BC) Greek playwright. *Fragments* (406? BC)

26 Hope flares like a bit of straw in the stable.

Paul Verlaine (1844–96) French poet. *Sagesse* (1881)

27 When we stop hoping, that which we fear will certainly come.

Christa Wolf (b. 1929) German writer. *No Place on Earth* (1979)

Horror

see also **Fear, The Supernatural**

1 The horror! The horror!

Joseph Conrad (1857–1924) Polish-born British novelist. *Heart of Darkness* (1902), ch. 3

2 Mankind is resilient: the atrocities that horrified us a week ago become acceptable tomorrow.

Joseph Heller (1923–99) US novelist. *Picture This* (1988), ch. 37

Houses

see also **Architecture, Home**

1 He that builds a fair house upon an ill seat, committeth himself to prison.

Francis Bacon (1561–1626) English philosopher, statesman, and lawyer. 'Of Building', *Essays* (1625)

2 When your house contains . . . so many services that the hardware could stand up by itself without any assistance from the house, why have a house to hold it up?

Reyner Banham (1922–88) British design historian and theorist. April 1965. Quoted in 'Art in America', *Modern Movements in Architecture* (Charles Jencks; 1973)

3 One day houses will be turned inside out like gloves.

Paul Éluard (1895–1952) French surrealist poet. *Le Surréalisme au Service de la Révolution* (1933)

4 A house is a machine for living in.
Le Corbusier (1887–1965) Swiss-born French architect. 1923. *Towards a New Architecture* (Frederick Etchells, tr.; 1927)

5 Houses are like sentinels in the plain, old keepers of the weather watch . . . All colors wear soon away in the wind and rain, and then the wood is burned gray and the grain appears and the nails turn red with rust.
N. Scott Momaday (b. 1934) Native American writer. *The Way to Rainy Mountain* (1969), Introduction, quoted in *The Heath Anthology of American Literature* (Paul Lauter, ed.; 1998), vol. 2

6 If you want a golden rule that will fit everybody, this is it: Have nothing in your houses that you do not know to be useful, or believe to be beautiful.
William Morris (1834–96) British designer, socialist reformer, and poet. *Hopes and Fears for Art? The Beauty of Life?* (1882)

Human Condition

see also **Character**, **Existence**, **Humankind**, **Human Nature**, **Life**

1 The human condition is such that pain and effort are not just symptoms which can be removed without changing life itself . . . For mortals, the 'easy life of the gods' would be a lifeless one.
Hannah Arendt (1906–75) German-born US philosopher and historian. 'Labor', *The Human Condition* (1958), ch. 16

2 Is it likely that whereas joiners and shoemakers have certain functions or activities, man as such has none, but has been left by nature a functionless being.
Aristotle (384–322 BC) Greek philosopher. *Nicomachean Ethics* (4th century BC), 1097b

3 Man is a history-making creature who can neither repeat his past nor leave it behind.
W. H. Auden (1907–73) British poet. 'D. H. Lawrence', *The Dyer's Hand* (1963)

4 Alone, alone, about the dreadful wood
Of conscious evil runs a lost mankind,
Dreading to find its Father.
W. H. Auden (1907–73) British poet. 1941–42. 'For the Time Being', *W. H. Auden: Collected Poems* (Edward Mendelson, ed.; 1991), pt. 3, st. 1, ll. 1–3

5 But men must know, that in this theatre of man's life it is reserved only for God and angels to be lookers on.
Francis Bacon (1561–1626) English philosopher, statesman, and lawyer. *The Advancement of Learning* (1605), bk. 2

6 No man needs curing of his individual sickness; his universal malady is what he should look to.
Djuna Barnes (1892–1982) US writer and illustrator. *Nightwood* (1936)

7 Man is not only of this world but of another world, not only of necessity, but of freedom.
Nikolai Berdyaev (1874–1948) Ukrainian philosopher. *The Meaning of the Creative Act* (Donald A. Lowrie, tr.; 1916)

8 For we brought nothing into this world, and it is certain we carry nothing out.
Bible. I Timothy, *King James Bible* (1611), 6:7

9 In the seventeenth century a dissociation of sensibility set in from which we have never recovered.
T. S. Eliot (1888–1965) US-born British poet and playwright. 'The Metaphysical Poets', *Selected Essays* (1932)

10 The existential split in man would be unbearable could he not establish a sense of unity within himself and with the natural and human world outside.
Erich Fromm (1900–80) German-born US psychoanalyst and philosopher. *The Anatomy of Human Destructiveness* (1973)

11 The weight of the world
is love.
Under the burden
of solitude, under the
burden of dissatisfaction.
Allen Ginsberg (1926–97) US poet. 'Song' (1954)

12 Oh wearisome condition of humanity!
Born under one law, to another bound.
Fulke Greville (1554–1628) English courtier and poet. *Mustapha* (1609), Act 5, Scene 4

13 Ancient Egyptians, medieval people and contemporary man all have a kinship in sharing the feeling that the world is too complicated for them.
Frederick Herzberg (b. 1923) US social psychologist. *Work and the Nature of Man* (1968)

14 We are not free, separate, and independent entities, but like links in a chain, and we could not by any means be what we are without those who went before us and showed us the way.
Thomas Mann (1875–1955) German writer. 1902. *Buddenbrooks: The Decline of a Family* (H. T. Lowe-Porter, tr.; 1924), pt.3, ch.10

15 Man is a master of contradictions, they exist through him, and so he is grander than they. Grander than death, too grand for it—that is the freedom of his head. Grander than life, too grand for it—that is the piety in his heart.
Thomas Mann (1875–1955) German writer. *The Magic Mountain* (1924)

16 Every man carries the entire form of human condition.
Michel de Montaigne (1533–92) French essayist. 'Of Repentance', *Essays* (1580–88), bk. 3, ch. 2

17 Modern man . . . can never for one moment forget that he is living in a world in which he is a means and whose end is not his business.
Alberto Moravia (1907–90) Italian novelist. *Man as an End* (Bernard Wall, tr.; 1964)

18 We are like sailors who must rebuild their ship on the open sea, never able to dismantle it in dry-dock and to reconstruct it there out of the best materials.
Otto Neurath (1882–1945) Austrian philosopher and social theorist. 'Protocol Sentences', *Logical Positivism* (A. J. Ayer, ed.; 1959)

19 JAQUES All the world's a stage,
And all the men and women merely players;
They have their exits and their entrances;
And one man in his time plays many parts,
His acts being seven ages.
William Shakespeare (1564–1616) English poet and playwright. *As You Like It* (1599), Act 2, Scene 7

20 The world is a penal settlement. People are brainwashed and don't know any more why they are punished. I am a postman who is bringing the mail without knowing what is in the letters.
Karlheinz Stockhausen (b. 1928) German composer. Referring to how he perceives himself as a composer. *Sunday Times* (1973)

21 There are no conditions of life to which a man cannot get accustomed, especially if he sees them accepted by *everyone* about him.
Leo Tolstoy (1828–1910) Russian writer. *Anna Karenina* (1875–77), pt. 7, sect. 13

22 We are all in the gutter, but some of us are looking at the stars.
Oscar Wilde (1854–1900) Irish poet, playwright, and wit. *Lady Windermere's Fan* (1892), Act 3

23 We're all of us guinea pigs in the laboratory of God. Humanity is just a work in progress.
Tennessee Williams (1911–83) US playwright. *Camino Real* (1953), block 12

Humankind

see also **Civilization, Evolution, Human Condition, Human Nature**

1 Either a beast or a god.
Aristotle (384–322 BC) Greek philosopher. *Politics* (335–322? BC), bk. 1

2 Man, when perfected, is the best of animals, but, when separated from law and justice, he is the worst of all.
Aristotle (384–322 BC) Greek philosopher. *Politics* (335–322? BC), bk. 1

3 Man is one: greatness and animal fused together. None of his acts is pure charity. None is pure bestiality.
Mariama Bâ (1929–81) Senegalese novelist and campaigner for women's rights. *So Long a Letter* (1979)

4 Man is neither good nor bad; he is born with instincts and abilities.
Honoré de Balzac (1799–1850) French writer. *La Comédie Humaine* (1842), vol. 1, Foreword

5 MAN, n. An animal so lost in rapturous contemplation of what he thinks he is as to overlook what he indubitably ought to be.
Ambrose Bierce (1842–1914?) US writer and journalist. *The Devil's Dictionary* (1911)

6 Man is a noble animal, splendid in ashes, and pompous in the grave.
Thomas Browne (1605–82) English physician and writer. *Urn Burial* (1658), ch. 5

7 Man's inhumanity to man
Makes countless thousands mourn!
Robert Burns (1759–96) Scottish poet and songwriter. 'Man Was Made to Mourn' (1786)

8 The true science and the true study of man is man.
Pierre Charron (1541–1603) French theologian and philosopher. *Traité de la Sagesse* (1601), bk. 1, ch. 1

9 Man is an exception, whatever else he is. If he is not the image of God, then he is a disease of the dust.
G. K. Chesterton (1874–1936) British writer and poet. 'Wine When It Is Red', *All Things Considered* (1908)

10 What the superior man seeks is in himself. What the mean man seeks is in others.
Confucius (551–479 BC) Chinese philosopher, administrator, and moralist. *Analects* (5th century BC)

11 Humanity i love you because
when you're hard up you pawn your
intelligence to buy a drink.
e. e. cummings (1894–1962) US poet and painter. 'La Guerre', *no.* 2 (1925)

12 Unless above himself he can
Erect himself, how poor a thing is man!
Samuel Daniel (1562–1619) English poet and playwright. 'To the Ladie Margret, Countesse of Cumberland' (1600?), quoted in *The Complete Works in Verse and Prose of Samuel Daniel* (Rev. Alexander B. Grosart, ed.; 1885), bk. 2, st. 12

13 Man is developed from an ovule, about 125th of an inch in diameter, which differs in no respect from the ovules of other animals.
Charles Darwin (1809–82) British naturalist. *The Descent of Man* (1871), ch. 1

14 We must, however, acknowledge, as it seems to me, that man with all his noble qualities . . . still bears in his bodily frame the indelible stamp of his lowly origin.
Charles Darwin (1809–82) British naturalist. Closing words. *The Descent of Man* (1871), ch. 21

15 A wonderful fact to reflect upon, that every human creature is constituted to be that profound secret and mystery to every other.
Charles Dickens (1812–70) British novelist. *A Tale of Two Cities* (1859), bk. 1, ch. 1

16 What is man, when you come to think upon him, but a minutely set, ingenious machine for turning, with infinite artfulness, the red wine of Shiraz into urine?
Isak Dinesen (1885–1962) Danish writer. 'The Dreamers', *Seven Gothic Tales* (1934)

17 Plato having defined man to be a two-legged animal without feathers, Diogenes plucked a cock and brought it into the Academy, and said, 'This is Plato's man'. On which account this addition was made to the definition—'with broad at nails'.
Diogenes Laërtius (*fl.* 3rd century) Greek historian and biographer. 'Plato', *Lives of the Philosophers* (3rd century?)

18 We are the hollow men
We are the stuffed men
Leaning together
Headpiece filled with straw. Alas!
T. S. Eliot (1888–1965) US-born British poet and playwright. *The Hollow Men* (1925)

19 Man is explicable by nothing less than all his history.
Ralph Waldo Emerson (1803–82) US poet and essayist. 'History', *Essays* (1841)

20 Man is physically as well as metaphysically a thing of shreds and patches, borrowed unequally from good and bad ancestors, and a misfit from the start.
Ralph Waldo Emerson (1803–82) US poet and essayist. 'Beauty', *The Conduct of Life* (1860)

21 I believe that man will not merely endure; he will prevail. He is immortal, not because he alone among creatures has an inexhaustible voice, but because he has a soul, a spirit capable of compassion and sacrifice and endurance.
William Faulkner (1897–1962) US novelist. December 10, 1949. On receiving a Nobel Prize for literature, Stockholm. Speech (1949), quoted in *Les Prix Nobel en 1950* (1951)

22 Human beings are like timid punctuation marks sprinkled among the incomprehensible sentences of life.
Jean Giraudoux (1882–1944) French playwright and writer. *Siegfried* (1922), ch. 2

23 Man is frequently overwhelmed by the immense and alien power of the universe. But within that immense and alien power the frail heart-beat of man is the never-ending fact of creation.
Wilson Harris (b. 1921) Guyanese-born writer. *Tradition, the Writer and Society* (1967)

24 Man is an intellectual animal, and therefore an everlasting contradiction to himself. His senses centre in himself, his ideas reach to the ends of the universe; so that he is torn in pieces between the two, without a possibility of its ever being otherwise.
William Hazlitt (1778–1830) British essayist and critic. *Characteristics* (1823)

25 Human endeavor clumsily betrays Humanity.
Anthony Hecht (b. 1923) US poet. 'Japan', *A Summoning of Stones* (1954), quoted in *The Penguin Book of American Verse* (Geoffrey Moore, ed.; 1977)

26 The life of man is of no greater importance to the universe than that of an oyster.
David Hume (1711–76) Scottish philosopher and historian. 'Of Suicide', *Essays, Moral and Political* (1741)

27 The human race will be the cancer of the planet.
Julian Huxley (1887–1975) British biologist. Attrib.

28 Out of the crooked timber of humanity no straight thing can ever be made.
Immanuel Kant (1724–1804) German philosopher. *Idea for a General History with a Cosmopolitan Purpose* (1784), Proposition 6

29 Man is exceedingly contentious.
The Koran (7th century), Sura 18, l. 55

30 Man is a masterpiece of creation; if only because no amount of determinism can prevent him from believing that he acts as a free being.
Georg Christoph Lichtenberg (1742–99) German physicist and writer. *Aphorisms* (1764–99)

31 That man is the noblest of all creatures may also be inferred from the fact that no other creature has yet denied him the title.
Georg Christoph Lichtenberg (1742–99) German physicist and writer. *Aphorisms* (1764–99)

32 Let Pascal say that man is a thinking reed. He is wrong; man is a thinking erratum. Each period in life is a new edition that corrects the preceding one and that in turn will be corrected by the next, until publication of the definitive edition, which the publisher donates to the worms.
Joaquim Maria Machado de Assis (1839–1908) Brazilian novelist and short-story writer. *Epitaph of a Small Winner* (1880)

33 Man has never been the same since God died. He has taken it very hard.
Edna St. Vincent Millay (1892–1950) US poet. 'Conversation at Midnight' (1937)

34 A human being, he wrote, is a whispering in the steam pipes on a cold night; dust sifted through a locked window; one or the other half of an unsolved equation; a pun made by God; an ingenious assembly of portable plumbing.
Christopher Darlington Morley (1890–1957) US writer and journalist. *Human Being* (1932), ch. 11

35 There are one hundred and ninety-three living species of monkeys and apes. One hundred and ninety-two of them are covered with hair. The exception is a naked ape self-named *Homo sapiens*.
Desmond Morris (b. 1928) British ethnologist and writer. *The Naked Ape* (1967), Introduction

36 A human is a comet streamed in language far down time.
Les Murray (b. 1938) Australian poet. 'From Where We Live on Presence', *Translations from the Natural World* (1993)

37 I teach you the Superman. Man is something that is to be surpassed.
Friedrich Wilhelm Nietzsche (1844–1900) German philosopher and poet. *Thus Spake Zarathustra* (1883–92)

38 Man is a rope, tied between beast and Superman—a rope over an abyss.
Friedrich Wilhelm Nietzsche (1844–1900) German philosopher and poet. *Thus Spake Zarathustra* (1883–92)

39 Man, as he is, is not a genuine article. He is an imitation of something, and a very bad imitation.
Peter Ouspensky (1878–1947) Russian philosopher. *The Psychology of Man's Possible Evolution* (1950), ch. 2

40 Now humanity does not know where to go because no one is waiting for it: not even God.
Antonio Porchia (1886–1968) Italian-born Argentinian writer. *Voces* (W. S. Merwin, tr.; 1968)

41 Man is the measure of all things.
Protagoras (480?–411? BC) Greek philosopher. 'On the Gods' (5th century BC)

42 Human beings were invented by water as a device for transporting itself from one place to another.
Tom Robbins (b. 1936) US writer. *Another Roadside Attraction* (1971)

43 The more we realise our minuteness and our impotence in the face of cosmic forces, the more amazing becomes what human beings have achieved.
Bertrand Russell (1872–1970) British philosopher and mathematician. *New Hopes for a Changing World* (1951)

44 Atoms for peace. Man is still the greatest miracle and the greatest problem on this earth.
David Sarnoff (1891–1971) Russian-born US broadcasting executive. January 27, 1954. First message sent with atomic power.

45 For mankind as a whole there are no exports. We did not start developing by obtaining foreign exchange from Mars or the moon. Mankind is a closed society.
E. F. Schumacher (1911–77) German-born British economist. *Small is Beautiful* (1973), ch. 14

46 HAMLET What a piece of work is a man! How noble in reason! how infinite in faculties! in form and moving, how express and admirable! in action, how like an angel! in apprehension, how like a god! the beauty of the world! the paragon of animals! And yet, to me, what is this quintessence of dust? Man delights not me—no, nor woman neither.
William Shakespeare (1564–1616) English poet and playwright. *Hamlet* (1601), Act 2, Scene 2

47 The salvation of mankind lies only in making everything the concern of all.
Alexander Solzhenitsyn (b. 1918) Russian novelist. Nobel lecture (1972)

48 Man, unlike any other thing organic or inorganic in the universe, grows beyond his work, walks up the stairs of his concepts, emerges ahead of his accomplishments.
John Steinbeck (1902–68) US novelist. *The Grapes of Wrath* (1939), ch. 14

49 The fish in the water is silent, the animal on the earth is noisy, the bird in the air is singing. But Man has in him the silence of the sea, the noise of the earth and the music of the air.
Rabindranath Tagore (1861–1941) Indian poet, writer, and philosopher. *Stray Birds* (1917), no. 43

50 I do not value any view of the universe into which man and the institutions of man enter very largely and absorb much of the attention. Man is but the place where I stand, and the prospect hence is infinite.
Henry David Thoreau (1817–62) US writer. *Journal* (April 2, 1852)

51 If the Eiffel Tower were now representing the world's age, the skin of paint on the pinnacle-knob at its summit would represent man's share of that age; and anybody would perceive that that skin was what the tower was built for.
Mark Twain (1835–1910) US writer and humorist. Mark Twain's riposte to Alfred Russel Wallace's 'anthropocentric' theory, that the universe was created specifically for the evolution of mankind. 'What Is Man?' (1903)

52 The noblest work of God? Man. Who found it out? Man.
Mark Twain (1835–1910) US writer and humorist. *Autobiography* (1924)

53 Man, by the very fact of being man, by possessing consciousness, is, in comparison with the ass or the crab, a diseased animal. Consciousness is a disease.
Miguel de Unamuno y Jugo (1864–1936) Spanish writer and philosopher. 'The Man of Flesh and Blood', *The Tragic Sense of Life in Men and Peoples* (1913)

54 We should expect the best and the worst from mankind, as from the weather.
Marquis de Vauvenargues (1715–47) French soldier and moralist. *Réflexions et Maximes* (1746)

55 Heaven has its seasons; Earth has its resources; Man has his government. This means that man is capable of forming a trinity with the other two.
Xunzi (300?–235? BC) Chinese philosopher. 3rd century BC. Quoted in *The Chinese Experience* (Raymond Dawson; 1978)

56 Of all the myriad created things, man is but one. And of all those who inhabit the land . . . an individual man is but one. Is not he, as compared with all creation, but as the tip of a hair upon a horse's skin?
Zhuangzi (369?–286 BC) Chinese philosopher and teacher. 'Autumn Floods', quoted in *Chuang Tzu* (Herbert A. Giles, tr.; 1980), ch. 17

Human Nature

see also Emotion, Human Condition, Humankind, Psychology

1 Human beings are more alike than unalike, and what is true anywhere is true everywhere, yet I encourage travel to as many destinations as possible for the sake of education as well as pleasure.
Maya Angelou (b. 1928) US writer. 'Passports to Understanding', *Wouldn't Take Nothing for My Journey Now* (1993)

2 There is in human nature generally more of the fool than of the wise.
Francis Bacon (1561–1626) English philosopher, statesman, and lawyer. 'Of Boldness', *Essays* (1625)

3 A man's nature runs either to herbs, or to weeds; therefore let him seasonally water the one, and destroy the other.
Francis Bacon (1561–1626) English philosopher, statesman, and lawyer. 'Of Nature in Men', *Essays* (1625)

4 Is a man a salvage at heart, skinned o'er with fragile Manners? Or is salvagery but a faint taint in the natural man's gentility, which erupts now and again like pimples on an angel's arse?
John Barth (b. 1930) US novelist. *The Sot-Weed Factor* (1960), Act 2

5 There is no surer way of calling the worst out of anyone than that of taking their worst as being their true selves; no surer way of bringing out the best than by only accepting that as being true of them.
E. F. Benson (1867–1940) British novelist. *Rex* (1925)

6 Cruelty has a Human Heart,
And Jealousy a Human Face;
Terror the Human Form Divine,
And Secrecy the Human Dress.
William Blake (1757–1827) British poet, painter, engraver, and mystic. Etched but not included in *Songs of Experience*. 'A Divine Image' (1791?)

7 Much of what we ascribe to human nature is no more than a reaction to the restraints put upon us by our civilization.
Franz Boas (1858–1942) German-born US anthropologist. Quoted in *Coming of Age in Samoa* (Margaret Mead; 1928)

8 Every man's a chasm. It makes you dizzy when you look down it.
Georg Büchner (1813–37) German dramatist. 1836. *Woyzeck* (1879), Scene 10

9 Nature's law,
That man was made to mourn!
Robert Burns (1759–96) Scottish poet and songwriter. 'Man Was Made to Mourn' (1786)

10 Every man is as Heaven made him, and sometimes a great deal worse.
Miguel de Cervantes (1547–1616) Spanish novelist and playwright. *Don Quixote* (1605–15), pt. 2, ch. 4

11 Men's natures are alike; it is their habits that carry them far apart.
Confucius (551–479 BC) Chinese philosopher, administrator, and moralist. *Analects* (5th century BC)

12 I got disappointed in human nature as well and gave it up because I found it too much like my own.
J. P. Donleavy (b. 1926) US novelist. *Fairy Tales of New York* (1960)

13 Many ancient, ancestral mechanisms persisting in modern man have to find some outlet, even if they no longer correspond to any real needs.
René Dubos (1901–82) French-born US bacteriologist. 1965. Quoted in *The Jingle Bell Principle* (Miroslav Holub; 1992)

14 History repeats itself in the large because human nature changes with geological leisureliness.
Will Durant (1885–1981) US historian. *The Lessons of History* (co-written with Ariel Durant; 1968)

15 Every man has a wild beast within him.
Frederick II (1712–86) Prussian monarch. Letter to Voltaire (1759)

16 Those who have looked deeply into human nature have recognized that our capacity for play is an expression of the highest seriousness.
Hans-Georg Gadamer (1900–2002) German philosopher. *The Play of Art* (1973)

17 I advocate a holistic recognition that biology and culture interpenetrate in an inextricable manner.
Stephen Jay Gould (1941–2002) US geologist and writer. *An Urchin in the Storm* (1987)

18 Human nature may change when it begins to comprehend the broken chains of Being in itself.
Wilson Harris (b. 1921) Guyanese-born writer. *Jonestown* (1996)

19 Human nature will not flourish, any more than a potato, if it be planted and replanted, for too long a series of generations, in the same worn-out soil.
Nathaniel Hawthorne (1804–64) US novelist and short-story writer. 'The Custom House', *The Scarlet Letter* (1850), Introduction

20 Man's chief goal in life is still to become and stay human, and defend his achievements against the encroachment of nature.
Eric Hoffer (1902–83) US philosopher and longshoreman. 'The Return of Nature', *The Temper of Our Time* (1967)

21 Be a good animal, true to your animal instincts.
D. H. Lawrence (1885–1930) British writer. *The White Peacock* (1911), pt. 2, ch. 2

22 Telling us to obey instinct is like telling us to obey 'people'. People say different things: so do instincts. Our instincts are at war . . . Each instinct, if you listen to it, will claim to be gratified at the expense of the rest.
C. S. Lewis (1898–1963) Irish-born British novelist. *The Abolition of Man* (1943)

23 The law of life is to do evil and good, to eat and be eaten, and the most supposedly innocuous good is, perhaps, also and occasionally violence in disguise.
David Mamet (b. 1947) US writer and film director. Lecture, Harvard University (December 11, 1988)

24 Our humanity rests upon a series of learned behaviors, woven together into patterns that are infinitely fragile and never directly inherited.
Margaret Mead (1901–78) US anthropologist. *Male and Female* (1949), ch. 9

25 The high sentiments always win in the end, the leaders who offer blood, toil, tears and sweat always get more out of their followers than those who offer safety and a good time. When it comes to the pinch, human beings are heroic.
George Orwell (1903–50) British writer. 'The Art of Donald McGill', *Horizon* (September 1941)

26 Man is not merely the sum of his masks. Behind the shifting face of personality is a hard nugget of self, a genetic gift.
Camille Paglia (b. 1947) US academic and author. *Sex, Art, and American Culture* (1992)

27 None of us can estimate what we do when we do it from instinct.
Luigi Pirandello (1867–1936) Italian dramatist, novelist, and short-story writer. *Henry IV* (Edward Storer, tr.; 1922)

28 So too with sex, anger, and all the desires, pleasures and pains which we say follow us in every activity. Poetic imitation fosters these in us. It nurtures and waters them when they ought to wither.
Plato (428?–347? BC) Greek philosopher. *The Republic* (370? BC)

29 To conduct great matters and never commit a fault is above the force of human nature.
Plutarch (46?–120?) Greek biographer and philosopher. 'Life of Fabius', *Parallel Lives* (1st–2nd century)

30 'Tis the way of all flesh.
Thomas Shadwell (1642?–92) English playwright and poet. *The Sullen Lovers* (1668), Act 5, Scene 2

31 AGRIPPA A rarer spirit never
Did steer humanity; but you, gods, will give us
Some faults to make us men.
William Shakespeare (1564–1616) English poet and playwright. *Antony and Cleopatra* (1606–07), Act 5, Scene 1

32 LEAR Thou art the thing itself; unaccommodated man is no more but such a poor, bare, forked animal as thou art. Off, off, you lendings! Come; unbutton here.
William Shakespeare (1564–1616) English poet and playwright. *King Lear* (1605–06), Act 3, Scene 4

33 Our nature is an illimitable space through which the intelligence moves without coming to an end.
Wallace Stevens (1879–1955) US poet. 'The Figure of the Youth as Virile Poet', *The Necessary Angel: Essays on Reality and the Imagination* (1951)

34 It is not the ape, nor the tiger in man that I fear, it is the donkey.
William Temple (1881–1944) British clergyman. Attrib.

35 I am a man, I count nothing human foreign to me.
Terence (185–159 BC) Roman playwright and poet. *The Self-Tormentor* (2nd century BC)

36 Alone among all creatures, the species that styles itself wise, *Homo sapiens*, has an abiding interest in its distant origins, knows that its allotted time is short, worries about the future, and wonders about the past.
John Noble Wilford (b. 1933) US journalist and author. *New York Times* (October 30, 1984)

37 If man's nature is evil, where do rites and justice spring from? They all derive from the fabrication of the sages.
Xunzi (300?–235? BC) Chinese philosopher. 3rd century BC. Quoted in *The Chinese Experience* (Raymond Dawson; 1978)

Human Rights

see also **Civil Rights, Equality, Freedom, Oppression, Women's Rights**

1 It is monstrous to say that for us man has no more right than lower animals or inanimate nature. It is also monstrous to say that these have no right as against him. The covering of a hideous world with the greatest possible number of inferior beings so long as they are human is not the end—even for us.
F. H. Bradley (1846–1924) British philosopher. Unpublished essay on Christian morality (undated), quoted in *A Dictionary of Philosophical Quotations* (A. J. Ayer and Jane O'Grady, eds.; 1992)

2 The right to be let alone—the most comprehensive of rights and the most valued by civilized men.
Louis D. Brandeis (1856–1941) US judge. Supreme Court opinion, *Olmstead v. United States* (1928)

3 Of course, if the nations which put their splendid signatures to the Universal Declaration of Human Rights . . . had had the slightest intention of honouring that Declaration, there would have been very little in the subject of Black and White for me or anyone else to write about.
Learie Constantine (1901–71) Trinidadian cricketer, barrister, and politician. *Colour Bar* (1954)

4   The offence of the political prisoner is his political boldness.

Angela Davis (b. 1944) US civil rights activist, educator, and writer. *If They Come in the Morning . . .* (1971)

5   A man who will not labor to gain his rights, is a man who would not, if he had them, prize and defend them.

Frederick Douglass (1817–95) US abolitionist, writer, and orator. *The North Star* (July 14, 1848)

6   A bill of rights is what the people are entitled to against every government on earth, general or particular, and what no just government should refuse to rest on inference.

Thomas Jefferson (1743–1826) US president. Letter to James Madison (December 20, 1787)

7   When there were no human rights, the exceptional individual had them. That was inhuman. Then equality was created by taking the human rights away from the exceptional individual.

Karl Kraus (1874–1936) Austrian writer. 1909. Quoted in 'Sprüche und Widersprüche', *Karl Kraus* (Harry Zohn; 1971)

8   Hating England is a form of self-defense. That kind of nationalism is nothing more than a local manifestation of a concern for human rights.

Naguib Mahfouz (b. 1911) Egyptian writer. Said by Kamal. *Palace of Desire* (1957)

9   Get up, stand up
Stand up for your rights
Get up stand up
Don't give up the fight.

Bob Marley (1945–81) Jamaican musician, singer, and songwriter. Song lyric. 'Get Up, Stand Up' (1980)

10 That all men are by nature equally free and independent, and have certain inherent rights, of which, when they enter into a state of society, they cannot by any compact deprive or divest their posterity; namely, the enjoyment of life and liberty, with the means of acquiring and possessing property, and pursuing and obtaining happiness and safety.

George Mason (1725–92) US statesman. *Virginia Bill of Rights* (June 12, 1776), Article 1

11 No man who knows aught, can be so stupid to deny that all men naturally were born free.

John Milton (1608–74) English writer. *The Tenure of Kings and Magistrates* (1649)

12 The right of a man to stand upright as a human being in his own country comes before questions of the kind of society he will create once he has that right.

Julius Kambarage Nyerere (1922–99) Tanzanian president. October 2, 1969. *Freedom and Development* (1973)

13 We expect them to work toward the elimination of human rights in accordance with the pursuit of justice.

Dan Quayle (b. 1947) US politician. February 3, 1989. Referring to government officials in El Salvador. Quoted in *Chicago Tribune* (February 4, 1989)

14 The most painful thing for me is seeing the fathers of human rights turning away from what is clearly genocide. By pulling the thread holding Bosnia together, they are pulling apart civilization in Europe.

Haris Silajdzic (b. 1945) Bosnian statesman. Referring to the role of the UN and Western governments in the wars of Yugoslav Succession (1991–95). Quoted in *Times* (December 29, 1993)

15 Dere's *two* things I've got a *right* to, and dese are, Death or Liberty—one or tother I mean to have.

Harriet Tubman (1820?–1913) US abolitionist. *Scenes in the Life of Harriet Tubman* (Sarah Bradford; 1869)

16 All human beings are born free and equal in dignity and rights.

Universal Declaration of Human Rights. Sometimes attributed to Eleanor Roosevelt. *Universal Declaration of Human Rights* (1948), Article 1

17 That's one of my Goddamn precious American rights, not to think about politics.

John Updike (b. 1932) US writer. *Rabbit Redux* (1971)

Humility

see also **Modesty, Selflessness**

1   When you're as great as I am, it's hard to be humble.

Muhammad Ali (b. 1942) US boxer. Attrib.

2   Often a mighty man is the humblest of creatures and a humble man is the mightiest of creatures.

Abu Abdullah Muhammad al-Harithi al-Baghdadi al-Mufid (*fl.* 10th century) Iraqi scholar and jurist. 10th century. 'The Life of the Commander of the Faithful', *The Book of Guidance into the Lives of the Twelve Imams* (I. K. A. Howard, tr.; 1981)

3   He that is down needs fear no fall;
He that is low, no pride.

John Bunyan (1628–88) English preacher and writer. Shepherd boy's song. *The Pilgrim's Progress* (1684), pt. 2

4   I am well aware that I am the 'umblest person going . . . My mother is likewise a very 'umble person. We live in a numble abode.

Charles Dickens (1812–70) British novelist. Said by Uriah Heep. *David Copperfield* (1850), ch. 16

5   It is difficult to be humble. Even if you aim at humility, there is no guarantee that when you have attained the state you will not be proud of the feat.

Bonamy Dobrée (1891–1974) British scholar and writer. *John Wesley* (1974)

6   If you hear that someone is speaking ill of you, instead of trying to defend yourself you should say: 'He obviously does not know me very well, since there are so many other faults he could have mentioned'.

Epictetus (55?–135?) Greek philosopher. *Enchiridion* (2nd century AD)

7   The meek shall inherit the earth but not the mineral rights.

J. Paul Getty (1892–1976) US oil magnate. Attrib.

8   Far from the madding crowd's ignoble strife
Their sober wishes never learn'd to stray;
Along the cool sequester'd vale of life
They kept the noiseless tenor of their way.

Thomas Gray (1716–71) British poet. 'Elegy Written in a Country Churchyard' (1751), st. 19

9   I succeed him; no one can replace him.

Thomas Jefferson (1743–1826) US president. Jefferson's reply to the question 'Is it you sir, who replaces Dr. Benjamin Franklin?'. Letter (1791)

10 All censure of a man's self is oblique praise. It is in order to shew how much he can spare.

Samuel Johnson (1709–84) British lexicographer and writer. April 25, 1778. Quoted in *Life of Samuel Johnson* (James Boswell; 1791)

11 Walk not on the earth exultantly, for thou canst not cleave the earth, neither shalt thou reach to the mountains in height.

The Koran (7th century), Sura 17, v. 37

12 Therefore hold to the things which are reliable. Look to simplicity; embrace purity; Lessen the self; diminish desire.

Laozi (570?–490? BC) Chinese philosopher. The *Daode Jing* is an early Chinese Taoist text. While attributed to Laozi, it probably dates from the 3rd century BC *Daode Jing* (Unknown), quoted in *Sacred Texts of the World* (Ninian Smart and Richard D. Hecht, eds.; 1982)

13 The meek do not inherit the earth unless they are prepared to fight for their meekness.

Harold Laski (1893–1950) British political theorist and economist. Attrib.

14 Teach thy tongue to say 'I do not know'.

Maimonides (1135–1204) Spanish-born Jewish philosopher and physician. Attrib.

15 One may be humble out of pride.

Michel de Montaigne (1533–92) French essayist. *Essays* (1580–88), bk. 2, ch. 17

16 Humility is not a peculiar habit of self-effacement, rather like having an inaudible voice, it is a selfless respect for reality and one of the most difficult and central of all the virtues.

Iris Murdoch (1919–99) Irish-born British novelist and philosopher. *The Sovereignty of Good* (1970)

17 Because there's no fourth class.

George Santayana (1863–1952) Spanish-born US philosopher, poet, and novelist. Referring to being asked why he always travelled third class. Quoted in *Living Biographies of Great Philosophers* (H. Thomas; 1946)

18 Humility is a virtue all preach, none practise, and yet everybody is content to hear. The master thinks it good doctrine for his servant, the laity for the clergy, and the clergy for the laity.

John Selden (1584–1654) English historian, jurist, and politician. 'Humility', *Table Talk* (1689)

19 Man does not live by words alone, despite the fact that sometimes he has to eat them.

Adlai Stevenson (1900–65) US statesman. Attrib.

20 Humility must always be doing its work like a bee making its honey in the hive: without humility all will be lost.

Saint Teresa of Ávila (1515–82) Spanish mystic, author, and nun. *The Interior Castle* (1577)

Humour

see also **Comedy, Laughter, Wit, Wordplay**

1 What god would be hanging around Terminal Two of Heathrow Airport trying to catch the 15.37 flight to Oslo?

Douglas Adams (1952–2001) British writer. *The Long Dark Tea-Time of the Soul* (1988), ch. 6

2 I have a fine sense of the ridiculous, but no sense of humour.

Edward Albee (b. 1928) US playwright. *Who's Afraid of Virginia Woolf?* (1962), Act 1

3 Mark my words, when a society has to resort to the lavatory for its humour the writing is on the wall.

Alan Bennett (b. 1934) British playwright, actor, and director. *Forty Years On* (1969)

4 A joke's a very serious thing.

Charles Churchill (1731–64) British poet. *The Ghost* (1763), bk. 4, l. 386

5 The trouble with Freud is that he never had to play the old Glasgow Empire on a Saturday night after Rangers and Celtic had both lost.

Ken Dodd (b. 1931) British entertainer. 1965. On Freud's attempt to investigate the psychology of humour. Quoted in many forms since 1965. Interview *Guardian* (April 30, 1991)

6 The comic is the perception of the opposite; humor is the feeling of it.

Umberto Eco (b. 1932) Italian writer and literary scholar. *Travels in Hyperreality* (William Weaver, tr.; 1986)

7 What do you mean, funny? Funny-peculiar or funny-ha-ha?

Ian Hay (1876–1952) Scottish novelist and playwright. *The Housemaster* (1938), Act 3

8 Humour is your own smile surprising you in the mirror.

Langston Hughes (1902–67) US novelist, playwright, and short-story writer. *The Book of Negro Folklore* (1958)

9 Humor is laughing at what you haven't got when you ought to have it.

Langston Hughes (1902–67) US novelist, playwright, and short-story writer. *The Book of Negro Humor* (1966)

10 Humor, a good sense of it, is to Americans what manhood is to Spaniards and we will go to great lengths to prove it.

Garrison Keillor (b. 1942) US writer and broadcaster. *We Are Still Married* (1989), Introduction

11 The coarse joke proclaims that we have here an animal which finds its own animality either objectionable or funny.

C. S. Lewis (1898–1963) Irish-born British novelist. *Miracles* (1947)

12 Please accept my resignation. I don't want to belong to any club that will accept me as a member.

Groucho Marx (1895–1977) US comedian and film actor. 1950? Resigning from the Friar's Club in Hollywood. *Groucho and Me* (1959), ch. 26

13 A sense of humor always withers in the presence of the messianic delusion, like justice and truth in front of patriotic passion.

H. L. Mencken (1880–1956) US journalist, critic, and editor. *Prejudices* (1919–27)

14 Good humour is the seasoning of truth.

Johann Heinrich Pestalozzi (1746–1827) Swiss educational reformer. Quoted in *The Education of Man: Aphorisms* (Heinz and Ruth Norden, trs.; 1951)

15 Good humour is a philosophic state of mind; it seems to say to Nature that we take her no more seriously than she takes us.

Ernest Renan (1823–92) French philosopher, philologist, and historian. *Feuilles Détachées* (1880)

16 Everything is funny, as long as it's happening to somebody else.

Will Rogers (1879–1935) US actor, writer, and humorist. *The Illiterate Digest* (1924)

17 ROSALINE A jest's prosperity lies in the ear Of him that hears it, never in the tongue Of him that makes it.

William Shakespeare (1564–1616) English poet and playwright. *Love's Labour's Lost* (1595), Act 5, Scene 2

18 Funny noises are not funny.

The Simpsons, US cartoon series. Lines written as punishment on a chalkboard during the opening credits of *The Simpsons*. The content of the lines changes with each episode. *The Simpsons* (Matt Groening; 1990–)

19 I live in a constant endeavour to fence against the infirmities of ill health, and other evils of life, by mirth.

Laurence Sterne (1713–68) Irish-born British writer and clergyman. *Tristram Shandy* (1759–67), Dedication

20 Humor is emotional chaos remembered in tranquility.

James Thurber (1894–1961) US writer, cartoonist, and humorist. *New York Post* (February 29, 1960)

21 Humour is the first of the gifts to perish in a foreign tongue.

Virginia Woolf (1882–1941) British novelist and critic. *The Common Reader: First Series* (1925)

Hunger

see also **Desire, Food**

1 The hungry belly and the full belly do not walk the same road.

Anonymous. Jamaican proverb.

2 The stomach is a bottomless pit, a hole as big as the world . . . No, there is nothing people will not do, and the sooner you learn that, the better off you will be.

Paul Auster (b. 1947) US writer. *In the Country of Last Things* (1987)

3 A dog starv'd at his Master's Gate
Predicts the ruin of the State.

William Blake (1757–1827) British poet, painter, engraver, and mystic. 'Auguries of Innocence' (1803?), ll. 9–10, quoted in *The Poetry and Prose of William Blake* (David V. Erdman, ed.; 1965)

4 When he told men to love their neighbour, their bellies were full. Nowadays things are different.

Bertolt Brecht (1898–1956) German playwright and poet. *Mother Courage and Her Children* (1941), Scene 2

5 When at noon his paunch grew mutinous
For a plate of turtle green and glutinous.

Robert Browning (1812–89) British poet. 'The Pied Piper of Hamelin', *Dramatic Lyrics* (1842), st. 4

6 Hunger and satisfaction are the two most intense states of consciousness, and they are very intimately connected.

John Dewey (1859–1952) US philosopher and educator. *Psychology* (1887)

7 Oliver Twist has asked for more.

Charles Dickens (1812–70) British novelist. *Oliver Twist* (1838), ch. 2

8 If only it were as easy to banish hunger by rubbing the belly as it is to masturbate.

Diogenes (412?–323 BC) Greek philosopher. 4th century BC. 'Diogenes', *Lives of the Philosophers* (Diogenes Läertius; 3rd century AD)

9 Hunger looks like the man that hunger is killing.

Eduardo Galeano (b. 1940) Uruguayan writer. 'Salgado, 17 Times', *An Uncertain Grace* (Sebastião Salgado; 1990)

10 I'm not interested in the bloody system! Why has he no food? Why is he starving to death?

Bob Geldof (b. 1954) Irish rock musician. *Observer* (October 27, 1985), 'Sayings of the Week'

11 Hunger is my native place in the land of the passions. Hunger for fellowship, hunger for righteousness—for a fellowship founded on righteousness, and a righteousness attained in fellowship.

Dag Hammarskjöld (1905–61) Swedish statesman and diplomat. *Markings* (Leif Sjöberg and W. H. Auden, trs.; 1964)

12 They that die by famine die by inches.

Matthew Henry (1662–1714) English clergyman. *An Exposition on the Old and New Testament* (1710), Psalm 59, v. 15, gloss 5

13 The war against hunger is truly mankind's war of liberation.

John Fitzgerald Kennedy (1917–63) US president. Speech at the World Food Congress (June 4, 1963)

14 A hungry stomach has no ears.

Jean de La Fontaine (1621–95) French writer and poet. 'Le Milan et le Rossignol', *Fables* (1668), bk. 9

15 The universe has not yet come to an end for lack of a few poems that have died aflower in a man's head, be the man illustrious or obscure, but . . . Humanity must eat.

Joaquim Maria Machado de Assis (1839–1908) Brazilian novelist and short-story writer. *Philosopher or Dog?* (Clotilde Wilson, tr.; 1892)

16 Timid roach, why be so shy? We are brothers, thou and I. In the midnight, like thyself, I explore the pantry shelf.

Christopher Darlington Morley (1890–1957) US writer and journalist. Attrib.

17 The only power poor people have is their hunger.

Ben Okri (b. 1959) Nigerian novelist, short-story writer, and poet. *The Famished Road* (1991)

18 Hunger will make a monkey eat pepper.

Haitian proverb.

19 LORD NORTHCLIFFE The trouble with you, Shaw, is that you look as if there were famine in the land.
G.B.S. The trouble with you, Northcliffe, is that you look as if you were the cause of it.

George Bernard Shaw (1856–1950) Irish playwright. Attrib.

20 The hungry hare has no frontiers and doesn't follow ideologies. The hungry hare goes where it finds the food. And the other hares don't block its passage with the tanks.

Lech Walesa (b. 1943) Polish trade union leader and president. Interview (1981)

21 I saw him even now going the way of all flesh, that is to say towards the kitchen.

John Webster (1578?–1632?) English playwright. *Westward Ho!* (co-written with Thomas Dekker; 1604?), Act 2, Scene 2

22 One man, his mind unhinged by slow starvation, killed his wife, 'powdered [salted] her, and had eaten part of her before it was knowne', for which he was hanged.

George F. Willison (1896–1972) US writer. Referring to the first winter (1607) in Jamestown, where four out of five died of starvation. *The American Heritage Cookbook* (1964)

Hypochondria

see also **Illness, Medicine, Paranoia**

1 I only take money from sick people.

Pierre Bretonneau (1778–1862) French physician. 19th century. Comment to a hypochondriac. *Bulletin of the New York Academy of Medicine*, 5: 154

2 This state I call the hypochondriac affection in men, and the hysteric in women . . . is a sort of waking dream, which, though a person be otherwise in sound health, makes him feel symptoms of every disease; and, though innocent, yet fills his mind with the blackest horrors of guilt.

William Heberden (1710–1801) British physician. *Commentaries on the History and Cure of Diseases* (W. Heberden the Younger, ed.; 1802), ch. 49

3 Hungry Joe collected lists of fatal diseases and arranged them in alphabetical order so that he could put his finger without delay on any one he wanted to worry about.

Joseph Heller (1923–99) US novelist. *Catch-22* (1961), ch. 17

4 I never read a patent medicine advertisement without being impelled to the conclusion that I am suffering from the particular disease therein dealt with in its most virulent form.

Jerome K. Jerome (1859–1927) British novelist and playwright. *Three Men in a Boat* (1889), ch. 1

5 Dear Doctor (said he one day to a common acquaintance, who lamented the tender state of his *inside*), do not be like the spider, man, and spin conversation thus incessantly out of thy own bowels.

Samuel Johnson (1709–84) British lexicographer and writer. Quoted in *Johnsonian Miscellanies* (G. B. Hill, ed.; 1897), vol. 1

6 Hypochondriacs squander large sums of time in search of nostrums by which they vainly hope they may get more time to squander.

Peter Ouspensky (1878–1947) Russian philosopher. *Lacon* (1920?), vol. 2

7 Hypochondria torments us not only with causeless irritation with the things of the present; not only with groundless anxiety on the score of future misfortunes entirely of our own manufacture; but also with unmerited self-reproach for our own past actions.

Arthur Schopenhauer (1788–1860) German philosopher. *Parerga and Paralipomena* (1851)

8 People who are always taking care of their health are like misers, who are hoarding a treasure which they have never spirit enough to enjoy.

Laurence Sterne (1713–68) Irish-born British writer and clergyman. Attrib.

9 The imaginary complaints of indestructible old ladies.

E. B. White (1899–1985) US writer and humorist. *Harper's Magazine* (November 1941)

Hypocrisy

see also Morality, Righteousness

1 It is the wisdom of the crocodiles that shed tears when they would devour.

Francis Bacon (1561–1626) English philosopher, statesman, and lawyer. 'Of Wisdom for a Man's Self', *Essays* (1625)

2 Beware of the scribes, which love to go in long clothing, and love salutations in the market places, and the chief seats in the synagogues, and the uppermost rooms at feasts: which devour widows' houses, and for a pretence make long prayers: these shall receive greater damnation.

Bible. Mark, *King James Bible* (1611), 12:38–40

3 O generation of vipers, how can ye, being evil, speak good things? for out of the abundance of the heart the mouth speaketh.

Bible. Matthew, *King James Bible* (1611), 12:34

4 Woe unto you, scribes and Pharisees, hypocrites! for ye are like unto whited sepulchres, which indeed appear beautiful outward, but are within full of dead men's bones, and of all uncleanness.

Bible. Matthew, *King James Bible* (1611), 23:27

5 Conventionality is not morality. Self-righteousness is not religion. To attack the first is not to assail the last. To pluck the mask from the face of the Pharisee, is not to lift an impious hand to the Crown of Thorns.

Charlotte Brontë (1816–55) British novelist. *Jane Eyre* (1847), Preface to the 2nd ed.

6 That vice pays homage to virtue is notorious; we call it hypocrisy.

Samuel Butler (1835–1902) British writer and composer. *The Way of All Flesh* (1903), ch. 19

7 Man is the only animal that can remain on friendly terms with the victims he intends to eat until he eats them.

Samuel Butler (1835–1902) British writer and composer. Quoted in *Note Books* (H. Festing Jones, ed.; 1912)

8 No man is a hypocrite in his pleasures.

Albert Camus (1913–60) Algerian-born French novelist, essayist, and playwright. *The Fall* (1956)

9 We ought to see far enough into a hypocrite to see even his sincerity.

G. K. Chesterton (1874–1936) British writer and poet. *Heretics* (1905), ch. 5

10 Stamps God's own name upon a lie just made, To turn a penny in the way of trade.

William Cowper (1731–1800) British poet. 'Table Talk' (1782), ll. 420–421

11 The louder he talked of his honour, the faster we counted our spoons.

Ralph Waldo Emerson (1803–82) US poet and essayist. 'Worship', *The Conduct of Life* (1860)

12 Can any man be a Christian who asserts that one part of the human race were ordained to be in perpetual bondage to another?

Olaudah Equiano (1745?–97) African-born British former slave. *Public Advertiser* (February 5, 1788)

13 Hypocrisy is the homage paid by vice to virtue.

François La Rochefoucauld (1613–80) French epigrammatist and moralist. *Reflections, or Sentences and Moral Maxims* (1665), no. 218

14 The man who murdered his parents, then pleaded for mercy on the grounds that he was an orphan.

Abraham Lincoln (1809–65) US president. Defining a hypocrite. Quoted in *Lincoln's Own Stories* (Anthony Gross, ed.; 1912)

15 Hypocrisy is the most difficult and nerve-racking vice that any man can pursue; it needs an unceasing vigilance and a rare detachment of spirit. It cannot, like adultery or gluttony, be practised at spare moments; it is a whole-time job.

Somerset Maugham (1874–1965) British writer. *Cakes and Ale* (1930), ch. 1

16 It is very unfair to expect a politician to live in private up to the statements he makes in public.

Somerset Maugham (1874–1965) British writer. *The Circle* (1921)

17 For neither man nor angel can discern Hypocrisy, the only evil that walks Invisible, except to God alone.

John Milton (1608–74) English writer. *Paradise Lost* (1667), bk. 3, ll. 682–684

18 We have, in fact, two kinds of morality side by side; one which we preach but do not practise, and another which we practise but seldom preach.

Bertrand Russell (1872–1970) British philosopher and mathematician. 'Eastern and Western Ideals of Happiness', *Sceptical Essays* (1928)

19 OPHELIA Do not, as some ungracious pastors do, Show me the steep and thorny way to heaven, Whiles, like a puff'd and reckless libertine, Himself the primrose path of dalliance treads And recks not his own rede.

William Shakespeare (1564–1616) English poet and playwright. *Hamlet* (1601), Act 1, Scene 3

20 HAMLET Goodnight—but go not to my uncle's bed; Assume a virtue, if you have it not.

William Shakespeare (1564–1616) English poet and playwright. *Hamlet* (1601), Act 3, Scene 4

21 RUMOUR I speak of peace, while covert enmity Under the smile of safety wounds the world.

William Shakespeare (1564–1616) English poet and playwright. *Henry IV, Part 2* (1597), Induction

22 PERICLES Few love to hear the sins they love to act.

William Shakespeare (1564–1616) English poet and playwright. *Pericles* (1606–08), Act 1, Scene 1

23 Most people sell their souls, and live with a good conscience on the proceeds.

Logan Pearsall Smith (1865–1946) US-born British writer. 'Other People', *Afterthoughts* (1931)

24 It's easy to love God. It's easy to love Jesus. It's easy to pray for the heathen African ten thousand miles from the house where you live. It's hard to call a lousy tramp your brother and set him down at your table.

Melvin Tolson (1900–66) US poet and teacher. April 2, 1938. Quoted in 'The Death of an Infidel', *Caviar and Cabbages: Selected Columns by Melvin B. Tolson* (Robert M. Farnsworth, ed.; 1982)

25 I hope you have not been leading a double life, pretending to be wicked and being really good all the time. That would be hypocrisy.

Oscar Wilde (1854–1900) Irish poet, playwright, and wit. *The Importance of Being Earnest* (1895), Act 2

I

Idealism

see also **Perfection, Romanticism**

1 A cause is like champagne and high heels—one must be prepared to suffer for it.
Arnold Bennett (1867–1931) British writer. *The Title* (1918)

2 You can't be a true idealist without being a true realist.
Jacques Delors (b. 1925) French statesman. Speech to the European Union Summit, Corfu (June 21, 1994)

3 I was in love with the whole world and all that lived in its rainy arms.
Louise Erdrich (b. 1954) US writer. 'The Good Tears', *Love Medicine* (1984)

4 There is within me an ideal so lofty that I will never achieve it. And I mean never because I have a cruel and deadly enemy—society.
Federico García Lorca (1899–1936) Spanish poet and playwright. 'Apunte', *A Dream of Life* (Leslie Stainton; 1998)

5 I must in the first place, guard my scheme from being treated as Utopian by superficial critics . . . this Utopia is far less attractive than any of those portrayed by Sir Thomas More.
Theodor Herzl (1860–1904) Hungarian-born Zionist leader. Referring to his plan for a Jewish homeland. *The Jewish State* (1896)

6 If a man hasn't discovered something that he will die for, he isn't fit to live.
Martin Luther King, Jr. (1929–68) US civil rights leader. Speech, Detroit, Michigan (June 23, 1963)

7 A woman whose sensuality never ceases and a man who constantly has ideas which mankind regards as sick: two human ideals.
Karl Kraus (1874–1936) Austrian writer. 1909. Quoted in 'Sprüche und Widersprüche', *Karl Kraus* (Harry Zohn; 1971)

8 Ideal mankind would abolish death, multiply itself million upon million, rear up city upon city, save every parasite alive, until the accumulation of mere existence is swollen to a horror.
D. H. Lawrence (1885–1930) British writer. *St. Mawr* (1925)

9 Imagine there's no heaven
It's easy if you try
No hell below us
Above us only sky
Imagine all the people
Living for today.
John Lennon (1940–80) British rock musician. 'Imagine' (1971)

10 I have cherished the ideal of a democratic and free society in which all persons live together in harmony and with equal opportunites . . . if needs be, it is an ideal for which I am prepared to die.
Nelson Mandela (b. 1918) South African president and lawyer. After his release from prison. Mandela was reiterating his words at his trial in 1964. Remark (February 11, 1990)

11 An idealist is one who, on noticing that a rose smells better than a cabbage, concludes that it will also make better soup.
H. L. Mencken (1880–1956) US journalist, critic, and editor. 1916. *The Vintage Mencken* (Alistair Cooke, ed.; 1955)

12 The world is not yet ripe for my ideal.
Friedrich von Schiller (1759–1805) German poet, playwright, and historian. *Don Carlos* (1787), Act 3, Scene 10

13 A liberal dreams of a better world, knowing the dream must ultimately be unattainable. Communism believed it was attainable and felt any means to reach it were justified. That was the corruption.
Mario Vargas Llosa (b. 1936) Peruvian writer. *Observer* (June 19, 1994), 'Sayings of the Week'

Ideas

see also **Creativity, Philosophy, Theory, Thinking**

1 Nothing is more dangerous than an idea, when you have only one idea.
Alain (1868–1951) French philosopher and essayist. *Propos sur la Religion* (1908–19), no. 74

2 One can live in the shadow of an idea without grasping it.
Elizabeth Bowen (1899–1973) Irish novelist and short-story writer. *The Heat of the Day* (1949)

3 Old ideas give way slowly; for they are more than abstract logical forms and categories. They are habits, predispositions, deeply engrained attitudes of aversion and preference.
John Dewey (1859–1952) US philosopher and educator. 'The Influence of Darwinism on Philosophy' (1909)

4 What would one not do in the hope of an idea!
Jean Henri Fabre (1823–1915) French entomologist. *Souvenirs Entomologiques* (1879–1907)

5 To die for an idea is to place a pretty high price upon conjectures.
Anatole France (1844–1924) French novelist, poet, and critic. *The Revolt of the Angels* (Mrs. Wilfrid Jackson, tr.; 1933)

6 Many ideas grow better when transplanted into another mind than in the one where they sprang up.
Oliver Wendell Holmes, Jr. (1841–1935) US judge. Quoted in *Yankee from Olympus* (C. Bowen; 1945)

7 Ideas are born, they struggle, triumph, change, and they are transformed; but there is a dead idea which in the end does not live on, transformed into a broader and clearer goal.
Eugenio María de Hostos (1839–1903) Puerto Rican educator, social reformer, and journalist. 'Hombres e Ideas', *Obras* (1939–54)

8 One can resist the invasion of an army; one cannot resist the invasion of ideas.
Victor Hugo (1802–85) French poet, novelist, and playwright. *Histoire d'un Crime* (1852), vol. 5, ch. 10

9 If nature has made any one thing less susceptible than all others of exclusive property, it is the action of the thinking power called an idea.
Thomas Jefferson (1743–1826) US president. Letter to Isaac McPherson (August 13, 1813)

10 Everything has been said, and we are more than seven thousand years of human thought too late.
Jean de La Bruyère (1645–96) French essayist and moralist. *Characters, or the Manners of the Age* (1688)

11 Whatsoever the Mind perceives in itself, or is the immediate object of Perception, Thought, or Understanding, that I call *Idea*.
John Locke (1632–1704) English philosopher. *An Essay Concerning Human Understanding* (1690), bk. 2

12 There is nothing worse than giving the longest of legs to the smallest of ideas.
Joaquim Maria Machado de Assis (1839–1908) Brazilian novelist and short-story writer. *Dom Casmurro* (1899)

13 God deliver you, dear reader, from a fixed idea . . . it is they that make both supermen and mad men.
Joaquim Maria Machado de Assis (1839–1908) Brazilian novelist and short-story writer. *Epitaph of a Small Winner* (1880)

14 The human mind treats a new idea in the same way the body treats a strange protein; it rejects it.
Peter Medawar (1915–87) Brazilian-born British biologist. Attrib.

15 The certainty of ideas is not the foundation of the certainty of perception but is, rather, based on it—in that it is perceptual experience which gives us the passage from one moment to the next and thus realizes the unity of time.
Maurice Merleau-Ponty (1908–61) French existentialist philosopher. Quoted in *The Essential Writings of Merleau-Ponty* (A. L. Fisher, ed.; 1969)

16 We are constantly hatching an enormous number of false ideas, conceits, Utopias, mystical explanations, suspicions, and megalomaniacal fantasies, which disappear when brought into contact with other people.
Jean Piaget (1896–1980) Swiss psychologist. 'Egocentrism of Thought in the Child' (1924), quoted in *The Essential Piaget* (H. E. Gruber and J. Jacques Vonèche, eds.; 1977)

17 The intensity of an idea depends upon the somatic excitation with which it is connected.
Wilhelm Reich (1897–1957) Austrian psychoanalyst. 1920. Quoted in *Reich Speaks of Freud* (M. Higgins, ed.; 1967)

18 The mind thinks, not with data, but with ideas whose creation and elaboration cannot be reduced to a set of predictable values.
Theodore Roszak (b. 1933) US writer and editor. *The Cult of Information* (1986)

19 There are very many thoughts which have value for him who thinks them, but only a few of them possess the power of engaging the interest of a reader after they have been written down.
Arthur Schopenhauer (1788–1860) German philosopher. *Parerga and Paralipomena* (1851)

20 It is the nature of an hypothesis, when once a man has conceived it, that it assimilates every thing to itself, as proper nourishment; and, from the first moment of your begetting it, it generally grows the stronger by every thing you see, hear, read, or understand. This is of great use.
Laurence Sterne (1713–68) Irish-born British writer and clergyman. *Tristram Shandy* (1759–67), bk. 2, ch. 19

21 The major abstraction is the idea of man
And major man is its exponent, abler
In the abstract than in his singular.
Wallace Stevens (1879–1955) US poet. 'Notes Toward a Supreme Fiction', *Selected Poems* (1955)

22 If an idea's worth having once, it's worth having twice.
Tom Stoppard (b. 1937) Czech-born British playwright and screenwriter. *Indian Ink* (1995)

23 Ideas that enter the mind under fire remain there securely and for ever.
Leon Trotsky (1879–1940) Russian revolutionary leader. *My Life* (1930), ch. 35

24 The true God, the mighty God, is the God of ideas.
Alfred de Vigny (1797–1863) French poet, novelist, and playwright. 'La Bouteille à la Mer' (1847)

25 Through metaphor to reconcile
the people and the stones.
Compose. (No ideas but in things.) Invent!
William Carlos Williams (1883–1963) US poet, novelist, and physician. 'A Sort of Song', *The Wedge* (1944)

Identity

see also **Character, Individuality, Names, The Self**

1 How does it feel
To be without a home
Like a complete unknown
Like a rolling stone?
Bob Dylan (b. 1941) US singer and songwriter. Song lyric. 'Like a Rolling Stone' (1965)

2 The identity crisis . . . occurs in that period of the life cycle when each youth must forge for himself some central perspective and direction, some working unity, out of the effective remnants of his childhood and the hopes of his anticipated adulthood.
Erik Erikson (1902–94) US psychoanalyst. *Young Man Luther* (1958)

3 I am a Jew to Catholics and a Catholic to Jews; an Englishman to the French and a Frenchman to the English.
James Goldsmith (1933–97) French-born British businessman and politician. Referring to his mixed ancestry as the son of a German-born Jewish father and a French Catholic mother. Quoted in *Times* (March 7, 1989)

4 I don't have a photograph, but you can have my footprints. They are upstairs in my socks.
Groucho Marx (1895–1977) US comedian and film actor. *A Night at the Opera* (George S. Kaufman and Morrie Ryskind; 1935)

5 I recognize that I am made up of several persons and that the person that at the moment has the upper hand will inevitably give place to another. But which is the real one? All of them or none?
Somerset Maugham (1874–1965) British writer. *A Writer's Notebook* (1949)

6 I want to know what is in my file. It is my file, yet I don't know where it is, and what is inside. My file is the basis for all levels of institutions and officials to judge, assess, and control me. If my file is lost, it means my disappearance in this society.
Mou Sen, Chinese theatre director. Quoted in 'File O', *China Review* (Fiona McConnon; Summer 1995)

7 Knowing who you are is good for one generation only.
Flannery O'Connor (1925–64) US novelist and short-story writer. 'Everything That Rises Must Converge', *Everything That Rises Must Converge* (1965)

8   O chestnut tree, great rooted blossomer,
    Are you the leaf, the blossom or the bole?
    O body swayed to music; O brightening glance,
    How can we know the dancer from the dance?
    W. B. Yeats (1865–1939) Irish poet and playwright. June 14, 1926.
    'Among School Children', *The Tower* (1928), pt. 8

Ignorance

see also **Foolishness, Forgetting, Knowledge, Stupidity**

1   Ignorance is an evil weed, which dictators may
    cultivate among their dupes, but which no
    democracy can afford among its citizens.
    William Henry Beveridge (1879–1963) British economist and social
    reformer. *Full Employment in a Free Society* (1944), pt. 4

2   If the blind lead the blind, both shall fall into the
    ditch.
    Bible. Matthew, *King James Bible* (1611), 15:14

3   IGNORAMUS, n. A person unacquainted with
    certain kinds of knowledge familiar to yourself,
    and having certain other kinds that you know
    nothing about.
    Ambrose Bierce (1842–1914?) US writer and journalist. *The Devil's
    Dictionary* (1911)

4   Let us all honestly own our ignorance when
    confronted with what we do not know.
    Deng To (1912–66) Chinese editor. *Evening Talks at Yenshan*
    (1961–62), quoted in *Literature of the People's Republic of
    China* (Kai-yu Hsu, ed.; 1980)

5   Say, like those wicked Turks, there is no What's-
    his-name but Thingummy, and What-you-may-
    call-it is his prophet!
    Charles Dickens (1812–70) British novelist. Said by Mrs. Skewton.
    Dombey and Son (1848), ch. 27

6   He declared that he knew nothing, except the
    fact of his ignorance.
    Diogenes Laertius (*fl.* 3rd century) Greek historian and biographer.
    Referring to Socrates. 'Socrates', *Lives of the Philosophers*
    (3rd century?)

7   To be conscious that you are ignorant is a great
    step to knowledge.
    Benjamin Disraeli (1804–81) British prime minister and writer. *Sybil*
    (1845), bk. 1, ch. 5

8   Ignorance is preferable to error; and he is less
    remote from the truth who believes nothing, than
    he who believes what is wrong.
    Thomas Jefferson (1743–1826) US president. *Notes on the State of
    Virginia* (1785)

9   Some minds remain open long enough for the
    truth not only to enter but to pass on through by
    way of a ready exit without pausing anywhere
    along the route.
    Elizabeth Kenny (1886–1952) Australian nurse. *And They Shall Walk*
    (co-written with Martha Ostenso; 1951)

10 Nothing in the world is more dangerous than
    sincere ignorance and conscientious stupidity.
    Martin Luther King, Jr. (1929–68) US civil rights leader. *Strength To
    Love* (1963)

11 The ignorant man always adores what he cannot
    understand.
    Cesare Lombroso (1836–1909) Italian physician and criminologist. *The
    Man of Genius* (1891), pt. 3, ch. 3

12 Society needs to condemn a little more and
    understand a little less.
    John Major (b. 1943) British prime minister. Interview, *Mail on
    Sunday* (February 21, 1993)

13 His ignorance was an Empire State Building of
    ignorance. You had to admire it for its size.
    Dorothy Parker (1893–1967) US writer and wit. Referring to Harold
    Ross. Attrib.

14 As geographers, Sosius, crowd into the edges of
    their maps parts of the world which they do not
    know about, adding notes in the margin to the effect
    that beyond this lies nothing but sandy deserts full of
    wild beasts, and unapproachable bogs.
    Plutarch (46?–120?) Greek biographer and philosopher. 'Aemilius
    Paulus', *Lives* (1st century), sect. 5

15 And even I can remember
    A day when the historians left blanks in their
    writings,
    I mean for things they didn't know.
    Ezra Pound (1885–1972) US poet, translator, and critic. *Cantos* (1954), no. 13

16 From ignorance our comfort flows,
    The only wretched are the wise.
    Matthew Prior (1664–1721) English diplomat and poet. 'To the Hon.
    Charles Montague' (1692), st. 9

17 I know not where I am going, I know not where
    I am.
    Racine (1639–99) French playwright. *Phèdre* (1677), Act 4, Scene 1

18 Hindu and Buddhist thinkers with a singular
    unanimity make out that *avidya* or ignorance is
    the source of our anguish, and *vidya* or wisdom,
    bodhi or enlightenment is our salvation.
    Sarvepalli Radhakrishnan (1888–1975) Indian philosopher and statesman.
    Eastern Religions and Western Thought (1939), ch. 2

19 Instead of acknowledging that in many areas we
    are ignorant, we have tended to say things like
    the Universe is permeated with the ineffable. A
    God of the Gaps is assigned responsibility for
    what we do not understand.
    Carl Sagan (1934–96) US astronomer and writer. Contrasting science
    and theology. *The Demon-Haunted World: Science as a
    Candle in the Dark* (1995)

20 NATHANIEL He hath never fed of the dainties that
    are bred in a book; he hath not eat paper, as it
    were; he hath not drunk ink; his intellect is not
    replenished.
    William Shakespeare (1564–1616) English poet and playwright. *Love's
    Labour's Lost* (1595), Act 4, Scene 2

21 Nowadays a parlourmaid as ignorant as Queen
    Victoria was when she came to the throne would
    be classed as mentally defective.
    George Bernard Shaw (1856–1950) Irish playwright. Attrib.

22 Have the courage to be ignorant of a great
    number of things, in order to avoid the calamity
    of being ignorant of everything.
    Sydney Smith (1771–1845) British clergyman, essayist, and wit. *The
    Letters of Peter Plymley* (1807)

23 Somebody else's ignorance is bliss.
    Jack Vance (b. 1916) US writer. *The Star King* (1964)

24 Beware of the man who works hard to learn
    something, learns it, and finds himself no wiser
    than before, Bokonon tells us. He is full of
    murderous resentment of people who are
    ignorant without having come by their ignorance
    the hard way.
    Kurt Vonnegut (b. 1922) US novelist. *Cat's Cradle* (1963)

25 Ignorance, arrogance, and racism have bloomed as
    Superior Knowledge in all too many universities.
    Alice Walker (b. 1944) US novelist and poet. 'A Talk: Convocation
    1972', *In Search of Our Mothers' Gardens* (1983)

26 Ignorance is like a delicate exotic fruit; touch it, and the bloom is gone.
Oscar Wilde (1854–1900) Irish poet, playwright, and wit. *The Importance of Being Earnest* (1895), Act 1

Illness

see also **Doctors, Hypochondria, Medicine**

1 That disease is called Incubus in which, when a person gets to sleep, he seems to have a heavy weight pressing on him, spirit oppressed, voice abolished, power to move impeded, throat obstructed almost to strangulation.
Avicenna (980–1037) Persian philosopher and physician. Many ancient texts on mental health refer to incubus in a similar vein. An incubus was also the term for the notion of a demon that has sex with a sleeping person. Attrib.

2 Diseases crucify the soul of man, attenuate our bodies, dry them, wither them, shrivel them up like old apples, make them so many anatomies.
Robert Burton (1577–1640) English scholar and churchman. *The Anatomy of Melancholy* (1621), pt. 1, sect. 2

3 I reckon being ill as one of the greatest pleasures of life, provided one is not too ill and is not obliged to work till one is better.
Samuel Butler (1835–1902) British writer and composer. *The Way of All Flesh* (1903), ch. 80

4 Disease is very old, and nothing about it has changed. It is we who change, as we learn to recognize what was formerly imperceptible.
Jean Martin Charcot (1825–93) French pathologist and neurologist. *De l'Expectation en Médecine* (1857)

5 Diseases of the soul are more dangerous and more numerous than those of the body.
Cicero (106–43 BC) Roman orator and statesman. *Tusculanae Disputationes* (45–44 BC), bk. 3

6 Too late for fruit, too soon for flowers.
Walter de la Mare (1873–1956) British poet and novelist. On being asked, as he lay seriously ill, whether he would like some fruit or flowers. Attrib. *The Faber Book of Anecdotes* (Clifton Fadiman; 1985)

7 To be conscious is an illness—a real thorough-going illness.
Fyodor Dostoyevsky (1821–81) Russian novelist. *Notes from the Underground* (1864)

8 Epidemics have often been more influential than statesmen and soldiers in shaping the course of political history, and diseases may also colour the moods of civilizations.
René Dubos (1901–82) French-born US bacteriologist. *The White Plague* (1953), ch. 5

9 If man thinks about his physical or moral state he usually discovers that he is ill.
Johann Wolfgang von Goethe (1749–1832) German poet, playwright, and scientist. *Sprüche in Prosa* (Rudolf Steiner, ed.; 1967), pt. 1, bk. 2

10 A bodily disease, which we look upon as whole and entire within itself, may, after all, be but a symptom of some ailment in the spiritual part.
Nathaniel Hawthorne (1804–64) US novelist and short-story writer. *The Scarlet Letter* (1850), ch. 10

11 By today's medical standards, Mozart would have written *La Clemenza di Tito* and the *Requiem* on dialysis, while awaiting a transplant.
Miroslav Holub (1923–98) Czech poet and immunologist. 'This Long Disease', *Shedding Life* (1997)

12 Some people are so sensitive they feel snubbed if an epidemic overlooks them.
Frank McKinney Hubbard (1868–1930) US caricaturist. *Abe Martin's Broadcast* (1930)

13 *Cough*. A convulsion of the lungs, vellicated by some sharp serosity.
Samuel Johnson (1709–84) British lexicographer and writer. *A Dictionary of the English Language* (1755)

14 A long illness seems to be placed between life and death, in order to make death a comfort both to those who die and to those who remain.
Jean de La Bruyère (1645–96) French essayist and moralist. *Characters, or the Manners of the Age* (1688)

15 How sickness enlarges the dimensions of a man's self to himself.
Charles Lamb (1775–1834) British essayist. 'The Convalescent', *Last Essays of Elia* (1833)

16 The earth is as full of brutality as the sea is full of motion. And some men are made sick by the one, and some by the other.
Jack London (1876–1916) US writer. Said by Wolf Larsen. *The Sea-Wolf* (1904)

17 One who is ill has not only the right but also the duty to seek medical aid.
Maimonides (1135–1204) Spanish-born Jewish philosopher and physician. Attrib.

18 Disease makes men more physical, it leaves them nothing but body.
Thomas Mann (1875–1955) German writer. *The Magic Mountain* (1924), ch. 4

19 Illness is in part what the world has done to a victim, but in a larger part it is what the victim has done with his world, and with himself.
Karl Menninger (1893–1990) US psychiatrist. *Illness as Metaphor* (Susan Sontag; 1978), ch. 6

20 Fever the eternal reproach to the physicians.
John Milton (1608–74) English writer. *Paradise Lost* (1667), bk. 11

21 It's better to be dead, or even perfectly well, than to suffer from the wrong affliction. The man who owns up to arthritis in a beriberi year is as lonely as a woman in a last month's dress.
Ogden Nash (1902–71) US humorist. *Saturday Evening Post* (October 14, 1933)

22 When God gives you a rash, he also gives you nails to scratch it with.
Flora Nwapa (1931–93) Nigerian novelist and educator. *Idu* (1970)

23 When meditating over a disease, I never think of finding a remedy for it, but, instead, a means of preventing it.
Louis Pasteur (1822–95) French scientist. Address to the Fraternal Association of Former Students of the École Centrale des Arts et Manufactures, Paris (May 15, 1884)

24 Thence I walked to the Tower; but Lord! how empty the streets are and how melancholy, so many poor sick people in the streets full of sores . . . in Westminster, there is never a physician and but one apothecary left, all being dead.
Samuel Pepys (1633–1703) English diarist and civil servant. Written during the Great Plague, the last major outbreak of bubonic plague in England, and the worst since the Black Death of 1348. *Diary* (September 16, 1665)

25 Nip disease in the bud.
Persius (34–62) Roman satirist. 1st century. *Satires* (Niall Rudd, tr.; 1973), no. 3, l. 64

26 It is in moments of illness that we are compelled
    to recognize that we live not alone but chained to
    a creature of a different kingdom, whole worlds
    apart, who has no knowledge of us and by
    whom it is impossible to make ourselves
    understood: our body.
    Marcel Proust (1871–1922) French novelist. 1921. Le Côté de
    Guermantes, À la Recherche du Temps Perdu (1913–27)

27 Diseases are the tax on pleasures.
    John Ray (1627–1705) English naturalist. English Proverbs (1670)

28 Every man who feels well is a sick man
    neglecting himself.
    Jules Romains (1885–1972) French writer. Knock, ou le Triomphe de
    la Médecine (1923)

29 The diseases which destroy a man are no less
    natural than the instincts which preserve him.
    George Santayana (1863–1952) Spanish-born US philosopher, poet, and
    novelist. Dialogues in Limbo (1926)

30 KING Diseases desperate grown
    By desperate appliance are relieved,
    Or not at all.
    William Shakespeare (1564–1616) English poet and playwright. Hamlet
    (1601), Act 4, Scene 3

31 Disease has social as well as physical, chemical,
    and biological causes.
    Henry E. Sigerist (1891–1957) Swiss medical historian. Attrib.

32 Everyone who is born holds dual citizenship, in
    the kingdom of the well and in the kingdom of
    the sick. Although we all prefer to use only the
    good passport, sooner or later each of us is
    obliged, at least for a spell, to identify ourselves
    as citizens of that other place.
    Susan Sontag (b. 1933) US writer. New York Review of Books
    (January 26, 1978)

33 The man of the present day would far rather
    believe that disease is connected only with
    immediate causes for the fundamental tendency
    in the modern view of life is always to seek what
    is more convenient.
    Rudolf Steiner (1861–1925) Austrian philosopher and scientist. 1910.
    The Manifestations of Karma (1925), lecture 3

34 Decay and disease are often beautiful, like the
    pearly tear of the shellfish and the hectic glow of
    consumption.
    Henry David Thoreau (1817–62) US writer. Journal (June 11, 1852),
    quoted in The Writings of Henry David Thoreau (1906)

35 Considering how common illness is . . . it
    becomes strange indeed that illness has not taken
    its place with love and battle and jealousy among
    the prime themes of literature.
    Virginia Woolf (1882–1941) British novelist and critic. The Moment (1947)

36 It has been days, and still this wind
    keeps coming to me from the sea.
    All night long, this raving wind delivers lobsters
    and jellyfish
    in the rope-baskets of sunken ships.
    Sa'di Yusuf (b. 1943) Iraqi poet. 'A State of Fever', Modern Arabic
    Poetry (Salma Khadra Jayyusi, ed.; 1987), ll. 1–5

Imagination

see also Consciousness, Creativity, Fantasy, Fiction, Mind,
Thinking

1   Is it lack of imagination that makes us come
    to imagined places, not just stay at home?
    Elizabeth Bishop (1911–79) US poet. 'Questions of Travel',
    Questions of Travel (1965)

2   What is now proved was once, only imagin'd.
    William Blake (1757–1827) British poet, painter, engraver, and mystic.
    'Proverbs of Hell', The Marriage of Heaven and Hell (1790–
    93), plate 8, l. 13

3   Imagination creates the real not the illusionary, it
    exists in the real not in nothingness. Imagination
    itself—not what it creates—is often illusionary.
    Edward Bond (b. 1934) British playwright. The Hidden Plot (2000)

4   Hope and imagination are the only consolations
    for the disappointments and sorrows of
    experience.
    Italo Calvino (1923–85) Cuban-born Italian novelist and short-story writer.
    1985. 'Exactitude', Six Memos for the Next Millennium
    (Patrick Creagh, tr.; 1992)

5   The Fancy is indeed no other than a mode of
    memory emancipated from the order of time and
    space.
    Samuel Taylor Coleridge (1772–1834) British poet. Biographia
    Literaria (1817), ch. 13

6   The primary imagination I hold to be the living
    Power and prime Agent of all human Perception,
    and as a repetition in the finite mind of the
    eternal act of creation in the infinite I AM.
    Samuel Taylor Coleridge (1772–1834) British poet. Biographia
    Literaria (1817), ch. 13

7   Imagination alone never did and never can
    produce works that are to stand by a comparison
    with realities.
    John Constable (1776–1837) English landscape painter. Lecture to the
    Royal Institution (1836)

8   Imagination may be defined as that operation of
    the intellect which embodies an idea in a
    particular form or image.
    John Dewey (1859–1952) US philosopher and educator. Psychology
    (1887)

9   Imagination is more important than knowledge.
    Knowledge is limited. Imagination encircles the
    world.
    Albert Einstein (1879–1955) German-born US physicist. 'What Life
    Means to Einstein: an Interview by George Sylvester Viereck',
    Saturday Evening Post (October 26, 1929)

10 Psychologists have hitherto failed to realize that
    imagination is a necessary ingredient of
    perception itself.
    Immanuel Kant (1724–1804) German philosopher. Critique of Pure
    Reason (1781), A 120

11 Heard melodies are sweet, but those unheard
    Are sweeter; therefore, ye soft pipes, play on;
    Not to the sensual ear, but, more endear'd,
    Pipe to the spirit ditties of no tone.
    John Keats (1795–1821) English poet. 'Ode on a Grecian Urn'
    (1820), st. 2

12 I am certain of nothing but the holiness of the
    heart's affections and the truth of imagination—
    what the imagination seizes as beauty must be
    truth—whether it existed before or not.
    John Keats (1795–1821) English poet. Letter to Benjamin Bailey
    (November 22, 1817), quoted in Letters of John Keats (H. E.
    Rollins, ed.; 1958), vol. 1

13 That alone is significant and fruitful which gives
    free play to the imagination.
    Gotthold Ephraim Lessing (1729–81) German playwright and critic.
    Laokoon (1766), ch. 3, quoted in Laocoon, Nathan the Wise
    and Minna von Barnhelm (W. A. Steel, ed.; 1930)

14 He who does not fill his world with phantoms
    remains alone.
    Antonio Porchia (1886–1968) Italian-born Argentinian writer. Voces
    (W. S. Merwin, tr.; 1968)

15 Imagination is not an empirical or superadded power of consciousness, it is the whole of consciousness as it realizes its freedom.
Jean-Paul Sartre (1905–80) French philosopher, playwright, and novelist. *The Psychology of Imagination* (1948)

16 Imaginative consciousness represents a certain type of thought; a thought which is constituted in and by its object.
Jean-Paul Sartre (1905–80) French philosopher, playwright, and novelist. *The Psychology of Imagination* (1948)

17 THESEUS The lunatic, the lover, and the poet, Are of imagination all compact.
William Shakespeare (1564–1616) English poet and playwright. *A Midsummer Night's Dream* (1595–96), Act 5, Scene 1

18 After the leaves have fallen, we return To a plain sense of things. It is as if We had come to an end of the imagination.
Wallace Stevens (1879–1955) US poet. 'Peter Quince at the Clavier', *Harmonium* (1923)

19 Imagination . . . is the irrepressible revolutionist.
Wallace Stevens (1879–1955) US poet. 'Imagination as Value', *The Necessary Angel: Essays on Reality and the Imagination* (1951)

20 It may be that the imagination is a miracle of logic and that its exquisite divinations are calculations beyond analysis, as the conclusions of reason are calculations wholly within analysis.
Wallace Stevens (1879–1955) US poet. 'Imagination as Value', *The Necessary Angel: Essays on Reality and the Imagination* (1951)

21 Of what value is anything to the solitary and those that live in misery and terror, except the imagination?
Wallace Stevens (1879–1955) US poet. 'Imagination as Value', *The Necessary Angel: Essays on Reality and the Imagination* (1951)

22 The imagination is the only genius. It is intrepid and eager and the extreme of its achievement lies in its abstraction. The achievement of the romantic, however, lies in minor wish-fulfillments and it is incapable of abstraction.
Wallace Stevens (1879–1955) US poet. 'Imagination as Value', *The Necessary Angel: Essays on Reality and the Imagination* (1951)

23 In countries where the imagination of the people, and the language they use, is rich and living, it is possible for a writer to be rich and copious in his words, and at the same time to give the reality, which is the root of all poetry, in a comprehensive and natural form.
J. M. Synge (1871–1909) Irish playwright. *The Playboy of the Western World* (1907), Preface

24 Don't let anybody tell you you're wasting your time when you're gazing into space. There is no other way to conceive an imaginary world . . . I daydream about my characters . . . take pen and paper and try to *report* what I've witnessed.
Stephen Vizinczey (b. 1933) Hungarian-born British writer, editor, and broadcaster. *Truth and Lies in Literature* (1986)

25 Imagination and fiction make up more than three quarters of our real life.
Simone Weil (1909–43) French philosopher, mystic, and political activist. 'Gravity and Grace' (1947)

Imitation

see also **Plagiarism, Similarity**

1 A lotta cats copy the Mona Lisa, but people still line up to see the original.
Louis Armstrong (1901–71) US jazz trumpeter. When asked whether he objected to people copying his style. Attrib.

2 Man is an idiot. He doesn't know how to do anything without copying, without imitating, without plagiarizing, without aping. It might even have been that man invented generation by coitus after seeing the grasshopper copulate.
Augusto Roa Bastos (b. 1917) Paraguayan writer. *I the Supreme* (1974)

3 Imitation is the sincerest form of flattery.
Charles Colton (1780–1832) British cleric and writer. *Lacon* (1820), vol. 1

4 Those who do not want to imitate anything, produce nothing.
Salvador Dalí (1904–89) Spanish surrealist painter. *Dalí by Dalí* (1970)

5 The pleasure of imitation, as the ancients knew, is one of the most innate in the human spirit.
Umberto Eco (b. 1932) Italian writer and literary scholar. *Travels in Hyperreality* (William Weaver, tr.; 1986)

6 O imitators, you slavish herd.
Horace (65–8 BC) Roman poet. *Epistles* (20? BC), bk. 1, no. 19, l. 19

Immortality

see also **Eternity, Life, Posterity, The Soul**

1 I don't want to achieve immortality through my work . . . I want to achieve it through not dying.
Woody Allen (b. 1935) US film actor and director. *Woody Allen and His Comedy* (Eric Lax; 1975)

2 The connection between history and nature is by no means an opposition. History receives into its remembrance those mortals who through deed and word have proved themselves worthy of nature, and their everlasting fame means that they . . . may remain in the company of the things that last forever.
Hannah Arendt (1906–75) German-born US philosopher and historian. *Between Past and Future: Six Exercises in Political Thought* (1961)

3 Immortality is what nature possesses without effort and without anybody's assistance, and immortality is what the mortals must therefore try to achieve if they want to live up to the world in which they were born.
Hannah Arendt (1906–75) German-born US philosopher and historian. *Between Past and Future: Six Exercises in Political Thought* (1961), ch. 2

4 Heaven and earth shall pass away, but my words shall not pass away.
Bible. Matthew, *King James Bible* (1611), 24:35

5 Sappho survives, because we sing her songs; And Aeschylus, because we read his plays!
Robert Browning (1812–89) British poet. 'Cleon', *Men and Women* (1855)

6 To live in hearts we leave behind Is not to die.
Thomas Campbell (1777–1844) Scottish poet. *Hallowed Ground* (1825)

7 One short sleep past, we wake eternally, And death shall be no more; Death, thou shalt die.
John Donne (1572?–1631) English metaphysical poet and divine. Holy Sonnets, *Divine Poems* (1633), no. 10, ll. 13–14

8 If you were to destroy in mankind the belief in immortality, not only love but every living force maintaining the life of the world would at once be dried up. Moreover, nothing then would be immoral, everything would be permissible, even cannibalism.
Fyodor Dostoyevsky (1821–81) Russian novelist. *The Brothers Karamazov* (1879–80), bk. 2, ch. 6

9 Oh may I join the choir invisible
Of those immortal dead who live again
In minds made better by their presence.

George Eliot (1819–80) British novelist. 'Oh May I Join the Choir Invisible' (1867)

10 Millions long for immortality who do not know what to do with themselves on a rainy Sunday afternoon.

Susan Ertz (1894?–1985) US-born British novelist and playwright. *Anger in the Sky* (1943)

11 He had decided to live for ever or die in the attempt.

Joseph Heller (1923–99) US novelist. *Catch-22* (1961), ch. 3

12 The man worthy of praise the Muse forbids to die.

Horace (65–8 BC) Roman poet. 23? BC. *Odes* (13? BC), bk. 4, no. 8, l. 28

13 I wish to believe in immortality—I wish to live with you for ever.

John Keats (1795–1821) English poet. Letter to Fanny Brawne (July 1820), quoted in *Letters of John Keats* (H. E. Rollins, ed.; 1958), vol. 2

14 There is an awful warmth about my heart like a load of immortality.

John Keats (1795–1821) English poet. Letter to John Hamilton Reynolds (September 22, 1818), quoted in *Letters of John Keats* (H. E. Rollins, ed.; 1958), vol. 2

15 Now I'm dead in the grave with my lips moving
And every schoolboy repeating my words by heart.

Osip Mandelstam (1891–1938) Russian poet, writer, and translator. 'Now I'm Dead in the Grave', *Poems* (1928), no. 306

16 'Tis true, 'tis certain; man though dead retains
Part of himself: the immortal mind remains.

Alexander Pope (1688–1744) English poet. *The Iliad of Homer* (1715–20), bk. 23, ll. 122–123

17 They live ill who expect to live always.

Publilius Syrus (*fl.* 1st century BC) Roman writer. *Moral Sayings* (1st century BC), 457

18 Immortality is to labour at an eternal task.

Ernest Renan (1823–92) French philosopher, philologist, and historian. 1848. *L'Avenir de la Science: Pensées de 1848* (1890), Preface

19 We feel and know that we are eternal.

Baruch Spinoza (1632–77) Dutch philosopher and theologian. *Ethics* (1677), pt. 4, prop. 23, note

20 A slumber did my spirit seal;
I had no human fears:
She seemed a thing that could not feel
The touch of earthly years.

William Wordsworth (1770–1850) English poet. 1799. One of the 'Lucy poems'. The identity of Lucy is uncertain. 'A Slumber Did My Spirit Seal', *Lyrical Ballads* (2nd ed.; 1800), ll.1–4

21 Hence in a season of calm weather
Though inland far we be,
Our souls have sight of that immortal sea
Which brought us hither.

William Wordsworth (1770–1850) English poet. 1802?–06. 'Ode: Intimations of Immortality from Recollections of Early Childhood', *Poems in Two Volumes* (1807), vol. 2, st. 9, ll. 165–168

22 All men think all men mortal, but themselves.

Edward Young (1683–1765) English poet. *The Complaint, or Night Thoughts on Life, Death, and Immortality* (1742–45), bk. 1, l. 424

Impatience

see **Haste, Procrastination**

Imperfection

see also **Failure, Mistakes**

1 You cannot carve rotten wood.

Anonymous. Spanish proverb. Quoted in *Understanding Motivation* (John Adair; 1990)

2 Even imperfection itself may have its ideal or perfect state.

Thomas De Quincey (1785–1859) British essayist and critic. 'Murder Considered as One of the Fine Arts', *Blackwood's Magazine* (1827)

3 Two half-truths do not make a truth, and two half-cultures do not make a culture.

Arthur Koestler (1905–83) Hungarian-born British writer and journalist. *The Ghost in the Machine* (1967), Preface

4 When the defects of others are perceived with so much clarity, it is because one possesses them oneself.

Jules Renard (1864–1910) French writer. 1908. *Journal* (1877–1910)

5 He is all fault who hath no fault at all:
For who loves me must have a touch of earth.

Alfred Tennyson (1809–92) British poet. 'Lancelot and Elaine', *Idylls of the King* (1859), ll. 132–134

Imperialism

see also **American Imperialism, British Imperialism, Capitalism, Globalization, Power**

1 Old and entire empires have been dissolved, and have lost their political being, whilst new ones have sprung up out of their ashes.

Andrés Bello (1781–1865) Chilean politician and writer. *Preliminary Remarks* (1812)

2 The day of small nations has long passed away. The day of Empires has come.

Joseph Chamberlain (1836–1914) British statesman. May 12, 1904. Speech, Birmingham, *Times* (May 13, 1904)

3 It is too often forgotten that when the Europeans gained enough maritime skill and gunpowder to conquer most of the world, they not only colonized the bulk of the world's people but they colonized the interpretation of history itself . . . The roots of modern racism can be traced to this conquest and colonization.

John Henrik Clarke (1915–98) US historian and educator. 'Race: An Evolving Issue in Western Thought', *Journal of Human Relations* (1970)

4 Exterminate all the brutes.

Joseph Conrad (1857–1924) Polish-born British novelist. Said by Kurtz. *Heart of Darkness* (1902), ch. 2

5 Imperialism is encrusted within the essence of every object, deep inside every material thing in America.

Ariel Dorfman (b. 1942) Chilean playwright and novelist. *Hard Rain* (1973)

6 All empire is no more than power in trust.

John Dryden (1631–1700) English poet, playwright, and literary critic. *Absalom and Achitophel* (1681), pt. 1, l. 411

7 The South creates the civilizations, the North conquers them, ruins them, borrows from them, spreads them: this is one summary of history.

Will Durant (1885–1981) US historian. *The Lessons of History* (co-written with Ariel Durant; 1968)

8 Advanced countries of today have reached their present affluence through domination of other races and countries . . . Their sheer ruthlessness, undisturbed by feelings of compassion or by abstract theories of freedom, equality or justice, gave them a head start.

Indira Gandhi (1917–84) Indian prime minister. Speech, Stockholm, Sweden (June 14, 1973)

9 It is forbidden ever to make peace with a monarch, a prince or a people who have not submitted.

Genghis Khan (1167?–1227) Mongol ruler and conqueror. Genghis Khan's military abilities were reinforced by a ruthless approach. He habitually used massacre as a tool of conquest. Laws (1206?)

10 The French and the Russians have shared out the land,
Britannia rules the oceans;
we reign unchallenged in the realm
of dreamy abstract notions.

Heinrich Heine (1797–1856) German poet. 1844. Deutschland. A Winter's Tale (T. J. Reed, tr.; 1986), st. 7

11 Every country should realize that its turn at world domination, domination because its rights coincided more or less with the character or progress of the epoch, must terminate with the change brought about by this progress.

Juan Ramón Jiménez (1881–1958) Spanish poet. 'Heroic Reason', Selected Writings (1957)

12 If it were necessary to give the briefest possible definition of imperialism we should have to say that imperialism is the monopoly stage of capitalism.

Vladimir Ilyich Lenin (1870–1924) Russian revolutionary leader. Imperialism, the Highest Stage of Capitalism (1916), ch. 7

13 Imperialist aggression shattered the fond dreams of the Chinese about learning from the West.

Mao Zedong (1893–1976) Chinese statesman. On People's Democratic Dictatorship (1949)

14 To sit in darkness here
Hatching vain empires.

John Milton (1608–74) English writer. Said by Beelzebub. Paradise Lost (1667), bk. 2, ll. 377–378

15 An empire founded by war has to maintain itself by war.

Montesquieu (1689–1755) French writer and jurist. Considérations sur les Causes de la Grandeur des Romains et de leur Décadence (1734), ch. 8

16 Never in the history of the world has an alien ruler granted self-rule to a people on a silver platter.

Kwame Nkrumah (1909–72) Ghanaian president. The Autobiography of Kwame Nkrumah (1959)

17 Imperialism knows no law beyond its own interests.

Kwame Nkrumah (1909–72) Ghanaian president. Towards Colonial Freedom (1947)

18 Alexander wept when he heard from Anaxarchus that there was an infinite number of worlds . . . 'Do you not think it a matter worthy of lamentation that when there is such a vast multitude of them, we have not yet conquered one?'

Plutarch (46?–120?) Greek biographer and philosopher. Referring to Alexander the Great. 'On the Tranquillity of the Mind' (1st–2nd century)

19 Providence has given to the French the empire of the land, to the English that of the sea, and to the Germans that of the air.

Jean Paul Richter (1763–1825) German novelist and humorist. Quoted in 'Richter', Critical and Miscellaneous Essays (Thomas Carlyle; 1827)

20 Imperialism, sane Imperialism, as distinguished from what I may call wild-cat Imperialism, is nothing but this—a larger patriotism.

Lord Rosebery (1847–1929) British prime minister and biographer. Speech at a City Liberal Club dinner, London (May 5, 1899)

21 Maps are always instruments of conquest; once projected, they are then implemented. Geography is therefore the art of war.

Edward W. Said (b. 1935) Palestinian-born US writer and educator. The Politics of Dispossession (1994), Epilogue

22 I am called
The richest monarch in the Christian world;
The sun in my dominion never sets.

Friedrich von Schiller (1759–1805) German poet, playwright, and historian. Originally said by Philip II. Don Carlos (1787), Act 1, Scene 6

23 This agglomeration which was called and which still calls itself the Holy Roman Empire was neither holy, nor Roman, nor an empire.

Voltaire (1694–1778) French writer and philosopher. Essai sur l'Histoire Générale et sur les Moeurs et l'Esprit des Nations (1756), ch. 70

24 But they know that my country
has known a thousand conquerors
and they know
that the thousand
have all melted away
like driven snow.

Tawfiq Zayyad (b. 1932) Palestinian poet. 'They Know', Modern Arabic Poetry (Salma Khadra Jayyusi, ed.; 1987), ll. 1–6

Impossibility

see also Futility, Pessimism

1 Probable impossibilities are to be preferred to improbable possibilities.

Aristotle (384–322 BC) Greek philosopher. Poetics (335–322? BC), ch. 24

2 There are three things you just can't do in life. You can't beat the phone company, you can't make a waiter see you until he is ready to see you, and you can't go home again.

Bill Bryson (b. 1951) US writer. The Lost Continent (1989), ch. 2

3 You may as well expect pears from an elm.

Miguel de Cervantes (1547–1616) Spanish novelist and playwright. Don Quixote (1605–15), pt. 2, ch. 40

4 Impossibilities are merely things of which we have not learned, or which we do not wish to happen.

Charles W. Chesnutt (1858–1932) US writer and educator. The Marrow of Tradition (1901)

5 The only way of finding the limits of the possible is by going beyond them into the impossible.

Arthur C. Clarke (b. 1917) British writer and scientist. The Lost Worlds of 2001 (1972)

6 Go, and catch a falling star,
Get with child a mandrake root,
Tell me, where all past years are,
Or who cleft the Devil's foot.

John Donne (1572?–1631) English metaphysical poet and divine. 'Song' ('Go, and Catch a Falling Star'), Songs and Sonnets (1635), ll. 1–4

7 At Godwin's they were disputing fiercely which was the best—Man as he was, or man as he is to be. 'Give me', says Lamb, 'man as he is not to be'.

William Hazlitt (1778–1830) British essayist and critic. Referring to Charles Lamb. 'My First Acquaintance with Poets', quoted in Hazlitt on English Literature (1913), ch. 17

Indecision

see also **Doubt, Procrastination**

1   We know what happens to people who stay in
    the middle of the road. They get run down.
    Aneurin Bevan (1897–1960) Welsh-born British politician. *Observer*
    (December 9, 1953)

2   Shall I part my hair behind? Do I dare to eat a
    peach?
    I shall wear white flannel trousers, and walk
    upon the beach.
    I have heard the mermaids singing, each to each.
    T. S. Eliot (1888–1965) US-born British poet and playwright. 'The Love
    Song of J. Alfred Prufrock', *Prufrock and Other Observations*
    (1917)

3   I sometimes think I'd rather crow
    And be a rooster than to roost
    And be a crow. But I dunno.
    Folk Verse. Quoted in 'I Sometimes Think I'd Rather Crow', *The
    Penguin Book of American Verse* (Geoffrey Moore, ed.; 1977)

4   The imagination of a boy is healthy, and the
    mature imagination of a man is healthy; but
    there is a space of life between, in which the soul
    is in a ferment, the character undecided, the way
    of life uncertain, the ambition thick-sighted.
    John Keats (1795–1821) English poet. *Endymion* (1818), Preface

5   The Right Hon. gentleman has sat so long on the
    fence that the iron has entered his soul.
    David Lloyd George (1863–1945) British prime minister. Referring to Sir
    John Simon. Attrib.

6   Nothing is so exhausting as indecision, and
    nothing is so futile.
    Bertrand Russell (1872–1970) British philosopher and mathematician. Attrib.

7   HAMLET But I am pigeon-liver'd, and lack gall
    To make oppression bitter, or ere this
    I should have fatted all the region kites
    With this slave's offal. Bloody, bawdy villain!
    Remorseless, treacherous, lecherous, kindless villain!
    William Shakespeare (1564–1616) English poet and playwright. *Hamlet*
    (1601), Act 2, Scene 2

8   I must have a prodigious quantity of mind; it
    takes me as much as a week, sometimes, to make
    it up.
    Mark Twain (1835–1910) US writer and humorist. *The Innocents
    Abroad* (1869), ch. 7

Independence

see also **Freedom, Liberty, Self-Confidence**

1   The landscape should belong to the people who
    see it all the time.
    Imamu Amiri Baraka (b. 1934) US author, editor, playwright, and political
    activist. 'The Legacy of Malcolm X, and the Coming of the
    Black Nation', *Home: Social Essays* (1966)

2   Complete independence through truth and non-
    violence means the independence of every unit, be
    it the humblest of the nation, without distinction
    of race, colour or creed.
    Mahatma Gandhi (1869–1948) Indian national leader. Quoted in *Questions
    in the Philosophy of Restraint* (Indira Rothermund; 1963)

3   Neither East nor West.
    Ruhollah Khomeini (1900–89) Iranian religious and political leader.
    Referring to his political philosophy, and his opposition to the
    superpowers, the United States and the Soviet Union. Quoted
    in *Living Islam* (Akbar Ahmed; 1993)

4   However painful the birth-pangs of progress may
    be, once a colony has taken the plunge along the
    road to self-government and self-determination,
    there can be no turning back.
    George Padmore (1902–59) Trinidadian campaigner. *Pan-Africanism*
    (1956)

5   In the name of God and of the dead generations
    from which she receives her old tradition of
    nationhood, Ireland . . . summons her children to
    her flag and strikes for her freedom . . . We
    hereby proclaim the Irish Republic as a Sovereign
    Independent State.
    Patrick Pearse (1879–1916) Irish poet and nationalist. 1916.
    Declaration signed and approved by Pearse and other
    republicans, and read on the steps of the General Post Office
    in Dublin. Quoted in *Rebels: The Irish Rising of 1916* (Peter
    de Rosa; 1990)

6   No one is a light unto himself, not even the sun.
    Antonio Porchia (1886–1968) Italian-born Argentinian writer. *Voces*
    (W. S. Merwin, tr.; 1968)

7   You who have never known a single day of joy
    and freedom in your lives . . . We offer you the
    fairest and most viable proposal from our
    standpoint today—autonomy, self-government—
    with all its advantages and limitations.
    Yitzhak Rabin (1922–95) Israeli statesman. Addressed to Palestinians.
    Speech to the Israeli Parliament, Tel Aviv (July 13, 1992),
    quoted in *Murder in the Name of God* (Michael Karpin and
    Ina Friedman; 1999)

8   In the first days of the revolt you must kill: to
    shoot down a European is to kill two birds with
    one stone, to destroy an oppressor and the man
    he oppresses at the same time: there remain a
    dead man, and a free man.
    Jean-Paul Sartre (1905–80) French philosopher, playwright, and novelist.
    1961. Referring to the liberation of colonized people from
    European imperial powers. Quoted in *The Wretched of the
    Earth* (F. Fanon; 1965), Preface

9   Self-determination is not a mere phrase. It is an
    imperative principle which statesmen will
    henceforth ignore at their peril.
    Woodrow Wilson (1856–1924) US president. Address to Congress
    (February 11, 1918)

India

see **Asian Countries**

Indifference

see also **Ignorance**

1   An indifferent spectator like myself watches the
    hyena, the spider, and the tree and understands
    them; a man with a sense of justice shoots the
    hyena, crushes the spider under his foot, and sits
    down under the shade of the tree, imagining that
    he has done a good deed.
    Pio Baroja (1872–1956) Basque writer. Said by Iturrioz. *The Tree of
    Knowledge* (1911)

2   Nothing is so fatal to religion as indifference,
    which is, at least, half infidelity.
    Edmund Burke (1729–97) Irish-born British statesman and political
    philosopher. Letter to William Smith (January 29, 1795)

3   We must not let the iron curtain be replaced with
    a veil of indifference.
    Bill Clinton (b. 1946) US president. Speech to NATO (January 10,
    1994)

4   O, she is the antidote to desire.

William Congreve (1670–1729) English playwright and poet. *The Way of the World* (1700), Act 4, Scene 14

5   Hippocleides doesn't care.

Hippocleides (b. 6th century? BC) Athenian aristocrat. Comment after Cleisthenes told him he had ruined his chances of marrying Cleisthenes' daughter. Quoted in *The Histories* (Herodotus; 450? BC), bk. 6, ch. 129, l. 4

6   Let them eat cake.

Marie-Antoinette (1755–93) Austrian-born French queen consort. 1780? On being told that the people had no bread to eat; in fact she was repeating a much older saying. Attrib.

7   They hanged Eichmann yesterday; my reaction was curious, rather shrugging . . . To execute a man and excite a reaction of indifference is to bring people too close to the way the Nazis felt about human life.

Mary McCarthy (1912–89) US writer. Referring to Adolf Eichmann. Letter to Hannah Arendt (June 1, 1962), quoted in *Between Friends: the Correspondence of Hannah Arendt and Mary McCarthy, 1949–75* (Carol Brightman, ed.; 1995)

8   Any battle or bombing raid or artillery barrage has the aesthetic purity of absolute moral indifference—a powerful, implacable beauty.

Tim O'Brien (b. 1946) US novelist. *The Things They Carried* (1990)

9   At length the morn and cold indifference came.

Nicholas Rowe (1674–1718) English playwright and poet. *The Fair Penitent* (1703), Act 1, Scene 1, Prologue

10 I regard you with an indifference closely bordering on aversion.

Robert Louis Stevenson (1850–94) Scottish novelist, essayist, and poet. 'The Rajah's Diamond: Story of the Bandbox', *The New Arabian Nights* (1882)

Individuality

see also Character, The Face, Identity, The Self

1   We have found the definition of 'person', namely, 'an individual substance of a rational nature'.

Boethius (480?–524?) Roman philosopher and statesman. *Contra Eutychen* (524?)

2   It is the common wonder of all men, how among so many million of faces, there should be none alike.

Thomas Browne (1605–82) English physician and writer. *Religio Medici* (1642), pt. 2

3   Did I ever tell you this snakeskin jacket is a symbol of my individuality and belief in personal freedom?

Nicolas Cage (b. 1964) US actor. As Sailor on marrying Lulu (played by Laura Dern). *Wild at Heart* (1990)

4   It appears that every man's insomnia is as different from his neighbor's as are their daytime hopes and aspirations.

F. Scott Fitzgerald (1896–1940) US writer. 'Sleeping and Waking', *The Crack-Up: with Other Uncollected Pieces, Note-Books and Unpublished Letters* (Edmund Wilson, ed.; 1945)

5   The memory of birth and the expectation of death always lurk within the human being, making him separate from his fellows and consequently capable of intercourse with them.

E. M. Forster (1879–1970) British novelist. 'What I Believe', *Two Cheers For Democracy* (1951)

6   Untalented individuality is as useless as bad imitation.

Natalia Goncharova (1881–1962) Russian painter, printmaker, and stage designer. 1913. 'Natalia Goncharova', *Feminist Art Journal* (Gloria Fenman Orenstein; Summer 1974)

7   The essential nature of individuality lies in the universal element of mind.

G. W. F. Hegel (1770–1831) German philosopher. 1807. *The Phenomenology of Mind* (J. B. Baillie, tr.; 1910)

8   You behold in me, said Stephen with grim displeasure, a horrible example of free thought.

James Joyce (1882–1941) Irish writer. *Ulysses* (1922)

9   Each age has its own characteristic depravity. Ours is perhaps not pleasure or indulgence or sensuality, but rather a dissolute pantheistic contempt for the individual man.

Søren Kierkegaard (1813–55) Danish philosopher. *Concluding Unscientific Postscript* (1846)

10 There are two major forces in society: love, which multiplies the species, and the nose, which subordinates it to the individual.

Joaquim Maria Machado de Assis (1839–1908) Brazilian novelist and short-story writer. *Epitaph of a Small Winner* (1880)

11 The only part of the conduct of any one, for which he is amenable to society, is that which concerns others. In the part which merely concerns himself, his independence is, of right, absolute. Over himself, over his own body and mind, the individual is absolute.

John Stuart Mill (1806–73) British philosopher and social reformer. *On Liberty* (1859)

12 Obsessed, bewildered
    By the shipwreck
    Of the singular
    We have chosen the meaning
    Of being numerous.

George Oppen (1908–84) US poet. 'Of Being Numerous', *Of Being Numerous* (1968), quoted in *The Norton Anthology of American Literature* (Nina Baym, ed.; 1998), vol. 2

13 Grand, gloomy, and peculiar, he sat upon the throne a sceptred hermit, wrapped in the solitude of his own originality.

Charles Phillips (1789–1859) British barrister and writer. Referring to Napoleon. *An Historical Character of Napoleon* (1816)

14 They will say that you are on the wrong road, if it is your own.

Antonio Porchia (1886–1968) Italian-born Argentinian writer. *Voces* (W. S. Merwin, tr.; 1968)

15 If a man does not keep pace with his companions, perhaps it is because he hears a different drummer. Let him step to the music which he hears, however measured or far away.

Henry David Thoreau (1817–62) US writer. 'Conclusion', *Walden, or, Life in the Woods* (1854)

Inequality

see also Civil Rights, Equality, Human Rights, Injustice, Women's Rights

1   Where some people are very wealthy and others have nothing the result will be either extreme democracy or absolute oligarchy, or despotism will come from either of those excesses.

Aristotle (384–322 BC) Greek philosopher. *Politics* (335–322? BC), bk. 4

2   If a society consisting of men and women is content to apply progress and education to one half of itself, such a society is weakened by half.

Kemal Atatürk (1881–1938) Turkish statesman. Referring to the need for women's education. Speech (1926)

3   All inequality that has no special utility to justify
    it is injustice.
    Jeremy Bentham (1748–1832) British philosopher, economist, jurist, and
    social reformer. 'Supply Without Burthen or Escheat Vice
    Taxation', *Jeremy Bentham's Economic Writings* (W. Stark,
    ed.; 1952)

4   There are only two families in the world, my old
    grandmother used to say, The *Haves* and the
    Have-Nots.
    Miguel de Cervantes (1547–1616) Spanish novelist and playwright. *Don
    Quixote* (1605–15), pt. 2, ch. 20

5   Inequality is not only about income, where real
    poverty has grown, it is about self-esteem.
    Will Hutton (b. 1950) British author and newspaper editor. *The State
    We're In* (1995)

6   The more education a woman has, the wider the
    gap between men's and women's earnings for the
    same work.
    Sandra Day O'Connor (b. 1930) US Supreme Court justice. *Phoenix
    Magazine* (1971)

7   It is a reproach to religion and government to
    suffer so much poverty and excess.
    William Penn (1644–1718) English preacher and colonialist. *Some Fruits
    of Solitude* (1693), pt. 1, no. 52

8   The rich have become richer, and the poor have
    become poorer; and the vessel of the state is
    driven between the Scylla and Charybdis of
    anarchy and despotism.
    Percy Bysshe Shelley (1792–1822) English poet. *A Defence of Poetry*
    (1821), quoted in *Essays, Letters from Abroad, Translations
    and Fragments* (Mrs. Shelley, ed.; 1840)

Infidelity

see also **Adultery, Betrayal, Faithfulness**

1   But I wasn't kissing her. I was whispering in her
    mouth.
    Chico Marx (1891–1961) US comedian and film actor. Response when
    his wife caught him kissing a chorus girl. *The Marx Brothers
    Scrapbook* (G. Marx and R. Anobile; 1974), ch. 24

2   Madame, you must really be more careful. Suppose
    it had been someone else who found you like this.
    Armand-Emmanuel du Plessis (1766–1822) French soldier and statesman.
    Discovering his wife with her lover. Quoted in *The Book of
    Lists* (David Wallechinsky, Irving Wallace, and Amy Wallace,
    eds.; 1977)

3   Monogamy is the Western custom of one wife
    and hardly any mistresses.
    Saki (1870–1916) British short-story writer. *Reginald in Russia* (1910)

Infinity

see also **Eternity, The Universe**

1   To see a World in a Grain of Sand
    And a Heaven in a Wild Flower,
    Hold Infinity in the palm of your hand
    And Eternity in an hour.
    William Blake (1757–1827) British poet, painter, engraver, and mystic.
    'Auguries of Innocence' (1803?), ll. 1–4, quoted in *The Poetry
    and Prose of William Blake* (David V. Erdman, ed.; 1965)

2   They cannot scare me with their empty spaces
    Between stars—on stars where no human race is
    I have it in me so much nearer home
    To scare myself with my own desert places.
    Robert Frost (1874–1963) US poet. 'Desert Places', *A Further Range*
    (1936)

3   From space to the sky, from the sky to the hills,
    and the sea; to every blade of grass, to every leaf,
    to the smallest insect, to the million waves of
    ocean . . . this earth itself appears but a mote in
    that sunbeam by which we are conscious of one
    narrow streak in the abyss.
    Richard Jefferies (1848–87) British naturalist and writer. *The Story of
    My Heart* (1883)

4   I cannot help it;—in spite of myself, infinity
    torments me.
    Alfred de Musset (1810–57) French poet and playwright. 'L'Espoir en
    Dieu' (1834)

5   All finite things reveal infinitude.
    Theodore Roethke (1908–63) US poet. *The Far Field* (1964)

6   I learned not to fear infinity,
    The far field, the windy cliffs of forever,
    The dying of time in the white light of
    tomorrow.
    Theodore Roethke (1908–63) US poet. 'The Far Field', *The Far Field*
    (1964)

7   Both small and great things must equally possess
    form. The mind cannot picture to itself a thing
    without form, nor conceive a form of unlimited
    dimensions.
    Zhuangzi (369?–286 BC) Chinese philosopher and teacher. 'Autumn
    Floods', quoted in *Chuang Tzu* (Herbert A. Giles, tr.; 1980),
    ch. 17

Influence

see also **Manipulation, Power**

1   As I have often said, I am easily influenced.
    Compared with me a weather vane is Gibraltar.
    Franklin P. Adams (1881–1960) US journalist. Quoted in *Wit's End*
    (Robert E. Drennan; 1973)

2   I believe in the immortality of influence.
    Luther Burbank (1849–1926) US botanist. *The Harvest of the Years*
    (co-written with Wilbur Hale; 1927)

3   How to Win Friends and Influence People
    Dale Carnegie (1888–1955) US writer and speaker. Book title. (1936)

4   He who influences the thought of his times,
    influences all the times that follow. He has made
    his impress on eternity.
    Hypatia (370?–415) Greek philosopher, mathematician, and astronomer.
    Quoted in 'Hypatia', *Little Journeys to the Homes of Great
    Teachers* (Elbert Hubbard; 1908)

5   I could always hypnotize people. Even when I
    lost sight of God, I could hypnotize with music.
    Charles Mingus (1922–79) US jazz musician. *Beneath the Underdog*
    (1971), ch. 30

6   A cock has great influence on his own dunghill.
    Publilius Syrus (*fl.* 1st century BC) Roman writer. 1st century BC.
    Maxims (Darius Lyman, tr.), 357

7   If I were the son of a nursery gardener, I would
    probably know a great deal about trees, and I
    would have an extraordinary taste for gardens.
    But I'm the son of a painter, so I'm more or less
    influenced by the painters who surrounded me . . .
    when I was young.
    Jean Renoir (1894–1979) French film director. Quoted in *Jean Renoir:
    Projections of Paradise* (Ronald Bergan; 1992)

8   Ah, you flavour everything; you are the vanilla of
    society.
    Sydney Smith (1771–1845) British clergyman, essayist, and wit. Quoted
    in *A Memoir of the Rev. Sydney Smith* (Lady Holland; 1855),
    vol. 1, ch. 9

9 True influence over another comes not from a moment's eloquence nor from any happily chosen word, but from the accumulation of a lifetime's thoughts stored up in the eyes.

Thornton Wilder (1897–1975) US novelist and playwright. *The Woman of Andros* (1930)

Information

see also Facts, Knowledge

1 Lord help you! Tell 'em Queen Anne's dead.

George Colman (1762–1836) British playwright and theatre owner. A phrase which came to be applied to news everyone already knows. *The Heir at Law* (1797), Act 1, Scene 1

2 Withholding information from someone is an act of intellectual imperialism. Not bothering to seek accurate information is an act of intellectual recklessness.

Nancy Kline, US author. *Time to Think* (1999)

3 In the long run, no ideas, no information.

Theodore Roszak (b. 1933) US writer and editor. *The Cult of Information* (1986)

4 Information and knowledge are the thermonuclear weapons of our time.

Thomas A. Stewart (b. 1948) US journalist. *Intellectual Capital* (1997)

Ingenuity

see Creativity, Innovation, Intelligence

Injustice

see also Exploitation, Inequality, Oppression

1 Hanged privily by night or in the luncheon hour.

Anonymous. Referring to abuses of the procedure for trying clerics. *From Domesday Book to Magna Carta* (Austin L. Poole; 1951)

2 In doing good, we are generally cold, and languid, and sluggish; and of all things afraid of being too much in the right. But the works of malice and injustice are quite in another style. They are finished with a bold, masterly hand.

Edmund Burke (1729–97) Irish-born British statesman and political philosopher. Speech, Bristol (1780), quoted in *The Writings and Speeches of Edmund Burke* (H. G. Bohn; 1855)

3 No man can mortgage his injustice as a pawn for his fidelity.

Edmund Burke (1729–97) Irish-born British statesman and political philosopher. *Reflections on the Revolution in France* (1790)

4 When one has been threatened with a great injustice, one accepts a smaller as a favour.

Jane Carlyle (1801–66) Scottish diarist. *Journal* (November 21, 1855)

5 Extreme justice is extreme injustice.

Cicero (106–43 BC) Roman orator and statesman. *De Officiis* (44 BC)

6 It is the government that should ask me for a pardon.

Eugene Victor Debs (1855–1926) US trade union leader, socialist, and pacifist. When released from prison (1921) on the orders of President Harding after being jailed for sedition (1918). *The People's Almanac* (D. Wallechinsky; 1921)

7 To disarm the strong and arm the weak would be to change the social order which it's my job to preserve. Justice is the means by which established injustices are sanctioned.

Anatole France (1844–1924) French novelist, poet, and critic. *Crainquebille* (1901)

8 National injustice is the surest road to national downfall.

William Ewart Gladstone (1809–98) British statesman. Speech at Plumstead, London (1878), quoted in *Gladstone's Speeches* (A. Tilney Bassett; 1916)

9 To have a grievance is to have a purpose in life.

Eric Hoffer (1902–83) US philosopher and longshoreman. *The Passionate State of Mind* (1954)

10 Undeservedly you will atone for the sins of your fathers.

Horace (65–8 BC) Roman poet. *Odes* (23? BC), bk. 3, no. 6, l. 1

11 The injustice done to an individual is sometimes of service to the public.

Junius (fl. 1769–72) British unidentified polemicist. Letter, *Public Advertiser* (November 14, 1770)

12 Injustice anywhere is a threat to justice everywhere.

Martin Luther King, Jr. (1929–68) US civil rights leader. Letter from Birmingham Jail, Alabama (April 16, 1963), quoted in *Right Thinking* (Edward Leigh; 1979)

13 We are out to defeat injustice and not white persons who may be unjust.

Martin Luther King, Jr. (1929–68) US civil rights leader. *Stride Toward Freedom* (1964)

14 The dispensing of injustice is always in the right hands.

Stanislaw Lec (1909–66) Polish writer. *Unkempt Thoughts* (1962)

15 Injustice, swift, erect, and unconfin'd,
Sweeps the wide earth, and tramples o'er mankind,
While prayers, to heal her wrongs, move slow behind.

Alexander Pope (1688–1744) English poet. *The Iliad of Homer* (1715–20), bk. 9, ll. 628–630

16 LEAR I am a man
More sinn'd against than sinning.

William Shakespeare (1564–1616) English poet and playwright. *King Lear* (1605–06), Act 3, Scene 2

17 OTHELLO I swear 'tis better to be much abused
Than but to know 't a little.

William Shakespeare (1564–1616) English poet and playwright. *Othello* (1602–04), Act 3, Scene 3

18 Rigorous law is often rigorous injustice.

Terence (185–159 BC) Roman playwright and poet. *The Self-Tormentor* (2nd century BC)

19 I sit on a man's back, choking him and making him carry me, and yet assure myself and others that I am very sorry for him and wish to ease his lot by all possible means—except by getting off his back.

Leo Tolstoy (1828–1910) Russian writer. *What Then Must We Do?* (1886), ch. 16

20 No injustice is done to someone who wants that thing done.

Ulpian (170?–228?) Roman jurist. Usually, 'Volenti non fit iniuria': To someone who wants it no injustice occurs. *Corpus Iuris Civilis* (212–217), Digests 47, X, i, 5

21 Injustice which lasts for three long centuries and which exists among millions of people over thousands of square miles of territory, is injustice no longer; it is an accomplished fact of life.

Richard Wright (1908–60) US novelist. Referring to slavery. *Native Son* (1940)

Innocence

see also **Childhood, Guilt**

1 There is nothing innocuous left . . . Even the blossoming tree lies the moment its bloom is seen without the shadow of terror; even the innocent 'How lovely!' becomes an excuse for an existence outrageously unlovely.
Theodor Adorno (1903–69) German philosopher, sociologist, and musicologist. *Minima Moralia* (E. F. N. Jephcott, tr.; 1951)

2 People who shut their eyes to reality simply invite their own destruction, and anyone who insists on remaining in a state of innocence long after that innocence is dead turns himself into a monster.
James Baldwin (1924–87) US writer and civil rights activist. 'Stranger in the Village', *Notes of a Native Son* (1955)

3 The secret motive of the absent-minded is to be innocent while guilty. Absent-mindedness is spurious innocence.
Saul Bellow (b. 1915) Canadian-born US writer. *More Die of Heartbreak* (1987)

4 No, it is not only our fate but our business to lose innocence, and once we have lost that, it is futile to attempt a picnic in Eden.
Elizabeth Bowen (1899–1973) Irish novelist and short-story writer. 'Out of a Book', *Orion III* (Rosamund Lehmann et al, eds.; 1946)

5 Ralph wept for the end of innocence, the darkness of man's heart, and the fall through the air of the true, wise friend called Piggy.
William Golding (1911–93) British novelist. *Lord of the Flies* (1954), ch. 12

6 Innocence is a kind of insanity.
Graham Greene (1904–91) British novelist. *The Quiet American* (1955)

7 Too near the ancient troughs of blood
Innocence is no earthly weapon.
Geoffrey Hill (b. 1932) British poet. 'Ovid in the Third Reich', *King Log* (1968), st. 1, ll. 3–4

8 Was there anything so loathsome as a wilfully innocent man? Hardly. An innocent man is a sin before God. Inhuman and therefore unworthy. No man should live without absorbing the sins of his kind.
Toni Morrison (b. 1931) US novelist. *Tar Baby* (1981)

9 It is innocence that is full and experience that is empty. It is innocence that wins and experience that loses.
Charles Pierre Péguy (1873–1914) French writer and poet. 'Innocence and Experience', *Basic Verities* (A. and J. Green, trs.; 1943)

10 He's arm'd without that's innocent within.
Alexander Pope (1688–1744) English poet. *Satires, Epistles, and Odes of Horace* (1737), bk. 1, Epistle 1, l. 94

11 Now my innocence begins to weigh me down.
Racine (1639–99) French playwright. *Andromaque* (1667), Act 3, Scene 1

12 SHYLOCK What judgment shall I dread, doing no wrong?
William Shakespeare (1564–1616) English poet and playwright. *The Merchant of Venice* (1596–98), Act 4, Scene 1

13 I am one hundred percent not guilty.
O. J. Simpson (b. 1947) US American football player, broadcaster, and actor. Read on television and often repeated. Open letter (June 17, 1994)

14 And the wild boys innocent as strawberries.
Dylan Thomas (1914–53) Welsh poet, playwright, and short-story writer. 'The Hunchback in the Park', *Deaths and Entrances* (1946), l. 40

15 The innocent and the beautiful
Have no enemy but time.
W. B. Yeats (1865–1939) Irish poet and playwright. October 1927. 'In Memory of Eva Gore-Booth and Con Markiewicz', *The Winding Stair and Other Poems* (1933), st. 2

Innovation

see also **Creativity, Experiments, Inventions, Originality**

1 The new always happens against the overwhelming odds of statistical laws and their probability . . . the new therefore always appears in the guise of a miracle.
Hannah Arendt (1906–75) German-born US philosopher and historian. *The Human Condition* (1958), pt. 5, ch. 24

2 As the births of living creatures at first are ill-shapen, so are all innovations, which are the births of time.
Francis Bacon (1561–1626) English philosopher, statesman, and lawyer. 'Of Innovations', *Essays* (1625)

3 It is not learning how to do something which people will call art, but rather inventing something that is absolutely necessary for the progress of our existence.
Robert Henri (1865–1929) US painter and teacher. 'The New York Exhibition of Independent Artists', *The Craftsman* (1910)

4 Invention is the process by which a new idea is discovered or created. In contrast, innovation occurs when that new idea is adopted.
Everett Rogers (b. 1931) US sociologist. Attrib.

5 Rules freeze companies inside a glacier; innovation lets them ride sleighs over it.
Ricardo Semler, Brazilian business executive. *Maverick!* (1993)

Insincerity

see **Artifice, Deception, Lying**

Inspiration

see also **Genius, Originality**

1 When I composed that, I was conscious of being inspired by God Almighty. Do you think I can consider your puny little fiddle when He speaks to me?
Ludwig van Beethoven (1770–1827) German composer. Said when a violinist complained that a passage was unplayable. *Music All Around Me* (Anthony Hopkins; 1967)

2 I tell poets that when a line just floats into your head, don't pay attention 'cause it probably has floated into somebody else's head.
Gwendolyn Brooks (1917–2000) US poet and novelist. *I Dream a World: Portraits of Black Women Who Changed America* (Brian Lanker; 1989)

3 For painters, poets and builders have very high flights, but they must be kept down.
Sarah Churchill (1660–1744) English courtier. Letter to the Duchess of Bedford (June 21, 1734)

4 His thoughts did not seem to come with labour and effort; but as if borne on the gusts of genius, and as if the wings of his imagination lifted him from off his feet.
William Hazlitt (1778–1830) British essayist and critic. Referring to Samuel Taylor Coleridge. 'On the Living Poets', *Lectures on the English Poets* (1818), Lecture 8

5 The deep well of unconscious cerebration.

Henry James (1843–1916) US-born British writer and critic. 'The American', *Prefaces* (1909)

6 O, for a draught of vintage! that hath been Cool'd a long age in the deep-delvéd earth.

John Keats (1795–1821) English poet. 'Ode to a Nightingale' (1820), st. 2

7 Deprivation is for me what daffodils were for Wordsworth.

Philip Larkin (1922–85) British poet. *Required Writing* (1983)

8 What in me is dark
Illumine, what is low raise and support;
That to the highth of this great argument
I may assert eternal providence,
And justify the ways of God to men.

John Milton (1608–74) English writer. The poet's invocation to God. *Paradise Lost* (1667), bk. 1, ll. 22–26

9 There are some times in your life when you have to call upon the best of all God gave you—and the best of what He didn't.

Gloria Naylor (b. 1950) US novelist, producer, and playwright. *Mama Day* (1988)

10 He who would have you believe that he is waiting for the inspiration of genius, is in reality at a loss how to begin, and is at last delivered of his monsters, with difficulty and pain.

Sir Joshua Reynolds (1723–92) British painter and writer. 1769. Quoted in *Discourses* (Pat Rogers, ed.; 1992)

11 'From the great Story Sea', he'd reply. 'I drink the warm Story Waters and then I feel full of steam'.

Salman Rushdie (b. 1947) Indian-born British novelist. Said by the storyteller Rashid Khalifa, explaining to his son Haroun where his stories come from. *Haroun and the Sea of Stories* (1990)

12 Imitation is not inspiration, and inspiration only can give birth to a work of art. The least of man's original emanation is better than the best of a borrowed thought.

Albert Pinkham Ryder (1847–1917) US painter. Quoted in *Albert Pinkham Ryder* (John Sherman; 1920)

13 You're best when you're not in charge. The ego locks the muse.

Robin Williams (b. 1951) US actor and comedian. *Premiere* (January 1988)

Insults

see also **Literary Insults**, **Political Insults**, **Ridicule**

1 Quite so. But I have not been on a ship for fifteen years and they still call me 'Admiral'.

Anonymous. Italian admiral to whom Eva Perón had complained that she had been called a 'whore' on an Italian visit.

2 An imitation rough diamond.

Margot Asquith (1865–1945) British political hostess and writer. Referring to an American general. *As I Remember* (1922)

3 Slander away, slander away; something will always stick.

Pierre-Augustin Caron de Beaumarchais (1732–99) French playwright. *The Barber of Seville* (1775), Act 3, Scene 13

4 I mock thee not, though I by thee am mockèd;
Thou call'st me madman, but I call thee blockhead.

William Blake (1757–1827) British poet, painter, engraver, and mystic. Remark to the British sculptor and illustrator John Flaxman. *Manuscript Notebooks* (1811), no. 10

5 If there is anyone here whom I have not insulted, I beg his pardon.

Johannes Brahms (1833–97) German composer. Said on leaving a gathering of friends. Attrib.

6 The petrifactions of a plodding brain.

Lord Byron (1788–1824) British poet. *English Bards and Scotch Reviewers* (1809), l. 416

7 Chevy Chase couldn't ad-lib a fart after a baked-bean dinner.

Johnny Carson (b. 1925) US chat-show host. Referring to the actor and comedian Chevy Chase. Attrib.

8 An injury is much sooner forgotten than an insult.

Lord Chesterfield (1694–1773) English statesman and writer. October 9, 1746. *Letters to his Son* (1774)

9 If you were my wife, I'd drink it.

Winston Churchill (1874–1965) British prime minister and writer. Replying to Lady Astor who had said, 'If you were my husband, I'd put poison in your coffee'. Attrib. *Nancy Astor and Her Friends* (E. Langhorne; 1974)

10 The only time in his life he ever put up a fight was when we asked him for his resignation.

Georges Clemenceau (1841–1929) French prime minister and journalist. Referring to Marshal Joffre. *Here I Lie* (A. M. Thomson; 1937)

11 How strange, when I saw you acting in *The Glorious Adventure* I laughed all the time.

Noël Coward (1899–1973) British playwright, actor, and songwriter. Said to Lady Diana Cooper who said she had not laughed once at his comedy *The Young Idea*. *The Noël Coward Diaries* (Graham Payn and Sheridan Morley, eds.; 1982)

12 The finest collection of frames I ever saw.

Humphry Davy (1778–1829) British chemist. When asked what he thought of the Paris art galleries. Attrib.

13 The words she spoke of Mrs. Harris, lambs could not forgive . . . nor worms forget.

Charles Dickens (1812–70) British novelist. Referring to Mrs. Gamp. *Martin Chuzzlewit* (1844), ch. 49

14 He is not only dull in himself, but the cause of dullness in others.

Samuel Foote (1720–77) British actor and playwright. Referring to a dull law lord. Parody of Falstaff's famous line in *Henry IV, Part 2*: 'I am not only witty in myself, but the cause that is wit in other men'. *Life of Samuel Johnson* (James Boswell; 1791), Sunday 30 March, 1783, Aetat. 74

15 You bubble-mouthing, fog-blathering, Chin-chuntering, chap-flapping, liturgical, Turgidical, base old man!

Christopher Fry (b. 1907) British playwright. *The Lady's Not for Burning* (1948), Act 1

16 The reason so many people showed up at his funeral was because they wanted to make sure he was dead.

Samuel Goldwyn (1882–1974) Polish-born US film producer. Referring to Louis B. Mayer; often attributed to others. Quoted in *Hollywood Rajah: the Life and Times of Louis B. Mayer* (Bosley Crowther; 1960)

17 Will no one rid me of this turbulent priest?

Henry II (1133–89) English monarch. Referring to Thomas à Becket, Archbishop of Canterbury, who opposed his attempts to remove the legal immunity of priests. Four of Henry's knights took his words literally and killed Becket in Canterbury Cathedral (December 1170). Remark (1170), quoted in *History of the Life of King Henry II* (G. Lyttleton; 1769), pt. 4

18 Sir, you are like a pin, but without either its head or its point.

Douglas Jerrold (1803–57) British playwright. Speaking to a small thin man who was boring him. Attrib.

19   Difficult do you call it, Sir? I wish it were impossible.

Samuel Johnson (1709–84) British lexicographer and writer. Said on hearing a famous violinist. Quoted in *Supplement to the Anecdotes of Distinguished Persons* (William Seward; 1797)

20   Calumnies are answered best with silence.

Ben Jonson (1572–1637) English playwright and poet. *Volpone* (1606), Act 2, Scene 2

21   Calling somebody a Communist is an entirely respectable, and popular, middle-class way to call somebody a low-down dirty dog.

June Jordan (b. 1936) US journalist, writer, and activist. *Where Are We and Whose Country Is This Anyway?* (1986)

22   Oh, well, you play Bach *your* way. I'll play him *his*.

Wanda Landowska (1877–1959) Polish-born harpsichordist and teacher. Remark to fellow musician. Quoted in *The Faber Book of Anecdotes* (Clifton Fadiman; 1985)

23   He looked at me as if I was a side dish he hadn't ordered.

Ring Lardner (1885–1933) US humorist and writer. Referring to William Howard Taft. Attrib.

24   The answer is in the plural and they bounce.

Edwin Landseer Lutyens (1869–1944) British architect. Attrib.

25   I never forget a face, but I'll make an exception in your case.

Groucho Marx (1895–1977) US comedian and film actor. *Guardian* (June 18, 1965)

26   You are the pits.

John McEnroe (b. 1959) US tennis player and broadcaster. Said to an umpire at Wimbledon. *Sunday Times* (June 24, 1981)

27   I could eat alphabet soup and *shit* better lyrics.

Johnny Mercer (1909–76) US lyricist and composer. Describing a British musical. Attrib.

28   Frankly, my dear, I don't give a damn.

Margaret Mitchell (1900–49) US novelist. Rhett Butler to Scarlett O'Hara. *Gone with the Wind* (screen version) (Sidney Howard; 1939)

29   This is adding insult to injuries.

Edward Moore (1712–57) English playwright. *The Foundling* (1747–48), Act 5

30   I don't have to take this abuse from you. I've got hundreds of people waiting to abuse me.

Bill Murray (b. 1950) US comedian and actor. As Dr. Peter Venkman. *Ghostbusters* (Dan Ackroyd and Harold Ramis; 1984)

31   Where does she find them?

Dorothy Parker (1893–1967) US writer and wit. Replying to the remark, 'Anyway, she's always very nice to her inferiors'. Quoted in *The Lyttelton Hart-Davis Letters* (Rupert Hart-Davis, ed.; 1978)

32   Pearls before swine.

Dorothy Parker (1893–1967) US writer and wit. Clare Booth Luce, going through a door with her, said, 'Age before beauty'. Quoted in *You Might As Well Live* (John Keats; 1970)

33   She ran the whole gamut of the emotions from A to B.

Dorothy Parker (1893–1967) US writer and wit. Referring to a first-night performance by Katherine Hepburn on Broadway. Attrib.

34   One does not insult the river god while crossing the river.

Chinese proverb.

35   The worst libel is the truth.

Yiddish proverb.

36   You really are an asshole, Lester. You went past assholism into some kinda urinary tract.

Lou Reed (b. 1942) US rock singer and songwriter. Said during an interview with the rock journalist Lester Bangs. Quoted in *Beyond the Velvet Underground* (Dave Thomson; 1974)

37   You killed Ted, you medieval dickweed!

Keanu Reeves (b. 1965) US film actor. As Bill, addressing Death. *Bill and Ted's Excellent Adventure* (Chris Matheson and Ed Solomon; 1988)

38   Sir, to be facetious it is not necessary to be indecent.

Thorold Rogers (1823–90) British political economist. Also attributed to Birkbeck Hill. Quoted in 'In Imitation of Samuel Johnson', *Dr. Johnson and His Circle* (John Bailey; 1913)

39   KENT Thou whoreson zed! thou unnecessary letter!

William Shakespeare (1564–1616) English poet and playwright. *King Lear* (1605–06), Act 2, Scene 2

40   ALBANY You are not worth the dust which the rude wind
Blows in your face.

William Shakespeare (1564–1616) English poet and playwright. *King Lear* (1605–06), Act 4, Scene 2

41   BENEDICK She speaks poniards, and every word stabs: if her breath were as terrible as her terminations, there were no living near her; she would infect to the north star.

William Shakespeare (1564–1616) English poet and playwright. *Much Ado About Nothing* (1598–99), Act 2, Scene 1

42   Better never than late.

George Bernard Shaw (1856–1950) Irish playwright. Responding to an offer by a producer to present one of his plays after an earlier rejection of it. Quoted in *The Unimportance of Being Oscar* (Oscar Levant; 1968)

43   You silly moo.

Johnny Speight (b. 1920) British television scriptwriter. Alf Garnett's catch phrase in the television comedy series. *Till Death Do Us Part* (BBC television; 1972)

44   My nose bleeds for you.

Herbert Beerbohm Tree (1853–1917) British actor and theatrical impresario. Attrib. *Beerbohm Tree* (Hesketh Pearson; 1956)

45   You have Van Gogh's ear for music.

Billy Wilder (1906–2002) Austrian-born US film director and screenwriter. Said to Cliff Osmond. Attrib.

46   If I had had to choose between him and a cockroach as a companion for a walking-tour, the cockroach would have had it by a short head.

P. G. Wodehouse (1881–1975) British-born US humorous writer. *My Man Jeeves* (1919)

Integrity

see also **Conscience, Morality, Sincerity**

1   We voted to die with dignity.

Anonymous. Said by a reporter on *The Buffalo Courier Express*, whose unions had refused to accept the scale of cuts Rupert Murdoch demanded to buy the paper. The paper shut down when the deal fell through. Quoted in *Rupert Murdoch: Ringmaster of the Information Circus* (William Shawcross; 1993)

2   Integrity without knowledge is weak and useless, and knowledge without integrity is dangerous and dreadful.

Samuel Johnson (1709–84) British lexicographer and writer. *Rasselas* (1759), ch. 41

3   HAMLET And blest are those
     Whose blood and judgement are so well
     comeddled
     That they are not a pipe for Fortune's finger
     To sound what stop she please.
     William Shakespeare (1564–1616) English poet and playwright. *Hamlet*
     (1601), Act 3, Scene 2

4   Man's word is God in man.
     Alfred Tennyson (1809–92) British poet. 'The Coming of Arthur',
     Idylls of the King (1869), l. 132

Intellect

see also Creativity, Intellectuals, Intelligence, Thinking

1   Intellectual virtue owes both its birth and its
     growth to teaching . . . while moral growth
     comes about as a result of habit.
     Aristotle (384–322 BC) Greek philosopher. *Nicomachean Ethics* (4th
     century BC), 1103a

2   Our age is the age of the nationalization of
     intellect in political hatreds.
     Julien Benda (1867–1956) French philosopher and essayist. *La Trahison
     des Clercs* (1927)

3   We should take care not to make the intellect our
     god; it has, of course, powerful muscles, but no
     personality.
     Albert Einstein (1879–1955) German-born US physicist. *Out of My
     Later Years* (1950)

4   It is an unscrupulous intellect that does not pay
     to antiquity its due reverence . . . There are many
     kinds of genius; each age has its different gifts.
     Desiderius Erasmus (1466?–1536) Dutch humanist, scholar, and writer.
     Works of Hilary (1523), Preface

5   Bodies devoid of mind are as statues in the
     marketplace.
     Euripides (480?–406? BC) Greek playwright. *Electra* (5th century BC),
     l. 386

6   The voice of the intellect is a soft one, but it does
     not rest till it has gained a hearing.
     Sigmund Freud (1856–1939) Austrian psychoanalyst. *The Future of an
     Illusion* (1927)

7   A towering intellect, grand in its achievements,
     and glorious in its possibilities, may, with the
     moral and spiritual faculties held in abeyance, be
     one of the most dangerous and mischievous
     forces in the world.
     Frances E. W. Harper (1825–1911) US writer and social reformer. 'A
     Factor in Human Progress', *African Methodist Episcopal
     Church Review* (1885)

8   Little minds are interested in the extraordinary;
     great minds in the commonplace.
     Elbert Hubbard (1856–1915) US writer, printer, and editor. *A Thousand
     and One Epigrams* (1911)

9   We are thinking beings, and we cannot exclude the
     intellect from participating in any of our functions.
     William James (1842–1910) US psychologist and philosopher. *The
     Varieties of Religious Experience* (1902)

10   We are perpetually moralists, but we are
     geometricians only by chance. Our intercourse with
     intellectual nature is necessary; our speculations
     upon matter are voluntary, and at leisure.
     Samuel Johnson (1709–84) British lexicographer and writer. 'Milton',
     Lives of the English Poets (1779–81)

11   The intellect is always fooled by the heart.
     François La Rochefoucauld (1613–80) French epigrammatist and moralist.
     Reflections, or Sentences and Moral Maxims (1665), no. 102

12   The height of cleverness is to be able to conceal it.
     François La Rochefoucauld (1613–80) French epigrammatist and moralist.
     Reflections, or Sentences and Moral Maxims (1665), no. 245

13   The highest intellects, like the tops of mountains,
     are the first to catch and to reflect the dawn.
     Thomas Babington Macaulay (1800–59) British politician, historian, and
     writer. 'Sir James Mackintosh', *Essays Contributed to the
     Edinburgh Review* (1843)

14   It is good to rub and polish our brain against
     that of others.
     Michel de Montaigne (1533–92) French essayist. *Essays* (1580–88),
     bk. 1

15   Intellect is invisible to the man who has none.
     Arthur Schopenhauer (1788–1860) German philosopher. *Aphorismen zur
     Lebensweisheit* (1919)

16   Disinterested intellectual curiosity is the life blood
     of real civilisation.
     G. M. Trevelyan (1876–1962) British historian. *English Social History*
     (1942), Preface

17   The intellect is part of life—not its counterpart.
     Kurt Tucholsky (1890–1935) German philosopher. Quoted in 'Selected
     Aphorisms', *Kurt Tucholsky. The Ironic Sentimentalist* (Bryan
     P. Grenville; 1981)

18   Our meddling intellect
     Misshapes the beauteous forms of things:
     We murder to dissect.
     William Wordsworth (1770–1850) English poet. May 23, 1798.
     Subtitled 'An Evening Piece on the Same Subject', referring to
     'Expostulation and Reply', to which it is a companion piece.
     'The Tables Turned', *Lyrical Ballads* (1798), ll. 26–28

19   An intellectual hatred is the worst.
     W. B. Yeats (1865–1939) Irish poet and playwright. June 1919. 'A
     Prayer for My Daughter', *Michael Robartes and the Dancer*
     (1921), st. 8

Intellectuals

see also Intellect, Intelligence

1   An intellectual is a man who doesn't know how
     to park a bike.
     Spiro T. Agnew (1918–96) US politician. Attrib.

2   He's very clever, but sometimes his brains go to
     his head.
     Margot Asquith (1865–1945) British political hostess and writer.
     Referring to the politician F. E. Smith. *As I Remember* (1922)

3   To the man-in-the-street, who, I'm sorry to say
     Is a keen observer of life,
     The word Intellectual suggests straight away
     A man who's untrue to his wife.
     W. H. Auden (1907–73) British poet. 'Note on Intellectuals' (1941)

4   I've been called many things, but never an
     intellectual.
     Tallulah Bankhead (1903–68) US actor. *Tallulah* (1952), ch. 15

5   The intellectuals' chief cause of anguish are one
     another's works.
     Jacques Barzun (b. 1907) French-born US writer, cultural critic, and
     educator. *The House of Intellect* (1959)

6   When Napoleon gave the French intellectuals
     ribbons stars and baubles, he knew what he was
     doing . . . From the time of Richelieu and earlier,
     the French had been big in the culture business.
     Saul Bellow (b. 1915) Canadian-born US writer. *Humboldt's Gift*
     (1975)

7   Intellectuals are people who believe that ideas are of more importance than values. That is to say, their own ideas and other people's values.
Gerald Brenan (1894–1987) Maltese-born British writer and novelist. 'Life', *Thoughts in a Dry Season* (1978)

8   An intellectual is a man who says a simple thing in a difficult way; an artist is a man who says a difficult thing in a simple way.
Charles Bukowski (1920–94) German-born US writer. *Notes of a Dirty Old Man* (1969)

9   In the US you have to be a deviant or exist in extreme boredom . . . Make no mistake; all intellectuals are deviants in the US.
William S. Burroughs (1914–97) US writer. *Yage Letters* (co-written with Allen Ginsberg; 1963)

10 An intellectual is someone whose mind watches itself.
Albert Camus (1913–60) Algerian-born French novelist, essayist, and playwright. *Notebooks* (1935–42)

11 Every intellectual who is called before one of the committees ought to refuse to testify, i.e., he must be prepared . . . for the sacrifice of his personal welfare in the interest of the cultural welfare of the country . . . This kind of inquisition violates the spirit of the Constitution.
Albert Einstein (1879–1955) German-born US physicist. May 16, 1953. Referring to the Senate Internal Security Subcommittee. Letter to William Frauenglass, *New York Times* (June 12, 1953)

12 It is ironic that the United States should have been founded by intellectuals; for throughout most of our political history the intellectual has been for the most part either an outsider, a servant, or a scapegoat.
Richard Hofstadter (1916–70) US historian. *Anti-Intellectualism in American Life* (1963)

13 Intellectual slavery masquerading as sophistication is the worst form of slavery.
Ngugi wa Thiongo (b. 1938) Kenyan writer. *Detained, A Writer's Prison Diary* (1981)

14 The trouble with me is, I belong to a vanishing race. I'm one of the intellectuals.
Robert E. Sherwood (1896–1955) US playwright. *The Petrified Forest* (1935)

Intelligence

see also **Consciousness, Mind, Thinking, Understanding**

1   No tool is more beneficial than intelligence. No enemy is more harmful than ignorance.
Abu Abdullah Muhammad al-Harithi al-Baghdadi al-Mufid (*fl.* 10th century) Iraqi scholar and jurist. 10th century. 'The Life of the Commander of the Faithful', *The Book of Guidance into the Lives of the Twelve Imams* (I. K. A. Howard, tr.; 1981)

2   Sublime moments, heroic acts, are rather the deeds of an exalted intelligence than of the will.
Pio Baroja (1872–1956) Basque writer. *The Quest* (Isaac Goldberg, tr.; 1922)

3   Intelligence is characterized by a natural incomprehension of life.
Henri-Louis Bergson (1859–1941) French philosopher. *Creative Evolution* (1907), ch. 2

4   Intelligence is almost useless to the person whose only quality it is.
Alexis Carrel (1873–1944) French biologist and surgeon. *Man, the Unknown* (1935)

5   To pretend to be less intelligent than one is deceives nobody and begets dislike, for intelligence cannot be hidden; like a cough, it will out, stifle it how you may.
Robertson Davies (1913–95) Canadian novelist and critic. *A Voice from the Attic* (1960)

6   Intelligence begins with the external and least representative state, and advances to the *internal* and most *symbolic*.
John Dewey (1859–1952) US philosopher and educator. *Psychology* (1887)

7   The test of a first-rate intelligence is the ability to hold two opposed ideas in the mind at the same time, and still retain the ability to function.
F. Scott Fitzgerald (1896–1940) US writer. 1936. *The Crack-Up: with Other Uncollected Pieces, Note-Books and Unpublished Letters* (Edmund Wilson, ed.; 1945)

8   No one ever went broke underestimating the intelligence of the American people.
H. L. Mencken (1880–1956) US journalist, critic, and editor. Attrib.

9   A really intelligent man feels what other men only know.
Montesquieu (1689–1755) French writer and jurist. *Essai sur les Causes qui Peuvent Affecter les Esprits et les Caractères* (1736)

10 We may have trouble defining intelligence but we recognize it when we see it.
Steven Pinker (b. 1954) US cognitive scientist and author. *How the Mind Works* (1997)

11 Is an intelligent human being likely to be much more than a large-scale manufacturer of misunderstanding?
Philip Roth (b. 1933) US novelist. *The Counterlife* (1986)

12 Give me the young man who has brains enough to make a fool of himself!
Robert Louis Stevenson (1850–94) Scottish novelist, essayist, and poet. *Virginibus Puerisque* (1881)

13 Intelligence becomes an asset when some useful order is created out of free-floating brainpower.
Thomas A. Stewart (b. 1948) US journalist. *Intellectual Capital* (1997)

14 Intelligence is quickness to apprehend as distinct from ability, which is capacity to act wisely on the thing apprehended.
A. N. Whitehead (1861–1947) British philosopher and mathematician. *Dialogues* (1954), ch. 135

International Relations

see **Diplomacy, Globalization, Imperialism**

Internet

see also **Communication, Computers, Media, Technology**

1   Online conversation is . . . talking by writing.
John Coate, US academic. Quoted in 'Cyberspace Innkeeping', *Reinventing Technology* (Philip E. Agre and Douglas Schuler, eds.; 1997)

2   The Internet is still a technology in search of a strategy.
Mary J. Cronin, US author. Quoted in *Opening Digital Markets* (Walid Mougayar; 1997)

3 There is no space or time out here, or in here . . . There are only connections. Everything is connected. All human knowledge gathered and linked . . . this site leading to that, this fact referenced to that, a keystroke, a mouse-click, a password—world without end, amen.

Don DeLillo (b. 1936) US novelist. *Underworld* (1998)

4 The Internet is becoming the town square for the global village of tomorrow.

Bill Gates (b. 1955) US business executive. *Business@the Speed of Thought: Using a Digital Nervous System* (co-written with Collins Hemingway; 1999)

5 Cyberspace does allow people to freely communicate with everybody else who is on-line . . . but it is largely owned and controlled by transnational corporations and regulated within current government policies.

Robert Kitchin, US author and academic. *Cyberspace* (1998)

6 The Net . . . provides the first totally unrestricted, totally uncensored communication system—*ever*. It is the embodiment of the open market in ideas.

John Naughton, British writer and journalist. 1990. *A Brief History of the Future* (1999)

7 Cyberspace is a topology, not a topography. There are no physical constructs like 'beside', 'above', 'to the north of'.

Nicholas Negroponte, US business executive and writer. Quoted in *Opening Digital Markets* (Walid Mougayar; 1997)

8 The Net still resembles a congested street: because users pay only for their car and fuel, rather than for the inconvenience their presence on the road imposes on others, they have no incentive to limit the use of their car to avoid traffic jams.

Newspapers. *Economist* (October 19, 1996)

9 The most participatory form of mass speech yet developed . . . a never-ending worldwide conversation.

Newspapers. Referring to the Internet. *Guardian* (December 5, 1996)

10 The hyperlinks which will enable any number of computer databases to exchange information, which, at the touch of a finger, give mankind access to a library of libraries, to an all-inclusive picture gallery or science museum . . . to a planetary noticeboard open to everyman, make for what can soberly be qualified as a new world.

George Steiner (b. 1929) US scholar and critic. *Grammars of Creation* (2001)

11 You're entering a non-existent universe. Consider the consequences.

Clifford Stoll, US astronomer and author. His warning to people using the Internet. *Silicon Snake Oil* (1995)

12 For all its egalitarian promise, whole groups of people hardly show up on the network. Women, blacks, elderly, and the poor are all underrepresented.

Clifford Stoll, US astronomer and author. Referring to the Internet. *Silicon Snake Oil* (1995)

13 This is a virtual world. This is a world inventing itself. Daily, new landmasses form and then submerge. New continents of thought break off from the mainland. Some benefit from a trade wind, some sink without trace. Others are like Atlantis—fabulous, talked about, but never found.

Jeanette Winterson (b. 1959) British novelist. Referring to the Internet. *The PowerBook* (2000)

Introductions

see also **Friendship, Greetings**

1 'You look a little shy; let me introduce you to that leg of mutton', said the Red Queen. 'Alice—Mutton; Mutton—Alice'.

Lewis Carroll (1832–98) British writer and mathematician. *Through the Looking-Glass and What Alice Found There* (1871), ch. 9

2 Do you suppose I could buy back my introduction to you?

Groucho Marx (1895–1977) US comedian and film actor. *Monkey Business* (S. J. Perelman, Will B. Johnstone, and Arthur Sheekman; 1931)

Inventions

see also **Creativity, Innovation, Technology**

1 I don't think necessity is the mother of invention—invention, in my opinion, arises directly from idleness, possibly also from laziness. To save oneself trouble.

Agatha Christie (1890–1976) English novelist and playwright. *An Autobiography* (1977)

2 Keep on the lookout for novel ideas that others have used successfully. Your idea has to be original only in its adaption to the problem you're working on.

Thomas Alva Edison (1847–1931) US inventor. Quoted in *A Kick in the Seat of the Pants* (Roger von Oech; 1986)

3 If a man make a better mouse-trap than his neighbor, though he build his house in the woods, the world will make a beaten path to his door.

Ralph Waldo Emerson (1803–82) US poet and essayist. Often rendered as 'The world will beat a path . . . ' Attrib. *Borrowings* (Sarah S. B. Yule; 1889)

4 What is the use of a new-born child?

Benjamin Franklin (1706–90) US statesman and scientist. Response when asked the use of a new invention. Quoted in *Life and Times of Benjamin Franklin* (J. Parton; 1864), pt. 4, ch. 17

5 I just invent, then wait until man comes round to needing what I've invented.

R. Buckminster Fuller (1895–1983) US architect, designer, and inventor. *Time* (June 10, 1964)

6 The wisest invention in the world is the flush mechanism for the toilet whose chain turns us all, when we pull it, into a miraculous Moses.

Ramón Gómez de la Serna (1888–1963) Spanish novelist. Quoted in 'El Problema de la Greguería' (A. Hoyle; 1989)

7 Being the inventor of sex would seem to be a sufficient distinction for a creature just barely large enough to be seen by the naked eye.

Joseph Wood Krutch (1893–1970) US essayist and naturalist. Referring to Volvox, a microscopic freshwater organism, indeterminately both plant and animal in its reproductive cycle. *The Great Chain of Life* (1957)

8 Ask dumb questions. 'How come computer commands all come from keyboards?' Somebody asked that one first; hence, the mouse.

Tom Peters (b. 1942) US management consultant and author. *Liberation Management* (1992)

9 'I didn't think people invented anymore', said Oedipa . . . 'I mean, who's there been, really, since Thomas Edison? Isn't it all teamwork now?'

Thomas Pynchon (b. 1937) US novelist. *The Crying of Lot 49* (1966), ch. 4

10 An inventor is not just someone who comes up
with ideas. Most people have ideas. The
difference between the average person and the
inventor is that the inventor for some reason has
the urge to see his ideas through to fruition.
Clive Sinclair (b. 1940) British inventor and entrepreneur. Quoted in
'Creativity and Inventiveness', *The Roots of Excellence*
(Ronnie Lessem; 1985), ch. 5

11 Invention is the mother of necessity.
Thorstein Bunde Veblen (1857–1929) US social scientist and economist.
Quoted in *The Oxford Book of Aphorisms* (John Gross, ed.;
1983)

12 I have seriously considered the possibility of
giving up my scientific productive effort because I
know of no way to publish without letting my
inventions go to the wrong hands.
Norbert Weiner, US business executive. Quoted in *The Cult of
Information* (Theodore Roszak; 1986)

Ireland

see also **Europe, European Cities, Northern Ireland**

1 We want him to be the last British Prime
Minister with jurisdiction in Ireland.
Gerry Adams (b. 1948) Northern Irish politician. Referring to Tony
Blair. *Irish Times* (October 18, 1997)

2 What constitutes the charm of our country, apart
of course from the scant population, and this
without help of the meanest contraceptive, is that
it is all derelict.
Samuel Beckett (1906–89) Irish playwright, novelist, and poet. 1946.
Referring to Ireland. *First Love* (1973)

3 Don't you realize that, if you sign this thing, you
will split Ireland from top to bottom?
Cathal Brugha (1874–1922) Irish politician. Referring to the treaty
establishing the Irish Free State, after which civil war did
indeed follow. Comment to Eamon de Valera (December
1921), quoted in *Erskine Childers* (Jim Ring; 1996)

4 The government of Ireland by England rests on
restraint, and not on law; and since it demands
no love it can evoke no loyalty.
Roger Casement (1864–1916) Irish nationalist. Speech, after being
found guilty of treason (1916)

5 Not in vain is Ireland pouring itself all over the
earth . . . The Irish, with their glowing hearts
and reverent credulity, are needed in this cold age
of intellect and skepticism.
Lydia Maria Child (1802–80) US abolitionist, suffrage campaigner, and
writer. December 8, 1842. *Letters from New York* (1852),
vol. 1, no. 33

6 Think—what have I got for Ireland? Something
which she has wanted these past seven hundred
years . . . I tell you this—early this morning I
signed my death warrant.
Michael Collins (1890–1922) Irish politician. Referring to signing the
agreement with Great Britain that established the Irish Free
State. He was assassinated in an ambush some months later.
Letter to John O'Kane (December 6, 1921), quoted in *Michael
Collins and the Treaty* (T. R. Dwyer; 1981)

7 This oppression did of force and necessity make
the Irish a craftie people, for such as are
oppressed and live in slavery are ever put to their
shifts.
John Davies (1569–1626) English poet and jurist. 1612? Quoted in
The Oxford Illustrated History of Ireland (R. F. Foster, ed.;
1989)

8 And then I prayed I yet might see
Our fetters rent in twain,
And Ireland, long a province, be
A Nation once again.
Thomas Davis (1814–45) Irish writer and nationalist. 'A Nation Once
Again' (1846)

9 Future Volunteers would have to wade through
Irish blood, through the blood of the soldiers of
the Irish Government, perhaps, the blood of some
of the members of Government in order to get
Irish freedom.
Eamon de Valera (1882–1975) US-born Irish statesman. Known as the
'rivers of blood' speech, advocating civil war. Speech, Thurles
(March 17, 1922), quoted in *Phrases Make History Here*
(Conor O'Clery; 1986)

10 Whenever I wanted to know what the Irish
people wanted, I had only to examine my own
heart and it told me straight off what the Irish
people wanted.
Eamon de Valera (1882–1975) US-born Irish statesman. Speech to the
Irish Parliament (January 6, 1922), quoted in *Phrases Make
History Here* (Conor O'Clery; 1986)

11 Thus you have a starving population, an absentee
aristocracy, and an alien Church, and in addition
the weakest executive in the world. That is the
Irish Question.
Benjamin Disraeli (1804–81) British prime minister and writer. Speech in
Parliament, *Hansard* (February 16, 1844), col. 1016

12 There was no sex in Ireland before television.
Oliver J. Flanagan (1920–87) Irish auctioneer and politician. Attrib.

13 I never met anyone in Ireland who understood
the Irish question, except one Englishman who
had only been there a week.
Keith Fraser (1867–1935) British politician. Speech to Parliament
(May 1919)

14 Ireland, Ireland! That cloud in the west, that
coming storm, the minister of God's retribution
upon cruel and inveterate and but half-atoned
injustice.
William Ewart Gladstone (1809–98) British statesman. Letter to his
wife (October 12, 1845)

15 We are bound to lose Ireland in consequence of
years of cruelty, stupidity and misgovernment
and I would rather lose her as a friend than as a
foe.
William Ewart Gladstone (1809–98) British statesman. Quoted in *More
Memories* (Margot Asquith; 1933), ch. 8

16 We have brought back the flag; we have brought
back the evacuation of Ireland after 700 years by
British troops and the formation of an Irish
army. We have brought back to Ireland her full
rights.
Arthur Griffith (1872–1922) Irish nationalist. Supporting the Anglo-
Irish Treaty. Speech, Dáil Éireann (Irish Parliament; December
1921)

17 It seems that the historic inability in Britain to
comprehend Irish feelings and sensitivities still
remains.
Charles Haughey (b. 1925) Irish prime minister. Speech (February
1988)

18 Every party in Ireland was founded on the gun.
John Hume (b. 1937) Northern Irish politician. 1995. Attrib.

19 Ireland is the old sow that eats her farrow.
James Joyce (1882–1941) Irish writer. *A Portrait of the Artist as a
Young Man* (1916), ch. 5

20 It is a symbol of Irish art. The cracked looking glass of a servant.

James Joyce (1882–1941) Irish writer. *Ulysses* (1922)

21 Ireland is a little Russia in which the longest way round is the shortest way home.

George Moore (1852–1933) Irish writer. *Hail and Farewell* (1911–14)

22 One of Ireland's many tricks is to fade away to a little speck down on the horizon of our lives, and then to return suddenly in tremendous bulk, frightening us.

George Moore (1852–1933) Irish writer. *Hail and Farewell* (1911–14)

23 The 1916 myth, like malaria, is in my bloodstream.

Dervla Murphy (b. 1931) Irish travel writer. Referring to the Easter Rising (Easter Rebellion) of 1916, an armed uprising of Irish nationalists against British rule. *A Place Apart* (1978)

24 I ran into a characteristic Irishman and before I had time to run out again, he had taken me nappertandy by the hand and started to talk.

Flann O'Brien (1911–66) Irish novelist and journalist. 'Our Sad Country', *The Best of Myles* (1968)

25 Our ancestors believed in magic, prayers, trickery, browbeating and bullying: I think it would be fair to sum that list up as 'Irish politics'.

Flann O'Brien (1911–66) Irish novelist and journalist. *The Hair of the Dogma* (Kevin O'Nolan, ed.; 1977)

26 I believe in the freedom of Ireland and that England has no right to be here. But I draw the line when I hear the gunmen blowin' about dyin' for the people, when it's the people that are dyin' for the gunmen.

Sean O'Casey (1880–1964) Irish playwright. *The Shadow of a Gunman* (1923)

27 The Union . . . was a crime, and it must still be criminal unless it shall be ludicrously pretended that crime, like wine, improves by old age.

Daniel O'Connell (1775–1847) Irish politician. Referring to the Act of Union of 1800, which joined Great Britain and Ireland. Repeal speech (1809)

28 This struggle for Irish national freedom often expresses itself in profoundly Oedipal terms. For if motherhood in our history is associated with revolution, fatherhood is often linked with authority.

Joseph O'Connor (b. 1963) Irish writer. 'Playboys on Crutches', *The Secret World of the Irish Male* (1994)

29 Parnell may be the Uncrowned King of Ireland; he is not the infallible Pope of Rome.

John O'Leary (1830–1907) Irish rebel. Charles Stewart Parnell's nickname was the 'Uncrowned King of Ireland'. Speech, Mullinahone, Ireland (August 1885), quoted in *A Book of Irish Quotations* (Sean McMahon, ed.; 1984)

30 No man has a right to fix the boundary of the march of a nation; no man has a right to say to his country—thus far shalt thou go and no further.

Charles Stewart Parnell (1846–91) Irish politician. Speech, Cork (January 21, 1885)

31 I have a parliament for Ireland within the hollow of my hand.

Charles Stewart Parnell (1846–91) Irish politician. Speech, Galway, Ireland (February 10, 1886), quoted in *Phrases Make History Here* (Conor O'Clery; 1986)

32 Ireland has been knocking at the English door long enough with kid gloves, and now she will knock with a mailed hand.

Charles Stewart Parnell (1846–91) Irish politician. Speech, Liverpool (1885), quoted in 'Tuam Herald', *A Book of Irish Quotations* (Sean McMahon, ed.; 1984)

33 The clear true eyes of this man almost alone in his day visioned Ireland as we of today would surely have her: not free merely, but Gaelic as well; not Gaelic merely, but free as well.

Patrick Pearse (1879–1916) Irish poet and nationalist. Funeral address for the Irish nationalist O'Donovan Rossa (August 1, 1915)

34 Ireland unfree shall never be at peace.

Patrick Pearse (1879–1916) Irish poet and nationalist. Funeral address for the Irish nationalist O'Donovan Rossa. Speech (August 1, 1915)

35 We declare the right of the people of Ireland to the ownership of Ireland, and to the unfettered control of Irish destinies, to be sovereign and indefeasible.

Provisional Government of the Irish Republic. 'Proclamation of the Irish Republic' (April 24, 1916)

36 I will drive a coach and six horses through the Act of Settlement.

Stephen Rice (1637–1715) Irish lawyer. Also given as 'I will drive a coach and six through the Act of Parliament'. Quoted in *State of the Protestants of Ireland* (W. King; 1672), ch. 3, sect. 8

37 Instead of rocking the cradle, they rocked the system.

Mary Robinson (b. 1944) Irish stateswoman. Paying tribute to Irish women who voted for her, helping her to become Ireland's first female president (1990–97). Victory speech following her election as President of the Republic of Ireland (November 10, 1990)

38 The English should give Ireland home rule—and reserve the motion picture rights.

Will Rogers (1879–1935) US actor, writer, and humorist. *The Autobiography of Will Rogers* (1949)

39 Gladstone spent his declining years trying to guess the answer to the Irish Question; unfortunately, whenever he was getting warm, the Irish secretly changed the question.

W. C. Sellar (1898–1951) British humorous writer. Referring to William Ewart Gladstone. *1066 and All That* (co-written with R. J. Yeatman; 1930), ch. 57

40 The moment the very name of Ireland is mentioned, the English seem to bid adieu to common feeling, common prudence, and common sense, and to act with the barbarity of tyrants, and the fatuity of idiots.

Sydney Smith (1771–1845) British clergyman, essayist, and wit. *The Letters of Peter Plymley* (1807), Letter 2

41 Rather on this bleaky shore
Where loudest winds incessant roar
Where neither herb nor tree will thrive,
Where nature hardly seems alive,
I'd go in freedom to my grave,
Than Rule yon Isle and be a Slave.

Jonathan Swift (1667–1745) Irish writer and clergyman. Expressing despair at having to return to Ireland. 'Holyhead, Sept. 25th, 1727' (1727)

42 Whatever I have said, written, or thought on the subject of Ireland I now reiterate: looking upon the connexion with England to have been her bane I have endeavoured by every means in my power to break that connexion.

Wolfe Tone (1763–98) Irish nationalist. Speech at his court martial (November 10, 1798), quoted in *Wolfe Tone: Prophet of Irish Independence* (Marianne Elliott; 1989)

43 A disease in the family that is never mentioned.
William Trevor (b. 1928) Irish novelist, short-story writer, and playwright. Referring to the 'Troubles' in Northern Ireland. *Observer* (November 1990)

44 Behind Ireland fierce and militant, is Ireland poetic, passionate, remembering, idyllic, fanciful and always patriotic.
W. B. Yeats (1865–1939) Irish poet and playwright. *Popular Ballad Poetry of Ireland* (1889)

Irony

see also **Humour, Satire**

1 Irony is the very substance of Providence.
Honoré de Balzac (1799–1850) French writer. *Eugénie Grandet* (1833)

2 Irony is humanity's sense of propriety.
Jules Renard (1864–1910) French writer. April 30, 1892. *Journal* (1877–1910)

3 You have to treat everything with irony, especially the things you hold dear. There's more of a chance then that they'll survive. That is perhaps one of the greatest secrets of our life.
Dmitri Shostakovich (1906–75) Russian composer. 1971–75. *Testimony: The Memoirs of Shostakovich* (Solomon Volkov, ed., Antonina W. Bouis, tr.; 1979), ch. 3

Islam

see also **God, Middle East, Religion**

1 Egalitarianism in Islam is more pronounced than in any other religion in the world.
Akbar Ahmed (b. 1943) British academic. *Living Islam* (1993)

2 In order to appreciate Islam, Europe must come to terms with its own past.
Akbar Ahmed (b. 1943) British academic. *Living Islam* (1993)

3 The verses of the Koran, in relation to intelligence, have the value of sunlight in relation to the eyesight, to wit, it is by this sunlight that the act of seeing is accomplished.
al-Ghazali (1058–1111) Islamic philosopher and theologian. *The Niche for Lights* (11th–12th century), quoted in *Four Sufi Classics* (Idris Shah, ed.; 1980)

4 How could they say that my religion, Islam, was a 'race hate' religion after all the plunder and enslavement and domination of my people by white Christians in the name of white supremacy?
Muhammad Ali (b. 1942) US boxer. *The Greatest: My Own Story* (co-written with Richard Durham; 1976)

5 I am neither a Moslem nor a Christian, but I owe a great deal to Islam and could never have made my connection with God ANYWHERE EXCEPT HERE.
William S. Burroughs (1914–97) US writer. Referring to Morocco. Letter to Allen Ginsberg (1957), quoted in *The Letters of William S. Burroughs* (Oliver Harris, ed.; 1993)

6 Islam is the blueprint of a social order.
Ernest Gellner (1925–95) British anthropologist and philosopher. *Muslim Society* (1981)

7 If more radical changes took place, it seemed more likely that in the 1980s they would take place in the name of an Islamic idea of the justice of God in the world. There was not one idea of Islam only, but a whole spectrum of them.
Albert Hourani (1915–93) Egyptian historian and author. Referring to the role of Islam in Middle Eastern politics. *A History of the Arab Peoples* (1991)

8 Islam, at the end of the twentieth century, has been made into the religion the West loves to hate; a seething cauldron of sexism, and a dumping ground for all blame.
Rana Kabbani (b. 1958) Syrian cultural historian. *Imperial Fictions: Europe's Myths of the Orient* (1994)

9 Islam is the religion of militant individuals who are committed to truth and justice. It is the religion of those who desire freedom and independence. It is the school of those who struggle against imperialism.
Ruhollah Khomeini (1900–89) Iranian religious and political leader. 1971. 'Islamic Government', *Islam and Revolution* (H. Algar, tr.; 1985)

10 A part of the excellence of a man's Islam is his leaving alone what does not concern him.
Muhammad (570?–632?) Arab religious leader and prophet. Originally reported as a saying of Muhammad by Abu Hurairah, one of his companions. Reported as spoken by Muhammad by Abu Dharr al-Ghifari. Quoted in *The Complete Forty Hadith* (Muhyid-Din al-Nawawi; 13th century), 12th Hadith

11 What I know of Islam is that tolerance, compassion and love are at its very heart.
Salman Rushdie (b. 1947) Indian-born British novelist. *Imaginary Homelands* (1991), pt. 12, ch. 5

12 The major capitalist countries resist Islam where it is an instrument of progress and unity, and encourage it whenever it serves to divide and weaken . . . one of the sources of severe contradiction in the lives and struggles of Arab women.
Nawal el-Saadawi (b. 1931) Egyptian novelist. 'Arab Women and Politics', *The Nawal el-Saadawi Reader* (1997)

Israel

see **Middle East**

Istanbul

see **European Cities**

Italy

see **Europe, European Countries**

J

Jazz

see also **Music, Popular Music**

1 Jazz . . . and its sources were *secret* as far as the rest of America was concerned, in much the same sense that the actual life of the black man in America was secret to the white American.
Imamu Amiri Baraka (b. 1934) US author, editor, playwright, and political activist. 1963. Referring to the emergence of jazz in the United States at the turn of the 20th century. 'Jazz and the White Critic', *Black Music* (1969), ch. 1

2 After emancipation . . . all those people who had been slaves, they needed the music more than ever now; it was like they were trying to find out in this music what they were supposed to do with this freedom.
Sidney Bechet (1897–1959) US jazz musician. Referring to jazz. *Treat It Gentle* (1960)

3 Jazz is about the only form of art existing today in which there is freedom of the individual without the loss of group contact.
Dave Brubeck (b. 1920) US jazz pianist, composer, and bandleader. Quoted in *The Jazz Book* (Joachim Berendt; 1982)

4 There is no more potent example of the equation between jazz and freedom in modern European history than . . . the ghetto Swingers and the Killer Drillers—which played in the concentration camps, where several of their members perished.
James Campbell (b. 1951) Scottish writer. Referring to the Nazi concentration camps during the German occupation of Czechoslovakia at the time of World War II. *The Picador Book of Blues and Jazz* (1995), Introduction

5 Jazz is an international music . . . of such extraordinary variety that it is most consistently recognizable by its rhythmic vitality.
Duke Ellington (1899–1974) US jazz bandleader, pianist, and composer. *Music is My Mistress* (1973)

6 If we had had Count Basie at the piano, and Freddie Green on guitar . . . Well, I don't know, maybe we might have scorched the moon.
Duke Ellington (1899–1974) US jazz bandleader, pianist, and composer. Referring to his band's success at the Newport Jazz Festival (1956). *Music is My Mistress* (1973)

7 'Asking for jazz in 3/4 time', he stated firmly, 'is like asking for a red piece of green chalk'.
Leonard G. Feather (1914–94) British musical arranger, composer, and writer. Referring to the reply by the editor of the magazine *Melody Maker* (London) to a letter from Feather. 'London', *The Jazz Years* (1986), pt. 1

8 Though the Jazz Age continued, it became less and less an affair of youth.
The sequel was like a children's party taken over by the elders.
F. Scott Fitzgerald (1896–1940) US writer. 1931. 'Echoes of the Jazz Age', *The Crack-Up: with Other Uncollected Pieces, Note-Books and Unpublished Letters* (Edmund Wilson, ed.; 1945)

9 He is so honest about music that he wants to catch the kernel of creativity as it's being created. If you rehearse too much, you're not going to get it.
Herbie Hancock (b. 1940) US jazz musician. Referring to Miles Davis, with whom Herbie Hancock worked during the 1960s. Quoted in 'Herbie Hancock', *Off the Record: An Oral History of Popular Music* (Joe Smith; 1988)

10 Boom, kick, that drummer was kicking his drums to the cellar and rolling the beat back upstairs with his murderous sticks, rattlety-boom!
Jack Kerouac (1922–69) US writer. Referring to jazz in San Francisco. *On the Road* (1957), ch. 4

11 It came from angelical smiling lips upon the mouthpiece and it was a soft, sweet, fairy-tale solo on an alto. Lonely as America, a throatpierced sound in the night.
Jack Kerouac (1922–69) US writer. Referring to jazz in Chicago. *On the Road* (1957), ch. 10

12 Parker was a modern jazz player just as Picasso was a modern painter and Pound a modern poet . . . Jazz had gone from Lascaux to Jackson Pollock in fifty years.
Philip Larkin (1922–85) British poet. Referring to the radical innovations achieved by Charlie Parker. *All What Jazz: a Record Diary* (1970), Introduction

13 My experience is that jazzmen, particularly those who have fought their way almost single-handedly to the top of their profession, are as cuddly as man-eating tigers.
Humphrey Lyttelton (b. 1921) British jazz trumpeter. *Take It From the Top* (1975), pt. 3, ch. 7

14 Jazz is music that really deals with what it means to be American . . . Louis Armstrong, the grandson of a slave, is the one more than anybody else who could translate into music that feeling of what it is to be an American.
Wynton Marsalis (b. 1961) US trumpet player and jazz musician. 'We Must Preserve Our Jazz Heritage', *Ebony* (Chicago; February 1986)

15 Modern jazz was like the Roman Catholic Church at the time of the Reformation. It had developed historically from the origins of jazz but had, in the eyes of the early revivalists, become decadent.
George Melly (b. 1926) British jazz singer and author. Referring to the revival of New Orleans jazz in the 1950s. *Owning Up* (1965), ch. 11

16 Get this straight, we pure-and-simple jazzmen didn't scoff at the serious composers exactly, but . . . symphony means slavery in any jazzman's dictionary. Jazz and freedom are synonymous.
Mezz Mezzrow (1899–1972) US jazz musician. *Really the Blues* (1946), ch. 8

17 Bix played a cornet . . . that looked like it came from the junkpile . . . The whiskey fumes that he blew out of that beat-up old cornet almost gassed me.

Mezz Mezzrow (1899–1972) US jazz musician. Referring to Bix Beiderbecke. *Really the Blues* (1946), ch. 8

18 Nothing could hold us back now. King Jazz was moving in, heading up his whole army of horn-tooters and skin-beaters, and I was right in there with them, ready to cover all spots.

Mezz Mezzrow (1899–1972) US jazz musician. Referring to the exodus of musicians to New York in 1928 after the suppression of Chicago's speakeasies. *Really the Blues* (1946), ch. 9

19 He breathed in air, he breathed out light. Charlie Parker was my delight.

Adrian Mitchell (b. 1932) British poet and playwright. 'Goodbye', *Poems* (1964)

20 I hit the piano with my elbow sometimes because of a certain sound I want to hear. You can't hit that many notes with your hands.

Thelonious Monk (1920–82) US jazz composer and pianist. Quoted in 'Round About Monk', *Jazz People* (Valerie Wilmer; 1970), ch. 4

21 It is evidently known, beyond contradiction, that New Orleans is the cradle of *jazz*, and I, myself, happened to be the creator in the year 1902 . . . *Jazz* music is a style, not compositions; any kind of music may be played in *jazz*, if one has the knowledge.

Jelly Roll Morton (1885–1941) US jazz pianist, composer, and bandleader. *Downbeat* (August 1938)

22 Jazz did not issue from the individual efforts of one composer, but from the spontaneous urge of a whole people.

Hugues Panassie (1912–74) French jazz writer and impresario. *The Real Jazz* (1942), ch. 1

23 Jazz is a music which is perpetually in motion, a *living* music which will never fall . . . into the funereal sleep of many *chefs d'oeuvre* which often give the impression of having been imprisoned in a pickle jar.

Hugues Panassie (1912–74) French jazz writer and impresario. *The Real Jazz* (1942), ch. 2

24 Bird was the supreme hipster. He made his own laws. His arrogance was enormous, his humility profound.

Robert Reisner (1921–74) US writer and humorist. Referring to Charlie 'Bird' Parker. *Bird: the Legend of Charlie Parker* (1962), ch. 1

25 Polyphony, flatted fifths, half-tones—they don't mean a thing. I just pick up my horn and play what I feel.

Jack Teagarden (1905–64) US jazz musician. *New York Times* (January 16, 1964)

26 As for my jazz ability, it reminds me of that old saying, 'Do you read music?' and the guy would say, 'Not enough to hurt my playing'.

Clark Terry (b. 1936) US jazz musician. Quoted in 'The Sweet Smell of Success', *Jazz People* (Valerie Wilmer; 1970), ch. 9

27 We had to deliver all our musical instruments to the Gestapo . . . I soaked the valves in sulphuric acid to prevent anyone from playing military marches on the horn used to play jazz.

Eric Vogel, Czechoslovakian jazz musician. *Down Beat Jazz* (December 1961), quoted in *The Picador Book of Blues and Jazz* (James Campbell, ed.; 1995)

28 Jazz isn't *what* you do, it's *how* you do it.

Fats Waller (1904–43) US jazz pianist, singer, and bandleader. *The Jazz Book* (Joachim E. Berendt; 1983)

Jealousy

see also **Envy**

1 Jealousy in romance is like salt in food. A little can enhance the savor, but too much can spoil the pleasure and, under certain circumstances, can be life-threatening.

Maya Angelou (b. 1928) US writer. 'Jealousy', *Wouldn't Take Nothing for My Journey Now* (1993)

2 The 'Green-Eyed Monster' causes much woe, but the absence of this ugly serpent argues the presence of a corpse whose name is Eros.

Minna Antrim (1856–1950) US writer. *Naked Truth and Veiled Allusions* (1902)

3 Jealousy is no more than feeling alone against smiling enemies.

Elizabeth Bowen (1899–1973) Irish novelist and short-story writer. *The House in Paris* (1935), pt. 2, ch. 8

4 It is with jealousy as with the gout. When such distempers are in the blood, there is never any security against their breaking out; and that often on the slightest occasions, and when least suspected.

Henry Fielding (1707–54) British novelist and playwright. *Tom Jones* (1749), bk. 2, ch. 3

5 Jealousy is all the fun you *think* they had.

Erica Jong (b. 1942) US writer. *How to Save Your Own Life* (1977)

6 Comparisouns doon offte gret greuaunce.

John Lydgate (1370?–1451?) English poet. *The Fall of Princes* (1431–38), bk. 3, l. 2188

7 To jealousy, nothing is more frightful than laughter.

Françoise Sagan (b. 1935) French writer. *La Chamade* (1965), ch. 9

8 If someone with whom one is having an affair keeps on mentioning some woman whom he knew in the past, however long ago it is since they separated, one is always irritated.

Sei Shonagon (966?–1013) Japanese diarist. *The Pillow Book* (1002?), quoted in *Anthology of Japanese Literature* (Donald Keene, ed.; 1968)

9 IAGO O, beware, my lord, of jealousy;
It is the green-ey'd monster which doth mock
The meat it feeds on.

William Shakespeare (1564–1616) English poet and playwright. *Othello* (1602–04), Act 3, Scene 3

10 OTHELLO If she be false, O! then heaven mocks itself.
I'll not believe it.

William Shakespeare (1564–1616) English poet and playwright. *Othello* (1602–04), Act 3, Scene 3

11 EMILIA Jealous souls will not be answer'd so;
They are not ever jealous for the cause,
But jealous for they are jealous.

William Shakespeare (1564–1616) English poet and playwright. *Othello* (1602–04), Act 3, Scene 4

12 IAGO He hath a daily beauty in his life.
That makes me ugly.

William Shakespeare (1564–1616) English poet and playwright. Referring to Cassio, Othello's lieutenant, of whose preferment Iago is jealous. *Othello* (1602–04), Act 5, Scene 1

13 LUCIANA How many fond fools serve mad jealousy!

William Shakespeare (1564–1616) English poet and playwright. *The Comedy of Errors* (1594), Act 2, Scene 1

14 ABBESS The venom clamours of a jealous woman Poison more deadly than a mad dog's tooth.

William Shakespeare (1564–1616) English poet and playwright. *The Comedy of Errors* (1594), Act 5, Scene 1

15 What is life like with another,— Simpler, no?—The stroke of an oar— Did the memory of me soon Fade away, a floating island.

Marina Tsvetaeva (1892–1941) Russian poet. 'An Attempt at Jealousy' (Peter Norman, tr.; 1924), ll. 1–4, quoted in *Leopard II: Turning the Page* (Christopher MacLehose, ed.; 1993)

Jobs

see Occupations

Journalism

see also Media, Newspapers, Publishing

1 Journalists say a thing that they know isn't true, in the hope that if they keep on saying it long enough it will be true.

Arnold Bennett (1867–1931) British writer. *The Title* (1918)

2 No news is good news; no journalists is even better.

Nicolas Bentley (1907–78) British cartoonist and writer. Attrib.

3 Mr. Luce's unique contribution to American journalism is that he placed into the hands of the people yesterday's newspaper and today's garbage homogenized into one package.

Herbert Lawrence Block (1909–2001) US cartoonist. Referring to the publisher Henry Luce, founder of *Time* (1923), *Fortune* (1929), and *Life* (1936) magazines. Attrib.

4 When a dog bites a man that is not news, but when a man bites a dog that is news.

John B. Bogart (1845–1921) US journalist. 1882. Sometimes attributed to Charles Dana and Amos Cummings. Attrib.

5 It was long ago in my life as a simple reporter that I decided that facts must never get in the way of truth.

James Cameron (1911–85) British journalist and broadcaster. Attrib.

6 Journalism is the only job that requires no degrees, no diplomas and no specialised knowledge of any kind.

Patrick Campbell (1913–80) British humorous writer and editor. *My Life and Easy Times* (1967)

7 When the seagulls are following a trawler, it's because they think sardines are going to be thrown into the sea.

Eric Cantona (b. 1966) French football player. Referring to journalists' relationship with their subjects. *Independent* (January 27, 1995)

8 Journalism largely consists of saying 'Lord Jones is dead' to people who never knew Lord Jones was alive.

G. K. Chesterton (1874–1936) British writer and poet. Attrib.

9 I hesitate to say what the functions of the modern journalist may be; but I imagine that they do not exclude the intelligent anticipation of facts even before they occur.

George Nathaniel Curzon (1859–1925) British statesman. Speech to Parliament (March 29, 1898)

10 The only thing I don't like about the press is I can give as many answers as you want, and be totally honest, but finally it's you who shapes the final product . . . often what comes out isn't what I meant at all.

Roddy Doyle (b. 1958) Irish novelist and playwright. *Observer* (May 1, 1994)

11 The life of the journalist is poor, nasty, brutish and short. So is his style.

Stella Gibbons (1902–89) British poet and novelist. *Cold Comfort Farm* (1933), Foreword

12 Backward ran sentences until reeled the mind.

Wolcott Gibbs (1902–58) US writer. Parodying the style of *Time* magazine. *More in Sorrow* (1958)

13 Perhaps if I wanted to be understood or to understand I would bamboozle myself into belief, but I am a reporter. God exists only for leader-writers.

Graham Greene (1904–91) British novelist. *The Quiet American* (1955)

14 Good taste is, of course, an utterly dispensable part of any journalist's equipment.

Michael Hogg (b. 1925) British journalist. *Daily Telegraph* (December 2, 1978)

15 EDITOR: a person employed by a newspaper whose business it is to separate the wheat from the chaff and to see that chaff is printed.

Elbert Hubbard (1856–1915) US writer, printer, and editor. *The Roycroft Dictionary* (1914)

16 A journalist is stimulated by a deadline. He writes worse when he has time.

Karl Kraus (1874–1936) Austrian writer. 1912. Quoted in 'Pro domo et mundo', *Karl Kraus* (Harry Zohn; 1971)

17 The making of a journalist: no ideas and the ability to express them.

Karl Kraus (1874–1936) Austrian writer. 1912. Quoted in 'Pro domo et mundo', *Karl Kraus* (Harry Zohn; 1971)

18 More attentive to the minute hand of history than to the hour hand.

Desmond MacCarthy (1878–1952) British poet and writer. Referring to journalism. Quoted in *Curtains* (K. Tynan; 1961)

19 Mailer's sexual journalism reads like the sporting news grafted on to a series of war dispatches.

Kate Millett (b. 1934) US feminist and writer. Referring to Norman Mailer. *Washington Post* (July 30, 1970)

20 The industry is just rife with jealousy and hatred. Everybody in it is a failed bassist.

Morrissey (b. 1959) British singer and songwriter. Referring to music journalism. Interview, *Time Out* (March 1985)

21 She can gain more readily as an interviewer access to both sexes. Women know best how to deal with women and the inborn chivalry of a gentleman leads him to grant her request when a man might have been repulsed without compunction.

Mrs. N. F. Mossell (1855–1948) US journalist. Referring to the advantages of a female reporter over her male counterpart. *The Work of the Afro-American Woman* (1894)

22 I am not going to claim that we fought the Battle of Wapping because we wanted to bring a silver age to British journalism.

Rupert Murdoch (b. 1931) Australian-born US media entrepreneur. Referring to the conflict between his company, News International, and the union at the *Times* newspaper over the introduction of new printing technology. Wapping was the site of new computer equipment, and was picketed by over 10,000 former employees. Speech, New York City (1989)

23 A reporter is a man who has renounced everything in life but the world, the flesh, and the devil.

David Murray (1888–1962) British journalist and writer. *Observer* (July 5, 1931), 'Sayings of the Week'

24 There are just two people entitled to refer to themselves as 'we'; one is a newspaper editor and the other is a fellow with a tapeworm.

Bill Nye (1850–96) US humorist. Attrib.

25 Journalists belong in the gutter because that is where ruling classes throw their guilty secrets.

Gerald Priestland (1927–91) British broadcaster and writer. *Times* (May 22, 1988)

26 Its primary office is the gathering of news. At the peril of its soul it must see that the supply is not tainted . . . Comment is free but facts are sacred.

C. P. Scott (1846–1932) British journalist. 1921. Referring to journalism. *Manchester Guardian* (May 5, 1922)

27 He's someone who flies around from hotel to hotel and thinks the most interesting thing about any story is the fact that he has arrived to cover it.

Tom Stoppard (b. 1937) Czech-born British playwright and screenwriter. Referring to foreign correspondents. *Night and Day* (1978), Act 1

28 We tell the public which way the cat is jumping. The public will take care of the cat.

Arthur Hays Sulzberger (1891–1968) US newspaper proprietor. Referring to journalism. *Time* (May 8, 1950)

29 If I'd written all the truth I knew for the past ten years, about 600 people—including me—would be rotting in prison cells from Rio to Seattle today. Absolute truth is a very rare and dangerous commodity in the context of professional journalism.

Hunter S. Thompson (b. 1939) US writer and journalist. 'Fear and Loathing at the Superbowl', *Rolling Stone* (February 15, 1973), quoted in *The Great Shark Hunt* (Hunter S. Thompson; 1979), pt. 1

30 The only qualities essential for real success in journalism are rat-like cunning, a plausible manner, and a little literary ability.

Nicholas Tomalin (1931–73) British journalist. *Sunday Times* (October 26, 1969)

31 It rots a writer's brain, it cretinizes you. You say the same thing again and again, and when you do that happily you're well on the way to being a cretin. Or a politician.

John Updike (b. 1932) US writer. Referring to being interviewed. Interview, *Observer* (Martin Amis; August 30, 1987)

32 Journalism—an ability to meet the challenge of filling the space.

Rebecca West (1892–1983) Irish-born British novelist, critic, and journalist. *New York Herald Tribune* (April 22, 1956)

33 There is much to be said in favour of modern journalism. By giving us the opinions of the uneducated, it keeps us in touch with the ignorance of the community.

Oscar Wilde (1854–1900) Irish poet, playwright, and wit. 'The Critic as Artist', *Intentions* (1891), pt. 2

34 The farmers of journalism . . . who love the good rich soil . . . and like to plunge their hands into the dirt.

Tom Wolfe (b. 1930) US journalist and novelist. Referring to tabloid journalists. *The Painted World* (1975)

35 People who can't talk interviewed by people who can't write for people who can't read.

Frank Zappa (1940–93) US rock musician and composer. Referring to music journalism. Quoted in *Mother! The Frank Zappa Story* (Michael Gray; 1993)

Journeys

see **Exploration, Travel**

Judaism

see also **God, Middle East, Religion**

1 All the good things that we have been led to believe existed only in Socialism and in Marxism, and in Communism, too, we found to exist in our own tradition and at a more refined, civilized level.

Aharon Appelfield (b. 1932) Israeli writer. September 25, 1986. Comparing the virtues of Communism, Socialism, and Marxism with those of the Jewish tradition. Quoted in Interview, *Voices of Israel* (Joseph Cohen; 1990)

2 And God said unto Moses, I AM THAT I AM: and he said, Thus shalt thou say unto the children of Israel, I AM hath sent me unto you.

Bible. Exodus, *King James Bible* (1611), 3:14

3 I will set thy bounds from the Red Sea even unto the sea of the Philistines, and from the desert unto the river: for I will deliver the inhabitants of the land into your hand; and thou shalt drive them out before thee.

Bible. One of a series of promises by God, in this case to Moses, setting out the boundaries of the 'Promised Land' after the escape of the Hebrews from Egypt. Some interpret this passage as the justification for the territorial claims of the modern State of Israel. Exodus, *King James Bible* (1611), 23:31

4 And the Lord said unto Moses, Come up to me into the mount, and be there: and I will give thee tables of stone, and a law, and commandments which I have written; that thou mayest teach them.

Bible. Exodus, *King James Bible* (1611), 24:12

5 They shall make an ark of shittim wood: two cubits and a half shall be the length thereof, and a cubit and a half the breadth thereof, and a cubit and a half the height thereof. And they shall overlay it with pure gold . . . and shalt make upon it a crown of gold round about.

Bible. The Ark of the Covenant, the portable shrine which was the most important focus for Hebrew worship. It had its own tent until King Solomon built the Temple in Jerusalem to house it. Exodus, *King James Bible* (1611), 25:10–11

6 Son of man, I have made thee a watchman unto the house of Israel: therefore hear the word at my mouth, and give them warning from me.

Bible. The definition of the prophet Ezekiel's role among the Hebrews in exile in Babylonia after the destruction of Jerusalem. Ezekiel, *King James Bible* (1611), 4:17

7 For Judaism, God is not a Kantian idea but an elementally present spiritual reality—neither something conceived by pure reason nor something postulated by practical reason, but emanating from the immediacy of existence as such.

Martin Buber (1878–1965) Austrian-born Israeli philosopher of religion and Zionist. 1923. Quoted in *On Judaism* (N. Glazer, ed., Eva Jose et al., trs.; 1967)

8 Messianism is Judaism's most profoundly original idea.

Martin Buber (1878–1965) Austrian-born Israeli philosopher of religion and Zionist. 1923. Quoted in *On Judaism* (N. Glazer, ed., Eva Jose et al., trs.; 1967)

9 This knowledge . . . —that the world is a devastated house that must be restored for the spirit; and that so long as this remains unaccomplished, the spirit has no dwelling place—is Jesus' most deep-seated Judaism.

Martin Buber (1878–1965) Austrian-born Israeli philosopher of religion and Zionist. 1923. Quoted in *On Judaism* (N. Glazer, ed., Eva Jose et al., trs.; 1967)

10 Zionism is our return to Judaism even before our return to the Jewish land!

Theodor Herzl (1860–1904) Hungarian-born Zionist leader. Speech, First Zionist Congress, Basel (August 29, 1897)

11 Judaism is the sustained attempt to bring the Divine presence from the soul to the body, from poetry to prose, from the innermost mind to the public domain, from exalted moments into the texture of everyday life.

Jonathan Sacks (b. 1948) British chief rabbi. *Community of Faith* (1995)

12 Where once nine Jews in ten lived, today there are fewer than one in five. Jewish life has moved from Europe to Israel and the United States.

Jonathan Sacks (b. 1948) British chief rabbi. *Community of Faith* (1995)

13 If a Jew is fascinated by Christians it is not because of their virtues, which he values little, but because they represent anonymity, humanity without race.

Jean-Paul Sartre (1905–80) French philosopher, playwright, and novelist. *Anti-Semite and Jew* (George J. Becker, tr.; 1976)

14 Death is the Messiah. That's the real truth.

Isaac Bashevis Singer (1904–91) Polish-born US writer. Closing lines. *The Family Moskat* (H. R. Gross, tr.; 1950)

Judgment

see also **Decision, Justice, Law**

1 Fortune is for all; judgment is theirs who have won it for themselves.

Aeschylus (525?–456 BC) Greek tragedian and dramatist. *Fragments* (5th century BC), fragment 217

2 For judgement I am come into this world, that they which see not might see; and that they which see might be made blind.

Bible. John, *King James Bible* (1611), 9:39

3 Judge not, that ye be not judged.

Bible. Matthew, *King James Bible* (1611), 7:1

4 And I saw the dead, small and great, stand before God; and the books were opened: and another book was opened, which is the book of life: and the dead were judged out of those things which were written in the books, according to their works.

Bible. Revelation, *King James Bible* (1611), 20:12

5 The catterpiller on the Leaf
Repeats to thee thy Mother's grief.
Kill not the Moth nor Butterfly
For the Last Judgment draweth nigh.

William Blake (1757–1827) British poet, painter, engraver, and mystic. 'Auguries of Innocence' (1803?), ll. 37–40, quoted in *The Poetry and Prose of William Blake* (David V. Erdman, ed.; 1965)

6 In the hour of death, and in the day of judgement.

Book of Common Prayer. The Litany (1662)

7 Perhaps your fear in passing judgment is greater than mine in receiving it.

Giordano Bruno (1548?–1600) Italian philosopher and poet. Said to the cardinals who excommunicated him. Attrib.

8 The cold neutrality of an impartial judge.

Edmund Burke (1729–97) Irish-born British statesman and political philosopher. 'Translator's Preface', *To His Constituents* (J. P. Brissot; 1794)

9 Don't wait for the Last Judgement. It takes place every day.

Albert Camus (1913–60) Algerian-born French novelist, essayist, and playwright. *The Fall* (1956)

10 You shall judge of a man by his foes as well as by his friends.

Joseph Conrad (1857–1924) Polish-born British novelist. *Lord Jim* (1900)

11 Judgment is the typical act of intelligence . . . Perception is a judgment of place; memory, a judgment of time; imagination, a judgment of ideal worth.

John Dewey (1859–1952) US philosopher and educator. *Psychology* (1887)

12 I expect a judgment. Shortly. On the Day of Judgment.

Charles Dickens (1812–70) British novelist. Said by Miss Flite. *Bleak House* (1853), ch. 3

13 Let me remind you of the old maxim: people under suspicion are better moving than at rest, since at rest they may be sitting in the balance without knowing it, being weighed together with their sins.

Franz Kafka (1883–1924) Czech writer. *The Trial* (Edwin and Willa Muir, trs.; 1953), ch. 8

14 We judge ourselves by what we feel capable of doing, while others judge us by what we have already done.

Henry Wadsworth Longfellow (1807–82) US poet. *Kavanagh* (1849), ch. 1

15 Discretion is the better part of reading people . . . If you let them know what you know, you will blow any chance of using your own insight effectively.

Mark McCormack (b. 1930) US sports agent, promoter, and lawyer. *What They Don't Teach You at Harvard Business School* (1984)

16 He who knows only his own side of the case knows little of that.

John Stuart Mill (1806–73) British philosopher and social reformer. *On Liberty* (1859), ch. 2

17 A judge is not supposed to know anything about the facts of life until they have been presented in evidence and explained to him at least three times.

Hubert Lister Parker (1900–72) British judge. *Observer* (March 12, 1961), 'Sayings of the Week'

18 They have a right to censure, that have a heart to help.
William Penn (1644–1718) English preacher and colonialist. *Some Fruits of Solitude* (1693)

19 'Tis with our judgments as our watches, none Go just alike, yet each believes his own.
Alexander Pope (1688–1744) English poet. *An Essay on Criticism* (1711)

20 Nothing indicates the soundness of a man's judgment so much as knowing how to choose between two disadvantages.
Cardinal de Retz (1613–79) French ecclesiastic and politician. *Mémoires* (1717)

21 Do not judge, and you will never be mistaken.
Jean-Jacques Rousseau (1712–78) French philosopher and writer. *Émile* (1762), bk. 3

22 The general will is always straight, but the judgment that guides it is not always enlightened.
Jean-Jacques Rousseau (1712–78) French philosopher and writer. Attrib.

23 POLONIUS Give every man thy ear, but few thy voice;
Take each man's censure, but reserve thy judgement.
William Shakespeare (1564–1616) English poet and playwright. *Hamlet* (1601), Act 1, Scene 3

24 IAGO For I am nothing if not critical.
William Shakespeare (1564–1616) English poet and playwright. *Othello* (1602–04), Act 2, Scene 1

25 Crime has its heroes, error has its martyrs:
Of true zeal and false, what vain judges we are.
Voltaire (1694–1778) French writer and philosopher. *Henriade* (1728), chant 5

26 One cool judgment is worth a thousand hasty councils.
Woodrow Wilson (1856–1924) US president. Speech at Pittsburgh (January 29, 1916), quoted in *The Public Papers* (Ray S. Stannard and William E. Dodd, eds.; 1925)

Justice

see also Civil Rights, Human Rights, Injustice, Law

1 The place of justice is a hallowed place.
Francis Bacon (1561–1626) English philosopher, statesman, and lawyer. 'Of Judicature', *Essays* (1625)

2 Justice is a human illusion: essentially everything is destruction and creation.
Pío Baroja (1872–1956) Basque writer. *The Tree of Knowledge* (1911)

3 When I came back to Dublin, I was courtmartialled in my absence and sentenced to death in my absence, so I said they could shoot me in my absence.
Brendan Behan (1923–64) Irish playwright and author. *The Hostage* (1958), Act 2

4 Justice! Custodian of the world! But since the world errs, justice must be the custodian of the world's errors.
Ugo Betti (1892–1953) Italian playwright and poet. *The Gambler* (Gino Rizzo, tr.; 1950)

5 It is better that ten guilty persons escape than one innocent suffer.
William Blackstone (1723–80) British jurist. *Commentaries on the Laws of England* (1765–69), bk. 4, ch. 27

6 You want justice, but do you want to pay for it, hm? When you go to a butcher you know you have to pay, but you people go to a judge as if you were off to a funeral supper.
Bertolt Brecht (1898–1956) German playwright and poet. *The Caucasian Chalk Circle* (1948), Act 4

7 I believe that in social matters one must start from an absolute principle of *justice*, seek the development of a new life and spirit in the *people*, and let the decrepit society of today go to the devil.
Georg Büchner (1813–37) German dramatist. 1836. Quoted in *Complete Plays, Lenz and Other Writings* (John Reddick, tr.; 1993)

8 Justice is being allowed to do whatever I like. Injustice is whatever prevents my doing it.
Samuel Butler (1835–1902) British writer and composer. Quoted in *Note Books* (H. Festing Jones, ed.; 1912)

9 We have chosen to accept human justice with its terrible imperfections, careful only to correct it through a desperately maintained honesty.
Albert Camus (1913–60) Algerian-born French novelist, essayist, and playwright. 1944. Article in the wartime French resistance movement newspaper, *Combat*, that Camus joined in 1943. Quoted in *Camus, a Biography* (H. R. Lottman; 1979), 'First Combats'

10 Justice is not to be taken by storm. She is to be wooed by slow advances.
Benjamin Cardozo (1870–1938) US Supreme Court justice. *The Growth of the Law* (1924)

11 Recompense injury with justice, and recompense kindness with kindness.
Confucius (551–479 BC) Chinese philosopher, administrator, and moralist. *Analects* (5th century BC)

12 Let justice be done, though the world perish.
Ferdinand I (1503–64) Spanish-born monarch. Motto. *Locorum Communium Collectanea* (Johannes Manlius; 1563), vol. 2

13 Justice . . . limps along, but it gets there all the same.
Gabriel García Márquez (b. 1928) Colombian novelist. Said by Guardiola to Judge Arcadio. *In Evil Hour* (1968)

14 I have loved justice and hated iniquity; therefore I die in exile.
Saint Gregory VII (1020?–85) Italian-born pope. 1085. Said to be his last words. Quoted in *The Life and Pontificate of Gregory VII* (J. W. Bowden; 1840), vol. 2, bk. 3, ch. 20

15 Justice is the end of government. It is the end of civil society. It ever has been and ever will be pursued until it be obtained, or until liberty be lost in the pursuit.
Alexander Hamilton (1757–1804) US statesman. *The Federalist* (co-written with James Madison and John Jay; 1787–88)

16 Justice should not only be done, but should manifestly and undoubtedly be seen to be done.
Gordon Hewart (1870–1943) British lawyer and politician. Quoted in *The Chief* (Robert Jackson; 1959)

17 There is no judge over us, and therefore we must do justice upon ourselves.
Henrik Ibsen (1828–1906) Norwegian playwright. *Rosmersholm* (1886), Act 4

18 As he brews, so shall he drink.
Ben Jonson (1572–1637) English poet and playwright. *Every Man in His Humour* (1598), Act 2, Scene 1

19 Justice is the constant and perpetual wish to render to everyone his due.
Justinian I (483–565) Byzantine emperor. *Institutes* (533?), bk. 1, ch. 1, para. 1

20 Yes, if you want to say that I was a drum major, say that I was a drum major for justice; say that I was a drum major for righteousness. And all of the other shallow things will not matter.
Martin Luther King, Jr. (1929–68) US civil rights leader. Comment (February 4, 1968)

21 The duty of a judge is to administer justice, but his practice is to delay it.
Jean de La Bruyère (1645–96) French essayist and moralist. Attrib.

22 The love of justice in most men is simply the fear of suffering injustice.
François La Rochefoucauld (1613–80) French epigrammatist and moralist. *Reflections, or Sentences and Moral Maxims* (1665), no. 78

23 Justice is such a fine thing that we cannot pay too dearly for it.
Alain René Lesage (1668–1747) French writer. *Crispin Rival de son Maître* (1707), pt. 9

24 To none will we sell, to none deny or delay, right or justice.
Magna Carta. 1215. The Magna Carta was a charter granted by King John to the English barons, subsequently regarded as the basis of English constitutional liberties.

25 Consider what you think justice requires, and decide accordingly. But never give your reasons; for your judgement will probably be right, but your reasons will certainly be wrong.
William Murray Mansfield (1705–93) Scottish-born British judge and politician. 18th century. Advice given to a new colonial governor ignorant in the law. *Lives of the Chief Justices of England* (Campbell; 1849), vol. 2, ch. 40

26 In England, Justice is open to all, like the Ritz hotel.
James Mathew (1830–1908) British judge. 1870? Quoted in *Miscellany-at-Law* (R. E. Megarry; 1955)

27 Justice must not only be seen to be done but has to be seen to be believed.
J. C. Morton (1893–1979) British journalist and writer. Attrib.

28 I thought that there might be some justice for a black man if he had the money to grease it. Money isn't a sure bet but it's the closest to God that I've seen in this world.
Walter Mosley (b. 1952) US novelist. *Devil in a Blue Dress* (1990), ch. 18

29 Justice without force is impotent, force without justice is tyranny.
Blaise Pascal (1623–62) French philosopher, mathematician, and physicist. *Pensées* (1669), no. 298

30 It is better to have a war for justice than peace in injustice.
Charles Pierre Péguy (1873–1914) French writer and poet. 'The Rights of Man', *Basic Verities* (A. and J. Green, trs.; 1943)

31 Each person possesses an inviolability founded on justice that even the welfare of society as a whole cannot override.
John Rawls (b. 1921) US philosopher. *A Theory of Justice* (1971)

32 There is a justice, but we do not always see it. Discreet, smiling, it is there, to one side, a little behind injustice, which makes a big noise.
Jules Renard (1864–1910) French writer. December 1906. *Journal* (1877–1910)

33 When in a town they close the doors of justice, they open the doors of the Revolution.
Práxedes Sagasta (1825–1903) Spanish politician. Quoted in *The Spanish Labyrinth* (Gerald Brenan; 1943)

34 EDGAR The gods are just, and of our pleasant vices
Make instruments to plague us.
William Shakespeare (1564–1616) English poet and playwright. *King Lear* (1605–06), Act 5, Scene 3

35 DUKE VINCENTIO Haste still pays haste, and leisure answers leisure;
Like doth quit like, and Measure still for Measure.
William Shakespeare (1564–1616) English poet and playwright. *Measure for Measure* (1604), Act 5, Scene 1

36 In a just cause the weak o'ercome the strong.
Sophocles (496?–406? BC) Greek playwright. *Oedipus at Colonus* (5th century BC), l. 880

37 This is a British murder inquiry and some degree of justice must be seen to be more or less done.
Tom Stoppard (b. 1937) Czech-born British playwright and screenwriter. *Jumpers* (1972), Act 2

K

Killing

see also **Crime, Death and Dying, Murder**

1   Killing is the lowest form of survival.
    Elias Canetti (1905–94) Bulgarian-born writer. *Crowds and Power* (1960)

2   One does not learn how to die by killing others.
    René Chateaubriand (1768–1848) French writer and statesman. *Mémoires d'Outre-tombe* (1849–50)

3   In the mere state of nature, if you have a mind to kill, that state itself affords you a right.
    Thomas Hobbes (1588–1679) English philosopher and political thinker. *Philosophical Rudiments: Concerning Government and Society* (1642)

4   What will we do
    when there is nobody left
    to kill?
    June Jordan (b. 1936) US journalist, writer, and activist. 'Poem for Nana', *Haruko/Love Poems* (1993)

5   The pellet with the poison's in the vessel with the pestle, and the chalice from the palace has the brew that is true.
    Danny Kaye (1913–87) US stage, film, and television entertainer. *The Court Jester* (1956)

6   Killing
    Is the ultimate simplification of life.
    Hugh MacDiarmid (1892–1978) Scottish poet and writer. 'England's Double Knavery' (1969)

7   There's no difference between one's killing and making decisions that will send others to kill. It's exactly the same thing, or even worse.
    Golda Meir (1898–1978) Russian-born Israeli prime minister. Quoted in *L'Europeo* (Oriana Fallaci; 1973)

8   Whenever you kill a human being you are killing a source of thought too. A human being is a collection of ideas, and these ideas take moral precedence over a society. Ideas are patterns of value.
    Robert T. Pirsig (b. 1928) US writer. *Lila: an Inquiry into Morals* (1991)

9   Kill a man, and you are a murderer. Kill millions of men, and you are a conqueror. Kill everyone, and you are a god.
    Jean Rostand (1894–1977) French biologist and writer. *Thoughts of a Biologist* (1955)

10 Patriots always talk of dying for their country, and never of killing for their country.
    Bertrand Russell (1872–1970) British philosopher and mathematician. 1967. Attrib.

11 The world soon kills
    what it cannot suffer.
    William Wantling (1933–74) US poet and novelist. 'For Lenny Bruce, For Us', *The Awakening* (1969)

12 Yet each man kills the thing he loves,
    By each let this be heard,
    Some do it with a bitter look,
    Some with a flattering word.
    The coward does it with a kiss,
    The brave man with a sword!
    Oscar Wilde (1854–1900) Irish poet, playwright, and wit. *The Ballad of Reading Gaol* (1898), pt. 1, st. 7

Kindness

see also **Friendship, Generosity, Help**

1   A word of kindness is better than a fat pie.
    Anonymous. Russian proverb.

2   The Master said, 'Is benevolence really far away? No sooner do I desire it than it is here'.
    Confucius (551–479 BC) Chinese philosopher, administrator, and moralist. 6th–5th century BC. Quoted in *The Analects* (D. C. Lau, tr.; 1979), bk. 7, no. 30

3   I love thee for a heart that's kind—
    Not for the knowledge in thy mind.
    W. H. Davies (1871–1940) British poet. 'Sweet Stay-at-Home', *Foliage* (1913)

4   True kindness presupposes the faculty of imagining as one's own the suffering and joy of others.
    André Gide (1869–1951) French novelist and critic. 'Pretexts', *Portraits and Aphorisms* (1903)

5   Always, Sir, set a high value on spontaneous kindness. He whose inclination prompts him to cultivate your friendship of his own accord, will love you more than one whom you have been at pains to attach to you.
    Samuel Johnson (1709–84) British lexicographer and writer. May 1781. Quoted in *Life of Samuel Johnson* (James Boswell; 1791)

6   The greatest pleasure I know, is to do a good action by stealth, and to have it found out by accident.
    Charles Lamb (1775–1834) British essayist. 'Table Talk by the Late Elia', *The Athenaeum* (January 4, 1834)

7   Do not feel badly if your kindness is rewarded with ingratitude; it is better to fall from your dream clouds than from a third-story window.
    Joaquim Maria Machado de Assis (1839–1908) Brazilian novelist and short-story writer. *Epitaph of a Small Winner* (1880)

8   Do not ask me to be kind; just ask me to act as though I were.
    Jules Renard (1864–1910) French writer. April 1898. *Journal* (1877–1910)

9   Here, at whatever hour you come, you will find light and help and human kindness.
    Albert Schweitzer (1875–1965) German theologian, philosopher, physician, and musicologist. Inscription on the lamp outside his hospital at Lambaréné (1913–65)

10 PETRUCHIO This is a way to kill a wife with kindness.

William Shakespeare (1564–1616) English poet and playwright. *The Taming of the Shrew* (1592), Act 4, Scene 1

11 The whole worth of a kind deed lies in the love that inspires it.

The Talmud (4th century? BC)

12 Kind hearts are more than coronets,
And simple faith than Norman blood.

Alfred Tennyson (1809–92) British poet. 'Lady Clara Vere de Vere', *Poems* (1842), st. 7

Kissing

see also **Declarations of Love, Love, Seduction**

1 Kiss till the cow comes home.

Beaumont & Fletcher, English playwrights. *The Scornful Lady* (1616), Act 2, Scene 2

2 What of soul was left, I wonder, when the kissing had to stop?

Robert Browning (1812–89) British poet. 'A Toccata of Galuppi's', *Men and Women* (1855), st. 14

3 The tongue in the ear is always the most persuasive of kisses . . . the tongue that probes and disarms, whispers and kisses, that almost obliges.

Javier Marías (b. 1951) Spanish novelist. *A Heart So White* (Margaret Jull Costa, tr.; 1995)

4 Whoever named it necking was a poor judge of anatomy.

Groucho Marx (1895–1977) US comedian and film actor. Remark (1950?), attrib.

5 When women kiss, it always reminds me of prize-fighters shaking hands.

H. L. Mencken (1880–1956) US journalist, critic, and editor. *A Mencken Chrestomathy* (1949), ch. 30

6 A kiss is but a kiss now! and no wave
Of a great flood that whirls me to the sea
But, as you will! we'll sit contentedly,
And eat our pot of honey on the grave.

George Meredith (1828–1909) British novelist and poet. 'Modern Love' (1862)

7 He kissed me and now I am someone else.

Gabriela Mistral (1889–1957) Spanish poet, diplomat, and educator. 'He Kissed Me', *Desolación* (1922)

8 Whenever you kiss a man, remember your last communion and think to yourself 'Could the Sacred Host and the lips of this man come together on my lips without sacrilege?'

Quentin de Sariegos, Spanish Capuchin friar. Advice on premarital contact between the sexes. Attrib.

9 Sweet red splendid kissing mouth.

Algernon Charles Swinburne (1837–1909) British poet. 'Complaint of the Fair Amouress', *The Poems of Algernon Swinburne* (1905)

10 A man had given all other bliss,
And all his worldly worth for this,
To waste his whole heart in one kiss
Upon her perfect lips.

Alfred Tennyson (1809–92) British poet. Subtitled 'A Fragment'. 'Sir Launcelot and Queen Guinevere', *Poems* (1842), st. 5

11 Once
twenty years ago
in the air-conditioned train
I kissed her the whole night long.

Sa'di Yusuf (b. 1943) Iraqi poet. 'A Woman', *Modern Arabic Poetry* (Salma Khadra Jayyusi, ed.; 1987), ll. 13–16

Knowledge

see also **Education, Information, Intelligence, Learning, Memory**

1 Much knowledge if out of proportion to the disposition of forces, is invalid, however formally correct it may be.

Theodor Adorno (1903–69) German philosopher, sociologist, and musicologist. *Minima Moralia* (E. F. N. Jephcott, tr.; 1951)

2 Everyman, I will go with thee, and be thy guide,
In thy most need to go by thy side.

Anonymous. Spoken by Knowledge in the morality play, *Everyman*. Used as the motto of the British publishing imprint, Everyman Library (founded 1906). *Everyman* (1509?–19?), pt. 1

3 The fox knows many things—the hedgehog knows one *big* thing.

Archilochus (680?–640? BC) Greek poet. Attrib.

4 I have taken all knowledge to be my province.

Francis Bacon (1561–1626) English philosopher, statesman, and lawyer. Letter to Lord Burghley (1592)

5 Knowledge itself is power.

Francis Bacon (1561–1626) English philosopher, statesman, and lawyer. 'De Haeresibus' ('Of Heresies'), *Meditationes Sacrae* (Religious Meditations; 1597)

6 The end of our foundation is the knowledge of causes, and secret motions of things; and the enlarging of the bounds of human Empire, to the effecting of all things possible.

Francis Bacon (1561–1626) English philosopher, statesman, and lawyer. *New Atlantis* (1627)

7 Knowledge, like Nature, feeds on ruins, and while systems are born and grow and wither and die, it will rise again, fresh and flourishing on its ashes, and will resume eternal youth.

Andrés Bello (1781–1865) Chilean politician and writer. 'The Craft of History' (1848)

8 And when the woman saw that the tree was good for food, and that it was pleasant to the eyes, and a tree to be desired to make one wise, she took of the fruit thereof, and did eat, and gave also unto her husband with her; and he did eat.
And the eyes of them both were opened, and they knew that they were naked; and they sewed fig leaves together; and made themselves aprons.

Bible. Genesis, *King James Bible* (1611), 3:6–7

9 'All that we know is, nothing can be known'.

Lord Byron (1788–1824) British poet. *Childe Harold's Pilgrimage* (1812–18), can. 2, st. 7

10 Not many people know that.

Michael Caine (b. 1933) British actor. Caine's catch phrase, which was made the title of his memoirs, is said to have been his comment when habitually offering information garnered from *The Guinness Book of Records*. Attrib.

11 The knowledge of the world is only to be acquired in the world, and not in a closet.

Lord Chesterfield (1694–1773) English statesman and writer. October 4, 1746. *Letters to His Son* (1774)

12 The dwarf sees farther than the giant, when he has the giant's shoulder to mount on.

Samuel Taylor Coleridge (1772–1834) British poet. 'On the Principles of Political Knowledge', *The Friend* (1818), vol. 2

13 Real knowledge is to know the extent of one's ignorance.

Confucius (551–479 BC) Chinese philosopher, administrator, and moralist. *Analects* (5th century BC)

14 Shall I teach you what knowledge is? When you know a thing, to hold that you know it; and when you do not know a thing, to allow that you do not know it. This is knowledge.
Confucius (551–479 BC) Chinese philosopher, administrator, and moralist. Quoted in *The Sayings of Confucius* (Lionel Giles, ed.; 1993)

15 Knowledge . . . resembles a statue of marble which stands in the desert and is continuously threatened with burial by the shifting sands. The hands of science must ever be at work in order that the marble column continue everlastingly to shine in the sun.
Albert Einstein (1879–1955) German-born US physicist. 'On Education', address to the State University of New York, Albany, *Ideas and Opinions* (1954)

16 You know I know you know I know you know.
Thom Gunn (b. 1929) British poet. 'Carnal Knowledge', *Fighting Terms* (1954)

17 Knowledge can be communicated but not wisdom.
Hermann Hesse (1877–1962) German-born Swiss novelist and poet. *Siddhartha* (1922)

18 Knowledge is proportionate to being . . . You know in virtue of what you are.
Aldous Huxley (1894–1963) British novelist and essayist. *Time Must Have a Stop* (1944), ch. 26

19 If a little knowledge is dangerous, where is the man who has so much as to be out of danger?
T. H. Huxley (1825–95) British biologist. Referring to Alexander Pope's famous line: 'A little learning is a dang'rous thing' (*An Essay on Criticism*, 1711). *On Elementary Instruction in Physiology* (1877)

20 There was never an age in which useless knowledge was more important than in our own.
C. E. M. Joad (1891–1953) British philosopher. *Observer* (September 30, 1951), 'Sayings of the Week'

21 Knowledge is of two kinds. We know a subject ourselves, or we know where we can find information upon it.
Samuel Johnson (1709–84) British lexicographer and writer. April 18, 1775. Quoted in *Life of Samuel Johnson* (James Boswell; 1791)

22 All our knowledge falls within the bounds of possible experience.
Immanuel Kant (1724–1804) German philosopher. *Critique of Pure Reason* (1781), A 146, B 185

23 I have therefore found it necessary to deny *knowledge* in order to make room for *faith*.
Immanuel Kant (1724–1804) German philosopher. *Critique of Pure Reason* (1781), B 30

24 The greater our knowledge increases the more our ignorance unfolds.
John Fitzgerald Kennedy (1917–63) US president. Speech, Rice University (September 12, 1962)

25 What we know is not much. What we do not know is immense.
Pierre Simon Laplace (1749–1827) French mathematician and astronomer. 1827. Alleged last words. Quoted in *Budget of Paradoxes*, (8th ed.) (Augustus De Morgan; 1872)

26 The genuine knowledge originates in direct experience.
Mao Zedong (1893–1976) Chinese statesman. *On Practice* (1937)

27 Specialist—A man who knows more and more about less and less.
William James Mayo (1861–1939) US physician. Also attributed to Nicholas Butler. *Modern Hospital* (September 1939)

28 What do I know?
Michel de Montaigne (1533–92) French essayist. *Essays* (1580–88), bk. 2, ch. 12

29 We are finite beings, and even if each of us possesses a large dormant capacity for objective self-transcendence, our knowledge of the world will always be fragmentary, however much we extend it.
Thomas Nagel (b. 1937) Yugoslavian-born US philosopher and educator. *The View from Nowhere* (1986)

30 The open society, the unrestricted access to knowledge, the unplanned and uninhibited association of men for its furtherance—these are what may make a vast, complex, ever growing, ever changing, ever more specialized and expert technological world, nevertheless a world of human community.
J. Robert Oppenheimer (1904–67) US nuclear physicist. *Science and the Common Understanding* (1953)

31 The true lover of knowledge naturally strives for truth, and is not content with common opinion, but soars with undimmed and unwearied passion till he grasps the essential nature of things.
Plato (428?–347? BC) Greek philosopher. *The Republic* (370? BC)

32 Our knowledge can only be finite, while our ignorance must necessarily be infinite.
Karl Popper (1902–94) Austrian-born British philosopher. *Conjectures and Refutations* (1963)

33 Until knowledge is understood in human and political terms as something to be won to the service of coexistence and community, not of particular races, nations, or religions, the future augurs badly.
Edward W. Said (b. 1935) Palestinian-born US writer and educator. *Covering Islam* (1981)

34 His had been an intellectual decision founded on his conviction that if a little knowledge was a dangerous thing, a lot was lethal.
Tom Sharpe (b. 1928) British novelist. *Porterhouse Blue* (1974), ch. 18

35 Taste all, and hand the knowledge down.
Gary Snyder (b. 1930) US poet, essayist, and translator. 'Ethnobotany', *Turtle Island* (1975)

36 We are creating and using up ideas and images at a faster and faster pace. Knowledge, like people, places, things, and organizational forms, is becoming dispensable.
Alvin Toffler (b. 1928) US writer. *Future Shock* (1970)

37 Beware you be not swallowed up in books! An ounce of love is worth a pound of knowledge.
John Wesley (1703–91) English religious leader. Quoted in *Life of Wesley* (R. Southey; 1820), ch. 16

38 Our knowledge forms an enormous system. And only within this system has a particular bit the value we give it.
Ludwig Wittgenstein (1889–1951) Austrian philosopher. 1950. Quoted in *On Certainty* (G. E. E. Anscombe, ed.; 1969)

L

Landscapes

see also Ecology, The Environment, Mountains, Nature

1 Spanish geography encourages a scepticism towards the visible. No sense can be found there. The essence lies elsewhere. The visible is a form of desolation.

John Berger (b. 1926) British novelist, essayist, and art critic. 'A Story for Aesop', *Keeping a Rendezvous* (1992)

2 The desert, the abode of enforced sterility, the dehydrated sea of infertility, the post-menopausal part of the earth.

Angela Carter (1940–92) British novelist, essayist, and short-story writer. *The Passion of New Eve* (1977), ch. 3

3 The mesa plain had an appearance of great antiquity, and of incompleteness; as if with all the materials for world-making assembled, the Creator had . . . gone away and left everything . . . The country was still waiting to be made into a landscape.

Willa Cather (1873–1947) US novelist, poet, and journalist. Referring to the landscape of Acoma, New Mexico. Founded about 1075, it is the oldest continuously inhabited settlement in the United States and a National Historic Landmark. *Death Comes for the Archbishop* (1927), ch. 3

4 The ice was here, the ice was there,
The ice was all around:
It cracked and growled, and roared and howled,
Like noises in a swound!

Samuel Taylor Coleridge (1772–1834) British poet. 'The Rime of the Ancient Mariner', *Lyrical Ballads* (1798), pt. 1

5 It is the drawback of all sea-side places that half the landscape is unavailable for purposes of human locomotion, being covered by useless water.

Norman Douglas (1868–1952) British writer. 'Mentone', *Alone* (1921)

6 The wondrous, beautiful prairies,
Billowy bays of grass ever rolling in shadow and in sunshine,
Bright with luxuriant clusters of roses and purple amorphae.

Henry Wadsworth Longfellow (1807–82) US poet. *Evangeline* (1847), pt. 2

7 The whole landscape a manuscript
We had lost the skill to read.

John Montague (b. 1929) US-born Irish poet. 1972. 'A Lost Tradition', *Collected Poems* (1995), ll. 16–17

8 Uncultivated paths intersect into the distance;
Cocks crow and dogs bark to one another.
Ritual vessels are still of ancient pattern;
In clothes there are no new fashions.

Tao Qian (365–427) Chinese poet. 'Poem', *Peach Blossom Spring* (4th–5th century), ll. 13–16

9 On either side the river lie
Long fields of barley and of rye,
That clothe the wold and meet the sky;
And thro' the field the road runs by
To many-tower'd Camelot.

Alfred Tennyson (1809–92) British poet. 'The Lady of Shalott', *Poems* (1832), pt. 1, st. 1

10 A LADY This landscape reminds me of your work.
WHISTLER Yes madam, Nature is creeping up.

James Abbott McNeill Whistler (1834–1903) US painter and etcher. Quoted in *Whistler Stories* (D. C. Seitz; 1913)

11 I love the look, austere, immaculate,
Of landscapes drawn in pearly monotones.

Elinor Wylie (1885–1928) US poet and writer. 'Wild Peaches' (1921)

Language

see also Communication, European Languages, Grammar, Poetry, Speech, Wordplay, Words, World English

1 Hebrew and Arabic,
which are like stones on the tongue and sand on the throat,
have softened for tourists like oil.

Yehuda Amichai (b. 1924) German-born Israeli poet. 'Patriotic Songs', *Amen* (1978), ll. 5–7

2 Is wartime the occasion to play about with letters?

Kemal Ataturk (1881–1938) Turkish statesman. Referring to his plans for reformation of the Turkish language at the time of World War I. Quoted in *Ataturk and the Modernization of Turkey* (Jacob M. Landau, ed.; 1984)

3 It survived, this stubborn language, by withdrawing,
by hiding away like a hedgehog in a place,
which, thanks to the traces it left behind there,
the world named the Basque country, or *Euskal Herria*.

Bernardo Atxaga (b. 1951) Basque writer. Referring to the Basque language, that has repeatedly been outlawed by Spanish nationalists. *Obabakoak* (Margaret Jull Costa, tr.; 1989)

4 Any semiology postulates a relation between two terms, a signifier and a signified. This relation concerns objects which belong to different categories, and this is why it is not one of equality but of equivalence.

Roland Barthes (1915–80) French philosopher and writer. *Mythologies* (Annette Lavers, tr.; 1957)

5 And the whole earth was of one language, and of one speech.

Bible. Genesis, *King James Bible* (1611), 11:1

6 Therefore is the name of it called Babel; because the Lord did there confound the language of all the earth: and from thence did the Lord scatter them abroad upon the face of all the earth.

Bible. Genesis, *King James Bible* (1611), 11:9

7   A Babylonish dialect
    Which learned pedants much affect.
    Samuel Butler (1612–80) English satirist. *Hudibras* (1663), pt. 1,
    can. 1, ll. 93–94

8   Language is called the garment of thought:
    however, it should rather be, language is the
    flesh-garment, the body, of thought.
    Thomas Carlyle (1795–1881) Scottish historian and essayist. *Sartor
    Resartus* (1833–34), bk. 1, ch. 11

9   Finding in 'primitive' languages a dearth of
    words for moral ideas, many people assumed
    these ideas did not exist. But the concepts of
    'good' or 'beautiful', so essential to Western
    thought, are meaningless unless they are rooted
    in things.
    Bruce Chatwin (1940–89) British writer and traveller. *In Patagonia*
    (1977)

10 Until we learn the use of living words we shall
    continue to be waxworks inhabited by
    gramophones.
    Walter de la Mare (1873–1956) British poet and novelist. *Observer*
    (May 12, 1929), 'Sayings of the Week'

11 We have no language—no syntax and no
    lexicon—which is foreign to this history; we can
    pronounce not a single destructive proposition
    which has not already had to slip into the form,
    the logic, and the implicit postulations of that
    which it seeks to contest.
    Jacques Derrida (b. 1930) Algerian-born French philosopher. *Writing and
    Difference* (1967)

12 Language is not an excrescence of mind or graft
    upon it, but . . . an essential mode of the
    expression of its activity . . . The abstract idea is
    projected into real existence through the medium
    of language.
    John Dewey (1859–1952) US philosopher and educator. *Psychology*
    (1887)

13 Polyphiloprogenitive
    The sapient sutlers of the Lord
    Drift across window-panes
    In the beginning was the Word.
    T. S. Eliot (1888–1965) US-born British poet and playwright. 'Mr Eliot's
    Sunday Morning Service', *Poems* (1919)

14 To speak a language is to take on a world, a
    culture.
    Frantz Fanon (1925–61) Martiniquan social scientist, physician, and
    psychiatrist. *Black Skin, White Masks* (1952)

15 It can happen that a civilisation can be
    imprisoned in a linguistic contour which no
    longer matches the landscape of . . . fact.
    Brian Friel (b. 1929) Irish dramatist. *Translations* (1980), Act 2

16 Things want to tell us something but . . . they are
    unable to find a single mouth to speak with a
    single language.
    Ramón Gómez de la Serna (1888–1963) Spanish novelist. Referring to
    physical objects. *Ismos* (1931)

17 The language in which we are speaking is his
    before it is mine. How different are the words
    home, Christ, ale, master, on his lips and on mine.
    James Joyce (1882–1941) Irish writer. Referring to the English
    language. *A Portrait of the Artist as a Young Man* (1916)

18 The baby doesn't understand English and the
    Devil knows Latin.
    Ronald Knox (1888–1957) British priest and writer. Said when asked to
    conduct a baptism service in English. Quoted in *The Life of
    Ronald Knox* (Evelyn Waugh; 1962), pt. 1, ch. 5

19 I master the language of others. Mine does what
    it wants with me.
    Karl Kraus (1874–1936) Austrian writer. 1918. Quoted in *Karl Kraus*
    (Harry Zohn; 1971)

20 Language is the material of the literary artist, but
    it does not belong to him alone, whereas colour
    belongs exclusively to the painter. Therefore
    people ought to be prohibited from talking. Sign
    language would be entirely sufficient for the ideas
    which they have to communicate to one another.
    Karl Kraus (1874–1936) Austrian writer. 1909. Quoted in 'Sprüche
    und Widersprüche', *Karl Kraus* (Harry Zohn; 1971)

21 Language is a form of human reason and has its
    reasons which are unknown to man.
    Claude Lévi-Strauss (b. 1908) French anthropologist. *The Savage Mind*
    (1966)

22 The only living language is the language in which
    we think and have our being.
    Antonio Machado (1875–1939) Spanish poet and playwright. *Juan de
    Mairena* (1943)

23 If Aristotle had spoken Chinese or Dakota, he
    would have had to adopt an entirely different
    Logic, or at any rate an entirely different theory
    of categories.
    Fritz Mauthner (1849–1923) German writer. *Beiträge zu einer Kritik
    der Sprache* (1902), vol. 3

24 Language is how ghosts enter the world.
    They twist into awkward positions
    to squeeze through the blank spaces.
    Anne Michaels (b. 1958) Canadian poet and novelist. 'What the Light
    Teaches', *Skin Divers* (1999)

25 If the English language had been properly
    organized . . . then there would be a word which
    meant both 'he' and 'she', and I could write, 'If
    John or Mary comes heesh will want to play
    tennis', which would save a lot of trouble.
    A. A. Milne (1882–1956) British writer. *The Christopher Robin
    Birthday Book* (1930)

26 The simpler the alphabet, the easier it is to read.
    Joan Miró (1893–1983) Catalan painter. Interview, *El País* (Madrid;
    June 18, 1978)

27 Language is the autobiography of the human mind.
    Max Müller (1823–1900) German-born British philologist. Quoted in
    Scholar Extraordinary (Nirad Chaudhuri; 1974)

28 I know of only four languages, viz: Latin, Irish,
    Greek and Chinese. These are languages because
    they are the instruments of integral civilisations.
    English and French are not languages: they are
    mercantile codes.
    Flann O'Brien (1911–66) Irish novelist and journalist. 'Criticism',
    Further Cuttings from Cruiskeen Lawn (1989)

29 The metaphor is probably the most fertile power
    possessed by man.
    José Ortega y Gasset (1883–1955) Spanish writer and philosopher. *The
    Dehumanization of Art* (1925)

30 One ought to recognize that the present political
    chaos is connected with the decay of language,
    and that one can probably bring about some
    improvement by starting at the verbal end.
    George Orwell (1903–50) British writer. 'Politics and the English
    Language', *Shooting an Elephant* (1950)

31 The great enemy of clear language is insincerity.
    When there is a gap between one's real and one's
    declared aims, one turns as it were instinctively
    to long words and exhausted idioms, like a
    cuttlefish squirting out ink.
    George Orwell (1903–50) British writer. 'Politics and the English
    Language', *Shooting an Elephant* (1950)

32 My friends, I lament the old language
and the old books.
I lament
our perforated words, like old shoes,
the phrases of debauchery, slander, and insult.

Nizar Qabbani (b. 1923) Syrian poet. 'Marginal Notes on the Book of Defeat' (1967), pt. 1, ll. 1–5, quoted in *When the Words Burn* (John Mikhail Asfour, ed., tr.; 1988)

33 Black A, white E, red I, green U, blue O: vowels,
Some day I shall recount your latent births.

Arthur Rimbaud (1854–91) French poet. 'Voyelles' (1871)

34 In a logically perfect language, there will be one word and no more for every simple object, and everything that is not simple will be expressed by a combination of words.

Bertrand Russell (1872–1970) British philosopher and mathematician. 'The Philosophy of Logical Atomism', *Logic and Knowledge* (1955)

35 CALIBAN You taught me language; and my profit on't
Is, I know how to curse: the red plague rid you
For learning me your language!

William Shakespeare (1564–1616) English poet and playwright. *The Tempest* (1611), Act 1, Scene 2

36 Language can be created only by talking to oneself, groaning, raving, crying, and even keeping silence.

Song Lin (b. 1959) Chinese writer. 'Prison Letter' (1991)

37 Finding language that will allow people to act together while cherishing each other's individuality is probably the most feminist and therefore truly revolutionary function of writers.

Gloria Steinem (b. 1934) US writer and feminist. *Outrageous Acts and Everyday Rebellions* (1983), Introduction

38 Language can only deal meaningfully with a special, restricted segment of reality. The rest, and it is presumably the much larger part, is silence.

George Steiner (b. 1929) US scholar and critic. 'The Retreat from the Word', *Language and Silence* (1967)

39 Language grows out of life, out of its needs and experiences.

Anne Sullivan (1866–1936) US teacher. Speech to the American Association to Promote the Teaching of Speech to the Deaf (July 1894)

40 The resignation to a language that would retard us discovers the fictiveness of dying.

Jenaro Talens (b. 1946) Spanish educator and poet. Closing lines. 'Interdum Iuvat Insanne', *A Bilingual Anthology of Contemporary Spanish Poetry* (Luis A. Ramos-García, ed.; 1997)

Last Words

see also **Death and Dying**

1 Jakie, is it my birthday or am I dying?

Nancy Astor (1879–1964) US-born British politician. 1964. To her son on her death bed. He replied, 'A bit of both, Mum'. Attrib.

2 It is finished.

Bible. John, *Vulgate* (404?), 19:30

3 Goodnight, my darlings. I'll see you tomorrow.

Noël Coward (1899–1973) British playwright, actor, and songwriter. *The Life of Noël Coward* (Cole Lesley; 1976)

4 Thou wilt show my head to the people: it is worth showing.

Georges Jacques Danton (1759–94) French revolutionary leader. April 5, 1794. Said as he mounted the scaffold. *The French Revolution* (Thomas Carlyle; 1837), vol. 3, bk. 6, ch. 2

5 How is the Empire?

George V (1865–1936) British monarch. Reputed last words. *Times* (January 21, 1936)

6 Bugger Bognor.

George V (1865–1936) British monarch. His alleged last words, when his doctor promised him he would soon be well enough to visit the coastal resort of Bognor Regis. Quoted in *King George V* (Kenneth Rose; 1983), ch. 9

7 Only one man ever understood me . . . And he didn't understand me.

G. W. F. Hegel (1770–1831) German philosopher. Said on his deathbed. Remark (1831), quoted in *Famous Last Words* (Barnaby Conrad; 1962)

8 Turn up the lights, I don't want to go home in the dark.

O. Henry (1862–1910) US short-story writer. His last words, quoting a popular song of the time, 'I'm Afraid To Go Home in the Dark'. Last words (1910), quoted in *O. Henry* (C. A. Smith; 1916), ch. 9

9 Thank God, I have done my duty. Kiss me, Hardy.

Horatio Nelson (1758–1805) English naval commander. October 21, 1805. Dying words at Battle of Trafalgar, to Captain Hardy of *The Victory*. Quoted in *Life of Nelson* (Robert Southey; 1813), ch. 9

10 I am just going outside and may be some time.

Lawrence Oates (1880–1912) British explorer. Last words before leaving the tent and vanishing into the blizzard on the British expedition to the South Pole (1912). Journal (March 17, 1912)

11 Die, my dear Doctor, that's the last thing I shall do!

Lord Palmerston (1784–1865) British prime minister. Last words (1865), quoted in *Famous Sayings and Their Authors* (E. Latham; 1904)

12 I am curious to see what happens in the next world to one who dies unshriven.

Perugino (1445?–1523) Italian painter. Giving his reasons for refusing to see a priest as he lay dying. Remark (1523)

13 I have not told half of what I saw.

Marco Polo (1254–1324) Venetian merchant and traveller. Remark (1324), quoted in *The Story of Civilization* (William Durant; 1935), vol. 1

14 Bring down the curtain, the farce is over.

François Rabelais (1494?–1553?) French humanist and satirist. 1553? Last words. A number of different quotations are attributed to Rabelais as his last words. Attrib.

15 Everybody has got to die, but I have always believed an exception would be made in my case. Now what?

William Saroyan (1908–81) US novelist. 1981. Last words. Quoted in *Time* (January 16, 1984)

16 If this is dying, I don't think much of it.

Lytton Strachey (1880–1932) British writer. 1932. Last words. Quoted in *Lytton Strachey* (Michael Holroyd; 1967–68), pt. 5, ch. 17

17 Even in the valley of the shadow of death, two and two do not make six.

Leo Tolstoy (1828–1910) Russian writer. November 1910. Refusing to reconcile himself with the Russian Orthodox Church as he lay dying. Attrib.

18 Either that wallpaper goes, or I do.

Oscar Wilde (1854–1900) Irish poet, playwright, and wit. 1900. Last words, as he lay dying in a drab Paris hotel bedroom. Attrib.

Latin America

see **South America**

Laughter

see also **Comedy, Humour**

1   The difference between the maniac and the
    schizophrenic laugh is—mania and the world laughs
    with you, schizophrenia and you smile alone.
    Richard Asher (1912–69) British psychiatrist. Quoted in *A Sense of
    Asher* (Ruth Holland, ed.; 1984)

2   I make myself laugh at everything, so that I do
    not weep.
    Pierre-Augustin Caron de Beaumarchais (1732–99) French playwright. *The
    Barber of Seville* (1775), Act 1, Scene 2

3   No man who has once heartily and wholly
    laughed can be altogether irreclaimably bad.
    Thomas Carlyle (1795–1881) Scottish historian and essayist. *Sartor
    Resartus* (1833–34), bk. 1, ch. 4

4   For there is nothing sillier than a silly laugh.
    Catullus (84?–54? BC) Roman poet. *Carmina* (60? BC), 39

5   There is nothing more unbecoming a man of
    quality than to laugh; Jesu, 'tis such a vulgar
    expression of the passion!
    William Congreve (1670–1729) English playwright and poet. *The Double
    Dealer* (1694), Act 1, Scene 4

6   But laughter is weakness, corruption, the
    foolishness of our flesh.
    Umberto Eco (b. 1932) Italian writer and literary scholar. *The Name of
    the Rose* (William Weaver, tr.; 1980)

7   Perhaps the mission of those that love mankind is
    to make people laugh at the truth, *to make truth
    laugh*, because the only truth lies in learning to
    free ourselves from insane passion for the truth.
    Umberto Eco (b. 1932) Italian writer and literary scholar. *The Name of
    the Rose* (William Weaver, tr.; 1980), Seventh Day: Night (2)

8   Nothing is so impenetrable as laughter in a
    language you don't understand.
    William Golding (1911–93) British novelist. *An Egyptian Journal* (1985)

9   Laughter is nothing else but sudden glory arising
    from some sudden conception of some eminency
    in ourselves, by comparison with the infirmity of
    others, or with our own formerly.
    Thomas Hobbes (1588–1679) English philosopher and political thinker.
    Human Nature (1650), ch. 9, sect. 13

10 Laughter is an affection arising from the sudden
    transformation of a strained expectation into
    nothing.
    Immanuel Kant (1724–1804) German philosopher. *Critique of
    Judgment* (1790)

11 One must laugh before one is happy, or one may
    die without ever laughing at all.
    Jean de La Bruyère (1645–96) French essayist and moralist. *Characters,
    or the Manners of the Age* (1688)

12 Laughter is pleasant, but the exertion is too
    much for me.
    Thomas Love Peacock (1785–1866) British novelist and poet. Said by the
    Hon. Mr. Listless. *Nightmare Abbey* (1818), ch. 5

13 To laugh, if but for an instant only, has never
    been granted to man before the fortieth day from
    his birth, and then it is looked upon as a miracle
    of precocity.
    Pliny the Elder (23?–79) Roman scholar. *Natural History* (77), bk. 7,
    sect. 2

14 He who laughs on Friday will cry on Sunday.
    Racine (1639–99) French playwright. *Les Plaideurs* (1668), Act 1,
    Scene 1

15 We are in the world to laugh. In purgatory or in
    hell we shall no longer be able to do so. And in
    heaven it would not be proper.
    Jules Renard (1864–1910) French writer. June 1907. *Journal* (1877–
    1910)

16 Laughter is as ridiculous as it is deceptive.
    Paul Verlaine (1844–96) French poet. *Poèmes Saturniens* (1866),
    Prologue

17 Laugh, and the world laughs with you;
    Weep, and you weep alone,
    For the sad old earth must borrow its mirth,
    But has trouble enough of its own.
    Ella Wheeler Wilcox (1850–1919) US poet. 'Solitude' (1917)

Law

see also **Government, Justice**

1   Many dues imposed by law are hostile to nature.
    Antiphon (*fl.* 5th century BC) Greek philosopher. Quoted in *The
    Presocratics* (Edward Hussey; 1972)

2   Laws can be unjust because they are contrary to
    the divine good . . . In no way is it permissible to
    observe them.
    Thomas Aquinas (1225–74) Italian theologian and philosopher. *Summa
    Theologica* (1266–73), I, pt. 1.2

3   Laws and institutions are constantly tending to
    gravitate. Like clocks, they must be occasionally
    cleansed, and wound up, and set to true time.
    Henry Ward Beecher (1813–87) US cleric and abolitionist. *Life Thoughts*
    (1863)

4   Laws are not masters but servants, and he rules
    them who obeys them.
    Henry Ward Beecher (1813–87) US cleric and abolitionist. *Proverbs
    from Plymouth Pulpit* (1887)

5   Every law is an evil, for every law is an
    infraction of liberty.
    Jeremy Bentham (1748–1832) British philosopher, economist, jurist, and
    social reformer. *An Introduction to the Principles of Morals and
    Legislation* (1789), Introduction

6   Bad laws are the worst sort of tyranny.
    Edmund Burke (1729–97) Irish-born British statesman and political
    philosopher. 1780. Speech at Bristol previous to the 1780
    election when he lost his parliamentary seat; he had been MP
    for Bristol since 1774.

7   'That's not a regular rule: you invented it just
    now'. 'It's the oldest rule in the book', said the
    King. 'Then it ought to be Number One', said
    Alice.
    Lewis Carroll (1832–98) British writer and mathematician. *Alice's
    Adventures in Wonderland* (1865), ch. 12

8   The law isn't justice. It's a very imperfect
    mechanism. If you press exactly the right buttons
    and are also lucky, justice may also turn up in
    the answer.
    Raymond Chandler (1888–1959) US novelist. *The Long Goodbye*
    (1953)

9   We do not get good laws to restrain bad people.
    We get good people to restrain bad laws.
    G. K. Chesterton (1874–1936) British writer and poet. *All Things
    Considered* (1908)

10 Possession is eleven points in the law.
    Colley Cibber (1671–1757) British actor and playwright. *Woman's Wit*
    (1697), Act 1

11 Law is founded not on theory but upon nature.
Cicero (106–43 BC) Roman orator and statesman. *De Legibus* (1st century BC), bk. 1, ch. 10, sect. 28

12 The good of the people is the chief law.
Cicero (106–43 BC) Roman orator and statesman. *De Legibus* (1st century BC), bk. 3, ch. 3, sect. 8

13 I don't want to know what the law is, I want to know who the judge is.
Roy Cohn (1927–86) US lawyer. Attrib. *American Heritage: Dictionary of American Quotations* (Margaret Miner and Hugh Rawson, eds.; 1997)

14 The law is simply expediency wearing a long white dress.
Quentin Crisp (1908–99) British writer. *Manners from Heaven* (1984), ch. 8

15 The law-courts of England are open to all men, like the doors of the Ritz Hotel.
Charles John Darling (1849–1936) British judge and writer. Attrib.

16 'If the law supposes that', said Mr. Bumble . . . , 'the law is a ass—a idiot'.
Charles Dickens (1812–70) British novelist. *Oliver Twist* (1838), ch. 51

17 As in law so in war, the longest purse finally wins.
Mahatma Gandhi (1869–1948) Indian national leader. Paper read to the Bombay Provincial Co-operative Conference (September 17, 1917)

18 There's no better way of exercising the imagination than the study of law. No poet ever interpreted nature as freely as a lawyer interprets the truth.
Jean Giraudoux (1882–1944) French playwright and writer. *Tiger at the Gates* (1935), Act 1

19 Law grinds the poor, and rich men rule the law.
Oliver Goldsmith (1730–74) Irish-born British novelist, playwright, and poet. *The Traveller* (1764), l. 386

20 I know no method to secure the repeal of bad or obnoxious laws so effective as their stringent execution.
Ulysses S. Grant (1822–85) US general. Inaugural address (March 4, 1869), quoted in *The Life and Campaigns of Lieut. Gen. U. S. Grant* (P. C. Headley; 1886), ch. 29

21 The law is the witness and external deposit of our moral life. Its history is the history of the moral development of the race.
Oliver Wendell Holmes, Jr. (1841–1935) US judge. Speech, Boston (January 8, 1897)

22 I have come to regard the law courts not as a cathedral but rather as a casino.
Richard Ingrams (b. 1937) British journalist. *Guardian* (July 30, 1977)

23 The Law of the Jungle—which is by far the oldest law in the world—has arranged for almost every kind of accident that may befall the Jungle People, till now its code is as perfect as time and custom can make it.
Rudyard Kipling (1865–1936) Indian-born British writer and poet. 'How Fear Came', *The Second Jungle Book* (1895)

24 Freedom of men under government is to have a standing rule to live by, common to every one in that society . . . and not to be subject to the inconstant, uncertain, unknown, arbitrary will of another man.
John Locke (1632–1704) English philosopher. *Second Treatise on Civil Government* (1690)

25 The man who does no wrong needs no law.
Menander (342?–291? BC) Greek playwright and poet. *Fragments*, no. 845

26 A judge is a law student who marks his own examination papers.
H. L. Mencken (1880–1956) US journalist, critic, and editor. Attrib.

27 Laws were made to be broken.
Christopher North (1785–1854) Scottish poet, essayist, and critic. 'Noctes Ambrosianae', *Blackwood's Magazine* (May 24, 1830), no. 49

28 Where laws end, tyranny begins.
William Pitt the Elder (1708–78) British prime minister. Referring to the trial of John Wilkes, regarded by many as a champion of freedom of the press. He was imprisoned for seditious libel (1769), elected an alderman (1770), and became lord mayor of London (1771). Speech to the House of Lords (January 9, 1770)

29 To make a law, yet not see that it is enforced, is to authorize what you have yourself forbidden.
Cardinal Richelieu (1585–1642) French churchman and statesman. 1641. *Testament Politique* (1688), maxims

30 There is only one law which by its nature requires unanimous assent. This is the social pact: for the civil association is the most voluntary act in the world; every man having been born free and master of himself, no one else may on any pretext whatsoever subject him without his consent.
Jean-Jacques Rousseau (1712–78) French philosopher and writer. *The Social Contract* (1762)

31 ANGELO We must not make a scarecrow of the law,
Setting it up to fear the birds of prey,
And let it keep one shape, till custom make it
Their perch and not their terror.
William Shakespeare (1564–1616) English poet and playwright. *Measure for Measure* (1604), Act 2, Scene 1

32 The big print giveth and the fine print taketh away.
Fulton J. Sheen (1895–1979) US Roman Catholic clergyman and broadcaster. Referring to his contract for a television appearance. Attrib.

33 Laws are like spiders' webs: if some poor weak creature come up against them, it is caught; but a bigger one can break through and get away.
Solon (638?–559? BC) Greek statesman. Quoted in *Lives of the Philosophers* (Diogenes Laërtius; 3rd century), bk. 1, ch. 58

34 Laws are like cobwebs, which may catch small flies, but let wasps and hornets break through.
Jonathan Swift (1667–1745) Irish writer and clergyman. 'A Critical Essay upon the Faculties of the Mind' (1709)

35 To the right wing 'law and order' is often just a code phrase, meaning 'get the nigger'. To the left wing it often means political oppression.
Gore Vidal (b. 1925) US novelist and essayist. 1975. Quoted in *The Cynic's Lexicon* (Jonathon Green, ed.; 1984)

Leadership

see also Decision, Power

1 The art of leadership is to work with the natural grain of the particular wood of humanity which comes to hand.
John Adair (b. 1934) British business writer. *Understanding Motivation* (1990)

2 Leaders learn by leading, and they learn best by leading in the face of obstacles. As weather shapes mountains, problems shape leaders.
Warren Bennis (b. 1925) US educationalist and writer. *On Becoming a Leader* (1988)

3 The art of leadership is saying no, not yes. It is very easy to say yes.
Tony Blair (b. 1953) British prime minister. *Mail on Sunday* (October 2, 1994)

4 No man will make a great leader who wants to do it all himself, or to get all the credit for doing it.
Andrew Carnegie (1835–1919) Scottish-born US industrialist and philanthropist. Quoted in 'Noteworthy Quotes', *Strategy and Business* (1999)

5 I have nothing to offer but blood, toil, tears and sweat.
Winston Churchill (1874–1965) British prime minister and writer. Said on becoming prime minister. Speech to Parliament (May 13, 1940)

6 The aim of leadership should be to improve the performance of man and machine, to improve quality, to increase output, and simultaneously to bring pride of workmanship to people.
W. Edwards Deming (1900–93) US management expert. *Out of the Crisis* (1982)

7 The first responsibility of a leader is to define reality. The last is to say thank you.
Max de Pree (b. 1924) US business executive and author. *Leadership is an Art* (1994)

8 Ninety percent of leadership is the ability to communicate something people want.
Dianne Feinstein (b. 1933) US politician. Quoted in *Time* (June 18, 1990)

9 Leadership is the priceless gift that you earn from the people who work for you. I have to earn the right to that gift and have to continuously re-earn that right.
John Harvey-Jones (b. 1924) British business executive and author. Quoted in *International Management* (September 1985)

10 As the Prime Minister put it to me . . . he saw his role as being that of Moses.
Peter Jay (b. 1937) British economist and broadcaster. Referring to a conversation with James Callaghan. *Guardian Weekly* (September 18, 1977)

11 You don't lead by pointing a finger and telling people some place to go. You lead by going to that place and making a case.
Ken Kesey (b. 1935) US writer. Interview, *Esquire* (June 1970)

12 Let me pass, I have to follow them, I am their leader.
Alexandre Auguste Ledru-Rollin (1807–74) French lawyer and politician. 1848. Trying to force his way through a mob during the Revolution of 1848, of which he was one of the chief instigators. Quoted in *Les Contemporains* (E. de Mirecourt; 1857), vol. 14, 'Ledru-Rollin'

13 Only one man in a thousand is a leader of men— the other 999 follow women.
Groucho Marx (1895–1977) US comedian and film actor. Attrib.

14 A leader who doesn't hesitate before he sends his nation into battle is not fit to be a leader.
Golda Meir (1898–1978) Russian-born Israeli prime minister. Quoted in *As Good as Golda* (Israel and Mary Shenker, eds.; 1967)

15 The most effective leader is the one who satisfies the psychological needs of his followers.
David Ogilvy (1911–99) US advertising executive. *Ogilvy on Advertising* (1983)

16 Leadership is the art of accomplishing more than the science of management says is possible.
Colin Powell (b. 1937) US military leader and politician. *A Soldier's Way* (1995)

17 Leadership, above all, consists of telling the truth, unpalatable though it may be. It is better to go down with the truth on one's lips than to rise high by innuendo and doubletalk.
Alfred Robens (b. 1910) British trade union leader and industrialist. Speech, Institute of Directors Annual Convention (November 7, 1974)

18 KING RICHARD II We were not born to sue, but to command.
William Shakespeare (1564–1616) English poet and playwright. *Richard II* (1595), Act 1, Scene 1

19 A leader is a man who has the ability to get other people to do what they don't want to do, and like it.
Harry S. Truman (1884–1972) US president. Quoted in *Key Management Ideas* (Stuart Crainer; 1996)

20 The leader's unending responsibility must be to remove every detour, every barrier to ensure that vision is first clear, then real.
Jack Welch (b. 1935) US electronics executive. Speech to the Bay Area Council, San Francisco (July 6, 1989)

21 I used to say of him that his presence on the field made the difference of forty thousand men.
Duke of Wellington (1769–1852) Irish-born British general and prime minister. November 2, 1831. Referring to Napoleon Bonaparte. *Notes of Conversations with the Duke of Wellington* (Philip Henry Stanhope; 1888)

22 Every man who takes office in Washington either grows or swells, and when I give a man office I watch him carefully to see whether he is growing or swelling.
Woodrow Wilson (1856–1924) US president. Speech (May 15, 1916)

Learning

see also **Education, Knowledge, Research, Teachers**

1 By studying the masters—not their pupils.
Niels Henrik Abel (1802–29) Norwegian mathematician. 1825? When asked how he had become a great mathematician so quickly. Quoted in *Men of Mathematics* (E. T. Bell; 1937)

2 They know enough who know how to learn.
Henry Adams (1838–1918) US historian. 1904. *The Education of Henry Adams* (1907)

3 It is always the season for the old to learn.
Aeschylus (525?–456 BC) Greek tragedian and dramatist. *Fragments* (5th century? BC)

4 What we have to learn to do, we learn by doing.
Aristotle (384–322 BC) Greek philosopher. *Nicomachean Ethics* (4th century BC), bk. 2

5 Histories make men wise; poets, witty; the mathematics, subtile; natural philosophy, deep; moral, grave; logic and rhetoric, able to contend.
Francis Bacon (1561–1626) English philosopher, statesman, and lawyer. 'Of Studies', *Essays* (1625)

6 They perfect nature and are perfected by experience.
Francis Bacon (1561–1626) English philosopher, statesman, and lawyer. 'Of Studies', *Essays* (1625)

7 Whatsoever things were written aforetime were written for our learning, that we through patience and comfort of the scriptures might have hope.
Bible. Romans, *King James Bible* (1611), 15:4

8 Read, mark, learn and inwardly digest.

Book of Common Prayer. Collect, 2nd Sunday in Advent (1662)

9 Learning, that cobweb of the brain,
Profane, erroneous, and vain.

Samuel Butler (1612–80) English satirist. *Hudibras* (1663), pt. 1, can. 3, ll. 1339–40

10 Learning had made us not more human, but less so. Learning had not increased our knowledge of good and evil, but intensified and made more rational and deadly our greed for gain.

Jan Carew (b. 1922) Guyanese-born novelist, actor, and newspaper editor. *Black Midas* (1969)

11 LIBOV ANDREEVNA Are you still a student?
TROFIMOV I expect I shall be a student to the end of my days.

Anton Chekhov (1860–1904) Russian playwright and short-story writer. *The Cherry Orchard* (1904), Act 1

12 My own suggestion is that a central part of what we call 'learning' is actually better understood as the growth of cognitive structures . . . We may usefully think of the language faculty, the number faculty, and others, as 'mental organs'.

Noam Chomsky (b. 1928) US linguist and political activist. *Rules and Representations* (1980)

13 I am always ready to learn although I do not always like being taught.

Winston Churchill (1874–1965) British prime minister and writer. *Observer* (November 9, 1952)

14 Study more and criticize less. This is a correct attitude toward learning.

Deng To (1912–66) Chinese editor. *Evening Talks at Yenshan* (1961–62), quoted in *Literature of the People's Republic of China* (Kai-yu Hsu, ed.; 1980)

15 That one gets used to everything—
one gets used to that.
The usual name for it is
a learning process.

Hans Enzensberger (b. 1929) German poet. 1971. 'The Force of Habit', *Poems 1955–70* (Michael Hamburger, tr.; 1977)

16 Whoso neglects learning in his youth,
Loses the past and is dead for the future.

Euripides (480?–406? BC) Greek playwright. *Phrixus* (5th century BC), fragment 927

17 Learning hath gained most by those books by which the printers have lost.

Thomas Fuller (1608–61) English historian. *The Holy State and the Profane State* (1642)

18 It is not knowledge, but the act of learning, not possession but the act of getting there, which grants the greatest enjoyment.

Carl Friedrich Gauss (1777–1855) German mathematician and astronomer. Letter to Farkas Bolyai (1808)

19 Whence is thy learning? Hath thy toil
O'er books consum'd the midnight oil?

John Gay (1685–1732) English poet and playwright. *Fables* (1727), Introduction, ll. 15–16

20 It is the true nature of mankind to learn from mistakes, not from example.

Fred Hoyle (1915–2001) British astronomer, mathematician, and writer. *Into Deepest Space* (1975)

21 The ink of the scholar is more sacred than the blood of the martyr.

Muhammad (570?–632?) Arab religious leader and prophet. Attrib.

22 I have had to learn the simplest things last.

Charles Olson (1910–70) US poet. 'I, Maximus to Himself', *The Maximus Poems 1–10* (1953)

23 Learning is not worth a penny when courage and joy are lost along the way.

Johann Heinrich Pestalozzi (1746–1827) Swiss educational reformer. Quoted in *The Education of Man: Aphorisms* (Heinz and Ruth Norden, trs.; 1951)

24 A little learning is a dangerous thing;
Drink deep, or taste not the Pierian spring:
There shallow draughts intoxicate the brain,
And drinking largely sobers us again.

Alexander Pope (1688–1744) English poet. *An Essay on Criticism* (1711), ll. 215–218

25 The learn'd is happy nature to explore,
The fool is happy that he knows no more.

Alexander Pope (1688–1744) English poet. *An Essay on Man* (1733), Epistle 2, ll. 263–264

26 Love seldom haunts the breast where learning lies,
And Venus sets ere Mercury can rise.

Alexander Pope (1688–1744) English poet. Written in imitation of Chaucer's *Canterbury Tales. The Wife of Bath. Her Prologue*, ll. 369–370, quoted in *The Works of Alexander Pope* (1736)

27 BEROWNE For where is any author in the world
Teaches such beauty as a woman's eye?
Learning is but an adjunct to oneself.

William Shakespeare (1564–1616) English poet and playwright. *Love's Labour's Lost* (1595), Act 4, Scene 3

28 TRANIO No profit grows where is no pleasure ta'en;
In brief, sir, study what you most affect.

William Shakespeare (1564–1616) English poet and playwright. *The Taming of the Shrew* (1592), Act 1, Scene 1

29 He who adds not to his learning diminishes it.

The Talmud (4th century? BC)

30 Learning is a common journey that binds leaders and employers together . . . Learning unites leaders and followers in a common journey of self-discovery and team development.

Dean Tjosvold, US psychologist and author. *Psychology for Leaders* (co-written with Mary M. Tjosvold; 1995)

Liberalism

see also **Freedom, Liberty, Politics**

1 You Liberals think that goats are just sheep from broken homes.

Malcolm Bradbury (1932–2000) British academic, novelist, and critic. Three plays for television. *The After Dinner Game* (1982)

2 To be absolutely honest, what I feel really bad about is that I don't feel worse. There's the ineffectual liberal's problem in a nutshell.

Michael Frayn (b. 1933) British journalist, novelist, and playwright. *Observer* (August 8, 1965)

3 The permissive society has been allowed to become a dirty phrase. A better phrase is the civilized society.

Roy Jenkins (b. 1920) British statesman. Speech, Abingdon, Oxfordshire (July 19, 1969)

4 When a liberal is abused, he says: Thank God they didn't beat me. When he is beaten, he thanks God they didn't kill him. When he is killed, he will thank God that his immortal soul has been delivered from its mortal clay.

Vladimir Ilyich Lenin (1870–1924) Russian revolutionary leader. December 1906. Lenin heard this characterization at a meeting, and repeated it with approval. 'Proletary', *The Government's Falsification of the Duma and the Tasks of the Social-Democrats* (1906)

5 Sadly I have come to realize that a great many so-called liberals aren't liberal—they will defend to the death your right to agree with them.

Ronald Reagan (b. 1911) US president and actor. *Where's the Rest of Me?* (1965)

6 He was learning for himself the truth of the saying, 'A liberal is a conservative who has been arrested'.

Tom Wolfe (b. 1930) US journalist and novelist. *The Bonfire of the Vanities* (1987)

Liberty

see also **Civil Rights, Freedom, Human Rights**

1 A day, an hour, of virtuous liberty
Is worth a whole eternity in bondage.

Joseph Addison (1672–1719) English essayist, poet, and statesman. *Cato* (1713), Act 1, Scene 2

2 Only reason can convince us of those three fundamental truths without a recognition of which there can be no effective liberty: that what we believe is not necessarily true; that what we like is not necessarily good; and that all questions are open.

Clive Bell (1881–1964) British art critic. *Civilization* (1928), ch. 5

3 Liberty then is neither more nor less than the absence of coercion . . . It exists without Law, and not by means of Law.

Jeremy Bentham (1748–1832) British philosopher, economist, jurist, and social reformer. Attrib.

4 Experience should teach us to be most on our guard to protect liberty when the Government's purposes are beneficent.

Louis D. Brandeis (1856–1941) US judge. *Olmstead vs. United States* (1928)

5 The people never give up their liberties but under some delusion.

Edmund Burke (1729–97) Irish-born British statesman and political philosopher. 'Except' is sometimes substituted for 'but'. Speech at a county meeting, Buckinghamshire (1784)

6 The only liberty I mean, is a liberty connected with order; that not only exists along with order and virtue, but which cannot exist at all without them.

Edmund Burke (1729–97) Irish-born British statesman and political philosopher. Edmund Burke was elected MP for Bristol in 1774. Speech on his arrival at Bristol (1774)

7 I flatter myself that I love a manly, moral, regulated liberty as well as any gentleman.

Edmund Burke (1729–97) Irish-born British statesman and political philosopher. *Reflections on the Revolution in France* (1790)

8 Liberty's in every blow!
Let us do or die!

Robert Burns (1759–96) Scottish poet and songwriter. Also known as 'Robert Bruce's March to Bannockburn'. 'Scots, Wha Hae' (1799)

9 There are two kinds of restrictions upon human liberty—the restraint of law and that of custom. No written law has ever been more binding than unwritten custom supported by popular opinion.

Carrie Chapman Catt (1859–1947) US women's rights campaigner and pacifist. Speech (February 1900), quoted in *History of Woman Suffrage* (Elizabeth C. Stanton, Susan B. Anthony, and Matilda J. Gage, eds.; 1902), vol. 4

10 The condition upon which God hath given liberty to man is eternal vigilance; which condition if he break, servitude is at once the consequence of his crime and the punishment of his guilt.

John Philpot Curran (1750–1817) Irish judge and orator. On the Right of Election of Lord Mayor. Speech, Dublin (July 10, 1790), quoted in *Speeches* (John Philpot Curran; 1808)

11 My government will protect all liberties but one—the liberty to do away with other liberties.

Gustavo Díaz Ordaz (1911–79) Mexican president. Inaugural speech as president (1964)

12 The price of Liberty is eternal vigilance.

Frederick Douglass (1817–95) US abolitionist, writer, and orator. *Douglass' Monthly* (January 1863)

13 The whole history of the progress of human liberty shows that all concessions yet made to her august claims have been born of earnest struggle.

Frederick Douglass (1817–95) US abolitionist, writer, and orator. Attrib. *The Meaning of History* (N. Gordon and Joyce Carper; 1991)

14 Climb ye the heights of liberty and cease not in well doing until you have planted the banner of the Red, the Black and the Green on the hilltops of Africa.

Marcus Garvey (1887–1940) Jamaican-born black nationalist leader and publisher. 1923. The Red, Black, and Green were the colours of Marcus Garvey's Back to Africa movement. Attrib.

15 I would remind you that extremism in the defence of liberty is no vice. And let me remind you also that moderation in the pursuit of justice is no virtue!

Barry Goldwater (1909–98) US politician. July 16, 1964. Acceptance speech for the Republican presidential nomination, San Francisco, *New York Times* (July 17, 1964)

16 Liberty of action, liberty of movement.

Jean-Claude-Marie-Vincent de Gournay (1712–59) French economist. He reputedly first used the phrase in an economic context. Speech (September 1758)

17 When the People contend for their Liberty, they seldom get anything by their Victory but new masters.

George Savile Halifax (1633–95) English statesman. 'Of Prerogative, Power and Liberty', *Political, Moral and Miscellaneous Thoughts and Reflections* (1750)

18 Liberty is so much latitude as the powerful choose to accord to the weak.

Learned Hand (1872–1961) US jurist. Address to University of Pennsylvania Law School (May 21, 1944)

19 The love of liberty is the love of others; the love of power is the love of ourselves.

William Hazlitt (1778–1830) British essayist and critic. 'Political Essays', *Times* (1819)

20 A just society would be one in which liberty for one person is constrained only by the demands created by equal liberty for another.

Ivan Illich (b. 1926) Austrian-born US educator and researcher. *Tools for Conviviality* (1973)

21 The tree of liberty must be refreshed from time to time with the blood of patriots and tyrants. It is its natural manure.

Thomas Jefferson (1743–1826) US president. Letter to William Stevens Smith (November 13, 1787)

22 It is true that liberty is precious—so precious that it must be rationed.

Vladimir Ilyich Lenin (1870–1924) Russian revolutionary leader. Attrib. *Soviet Communism* (Sidney and Beatrice Webb; 1936)

23 It is not our frowning battlements . . . or the strength of our gallant and disciplined army. These are not our reliance against a resumption of tyranny . . . Our defense is in the preservation of the spirit which prizes liberty as the heritage of all men, in all lands, everywhere.
Abraham Lincoln (1809–65) US president. Speech (September 11, 1858)

24 The Liberty of Man, in Society, is to be under no other Legislative Power, but that established by consent, in the Common-wealth, nor under the Domination of any Will, or Restraint of any Law, but what the Legislative shall enact, according to the trust put in it.
John Locke (1632–1704) English philosopher. *Two Treatises of Government* (1690)

25 Without dignity there is no liberty, without justice there is no dignity, and without independence there are no free men.
Patrice Lumumba (1925–61) Congolese prime minister. 1960. Letter to his wife, *Congo, My Country* (1962)

26 Liberty is won with the edge of the machete: it is not asked for. To beg for rights is the domain of cowards incapable of exercising these rights.
Antonio Maceo (1845–96) Cuban soldier and revolutionary leader. *Journal of the Knights of Labor* (November 5, 1896), quoted in *Antonio Maceo: The 'Bronze Titan' of Cuba's Struggle for Independence* (Philip S. Foner; 1977)

27 The liberty of the individual must be thus far limited; he must not make himself a nuisance to other people.
John Stuart Mill (1806–73) British philosopher and social reformer. *On Liberty* (1859), ch. 3

28 Yet know withal,
Since thy original lapse, true liberty
Is lost, which always with right reason dwells
Twinned, and from her hath no dividual being.
John Milton (1608–74) English writer. *Paradise Lost* (1667), bk. 12, ll. 82–85

29 Liberty is the right to do everything which the laws allow.
Montesquieu (1689–1755) French writer and jurist. *L'Esprit des Lois* (1748)

30 I sometimes think that the price of liberty is not so much eternal vigilance as eternal dirt.
George Orwell (1903–50) British writer. *The Road to Wigan Pier* (1937), ch. 4

31 Liberty is to Science what air is to the animal.
Jules Henri Poincaré (1854–1912) French mathematician and scientist. *Dernières Pensées* (1913), Appendix

32 Liberation will only arrive when the poor are the controllers of, and protagonists in, their own struggle and liberation.
Oscar Romero (1917–80) Salvadoran archbishop. Sermon, San Salvador (February 2, 1980), quoted in *The War of Gods* (Michael Löwy; 1996)

33 DUKE VINCENTIO Liberty plucks justice by the nose.
William Shakespeare (1564–1616) English poet and playwright. *Measure for Measure* (1604), Act 1, Scene 3

34 Liberty means responsibility. That is why most men dread it.
George Bernard Shaw (1856–1950) Irish playwright. Attrib.

35 Loss of liberty is a human disaster and to have liberty taken away is to be caught up in a process which, completed, encompasses the beginnings and ends of human life.
Song Lin (b. 1959) Chinese writer. 'Prison Letter' (1991)

36 The liberty the citizen enjoys is to be measured not by the governmental machinery he lives under, whether representative or other, but by the paucity of restraints it imposes on him.
Herbert Spencer (1820–1903) British philosopher. *The Man Versus the State* (1884)

37 Liberty is the right of any person to stand up anywhere and say anything whatsoever that everybody thinks.
Lincoln Steffens (1866–1936) US journalist. *Autobiography* (1931)

38 Europe made the revolution in order to conquer liberty, of which she was deprived. We, on the other hand, want to make it because we suffer from an excess of liberty.
Sun Yat-sen (1866–1925) Chinese revolutionary and nationalist leader. Quoted in *The Chinese* (Alain Peyrefitte; Graham Webb, tr.; 1977)

39 In overthrowing me, you have cut down in San Domingo only the trunk of the tree of liberty. It will spring up again by the roots for they are numerous and deep.
Toussaint L'Ouverture (1743–1803) Haitian revolutionary leader and general. June 1802. *The Black Jacobins* (C. L. R. James; 1938)

40 Liberty is the hardest test that one can inflict on a people. To know how to be free is not given equally to all men and all nations.
Paul Valéry (1871–1945) French poet and philosopher. 'On the Subject of Dictatorship', *Reflections on the World Today* (1933)

41 Liberty does not consist in mere declarations of the rights of man. It consists in the translation of those declarations into definite action.
Woodrow Wilson (1856–1924) US president. Speech (July 4, 1914)

42 Two voices are there; one is of the sea,
One of the mountains; each a mighty voice:
In both from age to age thou didst rejoice,
They were thy chosen music, Liberty!
William Wordsworth (1770–1850) English poet. 'Thought of a Briton on the Subjugation of Switzerland', *Poems in Two Volumes* (1807), vol. 1, ll. 1–4

Libraries

see also **Books, Knowledge, Learning, Research, University**

1 I keep my books at the British Museum and at Mudie's.
Samuel Butler (1835–1902) British writer and composer. The British Museum was, until 1998, the home of the British Library, and Mudie's was one of the main British subscription lending libraries towards the end of the 19th century. *The Humour of Homer, And Other Essays* (1913), 'Ramblings in Cheapside'

2 The true University of these days is a collection of books.
Thomas Carlyle (1795–1881) Scottish historian and essayist. 'The Hero as a Man of Letters', *On Heroes, Hero-Worship, and the Heroic in History* (1841)

3 A man will turn over half a library to make one book.
Samuel Johnson (1709–84) British lexicographer and writer. April 6, 1775. Quoted in *Life of Samuel Johnson* (James Boswell; 1791)

4 A library is thought in cold storage.
Herbert Samuel (1870–1963) British statesman and philosopher. *A Book of Quotations* (1947)

Life

see also **Being, Existence, Experience, Vitality**

1   The man who views the world at 50 the same as
    he did at 20 has wasted 30 years of his life.
    Muhammad Ali (b. 1942) US boxer. Interview, *Playboy* (November
    1975)

2   Life, the permission to know death.
    Djuna Barnes (1892–1982) US writer and illustrator. *Nightwood*
    (1936)

3   Your whole life is on the other side of the glass.
    And there is nobody watching.
    Alan Bennett (b. 1934) British playwright, actor, and director. *The Old
    Country* (1978), Act 1

4   A man of sixty has spent twenty years in bed and
    over three years eating.
    Arnold Bennett (1867–1931) British writer. *Bartlett's Unfamiliar
    Quotations* (Leonard Louis Levinson; 1972)

5   Life is a partial, continuous, progressive,
    multiform and conditionally interactive self-
    realization of the potentialities of atomic electron
    states.
    John Desmond Bernal (1901–71) Irish crystallographer. *The Origin of
    Life* (1967)

6   Life is the ensemble of functions that resist death.
    Marie François Bichat (1771–1802) French anatomist and physiologist.
    Recherches Physiologiques sur la Vie et la Mort (1800)

7   For everything that lives is holy, life delights in
    life.
    William Blake (1757–1827) British poet, painter, engraver, and mystic.
    America: A Prophecy (1793), pt. 8, l. 13

8   Life itself is but the shadow of death, and souls
    but the shadows of the living. All things fall
    under this name. The sun itself is but the dark
    simulacrum, and light but the shadow of God.
    Thomas Browne (1605–82) English physician and writer. *The Garden of
    Cyrus* (1658), ch. 4

9   Is life worth living? This is a question for an
    embryo, not for a man.
    Samuel Butler (1835–1902) British writer and composer. Quoted in
    Note Books (H. Festing Jones, ed.; 1912)

10 To live is like love, all reason is against it, and
    all healthy instinct for it.
    Samuel Butler (1835–1902) British writer and composer. Quoted in
    Note Books (H. Festing Jones, ed.; 1912)

11 Life is a dusty corridor, I say,
    Shut at both ends.
    Roy Campbell (1901–57) South African-born poet, translator, and
    journalist. *The Flaming Terrapin* (1924)

12 Life is a tragedy when seen in close-up, but a
    comedy in long-shot.
    Charlie Chaplin (1889–1977) British actor and director. *Guardian*
    (December 28, 1977), Obituary

13 One doesn't recognize in one's life the really
    important moments—not until it's too late.
    Agatha Christie (1890–1976) English novelist and playwright. *Endless
    Night* (1967), bk. 2, ch. 14

14 Life is a maze in which we take the wrong
    turning before we have learnt to walk.
    Cyril Connolly (1903–74) British writer and journalist. *The Unquiet
    Grave* (1944)

15 Men deal with life as children with their play,
    Who first misuse, then cast their toys away.
    William Cowper (1731–1800) British poet. 'Hope' (1782), ll. 127–128

16 Life was a funny thing that happened to me on
    the way to the grave.
    Quentin Crisp (1908–99) British writer. *The Naked Civil Servant*
    (1968)

17 Life is as the sea, art a ship in which man
    conquers life's crushing formlessness, reducing it
    to a course, a series of swells, tides and wind
    currents inscribed on a chart.
    Ralph Ellison (1914–94) US writer, jazz musician, and photographer.
    'Richard Wright's Blues', *Shadow and Act* (1964)

18 That was life, she said to herself. Be as cunning
    as a serpent and as harmless as a dove.
    Buchi Emecheta (b. 1944) Nigerian novelist and publisher. *Second-Class
    Citizen* (1974)

19 Life is a kiln in which one bakes one's
    experiences: some are taken out half done, some
    underdone and some undone.
    Nuruddin Farah (b. 1945) Somali novelist, playwright, and teacher.
    Sardines (1981)

20 As I get older I perceive
    Life has its tale in its mouth.
    Lawrence Ferlinghetti (b. 1919) US poet. 'Poet as Fisherman' (1988)

21 Life is a fatal complaint, and an eminently
    contagious one.
    Oliver Wendell Holmes (1841–1935) US judge. *The Poet at the
    Breakfast-Table* (1872), ch. 12

22 To live is to climb the Andes: the more one
    climbs, the steeper become the precipices.
    Eugenio María de Hostos (1839–1903) Puerto Rican educator, social
    reformer, and journalist. 'Hombres e Ideas', *Obras* (1939–54)

23 Life isn't all beer and skittles.
    Thomas Hughes (1822–96) British writer. *Tom Brown's Schooldays*
    (1857), pt. 1, ch. 2

24 Life exists in the universe only because the
    carbon atom possesses certain exceptional
    properties.
    James Jeans (1877–1946) British mathematician, physicist, and
    astronomer. *The Mysterious Universe* (1930), ch. 1

25 I do not cut my life up into days but my days
    into lives, each day, each hour, an entire life.
    Juan Ramón Jiménez (1881–1958) Spanish poet. 'Heroic Reason',
    Selected Writings (1957)

26 Every life is many days, day after day. We walk
    through ourselves, meeting robbers, ghosts,
    giants, old men, young men, wives, widows,
    brothers-in-love. But always meeting ourselves.
    James Joyce (1882–1941) Irish writer. *Ulysses* (1922)

27 A man's life of any worth is a continual allegory.
    John Keats (1795–1821) English poet. Letter to George and
    Georgiana Keats (February 18, 1819), quoted in *Letters of
    John Keats* (H. E. Rollins, ed.; 1958), vol. 2

28 There are only three events in a man's life; birth,
    life, and death; he is not conscious of being born,
    he dies in pain, and he forgets to live.
    Jean de La Bruyère (1645–96) French essayist and moralist. *Characters,
    or the Manners of the Age* (1688)

29 Life is what happens to you while you're busy
    making other plans.
    John Lennon (1940–80) British rock musician. 'Beautiful Boy' (1979)

30 While I thought that I was learning how to live, I
    have been learning how to die.
    Leonardo da Vinci (1452–1519) Italian artist, engineer, and inventor.
    Notebooks (1508–18), quoted in *Selections from the
    Notebooks of Leonardo da Vinci* (Irma A. Richter, ed.; 1952)

31 Life is so beautiful that the idea of death must itself arise first before it can be fulfilled.

Joaquim Maria Machado de Assis (1839–1908) Brazilian novelist and short-story writer. *Dom Casmurro* (1899)

32 I think if you have lived through a war
or have made your home in a country
not your own, of if you've learned to love one man,
then your life is a story.

Anne Michaels (b. 1958) Canadian poet and novelist. 'Blue Vigour', *Miner's Pond* (1991), ll. 1–5

33 The aim of life is to live, and to live means to be aware, joyously, drunkenly, serenely, divinely aware.

Henry Miller (1891–1980) US novelist. 'Creative Death', *The Wisdom of the Heart* (1941)

34 Life is a kind doctor who gives us death
in small daily doses
so that when at last, we drink
death's dark wine,
we have already tasted its bitterness.

Anna Sujartha Modayil (b. 1934) Indian poet. 'Stones', *The Voice of the Indian Poets* (Pranab Bandyopadhyay, ed.; 1975)

35 Life is a foreign language: all men mispronounce it.

Christopher Darlington Morley (1890–1957) US writer and journalist. *Thunder on the Left* (1925), ch. 14

36 Life is the only art that we are required to practice without preparation, and without being allowed the preliminary trials, the failures and botches, that are essential for training.

Lewis Mumford (1895–1990) US social philosopher and urban planner. Attrib.

37 The cradle rocks above an abyss, and common sense tells us that our existence is but a brief crack of light between two eternities of darkness.

Vladimir Nabokov (1899–1977) Russian-born US novelist, poet, and critic. *Speak, Memory* (1967)

38 Life is perhaps most wisely regarded as a bad dream between two awakenings and every day is a life in miniature.

Eugene O'Neill (1888–1953) US playwright. *Marco Millions* (1928)

39 In order to master the unruly torrent of life the learned man meditates, the poet quivers, and the political hero erects the fortress of his will.

José Ortega y Gasset (1883–1955) Spanish writer and philosopher. *Meditations on Quixote* (1914)

40 Life is the eternal text, the burning bush by the edge of the path from which God speaks.

José Ortega y Gasset (1883–1955) Spanish writer and philosopher. *Meditations on Quixote* (1914)

41 Life is our reaction to the basic insecurity which constitutes its substance.

José Ortega y Gasset (1883–1955) Spanish writer and philosopher. 'In Search of Goethe from Within', *Partisan Review* (December 1949)

42 Living is like working out one long addition sum, and if you make a mistake in the first two totals you will never find the right answer. It means involving oneself in a complicated chain of circumstances.

Cesare Pavese (1908–50) Italian novelist and poet. May 5, 1936. *The Burning Brand: Diaries 1935–50* (1952)

43 Life is full of infinite absurdities, which, strangely enough, do not even need to appear plausible, since they are true.

Luigi Pirandello (1867–1936) Italian dramatist, novelist, and short-story writer. *Six Characters in Search of an Author* (Edward Storer, tr.; 1921)

44 Like following life through creatures you dissect,
You lose it in the moment you detect.

Alexander Pope (1688–1744) English poet. *Moral Essays* (1735)

45 We spend our lives talking about this mystery: our life.

Jules Renard (1864–1910) French writer. April 1894. *Journal* (1877–1910)

46 To live is to be slowly born.

Antoine de Saint-Exupéry (1900–44) French writer and aviator. *Flight to Arras* (1942)

47 Life is not a spectacle or a feast; it is a predicament.

George Santayana (1863–1952) Spanish-born US philosopher, poet, and novelist. Quoted in *The Perpetual Pessimist* (Sagittarius and George; 1963)

48 It is only in the microscope that our life looks so big. It is an indivisible point, drawn out and magnified by the powerful lenses of Time and Space.

Arthur Schopenhauer (1788–1860) German philosopher. *Parerga and Paralipomena* (1851)

49 We begin in the madness of carnal desire and the transport of voluptuousness, we end in the dissolution of all our parts and the musty stench of corpses.

Arthur Schopenhauer (1788–1860) German philosopher. *Parerga and Paralipomena* (1851)

50 MACBETH Life's but a walking shadow, a poor player,
That struts and frets his hour upon the stage,
And then is heard no more; it is a tale
Told by an idiot, full of sound and fury,
Signifying nothing.

William Shakespeare (1564–1616) English poet and playwright. *Macbeth* (1606), Act 5, Scene 5

51 Life is a disease; and the only difference between one man and another is the stage of the disease at which he lives.

George Bernard Shaw (1856–1950) Irish playwright. 'Gospel of the Brothers Barnabas', *Back to Methuselah* (1921)

52 Life, like a dome of many-coloured glass,
Stains the white radiance of eternity.

Percy Bysshe Shelley (1792–1822) English poet. An elegy on the death of John Keats. *Adonais* (1821), st. 52

53 Living well and beautifully and justly are all one thing.

Socrates (470?–399? BC) Greek philosopher. 399? BC. Quoted in *Crito* (Plato)

54 Life is a gamble, at terrible odds—if it was a bet, you wouldn't take it.

Tom Stoppard (b. 1937) Czech-born British playwright and screenwriter. *Rosencrantz and Guildenstern Are Dead* (1966), Act 3

55 Life is an offensive, directed against the repetitive mechanism of the Universe.

A. N. Whitehead (1861–1947) British philosopher and mathematician. 1928. *Adventures of Ideas* (1933)

56 The life of man passes like a galloping horse, changing at every turn, at every hour. What should he do, or what should he not do, other than let his decomposition go on?

Zhuangzi (369?–286 BC) Chinese philosopher and teacher. 'Autumn Floods', quoted in *Chuang Tzu* (Herbert A. Giles, tr.; 1980), ch. 17

Light

see also **Darkness, Morning, The Sun**

1 Let there be light.
   Bible. Genesis, *Vulgate* (404?), 1:3

2 Water, glass, metal, match light in their raptures,
   Flashing their many answers to the one.
   What captures light belongs to what it captures:
   The whole side of a world facing the sun.
   Thom Gunn (b. 1929) British poet. 'Sunlight', *Moly* (1971)

3 Your voice of white fire
   in the universe of water, the ship, the sky,
   marking out the roads with delight,
   engraving for me with a blazing light my firm orbit.
   Juan Ramón Jiménez (1881–1958) Spanish poet. 'Full Consciousness',
   Roots and Wings: Poetry from Spain, 1900–75 (Hardie St.
   Martin, ed.; 1976)

4 'Tis not necessary to light a candle to the sun.
   Algernon Sidney (1622–83) English politician. *Discourses Concerning
   Government* (1698), ch. 2, pt. 23

5 Light breaks where no sun shines;
   Where no sea runs, the waters of the heart
   Push in their tides.
   Dylan Thomas (1914–53) Welsh poet, playwright, and short-story writer.
   'Light Breaks Where No Sun Shines', *18 Poems* (1934), ll. 1–3

Literacy

see also **Language, Reading, Writing**

1 To deliver the nation from illiteracy no other
   course is open than to abandon the Arabic
   letters . . . and to accept the Turkish letters,
   based on the Latin.
   Kemal Ataturk (1881–1938) Turkish statesman. Referring to the
   reform of the written language in Turkey after the abolition
   of the Sultanate in 1922. Statement (August 25, 1928)

2 In honest hands, literacy is the surest and the
   most effective means to true education. In
   dishonest hands, it may be a most dangerous, in
   fact a suicidal, acquisition.
   Obafemi Awolowo (1909–87) Nigerian lawyer and politician. *Voice of
   Reason: Selected Speeches of Chief Obafemi Awolowo* (1981),
   vol. 1

3 "Do you spell it with a 'V' or a 'W'?" inquired
   the judge. 'That depends upon the taste and
   fancy of the speller, my Lord', replied Sam.
   Charles Dickens (1812–70) British novelist. *The Pickwick Papers*
   (1837), ch. 34

4 A lonesome man on a rainy day who does not
   know how to read.
   Benjamin Franklin (1706–90) US statesman and scientist. On being
   asked what condition of man he considered the most pitiable.
   Wit, Wisdom and Foibles of the Great (C. A. Shriner; 1918)

5 Now I remember the name
   but have forgotten the flower.
   —The curse of literacy.
   Norman McCaig (1910–96) Scottish poet. '1,800 Feet Up' (1977)

6 The ratio of literacy to illiteracy is constant, but
   nowadays the illiterates can read and write.
   Alberto Moravia (1907–90) Italian novelist. *Observer* (October 14,
   1979)

7 He intended, he said, to devote the rest of his life
   to learning the remaining twenty-two letters of
   the alphabet.
   George Orwell (1903–50) British writer. Referring to Boxer, the farm
   horse. *Animal Farm* (1945), ch. 9

8 DOGBERRY To be a well-favoured man is the gift
   of fortune; but to write and read comes by
   nature.
   William Shakespeare (1564–1616) English poet and playwright. *Much
   Ado About Nothing* (1598–99), Act 3, Scene 3

Literary Insults

see also **Insults, Writers**

1 As a contribution to natural history, the work is
   negligible.
   Anonymous. Referring to Kenneth Grahame's *The Wind in the
   Willows* (1908). Book review, *Times Literary Supplement*
   (1908), quoted in *The Life of Kenneth Grahame* (Peter
   Morris Green; 1959)

2 The difference between genuine poetry and the
   poetry of Dryden, Pope, and all their school, is
   briefly this: their poetry is conceived and
   composed in their wits, genuine poetry is
   conceived and composed in the soul.
   Matthew Arnold (1822–88) British poet and critic. 'Thomas Gray',
   Essays in Criticism, Second Series (1888)

3 It is a pretty poem, Mr. Pope, but you must not
   call it Homer.
   Richard Bentley (1662–1742) English classical scholar. Referring to
   Alexander Pope's translation of the *Iliad*. Quoted in 'The Life
   of Pope', *The Works of Samuel Johnson* (Samuel Johnson;
   1787), vol. 4

4 That sovereign of insufferables.
   Ambrose Bierce (1842–1914?) US writer and journalist. Referring to
   Oscar Wilde. *Wasp* (1882)

5 Gibbon is an ugly, affected, disgusting fellow,
   and poisons our literary club for me. I class him
   among infidel wasps and venomous insects.
   James Boswell (1740–95) Scottish lawyer and biographer. Referring to
   Edward Gibbon. Diary entry (1779)

6 Miller is not really a writer but a non-stop talker
   to whom someone has given a typewriter.
   Gerald Brenan (1894–1987) Maltese-born British writer and novelist.
   Referring to Henry Miller. 'Literature', *Thoughts in a Dry
   Season* (1978)

7 I had not seen *Pride and Prejudice* till I read that
   sentence of yours, and then I got the book. And
   what did I find? An accurate daguerreotyped
   portrait of a commonplace face; a carefully
   fenced, highly cultivated garden, with neat
   borders and delicate flowers; but no glance of a
   bright, vivid physiognomy, no open country, no
   fresh air, no blue hill, no bonny beck. I should
   hardly like to live with her ladies and gentlemen,
   in their elegant but confined houses.
   Charlotte Brontë (1816–55) British novelist. Referring to Jane Austen.
   Letter to S. H. Lewes (January 12, 1848)

8 Listen, dear, you couldn't write fuck on a dusty
   venetian blind.
   Coral Browne (1913–91) Australian-born actor. Said to a Hollywood
   writer who had criticized the playwright Alan Bennett.
   Sunday Times Magazine (1984)

9 The book, when it came out in 1965, was
   considered an instant classic, largely because
   Capote told everyone it was.
   Bill Bryson (b. 1951) US writer. Referring to Truman Capote's *In
   Cold Blood* (1965). *The Lost Continent* (1989), ch. 20

10 An inspired idiot.
    George Byng (1663–1733) English admiral. Referring to Oliver
    Goldsmith. Attrib.

11 Let simple Wordsworth chime his childish verse,
And brother Coleridge lull the babe at nurse.

Lord Byron (1788–1824) British poet. Referring to Samuel Taylor Coleridge and William Wordsworth. 'English Bards and Scotch Reviewers' (1809), ll. 917–918

12 That's not writing, that's typing.

Truman Capote (1924–84) US novelist. Referring to Jack Kerouac's novel *On the Road*. Attrib.

13 A crawling and disgusting parasite, a base scoundrel, and pander to unnatural passions.

William Cobbett (1763–1835) British writer, journalist, and reformer. Referring to Virgil. Attrib.

14 He could not blow his nose without moralising on the state of the handkerchief industry.

Cyril Connolly (1903–74) British writer and journalist. Referring to George Orwell. *The Evening Colonnade* (1973)

15 He seems to me the most *vulgar-minded* genius that ever produced a great effect in literature.

George Eliot (1819–80) British novelist. Referring to Lord Byron. Letter (September 21, 1869)

16 Henry James has a mind so fine that no idea could violate it.

T. S. Eliot (1888–1965) US-born British poet and playwright. Attrib.

17 Mr. Huxley is perhaps one of those people who have to perpetrate thirty bad novels before producing a good one.

T. S. Eliot (1888–1965) US-born British poet and playwright. Referring to Aldous Huxley. Attrib.

18 Miss Austen's novels . . . seem to me vulgar in tone, sterile in artistic invention, imprisoned in the wretched conventions of English society, without genius, wit, or knowledge of the world. Never was life so pinched and narrow. The one problem in the mind of the writer . . . is marriageableness.

Ralph Waldo Emerson (1803–82) US poet and essayist. 1866. Referring to Jane Austen. *Journals* (1860–66)

19 Henry James was one of the nicest old ladies I ever met.

William Faulkner (1897–1962) US novelist. Quoted in *The Battle and the Books: Some Aspects of Henry James* (Edward Stone; 1964)

20 He has never been known to use a word that might send a reader to the dictionary.

William Faulkner (1897–1962) US novelist. Referring to Ernest Hemingway. Attrib.

21 Lunched with Pinker to meet D. H. Lawrence, that provincial genius. Interesting, but a type I could not get on with. Obsessed with self. Dead eyes, and a red beard, long pale narrow face. A strange bird.

John Galsworthy (1867–1933) British novelist and playwright. Quoted in *The Life and Letters of John Galsworthy* (H. V. Marrot; 1935)

22 He writes indexes to perfection.

Oliver Goldsmith (1730–74) Irish-born British novelist, playwright, and poet. *A Citizen of the World* (1762), Letter 29

23 He never hit a ball out of the infield in his life.

Ernest Hemingway (1899–1961) US writer. 1950. Referring to T. S. Eliot in a letter. 'The Pastime and the Literati', *New York Times* (April 8, 1981)

24 He likes to look on the bile when it is black.

Aldous Huxley (1894–1963) British novelist and essayist. Referring to T. S. Eliot. Quoted in *Ambrosia and Small Beer* (Edward Marsh; 1964)

25 He has a gross and repulsive face but appears *bon enfant* when you talk to him. But he is the dullest Briton of them all.

Henry James (1843–1916) US-born British writer and critic. Referring to Anthony Trollope. Letter to his family (November 1, 1875)

26 He was imperfect, unfinished, inartistic; he was worse than provincial—he was parochial.

Henry James (1843–1916) US-born British writer and critic. Referring to Henry David Thoreau. *Hawthorne* (1879), ch. 4

27 At his worst he is a sort of *idiot savant* of language.

Randall Jarrell (1914–65) US author and poet. 1940. Referring to Dylan Thomas. 'Poetry in a Dry Season', *Kipling, Auden, & Co.: Essays and Reviews, 1935–64* (1981)

28 It is burning a farthing candle at Dover, to shew light at Calais.

Samuel Johnson (1709–84) British lexicographer and writer. Referring to the impact of Richard Brinsley Sheridan's works upon the English language. Quoted in *Life of Samuel Johnson* (James Boswell; 1791)

29 He was dull in a new way, and that made many people think him *great*.

Samuel Johnson (1709–84) British lexicographer and writer. March 28, 1775. Referring to the poet Thomas Gray. Quoted in *Life of Samuel Johnson* (James Boswell; 1791)

30 They are forced plants, raised in a hot-bed; and they are poor plants; they are but cucumbers after all.

Samuel Johnson (1709–84) British lexicographer and writer. 1780. Referring to the poet Thomas Gray's *Odes*. Quoted in *Life of Samuel Johnson* (James Boswell; 1791)

31 Sir, there is no settling the point of precedency between a louse and a flea.

Samuel Johnson (1709–84) British lexicographer and writer. 1783. Said when Maurice Morgann asked him who he considered to be the better poet—Christopher Smart or Samuel Derrick. Quoted in *Life of Samuel Johnson* (James Boswell; 1791)

32 They sway'd about upon a rocking horse,
And thought it Pegasus.

John Keats (1795–1821) English poet. 1817. Referring to the Augustan poets, including Alexander Pope. 'Sleep and Poetry' (1820), l. 186

33 Mad, bad, and dangerous to know.

Caroline Lamb (1785–1828) British novelist. Her impression of Lord Byron when first meeting him in March 1812. *Journal* (1812)

34 My God, what a clumsy *olla putrida* James Joyce is! Nothing but old fags and cabbage stumps of quotations from the Bible and the rest, stewed in the juice of deliberate, journalistic dirty-mindedness.

D. H. Lawrence (1885–1930) British writer. Letter to Aldous Huxley (August 15, 1928)

35 So you're the little woman who wrote the book that made this great war!

Abraham Lincoln (1809–65) US president. Said on meeting Harriet Beecher Stowe, the author of *Uncle Tom's Cabin* (1852), which stimulated opposition to slavery before the American Civil War. Remark (1860?), quoted in *Abraham Lincoln: The War Years* (Carl Sandburg; 1936), vol. 2, ch. 39

36 There comes Poe, with his raven, like Barnaby Rudge,
Three fifths of him genius and two fifths sheer fudge.

James Russell Lowell (1819–91) US poet, editor, essayist, and diplomat. Referring to Edgar Allan Poe's poem 'The Raven' (1845). 'Poe', *A Fable for Critics* (1848), quoted in *The Penguin Book of American Verse* (Geoffrey Moore, ed.; 1977)

37 His imagination resembled the wings of an ostrich. It enabled him to run, though not to soar.

Thomas Babington Macaulay (1800–59) British politician, historian, and writer. 1828. Referring to John Dryden. 'On John Dryden', *Essays Contributed to the Edinburgh Review* (1843)

38 From the moment I picked up your book until I laid it down, I was convulsed with laughter. Some day I intend reading it.

Groucho Marx (1895–1977) US comedian and film actor. Quoted in *The Last Laugh* (S. J. Perelman; 1981)

39 Mr. Waugh, I always feel, is an antique in search of a period, a snob in search of a class, perhaps even a mystic in search of a beatific vision.

Malcolm Muggeridge (1903–90) British journalist. Referring to Evelyn Waugh. *The Most of Malcolm Muggeridge* (1966)

40 Poor Knight! he really had two periods, the first—a dull man writing broken English, the second—a broken man writing dull English.

Vladimir Nabokov (1899–1977) Russian-born US novelist, poet, and critic. *The Real Life of Sebastian Knight* (1941), ch. 1

41 He was retiring and yet craved to be seen, he was sincerely shy and naively exhibitionist. He had to rise above others and then humble himself, and in his self-inflicted humiliation demonstrate his superiority.

Lewis Bernstein Namier (1888–1960) Polish-born British educator and historian. Referring to T. E. Lawrence. Quoted in *T. E. Lawrence by His Friends* (A. W. Lawrence, ed.; 1937)

42 Emerson is one who lives instinctively on ambrosia—and leaves everything indigestible on his plate.

Friedrich Wilhelm Nietzsche (1844–1900) German philosopher and poet. Referring to Ralph Waldo Emerson. Attrib.

43 English literature's performing flea.

Sean O'Casey (1880–1964) Irish playwright. Referring to P. G. Wodehouse. Attrib.

44 This is not a novel to be tossed aside lightly. It should be thrown with great force.

Dorothy Parker (1893–1967) US writer and wit. Book review. Quoted in *Wit's End: Days and Nights of the Algonquin Round Table* (James R. Gaines; 1977)

45 To speak algebraically, Mr. M. is execrable, but Mr. C. is (x + 1)-ecrable.

Edgar Allan Poe (1809–49) US poet and writer. Referring to the writers Cornelius Mathews and William Ellery Channing. Quoted in *Mathematical Maxims and Minims* (N. Rose; 1988)

46 Mr. Wordsworth, a stupid man, with a decided gift for portraying nature in vignettes, never yet ruined anyone's morals, unless, perhaps, he has driven some susceptible persons to crime in a very fury of boredom.

Ezra Pound (1885–1972) US poet, translator, and critic. *Future* (November 1917)

47 I remember coming across him at the Grand Canyon and finding him peevish, refusing to admire it or even look at it properly. He was jealous of it.

J. B. Priestley (1894–1984) British writer. Referring to George Bernard Shaw. *Thoughts in the Wilderness* (1957)

48 His excessive emphasis on sex was due to the fact that in sex alone he was compelled to admit that he was not the only human being in the universe.

Bertrand Russell (1872–1970) British philosopher and mathematician. Referring to D. H. Lawrence. *The Autobiography of Bertrand Russell* (1967–69)

49 Waldo is one of those people who would be enormously improved by death.

Saki (1870–1916) British short-story writer. Referring to Ralph Waldo Emerson. 'The Feast of Nemesis', *Beasts and Super Beasts* (1914)

50 Sherard Blaw, the dramatist who had discovered himself, and who had given so ungrudgingly of his discovery to the world.

Saki (1870–1916) British short-story writer. Referring to George Bernard Shaw. *The Unbearable Bassington* (1912), ch. 13

51 I enjoyed talking to her, but thought *nothing* of her writing. I considered her 'a beautiful little knitter'.

Edith Sitwell (1887–1964) British poet, critic, and writer. Referring to Virginia Woolf. Letter to Geoffrey Singleton (July 11, 1955), quoted in *Selected Letters* (John Lehmann and Derek Palmer, eds.; 1970)

52 Two voices are there: one is of the deep . . .
And one is of an old half-witted sheep . . .
And, Wordsworth, both are thine.

James Kenneth Stephen (1859–92) British writer. 'A Sonnet', *Lapsus Calami* (1891)

53 Will there never come a season
Which shall rid us from the curse
Of a prose which knows no reason
And an unmelodious verse?
When there stands a muzzled stripling,
Mute, beside a muzzled bore:
When the Rudyards cease from Kipling
And the Haggards Ride no more.

James Kenneth Stephen (1859–92) British writer. Referring to Rudyard Kipling and H. Rider Haggard. 'To R. K.', *Lapsus Calami* (1891)

54 A monster gibbering, shrieking and gnashing imprecations against mankind.

William Makepeace Thackeray (1811–63) British novelist. Referring to Jonathan Swift. Attrib.

55 Wordsworth was a tea-time bore . . . the platitudinary reporter of Nature in his dullest moods. Open him at any page: and there lies the English language not, as George Moore said of Pater, in a glass coffin, but in a large, sultry, and unhygienic box.

Dylan Thomas (1914–53) Welsh poet, playwright, and short-story writer. Referring to William Wordsworth. Attrib.

56 All right, then, I'll say it: Dante makes me sick.

Lope de Vega (1562–1635) Spanish playwright and poet. 1635. Said on being informed he was about to die. Attrib.

57 Every other inch a gentleman.

Rebecca West (1892–1983) Irish-born British novelist, critic, and journalist. Referring to the writer Michael Arlen. Quoted in *Rebecca West* (Victoria Glendinning; 1987), pt. 3, ch. 5

58 Mr Bernard Shaw has no enemies but is intensely disliked by all his friends.

Oscar Wilde (1854–1900) Irish poet, playwright, and wit. Quoted in *Sixteen Self Sketches* (George Bernard Shaw; 1949), ch. 17

59 Trivial personalities decomposing in the eternity of print.

Virginia Woolf (1882–1941) British novelist and critic. Referring to *Jane Eyre* by Charlotte Brontë. 'Jane Eyre', *The Common Reader: First Series* (1925)

60 He is not a proper person to be admitted into respectable society, being the most perverse and malevolent creature that ill-luck has thrown my way.

William Wordsworth (1770–1850) English poet. Referring to William Hazlitt. Letter to B. R. Landon (April 1817)

61 But was there ever dog that praised his fleas?

W. B. Yeats (1865–1939) Irish poet and playwright. April 1909. 'To a Poet Who Would Have Me Praise Certain Bad Poets, Imitators of His and Mine', *The Green Helmet and Other Poems* (1910), l. 4

62 I see a schoolboy when I think of him,
With face and nose pressed to a sweetshop window.

W. B. Yeats (1865–1939) Irish poet and playwright. Referring to John Keats, and questioning what lay behind his 'deliberate happiness'. 'Ego Dominus Tuus', *The Wild Swans at Coole* (1919), ll. 55–56

Literary Style

see also **Poetry, Style, Writing**

1 Style, like sheer silk, too often hides eczema.

Albert Camus (1913–60) Algerian-born French novelist, essayist, and playwright. *The Fall* (1956)

2 A very simple way of saying complicated things.

Jean Cocteau (1889–1963) French film director, novelist, and playwright. A definition of style. *Le Secret Professionnel* (1924)

3 An author arrives at a good style when his language performs what is required of it without shyness.

Cyril Connolly (1903–74) British writer and journalist. *Enemies of Promise* (1938), ch. 3

4 I seek a form that my style cannot discover, a bud of thought that wants to be a rose; it is heralded by a kiss that is placed on my lips in the impossible embrace of the Venus de Milo.

Rubén Darío (1867–1916) Nicaraguan poet, journalist, and diplomat. 'Yo Persigo una Forma . . . ', *Prosas Profanas* (1896)

5 The literature which called itself 'realistic' was just as formalized and imaginary as the bucolic romances of the eighteenth century.

Vasily Grossman (1905–64) Russian writer. Referring to Socialist Realism. *Forever Flowing* (Thomas P. Whitney, tr.; 1970), ch. 11

6 Does he really think big emotions come from big words? He thinks I don't know the ten-dollar words . . . there are older and simpler and better words, and those are the ones I use.

Ernest Hemingway (1899–1961) US writer. In response to William Faulkner's jibe: 'He has never been known to use a word that might send a reader to the dictionary'. Quoted in *Papa Hemingway* (A. E. Hotchner; 1966), pt. 1, ch. 4

7 The pastoral is an aesthetic category for aristocrats and city folk, not for stable hands.

Miroslav Holub (1923–98) Czech poet and immunologist. 'By Nature Alone', *Shedding Life* (1997)

8 A good stylist should have a narcissistic enjoyment as he works. He must be able to objectivize his work to such an extent that he catches himself feeling envious . . . In short, he must display that highest degree of objectivity which the world calls vanity.

Karl Kraus (1874–1936) Austrian writer. 1909. Quoted in 'Sprüche und Widersprüche', *Karl Kraus* (Harry Zohn; 1971)

9 Poor style reflects imperfect thought.

Jules Renard (1864–1910) French writer. 1898. *Journal* (1877–1910)

10 One must be absolutely modern.

Arthur Rimbaud (1854–91) French poet. 'Adieu', *Une Saison en Enfer* (1873)

11 I depict men as they ought to be, but Euripides portrays them as they are.

Sophocles (496?–406? BC) Greek playwright. Quoted in *Poetics* (Aristotle; 340? BC)

12 Proper words in proper places, make the true definition of a style.

Jonathan Swift (1667–1745) Irish writer and clergyman. 'Letter to a Young Gentleman Lately Entered into Holy Orders' (January 9, 1720)

13 I will not have in my writing any elegance, or effect . . . to hang in the way between me and the rest like curtains . . . What I tell I tell for precisely what it is.

Walt Whitman (1819–92) US poet. *Leaves of Grass* (1855), Preface

14 Writers can't back off from realism, just as an ambitious engineer cannot back off from electricity.

Tom Wolfe (b. 1930) US journalist and novelist. *US News and World Report* (November 23, 1987)

Literature

see also **American Literature, Books, European Literature, Fiction, World Literature, Writing**

1 A literary movement: five or six people who live in the same town and hate each other.

Æ (George William Russell; 1867–1935) Irish poet. 1984. Attrib.

2 The story is a piece of work. The novel is a way of life.

Toni Cade Bambara (1939–95) US novelist, short-story writer, and educator. 'What It Is I Think I'm Doing Anyhow', *The Writer on Her Work* (Janet Sternburg, ed.; 1981), vol. 1

3 In the novel as in literature as a whole, the problem is how to invent; above all how to invent characters who have life.

Pío Baroja (1872–1956) Basque writer. Quoted in *The Spanish Avant-Garde* (Derek Harris; 1995)

4 Our literature is characterized by the pitiless divorce between the producer of the text and its user, between its owner and its customer, between its author and its reader.

Roland Barthes (1915–80) French philosopher and writer. *S/Z* (Richard Miller, tr.; 1990)

5 We know now that a text consists not of a line of words, releasing a single 'theological' meaning (the 'message' of the Author-God), but of a multi-dimensional space in which are married and contested several writings.

Roland Barthes (1915–80) French philosopher and writer. Posthumously published. *The Rustle of Language* (Richard Howard, tr.; 1984)

6 Where is the Proust of Papua? When the Zulus have a Tolstoy, we will read him.

Saul Bellow (b. 1915) Canadian-born US writer. *Harper's Magazine* (November 1994)

7 A losing trade, I assure you, sir: literature is a drug.

George Henry Borrow (1803–81) British writer and traveller. *Lavengro* (1851), ch. 30

8 In real life, of course, it is the hare who wins. Every time. Look around you. And in any case it is my contention that Aesop was writing for the tortoise market . . . Hares have no time to read. They are too busy winning the game.

Anita Brookner (b. 1928) British novelist and art historian. *Hotel du Lac* (1984)

9 Literature is never the product of a single subject. There are always at least three actors: the hand that writes, the voice that speaks, the god who watches over and compels.

Roberto Calasso, Italian writer. *Literature and the Gods* (Tim Parks, tr.; 2001)

10 The gods are fugitive guests of literature. They cross it with the trail of their names and are soon gone. Every time the writer sets down a word, he must fight to win them back.

Roberto Calasso, Italian writer. *Literature and the Gods* (Tim Parks, tr.; 2001)

11 The things that the novel does not say are necessarily more numerous than those it does say and only a special halo around what is written can give the illusion that you are reading also what is not written.

Italo Calvino (1923–85) Cuban-born Italian novelist and short-story writer. *If on a Winter's Night a Traveller* (William Weaver, tr.; 1979), ch. 10

12 All literature wavers between nature and paradise and loves to mistake one for the other.

Elias Canetti (1905–94) Bulgarian-born writer. *The Agony of Flies* (1992)

13 Literary men are . . . a perpetual priesthood

Thomas Carlyle (1795–1881) Scottish historian and essayist. 'The State of German Literature', *Critical and Miscellaneous Essays* (1838)

14 No literature can outdo the cynicism of real life; you won't intoxicate with one glass someone who has already drunk up a whole barrel.

Anton Chekhov (1860–1904) Russian playwright and short-story writer. Letter (1887)

15 A good novel tells us the truth about its hero; but a bad novel tells us the truth about its author.

G. K. Chesterton (1874–1936) British writer and poet. *Heretics* (1905), ch. 15

16 Literature is the art of writing something that will be read twice; journalism what will be grasped at once.

Cyril Connolly (1903–74) British writer and journalist. *Enemies of Promise* (1938), ch. 3

17 A work that aspires, however humbly, to the condition of art should carry its justification in every line.

Joseph Conrad (1857–1924) Polish-born British novelist. *The Nigger of the Narcissus* (1897), Preface

18 The unusual is only found in a very small percentage, except in literary creations, and that is exactly what makes literature.

Julio Cortázar (1914–84) Argentinian writer. *The Winners* (1960), ch. 31

19 Historians of literature like to regard a century as a series of ten faces, each grimacing in a different way.

Richard Ellmann (1918–87) US literary critic. Quoted in *New York Times* (February 5, 1967)

20 There shouldn't be opposition between the classical Canon and the multicultural cause. Historically, things have always changed.

James Fenton (b. 1949) British poet. *Independent* (November 21, 1994)

21 Yes—oh dear, yes—the novel tells a story.

E. M. Forster (1879–1970) British novelist. *Aspects of the Novel* (1927), ch. 2

22 Literature is a world that we try to build up and enter at the same time.

Northrop Frye (1912–91) Canadian academic. 'The Motive for Metaphor', *The Educated Imagination* (1964)

23 Ultimately, literature is nothing but carpentry. With both you are working with reality, a material just as hard as wood.

Gabriel García Márquez (b. 1928) Colombian novelist. Quoted in *Writers at Work* (George Plimpton, ed.; 1985)

24 He knew everything about literature except how to enjoy it.

Joseph Heller (1923–99) US novelist. *Catch-22* (1961), ch. 8

25 That was the chief difference between literature and life. In books, the proportion of exceptional to commonplace people is high; in reality, very low.

Aldous Huxley (1894–1963) British novelist and essayist. *Eyeless in Gaza* (1936)

26 Literature flourishes best when it is half a trade and half an art.

William Ralph Inge (1860–1954) British churchman. 'The Victorian Age' (1922)

27 It takes a great deal of history to produce a little literature.

Henry James (1843–1916) US-born British writer and critic. *Hawthorne* (1879), ch. 1

28 Literature is a state of culture, poetry is a state of grace, before and after culture.

Juan Ramón Jiménez (1881–1958) Spanish poet. 'Poetry and Literature', *Selected Writings* (1957)

29 What a man most wishes to hide, revise, and unsay, is precisely what literature is waiting and bleeding for. Every doctor knows, every Prophet knows the convulsion of truth.

Jack Kerouac (1922–69) US writer. Letter to Malcolm Cowley, *Selected Letters 1940–56* (Ann Cowley, ed.; 1996)

30 In the beginning was the review copy, and a man received it from the publisher. Then he wrote a review. Then he wrote a book which the publisher accepted and sent on to someone else as a review copy. The man who received it did likewise. This is how modern literature came into being.

Karl Kraus (1874–1936) Austrian writer. 1909. Quoted in 'Sprüche und Widersprüche', *Karl Kraus* (Harry Zohn; 1971)

31 The novel's spirit is the spirit of complexity. Every novel says to the reader 'Things are not as simple as you think'.

Milan Kundera (b. 1929) Czech novelist. *The Art of the Novel* (1986)

32 The classics are only primitive literature. They belong in the same class as primitive machinery and primitive music and primitive medicine.

Stephen Leacock (1869–1944) British-born Canadian writer and economist. 'Homer and Humbug', *Behind the Beyond* (1913)

33 Literature is mostly about having sex and not much about having children; life is the other way round.

David Lodge (b. 1935) British novelist and critic. *The British Museum is Falling Down* (1965), ch. 4

34 Suddenly I realized this literary stuff doesn't just come out of a hat. It has a mechanism which you can take apart like a watch.

David Lodge (b. 1935) British novelist and critic. *Times Educational Supplement* (May 18, 1990)

35 You understand *Epipsychidion* best when you are in love; *Don Juan* when anger is subsiding into indifference. Why not Strindberg when you have a temperature?

Desmond MacCarthy (1878–1952) British poet and writer. Referring to the works of Percy Bysshe Shelley, Lord Byron, and August Strindberg. 'Miss Julie and the Pariah', *Theatre* (1954)

36 In those days modern literature (like 'creative writing') was not taught in school *or* in college . . . As with Prohibition liquor, you had to know somebody to get hold of the good stuff. Professional librarians were no help.
Mary McCarthy (1912–89) US writer. *How I Grew* (1986), ch. 2

37 Every man with a belly full of the classics is an enemy to the human race.
Henry Miller (1891–1980) US novelist. 'Dijon', *Tropic of Cancer* (1934)

38 Great works of literature, perhaps the greatest— the Oresteia, Hamlet, even the Bible—have been stories of mystery and crime.
John Mortimer (b. 1923) British lawyer, novelist, and playwright. *Sunday Times* (April 1, 1990)

39 Literature and butterflies are the two sweetest passions known to man.
Vladimir Nabokov (1899–1977) Russian-born US novelist, poet, and critic. *Radio Times* (October 1962)

40 Literature is the honey of a nation's soul, preserved for her children to taste forever, a little at a time!
Ngugi wa Thiongo (b. 1938) Kenyan writer. *Devil on the Cross* (1982)

41 A novel is a river, but a short story is a glass of water. A novel is a forest, but the short story is a seed. It is more atomic. The atom may contain the secret structures of the universe.
Ben Okri (b. 1959) Nigerian novelist, short-story writer, and poet. Quoted in *Talking with African Writers* (Jane Wilkinson; 1992)

42 A novel can be approached in two ways: either by studying the image represented by the artist . . . or by studying life itself.
Benito Pérez Galdós (1843–1920) Spanish novelist and playwright. 'Present Day Society as Material for the Novel' (1897)

43 True ease in writing comes from art, not chance, As those move easiest who have learn'd to dance. 'Tis not enough no harshness gives offence, The sound must seem an echo to the sense.
Alexander Pope (1688–1744) English poet. *An Essay on Criticism* (1711), ll. 362–365

44 Literature is news that STAYS news.
Ezra Pound (1885–1972) US poet, translator, and critic. *ABC of Reading* (1934), ch. 1

45 Great Literature is simply language charged with meaning to the utmost possible degree.
Ezra Pound (1885–1972) US poet, translator, and critic. *How to Read* (1931), pt. 2

46 Make way, you Roman writers, make way, Greeks! Something greater than the *Iliad* is born.
Sextus Propertius (50?–15? BC) Roman poet. Referring to Virgil's *Aeneid*. *Elegies* (1st century BC), bk. 2, no. 34

47 It would be stretching the point to claim the Odyssey and the Book of Exodus as early travel books; but they help to underline the fact that as long as narrative literature has existed, it has taken the form of a journey, real or imagined, or . . . partly reported and partly invented.
Jonathan Raban (b. 1942) British author. 1991. Quoted in *Writers Abroad* (The British Council; 1992)

48 Your true lover of literature is never fastidious.
Robert Southey (1774–1843) English poet and writer. *The Doctor* (1812), ch. 17

49 A novel is a mirror which passes over a highway. Sometimes it reflects to your eyes the blue of the skies, at others the churned-up mud of the road.
Stendhal (1783–1842) French writer. *The Red and the Black* (1830), bk. 2, ch. 19

50 Something that everybody wants to have read and nobody wants to read.
Mark Twain (1835–1910) US writer and humorist. Definition of a literary classic. *New York Journal* (November 20, 1900)

51 The novel being dead, there is no point to writing made-up stories. Look at the French who will not and the Americans who cannot.
Gore Vidal (b. 1925) US novelist and essayist. *Myra Breckinridge* (1968), ch. 2

52 I am tired of words, and literature is an old couch stuffed with fleas, of culture stuffed in the taxidermist's hides.
Derek Walcott (b. 1930) St. Lucian poet and playwright. 'North and South', *The Fortunate Traveller* (1982)

53 All my novels are an accumulation of detail. I'm a bit of a bower-bird.
Patrick White (1912–90) British-born Australian novelist. *Southerly: The Magazine of the Australian English Association*, attrib.

54 Literature is strewn with the wreckage of men who have minded beyond reason the opinions of others.
Virginia Woolf (1882–1941) British novelist and critic. *A Room of One's Own* (1929)

London

see **British Cities**

Loneliness

see also **The Self**, **Solitude**

1 Alone, alone, all, all alone, Alone on a wide wide sea! And never a saint took pity on My soul in agony.
Samuel Taylor Coleridge (1772–1834) British poet. 'The Rime of the Ancient Mariner', *Lyrical Ballads* (1798), pt. 4

2 Loneliness seems to have become the great American disease.
John Corry, US writer. *New York Times* (April 25, 1984)

3 Lone goose, not drinking or pecking for food, it cries out in flight, voice yearns for the flock.
Du Fu (712–770) Chinese poet. 'Lone Wild Goose' (8th century), quoted in *An Anthology of Chinese Literature* (Stephen Owen, tr.; 1996)

4 The deepest need of man is the need to overcome his separateness, to leave the prison of his aloneness.
Erich Fromm (1900–80) German-born US psychoanalyst and philosopher. *The Art of Loving* (1956)

5 To feel completely alone and isolated leads to mental disintegration just as physical starvation leads to death.
Erich Fromm (1900–80) German-born US psychoanalyst and philosopher. *The Fear of Freedom* (1942)

6 In despair as in love, we are above all else, alone.
Marita Golden (b. 1950) US writer and teacher. *A Woman's Place* (1986)

7 Pray that your loneliness may spur you into finding something to live for, great enough to die for.
Dag Hammarskjöld (1905–61) Swedish statesman and diplomat. *Markings* (Leif Sjöberg and W. H. Auden, trs.; 1964)

8 You'll Never Walk Alone

Oscar Hammerstein II (1895–1960) US lyricist and librettist. Song title. *Carousel* (music by Richard Rodgers; 1945)

9 I remember my grandfather telling me how each of us must live with a full measure of loneliness that is inescapable, and we must not destroy ourselves with our passion to escape this aloneness.

Jim Harrison (b. 1937) US novelist and screenwriter. *Dalva* (1989)

10 It's probably a reflection of my own, if I may say, loneliness . . . It could be the whole human condition.

Edward Hopper (1882–1967) US painter. Referring to his paintings, many of which depict stark, lonely scenes. Quoted in *Washington Post* (June 25, 1995)

11 So lonely am I
My body is a floating weed
Severed at the roots.
Were there water to entice me,
I would follow it, I think.

Komachi (834–880) Japanese poet. *Kokinshu* (9th century), quoted in *Anthology of Japanese Literature* (Donald Keene, ed.; 1968)

12 Waits at the window, wearing the face that she keeps in a jar by the door.
Who is it for? All the lonely people, where do they all come from?
All the lonely people, where do they all belong?

Lennon & McCartney, British rock musicians. Song lyric. 'Eleanor Rigby' (1966)

13 Can you say over and over again
'Love', till its incantation makes us
Forget how much we are alone?

Norman McCaig (1910–96) Scottish poet. 'After' (1955)

14 I grow lean
in loneliness,
like a water lily
gnawed by a beetle.

Kaccipettu Nannakaiyar (*fl.* 3rd century) Indian poet. *Interior Landscape: Love Poems from a Tamil Anthology* (A. K. Ramanujan, ed.; 1967)

15 No man is born unto himself alone;
Who lives unto himself, he lives to none.

Francis Quarles (1592–1644) English poet. *Esther* (1621), sect. 1, Meditation 1

16 My heart is a lonely hunter that hunts on a lonely hill.

William Sharp (1856–1905) Scottish poet and writer. 1896. 'The Lonely Hunter', *Poems and Dramas by 'Fiona MacLeod'* (1910), st. 6

17 Don't think you can frighten me by telling me I am alone. France is alone; and God is alone; and what is my loneliness before the loneliness of my country and my God?

George Bernard Shaw (1856–1950) Irish playwright. *Saint Joan* (1924)

18 My living in Yorkshire was so far out of the way, that it was actually twelve miles from a lemon.

Sydney Smith (1771–1845) British clergyman, essayist, and wit. Quoted in *A Memoir of the Rev. Sydney Smith* (Lady Holland; 1855), vol. 1, ch. 9

19 Language has created the word loneliness to express the pain of being alone, and the word solitude to express the glory of being alone.

Paul Tillich (1886–1965) German-born US theologian and philosopher. 'Loneliness and Solitude', *The Eternal Now* (1963)

Longevity

see also **Immortality, Old Age**

1 And all the days of Methuselah were nine hundred sixty and nine years: and he died.

Bible. Genesis, *King James Bible* (1611), 5:27

2 LONGEVITY, n. Uncommon extension of the fear of death.

Ambrose Bierce (1842–1914?) US writer and journalist. *The Devil's Dictionary* (1911)

3 If I'd known I was gonna live this long, I'd have taken better care of myself.

Eubie Blake (1883–1983) US pianist and composer. *Observer* (February 13, 1983), 'Sayings of the Week'

4 God has forgotten me.

Jeanne Calment (1875–1997) French citizen. Referring to her long life (she was 120 at the time). *Daily Telegraph* (October 1995)

5 Longevity is the revenge of talent upon genius.

Cyril Connolly (1903–74) British writer and journalist. *Sunday Times* (June 19, 1966)

6 Have a chronic disease and take care of it.

Oliver Wendell Holmes (1841–1935) US judge. His formula for longevity. Attrib.

7 Life protracted is protracted woe.

Samuel Johnson (1709–84) British lexicographer and writer. 'The Vanity of Human Wishes' (1749)

8 Get your room full of good air, then shut up the windows and keep it. It will keep for years. Anyway, don't keep using your lungs all the time. Let them rest.

Stephen Leacock (1869–1944) British-born Canadian writer and economist. 'How To Live To Be 200', *Literary Lapses* (1910)

9 Do not try to live forever. You will not succeed.

George Bernard Shaw (1856–1950) Irish playwright. 'Preface on Doctors', *The Doctor's Dilemma* (1911)

10 If you live long enough, the venerability factor creeps in; you get accused of things you never did and praised for virtues you never had.

I. F. Stone (1907–89) US journalist and publisher. Attrib.

11 Keep breathing.

Sophie Tucker (1884–1966) Russian-born US singer and entertainer. Her reply, at the age of 80, when asked the secret of her longevity. Remark (1964)

Los Angeles

see **American Cities**

Loss

see also **Absence, Failure**

1 The art of losing isn't hard to master;
so many things seem filled with the intent
to be lost that their loss is no disaster.

Elizabeth Bishop (1911–79) US poet. 'One Art', *Geography III* (1976)

2 I hate to lose more than I like to win. I hate to see the happiness on their faces when they beat me.

Jimmy Connors (b. 1952) US tennis player. *New York Times* (January 24, 1977)

3 Are you the gentleman who has lost his nose?
Yes, that's me.
It's been found . . . We caught it just as it was
about to drive off in the Riga stagecoach.
Nikolay Gogol (1809–52) Russian novelist and playwright. 'The Nose'
(1836), quoted in *Diary of a Madman and Other Stories*
(Ronald Wilks, tr.; 1972)

4 The punctuation of anniversaries is terrible, like
the closing of doors, one after another between
you and what you want to hold on to.
Anne Morrow Lindbergh (1906–2001) US writer. On the first
anniversary of her son's kidnapping. Diary entry (1933)

5 Lost, yesterday, somewhere between sunrise and
sunset, two golden hours, each set with sixty
diamond minutes. No reward is offered, for they
are gone forever.
Horace Mann (1796–1859) US educator. Attrib.

6 This taught me a lesson, but I'm not sure what
it is.
John McEnroe (b. 1959) US tennis player and broadcaster. Referring to
losing the Ebel US Pro Indoor Championships to Tim
Mayotte. *New York Times* (February 9, 1987)

7 There are occasions when it is undoubtedly better
to incur loss than to make gain.
Plautus (254?–184 BC) Roman comic playwright. *Captivi* (3rd–2nd
century BC), Act 2, Scene 2

8 No man can lose what he never had.
Izaak Walton (1593–1683) English writer. *The Compleat Angler*
(1653), pt. 1, ch. 5

Love

see also **Commitment in Love, Declarations of Love, Desire,
Friendship, Relationships, Sex**

1 Oh, love is real enough, you will find it some
day, but it has one arch-enemy—and that is life.
Jean Anouilh (1910–87) French playwright. *Ardèle* (1948)

2 Love, by reason of its passion, destroys the
inbetween which relates us to and separates us
from the other.
Hannah Arendt (1906–75) German-born US philosopher and historian. *The
Human Condition* (1958), pt. 5, ch. 33

3 *Falling in love*, we said; *I fell for him.* We were
falling women. We believed in it, this downward
motion: so lovely, like flying, and yet at the same
time so dire, so extreme, so unlikely.
Margaret Atwood (b. 1939) Canadian novelist and poet. *The
Handmaid's Tale* (1985)

4 Will it come like a change in the weather?
Will its greeting be courteous or rough?
Will it alter my life altogether?
O tell me the truth about love.
W. H. Auden (1907–73) British poet. 1938. 'Twelve Songs',
Collected Poems (Edward Mendelson, ed.; 1991), no. 12,
st. 7, ll. 5–8

5 Nuptial love maketh mankind; friendly love
perfecteth it; but wanton love corrupteth and
embaseth it.
Francis Bacon (1561–1626) English philosopher, statesman, and lawyer.
'Of Love', *Essays* (1625)

6 The trick is to love somebody . . . If you love one
person, you see everybody else differently.
James Baldwin (1924–87) US writer and civil rights activist. Attrib.

7 Love is just a system for getting someone to call
you darling after sex.
Julian Barnes (b. 1946) British writer. *Talking It Over* (1991), ch. 16

8 Those have most power to hurt us that we love.
Beaumont & Fletcher, English playwrights. *The Maid's Tragedy*
(1611), Act 5, Scene 6

9 All those lips that had kissed me, those hearts
that had loved me (it is with the heart one loves,
is it not, or am I confusing it with something
else?).
Samuel Beckett (1906–89) Irish playwright, novelist, and poet. 1946.
First Love (1973)

10 Love ceases to be a pleasure, when it ceases to be
a secret.
Aphra Behn (1640?–89) English novelist and playwright. 'Four O'clock.
General Conversation', *The Lover's Watch* (1686)

11 Romantic love, in the modern sense, is a love
uniting or hoping to unite two displaced persons.
John Berger (b. 1926) British novelist, essayist, and art critic. *And Our
Faces, My Heart, Brief as Photos* (1984)

12 Beloved, let us love one another: for love is of
God; and every one that loveth is born of God,
and knoweth God.
He that loveth not knoweth not God; for God is
love.
Bible. I John, *King James Bible* (1611), 4:7–8

13 To fall in love is to create a religion that has a
fallible god.
Jorge Luis Borges (1899–1986) Argentinian writer and poet. 'The
Meeting in a Dream', *Other Inquisitions* (R. L. Simms, tr.;
1952)

14 Our pleasure in any one who in some way
resembles those we love should warn us that love
is in its essence not individual.
F. H. Bradley (1846–1924) British philosopher. *Aphorisms* (1930)

15 Love is like a motor that's going, you have such
vitality to do things, big things, because love is
goosing you all the time
Fanny Brice (1891–1951) US entertainer. Quoted in *The Fabulous
Fanny* (Norman Katlov; 1953)

16 How do I love thee? Let me count the ways.
I love thee to the depth and breadth and height
My soul can reach, when feeling out of sight
For the ends of Being and ideal Grace.
Elizabeth Barrett Browning (1806–61) British poet. No. 43, *Sonnets
from the Portuguese* (1850)

17 O lyric Love, half-angel and half-bird
And all a wonder and a wild desire.
Robert Browning (1812–89) British poet. 1868. *The Ring and the
Book* (1868–69), bk. 1, l. 1391–92

18 Love leaped out at us like a murderer jumping
out of a dark alley. It shocked us both—the
shock of a stroke of lightning, the shock of a
flick-knife.
Mikhail Bulgakov (1891–1940) Russian novelist and playwright. 1929–
40. *The Master and Margarita* (Michael Glenny, tr.; 1966),
ch. 1

19 My luve's like a red red rose
That's newly sprung in June:
My luve's like the melodie
That's sweetly play'd in tune.
Robert Burns (1759–96) Scottish poet and songwriter. Derived from
many folk songs. 'A Red Red Rose' (1796)

20 Love, in the form in which it exists in society, is nothing but the exchange of two fantasies and the superficial contact of two bodies.

Nicolas Chamfort (1741–94) French writer. *Maximes et Pensées* (1795), ch. 6

21 Can one love so fleetingly? Can love be as brief as a drink after a game of dominoes? Shouldn't we dig a trench between what we get from the balls and what comes from the heart?

Patrick Chamoiseau (b.1953) Martiniquan writer. *Solibo Magnificent* (1999)

22 To love a thing means wanting it to live.

Confucius (551–479 BC) Chinese philosopher, administrator, and moralist. *Analects* (5th century BC)

23 Love is a growing, or full constant light;
And his first minute, after noon, is night.

John Donne (1572?–1631) English metaphysical poet and divine. 'A Lecture upon the Shadow', *Songs and Sonnets* (1635), ll. 25–26

24 I am the Love that dare not speak its name.

Alfred Douglas (1870–1945) British writer and poet. Referring to homosexual love. 'Two Loves' (1896)

25 I think of the postmodern attitude as that of a man who loves a very cultivated woman and knows he cannot say to her, 'I love you madly', because he knows that she knows (and that she knows that he knows) that these words have already been used by Barbara Cartland.

Umberto Eco (b. 1932) Italian writer and literary scholar. 'Postmodernism, Irony, the Enjoyable', *Reflections on the Name of the Rose* (William Weaver, tr.; 1983)

26 Love is like linen often chang'd, the sweeter.

Phineas Fletcher (1582–1650) English clergyman and poet. *Sicelides* (1614), Act 3, Scene 4

27 Love is among the most pernicious and contagious of diseases. We who are afflicted with it can be detected by anyone. Dark circles under our eyes show that we never sleep, kept awake night after night by embraces or by their absence. We suffer from devastating fevers and have an irresistible urge to say stupid things.

Eduardo Galeano (b. 1940) Uruguayan writer. *The Book of Embraces* (1989)

28 Love Is Here To Stay

Ira Gershwin (1896–1983) US lyricist. Song title. *The Goldwyn Follies* (1937)

29 Oh mighty love! Man is one world, and hath Another to attend him.

George Herbert (1593–1633) English poet and cleric. 'Man', *The Temple: Sacred Poems and Private Ejaculations* (1633), ll. 47–48

30 The love we give away is the only love we keep.

Elbert Hubbard (1856–1915) US writer, printer, and editor. *The Note Book* (1927)

31 Love, I find, is like singing. Everybody can do enough to satisfy themselves, though it may not impress the neighbours as being very much.

Zora Neale Hurston (1891?–1960) US writer and folklorist. *Dust Tracks on a Road* (1942)

32 Only one who has loved knows the power of love.

Hu Shi (1891–1962) Chinese reformer and philosopher. *Dreams and Poetry* (1920), quoted in *Anthology of Modern Chinese Poetry* (Michelle Yeh, ed. and tr.; 1992)

33 Love's like the measles—all the worse when it comes late in life.

Douglas Jerrold (1803–57) British playwright. 'A Philanthropist', *Wit and Opinions* (Blanchard Jerrold, ed.; 1859)

34 Love is the wisdom of the fool and the folly of the wise.

Samuel Johnson (1709–84) British lexicographer and writer. Quoted in *Johnsonian Miscellanies* (G. B. Hill, ed.; 1897), vol. 2

35 Love is my religion—I could die for that.

John Keats (1795–1821) English poet. Letter to Fanny Brawne (October 13, 1819), quoted in *Letters of John Keats* (H. E. Rollins, ed.; 1958), vol. 2

36 What will survive of us is love.

Philip Larkin (1922–85) British poet. 'An Arundel Tomb', *The Whitsun Weddings* (1964)

37 To love is to find pleasure in the perfection of another.

Gottfried Wilhelm Leibniz (1646–1716) German philosopher and mathematician. 'Felicity', *Leibniz: Political Writings* (Patrick Riley; ed. and tr.; 1988)

38 All You Need Is Love

Lennon & McCartney, British rock musicians. Song title. *Magical Mystery Tour* (1968?)

39 Two souls with but a single thought,
Two hearts that beat as one.

Maria Lovell (1803–77) British actor and dramatist. Translated from Friedrich Halm's *Der Sohn der Wildniss* (1843). *Ingomar the Barbarian* (1855), Act 2

40 How alike are the groans of love to those of the dying.

Malcolm Lowry (1909–57) British novelist. *Under the Volcano* (1947), ch. 12

41 It is very rarely that a man loves
And when he does it is nearly always fatal.

Hugh MacDiarmid (1892–1978) Scottish poet and writer. 'The International Brigade' (1957)

42 The breeze of love blows for an hour and makes amends for the ill winds of the whole of a lifetime.

Naguib Mahfouz (b. 1911) Egyptian writer. Said by Sheikh Abd-Rabbih al-Ta-ih. *Echoes of an Autobiography* (1994)

43 I learned that love was only the dirty trick played on us to achieve continuation of the species.

Somerset Maugham (1874–1965) British writer. *A Writer's Notebook* (1949)

44 Love is the difficult realization that something other than oneself is real.

Iris Murdoch (1919–99) Irish-born British novelist and philosopher. 'The Sublime and the Good', *Chicago Review* (1959)

45 When a man is in love he endures more than at other times; he submits to everything.

Friedrich Wilhelm Nietzsche (1844–1900) German philosopher and poet. *The Antichrist* (1888)

46 They that love beyond the world cannot be separated by it. Death is but crossing the world, as friends do the seas; they live in one another still.

William Penn (1644–1718) English preacher and colonialist. *Some Fruits of Solitude* (1693)

47 Love is not the dying moan of a distant violin—it's the triumphant twang of a bedspring.

S. J. Perelman (1904–79) US humorist. Quoted in *Quotations for Speakers and Writers* (Allen Andrews; 1969)

48 Love is the sole and everlasting foundation on which our nature can be trained to humaneness.

Johann Heinrich Pestalozzi (1746–1827) Swiss educational reformer. Quoted in *The Education of Man: Aphorisms* (Heinz and Ruth Norden, trs.; 1951)

49 There can be no peace of mind in love, since the advantage one has secured is never anything but a fresh starting-point for further desires.

Marcel Proust (1871–1922) French novelist. 1918. À l'Ombre des Jeunes Filles en Fleurs, À la Recherche du Temps Perdu (1913–27)

50 If all the world and love were young,
And truth in every shepherd's tongue,
These pretty pleasures might me move
To live with thee, and be thy love.

Walter Raleigh (1554–1618) British explorer, courtier, and writer. Written in response to Christopher Marlowe's poem, 'The Passionate Shepherd to His Love'. 'The Nymph's Reply to the Shepherd' (1600), st. 1

51 Once the realization is accepted that even between the *closest* human beings infinite distances continue to exist, a wonderful living side by side can grow up, if they succeed in loving the distance between them.

Rainer Maria Rilke (1875–1926) Austrian poet and novelist. *Letters of Rainer Maria Rilke* (Jane Bannard Greene and M. D. Norton, trs.; 1945)

52 To fear love is to fear life, and those who fear life are already three parts dead.

Bertrand Russell (1872–1970) British philosopher and mathematician. *Marriage and Morals* (1929)

53 Love does not consist in gazing at each other but in looking together in the same direction.

Antoine de Saint-Exupéry (1900–44) French writer and aviator. *Wind, Sand and Stars* (1939), ch. 8

54 Love is only known by him who hopelessly persists in love.

Friedrich von Schiller (1759–1805) German poet, playwright, and historian. *Don Carlos* (1787), Act 3, Scene 8

55 Love is not love
Which alters when it alteration finds,
Or bends with the remover to remove.
O, no! it is an ever-fixed mark,
That looks on tempests and is never shaken.

William Shakespeare (1564–1616) English poet and playwright. Sonnet 116 (1609)

56 True Love in this differs from gold and clay,
That to divide is not to take away.

Percy Bysshe Shelley (1792–1822) English poet. *Epipsychidion* (1821), pt. 1, ll. 160–161

57 Love is above the laws, above the opinion of men; it is the truth, the flame, the pure element, the primary idea of the moral world.

Madame de Staël (1766–1817) French writer and intellectual. *Zulma and Other Tales* (1813)

58 Accustom yourself continually to make many acts of love, for they enkindle and melt the soul.

Saint Teresa of Ávila (1515–82) Spanish mystic, author, and nun. 'Maxims for Her Nuns' (1566?), quoted in *Selected Writings of St. Teresa of Avila* (William J. Doheny, ed.; 1950)

59 I have learned that every man lives not through care of himself, but by love.

Leo Tolstoy (1828–1910) Russian writer. *Anna Karenina* (1875–77), pt. 8, sect. 10

60 Nothing is too much trouble for love.

Desmond Tutu (b. 1931) South African clergyman and civil rights activist. *The Words of Desmond Tutu* (Naomi Tutu, ed.; 1989)

61 Love conquers all things: let us too give in to Love.

Virgil (70–19 BC) Roman poet. *Eclogues* (37 BC), no. 10, l. 69

62 Break a vase, and the love that reassembles the fragments is stronger than that love which took its symmetry for granted.

Derek Walcott (b. 1930) St. Lucian poet and playwright. 'Dissolving the Sigh of History', *Guardian* (December 16, 1992)

63 Could we forbear dispute and practise love,
We should agree as angels do above.

Edmund Waller (1606–87) English poet. 'Divine Love', *The Poems of Edmund Waller* (G. Thorn Drury; 1893), can. 3

64 Love conquers all things except poverty and toothache.

Mae West (1892–1980) US actor and comedian. Attrib.

65 'Tis said that some have died for love.

William Wordsworth (1770–1850) English poet. ''Tis Said That Some Have Died', *Lyrical Ballads* (2nd ed.; 1800), l. 1

66 Murmur, a little sadly, how Love fled
And paced upon the mountains overhead
And hid his face amid a crowd of stars.

W. B. Yeats (1865–1939) Irish poet and playwright. October 21, 1891. 'When You Are Old', *The Rose* (1893), st. 3

67 The most wonderful thing in life is to be delirious and the most wonderful kind of delirium is being in love.

Yevgeny Zamyatin (1884–1937) Russian writer. 'The Fisher of Men' (1918), quoted in *Islanders and the Fisher of Men* (Sophie Fuller and Julian Sacchi; eds. and trs.; 1984)

Lovers

see also Love, Relationships

1 One lover is always more moved than the other.

Saul Bellow (b. 1915) Canadian-born US writer. *Herzog* (1964)

2 My beloved is mine, and I am his: he feedeth among the lilies.
Until the day break, and the shadows flee away, turn, my beloved, and be thou like a roe or a young hart upon the mountains of Bether.

Bible. Song of Solomon, *King James Bible* (1611), 2:16–17

3 I was born when she kissed me. I died when she left me. For a few weeks I was alive while she loved me.

Humphrey Bogart (1899–1957) US actor. Said as Dixon Steele. *In a Lonely Place* (Andrew Salt; 1950)

4 They were like two migrating birds, male and female, who had been caught and forced to live in separate cages.

Anton Chekhov (1860–1904) Russian playwright and short-story writer. 'Lady with Lapdog' (1899), sect. 4

5 Where, like a pillow on a bed,
A pregnant bank swelled up, to rest
The violet's reclining head,
Sat we two, one another's best.

John Donne (1572?–1631) English metaphysical poet and divine. 'The Ecstasy', *Songs and Sonnets* (1635)

6 I wonder by my troth, what thou, and I
Did, till we lov'd? were we not wean'd till then?
But suck'd on country pleasures, childishly?
Or snorted we in the Seven Sleepers den?

John Donne (1572?–1631) English metaphysical poet and divine. 'The Good-Morrow', *Songs and Sonnets* (1635), ll. 1–4

7 Busy old fool, unruly Sun,
Why dost thou thus,
Through windows, and through curtains call on us?
Must to thy motions lovers' seasons run?

John Donne (1572?–1631) English metaphysical poet and divine. 'The Sun Rising', *Songs and Sonnets* (1635), ll. 1–4

8 A lover without indiscretion is no lover at all.

Thomas Hardy (1840–1928) British novelist and poet. *The Hand of Ethelberta* (1876), ch. 20

9 I have begun to pace
the Hadrian's Wall
of her shoulder, dreaming
of Maiden Castle.

Seamus Heaney (b. 1939) Irish poet. 'Bone Dreams', *North* (1975), st. 5

10 With you I should love to live, with you be ready to die.

Horace (65–8 BC) Roman poet. *Odes* (23? BC), bk. 3, no. 9, last line

11 And soft adorings from their loves receive
Upon the honey'd middle of the night.

John Keats (1795–1821) English poet. 'The Eve of Saint Agnes' (1820), st. 6, ll. 3–4

12 Ye gods! annihilate but space and time.
And make two lovers happy.

Alexander Pope (1688–1744) English poet. *The Art of Sinking in Poetry* (1727), ll. 11–12

13 TOUCHSTONE We that are true lovers run into strange capers.

William Shakespeare (1564–1616) English poet and playwright. *As You Like It* (1599), Act 2, Scene 4

14 CELIA It is as easy to count atomies as to resolve the propositions of a lover.

William Shakespeare (1564–1616) English poet and playwright. *As You Like It* (1599), Act 3, Scene 2

15 JULIET O Romeo, Romeo! wherefore art thou Romeo?

William Shakespeare (1564–1616) English poet and playwright. *Romeo and Juliet* (1595), Act 2, Scene 2

16 No oath too binding for a lover.

Sophocles (496?–406? BC) Greek playwright. *Phaedra* (5th century BC), fragment 848

17 The quarrels of lovers are the renewal of love.

Terence (185–159 BC) Roman playwright and poet. *Heauton Timoroumenos* (2nd century BC)

18 I doubt whether any girl would be satisfied with her lover's mind if she knew the whole of it.

Anthony Trollope (1815–82) British novelist. *The Small House at Allington* (1864), ch. 4

19 She was more beautiful than thy first love,
This lady by the trees.

W. B. Yeats (1865–1939) Irish poet and playwright. In the final version the second line reads: 'But now lies under boards'. 'A Dream of Death', *The Rose* (1893), early version, ll. 11–12

Loyalty

see also **Betrayal**, **Faith**, **Friendship**, **Trust**

1 Total loyalty is possible only when fidelity is emptied of all concrete content, from which changes of mind might naturally arise.

Hannah Arendt (1906–75) German-born US philosopher and historian. *The Origins of Totalitarianism* (1951), ch. 10, sect. 1

2 True as the needle to the pole,
Or as the dial to the sun.

Barton Booth (1681–1733) English tragic actor. 'Song' (18th century), quoted in *The Oxford Book of Eighteenth Century Verse* (David Nichol Smith, ed.; 1926)

3 O fie miss, you must not kiss and tell.

William Congreve (1670–1729) English playwright and poet. *Love for Love* (1695), Act 2, Scene 10

4 An ounce of loyalty is worth a pound of cleverness.

Elbert Hubbard (1856–1915) US writer, printer, and editor. *The Note Book* (1927)

5 Pray for the dead and fight like hell for the living.

Mother Jones (1830–1930) Irish-born US trade union leader. *Autobiography* (1925)

6 We are all the President's men.

Henry Kissinger (b. 1923) German-born US politician and diplomat. Said with reference to the invasion of Cambodia (1970). *Sunday Times Magazine* (May 4, 1975)

7 It is best not to swap horses in mid-stream.

Abraham Lincoln (1809–65) US president. June 9, 1864. Reply to the National Union League. *Collected Works of Abraham Lincoln* (R. P. Baster, ed.; 1953), vol. 7

8 I'll speak for the man, or against him, whichever will do him most good.

Richard Nixon (1913–94) US president. When agreeing to support a politician. Attrib.

9 ANGUS Those he commands move only in command,
Nothing in love; now does he feel his title
Hang loose about him, like a giant's robe
Upon a dwarfish thief.

William Shakespeare (1564–1616) English poet and playwright. *Macbeth* (1606), Act 5, Scene 2

10 Grant stood by me when I was crazy and I stood by him when he was drunk.

William Tecumseh Sherman (1820–91) US general. Referring to Ulysses S. Grant. Quoted in *Abraham Lincoln: The War Years* (Carl Sandburg; 1939)

Luck

see **Chance**, **Fate**

Lust

see also **Desire**, **Passion**, **Sex**

1 Oh would I could subdue the flesh
Which sadly troubles me!
And then perhaps could view the flesh
As though I never knew the flesh
And merry misery.

John Betjeman (1906–84) British poet and broadcaster. 'Senex', *Old Lights for New Chancels* (1940), st. 1

2 Jupiter himself was turned into a satyr, a shepherd, a bull, a swan, a golden shower, and what not for love.

Robert Burton (1577–1640) English scholar and churchman. *The Anatomy of Melancholy* (1621), pt. 3, sect. 2

3 I for one venerate a petticoat.

Lord Byron (1788–1824) British poet. *Don Juan* (1819–24), can. 14, st. 26

4 What is commonly called love, namely the desire of satisfying a voracious appetite with a certain quantity of delicate white human flesh.

Henry Fielding (1707–54) British novelist and playwright. *Tom Jones* (1749), bk. 6, ch. 1

5 Kept a hearth-girl in his house who kindled his fire but extinguished his virtue.

Gerald of Wales (1146?–1223?) Welsh topographer, archdeacon, and writer. Referring to the parish priest. *Gemma Ecclesiastica* (1210?), quoted in *Giraldus Cambrensis Opera* (8 vols.) (J. S. Brewer, J. F. Dimmock, and G. F. Warner, eds.; 1861–91)

6 I'll come no more behind your scenes, David; for the silk stockings and white bosoms of your actresses excite my amorous propensities.

Samuel Johnson (1709–84) British lexicographer and writer. 1750. Said to the actor-manager David Garrick. What Johnson was actually reported as saying was: 'I'll come no more behind your scenes, David, for the white bubbies and silk stockings of your actresses excite my genitals'. Quoted in *Life of Samuel Johnson* (James Boswell; 1791)

7 In the midst of the fountain of bliss there arises something bitter, which stings him even amid the very flowers.

Lucretius (99?–55? BC) Roman philosopher and poet. Referring to sexual lust poisoning a man's happiness. *De Rerum Natura* (1st century BC), pt. 4, l. 1133

8 Delight of lust is gross and brief
And weariness treads on desire.

Petronius Arbiter (d. 66) Roman writer. 1st century. Quoted in *Poetae Latinae Minores* (A. Baehrens, ed.; 1882), vol. 4, no. 101

9 Th' expense of spirit in a waste of shame
Is lust in action; and till action, lust
Is perjur'd, murd'rous, bloody, full of blame,
Savage, extreme, rude, cruel, not to trust;
Enjoy'd no sooner but despised straight.

William Shakespeare (1564–1616) English poet and playwright. Sonnet 129 (1609)

10 GHOST O wicked wit and gifts, that have the power
So to seduce!—won to his shameful lust
The will of my most seeming-virtuous Queen.

William Shakespeare (1564–1616) English poet and playwright. *Hamlet* (1601), Act 1, Scene 5

11 HAMLET For the power of beauty will sooner transform honesty from what it is to a bawd than the force of honesty can translate beauty into his likeness.

William Shakespeare (1564–1616) English poet and playwright. *Hamlet* (1601), Act 3, Scene 1

12 Outside every thin girl there is a fat man trying to get in.

Katharine Whitehorn (b. 1926) British journalist and writer. Attrib.

Luxury

see also **Extravagance, Wealth**

1 I agree with one of your reputable critics that a taste for drawing rooms has spoiled more poets than ever did a taste for gutters.

Thomas Beer (1888?–1940) US author. *The Mauve Decade* (1926)

2 And still she slept an azure-lidded sleep,
In blanched linen, smooth, and lavender'd,
While he from forth the closet brought a heap
Of candied apple, quince, and plum, and gourd . . .
Manna and dates, in argosy transferr'd
From Fez; and spiced dainties, every one,
From silken Samarcand to cedar'd Lebanon.

John Keats (1795–1821) English poet. Fez is Morocco, and Samarcand (Samarqand) and Lebanon were places associated with luxury and wealth. 'The Eve of Saint Agnes' (1820), st. 30

3 What this country needs is a really good 5-cent cigar.

Thomas R. Marshall (1854–1925) US vice president. *New York Tribune* (January 4, 1920)

4 Give us the luxuries of life, and we will dispense with its necessities.

John Lothrop Motley (1814–77) US historian and diplomat. Quoted in *The Autocrat of the Breakfast Table* (O. W. Holmes; 1905), ch. 6

5 Every luxury was lavished on you—atheism, breast-feeding, circumcision. I had to make my own way.

Joe Orton (1933–67) British playwright. *Loot* (1966)

6 Diamonds Are A Girl's Best Friend

Leo Robin (1895–1984) US songwriter. 1949. Title of song sung by Marilyn Monroe in the film *Gentlemen Prefer Blondes* (1953).

Lying

see also **Deception, Hypocrisy**

1 The lie has long since lost its honest function of misrepresenting reality. Nobody believes anybody, everyone is in the know. Lies are told only to convey to someone that one has no need either of him or his good opinion.

Theodor Adorno (1903–69) German philosopher, sociologist, and musicologist. *Minima Moralia* (E. F. N. Jephcott, tr.; 1951)

2 The boy cried 'Wolf, wolf!' and the villagers came out to help him.

Aesop (620?–560 BC) Greek writer. 'The Shepherd's Boy', *Aesop's Fables* (6th century BC)

3 With lies you will go far, but not back again.

Anonymous. Yiddish proverb.

4 It contains a misleading impression, not a lie. I was being economical with the truth.

Robert Armstrong (b. 1927) British civil servant. Giving evidence on behalf of the British Government in an Australian court case. Armstrong was, in fact, quoting Edmund Burke (1729–97). *Evidence* (November 1986)

5 She tells enough white lies to ice a wedding cake.

Margot Asquith (1865–1945) British political hostess and writer. Referring to Lady Desborough. Quoted in 'Margot Oxford', *Listener* (Lady Violet Bonham Carter; June 11, 1953)

6 A mixture of a lie doth ever add pleasure.

Francis Bacon (1561–1626) English philosopher, statesman, and lawyer. 'Of Truth', *Essays* (1625)

7 It is not the lie that passeth through the mind, but the lie that sinketh in, and settleth in it, that doth the hurt.

Francis Bacon (1561–1626) English philosopher, statesman, and lawyer. 'Of Truth', *Essays* (1625)

8 If we live all our lives under lies, it becomes difficult to see *anything* if it does not have anything to do with these lies.

Imamu Amiri Baraka (b. 1934) US author, editor, playwright, and political activist. 'Cuba Libre', *Home: Social Essays* (1966)

9 Matilda told such Dreadful Lies
It made one Gasp and Stretch one's Eyes.

Hilaire Belloc (1870–1953) French-born British writer. 'Matilda', *Cautionary Tales for Children* (1907), quoted in *Complete Verse* (1991)

10 For every time She shouted 'Fire!'
They only answered 'Little Liar!'
And therefore when her Aunt returned,
Matilda, and the House, were burned.

Hilaire Belloc (1870–1953) French-born British writer. 'Matilda', *Cautionary Tales for Children* (1907), quoted in *Complete Verse* (1991)

11 A lie can be half-way round the world before the truth has got its boots on.

Jim Callaghan (b. 1912) British prime minister. Speech to Parliament (November 1, 1976)

12 A liar is always lavish of oaths.

Corneille (1606–84) French playwright. *Le Menteur* (1644), Act 3, Scene 5

13 A good memory is needed after one has lied.

Corneille (1606–84) French playwright. *Le Menteur* (1644), Act 4, Scene 5

14 The lie that flatters I abhor the most.

William Cowper (1731–1800) British poet. 'Table Talk' (1782), l. 88, quoted in *The Works of William Cowper* (Robert Southey, ed.; 1835–37)

15 There are three kinds of lies: lies, damned lies and statistics.

Benjamin Disraeli (1804–81) British prime minister and writer. Attrib. *Autobiography* (Mark Twain; 1924), vol. 1

16 Without lies humanity would perish of despair and boredom.

Anatole France (1844–1924) French novelist, poet, and critic. *The Bloom of Life* (1922)

17 Whoever would lie usefully should lie seldom.

John Hervey (1696–1743) English writer and pamphleteer. *Memoirs of the Reign of George II* (J. W. Croker, ed.; 1848), vol. 1, ch. 19

18 The broad mass of a nation . . . will more easily fall victim to a big lie than to a small one.

Adolf Hitler (1889–1945) Austrian-born German dictator. *Mein Kampf* (1933), ch. 10

19 There is no worse lie than a truth misunderstood by those who hear it.

William James (1842–1910) US psychologist and philosopher. *The Varieties of Religious Experience* (1902)

20 Lying is the beginning of fiction.

Jamaica Kincaid (b. 1949) Antiguan-born US novelist, short-story writer, and journalist. *New York Times* (October 7, 1990)

21 The first rule of politics is not to lie to somebody unless it is absolutely necessary.

Russell B. Long (b. 1918) US politician. Attrib.

22 In justice to my father, one should note that he resorted to elaborate invention only after first experimenting with simple falsehood.

Joaquim Maria Machado de Assis (1839–1908) Brazilian novelist and short-story writer. *Epitaph of a Small Winner* (1880)

23 Each day a few more lies eat into the seed with which we are born, little institutional lies from the print of newspapers, the shock waves of television, and the sentimental cheats of the movie screen.

Norman Mailer (b. 1923) US novelist and journalist. 'First Advertisement for Myself', *Advertisements for Myself* (1959)

24 She's too crafty a woman to invent a new lie when an old one will serve.

Somerset Maugham (1874–1965) British writer. *The Constant Wife* (1926), Act 2

25 It is hard to believe that a man is telling the truth when you know that you would lie if you were in his place.

H. L. Mencken (1880–1956) US journalist, critic, and editor. *Prejudices* (1919–27)

26 Unless a man feels he has a good enough memory, he should never venture to lie.

Michel de Montaigne (1533–92) French essayist. *Essays* (1580–88), bk. 1

27 He led a double life. Did that make him a liar? He did not feel a liar. He was a man of two truths.

Iris Murdoch (1919–99) Irish-born British novelist and philosopher. *The Sacred and Profane Love Machine* (1974)

28 He who does not need to lie is proud of not being a liar.

Friedrich Wilhelm Nietzsche (1844–1900) German philosopher and poet. *Nachgelassene Fragmente* (1882–89)

29 The rulers of the State are the only ones who should have the privilege of lying, whether at home or abroad; they may be allowed to lie for the good of the State.

Plato (428?–347? BC) Greek philosopher. *The Republic* (370? BC)

30 He who cheats with an oath acknowledges that he is afraid of his enemy, but that he thinks little of God.

Plutarch (46?–120?) Greek biographer and philosopher. 'Lysander' (1st–2nd century), 8

31 A liar should have a good memory.

Quintilian (35?–95?) Roman rhetorician. *Institutio Oratoria* (90?)

32 The wicked always have recourse to perjury.

Racine (1639–99) French playwright. *Phèdre* (1677), Act 2, Scene 4

33 He would, wouldn't he?

Mandy Rice-Davies (b. 1944) Welsh model and showgirl. June 29, 1963. Said on being told, during the trial of Stephen Ward, that Lord Astor had denied her account of his involvement in orgies at Cliveden House.

34 OLD LADY The best thing others can do for us is to tell us lies.

Gabriela Roepke Bahamonde (b. 1920) Chilean playwright. *A White Butterfly* (1960)

35 Long ago, someone had told Grossbart the sad law that only lies can get the truth.

Philip Roth (b. 1933) US novelist. 'Defender of the Faith', *Goodbye, Columbus* (1959)

36 I have never but once succeeded in making him tell a lie and that was by a subterfuge. 'Moore', I said, 'Do you *always* tell the truth?' 'No', he replied. I believe this to be the only lie he ever told.

Bertrand Russell (1872–1970) British philosopher and mathematician. Referring to George Edward Moore. *The Autobiography of Bertrand Russell* (1967–69)

37 A little inaccuracy sometimes saves tons of explanation.

Saki (1870–1916) British short-story writer. 'The Square Egg', *Clovis and the Alleged Business of Romance* (1924)

38 PRINCE HENRY For my part, if a lie may do thee grace,
I'll gild it with the happiest terms I have.

William Shakespeare (1564–1616) English poet and playwright. Referring to Falstaff, whom he mistakenly believes has been killed in the battle. *Henry IV, Part 1* (1597), Act 5, Scene 4

39 FALSTAFF Lord, Lord! how subject we old men are to this vice of lying.

William Shakespeare (1564–1616) English poet and playwright. *Henry IV, Part 2* (1597), Act 3, Scene 2

40 Optimistic lies have such immense therapeutic value that a doctor who cannot tell them convincingly has mistaken his profession.

George Bernard Shaw (1856–1950) Irish playwright. *Misalliance* (1914), Preface

41 A lie is an abomination unto the Lord and a very present help in trouble.

Adlai Stevenson (1900–65) US statesman. Speech, Springfield (January 1951)

42 The cruellest lies are often told in silence.

Robert Louis Stevenson (1850–94) Scottish novelist, essayist, and poet. 'Virginibus Puerisque', *Virginibus Puerisque* (1881), pt. 4

43 That a lie which is all a lie may be met and fought with outright,
But a lie which is part a truth is a harder matter to fight.

Alfred Tennyson (1809–92) British poet. July 16, 1859. 'The Grandmother', *Enoch Arden* (1864), st. 8

44 That's the story of our life—men tell lies and women believe them.

Vladimir Voinovich (b. 1932) Russian novelist. *The Life and Extraordinary Adventures of Private Ivan Chonkin* (Richard Lourie, tr.; 1969), pt. 1, ch. 7

45 In exceptional circumstances it is necessary to say something that is untrue in the House of Commons.

William Waldegrave (b. 1946) British politician. Referring to the arms to Iraq scandal, in which he was implicated. *Guardian* (July 15, 1985)

46 Most people know things. All they want is a lie plausible enough to believe.

John A. Williams (b. 1925) US writer. *The Man Who Cried I Am* (1968)

47 Someone who knows too much finds it hard not to lie.

Ludwig Wittgenstein (1889–1951) Austrian philosopher. 1947. Quoted in *Culture and Value* (G. H. von Wright and Heikki Nyman, eds.; 1980)

M

Machines

see also **Computers**, **Technology**

1 The more we reduce ourselves to machines in the lower things, the more force we shall set free to use in the higher.
Anna C. Brackett (1836–1911) US writer. *The Technique of the Rest* (1892)

2 Machines from the Maxim gun to the computer, are for the most part means by which a minority can keep free men in subjection.
Kenneth Clark (1903–83) British art historian. *Civilisation* (1969)

3 The inventor of the Xerox machine will, I am sure, find a special place reserved for him on one of the inner circles of Dante's Inferno.
Nicholas Goodison (b. 1934) British business executive. Quoted in *How to Manage* (Ray Wild; 1982)

4 One machine can do the work of fifty ordinary men. No machine can do the work of one extraordinary man.
Elbert Hubbard (1856–1915) US writer, printer, and editor. *A Thousand and One Epigrams* (1911)

5 But remember, please, the Law by which we live,
We are not built to comprehend a lie,
We can neither love nor pity nor forgive,
If you make a slip in handling us you die!
Rudyard Kipling (1865–1936) Indian-born British writer and poet. 'The Secret of Machines', quoted in *A History of England* (C. R. L. Fletcher; 1911)

6 A man who says that men are machines may be a great scientist. A man who says he *is* a machine is 'depersonalized' in psychiatric jargon.
R. D. Laing (1927–89) Scottish psychiatrist. *The Divided Self* (1965), Preface

7 You cannot endow even the best machine with initiative. The jolliest steam-roller will not plant flowers.
Walter Lippmann (1889–1974) US writer and editor. *A Preface to Politics* (1913)

8 Projecting current trends, the love machine would appear a natural development in the near future—not just the computerized datefinder, but a machine whereby ultimate orgasm is achieved by direct mechanical stimulation of the pleasure circuits of the brain.
Marshall McLuhan (1911–80) Canadian sociologist. *Playboy* (March 1969)

9 Machines need to talk easily to one another in order to better serve people.
Nicholas Negroponte, US business executive and writer. *Being Digital* (1995)

10 A motorcycle functions entirely in accordance with the laws of reason, and a study of the art of motorcycle maintenance is really a miniature study of the art of rationality itself.
Robert T. Pirsig (b. 1928) US writer. *Zen and the Art of Motorcycle Maintenance* (1974)

11 It has suddenly become cheaper to have a machine to do a mental task than for a man to do it . . . Just as men's muscles were replaced in the first industrial revolution, men's minds will be replaced in this second one.
Clive Sinclair (b. 1940) British inventor and entrepreneur. Quoted in 'Creativity and Inventiveness', *The Roots of Excellence* (Ronnie Lessem; 1985), ch. 5

12 The real problem is not whether machines think but whether men do.
B. F. Skinner (1904–90) US psychologist. *Contingencies of Reinforcement* (1969), ch. 9

13 Sirs, I have tested your machine. It adds a new terror to life and makes death a long-felt want.
Herbert Beerbohm Tree (1853–1917) British actor and theatrical impresario. Referring to a gramophone. Attrib. *Beerbohm Tree* (Hesketh Pearson; 1956)

Madness

see also **Neurosis**, **Psychiatry**, **Sanity**

1 In a totally sane society, madness is the only freedom.
J. G. Ballard (b. 1930) Chinese-born British writer. *Running Wild* (1988)

2 We all are born mad. Some remain so.
Samuel Beckett (1906–89) Irish playwright, novelist, and poet. *Waiting for Godot* (1954), Act 2

3 Of course, in an age of madness, to expect to be untouched by madness is a form of madness. But the pursuit of sanity can be a form of madness, too.
Saul Bellow (b. 1915) Canadian-born US writer. *Henderson, The Rain King* (1959)

4 All of us are mad. If it weren't for the fact every one of us is slightly abnormal, there wouldn't be any point in giving each person a separate name.
Ugo Betti (1892–1953) Italian playwright and poet. *The Fugitive* (G. H. McWilliam, tr.; 1953)

5 The mad know one thing and it drives them mad because they know it with piercing insight: society is mad.
Edward Bond (b. 1934) British playwright. *The Hidden Plot* (2000)

6 There is another kinde of madnesse named lunaticus, the whiche is madnesse that dothe infest a man ones in a mone, the whiche doth cause one to be geryshe changeable and waveringe witted, not constant, but fantasticall.
Andrew Boorde (1490?–1549) English physician, writer, and monk. *The Breviary of Healthe* (1597)

7 Of its own beauty is the mind diseased
And fevers into false creation.
Lord Byron (1788–1824) British poet. *Childe Harold's Pilgrimage* (1812–18), can. 4, st. 122

8 Who e're is mad, he first had Wit to lose;
Betwixt Fool and Physitian wink and chuse.
James Carkesse, British clerk. *Lucida Intervalla: containing divers Miscellaneous poems written at Finsbury and Bethlem by the Doctors Patient Extraordinary* (1679)

9 I was out of work, drinking, and crazy. My kids were crazy, and my wife was crazy and having a 'thing' with an unemployed aerospace engineer she'd met at AA. He was crazy too.
Raymond Carver (1938–88) US poet, short-story writer, and essayist. 'Where Is Everyone?', *Fires: Essays, Stories, and Poems* (1983)

10 A knight errant who turns mad for a reason deserves neither merit nor thanks. The thing is to do it without cause.
Miguel de Cervantes (1547–1616) Spanish novelist and playwright. *Don Quixote* (1605–15), pt. 1, ch. 25

11 He is as mad as a March hare.
Miguel de Cervantes (1547–1616) Spanish novelist and playwright. *Don Quixote* (1605–15), pt. 2, ch. 33

12 The madman is not the man who has lost his reason. The madman is the man who has lost everything except his reason.
G. K. Chesterton (1874–1936) British writer and poet. *Orthodoxy* (1909), ch. 1

13 Madness is a final distillation of self, a final editing down. It's the drowning out of false voices.
Don DeLillo (b. 1936) US novelist. Said by Owen Brademas. *The Names* (1982)

14 Much Madness is divinest Sense—
To a discerning Eye—
Much Sense—the starkest Madness.
Emily Dickinson (1830–86) US poet. No. 435 (1862?), st. 1, ll. 1–3, quoted in *The Complete Works of Emily Dickinson* (Thomas H. Johnson, ed.; 1970)

15 There is less harm to be suffered in being mad among madmen than in being sane all by oneself.
Denis Diderot (1713–84) French encyclopedist and philosopher. *Supplément au Voyage de Bougainville* (1935)

16 I had rather be mad than delighted.
Diogenes (412?–323 BC) Greek philosopher. Attrib.

17 There is a pleasure sure
In being mad which none but madmen know.
John Dryden (1631–1700) English poet, playwright, and literary critic. *The Spanish Friar* (1681), Act 1, Scene 1

18 Whom God wishes to destroy, he first makes mad.
Euripides (480?–406? BC) Greek playwright. Attrib.

19 For the nineteenth century, the initial model of madness would be to believe oneself to be God, while for the preceding centuries it had been to deny God.
Michel Foucault (1926–84) French philosopher. *Madness and Civilization* (1967)

20 All forms of psychosis show the inability to be objective, to an extreme degree. For the insane person the only reality that exists is that within him, that of his fears and desires.
Erich Fromm (1900–80) German-born US psychoanalyst and philosopher. *The Art of Loving* (1956)

21 What is madness
To those who only observe, is often wisdom
To those to whom it happens.
Christopher Fry (b. 1907) British playwright. *A Phoenix Too Frequent* (1946)

22 I saw the best minds of my generation destroyed by madness, starving hysterical naked.
Allen Ginsberg (1926–97) US poet. *Howl and Other Poems* (1956)

23 The world is so full of simpletons and madmen, that one need not seek them in a madhouse.
Johann Wolfgang von Goethe (1749–1832) German poet, playwright, and scientist. March 17, 1830. Quoted in *Conversations with Goethe* (Johann Peter Eckermann; 1836–48)

24 The opinions of the world, both in ancient and later ages, concerning the cause of madness, have been two. Some, deriving them from the passions; some from demons, or spirits, either good or bad, which they thought might enter into a man, possess him, and move his organs in such strange, and uncouth manner.
Thomas Hobbes (1588–1679) English philosopher and political thinker. *Leviathan* (1651)

25 Insanity is often the logic of an accurate mind overtaxed.
Oliver Wendell Holmes (1841–1935) US judge. *The Autocrat of the Breakfast-Table* (1858), ch. 2

26 Because the only people for me are the mad ones . . . the ones who never yawn or say a commonplace thing, but burn, burn, burn, like fabulous yellow roman candles exploding like spiders across the stars and in the middle you see the blue centerlight pop and everybody goes 'Awww!'
Jack Kerouac (1922–69) US writer. *On the Road* (1957), pt. 1

27 Every one is more or less mad on one point.
Rudyard Kipling (1865–1936) Indian-born British writer and poet. 'On the Strength of a Likeness', *Plain Tales from the Hills* (1888)

28 Madness need not be all breakdown. It may also be break-through. It is potential liberation and renewal as well as enslavement and existential death.
R. D. Laing (1927–89) Scottish psychiatrist. *The Politics of Experience* (1967), ch. 16

29 The world is becoming like a lunatic asylum run by lunatics.
David Lloyd George (1863–1945) British prime minister. 1933. *Observer* (January 8, 1953), 'Sayings of Our Times'

30 Madmen do not appear to me to have lost the faculty of reasoning, but having joined together some of the ideas very wrongly, they mistake them for truths . . . For, by the violence of their imaginations, having taken their fancies for realities, they make right deductions from them.
John Locke (1632–1704) English philosopher. *An Essay Concerning Human Understanding* (1690), bk. 2

31 Man is quite insane. He wouldn't know how to create a maggot and he creates Gods by the dozen.
Michel de Montaigne (1533–92) French essayist. *Essays* (1580–88), bk. 2, ch. 12

32 The great proof of madness is the disproportion of one's designs to one's means.
Napoleon I (1769–1821) French emperor. Quoted in *Maximes de Napoléon* (A. G. de Liancourt, ed.; 1842)

33 Insanity in individuals is something rare—but in groups, parties, nations, and epochs it is the rule.

Friedrich Wilhelm Nietzsche (1844–1900) German philosopher and poet. *Beyond Good and Evil* (1886)

34 Men are so necessarily mad, that not to be mad would amount to another form of madness.

Blaise Pascal (1623–62) French philosopher, mathematician, and physicist. *Pensées* (1669), no. 414

35 His father's sister had bats in the belfry and was put away.

Eden Phillpotts (1862–1960) British writer. 'My First Murder', *Peacock House* (1926)

36 The insane person is running a private unapproved film which he happens to *like* better than the current cultural one.

Robert T. Pirsig (b. 1928) US writer. *Lila: an Inquiry into Morals* (1991)

37 The madman thinks the rest of the world crazy.

Publilius Syrus (*fl.* 1st century BC) Roman writer. *Moral Sayings* (1st century BC), 386

38 What's madness but nobility of soul
At odds with circumstance?

Theodore Roethke (1908–63) US poet. 'In a Dark Time', *The Far Field* (1964), ll. 7–8

39 A body seriously out of equilibrium, either with itself or with its environment, perishes outright. Not so a mind. Madness and suffering can set themselves no limit.

George Santayana (1863–1952) Spanish-born US philosopher, poet, and novelist. 'Reason in Common Sense', *The Life of Reason* (1905–06)

40 HAMLET I am but mad north-north-west; when the wind is southerly, I know a hawk from a handsaw.

William Shakespeare (1564–1616) English poet and playwright. *Hamlet* (1601), Act 2, Scene 2

41 POLONIUS Though this be madness, yet there is method in't.

William Shakespeare (1564–1616) English poet and playwright. *Hamlet* (1601), Act 2, Scene 2

42 KING Madness in great ones must not unwatch'd go.

William Shakespeare (1564–1616) English poet and playwright. *Hamlet* (1601), Act 3, Scene 1

43 QUEEN Mad as the sea and wind when both contend Which is the mightier.

William Shakespeare (1564–1616) English poet and playwright. *Hamlet* (1601), Act 4, Scene 1

44 FOOL He's mad that trusts in the tameness of a wolf, a horse's health, a boy's love, or a whore's oath.

William Shakespeare (1564–1616) English poet and playwright. *King Lear* (1605–06), Act 3, Scene 6

45 We want a few mad people now. See where the sane ones have landed us!

George Bernard Shaw (1856–1950) Irish playwright. *Saint Joan* (1924)

46 Madness isn't just an illness: it can also uncover areas of thinking which are normally shrouded in darkness.

Antoni Tàpies (b. 1923) Spanish painter. Quoted in *Conversations with Antoni Tàpies* (Barbara Catoir; 1991)

47 When we remember that we are all mad, the mysteries disappear and life stands explained.

Mark Twain (1835–1910) US writer and humorist. Attrib.

48 Men will always be mad and those who think they can cure them are the maddest of all.

Voltaire (1694–1778) French writer and philosopher. Letter (1762)

49 What is madness? To have erroneous perceptions and to reason correctly from them.

Voltaire (1694–1778) French writer and philosopher. 'Madness', *Dictionnaire Philosophique* (1764)

50 He knew now what this thing was—hysteria, a snake whose scales are tiny mirrors in which the dead world takes on a semblance of life.

Nathanael West (1903–40) US novelist and screenwriter. 'Miss Lonelyhearts and the Lamb', *Miss Lonelyhearts* (1933)

51 I shudder and I sigh to think
That even Cicero
And many-minded Homer were
Mad as the mist and snow.

W. B. Yeats (1865–1939) Irish poet and playwright. February 12, 1929. 'Mad as the Mist and Snow', *The Winding Stair and Other Poems* (1933), 'Words for Music Perhaps', no. 18, st. 3

Madrid

see **European Cities**

Magic

see also **The Supernatural, Wonder**

1 Open Sesame!

The Arabian Nights. The *Arabian Nights* derives from a sequence of Persian tales, translated into Arabic (850?), and later from Arabic into English. *Arabian Nights* (early 16th century), 'The History of Ali Baba'

2 I'm really a very good man; but I'm a very bad Wizard.

L. Frank Baum (1856–1919) US writer. Said by the Wizard of Oz. *The Wonderful Wizard of Oz* (1900), ch. 15

3 The human tendency to search for panaceas and magic solutions is well represented among politicians and economists.

William Keegan (b. 1938) British author and journalist. *The Spectre of Capitalism* (1992)

4 That old black magic has me in its spell.

Johnny Mercer (1909–76) US lyricist and composer. Song lyric. 'That Old Black Magic' (1942)

5 Enter these enchanted woods,
You who dare.

George Meredith (1828–1909) British novelist and poet. 'The Woods of Westermain' (1883), st. 1

6 Off-shore, by islands hidden in the blood
jewels & miracles, I, Maximus
a metal hot from boiling water, tell you
what is a lance, who obeys the figures of
the present dance.

Charles Olson (1910–70) US poet. 'I, Maximus of Gloucester, to You', *The Maximus Poems 1–10* (1953)

7 He opened his basket and took out a coil of rope, hundreds of feet in length. He grasped one end of this and threw it up, whereupon the rope stood straight up in the air as if suspended to something. It went higher and higher till it was lost in the clouds.

Pu Songling (1640–1715) Chinese writer of ghost stories. 'The Rope Trick' (17th–18th century), quoted in *Selected Tales of Liaozhai* (Yang Xianyi and Gladys Yang, trs.; 1981)

8 FIRST FAIRY You spotted snakes with double tongue,
Thorny hedgehogs, be not seen;
Newts and blind-worms, do no wrong,
Come not near our fairy Queen.

William Shakespeare (1564–1616) English poet and playwright. *A Midsummer Night's Dream* (1595–96), Act 2, Scene 1

9 PUCK I'll put a girdle round about the earth
In forty minutes.
William Shakespeare (1564–1616) English poet and playwright. *A Midsummer Night's Dream* (1595–96), Act 2, Scene 1

10 WITCHES Fair is foul, and foul is fair;
Hover through the fog and filthy air.
William Shakespeare (1564–1616) English poet and playwright. *Macbeth* (1606), Act 1, Scene 1

11 SECOND WITCH Eye of newt, and toe of frog,
Wool of bat, and tongue of dog,
Adder's fork, and blind-worm's sting,
Lizard's leg, and howlet's wing,
For a charm of powerful trouble,
Like a hell-broth boil and bubble.
William Shakespeare (1564–1616) English poet and playwright. *Macbeth* (1606), Act 4, Scene 1

12 CALIBAN Be not afeard. The isle is full of noises,
Sounds, and sweet airs, that give delight, and
hurt not.
William Shakespeare (1564–1616) English poet and playwright. *The Tempest* (1611), Act 3, Scene 2

13 PROSPERO I'll break my staff,
Bury it certain fathoms in the earth,
And deeper than did ever plummet sound
I'll drown my book.
William Shakespeare (1564–1616) English poet and playwright. *The Tempest* (1611), Act 5, Scene 1

Majority

see also **Democracy**, **Popularity**

1 Only the majority is sovereign; he who takes the
place of the people is a tyrant and his power is
usurpation.
Simón Bolívar (1783–1830) Venezuelan soldier and statesman. Proclamation to Venezuelans (December 16, 1826)

2 One with the law is a majority.
Calvin Coolidge (1872–1933) US president. Vice-presidential nomination acceptance speech to the Republican National Convention (July 27, 1920)

3 When great changes occur in history, when great
principles are involved, as a rule the majority are
wrong. The minority are right.
Eugene Victor Debs (1855–1926) US trade union leader, socialist, and pacifist. 1918. From a speech at his trial for sedition in Cleveland, Ohio. *Speeches* (1928)

4 The worst enemy of truth and freedom in our
society is the compact majority. Yes, the damned,
compact, liberal majority.
Henrik Ibsen (1828–1906) Norwegian playwright. *An Enemy of the People* (1882), Act 4

5 A man with God is always in the majority.
John Knox (1513?–72) Scottish religious reformer. Inscription on Reformation monument, Geneva, Switzerland (16th century)

6 One on God's side is a majority.
Wendell Phillips (1811–84) US reformer. Lecture, Brooklyn (November 1, 1859)

Manipulation

see also **Exploitation**, **Influence**, **Power**

1 If the means you employ to motivate others are
hidden from them or seek to bypass their
conscious minds, then one is becoming a
manipulator rather than a motivator.
John Adair (b. 1934) British business writer. *Understanding Motivation* (1990)

2 HAMLET You would play upon me; you would
seem to know my stops; you would pluck out the
heart of my mystery; you would sound me from
my lowest note to the top of my compass.
William Shakespeare (1564–1616) English poet and playwright. *Hamlet* (1601), Act 3, Scene 2

Manners

1 Manner is all in all, whate'er is writ,
The substitute for genius, sense, and wit.
William Cowper (1731–1800) British poet. 'Table Talk' (1782), ll. 542–543

2 At one early, glittering dinner party at
Buckingham Palace, the trembling hand of a
nervous waiter spilled a spoonful of decidedly
hot soup down my neck. How could I manage to
ease his mind . . . except to . . . say, without
thinking: 'Never darken my Dior again!'
Beatrice Lillie (1894–1989) Canadian-born British actor. *Every Other Inch a Lady* (1972), ch. 14

3 For to write good prose is an affair of good
manners. It is, unlike verse, a civil art. Poetry is
baroque.
Somerset Maugham (1874–1965) British writer. *The Summing Up* (1938)

4 An Englishman, even if he is alone, forms an
orderly queue of one.
George Mikes (1912–87) Hungarian-born British writer and humorist. *How to be an Alien* (1946)

5 We could not lead a pleasant life,
And 'twould be finished soon,
If peas were eaten with the knife,
And gravy with the spoon.
Eat slowly: only men in rags
And gluttons old in sin
Mistake themselves for carpet bags
And tumble victuals in.
Walter Alexander Raleigh (1861–1922) British critic and essayist. 'Stans puer ad mensam', *Laughter from a Cloud* (1923)

6 I think she must have been very strictly brought
up, she's so desperately anxious to do the wrong
thing correctly.
Saki (1870–1916) British short-story writer. 'Reginald on Worries', *Reginald* (1904)

7 Good breeding consists in concealing how much
we think of ourselves and how little we think of
the other person.
Mark Twain (1835–1910) US writer and humorist. *Notebooks* (1935)

8 Politeness is organized indifference.
Paul Valéry (1871–1945) French poet and philosopher. *Tel Quel* (1943)

Marketing

see also **Advertising**, **Business**, **Communication**

1 Only constant repetition will finally succeed in
imprinting an idea on the memory of the crowd.
Adolf Hitler (1889–1945) Austrian-born German dictator. *Mein Kampf* (1933), ch. 6

2 All the cosmetics' names seemed obscenely
obvious to me in their promise of sexual bliss.
They were all firming or uplifting or invigorating.
They made you *tingle*. Or *glow*. Or feel *young*.
Erica Jong (b. 1942) US writer. *How to Save your Own Life* (1977)

3 No great marketing decisions have ever been made on quantitative data.
John Sculley (b. 1939) US business executive. Quoted in *The Intuitive Manager* (Roy Rowan; 1986)

4 The customer is not always right and we let them know it from time to time.
Alan Sugar (b. 1947) British entrepreneur. Speech, City University Business School, London (April 1987)

5 Is it not singular how some men continue to obtain the reputation of popular authorship without adding a word to the literature of their country worthy of note? . . . To puff and to get one's self puffed have become different branches of a new profession.
Anthony Trollope (1815–82) British novelist. *The Way We Live Now* (1875), ch. 1

6 When the whale comes to the surface and spouts, that's when he gets harpooned.
John Livingston Weinberg (b. 1925) US investment banker. Referring to investment company Goldman Sachs' dislike of publicity. *Independent on Sunday* (September 9, 1990)

Marriage

see also **Commitment in Love, Love, Relationships**

1 Our people say a bad marriage kills the soul. Mine is fit for burial.
Ama Ata Aidoo (b. 1942) Ghanaian writer. 'No Sweetness Here', *No Sweetness Here* (1970)

2 Bigamy is having one wife too many. Monogamy is the same thing.
Anonymous

3 It is a truth universally acknowledged, that a single man in possession of a good fortune must be in want of a wife.
Jane Austen (1775–1817) British novelist. Opening words. *Pride and Prejudice* (1813)

4 A woman must marry the man who loves her but never the one she loves; that is the secret of lasting happiness.
Mariama Bâ (1929–81) Senegalese novelist and campaigner for women's rights. *So Long a Letter* (1979)

5 He was reputed one of the wise men, that made answer to the question, when a man should marry? A young man not yet, an elder man not at all.
Francis Bacon (1561–1626) English philosopher, statesman, and lawyer. 'Of Marriage and the Single Life', *Essays* (1625)

6 No man should marry until he has studied anatomy and dissected at least one woman.
Honoré de Balzac (1799–1850) French writer. *La Physiologie du Mariage* (1829)

7 Wherefore they are no more twain, but one flesh. What therefore God hath joined together, let not man put asunder.
Bible. Matthew, *King James Bible* (1611), 19:6

8 MARRIAGE, n. The state or condition of a community consisting of a master, a mistress and two slaves, making in all two.
Ambrose Bierce (1842–1914?) US writer and journalist. *The Devil's Dictionary* (1911)

9 In a happy marriage it is the wife who provides the climate, the husband the landscape.
Gerald Brenan (1894–1987) Maltese-born British writer and novelist. *Thoughts in a Dry Season* (1978)

10 It was very good of God to let Carlyle and Mrs Carlyle marry one another and so make only two people miserable instead of four, besides being very amusing.
Samuel Butler (1835–1902) British writer and composer. Referring to Thomas Carlyle. Letter to Miss Savage (November 21, 1884), quoted in *Letters Between Samuel Butler and Miss E. M. A. Savage* (1935)

11 Why don't they knead two virtuous souls for life Into that moral centaur, man and wife?
Lord Byron (1788–1824) British poet. *Don Juan* (1819–24), can. 5, st. 158

12 Marriage is a result of the longing for the deep, deep peace of the double bed after the hurly-burly of the chaise-longue.
Mrs. Patrick Campbell (1865–1940) British actor. Referring to her recent marriage. Quoted in *While Rome Burns* (Alexander Woollcott; 1934), 'The First Mrs Tanqueray'

13 They call it 'serial monogamy'.
Angela Carter (1940–92) British novelist, essayist, and short-story writer. *Wise Children* (1991)

14 She was a worthy womman al hir lyve, Housbondes at chirche dore she hadde fyve, Withouten other compaignye in youthe.
Geoffrey Chaucer (1343?–1400) English poet. Referring to the wife of Bath. 'The General Prologue', *The Canterbury Tales* (1390?), ll. 459–461, quoted in *The Works of Geoffrey Chaucer* (F. N. Robinson, ed.; 1957)

15 The most happy marriage I can picture or imagine to myself would be the union of a deaf man to a blind woman.
Samuel Taylor Coleridge (1772–1834) British poet. *Table Talk* (1835)

16 Tho' marriage makes man and wife one flesh, it leaves 'em still two fools.
William Congreve (1670–1729) English playwright and poet. *The Double Dealer* (1694), Act 2, Scene 3

17 Marriage is a wonderful invention; but then again so is a bicycle repair kit.
Billy Connolly (b. 1942) Scottish comedian and actor. *Billy Connolly* (Duncan Campbell; 1976)

18 Daisy, Daisy, give me your answer, do! I'm half crazy, all for the love of you! It won't be a stylish marriage, I can't afford a carriage, But you'll look sweet upon the seat Of a bicycle made for two!
Harry Dacre (1860–1922) British songwriter. Song lyric. 'Daisy Bell' (1892)

19 Marriage is a lottery in which men stake their liberty and women their happiness.
Virginie des Rieux, French writer. *La Satyre* (1967)

20 Every woman should marry—and no man.
Benjamin Disraeli (1804–81) British prime minister and writer. *Lothair* (1870), ch. 30

21 It seems to me that if the marriage ceremony is needed as a protection to ensure the enforced support of children, then you are marrying a man who, you suspect, would, under certain conditions, refuse to support his children, and it is a pretty low-down proposition.
Isadora Duncan (1877–1927) US dancer. *My Life* (1927)

22 The association of man and woman In daunsinge, signifying matrimonie— A dignified and commodious sacrament.
T. S. Eliot (1888–1965) US-born British poet and playwright. 'East Coker', *Four Quartets* (1940)

23 His designs were strictly honourable, as the phrase is; that is, to rob a lady of her fortune by way of marriage.

Henry Fielding (1707–54) British novelist and playwright. *Tom Jones* (1749), bk. 11, ch. 4

24 Most marriages don't add two people together. They subtract one from the other.

Ian Fleming (1908–64) British writer. *Diamonds Are Forever* (1956)

25 Married life requires shared mystery even when all the facts are known.

Richard Ford (b. 1944) US writer. *The Sportswriter* (1986)

26 A man in love is incomplete until he has married. Then he's finished.

Zsa Zsa Gabor (b. 1918) Hungarian-born US film actor. *Newsweek* (March 28, 1960)

27 The problem with marriage is that it ends every night after making love, and it must be rebuilt every morning before breakfast.

Gabriel García Márquez (b. 1928) Colombian novelist. *Love in the Time of Cholera* (1985)

28 Why have such scores of lovely, gifted girls Married impossible men? Simple self-sacrifice may be ruled out, And missionary endeavour, nine times out of ten.

Robert Graves (1895–1985) British poet and novelist. 'A Slice of Wedding Cake', *Robert Graves: Collected Poems* (1975)

29 Those who marry God . . . can become domesticated too—it's just as humdrum a marriage as all the others.

Graham Greene (1904–91) British novelist. *A Burnt Out Case* (1961), ch. 1

30 The others were only my wives. But you, my dear, will be my widow.

Sacha Guitry (1885–1957) Russian-born French actor and playwright. Allaying his fifth wife's jealousy of his previous wives. Attrib.

31 He loves his bonds, who, when the first are broke, Submits his neck unto a second yoke.

Robert Herrick (1591–1674) English poet. About a second marriage. 'To Love', *Hesperides* (1648)

32 Then, Madam, we must live in the same room and sleep in the same bed, dear Madam. Perhaps that is where we have met before.

Eugène Ionesco (1909–94) Romanian-born French playwright. The character is speaking to his own wife. *The Bald Prima Donna* (1950)

33 The triumph of hope over experience.

Samuel Johnson (1709–84) British lexicographer and writer. 1770. Referring to the hasty remarriage of an acquaintance following the death of his first wife, with whom he had been most unhappy. Quoted in *Life of Samuel Johnson* (James Boswell; 1791)

34 Love is moral even without legal marriage, but marriage is immoral without love.

Ellen Key (1849–1926) Swedish reformer and educationalist. 'The Morality of Woman', *The Morality of Woman and Other Essays* (1911)

35 In every house of marriage there's room for an interpreter.

Stanley Kunitz (b. 1905) US poet. 'Route Six' (1979)

36 Nothing is to me more distasteful than that entire complacency and satisfaction which beam in the countenances of a new-married couple.

Charles Lamb (1775–1834) British essayist. 'A Bachelor's Complaint of the Behaviour of Married People', *Essays of Elia* (1823)

37 Marriage is a wonderful institution, but who wants to live in an institution?

Groucho Marx (1895–1977) US comedian and film actor. Also attributed to Mae West. Attrib.

38 Marrying a man is a way of letting him know you want to be with him forever. It don't make no different if it don't last but two weeks.

Terry McMillan (b. 1951) US novelist and teacher. *Mama* (1987)

39 It's not that marriage itself is bad; it's the people we marry who give it a bad name.

Terry McMillan (b. 1951) US novelist and teacher. *Waiting to Exhale* (1992)

40 Marriage is like a cage; one sees the birds outside desperate to get in, and those inside equally desperate to get out.

Michel de Montaigne (1533–92) French essayist. *Essays* (1580–88), bk. 3

41 Why did He not marry? Could the answer be that Jesus was not by nature the marrying sort?

Hugh Montefiore (b. 1920) British bishop and author. Remark at a conference, Oxford (July 26, 1967)

42 It doesn't much signify whom one marries, for one is sure to find next morning that it was someone else.

Samuel Rogers (1763–1855) British poet and art collector. Quoted in *Table Talk of Samuel Rogers* (Alexander Dyce, ed.; 1860)

43 A married couple are well suited when both partners usually feel the need for a quarrel at the same time.

Jean Rostand (1894–1977) French biologist and writer. *Marriage* (1927)

44 It takes two to make a marriage a success and only one a failure.

Herbert Samuel (1870–1963) British statesman and philosopher. *A Book of Quotations* (1947)

45 CLOWN Many a good hanging prevents a bad marriage.

William Shakespeare (1564–1616) English poet and playwright. *Twelfth Night* (1601), Act 1, Scene 5

46 Marriage is popular because it combines the maximum of temptation with the maximum of opportunity.

George Bernard Shaw (1856–1950) Irish playwright. 'Maxims for Revolutionists', *Man and Superman* (1903)

47 My definition of marriage: . . . it resembles a pair of shears, so joined that they cannot be separated; often moving in opposite directions, yet always punishing anyone who comes between them.

Sydney Smith (1771–1845) British clergyman, essayist, and wit. Quoted in *A Memoir of the Rev. Sydney Smith* (Lady Holland; 1855), vol. 1, ch. 11

48 Even if we take matrimony at its lowest, even if we regard it as no more than a sort of friendship recognized by the police.

Robert Louis Stevenson (1850–94) Scottish novelist, essayist, and poet. 'Virginibus Puerisque', *Virginibus Puerisque* (1881), pt. 1

49 Every marriage tends to consist of an aristocrat and a peasant. Of a teacher and a learner.

John Updike (b. 1932) US writer. *Couples* (1968), ch. 1

50 Marriage isn't a word . . . it's a *sentence*!

King Vidor (1894–1982) US film director. Caption between scenes. *The Crowd* was a silent film. *The Crowd* (1928)

51 In married life three is company and two is none.

Oscar Wilde (1854–1900) Irish poet, playwright, and wit. *The Importance of Being Earnest* (1895), Act 1

52 Marriage is a bribe to make the housekeeper think she's a householder.

Thornton Wilder (1897–1975) US novelist and playwright. *The Merchant of Yonkers* (1939), Act 1

53 Marriage isn't a process of prolonging the life of love, but of mummifying the corpse.

P. G. Wodehouse (1881–1975) British-born US humorous writer. *Bring on the Girls* (co-written with Guy Bolton; 1953)

54 Wondering why one's friends chose to marry the people they did is unprofitable, but recurrent. One could so often have done so much better for them.

John Wyndham (1903–69) British science-fiction writer. *The Kraken Wakes* (1953)

Martyrdom

see also **Death and Dying, Fanaticism, Sacrifice**

1 To die for a religion is easier than to live it absolutely.

Jorge Luis Borges (1899–1986) Argentinian writer and poet. 1953? *Labyrinths* (1962), quoted in *Labyrinths: Selected Stories and Other Writings* (Donald A. Yates and James E. Irby, eds.; 1962)

2 I am fully persuaded that I am worth inconceivably more to hang than for any other purpose.

John Brown (1800–59) US abolitionist. Said before his execution. Remark (November 2, 1859), quoted in *The Home Book of Quotations* (Burton Stevenson; 1984)

3 This land absorbs the skins of martyrs. This land promises wheat and stars. Worship it! We are its salt and its water. We are its wound, but a wound that fights.

Mahmoud Darwish (b. 1942) Palestinian poet. 'Diary of a Palestinian Wound', *Modern Arabic Poetry* (Salma Khadra Jayyusi, ed.; 1987), no. 11

4 As a man, I undertake to face the possibility of annihilation in order that two or three truths may cast their eternal brilliance over the world.

Frantz Fanon (1925–61) Martinican social scientist, physician, and psychiatrist. *Black Skin, White Masks* (1952)

5 A patron of play-actors and a follower of hounds to become a shepherd of souls.

Herbert of Bosham (*fl.* 12th century) British chaplain and biographer of Thomas Becket. Referring to Thomas à Becket. *Vita Sancti Thomae* (12th century)

6 I dreamt that I died for my country. And right away a coffin-lid opener was there, holding out his hand for a tip.

Karl Kraus (1874–1936) Austrian writer. 1912. Quoted in 'Pro domo et mundo', *Karl Kraus* (Harry Zohn; 1971)

7 'Dying for an idea', again, sounds well enough, but why not let the idea die instead of you?

Wyndham Lewis (1882–1957) British novelist and painter. *The Art of Being Ruled* (1926), pt. 1, ch. 1

8 So greatly did she care for freedom that she died for it. So dearly did she love women that she offered her life as their ransom. That is the verdict given at the great Inquest of the Nation on the death of Emily Wilding Davison.

Christabel Pankhurst (1880–1958) British suffragette. Emily Davison threw herself under the king's racehorse during a race in protest at the imprisoning of suffragettes. *The Suffragette* (June 13, 1913)

9 Martyrdom is a grace of God which I do not think that I deserve. But if God accepts the sacrifice of my life, let my blood be a seed of freedom and the sign that hope will soon become reality.

Oscar Romero (1917–80) Salvadoran archbishop. Oscar Romero was murdered by paramilitary death squads (March 24, 1980). Quoted in *The War of Gods* (Michael Löwy; 1996)

10 The blood of the martyrs is the seed of the Church.

Tertullian (160?–220?) Carthaginian theological writer. Traditional misquotation: more accurately, 'Our numbers increase as often as you cut us down: the blood of Christians is the seed'. *Apologeticus* (197?), ch. 50, sect. 13

11 A thing is not necessarily true because a man dies for it.

Oscar Wilde (1854–1900) Irish poet, playwright, and wit. Quoted in *Oscariana* (1910)

Marxism

see also **Communism, Economics, Politics, Socialism**

1 The Marxist analysis has got nothing to do with what happened in Stalin's Russia; it's like blaming Jesus Christ for the Inquisition in Spain.

Tony Benn (b. 1925) British politician and author. *Observer* (April 27, 1980)

2 The intellectual rigour of Marxism proved to be far inferior to its emotive power . . . Marx had unwittingly provided . . . yet another substitute religion.

Norman Davies (b. 1939) British historian and writer. *Europe: A History* (1996), ch. 10

3 Ask anyone committed to Marxist analysis how many angels on the head of a pin, and you will be asked in return to never mind the angels, tell me who controls the production of pins.

Joan Didion (b. 1934) US journalist and writer. 1972. 'The Women's Movement', *The White Album* (1979), pt. 3

4 Just as Darwin discovered the law of evolution of organic matter, so Marx discovered the law of evolution of human history.

Friedrich Engels (1820–95) German socialist. Said at the funeral of Karl Marx. Remark (1883), quoted in *Europe Since 1870* (James Joll; 1976), ch. 3

5 Said Marx: 'Don't be snobbish, we seek to abolish The 3rd Class, not the 1st'.

Christopher Logue (b. 1926) British poet, playwright, and actor. 'M', *Abecedary* (1977)

6 Marxism is like a classical building that followed the Renaissance; beautiful in its way, but incapable of growth.

Harold Macmillan (1894–1986) British prime minister. Speech to the Primrose League (April 29, 1981)

7 What I did that was new was to prove . . . that class struggle necessarily leads to the dictatorship of the proletariat.

Karl Marx (1818–83) German philosopher. Letter to Georg Weydemeyer (March 5, 1852)

8 All I know is that I am not a Marxist.

Karl Marx (1818–83) German philosopher. Attrib.

9 The elderly Bektasi masters in Albania who got together with the party leadership . . . had no inkling that it wasn't the mysteries of the order that were being recited at the ceremonies, but exuberant Marxist-Leninist analyses.

Orhan Pamuk (b. 1952) Turkish novelist. *The Black Book* (Guneli Gun, tr.; 1990)

10 The cold metal of economic theory is in Marx's pages immersed in such a wealth of steaming phrases as to acquire a temperature not naturally its own.
Joseph Alois Schumpeter (1883–1950) Austrian-born US economist. *Capitalism, Socialism, and Democracy* (1942)

11 Dialectics is the soul of Marxism.
Joseph Stalin (1879–1953) Soviet dictator. *Problems of Leninism* (1940)

12 But not even Marx is more precious to us than the truth.
Simone Weil (1909–43) French philosopher, mystic, and political activist. 1933. 'Revolution proletarienne', *Oppression and Liberty* (1958)

Masculinity

see Men, Sexuality

Masturbation

see also Sex

1 Don't knock it, it's sex with someone you love.
Woody Allen (b. 1935) US film actor and director. Referring to masturbation. *Annie Hall* (1977)

2 You're treating your body like an amusement park!
Larry David, US television producer, screenwriter, and actor. As George, recounting what his mother said on discovering him masturbating. 'The Contest', *Seinfeld* (November 1992)

3 Masturbation is the thinking man's television.
Christopher Hampton (b. 1946) British playwright. *The Philanthropist* (1970)

4 Masturbation: the primary sexual activity of mankind. In the nineteenth century it was a disease; in the twentieth, it's a cure.
Thomas Szasz (b. 1920) Hungarian-born US psychiatrist. 'Sex', *The Second Sin* (1973)

Materialism

see also Business, Capitalism, Economics

1 The consumption explosion in the West, specially in the United States, is much more dangerous than the population 'explosion' in terms of putting pressure on natural resources . . . and yet the poor of developing countries . . . are now being blamed for the destruction of the environment.
Farida Akhter, Bangladeshi academic. *Depopulating Bangladesh* (1992)

2 Why grab possessions like thieves, or divide them like socialists, when you can ignore them like wise men?
Natalie Clifford Barney (1876–1972) US writer and literary hostess. 'Adam' (1962), no. 299

3 Before the time of our Ford.
Aldous Huxley (1894–1963) British novelist and essayist. In Huxley's futuristic anti-utopian satire, Henry Ford has become the presiding deity, with the president known as 'his Fordship'. *Brave New World* (1932), ch. 3

4 Man must choose whether to be rich in things or in the freedom to use them.
Ivan Illich (b. 1926) Austrian-born US educator and researcher. *Deschooling Society* (1971), ch. 4

5 The people long eagerly for just two things— bread and circuses.
Juvenal (65?–128?) Roman poet. *Satires* (98?–128?), no. 10, l. 80

6 Kissing your hand may make you feel very very good but a diamond and sapphire bracelet lasts forever.
Anita Loos (1888–1981) US writer. *Gentlemen Prefer Blondes* (1925), ch. 4

7 The devaluation of the world of men is in direct proportion to the increasing value of the world of things.
Karl Marx (1818–83) German philosopher. *Economic and Philosophic Manuscripts* (1844)

8 Years ago a person, he was unhappy, didn't know what to do with himself—he'd go to church, start a revolution—something. Today you're unhappy? Can't figure it out? What is the salvation? Go shopping.
Arthur Miller (b. 1915) US playwright. *The Price* (1968), Act 1

9 Only when he has ceased to need things can a man truly be his own master and so really exist.
Anwar al-Sadat (1918–81) Egyptian statesman. *In Search of Identity* (1978)

10 The want of a thing is perplexing enough, but the possession of it is intolerable.
John Vanbrugh (1664–1726) English architect and playwright. *The Confederacy* (1705), Act 1, Scene 2

11 Conspicuous consumption of valuable goods is a means of reputability to the gentleman of leisure.
Thorstein Bunde Veblen (1857–1929) US social scientist and economist. *The Theory of the Leisure Class* (1899), ch. 4

Mathematics

see also Physics, Science

1 The imagination in a mathematician who creates makes no less difference than in a poet who invents . . . Of all the great men of antiquity, Archimedes may be the one who most deserves to be placed beside Homer.
Jean le Rond d' Alembert (1717–83) French scientist, mathematician, and philosopher. *Discours Preliminaire de l'Encyclopédie* (1751)

2 There are very few things which we know, which are not capable of being reduc'd to a Mathematical Reasoning; and when they cannot it's a sign our knowledge of them is very small and confus'd.
John Arbuthnot (1667–1735) Scottish writer and physician. *Of the Laws of Chance* (1692)

3 For the things of this world cannot be made known without a knowledge of mathematics.
Roger Bacon (1220?–92) English monk, philosopher, and scientist. 'Distincta Prima', *Opus Majus* (1266–67), pt. 4

4 What is algebra exactly; is it those three-cornered things?
J. M. Barrie (1860–1937) British playwright and novelist. *Quality Street* (1901), Act 2, Scene 1

5 The longer mathematics lives the more abstract— and therefore, possibly also the more practical—it becomes.
Eric Temple Bell (1883–1960) Scottish-born US mathematician. Quoted in *The Mathematical Intelligencer* (1991), vol. 13

6 Out of nothing I have created a strange new universe.
János Bolyai (1802–60) Hungarian mathematician. Referring to non-Euclidean geometry. Attrib.

7 And wisely tell what hour o' the day
The clock does strike, by algebra.

Samuel Butler (1612–80) English satirist. *Hudibras* (1663), pt. 1,
can. 1, ll. 125–6

8 Every new body of discovery is mathematical in
form, because there is no other guidance we can
have.

Charles Darwin (1809–82) British naturalist. Quoted in *Mathematical
Maxims and Minims* (N. Rose, ed.; 1988)

9 The formula 'Two and two make five' is not
without its attractions.

Fyodor Dostoyevsky (1821–81) Russian novelist. *Notes from the
Underground* (1864)

10 We used to think that if we knew one, we knew
two, because one and one are two. We are finding
that we must learn a great deal more about 'and'.

Arthur Eddington (1882–1944) British astronomer and physicist. Quoted
in *Mathematical Maxims and Minims* (N. Rose, ed.; 1988)

11 Equations are more important to me, because
politics is for the present, but an equation is
something for eternity.

Albert Einstein (1879–1955) German-born US physicist. 1952? Quoted
in *A Brief History of Time* (Stephen Hawking; 1988)

12 As far as the laws of mathematics refer to reality,
they are not certain, and as far as they are
certain, they do not refer to reality.

Albert Einstein (1879–1955) German-born US physicist. *The Tao of
Physics* (F. Capra; 1975), ch. 2

13 When we reach the sphere of mathematics we are
among processes which seem to some the most
inhuman of all human activities and the most
remote from poetry. Yet it is here that the artist
has fullest scope for his imagination.

Havelock Ellis (1859–1939) British psychologist. *The Dance of Life*
(1923)

14 Which was to be proved.

Euclid (*fl.* 300 BC) Greek mathematician. The Latin version of this
phrase is *Quod erat demonstrandum*, hence Q.E.D. *Elements*
(300? BC), bk. 1, proposition 5

15 To divide a cube into two other cubes, a fourth
power or in general any power whatever into
two powers of the same denomination above the
second is impossible, and I have assuredly found
an admirable proof of this, but the margin is too
narrow to contain it.

Pierre de Fermat (1601–65) French mathematician. 1665. 'Fermat's
Last Theorem' was written in the margin of his copy of
Diophantus' *Arithmetica*. A proof of the same was discovered
in 1997. Attrib.

16 God does arithmetic.

Carl Friedrich Gauss (1777–1855) German mathematician and astronomer.
Attrib.

17 The layman finds such a law as dx/dt = K(d^2x/
dy^2) much less simple than 'it oozes', of which
it is the mathematical statement.

J. B. S. Haldane (1892–1964) British geneticist. *Possible Worlds*
(1927)

18 I am interested in mathematics only as a creative art.

Godfrey Harold Hardy (1877–1947) British mathematician. *A
Mathematician's Apology* (1941)

19 There exists, if I am not mistaken, an entire
world which is the totality of mathematical
truths, to which we have access only with our
mind, just as a world of physical reality exists,
the one like the other independent of ourselves,
both of divine creation.

Charles Hermite (1822–1901) French mathematician. Quoted in *The
Mathematical Intelligencer*, vol. 5, no. 4

20 Mathematics is the science of what is clear by
itself.

Karl Gustav Jakob Jacobi (1804–51) German mathematician. Quoted in
The World of Mathematics (J. R. Newman, ed.; 1956)

21 Where there is matter, there is geometry.

Johannes Kepler (1571–1630) German astronomer. Quoted in *Solid
Shape* (J. Koenderink; 1990)

22 Number theorists are like lotus-eaters—having
once tasted of this food they can never give it up

Leopold Kronecker (1823–91) German mathematician. Quoted in
Mathematical Circles Squared (H. Eves; 1972)

23 A good calculator does not need artificial aids.

Laozi (570?–490? BC) Chinese philosopher. The *Daode Jing* is an
early Chinese Taoist text. While attributed to Laozi, it
probably dates from the 3rd century BC *Daode Jing*
(Unknown)

24 The shortest distance between two points is not
always a straight line.

Nikolay Lobachevsky (1793–1856) Russian mathematician. Quoted in
The Jingle Bell Principle (Miroslav Holub; 1992)

25 Today, it is not only that our kings do not know
mathematics, but our philosophers do not know
mathematics and—to go a step further—our
mathematicians do not know mathematics.

J. Robert Oppenheimer (1904–67) US nuclear physicist. 'The Tree of
Knowledge', *Harper's Magazine* (1958)

26 Let no one ignorant of mathematics enter here.

Plato (428?–347? BC) Greek philosopher. 387 BC. Inscription written
over the entrance to the Academy. Quoted in *Biographical
Encyclopedia* (I. Asimov; 1966)

27 MOHAN One-two-three-four-five-six-seven-eight-
nine—zero! You put a zero after one and it
becomes more than nine. Every zero added
multiplies it ten times. Isn't that wonderful? Well
we discovered that zero—an unknown Indian.

Satyajit Ray (1921–92) Indian film director. *The Alien* (1967)

28 To a mind of sufficient intellectual power, the
whole of mathematics would appear trivial, as
trivial as the statement that a four-footed animal
is an animal.

Bertrand Russell (1872–1970) British philosopher and mathematician. *My
Philosophical Development* (1959)

29 Mathematics, rightly viewed, possesses not only
truth, but supreme beauty—a beauty cold and
austere, like that of sculpture.

Bertrand Russell (1872–1970) British philosopher and mathematician.
1902. *Philosophical Essays* (1910), no. 4

30 The fact that all Mathematics is Symbolic Logic
is one of the greatest discoveries of our age; and
when this fact has been established, the
remainder of the principles of mathematics
consists in the analysis of Symbolic Logic itself.

Bertrand Russell (1872–1970) British philosopher and mathematician.
Principia Mathematica (co-written with A. N. Whitehead;
1913)

31 I like mathematics because it is *not* human and
has nothing particular to do with this planet or
with the whole accidental universe—because, like
Spinoza's God, it won't love us in return.

Bertrand Russell (1872–1970) British philosopher and mathematician.
Attrib.

32 There are no sects in geometry.

Voltaire (1694–1778) French writer and philosopher. Quoted in *The
Viking Book of Aphorisms* (W. H. Auden and L.
Kronenberger, eds.; 1962)

33 God exists since mathematics is consistent, and the Devil exists since we cannot prove it.

André Weil (b. 1906) French-born US mathematician. Quoted in *Mathematical Circles Adieu* (H. Eves; 1977)

34 Numbers constitute the only universal language.

Nathanael West (1903–40) US novelist and screenwriter. *Miss Lonelyhearts* (1933)

35 Mathematics is thought moving in the sphere of complete abstraction from any particular instance of what it is talking about.

A. N. Whitehead (1861–1947) British philosopher and mathematician. *Science and the Modern World* (1925)

Meaning

see also **Language, Words**

1 The significance of man is that he is that part of the universe that asks the question, What is the significance of Man?

Carl Becker (1873–1945) US historian. *Progress and Power* (1936), ch. 3

2 The title means exactly what the words say: NAKED Lunch—a frozen moment when everyone sees what is on the end of every fork.

William S. Burroughs (1914–97) US writer. *The Naked Lunch* (1959), Introduction

3 'Take some more tea', the March Hare said to Alice, very earnestly.
'I've had nothing yet', Alice replied in an offended tone, 'so I can't take more'.
'You mean you can't take *less*', said the Hatter: 'it's very easy to take *more* than nothing'.

Lewis Carroll (1832–98) British writer and mathematician. *Alice's Adventures in Wonderland* (1865), ch. 7

4 Take care of the sense, and the sounds will take care of themselves.

Lewis Carroll (1832–98) British writer and mathematician. *Alice's Adventures in Wonderland* (1865), ch. 9

5 'I don't know what you mean by "glory"', Alice said. Humpty Dumpty smiled contemptuously. 'Of course you don't—till I tell you. I meant "there's a nice knock-down argument for you"!' 'But glory doesn't mean "a nice knock-down argument"', Alice objected.

Lewis Carroll (1832–98) British writer and mathematician. *Through the Looking-Glass and What Alice Found There* (1871)

6 Meaning implies that something is happening; you can say meaning is determined by the use of the thing, the way an audience uses a painting once it is put in public.

Jasper Johns (b. 1930) US painter. Quoted in 'What is Pop Art? Interviews with Eight Painters', *Art News* (G. R. Swenson; February 1964), issue 62, no. 10

7 The least of things with a meaning is worth more in life than the greatest of things without it.

Carl Gustav Jung (1875–1961) Swiss psychoanalyst. *Modern Man in Search of a Soul* (1933)

8 Fortunately, in her kindness and patience, Nature has never put the fatal question as to the meaning of their lives into the mouths of most people. And where no one asks, no one needs to answer.

Carl Gustav Jung (1875–1961) Swiss psychoanalyst. *The Development of Personality* (1934)

9 The sea rips in between two claws of stone Or races out, as meaning does with words.

Norman McCaig (1910–96) Scottish poet. 'Ardmore' (1960)

10 Where more is meant than meets the ear.

John Milton (1608–74) English writer. 'Il Penseroso', *Poems of Mr. John Milton* (1645), l. 120

11 Any general statement is like a check drawn on a bank. Its value depends on what is there to meet it.

Ezra Pound (1885–1972) US poet, translator, and critic. *ABC of Reading* (1934), ch. 1

12 What's the short meaning of this long harangue?

Friedrich von Schiller (1759–1805) German poet, playwright, and historian. *Piccolomini* (1800), Act 1, Scene 2

13 Semantic inflation.

Thomas Szasz (b. 1920) Hungarian-born US psychiatrist. Referring to the increasing hyperbole in language, for example, describing the common cold as 'flu', a bad day as a 'traumatic' one. Quoted in 'A Sickness Called Therapy', *Guardian* (Dylan Evans; August 28, 1999)

14 When Levin puzzled over what he was and what he was living for, he could find no answer and fell into despair; but when he left off worrying about the problem of his existence he seemed to know both what he was and for what he was living, for he acted and lived resolutely and unfalteringly.

Leo Tolstoy (1828–1910) Russian writer. *Anna Karenina* (1875–77), pt. 8, sect. 10

Media

see also **Communication, Internet, Journalism, Newspapers, Publishing, Television**

1 Broadcasting is really too important to be left to the broadcasters and somehow we must find some new way of using radio and television to allow us to talk to each other.

Tony Benn (b. 1925) British politician and author. Similar remarks were made by Georges Clemenceau and Charles de Gaulle. Speech, Bristol (October 18, 1968)

2 We are bombarded today by such a quantity of images that we can no longer distinguish direct experience from what we have seen for a few seconds on television. The memory is littered with bits and pieces of images, like a rubbish dump.

Italo Calvino (1923–85) Cuban-born Italian novelist and short-story writer. 1985. 'Visibility', *Six Memos for the Next Millennium* (Patrick Creagh, tr.; 1992)

3 Burke said that there were Three Estates in Parliament; but, in the Reporters' Gallery yonder, there sat a *Fourth Estate*, more important far than they all.

Thomas Carlyle (1795–1881) Scottish historian and essayist. Referring to Edmund Burke. 'The Hero as Man of Letters', *On Heroes, Hero-Worship, and the Heroic in History* (1841)

4 To starve is to be of media interest these days.

Nuruddin Farah (b. 1945) Somali novelist, playwright, and teacher. *Gifts* (1993)

5 Media is a word that has come to mean bad journalism.

Graham Greene (1904–91) British novelist. *Ways of Escape* (1981)

6 The idea that the media is there to educate us, or to inform us, is ridiculous because that's about tenth or eleventh on their list. The first purpose of the media is to sell us shit.

Abbie Hoffman (1936–89) US political activist. Speech, University of South Carolina (September 16, 1987)

7　As agents of the unification of the planet's history, the media amplify and channel the reduction process; they distribute throughout the world the same simplifications and stereotypes easily acceptable by the greatest number, by everyone, by all mankind.

Milan Kundera (b. 1929) Czech novelist. *The Art of the Novel* (1986)

8　One way to look at the future being digital is to ask if the quality of one medium can be transposed to another.

Nicholas Negroponte, US business executive and writer. *Being Digital* (1995)

9　We spend all day broadcasting on the radio and TV telling people back home what's happening here. And we learn about what's happening here by spending all day monitoring the radio and TV broadcasts from back home.

P. J. O'Rourke (b. 1947) US writer and humorist. Referring to the media during the Gulf War. Remark (January 31, 1991)

10　Never lose your temper with the Press or the public is a major rule of political life.

Christabel Pankhurst (1880–1958) British suffragette. *Unshackled* (1959), ch. 5

11　Nation shall speak peace unto nation.

Montague John Rendall (1862–1950) British headteacher. 1927. Motto of the British Broadcasting Corporation (BBC).

12　The media. It sounds like a convention of spiritualists.

Tom Stoppard (b. 1937) Czech-born British playwright and screenwriter. *Night and Day* (1978), Act 1

Medicine

see also **Doctors, Health and Healthy Living, Illness, Remedies, Science**

1　Medicine would be the ideal profession if it did not involve giving pain.

Samuel Hopkins Adams (1871–1958) US journalist. *The Health Master* (1913), ch. 3

2　In treating a patient, let your first thought be to strengthen his natural vitality.

Al-Razi (865?–928?) Persian physician and philosopher. Attrib.

3　Medicinal discovery,
It moves in mighty leaps,
It leapt straight past the common cold
And gave it us for keeps.

Pam Ayres (b. 1947) British poet. 'Oh No, I Got a Cold', *Some of Me Poetry* (1976)

4　Cure the disease and kill the patient.

Francis Bacon (1561–1626) English philosopher, statesman, and lawyer. 'Of Friendship', *Essays* (1625)

5　The poets did well to conjoin Music and Medicine in Apollo, because the office of Medicine is but to tune this curious harp of man's body and to reduce it to harmony.

Francis Bacon (1561–1626) English philosopher, statesman, and lawyer. *The Advancement of Learning* (1605), bk. 2

6　DIAGNOSIS, n. A physician's forecast of disease by the patient's pulse and purse.

Ambrose Bierce (1842–1914?) US writer and journalist. *The Devil's Dictionary* (1911)

7　Medicine . . . the only profession that labours incessantly to destroy the reason for its own existence.

James Bryce (1838–1922) British politician, jurist, and historian. Attrib.

8　Vaccination is the medical sacrament corresponding to baptism.

Samuel Butler (1835–1902) British writer and composer. Quoted in *Note Books* (H. Festing Jones, ed.; 1912)

9　The feasibility of an operation is not the *best* indication for its performance.

Henry Cohen (1900–77) British surgeon. *Annals of the Royal College of Surgeons of England* (1950)

10　Medicine is a conjectural art.

Jean Nicolas Corvisart des Marets (1755–1821) French physician. Attrib.

11　To a physician, each man, each woman, is an amplification of one organ.

Ralph Waldo Emerson (1803–82) US poet and essayist. *Bartlett's Unfamiliar Quotations* (Leonard Louis Levinson, ed.; 1972)

12　The practice of medicine is a thinker's art; the practice of surgery a plumber's.

Martin H. Fischer (1879–1962) German-born US physician and author. *Fischerisms* (Howard Fabing and Ray Marr, eds.; 1944)

13　Before undergoing a surgical operation arrange your temporal affairs—you may live.

Rémy de Gourmont (1858–1915) French poet, novelist, and critic. Attrib.

14　The foundation of the study of Medicine, as of all scientific inquiry, lies in the belief that every natural phenomenon, trifling as it may seem, has a fixed and invariable meaning.

William Withey Gull (1815–90) British physician. 'Study of Medicine', *A Collection of the Published Writings of W. W. Gull* (T. D. Acland, ed.; 1894)

15　The life so short, the craft so long to learn.

Hippocrates (460?–377? BC) Greek physician. Describing medicine. It is often quoted in Latin as *Ars longa, vita brevis*, and interpreted as 'Art lasts; life is short'. *Aphorisms* (415? BC), sect. 1

16　The lancet was the magician's wand of the dark ages of medicine.

Oliver Wendell Holmes (1841–1935) US judge. 'Some of My Early Teachers', *Medical Essays (1842–82)* (1891)

17　To a human being who is allowed to go on living and pursuing questions about the meaning of life by means of a heart or kidney transplant and the discovery of cyclosporin A, the problem of interference with the wisdom of nature may appear to be rather an abstract question.

Miroslav Holub (1923–98) Czech poet and immunologist. 'From the Amoeba to the Philosopher', *Shedding Life* (1997)

18　The only sure foundations of medicine are, an intimate knowledge of the human body, and observation on the effects of medicinal substances on that.

Thomas Jefferson (1743–1826) US president. Letter to Dr. Casper Wistar (June 21, 1807)

19　We are too much accustomed to attribute to a single cause that which is the product of several, and the majority of our controversies come from that.

Justus Liebig (1803–73) German chemist and educator. Attrib.

20　Medical practice is not knitting and weaving and the labor of the hands, but it must be inspired with soul and be filled with understanding and equipped with the gift of keen observation; these together with accurate scientific knowledge are the indispensable requisites for proficient medical practice.

Maimonides (1135–1204) Spanish-born Jewish philosopher and physician. *Bulletin of the Institute of the History of Medicine* (1935), vol. 3

21 Once on this August day, an exiled man
Striving to read the hieroglyphics spelled
By changing speckles upon glass, beheld
A secret hidden since the world began.
John Masefield (1878–1967) British poet and playwright. Referring to the 60th anniversary of the discovery by Ronald Ross of the transmission of malaria by the mosquito *Anopheles stephensi*. *Times* (August 20, 1957)

22 A possible apprehension now is that the surgeon be sometimes tempted to supplant instead of aiding Nature.
Henry Maudsley (1835–1918) British psychiatrist. Attrib.

23 The aim of medicine is to prevent disease and prolong life, the ideal of medicine is to eliminate the need of a physician.
William James Mayo (1861–1939) US physician. *National Education Association: Proceedings and Addresses* (1928)

24 Medicine may be defined as the art or the science of keeping a patient quiet with frivolous reasons for his illness and amusing him with remedies good or bad until nature kills him or cures him.
Gilles Ménage (1613–92) French scholar, lawyer, and cleric. *Ménagiana* (1693), pt. 3

25 GERONTE There was just one thing which surprised me—that was the positions of the liver and the heart. It seemed to me that you got them the wrong way about, that the heart should be on the left side, and the liver on the right.
SGANARELLE Yes, it used to be so but we have changed all that. Everything's quite different in medicine nowadays.
Molière (1622–73) French playwright. *Le Médecin Malgré Lui* (1667), Act 2, Scene 4

26 Medicine is a collection of uncertain prescriptions, the results of which, taken collectively, are more fatal than useful to mankind. Water, air, and cleanliness are the chief articles in my pharmacopeia.
Napoleon I (1769–1821) French emperor. Attrib.

27 The trained nurse has become one of the great blessings of humanity, taking a place beside the physician and the priest, and not inferior to either in her mission.
William Osler (1849–1919) Canadian physician. 'Nurse and Patient', *Aequanimitas, with Other Addresses* (1889)

28 The art of medicine is my discovery. I am called Help-Bringer throughout the world, and all the potency of herbs is known to me.
Ovid (43 BC–AD 17?) Roman poet. Said by Apollo. *Metamorphoses* (AD 8?)

29 The book of Nature is that which the physician must read; and to do so he must walk over the leaves.
Paracelsus (1493–1541) German alchemist and physician. Quoted in *Encyclopædia Britannica*, vol. 28

30 This basis of medicine is sympathy and the desire to help others, and whatever is done with this end must be called medicine.
Frank Payne (1840–1910) British physician. *English Medicine in the Anglo-Saxon Times* (1904)

31 Medicine is an art, and attends to the nature and constitution of the patient, and has principles of action and reason in each case.
Plato (428?–347? BC) Greek philosopher. *Gorgias* (4th century BC)

32 Medicine, to produce health, has to examine disease.
Plutarch (46?–120?) Greek biographer and philosopher. 'Demetrius', *Parallel Lives* (1st–2nd century)

33 Nature, time and patience are the three great physicians.
Proverb.

34 Medicine for the dead is too late.
Quintilian (35?–95?) Roman rhetorician. Attrib.

35 CYMBELINE By medicine life may be prolonged, yet death
Will seize the doctor too.
William Shakespeare (1564–1616) English poet and playwright. *Cymbeline* (1609–10), Act 5, Scene 5

36 The technology of medicine has outrun its sociology.
Henry E. Sigerist (1891–1957) Swiss medical historian. *Medicine and Human Welfare* (1941), ch. 3

37 Formerly, when religion was strong and science weak, men mistook magic for medicine, now, when science is strong and religion weak, men mistake medicine for magic.
Thomas Szasz (b. 1920) Hungarian-born US psychiatrist. 'Science and Scientism', *The Second Sin* (1973)

38 The art of medicine consists of amusing the patient while Nature cures the disease.
Voltaire (1694–1778) French writer and philosopher. Attrib.

Mediocrity

1 The English instinctively admire any man who has no talent and is modest about it.
James Agate (1877–1947) British theatre critic. Attrib.

2 The most insidious influence on the young is not violence, drugs, tobacco, drink or sexual perversion, but our pursuit of the trivial and our tolerance of the third rate.
Eric Anderson (b. 1936) British teacher. *Observer* (June 12, 1994), 'Sayings of the Week'

3 It's my deserts; I'm a second eleven sort of chap.
J. M. Barrie (1860–1937) British playwright and novelist. *The Admirable Crichton* (1902), Act 3

4 Only mediocrity can be trusted to be always at its best.
Max Beerbohm (1872–1956) British essayist, critic, and caricaturist. *Conversations with Max* (S. N. Behrman; 1960)

5 If a thing is worth doing, it is worth doing badly.
G. K. Chesterton (1874–1936) British writer and poet. 'Folly and Female Education', *What's Wrong with the World* (1910), pt. 4

6 Some men are born mediocre, some men achieve mediocrity, and some men have mediocrity thrust upon them. With Major Major it had been all three.
Joseph Heller (1923–99) US novelist. Paraphrase of William Shakespeare's: 'Some are born great, some achieve greatness, and some have greatness thrust upon 'em'. (*Twelfth Night*, Act 2, Scene 5). *Catch-22* (1961), ch. 9

7 Not gods, nor men, nor even booksellers have put up with poets being second-rate.
Horace (65–8 BC) Roman poet. *Ars Poetica* (19–8 BC), l. 372

8 It is an infallible sign of the second-rate in nature and intellect to make use of everything and everyone.
Ada Leverson (1862–1933) British writer and journalist. *The Limit* (1911)

9 I'm afraid you've got a bad egg, Mr. Jones. Oh no, my Lord, I assure you! Parts of it are excellent!
Newspapers. The origin of the expression, 'a curate's egg'. *Punch* (1895), vol. 109

MEMORY

285

10 It isn't evil that is ruining the earth, but
mediocrity. The crime is not that Nero played
while Rome burned, but that he played badly.
Ned Rorem (b. 1923) US composer and writer. *The Final Diary* (1974)

11 HAMLET A king of shreds and patches.
William Shakespeare (1564–1616) English poet and playwright. *Hamlet*
(1601), Act 3, Scene 4

12 A man of great common sense and good taste,—
meaning thereby a man without originality or
moral courage.
George Bernard Shaw (1856–1950) Irish playwright. Referring to Julius
Caesar. *Caesar and Cleopatra* (1901), Notes

13 Much of a muchness.
John Vanbrugh (1664–1726) English architect and playwright. *The
Provok'd Husband* (1728), Act 1, Scene 1

Melancholy

see also **Depression, Sorrow**

1 Melancholy is sensing the distance of one's being
from its own possible, attainable ideals!
Peter Altenberg (1859–1919) Austrian writer. *Prodomos* (Andrew
Barker, tr.; 1905)

2 Melancholy is a humour, boystrous & thycke,
and is bredde of troubled drastes of blode; &
hath his name of melon—that is black, & colim,
that is humor: wheruacon it is called melancolia,
as it were a black humor.
Bartholomaeus Anglicus (fl. 1230–50) English theologian and friar. *De
Proprietatibus Rerum* (1483)

3 Other men get their knowledge from books: I get
mine from melancholizing.
Robert Burton (1577–1640) English scholar and churchman. *The
Anatomy of Melancholy* (1621)

4 If there is a hell upon earth, it is to be found in a
melancholy man's heart.
Robert Burton (1577–1640) English scholar and churchman. *The
Anatomy of Melancholy* (1621)

5 All my joys to this are folly,
Naught so sweet as Melancholy.
Robert Burton (1577–1640) English scholar and churchman. 'Author's
Abstract of Melancholy', *The Anatomy of Melancholy* (1621)

6 Tell us, pray, what devil
This melancholy is, which can transform
Men into monsters.
John Ford (1586–1640?) English playwright. *The Lady's Trial* (1639),
Act 3, Scene 1

7 My heart aches, and a drowsy numbness pains
My sense, as though of hemlock I had drunk.
John Keats (1795–1821) English poet. The opening lines of the
poem. 'Ode to a Nightingale' (1820)

8 Deep in the shady sadness of a vale
Far sunken from the healthy breath of morn,
Far from the fiery noon, and eve's one star,
Sat gray-hair'd Saturn, quiet as a stone.
John Keats (1795–1821) English poet. The opening lines of the
poem. *Hyperion: A Fragment* (1820)

9 Wrapt in a pleasing fit of melancholy.
John Milton (1608–74) English writer. *Comus* (1637), l. 545

10 When we call this a case of Melancholia, we
understand that it is an affection of the brain; it
is the brain then that is at fault, but to what is it
due?
Montanus (fl. 2nd century) Phrygian prophet and religious leader.
Consultationes medicae (200?)

11 I am the darkly shaded, the bereaved, the
unconsoled,
The Prince of Aquitaine, with the blasted tower:
My only star is dead, and my star-studded lute
Wears the black sun of melancholy.
Gérard de Nerval (1808–55) French symbolist writer. 'El Desdichado',
Les Chimères (1854)

12 JAQUES I can suck melancholy out of a song,
as a weasel sucks eggs.
William Shakespeare (1564–1616) English poet and playwright. *As You
Like It* (1599), Act 2, Scene 5

13 KING There's something in his soul
O'er which his melancholy sits on brood.
William Shakespeare (1564–1616) English poet and playwright. *Hamlet*
(1601), Act 3, Scene 1

Memorials

see also **Death and Dying, Memory**

1 Who will remember, passing through this gate
The unheroic dead who fed the guns?
Who shall absolve the foulness of their fate—
Those doomed, conscripted, unvictorious ones?
Siegfried Sassoon (1886–1967) British poet and writer. 'On Passing the
New Menin Gate' (1928)

2 Remembrance is the secret of reconciliation.
Rudolf Scharping (b. 1947) German politician. *Observer* (April 17,
1994), 'Sayings of the Week'

3 ANTONY Friends, Romans, countrymen, lend me
your ears
I come to bury Caesar, not to praise him.
William Shakespeare (1564–1616) English poet and playwright. *Julius
Caesar* (1599), Act 3, Scene 2

4 Remember, now, Lawrence dead.
Blue squills in bloom—to
the scorched aridity of
the Mexican plateau.
William Carlos Williams (1883–1963) US poet, novelist, and physician.
'An Elegy for D. H. Lawrence', *An Early Martyr and other
Poems* (1935), quoted in *The Penguin Book of American
Verse* (Geoffrey Moore, ed.; 1977)

5 Each time a tragedy ends
People return to their homes one by one
And set up a grey memorial
In another new ruin.
Wu Yingtao (1916–71) Taiwanese poet. 'The Ruins', *Anthology of
Modern Chinese Poetry* (Michelle Yeh, ed., tr.; 1992)

Memory

see also **Forgetting, History, The Past**

1 There is a dark memory on which the noise of
Playing children is scattered like powdered sugar.
Yehuda Amichai (b. 1924) German-born Israeli poet. 'Sadness of the
Eyes and Descriptions of a Journey', *Amen* (1978), ll. 1–2

2 Memories are hunting horns whose sound dies
on the wind.
Guillaume Apollinaire (1880–1918) Italian-born French poet. 'Cors de
Chasse' (1912)

3 It is so surprising, is it not, how even the worst
happenings of the past acquire a sweetness in the
memory. Old harsh distresses are now merely
pictures and tastes which hurt no more, like
itching scars which can only give pleasure now.
Ayi Kwei Armah (b. 1939) Ghanaian writer and educator. *The Beautyful
Ones Are Not Yet Born* (1968)

4 Memory is not an act of will, after all. It is
something that happens in spite of oneself, and
when too much is changing all the time . . .
things are bound to slip through it.
Paul Auster (b. 1947) US writer. *In the Country of Last Things*
(1987)

5 God gave us our memories so that we might
have roses in December.
J. M. Barrie (1860–1937) British playwright and novelist. Rectorial
address, St. Andrews University (May 3, 1922)

6 The things that have come into being change
continually. The man with a good memory
remembers nothing because he forgets nothing.
Augusto Roa Bastos (b. 1917) Paraguayan writer. *I the Supreme* (1974)

7 I have more memories than if I were a thousand
years old.
Charles Baudelaire (1821–67) French poet. *Spleen* (1869)

8 Memories are like stones, time and distance erode
them like acid.
Ugo Betti (1892–1953) Italian playwright and poet. *Goat Island* (1946)

9 Far away now in the mountains . . . a
photograph guards the memory of a man. The
photograph is all alone out there. The snow is
falling eighteen years after his death. It covers up
the door.
Richard Brautigan (1935?–84) US novelist and poet. *Trout Fishing in
America* (1967)

10 Memory is often the attribute of stupidity; it
generally belongs to heavy spirits whom it makes
even heavier by the baggage it loads them down
with.
René Chateaubriand (1768–1848) French writer and statesman.
Mémoires d'Outre-tombe (1849–50)

11 Oon ere it herde, at tother out it wente.
Geoffrey Chaucer (1343?–1400) English poet. *Troilus and Criseyde*
(1380–86), bk. 4, 1. 434, quoted in *The Works of Geoffrey
Chaucer* (F. N. Robinson, ed.; 1957)

12 I got a long memory and I came from a line of
black and goin on women.
Lucille Clifton (b. 1936) US novelist and poet. 'For De Lawd', *Good
Times* (1969)

13 My memory is loyal to me, more loyal than my
best friends.
Dai Wangshu (1905–50) Chinese writer. 'My Memory', *Anthology of
Modern Chinese Poetry* (Michelle Yeh, ed., tr.; 1992)

14 It is very good to copy what one sees; it is much
better to draw what you can't see any more but
is in your memory. It is a transformation in
which imagination and memory work together.
You only reproduce what struck you, that is to
say the necessary.
Edgar Degas (1834–1917) French artist. *Degas by Himself: Drawings,
Prints, Paintings, Writings* (Richard Kendall, ed.; 1987)

15 He said that men ought to remember those
friends who were absent as well as those who
were present.
Diogenes Laërtius (fl. 3rd century) Greek historian and biographer.
Referring to Thales. 'Thales', *Lives of the Philosophers* (3rd
century?)

16 A man should keep his little brain attic stocked
with all the furniture that he is likely to use, and
the rest he can put away in the lumber room of
his library, where he can get it if he wants it.
Arthur Conan Doyle (1859–1930) Scottish-born British writer and physician.
'Five Orange Pips', *The Adventures of Sherlock Holmes* (1892)

17 Footfalls echo in the memory
Down the passage which we did not take
Towards the door we never opened
Into the rose-garden. My words echo
Thus, in your mind.
T. S. Eliot (1888–1965) US-born British poet and playwright. 'Burnt
Norton', *Four Quartets* (1935)

18 Every street-lamp that I pass
Beats like a fatalistic drum,
And through the spaces of the dark
Midnight shakes the memory
As a madman shakes a dead geranium.
T. S. Eliot (1888–1965) US-born British poet and playwright. 'Rhapsody
on a Windy Night', *Prufrock and Other Observations* (1917)

19 Memory believes before knowing remembers.
Believes longer than recollects, longer than
knowing even wonders.
William Faulkner (1897–1962) US novelist. *Light in August* (1932)

20 Idiot memory repeats itself as tragic litany. Lively
memory, on the other hand, is born every day,
springing from the past and set against it.
Eduardo Galeano (b. 1940) Uruguayan writer. *The Book of Embraces*
(1989)

21 It was inevitable: the scent of bitter almonds
always reminded him of the fate of unrequited
love.
Gabriel García Márquez (b. 1928) Colombian novelist. Opening words.
Love in the Time of Cholera (1985)

22 Only if a horse's muzzle appeared from out of
nowhere, propped itself on his shoulder and
fanned his cheek with a gust from its nostrils—
only then did he realize he was not in the middle
of a sentence but in the middle of the street.
Nikolay Gogol (1809–52) Russian novelist and playwright. Referring to
an overworked clerk, the hero of the story. 'The Overcoat'
(1842), quoted in *Diary of a Madman and Other Stories*
(Ronald Wilks, tr.; 1972)

23 What a strange thing is memory, and hope; one
looks backward, the other forward. The one is of
today, the other is the Tomorrow. Memory is
history recorded in our brain, memory is a
painter, it paints pictures of the past and of the
day.
Grandma Moses (1860–1961) US artist. *Grandma Moses, My Life's
History* (Aotto Kallir, ed.; 1947), ch. 1

24 Memory is the thread of personal identity,
history of public identity.
Richard Hofstadter (1916–70) US historian. *The Progressive
Historians* (1968)

25 This theory that memory images were stored in
different parts of the brain was surely the origin
of my belief that my mother's memories were still
intact, like a butterfly collection left behind in the
attic of an abandoned house.
Michael Ignatieff (b. 1947) Canadian-born British writer and broadcaster.
Describing his mother's dementia. *Scar Tissue* (1993)

26 The machinery of recall is thus the same as the
machinery of association, and the machinery of
association . . . is nothing but the elementary law
of habit in the nerve centers.
William James (1842–1910) US psychologist and philosopher. *The
Principles of Psychology* (1890), vol. 1

27 And when he is out of sight, quickly also is he
out of mind.
Thomas à Kempis (1379?–1471) German monk and religious writer.
Referring to death. *The Imitation of Christ* (1415–24?), bk. 1,
ch. 23

28 Everyone complains of his memory, but no one complains of his judgement.

François La Rochefoucauld (1613–80) French epigrammatist and moralist. *Reflections, or Sentences and Moral Maxims* (1665), no. 89

29 If you desire something more than their aroma, I am sorry to have to tell you that I have kept neither portraits, nor letters, nor memories; even the emotion has vanished.

Joaquim Maria Machado de Assis (1839–1908) Brazilian novelist and short-story writer. Referring to past loves. *Epitaph of a Small Winner* (1880)

30 Only stay quiet while my mind remembers
The beauty of fire from the beauty of embers.

John Masefield (1878–1967) British poet and playwright. 'On Growing Old', *The Collected Poems of John Masefield* (1923), st. 1, ll. 13–14

31 We do not descend, but rise from our histories.
If cut open, memory would resemble a cross-section of the earth's core,
a table of geographical time.

Anne Michaels (b. 1958) Canadian poet and novelist. 'Lake of Two Rivers', *The Weight of Oranges* (1986), sect. 4, ll. 31–32.

32 It has memory's ear
that can hear without
having to hear.

Marianne Moore (1887–1972) US poet. 'The Mind is an Enchanting Thing', *Nevertheless* (1944), ll. 13–15

33 If you can remember the sixties, you weren't really there.

Newspapers. Quoted in *Guardian* (June 2, 1987)

34 'I have done that', says my memory. 'I cannot have done that', says my pride, and remains inexorable. Eventually—memory yields.

Friedrich Wilhelm Nietzsche (1844–1900) German philosopher and poet. *Beyond Good and Evil* (1886)

35 The chain of memory is resurrection.

Charles Olson (1910–70) US poet. "A Newly Discovered 'Homeric' Hymn", *Charles Olson: Selected Poems* (Robert Creeley, ed.; 1993)

36 To be confronted with the trace instead of the memory itself is like looking through tears at the indentations on the armchair left there by your lover who has abandoned you and will never return.

Orhan Pamuk (b. 1952) Turkish novelist. *The Black Book* (Guneli Gun, tr.; 1990)

37 There are things I remember which may never have happened but as I recall them so they take place.

Harold Pinter (b. 1930) British playwright, theatre director, and screenwriter. *Old Times* (1971)

38 One lives in the hope of becoming a memory.

Antonio Porchia (1886–1968) Italian-born Argentinian writer. *Voces* (W. S. Merwin, tr.; 1968)

39 The taste was that of the little crumb of madeleine which on Sunday mornings at Combray . . . when I used to say good-day to her in her bedroom, my aunt Léonie used to give me, dipping it first in her own cup of real or of lime-flower tea.

Marcel Proust (1871–1922) French novelist. 1913. Du Côté de Chez Swann, *À la Recherche du Temps Perdu* (1913–27)

40 Thanks for the Memory

Leo Robin (1895–1984) US songwriter. Song title. Co-written with Ralph Rainger. (1938)

41 Remember me when I am gone away,
Gone far away into the silent land.

Christina Rossetti (1830–94) British poet. 'Remember' (1862)

42 OPHELIA There's rosemary, that's for remembrance; pray, love, remember: and there is pansies, that's for thoughts.

William Shakespeare (1564–1616) English poet and playwright. *Hamlet* (1601), Act 4, Scene 5

43 Yes. I remember Adlestrop—
The name, because one afternoon
Of heat the express train drew up there
Unwontedly. It was late June.

Edward Thomas (1878–1917) British poet, biographer, and critic. Originally published under the pseudonym Edward Eastaway. 'Adlestrop', *Poems* (1917)

44 The nice thing about having memories is that you can choose.

William Trevor (b. 1928) Irish novelist, short-story writer, and playwright. *Matilda's England* (1995)

45 The play is memory. Being a memory play, it is dimly lighted, it is sentimental, it is not realistic. In memory everything seems to happen to music. That explains the fiddle in the wings.

Tennessee Williams (1911–83) US playwright. *The Glass Menagerie* (1945), Scene 1

46 Memories are like mulligatawny soup in a cheap restaurant. It is best not to stir them.

P. G. Wodehouse (1881–1975) British-born US humorous writer. *Bring on the Girls* (co-written with Guy Bolton; 1953)

47 Even if my memory were to fail me in the future, I would still be able to retrace with certainty the footsteps of my soul.

Ye Si (b. 1948) Hong Kong-born Chinese writer. 'Transcendence and the Fax Machine' (Jeanne Tai, tr.; 1990)

Men

see also **The Sexes**, **Sexuality**, **Women**

1 I will have nothing to do with a man who can blow hot and cold with the same breath.

Aesop (620?–560 BC) Greek writer. 'The Man and the Satyr', *Aesop's Fables* (6th century BC)

2 A gentleman is any man who wouldn't hit a woman with his hat on.

Fred Allen (1894–1956) US comedian. Attrib. *Peter's Quotations* (Laurence J. Peter; 1978)

3 In passing, also, I would like to say that the first time Adam had a chance he laid the blame on woman.

Nancy Astor (1879–1964) US-born British politician. Attrib.

4 Man is defined as a human being and woman as a female—whenever she behaves as a human being she is said to imitate the male.

Simone de Beauvoir (1908–86) French writer and feminist theorist. *The Second Sex* (1949)

5 The most mediocre of males feels himself a demigod as compared with women.

Simone de Beauvoir (1908–86) French writer and feminist theorist. *The Second Sex* (1949)

6 There is an absolute human type, the masculine . . . Man superbly ignores the fact that his anatomy also includes glands, such as the testicles, and that they secrete hormones . . . He believes he apprehends objectivity.

Simone de Beauvoir (1908–86) French writer and feminist theorist. *The Second Sex* (1949)

7 It is probably true to say that the largest scope for change still lies in men's attitude to women, and in women's attitude to themselves.

Vera Brittain (1893–1970) British writer and feminist. *Lady into Woman* (1953), ch. 15

8 Do you know why God withheld the sense of humour from women? That we may love you instead of laughing at you.

Mrs. Patrick Campbell (1865–1940) British actor. Quoted in *Mrs. Pat: the Life of Mrs Patrick Campbell* (Margot Peters; 1984)

9 The male ego with few exceptions is elephantine to start with.

Bette Davis (1908–89) US actor. Attrib.

10 The average man is more interested in a woman who is interested in him than he is in a woman—any woman—with beautiful legs.

Marlene Dietrich (1901–92) German-born US actor and singer. Attrib.

11 Men are but children of a larger growth;
Our appetites as apt to change as theirs,
And full as craving too, and full as vain.

John Dryden (1631–1700) English poet, playwright, and literary critic. *All for Love* (1678), Act 4

12 A man is seldom ashamed of feeling that he cannot love a woman so well when he sees a certain greatness in her: nature having intended greatness for men.

George Eliot (1819–80) British novelist. *Middlemarch* (1871–72), ch. 39

13 All men are rapists and that's all they are. They rape us with their eyes, their laws, and their codes.

Marilyn French (b. 1929) US novelist and feminist. *The Women's Room* (1977)

14 The dark flame of his male pride was a little suspicious of having its leg pulled.

Stella Gibbons (1902–89) British poet and novelist. *Cold Comfort Farm* (1933), ch. 7

15 Probably the only place where a man can feel really secure is in a maximum security prison, except for the imminent threat of release.

Germaine Greer (b. 1939) Australian-born British writer and academic. 'Security', *The Female Eunuch* (1970)

16 Men will say (and accept) anything in order to foster national pride or soothe a troubled conscience.

C. L. R. James (1901–89) Trinidadian writer, political theorist, and educator. *The Black Jacobins* (1938)

17 Men peak at age nineteen and go downhill.

Garrison Keillor (b. 1942) US writer and broadcaster. *Leaving Home* (1987)

18 One realizes with horror, that the race of men is almost extinct in Europe. Only Christ-like heroes and woman-worshipping Don Juans, and rabid equality-mongrels.

D. H. Lawrence (1885–1930) British writer. *Sea and Sardinia* (1921)

19 The last gentleman in Europe.

Ada Leverson (1862–1933) British writer and journalist. Referring to Oscar Wilde. 'Reminiscences', *Letters to the Sphinx* (1930)

20 Unfortunately, most men are deaf.

Terry McMillan (b. 1951) US novelist and teacher. *Waiting to Exhale* (1992)

21 Many a man has been a wonder to the world, whose wife and valet have seen nothing in him that was even remarkable. Few men have been admired by their servants.

Michel de Montaigne (1533–92) French essayist. *Essays* (1580–88), bk. 3, ch. 2

22 I'm a lumberjack and I'm OK,
I sleep all night and I work all day,
I cut down trees, I skip and jump,
I like to press wild flowers.
I put on women's clothing,
And hang around in bars.

Monty Python's Flying Circus, British television series. Song lyric. 'The Lumberjack Song', *Monty Python's Flying Circus* (co-written by John Cleese, Michael Palin, Eric Idle, Graham Chapman, Terry Jones and Terry Gilliam; 1969–74)

23 Men know they are sexual exiles. They wander the earth seeking satisfaction, craving and despising, never content. There is nothing in that anguished motion for women to envy.

Camille Paglia (b. 1947) US academic and author. *Sexual Personae* (1990)

24 He may have hair upon his chest
But, sister, so has Lassie.

Cole Porter (1893–1964) US songwriter and composer. 'I Hate Men', *Kiss Me Kate* (1948)

25 I wonder if what makes men walk lordlike and speak so masterfully is having the love of women.

Alma Routsong (b. 1924) US writer and feminist. *A Place For Us* (1969)

26 The more I see of men, the more I admire dogs.

Madame de Sévigné (1626–96) French writer. Attrib.

27 MACBETH I dare do all that may become a man;
Who dares do more is none.

William Shakespeare (1564–1616) English poet and playwright. *Macbeth* (1606), Act 1, Scene 7

28 MARIANA They say best men are moulded out of faults
And, for the most, become much more the better
For being a little bad.

William Shakespeare (1564–1616) English poet and playwright. *Measure for Measure* (1604), Act 5, Scene 1

29 What would happen if . . . men could menstruate and women could not? Clearly, menstruation would become an enviable, boast-worthy, masculine event: Men would brag about how long and how much. Young boys would talk about it as the envied beginning of manhood.

Gloria Steinem (b. 1934) US writer and feminist. 'If Men Could Menstruate' (1978)

30 He is a man of brick. As if he was born as a baby literally of clay and decades of exposure have baked him to the colour and hardness of brick.

John Updike (b. 1932) US writer. *Rabbit, Run* (1960)

31 Sometimes I think if there was a third sex men wouldn't get so much as a glance from me.

Amanda Vail (1921–66) US writer. *Love Me Little* (1957), ch. 6

32 Men use thought only to justify their injustices, and speech only to conceal their thoughts.

Voltaire (1694–1778) French writer and philosopher. 'Le Chapon et la poularde', *Dialogue* (1763)

33 Take off they pants, I say, and men look like frogs to me. No matter how you kiss 'em, as far as I'm concern, frogs is what they stay.

Alice Walker (b. 1944) US novelist and poet. *The Color Purple* (1982)

34 I base everything on the idea that all men are basically just seven years old.

John Waters (b. 1946) US film director. Attrib.

35   A man who reads, who thinks, or who calculates, belongs to the species and not to the sex; in his better moments, he even escapes being human.
Marguerite Yourcenar (1903–87) Belgian-born French writer. *Memoirs of Hadrian* (1951)

Metamorphosis

see also **Change, Evolution**

1   Now I am ready to tell how bodies are changed into different bodies.
Ted Hughes (1930–98) British writer and poet. Opening words. *Tales from Ovid* (1997)

2   Gregory Samsa woke from uneasy dreams one morning to find himself changed into a giant bug.
Franz Kafka (1883–1924) Czech writer. 1913. Opening words. 'The Metamorphosis', *Franz Kafka: Stories 1904–24* (J. A. Underwood, tr.; 1981)

3   The universe is transformation; our life is what our thoughts make it.
Marcus Aurelius (121–180) Roman emperor and philosopher. *Meditations* (170–180), bk. 4, sect. 35

4   The longer you look at a thing
the more it transforms.
Anne Michaels (b. 1958) Canadian poet and novelist. 'Lake of Two Rivers', *The Weight of Oranges* (1986), sect. 4, ll. 1–2

5   In a metamorphosis the essential truth overruns the external illusion of truth: as you are, so you become. If you are insensitive to the world you turn into a rhinocerous.
Ben Okri (b. 1959) Nigerian novelist, short-story writer, and poet. *A Way of Being Free* (1997)

6   Of shapes transformed to bodies strange I purpose to entreat.
Ovid (43 BC–AD 17?) Roman poet. Opening words. *Metamorphoses* (AD 8?)

7   It would be very interesting to preserve photographically not the stages, but the metamorphoses of a picture. Possibly one might then discover the path followed by the brain in materializing a dream.
Pablo Picasso (1881–1973) Spanish painter and sculptor. Quoted in *Success and Failure of Picasso* (John Berger; 1965)

Metaphysics

see also **Philosophy, Theory**

1   I had rather believe all the fables in the legend, and the Talmud, and the Alcoran, than that this universal frame is without a mind.
Francis Bacon (1561–1626) English philosopher, statesman, and lawyer. 'Of Atheism', *Essays* (1625)

2   A blind man in a dark room—looking for a black hat—which isn't there.
Charles Bowen (1835–94) British judge. Characterization of a metaphysician. Attrib.

3   Metaphysics is the finding of bad reasons for what we believe upon instinct; but to find these reasons is no less an instinct.
F. H. Bradley (1846–1924) British philosopher. *Appearance and Reality* (1893), Preface

4   The human mind has created celestial and terrestrial physics, mechanics and chemistry, vegetable and animal physics, we might say, but we still have to complete the system of observational sciences with *social physics*.
Auguste Comte (1798–1857) French philosopher and sociologist. *Course in Positive Philosophy* (M. Clarke, tr.; 1830–42)

5   All metaphysics, including its opponent, positivism, speaks the language of Plato.
Martin Heidegger (1889–1976) German philosopher. *The End of Philosophy* (Joan Stambaugh, tr.; 1973)

6   The unrest which keeps the never stopping clock of metaphysics going is the thought that the non-existence of the world is just as possible as its existence.
William James (1842–1910) US psychologist and philosopher. *Some Problems of Philosophy* (1911)

7   Metaphysics is almost always an attempt to prove the incredible by an appeal to the unintelligible.
H. L. Mencken (1880–1956) US journalist, critic, and editor. 'Minority Report', *Notebooks* (1956)

Mexico

see **Central America**

Middle Age

see also **Adulthood, Age, Parents**

1   Years ago we discovered the exact point the dead center of middle age. It occurs when you are too young to take up golf and too old to rush up to the net.
Franklin P. Adams (1881–1960) US journalist. *Nods and Becks* (1944)

2   I am past thirty, and three parts iced over.
Matthew Arnold (1822–88) British poet and critic. Letter to Arthur Hugh Clough (February 12, 1853), quoted in *The Life and Correspondence of Thomas Arnold* (Penrhyn Stanley; 1844), vol. 1

3   Middle age is youth without its levity,
And age without decay.
Daniel Defoe (1660–1731) English novelist and journalist. Attrib.

4   The years between fifty and seventy are the hardest. You are always being asked to do things, and you are not yet decrepit enough to turn them down.
T. S. Eliot (1888–1965) US-born British poet and playwright. *Time* (October 23, 1950)

5   Middle age is when your age starts to show around the middle.
Bob Hope (b. 1903) British-born US comedian and film actor. Attrib.

6   Middle age snuffs out more talent than even wars or sudden deaths do.
Richard Hughes (1900–76) British writer. *The Fox in the Attic* (1961)

7   I think middle age is the best time, if we can escape the fatty degeneration of the conscience which often sets in at about fifty.
William Ralph Inge (1860–1954) British churchman. *Observer* (June 8, 1930)

8 Age became middle: the habits
  Made themselves at home, they were dressed
  In quilted dressing-gowns and carried
  A decanter, a siphon, and a tranquilliser.

  Louis MacNeice (1907–63) Irish-born British poet. 'The Habits', *The Burning Perch* (1963), ll. 16–19

9 Middle age is when you've met so many people
  that every new person you meet reminds you of
  someone else.

  Ogden Nash (1902–71) US humorist. *Versus* (1949)

10 At 50, everyone has the face he deserves.

  George Orwell (1903–50) British writer. Manuscript notebook (April 17, 1949)

11 One of the pleasures of middle age is to *find out*
  that one WAS right, and that one was much
  righter than one knew at say 17 or 23.

  Ezra Pound (1885–1972) US poet, translator, and critic. *ABC of Reading* (1934), ch. 1

12 Forty is the old age of youth; fifty is the youth of
  old age.

  Proverb.

13 For certain people, after fifty, litigation takes the
  place of sex.

  Gore Vidal (b. 1925) US novelist and essayist. *Evening Standard* (1981)

14 In a man's middle years there is scarcely a part
  of the body he would hesitate to turn over to the
  proper authorities.

  E. B. White (1899–1985) US writer and humorist. 'A Weekend with the Angels', *The Second Tree from the Corner* (1954)

15 By age forty you were either making a million a
  year or you were timid and incompetent.

  Tom Wolfe (b. 1930) US journalist and novelist. Referring to the narrator's assessment of career expectations on Wall Street in the 1980s. *The Bonfire of the Vanities* (1987)

Middle East

see also Islam, Judaism

1 For many Arabs who opposed Saddam Hussein
  and his policies their paradoxical support of Iraq
  was a gesture of defiance against the West.

  Akbar Ahmed (b. 1943) British academic. *Living Islam* (1993)

2 In almost all Arab countries the veil has been
  abolished, but not by force or by occidental
  criticism. It has been abolished by the women who
  decided one day that they did not want it any more.

  Nouha Alhegelan, Saudi Arabian writer. 'Women in the Arab World', *Irish Arab World* (1978)

3 They are burning the photographs
  of divided Jerusalem, and those
  beautiful love letters of a silent love.

  Yehuda Amichai (b. 1924) German-born Israeli poet. 'Patriotic Songs', *Amen* (1978), no. 24, ll. 1–3

4 Beirut will be the Hanoi and Stalingrad of the
  Israeli army.

  Yasir Arafat (b. 1929) Palestinian political and military leader. Referring to the Israeli invasion of Lebanon and the encirclement of Beirut. Drawing a comparison with the Soviet defeat at the Battle of Stalingrad (1942–43) during World War II, and the resistance of Hanoi to the US army during the Vietnam War (1959–75). Radio broadcast (1982), quoted in *Arafat: From Defender to Dictator* (Saïd Aburish; 1998)

5 It's not good enough to have just any old state, a
  replica of a Third World state, an instrument of
  Israeli domination.

  Hanan Ashrawi (b. 1946) Palestinian politician. Referring to the creation of a Palestinian state. *Independent* (May 31, 1995)

6 His Majesty's Government views with favour the
  establishment in Palestine of a national home for
  the Jewish people.

  Arthur Balfour (1848–1930) British prime minister. The so-called 'Balfour Declaration'. Letter to Lionel Walter, Lord Rothschild (November 2, 1917)

7 It is not possible to create peace in the Middle
  East by jeopardising the peace of the world.

  Aneurin Bevan (1897–1960) Welsh-born British politician. Remark made at a rally protesting against Britain's armed intervention in the Suez dispute. Speech, Trafalgar Square, London (November 4, 1956)

8 I will draw a line in the sand.

  George Bush (b. 1924) US president. Referring to the defence of Saudi Arabia by US forces following the Iraqi invasion of Kuwait. Remark at a press conference (1990)

9 My fear will be that in 15 years time, Jerusalem,
  Bethlehem, once centres of strong Christian
  presence, might become a kind of Walt Disney
  Theme Park.

  George Carey (b. 1935) British Anglican bishop. *Observer* (January 12, 1992)

10 Throughout the Middle East, there is a great
  yearning for the quiet miracle of a normal life.

  Bill Clinton (b. 1946) US president. Referring to the Israeli-PLO peace accord. *Times* (September 14, 1993)

11 The whole religious complexion of the modern
  world is due to the absence from Jerusalem of a
  lunatic asylum.

  Havelock Ellis (1859–1939) British psychologist. *Impressions and Comments* (1914)

12 We feel that the Arabs and the Jews are cousins
  in race, having suffered similar oppression at the
  hands of powers stronger than ourselves.

  Faisal (1905–75) Saudi Arabian monarch. Quoted in *Dawn of the Promised Land* (Ben Wicks; 1997)

13 Zionism . . . is a moral, lawful, humanitarian
  movement, directed towards the long yearned-for
  goal of our people.

  Theodor Herzl (1860–1904) Hungarian-born Zionist leader. Address to the First Zionist Congress, Basel, Switzerland (August 29, 1897)

14 This plan . . . is a reserve against more evil days.

  Theodor Herzl (1860–1904) Hungarian-born Zionist leader. Referring to the plan for a Jewish homeland. Letter to Rabbi Gudemann, Chief Rabbi of Vienna (1895)

15 And if it should occur that men of other creeds
  and different nationalities come to live amongst
  us, we should accord them honorable protection
  and equality before the law.

  Theodor Herzl (1860–1904) Hungarian-born Zionist leader. *The Jewish State* (1896)

16 The Promised Land, where we can have hooked
  noses, black or red beards, and bow legs, without
  being despised for it.

  Theodor Herzl (1860–1904) Hungarian-born Zionist leader. *The Jewish State* (1896)

17 We shall keep our priests within the confines of
  their temples in the same way as we shall keep
  our professional army within the confines of their
  barracks . . . they must not interfere in the
  administration of the state.

  Theodor Herzl (1860–1904) Hungarian-born Zionist leader. *The Jewish State* (1896)

18 Arabs today . . . see a travesty of modernism,
  neither genuinely Western nor properly Eastern,
  and certainly not satisfactory. The frenzy of
  Islamic revivalism must surely be a reaction to
  this state of affairs.

  Rana Kabbani (b. 1958) Syrian cultural historian. *A Letter to Christendom* (1989)

19 The Israelis are now what we call the 'enemy-friends'.
Rose Macaulay (1881–1958) British poet, novelist, and essayist. Quoted in *Independent* (July 5, 1994)

20 No country will more quickly dissipate romantic expectations than Palestine—particularly Jerusalem . . . Is the desolation of the land the result of the fatal embrace of the Deity? Hapless are the favorites of heaven.
Herman Melville (1819–91) US novelist. January 25, 1857. Quoted in *Journal of a Visit to Europe and the Levant* (H. C. Horsford, ed.; 1955)

21 Western democracy, although it seems to carry within it the seeds of life, is too linked in our history with the seeds of death.
Fatima Mernissi (b. 1941) Moroccan writer. *Islam and Democracy* (1992)

22 City of my birth. City of my dreams . . . And here I was, stalking its streets clutching a submachine gun, like a figure in one of my childhood nightmares: an alien man in an alien city.
Amos Oz (b. 1939) Israeli writer. 1968. 'An Alien City', *Under This Blazing Light* (1979)

23 The new Israel is not a reconstruction of the kingdom of David and Solomon . . . or the *shtetl* borne to the hills of Canaan on the wings of Chagall.
Amos Oz (b. 1939) Israeli writer. 1967. 'The Meaning of Homeland', *Under This Blazing Light* (1979)

24 The Zionist enterprise has no other objective justification than the right of a drowning man to grasp the only plank that can save him.
Amos Oz (b. 1939) Israeli writer. 1967. 'The Meaning of Homeland', *Under This Blazing Light* (1979)

25 I believe in . . . a Zionism that recognizes both the spiritual implications and the political consequences of the fact that this small tract of land is the homeland of two peoples fated to live facing each other.
Amos Oz (b. 1939) Israeli writer. 1967. Referring to the Israelis and the Palestinians. 'The Meaning of Homeland', *Under This Blazing Light* (1979)

26 My poor country,
you have changed me in a moment
from a poet who writes of love and longing
to a poet who writes with a knife.
Nizar Qabbani (b. 1923) Syrian poet. 'Marginal Notes on the Book of Defeat' (1967), pt. 3, quoted in *When the Words Burn* (John Mikhail Asfour, ed., tr.; 1988)

27 The acacia is drooping,
the door of a house in Rafah
opens like a wound
. . . Five Guns
She stares wide-eyed.
Samih Qasim (b. 1939) Palestinian poet. 'Girl from Rafah', *Modern Arabic Poetry* (Salma Khadra Jayyusi, ed.; 1987), ll. 12–14, ll. 24–25

28 No longer are we necessarily 'a people that dwells alone', and no longer is it true that 'the whole world's against us'. We must overcome the sense of isolation that has held us in its thrall for almost half a century.
Yitzhak Rabin (1922–95) Israeli statesman. Speech to the Israeli parliament, Tel Aviv (July 13, 1992), quoted in *Murder in the Name of God* (Michael Karpin and Ina Friedman; 1999)

29 We have been fated to live together on the same patch of land, in the same country . . . One hundred years of your bloodshed and terror against us have brought you only suffering, humiliation, bereavement, and pain.
Yitzhak Rabin (1922–95) Israeli statesman. Addressed to Palestinians. Speech to the Israeli parliament, Tel Aviv (July 13, 1992), quoted in *Murder in the Name of God* (Michael Karpin and Ina Friedman; 1999)

30 Israel is a people at whose centre is the space we make for God.
Jonathan Sacks (b. 1948) British chief rabbi. *Community of Faith* (1995)

31 A brilliant soldier who hated war, he was a man of battle who longed for peace.
Jonathan Sacks (b. 1948) British chief rabbi. Referring to Yitzhak Rabin. *Times Magazine* (December 30, 1995)

32 There is no such thing as partial independence or limited autonomy. Without political independence there is neither sovereignty nor real freedom, and certainly not equality.
Edward W. Said (b. 1935) Palestinian-born US writer and educator. Referring to the desire for an independent Palestinian state. *The Politics of Dispossession* (1994), epilogue

33 The Arabs have the reputation of being uneducated, the people of camels, petrol, terrorism, etc. So how can a Westerner believe that Arabs have culture, literature, and woman writers?
Hanan al-Shaykh (b. 1945) Palestinian writer. Interview, *Michigan Quarterly Review* (Fall 1992)

34 Why did my country become a gateway to hell? Since when are apples bitter? When did moonlight stop bathing orchards?
Fadwa Tuqan (b. 1917) Palestinian poet. 'Face Lost in the Wilderness', *Modern Arabic Poetry* (Salma Khadra Jayyusi, ed.; 1987), ll. 32–34

35 All of us, all hostages, would plead with those who are holding the people of South Lebanon, innocent people being held as hostages, to release them soon; to put an end to this problem; to put an end to terrorism, and to find peaceful, humane and civilized ways of resolving the very complex problems that face the Middle East.
Terry Waite (b. 1939) British religious adviser. 1991. *Times* (November 19, 1991)

36 I am anxious not for the survival of the Diaspora . . . but for the survival of Israel.
A. B. Yehoshua (b. 1936) Israeli novelist. Interview (March 7, 1985), quoted in *Voices of Israel* (Joseph Cohen; 1990)

37 Our region is not the Middle East so much as it is a region of the Mediterranean. It is Greece and Italy and Egypt and Malta and Turkey.
A. B. Yehoshua (b. 1936) Israeli novelist. Interview (March 7, 1985), quoted in *Voices of Israel* (Joseph Cohen; 1990)

38 Those perfect German Orientalists who know all the mysteries of the Koran but are unable to go to an Arab village and ask for a coffee.
A. B. Yehoshua (b. 1936) Israeli novelist. Interview (March 7, 1985), quoted in *Voices of Israel* (Joseph Cohen; 1990)

Mind

see also **Consciousness, Psychology, Thinking, Understanding**

1 My mind is not a bed to be made and re-made.
James Agate (1877–1947) British theatre critic. *Ego* (June 9, 1943)

2 In everything there is a portion of everything except Mind.

Anaxagoras (500?–428? BC) Greek philosopher. Quoted in *The Presocratic Philosophers* (G. S. Kirk, J. E. Raven, and M. Schofield; 1983)

3 The mind is properly conceived as an inner principle, but a principle that is identified in terms of the outward behaviour it is apt for bringing about.

D. M. Armstrong (b. 1926) Australian philosopher. An attempt to reconcile behaviourism and classical philosophy. *The Nature of Mind* (1980)

4 I call the soul or mind thinking substance. Thinking, knowing, and perceiving are all the same thing. I also take the idea of an object and the perception of an object to be the same thing.

Antoine Arnauld (1612–94) French philosopher, lawyer, mathematician, and priest. *Des Vraies et Fausses Idées* (1683), 38

5 Murphy's mind pictured itself as a large hollow sphere, hermetically closed to the universe without.

Samuel Beckett (1906–89) Irish playwright, novelist, and poet. *Murphy* (1938), ch. 6

6 BRAIN, n. An apparatus with which we think that we think.

Ambrose Bierce (1842–1914?) US writer and journalist. *The Devil's Dictionary* (1911)

7 Measure your mind's height by the shade it casts!

Robert Browning (1812–89) British poet. *Paracelsus* (1835), pt. 3, l. 821

8 No mind is thoroughly well organized that is deficient in a sense of humour.

Samuel Taylor Coleridge (1772–1834) British poet. 1833. *Table Talk* (1835)

9 Babylon in all its desolation is a sight not so awful as that of the human mind in ruins.

Scrope Davies (1783?–1852) British dandy. Letter to Thomas Raikes (May 25, 1835), quoted in *Journal, 1831–47* (T. Raikes, ed.; 1856), vol. 2

10 There is a great difference between the mind and the body, inasmuch as the body is by its very nature always divisible, while the mind is utterly indivisible.

René Descartes (1596–1650) French philosopher and mathematician. *Meditations on First Philosophy* (1641), Sixth Meditation

11 We know the human brain is a device to keep the ears from grating on one another.

Peter De Vries (1910–93) US novelist. *Comfort Me With Apples* (1956), ch. 1

12 The various fine arts, architecture, sculpture, painting, music, and poetry, are the successive attempts of the mind adequately to express its own ideal nature.

John Dewey (1859–1952) US philosopher and educator. *Psychology* (1887)

13 The mind is an iceberg; it floats with only 17% of its bulk above water.

Sigmund Freud (1856–1939) Austrian psychoanalyst. *Bartlett's Unfamiliar Quotations* (Leonard Louis Levinson, ed.; 1972)

14 My life and work has been aimed at one goal only: to infer or guess how the mental apparatus is constructed and what forces interplay and counteract in it.

Sigmund Freud (1856–1939) Austrian psychoanalyst. Quoted in *Sigmund Freud: Life and Work* (3 vols.) (Ernest Jones; 1953–55)

15 The force of mind is only as great as its expression; its depth only as deep as its power to expand and lose itself.

G. W. F. Hegel (1770–1831) German philosopher. 1807. *The Phenomenology of Mind* (J. B. Baillie, tr.; 1910)

16 All men should know that the brain, and the brain only, is responsible for, and is the seat of, all our joys and happiness, our pain and sadness; here is seated wisdom, understanding, and the knowledge of the difference between good and evil.

Hippocrates (460?–377? BC) Greek physician. *Sacred Disease* (5th century? BC)

17 The mind, once expanded to the dimensions of larger ideas, never returns to its original size.

Oliver Wendell Holmes (1841–1935) US judge. Attrib.

18 If there is anything the matter with your eyes, you hasten to get it put right; but if anything is the matter with your mind, you put off treatment for a year.

Horace (65–8 BC) Roman poet. *Epistles* (20? BC), bk. 1, no. 2, l. 38

19 When very fresh, our minds carry an immense horizon with them. The present image shoots its perspective far before it, irradiating in advance the regions in which lie the thoughts as yet unborn.

William James (1842–1910) US psychologist and philosopher. *The Principles of Psychology* (1890), vol. 1

20 Bodily decay is gloomy in prospect, but of all human contemplations the most abhorrent is body without mind.

Thomas Jefferson (1743–1826) US president. Letter to John Adams (August 1, 1816)

21 The pendulum of the mind oscillates between sense and nonsense, not between right and wrong.

Carl Gustav Jung (1875–1961) Swiss psychoanalyst. *Memories, Dreams, Reflections* (1962), ch. 5

22 The human mind *has* to ask 'Who, what, whence, whither, why am I?' And it is very doubtful if the human mind can answer any of these questions.

R. D. Laing (1927–89) Scottish psychiatrist. *Wisdom, Madness and Folly: The Making of a Psychiatrist, 1927–57* (1985)

23 The brain has muscles for thinking as the legs have muscles for walking.

Julien Offroy de La Mettrie (1709–51) French philosopher and physician. *The Man-Machine* (1747)

24 Our minds are lazier than our bodies.

François La Rochefoucauld (1613–80) French epigrammatist and moralist. *Reflections, or Sentences and Moral Maxims* (1665), no. 490

25 The highest function of *mind* is its function of messenger.

D. H. Lawrence (1885–1930) British writer. *Kangaroo* (1923)

26 In four hours by the swimming pool in Cuernavaca I learned more about the mind, the brain, and its structure than I did in the preceding fifteen as a diligent psychologist.

Timothy Leary (1920–96) US psychologist and guru. Referring to his first experience of psychedelic drugs. *Flashbacks: an Autobiography* (1983)

27 Let us then suppose the Mind to be, as we say, white Paper, void of all Characters, without any *Ideas*; How comes it to be furnished? . . . Whence has it all the materials of Reason and Knowledge? To this I answer, in one word, From *Experience*.

John Locke (1632–1704) English philosopher. *An Essay Concerning Human Understanding* (1690), bk. 2

28 The most merciful thing in the world, I think, is the inability of the human mind to correlate all its contents.
H. P. Lovecraft (1890–1937) US writer. *The Call of Cthulhu* (1928), ch. 1

29 The mind like a sick body can be healed and changed by medicine.
Lucretius (99?–55? BC) Roman philosopher and poet. *De Rerum Natura* (1st century BC), pt. 3

30 The beauty of Bertrand Russell's beautiful mathematical mind is absolute, like the third movement of Beethoven's A Minor Quartet.
Ethel Mannin (1900–84) British writer. *Confessions and Impressions* (1930)

31 I took my mind a walk
or my mind took me a walk—
whichever was the truth of it.
Norman McCaig (1910–96) Scottish poet. 'An Ordinary Day' (1966)

32 A mind not to be changed by place or time.
The mind is its own place, and in itself
Can make a heaven of hell, a hell of heaven.
John Milton (1608–74) English writer. Said by Satan. *Paradise Lost* (1667), bk. 1, ll. 253–255

33 The mind has great influence over the body, and maladies often have their origin there.
Molière (1622–73) French playwright. *Le Médecin Malgré Lui* (1667), Act 3

34 The Mind is an Enchanting Thing
is an enchanted thing
like the glaze on a
katydid-wing.
Marianne Moore (1887–1972) US poet. A katydid is a kind of grasshopper. 'The Mind is an Enchanting Thing', *Nevertheless* (1944), ll. 1–3

35 It is the mind that makes the man, and our vigour is in our immortal soul.
Ovid (43 BC–AD 17?) Roman poet. *Metamorphoses* (AD 8?), bk. 13

36 The discovery by cognitive science . . . of the technical challenges overcome by our mundane mental activity is . . . an awakening of the imagination comparable to learning that the universe is made up of billions of galaxies.
Steven Pinker (b. 1954) US cognitive scientist and author. *How the Mind Works* (1997)

37 Mind is ever the ruler of the universe.
Plato (428?–347? BC) Greek philosopher. *Philebus* (4th century? BC)

38 Alas! in truth the man but chang'd his mind, Perhaps was sick, in love, or had not din'd.
Alexander Pope (1688–1744) English poet. 'To Lord Cobham', *Epistles to Several Persons* (1734), ll. 127–128

39 As long as our brain is a mystery, the universe, the reflection of the structure of the brain, will also be a mystery.
Santiago Ramón y Cajal (1852–1934) Spanish scientist. *Charlas de Café* (1920)

40 The dogma of the Ghost in the Machine.
Gilbert Ryle (1900–76) British philosopher. Referring to Descartes' mental-conduct concepts. *The Concept of Mind* (1949), ch. 1

41 If it is for mind that we are searching the brain, then we are supposing the brain to be much more than a telephone-exchange. We are supposing it a telephone-exchange along with the subscribers as well.
Charles Scott Sherrington (1857–1952) British physiologist. *Man on his Nature* (1940)

42 The mind has added nothing to human nature. It is a violence from within that protects us from a violence without.
Wallace Stevens (1879–1955) US poet. 'The Noble Rider and the Sound of Words', *The Necessary Angel: Essays on Reality and the Imagination* (1951)

43 Untilled soil, however fertile it may be, will bear thistles and thorns; and so it is with man's mind.
Saint Teresa of Ávila (1515–82) Spanish mystic, author, and nun. 'Maxims for Her Nuns' (1566?), quoted in *Selected Writings of St. Teresa of Avila* (William J. Doheny, ed.; 1950)

44 The brain is the means by which we think we think.
Julian Tuwim (1894–1953) Polish poet. Quoted in *The Jingle Bell Principle* (Miroslav Holub; 1992)

45 Once we are destined to live out our lives in the prison of our mind, our one duty is to furnish it well.
Peter Ustinov (b. 1921) British actor, director, and writer. *Dear Me* (1977), ch. 20

46 I have no castle; I make unmovable mind my castle. I have no sword; I make the sleep of the mind my sword.
Alan Watts (1915–73) British-born US mystic and writer. Extract from the Samurai creed, referring to the condition of detachment known as 'Muga'. *The Spirit of Zen* (1936)

47 Mind is the great lever of all things; human thought is the process by which human ends are ultimately answered.
Daniel Webster (1782–1852) US lawyer, politician, and orator. 1825. Address on laying the cornerstone of the Bunker Hill Monument, quoted in *The Writings and Speeches of Daniel Webster* (J. W. McIntyre, ed.; 1903), vol. 1

48 The mind can also be an erogenous zone.
Raquel Welch (b. 1940) US film actor. Quoted in *Colombo's Hollywood* (J. R. Colombo; 1979)

49 The human mind is a device for survival and reproduction, and reason is just one of its various techniques.
Edward O. Wilson (b. 1929) US evolutionary biologist. 'Dilemma', *On Human Nature* (1978)

50 Nor less I deem that there are Powers
Which of themselves our minds impress;
That we can feed this mind of ours
In a wise passiveness.
William Wordsworth (1770–1850) English poet. May 23, 1798. Companion piece to 'The Tables Turned'. 'Expostulation and Reply', *Lyrical Ballads* (1798), ll. 21–24

Misanthropy

see also **Contempt, Hate**

1 People are worms, and even the God who created them is immensely bored with their antics.
Ama Ata Aidoo (b. 1942) Ghanaian writer. 'Two Sisters', *No Sweetness Here* (1970)

2 I do not want people to be very agreeable, as it saves me the trouble of liking them a great deal.
Jane Austen (1775–1817) British novelist. Letter (December 24, 1798)

3 Many people believe that they are attracted by God, or by Nature, when they are only repelled by man.
William Ralph Inge (1860–1954) British churchman. *More Lay Thoughts of a Dean* (1931), pt. 4, ch. 1

4 Upon the whole I dislike mankind: whatever people on the other side of the question may advance, they cannot deny that they are always surprised at hearing of a good action and never of a bad one.

John Keats (1795–1821) English poet. Letter to Georgiana Keats (January 13, 15, 17, and 28, 1820), quoted in *Letters of John Keats* (Robert Gittings, ed.; 1970)

5 I am not for women but against men.

Karl Kraus (1874–1936) Austrian writer. 1912. Quoted in 'Pro domo et mundo', *Karl Kraus* (Harry Zohn; 1971)

6 I'm hostile to men, I'm hostile to women. I'm hostile to cats, to poor cockroaches, I'm afraid of horses.

Norman Mailer (b. 1923) US novelist and journalist. 'Sixth Presidential Paper—A Kennedy Miscellany: An Impolite Interview', *The Presidential Papers* (1963)

7 He who is the friend of all humanity is not my friend.

Molière (1622–73) French playwright. *Le Misanthrope* (1666), Act 1, Scene 1

8 A young, earnest American brought up the subject of nuclear warfare which, he said might well destroy the entire human race. 'I can't wait', P. G. Wodehouse murmured.

Malcolm Muggeridge (1903–90) British journalist. *Tread Softly For You Tread on My Jokes* (1966)

9 So that's what Hell is. I'd never have believed it . . . Do you remember, brimstone, the stake, the gridiron? What a joke! No need of a gridiron—Hell is other people.

Jean-Paul Sartre (1905–80) French philosopher, playwright, and novelist. *Huis Clos* (1944), Scene 5

10 Other people are quite dreadful. The only possible society is oneself.

Oscar Wilde (1854–1900) Irish poet, playwright, and wit. *An Ideal Husband* (1895), Act 2

Misfortune

see also **Disaster, Fate, Sorrow**

1 Calamity is man's true touchstone.

Beaumont & Fletcher, English playwrights. *Four Plays in One: The Triumph of Honour* (performed 1647), Scene 1

2 Calamities are of two kinds: misfortune to ourselves, and good fortune to others.

Ambrose Bierce (1842–1914?) US writer and journalist. *The Devil's Dictionary* (1911)

3 Ill-luck, you know, seldom comes alone.

Miguel de Cervantes (1547–1616) Spanish novelist and playwright. *Don Quixote* (1605–15), pt. 1, bk. 3, ch. 6

4 Ill news hath wings, and with the wind doth go, Comfort's a cripple and comes ever slow.

Michael Drayton (1563–1631) English poet. *The Barons' Wars* (1603), can. 2, st. 27

5 'The Army of Misfortune'. Why should we always think of this as meaning 'The Others'?

Dag Hammarskjöld (1905–61) Swedish statesman and diplomat. *Markings* (Leif Sjöberg and W. H. Auden, trs.; 1964)

6 Depend upon it that if a man talks of his misfortunes there is something in them that is not disagreeable to him; for where there is nothing but pure misery there never is any recourse to the mention of it.

Samuel Johnson (1709–84) British lexicographer and writer. 1780. Quoted in *Life of Samuel Johnson* (James Boswell; 1791)

7 We are all strong enough to bear the misfortunes of others.

François La Rochefoucauld (1613–80) French epigrammatist and moralist. *Reflections, or Sentences and Moral Maxims* (1665), no. 19

8 In the misfortune of our best friends, we always find something which is not displeasing to us.

François La Rochefoucauld (1613–80) French epigrammatist and moralist. *Reflections, or Sentences and Moral Maxims* (1665), no. 99

9 Using one's imagination avoids many misfortunes . . . the person who anticipates his own death rarely kills himself.

Javier Marías (b. 1951) Spanish novelist. *A Heart So White* (Margaret Jull Costa, tr.; 1995)

10 KING When sorrows come, they come not single spies,
But in battalions!

William Shakespeare (1564–1616) English poet and playwright. *Hamlet* (1601), Act 4, Scene 5

11 EDMUND This is the excellent foppery of the world, that, when we are sick in fortune, often the surfeit of our own behaviour, we make guilty of our disasters the sun, the moon, and stars.

William Shakespeare (1564–1616) English poet and playwright. *King Lear* (1605–06), Act 1, Scene 2

12 To lose one parent, Mr. Worthing, may be regarded as a misfortune; to lose both looks like carelessness.

Oscar Wilde (1854–1900) Irish poet, playwright, and wit. *The Importance of Being Earnest* (1895), Act 2

Misogyny

see also **Hate, Prejudice, Sexism, Women**

1 I'd be equally as willing
For a dentist to be drilling
Than to ever let a woman in my life.

Alan Jay Lerner (1918–86) US lyricist and librettist. Song lyric. *My Fair Lady* (1956), Act 1, Scene 2

2 It had taken him . . . three divorces and four wives to decide that some female phenomena could be explained by no hypothesis less thoroughgoing than the absolute existence of witches.

Norman Mailer (b. 1923) US novelist and journalist. 'History as Novel: The Steps of the Pentagon', *The Armies of the Night* (1968), bk. 1, pt. 3, ch. 5

3 There may be some argument for suffrage for unfortunate females, such as widows and hopeless spinsters, but such status is not contemplated as a normal social relation.

Kelly Miller (1863–1939) US sociologist, educator, and civil rights activist. 'The Risk of Woman Suffrage', *The Crisis* (November 1915)

4 One tongue is sufficient for a woman.

John Milton (1608–74) English writer. On being asked whether he would allow his daughters to learn foreign languages. Attrib.

5 There are already so many women in the world! Why then . . . was I born a woman, to be scorned by men in words and deeds?

Isotta Nogarola (1418–66) Italian scholar and author. Letter to Guarino Veronese (15th century)

6 And do you know that you are an Eve? God's sentence hangs over all your sex and His punishment weighs down upon you. You are the devil's gateway; it was you who first violated the forbidden tree and broke God's law . . . You should always go in mourning and rags.

Tertullian (160?–220?) Carthaginian theological writer. *De Cultu Feminarum* (2nd–3rd century)

7 With many women I doubt whether there be any
   more effectual way of touching their hearts than
   ill-using them and then confessing it. If you wish
   to get the sweetest fragrance from the herb at
   your feet, tread on it and bruise it.
   Anthony Trollope (1815–82) British novelist. *Miss Mackenzie* (1865),
   ch. 10

8 MARIA Men rail at weakness themselves create,
   And boldly stigmatize the female mind,
   As though kind nature's just impartial hand
   Had form'd its features in a baser mold.
   Mercy Warren (1728–1814) US writer. Poems Dramatic and
   Miscellaneous, *The Ladies of Castile* (1790), Act 1, Scene 5

Mistakes

see also Failure, Imperfection, Loss

1 If you board the wrong train, it is no use running
   along the corridor in the other direction.
   Dietrich Bonhoeffer (1906–45) German theologian. *The Way to
   Freedom: Letters, Lectures and Notes* (1935–39)

2 A man who has committed a mistake and doesn't
   correct it, is committing another mistake.
   Confucius (551–479 BC) Chinese philosopher, administrator, and moralist.
   Analects (5th century BC)

3 To be wrong is nothing unless you continue to
   remember it.
   Confucius (551–479 BC) Chinese philosopher, administrator, and moralist.
   Analects (5th century BC)

4 The proactive approach to a mistake is to
   acknowledge it instantly, correct and learn from
   it. This literally turns a failure into a success.
   Stephen R. Covey (b. 1932) US educator, leadership consultant, author,
   and academic. *The Seven Habits of Highly Effective People*
   (1989)

5 I beseech you, in the bowels of Christ, think it
   possible you may be mistaken.
   Oliver Cromwell (1599–1658) English soldier and statesman. August 3,
   1650. Letter to the General Assembly of the Church of
   Scotland, quoted in *Oliver Cromwell's Letters and Speeches*
   (Thomas Carlyle, ed.; 1845)

6 Errors look so very ugly in persons of small
   means—one feels they are taking quite a liberty
   in going astray; whereas people of fortune may
   naturally indulge in a few delinquencies.
   George Eliot (1819–80) British novelist. 'Janet's Repentance', *Scenes
   of Clerical Life* (1858), ch. 25

7 Honorable errors do not count as failures in
   science, but as seeds for progress in the
   quintessential activity of correction.
   Stephen Jay Gould (1941–2002) US geologist and writer. *Leonardo's
   Mountain of Clams and the Diet of Worms: Essays on
   Natural History* (1998)

8 Generally speaking, the errors in religion are
   dangerous; those in philosophy only ridiculous.
   David Hume (1711–76) Scottish philosopher and historian. *A Treatise of
   Human Nature* (1739–40)

9 A new maxim is often a brilliant error.
   Chrétien de Malesherbes (1721–94) French statesman. *Pensées et
   Maximes* (18th century)

10 Erratum. In my article on the Price of Milk,
   'Horses' should have read 'Cows' throughout.
   J. C. Morton (1893–1979) British journalist and writer. *The Best of
   Beachcomber* (1963)

11 The mid-point being passed, the pattern is clear.
   This road I had taken for a good byway
   Is the main thoroughfare.
   Bernard O'Donoghue (b. 1945) Irish poet and academic. 'Nel Mezzo
   del Cammin', *Gunpowder* (1995)

12 The man who makes no mistakes does not
   usually make anything.
   Edward John Phelps (1822–1900) US lawyer and diplomat. Speech,
   Mansion House, London (January 24, 1899)

13 For to err in opinion, though it be not the part
   of wise men, is at least human.
   Plutarch (46?–120?) Greek biographer and philosopher. 'Against
   Colotes', *Moralia* (1st–2nd century)

14 A man should never be ashamed to own he has
   been in the wrong which is but saying, in other
   words, that he is wiser to-day than he was
   yesterday.
   Alexander Pope (1688–1744) English poet. 'Thoughts on Various
   Subjects', *Miscellanies* (1727)

15 I stand by all the misstatements that I've made.
   Dan Quayle (b. 1947) US politician. August 17, 1989. Quoted in
   Esquire (August 1992)

16 The man who can own up to his error is greater
   than he who merely knows how to avoid making
   it.
   Cardinal de Retz (1613–79) French ecclesiastic and politician. *Mémoires*
   (1717)

17 HAMLET Thou wretched, rash, intruding fool,
   farewell!
   I took thee for thy better.
   William Shakespeare (1564–1616) English poet and playwright. On
   discovering that he has killed Polonius, who had been hiding
   in his mother's bedroom behind a tapestried wall hanging.
   Hamlet (1601), Act 3, Scene 4

18 Human blunders usually do more to shape
   history than human wickedness.
   A. J. P. Taylor (1906–90) British historian. *The Origins of the Second
   World War* (1961), ch. 10

19 Well, if I called the wrong number, why did you
   answer the phone?
   James Thurber (1894–1961) US writer, cartoonist, and humorist. Cartoon
   caption, *New Yorker* (June 5, 1937)

20 If we had had more time for discussion we
   should probably have made a great many more
   mistakes.
   Leon Trotsky (1879–1940) Russian revolutionary leader. *My Life* (1930)

21 Had silicon been a gas I'would have been a
   major-general.
   James Abbott McNeill Whistler (1834–1903) US painter and etcher.
   Referring to his failure in the chemistry paper of an entrance
   exam to West Point Military Academy. Quoted in *The Life of
   James McNeill Whistler* (Joseph Pennell; 1908)

Moderation

see also Conservatism, Excess, Prudence

1 I know many have been taught to think that
   moderation, in a case like this, is a sort of
   treason.
   Edmund Burke (1729–97) Irish-born British statesman and political
   philosopher. Letter to the Sheriffs of Bristol (1777)

2 Half the vices which the world condemns most
   loudly have seeds of good in them and require
   moderate use rather than total abstinence.
   Samuel Butler (1835–1902) British writer and composer. *The Way of
   All Flesh* (1903)

3 As some say, Solon was the author of the
   apophthegm, 'Nothing in excess'.
   Diogenes Laërtius (*fl.* 3rd century) Greek historian and biographer.
   'Solon', *Lives of the Philosophers* (3rd century?)

4 Eat not to dullness; drink not to elevation.
   Benjamin Franklin (1706–90) US statesman and scientist. 1771–90.
   The Autobiography (1868), ch. 6

5 Moderation is a virtue only in those who are
   thought to have an alternative.
   Henry Kissinger (b. 1923) German-born US politician and diplomat.
   Observer (January 24, 1982)

6 What have I gained by health? intolerable
   dullness. What by early hours and moderate
   meals?—a total blank.
   Charles Lamb (1775–1834) British essayist. Letter to William
   Wordsworth (January 22, 1830)

7 Temperance is the love of health, or the inability
   to overindulge.
   François La Rochefoucauld (1613–80) French epigrammatist and moralist.
   Reflections, or Sentences and Moral Maxims (1665), no. 583

8 Early to rise and early to bed makes a male
   healthy and wealthy and dead.
   James Thurber (1894–1961) US writer, cartoonist, and humorist. 'The
   Shrike and the Chipmunks', *Fables for Our Time* (1940)

9 Temperance is the nurse of chastity.
   William Wycherley (1640–1716) English playwright. *Love in a Wood*
   (1671), Act 3, Scene 3

Modernity

see also **Civilization, The Present, Twentieth Century, Twenty-
first Century**

1 This strange disease of modern life,
   With its sick hurry, its divided aims.
   Matthew Arnold (1822–88) British poet and critic. 'The Scholar-Gipsy'
   (1853)

2 There is only one way left to escape the alienation
   of present day society: *to retreat ahead of it.*
   Roland Barthes (1915–80) French philosopher and writer. *Mythologies*
   (1957)

3 If modern man has often become a victim of his
   own positivism, the process starts . . . with the
   denial or abolition of the time created by the
   event of consciousness.
   John Berger (b. 1926) British novelist, essayist, and art critic. *And Our
   Faces, My Heart, Brief as Photos* (1984)

4 A single sentence will suffice for modern man: he
   fornicated and read the papers.
   Albert Camus (1913–60) Algerian-born French novelist, essayist, and
   playwright. *The Fall* (1956)

5 The three great elements of modern civilization,
   Gunpowder, Printing, and the Protestant
   Religion.
   Thomas Carlyle (1795–1881) Scottish historian and essayist. 'The State of
   German Literature', *Critical and Miscellaneous Essays* (1838)

6 The modern world . . . has no notion except that
   of simplifying something by destroying nearly
   everything.
   G. K. Chesterton (1874–1936) British writer and poet. 'All I Survey', *A
   Book of Essays* (1933)

7 It is so stupid of modern civilization to have
   given up believing in the devil when he is the
   only explanation of it.
   Ronald Knox (1888–1957) British priest and writer. *Let Dons Delight*
   (1939)

8 The closed operational universe of advanced
   industrial civilization with its terrifying harmony
   of freedom and oppression, productivity and
   destruction, growth and regression is pre-
   designed in this idea of Reason as a specific
   historical project.
   Herbert Marcuse (1898–1979) German-born US philosopher. *One-
   dimensional Man* (1964)

9 The modern world lacks not only hiding places,
   but certainties.
   Salman Rushdie (b. 1947) Indian-born British novelist. 'Outside the
   Whale', *Imaginary Homelands* (1991)

10 Almost everything that distinguishes the modern
   world from earlier centuries is attributable to
   science, which achieved its most spectacular
   triumphs in the seventeenth century.
   Bertrand Russell (1872–1970) British philosopher and mathematician. *A
   History of Western Philosophy* (1945)

Modesty

see also **Humility, Selflessness**

1 It is, of course, a bit of a drawback that science
   was invented after I left school.
   Lord Carrington (b. 1919) British politician. *Observer* (January 23,
   1983)

2 I should never have entered the church on that
   day, though it was an important feast, could I
   have known the Pope's intention in advance.
   Charlemagne (742?–814) Frankish monarch. Referring to his
   coronation as emperor. Attrib. (December 25, 800)

3 Be wiser than other people if you can, but do not
   tell them so.
   Lord Chesterfield (1694–1773) English statesman and writer. November
   19, 1745. *Letters to his Son* (1774)

4 On their own merits modest men are dumb.
   George Colman (1762–1836) British playwright and theatre owner. 1797.
   The Heir at Law (1808), Epilogue

5 Yes, I had two strings to my bow; both golden
   ones, egad! and both cracked.
   Henry Fielding (1707–54) British novelist and playwright. *Love in
   Several Masques* (1728), Act 5, Scene 13

6 In everything that relates to science, I am a whole
   Encyclopaedia behind the rest of the world.
   Charles Lamb (1775–1834) British essayist. 'The Old and the New
   Schoolmaster', *Essays of Elia* (1823)

7 To refuse praise reveals a desire to be praised
   twice over.
   François La Rochefoucauld (1613–80) French epigrammatist and moralist.
   Reflections, or Sentences and Moral Maxims (1665), no. 149

8 Be modest! It is the kind of pride least likely to
   offend.
   Jules Renard (1864–1910) French writer. 1895. *Journal* (1877–1910)

9 There is false modesty, but there is no false pride.
   Jules Renard (1864–1910) French writer. 1909. *Journal* (1877–1910)

10 I have often wished I had time to cultivate
   modesty . . . But I am too busy thinking about
   myself.
   Edith Sitwell (1887–1964) British poet, critic, and writer. *Observer*
   (April 30, 1950), 'Sayings of the Week'

11 I am a parcel of vain strivings tied
   By a chance bond together.
   Henry David Thoreau (1817–62) US writer. 'I Am a Parcel of Vain
   Strivings Tied', *The Penguin Book of American Verse*
   (Geoffrey Moore, ed.; 1977)

Monarchy

see also **Government, Republicanism**

1 The mystic reverence, the religious allegiance, which are essential to a true monarchy, are imaginative sentiments that no legislature can manufacture in any people.
Walter Bagehot (1826–77) British economist and journalist. 'The Cabinet', *The English Constitution* (1867)

2 It has been said, not truly, but with a possible approximation to truth, 'that in 1802 every hereditary monarch was insane'.
Walter Bagehot (1826–77) British economist and journalist. 'The House of Lords', *The English Constitution* (1867)

3 At the moment of decision the masses will stand on the side of kingship, regardless of whether the latter happens to follow a liberal or a conservative tendency.
Prince Otto von Bismarck (1815–98) German chancellor. Remark (1866), quoted in *Germany, 1866–1945* (Gordon A. Craig; 1978), ch. 2

4 That the king can do no wrong, is a necessary and fundamental principle of the English constitution.
William Blackstone (1723–80) British jurist. *Commentaries on the Laws of England* (1765–69), bk. 3, ch. 17

5 All your work is done on paper, which does not mind how you treat it . . . But I, poor Empress, must work upon human skin, which is much more ticklish and irritable.
Catherine the Great (1729–96) German-born Russian empress. Comparing her relationship with her political subjects with that of Denis Diderot to his writing. Letter to Denis Diderot (1770)

6 I personally would much rather see my title as Defender of Faith, not the Faith, because it means just one interpretation of the faith, which I think is sometimes something that causes a great deal of a problem.
Prince Charles (b. 1948) British prince. ITV television programme, 'Charles: The Private Man, the Public Role' (June 29, 1994)

7 The monarchy is the oldest profession in the world.
Prince Charles (b. 1948) British prince. Attrib.

8 You had better have one King than five hundred.
Charles II (1630–85) English monarch. After saying which he did not summon Parliament again. Speech (March 28, 1681)

9 Loss of the Royal Family's symbolism together with Britain's other problems may have serious outcomes. Those are pre-fascist conditions.
Noam Chomsky (b. 1928) US linguist and political activist. *Independent* (October 18, 1994)

10 Everyone likes flattery; and when you come to Royalty you should lay it on with a trowel.
Benjamin Disraeli (1804–81) British prime minister and writer. Said to Matthew Arnold. Quoted in *Collections and Recollections* (G. W. E. Russell; 1898), ch. 23

11 War is the trade of kings.
John Dryden (1631–1700) English poet, playwright, and literary critic. *King Arthur* (1691), Act 2, Scene 2

12 The influence of the Crown has increased, is increasing, and ought to be diminished.
John Dunning (1731–83) British lawyer and politician. Defending the motion passed by parliament. (April 6, 1780)

13 Let a king recall that to improve his realm is better than to increase his territory.
Desiderius Erasmus (1466?–1536) Dutch humanist, scholar, and writer. *Querela Pacis* (July 1517)

14 Soon there will be only five kings left—the Kings of England, Diamonds, Hearts, Spades, and Clubs.
Farouk I (1920–65) Egyptian monarch. 1948. Remark made to Lord Boyd-Orr at a conference in Cairo. *As I Recall* (Lord Boyd-Orr; 1966), ch. 21

15 A crown is merely a hat that lets the rain in.
Frederick II (1712–86) Prussian monarch. Attrib.

16 There are kings enough in England. I am nothing there, I am old and want rest and should only go to be plagued and teased there about that damned House of Commons.
George II (1683–1760) German-born British monarch. Reply when urged to leave Hanover and return to England. Quoted in Letter from Earl of Holderness to Duke of Newcastle (August 3, 1755)

17 We're not a family; we're a firm.
George VI (1895–1952) British monarch. Quoted in *Our Future King* (Peter Lane; 1978)

18 The personality conveyed by the utterances which are put into her mouth is that of a priggish schoolgirl, captain of the hockey team, a prefect, and a recent candidate for confirmation. It is not thus that she will be able to come into her own as an independent and distinctive character.
John Grigg (b. 1924) British writer. Referring to Queen Elizabeth II. *National and English Review* (August 1958)

19 The tourists who come to our island take in the Monarchy along with feeding the pigeons in Trafalgar Square.
William Hamilton (b. 1917) Scottish politician. *My Queen and I* (1975), ch. 9

20 An illiterate king is a crowned ass.
Henry I (1068–1135) English monarch. Attrib. *Quotations in History* (Alan and Veronica Palmer; 1976)

21 I order you to hold a free election, but forbid you to elect anyone but Richard my clerk.
Henry II (1133–89) English monarch. Referring to the election of a new bishop. Richard d'Ilchester was one of the king's trusted servants. Writ to the electors of the See of Winchester, *Recueil des Historiens des Gaules et de la France* (J. J. Brial; 1806–22)

22 The kings of England in times past never had any superior but God. Wherefore know you that we will maintain the rights of the Crown . . . as any of our progenitors.
Henry VIII (1491–1547) English monarch. Refusing to allow an ecclesiastical dispute to be referred to Rome. Remark (1515)

23 Did I ascend the throne by robbery or armed bloodshed? I was born to rule by the grace of God; and I do not even remember my father bequeathing the kingdom to me and blessing me—I grew up upon the throne.
Ivan IV (1530–84) Russian monarch. Letter to Prince Kurbsky (September 1577)

24 The state of monarchy is the supremest thing upon earth; for kings are not only God's Lieutenants upon earth, and sit upon God's throne, but even by God himself they are called Gods.
James I (1566–1625) English monarch. Speech to Parliament (March 21, 1609)

25 This haughty, vigilant, resolute, sagacious blue-stocking, half Mithridates and half Trissotin, bearing up against a world in arms.
Thomas Babington Macaulay (1800–59) British politician, historian, and writer. Referring to Frederick the Great. 'Frederick the Great', *Collected Essays* (1843)

26 I must have wanton poets, pleasant wits,
Musicians, that with touching of a string
May draw the pliant king which way I please.
Christopher Marlowe (1564–93) English playwright and poet. *Edward II* (1593), Act 1, Scene 1

27 The power of kings and magistrates is nothing else, but what only is derivative, transformed and committed to them in trust from the people to the common good of them all, in whom the power yet remains fundamentally, and cannot be taken from them, without a violation of their natural birthright.
John Milton (1608–74) English writer. *The Tenure of Kings and Magistrates* (1649)

28 I shall maintain the principle of autocracy just as firmly and unflinchingly as it was upheld by my own ever to be remembered dead father.
Nicholas II (1868–1918) Russian monarch. Declaration to representatives of Tver (January 17, 1896)

29 Whenever kingship approaches tyranny it is near its end, for by this it becomes ripe for division, change of dynasty, or total destruction, especially in a temperate climate . . . where men are habitually, morally, and naturally free.
Nicole d'Oresme (1325?–82?) French prelate. *De Moneta* (Charles Johnson, tr.; 1956)

30 But methought it lessened my esteem of a king, that he should not be able to command the rain.
Samuel Pepys (1633–1703) English diarist and civil servant. *Diary* (July 19, 1662)

31 The monarchy is part of the fabric of the country. And, as the fabric alters, so the monarchy and its people's relations to it alters.
Prince Philip (b. 1921) Greek-born British consort of Queen Elizabeth II. March 20, 1968. Attrib.

32 He is the most potent man, as regards forces and lands and treasure that exists in the world.
Marco Polo (1254–1324) Venetian merchant and traveller. Referring to Kublai Khan, Emperor of China. *The Travels of Marco Polo* (1298–99)

33 The Right Divine of Kings to govern wrong.
Alexander Pope (1688–1744) English poet. *The Dunciad* (1742), bk. 4, l. 187

34 What is a King?—a man condemned to bear
The public burden of the nation's care.
Matthew Prior (1664–1721) English diplomat and poet. *Solomon* (1718), bk. 3, ll. 275–276

35 God and my right.
Richard I (1157–99) English monarch. This later became the motto of the royal arms of England. *Battle-cry* (September 1198)

36 As the earth darkens when the sun departs, so the face of this kingdom was changed by the absence of the king. All the barons were restless, castles were strengthened, towns fortified, moats dug.
Richard of Devizes (fl. 1190) English monk and chronicler. Referring to the absence of Richard I at the Crusades. *Chronicon de rebus gestis Ricardo Prim* (1192)

37 To know how to dissimulate is the knowledge of kings.
Cardinal Richelieu (1585–1642) French churchman and statesman. *Testament Politique* (1688), maxims

38 KING HENRY IV Uneasy lies the head that wears a crown.
William Shakespeare (1564–1616) English poet and playwright. *Henry IV, Part 2* (1597), Act 3, Scene 1

39 PERICLES Kings are earth's gods; in vice their law's their will.
William Shakespeare (1564–1616) English poet and playwright. *Pericles* (1606–08), Act 1, Scene 1

40 KING RICHARD What must the king do now?
Must he submit?
The king shall do it: must he be depos'd?
The king shall be contented: must he lose
The name of king? A God's name, let it go.
William Shakespeare (1564–1616) English poet and playwright. *Richard II* (1595), Act 3, Scene 3

41 Kings are not born, they are made by artificial hallucination.
George Bernard Shaw (1856–1950) Irish playwright. *Man and Superman* (1903)

42 The king reigns, and the people govern themselves.
Adolphe Thiers (1797–1877) French statesman and historian. In an unsigned article attributed to Thiers. *Le National* (January 20, 1830)

Money

see also **Business, Capitalism, Wealth**

1 Money is better than poverty, if only for financial reasons.
Woody Allen (b. 1935) US film actor and director. *Without Feathers* (1976)

2 There is no such thing as a free lunch.
Anonymous. Often attributed to Milton Friedman.

3 Money, of course, is never just money. It's always something else, and it's always something more, and it always has the last word.
Paul Auster (b. 1947) US writer. *Hand to Mouth* (1997)

4 Money is like muck, not good except it be spread.
Francis Bacon (1561–1626) English philosopher, statesman, and lawyer. 'Of Seditions and Troubles', *Essays* (1625)

5 Money, it turned out, was exactly like sex, you thought of nothing else if you didn't have it and thought of other things if you did.
James Baldwin (1924–87) US writer and civil rights activist. *Nobody Knows My Name* (1961)

6 If you would know what the Lord God thinks of money, you have only to look at those to whom He gives it.
Maurice Baring (1874–1945) British writer and journalist. Attrib.

7 Money speaks sense in a language all nations understand.
Aphra Behn (1640?–89) English novelist and playwright. *The Rover* (1678), pt. 2, Act 3, Scene 1

8 I'm tired of Love: I'm still more tired of Rhyme.
But Money gives me pleasure all the Time.
Hilaire Belloc (1870–1953) French-born British writer. 'Fatigued' (1923)

9 MONEY, n. A blessing that is of no advantage to us excepting when we part with it.

Ambrose Bierce (1842–1914?) US writer and journalist. *The Devil's Dictionary* (1911)

10 Rob Peter, and pay Paul.

Robert Burton (1577–1640) English scholar and churchman. 'Democritus to the Reader', *The Anatomy of Melancholy* (1621)

11 It has been said that the love of money is the root of all evil. The want of money is so quite as truly.

Samuel Butler (1835–1902) British writer and composer. *Erewhon* (1872), ch. 20

12 Keeping neat records and overspending is not money management.

Philip B. Crosby (b. 1926) US business executive. *The Art of Getting Your Own Sweet Way* (1981)

13 Money, it has been said, has two properties. It is flat so that it can be piled up. But it is also round so that it can circulate.

Geoffrey Crowther (1907–72) British economist. *An Outline of Money* (1941), ch. 2

14 Money is the sinews of love, as of war.

George Farquhar (1678–1707) Irish playwright. *Love and a Bottle* (1698), Act 2, Scene 1

15 Penny saved is a penny got.

Henry Fielding (1707–54) British novelist and playwright. *The Miser* (1733), Act 3, Scene 12

16 MONEY Cause of all evil . . . Politicians call it emoluments; lawyers, retainers; doctors, fees; employees, salary; workmen, pay; servants, wages.

Gustave Flaubert (1821–80) French novelist. Quoted in *Le Dictionnaire des Idées Reçues* (1911)

17 Money is like an arm or a leg—use it or lose it.

Henry Ford (1863–1947) US car manufacturer. *New York Times* (1931)

18 Money differs from an automobile, a mistress, or cancer in being equally important to those who have it and those who do not.

J. K. Galbraith (b. 1908) Canadian-born US economist. Attrib.

19 He knew the value of money, because he had never had any.

Roy A. K. Heath (b. 1926) Guyanese novelist and teacher. *Kwaku* (1982)

20 If possible honestly, if not, somehow, make money.

Horace (65–8 BC) Roman poet. *Epistles* (20? BC), bk. 1, no. 1, l. 66

21 Money is not, properly speaking, one of the subjects of commerce, but only the instrument which men have agreed upon to facilitate the exchange of one commodity for another.

David Hume (1711–76) Scottish philosopher and historian. 'Of Money' (1752)

22 'To make money', said Mr. Porteous, 'one must be really interested in money'.

Aldous Huxley (1894–1963) British novelist and essayist. *Antic Hay* (1923)

23 Money's a horrid thing to follow, but a charming thing to meet.

Henry James (1843–1916) US-born British writer and critic. *The Portrait of a Lady* (1881), ch. 35

24 Money and time are the heaviest burdens of life, and . . . the unhappiest of all mortals are those who have more of either than they know how to use.

Samuel Johnson (1709–84) British lexicographer and writer. *The Idler* (November 11, 1758), no. 30

25 For I don't care too much for money,
For money can't buy me love.

Lennon & McCartney, British rock musicians. 'Can't Buy Me Love', *A Hard Day's Night* (1964)

26 Money is the instrument by which men's wants are supplied, and many who possess it will part with it for that purpose, who would not gratify themselves at the expense of their visible property.

James Madison (1751–1836) US president. *The National Gazette* (1791)

27 I must say I hate money but it's the lack of it I hate most.

Katherine Mansfield (1888–1923) New Zealand-born British short-story writer and poet. Quoted in *Katherine Mansfield* (Anthony Alpers; 1954)

28 Money is the external, universal means and power (not derived from man as man nor from human society as society) to change representation into reality and reality into mere representation.

Karl Marx (1818–83) German philosopher. 1844. Quoted in *Economical and Philosophical Manuscripts* (T. B. Bottomore, tr.; 1963)

29 Money is like a sixth sense without which you cannot make a complete use of the other five.

Somerset Maugham (1874–1965) British writer. *Of Human Bondage* (1915), ch. 51

30 Money is a poor man's credit card.

Marshall McLuhan (1911–80) Canadian sociologist. Quoted in *Maclean's Magazine* (Toronto) (Peter C. Newman, ed.; June 1971)

31 Money can't buy friends, but you can get a better class of enemy.

Spike Milligan (1918–2002) Indian-born British humorist, writer, and actor. *Puckoon* (1963)

32 Money is like manure. If you spread it around it does a lot of good. But if you pile it up in one place it stinks like hell.

Clint Murchison (1895–1969) US industrialist. *Time* (June 16, 1961)

33 Some people's money is merited
And other people's is inherited.

Ogden Nash (1902–71) US humorist. 'The Terrible People' (1933)

34 Better mankind born without mouths and stomachs than always to worry about money to buy, to shop, to fix, to cook, to wash, to clean.

Tillie Olsen (b. 1913) US writer. *Tell me a Riddle* (1961)

35 Money demands that you sell, not your weakness to men's stupidity, but your talent to their reason.

Ayn Rand (1905–82) Russian-born US writer and philosopher. *Atlas Shrugged* (1957)

36 Money is good for bribing yourself through the inconveniences of life.

Gottfried Reinhardt (1913–94) German-born US film producer. Quoted in 'Looks Like We're Still in Business', *Picture* (Lillian Ross; 1997)

37 Money is the seed of money, and the first franc is sometimes more difficult to acquire than the second million.
Jean-Jacques Rousseau (1712–78) French philosopher and writer. *Discourse on the Origin and Foundation of Inequality Among Men* (1754)

38 Money doesn't make you happy. I now have $50 million but I was just as happy when I had $48 million.
Arnold Schwarzenegger (b. 1947) Austrian-born US bodybuilder and film actor. Attrib.

39 CORIN He that wants money, means, and content, is without three good friends.
William Shakespeare (1564–1616) English poet and playwright. *As You Like It* (1599), Act 3, Scene 2

40 The surest way to ruin a man who doesn't know how to handle money is to give him some.
George Bernard Shaw (1856–1950) Irish playwright. *Heartbreak House* (1919)

41 Lack of money is the root of all evil.
George Bernard Shaw (1856–1950) Irish playwright. 'Maxims for Revolutionists', *Man and Superman* (1903)

42 There are few sorrows, however poignant, in which a good income is of no avail.
Logan Pearsall Smith (1865–1946) US-born British writer. 'Life and Human Nature', *Afterthoughts* (1931)

43 Money, the life-blood of the nation, Corrupts and stagnates in the veins, Unless a proper circulation Its motion and its heat maintains.
Jonathan Swift (1667–1745) Irish writer and clergyman. 1720. 'The Run upon the Bankers', *Poems* (1735)

44 The easiest way for your children to learn about money is for you not to have any.
Katharine Whitehorn (b. 1926) British journalist and writer. *How to Survive Children* (1975)

The Moon

see also Astronomy, Space

1 Beautiful! Beautiful! Magnificent desolation!
Buzz Aldrin (b. 1930) US astronaut. Said on joining Neil Armstrong for the first moon walk. Remark (July 20, 1969)

2 That's one small step for man, one giant leap for mankind.
Neil Armstrong (b. 1930) US astronaut. Remark after having stepped onto the moon. Armstrong later claimed that he had said, 'small step for a man . . . ', but that the 'a' had been lost in the radio transmission. *New York Times* (July 21, 1969)

3 Do I carry the moon in my pocket?
Robert Browning (1812–89) British poet. 'Master Hugues of Saxe-Gotha', *Men and Women* (1855), st. 29

4 who knows if the moon's a balloon, coming out of a keen city in the sky—filled with pretty people?
e. e. cummings (1894–1962) US poet and painter. 1925. Used as the title of David Niven's first volume of autobiography, *The Moon's a Balloon*, about his experiences in the film industry. 'Seven Poems', *Complete Poems 1913–35* (1968), no. 7, st. 1, ll. 1–3

5 So sicken waning moons too near the sun, And blunt their crescents on the edge of day.
John Dryden (1631–1700) English poet, playwright, and literary critic. 'Annus Mirabilis' (1667)

6 The moon is nothing But a circumambulating aphrodisiac Divinely subsidized to provoke the world Into a rising birth-rate.
Christopher Fry (b. 1907) British playwright. *The Lady's Not for Burning* (1949), Act 3

7 I feel sure that the surface of the Moon is not perfectly smooth, free from inequalities and exactly spherical . . . on the contrary, it is full of inequalities, uneven, full of hollows and protuberances, just like the surface of the Earth itself, which is varied everywhere by lofty mountains and deep valleys.
Galileo (1564–1642) Italian scientist. Referring to his observations with a telescope he had made. *The Starry Messenger* (March 1610)

8 God, what a dancing spectre seems the moon.
George Meredith (1828–1909) British novelist and poet. 'Modern Love' (1862)

9 For years politicians have promised the moon, I'm the first one to be able to deliver it.
Richard Nixon (1913–94) US president. July 20, 1969. About the first moon landing. Attrib.

10 Hear all, the newmoon new in all the ancient sky.
Charles Olson (1910–70) US poet. Closing lines. 'Celestial Evening, October 1967' (1975)

11 The lilac moon of the earth's backyard which gives silence to the whole house falls down out of the sky over the fence.
Charles Olson (1910–70) US poet. 'May 31, 1961', *Charles Olson: Selected Poems* (Robert Creeley, ed.; 1993)

12 Pancake in cream The moon slithers sideways, Tantalizing The pursuing sleigh.
Boris Pasternak (1890–1960) Russian poet and novelist. 'Tracks in the Snow' (Michael Harari, tr.; 1955–56)

13 A trip to the moon on gossamer wings.
Cole Porter (1893–1964) US songwriter and composer. 'Just One of Those Things', *Jubilee* (1935)

14 KALYANI But they won't be the same anymore— the nursery rhymes. Uncle Moon! How could Uncle Moon ever be the same with those Americans trampling all over him.
Satyajit Ray (1921–92) Indian film director. *The Alien* (1967)

15 LORENZO How sweet the moonlight sleeps upon this bank! Here will we sit, and let the sounds of music Creep in our ears; soft stillness and the night Become the touches of sweet harmony.
William Shakespeare (1564–1616) English poet and playwright. *The Merchant of Venice* (1596–98), Act 5, Scene 1

16 Nothing is more symptomatic of the enervation, of the decompression of the Western imagination, than our incapacity to respond to the landings on the Moon. Not a single great poem, picture, metaphor has come of this breathtaking act, of Prometheus' rescue of Icarus or of Phaeton in flight towards the stars.
George Steiner (b. 1929) US scholar and critic. 'Modernity, Mythology, and Magic', lecture, Salzburg Festival, *Guardian* (August 6, 1994)

17   This shows the moon is basically right there as a stepping stone, and calling us.

Rick Tomlinson, US campaigner for space exploration. Referring to the discovery of large deposits of ice at the moon's poles by the NASA space probe *Lunar Prospector*. *Guardian* (March 6, 1998)

Morality

see also **Choice, Evil, Freedom, Good**

1   Nature has placed mankind under the governance of two sovereign masters, *pain* and *pleasure*. It is for them alone to point out what we ought to do, as well as to determine what we shall do.

Jeremy Bentham (1748–1832) British philosopher, economist, jurist, and social reformer. *An Introduction to the Principles of Morals and Legislation* (1789)

2   Morality's not practical. Morality's a gesture. A complicated gesture learnt from books.

Robert Bolt (1924–95) British playwright. *A Man for All Seasons* (1960)

3   The propriety of some persons seems to consist in having improper thoughts about their neighbours.

F. H. Bradley (1846–1924) British philosopher. *Aphorisms* (1930)

4   First comes the grub, then comes the morals.

Bertolt Brecht (1898–1956) German playwright and poet. "Ballad about the Question: 'What Keeps a Man Alive?'", *The Threepenny Opera* (1929)

5   Everything's got a moral, if only you can find it.

Lewis Carroll (1832–98) British writer and mathematician. *Alice's Adventures in Wonderland* (1865), ch. 9

6   When morality comes up against profit, it is seldom that profit loses.

Shirley Chisholm (b. 1924) US state legislator, educator, and US representative. *Unbought and Unbossed* (1970)

7   Values are determined by systems, contexts and circumstances.

Edward de Bono (b. 1933) Maltese-born British psychologist and writer. *Parallel Thinking: From Socratic to de Bono Thinking* (1994)

8   My life's principle . . . was to desire and to strive to achieve ethical values. From a particular moment, however, I was prevented by the State from living according to this principle. I had to switch from the unity of ethics to one of multiple morals. I had to yield to the inversion of values which was prescribed by the State.

Adolf Eichmann (1906–62) German Nazi war criminal. Final plea at his trial (1961)

9   A man's ethical behavior should be based effectually on sympathy, education, and social ties and needs; no religious basis is necessary. Man would indeed be in a poor way if he had to be restrained by fear of punishment and hope of reward after death.

Albert Einstein (1879–1955) German-born US physicist. 'Religion and Science', *New York Times* (November 9, 1930)

10   Eating people is wrong.

Michael Flanders (1922–75) British comedian and songwriter. Song. 'The Reluctant Cannibal' (1956)

11   What is moral is what you feel good after, and what is immoral is what you feel bad after.

Ernest Hemingway (1899–1961) US writer. *Death in the Afternoon* (1932), ch. 1

12   We must rule out as irrelevant the conception of the hero as a morally worthy man, not because ethical judgments are illegitimate in history, but because so much of it has been made by the wicked.

Sidney Hook (1902–89) US philosopher and educator. Attrib.

13   As a result of innumerable outstanding contradictions in our civilization a general numbness of moral perception has developed.

Karen Horney (1885–1952) German-born US psychoanalyst. *Our Inner Conflicts* (1945)

14   Morals excite passions, and produce or prevent actions. Reason of itself is utterly impotent in this particular. The rules of morality, therefore, are not conclusions for reason.

David Hume (1711–76) Scottish philosopher and historian. *A Treatise of Human Nature* (1739–40)

15   Good and ill, both natural and moral, are entirely relative to human sentiment and affection.

David Hume (1711–76) Scottish philosopher and historian. 'The Sceptic', *Essays, Moral and Political* (1741)

16   The quality of moral behaviour varies in inverse ratio to the number of human beings involved.

Aldous Huxley (1894–1963) British novelist and essayist. *Grey Eminence: A Study in Religion and Politics* (1941), ch. 10

17   The great temptation in these difficult days of racial polarization and economic injustice is to make political arguments black and white and miss the moral imperative of wrong and right. Vanity asks, 'Is it popular?' Politics asks 'Will it win?' Morality and conscience ask, 'Is it right?'

Jesse Jackson (b. 1941) US clergyman, civil rights leader, and politician. Speech to the US Democratic National Convention (July 14, 1992)

18   But if he does really think that there is no distinction between virtue and vice, why, Sir, when he leaves our houses let us count our spoons.

Samuel Johnson (1709–84) British lexicographer and writer. July 14, 1763. Referring to an 'impudent fellow' from Scotland. Quoted in *Life of Samuel Johnson* (James Boswell; 1791)

19   Even on the highest peak we shall never be 'beyond good and evil', and the more we experience of their inextricable entanglement the more uncertain and confused will our moral judgement be.

Carl Gustav Jung (1875–1961) Swiss psychoanalyst. 1958. 'A Psychological Approach to the Dogma of the Trinity', *Collected Works* (1969), vol. 2

20   We do not need science and philosophy to know what we should do to be honest and good, yea, even wise and virtuous.

Immanuel Kant (1724–1804) German philosopher. *Fundamental Principles of the Metaphysics of Ethics* (1785)

21   The moral problem of our age is concerned with the love of money.

John Maynard Keynes (1883–1946) British economist. *Essays in Persuasion* (1925)

22   Moral principles have lost their distinctiveness. For modern man, absolute right and absolute wrong are a matter of what the majority is doing.

Martin Luther King, Jr. (1929–68) US civil rights leader. *Strength To Love* (1963)

23 Moral responsibility is what is lacking in a man when he demands it of a woman.

Karl Kraus (1874–1936) Austrian writer. 1909. Quoted in 'Sprüche und Widersprüche', *Karl Kraus* (Harry Zohn; 1971)

24 The triumph of morality: A thief who has broken into a bedroom claims his sense of shame has been outraged, and by threatening the occupants with exposure of an immoral act he blackmails them into not bringing charges for burglary.

Karl Kraus (1874–1936) Austrian writer. 1909. Quoted in 'Sprüche und Widersprüche', *Karl Kraus* (Harry Zohn; 1971)

25 Morality which is based on ideas, or on an ideal, is an unmitigated evil.

D. H. Lawrence (1885–1930) British writer. *Fantasia of the Unconscious* (1922), ch. 7

26 We can only tolerate miracles in the physical world; in the moral everything must retain its neutral course, because the theatre is to be the school of the moral.

Gotthold Ephraim Lessing (1729–81) German playwright and critic. 1767. Quoted in *Hamburg Dramaturgy* (Victor Lange, ed.; 1962), no. 2

27 Somewhere between my ambition and my ideals, I lost my ethical compass.

Jeb Magruder (b. 1934) US political aide. He was giving evidence to the Congressional investigation into Watergate. Quoted in *Time* (June 3, 1974)

28 Human moral capacities are just what could be expected to evolve when a highly social creature becomes intelligent enough to become aware of profound conflicts among his motives.

Mary Midgley (b. 1919) British philosopher. *The Ethical Primate* (1994)

29 The assertion 'I am morally bound to perform this action' is identical with the assertion, 'This action will produce the greatest possible amount of good in the Universe'.

G. E. Moore (1873–1958) British philosopher. *Principia Ethica* (1903)

30 Morality in Europe today is herd-morality.

Friedrich Wilhelm Nietzsche (1844–1900) German philosopher and poet. *Beyond Good and Evil* (1886)

31 Moral, like physical, cleanliness is not acquired once and for all: it can only be kept and renewed by a habit of constant watchfulness and discipline.

Victoria Ocampo (1891–1979) Argentinian writer and publisher. 'Scruples and Ambitions' (1947)

32 Man is only a reed, the weakest in nature, but he is a thinking reed . . . Let us then strive to think well; that is the basic principle of morality.

Blaise Pascal (1623–62) French philosopher, mathematician, and physicist. *Pensées* (1669), no. 200

33 Always act in such a way as to secure the love of your neighbour.

Pliny the Elder (23?–79) Roman scholar. *Natural History* (77), bk. 18, sect. 44

34 There can be no scientific morality; but then neither can science be immoral.

Jules Henri Poincaré (1854–1912) French mathematician and scientist. *Dernières Pensées* (1913), ch. 8

35 Morality, like language, is an invented structure for conserving and communicating order. And morality is learned, like language, by mimicking and remembering.

Jane Rule (b. 1931) US-born Canadian writer. 'Myth and Morality, Sources of Law and Prejudice', *Lesbian Images* (1975)

36 All universal moral principles are idle fancies.

Marquis de Sade (1740–1814) French philosopher and novelist. *The 120 Days of Sodom* (1785)

37 Without doubt the greatest injury . . . was done by basing morals on myth, for sooner or later myth is recognized for what it is, and disappears. Then morality loses the foundation on which it has been built.

Herbert Samuel (1870–1963) British statesman and philosopher. Romanes lecture (1947)

38 I distrust an immediate morality, it involves too much bad faith, all the tepidness of ignorance.

Jean-Paul Sartre (1905–80) French philosopher, playwright, and novelist. *Notebooks for an Ethics* (1983)

39 He never does a proper thing without giving an improper reason for it.

George Bernard Shaw (1856–1950) Irish playwright. *Major Barbara* (1907), Act 3

40 DUBEDAT Morality consists in suspecting other people of not being legally married.

George Bernard Shaw (1856–1950) Irish playwright. Said by the artist to the doctors diagnosing him, who jump to the conclusion that he's not married to his wife. *The Doctor's Dilemma* (1911), Act 2

41 The so-called new morality is too often the old immorality condoned.

Lord Shawcross (b. 1902) German-born British politician and lawyer. *Observer* (November 17, 1963)

42 If your morals make you dreary, depend upon it, they are wrong.

Robert Louis Stevenson (1850–94) Scottish novelist, essayist, and poet. *Across the Plains* (1892)

43 Do not be too moral. You may cheat yourself out of much of life. So aim above morality. Be not simply good; be good for something.

Henry David Thoreau (1817–62) US writer. Letter to Harrison Blake (March 27, 1848)

44 When men are weak, they become moral. When men and nations are strong, they don't give a damn about morality.

Melvin Tolson (1900–66) US poet and teacher. 'The Weapon of the Weak to Curb the Power of the Strong' (September 7, 1940)

45 The end may justify the means as long as there is something that justifies the end.

Leon Trotsky (1879–1940) Russian revolutionary leader. Attrib.

46 The condition of all human ethics can be summed up in two sentences: We ought to. But we don't.

Kurt Tucholsky (1890–1935) German philosopher. Quoted in 'Selected Aphorisms', *Kurt Tucholsky. The Ironic Sentimentalist* (Bryan P. Grenville; 1981)

47 Morals are an acquirement—like music, like a foreign language, like piety, poker, paralysis—no man is born with them.

Mark Twain (1835–1910) US writer and humorist. *Seventieth Birthday* (1907)

48 What is morality in any given time or place? It is what the majority then and there happen to like and immorality is what they dislike.

A. N. Whitehead (1861–1947) British philosopher and mathematician. *Dialogues* (1954)

Morning

see also **Beginning**, **Light**

1 Yet, behind the night,
   Waits for the great unborn, somewhere far
   Some white tremendous daybreak.

Rupert Brooke (1887–1915) British poet. 1908. 'Second Best', *The Poetical Works of Rupert Brooke* (Geoffrey Keynes, ed.; 1970)

2 And all small fowlys singis on the spray:
Welcum the lord of lycht and lamp of day.
Gawin Douglas (1474?–1522) Scottish poet and bishop. *Eneados*
(1513?), bk. 12, Prologue, ll. 251–252

3 Awake! for Morning in the Bowl of Night
Has flung the Stone that puts the Stars to Flight:
And Lo! the Hunter of the East has caught
The Sultán's Turret in a Noose of Light.
Edward FitzGerald (1809–83) British poet and translator. *The Rubáiyát
of Omar Khayyám* (1859), st. 1

4 Oh, what a beautiful mornin'!
Oh, what a beautiful day!
Oscar Hammerstein II (1895–1960) US lyricist and librettist. Song lyric.
'Oh, What a Beautiful Mornin'', *Oklahoma!* (music by
Richard Rodgers; 1943)

5 Get up, get up for shame, the blooming morn
Upon her wings presents the god unshorn.
Robert Herrick (1591–1674) English poet. 'Corinna's Going a-
Maying', *Hesperides* (1648), ll. 1–2

6 The dawn speeds a man on his journey, and
speeds him too in his work.
Hesiod (*fl.* 8th century BC) Greek poet. *Theogony* (750? BC), l. 579

7 Daybreak
has that sadness of arriving
by train at a station that's not yours.
Juan Ramón Jiménez (1881–1958) Spanish poet. 'Daybreak', *Roots
and Wings: Poetry from Spain, 1900–75* (Hardie St. Martin,
ed.; 1976)

8 Stately, plump Buck Mulligan came from the
stairhead, bearing a bowl of lather on which a
mirror and a razor lay crossed.
James Joyce (1882–1941) Irish writer. Opening sentence. *Ulysses*
(1922)

9 The average, healthy, well-adjusted adult gets up
at seven-thirty in the morning feeling just plain
terrible.
Jean Kerr (b. 1923) US playwright and humorist. *Please Don't Eat the
Daisies* (1960)

10 Believe me, you have to get up early if you want
to get out of bed.
Groucho Marx (1895–1977) US comedian and film actor. *The Cocoanuts*
(George S. Kaufman and Morrie Ryskind; 1929)

11 Under the opening eye-lids of the morn.
John Milton (1608–74) English writer. 1638. 'Lycidas', *Poems of Mr.
John Milton* (1645), l. 26

12 Rosy-fingered dawn.
Alexander Pope (1688–1744) English poet. This phrase first appears
in book 2, and is used throughout to describe Eos, the
goddess of dawn. *The Odyssey of Homer* (1725), bk. 2, l. 1
and elsewhere

13 As cool as the pale wet leaves
of lily-of-the-valley
She lay beside me in the dawn.
Ezra Pound (1885–1972) US poet, translator, and critic. 'A Pact',
Dramatis Personae (1926), quoted in *The Penguin Book of
American Verse* (Geoffrey Moore, ed.; 1977)

14 I have embraced the summer dawn.
Arthur Rimbaud (1854–91) French poet. 'Aube', *Illuminations* (1886)

15 Full many a glorious morning have I seen
Flatter the mountain-tops with sovereign eye.
William Shakespeare (1564–1616) English poet and playwright. Sonnet
33 (1609)

16 Hark, hark! the lark at heaven's gate sings
And Phoebus 'gins arise,
His steeds to water at those springs
On chalic'd flow'rs that lies;
And winking Mary-buds begin
To ope their golden eyes.
William Shakespeare (1564–1616) English poet and playwright.
Cymbeline (1609–10), Act 2, Scene 3

17 The principality of the sky lightens now, over our
green hill, into spring morning larked and
crowed and belling.
Dylan Thomas (1914–53) Welsh poet, playwright, and short-story writer.
Thomas's 'play for voices', written for the BBC and first
broadcast on January 25, 1954. *Under Milk Wood* (1954)

18 And when the rising sun has first breathed on us
with his panting horses, over there the red
evening-star is lighting his late lamps.
Virgil (70–19 BC) Roman poet. *Georgics* (29 BC), no. 1, l. 250

19 For what human ill does not dawn seem to be an
alternative?
Thornton Wilder (1897–1975) US novelist and playwright. *The Bridge of
San Luis Rey* (1927)

Mortality

see also **Death and Dying**, **Time**, **Transience**

1 One day we were born, one day we shall die, the
same day, the same second, is that not enough
for you? (*Calmer.*) They give birth astride of a
grave.
Samuel Beckett (1906–89) Irish playwright, novelist, and poet. *Waiting
for Godot* (1954), Act 2

2 Man's life is like unto a winter's day,
Some break their fast and so depart away;
Others stay dinner, then depart full fed;
The longest age but sups and goes to bed.
O reader, then behold and see!
As we are now, so must you be.
Joseph Henshaw (1603–79) English prelate. *Horae Sucissivae* (1631)

3 The payment for life is death.
George Jackson (1941–71) US political activist and writer. April 18,
1965. Letter to his father, *Soledad Brother* (1970)

4 When I have fears that I may cease to be
Before my pen has glean'd my teeming brain.
John Keats (1795–1821) English poet. 'When I Have Fears' (1818),
quoted in *Life, Letters, and Literary Remains of John Keats*
(R. M. Milnes, ed.; 1848)

5 And life is given to none freehold, but it is
leasehold for all.
Lucretius (99?–55? BC) Roman philosopher and poet. *De Rerum
Natura* (1st century BC), pt. 3, l. 971

6 He turned and saw the accusing clock
Race like a torrent round a rock.
Louis MacNeice (1907–63) Irish-born British poet. 'The Slow Starter',
Solstices (1961), ll. 23–24

7 My candle burns at both ends;
It will not last the night;
But ah, my foes, and oh, my friends—
It gives a lovely light!
Edna St. Vincent Millay (1892–1950) US poet. 'First Fig', *A Few Figs
from Thistles* (1920)

8 Man has given a false importance to death
   Any animal plant or man who dies
   adds to Nature's compost heap
   becomes the manure without which
   nothing could grow nothing could be created
   Death is simply part of the process.
   Peter Weiss (1916–82) German-born Swedish novelist and playwright. *The
   Persecution and Assassination of Marat as Performed by the
   Inmates of the Asylum of Charenton Under the Direction of
   the Marquis de Sade* (1964), Act 1, Scene 12

Moscow

see European Cities

Mothers

see also Children, Family, Parents, Pregnancy

1 Motherhood meant I have written four fewer
   books, but I know more about life.
   A. S. Byatt (b. 1936) British novelist and academic. *Sunday Times*
   (October 21, 1990)

2 A mother is a mother still,
   The holiest thing alive.
   Samuel Taylor Coleridge (1772–1834) British poet. 'The Three Graves'
   (1798)

3 The mother-child relationship is paradoxical and,
   in a sense, tragic. It requires the most intense
   love on the mother's side, yet this very love must
   help the child grow away from the mother and to
   become fully independent.
   Erich Fromm (1900–80) German-born US psychoanalyst and philosopher.
   Attrib.

4 Mother is the dead heart of the family, spending
   father's earnings on consumer goods to enhance
   the environment in which he eats, sleeps, and
   watches the television.
   Germaine Greer (b. 1939) Australian-born British writer and academic.
   The Female Eunuch (1970)

5 Being a mother is a noble status, right? Right. So
   why does it change when you put 'unwed' or
   'welfare' in front of it?
   Florynce R. Kennedy (1916–2000) US lawyer and activist. 1973. Quoted
   in 'The Verbal Karate of Florynce R. Kennedy, Esq.', *Ms.*'
   (Gloria Steinem; March 1973)

6 Nobody loves me but my mother,
   And she could be jiving, too.
   B. B. King (b. 1925) US blues singer and guitarist. Song lyric. Attrib.

7 Mothers? Hell, they seldom die!
   Paule Marshall (b. 1929) US novelist, teacher, and journalist. *Brown
   Girl, Brownstones* (1954)

8 I am old enough to be—in fact am—your
   mother.
   A. A. Milne (1882–1956) British writer. *Belinda* (1922)

9 My grief and my smile begin in your face, my
   son.
   Gabriela Mistral (1889–1957) Spanish poet, diplomat, and educator.
   'Poem of the Son', *Desolación* (1922)

10 It is not that I half knew my mother. I knew half
    of her: the lower half—her lap, legs, feet, her
    hands and wrists as she bent forward.
    Flann O'Brien (1911–66) Irish novelist and journalist. *The Hard Life*
    (1961)

11 You
    are my mother and your love's my bondage.
    I spent my childhood to this lofty,
    incurable sense of immense commitment.
    Pier Paolo Pasolini (1922–75) Italian filmmaker. 'Prayer To My
    Mother' (1964)

12 No matter how old a mother is she watches her
    middle-aged children for signs of improvement.
    Florida Scott-Maxwell (1883–?) US-born British writer. *The Measure of
    My Days* (1968)

13 She regarded me as a piece of fiction—like one of
    her novels—that she could edit and improve.
    Anthony West (1914–87) British journalist and writer. Referring to his
    mother, Rebecca West. *Heritage* (1984)

Motive

see also Ambition, Desire, Determination, Purpose

1 Never ascribe to an opponent motives meaner
   than your own.
   J. M. Barrie (1860–1937) British playwright and novelist. Rectorial
   address, St. Andrews University (May 3, 1922)

2 Any man who has known real loves, real revolts,
   real desires, and real will knows quite well that
   he has no need of any guarantee to be sure of his
   goals; their certitude comes from his own drive.
   Simone de Beauvoir (1908–86) French writer and feminist theorist. *The
   Ethics of Ambiguity* (1948)

3 Reasons are not like garments, the worse for
   wearing.
   Robert Devereux (1566–1601) English soldier. Letter to Lord
   Willoughby (January 4, 1599), quoted in *Notes & Queries,
   10th series, vol. 2*

4 The winds of the people,
   Spreading within my heart.
   The winds of the people impel me,
   and roar in my very throat.
   Miguel Hernandez, Spanish poet. 'The Winds of the People', *Roots
   and Wings: Poetry from Spain (1900–75)* (Hardie St. Martin,
   ed.; 1976), ll. 1–4

5 Dreams are the most powerful motivators of all.
   Nick Thornely, British author. *Leadership: the Art of Motivation*
   (co-written with Dan Lees; 1993)

6 The story of motivation has been that of a
   gradual return to the principle of motivating by
   pleasure.
   Nick Thornely, British author. *Leadership: the Art of Motivation*
   (co-written with Dan Lees; 1993)

Mountains

see also Exploration, Landscapes

1 Mountains interposed
   Make enemies of nations, who had else,
   Like kindred drops, been mingled into one.
   William Cowper (1731–1800) British poet. 'The Time-piece', *The Task*
   (1785), bk. 2, ll. 17–19

2 Sometimes we see these mountains rising up at
   once, from the lowest valleys, to the highest
   summits which makes the height look horrid and
   frightful, even worse than those mountains
   abroad.
   Daniel Defoe (1660–1731) English novelist and journalist. 1725.
   Referring to the Welsh mountains. Quoted in *A Tour
   Through the Whole Island of Great Britain* (Pat Rogers, ed.;
   1971), vol.2, letter 6

3   Well, we knocked the bastard off!

Edmund Hillary (b. 1919) New Zealand mountaineer. May 29, 1953.
Referring to reaching the summit of Mount Everest with Tenzing
Norgay. *Nothing Venture, Nothing Win* (1975), ch. 10

4   I see the Pyrenees, the gilded peaks of snow,
and all of Catalonia, stretched out at their feet,
And I feel drawn.

Joan Maragall (1860–1911) Catalan poet. 'Oda Nova a Barcelona',
quoted in *Barcelona* (Felipe Fernández-Armesto; 1992)

5   Climb Electric Peak when a big bossy, well-charged
thunder-cloud is on it, to breathe the ozone set free,
and get yourself kindly shaken and shocked . . .
Every hair of your head will stand up and hum and
sing like an enthusiastic congregation.

John Muir (1838–1914) US naturalist and explorer. *Our National
Parks* (1901), quoted in *John Muir: The Eight Wilderness
Discovery Books* (1992)

6   Climb the mountains and get their good tidings.
Nature's peace will flow into you as sunshine
flows into trees. The winds will blow their own
freshness into you, and the storms their energy,
while cares will drop off like autumn leaves.

John Muir (1838–1914) US naturalist and explorer. Attrib.

7   Mountains are the beginning and the end of all
natural scenery.

John Ruskin (1819–1900) British art critic, writer, and reformer. *Modern
Painters* (1856), vol. 4, pt. 5, ch. 20

8   They say that if the Swiss had designed these
mountains they'd be rather flatter.

Paul Theroux (b. 1941) US writer. Referring to the Alps. *The Great
Railway Bazaar* (1975), ch. 28

Mourning

see **Bereavement, Death and Dying, Sorrow**

Murder

see also **Crime, Death and Dying, Killing**

1   Murderers, in general, are people who are
consistent, people who are obsessed with one
idea and nothing else.

Ugo Betti (1892–1953) Italian playwright and poet. *Struggle Till Dawn*
(G. H. McWilliam, tr.; 1949)

2   No actions are bad in themselves, even murder
can be justified.

Dietrich Bonhoeffer (1906–45) German theologian. 1928–36. Quoted in
No Rusty Swords (Edwin H. Rosenbaum, ed.; 1970)

3   I've been accused of every death except the
casualty list of the World War.

Al Capone (1899–1947) Italian-born US gangster. *The Bootleggers*
(Kenneth Allsop; 1961), ch. 11

4   I didn't want to harm the man. I thought he was
a very nice gentleman. Soft-spoken. I thought so
right up to the moment I cut his throat.

Truman Capote (1924–84) US novelist. *In Cold Blood* (1966)

5   Mordre wol out, that see we day by day.

Geoffrey Chaucer (1343?–1400) English poet. 'The Nun's Priest's
Tale', *The Canterbury Tales* (1390?), quoted in *The Works of
Geoffrey Chaucer* (F. N. Robinson, ed.; 1957)

6   I have never yet heard of a murderer who was
not afraid of a ghost.

John Philpot Curran (1750–1817) Irish judge and orator. Said to an
Irish peer who hated the sight of the late Irish Parliament
building, for whose abolition he had voted. Attrib. *A Book of
Irish Quotations* (Sean McMahon, ed.; 1984)

7   To kill a human being is, after all, the least
injury you can do him.

Henry James (1843–1916) US-born British writer and critic. *My Friend
Bingham* (1867)

8   I murdered my grandmother this morning.

Franklin D. Roosevelt (1882–1945) US president. His habitual remark
to any guest at the White House he suspected of paying no
attention to what he said. Quoted in *Ear on Washington*
(Diana McClellan; 1982)

9   GHOST Murder most foul, as in the best it is;
But this most foul, strange, and unnatural.

William Shakespeare (1564–1616) English poet and playwright. *Hamlet*
(1601), Act 1, Scene 5

10 MACBETH Is this a dagger which I see before me,
The handle toward my hand? Come, let me
clutch thee:
I have thee not, and yet I see thee still.

William Shakespeare (1564–1616) English poet and playwright. *Macbeth*
(1606), Act 2, Scene 1

11 OTHELLO I kiss'd thee ere I kill'd thee, no way
but this,
Killing myself to die upon a kiss.

William Shakespeare (1564–1616) English poet and playwright. *Othello*
(1602–04), Act 5, Scene 2

12 Nothing is ever done in this world until men are
prepared to kill each other if it is not done.

George Bernard Shaw (1856–1950) Irish playwright. *Major Barbara*
(1907), Act 3

13 I met Murder on the way—
He had a mask like Castlereagh.

Percy Bysshe Shelley (1792–1822) English poet. Viscount Castlereagh
(1769–1822) was British foreign secretary (1812–22). He was
highly unpopular and became identified with such
controversial events as the Peterloo massacre of 1819. 'The
Masque of Anarchy' (1819), st. 2

14 Other sins only speak; murder shrieks out.

John Webster (1578?–1632?) English playwright. *The Duchess of Malfi*
(1623), Act 4, Scene 2

15 The person by far the most likely to kill you is
yourself.

Jock Young, British criminologist. *Observer* (May 8, 1994), 'Sayings
of the Week'

Music

see also **The Arts, Jazz, Musicians, Popular Music, Songs**

1   Music, the greatest good that mortals know,
And all of heaven we have below.

Joseph Addison (1672–1719) English essayist, poet, and statesman. 'A
Song for St. Cecilia's Day' (1694), st. 3

2   I can't listen to that much Wagner. I start getting
the urge to conquer Poland.

Woody Allen (b. 1935) US film actor and director. *Manhattan Murder
Mystery* (1993)

3   Music has the power of producing a certain
effect on the moral character of the soul.

Aristotle (384–322 BC) Greek philosopher. *Politics* (335–322? BC)

4   Folk music? Why, daddy, I don't know no other
kind of music *but* folk music. I ain't never heard
a horse sing a song.

Louis Armstrong (1901–71) US jazz trumpeter. *The Jazz Book*
(Joachim E. Berendt; 1983)

5   Music is the best means we have of digesting
time.

W. H. Auden (1907–73) British poet. Quoted in *Stravinsky:
Chronicle of a Friendship* (Robert Craft; 1972)

6 Music is edifying, for from time to time it sets the soul in operation.
John Cage (1912–92) US composer. *Silence* (1961)

7 Music is well said to be the speech of angels.
Thomas Carlyle (1795–1881) Scottish historian and essayist. *The Opera* (1852)

8 The heart of the melody can never be put down on paper.
Pablo Casals (1876–1973) Catalan cellist, conductor, and composer. *Conversations* (1955)

9 If the music doesn't say it, how can words say it *for* the music?
John Coltrane (1926–67) US jazz musician, composer, and bandleader. *Jazz Is* (Nat Hentoff; 1976)

10 The greatest moments of the human spirit may be deduced from the greatest moments in music.
Aaron Copland (1900–90) US composer. From a radio broadcast. 'Music as an Aspect of the Human Spirit' (1954)

11 Music is a sum total of scattered forces.
Claude Debussy (1862–1918) French composer. *Monsieur Croche, Antidilettante* (1921)

12 Music was invented to confirm human loneliness.
Lawrence Durrell (1912–90) British novelist and poet. *Clea* (1960)

13 There is music in the air, music all round us: the world is full of it, and you simply take as much as you require.
Edward Elgar (1857–1934) British composer, conductor, and violinist. *Sir Edward Elgar* (R. J. Buckley; 1905)

14 When it sounds good, it *is* good.
Duke Ellington (1899–1974) US jazz bandleader, pianist, and composer. *Music is My Mistress* (1973)

15 The music of what happens . . . that is the finest music in the world.
Fionn MacCool (*fl.* 2nd century) mythical Irish chieftain. 2nd century. Quoted in *Irish Fairy Tales* (James Stephens; 1920)

16 I frequently hear music in the heart of noise.
George Gershwin (1898–1937) US composer. Quoted in *George Gershwin* (Isaac Goldberg; 1931)

17 Music is going to break the way. It's like the waves of the ocean. You can't just cut out the perfect wave and take it home with you. It's constantly moving all the time.
Jimi Hendrix (1942–70) US rock musician. Quoted in *The Face of Black Music* (Valerie Wilmer; 1976)

18 Music is one of the ways God has of beating in on man.
Charles Ives (1874–1954) US composer. 'Epitaph for David Twitchell' (1924)

19 The music, yearning like a God in pain.
John Keats (1795–1821) English poet. 'The Eve of Saint Agnes' (1820), st. 7, l. 2

20 Music is not written in red, white and blue. It is written in the heart's blood of the composer.
Nellie Melba (1861–1931) Australian operatic soprano. *Melodies and Memories* (1925)

21 Music creates order out of chaos; for rhythm imposes unanimity upon the divergent, melody imposes continuity upon the disjointed, and harmony imposes compatibility upon the incongruous.
Yehudi Menuhin (1916–99) US-born British violinist. *Sunday Times* (October 10, 1976)

22 Music is capable of going directly to the source of the mystery. It doesn't have to explain it. It can simply celebrate it.
Marsha Norman (b. 1947) US playwright. Quoted in 'Marsha Norman', *Interviews with Contemporary Women Playwrights* (Kathleen Betsko and Rachel Koenig; 1987)

23 Music is your own experience, your thoughts, your wisdom. If you don't live it, it won't come out of your horn.
Charlie Parker (1920–55) US jazz saxophonist and composer. Quoted in *Hear Me Talkin' to Ya* (Nat Shapiro and Nat Hentoff; 1955)

24 Music begins to atrophy when it departs too far from the dance; . . . poetry begins to atrophy when it gets too far from music.
Ezra Pound (1885–1972) US poet, translator, and critic. 'Warning', *ABC of Reading* (1934)

25 The music is all. People should die for it. People are dying for everything else, so why not the music?
Lou Reed (b. 1942) US rock singer and songwriter. Quoted in *Lou Reed: Between the Lines* (Michael Wrenn; 1993)

26 ORSINO If music be the food of love, play on, / Give me excess of it, that, surfeiting, / The appetite may sicken and so die.
William Shakespeare (1564–1616) English poet and playwright. *Twelfth Night* (1601), Act 1, Scene 1

27 Without music we shall surely perish of drink, morphia, and all sorts of artificial exaggerations of the cruder delights of the senses.
George Bernard Shaw (1856–1950) Irish playwright. 'The Religion of the Pianoforte', *Fortnightly Review* (1894)

28 Can music be something more than shadows made to the measure of an idea, engraved on glass by one who forgets that he causes a god to come forth from among his notes?
Jaime Siles, Spanish writer and critic. 'Interiors', *A Bilingual Anthology of Contemporary Spanish Poetry* (Luis A. Ramos-García, ed.; 1997), pt. 2

29 Music revives the recollections it would appease.
Madame de Staël (1766–1817) French writer and intellectual. *Corinna, or Italy* (1807)

30 Just as my fingers on these keys / Make music, so the selfsame sounds / On my spirit make a music, too.
Wallace Stevens (1879–1955) US poet. 'Peter Quince at the Clavier', *Harmonium* (1923), st. 1

31 Today one composes because of an interior impulse; music has no other sources of improvisation any longer, apart from our own spirit.
Karlheinz Stockhausen (b. 1928) German composer. 1981. Quoted in 'In the Service of Music: The Quest for Perfection', *Conversations with Stockhausen* (Mya Tannenbaum; 1987)

32 Too many pieces of music finish too long after the end.
Igor Stravinsky (1882–1971) Russian-born US composer. Attrib.

33 Music that gentlier on the spirit lies, / Than tir'd eyelids upon tir'd eyes.
Alfred Tennyson (1809–92) British poet. 1830–32. 'The Lotos-Eaters', *Poems* (1832), 'Choric Song', st. 1

34 Music is the crystallization of sound.
Henry David Thoreau (1817–62) US writer. *Journal* (1841), quoted in *The Journal of Henry David Thoreau* (Bradford Torrey and Francis H. Allen, eds.; 1962)

35 When I hear music, I fear no danger. I am invulnerable. I see no foe. I am related to the earliest times and to the latest.

Henry David Thoreau (1817–62) US writer. *Journal* (1857), quoted in *The Journal of Henry David Thoreau* (Bradford Torrey and Francis H. Allen, eds.; 1962)

36 It is a truth for ever, that where the speech of man stops short there Music's reign begins.

Richard Wagner (1813–83) German composer. 'A Happy Evening' (1841), quoted in *Pilgrimage to Beethoven* (W. A. Ellis, tr.; 1994)

37 If one hears bad music, it is one's duty to drown it by one's conversation.

Oscar Wilde (1854–1900) Irish poet, playwright, and wit. *The Picture of Dorian Gray* (1891)

38 Let me sum it up for you. Information is not knowledge. Knowledge is not wisdom. Wisdom is not truth. Truth is not beauty. Beauty is not love. Love is not music. Music is the best.

Frank Zappa (1940–93) US rock musician and composer. Quoted in *Mother! The Frank Zappa Story* (Michael Gray; 1993)

Musicians

see also **Music, Singers and Singing**

1 Knowing how to play an instrument is the barest superficiality if one is thinking of becoming a musician. It is the ideas that one utilizes *instinctively* that determine the degree of profundity any artist reaches.

Imamu Amiri Baraka (b. 1934) US author, editor, playwright, and political activist. 1961. 'The Jazz Avant-Garde', *Black Music* (1969), ch. 10

2 A bird of brilliant plumage, fluttering over the horrors of the abyss.

Charles Baudelaire (1821–67) French poet. Comment on the music of Frédéric Chopin, who was a friend. Quoted in 'The Fallacies of Hope', *Civilisation* (Kenneth Clark; 1969)

3 It's assumed that a lot of musicians are speaking for someone else—speaking for the steelworkers or for the underprivileged—whereas a lot of musicians are privileged people.

David Byrne (b. 1952) US musician. Interview, *New Musical Express* (December 8, 1984), quoted in *Shots from the Hip* (Charles Shaar Murray; 1993)

4 A lot of notes lying around on that old piano. I just pick at the ones I like.

Nat King Cole (1919–65) US singer and jazz pianist. Describing his style of piano playing. *Saturday Evening Post* (1943)

5 The attraction of the virtuoso for the public is very like that of the circus for the crowd. There is always the hope that something dangerous may happen.

Claude Debussy (1862–1918) French composer. *Monsieur Croche, Antidilettante* (1921)

6 The heroines of her lyrics are Amazonian and Junoesque, indefatigably sexual; her voice and Louis' trumpet exchange brazen and derisive comment.

Elaine Feinstein (b. 1930) British poet and novelist. Referring to Bessie Smith's performances with Louis Armstrong. *Bessie Smith: Empress of the Blues* (1985), ch. 1

7 A musician, if he's a messenger, is like a child who hasn't been handled too many times by man, hasn't had too many fingerprints across his brain.

Jimi Hendrix (1942–70) US rock musician. *Life* (1969)

8 Sometimes, I think, not so much am I a pianist, but a vampire. All my life I have lived off the blood of Chopin.

Arthur Rubinstein (1887–1982) Polish-born US pianist. 1977. Comment on turning 90. Attrib.

9 Brahms is just like Tennyson, an extraordinary musician with the brains of a third-rate village policeman.

George Bernard Shaw (1856–1950) Irish playwright. April 4, 1893. Attrib.

10 Madam, there you sit with that magnificent instrument between your legs, and all you can do is *scratch* it!

Arturo Toscanini (1867–1957) Italian conductor. Rebuking a cellist. Attrib.

11 Please do not shoot the pianist. He is doing his best.

Oscar Wilde (1854–1900) Irish poet, playwright, and wit. 1883. 'Leadville', *Personal Impressions of America* (1893)

Mysticism

see also **Religion, Thinking**

1 We make assertions and denials of what is next to it, but never of it, for it is both beyond every assertion, being the perfect and unique cause of all things, and, by virtue of its preeminently simple and absolute nature, free of every limitation, beyond every limitation; it is also beyond every denial.

Dionysius the Areopagite (fl. 1st century) Greek church leader and martyr. 1st century AD. Some modern scholars now identify the work attributed to Dionysius to a 6th-century Neoplatonist known as Pseudo-Dionysius. Quoted in 'The Mystical Theology', *Pseudo-Dionysius, The Complete Works* (C. Luibheid, tr.; 1987), ch. 5

2 At the still point of the turning world. Neither flesh nor fleshless;
Neither from nor towards; at the still point, there the
dance is,
But neither arrest nor movement.

T. S. Eliot (1888–1965) US-born British poet and playwright. 'Burnt Norton', *Four Quartets* (1935), pt. 2

3 The dark night of the soul.

Saint John of the Cross (1542–91) Spanish poet, mystic, and Doctor of the Church. 'Noche obscura del alma' (1578?)

4 The mystic sees the ineffable, and the psychopathologist the unspeakable.

Somerset Maugham (1874–1965) British writer. *The Moon and Sixpence* (1919), ch. 1

5 And looks commercing with the skies,
Thy rapt soul sitting in thine eyes.

John Milton (1608–74) English writer. 'Il Penseroso', *Poems of Mr. John Milton* (1645), ll. 39–40

6 I regard mysticism as a state of mind which is necessary to scientific thinking, as well as to art: it enables one to discover things which cannot be found by any other means.

Antoni Tàpies (b. 1923) Spanish painter. Quoted in *Conversations with Antoni Tàpies* (Barbara Catoir; 1991)

7 Mystics always hope that science will some day overtake them.

Booth Tarkington (1869–1946) US novelist. *Looking Forward, and Others* (1926)

8 Mysticism is simply the insistence upon a direct and present religious experience.

Ernst Troeltsch (1865–1923) German theologian and scholar. *The Social Teaching of the Christian Church* (O. Wyon, tr.; 1912)

9 Whither is fled the visionary gleam?
Where is it now, the glory and the dream?

William Wordsworth (1770–1850) English poet. 1802?–06. 'Ode: Intimations of Immortality from Recollections of Early Childhood', *Poems in Two Volumes* (1807), vol. 2, st. 4, ll. 56–57

Myths

see also **Fantasy, Fiction, History**

1 One is tempted to say that old myths never die; they just become embedded in the textbooks.

Thomas A. Bailey (1902–83) US historian. 'The Mythmakers of American History', *Journal of American History* (June 1968)

2 And they went in unto Noah into the ark, two and two of all flesh, wherein is the breath of life . . .
And the flood was forty days upon the earth; and the waters increased, and bare up the ark, and it was lifted up above the earth.

Bible. Genesis, *King James Bible* (1611), 7:15–17

3 A world that can be explained even with bad reasons is a familiar world. But in a universe suddenly divested of illusions and lights, man feels an alien, a stranger.

Albert Camus (1913–60) Algerian-born French novelist, essayist, and playwright. *The Myth of Sisyphus* (1942)

4 I believe that all myths are products of the human mind and reflect only aspects of material human practice. I'm in the demythologising business.

Angela Carter (1940–92) British novelist, essayist, and short-story writer. 'Notes From the Front Line', *Shaking A Leg: Journalism and Writings* (1983)

5 Myth deals in false universals, to dull the pain of particular circumstances.

Angela Carter (1940–92) British novelist, essayist, and short-story writer. 'Polemical Preface', *The Sadeian Woman* (1979)

6 At the centre of every myth is another: that of the people who created it.

Nuruddin Farah (b. 1945) Somali novelist, playwright, and teacher. *Gifts* (1993)

7 For who could see the passage of a goddess unless she wished his mortal eyes aware?

Homer (*fl.* 8th century BC) Greek poet. Late 8th century BC. *Odyssey* (Robert Fitzgerald, tr.), bk. 10, ll. 575–576

8 The world of poetry, mythology, and religion represents the world as a man would like to have it, while science represents the world as he gradually comes to discover it.

Joseph Wood Krutch (1893–1970) US essayist and naturalist. *The Modern Temper* (1929)

9 Contemporary man has rationalized the myths, but he has not been able to destroy them.

Octavio Paz (1914–98) Mexican author and poet. *The Labyrinth of Solitude* (Lysander Kemp, tr.; 1985)

10 I wonder if we could contrive . . . some magnificent myth that would in itself carry conviction to our whole community.

Plato (428?–347? BC) Greek philosopher. *The Republic* (370? BC), bk. 5

11 A myth is, of course, not a fairy story. It is the presentation of facts belonging to one category in the idioms appropriate to another. To explode a myth is accordingly not to deny the facts but to re-allocate them.

Gilbert Ryle (1900–76) British philosopher. *The Concept of Mind* (1949), Introduction

12 An arm
Rose up from out the bosom of the lake,
Clothed in white samite, mystic, wonderful.

Alfred Tennyson (1809–92) British poet. 'The Passing of Arthur', *Idylls of the King* (1869), ll. 197–199

13 Plato means by 'myth' a form of expression to which one turns when the resources of the intellect have been exhausted.

Arnold Toynbee (1889–1975) British historian. 'What are the Criteria for Comparisons between Religions?', *Christianity Among the Religions of the World* (1958), pt. 1

14 Freud . . . has not given an explanation of the ancient myth. What he has done is to propound a new myth.

Ludwig Wittgenstein (1889–1951) Austrian philosopher. Referring to Sigmund Freud's work with myth in such areas as the Oedipus complex. Quoted in *Lectures and Conversations* (Cyril Barnett, ed.; 1966)

N

Nakedness

see also **The Body**

1 'But the Emperor has nothing on at all!' cried a little child.
Hans Christian Andersen (1805–75) Danish writer. 1837. 'The Emperor's New Clothes', *Tales, Told for Children* (1843)

2 a pretty girl who naked is
is worth a million statues.
e. e. cummings (1894–1962) US poet and painter. *Collected Poems* (1938)

3 No woman so naked as one you can see to be naked underneath her clothes.
Michael Frayn (b. 1933) British journalist, novelist, and playwright. *Constructions* (1974)

4 To see you naked is to recall the Earth.
Federico García Lorca (1899–1936) Spanish poet and playwright. 'Casida of the Woman Prone', *Divan of the Tamarit* (1936)

5 I give you my naked soul
Like a statue unveiled.
Juana de Ibarbourou (1895–1989) Uruguayan poet. 'The Hour', *Diamond Tongues* (1919)

6 The part never calls for it. And I've never ever used that excuse. The box office calls for it.
Helen Mirren (b. 1945) British actor. Referring to nudity. *Observer* (March 27, 1994), 'Sayings of the Week'

7 JOURNALIST Didn't you have anything on?
M. M. I had the radio on.
Marilyn Monroe (1926–62) US film actor. Attrib.

8 There's more enterprise
In walking naked.
W. B. Yeats. (1865–1939) Irish poet and playwright. 'A Coat', *Responsibilities and Other Poems* (1916)

Names

see also **Identity**

1 With a name like that he was made from an early age—all he needed was a hustle.
Anonymous. Referring to the jazz musician Thelonius Sphere Monk. Quoted in 'Round About Monk', *Jazz People* (Valerie Wilmer; 1970), ch. 4

2 Nicknames . . . give away the whole drama of man. They fall into many classes; the three most current are: those we invent to make a person what he should be . . . those we invent to make him appear what he is not . . . and those we invent to more tightly wrap him in that which he is.
Djuna Barnes (1892–1982) US writer and illustrator. 'The Psychology of Nicknames', *Ryder* (1928), ch. 29

3 I don't like your Christian name. I'd like to change it.
Thomas Beecham (1879–1961) British conductor and impresario. Said to his future wife. She replied, 'You can't, but you can change my surname'. Attrib.

4 I have fallen in love with American names,
The sharp names that never get fat,
The snakeskin-titles of mining-claims,
The plumed war-bonnet of Medicine Hat,
Tucson and Deadwood and Lost Mule Flat.
Stephen Vincent Benét (1898–1943) US poet and novelist. 'American Names' (1927)

5 The act of naming is the great and solemn consolation of mankind.
Elias Canetti (1905–94) Bulgarian-born writer. *The Agony of Flies* (1992)

6 With a name like yours, you might be any shape, almost.
Lewis Carroll (1832–98) British writer and mathematician. Said by Humpty Dumpty to Alice. *Through the Looking-Glass and What Alice Found There* (1871), ch. 6

7 Everybody has a right to pronounce foreign names as he chooses.
Winston Churchill (1874–1965) British prime minister and writer. *Observer* (August 5, 1951), 'Sayings of the Week'

8 The Naming of Cats is a difficult matter
It isn't just one of your holiday games.
T. S. Eliot (1888–1965) US-born British poet and playwright. 'The Naming of Cats', *Old Possum's Book of Practical Cats* (1939)

9 Although my father wanted me to become an engineer and my mother a bishop, I myself am quite contented to have become an adjective.
Federico Fellini (1920–93) Italian film director. Referring to the usage of the term 'Felliniesque', meaning to blend fantasy and reality as Fellini does in his movies. Quoted in *Halliwell's Filmgoer's Companion* (Leslie Halliwell; 1993)

10 A nickname is the heaviest stone that the devil can throw at a man.
William Hazlitt (1778–1830) British essayist and critic. 'Nicknames', *Sketches and Essays* (William Carew Hazlitt, ed.; 1839)

11 All the names that I gave
to the universe that I created again for you
are now turning into one name, into one god.
Juan Ramón Jiménez (1881–1958) Spanish poet. 'The Name Drawn From the Names', *Roots and Wings: Poetry from Spain, 1900–75* (Hardie St. Martin, ed.; 1976)

12 Dr. Simpson's first patient, a doctor's wife in 1847, had been so carried away with enthusiasm that she christened her child, a girl, 'Anaesthesia'.
Elizabeth Longford (b. 1906) British writer. *Queen Victoria* (1964), ch. 17

13 No, Groucho is not my real name. I'm breaking it in for a friend.
Groucho Marx (1895–1977) US comedian and film actor. Remark (1950?), attrib.

14 There is no counting the names, that surgeons and anatomists give to the various parts of the human body . . . which keep increasing every day, and hour . . . But people seem to have a great love for names; for to know a great many names seems to look like knowing a good many things.
Herman Melville (1819–91) US novelist. *Redburn* (1849), ch. 13

15 PROCTOR How may I live without my name?
Arthur Miller (b. 1915) US playwright. Considering whether ignominiously to confess to witchcraft and thus escape execution. *The Crucible* (1953), Act 4

16 Because he spills his seed on the ground.
Dorothy Parker (1893–1967) US writer and wit. Referring to naming her canary 'Onan'; referring to Genesis 38:9, 'And Onan knew that the seed should not be his; and it came to pass, when he went in unto his brother's wife, that he spilled it on the ground'. Quoted in *You Might As Well Live* (John Keats; 1970)

17 ROMEO What's in a name? That which we call a rose
By any other name would smell as sweet.
William Shakespeare (1564–1616) English poet and playwright. *Romeo and Juliet* (1595), Act 2, Scene 2

18 Names should be charms . . . I used to hope that, by saying some of them often enough, I might evoke reality.
Patrick White (1912–90) British-born Australian novelist. *Voss* (1957)

Narcissism

see also **Pride, The Self, Vanity**

1 Most people enjoy the sight of their own handwriting as they enjoy the smell of their own farts.
W. H. Auden (1907–73) British poet. 'Writing', *The Dyer's Hand* (1963)

2 He is, after all, the reflection of the tenderness I bear for myself. It is always ourselves we love.
Beryl Bainbridge (b. 1934) British author and journalist. 'Maggie', *A Weekend with Claud* (1967)

3 He that falls in love with himself, will have no rivals.
Benjamin Franklin (1706–90) US statesman and scientist. *Poor Richard's Almanack* (1787)

4 Narcissism is the earliest stage of human development, and the person who in later life has returned to this stage is incapable of love; in the extreme case he is insane.
Erich Fromm (1900–80) German-born US psychoanalyst and philosopher. *The Art of Loving* (1956)

5 Narcissus leant over the spring, enchanted by his own ugliness, which he prided himself upon having the courage to admit.
Dag Hammarskjöld (1905–61) Swedish statesman and diplomat. *Markings* (Leif Sjöberg and W. H. Auden, trs.; 1964)

6 A Grecian lad, as I hear tell,
One that many loved in vain,
Looked into a forest well
And never looked away again.
A. E. Housman (1859–1936) British poet and classicist. Referring to Narcissus. *A Shropshire Lad* (1896), quoted in *The Collected Poems of A. E. Housman* (John Carter, ed.; 1967)

7 We never remark any passion or principle in others, of which, in some degree or other, we may not find a parallel in ourselves.
David Hume (1711–76) Scottish philosopher and historian. *A Treatise of Human Nature* (1739–40)

8 A narcissist is someone better looking than you are.
Gore Vidal (b. 1925) US novelist and essayist. Quoted in *San Francisco Chronicle* (April 12, 1981)

Nations

see also **African Countries, Asian Countries, Australia, The Caribbean, Central America, European Countries, Russia, South America, United States**

1 We must free ourselves from thinking in terms of nation states.
Konrad Adenauer (1876–1967) West German chancellor. Speech (May 1953)

2 In the youth of a state arms do flourish; in the middle age of a state, learning; and then both of them together for a time; in the declining age of a state, mechanical arts and merchandise.
Francis Bacon (1561–1626) English philosopher, statesman, and lawyer. 'Of Vicissitude of Things', *Essays* (1625)

3 Have the Kurdish people committed such crimes that every nation in the world should be against them?
Mustafa Barzani (1903–79) Kurdish political and military leader. Remark (1975), quoted in *Kurdistan* (Jonathan C. Randal; 1998)

4 Since individuals are by nature equal, the groups of persons who compose universal society are also equal. Even the weakest republic enjoys the same rights and is subject to the same obligations as the most powerful empire.
Andrés Bello (1781–1865) Chilean politician and writer. 'Principles of International Law' (1864)

5 Nations, like men, have their infancy.
Henry St. John Bolingbroke (1678–1751) English statesman. *Letters on the Study and Use of History* (1752), Letter 4

6 A nation must be willing to look dispassionately at its own history.
Willy Brandt (1913–92) German statesman. Declaration on the 25th anniversary of the end of World War II (May 8, 1970), quoted in *Willy Brandt, Peace* (Klaus Reiff, ed.; 1971)

7 Things are getting back to a wholesome state. Every nation for itself, and God for us all.
George Canning (1770–1827) British prime minister. Canning supported nationalist movements in South America and Europe. Quoted in *Europe: A History* (Norman Davies; 1996), ch. 10

8 We have a country full of words. Speak, speak so that I can rest my road against a rock.
We have a country full of words. Speak, speak, so that we may know what is the limit of this travelling.
Mahmoud Darwish (b. 1942) Palestinian poet. 'We Travel like Other People', *Modern Arabic Poetry* (Salma Khadra Jayyusi, ed.; 1987), ll. 9–10

9 The present, after all, is merely a nation's skin, its body is the past.
Carl N. Degler (b. 1921) US historian. 'Remaking American History', *Journal of American History* (June 1980)

10 The nation is rapidly ceasing to be the real defining unit of society.
Northrop Frye (1912–91) Canadian academic. *The Modern Century* (1967)

11 Although they are an occupied nation
and their only border is an inland one
they yield to nobody in their belief
that the country is an island.
Seamus Heaney (b. 1939) Irish poet. 'Parable Island', *The Haw Lantern* (1987), ll. 1–4

12 The essential thing is the formation of the political will of the nation: that is the starting point for political action.

Adolf Hitler (1889–1945) Austrian-born German dictator. Speech, Düsseldorf (January 27, 1932)

13 The nations which have put mankind and posterity most in their debt have been small states—Israel, Athens, Florence, Elizabethan England.

William Ralph Inge (1860–1954) British churchman. 'State, Visible and Invisible', *Outspoken Essays* (1922), Second Series

14 Peace, commerce, and honest friendship with all nations, entangling alliances with none.

Thomas Jefferson (1743–1826) US president. Inaugural address, Washington, D.C. (March 4, 1801)

15 Blest is that nation whose silent course of happiness furnishes nothing for history to say.

Thomas Jefferson (1743–1826) US president. Letter to Diodati (1807)

16 A nation, like a person, not conscious of its own past is adrift without purpose or protection against the contending forces of dissolution.

Lyndon Baines Johnson (1908–73) US president. Thanksgiving Day proclamation (November 25, 1964)

17 The great nations have always acted like gangsters, and the small nations like prostitutes.

Stanley Kubrick (1928–99) US film director. *Guardian* (June 5, 1963)

18 A nation is the universality of citizens speaking the same tongue.

Giuseppe Mazzini (1805–72) Italian revolutionary and political theorist. *La Giovine Italia* (1831)

19 The struggle of any nation in its successive generations is a structure that rises one stone upon another.

Gamal Abdel Nasser (1918–70) Egyptian statesman. *The Philosophy of the Revolution* (1952)

20 A nation has character only when it is free.

Madame de Staël (1766–1817) French writer and intellectual. *De la Littérature* (1800)

21 Nationalism is a form of lack of culture that pervades all cultures and coexists with all ideologies, a chameleon resource at the service of politicians of every persuasion.

Mario Vargas Llosa (b. 1936) Peruvian writer. 'Nations, Fictions' (1992)

22 If people behaved in the way nations do they would all be put in straitjackets.

Tennessee Williams (1911–83) US playwright. Attrib.

Nature

see also **Evolution, Genetics, Landscapes, Science**

1 Nature is often hidden, sometimes overcome, seldom extinguished.

Francis Bacon (1561–1626) English philosopher, statesman, and lawyer. 'Of Nature in Men', *Essays* (1625)

2 Nature, to be commanded, must be obeyed.

Francis Bacon (1561–1626) English philosopher, statesman, and lawyer. *Novum Organum* (1620), aphorism 129

3 Nature is not easy to live with. It is hard to have rain on your cut hay, or floodwater over your cropland, or coyotes in your sheep . . . nature does not respect your intentions.

Wendell Berry (b. 1934) US poet, novelist, and essayist. 1985. 'Preserving Wildness', *The Landscape of Harmony* (1987)

4 Go forth under the open sky, and list
To Nature's teachings.

William Cullen Bryant (1794–1878) US poet and journalist. 'Thanatopsis' (1817), ll. 14–15

5 There is a pleasure in the pathless woods,
There is a rapture on the lonely shore,
There is society, where none intrudes,
By the deep Sea, and music in its roar:
I love not Man the less, but Nature more.

Lord Byron (1788–1824) British poet. *Childe Harold's Pilgrimage* (1812–18), can. 4, st. 178

6 Nature admits no lie.

Thomas Carlyle (1795–1881) Scottish historian and essayist. *Latter-Day Pamphlets* (1850), 5

7 Nature, exerting an unwearied pow'r,
Forms, opens, and gives scent to ev'ry flow'r;
Spreads the fresh verdure of the field, and leads
The dancing Naiads through the dewy meads.

William Cowper (1731–1800) British poet. 'Table Talk' (1782), ll. 690–693, quoted in *The Works of William Cowper* (Robert Southey, ed.; 1835–37)

8 Nature is but a name for an effect
Whose cause is God.

William Cowper (1731–1800) British poet. 'The Winter Walk at Noon', *The Task* (1785), bk. 6, ll. 223–224

9 When it occurs to a man that nature does not regard him as important, and that she feels she would not maim the universe by disposing of him, he at first wishes to throw books at the temple, and he hates deeply the fact that there are no bricks and no temples.

Stephen Crane (1871–1900) US writer and journalist. 1897. 'The Open Boat', *The Open Boat and Other Stories* (1898)

10 Nature can do more than physicians.

Oliver Cromwell (1599–1658) English soldier and statesman. Attrib.

11 Nature tells every secret once.

Ralph Waldo Emerson (1803–82) US poet and essayist. 'Behavior', *The Conduct of Life* (1860)

12 All Nature wears one universal grin.

Henry Fielding (1707–54) British novelist and playwright. *Tom Thumb the Great* (1731), Act 1, Scene 1

13 Something there is that doesn't love a wall.
And wants it down.

Robert Frost (1874–1963) US poet. 'Mending Wall', *North of Boston* (1914)

14 Nature is all very well in her place, but she must not be allowed to make things untidy.

Stella Gibbons (1902–89) British poet and novelist. *Cold Comfort Farm* (1933), ch. 6

15 Nature is amoral, not immoral . . . It existed for eons before we arrived, didn't know we were coming, and doesn't give a damn about us.

Stephen Jay Gould (1941–2002) US geologist and writer. *Rocks of Ages: Science and Religion in the Fullness of Life* (1999)

16 Nature, Mr. Allnut, is what we are put into this world to rise above.

Katharine Hepburn (b. 1907) US actor. As the missionary, Rosie Sayer. Charlie Allnut, captain of the river boat *The African Queen*, was played by Humphrey Bogart. *The African Queen* (James Agee and John Huston; 1951)

17 You may drive out nature with a pitchfork, yet she'll be constantly running back.

Horace (65–8 BC) Roman poet. *Epistles* (20? BC), bk. 1, no. 10, l. 24

18 Nature is as wasteful of promising young men as she is of fish spawn.

Richard Hughes (1900–76) British writer. *The Fox in the Attic* (1961)

19 Art may make a suit of clothes: but Nature must produce a man.

David Hume (1711–76) Scottish philosopher and historian. 'The Epicurean', *Essays, Moral and Political* (1741)

20 The whole of nature is a conjugation of the verb to eat, in the active and the passive.

William Ralph Inge (1860–1954) British churchman. *Outspoken Essays* (1919), First Series

21 In nature there are neither rewards nor punishments—there are consequences.

Robert G. Ingersoll (1833–99) US lawyer. *Some Reasons Why* (1881), pt. 8, 'The New Testament'

22 Nature uses as little as possible of anything.

Johannes Kepler (1571–1630) German astronomer. *Harmonice mundi* (1619)

23 Now this is the Law of the Jungle—as old and as true as the sky;
And the Wolf that shall keep it may prosper, but the Wolf that shall break it must die.

Rudyard Kipling (1865–1936) Indian-born British writer and poet. 'The Law of the Jungle', *The Second Jungle Book* (1895)

24 Nature did not care. To life she set one task, gave one law. To perpetuate was the task of life, its law was death.

Jack London (1876–1916) US writer. 'The Law of Life' (1901)

25 Notwithstanding, therefore, that we have not witnessed within the last three thousand years the devastation by deluge of a large continent, yet, as we may predict the future occurrence of such catastrophes, we are authorized to regard them as part of the present order of Nature.

Charles Lyell (1797–1875) British geologist. *Principles of Geology* (1830–33)

26 Accuse not nature, she hath done her part;
Do thou but thine.

John Milton (1608–74) English writer. Raphael to Adam. *Paradise Lost* (1667), bk. 8, ll. 561–562

27 To look nature in the face and *dominate it* is enormously attractive and exciting. It's as though by the strength of your eyes you bring down a panther at your feet in the middle of the jungle.

Joan Miró (1893–1983) Catalan painter. Letter to Pierre Matisse (February 12, 1937)

28 Nature is very consonant and conformable with herself.

Isaac Newton (1642–1727) English mathematician and physicist. *Opticks* (1704), bk. 3

29 There are no accidents, only nature throwing her weight around . . . After the bomb, nature will pick up the cards we have spilled, shuffle them, and begin her game again.

Camille Paglia (b. 1947) US academic and author. *Sexual Personae* (1990)

30 It is far from easy to determine whether she has proved a kind parent to man or a merciless step-mother.

Pliny the Elder (23?–79) Roman scholar. Referring to nature. *Natural History* (77), bk. 7

31 Nature abhors a vacuum.

François Rabelais (1494?–1553?) French humanist and satirist. Quoting an article of classical wisdom. *Gargantua* (1534), bk. 1, ch. 5

32 Certainly nothing is unnatural that is not physically impossible.

Richard Brinsley Sheridan (1751–1816) Irish-born British playwright and politician. *The Critic* (1779), Act 2, Scene 1

33 Forest equals crop Scenery equals recreation Public equals money: The shopkeeper's view of nature.

Gary Snyder (b. 1930) US poet, essayist, and translator. June 27, 1953. 'Lookout's Journal: Sourdough', *Earth House Hold* (1969)

34 Only to the white man was nature a 'wilderness' . . . To us it was tame. Earth was bountiful and we were surrounded with the blessings of the Great Mystery.

Luther Standing Bear (1868?–1939?) US Native American leader and writer. The Great Mystery, Wakan Tanka, is the Sioux's one and omnipotent god. *Land of the Spotted Eagle* (1933)

35 Life consists with wildness. The most alive is the wildest. Not yet subdued to man, its presence refreshes him.

Henry David Thoreau (1817–62) US writer. 'Walking', *Excursions* (1863)

36 In nature there are no rewards or punishments; there are consequences.

Horace Annesley Vachell (1861–1955) British writer. *The Face of Clay* (1906), ch. 10

37 Nature has always had more power than education.

Voltaire (1694–1778) French writer and philosopher. *Vie de Molière* (1733–34)

38 Through nature one came to love the absence of philosophy, and fatally, perhaps, the beauty of certain degradations.

Derek Walcott (b. 1930) St. Lucian poet and playwright. *What the Twilight Says* (1998)

39 Nature contains the elements, in colour and form, of all pictures, as the keyboard contains the notes of all music.

James Abbott McNeill Whistler (1834–1903) US painter and etcher. *The Gentle Art of Making Enemies* (1890)

40 After you have exhausted what there is in business, politics, conviviality, and so on—have found that none of these finally satisfy, or permanently wear—what remains? Nature remains.

Walt Whitman (1819–92) US poet. 'New Themes Entered Upon', *Specimen Days and Collect* (1882)

41 For I have learned
To look on nature, not as in the hour
Of thoughtless youth; but hearing often-times
The still, sad music of humanity.

William Wordsworth (1770–1850) English poet. July 13, 1798. Subtitled: 'On Revisiting the Banks of the Wye During a Tour, July 13, 1798'. 'Lines Composed a Few Miles Above Tintern Abbey', *Lyrical Ballads* (1798), ll. 88–91

42 Knowing that Nature never did betray
The heart that loved her.

William Wordsworth (1770–1850) English poet. July 13, 1798. Subtitled: 'On Revisiting the Banks of the Wye During a Tour, July 13, 1798'. 'Lines Composed a Few Miles Above Tintern Abbey', *Lyrical Ballads* (1798), ll. 122–123

43 Come forth into the light of things,
Let Nature be your Teacher.

William Wordsworth (1770–1850) English poet. May 23, 1798. Subtitled 'An Evening Piece on the Same Subject', referring to 'Expostulation and Reply', to which it is a companion piece. 'The Tables Turned', *Lyrical Ballads* (1798), ll. 15–16

Necessity

see also **Desires, Hunger**

1   You gotta have a swine to show you where the truffles are.
    Edward Albee (b. 1928) US playwright. *Who's Afraid of Virginia Woolf?* (1962), Act 1

2   It is necessary to assume something which is necessary of itself, and has no cause of its necessity outside itself but is rather the cause of necessity in other things. And this all men call God.
    Thomas Aquinas (1225–74) Italian theologian and philosopher. *Summa Theologica* (1266–73), I, pt. 1

3   Man cannot be free if he does not know that he is subject to necessity, because his freedom is always won in his never wholly successful attempts to liberate himself from necessity.
    Hannah Arendt (1906–75) German-born US philosopher and historian. *The Human Condition* (1958), pt. 3, ch. 16

4   We have almost succeeded in leveling all human activities to the common denominator of securing the necessities of life and providing for their abundance.
    Hannah Arendt (1906–75) German-born US philosopher and historian. *The Human Condition* (1958), pt. 3, ch. 17

5   Everything necessarily is or is not, and will be or will not be; but one cannot divide and say that one or the other is necessary.
    Aristotle (384–322 BC) Greek philosopher. *De Interpretatione* (4th century BC), 19a

6   Make a virtue of necessity.
    Robert Burton (1577–1640) English scholar and churchman. *The Anatomy of Melancholy* (1621), pt. 3, sect. 3

7   They must needs go whom the Devil drives.
    Miguel de Cervantes (1547–1616) Spanish novelist and playwright. *Don Quixote* (1605–15), pt. 1, bk. 4, ch. 4

8   Thanne is it wysdom, as it thynketh me,
    To maken vertue of necessitee.
    Geoffrey Chaucer (1343?–1400) English poet. 'The Knight's Tale', *The Canterbury Tales* (1390?), ll. 3041–42

9   Necessity makes an honest man a knave.
    Daniel Defoe (1660–1731) English novelist and journalist. *The Serious Reflections of Robinson Crusoe* (1720), ch. 2

10 Necessity knows no law and discriminates in favor of no man or race.
    Timothy Thomas Fortune (1856–1928) US journalist and orator. *Black and White: Land, Labor and Politics in the South* (1884)

11 Necessity has the face of a dog.
    Gabriel García Márquez (b. 1928) Colombian novelist. *In Evil Hour* (1968)

12 And with necessity,
    The tyrant's plea, excus'd his devilish deeds.
    John Milton (1608–74) English writer. Satan plots humankind's downfall. *Paradise Lost* (1667), bk. 4, l. 393

13 The true creator is necessity, which is the mother of invention.
    Plato (428?–347? BC) Greek philosopher. *The Republic* (370? BC)

14 Necessity knows no law.
    Publilius Syrus (*fl.* 1st century BC) Roman writer. 1st century BC. Attrib.

15 LEAR The art of our necessities is strange,
    That can make vile things precious.
    William Shakespeare (1564–1616) English poet and playwright. *King Lear* (1605–06), Act 3, Scene 2

16 GAUNT Teach thy necessity to reason thus:
    There is no virtue like necessity.
    William Shakespeare (1564–1616) English poet and playwright. *Richard II* (1595), Act 1, Scene 3

17 KING RICHARD II I am sworn brother, sweet,
    To grim Necessity, and he and I
    Will keep a league till death.
    William Shakespeare (1564–1616) English poet and playwright. *Richard II* (1595), Act 5, Scene 1

Neurosis

see also **Madness, Psychiatry, Psychoanalysis**

1   The neurotic individual is the typical killjoy and peace destroyer. He is misled by his megalomaniac ideal . . . and is always busy trying to hypostasize and deify his own guiding line, and to cross those of others.
    Alfred Adler (1870–1937) Austrian psychiatrist. 1912. *The Neurotic Constitution* (1921)

2   A mistake which is commonly made about neurotics is to suppose that they are interesting. It is not interesting to be always unhappy, engrossed with oneself, malignant and ungrateful, and never quite in touch with reality.
    Cyril Connolly (1903–74) British writer and journalist. *The Unquiet Grave* (1944)

3   Neurosis is a spontaneous archaeology of the libido.
    Michel Foucault (1926–84) French philosopher. 1962. *Mental Illness and Psychology* (1976)

4   Neurotic nuclei are found in the minds of normal people as regularly as large areas of usual functioning are part of the makeup of every neurotic.
    Anna Freud (1895–1982) Austrian-born British psychoanalyst. *Problems of Analytic Technique and Therapy* (1972)

5   Neurosis can be understood best as the battle between two tendencies within an individual; deep character analysis leads, if successful, to the progressive solution.
    Erich Fromm (1900–80) German-born US psychoanalyst and philosopher. *The Anatomy of Human Destructiveness* (1973)

6   All the pretenses to which a neurotic resorts in order to bridge the gap between his real self and his idealized image serve in the end only to widen it.
    Karen Horney (1885–1952) German-born US psychoanalyst. *Our Inner Conflicts* (1945)

7   Every person, to the extent that he is neurotic, is like an airplane directed by remote control.
    Karen Horney (1885–1952) German-born US psychoanalyst. *Our Inner Conflicts* (1945)

8   The neurotic striving for power . . . is born out of anxiety, hatred, and feelings of inferiority.
    Karen Horney (1885–1952) German-born US psychoanalyst. *The Neurotic Personality of Our Time* (1936)

9   Neurosis is always a substitute for legitimate suffering.
    Carl Gustav Jung (1875–1961) Swiss psychoanalyst. Attrib.

10 The impulse to control other people is . . . an essential element in obsessional neurosis. The need to control others can to some extent be explained by a deflected drive to control parts of the self.
    Melanie Klein (1882–1960) Austrian psychoanalyst. 'Notes on Some Schizoid Mechanisms' (1946), quoted in *The Selected Melanie Klein* (Juliet Mitchell, ed.; 1986)

11 This is, I think, very much the Age of Anxiety, the age of the neurosis, because along with so much that weighs on our minds there is perhaps even more that grates on our nerves.
Louis Kronenberger (1904–80) US writer and critic. 'The Spirit of the Age', *Company Manners* (1954)

12 Modern neurosis began with the discoveries of Copernicus. Science made man feel small by showing him that the earth was not the center of the universe.
Mary McCarthy (1912–89) US writer. 'Tyranny of the Orgasm', *On the Contrary* (1961)

13 Neurotic means he is not as sensible as I am, and psychotic means he's even worse than my brother-in-law.
Karl Menninger (1893–1990) US psychiatrist. Attrib.

14 The neurotic is the flounder that lies on the bed of the river, securely settled in the mud, waiting to be speared. For him death is the only certainty, and the dread of that grim certainty immobilizes him.
Henry Miller (1891–1980) US novelist. *Sexus* (1949)

15 Freud is all nonsense; the secret of neurosis is to be found in the family battle of wills to see who can refuse longest to help with the dishes.
Julian Mitchell (b. 1935) British writer and playwright. *As Far as You Can Go* (1963), pt. 1, ch. 1

16 Everything great in the world is done by neurotics; they alone founded our religions and created our masterpieces.
Marcel Proust (1871–1922) French novelist. 1921. Le Côté de Guermantes, *À la Recherche du Temps Perdu* (1913–27)

17 Neurosis has an absolute genius for malingering. There is no illness which it cannot counterfeit perfectly . . . If it is capable of deceiving the doctor, how should it fail to deceive the patient?
Marcel Proust (1871–1922) French novelist. 1921. Le Côté de Guermantes, *À la Recherche du Temps Perdu* (1913–27)

18 Neurosis is the way of avoiding non-being by avoiding being.
Paul Tillich (1886–1965) German-born US theologian and philosopher. *The Courage to Be* (1952), pt. 2, ch. 3

Newspapers

see also **Journalism, Media, Publishing**

1 Have you noticed that life, real honest to goodness life, with murders and catastrophes and fabulous inheritances, happens almost exclusively in newspapers?
Jean Anouilh (1910–87) French playwright. *The Rehearsal* (1950)

2 What the proprietorship of these papers is aiming at is power, and power without responsibility— the prerogative of the harlot through the ages.
Stanley Baldwin (1867–1947) British prime minister. Speech at election rally, March 18, 1931, attacking the press barons Lords Rothermere and Beaverbrook. (March 18, 1931)

3 The newspaper . . . denies itself any other form of organisation than that imposed on it by the reader's impatience.
Walter Benjamin (1892–1940) German writer and critic. 'The Author as Producer', *Reflections* (Peter Demetz, ed.; 1986)

4 If I rescued a child from drowning, the Press would no doubt headline the story 'Benn grabs child'.
Tony Benn (b. 1925) British politician and author. *Observer* (March 2, 1975), 'Sayings of the Week'

5 Deleted by French censor.
James Gordon Bennett, Jr. (1841–1918) US newspaper owner and editor. Used to fill empty spaces in his papers during World War I when news was lacking. *Americans in Paris* (Brian Morton; 1984)

6 I read the newspapers avidly. It is my one form of continuous fiction.
Aneurin Bevan (1897–1960) Welsh-born British politician. *Times* (March 29, 1960)

7 Reading someone else's newspaper is like sleeping with someone else's wife. Nothing seems to be precisely in the right place, and when you find what you are looking for, it is not clear then how to respond to it.
Malcolm Bradbury (1932–2000) British academic, novelist, and critic. *Stepping Westward* (1965), bk. 1, ch. 1

8 I believe it has been said that one copy of *The Times* contains more useful information than the whole of the historical works of Thucydides.
Richard Cobden (1804–65) British economist and politician. Speech, Manchester (December 27, 1850)

9 If the Press, a 'FREE PRESS', be a foe to the tyrant—if its blessings be so great and innumerable, the Question naturally presents itself, why may we not have one of our own?
Samuel Eli Cornish (1795?–1858) US clergyman and newspaper editor. *A Documentary History of the Negro People in the United States* (Herbert Aptheker; 1951), vol. 1

10 A newspaper is a collection of half-injustices
 . . . A newspaper is a court,
Where every one is unkindly and unfairly tried
By a Squalor of honest men.
Stephen Crane (1871–1900) US writer and journalist. 'A Newspaper is a Collection of Half-Injustices', *War Is Kind* (1899), quoted in *The Penguin Book of American Verse* (Geoffrey Moore, ed.; 1977)

11 All the wickedness of the world is print to him.
Charles Dickens (1812–70) British novelist. Said by Mrs. Gamp. *Martin Chuzzlewit* (1844), ch. 26

12 A good newspaper is never nearly good enough but a lousy newspaper is a joy forever.
Garrison Keillor (b. 1942) US writer and broadcaster. 'That Old Picayune-Moon', *Harper's* (September 1990)

13 It is the mission of the press to disseminate intellect and at the same time destroy the receptivity of it.
Karl Kraus (1874–1936) Austrian writer. 1909. Quoted in 'Sprüche und Widersprüche', *Karl Kraus* (Harry Zohn; 1971)

14 Newspapers always excite curiosity. No one ever lays one down without a feeling of disappointment.
Charles Lamb (1775–1834) British essayist. 'Detached Thoughts on Books and Reading', *Last Essays of Elia* (1833)

15 The gallery in which the reporters sit has become a fourth estate of the realm.
Thomas Babington Macaulay (1800–59) British politician, historian, and writer. 1824. Referring to the press gallery in Parliament. 'On Hallam's *Constitutional History*', *Essays Contributed to the Edinburgh Review* (1843)

16 A good newspaper, I suppose, is a nation talking to itself.

Arthur Miller (b. 1915) US playwright. *Observer* (November 26, 1961), 'Sayings of the Week'

17 SIXTY HORSES WEDGED IN A CHIMNEY
The story to fit this sensational headline has not turned up yet.

J. C. Morton (1893–1979) British journalist and writer. 1936. 'Mr Justice Cocklecarrot: Home Life', *The Best of Beachcomber* (1963)

18 If the newspapers of a country are filled with good news, the jails will be filled with good people.

Daniel Patrick Moynihan (b. 1927) US academic and politician. Attrib.

19 Never believe in mirrors or newspapers.

John Osborne (1929–94) British playwright and screenwriter. *The Hotel in Amsterdam* (1968)

20 Homer is new this morning, and perhaps nothing is as old as today's newspaper.

Charles Pierre Péguy (1873–1914) French writer and poet. 'Note sur M. Bergson et la Philosophie Bergsonienne', *Cahiers de la Quinzaine* (April 8–26, 1914)

21 The newspapers! Sir, they are the most villainous—licentious—abominable—infernal— Not that I ever read them—No—I make it a rule never to look into a newspaper.

Richard Brinsley Sheridan (1751–1816) Irish-born British playwright and politician. *The Critic* (1779), Act 1, Scene 1

22 If Moses had been paid newspaper rates for the Ten Commandments, he might have written the Ten Thousand Commandments.

Isaac Bashevis Singer (1904–91) Polish-born US writer. *New York Times* (June 30, 1985)

23 News is what a chap who doesn't care much about anything wants to read. And it's only news until he's read it. After that it's dead.

Evelyn Waugh (1903–66) British novelist. *Scoop* (1938), bk. 1, ch. 5

24 The great public bath, vat, spa, regional physiotherapy tank, White Sulphur Springs, Marienbad, Ganges, River Jordan for a million souls . . . the Sunday *New York Times*.

Tom Wolfe (b. 1930) US journalist and novelist. *The Painted World* (1975)

New York City

see American Cities

Night

see also Darkness, Evening

1 Parting day
Dies like the dolphin, whom each pang imbues
With a new colour as it gasps away,
The last still loveliest, till—'t is gone, and all is gray.

Lord Byron (1788–1824) British poet. *Childe Harold's Pilgrimage* (1812–18), can. 4, st. 29

2 During the day beings live, at night things live.

Alphonse Daudet (1840–97) French writer. 'Les Étoiles', *Lettres de Mon Moulin* (1869)

3 All the things that are in me and outside of me became evident with the coming of the dark.
It is a probing surge against the world
in the shape of hand, foot, and thought.

Fazil Hüsnü Dag larca (b. 1914) Turkish poet. 'Three Poems from the Legend of Chakir', *Modern Turkish Poetry* (Feyyaz Kayacan Fergar, ed.; 1992), no. 1

4 The heaventree of stars hung with humid nightblue fruit.

James Joyce (1882–1941) Irish writer. *Ulysses* (1922)

5 The night roared like a lion with a poisoned spear stuck in its throat.

Stephen King (b. 1947) US novelist. *Needful Things* (1991)

6 Night hath a thousand eyes.

John Lyly (1554?–1606) English writer. *Maides Metamorphose* (1600), Act 3, Scene 1

7 In the country the darkness of night is friendly and familiar, but in a city, with its blaze of lights, it is unnatural, hostile and menacing. It is like a monstrous vulture that hovers, biding its time.

Somerset Maugham (1874–1965) British writer. *A Writer's Notebook* (1949)

8 Midnight brought on the dusky hour
Friendliest to sleep and silence.

John Milton (1608–74) English writer. *Paradise Lost* (1667), bk. 5, ll. 667–668

9 In the night reason disappears, only the lives of things remaining.

Antoine de Saint-Exupéry (1900–44) French writer and aviator. *Vol de Nuit* (1931)

10 BOLINGBROKE Deep night, dark night, the silent of the night,
The time of night when Troy was set on fire,
The time when screech-owls cry, and ban-dogs howl,
And spirits walk, and ghosts break up their graves;
That time best fits the work we have in hand.

William Shakespeare (1564–1616) English poet and playwright. *Henry VI, Part 2* (1592), Act 1, Scene 4

11 ROMEO Night's candles are burnt out, and jocund day
Stands tiptoe on the misty mountain tops.

William Shakespeare (1564–1616) English poet and playwright. *Romeo and Juliet* (1595), Act 3, Scene 5

12 It is spring, moonless night in the small town, starless and bible-black, the cobblestreets silent and the hunched, courters'-and-rabbits' wood limping invisible down to the sloeblack, slow, black, crowblack, fishingboat-bobbing sea.

Dylan Thomas (1914–53) Welsh poet, playwright, and short-story writer. Thomas's 'play for voices', written for the BBC and first broadcast on January 25, 1954. *Under Milk Wood* (1954)

13 The City is of Night; perchance of Death,
But certainly of Night.

James Thomson (1834–82) British poet. 'The City of Dreadful Night' (1874), can. 1

Nihilism

see also Futility, Nothingness, Pessimism

1 I proclaim that I believe in nothing and that everything is absurd, but I cannot doubt the validity of my own proclamation and I am compelled to believe, at least, in my own protest. The first and only datum . . . within absurdist experience, is rebellion.

Albert Camus (1913–60) Algerian-born French novelist, essayist, and playwright. *The Rebel* (1951)

2 One cannot be a part-time nihilist.

Albert Camus (1913–60) Algerian-born French novelist, essayist, and playwright. *The Rebel* (1951)

3 Nothing in the world matters; not even success in America but just void and emptiness await the career of a soul of a man.

Jack Kerouac (1922–69) US writer. 1951–52. *Visions of Cody* (1972)

4 What I am doing is to recount the history of the next two centuries. I am describing what is coming, what can no longer come in any other form: the rise of nihilism.

Friedrich Wilhelm Nietzsche (1844–1900) German philosopher and poet. Quoted in *Europe Since 1870* (James Joll; 1973)

5 A spectre haunts the intellectual world.
Who are you?
I am Man.

Wang Ruoshui (b. 1926) Chinese journalist. 'Humanity' (1983)

Nonsense

see also **Foolishness, Stupidity**

1 Nothing is capable of being well set to music that is not nonsense.

Joseph Addison (1672–1719) English essayist, poet, and statesman. *Spectator* (1711), no. 18

2 Twinkle, twinkle, little bat!
How I wonder what you're at!
Up above the world you fly!
Like a teatray in the sky.

Lewis Carroll (1832–98) British writer and mathematician. *Alice's Adventures in Wonderland* (1865), ch. 7

3 'Will you walk a little faster?' said a whiting to a snail,
'There's a porpoise close behind us, and he's treading on my tail'.

Lewis Carroll (1832–98) British writer and mathematician. *Alice's Adventures in Wonderland* (1865), ch. 10

4 'Tis the voice of the lobster; I heard him declare,
'You have baked me too brown, I must sugar my hair'.

Lewis Carroll (1832–98) British writer and mathematician. *Alice's Adventures in Wonderland* (1865), ch. 10

5 'Twas brillig, and the slithy toves
Did gyre and gimble in the wabe;
All mimsy were the borogoves,
And the mome raths outgrabe.
'Beware the Jabberwock, my son!
The jaws that bite, the claws that catch!'

Lewis Carroll (1832–98) British writer and mathematician. *Through the Looking-Glass and What Alice Found There* (1871), ch. 1

6 'The time has come', the Walrus said,
'To talk of many things:
Of shoes—and ships—and sealing-wax—
Of cabbages—and kings—
And why the sea is boiling hot—
And whether pigs have wings'.

Lewis Carroll (1832–98) British writer and mathematician. *Through the Looking-Glass and What Alice Found There* (1871), ch. 4

7 A little nonsense now and then is treasured by the best of men.

Phil Donahue (b. 1935) US television chat-show host. Quoted in *Speaking Freely—a Guided Tour of American English* (Stuart Berg Flexner and Anne H. Soukhanov; 1997)

8 To die for faction is a common evil,
But to be hanged for nonsense is the Devil.

John Dryden (1631–1700) English poet, playwright, and literary critic. *Absalom and Achitophel* (1681), pt. 2

9 Whenever a poet or preacher, chief or wizard spouts gibberish, the human race spends centuries deciphering the message.

Umberto Eco (b. 1932) Italian writer and literary scholar. *Foucault's Pendulum* (William Weaver, tr.; 1988)

10 If all the world were paper,
And all the sea were ink,
And all the trees were bread and cheese,
What should we do for drink?

Folk Verse. 17th century. 'If All the World were Paper'

11 And those who watch at that midnight hour
From Hall or Terrace, or lofty Tower,
Cry, as the wild light passes along,—
'The Dong!—the Dong!
The wandering Dong through the forest goes!
The Dong! the Dong!
The Dong with a luminous Nose!'

Edward Lear (1812–88) British writer and artist. 'The Dong with a Luminous Nose', *Laughable Lyrics* (1877), ll. 19–25, quoted in *The Complete Nonsense of Edward Lear* (Holbrook Jackson, ed.; 1947)

12 The Owl and the Pussy-Cat went to sea
In a beautiful pea-green boat,
They took some honey, and plenty of money,
Wrapped up in a five-pound note.

Edward Lear (1812–88) British writer and artist. 'The Owl and the Pussy-Cat', *Nonsense Songs* (1871), st. 1, quoted in *The Complete Nonsense of Edward Lear* (Holbrook Jackson, ed.; 1947)

13 One morning I shot an elephant in my pajamas. How he got into my pajamas I'll never know.

Groucho Marx (1895–1977) US comedian and film actor. From a musical written by Morrie Ryskind and George S. Kaufman. *Animal Crackers* (Morrie Ryskind; 1930)

14 SEAGOON I want you to accompany me on the safari.
BLOODNOCK Gad sir, I'm sorry, I've never played one.

Spike Milligan (1918–2002) Indian-born British humorist, writer, and actor. BBC radio series. *The Goon Show* (1951–59)

Normality

see also **Conformity, Orthodoxy**

1 Depend upon it, there is nothing so unnatural as the commonplace.

Arthur Conan Doyle (1859–1930) Scottish-born British writer and physician. 'A Case of Identity', *The Adventures of Sherlock Holmes* (1892)

2 Living is abnormal.

Eugène Ionesco (1909–94) Romanian-born French playwright. *Rhinoceros* (1959), Act 1

3 It's deadly commonplace, but, after all, the commonplaces are the great poetic truths.

Robert Louis Stevenson (1850–94) Scottish novelist, essayist, and poet. *The Weir of Hermiston* (1896), ch. 6

Northern Ireland

see also **Britain, Europe, Ireland**

1 It's like stew—you can have all the right ingredients but you have to cook it properly.

Gerry Adams (b. 1948) Northern Irish politician. Referring to all-party negotiations on the political future of Northern Ireland. Interview, *The World at One* (BBC radio; April 7, 1998)

2 The two governments of Ireland . . . affirm that any change in the status of Northern Ireland would only come about with the consent of a majority of the people of Northern Ireland.

Anonymous. The agreement on security cooperation between the Irish Republic and the United Kingdom, signed by Garrett Fitzgerald and Margaret Thatcher. *Anglo-Irish Agreement* (November 15, 1985), Article 1

3 They are part of Ireland. They have always been part of Ireland, and their people, Catholic and Protestant, are our people.

Eamon de Valera (1882–1975) US-born Irish statesman. Referring to the six counties of Northern Ireland. Letter to Winston Churchill (May 26, 1941)

4 If you were to elect the head of the Orange Order as President of this Republic, the Unionists would still find we are doing something dishonest, deceitful and totally unacceptable to them.

Charles Haughey (b. 1925) Irish prime minister. The Orange Order is a group of Northern Irish Protestants who support Northern Ireland's continuing role in the United Kingdom, and are in opposition to a united Irish Republic. At the time of saying this Charles Haughey was an opposition leader in the Irish parliament. Quoted in *Irish Times* (June 30, 1986)

5 The cynical experiment of partitioning Ireland has ended in total, tragic failure.

Charles Haughey (b. 1925) Irish prime minister. Quoted in *Irish Times* (August 12, 1971)

6 I have never and never will accept the right of a minority who happen to be a majority in a small part of the country to opt out of a nation.

Jack Lynch (b. 1917) Irish prime minister. Referring to Loyalists in Northern Ireland. *Irish Times* (November 14, 1970), 'This Week They Said'

7 We cannot go on spilling blood in the name of the past. There is no excuse, no justification and no future for the use of violence in Northern Ireland.

John Major (b. 1943) British prime minister. Referring to the Anglo-Irish peace initiative. Press conference (December 15, 1993)

8 The mainstream male politics of Northern Ireland have been not only macho in style but macho in agenda.

Monica McWilliams, Irish sociologist. *Irish Times* (October 25, 1997), 'This Week They Said'

9 In bowler hats and Sunday suits
Orange sashes, polished boots,
Atavistic trainbands come
To blow the fife and beat the drum.

Richard Murphy (b. 1927) Irish poet. Referring to the Orange Order, who support the continuation of British rule in Northern Ireland. William III (William of Orange) defeated the Irish at Aughrim in 1691. 'Orange March', *The Battle of Aughrim* (1968)

10 The Catholics have been intervening in Ulster affairs since 1641.

Ian Paisley (b. 1926) Northern Irish politician. In 1641, the Irish, led by the chieftain Rory O'More, succeeded in driving English and Scottish settlers out of Ulster. Remark (1970s)

11 Trusting in the God of our fathers and confident that our cause is just, we will never surrender our heritage.

Ian Paisley (b. 1926) Northern Irish politician. *Guardian* (August 21, 1968)

12 You have sold Ulster to buy off the fiendish republican scum. You will learn in a bitter school that all appeasement of these monsters is self-destructive.

Ian Paisley (b. 1926) Northern Irish politician. Referring to John Major's Anglo-Irish peace initiative. *Independent* (December 16, 1993)

13 I would rather be British than just.

Ian Paisley (b. 1926) Northern Irish politician. *Sunday Times* (December 12, 1971)

14 It was an old society, with a long memory . . . 1690 was considered just yesterday by people who were not sure whether they had their bus fare home tonight.

Paul Theroux (b. 1941) US writer. Referring to the Protestant community in Northern Ireland. *The Kingdom by the Sea* (1983)

Nostalgia

see also **Memory, The Past**

1 Nostalgia isn't what it used to be.

Anonymous. Grafitti.

2 Oh the after-tram-ride quiet, when we heard a mile beyond,
Silver music from the bandstand, barking dogs by Highgate Pond.

John Betjeman (1906–84) British poet and broadcaster. 'Parliament Hill Fields', *New Bats in Old Belfries* (1945), st. 4, quoted in *Collected Poems* (1971)

3 Play it, Sam. Play 'As Time Goes By'.

Humphrey Bogart (1899–1957) US actor. Often misquoted as 'Play it again, Sam'. Also said by Ingrid Bergman in the character of Ilsa Lund. *Casablanca* (Julius J. Epstein, Philip G. Epstein, Howard Koch; 1942)

4 How sad and bad and mad it was!
But then, how it was sweet!

Robert Browning (1812–89) British poet. 'Confessions', *Dramatis Personae* (1864), st. 9

5 The 'good old times'—all times when old are good—
Are gone.

Lord Byron (1788–1824) British poet. *The Age of Bronze* (1823), st. 1, ll. 1–2

6 Into my heart an air that kills
From yon far country blows:
What are those blue remembered hills,
What spires, what farms are those?

A. E. Housman (1859–1936) British poet and classicist. 'The Welsh Marches', *A Shropshire Lad* (1896), no. 40, quoted in *The Collected Poems of A. E. Housman* (John Carter, ed.; 1967)

7 The glamour
Of childish days is upon me, my manhood is cast
Down in the flood of remembrance, I weep like a child for the past.

D. H. Lawrence (1885–1930) British writer. 'Piano', *Poetry of the Present* (1918), Introduction to the US edition of *New Poems*

8 Yesterday, all my troubles seemed so far away.

Lennon & McCartney, British rock musicians. 'Yesterday', *Rubber Soul* (1965)

9 Unenlightened reader, if you do not keep the letters of your youth you will never enjoy the pleasure of seeing yourself, far off in the flatteringly dim light, with a three-cornered hat, seven-league boots, and curled mustachios, dancing at a ball to the music of Anacreontic pipes.

Joaquim Maria Machado de Assis (1839–1908) Brazilian novelist and short-story writer. *Epitaph of a Small Winner* (1880)

10 What good is roots if you can't go back to 'em?

Terry McMillan (b. 1951) US novelist and teacher. *Mama* (1987)

11 The nostalgia I have been cherishing all these
years is a hypertrophied sense of lost childhood,
not sorrow for lost banknotes.
Vladimir Nabokov (1899–1977) Russian-born US novelist, poet, and critic.
Speak, Memory (1967), ch. 3, sect. 5

12 Before the war, and especially before the Boer
War, it was summer all the year round.
George Orwell (1903–50) British writer. *Coming Up for Air* (1939),
pt. 2, ch. 1

13 They spend their time mostly looking forward to
the past.
John Osborne (1929–94) British playwright and screenwriter. *Look Back
in Anger* (1956), Act 2, Scene 1

14 Sweet Memory! wafted by thy gentle gale,
Oft up the stream of Time I turn my sail.
Samuel Rogers (1763–1855) British poet and art collector. *The
Pleasures of Memory* (1792), pt. 2

15 Gentle ladies, you will remember till old age
what we did together in our brilliant youth.
Sappho (610?–580? BC) Greek poet. Quoted in *Distinguished
Women Writers* (Virginia Moore; 1934)

16 FLAVIUS We have seen better days.
William Shakespeare (1564–1616) English poet and playwright. *Timon of
Athens* (1607?), Act 4, Scene 2

17 Dear as remember'd kisses after death,
And sweet as those by hopeless fancy feign'd
On lips that are for others: deep as love,
Deep as first love, and wild with all regret;
O Death in Life, the days that are no more.
Alfred Tennyson (1809–92) British poet. 'Tears, Idle Tears, I Know
Not What They Mean', *The Princess* (1847), pt. 4, song,
ll. 1–5

18 The Sixties were an era of extreme reality. I miss
the smell of teargas. I miss the fear of getting
beaten.
Hunter S. Thompson (b. 1939) US writer and journalist. *Independent on
Sunday* (October 12, 1997)

19 But where are the snows of yesteryear?
François Villon (1431?–63?) French poet. 1461. 'Ballade des
Dames du Temps Jadis', *Le Grand Testament* (D. G.
Rossetti, tr.), l. 16

Nothingness

see also **Absence, Futility, Nihilism**

1 What happens to the hole when the cheese is
gone?
Bertolt Brecht (1898–1956) German playwright and poet. *Mother
Courage and Her Children* (1941), Scene 6

2 Those who truly have a taste for nothingness
burn their clothes before dying.
René Char (1907–88) French poet. 'Artine: La Manne de Lola
Abba', *Le Marteau sans Maître* (1934)

3 It is contrary to reason to say that there is a
vacuum or space in which there is absolutely
nothing.
René Descartes (1596–1650) French philosopher and mathematician.
Principia Philosophiae (1644), pt. 2, sect. 16

4 Nothing can be produced out of nothing.
Diogenes Läertius (*fl.* 3rd century) Greek historian and biographer.
'Diogenes of Apollonia', quoted in *Lives and Opinions of the
Eminent Philosophers* (C. D. Yonge, tr.; 1853)

5 I can connect
Nothing with nothing.
The broken fingernails of dirty hands.
My people humble people who expect
Nothing.
T. S. Eliot (1888–1965) US-born British poet and playwright. 'The Fire
Sermon', *The Waste Land* (1922)

6 A vacuum can only exist, I imagine, by the things
which enclose it.
Zelda Fitzgerald (1900–48) US writer. *Journal* (1932)

7 Cut out doors and windows in order to make a
room. Adapt the nothing therein to the purpose
in hand, and you will have the use of the room.
Laozi (570?–490? BC) Chinese philosopher. The *Daode Jing* is an
early Chinese Taoist text. While attributed to Laozi, it
probably dates from the 3rd century BC *Daode Jing*, quoted
in *Tao Te Ching* (D. C. Lau, tr.; 1963), bk. 1, pt. 11

8 Nothing, like something, happens anywhere.
Philip Larkin (1922–85) British poet. 1954. 'I Remember, I
Remember', *Philip Larkin Collected Poems* (Anthony
Thwaite, ed.; 1988), st. 8

9 Nothing can be created out of nothing.
Lucretius (99?–55? BC) Roman philosopher and poet. *De Rerum
Natura* (1st century BC), pt. 1, l. 101

10 Well, it's when people call out at you just as
you're going off to do it, 'What are you going to
do, Christopher Robin?' and you say 'Oh,
nothing', and then you go and do it.
A. A. Milne (1882–1956) British writer. In reply to Piglet's question,
'How do you do Nothing?' 'An Enchanted Place', *The House
at Pooh Corner* (1928)

Novelty

see also **Innovation, Originality**

1 There are three things which the public will
always clamour for, sooner or later: namely,
Novelty, novelty, novelty.
Thomas Hood (1799–1845) British poet and humorist. *Comic Annual*
(1836)

2 If we do not find anything pleasant, at least we
shall find something new.
Voltaire (1694–1778) French writer and philosopher. *Candide* (1759),
ch. 17

Nuclear War

see also **Nuclear Weapons, War, Weapons**

1 Now we are all sons of bitches.
Kenneth T. Bainbridge (1904–96) US physicist. July 16, 1945. After
the first atomic bomb test near Alamogordo, New Mexico, on
July 16, 1945. *The Decision to Drop the Atomic Bomb*
(Dennis D. Wainstock; 1996)

2 The way to win an atomic war is to make certain
it never starts.
Omar Bradley (1893–1981) US general. *Observer* (April 20, 1952),
'Sayings of the Week'

3 The notion that our only strategic choice is
MAD—mutually assured destruction—which
means nothing less than an unstable pact to
commit instant and total mutual suicide in the
event of war—is irrational, immoral, and
unnecessary.
Zbigniew Brzezinski (b. 1928) Polish-born US political scientist and
politician. 'Entering the Age of Defense', *Washington Post*
(October 2, 1988)

4 An optimist, in the atomic age, thinks the future is uncertain.

Russell M. Crouse (1893–1966) US writer. *State of the Union* (1946)

5 A Hard Rain's A-Gonna Fall

Bob Dylan (b. 1941) US singer and songwriter. Song title. 'A Hard Rain's A-Gonna Fall' (1963)

6 The discovery of nuclear chain reactions need not bring about the destruction of mankind . . . We only must do everything in our power to safeguard against its abuse. Only a supranational organization, equipped with a sufficiently strong executive power, can protect us.

Albert Einstein (1879–1955) German-born US physicist. Referring to the United Nations. Open letter (1953)

7 In our nuclear age, the lack of a sense of history could have mortal consequences.

Hubert H. Humphrey (1911–78) US vice president. 'What My Students Taught Me', *Today's Health* (August 1971)

8 Dig a hole, cover it with a couple of doors and then throw three feet of dirt on top . . . It's the dirt that does it . . . You know, dirt is just great stuff . . . If there are enough shovels to go round, everybody's going to make it.

Thomas K. Jones, US public official. Referring to civil defence precautions in the event of a nuclear war. Quoted in *With Enough Shovels: Reagan, Bush and Nuclear War* (Robert Scheer; 1981)

9 Today . . . every man, woman and child lives under a nuclear sword of Damocles, hanging by the slenderest of threads, capable of being cut at any moment by accident or miscalculation or madness.

John Fitzgerald Kennedy (1917–63) US president. Speech to the United Nations General Assembly, New York (September 1961)

10 The dangers of atomic war are underrated. It would be hard on little, concentrated countries like England. In the United States we have lots of space.

Robert Rutherford McCormick (1880–1955) US editor and publisher. *Chicago Tribune* (February 23, 1950)

11 As a military man who has given half a century of active service, I say in all sincerity that the nuclear arms race has no military purpose. Wars cannot be fought with nuclear weapons; their existence only adds to our perils because of the illusions which they have generated.

Lord Mountbatten (1900–79) British naval commander and statesman. Speech, Strasbourg (May 11, 1979)

12 I am become death, the destroyer of worlds.

J. Robert Oppenheimer (1904–67) US nuclear physicist. July 16, 1945. Quoting Vishnu from the Indian religious text the Bhagavad-Gita, at the first atomic test in New Mexico. Quoted in *The Decision to Drop the Bomb* (Len Giovanitti and Fred Freed; 1965)

13 My fellow Americans, I am pleased to tell you I have signed legislation which outlaws Russia for ever. We begin bombing in five minutes.

Ronald Reagan (b. 1911) US president and actor. August 11, 1984. Testing a radio microphone while on air. Reported in *New York Times* (August 13, 1984)

14 You may reasonably expect a man to walk a tightrope safely for ten minutes; it would be unreasonable to do so without accident for two hundred years.

Bertrand Russell (1872–1970) British philosopher and mathematician. On the subject of nuclear war between the United States and the Soviets. Quoted as an epigraph in *The Tightrope Men* (D. Bagley; 1973)

15 I don't say we wouldn't get our hair mussed, but I do say no more than ten to twenty million people killed.

George C. Scott (b. 1927) US actor. As General, referring to nuclear war with the USSR. *Dr. Strangelove, or How I Learned to Stop Worrying and Love the Bomb* (Stanley Kubrick, Terry Southern, and Peter George; 1963)

16 Following a nuclear attack on the United States, the US Postal Service plans to distribute Emergency Change of Address Cards.

United States Federal Emergency Management Agency. Executive Order 11490 (1969)

17 Every effort will be made to clear trans-nuclear attack checks, including those drawn on destroyed banks. You will be encouraged to buy US Savings Bonds.

United States Federal Emergency Management Agency. Referring to provision for nuclear attack. Executive Order 11490 (1969)

18 The atomic threat . . . must . . . have brought us to the brink of silence . . . to the brink of endurance, to the brink of reserve about our fear and anxiety, and our true opinions.

Christa Wolf (b. 1929) German writer. 1983. 'A Work Diary', *Cassandra. A Novel and Four Essays* (Jan van Heurck, tr.; 1984)

Nuclear Weapons

see also **Nuclear War**, **Weapons**

1 It is not some peaceful use of atomic energy with some heating applications. It is a red bomb that spouts a great white cloud like some thunder god of ancient Eurasia.

Don DeLillo (b. 1936) US novelist. *Underworld* (1998)

2 I was ten years old when 'the atomic age' . . . came forcibly to the world's notice . . . I recall being told that the device which ended World War II was 'the size of a lemon' (this was not true).

Joan Didion (b. 1934) US journalist and writer. 1991. 'Pacific Distances', *Sentimental Journeys* (1992)

3 Some recent work by E. Fermi and L. Szilard . . . leads me to expect that the element uranium may be turned into a new and important source of energy in the immediate future. Certain aspects . . . call for watchfulness and, if necessary, quick action on the part of the Administration.

Albert Einstein (1879–1955) German-born US physicist. Referring to Enrico Fermi and Leo Szilard. Albert Einstein was expressing concern about possible Nazi development of an atomic bomb. His letter helped convince President Franklin D. Roosevelt to initiate the Manhattan Project to develop atomic weapons in the United States. Letter to President Franklin D. Roosevelt (August 2, 1939)

4 If I had known that the Germans would not succeed in constructing the atom bomb, I would never have lifted a finger.

Albert Einstein (1879–1955) German-born US physicist. 1947. Quoted in *Brighter Than a Thousand Suns* (Robert Jungk; 1958)

5 We thus denounce the false and dangerous programme of the arms race, of the secret rivalry between peoples for military superiority.

John Paul II (b. 1920) Polish pope. *Observer* (December 19, 1976), 'Sayings of the Week'

6 Preparing for suicide is not a very intelligent means of defence.

Bruce Kent (b. 1929) British peace campaigner and cleric. Referring to the nuclear deterrent. *Observer* (August 10, 1986), 'Sayings of the Week'

7 The statesmen of the world who boast and
   threaten that they have Doomsday weapons are
   far more dangerous, and far more estranged from
   'reality', than many of the people on whom the
   label 'psychotic' is affixed.
   R. D. Laing (1927–89) Scottish psychiatrist. *The Divided Self* (1965),
   Preface

8 At first it was a giant column that soon took the
   shape of a supramundane mushroom.
   William L. Laurence (1888–1977) US journalist. July 16, 1945.
   Referring to the explosion of the first atomic bomb in New
   Mexico. *New York Times* (September 26, 1945)

9 The hazards of nuclear and of ultra-violet
   radiation are much in mind these days and some
   fear that they may destroy all life on Earth. Yet
   the very womb of life was flooded by the light of
   these fierce energies.
   James Lovelock (b. 1919) British scientist. *Gaia: A New Look at Life
   on Earth* (1979)

10 The atom bomb is a paper tiger which the United
   States reactionaries use to scare people.
   Mao Zedong (1893–1976) Chinese statesman. August 1946.
   Interview, *Selected Works* (1961), vol. 4

11 One cannot fashion a credible deterrent out of an
   incredible action.
   Robert McNamara (b. 1916) US politician and business executive.
   Referring to nuclear weapons. *The Essence of Security:
   Reflections in Office* (1968)

12 We knew the world would not be the same. A
   few people laughed, a few people cried. Most
   people were silent.
   J. Robert Oppenheimer (1904–67) US nuclear physicist. Referring to the
   first atomic bomb test at Alamagordo, New Mexico. Quoted
   in *The Decision to Drop the Bomb* (Len Giovanitti and Fred
   Freed; 1965)

13 The atomic bomb . . . made the prospect of
   future war unendurable. It has led us up those
   last few steps to the mountain pass; and beyond
   there is a different country.
   J. Robert Oppenheimer (1904–67) US nuclear physicist. Quoted in *The
   Making of the Atomic Bomb* (Richard Rhodes; 1987)

14 Building up arms is not a substitute for diplomacy.
   Samuel Pisar (b. 1929) Polish-born US writer and lawyer. *Of Blood and
   Hope* (1980)

15 The lie that we have all come to live—the
   pretence that life lived on top of a nuclear
   stockpile can last.
   Jonathan Schell (b. 1943) US author. *The Fate of the Earth* (1982)

16 If our economy were to produce a wonderful
   abundance of silverware, glasses, and table
   napkins but no food, people would quickly rebel
   and insist on a different system.
   Jonathan Schell (b. 1943) US author. Alluding to the nuclear arms
   industry. *The Fate of the Earth* (1982)

17 Vertical disarmament makes a catastrophe,
   should it ever occur, smaller. Horizontal
   disarmament makes a catastrophe of any size less
   likely to occur. The verticalist looks at the size of
   the arsenals. The horizontalist looks at its
   operation.
   Jonathan Schell (b. 1943) US author. Referring to alternative types
   of nuclear disarmament. *The Gift of Time* (1998), ch. 3

18 Man has wrested from nature the power to make
   the world a desert or to make the deserts bloom.
   There is no evil in the atom, only in men's souls.
   Adlai Stevenson (1900–65) US statesman. Speech, Hartford,
   Connecticut (September 18, 1952), quoted in 'The Atomic
   Future', *Speeches* (1952)

19 For Hon. Members opposite the deterrent is a
   phallic symbol. It convinces them that they are
   men.
   George Wigg (1900–76) British politician. *Observer* (March 8,
   1964), 'Sayings of the Week'

20 A bigger bang for a buck.
   Charles E. Wilson (1890–1961) US politician and businessman. 1954.
   Referring to testing the hydrogen bomb at Bikini (1954).
   Quoted in *Safire's Political Dictionary* (William Safire; 1978)

Nurturing

see Childhood, Children, Parents

O

Obedience

see also **Loyalty**

1　Obedience is the mother of success and the wife of safety.
Aeschylus (525?–456 BC) Greek tragedian and dramatist. *The Libation Bearers* (458 BC)

2　Acts of disobedience are the postal service of disbelief.
Muhyid-Din Abu Zakariyya ibn Sharaf al-Nawawi (1233–77) Syrian Islamic scholar. 13th century. *The Complete Forty Hadith* (Abdassamad Clarke, tr.; 1988), 6th Hadith

3　I have within me an impossibility of obeying.
René Chateaubriand (1768–1848) French writer and statesman. *Mémoires d'Outre-tombe* (1849–50), bk. 2, ch. 8

4　What we call morals is simply blind obedience to words of command.
Havelock Ellis (1859–1939) British psychologist. *The Dance of Life* (1923)

5　Authority compels people to obedience, but reason persuades them to it.
Cardinal Richelieu (1585–1642) French churchman and statesman. *Testament Politique* (1688), ch. 2

6　POSTHUMUS Every good servant does not all commands.
William Shakespeare (1564–1616) English poet and playwright. *Cymbeline* (1609–10), Act 5, Scene 1

Obituaries

see also **Death and Dying**, **Funerals**, **Memorials**

1　There's no such thing as bad publicity except your own obituary.
Brendan Behan (1923–64) Irish playwright and author. Quoted in *My Brother Brendan* (Dominic Behan; 1965)

2　I've just read that I am dead. Don't forget to delete me from your list of subscribers.
Rudyard Kipling (1865–1936) Indian-born British writer and poet. Writing to a magazine that had mistakenly published an announcement of his death. Attrib.

3　John Le Mesurier wishes it to be known that he conked out on November 15th. He sadly misses family and friends.
John Le Mesurier (1912–83) British actor. His death announcement. *Times* (November 15, 1983)

4　You should have known that it was not easy for me to die. But, tell me, were my obituaries good?
Makarios III (1913–77) Greek Cypriot president. After mistaken reports of his death. Attrib.

5　The report of my death was an exaggeration.
Mark Twain (1835–1910) US writer and humorist. Usually quoted as 'Reports of my death have been greatly exaggerated'. Note to the London office of the *New York Journal* on learning that his obituary had been published there. *New York Journal* (June 2, 1897)

Obsessions

see also **Addiction**, **Fanaticism**

1　Obsession of all the beds in all the pigeonhole bedrooms . . . Obsession of feet creaking on the stairs of lodginghouses, hands fumbling at doorknobs. Obsession of pounding temples and solitary bodies rigid on their beds.
John Dos Passos (1896–1970) US novelist. *Manhattan Transfer* (1925), pt. 2

2　I can't sleep. There is a woman stuck between my eyelids. I would tell her to get out if I could. But there is a woman stuck in my throat.
Eduardo Galeano (b. 1940) Uruguayan writer. *The Book of Embraces* (1989)

3　*Papyromania*—compulsive accumulation of papers . . .
Papyrophobia—abnormal desire for 'a clean desk'.
Laurence J. Peter (1919–90) Canadian writer. *The Peter Principle* (1969), Glossary

4　Fetiches may be fragments of bone or shell, the tips of the tails of animals, the claws of birds or beasts, perhaps dried hearts of little warblers, shards of beetles, leaves powdered and held in bags, or crystals from the rocks—anything curious may become a fetich.
John Wesley Powell (1834–1902) US ethnologist, geologist, and explorer. 'Sketch of the Mythology of the North American Indians', *First Annual Report of the Bureau of Ethnology* (1881)

5　MR PRITCHARD I must dust the blinds and then I must raise them.
MRS OGMORE-PRITCHARD And before you let the sun in, mind it wipes its shoes.
Dylan Thomas (1914–53) Welsh poet, playwright, and short-story writer. Thomas's 'play for voices', written for the BBC and first broadcast on January 25, 1954. *Under Milk Wood* (1954)

6　I was seized by the stern hand of Compulsion, that dark, unseasonable Urge that impels women to clean house in the middle of the night.
James Thurber (1894–1961) US writer, cartoonist, and humorist. 'There's a Time for Flags', *Alarms and Diversions* (1957)

Occupations

see also **Academics**, **Acting and Actors**, **Artists**, **Doctors**, **Scientists**, **Teachers**, **Writers**

1　The price one pays for pursuing any profession or calling is an intimate knowledge of its ugly side.
James Baldwin (1924–87) US writer and civil rights activist. *Nobody Knows My Name* (1961)

2　Soldiers in peace are like chimneys in summer.
William Cecil (1520–98) English statesman. Attrib.

3 One of the unpardonable sins, in the eyes of most people, is for a man to go about unlabelled. The world regards such a person as the police do an unmuzzled dog, not under proper control.

T. H. Huxley (1825–95) British biologist. *Evolution and Ethics* (1893)

4 It is brought home to you . . . that it is only because miners sweat their guts out that superior persons can remain superior.

George Orwell (1903–50) British writer. *The Road to Wigan Pier* (1937), ch. 2

5 A doctor who doesn't say too many foolish things is a patient half-cured, just as a critic is a poet who has stopped writing verse and a policeman a burglar who has retired from practice.

Marcel Proust (1871–1922) French novelist. 1921. Le Côté de Guermantes, *À la Recherche du Temps Perdu* (1913–27)

6 Doctors bury their mistakes. Lawyers hang them. But journalists put theirs on the front page.

Proverb.

7 A lawyer without history or literature is a mechanic, a mere working mason; if he possesses some knowledge of these, he may venture to call himself an architect.

Sir Walter Scott (1771–1832) Scottish novelist. *Guy Mannering* (1815), ch. 37

8 A good farmer is nothing more nor less than a handy man with a sense of humus.

E. B. White (1899–1985) US writer and humorist. 'The Practical Farmer', *One Man's Meat* (1942)

Old Age

see also Age, Longevity

1 The principal objection to old age is that there's no future in it.

Anonymous

2 Old men are children for a second time.

Aristophanes (448? BC–385? BC) Greek playwright. *The Clouds* (423 BC)

3 When men desire old age, what else do they desire but prolonged infirmity?

Saint Augustine of Hippo (354–430) Numidian Christian theologian and Doctor of the Church. 'Of the Catechizing of the Unlearned' (400?)

4 You grew old first not in your own eyes, but in other people's eyes; then, slowly, you agreed with their opinion of you.

Julian Barnes (b. 1946) British writer. *Staring at the Sun* (1988)

5 I will never be an old man. To me, old age is always fifteen years older than I am.

Bernard Mannes Baruch (1870–1965) US financier, statesman, and philanthropist. *Observer* (August 21, 1955), 'Sayings of the Week'

6 Age is deformed, youth unkind,
We scorn their bodies, they our mind.

Thomas Bastard (1566–1618) English poet and cleric. *Chrestoleros* (1598), bk. 7, epigram 9

7 Old age comes on apace to ravage all the clime.

James Beattie (1735–1803) Scottish poet and philosopher. *The Minstrel* (1771), bk. 1, st. 25

8 To be old is to be part of a huge and ordinary multitude . . . the reason why old age was venerated in the past was because it was extraordinary.

Ronald Blythe (b. 1922) British writer. *The View in Winter* (1979)

9 Old age takes away from us what we have inherited and gives us what we have earned.

Gerald Brenan (1894–1987) Maltese-born British writer and novelist. 'Life', *Thoughts in a Dry Season* (1978)

10 I was brought up to respect my elders and now I don't have to respect *anybody*.

George Burns (1896–1996) US comedian and actor. Remark at the age of 87 (1983)

11 Years steal
Fire from the mind as vigour from the limb,
And life's enchanted cup but sparkles near the brim.

Lord Byron (1788–1824) British poet. *Childe Harold's Pilgrimage* (1812–18), can. 3, st. 8

12 It is the misfortune of an old man that though he can put things out of his head he can't put them out of his feelings.

Joyce Cary (1888–1957) Irish-born British novelist. *To be a Pilgrim* (1942), ch. 8

13 He watched him grow old. It was nothing: a stiffness of the back, a misshapen silhouette, the constant shaking of an ear.

Patrick Chamoiseau (b. 1953) Martiniquan writer. *Childhood* (1993)

14 An archaeologist is the best husband any woman can have: the older she gets, the more interested he is in her.

Agatha Christie (1890–1976) English novelist and playwright. March 8, 1954. Attrib.

15 Old age is a shipwreck.

Charles de Gaulle (1890–1970) French president. *The Life of Arthur Ransome* (Hugh Brogan; 1984)

16 When a man fell into his anecdotage it was a sign for him to retire from the world.

Benjamin Disraeli (1804–81) British prime minister and writer. *Lothair* (1870), ch. 28

17 I grow old . . . I grow old . . .
I shall wear the bottoms of my trousers rolled.

T. S. Eliot (1888–1965) US-born British poet and playwright. 'The Love Song of J. Alfred Prufrock', *Prufrock and Other Observations* (1917)

18 According to the doctors, I'm only suffering from a light form of premature baldness.

Federico Fellini (1920–93) Italian film director. After spending four days in a clinic in Rome. *Variety* (1986)

19 A man knows when he is growing old because he begins to look like his father.

Gabriel García Márquez (b. 1928) Colombian novelist. *Love in the Time of Cholera* (1985)

20 The secret of good old age is simply an honorable pact with solitude.

Gabriel García Márquez (b. 1928) Colombian novelist. Said by Aureliano Buendía. *One Hundred Years of Solitude* (1967)

21 You will recognize, my boy, the first sign of old age: it is when you go out into the streets of London and realize for the first time how young the policemen look.

Seymour Hicks (1871–1949) British actor-manager. Quoted in *They Were Singing* (C. Pulling; 1952), ch. 7

22 Oh, to be seventy again!

Oliver Wendell Holmes, Jr. (1841–1935) US judge. 1928. Said in his 87th year, while watching a pretty girl. Quoted in *The American Treasury* (Clifton Fadiman; 1955)

23 A medical revolution has extended the life of our elder citizens without providing the dignity and security those later years deserve.

John Fitzgerald Kennedy (1917–63) US president. Speech at the Democratic National Convention, Los Angeles (July 15, 1960)

24 Perhaps being old is having lighted rooms
Inside your head, and people in them, acting.
People you know, yet can't quite name.
Philip Larkin (1922–85) British poet. 'The Old Fools' (1973), st. 3,
ll. 1–3, quoted in *Philip Larkin Collected Poems* (Anthony
Thwaite, ed.; 1988)

25 Will you still need me, will you still feed me
When I'm sixty-four?
Lennon & McCartney, British rock musicians. 'When I'm Sixty-Four',
Sergeant Pepper's Lonely Hearts Club Band (1967)

26 What makes old age hard to bear is not the
failing of one's faculties, mental and physical, but
the burden of one's memories.
Somerset Maugham (1874–1965) British writer. *Points of View*
(1958), ch. 1

27 Growing old is no more than a bad habit which
a busy man has no time to form.
André Maurois (1885–1967) French writer. 'The Art of Growing Old',
The Art of Living (1940)

28 Like dolmens round my childhood, the old
people.
John Montague (b. 1929) US-born Irish poet. 1972. 'Like Dolmens
Round My Childhood', *Collected Poems* (1995), l. 1

29 Old age puts more wrinkles in our minds than
on our faces.
Michel de Montaigne (1533–92) French essayist. 'Of Repentance',
Essays (1580–88), bk. 3, ch. 2

30 Old age is an island surrounded by death.
Juan Montalvo (1832–89) Ecuadorian writer. Attrib.

31 Body and mind, like man and wife, do not
always agree to die together.
Peter Ouspensky (1878–1947) Russian philosopher. *Lacon* (1920?), vol. 1

32 An old doting fool, with one foot already in the
grave.
Plutarch (46?–120?) Greek biographer and philosopher. 'Of the Training
of Children' (1st–2nd century)

33 A green old age, unconscious of decays,
That proves the hero born in better days.
Alexander Pope (1688–1744) English poet. *The Iliad of Homer*
(1715–20), bk. 23, ll. 929–930

34 Just like those who are incurably ill, the aged know
everything about their dying except exactly when.
Philip Roth (b. 1933) US novelist. 'Opening letter to Zuckerman',
The Facts (1988)

35 If you want to be a dear old lady at seventy, you
should start early, say about seventeen.
Maud Royden (1876–1956) British woman suffrage campaigner and writer.
Attrib.

36 Old age is a disease which we cannot cure.
Seneca, 'the Younger' (4? BC–AD 65) Roman writer, philosopher, and
statesman. *Epistulae Morales* (63?), no. 108

37 You're Only Old Once!
Dr. Seuss (1904–91) US writer and illustrator. 1986. Book title.

38 In a dream you are never eighty.
Anne Sexton (1928–74) US poet. 'Old', *All My Pretty Ones* (1962)

39 When forty winters shall besiege thy brow,
And dig deep trenches in thy beauty's field.
William Shakespeare (1564–1616) English poet and playwright. Sonnet 2
(1609)

40 JAQUES Last scene of all,
That ends this strange eventful history,
Is second childishness and mere oblivion;
Sans teeth, sans eyes, sans taste, sans everything.
William Shakespeare (1564–1616) English poet and playwright. *As You
Like It* (1599), Act 2, Scene 7

41 LEAR I am a very foolish, fond old man,
Fourscore and upward, not an hour more or less;
And, to deal plainly,
I fear I am not in my perfect mind.
William Shakespeare (1564–1616) English poet and playwright. *King
Lear* (1605–06), Act 4, Scene 7

42 Old men are dangerous; it doesn't matter to them
what is going to happen to the world.
George Bernard Shaw (1856–1950) Irish playwright. *Heartbreak House*
(1919)

43 The denunciation of the young is a necessary part
of the hygiene of older people, and greatly assists
the circulation of their blood.
Logan Pearsall Smith (1865–1946) US-born British writer. 'Age and
Death', *Afterthoughts* (1931)

44 Being over seventy is like being engaged in a war.
All our friends are going or gone and we survive
amongst the dead and the dying as on a
battlefield.
Muriel Spark (b. 1918) British novelist. *Memento Mori* (1959), ch. 4

45 Old men and comets have been reverenced for
the same reason; their long beards, and pretences
to foretell events.
Jonathan Swift (1667–1745) Irish writer and clergyman. *Thoughts on
Various Subjects* (1727 edition)

46 Hope I die before I get old.
Pete Townshend (b. 1945) British rock musician. Song lyric. 'My
Generation' (1965)

47 Old age is the most unexpected of all the things
that happen to a man.
Leon Trotsky (1879–1940) Russian revolutionary leader. *Diary in Exile*
(May 8, 1935)

48 Now that I am sixty, I see why the idea of elder
wisdom has passed from currency.
John Updike (b. 1932) US writer. *New Yorker* (1992)

49 Man can have only a certain number of teeth,
hair, and ideas; there comes a time when he
necessarily loses his teeth, hair, and ideas.
Voltaire (1694–1778) French writer and philosopher. 'Fate',
Dictionnaire Philosophique (1764)

50 It is a terrible thing for an old woman to outlive
her dogs.
Tennessee Williams (1911–83) US playwright. *Camino Real* (1953),
Prologue

51 He was either a man of about a hundred and
fifty who was rather young for his years or a
man of about a hundred and ten who had been
aged by trouble.
P. G. Wodehouse (1881–1975) British-born US humorous writer. Quoted
in *Wodehouse at Work to the End* (Richard Usborne; 1961),
ch. 6

Opera

see also Music, Singers and Singing

1 I do not mind what language an opera is sung in
so long as it is a language I don't understand.
Edward Victor Appleton (1892–1965) British physicist. Attrib. *Observer*
(August 28, 1955), 'Sayings of the Week'

2 No good opera plot can be sensible, for people
do not sing when they are feeling sensible.
W. H. Auden (1907–73) British poet. *Time* (December 29, 1961)

3 Today, if something is not worth saying, people
sing it.
Pierre-Augustin Caron de Beaumarchais (1732–99) French playwright. *The
Barber of Seville* (1775), Act 1, Scene 2

4 The opera ain't over till the fat lady sings.
Daniel John Cook (b. 1926) US journalist. *Washington Post* (June 13, 1978)

5 People are wrong when they say the opera isn't what it used to be. It is what it used to be. That's what's wrong with it.
Noël Coward (1899–1973) British playwright, actor, and songwriter. *Design for Living* (1933)

6 Opera is when a guy gets stabbed in the back and instead of bleeding he sings.
Ed Gardner (1904–63) US radio comedian. *Duffy's Tavern* (US radio show; 1940)

7 Opera in English is, in the main, just about as sensible as baseball in Italian.
H. L. Mencken (1880–1956) US journalist, critic, and editor. 1950? Quoted in *The Frank Muir Book: An Irreverent Companion to Social History* (Frank Muir; 1976)

8 Going to the opera, like getting drunk, is a sin that carries its own punishment with it.
Hannah More (1745–1833) British writer and philanthropist. Letter to her sister (1775), quoted in *The Letters of Hannah More* (R. Brimley Johnson, ed.; 1925)

9 I sometimes wonder which would be nicer—an opera without an interval, or an interval without an opera.
Ernest Newman (1868–1959) English music critic. Quoted in *Berlioz, Romantic and Classic* (Peter Heyworth, ed.; 1972)

10 What bothered Stalin in *Boris*? That the blood of the innocent will sooner or later rise from the soil. That's the ethical centre of the opera.
Dmitri Shostakovich (1906–75) Russian composer. 1971–75. Referring to Modest Mussorgsky's opera *Boris Godunov* (1874). *Testimony: The Memoirs of Shostakovich* (Solomon Volkov, ed., Antonina W. Bouis, tr.; 1979), ch. 7

11 An unalterable and unquestioned law of the musical world required that the German text of French operas sung by Swedish artists should be translated into Italian for the clearer understanding of English-speaking audiences.
Edith Wharton (1862–1937) US novelist. *The Age of Innocence* (1920), bk. 1, ch. 1

Opinions

see also **Conversation, Gossip, Ideas**

1 We must say that the same opinions have arisen among men in cycles, not once, twice, nor a few times, but infinitely often.
Aristotle (384–322 BC) Greek philosopher. *Meteorologica* (335–322? BC)

2 Because half a dozen grasshoppers under a fern make the field ring with their importunate chink, whilst thousands of great cattle, reposed beneath the shadow of the British oak, chew the cud and are silent, pray do not imagine that those who make noise are the only inhabitants of the field; that, of course, they are many in number; or that, after all, they are other than the little shrivelled, meagre, hopping, though loud and troublesome insects of the hour.
Edmund Burke (1729–97) Irish-born British statesman and political philosopher. *Reflections on the Revolution in France* (1790), vol. 3

3 I have opinions of my own—strong opinions— but I don't always agree with them.
George Bush (b. 1924) US president. Attrib.

4 The wish to spread those opinions that we hold conducive to our own welfare is so deeply rooted in the English character that few of us can escape its influence.
Samuel Butler (1835–1902) British writer and composer. *Erewhon* (1872), ch. 20

5 The public buys its opinions as it buys its meat, or takes in its milk, on the principle that it is cheaper to do this than to keep a cow. So it is, but the milk is more likely to be watered.
Samuel Butler (1835–1902) British writer and composer. Quoted in *Note Books* (H. Festing Jones, ed.; 1912)

6 A man's opinion on tramcars matters; his opinion on Botticelli matters; his opinion on all things does not matter.
G. K. Chesterton (1874–1936) British writer and poet. *Heretics* (1905)

7 I do not want to use the word 'true'. There are only opinions, some of which are preferable to others. One cannot say: 'Ah, if it is just a matter of preference to hell with it'. . . . One can die for an opinion which is only preferable.
Umberto Eco (b. 1932) Italian writer and literary scholar. *Index on Censorship* (May/June 1994), vol. 23

8 Any stigma will do to beat a dogma.
Philip Guedalla (1889–1944) British writer. 'Ministers of State', *Masters and Men* (1923)

9 I have always found that the only kind of statement worth making is an overstatement. A half-truth, like half a brick, is always more forcible as an argument than a whole one. It carries further.
Stephen Leacock (1869–1944) British-born Canadian writer and economist. 'The Perfect Salesman', *The Garden of Folly* (1924)

10 Nothing is more conducive to peace of mind than not having an opinion.
Georg Christoph Lichtenberg (1742–99) German physicist and writer. *Aphorisms* (1764–99)

11 New opinions are always suspected, and usually opposed, without any other reason but because they are not already common.
John Locke (1632–1704) English philosopher. *An Essay Concerning Human Understanding* (1690), dedicatory epistle

12 Men are never so good or so bad as their opinions.
James Mackintosh (1765–1832) Scottish lawyer, philosopher, and historian. 'Jeremy Bentham', *Ethical Philosophy* (1830)

13 A point of view can be a dangerous luxury when substituted for insight and understanding.
Marshall McLuhan (1911–80) Canadian sociologist. *The Gutenberg Galaxy* (1962)

14 If all mankind minus one were of one opinion, and only one person were of the contrary opinion, mankind would be no more justified in silencing that one person, than he, if he had the power, would be justified in silencing mankind.
John Stuart Mill (1806–73) British philosopher and social reformer. *On Liberty* (1859), ch. 2

15 Ask no one's view but your own.
Persius (34–62) Roman satirist. 1st century. *Satires* (Niall Rudd, tr.; 1973), no.1, l. 7

16 The fact that an opinion has been widely held is no evidence whatever that it is not utterly absurd.
Bertrand Russell (1872–1970) British philosopher and mathematician. *Marriage and Morals* (1929)

17 The average man's opinions are much less foolish than they would be if he thought for himself.
Bertrand Russell (1872–1970) British philosopher and mathematician. *The Autobiography of Bertrand Russell* (1967–69)

18 Men seldom take the opinion of their equals, or of a man like themselves, on trust.
Alexis de Tocqueville (1805–59) French writer and politician. *Democracy in America* (1835–40)

19 I agree with no man's opinion. I have some of my own.
Ivan Turgenev (1818–83) Russian novelist. *Fathers and Sons* (1862), ch. 13

20 It is just when opinions universally prevail and we have added lip service to their authority that we become sometimes most keenly conscious that we do not believe a word that we are saying.
Virginia Woolf (1882–1941) British novelist and critic. *The Common Reader* (1929–35)

Opportunity

see also **Ambition, Chance, Possibility**

1 I would rather be an opportunist and float than go to the bottom with my principles round my neck.
Stanley Baldwin (1867–1947) British prime minister. Attrib.

2 Let us make hay while the sun shines.
Miguel de Cervantes (1547–1616) Spanish novelist and playwright. *Don Quixote* (1605–15), pt. 1, bk. 3, ch. 11

3 Man is not the creature of circumstances. Circumstances are the creatures of men.
Benjamin Disraeli (1804–81) British prime minister and writer. *Vivian Grey* (1826), bk. 6, ch. 7

4 Be careful still of the main chance.
John Dryden (1631–1700) English poet, playwright, and literary critic. *Satires of A. Persius Flaccus* (1693), Satire 6

5 Thou strong seducer, opportunity!
John Dryden (1631–1700) English poet, playwright, and literary critic. *The Conquest of Granada* (1680), pt. 2, Act 4, Scene 3

6 Seize the day, and put as little trust as you can in the morrow.
Horace (65–8 BC) Roman poet. *Odes* (23? BC), bk. 1, no. 11, l. 7

7 Opportunities are usually disguised as hard work, so most people don't recognize them.
Ann Landers (b. 1918) US journalist. Attrib.

8 One can present people with opportunities. One cannot make them equal to them.
Rosamond Lehmann (1901–90) British novelist. *The Ballad and the Source* (1945)

9 You should hammer your iron when it is glowing hot.
Publilius Syrus (*fl.* 1st century BC) Roman writer. 1st century BC. *Maxims* (Darius Lyman, tr.), 262

10 BRUTUS There is a tide in the affairs of men
Which, taken at the flood, leads on to fortune;
Omitted, all the voyage of their life
Is bound in shallows and in miseries.
On such a full sea are we now afloat,
And we must take the current when it serves,
Or lose our ventures.
William Shakespeare (1564–1616) English poet and playwright. As Mark Antony gathers forces against him at Philippi. *Julius Caesar* (1599), Act 4, Scene 3

11 KING JOHN How oft the sight of means to do ill deeds
Makes ill deeds done!
William Shakespeare (1564–1616) English poet and playwright. *King John* (1591–98), Act 4, Scene 2

12 PISTOL Why, then the world's mine oyster, Which I with sword will open.
William Shakespeare (1564–1616) English poet and playwright. *The Merry Wives of Windsor* (1597), Act 2, Scene 2

13 Hoist up saile while gale doth last,
Tide and wind stay no man's pleasure.
Robert Southwell (1561–95) English poet and martyr. 'St Peter's Complaint' (1595)

14 It is better to be at the right place with 10 men than absent with 10,000.
Tamerlane (1336–1405) Turkic ruler and conqueror. Attrib.

Oppression

see also **Authoritarianism, Exploitation, Persecution, Slavery, Torture, Totalitarianism, Tyranny**

1 Those who have had no share in the good fortunes of the mighty often have a share in their misfortunes.
Bertolt Brecht (1898–1956) German playwright and poet. *The Caucasian Chalk Circle* (1948), Scene 1

2 Oppression makes the wise man mad.
Robert Browning (1812–89) British poet. *Luria* (1846), Act 4, Scene 16, ll. 57

3 People crushed by law have no hopes but from power. If laws are their enemies, they will be enemies to laws; and those, who have much to hope and nothing to lose, will always be dangerous, more or less.
Edmund Burke (1729–97) Irish-born British statesman and political philosopher. Letter to Charles James Fox (October 8, 1777)

4 Nobody knows you. Nobody remembers you. You are not a man of steel. Even if you are a man of steel, we can break you and there's no one to come to your rescue. We have limitless manpower and unlimited time.
Thye Poh Chia (b. 1941) Singaporean dissident. Referring to the threats of his internal security interrogators. *Guardian* (February 7, 1992)

5 Where a system of oppression has become institutionalized it is unnecessary for individuals to be oppressive.
Florynce R. Kennedy (1916–2000) US lawyer and activist. Quoted in 'Institutionalized Oppression vs. the Female', *Sisterhood is Powerful* (Robin Morgan, ed.; 1970)

6 Those who deny freedom to others, deserve it not for themselves.
Abraham Lincoln (1809–65) US president. Letter to H. L. Pierce and others (April 6, 1859)

7 To overthrow oppression has been sanctioned by humanity and is the highest aspiration of every free man.
Nelson Mandela (b. 1918) South African president and lawyer. 1953. *The Struggle is My Life* (1990)

8 The government burns down whole cities while the people are forbidden to light lamps.
Mao Zedong (1893–1976) Chinese statesman. On his Nationalist opponents during a period of civil war. Attrib.

9 You have not converted a man because you have silenced him.

John Morley (1838–1923) British statesman and writer. *On Compromise* (1874), ch. 5

10 I was not born to blow rams' horns and liberate lands from the 'foreign yoke'. I can hear the groaning of oppressed people; I cannot hear the groaning of oppressed lands.

Amos Oz (b. 1939) Israeli writer. 1968. 'An Alien City', *Under This Blazing Light* (1979)

11 I would like to make a special appeal to the members of the Army . . . In the name of God, in the name of your tormented people whose cries rise up . . . I beseech you, I beg you, I command YOU: STOP THE REPRESSION!

Oscar Romero (1917–80) Salvadoran archbishop. Said on the day before his murder by paramilitary death squads. Sermon, San Salvador (March 23, 1980), quoted in *The War of Gods* (Michael Löwy; 1996)

12 3RD FISHERMAN Master, I marvel how the fishes live in the sea.
1ST FISHERMAN Why, as men do a-land—the great ones eat up the little ones.

William Shakespeare (1564–1616) English poet and playwright. *Pericles* (1606–08), Act 2, Scene 1

13 Forget the outside world. Life has different laws in here. This is Campland, an invisible country. It's not in the geography books, or the psychology books or the history books. This is the famous country where ninety-nine men weep while one laughs.

Alexander Solzhenitsyn (b. 1918) Russian novelist. Referring to the world of Soviet labour camps known as the Gulag Archipelago. *The Love-Girl and the Innocent* (1969), Act 1, Scene 3

14 We must remember that every 'mental' symptom is a veiled cry of anguish. Against what? Against oppression, or what the patient experiences as oppression. The oppressed speak a million tongues.

Thomas Szasz (b. 1920) Hungarian-born US psychiatrist. Attrib.

15 We cannot have the oppressors telling the oppressed how to rid themselves of the oppressor.

Kwame Touré (b. 1941) Trinidadian-born US civil rights activist. Speech, *Times* (September 15, 1966)

Optimism

see also **Hope**, **Pessimism**

1 Keep your sunny side up.

Lew Brown (1893–1958) US songwriter. Song lyric. 'Sunny Side Up' (co-written with Buddy De Silva; 1929)

2 Don't you know each cloud contains
Pennies from Heaven?

Johnny Burke (1908–64) US songwriter. 'Pennies from Heaven' (1936)

3 Be thou the rainbow to the storms of life!
The evening beam that smiles the clouds away,
And tints to-morrow with prophetic ray!

Lord Byron (1788–1824) British poet. *The Bride of Abydos* (1813), can. 2, st. 20

4 I am not an optimist but a meliorist.

George Eliot (1819–80) British novelist. Quoted in *A. E. H.* (Laurence Housman; 1937)

5 The place where optimism most flourishes is the lunatic asylum.

Havelock Ellis (1859–1939) British psychologist. *The Dance of Life* (1923)

6 Optimism is the content of small men in high places.

F. Scott Fitzgerald (1896–1940) US writer. 1936. *The Crack-Up: with Other Uncollected Pieces, Note-Books and Unpublished Letters* (Edmund Wilson, ed.; 1945)

7 Optimism is an alienated form of faith, pessimism an alienated form of despair.

Erich Fromm (1900–80) German-born US psychoanalyst and philosopher. *The Anatomy of Human Destructiveness* (1973)

8 The corn is as high as an elephant's eye.

Oscar Hammerstein II (1895–1960) US lyricist and librettist. Song lyric. 'Oh, What a Beautiful Mornin'', *Oklahoma!* (music by Richard Rodgers; 1943)

9 'Tis always morning somewhere in the world.

Richard Henry Horne (1803–84) British writer and colonialist. *Orion* (1843), bk. 3, can. 2

10 OPTIMISM: A kind of heart stimulant—the digitalis of failure.

Elbert Hubbard (1856–1915) US writer, printer, and editor. *The Roycroft Dictionary* (1914)

11 Cheer up, the worst is yet to come.

Philander Chase Johnson (1866–1939) US journalist. 'Shooting Stars', *Everybody's Magazine* (1920)

12 The supreme wisdom, united to a goodness that is no less infinite, cannot have chosen but the best . . . So it may be said that if this were not the best of all possible worlds, God would not have created any.

Gottfried Wilhelm Leibniz (1646–1716) German philosopher and mathematician. The origin of the notion 'the best of all possible worlds' as espoused by Doctor Pangloss in Voltaire's *Candide* (1759). *Essays in Theodicy on the Goodness of God, the Liberty of Man, and the Origin of Evil* (1710), bk. 1, sect. 8

13 That virgin, vital, fine day: today.

Stéphane Mallarmé (1842–98) French poet. 'Plusieurs Sonnets', *Poésies* (1887), no. 1

14 Well I know that, wey I figure seh, maybe things get worse for the better?

Bob Marley (1945–81) Jamaican musician, singer, and songwriter. 1980. Quoted in *Bob Marley: Conquering Lion of Reggae* (Stephen Davis; 1983)

15 an optimist is a guy
that never had
much experience.

Don Marquis (1878–1937) US journalist and writer. 'certain maxims of archy', *archy and mehitabel* (1927)

16 DUKE SENIOR Sweet are the uses of adversity,
Which like the toad, ugly and venomous,
Wears yet a precious jewel in his head;
And this our life, exempt from public haunt,
Finds tongues in trees, books in the running brooks,
Sermons in stones, and good in everything.

William Shakespeare (1564–1616) English poet and playwright. *As You Like It* (1599), Act 2, Scene 1

17 MIRANDA How beauteous mankind is! O brave new world
That has such people in't!

William Shakespeare (1564–1616) English poet and playwright. *The Tempest* (1611), Act 5, Scene 1

18 The latest definition of an optimist is one who fills up his crossword puzzle in ink.

Clement King Shorter (1857–1926) British journalist and literary critic. *Observer* (February 22, 1925), 'Sayings of the Week'

19 I am an optimist, unrepentant and militant. After all, in order not to be a fool an optimist must know how sad a place the world can be. It is only the pessimist who finds this out anew every day.
Peter Ustinov (b. 1921) British actor, director, and writer. *Dear Me* (1977), ch. 9

20 You will be home before the leaves have fallen from the trees.
William II (1859–1941) German monarch. August 1914. Said to troops leaving for the Front. Quoted in *The Guns of August* (Barbara W. Tuchman; 1962), ch. 9

21 I'm an optimist, but I'm an optimist who carries a raincoat.
Harold Wilson (1916–95) British prime minister. Attrib.

Order

see also **Government, Law**

1 Good order is the foundation of all good things.
Edmund Burke (1729–97) Irish-born British statesman and political philosopher. *Reflections on the Revolution in France* (1790)

2 Things are always best seen when they are a trifle mixed-up, a trifle disordered; the chilly administrative neatness of museums and filing cases, of statistics and cemeteries, is an inhuman and antinatural kind of order; it is, in a word, disorder. True order belongs to Nature, which never yet has produced two identical trees or mountains or horses.
Camilo José Cela (1916–2002) Spanish writer. *Journey to the Alcarria* (1948)

3 He who keeps danger in mind will rest safely in his seat; he who keeps ruin in mind will preserve his interests secure; he who sets the dangers of disorder before himself will maintain a state of order.
Confucius (551–479 BC) Chinese philosopher, administrator, and moralist. An idea frequently referred to by leaders in China and Singapore. Attrib.

4 Can you call order that fictitious peace which you obtain by cutting with the sword all that you are too stupid to organize with your limited intelligence?
Francisco Pi y Margall (1824–1901) Spanish politician and author. *La Reacción y La Revolución* (1854)

5 True order supposes cohesion, yet not a cohesion obtains by the presence of exterior causes, but an intimate and spontaneous cohesion which you with all your restrictions inevitably inhabit.
Francisco Pi y Margall (1824–1901) Spanish politician and author. *La Reacción y La Revolución* (1854)

6 Order is heaven's first law.
Alexander Pope (1688–1744) English poet. *An Essay on Man* (1733), Epistle 4, l. 49

7 In the long run, order imposes itself on things.
Raymond Radiguet (1903–23) French writer. *The Devil in the Flesh* (1923)

8 ULYSSES The heavens themselves, the planets, and this centre,
Observe degree, priority, and place,
Insisture, course, proportion, season, form,
Office, and custom, in all line of order.
William Shakespeare (1564–1616) English poet and playwright. *Troilus and Cressida* (1602), Act 1, Scene 3

9 A place for everything, and everything in its place.
Samuel Smiles (1812–1904) Scottish writer. *Thrift* (1875), ch. 5

10 Oh! Blessed rage for order, pale Ramon
The maker's rage to order words of the sea.
Wallace Stevens (1879–1955) US poet. 'The Idea of Order at Key West' (1935), quoted in *The Penguin Book of American Verse* (Geoffrey Moore, ed.; 1977)

Originality

see also **Creativity, Innovation, Novelty**

1 But I'm not original. The only way I could say I was original is if I created the English language. I did, man, but they don't believe me.
Lenny Bruce (1925–66) US comedian. 1960? Quoted in *The Essential Lenny Bruce* (John Cohen, ed.; 1967)

2 An original writer is not one who imitates nobody, but one whom nobody can imitate.
René Chateaubriand (1768–1848) French writer and statesman. *Génie du Christianisme* (1802)

3 A thought is often original, though you have uttered it a hundred times. It has come to you over a new route, by a new and express train of associations.
Oliver Wendell Holmes (1841–1935) US judge. *The Autocrat of the Breakfast-Table* (1858), ch. 1

4 All good things which exist are the fruits of originality.
John Stuart Mill (1806–73) British philosopher and social reformer. *On Liberty* (1859), ch. 3

5 The glass I drink from is not large, but at least it is my own.
Alfred de Musset (1810–57) French poet and playwright. 'La Coupe et les Lèvres' (1832), quoted in *Poésies Complètes* (Maurice Allem, ed.; 1933)

6 The more intelligence one has the more people one finds original. Commonplace people see no difference between men.
Blaise Pascal (1623–62) French philosopher, mathematician, and physicist. *Pensées* (1669), sect. 1, no. 7

7 Nothing has yet been said that's not been said before.
Terence (185–159 BC) Roman playwright and poet. 161 BC. *The Eunuch* (H. T. Riley, tr.), Prologue, l. 41

8 The notion of doing something impossibly new usually turns out to be an illusion.
Twyla Tharp (b. 1941) US choreographer and dancer. *Independent* (December 8, 1995)

9 Do a common thing in an uncommon way.
Booker T. Washington (1856–1915) US educator and political activist. *Daily Resolves* (1896)

10 Everything of importance has been said before by somebody who did not discover it.
A. N. Whitehead (1861–1947) British philosopher and mathematician. Quoted in *The World of Mathematics* (J. R. Newman; 1956)

Orthodoxy

see also **Conformity, Normality**

1 The difference between Orthodoxy or My-doxy and Heterodoxy or Thy-doxy.
Thomas Carlyle (1795–1881) Scottish historian and essayist. *The French Revolution* (1837), pt. 2, bk. 4, ch. 2

2 The word 'orthodoxy' not only no longer means being right; it practically means being wrong.

G. K. Chesterton (1874–1936) British writer and poet. *Heretics* (1905), ch. 1

3 To overturn orthodoxy is no easier in science than in philosophy, religion, economics, or any other disciplines through which we try to comprehend the world and the society in which we live.

Ruth Hubbard (b. 1924) US biologist. 'Have Only Men Evolved?', *Women Look at Biology Looking at Women* (co-written with Mary Sue Henfin and Barbara Fried, eds.; 1979)

4 Political correctness is a really inane concept. It automatically gives the impression that left-wing ideas are about toeing some line, it makes people think that being left-wing means being a Stalinist . . . Plus it makes the racists look like the rebels.

Mark Thomas, British comedian. February 1993. Attrib.

5 Orthodoxy is my doxy; heterodoxy is another man's doxy.

William Warburton (1698–1779) English theologian. Letter to Lord Sandwich. Quoted in *Memoirs* (Joseph Priestley; 1807), vol. 1

Oxford

see **British Cities**

P

Pacifism

see also **Diplomacy, Peace**

1 Extreme pacifism . . . amounts only to sitting back and getting yourself slaughtered.

Yehuda Amichai (b. 1924) German-born Israeli poet. April 10, 1984. Quoted in Interview, *Voices of Israel* (Joseph Cohen, ed.; 1990)

2 My pacifism is not based on any intellectual theory but on a deep antipathy to every form of cruelty and hatred.

Albert Einstein (1879–1955) German-born US physicist. 1914. Said on the outbreak of World War I. Attrib.

3 Non-violence is the law of our species as violence is the law of the brute. The spirit lies dormant in the brute and he knows no law but that of physical might. The dignity of man requires obedience to another law—to the strength of the spirit.

Mahatma Gandhi (1869–1948) Indian national leader. *Young India* (August 11, 1920)

4 It's possible to disagree with someone about the ethics of non-violence without wanting to kick his face in.

Christopher Hampton (b. 1946) British playwright. *Treats* (1976), Scene 4

5 Today a pacifist revolutionary is something akin to a vegetarian lion.

Juan Domingo Perón (1895–1974) Argentinian president. Quoted in *We Say No* (Eduardo Galeano; 1992)

6 I do not believe in moral issues being settled by physical force.

James S. Woodsworth (1874–1942) Canadian cleric, reformer, and politician. Speech, Winnipeg (June 4, 1916)

Pain

see also **Cruelty, Suffering, Torture**

1 The greatest evil is physical pain.

Saint Augustine of Hippo (354–430) Numidian Christian theologian and Doctor of the Church. *Soliloquies*, I

2 Significant pain isolates you . . . but under certain circumstances, it may be all you've got, and after great loss, you must use whatever's left, even if it isolates you from anyone else.

Russell Banks (b. 1940) US novelist. *The Sweet Hereafter* (1991)

3 Pain—has an Element of Blank—
It cannot recollect
When it began—or if there were
A time when it was not.

Emily Dickinson (1830–86) US poet. No. 650 (1862?), st. 1, ll. 1–4, quoted in *The Complete Works of Emily Dickinson* (Thomas H. Johnson, ed.; 1970)

4 People will not readily bear pain unless there is hope.

Michael Edwardes (b. 1930) South African-born British company executive. Speech (July 2, 1980)

5 Much of your pain is self-chosen.
It is the bitter potion by which the physician within you heals your sick self.

Kahlil Gibran (1883–1931) Lebanese-born US mystic, painter, and poet. 'On Pain', *The Prophet* (1923)

6 The art of life is the art of avoiding pain.

Thomas Jefferson (1743–1826) US president. Letter to Maria Cosway (October 12, 1786)

7 Pain is life—the sharper, the more evidence of life.

Charles Lamb (1775–1834) British essayist. Letter to Bernard Barton (January 9, 1824)

8 But pain is perfect misery, the worst
Of evils, and excessive, overturns
All patience.

John Milton (1608–74) English writer. *Paradise Lost* (1667), bk. 6, ll. 462–465

9 Pain is unjust, and all the arguments that do not soothe it only worsen suspicions.

Racine (1639–99) French playwright. *Brittanicus* (1669), Act 1, Scene 2

10 Pain is a more terrible lord of mankind than even death himself.

Albert Schweitzer (1875–1965) German theologian, philosopher, physician, and musicologist. *On the Edge of the Primeval Forest* (1922), ch. 5

11 Remember that pain has this most excellent quality: if prolonged it cannot be severe, and if severe it cannot be prolonged.

Seneca, 'the Younger' (4? BC–AD 65) Roman writer, philosopher, and statesman. *Epistulae Morales* (63?), no. 94

12 Pain is the correlative of some species of wrong—some kind of divergence from that course of action which perfectly fills all requirements.

Herbert Spencer (1820–1903) British philosopher. *The Data of Ethics* (1879), ch. 15

13 Nothing begins and nothing ends
That is not paid with moan;
For we are born in others' pain,
And perish in our own.

Francis Thompson (1859–1907) British poet and critic. 'Daisy', *Works* (Wilfred Meynell, ed.; 1913), st. 15, ll. 1–4

14 Pain with the thousand teeth.

William Watson (1858–1935) British poet. 'The Dream of Man', *The Poems of Sir William Watson* (1936)

Painting

see also **Art, Artistic Styles, Artists**

1 A graveyard for pleasure,
good taste, the urge
to fornicate with what's painted.
Les Demoiselles d'Avignon.

Rafael Alberti (1902–99) Spanish poet. Referring to Pablo Picasso's painting, *Les Demoiselles d'Avignon* (1907). 'Ballad of Les Demoiselles d'Avignon', *The Eight Names of Picasso* (1992), st. 5

2 Painting, like passion, is an emotion full of truth and rings a living sound like the roar coming from the lion's breast.
Karel Appel (b. 1921) Dutch painter. 1953. Quoted in 'My Paint is Like a Rocket', *Karel Appel Painter* (Hugo Claus; 1962)

3 To paint is to destroy what preceded. I never try to make a painting, but a chunk of life.
Karel Appel (b. 1921) Dutch painter. 1953. Quoted in 'My Paint is Like a Rocket', *Karel Appel Painter* (Hugo Claus; 1962)

4 When talking about the violence of paint, it's nothing to do with the violence of war. It's to do with an attempt to remake the violence of reality itself.
Francis Bacon (1909–92) Irish-born British artist. 1971. Quoted in *Interviews with Francis Bacon* (David Sylvester; 1980), Interview 3

5 All finished paintings, whether a year or five hundred years old, are now prophecies, received from the past, about what the spectator is seeing in front of the canvas at the present moment.
John Berger (b. 1926) British novelist, essayist, and art critic. *And Our Faces, My Heart, Brief as Photos* (1984)

6 The painted image delivers what it depicts to the here and now—Turner crosses the Alps and brings back an image of nature's awesomeness.
John Berger (b. 1926) British novelist, essayist, and art critic. 'Ev'ry Time We Say Goodbye', *Keeping a Rendezvous* (1991)

7 PAINTING, n. The art of protecting flat surfaces from the weather and exposing them to the critic.
Ambrose Bierce (1842–1914?) US writer and journalist. *The Devil's Dictionary* (1911)

8 The painting is finished when it has blotted out the idea.
Georges Braque (1882–1963) French painter and sculptor. Quoted in 'Late Lyrics: Braque', *Art in America* (Jed Perl; February 1983), vol. 71

9 The painter Orbaneja of Ubeda, if he chanced to draw a cock, he wrote under it, 'This is a cock', lest the people should take it for a fox.
Miguel de Cervantes (1547–1616) Spanish novelist and playwright. *Don Quixote* (1605–15)

10 Good painters imitate nature, bad ones spew it up.
Miguel de Cervantes (1547–1616) Spanish novelist and playwright. *El Licenciado Vidriera* (1613)

11 To paint well is to express one's own time where it is most progressive, to stand on the summit of the world, on the heights of humanity.
Paul Cézanne (1839–1906) French painter. Quoted in *Joachim Gasquet's Cézanne: A Memoir with Conversations* (Christopher Pemberton, tr.; 1991)

12 The day is coming when a single carrot, freshly observed, will set off a revolution.
Paul Cézanne (1839–1906) French painter. Attrib.

13 I do not paint a portrait to look like the subject, rather does the person grow to look like his portrait.
Salvador Dalí (1904–89) Spanish surrealist painter. *Diary of a Genius* (Richard Howard, tr.; 1966)

14 Every good painter who aspires to the creation of genuine masterpieces should first of all marry my wife.
Salvador Dalí (1904–89) Spanish surrealist painter. 1969. Quoted in *Surrealist Art* (Sarane Alexandrian; 1970)

15 Painting is only a bridge linking the painter's mind with that of the viewer.
Eugène Delacroix (1798–1863) French painter. October 8, 1822. *Journal* (1893–95)

16 The first virtue of a painting is to be a feast for the eyes.
Eugène Delacroix (1798–1863) French painter. *Journal* (1893–95)

17 Painting . . . is able to reproduce on a panel a far more perfect visible world than the real world can ever be.
Johann Wolfgang von Goethe (1749–1832) German poet, playwright, and scientist. *Theory of Colour* (1810)

18 Sometimes I see it and then paint it. Other times I paint it and then see it. Both are impure situations, and I prefer neither.
Jasper Johns (b. 1930) US painter. Quoted in *Sixteen Americans* (Dorothy C. Miller, ed.; 1959)

19 Never mind about my soul, just make sure you get my tie right.
James Joyce (1882–1941) Irish writer. Responding to the painter Patrick Tuohy's assertion that he wished to capture Joyce's soul in his portrait of him. Quoted in *James Joyce* (Richard Ellmann; 1959)

20 Painting is poetry which is seen and not heard, and poetry is a painting which is heard but not seen.
Leonardo da Vinci (1452–1519) Italian artist, engineer, and inventor. 'The Paragone', *First Part of the Book on Painting* (1651)

21 Whatever exists in the universe, whether in essence, in act, or in the imagination, the painter has first in his mind and then in his hands.
Leonardo da Vinci (1452–1519) Italian artist, engineer, and inventor. *Notebooks* (1508–18), quoted in *Treatise On Painting* (A. P. McMahon, tr.; 1956)

22 There is nothing more difficult for a truly creative painter than to paint a rose, because before he can do so he has first to forget all the roses that were ever painted.
Henri Matisse (1869–1954) French painter and sculptor. Quoted in Obituary (November 5, 1954)

23 Every painting is a way of saying goodbye.
Anne Michaels (b. 1958) Canadian poet and novelist. 'Modersohn—Becker', *Miner's Pond* (1991)

24 Poetry and painting are done in the same way you make love; it's an exchange of blood, a total embrace—without caution, without any thought of protecting yourself.
Joan Miró (1893–1983) Catalan painter. Interview, *Cahiers D'Art* (Paris) (Georges Duthuit; 1936)

25 A form is never something abstract; it is always a sign of something. It is always a man, a bird, or something else . . . painting is never form for form's sake.
Joan Miró (1893–1983) Catalan painter. Interview, *Partisan Review* (New York; February 1948)

26 What is of importance in painting is paint. Paint can be color. Paint becomes painting when color establishes surface.
Jules Olitski (b. 1922) Russian-born US painter and sculptor. 1966. 'Painting in Color', *Artforum* (January 1967)

27 I mix them with my brains, sir.
John Opie (1761–1807) British painter. When asked what he mixed his colours with. Quoted in *Self-Help* (Samuel Smiles; 1859), ch. 4

28 A picture has been said to be something between a thing and a thought.
Samuel Palmer (1805–81) British painter and etcher. Quoted in *William Blake* (Arthur Symons; 1907)

29 A well-painted picture gives us a pleasure that
raises us to the realm of celestial love by leading
us to its divine origin. For is there anyone who
delights in the small brook and hates the spring
where it is born?
Petrarch (1304–74) Italian poet and scholar. Quoted in *El arte de la
pintura* (Francisco Pacheco; 1649)

30 I paint objects as I think them, not as I see them.
Pablo Picasso (1881–1973) Spanish painter and sculptor. Quoted in
Cubism: a History and Analysis, 1907–14 (John Golding;
1959)

31 Painting is a blind man's profession. He paints
not what he sees, but what he feels, what he tells
himself about what he has seen.
Pablo Picasso (1881–1973) Spanish painter and sculptor. Quoted in
'Childhood', *The Journals of Jean Cocteau* (Wallace Fowlie,
tr.; 1957)

32 There are painters who transform the sun into a
yellow spot, but there are others who, thanks to
their art and intelligence, transform a yellow spot
into the sun.
Pablo Picasso (1881–1973) Spanish painter and sculptor. Attrib.

33 The thing that interests me today is that painters
do not have to go to a subject matter outside of
themselves. Most modern painters work from a
different source. They work from within.
Jackson Pollock (1912–56) US artist. 1951. Quoted in *Pollock: A
Catalogue Raisonné* (Francis V. O'Connor and Eugene Victor
Thaw, eds.; 1978)

34 Painting is nothing but the image of incorporeal
things, despite the fact that it depicts bodies, for
it represents only the arrangements, proportions
and shapes of things and is more concerned with
the idea of beauty than any other.
Nicolas Poussin (1594–1665) French painter. Quoted in *Lives of the
Modern Painters, Sculptors and Architects* (Giovanni Pietro
Bellori; 1672)

35 I realize that historically the function of painting
very large pictures has been grandiose and
pompous. The reason I paint them . . . I want to
be very intimate and human. To paint a small
picture is to . . . look upon an experience as a
stereopticon view with a reducing glass.
Mark Rothko (1903–70) Russian-born US painter. 'A Symposium on
How to Combine Architecture, Painting and Sculpture',
Interiors (May 1951), 110, no. 10

36 Every time I paint a portrait I lose a friend.
John Singer Sargent (1856–1925) US portrait painter. *Treasury of
Humorous Quotations* (N. Bentley and E. Esar; 1951)

37 A portrait is a picture in which there is
something wrong with the mouth.
Eugene Speicher (1883–1962) US painter. Attrib.

38 My business is to paint not what I know, but
what I see.
J. M. W. Turner (1775–1851) British painter. Responding to a
criticism of the fact that he had painted no portholes on the
ships in a view of Plymouth. Attrib.

39 A painter should not paint what he sees, but
what will be seen.
Paul Valéry (1871–1945) French poet and philosopher. *Mauvaises
Pensées et Autres* (1942)

40 As music is the poetry of sound so painting is the
poetry of sight, and the subject matter has
nothing to do with harmony of sound or colour.
James Abbott McNeill Whistler (1834–1903) US painter and etcher. *The
Gentle Art of Making Enemies* (1890)

41 No, I ask it for the knowledge of a lifetime.
James Abbott McNeill Whistler (1834–1903) US painter and etcher. 1878.
Replying to the taunt, during the John Ruskin trial, that he
was asking an exorbitant fee of 200 guineas for two days'
painting. Whistler had brought a libel action against Ruskin
for damning one of his paintings as 'flinging a pot of paint in
the public's face'. *The Gentle Art of Making Enemies* (1890)

Paradise

see **Heaven**

Paradox

1 For thence,—a paradox
Which comforts while it mocks.
Shall life succeed in that it seems to fail.
Robert Browning (1812–89) British poet. 'Rabbi Ben Ezra', *Dramatis
Personae* (1864), st. 7

2 Paradoxes are useful to attract attention to ideas.
Mandell Creighton (1843–1901) British churchman and historian. *The
Life and Letters of Mandell Creighton* (Louise Creighton;
1904)

3 He who confronts the paradoxical exposes
himself to reality.
Friedrich Dürrenmatt (1921–90) Swiss writer. *The Physicists* (1962)

4 Out of the tension of duality life always produces
a 'third' that seems somehow incommensurable
or paradoxical.
Carl Gustav Jung (1875–1961) Swiss psychoanalyst. 1958. Referring to
the psychological provenance of 'the idea of the Holy Ghost'.
'A Psychological Approach to the Dogma of the Trinity',
Collected Works (1969), vol. 2

5 The paradox is the source of the thinker's
passion, and the thinker without a paradox is
like a lover without feeling: a paltry mediocrity.
Søren Kierkegaard (1813–55) Danish philosopher. Attrib.

6 Rousseau says that man is born free, but is
everywhere in chains. That is like saying that
sheep are born carnivores, but are everywhere
herbivorous.
Joseph Marie de Maistre (1753–1821) French political philosopher and
diplomat. Referring to Jean-Jacques Rousseau. Attrib.

Paranoia

see *also* **Fear, Hypochondria, Neurosis**

1 You go into a strange diner in the South and
everything goes quiet, and you realize all the
other customers are looking at you as if they are
sizing up the risk involved in murdering you for
your wallet and leaving your body in a shallow
grave somewhere out in the swamps.
Bill Bryson (b. 1951) US writer. *The Lost Continent* (1989), ch. 1

2 I have a feeling I'm falling
on rare occasions
but most of the time I have my feet on the
ground
I can't help it if the ground itself is falling.
Lawrence Ferlinghetti (b. 1919) US poet. 'Mock Confessional' (1973)

3 Even a paranoid can have enemies.
Henry Kissinger (b. 1923) German-born US politician and diplomat. *Time*
(January 24, 1977)

4 In paranoia the characteristic defences are chiefly aimed at annihilating the 'persecutors', while anxiety on the ego's account occupies a prominent place in the picture.

Melanie Klein (1882–1960) Austrian psychoanalyst. 'The Psychogenesis of Manic-Depressive States' (1935), quoted in *The Selected Melanie Klein* (Juliet Mitchell, ed.; 1986)

5 Just because you're paranoid doesn't mean they're not out to get you.

Proverb.

6 Who organized this standing ovation?

Joseph Stalin (1879–1953) Soviet dictator. May 1944. Said on hearing that at a poetry reading in Moscow the whole audience had spontaneously risen at the appearance of the poet Anna Akhmatova. Quoted in *Hope Abandoned* (Nadezhda Mandelstam; 1972), ch. 31

Parents

see also **Children, Family, Fathers, Mothers**

1 And my parents finally realize that I'm kidnapped and they snap into action immediately: they rent out my room.

Woody Allen (b. 1935) US film actor and director. *Woody Allen and His Comedy* (Eric Lax; 1975)

2 The joys of parents are secret, and so are their griefs and fears.

Francis Bacon (1561–1626) English philosopher, statesman, and lawyer. 'Of Parents and Children', *Essays* (1625)

3 Parents are the last people on earth who ought to have children.

Samuel Butler (1835–1902) British writer and composer. Quoted in *Note Books* (H. Festing Jones, ed.; 1912)

4 If one is not going to take the necessary precautions to avoid having parents one must undertake to bring them up.

Quentin Crisp (1908–99) British writer. *The Naked Civil Servant* (1968)

5 There are times when parenthood seems nothing but feeding the mouth that bites you.

Peter De Vries (1910–93) US novelist. *The Tunnel of Love* (1954)

6 Possessive parents rarely live long enough to see the fruits of their selfishness.

Alan Garner (1934–96) British author. *The Owl Service* (1967)

7 They fuck you up, your mum and dad.
They may not mean to, but they do.
They fill you with the faults they had
And add some extra, just for you.

Philip Larkin (1922–85) British poet. 'This be the Verse' (1971), st. 1, ll. 1–4, quoted in *Philip Larkin Collected Poems* (Anthony Thwaite, ed.; 1988)

8 Parents are sometimes a bit of a disappointment to their children. They don't fulfil the promise of their early years.

Anthony Powell (1905–2000) British novelist. *A Buyer's Market* (1952), ch. 2

9 Parentage is a very important profession; but no test of fitness for it is ever imposed in the interest of children.

George Bernard Shaw (1856–1950) Irish playwright. *Everybody's Political What's What* (1944)

10 Everything is dear to its parent.

Sophocles (496?–406? BC) Greek playwright. *Oedipus at Colonus* (5th century BC), l. 1108

11 Parents learn a lot from their children about coping with life.

Muriel Spark (b. 1918) British novelist. *The Comforters* (1957), ch. 6

12 I wish either my father or my mother, or indeed both of them, as they were in duty both equally bound to it, had minded what they were about when they begot me.

Laurence Sterne (1713–68) Irish-born British writer and clergyman. *Tristram Shandy* (1759–67), bk. 1, ch. 1

13 Parents are the bones on which children sharpen their teeth.

Peter Ustinov (b. 1921) British actor, director, and writer. *Dear Me* (1977)

14 Don't hold your parents up to contempt. After all, you are their son, and it is just possible that you may take after them.

Evelyn Waugh (1903–66) British novelist. *The Tablet* (May 9, 1951)

Paris

see **European Cities**

Parliaments and Assemblies

see also **Democracy, Government**

1 The House of Lords is like a glass of champagne that has stood for five days.

Clement Attlee (1883–1967) British politician. Attrib.

2 The House of Lords is the British Outer Mongolia for retired politicians.

Tony Benn (b. 1925) British politician and author. Remark (1962)

3 England is the mother of parliaments.

John Bright (1811–89) British politician. January 18, 1865. *Times* (January 19, 1865)

4 Parliament is not a congress of ambassadors from different and hostile interests; which interests each must maintain . . . but parliament is a deliberative assembly of one nation, with one interest, that of the whole; where, not local purposes . . . ought to guide, but the general good, resulting from the general reason of the whole.

Edmund Burke (1729–97) Irish-born British statesman and political philosopher. Edmund Burke was elected MP for Bristol in 1774. Speech to the electors of Bristol (November 3, 1774)

5 The duty of an opposition is to oppose.

Randolph Churchill (1849–95) British statesman. 1880? *Lord Randolph Churchill* (W. S. Churchill; 1906)

6 The House of Lords is a model of how to care for the elderly.

Frank Field (b. 1942) British politician. *Observer* (1981)

7 Every man has a House of Lords in his own head. Fears, prejudices, misconceptions—those are the peers, and they are hereditary.

David Lloyd George (1863–1945) British prime minister. 1927. Speech, Cambridge

8 The Commons, faithful to their system, remained in a wise and masterly inactivity.

James Mackintosh (1765–1832) Scottish lawyer, philosopher, and historian. *Vindiciae Gallicae* (1791)

9 Instead of governing, for which it is radically unfit, the proper office of a representative assembly is to watch and control the government.

John Stuart Mill (1806–73) British philosopher and social reformer. *Representative Government* (1861)

10 A parliament can do any thing but make a man a woman, and a woman a man.
Earl of Pembroke (1534?–1601) English aristocrat. Quoted in a speech at Oxford by his son, the 4th Earl, on April 11, 1648. Quoted in *Harleian Miscellany* (1745), vol. 5

11 Parliaments are the great lie of our time.
Konstantin Pobedonostsev (1827–1907) Russian administrator. *Moskovskii Sbornik* (1896)

12 The House of Lords must be the only institution in the world which is kept efficient by the persistent absenteeism of most of its members.
Herbert Samuel (1870–1963) British statesman and philosopher. *News Review* (February 5, 1948)

13 The longest-running farce in the West End.
Cyril Smith (b. 1928) British Liberal politician. Referring to Parliament. *Big Cyril* (1977), ch. 8

14 The House of Lords, an illusion to which I have never been able to subscribe—responsibility without power, the prerogative of the eunuch throughout the ages.
Tom Stoppard (b. 1937) Czech-born British playwright and screenwriter. *Lord Malquist and Mr Moon* (1966), pt. 6, ch.1

Parties

see also **Festivals**

1 I'll tell you what game we'll play. We're done with Humiliate the Host . . . and we don't want to play Hump the Hostess . . . We'll play a round of Get the Guests.
Edward Albee (b. 1928) US playwright. *Who's Afraid of Virginia Woolf?* (1962)

2 The sooner every party breaks up the better.
Jane Austen (1775–1817) British novelist. *Emma* (1816), ch. 25

3 I was one of the few guests who had actually been invited. People were not invited—they went there.
F. Scott Fitzgerald (1896–1940) US writer. *The Great Gatsby* (1925), ch. 3

4 For one of the pleasures of having a rout, Is the pleasure of having it over.
Thomas Hood (1799–1845) British poet and humorist. 'Her Dream', *Miss Kilmansegg and Her Precious Leg* (1841–43)

5 HE Have you heard it's in the stars
Next July we collide with Mars?
SHE Well, did you evah! What a swell party this is.
Cole Porter (1893–1964) US songwriter and composer. 'Well, Did You Evah!', *High Society* (1956)

6 Good-bye, I've barely said a word to you, it is always like that at parties, we never see the people, we never say the things we should like to say, but it is the same everywhere in this life. Let us hope that when we are dead things will be better arranged.
Marcel Proust (1871–1922) French novelist. 1921. Sodome et Gomorrhe, *À la Recherche du Temps Perdu* (1913–27)

7 Certainly, there is nothing else here to enjoy.
George Bernard Shaw (1856–1950) Irish playwright. Said at a party when his hostess asked him whether he was enjoying himself. Quoted in *Pass the Port Again* (Oxfam; 1980)

8 The Life and Soul, the man who will never go home while there is one man, woman or glass of anything not yet drunk.
Katharine Whitehorn (b. 1926) British journalist and writer. 'Husband-Swapping', *Sunday Best* (1976)

Parting

see also **Divorce, Separation**

1 It is never any good dwelling on goodbyes. It is not the being together that it prolongs, it is the parting.
Elizabeth Charlotte Lucy Bibescu (1897–1945) British writer. Attrib.

2 I pray thee leave, love me no more,
Call home the heart you gave me
I but in vain the saint adore,
That can, but will not, save me.
Michael Drayton (1563–1631) English poet. 'To His Coy Love' (1619)

3 In every parting there is an image of death.
George Eliot (1819–80) British novelist. 'Amos Barton', *Scenes of Clerical Life* (1858), ch. 10

4 To go away is to die a little, it is to die to that which one loves: everywhere and always, one leaves behind a part of oneself.
Edmond Haraucourt (1857–1941) French poet. 'Rondel de l'Adieu', *Seul* (1891)

5 Parting is the younger sister of death.
Osip Mandelstam (1891–1938) Russian poet, writer, and translator. *Journey to Armenia* (Clarence Brown, tr.; 1931–32), ch. 3

6 I have studied the science of saying goodbye.
Osip Mandelstam (1891–1938) Russian poet, writer, and translator. 1918. 'Tristia', *Tristia* (Robert Tracy, tr.; 1922), l. 1

7 Had she come all the way for this,
To part at last without a kiss?
Yea, had she borne the dirt and rain
That her own eyes might see him slain
Beside the haystack in the floods?
William Morris (1834–96) British designer, socialist reformer, and poet. 'The Haystack in the Floods' (1858)

8 So, till to-morrow eve, my Own, adieu!
Parting's well-paid with soon again to meet,
Soon in your arms to feel so small and sweet,
Sweet to myself that am so sweet to you!
Coventry Patmore (1823–96) British poet. 'The Azalea', *The Unknown Eros* (1877), ll. 341–344

9 It is seldom indeed that one parts on good terms, because if one were on good terms one would not part.
Marcel Proust (1871–1922) French novelist. 1923. La Prisonnière, *À la Recherche du Temps Perdu* (1913–27)

10 We live our lives, for ever taking leave.
Rainer Maria Rilke (1875–1926) Austrian poet and novelist. 1923. 'The Eighth Elegy', *Duino Elegies* (J. B. Leishman and Stephen Spender, trs.; 1939)

11 Every parting gives a foretaste of death; every coming together again a foretaste of the resurrection.
Arthur Schopenhauer (1788–1860) German philosopher. *Gedanken über vielerlei Gegenstände* (1851), no. 26

12 JULIET Good night, good night! Parting is such sweet sorrow
That I shall say good night till it be morrow.
William Shakespeare (1564–1616) English poet and playwright. *Romeo and Juliet* (1595), Act 2, Scene 2

13 I remember the way we parted,
The day and the way we met;
You hoped we were both broken-hearted,
And knew we should both forget.
Algernon Charles Swinburne (1837–1909) British poet. 'An Interlude', *Poems and Ballads: First Series* (1866), st. 11

Partners

see **Lovers, Marriage, Relationships**

Passion

see also **Desire, Love, Lust, Vitality**

1 Nothing kills passion faster than an exploding harpoon in the guts.
Ben Elton (b. 1959) British comedian and writer. *Stark* (1992)

2 Passions fade when one removes them from their usual surroundings.
Gustave Flaubert (1821–80) French novelist. *L'Éducation Sentimentale* (1869), pt. 2, ch. 1

3 The scribbling modern philosophy holds passion in contempt; and yet passion is the culmination of existence for an existing individual—and we are all of us existing individuals.
Søren Kierkegaard (1813–55) Danish philosopher. *Concluding Unscientific Postscript* (1846)

4 We seriously undervalue the passion . . . a person brings to an enterprise. You can rent a brain, but you can't rent a heart.
Mark McCormack (b. 1930) US sports agent, promoter, and lawyer. *McCormack on Managing* (1985)

5 My first thought was that he had committed a crime, but soon I saw it was only a passion that had moved into his body like a stranger.
Arthur Miller (b. 1915) US playwright. *A View from the Bridge* (1955), Act 1

6 As far as the passionate spirit is concerned, it will always be easier for me to understand the man who kills three people because somebody's touched a hair of his wife's head than it will be to understand a French ménage à trois.
Joan Miró (1893–1983) Catalan painter. Interview, *La Publicitat* (Barcelona; July 14, 1928)

7 It is a difficult thing for a man to resist the natural necessity of mortal passions.
Plutarch (46?–120?) Greek biographer and philosopher. 'Of Those Whom God is Slow to Punish' (1st–2nd century)

8 And hence one master-passion in the breast, Like Aaron's serpent, swallows up the rest.
Alexander Pope (1688–1744) English poet. *An Essay on Man* (1733), Epistle 2, ll. 131–132

9 The ruling passion, be it what it will
The ruling passion conquers reason still.
Alexander Pope (1688–1744) English poet. 'To Lord Bathurst', *Epistles to Several Persons* (1734), ll. 155–156

10 It's no longer a burning within my veins: it's Venus entire latched onto her prey.
Racine (1639–99) French playwright. *Phèdre* (1677), Act 1, Scene 3

11 Our passions are most like to floods and streams: The shallow murmur, but the deep are dumb.
Walter Raleigh (1554–1618) British explorer, courtier, and writer. 'Sir Walter Raleigh to the Queen' (1599?), st. 1

12 Passion is like genius: a miracle.
Romain Rolland (1866–1944) French writer. 1912. 'Le Buisson ardent', *Jean-Christophe* (1903–12), vol. 9

13 Passion, you see, can be destroyed by a doctor. It cannot be created.
Peter Shaffer (b. 1926) British playwright. *Equus* (1973), Act 2, Scene 35

14 Yes, I am a fatal man, Madame Fribsbi. To inspire hopeless passion is my destiny.
William Makepeace Thackeray (1811–63) British novelist. *The History of Pendennis* (1848–50), ch. 23

15 Strange fits of passion have I known:
And I will dare to tell,
But in the lover's ear alone,
What once to me befell.
William Wordsworth (1770–1850) English poet. 1799. One of the 'Lucy poems'. The identity of Lucy is uncertain. 'Strange Fits of Passion', *Lyrical Ballads* (2nd ed.; 1800), ll. 1–4

The Past

see also **History**

1 Even a God cannot change the past.
Agathon (446?–401 BC) Greek tragic poet. 410? BC. Quoted in *Nicomachean Ethics* (Aristotle), bk. 6, para. 113

2 I hibernated in my past.
Guillaume Apollinaire (1880–1918) Italian-born French poet. 'La Chanson du Mal-aimé', *Alcools* (1913)

3 In other words, it is quite true that the past *haunts* us; it is the past's function to haunt us who are present and wish to live in the world as it really is, that is, *become* what it is now.
Hannah Arendt (1906–75) German-born US philosopher and historian. Quoted in *The Meaning of History* (N. Gordon and Joyce Carper; 1991)

4 Man has truly a past only when he is conscious of having one, for this consciousness alone introduces the possibility of dialogue and choice.
Raymond Aron (1905–83) French writer. *Dimensions de la Conscience Historique* (1962), pt. 1, ch. 1

5 We're dying from not knowing and not understanding our past.
Jacques Bainville (1879–1936) French journalist and historian. Journal (August 18, 1916)

6 To accept one's past—one's history—is not the same thing as drowning in it; it is learning how to use it. An uninvented past can never be used; it cracks and crumbles under the pressures of life like clay in a season of drought.
James Baldwin (1924–87) US writer and civil rights activist. *The Fire Next Time* (1963)

7 If we cannot be on familiar terms with our past, it is no good. We must have a past that is the product of all the present.
Carl Becker (1873–1945) US historian. 'Detachment and the Writing of History', *Atlantic Monthly* (October 1910)

8 The past is a kind of screen upon which we project our vision of the future; and it is indeed a moving picture, borrowing much of its form and color from our fears and aspirations.
Carl Becker (1873–1945) US historian. 'Detachment and the Writing of History', *Atlantic Monthly* (October 1910)

9 Duration is the continuous progress of the past which gnaws into the future and which swells as it advances.
Henri-Louis Bergson (1859–1941) French philosopher. *Creative Evolution* (Arthur Mitchell, tr.; 1907)

10 Nothing has happened to the present by becoming past except that fresh slices of existence have been added to the total history of the world. The past is thus as real as the present.
C. D. Broad (1887–1971) British philosopher. *Scientific Thought* (1923)

11 There was a house we all had in common and it
was called the past.
Angela Carter (1940–92) British novelist, essayist, and short-story writer.
Wise Children (1991)

12 Nothing recalls the past so potently as a smell.
Winston Churchill (1874–1965) British prime minister and writer. *My
Early Life* (1930)

13 Study the past, if you would divine the future.
Confucius (551–479 BC) Chinese philosopher, administrator, and moralist.
Analects (5th century BC)

14 We review the past, not in order to return to it,
but that we may find in what direction it points
to the future.
Calvin Coolidge (1872–1933) US president. Quoted in *The Meaning
of History* (N. Gordon and Joyce Carper; 1991)

15 When eras die, their legacies
Are left to strange police.
Professors in New England guard
The glory that was Greece.
Clarence Shepard Day (1874–1935) US writer. 'Thoughts on Deaths',
Thoughts Without Words (1928)

16 We, who are the living, possess the past.
Tomorrow is for our martyrs.
James Farmer (b. 1920) US civil rights leader. *Lay Bare The Heart:
An Autobiography of the Civil Rights Movement* (1985)

17 The past is never dead, it is not even past.
William Faulkner (1897–1962) US novelist. Attrib. *Newsweek*
(February 21, 1977)

18 So we beat on, boats against the current, borne
back ceaselessly into the past.
F. Scott Fitzgerald (1896–1940) US writer. Last line. *The Great
Gatsby* (1925)

19 The past is a foreign country: they do things
differently there.
L. P. Hartley (1895–1972) British novelist. *The Go-Between* (1953),
Prologue

20 The past is but a coarse and sensual prophecy of
the present and the future.
Nathaniel Hawthorne (1804–64) US novelist and short-story writer. *The
House of Seven Gables* (1851)

21 The Past lies upon the Present like a giant's dead
body.
Nathaniel Hawthorne (1804–64) US novelist and short-story writer. *The
House of Seven Gables* (1851)

22 Respect the past in the full measure of its deserts,
but do not make the mistake of confusing it with
the present nor seek in it the ideals of the future.
José Ingenieros (1877–1925) Argentinian psychiatrist, educator, and
politician. *Proposiciones Relativas al Porvenir de la Filosofía*
(1918)

23 Why doesn't the past decently bury itself, instead of
sitting and waiting to be admitted by the present?
D. H. Lawrence (1885–1930) British writer. *St. Mawr* (1925)

24 The past is a rich resource on which we can
draw in order to make decisions for the future,
but it does not dictate our choices. We should
look back at the past and select what is good,
and leave behind what is bad.
Nelson Mandela (b. 1918) South African president and lawyer. February
25, 1990. *The Struggle is My Life* (1990)

25 To excel the past we must not allow ourselves to
lose contact with it; on the contrary, we must feel it
under our feet because we raised ourselves upon it.
José Ortega y Gasset (1883–1955) Spanish writer and philosopher. 'In
Search of Goethe from Within', *Partisan Review* (December
1949)

26 The past is the *terra firma* of methods, of the
roads which we believe we have under our feet.
José Ortega y Gasset (1883–1955) Spanish writer and philosopher. 'In
Search of Goethe from Within', *Partisan Review* (New York;
December 1949)

27 The struggle with the past is not a hand-to-hand
fight. The future overcomes it by swallowing it. If
it leaves anything outside it is lost.
José Ortega y Gasset (1883–1955) Spanish writer and philosopher. *The
Revolt of the Masses* (1930)

28 The earth's about five thousand million years
old. Who can afford to live in the past?
Harold Pinter (b. 1930) British playwright, theatre director, and
screenwriter. *The Homecoming* (1965)

29 The past is the only dead thing that smells sweet.
Edward Thomas (1878–1917) British poet, biographer, and critic.
Originally published under the pseudonym Edward Eastaway.
'Early One Morning', *Poems* (1917)

30 What is past is not dead; it is not even past. We
cut ourselves off from it; we pretend to be
strangers.
Christa Wolf (b. 1929) German writer. *A Model Childhood*
(U. Molinaro and H. Rappott, trs.; 1976), ch. 1

Patience

1 Don't count your chickens before they are
hatched.
Aesop (620?–560 BC) Greek writer. 'The Milkmaid and her Pail',
Aesop's Fables (6th century BC)

2 ESTRAGON Let's go.
VLADIMIR We can't.
ESTRAGON Why not?
VLADIMIR We're waiting for Godot.
Samuel Beckett (1906–89) Irish playwright, novelist, and poet. *Waiting
for Godot* (1954), Act 1, passim

3 PATIENCE, n. A minor form of despair, disguised
as a virtue.
Ambrose Bierce (1842–1914?) US writer and journalist. *The Devil's
Dictionary* (1911)

4 The ability to wait while conditions develop is a
requisite of practical policy.
Prince Otto von Bismarck (1815–98) German chancellor. Remark
(February 1869), quoted in *Germany, 1866–1945* (Gordon A.
Craig; 1978), ch. 1

5 We've been waiting 700 years, you can have the
seven minutes.
Michael Collins (1890–1922) Irish politician. 1922. Said on being told
he was 7 minutes late for the hand-over of British military
jurisdiction to the Irish Free State. Attrib. *Michael Collins: A
Biography* (Tim Pat Coogan; 1990)

6 If you go slowly,
Time will walk behind you
Like a submissive ox.
Juan Ramón Jiménez (1881–1958) Spanish poet. 'To Miss Rápida',
Selected Writings (1957)

7 Job endured everything—until his friends came to
comfort him, then he grew impatient.
Søren Kierkegaard (1813–55) Danish philosopher. *Journal* (1849)

8 Patience and passage of time do more than
strength and fury.
Jean de La Fontaine (1621–95) French writer and poet. 'Le Lion et le
Rat', *Fables* (1668), bk. 2

9 There is a patience of the wild . . . that holds motionless for endless hours the spider in its web, the snake in its coils, the panther in its ambuscade; this patience belongs primarily to life when it hunts its living food.

Jack London (1876–1916) US writer. *The Call of the Wild* (1903)

10 Patience is the best remedy for every trouble.

Plautus (254?–184 BC) Roman comic playwright. *Rudens* (3rd–2nd century BC), Act 2, Scene 5

11 He that has patience may compass anything.

François Rabelais (1494?–1553?) French humanist and satirist. *Gargantua* (1534), bk. 4, ch. 48

12 NYM Though patience be a tired mare, yet she will plod.

William Shakespeare (1564–1616) English poet and playwright. *Henry V* (1599), Act 2, Scene 1

13 It is very strange . . . that the years teach us patience; that the shorter our time, the greater our capacity for waiting.

Elizabeth Taylor (1912–75) British novelist and short-story writer. *A Wreath of Roses* (1950)

14 A healthy male adult bore consumes each year one and a half times his own weight in other people's patience.

John Updike (b. 1932) US writer. 'Confessions of a Wild Bore', *Assorted Prose* (1965)

Patriotism

see also **Loyalty**, **Nations**

1 What pity is it
That we can die but once to serve our country!

Joseph Addison (1672–1719) English essayist, poet, and statesman. *Cato* (1713), Act 4, Scene 1

2 I am not one of those who left their land
For enemies to tear apart.

Anna Akhmatova (1888–1966) Russian poet. 'I am not one of those who left their land . . . ' (Peter Norman, tr.; June 22, 1939), quoted in *The Akhmatova Journals: 1938–41* (Lydia Chukovskaya, ed.; 1989), no. 41

3 It comes as a great shock around the age of five, six or seven to discover that the flag to which you have pledged allegiance . . . has not pledged allegiance to you . . . to see Gary Cooper killing off the Indians, and, although you are rooting for Gary Cooper . . . the Indians are you.

James Baldwin (1924–87) US writer and civil rights activist. February 1965. Speech at Cambridge Union Society, *The Price of the Ticket* (1985)

4 If I should die, think only this of me:
That there's some corner of a foreign field
That is forever England.

Rupert Brooke (1887–1915) British poet. 'The Soldier' (1914), quoted in *The Poetical Works of Rupert Brooke* (Geoffrey Keynes, ed.; 1970)

5 The religion of Hell is patriotism and the government is an enlightened democracy.

James Branch Cabell (1879–1958) US novelist and journalist. *Jurgen* (1919)

6 The love of one's country is a natural thing. But why should love stop at the border?

Pablo Casals (1876–1973) Catalan cellist, conductor, and composer. Quoted in *Joys and Sorrows* (Julian Lloyd Webber, ed.; 1970)

7 In Ireland alone, in this twentieth century, is loyalty held to be a crime.

Roger Casement (1864–1916) Irish nationalist. Speech, after being found guilty of treason (1916)

8 We love a country that brings the people happiness, not a country that demands the people sacrifice themselves.

Chen Duxiu (1879–1942) Chinese reformer. Remark (1915)

9 'My country, right or wrong' is a thing that no patriot would think of saying, except in a desperate case. It is like saying 'My mother, drunk or sober'.

G. K. Chesterton (1874–1936) British writer and poet. *The Defendant* (1901)

10 My country right or wrong.

John Crittenden (1787–1863) US politician. 1846. Responding to President James Polk's request for a declaration of war. Quoted in *Speaking Freely* (Stuart Berg Flexner and Anne H. Soukhanov; 1997)

11 Never was patriot yet, but was a fool.

John Dryden (1631–1700) English poet, playwright, and literary critic. *Absalom and Achitophel* (1681), pt. 1, l. 968

12 I hate the idea of causes, and if I had to choose between betraying my country and betraying my friend, I hope I should have the guts to betray my country.

E. M. Forster (1879–1970) British novelist. 'What I Believe', *Two Cheers for Democracy* (1951)

13 I have never understood why one's affections must be confined, as once with women, to a single country.

J. K. Galbraith (b. 1908) Canadian-born US economist. *A Life in our Times* (1981)

14 It is a sweet and seemly thing to die for one's country.

Horace (65–8 BC) Roman poet. *Odes* (23? BC), bk. 3, no. 2, l. 13

15 One of the great attractions of patriotism—it fulfils our worst wishes. In the person of our nation we are able, vicariously, to bully and to cheat. Bully and cheat, what's more, with a feeling that we are profoundly virtuous.

Aldous Huxley (1894–1963) British novelist and essayist. *Eyeless in Gaza* (1936)

16 Patriotism is the last refuge of a scoundrel.

Samuel Johnson (1709–84) British lexicographer and writer. April 7, 1775. Quoted in *Life of Samuel Johnson* (James Boswell; 1791)

17 My principle is: France before everything.

Napoleon I (1769–1821) French emperor. Letter to Eugène de Beauharnais (August 23, 1810)

18 Patriotism is often an arbitrary veneration of real estate above principles.

G. J. Nathan (1882–1958) US drama critic. *Testament of a Critic* (1930)

19 The *Daily Mirror* does not believe that patriotism had to be proved in blood. Especially someone else's blood.

Newspapers. Referring to the Falklands War (1982). *Daily Mirror* (April 1982)

20 The old Lie: Dulce et decorum est
Pro patria mori.

Wilfred Owen (1893–1918) British poet. 'Dulce et decorum est' (1914?), quoted in *The Collected Poems of Wilfred Owen* (C. Day Lewis, ed.; 1963)

21 The summer soldier and the sunshine patriot will, in this crisis, shrink from the service of their country.

Thomas Paine (1737–1809) English writer and political philosopher. George Washington ordered this paper to be read to his troops on the eve of the Battle of Trenton, New Jersey (December 26, 1776). *Pennsylvania Journal* (December 19, 1776)

22   Who dare to love their country, and be poor.

Alexander Pope (1688–1744) English poet. 'Verses on a Grotto by the River Thames at Twickenham, Composed of Marbles, Spars, and Minerals' (1740)

23   My father was a slave, and my people died to build this country, and I am going to stay here and have a piece of it, just like you.

Paul Robeson (1898–1976) US singer, actor, and civil rights activist. Statement to the House Committee on Un-American Activities (June 12, 1956)

24   KING HENRY V The game's afoot:
Follow your spirit; and, upon this charge
Cry 'God for Harry! England and Saint George!'

William Shakespeare (1564–1616) English poet and playwright. *Henry V* (1599), Act 3, Scene 1

25   You'll never have a quiet world till you knock the patriotism out of the human race.

George Bernard Shaw (1856–1950) Irish playwright. *O'Flaherty V.C.* (1919)

26   The Pledge of Allegiance does not end with 'Hail Satan'.

The Simpsons, US cartoon series. Lines written as punishment on a chalkboard during the opening credits of *The Simpsons*. The content of the lines changes with each episode. *The Simpsons* (Matt Groening; 1990–)

27   True patriotism is of no party.

Tobias Smollett (1721–71) Scottish novelist. *The Adventures of Sir Launcelot Greaves* (1762)

28   Patriotism to the Soviet state is a revolutionary duty, whereas patriotism to a bourgeois state is treachery.

Leon Trotsky (1879–1940) Russian revolutionary leader. Attrib.

29   The black man cannot protect a country, if the country doesn't protect him; and if, tomorrow, a war should arise, I would not raise a musket to defend a country where my manhood is denied.

Henry M. Turner (1834–1915) US politician and cleric. Speech in the House of Representatives (September 3, 1868), quoted in *A Documentary History of the Negro People in the United States* (Herbert Aptheker; 1951), vol. 2

30   There is one certain means by which I can be sure never to see my country's ruin; I will die in the last ditch.

William III (1650–1702) English monarch. Quoted in *History of England* (David Hume; 1757)

Peace

see also **Diplomacy, Pacifism**

1   Knowledge of peace
passes from country to country,
like children's games,
which are so much alike, everywhere.

Yehuda Amichai (b. 1924) German-born Israeli poet. 'Patriotic Songs', *Amen* (1978), no. 15, ll. 7–10

2   Now, after years of observation and enough courage to admit what I have observed, I try to plant peace if I do not want discord; to plant loyalty and honesty if I want to avoid betrayal and lies.

Maya Angelou (b. 1928) US writer. 'At Harvest Time', *Wouldn't Take Nothing for My Journey Now* (1993)

3   Let us be clear as to what is our ultimate aim. It is not just the negation of war but the creation of a world which is governed by justice and moral law.

Clement Attlee (1883–1967) British politician. Speech at the opening session of the first UN General Assembly (1945)

4   Perhaps there is nothing in the whole of creation that knows the meaning of peace. For is the soil not restless compared to the unyielding rock?

Ugo Betti (1892–1953) Italian playwright and poet. *The Fugitive* (G. H. McWilliam, tr.; 1953)

5   There is no peace, saith the Lord, unto the wicked.

Bible. Isaiah, *King James Bible* (1611), 48:22

6   They shall beat their swords into plowshares and their spears into pruning hooks: nation shall not lift up a sword against nation, neither shall they learn war any more. But they shall sit every man under his vine and under his fig tree; and none shall make them afraid.

Bible. Micah, *King James Bible* (1611), 4:3–4

7   PEACE, n. In international affairs, a period of cheating between two periods of fighting.

Ambrose Bierce (1842–1914?) US writer and journalist. *The Devil's Dictionary* (1911)

8   Peace, like freedom, is no original state which existed from the start; we shall have to make it, in the truest sense of the word.

Willy Brandt (1913–92) German statesman. Address given on the presentation of a Nobel Prize in peace (December 11, 1971), quoted in *Willy Brandt, Peace* (Klaus Reiff, ed.; 1971)

9   The struggle for peace and the struggle for human rights are inseparable.

Willy Brandt (1913–92) German statesman. Speech, Stockholm, the day after receiving a Nobel Prize in peace (December 12, 1971), quoted in *Willy Brandt, Peace* (Klaus Reiff, ed.; 1971)

10   Don't tell me peace has broken out.

Bertolt Brecht (1898–1956) German playwright and poet. *Mother Courage and Her Children* (1941), Scene 8

11   Draw back the rifles, draw back the machine-guns, draw back the cannons—trust in conciliation, in arbitration, in peace! . . . A country grows in history not only because of the heroism of its troops on the field of battle, it grows also when it turns to justice and to right for the conservation of its interests.

Aristide Briand (1862–1932) French statesman. Referring to Germany's admission to membership of the League of Nations. Speech, Geneva, Switzerland (September 10, 1926)

12   Mark! where his carnage and his conquests cease!
He makes a solitude, and calls it—peace!

Lord Byron (1788–1824) British poet. *The Bride of Abydos* (1813), can. 2, st. 20

13   This is the second time in our history that there has come back from Germany to Downing Street peace with honour. I believe it is peace for our time.

Neville Chamberlain (1869–1940) British prime minister. September 30, 1938. Speech from 10 Downing Street, home of the prime minister. *Times* (October 1, 1938)

14   The war ended, the explosions stopped.
The men surrendered their weapons
And hung around limply.
Peace took them all prisoner.

Ted Hughes (1930–98) British writer and poet. 'A Motorbike', *Earth-Numb* (1979), st. 2, ll. 1–4

15   Arms alone are not enough to keep the peace—it must be kept by men.

John Fitzgerald Kennedy (1917–63) US president. *Observer* (1962), 'Sayings of the Decade'

16 All we are saying is Give Peace a Chance.

John Lennon (1940–80) British rock musician. Song lyric. 'Give Peace A Chance' (1969)

17 They made peace between us; we embraced, and we have been mortal enemies ever since.

Alain René Lesage (1668–1747) French writer. *Le Diable Boiteux* (1707), ch. 3

18 Peace is indivisible.

Maxim Maximovich Litvinov (1876–1951) Soviet statesman. Speech to the League of Nations, Geneva (July 1, 1936)

19 I live in peace with men and at war with my innards.

Antonio Machado (1875–1939) Spanish poet and playwright. 'Proverbs and Songs', *Castilian Landscapes* (1907–17), no. 23

20 If man does find the solution for world peace it will be the most revolutionary reversal of his record we have ever known.

George Marshall (1880–1959) US military commander and politician. 1945. *Biennial Report of the Chief of Staff, United States Army* (September 1, 1945)

21 The Gulf War is over . . . life goes on. You are surprised to find yourself singing in the springtime, putting a flower in your hair, trying a new lipstick.

Fatima Mernissi (b. 1941) Moroccan writer. *Islam and Democracy* (1992)

22 Peace hath her victories
No less renowned than war.

John Milton (1608–74) English writer. 1652. 'To Oliver Cromwell', *Letters of State . . . Together with Several of his Poems* (1694), ll. 9–10

23 Perpetual peace is a dream, and not even a beautiful dream. War is part of God's order . . . In it, man's most noble virtues are displayed.

Helmuth Johannes von Moltke (1848–1916) German military commander. Letter to Dr. J. K. Bluntschi (December 11, 1880), quoted in *Europe: A History* (Norman Davies; 1996)

24 There is no way to peace. Peace is the way.

A. J. Muste (1885–1967) US author and pacifist. *New York Times* (November 16, 1967)

25 He accepted peace as if he had been defeated.

Napoleon I (1769–1821) French emperor. Referring to the Duke of Wellington. Attrib.

26 Peace is made with yesterday's enemies. What is the alternative?

Shimon Peres (b. 1923) Israeli prime minister. *Observer* (October 16, 1994), 'Sayings of the Week'

27 When peace has been broken anywhere, the peace of all countries everywhere is in danger.

Franklin D. Roosevelt (1882–1945) US president. September 3, 1939. Radio broadcast. 'Fireside Chat', *Public Papers* (1941), vol. 8

28 You may either win your peace or buy it; win it by resistance to evil; buy it by compromise with evil.

John Ruskin (1819–1900) British art critic, writer, and reformer. 'The Two Paths' (1859), lecture 5

29 Peace is much more precious than a piece of land.

Anwar al-Sadat (1918–81) Egyptian statesman. *In Search of Identity* (1978)

30 Peace is not only better than war, but infinitely more arduous.

George Bernard Shaw (1856–1950) Irish playwright. *Heartbreak House* (1919), Preface

31 To many men . . . the miasma of peace seems more suffocating than the bracing air of war.

George Steiner (b. 1929) US scholar and critic. 'Has Truth a Future?' (1978)

32 They make a wilderness and call it peace.

Tacitus (55?–117?) Roman historian. *De Vita Iulii Agricola* (98?), ch. 30

33 I want peace and I'm willing to fight for it.

Harry S. Truman (1884–1972) US president. Diary entry (May 22, 1945), quoted in *Off the Record* (Robert H. Ferrell; 1980)

34 Let him who desires peace, prepare for war.

Vegetius (*fl.* 4th century) Roman writer. *Epitome Rei Militaris* (373?), Prologue pt. 3

Perception

see also **Senses, Understanding**

1 No man ever looks at the world with pristine eyes. He sees it edited by a definite set of customs and institutions and ways of thinking.

Ruth Benedict (1887–1948) US anthropologist. *Patterns of Culture* (1934)

2 We see only the appearances, and not the real qualities of things . . . for aught we know, all we see, hear, and feel may be only phantom and vain chimera, and not all agree with the real things, existing in *rerum natura*.

Bishop Berkeley (1685–1753) Irish prelate and philosopher. *A Treatise Concerning the Principles of Human Knowledge* (1710)

3 If the doors of perception were cleansed every thing would appear to man as it is, infinite.

William Blake (1757–1827) British poet, painter, engraver, and mystic. 'A Memorable Fancy', *The Marriage of Heaven and Hell* (1790–93), plate 14

4 The first psychological difference between humans and animals resides in how we regard each other. Humans regard animals differently than animals regard animals (and humans), so a first step in restoring Eden would be to regain the animal eye.

James Hillman (b. 1926) US author. *Typologies* (1986)

5 All the perceptions of the human mind resolve themselves into two distinct kinds, which I shall call IMPRESSIONS and IDEAS.

David Hume (1711–76) Scottish philosopher and historian. *A Treatise of Human Nature* (1739–40)

6 If we believe, that fire warms, or water refreshes, 'tis only because it costs us too much pains to think otherwise.

David Hume (1711–76) Scottish philosopher and historian. *A Treatise of Human Nature* (1739–40)

7 Two men look out through the same bars:
One sees the mud, and one the stars.

Frederick Langbridge (1849–1922) British writer and priest. 'A Cluster of Quiet Thoughts' (1896)

8 If the only tool you have is a hammer, all problems begin to look like nails.

Abraham Maslow (1908–70) US psychologist. *Motivation and Personality* (1954)

9 Every object is the mirror of all other objects.

Maurice Merleau-Ponty (1908–61) French existentialist philosopher. *Phenomenology of Perception* (1945)

10 I saw it, but I did not realize it.

Elizabeth Peabody (1804–94) US educator. Giving a transcendentalist explanation for her accidentally walking into a tree. Quoted in *The Peabody Sisters of Salem* (Louise Tharp; 1950)

11 In a dark time, the eye begins to see.
Theodore Roethke (1908–63) US poet. 'In a Dark Time', *The Far Field* (1964), l. 1

12 One must have a mind of winter
To regard the frost and the boughs
Of the pine-trees crusted with snow.
Wallace Stevens (1879–1955) US poet. 'The Snow Man', *Harmonium* (1923)

13 Few people realize that they are looking at the world of their own thoughts and the world of their own feelings.
Wallace Stevens (1879–1955) US poet. 'The Figure of the Youth as Virile Poet', *The Necessary Angel: Essays on Reality and the Imagination* (1951)

14 Vision is the art of seeing things invisible.
Jonathan Swift (1667–1745) Irish writer and clergyman. 'Thoughts on Various Subjects' (1726)

15 Something I cannot see puts up libidinous prongs,
Seas of bright juice suffuse heaven.
Walt Whitman (1819–92) US poet. 1855. 'Song of Myself', *Leaves of Grass* (1881), st. 24

Perfection

see also **Excellence, Idealism**

1 The pursuit of perfection, then, is the pursuit of sweetness and light . . . He who works for sweetness and light united, works to make reason and the will of God prevail.
Matthew Arnold (1822–88) British poet and critic. *Culture and Anarchy* (1869), ch. 1

2 What's come to perfection perishes.
Things learned on earth, we shall practise in heaven.
Works done least rapidly, Art most cherishes.
Robert Browning (1812–89) British poet. 'Old Pictures in Florence', *Men and Women* (1855), st. 17

3 Faultless to a fault.
Robert Browning (1812–89) British poet. 1868. *The Ring and the Book* (1868–69), bk. 9, l. 1175

4 The very pink of perfection.
Oliver Goldsmith (1730–74) Irish-born British novelist, playwright, and poet. *She Stoops to Conquer* (1773), Act 1

5 Perfection is the child of Time.
Joseph Hall (1574–1656) British prelate and writer. *Works* (1625)

6 No one is perfect in this imperfect world.
Patrice Lumumba (1925–61) Congolese prime minister. *Congo, My Country* (1962)

7 Perfection has one grave defect; it is apt to be dull.
Somerset Maugham (1874–1965) British writer. *The Summing Up* (1938)

8 Only perfection was good enough for him, and on the rare occasions he encountered it, he reviewed it with astonished suspicion.
Ramón María Narváez (1800–68) Spanish general and politician. Referring to Harold W. Ross, editor of *New Yorker*. Quoted in *The Years with Ross* (James Thurber; 1957)

9 The essence of being human is that one does not seek perfection.
George Orwell (1903–50) British writer. 'Reflections on Gandhi', *Shooting an Elephant* (1950)

10 His only fault is that he has no fault.
Pliny the Younger (62–113) Roman politician and writer. Quoted in *The Letters of Pliny the Consul* (W. Melmoth, tr.; 1747), bk. 9, letter 16

11 All is for the best in the best of all possible worlds.
Voltaire (1694–1778) French writer and philosopher. *Candide* (1759), ch. 1

Performance

see also **Acting and Actors, The Arts, Music, Theatre**

1 The art of interpretation is not to play what is written.
Pablo Casals (1876–1973) Catalan cellist, conductor, and composer. Letter, *Times* (December 29, 1946), quoted in *The Song of the Birds* (Julian Lloyd Webber, ed.; 1985)

2 He played the King as though under momentary apprehension that someone else was about to play the ace.
Eugene Field (1850–95) US journalist and children's author. Referring to Creston Clarke's performance in the role of King Lear in Denver (1880?). *The Denver Tribune* (1880)

3 The only true performance is the one which attains madness.
Mick Jagger (b. 1943) British rock musician and songwriter. Quoted in *The Wit and Wisdom of Rock and Roll* (Maxim Jabukowski, ed.; 1983)

4 Almost every man wastes part of his life in attempts to display qualities which he does not possess, and to gain applause which he cannot keep.
Samuel Johnson (1709–84) British lexicographer and writer. *The Rambler* (1750–52)

5 The only time I really open up is onstage. The mask of performing gives it to me, a place where I hide myself then I can reveal myself.
Jim Morrison (1943–71) US rock singer and songwriter. Quoted in *No One Here Gets out Alive* (Jerry Hopkins and Danny Sugerman; 1980)

6 The notes I handle no better than many pianists. But the pauses between the notes—ah, that is where the art resides.
Artur Schnabel (1882–1951) Austrian pianist and composer. Quoted in *Chicago Daily News* (June 11, 1958)

7 When a piece gets difficult make faces.
Artur Schnabel (1882–1951) Austrian pianist and composer. Advice given to the pianist Vladimir Horowitz. Quoted in *The Unimportance of Being Oscar* (Oscar Levant; 1968)

Persecution

see also **Heresy, Oppression**

1 Persecution is a bad and indirect way to plant religion. There are many (questionless) canonized on earth, that shall never be Saints in Heaven.
Thomas Browne (1605–82) English physician and writer. *Religio Medici* (1642), pt. 1, sect. 26

2 Religious persecution may shield itself under the guise of a mistaken and over-zealous piety.
Edmund Burke (1729–97) Irish-born British statesman and political philosopher. Speech for the prosecution at the impeachment of Warren Hastings, former governor-general of India (February 18, 1788), quoted in *Speeches . . . in the Trial of Warren Hastings* (E. A. Bond; 1859), vol. 1

3 Persecution produced its natural effect on them. It found them a sect; it made them a faction.

Thomas Babington Macaulay (1800–59) British politician, historian, and writer. 1848. Referring to the early Puritans and Calvinists. *History of England from the Accession of James II* (1848–61), vol. 1, ch. 1

4 The witch-hunt was a perverse manifestation of the panic which set in among all classes when the balance began to turn toward greater individual freedom.

Arthur Miller (b. 1915) US playwright. Referring to the Salem witchcraft trials (1692). *The Crucible* (1953), Act 1, Overture

5 Wilde's captors were the police. But his persecutors were to be found on the letters page of the *Daily Telegraph*.

Matthew Parris (b. 1949) British journalist. Referring to Oscar Wilde. *Times* (April 7, 1993)

6 Because we do not make any distinction in rank and outward appearance, or wealth and education, or age and sex, they devise an accusation against us that we practice cannibalism and sexual perversions.

Tatian (120?–173) Syrian writer and Christian thinker. 160? Referring to the early Christian Church, which regarded as heretical his association with the ascetic religious community of Encratites, which combined Christianity and Stoicism. 'Oratio ad Graecos', *The Early Christians* (E. Arnold; 1970)

7 Anyone who denies that he is a Christian and actually proves this by worshipping our gods is pardoned on repentance, no matter how suspect his past may have been.

Trajan (53?–117) Roman emperor. 112. Quoted in Letters, Trajan with Pliny, *The Early Christians* (E. Arnold; 1970)

Persistence

see also Effort, Endurance

1 There must be a beginning of any great matter, but the continuing unto the end until it be thoroughly finished yields the true glory.

Francis Drake (1540?–96) English navigator and admiral. Despatch to Sir Francis Walsingham. *Navy Records Society* (May 17, 1587), vol. 11

2 For water continually dropping will wear hard rocks hollow.

Plutarch (46?–120?) Greek biographer and philosopher. 'Of the Training of Children' (1st–2nd century)

3 'Tis known by the name of perseverance in a good cause,—and of obstinacy in a bad one.

Laurence Sterne (1713–68) Irish-born British writer and clergyman. *Tristram Shandy* (1759–67), bk. 1, ch. 17

Perversity

see also Extremes, Normality, Orthodoxy

1 The cars in which she moved would become devices for exploiting every pornographic and erotic possibility, every conceivable sex-death and mutilation.

J. G. Ballard (b. 1930) Chinese-born British writer. *Crash* (1973)

2 In injust society deviance is the practice of freedom.

Edward Bond (b. 1934) British playwright. *The Hidden Plot* (2000)

3 Mr. Mercaptan went on to preach a brilliant sermon on that melancholy sexual perversion known as continence.

Aldous Huxley (1894–1963) British novelist and essayist. *Antic Hay* (1923), ch. 18

4 The instinct of acquisitiveness has more perverts, I believe, than the instinct of sex. At any rate people seem to be odder about money than about even their amours.

Aldous Huxley (1894–1963) British novelist and essayist. *Point Counter Point* (1928)

5 Perversity is not very inventive, my son, and if we had the entry book of hell to hand, we'd be bored reading it, so monotonous is it.

Benito Pérez Galdós (1843–1920) Spanish novelist and playwright. Said by the priest to Polo. *Inferno* (1884)

6 Thank heavens the sun has gone in and I don't have to go out and enjoy it.

Logan Pearsall Smith (1865–1946) US-born British writer. 'Myself', *Afterthoughts* (1931)

7 Perversity is the muse of modern literature.

Susan Sontag (b. 1933) US writer. 'Camus', *Against Interpretation* (1966)

Pessimism

see also Futility, Nihilism, Optimism

1 More than any other time in history, mankind faces a crossroads. One path leads to despair and utter hopelessness. The other, to total extinction. Let us pray we have the wisdom to choose correctly.

Woody Allen (b. 1935) US film actor and director. 'My Speech to the Graduates', *Side Effects* (1980)

2 Pessimism, when you get used to it, is just as agreeable as optimism.

Arnold Bennett (1867–1931) British writer. 'The Slump in Pessimism', *Things That Have Interested Me* (1921)

3 The pessimist is the man who believes things couldn't possibly be worse, to which the optimist replies 'Oh yes they could'.

Vladimir Bukovsky (b. 1942) Russian writer and scientist. *Guardian Weekly* (July 10, 1977)

4 The optimist proclaims that we live in the best of all possible worlds; and the pessimist fears this is true.

James Branch Cabell (1879–1958) US novelist and journalist. *The Silver Stallion* (1926), bk. 4, ch. 26

5 But you have no silver linings without a cloud.

Angela Carter (1940–92) British novelist, essayist, and short-story writer. *Wise Children* (1991)

6 We all agree that pessimism is a mark of superior intellect.

J. K. Galbraith (b. 1908) Canadian-born US economist. *Observer* (April 3, 1977), 'Sayings of the Week'

7 Nothing makes me more pessimistic than the obligation not to be pessimistic.

Eugène Ionesco (1909–94) Romanian-born French playwright. Attrib.

8 If we see light at the end of the tunnel it is the light of an oncoming train.

Robert Lowell (1917–77) US poet. 'Since 1939', *Day by Day* (1977)

9 The world degenerates and grows worse every day . . . The calamities inflicted on Adam . . . were light in comparison with those inflicted on us.

Martin Luther (1483–1546) German theologian and religious reformer. *Commentary on the Book of Genesis* (1545)

10 How many pessimists end up by desiring the things they fear, in order to prove that they are right.

Robert Mallet (b. 1915) French writer and academic. *Apostilles, ou l'Utile et le Futile* (1972)

11 A pessimist is a man who looks both ways before crossing a one-way street.

Laurence J. Peter (1919–90) Canadian writer. *Peter's Quotations* (1977)

12 HAMLET It is not, nor it cannot come to good.

William Shakespeare (1564–1616) English poet and playwright. *Hamlet* (1601), Act 1, Scene 2

13 EDGAR The worst is not
So long as we can say 'This is the worst'.

William Shakespeare (1564–1616) English poet and playwright. *King Lear* (1605–06), Act 4, Scene 1

14 I can endure my own despair,
But not another's hope.

William Walsh (1663–1708) English poet. 'Song: Of All the Torments', *The Poetical Works of William Walsh* (C. Cooke, ed.; 1797)

Philistinism

see also **Ignorance**

1 For this class we have a designation which now has become prety well known, and which we may as well still keep from them, the designation of Philistines.

Matthew Arnold (1822–88) British poet and critic. Referring to the middle class. *Culture and Anarchy* (1869), ch. 3

2 Yes we have. Humbug.

Lord Palmerston (1784–1865) British prime minister. In response to being told there was no English word for the French *sensibilité*. Attrib.

3 Particularly against books the Home Secretary is. If we can't stamp out literature in the country, we can at least stop it being brought in from outside.

Evelyn Waugh (1903–66) British novelist. *Vile Bodies* (1930), ch. 2

4 Listen! There never was an artistic period. There never was an art-loving nation.

James Abbott McNeill Whistler (1834–1903) US painter and etcher. 1885. Attrib.

Philosophy

see also **Being**, **Existence**, **Knowledge**, **Thinking**

1 The goal of philosophy is always the same, to assist men to understand themselves and thus operate in the open, and not wildly, in the dark.

Isaiah Berlin (1909–97) Latvian-born British philosopher and historian of ideas. *Concepts and Categories* (1978)

2 All are lunatics, but he who can analyze his delusion is called a philosopher.

Ambrose Bierce (1842–1914?) US writer and journalist. Epigram. Attrib.

3 Philosophy, like medicine, has plenty of drugs, few good remedies, and hardly any specific cures.

Nicolas Chamfort (1741–94) French writer. *Maximes et Pensées* (1795)

4 There is nothing so absurd but some philosopher has said it.

Cicero (106–43 BC) Roman orator and statesman. *De Divinatione* (44? BC), bk. 2, sect. 58

5 Socrates was the first to call philosophy down from the heavens and to place it in cities, and even to introduce it into homes and compel it to enquire about life and standards and good and ill.

Cicero (106–43 BC) Roman orator and statesman. *Tusculanae Disputationes* (45–44 BC)

6 Each of our principal conceptions, each branch of our knowledge passes successively through three different theoretical states: the theological, or fictitious; the metaphysical, or abstract; and the scientific, or positive.

Auguste Comte (1798–1857) French philosopher and sociologist. Referring to the unifying principle of Positivism. Quoted in *The Essential Comte* (S. Andreski, ed., M. Clarke, tr.; 1974)

7 Every question in philosophy is the mask of another question; and all these masking and masked questions require to be removed and laid aside, until the ultimate but *truly first* question has been reached.

James F. Ferrier (1808–64) British philosopher. 'The Theory of Knowing and Being', *Institutes of Metaphysic* (1854)

8 It often seems that the poet's derisive comment is not unjustified when he says of the philosopher: 'With his nightcaps and the tatters of his dressing-gown he patches up the gaps in the structure of the universe'.

Sigmund Freud (1856–1939) Austrian psychoanalyst. *New Introductory Lectures on Psychoanalysis* (James Strachey, tr.; 1933)

9 A cleric who loses his faith abandons his calling; a philosopher who loses his redefines his subject.

Ernest Gellner (1925–95) British anthropologist and philosopher. *Words and Things* (1968)

10 To a philosopher no circumstance, however trifling, is too minute.

Oliver Goldsmith (1730–74) Irish-born British novelist, playwright, and poet. *A Citizen of the World* (1762), Letter 29

11 What is rational is actual and what is actual is rational. On this conviction the plain man like the philosopher takes his stand, and from it philosophy starts in its study of the universe of mind as well as the universe of nature.

G. W. F. Hegel (1770–1831) German philosopher. 1821. *The Philosophy of Right* (T. M. Knox, tr.; 1952)

12 Philosophy . . . always comes on the scene too late to give it . . . The owl of Minerva spreads its wings only with the falling of the dusk.

G. W. F. Hegel (1770–1831) German philosopher. 1821. The owl of Minerva represents wisdom. *The Philosophy of Right* (T. M. Knox, tr.; 1952)

13 So long as man exists, philosophizing of some sort occurs. Philosophy—what we call philosophy—is metaphysics getting underway, in which philosophy comes to itself and to its explicit tasks.

Martin Heidegger (1889–1976) German philosopher. *What is Metaphysics?* (1929)

14 Be a philosopher; but, amidst all your philosophy, be still a man.

David Hume (1711–76) Scottish philosopher and historian. *A Treatise of Human Nature* (1739–40)

15 I doubt if the philosopher lives, or ever has lived, who could know himself to be heartily despised by a street boy without some irritation.

T. H. Huxley (1825–95) British biologist. *Evolution and Ethics* (1893)

16 It is precisely in knowing its limits that philosophy consists.

Immanuel Kant (1724–1804) German philosopher. *Critique of Pure Reason* (1781)

17 In relation to their systems most systematizers are like a man who builds an enormous castle and lives in a shack close by; they do not live in their own enormous systematic buildings.

Søren Kierkegaard (1813–55) Danish philosopher. *The Journals of Søren Kierkegaard* (Alexander Dru, tr.; 1938)

18 Philosophy does not exist. It is nothing but an hypostatized abstraction.

R. D. Laing (1927–89) Scottish psychiatrist. *Reason and Violence* (1964), ch. 1

19 Philosophy triumphs easily over past evils and future evils; but present evils triumph over it.

François La Rochefoucauld (1613–80) French epigrammatist and moralist. *Reflections, or Sentences and Moral Maxims* (1665), no. 22

20 Humanism must be denounced because it is not sufficiently human.

Emmanuel Levinas (1905–95) Lithuanian-born French philosopher. 1974. *Otherwise than Being, or Beyond Essence* (Alphonso Lingis, tr.; 1981)

21 We set out from real, active men, and on the basis of their real life process we demonstrate the development of the ideological reflexes and echoes of this life process.

Karl Marx (1818–83) German philosopher. Referring to the methodology of historical materialism. *The German Ideology* (1846)

22 Phenomenology . . . is a transcendental philosophy . . . for which the world is always 'already there' before reflection begins.

Maurice Merleau-Ponty (1908–61) French existentialist philosopher. *Phenomenology of Perception* (1945)

23 How charming is divine philosophy!
Not harsh, and crabbed as dull fools suppose,
But musical as is Apollo's lute,
And a perpetual feast of nectared sweets,
Where no crude surfeit reigns.

John Milton (1608–74) English writer. *Comus* (1637), ll. 475–479

24 Philosophy is the childhood of the intellect, and a culture that tries to skip it will never grow up.

Thomas Nagel (b. 1937) Yugoslavian-born US philosopher and educator. *The View from Nowhere* (1986)

25 Gradually it has become clear to me what every great philosophy so far has been: namely, the personal confession of its author and a kind of involuntary and unconscious memoir.

Friedrich Wilhelm Nietzsche (1844–1900) German philosopher and poet. *Beyond Good and Evil* (1886)

26 Philosophy, as I have so far understood and lived it, means living voluntarily among ice and high mountains—seeking out everything strange and questionable in existence, everything so far placed under a ban by morality.

Friedrich Wilhelm Nietzsche (1844–1900) German philosopher and poet. *Ecce Homo* (1888), Preface

27 Philosophy is not bad, either. Unfortunately it's like Russia: full of bogs and often invaded by Germans.

Roger Nimier (1925–62) French writer. *Le Hussard bleu* (1950), pt. 3

28 Why are philosophers intent on forcing others to believe things? Is that a nice way to behave towards someone?

Robert Nozick (b. 1938) US philosopher and political theorist. *Philosophical Explanations* (1981)

29 Philosophy has always gone astray by giving the name of 'I' to the most unlikely things but never to the thing you call 'I' in your daily life.

José Ortega y Gasset (1883–1955) Spanish writer and philosopher. 'In Search of Goethe from Within', *The Worlds of Existentialism* (M. Friedman, ed.; 1964)

30 French rhetorical models are too narrow for the English tradition . . . The Parisian is a provincial when he pretends to speak for the universe.

Camille Paglia (b. 1947) US academic and author. *Sexual Personae* (1990)

31 Not to care for philosophy is to be a true philosopher.

Blaise Pascal (1623–62) French philosopher, mathematician, and physicist. *Pensées* (1669), sect. 6, no. 430

32 A great philosophy is not a flawless philosophy, but a fearless one.

Charles Pierre Péguy (1873–1914) French writer and poet. 'Note sur M. Bergson et la Philosophie Bergsonienne', *Cahiers de la Quinzaine* (April 8–26, 1914)

33 It is a proof of philosophical mediocrity, today, to look for a philosophy.

Pierre Joseph Proudhon (1809–65) French writer and political theorist. *La Révolution sociale* (1852)

34 The chief danger to our philosophy, apart from laziness and woolliness, is *scholasticism*, the essence of which is treating what is vague as if it were precise and trying to fit it into an exact logical category.

Frank Ramsey (1903–30) British mathematical logician. 'The Foundations of Mathematics', *Philosophical Papers* (D. H. Mellor, ed.; 1990)

35 We thought philosophy ought to be patient and unravel people's mental blocks. Trouble with doing that is, once you've unravelled them, their heads fall off.

Frederic Raphael (b. 1931) British writer. 'A Double Life', *The Glittering Prizes* (1976), pt. 3, sect. 2

36 The point of philosophy is to start with something so simple as to seem not worth stating, and to end with something so paradoxical that no one will believe it.

Bertrand Russell (1872–1970) British philosopher and mathematician. *Logic and Knowledge* (1955)

37 It is a great advantage for a system of philosophy to be substantially true.

George Santayana (1863–1952) Spanish-born US philosopher, poet, and novelist. *The Unknowable* (1923)

38 The two main requirements for philosophizing are: firstly, to have the courage not to keep any question back; and secondly, to attain a clear consciousness of anything that goes without saying so as to comprehend it as a problem.

Arthur Schopenhauer (1788–1860) German philosopher. *Parerga and Paralipomena* (1851)

39 HAMLET There are more things in heaven and earth, Horatio,
Than are dreamt of in your philosophy.

William Shakespeare (1564–1616) English poet and playwright. *Hamlet* (1601), Act 1, Scene 5

40 Three-fourths of philosophy and literature is the talk of people trying to convince themselves that they really like the cage they were tricked into entering.

Gary Snyder (b. 1930) US poet, essayist, and translator. October 24, 1956. 'Japan First Time Around', *Earth House Hold* (1969)

41 Lee Chong is . . . an Asiatic planet held to its orbit by the pull of Lao Tze and held away from Lao Tze by the centrifugality of abacus and cash register.

John Steinbeck (1902–68) US novelist. 'Lao Tze' is Laozi, the semi-mythical early Taoist sage. *Cannery Row* (1945), ch. 2

42 There are now-a-days professors of philosophy but not philosophers.

Henry David Thoreau (1817–62) US writer. 'Economy', *Walden, or, Life in the Woods* (1854)

43 The safest general characterization of the European philosophical tradition is that it consists of a series of footnotes to Plato.
A. N. Whitehead (1861–1947) British philosopher and mathematician. *Process and Reality* (1929)

44 Philosophy, as we use the word, is a fight against the fascination which forms of expression exert upon us.
Ludwig Wittgenstein (1889–1951) Austrian philosopher. *The Blue Book* (1958)

45 I am in one sense making propaganda for one style of thinking as opposed to another. I am honestly disgusted with the other.
Ludwig Wittgenstein (1889–1951) Austrian philosopher. 1938. Referring to thinking which is not based on a naïve reliance on scientific certainty. Quoted in *Lectures and Conversations* (Cyril Barnett, ed.; 1966)

Photography

see also **Aesthetics, Art**

1 A photograph is not an accident, it is a concept. It exists at, or before, the moment of exposure of the negative. From that point on to the final print, the process is chiefly one of *craft*.
Ansel Adams (1902–84) US photographer. 'A Personal Credo', *The American Annual of Photography* (1944), vol. 58

2 There are things nobody would see if I didn't photograph them.
Diane Arbus (1923–71) US photographer. Quoted in *Diane Arbus* (1972)

3 For me, there is only one criterion for a good photograph: that it be unforgettable.
Brassaï (1889–1984) Hungarian-born French photographer. 1982. Quoted in 'Guest Speaker: Brassaï. The Three Faces of Paris', *Architectural Digest* (Avis Berman; July 1984)

4 For me the camera is a sketchbook, an instrument of intuition and spontaneity, the master of the instant which—in visual terms—questions and decides simultaneously.
Henri Cartier-Bresson (b. 1908) French photographer, painter, and writer. *Aperture* (1976)

5 In order to 'give a meaning' to the world, one has to feel oneself involved in what he frames through the viewfinder.
Henri Cartier-Bresson (b. 1908) French photographer, painter, and writer. *Aperture* (1976)

6 In a portrait, I'm looking for the silence in somebody.
Henri Cartier-Bresson (b. 1908) French photographer, painter, and writer. *Observer* (May 15, 1994), 'Sayings of the Week'

7 The camera cannot lie. But it can be an accessory to untruth.
Harold Evans (b. 1928) British-born US publisher and newspaper editor. *Pictures on a Page* (1978)

8 The camera is an instrument that teaches people how to see without a camera.
Dorothea Lange (1895–1965) US photographer. *Los Angeles Times* (August 13, 1978)

9 I have for instance among my purchases . . . several original Mona Lisas all painted (according to the Signature) by the great artist Kodak.
Spike Milligan (1918–2002) Indian-born British humorist, writer, and actor. 'Letters to Harry Secombe', *A Dustbin of Milligan* (1963)

10 A photograph is not only an image (as a painting is an image), an interpretation of the real; it is also a trace, something directly stencilled off the real, like a footprint or a death mask.
Susan Sontag (b. 1933) US writer. *On Photography* (1977)

Physics

see also **Mathematics, Science**

1 There is no democracy in physics. We can't say that some second-rate guy has as much right to an opinion as Fermi.
Luis Alvarez (b. 1911) US physicist. Referring to Enrico Fermi, who achieved the first controlled nuclear reaction. Quoted in *The Politics of Pure Science* (D. S. Greenberg; 1967)

2 Give me a firm place to stand, and I will move the earth.
Archimedes (287?–212 BC) Sicilian-born Greek mathematician and inventor. On the action of a lever. *Synagoge* (220? BC), bk. 8, proposition 10, section 11

3 Common sense drives us to accept quantum theory in place of classical physics as more consistent with common sense . . . When they are inspected, the explanations of classical physics fall apart, and are seen to be mere superficial delusions, like film-sets.
P. W. Atkins (b. 1940) British physical chemist. *Creation Revisited: The Origin of Space, Time and the Universe* (1992)

4 Physics becomes in those years the greatest collective work of science—no, more than that, the great collective work of art of the twentieth century.
Jacob Bronowski (1908–74) Polish-born British mathematician, poet, and humanist. Referring to the period around the turn of the century marked by the elucidation of atomic structure and the development of the quantum theory. *The Ascent of Man* (1973), ch. 10

5 A physical theory is not an explanation. It is a system of mathematical propositions, deduced from a small number of principles, which aim to represent as simply, as completely, and as exactly as possible a set of experimental laws.
Pierre Dühem (1861–1916) French physicist and philosopher. Quoted in *The Aim and Structure of Physical Theory* (P. P. Wiener, tr.; 1906)

6 I believe there are 15,747,724,136,275,002,577, 605,653,961,181,555,468,044,717,914,527,116, 709,366,231,425,076,185,631,031,296 protons in the universe and the same number of electrons.
Arthur Eddington (1882–1944) British astronomer and physicist. *The Philosophy of Physical Science* (1939)

7 Einstein said that if quantum mechanics is right, then the world is crazy. Well, Einstein was right. The world is crazy.
Daniel Greenberger, US physicist. Quoted in 'Quantum Philosophy', *Scientific American* (John Horgan; July 1992)

8 MASTER They split the atom by firing particles at it, at 5,500 miles a second.
BOY Good heavens. And they only split it?
Will Hay (1888–1949) British comic actor. 'The Inkstains Theory', *The Fourth Form at St Michael's* (1925)

9 Physics is much too hard for physicists.
David Hilbert (1862–1943) German mathematician and philosopher. Quoted in *Hilbert* (C. Reid; 1970)

10 It's as important an event as would be the transfer of the Vatican from Rome to the New World. The pope of Physics has moved and the United States will now become the center of the natural sciences.

Paul Langevin (1872–1946) French physicist. 1933. Referring to Albert Einstein's departure from Berlin to Princeton University, Princeton, New Jersey (1933). Quoted in *Brighter than a Thousand Suns* (Robert Jungk; 1958)

11 The physicists have known sin; and this is a knowledge which they cannot lose.

J. Robert Oppenheimer (1904–67) US nuclear physicist. Referring to the development of the nuclear bomb. Lecture at Massachusetts Institute of Technology (November 25, 1947)

12 All science is either physics or stamp collecting.

Ernest Rutherford (1871–1937) New Zealand-born British physicist. Quoted in *Rutherford at Manchester* (J. B. Birks; 1962)

13 Classical physics has been superseded by quantum theory: quantum theory is verified by experiments. Experiments must be described in terms of classical physics.

Carl Friedrich von Weizsäcker (b. 1912) German physicist and philosopher. Attrib.

Places

see also **Cities, Nations**

1 A neighborhood is where, when you go out of it, you get beat up.

Anonymous. Quoted in 'Group Dynamics', *America Comes of Middle Age* (Murray Kempton; 1963)

2 This doesn't look like Kansas, Toto.

L. Frank Baum (1856–1919) US writer. Dorothy's remark to her dog Toto on first arriving in the land of Oz, later made famous by the hugely successful musical film *The Wizard of Oz* (1939), starring Judy Garland. *The Wonderful Wizard of Oz* (1900)

3 The most serious charge which can be brought against New England is not Puritanism, but February.

Joseph Wood Krutch (1893–1970) US essayist and naturalist. 'February', *The Twelve Seasons* (1949)

4 If time imposes on us its evolution, place also imposes upon us its reality.

Gamal Abdel Nasser (1918–70) Egyptian statesman. *The Philosophy of the Revolution* (1952)

5 The Park throughout is a single work of art, and as such subject to the primary law of every work of art, namely, that it shall be framed upon a single, noble motive, to which the design of all its parts, in some more or less subtle way, shall be confluent and helpful.

Frederick Law Olmsted (1822–1903) US landscape architect. Referring to Central Park, New York City. Report (co-written with Calvert Vaux; April 28, 1858)

6 Show me a man who cares no more for one place than another, and I will show you in that same person one who loves nothing but himself. Beware of those who are homeless by choice.

Robert Southey (1774–1843) English poet and writer. *The Doctor* (1812), ch. 34

Plagiarism

see also **Imitation**

1 Plagiarism has many advantages over the labor of creation. It is much easier to carry out and less hard work. You can finish twenty works of plagiarism in the time it takes to produce one creative work.

Bernardo Atxaga (b. 1951) Basque writer. *Obabakoak* (Margaret Jull Costa, tr.; 1989)

2 They lard their lean books with the fat of others' works.

Robert Burton (1577–1640) English scholar and churchman. 'Democritus to the Reader', *The Anatomy of Melancholy* (1621)

3 We can say nothing but what hath been said. Our poets steal from Homer . . . Our story-dressers do as much; he that comes last is commonly best.

Robert Burton (1577–1640) English scholar and churchman. 'Democritus to the Reader', *The Anatomy of Melancholy* (1621)

4 Confound those who have said our remarks before us.

Aelius Donatus (*fl.* 4th century) Roman grammarian. *St. Jerome, Commentaries on Ecclesiastes* (4th century), bk. 1

5 Immature poets imitate; mature poets steal.

T. S. Eliot (1888–1965) US-born British poet and playwright. 'Philip Massinger', *The Sacred Wood* (1920)

6 We prefer to believe that the absence of inverted commas guarantees the originality of a thought, whereas it may be merely that the utterer has forgotten its source.

Clifton Fadiman (b. 1904) US writer, editor, and broadcaster. *Any Number Can Play* (1957)

7 We all steal but if we're smart we steal from great directors. Then, we can call it influence.

Krzysztof Kieslowski (1941–96) Polish film director. *7 Days* (May 6, 1990), quoted in *Chambers Film Quotes* (Tony Crawley, ed.; 1991)

8 When you steal from one author, it's plagiarism; if you steal from many, it's research.

Wilson Mizner (1876–1933) US playwright. Quoted in *The Legendary Mizners* (Alva Johnston; 1953)

9 If you must write prose poems
the words you use should be your own
don't plagiarise or take 'on loan'.
There's always someone, somewhere
with a big nose who knows.

Morrissey (b. 1959) British singer and songwriter. 'Cemetery Gates', *The Queen is Dead* (1986)

10 Of all my verse, like not a single line;
But like my title, for it is not mine.
That title from a better man I stole;
Ah, how much better, had I stol'n the whole!

Robert Louis Stevenson (1850–94) Scottish novelist, essayist, and poet. 'Foreword', *Underwoods* (1887)

11 I will be sufficiently rewarded if when telling it to others you will not claim the discovery as your own, but will say it was mine.

Thales (625?–546? BC) Greek philosopher. Quoted in *In Mathematical Circles* (H. Eves; 1969)

Playing

see **Competition, Performance, Sports and Games**

Pleasure

see also **Euphoria, Happiness**

1 One half of the world cannot understand the pleasures of the other.

Jane Austen (1775–1817) British novelist. *Emma* (1816), ch. 9

2 Variety is the soul of pleasure.

Aphra Behn (1640?–89) English novelist and playwright. *The Rover* (1678), pt. 2, Act 1

3 Pleasure after all is a safer guide than either right or duty.
Samuel Butler (1835–1902) British writer and composer. *The Way of All Flesh* (1903), ch. 19

4 Pleasure's a sin, and sometimes sin's a pleasure.
Lord Byron (1788–1824) British poet. *Don Juan* (1819–24), can. 1, st. 133

5 Though sages may pour out their wisdom's treasure,
There is no sterner moralist than Pleasure.
Lord Byron (1788–1824) British poet. *Don Juan* (1819–24), can. 3, st. 65

6 Pleasure is a lovely flame
That's soon converted into dust and ashes
By any wind that blows it.
Pedro Calderón de la Barca (1600–81) Spanish playwright and poet. *Life is a Dream* (1635), Act 3

7 Follow your bliss.
Joseph Campbell (1904–87) US writer, editor, and teacher. 1987. Motto. Published the year after Campbell's death. *The Power of Myth* (1988)

8 Nothing can permanently please, which does not contain in itself the reason why it is so, and not otherwise.
Samuel Taylor Coleridge (1772–1834) British poet. *Biographia Literaria* (1817), ch. 14

9 Pleasure is labour too, and tires as much.
William Cowper (1731–1800) British poet. 'Hope' (1782), l. 20, quoted in *The Works of William Cowper* (Robert Southey, ed.; 1835–37)

10 For present joys are more to flesh and blood
Than a dull prospect of a distant good.
John Dryden (1631–1700) English poet, playwright, and literary critic. *The Hind and the Panther* (1687), pt. 3, ll. 364–365

11 We begin every act of choice and avoidance from pleasure, and it is to pleasure that we return using our experience of pleasure as the criterion of every good thing.
Epicurus (341–270 BC) Greek philosopher. Quoted in *Hellenistic Philosophy* (A. A. Long; 1986)

12 Enjoyment is *not* a goal, it is a feeling that accompanies important ongoing activity.
Paul Goodman (1911–72) US writer, teacher, and psychotherapist. *Growing Up Absurd* (1960)

13 Girls in white dresses with blue satin sashes,
Snowflakes that stay on my nose and eyelashes,
Silver white winters that melt into springs,
These are a few of my favorite things.
Oscar Hammerstein II (1895–1960) US lyricist and librettist. Song lyric. 'My Favorite Things', *The Sound of Music* (music by Richard Rodgers; 1959)

14 The art of pleasing consists in being pleased.
William Hazlitt (1778–1830) British essayist and critic. 'On Manner', *The Round Table* (1817)

15 People must not do things for fun. We are not here for fun. There is no reference to fun in any Act of Parliament.
A. P. Herbert (1890–1971) British writer and politician. 'Is it a Free Country?', *Uncommon Law* (1935)

16 Look not on pleasures as they come, but go.
George Herbert (1593–1633) English poet and cleric. 'The Church Porch', *The Temple: Sacred Poems and Private Ejaculations* (1633), st. 77

17 He that will do anything for his pleasure, must engage himself to suffer all the pains attached to it.
Thomas Hobbes (1588–1679) English philosopher and political thinker. *Leviathan* (1651)

18 Pleasure is very seldom found where it is sought; our brightest blazes of gladness are commonly kindled by unexpected sparks.
Samuel Johnson (1709–84) British lexicographer and writer. *The Idler* (1758)

19 Give me books, fruit, French wine and fine weather and a little music out of doors, played by somebody I do not know.
John Keats (1795–1821) English poet. Letter to Fanny Keats (August 28, 1819), quoted in *Letters of John Keats* (Robert Gittings, ed.; 1970)

20 Pleasure is a knowledge or feeling of perfection, not only in ourselves, but also in others, for in this way some further perfection is aroused in us.
Gottfried Wilhelm Leibniz (1646–1716) German philosopher and mathematician. 'Felicity', *Leibniz: Political Writings* (Patrick Riley, ed., tr.; 1988)

21 Tight boots are one of the greatest goods in the world, for, by making feet hurt, they create an opportunity to enjoy the pleasure of taking off your boots.
Joaquim Maria Machado de Assis (1839–1908) Brazilian novelist and short-story writer. *Epitaph of a Small Winner* (1880)

22 Mirth, admit me of thy crew
To live with her, and live with thee,
In unreproved pleasures free.
John Milton (1608–74) English writer. 'L'Allegro', *Poems of Mr. John Milton* (1645), ll. 38–40

23 I shouldn't be surprised if the greatest rule of all weren't to give pleasure.
Molière (1622–73) French playwright. *La Critique de l'École des Femmes* (1663), Scene 7

24 Great lords have their pleasures, but the people have fun.
Montesquieu (1689–1755) French writer and jurist. *Pensées et Fragments Inédits* (1899), vol. 2, no. 992

25 Surely all God's people, however serious or savage, great or small, like to play; whales and elephants, dancing, humming gnats, and invisibly small mischievous microbes—all are warm with divine radium and must have lots of fun in them.
John Muir (1838–1914) US naturalist and explorer. *The Story of my Boyhood and Youth* (1913), quoted in *John Muir: The Eight Wilderness Discovery Books* (1992)

26 If you admit the Muse of sweet pleasure, whether in lyrics or epic, pleasure and pain will rule as monarchs in your city, instead of the law and that rational principle which is always and by all thought to be the best.
Plato (428?–347? BC) Greek philosopher. *The Republic* (370? BC)

27 Reason's whole pleasure, all the joys of sense,
Lie in three words, health, peace, and competence.
Alexander Pope (1688–1744) English poet. *An Essay on Man* (1733), Epistle 4, ll. 79–80

28 It's delightful, it's delicious, it's de-lovely.
Cole Porter (1893–1964) US songwriter and composer. 'It's De-Lovely', *Red, Hot and Blue* (1936)

29 Pleasure is nothing else but the intermission of pain.
John Selden (1584–1654) English historian, jurist, and politician. 'Pleasure', *Table Talk* (1689)

30 All the things I really like to do are either immoral, illegal, or fattening.
Alexander Woollcott (1887–1943) US writer and critic. Attrib.

31 Pleasures newly found are sweet
When they lie about our feet.

William Wordsworth (1770–1850) English poet. May 1, 1802.
Companion piece to 'To the Small Celandine (Pansies, Lilies,
Kingcups, Daisies)'. *Poems in Two Volumes* (1807), vol. 2,
ll. 1–2

Poetry

see also **Language, Literary Style, Poets, Writing**

1 I live between the fire and the plague
with my language—with this mute universe.

Adonis (b. 1929) Syrian poet. 'The Fall' (1961), quoted in *When
the Words Burn* (John Mikhail Asfour, ed., tr.; 1988)

2 To write poetry after Auschwitz is barbaric.

Theodor Adorno (1903–69) German philosopher, sociologist, and
musicologist. *Prisms* (Samuel and Sherry Weber, trs.; 1967)

3 I think it will be found that the grand style arises
in poetry, when a noble nature, poetically gifted,
treats with simplicity or with severity a serious
subject.

Matthew Arnold (1822–88) British poet and critic. Closing words. 'On
Translating Homer' (1861)

4 Poetry makes nothing happen, it survives
In the valley of its making.

W. H. Auden (1907–73) British poet. 'In Memory of W. B. Yeats'
(1940)

5 The complexities of poetry are destroyed by the
media. In the theatre, spoken language can be
defended and expanded.

Howard Barker (b. 1946) British playwright. *Times* (January 3, 1990)

6 Perhaps only poetry had the strength to rival the
attractions of narcotics, the magnetism of TV, the
excitements of sex, or the ecstasies of destruction.

Saul Bellow (b. 1915) Canadian-born US writer. *The Dean's December*
(1982)

7 Poetry can speak of immortality because it
abandons itself to language, in the belief that
language embraces all experience, past, present,
and future.

John Berger (b. 1926) British novelist, essayist, and art critic. *And Our
Faces, My Heart, Brief as Photos* (1984)

8 Too many people in the modern world view
poetry as a luxury, not a necessity like petrol.
But to me it's the oil of life.

John Betjeman (1906–84) British poet and broadcaster. *Observer*
(1974), 'Sayings of the Year'

9 Poetry is as much a part of the universe as
mathematics and physics. It is not a cleverer
device or recreation, unless the Eternal is clever.

Edmund Blunden (1896–1974) British poet and scholar. Speech on his
election as Professor of Poetry at Oxford University (1966)

10 I have nothing to say, I am saying it, and that is
poetry.

John Cage (1912–92) US composer. Quoted in *Sunday Times*
(September 10, 1972)

11 To search the heart is poetry's lifeblood.

Cai Qijiao (b. 1918) Chinese poet. 'Poetry' (1976), quoted in *The
Red Azalea* (Edward Morin, ed.; 1990)

12 Poetry is a weapon loaded with the future.

Gabriel Celaya (1911–91) Spanish poet. Quoted in *Spain:
Dictatorship to Democracy* (Raymond Carr and Juan Pablo
Fusi Aizpurna; 1979)

13 Poetry will steal death from me.

René Char (1907–88) French poet. 'La Bibliothèque est en Feu', *La
Parole en Archipel* (1961)

14 The poem is not made up of these letters that I
plant like nails, but of the white that remains on
the paper.

Paul Claudel (1868–1955) French writer and diplomat. 'Les Muses',
Cinq Grandes Odes (1910)

15 You don't make a poem with thoughts; you must
make it with words.

Jean Cocteau (1889–1963) French film director, novelist, and playwright.
Sunday Times (October 20, 1963)

16 I wish our clever young poets would remember
my homely definitions of prose and poetry; that
is, prose = words in their best order; poetry = the
best words in the best order.

Samuel Taylor Coleridge (1772–1834) British poet. July 12, 1827.
Table Talk (1835)

17 Poetry is the voice of a poet at its birth, the voice
of a people in its ultimate fulfilment as a
successful and useful work of art.

Guy Davenport (b. 1927) US writer, translator, and educator. 'Where
Poems Come From', *The Geography of the Imagination* (1984)

18 Poetry's unnat'ral; no man ever talked poetry
'cept a beadle on boxin' day.

Charles Dickens (1812–70) British novelist. *The Pickwick Papers*
(1837), ch. 33

19 The poem
feeds upon thought, feeling, impulse,
to breed itself,
a spiritual urgency at the dark ladders leaping.

Robert Duncan (1919–88) US poet. 'Poetry, a Natural Thing', *The
Opening of the Field* (1960), quoted in *The Penguin Book of
American Verse* (Geoffrey Moore, ed.; 1977)

20 I would define the poetic effect as the capacity
that a text displays for continuing to generate
different readings, without ever being completely
consumed.

Umberto Eco (b. 1932) Italian writer and literary scholar. 'Telling the
Process', *Reflections on the Name of the Rose* (William
Weaver, tr.; 1983)

21 These fragments I have shored against my ruin.

T. S. Eliot (1888–1965) US-born British poet and playwright. 'What the
Thunder Said', *The Waste Land* (1922)

22 Because it could do it well
the poem wants to glorify suffering.
I mistrust it.

Roy Fisher (b. 1930) British poet. 'It is Writing', *Poems, 1955–87*
(1988)

23 Poetry is what gets lost in translation. It is also
what is lost in interpretation.

Robert Frost (1874–1963) US poet. Quoted in *Robert Frost: A
Backward Look* (Louis Untermeyer; 1964), ch. 1

24 Poetry is the language in which man explores his
own amazement.

Christopher Fry (b. 1907) British playwright. *Time* (April 3, 1950)

25 If Galileo had said in verse that the world
moved, the Inquisition might have let him alone.

Thomas Hardy (1840–1928) British novelist and poet. Quoted in *The
Later Years of Thomas Hardy, 1892–1928* (Florence Hardy;
1930)

26 The function of language in much modern
poetry, and in much poetry admired by moderns,
is to talk about itself to itself.

Seamus Heaney (b. 1939) Irish poet. 'The Fire i' the Flint',
Preoccupations: Selected Prose 1968–78 (1980)

27 If a line of poetry strays into my memory, my
skin bristles so that the razor ceases to act.

A. E. Housman (1859–1936) British poet and classicist. Leslie Stephen
Lecture, University of Cambridge (May 9, 1933)

28 You might not think that these two interests, capturing animals and writing poems, have much in common. But the more I think back the more sure I am that with me the two interests have been one interest.

Ted Hughes (1930–98) British writer and poet. *Poetry in the Making* (1967)

29 If Poetry comes not as naturally as Leaves to a tree it had better not come at all.

John Keats (1795–1821) English poet. Countering his publisher's attempts to get him to amend *Endymion*. Letter to John Taylor (February 27, 1818), quoted in *Letters of John Keats* (H. E. Rollins, ed.; 1958), vol. 1

30 When power narrows the areas of man's concern, poetry reminds him of the richness and diversity of his existence.

John Fitzgerald Kennedy (1917–63) US president. Address at the Dedication of the Robert Frost Library (October 26, 1963)

31 Prose on certain occasions can bear a great deal of poetry: on the other hand, poetry sinks and swoons under a moderate weight of prose.

Walter Savage Landor (1775–1864) British poet and writer. 'Archdeacon Hare and Walter Landor', *Imaginary Conversations* (1853)

32 Those blessed structures, plot and rhyme—why are they no help to me now
I want to make
something imagined, not recalled?

Robert Lowell (1917–77) US poet. 'Epilogue', *Day by Day* (1977)

33 A poem should be wordless
As the flight of birds.

Archibald MacLeish (1892–1982) US poet and educator. 'Ars Poetica' (1926)

34 To *name* an object is to destroy three-quarters of the pleasure given by a poem, which is gained little by little: to *suggest* it, that is the ideal.

Stéphane Mallarmé (1842–98) French poet. *Réponses à des Enquêtes: Sur l'Évolution Littéraire* (1891)

35 The essential elements of our poetry will be courage, audacity, and revolt. We wish to exalt too aggressive movement, feverish insomnia, running the perilous leap, the cuff, the blow.

Filippo Tommaso Marinetti (1876–1944) Italian writer, poet, and political activist. 'Founding and First Manifesto of Futurism' (1909), quoted in *Cubism, Futurism and Constructivism* (J. M. Nash; 1974)

36 Today's poetry—is the poetry of strife.
Each word must, like a soldier in the army, be made of meat that is healthy, meat that is red! Those who have it—join us!

Vladimir Mayakovsky (1893–1930) Russian poet and playwright. 'We Also Want Meat!' (Helen Segall, tr.; 1914), quoted in *The Ardis Anthology of Russian Futurism* (Ellendea Proffer and Carl R. Proffer, eds.; 1980)

37 Poetry is a comforting piece of fiction set to more or less lascivious music.

H. L. Mencken (1880–1956) US journalist, critic, and editor. 'The Poet and his Art', *Prejudices* (1922)

38 The thing that makes poetry different from all of the other arts . . . is you're using language, which is what you use for everything else—telling lies and selling socks, advertising, and conducting law. Whereas we don't write little concerts or paint little pictures.

W. S. Merwin (b. 1927) US poet and writer. Said on receiving the $100,000 Tanning Prize for poetry. Quoted in *Washington Post* (September 30, 1994)

39 Yea, marry, now it is somewhat, for now it is rhyme; before, it was neither rhyme nor reason.

Thomas More (1478–1535) English statesman and writer. On reading an unremarkable book recently rendered into verse by a friend of his. Quoted in *Apophthegms New and Old* (Francis Bacon; 1625)

40 I've never read a political poem that's accomplished anything. Poetry makes things happen, but rarely what the poet wants.

Howard Nemerov (1920–91) US poet, novelist, and critic. *International Herald Tribune* (October 14, 1988)

41 Peace goes into the making of a poem as flour goes into the making of bread.

Pablo Neruda (1904–73) Chilean poet and diplomat. *Memoirs* (1974)

42 A poem is energy transferred from where the poet got it . . . by way of the poem itself to, all the way over to, the reader.

Charles Olson (1910–70) US poet. Quoted in *Norton Anthology of American Literature* (Nina Baym, ed.; 1998)

43 I have not and never did have any motive of poetry
But to achieve clarity.

George Oppen (1908–84) US poet. 'Route', *Of Being Numerous* (1968), quoted in *The Norton Anthology of American Literature* (Nina Baym, ed.; 1998), vol. 2

44 Poetry, I will swear by
You, and end up croaking:
You are not a posture of the liquid-throated,
You are summer, seated in a third-class coach;
A suburb, not a refrain.

Boris Pasternak (1890–1960) Russian poet and novelist. Quoted in 'Pasternak's Mission', *Pasternak* (Yury Tynyanov and Angela Livingston, eds.; Donald Davie, tr.; 1969)

45 It is the monster hiding in a child's dark room, it is the scar on a beautiful person's face. It is the last blade of grass being picked from the city park.

Brian Patten (b. 1946) British poet and playwright. Referring to poetry. 'Prose poem towards a definition of itself', *Grinning Jack* (1990)

46 And he, whose fustian's so sublimely bad,
It is not poetry, but prose run mad.

Alexander Pope (1688–1744) English poet. *Epistle to Dr. Arbuthnot* (1735), ll. 187–188

47 Poetry is the revelation of a feeling that the poet believes to be interior and personal but which the reader recognizes as his own.

Salvatore Quasimodo (1901–68) Italian poet and critic. *New York Times* (May 14, 1960)

48 A sonnet is a moment's monument—
Memorial from the Soul's eternity
To one dead deathless hour.

Dante Gabriel Rossetti (1828–82) British painter and poet. 'Introduction', *The House of Life* (1881)

49 What is poetry? . . . The suggestion, by the imagination, of noble grounds for the noble emotions.

John Ruskin (1819–1900) British art critic, writer, and reformer. *Modern Painters* (1856), vol. 3, pt. 4, ch. 1

50 Not marble, nor the gilded monuments
Of princes, shall outlive this powerful rhyme.

William Shakespeare (1564–1616) English poet and playwright. Sonnet 55 (1609)

51 quite simply a poem shd fill you up with something
cd make you swoon, stop in yr tracks, change yr mind, or make it up. a poem shd happen to you like cold water or a kiss.

Ntozake Shange (b. 1948) US poet, novelist, essayist, and playwright. 'i talk to myself', *nappy edges* (1978)

52 Poetry proves again and again that any single overall theory of anything doesn't work. Poetry is always the cat concert under the window of the room in which the official version of reality is being written.

Charles Simic (b. 1938) Yugoslav-born US poet and educator. Quoted in *The Best of the Best American Poetry 1988–97* (Harold Bloom, ed.; 1997)

53 Poetry is the supreme fiction, madame.
Take the moral law and make a nave of it
And from the nave build haunted heaven.

Wallace Stevens (1879–1955) US poet. 1923. 'A High-Toned Old Christian Woman', *The Collected Poems of Wallace Stevens* (1954), ll. 1–3

54 A poem is never finished; it's always an accident that puts a stop to it—that is to say, gives it to the public.

Paul Valéry (1871–1945) French poet and philosopher. *Littérature* (1930)

55 Poetry is to prose as dancing is to walking.

John Wain (1925–94) British novelist and poet. BBC Radio broadcast (January 13, 1976)

56 Because Rhyme remains the parentheses of palms shielding a candle's tongue, it is the language's desire to enclose the loved world in its arms.

Derek Walcott (b. 1930) St. Lucian poet and playwright. *Omeros* (1990)

57 Poetry . . . is perfection's sweat but which must seem as fresh as the raindrops on a statue's bow.

Derek Walcott (b. 1930) St. Lucian poet and playwright. *The New York Times* (December 8, 1992)

58 The fate of poetry is to fall in love with the world, in spite of History.

Derek Walcott (b. 1930) St. Lucian poet and playwright. *The New York Times* (December 8, 1992)

59 The process of poetry is one of excavation and of self-discovery.

Derek Walcott (b. 1930) St. Lucian poet and playwright. *The New York Times* (December 8, 1992)

60 So much depends
upon
a red wheel
barrow glazed with rain
water
beside the white
chickens.

William Carlos Williams (1883–1963) US poet, novelist, and physician. 'The Red Wheelbarrow' (1923)

61 Poetry is the spontaneous overflow of powerful feelings: it takes its origin from emotion recollected in tranquillity.

William Wordsworth (1770–1850) English poet. *Lyrical Ballads* (2nd ed.; 1800), Preface

62 Out of the quarrel with others we make rhetoric; out of the quarrel with ourselves we make poetry.

W. B. Yeats (1865–1939) Irish poet and playwright. 'Anima Hominis', *Essays* (1924), sect. 5

Poets

see also **Poetry**, **Writers**

1 But in the room of the poet in disgrace
Fear and the muse keep watch in turn.
The night presses on,
Which knows no dawn.

Anna Akhmatova (1888–1966) Russian poet. Dedicated to the poet Osip Mandelstam in exile. 'Voronezh' (Peter Norman, tr.; March 4, 1936), quoted in *The Akhmatova Journals: 1938–41* (Lydia Chukovskaya; 1989), no. 42

2 It is a sad fact about our culture that a poet can earn much more money writing or talking about his art than he can by practising it.

W. H. Auden (1907–73) British poet. *The Dyer's Hand* (1962), Foreword

3 The poet is like the prince of the clouds,
Who rides out the tempest and laughs at the archer.
But when he is exiled on the ground, amidst the clamour,
His giant's wings prevent him from walking.

Charles Baudelaire (1821–67) French poet. 'L'Albatross', *Les Fleurs du Mal* (1857)

4 VLADIMIR You should have been a poet.
ESTRAGON I was. (*Gestures towards his rags.*) Isn't that obvious.

Samuel Beckett (1906–89) Irish playwright, novelist, and poet. *Waiting for Godot* (1954), Act 1

5 Modern poets had more wonderful material than Homer or Dante. What they didn't have was a sane and steady idealization. To be Christian was impossible, to be pagan also. That left you-know-what.

Saul Bellow (b. 1915) Canadian-born US writer. *Humboldt's Gift* (1975)

6 It is not possible for a poet . . . to protect himself from the tragic elements in human life . . . Illness, old age, and death—subjects as ancient as humanity—these are the subjects that the poet must speak of very nearly from the first moment that he begins to speak.

Louise Bogan (1897–1970) US poet and critic. *Selected Criticism* (1958)

7 Poets and painters are outside the class system, or rather they constitute a special class of their own, like the circus people and the gipsies.

Gerald Brenan (1894–1987) Maltese-born British writer and novelist. 'Writing', *Thoughts in a Dry Season* (1978)

8 All the journeys he took—through lands, caves of the psyche, doctrines, creeds—served not so much to improve his argument as to expand his diction.

Joseph Brodsky (1940–96) Russian-born US poet and writer. Referring to W. H. Auden. 'To Please a Shadow', *Less Than One* (1986)

9 The great Metaquizzical poet.

Lord Byron (1788–1824) British poet. Referring to William Wordsworth. Letter to John Murray (January 19, 1821)

10 Or like a poet woo the moon,
Riding an armchair for my steed,
And with a flashing pen harpoon
Terrific metaphors of speed.

Roy Campbell (1901–57) South African-born poet, translator, and journalist. 'The Festivals of Flight', *Adamaster* (1930)

11 The poet lives by exaggeration and makes himself known through misunderstandings.

Elias Canetti (1905–94) Bulgarian-born writer. *The Agony of Flies* (1992)

12 A poet without love were a physical and metaphysical impossibility.

Thomas Carlyle (1795–1881) Scottish historian and essayist. 'Burns', *Edinburgh Review* (1828)

13 How does the poet speak to men with power, but by being still more a man than they?

Thomas Carlyle (1795–1881) Scottish historian and essayist. 'Burns', *Edinburgh Review* (1828)

14 You explain nothing, O poet, but thanks to you all things become explicable.

Paul Claudel (1868–1955) French writer and diplomat. *La Ville* (1890), Act 1

15 A true poet does not bother to be poetical. Nor does a nursery gardener scent his roses.

Jean Cocteau (1889–1963) French film director, novelist, and playwright. *Professional Secrets* (1922)

16 No man was ever yet a great poet, without being at the same time a profound philosopher.

Samuel Taylor Coleridge (1772–1834) British poet. *Biographia Literaria* (1817), ch. 15

17 A young Apollo, golden-haired,
Stands dreaming on the verge of strife,
Magnificently unprepared
For the long littleness of life.

Frances Cornford (1886–1960) British poet. 1910. Referring to Rupert Brooke. 'Youth', *Collected Poems* (1954)

18 He understood . . . the regeneration of truths which poetry effects in the face of the intellectual algebra which tends to conventionalize them.

Benedetto Croce (1866–1952) Italian philosopher, historian, and politician. Referring to Percy Bysshe Shelley. *The Defence of Poetry* (1933), quoted in *The Great Critics* (James Harry Smith and Edd Winfield Parks, eds.; 1951)

19 Tempt me no more; for I
Have known the lightning's hour,
The poet's inward pride,
The certainty of power.

Cecil Day-Lewis (1904–72) Irish-born British writer. *The Magnetic Mountain* (1933), pt. 3

20 But the poet's job is, after all, to translate God's poem (or is it the Fiend's?) into words.

Babette Deutsch (1895–1982) US writer and poet. 'Poetry at the Mid-Century', *The Writer's Book* (Helen Hull, ed.; 1950)

21 Ovid, the soft philosopher of love.

John Dryden (1631–1700) English poet, playwright, and literary critic. *Love Triumphant* (1694), Act 2, Scene 1

22 No poet, no artist of any sort, has his complete meaning alone. His significance, his appreciation is the appreciation of his relation to the dead poets and artists.

T. S. Eliot (1888–1965) US-born British poet and playwright. 'Tradition and the Individual Talent' (1920)

23 I am the poet, prying locksmith of invisible things
I am the angel of inquisition, steering life's funerals.

Necip Fazıl (1905–83) Turkish poet. 'Poet', *Modern Turkish Poetry* (Feyyaz Kayacan Fergar, ed.; 1992), ll. 1–2

24 Constantly risking absurdity
and death
whenever he performs
above the heads
of his audience
the poet like an acrobat
climbs on rime
to a high wire of his own making.

Lawrence Ferlinghetti (b. 1919) US poet. 'A Coney Island of the Mind' (1958), quoted in *The Penguin Book of American Verse* (Geoffrey Moore, ed.; 1977)

25 It was simple. She had come
to flesh out the memory of the poet
whose body was never found.

Carolyn Forché, US poet. Referring to a refugee returning to her homeland in El Salvador after the civil war (1979–80). 'The Island', *The Country Between Us* (1981)

26 In a century of zeppelins and stupid deaths I sob before my piano, dreaming in a Handelian mist, and I create verses very much my own, singing the same to Christ as to Buddha, to Mohammed, and to Pan . . . Why fight against the flesh when the terrifying problem of the spirit exists?

Federico García Lorca (1899–1936) Spanish poet and playwright. Letter to a friend (1918), quoted in 'Epistalario', *A Dream of Life* (Leslie Stainton; 1998), vol. 1

27 The poet is the medium
of Nature
who explains her grandeur
by means of words.

Federico García Lorca (1899–1936) Spanish poet and playwright. 1918. From a poem on the poet written as an inscription in a copy of Antonio Machado Ruiz's *Campos de Castilla* (1912), belonging to his friend Antonio Gallego Búrin. Quoted in *Collected Poems* (Christopher Maurer, ed.; 1990)

28 He repeated until his dying day that there was no one with more common sense, no stonecutter more obstinate, no manager more lucid or dangerous, than a poet.

Gabriel García Márquez (b. 1928) Colombian novelist. *Love in the Time of Cholera* (1985)

29 When the brave poet is afraid to die
his best poem is silence!

Ghazi al-Gosaibi (b. 1940) Saudi Arabian poet. 'Silence', *Modern Arabic Poetry* (Salma Khadra Jayyusi, ed.; 1987), ll. 12–13

30 Soaring falcon, noble Poet, come to my aid: bear me aloft to the realm of more luminous truths: one's true homeland is not the country of one's birth: man is not a tree: help me to live without roots: ever on the move: my only sustenance your nourishing language.

Juan Goytisolo (b. 1931) Spanish novelist and essayist. *Count Julian* (1970)

31 To be a poet is a condition rather than a profession.

Robert Graves (1895–1985) British poet and novelist. 1946. Reply to questionnaire. 'The Cost of Letters', *Horizon* (September 1946)

32 Shelley and Keats were the last English poets who were at all up to date in their chemical knowledge.

J. B. S. Haldane (1892–1964) British geneticist. *Daedalus, or, Science and the Future* (1924)

33 He had a fire in his eye, a fever in his blood, a maggot in his brain, a hectic flutter in his speech, which mark out the philosophic fanatic.

William Hazlitt (1778–1830) British essayist and critic. Referring to Percy Bysshe Shelley. 'On Criticism', *Table Talk* (1821–22)

34 Although at least one spirit of the age will probably be discernible in a poet's work, he should not turn his brain into a butterfly net to pursue it.

Seamus Heaney (b. 1939) Irish poet. 'Canticles to the Earth', *Preoccupations: Selected Prose 1968–78* (1980)

35 Many brave men lived before Agamemnon's time; but they are all, unmourned and unknown, covered by the long night, because they lack their sacred poet.

Horace (65–8 BC) Roman poet. 23? BC. *Odes* (13? BC), bk. 4, no. 9, l. 25

36 My feet, so deep in the earth!
My wings, so far into the heavens!
—And so much pain
in the heart torn between!

Juan Ramón Jiménez (1881–1958) Spanish poet. 'My Feet So Deep in the Earth', *Roots and Wings: Poetry from Spain, 1900–75* (Hardie St. Martin, ed.; 1976)

37 Milton, Madam, was a genius that could cut a Colossus from a rock; but could not carve heads upon cherry-stones.

Samuel Johnson (1709–84) British lexicographer and writer. June 13, 1784. When Miss Hannah More had wondered why Milton could write the epic *Paradise Lost* (1667) but only very poor sonnets. Quoted in *Life of Samuel Johnson* (James Boswell; 1791)

38 A Poet is the most unpoetical of anything in existence, because he has no Identity—he is continually infor(ming?)—and filling some other Body.

John Keats (1795–1821) English poet. Letter to Richard Woodhouse (October 27, 1818), quoted in *Letters of John Keats* (H. E. Rollins, ed.; 1958), vol. 1

39 On the day the world becomes good, the poet will cease to suffer, and not before; but at the same time he will also cease to be a poet.

Halldór Laxness (1902–98) Icelandic novelist. *World Light* (1969)

40 Here with a black suit and black briefcase; in the brief,
an abomination, Possum's hommage to Milton.

Robert Lowell (1917–77) US poet. According to Robert Lowell, Ezra Pound's assessment of T. S. Eliot ('Possum'), in St. Elizabeth's Hospital for the criminally insane (1946–58). 'Ezra Pound', *History* (1973), quoted in *The Penguin Book of American Verse* (Geoffrey Moore, ed.; 1977)

41 The great philosophers are poets who believe in the reality of their own poems.

Antonio Machado (1875–1939) Spanish poet and playwright. *Juan de Mairena* (1943)

42 Friends, carve a monument
out of dream stone
for the poet in the Alhambra,
over a fountain where the grieving water
shall say forever:
the crime was in Granada, his Granada.

Antonio Machado (1875–1939) Spanish poet and playwright. 1936. Referring to Federico García Lorca, who was assassinated by nationalists near Granada in 1936. 'The Crime Was in Granada', *Selected Poems* (Alan S. Trueblood, tr.; 1982), ll. 34–39

43 The courage of the poet is to keep ajar the door that leads to madness.

Christopher Darlington Morley (1890–1957) US writer and journalist. *Inward Ho* (1923)

44 An archaeologist of morning.

Charles Olson (1910–70) US poet. Referring to his own preoccupation with the origin of things. Quoted in *Norton Anthology of American Literature* (Nina Baym, ed.; 1998)

45 The poet begins where the man ends. The man's lot is to live his human life, the poet's to invent what is nonexistent.

José Ortega y Gasset (1883–1955) Spanish writer and philosopher. *The Dehumanization of Art* (1925)

46 All the poet can do today is to warn. That is why the true Poets must be truthful.

Wilfred Owen (1893–1918) British poet. 1918. 'Preface', *Poems* (1920)

47 Like a pilot, like a planet,
don't give way to drowsiness, poet.
You are the pledge we give to eternity
and so the slave of every second.

Boris Pasternak (1890–1960) Russian poet and novelist. Written recovering from a stroke. 'Night' (Craig Raine and Ann Pasternak Slater, trs.; 1956), ll. 37–40, quoted in *Leopard II: Turning the Page* (Christopher MacLehose, ed.; 1993)

48 I make a pact with you, Walt Whitman
I have detested you long enough
It was you that broke the new wood,
Now is a time for carving
We have one sap and one root
Let there be commerce between us.

Ezra Pound (1885–1972) US poet, translator, and critic. 'A Pact', *Lustra* (1916)

49 I say one must be a *seer*, make oneself *seer*. The poet makes himself a *seer* by an immense, long, deliberate *disordering* of the senses.

Arthur Rimbaud (1854–91) French poet. Letter to Paul Demeny (May 15, 1871), quoted in *Lettres du Voyant: 13 et 15 Mai 1871* (Gérald Schaeffer, ed.; 1975)

50 I mean they're not *real* poets. They're just people that write poems and get published and anthologized all over the place, but they're not *poets*.

J. D. Salinger (b. 1919) US novelist. Said by Franny, referring to the staff of her English department. 'Franny', *Franny and Zooey* (1961)

51 Popular poets are the parish priests of the Muse, retailing her ancient divinations to a long since converted public.

George Santayana (1863–1952) Spanish-born US philosopher, poet, and novelist. 'Reason in Art', *The Life of Reason* (1905–06)

52 In me the tiger sniffs the rose.

Siegfried Sassoon (1886–1967) British poet and writer. 'VII', *The Heart's Journey* (1928)

53 THESEUS The poet's eye, in a fine frenzy rolling,
Doth glance from heaven to earth, from earth to heaven;
And as imagination bodies forth
The forms of things unknown, the poet's pen
Turns them to shapes, and gives to airy nothing
A local habitation and a name.

William Shakespeare (1564–1616) English poet and playwright. *A Midsummer Night's Dream* (1595–96), Act 5, Scene 1

54 Milton's Devil as a moral being is far superior to his God . . . Milton has so far violated the popular creed . . . as to have alleged no superiority of moral virtue to his God over his Devil. And this bold neglect of direct moral purpose is the most decisive proof of Milton's genius.

Percy Bysshe Shelley (1792–1822) English poet. *A Defence of Poetry* (1821), quoted in *Essays, Letters from Abroad, Translations and Fragments* (Mrs. Shelley, ed.; 1840)

55 Poets are . . . the trumpets which sing to battle
and feel not what they inspire . . . Poets are the
unacknowledged legislators of the world.
Percy Bysshe Shelley (1792–1822) English poet. *A Defence of Poetry*
(1821), quoted in *Essays, Letters from Abroad, Translations
and Fragments* (Mrs. Shelley, ed.; 1840)

56 He hath awakened from the dream of life—
'Tis we, who lost in stormy visions, keep
With phantoms an unprofitable strife,
And in mad trance, strike with our spirit's knife
Invulnerable nothings.
Percy Bysshe Shelley (1792–1822) English poet. An elegy on the death
of John Keats. *Adonais* (1821), st. 23

57 The first time I saw Dylan Thomas I felt as if
Rubens had suddenly taken it into his head to
paint a youthful Silenus.
Edith Sitwell (1887–1964) British poet, critic, and writer. *Taken Care
Of: An Autobiography* (1965)

58 For poets, language is a maze, not a way
forward.
Song Lin (b. 1959) Chinese writer. 'Prison Letter' (1991)

59 The poet is the priest of the invisible.
Wallace Stevens (1879–1955) US poet. 'Adagia', *Opus Posthumous*
(1957)

60 A poet, starving in a garret,
Conning old topics like a parrot,
Invokes his mistress and his muse,
And stays at home for want of shoes.
Jonathan Swift (1667–1745) Irish writer and clergyman. 'To Stella Who
Collected and Transcribed his Poems' (1723?)

61 He is a writer of something occasionally like
English, and a man of something occasionally
like genius.
Algernon Charles Swinburne (1837–1909) British poet. Referring to
Walt Whitman. 'Whitmania' (1894)

62 Blake is the only poet who sees all temporal
things under a form of eternity . . . Where other
poets use reality as a spring-board into space, he
uses it as a foothold on his return from flight.
Arthur Symons (1865–1945) British poet and literary critic. Referring to
William Blake. *William Blake* (1907)

63 The poet may be used as the barometer, but let
us not forget he is also part of the weather.
Lionel Trilling (1905–75) US literary critic. 'The Sense of the Past',
The Liberal Imagination (1950)

64 The Poet of Immortal Youth.
Henry Van Dyke (1852–1933) US clergyman, poet, and theologian.
Referring to John Keats. Attrib.

65 It would be sacrilege to put a name there—it
would be like putting a name on the universe . . .
at most I am only a mouthpiece.
Walt Whitman (1819–92) US poet. Referring to the 1855 edition of
Leaves of Grass, which he initially published anonymously.
Attrib.

66 I would venture to guess that Anon, who wrote
so many poems without signing them, was often
a woman.
Virginia Woolf (1882–1941) British novelist and critic. *A Room of
One's Own* (1929)

67 That mighty orb of song, the divine Milton.
William Wordsworth (1770–1850) English poet. 'The Wanderer', *The
Excursion* (1814), bk. 1, ll. 249–250

68 A poet's autobiography is his poetry. Anything
else is just a footnote.
Yevgeny Yevtushenko (b. 1933) Russian poet. Attrib.

Poland

see **Europe, European Countries**

Political Insults

see also **Insults, Politicians**

1 The Mephistopheles of politics.
Henry Adams (1838–1918) US historian. Referring to Aaron Burr,
vice president to Thomas Jefferson (1800), who later killed his
main political opponent, the federalist Alexander Hamilton, in
a duel (1804). *History of the United States during the
Administrations of Thomas Jefferson and James Madison*
(1888–91), vol. 2

2 The doughty knight of the stuffed cravat.
John Quincy Adams (1767–1848) US president. Referring to the US
statesman Thomas Hart Benton. Quoted in *The First Ten*
(Alfred Steinberg; 1967)

3 That infernal creature who is the curse of all the
human race becomes every day more and more
abominable.
Alexander I (1777–1825) Russian monarch. Referring to Napoleon I.
Letter to his sister Catherine (January 5, 1812)

4 TO HELL WITH YOU. OFFENSIVE LETTER FOLLOWS.
Anonymous. Telegram to Sir Alec Douglas-Home

5 Lord George Brown drunk is a better man than
the prime minister sober.
Anonymous. *Times* (March 6, 1976)

6 The sort of woman who, if accidentally locked in
alone in the National Gallery, would start
rearranging the pictures.
Anonymous. Referring to Margaret Thatcher.

7 The only man who has ever run away from the
circus to become an accountant.
Anonymous. Referring to John Major, British prime minister
(1990–97), whose father had once been a trapeze artist.

8 Paddy Ashdown is the first trained killer to be a
party leader . . . Mrs Thatcher being self-taught.
Gilbert Archer, Scottish business executive. Paddy Ashdown, leader of
the Liberal Democrat Party (1988–99), was previously a
member of the Royal Marines. Remark (1992)

9 It is fitting that we should have buried the
Unknown Prime Minister by the side of the
Unknown Soldier.
Herbert Henry Asquith (1852–1928) British prime minister. Said at
Bonar Law's funeral at Westminster Abbey. Remark
(November 5, 1923), quoted in *The Unknown Prime Minister*
(Robert Blake; 1955)

10 Lloyd George could not see a belt without hitting
below it.
Margot Asquith (1865–1945) British political hostess and writer. 1936.
Quoted in 'Margot Oxford', *Listener* (Lady Violet Bonham
Carter; June 11, 1953)

11 The voice we heard was that of Mr Churchill but
the mind was that of Lord Beaverbrook.
Clement Attlee (1883–1967) British politician. June 5, 1945. Implying
that Winston Churchill's words were influenced by the press
baron Lord Beaverbrook, who owned *Express* newspapers
and *The London Evening Standard*. Quoted in Speech (BBC
radio), *A Prime Minister Remembers* (Francis Williams; 1961)

12 No man has come so near our definition of a
constitutional statesman—the powers of a first-
rate man and the creed of a second-rate man.
Walter Bagehot (1826–77) British economist and journalist. Referring to
Sir Robert Peel. 'The Character of Sir Robert Peel', *National
Review* (1856)

13 I served with Jack Kennedy. I knew Jack Kennedy. Jack Kennedy was a friend of mine. Senator, you're no Jack Kennedy.

Lloyd Bentsen (b. 1921) US politician. Replying to Dan Quayle's claim, in a television debate, that he had as much experience of Congress as Kennedy did on accession to the presidency. Remark (1988)

14 He is a man suffering from petrified adolescence.

Aneurin Bevan (1897–1960) Welsh-born British politician. Referring to Winston Churchill. Quoted in *Aneurin Bevan* (Vincent Brome; 1953), ch. 11

15 Listening to a speech by Chamberlain is like paying a visit to Woolworths; everything in its place and nothing over sixpence.

Aneurin Bevan (1897–1960) Welsh-born British politician. 1937. Referring to Neville Chamberlain. Quoted in *Aneurin Bevan* (Michael Foot; 1973), vol. 1, ch. 8

16 And he adores his maker.

John Bright (1811–89) British politician. Comment when informed that Disraeli should be admired for being a self-made man. Attrib.

17 My dog Millie knows more about foreign policy than these two bozos.

George Bush (b. 1924) US president. Referring to Bill Clinton and Al Gore, his Democratic opponents in the 1992 US presidential election. Remark (October 1992)

18 I can think of no better step to signalize the inauguration of the National Health service than that a person who so obviously needs psychiatric attention should be among the first of its patients.

Winston Churchill (1874–1965) British prime minister and writer. 1948. Referring to Aneurin Bevan who introduced the National Health Service (1948). Speech (July, 1948)

19 And you, madam, are ugly. But I shall be sober in the morning.

Winston Churchill (1874–1965) British prime minister and writer. Replying to the MP Bessie Braddock, who told him he was drunk. Attrib.

20 Abuse is in order, but it is best if it is supported by argument.

Robin Day (1923–2000) British journalist and broadcaster. *Election Call* BBC Radio (1987)

21 If a traveller were informed that such a man was leader of the House of Commons, he may well begin to comprehend how the Egyptians worshipped an insect.

Benjamin Disraeli (1804–81) British prime minister and writer. 1852. Referring to Lord John Russell. Attrib.

22 A semi-house-trained polecat.

Michael Foot (b. 1913) British politician and writer. Referring to Norman Tebbit. Speech in Parliament, quoted in *Hansard* (March 2, 1978)

23 He was the only man I knew who could make a curse sound like a caress.

Michael Foot (b. 1913) British politician and writer. Referring to Aneurin Bevan. *Aneurin Bevan 1897—1945* (1962), vol. 1

24 Attila the Hen.

Clement Freud (b. 1924) British broadcaster and writer. Referring to Margaret Thatcher. *News Quiz* (BBC Radio).

25 She approaches the problems of our country with all the one-dimensional subtlety of a comic-strip.

Denis Healey (b. 1917) British statesman. Referring to Margaret Thatcher. Speech to Parliament, *Hansard* (May 22, 1979)

26 Like being savaged by a dead sheep.

Denis Healey (b. 1917) British statesman. Referring to the criticism of his budget proposals by Conservative politician Geoffrey Howe. Speech to Parliament, *Hansard* (June 14, 1978)

27 For the past few months she has been charging about like some bargain-basement Boadicea.

Denis Healey (b. 1917) British statesman. November 1982. Referring to the behaviour of prime minister Margaret Thatcher during the Falklands War (1982). *Observer* (November 7, 1982), 'Sayings of the Week'

28 Ordinarily he is insane, but he has lucid moments when he is only stupid.

Heinrich Heine (1797–1856) German poet. A comment on Savoye, the French ambassador in Frankfurt. Remark (1848), attrib.

29 Kissinger brought peace to Vietnam the same way Napoleon brought peace to Europe: by losing.

Joseph Heller (1923–99) US novelist. Referring to Henry Kissinger and Napoleon I. *Good as Gold* (1979), ch. 7

30 Well, he seemed such a nice old gentleman, I thought I would give him my autograph as a souvenir.

Adolf Hitler (1889–1945) Austrian-born German dictator. Referring to Neville Chamberlain. Attrib.

31 He is the apostle of class-hatred, the founder of a Satanic anti-religion, which resembles some religions in its cruelty, fanaticism and irrationality.

William Ralph Inge (1860–1954) British churchman. Referring to Karl Marx. *Assessments and Anticipations* (1929)

32 She sounded like the Book of Revelation read out over a railway address system by a headmistress of a certain age wearing calico knickers.

Clive James (b. 1939) Australian writer and broadcaster. 1979. Referring to Margaret Thatcher's television broadcasts. Attrib.

33 President Robbins was so well adjusted to his environment that sometimes you could not tell which was the environment and which was President Robbins.

Randall Jarrell (1914–65) US author and poet. *Pictures from an Institution* (1954), pt. I, ch. 4

34 Jerry Ford is so dumb that he can't fart and chew gum at the same time.

Lyndon Baines Johnson (1908–73) US president. Referring to Gerald Ford. Quoted in *A Ford, Not a Lincoln: The Decline of American Political Leadership* (R. Reeves; 1976), ch. 1

35 This man I thought had been a Lord among wits; but, I find, he is only a wit among Lords.

Samuel Johnson (1709–84) British lexicographer and writer. 1754. Referring to Lord Chesterfield. Quoted in *Life of Samuel Johnson* (James Boswell; 1791)

36 One could forgive the fiend for becoming a torrent, but to become an earthquake was really too much.

Charles Joseph de Ligne (1735–1814) Belgian-born soldier, statesman, and writer. Referring to Napoleon I. Attrib.

37 Like a cushion, he always bore the impress of the last man who sat on him.

David Lloyd George (1863–1945) British prime minister. Referring to Lord Derby. This remark is also credited to Earl Haig. Quoted in *Listener* (September 7, 1978)

38 I see some rats have got in; let them squeal, it doesn't matter.

David Lloyd George (1863–1945) British prime minister. Said when suffragettes interrupted a meeting. Quoted in *The Faber Book of English History in Verse* (Kenneth Baker, ed.; 1988)

39 With him, words take the place of actions. He thinks that to say something is to do something, which is an imperfect view of administration.

Henry Cabot Lodge (1850–1924) US politician. Referring to William Jennings Bryan. Letter to Sturgis Bigelow (May 23, 1913)

40 You can't make a soufflé rise twice.

Alice Lee Longworth (1884–1980) US society figure. Referring to Thomas E. Dewey's nomination, in 1948. Quoted in *Mr. Republican, A Biography of Robert A. Taft* (James T. Patterson; 1972)

41 The best clerk I ever fired.

Douglas MacArthur (1880–1964) US general. Referring to Dwight D. Eisenhower. Attrib.

42 We have never said to the press that Clinton is a philandering, pot-smoking draft dodger.

Mary Matalin (b. 1953?) US political adviser. Remark (1992)

43 The wicked asp of Twickenham.

Mary Wortley Montagu (1689–1762) British writer. Referring to Alexander Pope. Attrib.

44 The rogue elephant among British prime ministers.

Kenneth Morgan (b. 1934) British historian. Referring to David Lloyd George. *Life of David Lloyd George* (1963)

45 He is not only a bore but he bores for England.

Malcolm Muggeridge (1903–90) British journalist. Referring to Sir Anthony Eden. Quoted in 'Boring for England', *New Statesmanship* (Edward Hyams; 1963)

46 Napoleon my arse, replied Zazie. He doesn't interest me at all, that puffed-up prick with his cuckold hat.

Raymond Queneau (1903–76) French writer. *Zazie dans le Métro* (1959), ch. 1

47 Like the sorry tapping of Neville Chamberlain's umbrella on the cobblestones of Munich.

Ronald Reagan (b. 1911) US president and actor. Referring to President Jimmy Carter's foreign policy. Attrib.

48 A life peer is like a mule—no pride of ancestry, no hope of posterity.

Lord Shackleton (1911–94) British politician. Attrib.

49 He not only overflowed with learning, but stood in the slop.

Sydney Smith (1771–1845) British clergyman, essayist, and wit. Referring to Lord Macaulay. Quoted in *A Memoir of the Rev. Sydney Smith* (Lady Holland; 1855), vol. 1, ch. 11

50 When political ammunition runs low inevitably the rusty artillery of abuse is always wheeled into action.

Adlai Stevenson (1900–65) US statesman. Referring to critical press opinion claiming he was a 'leftist egghead'. Speech, New York City (September 22, 1952)

51 A triumph of the embalmer's art.

Gore Vidal (b. 1925) US novelist and essayist. Referring to Ronald Reagan. Quoted in Interview, *Observer* (John Heilpern; April 26, 1981)

52 I cannot bring myself to vote for a woman who has been voice-trained to speak to me as though my dog has just died.

Keith Waterhouse (b. 1929) British journalist and novelist. Referring to Margaret Thatcher. Attrib.

53 A typical triumph of modern science to find the only part of Randolph that was not malignant and remove it.

Evelyn Waugh (1903–66) British novelist. March 1964. Remarking upon the news that Randolph Churchill had had a non-cancerous lung removed. 'Irregular Notes', *Diaries of Evelyn Waugh* (Michael Davie, ed.; 1976)

54 Simply a radio personality who outlived his prime.

Evelyn Waugh (1903–66) British novelist. Referring to Sir Winston Churchill. Quoted in *Evelyn Waugh: A Biography* (Christopher Syke; 1975)

Politicians

see also **Political Insults, Politics**

1 As in Italy, the TD is a kind of secular priest, interceding to the earthly powers as the priest intercedes to God.

Anonymous. Referring to the role of the Teachta Dala (TD), a deputy of the Dáil Éireann (lower house of the Irish Parliament), in representing constituents' grievances. Quoted in *Ireland and the Irish: Portrait of a Changing Society* (John Ardagh; 1994)

2 There are three classes which need sanctuary more than others—birds, wild flowers, and Prime Ministers.

Stanley Baldwin (1867–1947) British prime minister. 1925. *Observer* (May 24, 1925)

3 My mind is very, very open and so is my mouth.

Tony Banks, British politician. Referring to his appointment as minister for sport in the new Labour government (May 1997). *Observer* (December 28, 1997)

4 The politician is an acrobat. He keeps his balance by saying the opposite of what he does.

Maurice Barrès (1862–1923) French politician and novelist. *Mes Cahiers 1896–1923* (1963)

5 I am on the right wing of the middle of the road and with a strong radical bias.

Tony Benn (b. 1925) British politician and author. Attrib.

6 Your representative owes you, not his industry only, but his judgement; and he betrays instead of serving you if he sacrifices it to your opinion.

Edmund Burke (1729–97) Irish-born British statesman and political philosopher. Edmund Burke was elected MP for Bristol in 1774. Speech to the electors of Bristol (November 3, 1774)

7 Politics and the fate of mankind are shaped by men without ideas and without greatness. Men who have greatness within them don't go in for politics.

Albert Camus (1913–60) Algerian-born French novelist, essayist, and playwright. *Notebooks* (1935–42)

8 I come to galvanize the political corpse of Spain.

Antonio Cánovas del Castillo (1828–97) Spanish politician. He came to power after the failure of the 1868 revolution. Quoted in *The Spanish Labyrinth* (Gerald Brenan; 1943)

9 She is clearly the best man among them.

Barbara Castle (1911–2002) British politician. Referring to Margaret Thatcher. *The Castle Diaries* (1980)

10 The nation had the lion's heart. I had the luck to give the roar.

Winston Churchill (1874–1965) British prime minister and writer. Speech to both houses of Parliament on his 80th birthday (1954)

11 I know of no other man in our time, or indeed in recent history, who so convincingly demonstrated the power of the spirit over things material.

Stafford Cripps (1889–1952) British politician, lawyer, and economist. Referring to Mahatma Gandhi. Speech, Commonwealth Prime Ministers' Conference, London (October 1, 1948)

12 a politician is an arse upon which everyone has sat except a man.

e. e. cummings (1894–1962) US poet and painter. *1 x 1* (1944), no. 10

13 When I was a boy I was told that anybody could become President of the United States. I am beginning to believe it.

Clarence Darrow (1857–1938) US lawyer. Quoted in *Clarence Darrow for the Defense* (Irving Stone; 1941), ch. 6

14 In order to become the master, the politician poses as the servant.

Charles de Gaulle (1890–1970) French president. Attrib. (1969)

15 The opportunist thinks of me and today. The statesman thinks of us and tomorrow.

Dwight D. Eisenhower (1890–1969) US general and president. Speech, Lafayette College, Easton, Pennsylvania (November 1, 1946)

16 The difference between being an elder statesman
And posing successfully as an elder statesman
Is practically negligible.

T. S. Eliot (1888–1965) US-born British poet and playwright. *The Elder Statesman* (1959), Act 2

17 He needs a great deal of cutting and pruning, but we think him an infant Hercules.

Ralph Waldo Emerson (1803–82) US poet and essayist. Referring to George Bancroft. Quoted in *New England Quarterly* (Michael Kraus; December 1934)

18 'Do you pray for the senators, Dr. Hale?'
'No, I look at the senators and I pray for the country'.

Edward Everett Hale (1822–1909) US author and cleric. Quoted in *New England Indian Summer* (Van Wyck Brooks; 1940)

19 No man can be a Politician, except he be first an Historian or a Traveller; (for except he can see what must be, or what may be, he is no Politician).

James Harrington (1611–77) English political theorist. *The Commonwealth of Oceana* (1656)

20 I've been around so long now they know I don't eat babies.

Charles Haughey (b. 1925) Irish prime minister. Referring to the electorate's opinion of himself. In 1987 he was re-elected as Irish premier, after having been acquitted in a scandal trial. 'Eating babies' was made synonymous with political scandal in Ireland by Jonathan Swift, whose satirical 'A Modest Proposal' (1729) suggested that Ireland solve its hunger problems by consuming young children. Charles Haughey was later forced to resign as prime minister in February 1992, following allegations that he had known about the tapping of phones by his minister of justice in a previous administration. Quoted in *Irish Times* (Maeve Binchy; February 14, 1987)

21 A politician will do anything to keep his job—even become a patriot.

William Randolph Hearst (1863–1951) US newspaper publisher. Syndicated editorial (August 28, 1933)

22 There is one statesman of the present day, of whom I always say that he would have escaped making the blunders that he has made if he had only ridden more in omnibuses.

Arthur Helps (1813–75) British historian. 'On Government', *Friends in Council* (1859), vol. 2, ch. 9

23 A politician rises on the backs of his friends . . . but it is through his enemies he will have to govern afterwards.

Richard Hughes (1900–76) British writer. *The Fox in the Attic* (1961)

24 When a man assumes a public trust, he should consider himself as public property.

Thomas Jefferson (1743–1826) US president. Remark to Baron von Humboldt (1807), quoted in *Life of Jefferson* (B. L. Rayner; 1834)

25 A politician ought to be born a foundling and remain a bachelor.

Lady Bird Johnson (b. 1912) US first lady. *Time* (December 1, 1975)

26 Politicians are the same all over. They promise to build a bridge even where there's no river.

Nikita Khrushchev (1894–1971) Soviet statesman. Remark to journalists while on a visit to the United States (1960)

27 Political renegades always start their career of treachery as 'the best men of all parties' and end up in the Tory knackery.

Neil Kinnock (b. 1942) British politician. Speech to Welsh Labour Party Conference (1985)

28 He had grown up in a country run by politicians who sent the pilots to man the bombers to kill the babies to make the world safe for children to grow up in.

Ursula Le Guin (b. 1929) US writer. *The Lathe of Heaven* (1971)

29 Politicians tend to live *in character* and many a public figure has come to imitate the journalism which describes him.

Walter Lippmann (1889–1974) US writer and editor. *A Preface to Politics* (1913)

30 The problem is that many MPs never see the London that exists beyond the wine bars and brothels of Westminster.

Ken Livingstone (b. 1945) British politician. *Times* (February 19, 1987)

31 A politician is a person with whose politics you did not agree. When you did agree, he was a statesman.

David Lloyd George (1863–1945) British prime minister. Speech, Central Hall, Westminster, *Times* (July 2, 1935)

32 As a prince must be able to act just like a beast, he should learn from the fox and the lion; because the lion does not defend himself against traps, and the fox does not defend himself against wolves. So one has to be a fox in order to recognize traps, and a lion to frighten off wolves.

Niccolò Machiavelli (1469–1527) Italian historian, statesman, and political philosopher. *The Prince* (1513)

33 A politician in . . . trouble can give away the last of his soul in order not to be forced to witness how much he has given away already.

Norman Mailer (b. 1923) US novelist and journalist. 'The Siege of Chicago', *Miami and the Siege of Chicago* (1968)

34 One has to be a lowbrow, a bit of a murderer, to be a politician, ready and willing to see people sacrificed, slaughtered for the sake of an idea, whether a good one or a bad one.

Henry Miller (1891–1980) US novelist. Quoted in *Writers at Work* (Malcolm Crowley, ed.; 1958)

35 Your politicians will always be there when they need you.

Mottos and Slogans. US T-shirt slogan.

36 Old politicians, like old actors, revive in the limelight.

Malcolm Muggeridge (1903–90) British journalist. Attrib.

37 I have as my ideal the life of Jesus.

Richard Nixon (1913–94) US president. Quoted in *Nixon, A Life* (Jonathan Aitken; 1993)

38 The majority of the members of the Irish parliament are professional politicians, in the sense that otherwise they would not be given jobs minding mice at crossroads.

Flann O'Brien (1911–66) Irish novelist and journalist. *The Hair of the Dogma* (Kevin O'Nolan, ed.; 1977)

39 There will be no end to the troubles of states, or indeed, my dear Glaucon, of humanity itself, till philosophers become kings in this world, or till those we now call kings and rulers really and truly become philosophers.

Plato (428?–347? BC) Greek philosopher. *The Republic* (370? BC), bk. 5

40 A statesman is a politician who places himself at the service of the nation. A politician is a statesman who places the nation at his service.
Georges Pompidou (1911–74) French president. *Observer* (December 30, 1973), 'Sayings of the Year'

41 All political lives, unless they are cut off in mid-stream at a happy juncture, end in failure, because that is the nature of politics and of human affairs.
Enoch Powell (1912–98) British politician. *Joseph Chamberlain* (1977)

42 Politicians are people who, when they see light at the end of the tunnel, order more tunnel.
Sir John Quinton (b. 1929) British banker. Quoted in *Money* (June 1989)

43 I am reminded of four definitions. A radical is a man with both feet firmly planted—in the air; a conservative is a man with two perfectly good legs who, however, has never learned to walk; a reactionary is a somnambulist walking backwards; a liberal is a man who uses his legs and his hands at the behest of his head.
Franklin D. Roosevelt (1882–1945) US president. Radio broadcast (October 26, 1939)

44 Our great democracies still tend to think that a stupid man is more likely to be honest than a clever man, and our politicians take advantage of this prejudice by pretending to be even more stupid than nature has made them.
Bertrand Russell (1872–1970) British philosopher and mathematician. *New Hopes for a Changing World* (1951)

45 He knows nothing; and he thinks he knows everything. That points clearly to a political career.
George Bernard Shaw (1856–1950) Irish playwright. *Major Barbara* (1907), Act 3

46 All politicians have vanity. Some wear it more gently than others.
David Steel (b. 1938) Scottish politician. *Observer* (July 14, 1985), 'Sayings of the Week'

47 A politician is a statesman who approaches every question with an open mouth.
Adlai Stevenson (1900–65) US statesman. 1964. Also attributed to Arthur Goldberg. Quoted in *The Fine Art of Political Wit* (Leon Harris; 1966), ch. 10

48 Whoever could make two ears of corn or two blades of grass to grow upon a spot of ground where only one grew before would deserve better of mankind and do more essential service to his country than the whole race of politicians put together.
Jonathan Swift (1667–1745) Irish writer and clergyman. The king of Brobdingnag's opinion of politicians. 'A Voyage to Brobdingnag', *Gulliver's Travels* (1726), ch. 7

49 All politicians have selective memories; and this is most true of politicians who originally practised as historians.
A. J. P. Taylor (1906–90) British historian. *The Struggle for Mastery in Europe* (1954), bibliography

50 A career politician finally smelling the White House is not much different from a bull elk in the rut. He will stop at nothing, trashing anything that gets in his way; and anything he can't handle personally he will hire out—or, failing that, make a deal.
Hunter S. Thompson (b. 1939) US writer and journalist. *Fear and Loathing on the Campaign Trail, '72* (1972)

51 We should look for our brave men in prisons and for the fools among politicians.
David Trimble (b. 1944) Northern Irish politician. Said in support of a Catholic-Protestant power-sharing administration in Ulster, in opposition to Unionist politicians. Speech to the Northern Ireland constitutional convention (1997), quoted in 'Will he Stick his Neck out for Peace?', *Independent* (David McKittrick; July 22, 1997)

52 A politician is a man who understands government, and it takes a politician to run a government. A statesman is a politician who's been dead ten or fifteen years.
Harry S. Truman (1884–1972) US president. *New York World Telegram and Sun* (April 12, 1958)

53 The carefully packaged persona of the old-time movie star resembles nothing so much as the carefully packaged persona of today's politician. Was it not inevitable that the two would at last coincide in one person?
Gore Vidal (b. 1925) US novelist and essayist. Referring to George Bancroft. 'Ronnie and Nancy: A Life in Pictures', *Armageddon* (1987)

54 All those men have their price.
Sir Robert Walpole (1676–1745) English statesman. 1739. Said of fellow parliamentarians. *Memoirs of Sir Robert Walpole* (W. Coxe; 1798), vol. 1

55 Politicians can forgive almost anything in the way of abuse; they can forgive subversion, revolution, being contradicted, exposed as liars, even ridiculed, but they can never forgive being ignored.
Auberon Waugh (1939–2001) British novelist, journalist, and critic. *Observer* (October 11, 1981)

56 A politician is the devil's quilted anvil—He fashions all sins on him, and the blows Are never heard.
John Webster (1578?–1632?) English playwright. *The Duchess of Malfi* (1623), Act 3, Scene 2

Politics

see also Democracy, Government, Politicians

1 Practical politics consists in ignoring facts.
Henry Adams (1838–1918) US historian. 1904. *The Education of Henry Adams* (1907)

2 Man is by nature a political animal.
Aristotle (384–322 BC) Greek philosopher. *Politics* (335–322? BC), bk. 1

3 You will find in politics that you are much exposed to the attribution of false motives. Never complain and never explain.
Stanley Baldwin (1867–1947) British prime minister. Quoting Benjamin Disraeli, himself quoted in J. Morley, *Life of William Ewart Gladstone* (1903, vol. 1). Remark to Harold Nicolson (July 21, 1943)

4 I knew that politics would bring many strange experiences, but nothing in life can prepare a man to make small talk to a transsexual bird cage.
Martin Bell (b. 1938) British journalist and politician. Referring to Miss Moneypenny, a 7-ft transsexual election candidate who wore a bird cage on her head. *Independent* (May 10, 1997)

5 The connection between humbug and politics is too long established to be challenged.
Ronald Bell (1914–82) British politician. Remark (December 5, 1979)

6 The art of looking for trouble, finding it whether it exists or not, diagnosing it incorrectly, and applying the wrong remedy.
Ernest Benn (1875–1954) British publisher. Defining the art of politics. Attrib.

7 Injustice, poverty, slavery, ignorance—these may be cured by reform or revolution. But men do not live only by fighting evils. They live by positive goals, individual and collective, a vast variety of them, seldom predictable, at times incompatible.
Isaiah Berlin (1909–97) Latvian-born British philosopher and historian of ideas. 'Political Ideas in the Twentieth Century', *Four Essays on Liberty* (1969)

8 Politics is a blood sport.
Aneurin Bevan (1897–1960) Welsh-born British politician. 1950s. Quoted in *My Life with Nye* (Jennie Lee; 1980)

9 REFERENDUM, n. A law for submission of proposed legislation to a popular vote to learn the nonsensus of public opinion.
Ambrose Bierce (1842–1914?) US writer and journalist. *The Devil's Dictionary* (1911)

10 All politics reduce themselves to this formula: to try to be one of three, as long as the world is governed by an unstable equilibrium of five powers.
Prince Otto von Bismarck (1815–98) German chancellor. Remark to the Russian ambassador to Germany (January 1880), quoted in *Germany, 1866–1945* (Gordon A. Craig; 1978), ch. 4

11 Politics is the art of the possible.
Prince Otto von Bismarck (1815–98) German chancellor. August 11, 1867. Remark to Meyer von Waldeck. Quoted in *Bismarck-Worte* (H. Amelung; 1918)

12 My vision for the 21st century is of a popular politics reconciling themes which in the past have wrongly been viewed as antagonistic—patriotism and internationalism; rights and responsibilities; the promotion of enterprise and the attack on poverty and discrimination.
Tony Blair (b. 1953) British prime minister. Lecture to the Fabian Society, London (1998)

13 Those who seriously believe that we cannot improve on words written for the world of 1918 when we are now in 1995 are not learning from our history but living it.
Tony Blair (b. 1953) British prime minister. Referring to his proposal to revise Clause 4 of the Labour Party Constitution, which stated Labour's historic commitment to nationalization of major industries. Clause 4 was revised in 1995, with approval by party membership, stating a commitment to realize 'a community in which power, wealth and opportunity are in the hands of the many not the few'. *Independent* (January 11, 1995)

14 Politics are usually the executive expression of human immaturity.
Vera Brittain (1893–1970) British writer and feminist. *The Rebel Passion* (1964)

15 Magnanimity in politics is not seldom the truest wisdom; and a great empire and little minds go ill together.
Edmund Burke (1729–97) Irish-born British statesman and political philosopher. Speech to the British Parliament (March 22, 1775)

16 A state without the means of some change is without the means of its conservation.
Edmund Burke (1729–97) Irish-born British statesman and political philosopher. *Reflections on the Revolution in France* (1790)

17 I am not made for politics because I am incapable of wishing for, or accepting the death of my adversary.
Albert Camus (1913–60) Algerian-born French novelist, essayist, and playwright. *The Rebel* (1951)

18 Power politics is the diplomatic name for the law of the jungle.
Ely Culbertson (1891–1955) US bridge player. *Must We Fight Russia?* (1946)

19 You campaign in poetry. You govern in prose.
Mario Cuomo (b. 1932) US politician. *New Republic* (April 8, 1985)

20 Party is organized opinion.
Benjamin Disraeli (1804–81) British prime minister and writer. November 25, 1864. Said to the Society for Increasing Endowments of Small Livings in the Diocese of Oxford. *Times* (November 26, 1864)

21 The art of dividing a cake in such a way that everyone believes he has the biggest piece.
Ludwig Erhard (1897–1977) German economist and chancellor. Referring to politics. Attrib.

22 Politics is not the art of the possible. It consists in choosing between the disastrous and the unpalatable.
J. K. Galbraith (b. 1908) Canadian-born US economist. *Ambassador's Journal* (1969)

23 Politics is the reflex of the business and industrial world.
Emma Goldman (1869–1940) Lithuanian-born US anarchist. *The Tragedy of Women's Emancipation* (1911)

24 No party has a monopoly over what is right.
Mikhail Gorbachev (b. 1931) Russian statesman. Speech (March 1986)

25 Political genius consists in identifying oneself with a principle.
G. W. F. Hegel (1770–1831) German philosopher. *Constitution of Germany* (1802)

26 You can't adopt politics as a profession and remain honest.
Louis McHenry Howe (1871–1936) US presidential adviser. Speech, Columbia University (January 17, 1933)

27 The politics of the left and centre of this country are frozen in an out-of-date mould which is bad for the political and economic health of Britain and increasingly inhibiting for those who live within the mould. Can it be broken?
Roy Jenkins (b. 1920) British statesman. Launching the idea of the Social Democratic Party, which he co-founded the following year. Speech to the parliamentary press gallery (June 9, 1980)

28 If you're in politics and you can't tell when you walk into a room who's for you and who's against you, then you're in the wrong line of work.
Lyndon Baines Johnson (1908–73) US president. Quoted in *The Lyndon Johnson Story* (B. Mooney; 1956)

29 Politics is the clearing house of pressures.
Paul Keating (b. 1944) Australian statesman. *Sydney Morning Herald* (May 17, 1986), 'Sayings of the Week'

30 You don't play politics with people's jobs.
Neil Kinnock (b. 1942) British politician. Addressing the Labour Party's 'Militant Tendency'. Speech at the Labour Party Conference (October 1985)

31 Party loyalty lowers the greatest of men to the petty level of the masses.
Jean de La Bruyère (1645–96) French essayist and moralist. *Characters, or the Manners of the Age* (1688)

32   For us, sons of France, political sentiment is a
     passion; while, for the Englishmen, politics are a
     question of business.
     Wilfrid Laurier (1841–1919) Canadian statesman. Speech, Montreal
     (May 19, 1884)

33   Politics is opposed to morality, as philosophy to
     naïveté.
     Emmanuel Levinas (1905–95) Lithuanian-born French philosopher.
     Totality and Infinity (1969)

34   The man who pulls the plow gets the plunder in
     politics.
     Huey Long (1893–1935) US politician. Speech, US Senate (January
     30, 1934)

35   The first thing that one loses in politics is one's
     freedom.
     Joaquim Maria Machado de Assis (1839–1908) Brazilian novelist and
     short-story writer. *Philosopher or Dog?* (Clotilde Wilson, tr.;
     1892)

36   In politics, as in grammar, one should be able to
     tell the substantives from the adjectives. Hitler
     was a substantive; Mussolini only an adjective.
     Hitler was a nuisance. Mussolini was bloody.
     Together a bloody nuisance.
     Salvador de Madariaga y Rogo (1886–1978) Spanish diplomat and writer.
     Attrib.

37   I think that so long as politics is seen as the
     rather undignified contest between groups that
     are struggling for nothing more dignified than
     power, so long as that is true, then so long is
     shame the proper attitude to apply to the
     process.
     Michael Manley (1924–96) Jamaican prime minister. Speech (September
     12, 1974), quoted in *Michael Manley: The Making of a
     Leader* (Darrell E. Levi; 1989)

38   I hate politics and the belief in politics, because it
     makes men arrogant, doctrinaire, obstinate, and
     inhuman.
     Thomas Mann (1875–1955) German writer. *Reflections of a Non-
     Political Man* (1918)

39   A party of order or stability, and a party of
     progress or reform, are both necessary elements
     of a healthy state of political life.
     John Stuart Mill (1806–73) British philosopher and social reformer. *On
     Liberty* (1859), ch. 2

40   Anything that earnestly concerns the cultural
     health of a nation is political.
     Edwin Morgan (b. 1920) Scottish poet. 1972. 'The Resources of
     Scotland', *Crossing the Border* (1990)

41   Any party which takes credit for the rain must
     not be surprised if its opponents blame it for the
     drought.
     Dwight Whitney Morrow (1873–1931) US diplomat and politician. Speech
     (October 1930)

42   Ideas are great arrows, but there has to be a
     bow. And politics is the bow of idealism.
     Bill Moyers (b. 1934) US broadcast journalist. *Time* (October 29,
     1965)

43   Seek ye first the political kingdom and all things
     shall be added unto you.
     Kwame Nkrumah (1909–72) Ghanaian president. *The Autobiography
     of Kwame Nkrumah* (1959)

44   A bad cause will ever be supported by bad means
     and bad men.
     Thomas Paine (1737–1809) English writer and political philosopher. *The
     American Crisis* (January 13, 1777), no. 2

45   There are only three men who have ever
     understood it: one was Prince Albert, who is
     dead; the second was a German professor, who
     became mad. I am the third—and I have
     forgotten all about it.
     Lord Palmerston (1784–1865) British prime minister. Referring to the
     Schleswig-Holstein question. Quoted in *Britain in Europe
     1789–1914* (R. W. Seton-Watson; 1937), ch. 14

46   Politics is just like show business. You have a
     hell of an opening, coast for a while, and then
     have a hell of a close.
     Ronald Reagan (b. 1911) US president and actor. Remark to Stuart
     Spencer. Quoted in *There He Goes Again: Ronald Reagan's
     Reign of Error* (Mark Green and Gail MacColl; 1983)

47   Getting someone to do something for you.
     Charles Sanford, Jr. (b. 1936) US business executive. Defining politics.
     Economist (July 11, 1987)

48   Politics does work better when citizens are guided
     by a sense of right or wrong rather than sheer
     expediency.
     George Soros (b. 1930) Hungarian-born US investor and philanthropist.
     The Crisis of Global Capitalism (1998)

49   Politics is perhaps the only profession for which
     no preparation is thought necessary.
     Robert Louis Stevenson (1850–94) Scottish novelist, essayist, and poet.
     'Yoshida-Torajiro', *Familiar Studies of Men and Books* (1882)

50   A new world demands a new political science.
     Alexis de Tocqueville (1805–59) French writer and politician. *Democracy
     in America* (1835–40)

51   Politics is the art of preventing people from
     taking part in affairs which properly concern
     them.
     Paul Valéry (1871–1945) French poet and philosopher. *Tel Quel* (1943)

52   Real politics . . . has little to do with ideas,
     values, and imagination . . . and everything to do
     with manoeuvres, intrigues, plots, paranoias,
     betrayals, a great deal of calculation, no little
     cynicism, and every kind of con game.
     Mario Vargas Llosa (b. 1936) Peruvian writer. Quoted in *A Fish in the
     Water* (Helen Lane, tr.; 1994)

53   A week is a long time in politics.
     Harold Wilson (1916–95) British prime minister. 1964. Repeated on
     several occasions but first thought to have been said during
     the 1964 sterling crisis. Attrib.

54   For politicians, politics is the art of staying
     out of jail,
     for convicts it is the prospect of freedom.
     Can Yücel (b. 1926) Turkish poet. 'Poem 26', *Modern Turkish
     Poetry* (Feyyaz Kayacan Fergar, ed.; 1992), ll. 5–7

Pollution

see also **Ecology**, **The Environment**

1   Only You Can Prevent Forests.
    Anonymous. Sign in the quarters of US airmen spraying
    defoliants during the Vietnam War. Quoted in *A Soldier
    Reports* (William C. Westmoreland; 1976)

2   As crude a weapon as the cave man's club, the
    chemical barrage has been hurled against the
    fabric of life.
    Rachel Carson (1907–64) US ecologist. *Silent Spring* (1962)

3   They improvidentially piped growing volumes of
    sewage into the sea, the healing virtues of which
    were advertised on every railway station.
    Robert Cecil (1864–1958) British statesman. Referring to seaside
    resorts. *Life in Edwardian England* (1969)

4 This spring a lamb sips caesium on a Welsh hill.
A child, lifting her face to drink the rain,
Takes into her blood the poisoned arrow.

Gillian Clarke (b. 1937) Welsh poet. Written about the aftermath of
the Chernobyl disaster. 'Neighbours', *Letting in the Rumour*
(1989)

5 Reactors breed plutonium
bloodcells pay their dues
radiation keeps leaking & seeping
and i've got the Chernobyl Three Mile Island
Blues.

Jayne Cortez (b. 1936) US musician and poet. 'Deadly Radiation
Blues', *Poetic Magnetic* (1991)

6 The sea is the universal sewer.

Jacques Cousteau (1910–97) French film director and underwater explorer.
1971. Said to the US House Committee on Science and
Astronautics. Quoted in *Speaking Freely* (Stuart Berg Flexner
and Anne H. Soukhanov; 1997)

7 I am glad to have known our countryside before
its roads were too dangerous to walk on . . .
before its butterflies and wild flowers were
decimated by arsenical spray, before
Shakespeare's Avon frothed with detergents and
the fish floated belly-up in the Cam.

E. M. Forster (1879–1970) British novelist. *The Longest Journey*
(1984), introduction

8 Saying sulfates do not cause acid rain is the same
as saying that smoking does not cause lung
cancer.

Drew Lewis, US presidential envoy. 1985. Quoted in *Speaking Freely*
(Stuart Berg Flexner and Anne H. Soukhanov; 1997)

9 If emerging economies have to relive the entire
industrial revolution with all its waste, its energy
use, and its pollution, I think it's all over.

Robert B. Shapiro (b. 1938) US business executive. *Harvard Business
Review* (January-February 1997)

10 I've always thought that underpopulated
countries in Africa are vastly underpolluted.

Lawrence H. Summers (b. 1954) US politician and economist. Quoted in
Faith and Credit: The World Bank's Secular Empire (Fabrizio
Sabelli; 1994)

11 The economic logic behind dumping a load of
toxic waste in the lowest wage country is
impeccable and we should face up to it.

Lawrence H. Summers (b. 1954) US politician and economist. Quoted in
Faith and Credit: The World Bank's Secular Empire (Fabrizio
Sabelli; 1994)

Popularity

see also **Celebrity, Fame**

1 What's a cult? It just means not enough people
to make a minority.

Robert Altman (b. 1925) US film director. An interview. *Observer*
(April 11, 1981)

2 The time to worry is when everybody likes you.
When everybody likes you you've had it.

Adam Ant (b. 1954) British pop singer and songwriter. Quoted in *The
Wit and Wisdom of Rock and Roll* (Maxim Jabukowski, ed.;
1983)

3 The people would be just as noisy if they were
going to see me hanged.

Oliver Cromwell (1599–1658) English soldier and statesman. Referring
to a cheering crowd. Remark (1654)

4 Everybody hates me because I'm so universally
liked.

Peter De Vries (1910–93) US novelist. *The Vale of Laughter* (1967),
pt. 1

5 Popularity is a crime from the moment it is
sought; it is only a virtue where men have it
whether they will or no.

George Savile Halifax (1633–95) English statesman. 'Of Ambition',
Political, Moral and Miscellaneous Thoughts and Reflections
(1750)

6 Popularity? It's glory's small change.

Victor Hugo (1802–85) French poet, novelist, and playwright. *Ruy Blas*
(1838), Act 3, Scene 5

7 The worse I do, the more popular I get.

John Fitzgerald Kennedy (1917–63) US president. Referring to his
popularity following the failure of the US invasion of Cuba.
Quoted in *The People's Almanac* (D. Wallechinsky; 1962)

8 We're more popular than Jesus Christ now. I
don't know which will go first. Rock and roll or
Christianity.

John Lennon (1940–80) British rock musician. *Evening Standard*
(March 4, 1966)

9 Popularity is exhausting. The life of the party
almost always winds up in a corner with an
overcoat over him.

Wilson Mizner (1876–1933) US playwright. Attrib.

10 Dear Frank, we believe you; you have dined in
every house in London—once.

Oscar Wilde (1854–1900) Irish poet, playwright, and wit. Interrupting
Frank Harris's interminable account of the houses at which he
had dined. Attrib.

Popular Music

see also **Jazz, Music, Musicians, Singers and Singing**

1 It was three o'clock in the morning in New York.
It was pouring with rain, and it came to me . . .
'And now the end is near and so I face the final
curtain' . . . And I said wow that's it, that's for
Sinatra . . . and then I cried.

Paul Anka (b. 1941) US singer and songwriter. Remark on completing
the English lyrics of 'My Way', based on the Claude François
original, 'Comme d'habitude'. Attrib.

2 Do they merit vitriol, even a drop of it? Yes,
because they corrupt the young, persuading them
that the mature world, which produced
Beethoven and Schweitzer, sets an even higher
value on the transient anodynes of youth than
does youth itself . . . They are the Hollow Men.
They are electronic lice.

Anthony Burgess (1917–93) British writer and critic. Referring to disc
jockeys. *Punch* (September 20, 1967)

3 Simple songs, one-line lyrics, gimmicks, big smiles
and a dash of good clean filth for flavouring. It's
a format that's changed only fractionally with
time.

Nik Cohn, US journalist. Referring to successful pop music.
AwopbopaloobopAlopbamboom (1969)

4 An excuse for white teenagers in the Midwest
to . . . assume the posture without feeling the
pain.

Cheo Hodari Coker, US journalist. Referring to gangsta rap music's
depiction of urban violence and sexuality, and its appeal to
white American teenagers. 'Tupac. Thug Life Vol. 1', *Vibe*
(1994)

5 Sounds like a gameboy down a well.

Elvis Costello (b. 1955) British singer and songwriter. Referring to
techno music on a British television programme. *The O Zone*
(January 9, 1995)

6 Rap music is information that has never been delivered to people so young or poor. A rap song has three times as many words as a singing song . . . Rap music is the invisible TV station that black people never had.

Chuck D, US vocalist and writer. Speech, Black Expo Seminar on Rap, Indiana (July 22, 1989)

7 Don't be satisfied with just selling a song.

Chuck D, US vocalist and writer. Advising fans and artists alike to become politically active. 'Who's Gonna Take the Weight?', *Vibe* (February 1994)

8 Pop is the perfect religious vehicle. It's as if God had come down to earth and seen all the ugliness that was being created and chosen pop to be the great force for love and beauty.

Donovan, British folksinger. 1968. Quoted in *Rock 'n' Roll Babylon* (Gary Herman; 1994)

9 The blues is an art of ambiguity, an assertion of the irrepressibly human over all circumstance whether created by others or by one's own human failings.

Ralph Ellison (1914–94) US writer, jazz musician, and photographer. 'Remembering Jimmy', *Shadow and Act* (1964)

10 We'd always get in a van and go anywhere to play a gig, whereas your middle-class groups will say, 'I'm not doing that, I've got college in the morning'.

Noel Gallagher (b. 1967) British rock musician. *Guardian* (March 17, 1995)

11 Music, not sex, got me aroused.

Marvin Gaye (1939–84) US singer and songwriter. Quoted in *Divided Soul: The Life of Marvin Gaye* (David Ritz; 1985)

12 I'm not going to be dictated to by fans, certainly. I'm dictated enough to by my record company to last me a million years.

Marvin Gaye (1939–84) US singer and songwriter. Quoted in *Melody Maker* (Geoff Brown; October 9, 1976)

13 It is Hollywood who originated the, 'hip hop de hippy hop the body rock' that led to the rap-breaking graffiti scene labeled hip hop.

Nelson George, US journalist. Referring to DJ Hollywood, a South Bronx rapping disc jockey credited by many as the originator of hip hop. *Village Voice* (1980)

14 He turns revolt into a style, prolongs
The impulse to a habit of the time.

Thom Gunn (b. 1929) British poet. 'Elvis Presley', *The Sense of Movement* (1957)

15 The blues came from the man farthest down. The blues came from nothingness, from want, from desire. And when a man sang or played the blues, a small part of the want was satisfied from the music.

W. C. Handy (1873–1958) US composer, cornetist, and bandleader. Quoted in *Hear Me Talkin' to Ya* (Nat Shapiro and Nat Hentoff, eds.; 1955)

16 I made my own image, then I was trapped in it.

Deborah Harry (b. 1945) US singer and actor. Referring to being lead singer in the band Blondie. Interview, *Mail on Sunday* (July 11, 1993), You magazine

17 When we sing the blues, we're singin' out our hearts, we're singin' out our feelings. Maybe we're hurt and just can't answer back, then we sing or maybe even hum the blues.

Zora Neale Hurston (1891?–1960) US writer and folklorist. Quoted in *Hear Me Talkin' to Ya* (Nat Shapiro and Nat Hentoff, eds.; 1955)

18 I'd rather be dead than singing 'Satisfaction' when I'm 45.

Mick Jagger (b. 1943) British rock musician and songwriter. '(I Can't Get No) Satisfaction' was released in 1965. Quoted in *The Wit and Wisdom of Rock and Roll* (Maxim Jabukowski, ed.; 1983)

19 My little rebellion was to have my tie loose, with the top button of my shirt undone, but Paul'd always come up to me and put it straight.

John Lennon (1940–80) British rock musician. Quoted in *The Wit and Wisdom of Rock and Roll* (Maxim Jabukowski, ed.; 1983)

20 Pop music is just long hours, hard work, and lots of drugs.

Mama Cass (1941–74) US singer. 1970? Quoted in *Rock 'n' Roll Babylon* (Gary Herman; 1994)

21 Well, reggae music is a music created by Rasta people, and it carry earth force, people rhythm . . . it is a rhythm of working people, movement, a music of the masses, see?

Bob Marley (1945–81) Jamaican musician, singer, and songwriter. 1979. Quoted in *Bob Marley: Conquering Lion of Reggae* (Stephen Davis; 1983)

22 If we had a hundred Beatles we would not have any balance of payments problems.

Richard Marsh (b. 1928) British civil servant and politician. Referring to The Beatles. *Daily Mail* (June 17, 1965)

23 You had your Shakespeare and Marx and Freud and Einstein and Jesus Christ and Guy Lombardo but we came up with *jazz* . . . and all the pop music in the world today is from that primary cause.

Charles Mingus (1922–79) US jazz musician. *Beneath the Underdog* (1971), ch. 38

24 Punk was . . . a musical movement without music.

Morrissey (b. 1959) British singer and songwriter. Interview, *The Face* (1985)

25 I'd be interested to know how many people who say they're going to write a hit song actually do. I've never done it . . . I just write what comes out.

Randy Newman (b. 1944) US singer and songwriter. Quoted in 'Randy Newman', *Off the Record: An Oral History of Popular Music* (Joe Smith; 1988)

26 No one with the slightest knowledge of jazz music can pretend that the real, honest 'rock 'n' roll' does not belong to jazz. It was jazz *before* getting this name.

Hugues Panassie (1912–74) French jazz writer and impresario. *The Real Jazz* (1942), ch. 17

27 Every popular song has at least one line or sentence that is perfectly clear—the line that fits the music.

Ezra Pound (1885–1972) US poet, translator, and critic. Attrib.

28 Some people tap their feet, some people snap their fingers, and some people sway back and forth. I just sorta do 'em all together, I guess.

Elvis Presley (1935–77) US pop singer. Quoted in *Down at the End of Lonely Street: the Life and Death of Elvis Presley* (Pat S. Broeske and Peter Harry Brown; 1998)

29 When I'm recording I could have orgasm on my mind and my bass player could have pickles on his. It makes it a little rough when you listen back to a track and it's not played with the same intensity.

Prince (b. 1958) US rock singer and songwriter. Quoted in *The Wit and Wisdom of Rock and Roll* (Maxim Jabukowski, ed.; 1983)

30 Most bands don't think about the future. Most musicians can't even spell future. Lunch is how far we think ahead.
David Lee Roth (b. 1954) US musician. Quoted in 'David Lee Roth', *Off the Record: An Oral History of Popular Music* (Joe Smith; 1988)

31 We don't need a choir . . . We just turn this key, and there's the choir.
Florian Schneider (b. 1947) German musician. Referring to the ease with which synthesizers can create a wide variety of sounds. Interview, *Creem* (September 1975)

32 Every time the industry gets powerful, and corporate thinking dominates what the music is, then the music really pales.
Paul Simon (b. 1942) US singer and songwriter. Quoted in 'Paul Simon', *Off the Record: An Oral History of Popular Music* (Joe Smith; 1988)

33 All record companies prefer third-rate talents to true genius because they can push them around more easily, make them change their clothes or politics just to sell more records.
Nina Simone (b. 1933) US jazz singer, pianist, and songwriter. *I Put a Spell On You: The Autobiography* (1991)

34 We don't get groupies. We get teenagers who want to read us their poetry.
Michael Stipe (b. 1960) US rock musician and songwriter. *Q* (September 1, 1994)

35 It doesn't have anything to do with my life. It doesn't talk about kids. It doesn't talk about long-term relationships. I don't think there's any pop music directed at the peculiar class of anger women my age that I know feel.
Ariel Swartley, US music journalist. 'This Prince is No Pretender', *Real Paper* (March 1, 1980)

36 If Dylan had just been a poet with no guitar saying those same things, it wouldn't have worked; but you can't ignore poetry when it shoots into the Top Ten.
Andy Warhol (1928?–87) US artist and filmmaker. Referring to Bob Dylan. *Popism* (1980)

37 Since we're all capitalist enterprises, we have to capture the lowest possible denominator. What's wrong is that we have to cater to the rancid, infantile, pubescent tastes of the public.
Jerry Wexler (b. 1917) US record producer. Quoted in *The Wit and Wisdom of Rock and Roll* (Maxim Jabukowski, ed.; 1983)

38 I think I can tell a hit record as good as the next guy. It's from listening to the radio, not because of some musical ability.
Walter Yetnikoff, US record company executive. Quoted in 'Walter Yetnikoff', *Off the Record: An Oral History of Popular Music* (Joe Smith; 1988)

Pornography

1 When you're a kid you use the cards as a substitute for a real experience, and when you're older you use real experience as a substitute for the fantasy.
Edward Albee (b. 1928) US playwright. Said by Jerry, referring to pornographic playing cards. *The Zoo Story* (1958)

2 This is the kind of show that gives pornography a bad name.
Clive Barnes (b. 1927) British-born theatre and ballet critic. Review of *Oh, Calcutta!* Attrib.

3 Pornographers are the enemies of women only because our contemporary ideology of pornography does not encompass the possibility of change.
Angela Carter (1940–92) British novelist, essayist, and short-story writer. *The Sadeian Woman* (1979), ch. 1

4 I don't think pornography is very harmful, but it is terribly, terribly boring.
Noël Coward (1899–1973) British playwright, actor, and songwriter. *Observer* (September 24, 1972), 'Sayings of the Week'

5 She is the pin-up, the centerfold, the poster, the postcard, the dirty picture, naked, half-dressed, laid out, legs spread, breast or ass protruding. She is the thing she is supposed to be: the thing that makes him erect.
Andrea Dworkin (b. 1946) US writer and feminist. *Pornography: Men Possessing Women* (1981)

6 Pornography is the attempt to insult sex, to do dirt on it.
D. H. Lawrence (1885–1930) British writer. 'Pornography and Obscenity', *Phoenix* (1929)

7 Its avowed purpose is to excite sexual desire, which, I should have thought, is unnecessary in the case of the young, inconvenient in the case of the middle aged, and unseemly in the old.
Malcolm Muggeridge (1903–90) British journalist. Referring to pornography. *Tread Softly For You Tread on My Jokes* (1966)

8 What pornography is really about, ultimately, isn't sex but death.
Susan Sontag (b. 1933) US writer. 'The Pornographic Imagination', *Styles of Radical Will* (1969)

9 Erotica is about sexuality, but pornography is about power and sex-as-weapon—in the same way we have come to understand that rape is about violence, and not really about sex at all.
Gloria Steinem (b. 1934) US writer and feminist. 'Erotica and Pornography, A Clear and Present Difference', *Ms* (November 1978)

10 Pornographers subvert this last, vital privacy; they do our imagining for us. They take away the words that were of the night and shout them over the roof-tops, making them hollow.
George Steiner (b. 1929) US scholar and critic. 'Nightworks', *Language and Silence* (1967)

Possibility

see also **Chance, Impossibility, Opportunity**

1 'What is conceivable can happen too', Said Wittgenstein, who had not dreamt of you.
William Empson (1906–84) British poet and literary critic. Referring to Ludwig Wittgenstein. 'This Last Pain', *Collected Poems* (Michael Roberts and Donald Hall, eds.; 1955)

2 Under different circumstances, I could have been Leonardo da Vinci.
Chris Eubank (b. 1966) British boxer. *Observer* (August 21, 1994)

3 Some men see things as they are and say why? I dream things that never were and say 'Why not?'
Robert Kennedy (1925–68) US statesman. *Esquire* (1969)

4 Supposing Pooh, said Piglet, we were walking in the forest and a tree fell on us. Supposing it didn't, said Pooh after careful consideration.
A. A. Milne (1882–1956) British writer. *The House at Pooh Corner* (1928)

5 Everything may happen.

Seneca, 'the Younger' (4? BC–AD 65) Roman writer, philosopher, and statesman. *Epistulae Morales* (63?), no. 70

6 So many worlds, so much to do,
So little done, such things to be.

Alfred Tennyson (1809–92) British poet. 1833–49. 'A. H. H.' (Arthur Henry Hallam) was the fiancé of Tennyson's sister Emily and died suddenly in September 1833. *In Memoriam A. H. H.* (1850), can. 73, st. 1

Posterity

see also Fame, Immortality, Reputation

1 We are always doing something for posterity, but I would fain see posterity do something for us.

Joseph Addison (1672–1719) English essayist, poet, and statesman. *Spectator* (August 20, 1714), no. 583

2 Posterity is as likely to be wrong as anybody else.

Heywood Broun (1888–1939) US journalist. *Sitting on the World* (1924)

3 When a man is in doubt about this or that in his writing, it will often guide him if he asks himself how it will tell a hundred years hence.

Samuel Butler (1835–1902) British writer and composer. Quoted in *Note Books* (H. Festing Jones, ed.; 1912)

4 When the Present has latched its postern behind my tremulous stay,
And the May month flaps its glad green leaves like wings,
Delicate-filmed as new-spun silk, will the neighbours say,
'He was a man who used to notice such things'?

Thomas Hardy (1840–1928) British novelist and poet. 'Afterwards', *Moments of Vision* (1917), st. 1

5 Believe me, you who come after me!

Horace (65–8 BC) Roman poet. *Odes* (23? BC), bk. 2, no. 19, l. 2

6 I shall not altogether die.

Horace (65–8 BC) Roman poet. Referring to the immortality he anticipates his poetry will confer on his name. *Odes* (23? BC), bk. 3, no. 30, l. 6

7 Damn the age; I'll write for Antiquity.

Charles Lamb (1775–1834) British essayist. Describing his reaction to one of his sonnets being rejected. Letter to B. W. Proctor (1829)

8 What has posterity done for us?

Boyle Roche (1743–1807) Irish politician. Speech to the Irish Parliament (1780)

9 I write for today. I don't care about posterity.

Kurt Weill (1900–50) German-born US composer. Quoted in *American Composers* (David Ewen; 1982)

Poverty

see also Inequality, Wealth

1 Poverty is an anomaly to rich people. It is very difficult to make out why people who want dinner do not ring the bell.

Walter Bagehot (1826–77) British economist and journalist. Quoted in *Literary Studies* (Hartley Coleridge; 1879), vol. 2

2 A characteristic of Thatcherism is a reversion to the idea of nature, irreparable in its forces. Poverty and sickness are seen as part of an order.

Howard Barker (b. 1946) British playwright. *Times* (January 3, 1990)

3 Come away; poverty's catching.

Aphra Behn (1640?–89) English novelist and playwright. *The Rover* (1678), pt. 2, Act 1

4 If we could only imagine that the holes in our trousers were palace windows, we could live like kings; as it is, we're miserably cold.

Georg Büchner (1813–37) German dramatist. 1835. Quoted in *Complete Plays, Lenz and Other Writings* (John Reddick, tr.; 1993)

5 As long as I asked people to help the poor, I was called a saint. But when I asked the question: why is there so much poverty? I was called a communist.

Dom Helder Câmara, Brazilian cardinal. Quoted in *The War of Gods* (Michael Löwy; 1996)

6 We don't need a War on Poverty. What we need is a war on the rich.

Eldridge Cleaver (b. 1935) US writer and civil rights activist. 1967. *Eldridge Cleaver: Post-Prison Writings and Speeches* (Robert Scheer, ed.; 1968)

7 To be poor and independent is very nearly an impossibility.

William Cobbett (1763–1835) British writer, journalist, and reformer. *Advice to Young Men* (1829)

8 In a country well governed poverty is something to be ashamed of. In a country badly governed wealth is something to be ashamed of.

Confucius (551–479 BC) Chinese philosopher, administrator, and moralist. *Analects* (5th century BC)

9 The great curse of our modern society is not so much the lack of money as the fact that the lack of money condemns a man to a squalid and incomplete existence.

Christopher Dawson (1889–1970) US academic. *The Modern Dilemma* (1932)

10 The trouble with being poor is that it takes up all your time.

Willem de Kooning (1904–97) Dutch-born US painter and sculptor. Attrib.

11 'It's a wery remarkable circumstance, sir', said Sam, 'that poverty and oysters always seem to go together'.

Charles Dickens (1812–70) British novelist. *The Pickwick Papers* (1837), ch. 22

12 There is no scandal like rags, nor any crime so shameful as poverty.

George Farquhar (1678–1707) Irish playwright. *The Beaux' Stratagem* (1707), Act 1, Scene 1

13 It is only the poor who are forbidden to beg.

Anatole France (1844–1924) French novelist, poet, and critic. *Crainquebille* (1901)

14 To a people famishing and idle, the only acceptable form in which God can dare to appear is work and promise of food and wages.

Mahatma Gandhi (1869–1948) Indian national leader. *Young India* (October 13, 1921)

15 For every talent that poverty has stimulated, it has blighted a hundred.

John W. Gardner (1912–77) US writer and public official. *Excellence: Can We be Equal and Excellent Too?* (1961)

16 I got plenty o' nuttin'
And nuttin's plenty for me.

Ira Gershwin (1896–1983) US lyricist. Song lyric. 'I Got Plenty o' Nuttin'', *Porgy and Bess* (1935)

17 Ye friends to truth, ye statesmen who survey
The rich man's joys increase, the poor's decay,
'Tis yours to judge how wide the limits stand
Between a splendid and a happy land.

Oliver Goldsmith (1730–74) Irish-born British novelist, playwright, and poet. *The Deserted Village* (1770)

18 If there were no poor, how do you think rich men would live?

Rosa Guy (b. 1928) Trinidadian-born US writer. *My Love, My Love* (1985)

19 Resolve not to be poor: whatever you have, spend less. Poverty is a great enemy to human happiness; it certainly destroys liberty, and it makes some virtues impracticable and others extremely difficult.

Samuel Johnson (1709–84) British lexicographer and writer. December 7, 1782. Quoted in Letter to Boswell, *Life of Samuel Johnson* (James Boswell; 1791)

20 When I mock poorness, then heaven make me poor.

Ben Jonson (1572–1637) English playwright and poet. *The Case is Altered* (1599), Act 3, Scene 1

21 Problems reproduce themselves from generation to generation . . . I refer to this as a 'cycle of deprivation'.

Keith Joseph (1918–94) British politician. Speech to the Pre-School Playgroups Association (June 29, 1972)

22 Where poverty is shared it may be endured. Where poverty is mocked by extravagance it becomes the condition within which resentment smoulders.

Michael Manley (1924–96) Jamaican prime minister. *Jamaica: Struggle in the Periphery* (1982)

23 Look at me: I worked my way up from nothing to a state of extreme poverty.

Groucho Marx (1895–1977) US comedian and film actor. *Monkey Business* (S. J. Perelman, Will B. Johnstone, and Arthur Sheekman; 1931)

24 White people have often confused the symbol of our poverty with our culture.

Tom Mboya (1930–69) Kenyan nationalist leader. From an article written shortly before his death. *New York Times* (1969), quoted in *The Challenge of Nationhood* (Tom Mboya; 1970)

25 Our hearts are surviving at the poverty level. We're scared to death that getting 'too close' will cost us too much.

Terry McMillan (b. 1951) US novelist and teacher. *Essence* (May 1993)

26 Poverty of goods is easily cured; poverty of soul, impossible.

Michel de Montaigne (1533–92) French essayist. *Essays* (1580–88), bk. 3

27 Short of genius, a rich man cannot imagine poverty.

Charles Pierre Péguy (1873–1914) French writer and poet. 'Socialism and the Modern World', *Basic Verities* (A. and J. Green, trs.; 1943)

28 The heart of the matter, as I see it, is the stark fact that world poverty is primarily a problem of two million villages, and thus a problem of two thousand million villagers.

E. F. Schumacher (1911–77) German-born British economist. *Small is Beautiful* (1973), ch. 13

29 A hole is the accident of a day, while a darn is premeditated poverty.

Edward Shuter (1728–76) British actor. Explaining why he did not mend the holes in his stocking. Quoted in *Dictionary of National Biography* (1897)

30 Poverty is no disgrace to a man, but it is confoundedly inconvenient.

Sydney Smith (1771–1845) British clergyman, essayist, and wit. Quoted in *Sydney Smith: His Wit and Wisdom* (J. Potter Briscoe, ed.; 1900)

31 He was a gentleman who was generally spoken of as having nothing a-year, paid quarterly.

Robert S. Surtees (1803–64) British novelist. *Mr. Sponge's Sporting Tour* (1853), ch. 24

32 The poor are our brothers and sisters . . . people in the world who need love, who need care, who have to be wanted.

Mother Teresa of Calcutta (1910–97) Albanian-born nun. 'Saints Among Us', *Time* (December 29, 1975)

33 How good can freedom be if you're alone and broke, with just a few coins in the bottom of your purse, hidden in the lining, the forgotten coins nobody cares about.

Luisa Valenzuela (b. 1938) Argentinian writer. 'The Body' (1967)

Power

see also **Authoritarianism, Exploitation, Imperialism, Influence, Totalitarianism, Tyranny**

1 Power tends to corrupt, and absolute power corrupts absolutely. Great men are almost always bad men . . . There is no worse heresy than that the office sanctifies the holder of it.

Lord Acton (1834–1902) British historian. Often misquoted as 'Power corrupts . . . ' Letter to Bishop Mandell Creighton (April 3, 1887), quoted in *The Life and Letters of Mandell Creighton* (Louise Creighton; 1904), vol. 1, ch. 13

2 Nothing destroyeth authority so much as the unequal and untimely interchange of power pressed too far, and relaxed too much.

Francis Bacon (1561–1626) English philosopher, statesman, and lawyer. 'Of Empire', *Essays* (1625)

3 I sell here, Sir, what all the world desires to have—power.

Matthew Boulton (1728–1809) British engineer. March 22, 1775. Said to James Boswell, on his engineering works. Quoted in *The Life of Samuel Johnson* (James Boswell; 1791), vol. 2

4 The greater the power, the more dangerous the abuse.

Edmund Burke (1729–97) Irish-born British statesman and political philosopher. Speech to the British Parliament (February 7, 1771)

5 The slave begins by demanding justice and ends by wanting to wear a crown. He must dominate in his turn.

Albert Camus (1913–60) Algerian-born French novelist, essayist, and playwright. *The Rebel* (1951)

6 The less people know about what is really going on, the easier it is to wield power and authority.

Prince Charles (b. 1948) British prince. *Observer* (March 2, 1975), 'Sayings of the Week'

7 Headmasters have powers at their disposal with which Prime Ministers have never yet been invested.

Winston Churchill (1874–1965) British prime minister and writer. *My Early Life* (1930), ch. 2

8 Who is all-powerful should fear all things.

Corneille (1606–84) French playwright. *Cinna* (1641), Act 2, Scene 2

9 Nothing is more common in the world than man's eagerness for power, and his pride in the possession of it. It is a sad reflection, however, that a sense of the responsibility which comes with power is the rarest of things.

Alexander Crummell (1819–98) US clergyman, teacher, and missionary. *The Greatness of Christ and other Sermons* (1882)

10 Will and wisdom are both mighty leaders. Our times worship will.

Clarence Shepard Day (1874–1935) US writer. 'Humpty Dumpty and Adam', *The Crow's Nest* (1921)

11 Power concedes nothing without demand. It never did and it never will . . . The limits of tyrants are prescribed by the endurance of those whom they oppress.

Frederick Douglass (1817–95) US abolitionist, writer, and orator. West India Emancipation speech, Canandaigua, New York (August 4, 1856), quoted in *The Life and Writings of Frederick Douglass* (Philip S. Foner, ed.; 1950), vol. 2

12 Power must always be balanced by responsibility. Otherwise it is tyranny.

Peter Drucker (b. 1909) Austrian-born US management consultant. *Post-capitalist Society* (1993)

13 The greatest power available to man is not to use it.

Meister Eckhart (1260?–1328?) German theologian and mystic. Quoted in *The Jingle Bell Principle* (Miroslav Holub; 1992)

14 Obtain power, then, by all means; power is the law of man; make it yours.

Maria Edgeworth (1767–1849) British-born Irish novelist. 'An Essay on the Noble Science of Self-Justification', *Letters for Literary Ladies* (1795)

15 Power doesn't have to show off. Power is confident, self-assuring, self-starting and self-stopping, self-warming and self-justifying. When you have it, you know it.

Ralph Ellison (1914–94) US writer, jazz musician, and photographer. *Invisible Man* (1953)

16 Men of power have not time to read; yet men who do not read are unfit for power.

Michael Foot (b. 1913) British politician and writer. *Debts Of Honour* (1980)

17 What makes power hold good, what makes it accepted, is simply the fact that it does not only weigh on us as a force that says no, but that it traverses and produces things, it induces pleasure, forms knowledge, produces discourse.

Michel Foucault (1926–84) French philosopher. 1972–77. Quoted in *Power/Knowledge* (C. Gordon, ed., tr., L. Marshall, J. Mepham and K. Soper, trs.; 1980)

18 People have power when people think they have power.

William Wyche Fowler (b. 1940) US politician. Attrib.

19 For the owners of power who dream of a quiet world, history is subversive because it always changes.

Eduardo Galeano (b. 1940) Uruguayan writer. 'Fascism in Latin America: A Letter to a Mexican Editor', *We Say No* (1992)

20 Power is the only argument that satisfies man.

Marcus Garvey (1887–1940) Jamaican-born black nationalist leader and publisher. *The Philosophy and Opinions of Marcus Garvey* (Amy Jacques Garvey, ed.; 1923)

21 Power is so apt to be insolent and Liberty to be saucy, that they are seldom upon good Terms.

George Savile Halifax (1633–95) English statesman. 'Of Prerogative, Power and Liberty', *Political, Moral and Miscellaneous Thoughts and Reflections* (1750)

22 Force, if unassisted by judgment, collapses through its own mass.

Horace (65–8 BC) Roman poet. *Odes* (23? BC), bk. 3, no. 4, l. 65

23 The power of the people lies in its greater potential for violence.

George Jackson (1941–71) US political activist and writer. *Blood in My Eye* (1972)

24 Power at its best is love implementing the demands of justice. Justice at its best is love correcting everything that stands against love.

Martin Luther King, Jr. (1929–68) US civil rights leader. *Where Do We Go From Here: Chaos or Community?* (1967)

25 Power without responsibility—the prerogative of the harlot throughout the ages.

Rudyard Kipling (1865–1936) Indian-born British writer and poet. Better known for its subsequent use by Kipling's cousin, Stanley Baldwin, in 1931. Quoted in *Kipling Journal* (December 1971), vol. 38, no. 180

26 Power is the ultimate aphrodisiac.

Henry Kissinger (b. 1923) German-born US politician and diplomat. Sometimes quoted as 'Power is the great aphrodisiac'. *New York Times* (January 19, 1971)

27 Nothing causes self-delusion quite so readily as power.

Liu Binyan (b. 1925) Chinese writer. 1979. 'People or Monsters', *People or Monsters* (Perry Link, ed.; 1983)

28 Power? It's like a dead sea fruit; when you achieve it, there's nothing there.

Harold Macmillan (1894–1986) British prime minister. Quoted in *The New Anatomy of Britain* (Anthony Sampson; 1971), ch. 37

29 Power never takes a back step—only in the face of more power.

Malcolm X (1925–65) US Black activist. Quoted in *Malcolm X Speaks* (George Breitman, ed.; 1965)

30 Here we may reign secure, and in my choice
To reign is worth ambition though in hell:
Better to reign in hell, than serve in heaven.

John Milton (1608–74) English writer. *Paradise Lost* (1667), bk. 1, ll. 261–263

31 Power is my mistress. I have worked too hard in conquering her to allow anyone to take her from me, or even to covet her.

Napoleon I (1769–1821) French emperor. *The Journal of Roederer* (1804)

32 Power is not merely shouting aloud. Power is to act positively with all the components of power.

Gamal Abdel Nasser (1918–70) Egyptian statesman. *The Philosophy of the Revolution* (1952)

33 Who controls the past controls . . . the future: who controls the present controls the past.

George Orwell (1903–50) British writer. *Nineteen Eighty-Four* (1949), pt. 1, ch. 3

34 Unlimited power is apt to corrupt the minds of those who possess it.

William Pitt the Elder (1708–78) British prime minister. Speech to the House of Lords (January 9, 1770)

35 Since I cannot do without the system of votes, I shall universalize suffrage. Since I cannot do without supreme magistrates I shall make them as far as possible changeable. I shall divide and subdivide power, I shall make it changeable and will go on destroying it.

Francisco Pi y Margall (1824–1901) Spanish politician and author. *La Reacción y La Revolución* (1854)

36 Since power over human beings is shown in making them do what they would rather not do, the man who is activated by love of power is more apt to inflict pain than to permit pleasure.

Bertrand Russell (1872–1970) British philosopher and mathematician. Nobel Prize acceptance speech, 'Human Society in Ethics and Politics' (1950)

37 ANGELO O, it is excellent
To have a giant's strength! But it is tyrannous
To use it like a giant.
William Shakespeare (1564–1616) English poet and playwright. *Measure for Measure* (1604), Act 2, Scene 2

38 You only have power over people so long as you don't take *everything* away from them. But when you've robbed a man of everything, he's no longer in your power—he's free again.
Alexander Solzhenitsyn (b. 1918) Russian novelist. *The First Circle* (1968), ch. 17

39 The cold reality of power is, of course, that it has to be endured. Even when it is culpable and seen to be so, its effective reality is that it cannot be escaped for a duration.
Wole Soyinka (b. 1934) Nigerian novelist, playwright, poet, and lecturer. *The Man Died* (1975)

40 Power corrupts, but lack of power corrupts absolutely.
Adlai Stevenson (1900–65) US statesman. Parody of a remark by Lord Acton. *Observer* (January 1963)

41 Power buries those who wield it.
The Talmud (4th century? BC)

42 Athens holds sway over all Greece; I dominate Athens; my wife dominates me; our newborn son dominates her.
Themistocles (527?–460? BC) Athenian general and statesman. Explaining an earlier remark to the effect that his baby son ruled all Greece. Attrib.

43 Our supreme governors, the mob.
Horace Walpole (1717–97) British writer. Letter to Sir Horace Mann (September 7, 1743), quoted in *Correspondence* (Yale, ed.), vol. 18

44 The balance of power.
Sir Robert Walpole (1676–1745) English statesman. Speech to Parliament (February 13, 1741)

45 The wrong sort of people are always in power because they would not be in power if they were not the wrong sort of people.
Jon Wynne-Tyson (b. 1924) British writer. Attrib.

Praise

see also **Compliments, Flattery, Sycophancy**

1 There is no such whetstone, to sharpen a good wit and encourage a will to learning, as is praise.
Roger Ascham (1515–68) English humanist and scholar. *The Scholemaster* (1570)

2 Watch how a man takes praise and there you have the measure of him.
Thomas Burke (1886–1945) Scottish-born British writer. *T. P.'s Weekly* (June 8, 1928)

3 He who praises everybody praises nobody.
Samuel Johnson (1709–84) British lexicographer and writer. 1777. Quoted in *Life of Samuel Johnson* (James Boswell; 1791)

4 She is Venus when she smiles;
But she's Juno when she walks,
And Minerva when she talks.
Ben Jonson (1572–1637) English playwright and poet. 'Celebration of Charis. His Discourse with Cupid', *The Underwood* (1640)

5 You are one of the forces of nature.
Jules Michelet (1798–1874) French historian. Letter to Alexandre Dumas.

6 Fondly we think we honour merit then,
When we but praise ourselves in other men.
Alexander Pope (1688–1744) English poet. *An Essay on Criticism* (1711), ll. 454–455

7 Praise undeserv'd is scandal in disguise.
Alexander Pope (1688–1744) English poet. *Satires, Epistles, and Odes of Horace* (1737), bk. 2, Epistle 1, l. 413

8 Praise from a friend, or censure from a foe,
Are lost on hearers that our merits know.
Alexander Pope (1688–1744) English poet. *The Iliad of Homer* (1715–20), bk. 10, ll. 293–294

9 ENOBARBUS I will praise any man that will praise me.
William Shakespeare (1564–1616) English poet and playwright. *Antony and Cleopatra* (1606–07), Act 2, Scene 6

10 Nor e'er was to the bowers of bliss conveyed
A fairer spirit or more welcome shade.
Thomas Tickell (1686–1740) English poet. 'To the Earl of Warwick. On the Death of Mr. Addison' (1721), ll. 45–46

11 Of this blest man, let his just praise be given,
Heaven was in him, before he was in heaven.
Izaak Walton (1593–1683) English writer. 17th century. Inscription, referring to Dr. Richard Sibbes, in a copy of *The Returning Backslider* (in Salisbury Cathedral Library). *The Compleat Angler* (1653)

Pregnancy

see also **Babies, Birth, Mothers**

1 The baby bounced gently off the wall of her uterus. She opened her dressing gown and put her hands back on her belly. It moved again like a dolphin going through the water; that was the way she imagined it. Are yeh normal? she said.
Roddy Doyle (b. 1958) Irish novelist and playwright. *The Snapper* (1990)

2 In men nine out of ten abdominal tumors are malignant; in women nine out of ten abdominal swellings are the pregnant uterus.
Rutherford Morrison (1853–1939) British doctor. *The Practitioner* (October 1965)

3 Never neglect the history of a missed menstrual period.
Rutherford Morrison (1853–1939) British doctor. *The Practitioner* (October 1965)

4 A fetus is a benign tumor, a vampire who steals in order to live. The so-called miracle of birth is nature getting her own way.
Camille Paglia (b. 1947) US academic and author. *Sexual Personae* (1990)

Prejudice

see also **Bigotry, Ignorance, Xenophobia**

1 You can never beat prejudice by a frontal attack, because there is mere emotion at the root of it. Always flank it.
James Emman Kwegyir Aggrey (1875–1927) Ghanaian educator. Quoted in *Aggrey of Africa* (Edwin William Smith; 1956)

2 Prejudice is planted in childhood, learnt like table manners and cadences of speech, nurtured through fictions like *Uncle Tom's Cabin* and *Gone With the Wind*.
Beryl Bainbridge (b. 1934) British author and journalist. *Forever England North and South* (1987)

3 Common sense is the collection of prejudices acquired by age eighteen.

Albert Einstein (1879–1955) German-born US physicist. Quoted in *Mathematics, Queen and Servant of the Sciences* (E. T. Bell; 1952)

4 I am free of all prejudice. I hate everyone equally.

W. C. Fields (1879–1946) US entertainer. Attrib.

5 The hitherto strong-footed, but sore-eyed vixen, prejudice, is limping off, seeking the shade.

William Rowan Hamilton (1805–65) Irish mathematician. 1834. *Minutes of the Fourth Annual Convention, for the Improvement of the Free People of Colour* (June 2–13, 1834)

6 My corns ache, I get gouty, and my prejudices swell like varicose veins.

James Gibbons Huneker (1860–1921) US musician and critic. *Old Fogy: His Musical Opinions and Grotesques* (1913), ch. 1

7 Nothing is more narrow-minded than chauvinism or race hatred. To me all men are equal: there are jackasses everywhere, and I have the same contempt for all. No petty prejudices.

Karl Kraus (1874–1936) Austrian writer. 1909. Quoted in 'Sprüche und Widersprüche', *Karl Kraus* (Harry Zohn; 1971)

8 The tendency of the casual mind is to pick out or stumble upon a sample which supports or defines its prejudices, and then to make it representative of a whole class.

Walter Lippmann (1889–1974) US writer and editor. *Public Opinion* (1922)

9 Since my daughter is only half-Jewish, could she go in the water up to her knees?

Groucho Marx (1895–1977) US comedian and film actor. When excluded from a beach club on racial grounds. *Observer* (August 21, 1977)

10 We cannot, through ignorant prejudice, afford to under-use the talents and potential of half our citizens, merely because they are women.

Tom Mboya (1930–69) Kenyan nationalist leader. *The Challenge of Nationhood* (1970)

11 EDMUND Why bastard? wherefore base?
When my dimensions are as well compact,
My mind as generous, and my shape as true,
As honest madam's issue? Why brand they us
With base? with baseness? bastardy? base, base?
Who in the lusty stealth of nature take
More composition and fierce quality
Than doth, within a dull, stale, tired bed,
Go to creating a whole tribe of fops,
Got 'tween asleep and wake?

William Shakespeare (1564–1616) English poet and playwright. *King Lear* (1605–06), Act 1, Scene 2

12 SHYLOCK You call me misbeliever, cut-throat dog,
And spit upon my Jewish gaberdine,
And all for use of that which is mine own.

William Shakespeare (1564–1616) English poet and playwright. *The Merchant of Venice* (1596–98), Act 1, Scene 3

13 Minds like beds always made up,
(more stony than a shore)
unwilling or unable.

William Carlos Williams (1883–1963) US poet, novelist, and physician. *Paterson* (1946–58), bk. 1, Preface

The Present

see also **Modernity, Twenty-first Century**

1 The real universe. That's the present moment. The past is no good to us. The future is full of anxiety. Only the present is real—the here-and-now. Seize the day.

Saul Bellow (b. 1915) Canadian-born US writer. *Seize the Day* (1956), ch. 4

2 The present contains nothing more than the past, and what is found in the effect was already in the cause.

Henri-Louis Bergson (1859–1941) French philosopher. *Creative Evolution* (1907), ch. 1

3 You define the present in an arbitrary manner as *that which is*, whereas the present is simply *what is being made* . . . When we think this present as going to be, it exists not yet; and when we think it as existing, it is already past.

Henri-Louis Bergson (1859–1941) French philosopher. *Matter and Memory* (N. M. Paul and W. Scott Palmer, trs.; 1896)

4 PRESENT, n. That part of eternity dividing the domain of disappointment from the realm of hope.

Ambrose Bierce (1842–1914?) US writer and journalist. *The Devil's Dictionary* (1911)

5 But if we're to start living in the present isn't it abundantly clear that we've first got to redeem our past and make a clean break with it? And we can only redeem it by suffering and getting down to some real work for a change.

Anton Chekhov (1860–1904) Russian playwright and short-story writer. *The Cherry Orchard* (1904), Act 2

6 You don't run down the present, pursue it with baited hooks and nets. You wait for it, empty-handed, and you are filled. You'll have fish left over.

Annie Dillard (b. 1945) US writer. *Pilgrim at Tinker's Creek* (1974), ch. 6

7 What if this present were the world's last night?

John Donne (1572?–1631) English metaphysical poet and divine. Holy Sonnets, *Divine Poems* (1633), no. 13, l. 1

8 The present is the past rolled up for action, and the past is the present unrolled for understanding.

Will Durant (1885–1981) US historian. *The Lessons of History* (co-written with Ariel Durant; 1968)

9 The now, the here, through which all future plunges to the past.

James Joyce (1882–1941) Irish writer. *Ulysses* (1922)

10 We are always acting on what just finished happening. It happened at least one thirtieth of a second ago. We think we're in the present but we aren't. The present we know is only a movie of what happened in the past.

Ken Kesey (b. 1935) US writer. Quoted in *The Electric Kool-aid Acid Test* (Tom Wolfe; 1968)

11 The Present Is a Dangerous Place to Live

Keorapetse Kgositsile (b. 1938) South African poet, journalist, and teacher. Poem title. Quoted in *Contemporary African Literature* (Edris Makward and Leslie Lacy, eds; 1972)

12 The spirit of our time is firmly focused on a present that is so expansive and profuse that it shoves the past off our horizon and reduces time to the present moment only.

Milan Kundera (b. 1929) Czech novelist. *The Art of the Novel* (1986)

13 For what *is* passes so swiftly and irrevocably into what *was*, no human claim can be of the least significance.

Joyce Carol Oates (b. 1938) US writer. *What I Lived For* (1994), prologue

14 When the present is intolerable, the unknown harbours no risks.

Wole Soyinka (b. 1934) Nigerian novelist, playwright, poet, and lecturer. *The Bacchae of Euripides* (1973)

Pretension

see also **Artifice**, **Class**, **Manners**, **Self-Delusion**

1 Pretentious? *Moi?*

John Cleese (b. 1939) British comic actor and writer. As Basil Fawlty. *Fawlty Towers* (BBC Television) (co-written with Connie Booth; 1979)

Pride

see also **Boasts**, **Self-Confidence**, **Vanity**

1 Pride goeth before destruction, and an haughty spirit before a fall.

Bible. Proverbs, *King James Bible* (1611), 16:18

2 Ay, do despise me! I'm the prouder for it; I like to be despised.

Isaac Bickerstaffe (1735?–1812?) Irish playwright. *The Hypocrite* (1768), Act 5, Scene 1

3 I know of no case where a man added to his dignity by standing on it.

Winston Churchill (1874–1965) British prime minister and writer. Attrib.

4 I want to thank you for stopping the applause. It is impossible for me to look humble for any period of time.

Henry Kissinger (b. 1923) German-born US politician and diplomat. Attrib.

5 Tallchief commented succinctly that she didn't mind being listed alphabetically, she just didn't want to be treated alphabetically.

Donagh MacDonagh (1912–68) Irish playwright and broadcaster. Said about the New York City Ballet Company's policy of star billing. Maria Tallchief was a ballerina with the company. *George Balanchine* (1983)

6 Pride is My cloak and greatness My robe, and he who competes with Me in respect of either of them I shall cast into Hell-fire.

Muhammad (570?–632?) Arab religious leader and prophet. 610?–632? Reported as revealed through Muhammad by Abu Hurairah, one of his companions. Quoted in *Forty Hadith Qudsi* (E. Ibrahim and D. Johnson-Davies, eds., trs.; 1988), 19th Hadith

7 We are not ashamed of what we have done, because, when you have a great cause to fight for, the moment of greatest humiliation is the moment when the spirit is proudest.

Christabel Pankhurst (1880–1958) British suffragette. Speech, Albert Hall, London (March 19, 1908)

8 If I had not been born Perón, I would have liked to be Perón.

Juan Domingo Perón (1895–1974) Argentinian president. *Observer* (February 21, 1960), 'Sayings of the Week'

9 Of all the causes which conspire to blind
Man's erring judgment, and misguide the mind,
What the weak head with strongest bias rules,
Is Pride, the never-failing vice of fools.

Alexander Pope (1688–1744) English poet. *An Essay on Criticism* (1711)

10 Yes; I am proud, I must be proud to see
Men not afraid of God, afraid of me.

Alexander Pope (1688–1744) English poet. *Epilogue to the Satires* (1738), Dialogue 2, ll. 208–209

11 ISABELLA But man, proud man
Dress'd in a little brief authority,
Most ignorant of what he's most assur'd,
His glassy essence, like an angry ape,
Plays such fantastic tricks before high heaven
As makes the angels weep.

William Shakespeare (1564–1616) English poet and playwright. *Measure for Measure* (1604), Act 2, Scene 2

12 The French want no one to be their *superior*. The English want *inferiors*. The Frenchman constantly raises his eyes above him with anxiety. The Englishman lowers his beneath him with satisfaction. On either side it is pride, but understood in a different way.

Alexis de Tocqueville (1805–59) French writer and politician. May 8, 1835. *Voyage en Angleterre et en Irlande de 1835* (1835)

13 Pride is like a perfume. When it is worn, it radiates a sense of self the world reacts to.

Stevie Wonder (b. 1950) US singer, songwriter, and activist. *Essence* (January 1975)

Principles

see also **Morality**, **Righteousness**

1 It is easier to fight for one's principles than to live up to them.

Alfred Adler (1870–1937) Austrian psychiatrist. 1927? Quoted in *Alfred Adler: Apostle of Freedom* (Phyllis Bottome; 1939), ch. 5

2 If one sticks too rigidly to one's principles one would hardly see anybody.

Agatha Christie (1890–1976) English novelist and playwright. *Towards Zero* (1944)

3 To see what is right, and not do it, is want of courage, or of principle.

Confucius (551–479 BC) Chinese philosopher, administrator, and moralist. *Analects* (5th century BC)

4 Whenever two people argue over principles, they are both right.

Marie von Ebner-Eschenbach (1830–1916) Austrian novelist and poet. Quoted in *The New Quotable Woman* (Elaine Partnow; 1993)

5 There is only *one* principle that can be defended under *all* stages of human development. It is the principle: *anything goes.*

Paul K. Feyerabend (1924–94) German philosopher. *Against Method* (1975)

6 The proclamation and repetition of first principles is a constant feature of life in our democracy. Active adherence to these principles, however, has always been considered un-American.

David Mamet (b. 1947) US writer and film director. 'First Principles', *Writing in Restaurants* (1986)

7 I am not less life-loving than you are. But I cannot sell my birthright, nor am I prepared to sell the birthright of the people to be free.

Nelson Mandela (b. 1918) South African president and lawyer. Response to the offer of freedom from P. W. Botha. Remark (February 1985), quoted in *Part of My Soul Went With Him* (Winnie Mandela; 1985)

8 You can't learn too soon that the most useful thing about a principle is that it can always be sacrificed to expediency.

Somerset Maugham (1874–1965) British writer. *The Circle* (1921), Act 3

9 Nobody ever did anything very foolish except from some strong principle.

Lord Melbourne (1779–1848) British prime minister. Quoted in *The Young Melbourne* (Lord David Cecil; 1939)

Priorities

1 I can't afford to waste my time making money.
Louis Rodolphe Agassiz (1807–73) Swiss-born US naturalist. When asked to give a lecture for a fee. Attrib.

2 It has long been an axiom of mine that the little things are infinitely the most important.
Arthur Conan Doyle (1859–1930) Scottish-born British writer and physician. 'A Case of Identity', The Adventures of Sherlock Holmes (1892)

3 The world must be all fucked up when men travel first class and literature goes as freight.
Gabriel García Márquez (b. 1928) Colombian novelist. Said by the Catalan bookstore owner in Macondo. One Hundred Years of Solitude (1967)

4 'I believe I take precedence', he said coldly; 'you are merely the club Bore: I am the club Liar'.
Saki (1870–1916) British short-story writer. 'A Defensive Diamond', Beasts and Super-Beasts (1914)

Privacy

see also Freedom, Individuality, Secrecy

1 We never knows wot's hidden in each other's hearts; and if we had glass winders there, we'd need keep the shutters up, some on us, I do assure you!
Charles Dickens (1812–70) British novelist. Said by Mrs. Gamp. Martin Chuzzlewit (1844), ch. 29

2 The story of my life is about back entrances and side doors and secret elevators and other ways of getting in and out of places so that people won't bother you.
Greta Garbo (1905–90) Swedish-born US film actor. Attrib.

3 The business of everybody is the business of nobody.
Thomas Babington Macaulay (1800–59) British politician, historian, and writer. 1824. 'On Hallam's Constitutional History', Essays Contributed to the Edinburgh Review (1843)

4 Isn't it amazing that there's no copyright on your own life.
Sarah Miles (b. 1941) British actor. Observer (February 2, 1994), 'Sayings of the Week'

5 I oppose intrusions of the state into the private realm—as in abortion, sodomy, prostitution, pornography, drug use, or suicide, all of which I would strongly defend as matters of free choice in a representative democracy.
Camille Paglia (b. 1947) US academic and author. Sex, Art, and American Culture (1992), introduction

6 That should assure us of at least forty-five minutes of undisturbed privacy.
Dorothy Parker (1893–1967) US writer and wit. Pressing a button marked NURSE during a stay in hospital. Quoted in The Algonquin Wits (R. E. Drennan; 1968)

7 An affair wants to spill, to share its glory with the world. No act is so private it does not seek applause.
John Updike (b. 1932) US writer. Couples (1968), ch. 2

8 This is a free country, madam. We have a right to share your privacy in a public place.
Peter Ustinov (b. 1921) British actor, director, and writer. Romanoff and Juliet (1956), Act 1

9 He was meddling too much in my private life.
Tennessee Williams (1911–83) US playwright. Explaining why he had given up visiting his psychoanalyst. Attrib.

Privilege

see also Class, Luxury

1 The privileged man, whether politically or economically, is a man depraved in mind and heart. That is a social law which admits of no exception, and it is applicable to entire nations as to classes, corporations, and individuals.
Mikhail Bakunin (1814–76) Russian-born anarchist. Quoted in Bakunin on Anarchy (Sam Dolgoff, ed.; 1973)

2 Scratch a pessimist, and you find often a defender of privilege.
William Henry Beveridge (1879–1963) British economist and social reformer. Observer (December 17, 1943), 'Sayings of the Week'

3 Privilege is the greatest enemy of right.
Marie von Ebner-Eschenbach (1830–1916) Austrian novelist and poet. Quoted in The New Quotable Woman (Elaine Partnow; 1993)

4 A people that values its privileges above its principles soon loses both.
Dwight D. Eisenhower (1890–1969) US general and president. Inaugural address, Washington, D.C. (January 20, 1953)

5 A self-made man is one who believes in luck and sends his son to Oxford.
Christina Stead (1902–83) Australian writer. The House of All Nations (1938), 'Credo'

Procrastination

see also Indecision, Punctuality

1 No task is a long one but the task on which one dare not start. It becomes a nightmare.
Charles Baudelaire (1821–67) French poet. 'Mon Coeur Mis à Nu', Journaux Intimes (1887)

2 He who desires but acts not, breeds pestilence.
William Blake (1757–1827) British poet, painter, engraver, and mystic. 'Proverbs of Hell', The Marriage of Heaven and Hell (1790–93), l. 5

3 Delay always breeds danger.
Miguel de Cervantes (1547–1616) Spanish novelist and playwright. Don Quixote (1605–15), pt. 1, bk. 4, ch. 2

4 Defer not till to-morrow to be wise, To-morrow's sun to thee may never rise.
William Congreve (1670–1729) English playwright and poet. Letter to Cobham. 'Verses to the Right Honourable the Lord Viscount Cobham', Mr Congreve's Last Will and Testament, with Characters of his Writings (Dryden, Blackmore, Addison, Pack; 1729)

5 Never leave that till to-morrow which you can do to-day.
Benjamin Franklin (1706–90) US statesman and scientist. Poor Richard's Almanack (1757)

6 procrastination is the art of keeping up with yesterday.
Don Marquis (1878–1937) US journalist and writer. 'certain maxims of archy', archy and mehitabel (1927)

7 Delay is the deadliest form of denial.
Cyril Northcote Parkinson (1909–93) British political scientist, historian, and writer. Parkinson's Law of Delay (1958)

8 Next week, or next month, or next year I'll kill myself. But I might as well last out my month's rent, which has been paid up, and my credit for breakfast in the morning.
Jean Rhys (1894–1979) Dominican-born British novelist. Good Morning, Midnight (1939), pt. 2

9 Procrastination is the thief of time.

Edward Young (1683–1765) English poet. *The Complaint, or Night Thoughts on Life, Death, and Immortality* (1742–45), bk. 1, l. 393

Progress

see also **Change, Evolution, Modernity**

1 The people who live in the past must yield to the people who live in the future. Otherwise the world would begin to turn the other way round.

Arnold Bennett (1867–1931) British writer. *Milestones* (1912)

2 The twentieth-century struggle between capitalism and socialism is, at an ideological level, a fight about the content of progress.

John Berger (b. 1926) British novelist, essayist, and art critic. 1999. *Pig Earth* (1999 edition), Introduction

3 We have stopped believing in progress. What progress that is!

Jorge Luis Borges (1899–1986) Argentinian writer and poet. Attrib.

4 Progress, man's distinctive mark alone,
Not God's, and not the beasts': God is, they are,
Man partly is and wholly hopes to be.

Robert Browning (1812–89) British poet. 'A Death in the Desert', *Dramatis Personae* (1864), l. 586–88

5 Progress is
The law of life, man is not man as yet.

Robert Browning (1812–89) British poet. *Paracelsus* (1835)

6 Nothing in progression can rest on its original plan. We may as well think of rocking a grown man in the cradle of an infant.

Edmund Burke (1729–97) Irish-born British statesman and political philosopher. Letter to the Sheriffs of Bristol (1777)

7 All progress is based upon a universal innate desire on the part of every organism to live beyond its income.

Samuel Butler (1835–1902) British writer and composer. Quoted in *Note Books* (H. Festing Jones, ed.; 1912)

8 I am afraid I believe we delude ourselves if we think that humanity is becoming ever more civilised, ever more sophisticated and ever more reasonable. It's simply not the case.

Prince Charles (b. 1948) British prince. ITV television programme, 'Charles: The Private Man, the Public Role' (June 29, 1994)

9 As enunciated today, 'progress' is simply a comparative of which we have not settled the superlative.

G. K. Chesterton (1874–1936) British writer and poet. *Heretics* (1905)

10 pity this busy monster, manunkind,
not. Progress is a comfortable disease.

e. e. cummings (1894–1962) US poet and painter. *1 x 1* (1944), no.14

11 Praise progress—it's at least a moving target.

Bob Davis (b. 1943) US business executive and educator. Attrib.

12 If there is no struggle there is no progress.

Frederick Douglass (1817–95) US abolitionist, writer, and orator. West India Emancipation speech, Canandaigua, New York (August 4, 1856)

13 What we call progress is the exchange of one nuisance for another nuisance.

Havelock Ellis (1859–1939) British psychologist. *Impressions and Comments* (1914)

14 All that is human must retrograde if it does not advance.

Edward Gibbon (1737–94) British historian. *The Decline and Fall of the Roman Empire* (1776–88), ch. 71

15 'Progress' involves the systematic substitution of the technosphere or manmade world for the biosphere or natural world.

Edward Goldsmith (b. 1928) British business executive and ecologist. 'Biospheric Ethics' (1992), quoted in *The Future of Progress* (Helena Norberg-Hodge, Peter Goering and Steven Gorelick, eds.; 1992)

16 Our most noble byword: progress: colonizing the distant future by subjecting it to rigorous programming: thereby sacrificing a natural propensity for indolence and game-playing.

Juan Goytisolo (b. 1931) Spanish novelist and essayist. *Makbara* (1980)

17 The world owes all its onward impulse to men ill at ease. The happy man inevitably confines himself within ancient limits.

Nathaniel Hawthorne (1804–64) US novelist and short-story writer. *The House of Seven Gables* (1851), ch. 20

18 The means by which we live have outdistanced the ends for which we live. Our scientific power has outrun our spiritual power. We have guided missiles and misguided men.

Martin Luther King, Jr. (1929–68) US civil rights leader. *Strength To Love* (1963)

19 If you're not a part of the solution, then you're a part of the problem.

Martin Luther King, Jr. (1929–68) US civil rights leader. Attrib.

20 One step forward, two steps back . . . It happens in the lives of individuals, and it happens in the history of nations and in the development of parties.

Vladimir Ilyich Lenin (1870–1924) Russian revolutionary leader. *One Step Forward, Two Steps Back* (1904)

21 Progress has gone full circle to regress.

Taban Lo Liyong (b. 1939) Sudanese poet, novelist, and short-story writer. 'Why Be Good if Goodness Can Be Misused?', *Ballads of Underdevelopment* (1976)

22 The simplest schoolboy is now familiar with truths for which Archimedes would have sacrificed his life.

Ernest Renan (1823–92) French philosopher, philologist, and historian. *Souvenirs d'Enfance et de Jeunesse* (1883)

23 Organic life, we are told, has developed gradually from the protozoon to the philosopher, and this development, we are assured, is indubitably an advance. Unfortunately it is the philosopher, not the protozoon, who gives us this assurance.

Bertrand Russell (1872–1970) British philosopher and mathematician. *Mysticism and Logic* (1918)

24 Man's 'progress' is but a gradual discovery that his questions have no meaning.

Antoine de Saint-Exupéry (1900–44) French writer and aviator. Posthumously published as *Citadelle*. *The Wisdom of the Sands* (Stuart Gilbert, tr.; 1948)

25 Progress, far from consisting in change, depends on retentiveness. Those who cannot remember the past are condemned to repeat it.

George Santayana (1863–1952) Spanish-born US philosopher, poet, and novelist. *The Life of Reason* (1905–06)

26 It took us eighteen months to build the first nuclear power generator; it now takes twelve years; that's progress.

Edward Teller (b. 1908) Hungarian-born US physicist. Quoted in *Free to Choose* (Milton Friedman and Rose Friedman; 1979)

27 And step by step, since time began,
I see the steady gain of man.

John Greenleaf Whittier (1807–92) US poet. 'The Chapel of the Hermits',
The Poetical Works of John Greenleaf Whittier (1894)

28 Who does nothing, makes no mistakes; and who
makes no mistakes, never makes any progress.

Paul Winkler (1630–86) German lawyer and writer. *Drei Tausend gute
Gedanken* (1685)

Promises

1 Promises are the uniquely human way of ordering
the future, making it predictable and reliable to
the extent that this is humanly possible.

Hannah Arendt (1906–75) German-born US philosopher and historian.
'Civil Disobedience', *Crises of the Republic* (1972)

2 Never promise more than you can perform.

Publilius Syrus (*fl.* 1st century BC) Roman writer. 1st century BC.
Maxims (Darius Lyman, tr.), 528

3 Promises and pie-crust are made to be broken.

Jonathan Swift (1667–1745) Irish writer and clergyman. *Polite
Conversation* (1738), Dialogue 1

Propaganda

see also **Advertising, Communication, Marketing, Rhetoric**

1 Propaganda is that branch of the art of lying
which consists in nearly deceiving your friends
without quite deceiving your enemies.

F. M. Cornford (1874–1943) British philosopher. Attrib. *New
Statesman* (September 15, 1978)

2 The propagandist's purpose is to make one set of
people forget that certain other sets of people are
human.

Aldous Huxley (1894–1963) British novelist and essayist. *The Olive
Tree and Other Essays* (1936)

3 We all become so immersed in the habits of
American culture that if we are not careful we
mistake them for life itself.

Michael Manley (1924–96) Jamaican prime minister. *Jamaica: Struggle
in the Periphery* (1982)

4 Every method is used to prove to men that in
given political, economic, and social situations
they are bound to be happy, and those who are
unhappy are mad or criminals or monsters.

Alberto Moravia (1907–90) Italian novelist. *Man as an End* (Bernard
Wall, tr.; 1964)

5 In our country the lie has become not just a
moral category but a pillar of the State.

Alexander Solzhenitsyn (b. 1918) Russian novelist. *Observer* (December
29, 1974), 'Sayings of the Year'

Prophecy

see also **The Future**

1 Beware of false prophets, which come to you in
sheep's clothing, but inwardly they are ravening
wolves.

Bible. Matthew, *King James Bible* (1611), 7:15

2 How seldom does prediction fail, when evil!
How oft, foretelling good!

Pedro Calderón de la Barca (1600–81) Spanish playwright and poet. *Life
is a Dream* (1635), Act 2

3 A hopeful disposition is not the sole qualification
to be a prophet.

Winston Churchill (1874–1965) British prime minister and writer. Speech
to Parliament (April 10, 1927)

4 And 'mid this tumult Kubla heard from far
Ancestral voices prophesying war!

Samuel Taylor Coleridge (1772–1834) British poet. 'Kubla Khan'
(1797), ll. 29–30, quoted in *The Portable Coleridge*
(I. A. Richards, ed.; 1950)

5 Among all forms of mistake, prophecy is the
most gratuitous.

George Eliot (1819–80) British novelist. *Middlemarch* (1871–72),
ch. 10

6 You can only predict things after they've
happened.

Eugène Ionesco (1909–94) Romanian-born French playwright. *Rhinoceros*
(1959), Act 3

7 The prophet who fails to present a bearable
alternative and yet preaches doom is part of the
trap that he postulates.

Margaret Mead (1901–78) US anthropologist. *Culture and
Commitment* (1970), Introduction

8 At night they will think they have seen the sun,
when they see the half pig man: Noise, screams,
battle seen fought in the skies. The brute beasts
will be heard to speak.

Nostradamus (1503–66) French astrologer and physician. Thought to
foretell a 20th-century air-battle. *The Prophecies of
Nostradamus* (16th century), Century 1, st. 64

9 My doctor has advised me to cut back on
predictions.

Conor Cruise O'Brien (b. 1917) Irish historian, critic, and politician.
Newspaper column (November 11, 1994)

10 After us the deluge.

Madame de Pompadour (1721–64) French courtesan. 1757. Reputed
reply to Louis XV after the French defeat at the hands of
Frederick the Great. Quoted in *Mémoires* (Mme du Hausset;
1824)

11 Man has lost the capacity to foresee and to
forestall. He will end by destroying the earth.

Albert Schweitzer (1875–1965) German theologian, philosopher, physician,
and musicologist. Attrib.

12 The ordinary-sized stuff which is our lives . . . as
mysterious to us as the heavens were to the
Greeks. We're better at predicting events at the
edge of a galaxy or inside the nucleus of an atom
than whether it'll rain on auntie's garden party
three Sundays from now.

Tom Stoppard (b. 1937) Czech-born British playwright and screenwriter.
Arcadia (1993)

Protest

see also **Arguments, Civil Rights, Free Speech, Human Rights**

1 Keep asking me, no matter how long
On the war in Viet Nam, I sing this song
I ain't got no quarrel with the Viet Cong.

Muhammad Ali (b. 1942) US boxer. February 1966. *The Greatest:
My Own Story* (co-written with Richard Durham; 1976)

2 The defiance of established authority, religious
and secular, social and political, as a world-wide
phenomenon may well one day be accounted the
outstanding event of the last decade.

Hannah Arendt (1906–75) German-born US philosopher and historian.
'Civil Disobedience', *Crises of the Republic* (1972)

3 If we have committed all these crimes, it is solely because of our support for two gentlemen, Mr. Democracy, and Mr. Science. As supporters of Democracy, we are obliged to attack Confucianism, rituals, womanly chastity, traditional morality, and old-style politics.
Chen Duxiu (1879–1942) Chinese reformer. January 1919. Said in defence of his criticism of traditional Confucian culture. Quoted in *Origins of the Chinese Revolution, 1915–49* (Lucien Bianco; 1967), 'Intellectual Origins of the Revolution'

4 Even if they're functioning out of ignorance, they are still participating and must be suppressed. In China, even one million people can be considered a small sum.
Deng Xiaoping (1904–97) Chinese statesman. Referring to the prodemocracy demonstrators in Tiananmen Square. *Times* (June 5, 1989)

5 Can't Pay! Won't Pay!
Dario Fo (b. 1926) Italian playwright and actor. 1974. Play title.

6 It is better to be violent, if there is violence in our hearts, than to put on the cloak of non-violence to cover impotence.
Mahatma Gandhi (1869–1948) Indian national leader. *Non-Violence in Peace and War* (1948)

7 To create such a crisis and foster such a tension that a community which has constantly refused to negotiate is forced to confront the issue.
Martin Luther King, Jr. (1929–68) US civil rights leader. 1963. Referring to the objectives of nonviolent protest. Letter from Birmingham Jail, *History Today* (April 1998), vol. 48

8 Urban riots must now be recognized as a durable social phenomenon. They are a special form of violence . . . mainly intended to shock the white community.
Martin Luther King, Jr. (1929–68) US civil rights leader. *The American Psychologist* (1968)

9 A riot is at bottom the language of the unheard.
Martin Luther King, Jr. (1929–68) US civil rights leader. *Where Do We Go From Here: Chaos or Community?* (1967)

10 Make love not war.
Mottos and Slogans. 1960s. Anti-Vietnam War slogan.

11 Be realistic, demand the impossible.
Mottos and Slogans. May 1968. Paris Students' Revolt slogan.

12 What do we want? Radio 4! Where do we want it? Long wave! And what do we say? Please!
Newspapers. 1993. Chanted by protesters who successfully opposed the BBC's plans to broadcast Radio 4 on FM only. *Guardian* (April 5, 1993)

13 The voice of protest, of warning, of appeal is never more needed than when the clamor of fife and drum, echoed by the press and too often by the pulpit, is bidding all men fall in and keep step and obey in silence the tyrannous word of command.
Charles Eliot Norton (1827–1908) US writer, editor, and educator. *True Patriotism* (1898)

14 We have taken this action, because as women . . . we realize that the condition of our sex is so deplorable that it is our duty even to break the law in order to call attention to the reasons why we do so.
Emmeline Pankhurst (1858–1928) British suffragette. Speech in court (October 21, 1908), quoted in *Shoulder to Shoulder* (Midge Mackenzie, ed.; 1975)

15 It was not a riot. It was an open, unorganized protest against empty stomachs, overcrowded tenements, filthy sanitation, rotten foodstuffs, and chiseling landlords. It was not caused by Communists.
Adam Clayton Powell, Jr. (1908–72) US clergyman and civil rights leader. Referring to protests in Harlem, New York City. Letter to the editor, *New York Post* (1935)

16 I am making this statement as a wilful defiance of military authority because I believe that the War is being deliberately prolonged by those who have the power to end it.
Siegfried Sassoon (1886–1967) British poet and writer. *Memoirs of an Infantry Officer* (1930), pt. 10, ch. 3

17 We Shall Overcome
Pete Seeger (b. 1919) US folksinger and songwriter. 1962. Song title.

18 The long fight to save wild beauty represents democracy at its best. It requires citizens to practice the hardest of virtues—self-restraint.
Edwin Way Teale (1899–1980) US naturalist, writer, and photographer. 'February 2', *Circle of the Seasons* (1953)

Prudence

see also **Moderation**

1 For those that fly may fight again, Which he can never do that's slain.
Samuel Butler (1612–80) English satirist. *Hudibras* (1678), pt. 3, can. 3, ll. 243–4

2 'It's always best on these occasions to do what the mob do'. 'But suppose there are two mobs?' suggested Mr Snodgrass. 'Shout with the largest', replied Mr Pickwick.
Charles Dickens (1812–70) British novelist. *The Pickwick Papers* (1837), ch. 13

3 In skating over thin ice, our safety is in our speed.
Ralph Waldo Emerson (1803–82) US poet and essayist. 'Prudence', *Essays* (1841)

4 Be nice to people on your way up because you'll meet 'em on your way down.
Wilson Mizner (1876–1933) US playwright. 1920? Also attributed to Jimmy Durante. Quoted in *The Legendary Mizners* (Alva Johnston; 1953)

5 Self-denial is not a virtue; it is only the effect of prudence on rascality.
George Bernard Shaw (1856–1950) Irish playwright. 'Maxims for Revolutionists', *Man and Superman* (1903)

Psychiatry

see also **Madness**, **Mind**, **Psychoanalysis**, **Psychology**

1 I have myself spent nine years in a lunatic asylum and have never suffered from the obsession of wanting to kill myself; but I know that each conversation with a psychiatrist in the morning made me want to hang myself because I knew I could not strangle him.
Antonin Artaud (1896–1948) French actor, playwright, and writer. Attrib.

2 A mental stain can neither be blotted out by the passage of time nor washed away by any waters.
Cicero (106–43 BC) Roman orator and statesman. *De Legibus* (1st century BC), bk. 2

3 Schizophrenia is the price that Homo sapiens pays for language.

Tim J. Crow (b. 1938) British psychiatrist. *British Journal of Psychiatry* (1998), vol. 172

4 Freud . . . compared *psychotic* patients to crystals which, when broken up, reveal their structure by the manner in which they come apart.

Anna Freud (1895–1982) Austrian-born British psychoanalyst. *Problems of Analytic Technique and Therapy* (1972)

5 What the psychiatrist has learned so far are, as it were, the first single phrases of a foreign tongue which have to be linked up with each other, enlarged on, and built into the correct grammatical fabric of a language.

Anna Freud (1895–1982) Austrian-born British psychoanalyst. *Problems of Analytic Technique and Therapy* (1972)

6 Whatever the starting point and however tortuous the road, we must finally arrive at a disturbance of the personality as the source of psychic illness.

Karen Horney (1885–1952) German-born US psychoanalyst. *Our Inner Conflicts* (1945)

7 Successful psychiatrists necessarily correspond in their natures to the needs and desires of 'nervous patients', since the mass of patients decide who is to be the successful therapist, and not the actual value or correctness of the doctor's own views.

Karl Jaspers (1883–1969) German philosopher. 1913. *General Psychopathology* (J. Hoenig and M. Hamilton, trs.; 1963)

8 The relation between psychiatrists and other kinds of lunatics is more or less the relation of a convex folly to a concave one.

Karl Kraus (1874–1936) Austrian writer. 1972. Attrib.

9 Schizophrenic behaviour is a special strategy that a person invents in order to live in an unlivable situation.

R. D. Laing (1927–89) Scottish psychiatrist. *The Politics of Experience* (1967), ch. 5

10 A mental healer may be a psychiatrist. A psychiatrist may or may not be a mental healer.

R. D. Laing (1927–89) Scottish psychiatrist. *Wisdom, Madness and Folly: The Making of a Psychiatrist, 1927–57* (1985)

11 I remember remarks made in all seriousness by psychiatrists. 'Hamlet was just a badly conditioned rat'. 'If Lear had been given electric shocks there would have been no need for all that nonsense'.

R. D. Laing (1927–89) Scottish psychiatrist. *Wisdom, Madness and Folly: The Making of a Psychiatrist, 1927–57* (1985)

12 When our very lives are threatened we begin to live. Even the psychic invalid throws away his crutches in such moments.

Henry Miller (1891–1980) US novelist. *Sexus* (1949)

13 On the third day at Belle Vue I was sitting in the gymnasium writing a song called 'All The Things You Could Be If Sigmund Freud's Wife Was Your Mother', which I later recorded.

Charles Mingus (1922–79) US jazz musician. Referring to his period of psychiatric treatment in New York's Bellevue Hospital. *Beneath the Underdog* (1971), ch. 36

14 Psychiatric treatment was not a search for truth but the promulgation of a dogma. Psychiatrists seemed to fear the taint of insanity much as inquisitors once feared succumbing to the devil.

Robert T. Pirsig (b. 1928) US writer. *Lila: an Inquiry into Morals* (1991)

15 The new definition of psychiatry is the care of the id by the odd.

Proverb.

16 One should only see a psychiatrist out of boredom.

Muriel Spark (b. 1918) British novelist. Attrib.

17 A psychiatrist is a man who goes to the Folies-Bergères and looks at the audience.

Mervyn Stockwood (b. 1913) British Anglican cleric. *Observer* (October 15, 1961), 'Sayings of the Week'

18 Schizophrenia will continue to be a mystery so long as we fail to understand the forces and the organization which make for the wholeness of the personality.

Anthony Storr (b. 1920) British writer and psychiatrist. *The Integrated Personality* (1960)

19 As the primitive had spiritualized nature, so the psychiatrist now animalizes man . . . Who will correct the psychiatrist's mistake, and ours for supporting it?

Thomas Szasz (b. 1920) Hungarian-born US psychiatrist. *Insanity: The Idea and its Consequences* (1987)

20 In the past, men created witches: now they create mental patients.

Thomas Szasz (b. 1920) Hungarian-born US psychiatrist. *The Manufacture of Madness* (1970), Introduction

21 Psychiatrists classify a person as neurotic if he suffers from his problems in living, and a psychotic if he makes others suffer.

Thomas Szasz (b. 1920) Hungarian-born US psychiatrist. *The Second Sin* (1973)

22 If you talk to God, you are praying; if God talks to you, you have schizophrenia. If the dead talk to you, you are a spiritualist; if God talks to you, you are a schizophrenic.

Thomas Szasz (b. 1920) Hungarian-born US psychiatrist. 'Schizophrenia', *The Second Sin* (1973)

Psychoanalysis

see also **Consciousness, Mind, The Self, Therapy**

1 They were a tense and peculiar family, the Oedipuses, weren't they?

Max Beerbohm (1872–1956) British essayist, critic, and caricaturist. Quoted in *Max: A Biography* (D. Cecil; 1965)

2 Psychoanalysts are not occupied with the minds of their patients; they do not believe in the mind but in a cerebral intestine.

Bernard Berenson (1865–1959) Lithuanian-born US art historian. Quoted in *Conversations with Berenson* (Umberto Morra; 1963)

3 Psychoanalysis can provide a theory of 'progress', but only by viewing history as a neurosis.

Norman O. Brown (b. 1913) US writer and educator. *Life Against Death* (1959)

4 Psychoanalysis is confession without absolution.

G. K. Chesterton (1874–1936) British writer and poet. Attrib.

5 Or look at it this way. Psychoanalysis is a permanent fad.

Peter De Vries (1910–93) US novelist. Opening words. *Forever Panting* (1973)

6 The secret pathways between body and mind . . . remain invisible as such in adult patients unless they are brought to the surface by detailed analytic work.

Anna Freud (1895–1982) Austrian-born British psychoanalyst. *Problems of Analytic Technique and Therapy* (1972)

7 Psychoanalysis is in essence a cure through love.
Sigmund Freud (1856–1939) Austrian psychoanalyst. Letter to Carl Jung, quoted in *Freud and Man's Soul* (Bruno Bettelheim; 1982)

8 The sexual wishes in regard to the mother become more intense and the father is perceived as an obstacle to them; this gives rise to the Oedipus complex.
Sigmund Freud (1856–1939) Austrian psychoanalyst. *The Ego and the Id* (1923)

9 In psychoanalysis there is no choice for us but to assert that mental processes are in themselves unconscious, and to liken the perception of them by means of consciousness to the perception of the external world by means of the sense organs.
Sigmund Freud (1856–1939) Austrian psychoanalyst. Quoted in *The Essentials of Psycho-analysis* (Anna Freud, ed., James Strachey, tr.; 1986)

10 The goal of psychoanalysis is a cultural achievement somewhat like the draining of the Zuyder Zee.
Sigmund Freud (1856–1939) Austrian psychoanalyst. Attrib.

11 Psychoanalysis is essentially a theory of unconscious strivings, of resistance, of falsification of reality according to one's subjective needs and expectations.
Erich Fromm (1900–80) German-born US psychoanalyst and philosopher. *The Anatomy of Human Destructiveness* (1973)

12 One of the latent but supremely important aspects of psychoanalysis is that it provides the possibility of purchasing a regular supply of sustained, careful *attention*.
Ernest Gellner (1925–95) British anthropologist and philosopher. *The Psychoanalytic Movement* (1985)

13 Freud is midwife to the soul.
H. D. (pen name of Hilda Doolittle) (1886–1961) US-born British poet and writer. Referring to her psychoanalysis with Sigmund Freud (1933–34). Attrib.

14 Psychoanalysis cannot be considered a method of education if by education we mean the topiary art of clipping a tree into a beautiful artificial shape. But those who have a higher conception of education will prize most the method of cultivating a tree so that it fulfils to perfection its own natural conditions of growth.
Carl Gustav Jung (1875–1961) Swiss psychoanalyst. Attrib.

15 Psychoanalysis is the disease it purports to cure.
Karl Kraus (1874–1936) Austrian writer. *Die Fackel* (June 1913)

16 Psychoanalysts are father confessors who like to listen to the sins of the fathers as well.
Karl Kraus (1874–1936) Austrian writer. 1918. Quoted in *Karl Kraus* (Harry Zohn; 1971)

17 The greatest psychopathologist has been Freud. Freud was a hero. He descended to the 'Underworld' and met there stark terrors. He carried with him his theory as a Medusa's head which turned these terrors to stone.
R. D. Laing (1927–89) Scottish psychiatrist. *The Divided Self* (1965), ch. 1

18 Like Communism and Christianity, psychoanalysis was a revered orthodoxy that brought respectability and fortune to an elite.
Timothy Leary (1920–96) US psychologist and guru. *Flashbacks: an Autobiography* (1983)

19 Psychoanalysis . . . has raised understanding to an art so fine that it can actually be practiced as a legitimate occupation . . . A psychoanalyst is, therefore, nothing but an artist at understanding.
Robert Lindner (1915–56) US psychoanalyst. 1954. *The Fifty-Minute Hour* (1986), Foreword

20 Considered in its entirety, psychoanalysis won't do. It's an end product, moreover, like a dinosaur or a zeppelin; no better theory can ever be erected on its ruins, which will remain for ever one of the saddest and strangest of all landmarks in the history of twentieth century thought.
Peter Medawar (1915–87) Brazilian-born British biologist. 'Further Comments on Psychoanalysis', *The Hope of Progress* (1972)

21 It is psychoanalysis that has returned our myths to us. What will become of all this if the tamed sphinx soberly takes its place in a new philosophy of enlightenment?
Maurice Merleau-Ponty (1908–61) French existentialist philosopher. Quoted in *The Essential Writings of Merleau-Ponty* (A. L. Fisher, ed.; 1969)

22 The aim of psychoanalysis is very daring. It consists in rediscovering, in the individual's unconscious, the hidden tendencies which guide the person without his knowledge and which influence the actual contents of consciousness.
Jean Piaget (1896–1980) Swiss psychologist. 'Psychoanalysis and its Relations with Child Psychology' (1920), quoted in *The Essential Piaget* (H. E. Gruber and J. Jacques Vonèche, eds.; 1977)

23 A psychoanalyst is one who pretends he doesn't know everything.
Proverb.

Psychology

see also **Human Nature, Mind**

1 Psychology has a long past, but only a short history.
Hermann Ebbinghaus (1850–1909) German psychologist. *Summary of Psychology* (1885)

2 'Psychology' is merely a thin skin on the surface of the ethical world in which modern man seeks his truth—and loses it.
Michel Foucault (1926–84) French philosopher. 1962. *Mental Illness and Psychology* (1976)

3 Psychology can never tell the truth about madness because it is madness that holds the truth of psychology.
Michel Foucault (1926–84) French philosopher. *Mental Illness and Psychology* (1976)

4 A man like me cannot live without a hobby-horse, a consuming passion—in Schiller's words a tyrant. I have found my tyrant, and in his service I know no limits. My tyrant is psychology.
Sigmund Freud (1856–1939) Austrian psychoanalyst. Letter to William Fliess (1895)

5 Psychology as a science has its limitations, and, as the logical consequence of theology is mysticism, so the ultimate consequence of psychology is love.
Erich Fromm (1900–80) German-born US psychoanalyst and philosopher. *The Art of Loving* (1956)

6 The only thing which psychology has the right to postulate at the outset is the fact of thinking itself, and that must first be taken up and analyzed.

William James (1842–1910) US psychologist and philosopher. *The Principles of Psychology* (1890), vol. 1

7 The psychological observer ought to be more agile than the tightrope dancer in order to be able to insinuate himself under the skin of other people.

Søren Kierkegaard (1813–55) Danish philosopher. 1844. *The Concept of Dread* (W. Lowrie, tr.; 1957)

8 Psychology is as unnecessary as directions for using poison.

Karl Kraus (1874–1936) Austrian writer. Attrib.

9 Modern psychology, like modern man, does not like to see the sparse, wrinkled-skin facts about human transience. The personality chess game is blown up to compelling importance.

Timothy Leary (1920–96) US psychologist and guru. *The Politics of Ecstasy* (1968)

10 Psychology which explains everything
explains nothing,
and we are still in doubt.

Marianne Moore (1887–1972) US poet. 'Marriage', *Collected Poems* (1951)

11 An animal psychologist is a man who pulls habits out of rats.

Proverb.

12 A large part of the popularity and persuasiveness of psychology comes from its being a sublimated spiritualism: a secular, ostensibly scientific way of affirming the primacy of 'spirit' over matter.

Susan Sontag (b. 1933) US writer. *Illness as Metaphor* (1978), ch. 7

13 The object of psychology is to give us a totally different idea of the things we know best.

Paul Valéry (1871–1945) French poet and philosopher. *Tel Quel* (1943)

Publishing

see also **Books, Journalism, Media**

1 Publication is the male equivalent of childbirth.

Richard Acland (1906–90) British politician and writer. *Observer* (May 19, 1974), 'Sayings of the Week'

2 I'll publish, right or wrong:
Fools are my theme, let satire be my song.

Lord Byron (1788–1824) British poet. *English Bards and Scotch Reviewers* (1809)

3 I, according to my copy, have done set it in imprint, to the intent that noble men may see and learn the noble acts of chivalry, the gentle and virtuous deeds that some knights used in those days.

William Caxton (1422?–91) English printer. Quoted in *Le Morte D'Arthur* (Thomas Malory; 1485), Original Preface

4 As repressed sadists are supposed to become policemen or butchers so those with irrational fear of life become publishers.

Cyril Connolly (1903–74) British writer and journalist. *Enemies of Promise* (1938), ch. 3

5 My own motto is publish and be sued.

Richard Ingrams (b. 1937) British journalist. Referring to his editorship of *Private Eye*, a satirical magazine. Remark on BBC Radio (May 4, 1977)

6 Curse the blasted, jelly-boned swines, the slimy, the belly-wriggling invertebrates, the miserable sodding rutters, the flaming sods, the snivelling, dribbling, dithering, palsied, pulse-less lot that make up England today. They've got white of egg in their veins and their spunk is that watery it's a marvel they can breed.

D. H. Lawrence (1885–1930) British writer. On Heinemann's rejection of *Sons and Lovers*. Letter to Edward Garnet (July 13, 1912)

7 I don't mind your thinking slowly: I mind your publishing faster than you think.

Wolfgang Pauli (1900–58) Austrian-born US physicist. Attrib.

Punctuality

see also **Procrastination**

1 Punctuality is the politeness of kings.

Louis XVIII (1755–1824) French monarch. Attrib.

2 'Twenty-three and a quarter minutes past', Uncle Matthew was saying furiously, 'in precisely six and three-quarter minutes the damned fella will be late'.

Nancy Mitford (1904–73) British writer. *Love in a Cold Climate* (1949), pt. 1, ch.13

3 I have come too late into a world too old.

Alfred de Musset (1810–57) French poet and playwright. 'Rolla', *Poésies Nouvelles* (1833)

4 Punctuality is the virtue of the bored.

Evelyn Waugh (1903–66) British novelist. March 26, 1962. 'Irregular Notes', *Diaries of Evelyn Waugh* (Michael Davie, ed.; 1976)

Punishment

see also **Crime, Execution**

1 All punishment is mischief: all punishment in itself is evil.

Jeremy Bentham (1748–1832) British philosopher, economist, jurist, and social reformer. *An Introduction to the Principles of Morals and Legislation* (1789), ch. 13

2 But his wife looked back from behind him, and she became a pillar of salt.

Bible. Genesis, *King James Bible* (1611), 19:26

3 He that spareth his rod hateth his son: but he that loveth him chasteneth him betimes.

Bible. Proverbs, *King James Bible* (1611), 13:24

4 Hanging is too good for him, said Mr. Cruelty.

John Bunyan (1628–88) English preacher and writer. *The Pilgrim's Progress* (1678), pt. 1

5 This was the hand that wrote it, therefore it shall suffer first punishment.

Thomas Cranmer (1489–1556) English archbishop. March 21, 1556. Remark made at the stake, referring to the hand that signed his recantation. Quoted in *Short History of the English People* (John Richard Green; 1874)

6 Punishment has passed from being an art of unsupportable sensations to an economy of suspended rights.

Michel Foucault (1926–84) French philosopher. *Surveiller et Punir* (1975)

7 Punishment is not for revenge, but to lessen crime and reform the criminal.

Elizabeth Fry (1780–1845) British prison reformer. Quoted in *Women's Record: Sketches of All Distinguished Women* (Sarah Josepha Hale; 1853)

8 He never spoils the child and spares the rod,
But spoils the rod and never spares the child.

Thomas Hood (1799–1845) British poet and humorist. 'The Irish Schoolmaster', ll. 106–107, quoted in *The Works of Thomas Hood* (1862–63)

9 A whipping never hurts so much as the thought that you are being whipped.

Edgar Watson Howe (1853–1937) US novelist. *Country Town Sayings* (1911)

10 The power of punishment is to silence, not to confute.

Samuel Johnson (1709–84) British lexicographer and writer. *Sermons* (1788), no. 23

11 The refined punishments of the spiritual mode are usually much more indecent and dangerous than a good smack.

D. H. Lawrence (1885–1930) British writer. *Fantasia of the Unconscious* (1922), ch. 4

12 I will not sell land in Florida.

The Simpsons, US cartoon series. Lines written as punishment on a chalkboard during the opening credits of *The Simpsons*. The content of the lines changes with each episode. *The Simpsons* (Matt Groening; 1990–)

13 I'm all for bringing back the birch, but only between consenting adults.

Gore Vidal (b. 1925) US novelist and essayist. Said when asked by presenter David Frost in a British television interview for his views about corporal punishment. (1973)

Puns

see **Wordplay**

Puritanism

see also **Morality**, **Oppression**

1 The Puritans . . . ceased to need or to find pleasure in ritual and symbol or any representative art; their religious mysticism was reduced to a pale phosphorescence of renunciation.

Mary Austin (1868–1934) US novelist. 'Sex in American Literature' (1923), quoted in *A Mary Austin Reader* (E. F. Lanigan, ed.; 1996)

2 A puritan's a person who pours righteous indignation into the wrong things.

G. K. Chesterton (1874–1936) British writer and poet. Attrib.

3 A learned man who is not cleansed is more dangerous than an ignorant man.

Ruhollah Khomeini (1900–89) Iranian religious and political leader. Speech (July 6, 1980)

4 To the Puritan all things are impure, as somebody says.

D. H. Lawrence (1885–1930) British writer. 'Cerveteri', *Etruscan Places* (1932)

5 Puritanism—the haunting fear that someone, somewhere, may be happy.

H. L. Mencken (1880–1956) US journalist, critic, and editor. *A Mencken Chrestomathy* (1949), ch. 30

Purity

see also **Virtue**

1 No one is more dangerous than he who imagines himself pure in heart: for his purity, by definition, is unassailable.

James Baldwin (1924–87) US writer and civil rights activist. 'The Black Boy Looks at the White Boy', *Nobody Knows My Name* (1961)

2 I'm as pure as the driven slush.

Tallulah Bankhead (1903–68) US actor. *Observer* (February 24, 1957), 'Sayings of the Week'

3 Pure and disposed to mount unto the stars.

Dante Alighieri (1265–1321) Italian poet. 'Purgatorio', *The Divine Comedy* (1307?–21?), can. 33, l. 145

4 My strength is as the strength of ten,
Because my heart is pure.

Alfred Tennyson (1809–92) British poet. 'Sir Galahad', *Poems* (1842), st. 1

Purpose

see also **Ambition**, **Motive**

1 Purpose is the central ingredient of power.

Michael Eisner (b. 1942) US entertainment executive. *Strategy and Business* (1997), 'Noteworthy Quotes'

2 The purpose of population is not ultimately peopling earth. It is to fill heaven.

Graham Leonard (b. 1921) British churchman. Contribution to a debate on the Church and the Bomb. Remark, General Synod of the Church of England (February 10, 1983)

3 Wise men write many books, in words too hard to understand. But this, the purpose of our lives, the end of all our struggle, is beyond all human wisdom.

Alan Stewart Paton (1903–88) South African novelist and political activist. *Cry, The Beloved Country* (1948)

4 I have a mission only, no opinions.

Friedrich von Schiller (1759–1805) German poet, playwright, and historian. *The Robbers and Wallenstein* (1799), Act 1, Scene 5

5 MARIA My purpose is, indeed, a horse of that colour.

William Shakespeare (1564–1616) English poet and playwright. *Twelfth Night* (1601), Act 2, Scene 3

6 All dressed up, with nowhere to go.

William Allen White (1868–1944) US writer. 1916. Referring to members of the Progressive Party after Theodore Roosevelt's failed attempt to win the US presidential election (1916). Attrib.

Q

Questions

see also **Answers**, **Curiosity**

1 Life, the Universe and Everything.

Douglas Adams (1952–2001) British writer. The Ultimate Question, which the Earth was constructed to solve. *The Hitch Hiker's Guide to the Galaxy* (1979)

2 We do not solve them: we get over them.

John Dewey (1859–1952) US philosopher and educator. Referring to dealing with philosophical, and other, questions. 'The Influence of Darwinism on Philosophy' (1909)

3 Ask me no questions, and I'll tell you no fibs.

Oliver Goldsmith (1730–74) Irish-born British novelist, playwright, and poet. *She Stoops to Conquer* (1773), Act 3

4 Test every concept by the question, 'What sensible difference to anybody will its truth make?'

William James (1842–1910) US psychologist and philosopher. *Pragmatism: A New Name for Old Ways of Thinking* (1907)

5 Questioning is not the mode of conversation among gentlemen.

Samuel Johnson (1709–84) British lexicographer and writer. March 25, 1776. Quoted in *Life of Samuel Johnson* (James Boswell; 1791)

6 There are innumerable questions to which the inquisitive mind can in this state receive no answer: Why do you and I exist? Why was this world created? Since it was to be created, why was it not created sooner?

Samuel Johnson (1709–84) British lexicographer and writer. 1778. Quoted in *Life of Samuel Johnson* (James Boswell; 1791)

7 We have learned the answers, all the answers: It is the question that we do not know.

Archibald MacLeish (1892–1982) US poet and educator. 'The Hamlet of A. MacLeish' (1928)

8 The question of the ultimate meaning of life cannot be silenced as long as men are men.

Paul Tillich (1886–1965) German-born US theologian and philosopher. *Christianity and the Encounter of the World Religions* (1961), ch. 4

9 The man who sees both sides of a question is a man who sees absolutely nothing at all.

Oscar Wilde (1854–1900) Irish poet, playwright, and wit. 'The Critic as Artist', *Intentions* (1891), pt. 2

10 My advice to you is not to inquire why or whither, but just enjoy your ice cream while it's on your plate—that's my philosophy.

Thornton Wilder (1897–1975) US novelist and playwright. *The Skin of Our Teeth* (1942), Act 1

11 The philosopher's treatment of a question is like the treatment of an illness.

Ludwig Wittgenstein (1889–1951) Austrian philosopher. *Philosophical Investigations* (1953)

Quotations

see also **Plagiarism**, **Soundbites**

1 An aphorism is something which spares the writer an essay by way of commentary, but in consequence is deeply shocking to the reader.

Peter Altenberg (1859–1919) Austrian writer. *Prodomos* (Andrew Barker, tr.; 1905)

2 There is always the option of being emotionally lazy, that is, of quoting.

Alain de Botton (b. 1969) British writer. *Essays in Love* (1994)

3 When a thing has been said and said well, have no scruple. Take it and copy it.

Anatole France (1844–1924) French novelist, poet, and critic. Quoted in *The Routledge Dictionary of Quotations* (Robert Andrews, ed.; 1987)

4 Every quotation contributes something to the stability or enlargement of the language.

Samuel Johnson (1709–84) British lexicographer and writer. On citations used in a dictionary. *A Dictionary of the English Language* (1755), Preface

5 If with the literate I am
Impelled to try an epigram
I never seek to take the credit
We all assume that Oscar said it.

Dorothy Parker (1893–1967) US writer and wit. Referring to Oscar Wilde. 'Oscar Wilde', *Sunset Gun* (1928)

6 A facility for quotation covers the absence of original thought.

Dorothy L. Sayers (1893–1957) British writer. Said by Lord Peter Wimsey. *Gaudy Night* (1935)

7 A quotation at the right moment is like bread to the famished.

The Talmud (4th century? BC)

8 In the dying world I come from quotation is a national vice. It used to be the classics, now it's lyric verse.

Evelyn Waugh (1903–66) British novelist. *The Loved One* (1948)

9 I summed up all systems in a phrase, and all existence in an epigram.

Oscar Wilde (1854–1900) Irish poet, playwright, and wit. Written in Reading Prison. Letter to Lord Alfred Douglas (January–March 1897)

R

Racism

see also Apartheid, Bigotry, Civil Rights, Prejudice, Xenophobia

1 Some white people ought to be transformed into Negroes just for a few days, so as to feel what we feel and suffer what we suffer.
James Emman Kwegyir Aggrey (1875–1927) Ghanaian educator. Quoted in *Aggrey of Africa* (Edwin William Smith; 1956)

2 Sometimes, it's like a hair across your cheek. You can't see it, you can't find it with your fingers, but you keep brushing at it because the feel of it is irritating.
Marian Anderson (1897–1993) US opera singer. Referring to racial prejudice. *Ladies Home Journal* (September 1960)

3 Racism is an *ism* to which everyone in the world today is exposed; for or against, we must take sides. And the history of the future will differ according to the decision which we make.
Ruth Benedict (1887–1948) US anthropologist. *Race: Science and Politics* (1940), ch. 1

4 The gentleman will please remember that when his half-civilized ancestors were hunting the wild boar in Silesia, mine were princes of the earth.
Judah Benjamin (1811–84) Caribbean-born Confederate statesman and lawyer. Replying to a US senator of Germanic origin who had made an anti-Semitic remark. Attrib.

5 Here is a state that used to lynch people like me suddenly declaring my version of a song as its State Song.
Ray Charles (b. 1932) US pianist and singer. Referring to his version of the song, 'Georgia'. Quoted in 'Ray Charles', *Off the Record: An Oral History of Popular Music* (Joe Smith; 1988)

6 Hurry was one of those theorists who believed in the inferiority of all the human race who were not white. His notions on the subject were not very clear, nor were his definitions at all well settled; but his opinions were none the less dogmatical or fierce.
James Fenimore Cooper (1789–1851) US novelist. *The Deerslayer: Or the First War Path* (1841), quoted in *The Leatherstocking Saga* (Allan Nevins, ed.; 1955)

7 Racism, in the first place, is a weapon used by the wealthy to increase the profits they bring in—by paying Black workers less for their work.
Angela Davis (b. 1944) US civil rights activist, educator, and writer. *Angela Davis: An Autobiography* (1974)

8 Being a star has made it possible for me to get insulted in places where the average Negro could never hope to go and get insulted.
Sammy Davis, Jr. (1925–90) US singer and entertainer. *Yes I Can* (1965)

9 The fact is, white Americans find it hard to tell the truth about colored people. They see us with a dollar in their eyes.
Frederick Douglass (1817–95) US abolitionist, writer, and orator. *Douglass' Monthly* (May 1861)

10 I am an invisible man, I am a man of substance, of flesh and bone, fiber and liquids—and I might even be said to possess a mind. I am invisible, understand, simply because people refuse to see me.
Ralph Ellison (1914–94) US writer, jazz musician, and photographer. *Invisible Man* (1953), prologue

11 It is the racist who creates his inferior.
Frantz Fanon (1925–61) Martiniquan social scientist, physician, and psychiatrist. *Black Skin, White Masks* (1952)

12 Let's see now. They've broken the four-minute mile; the sixteen-foot pole vault—how 'bout clearing the color bar next?
Dick Gregory (b. 1932) US comedian and civil rights activist. *From the Back of the Bus* (1962)

13 Anti-Semitism of today . . . is for the most part a movement among civilized nations by which they try to chase away the spectres of their own past.
Theodor Herzl (1860–1904) Hungarian-born Zionist leader. *The Jewish State* (1896)

14 All those who are not racially pure are mere chaff.
Adolf Hitler (1889–1945) Austrian-born German dictator. *Mein Kampf* (1933), ch. 2

15 White people tend to grossly underestimate all blacks, out of habit. Blacks have been overestimating whites in a conditioned reflex.
George Jackson (1941–71) US political activist and writer. June 10, 1970. Letter, *Soledad Brother* (1970)

16 When we're unemployed, we're called lazy; when the whites are unemployed it's called a depression, which is the psycho-linguistics of racism.
Jesse Jackson (b. 1941) US clergyman, civil rights leader, and politician. Interview by David Frost, *The Americans* (1970)

17 The battle still remains the same. It is not anti-white, but anti-wrong.
Kenneth David Kaunda (b. 1924) Zambian president. 1961. Quoted in *Kenneth Kaunda* (Philip Brownrigg; 1989)

18 Being a Negro in America means trying to smile when you want to cry. It means trying to hold on to physical life amid psychological death. It means the pain of watching your children grow up with clouds of inferiority in their mental skies. It means having your legs cut off, and then being condemned for being a cripple.
Martin Luther King, Jr. (1929–68) US civil rights leader. *Where Do We Go From Here: Chaos or Community?* (1967)

19 San Francisco supplemented the anti-Chinese
state laws with . . . a queue tax, a 'cubic air
ordinance' requiring that every residence have so
many cubic feet of air per inhabitant, a pole law
prohibiting the use of carrying baskets on poles,
cigar taxes, shoe taxes, and laundry taxes.
Maxine Hong Kingston (b. 1940) US writer. *China Men* (1980)

20 I am not, nor ever have been, in favor of
bringing about in any way the social and political
equality of the white and black races—I am
not . . . in favor of making voters or jurors of
Negroes, nor of qualifying them to hold office.
Abraham Lincoln (1809–65) US president. The first Lincoln-Douglas
debate. Speech (August 21, 1858)

21 And if I can die having brought any light, having
exposed any meaningful truth that will help to
destroy the racist cancer that is malignant in the
body of America—then, all of the credit is due to
Allah. Only the mistakes have been mine.
Malcolm X (1925–65) US Black activist. *The Autobiography of
Malcolm X* (1965)

22 And I must walk the way of life a ghost
Among the sons of earth, a thing apart.
For I was born, far from my native clime,
Under the white man's menace, out of time.
Claude McKay (1890–1948) Jamaican-born US writer. 'Outcast', *Harlem
Shadows* (1922)

23 These white folks didn't actually hate colored
people, they just didn't like being too close to
them.
Terry McMillan (b. 1951) US novelist and teacher. *Mama* (1987)

24 One of the things that makes a Negro unpleasant
to white folk is the fact that he suffers from their
injustice. He is thus a standing rebuke to them.
H. L. Mencken (1880–1956) US journalist, critic, and editor. 'Minority
Report', *Notebooks* (1956)

25 The world said you spelled black with a capital
nothing.
Gloria Naylor (b. 1950) US novelist, producer, and playwright. *Linden
Hills* (1985)

26 Racial oppression of black people in America has
done what neither class oppression nor sexual
oppression, with all their perniciousness, has ever
done: destroyed an entire people and their
culture.
Eleanor Holmes Norton (b. 1937) US politician. 'For Sadie and
Maude', *Sisterhood is Powerful* (Robin Morgan, ed.; 1970)

27 He's really awfully fond of coloured people.
Well, he says himself, he wouldn't have white
servants.
Dorothy Parker (1893–1967) US writer and wit. 'Arrangements in
Black and White', *Collected Stories* (1939)

28 White folks is a miracle of affliction, say Sofia.
Alice Walker (b. 1944) US novelist and poet. *The Color Purple* (1982)

29 No race can wrong another race simply because
it has the power to do so without being
permanently in moral chaos. The Negro can
endure the temporary inconvenience, but the
injury to the white man is permanent. It is for
the white man to save himself from his
degradation that I plead.
Booker T. Washington (1856–1915) US educator and political activist.
Speech to the Institute of Arts and Sciences, New York
(September 30, 1896), quoted in *Selected Speeches of Booker
T. Washington* (E. Davidson Washington, ed.; 1932)

30 Some view our sable race with scornful eye;
'Their color is a diabolic dye.'
Remember, Christians, Negroes, black as Cain,
May be refined, and join th' angelic train.
Phillis Wheatley (1753?–84) Senegalese-born US poet. 'On Being
Brought from Africa to America', *Poems on Various Subjects,
Religious and Moral* (1773)

Radicalism

see also **Originality, Politics, Rebellion**

1 RADICALISM, n. The conservatism of to-morrow
injected into the affairs of to-day.
Ambrose Bierce (1842–1914?) US writer and journalist. *The Devil's
Dictionary* (1911)

2 'Moderate', 'liberal'. Bad words in a situation of
conflict. In any situation that requires nothing
less than militancy to redress wrongs done to any
section of a people. To be a liberal you have to
be white.
Es'kia Mphahlele (b. 1919) South African novelist, teacher, and political
activist. *The African Image* (1974)

3 The radical invents the views. When he has worn
them out, the conservative adopts them.
Mark Twain (1835–1910) US writer and humorist. *Notebooks* (1935)

Rationalism

see also **Philosophy, Reason**

1 The empiricist view is so deep-seated in our way
of looking at the human mind that it almost has
the character of a superstition.
Noam Chomsky (b. 1928) US linguist and political activist. Quoted in
Listener (May 30, 1968)

2 My chief desire is to let you see that there is that
which is rational, that which is irrational and
that which is non-rational—and to leave you
weltering in that morass thereafter.
Seamus Deane (b. 1940) Irish writer and academic. *Reading in the
Dark* (1996), ch. 5

3 Nothing is more fairly distributed than common
sense: for each man thinks he has enough of it.
René Descartes (1596–1650) French philosopher and mathematician. *Le
Discours de la Méthode* (1637)

4 I have always been astonished by the tendency of
so many academic psychologists, economists, and
even anthropologists to treat human beings as
entirely rational. My own experience has always
been that rationality is only one of many factors
governing human behaviour and by no means
always the dominant factor.
Murray Gell-Mann (b. 1929) US particle physicist. *The Quark and the
Jaguar* (1994)

5 What could an entirely rational being speak of
with another entirely rational being?
Emmanuel Levinas (1905–95) Lithuanian-born French philosopher.
Totality and Infinity (1969)

6 Let's break away from rationality as out of a
horrible husk . . . Let's give ourselves up to the
unknown, not out of desperation but to plumb
the depths of the absurd.
Filippo Tommaso Marinetti (1876–1944) Italian writer, poet, and political
activist. Quoted in *Cubism, Futurism and Constructivism*
(J. M. Nash; 1974)

Readers

see also **Books**, **Critics**, **Reading**

1   A reader seldom peruses a book with pleasure
    until he knows whether the writer of it be a
    black man or a fair man, of a mild or choleric
    disposition, married or a bachelor.
    Joseph Addison (1672–1719) English essayist, poet, and statesman.
    Spectator (March 1, 1711), no. 1

2   Hypocrite reader—my likeness—my brother.
    Charles Baudelaire (1821–67) French poet. 'Au Lecteur', *Les Fleurs
    du Mal* (1857)

3   The human race, to which so many of my
    readers belong.
    G. K. Chesterton (1874–1936) British writer and poet. *The Napoleon of
    Notting Hill* (1904), ch. 1

4   Readers may be divided into four classes: 1.
    Sponges, who absorb all they read and return it
    nearly in the same state, only a little dirtied. 2.
    Sand-glasses, who retain nothing, and are content
    to get through a book for the sake of getting
    through the time. 3. Strain-bags, who retain
    merely the dregs of what they read, and return it
    nearly in the same state, only a little dirtied. 4.
    Mogul diamonds, equally rare and valuable, who
    profit by what they read, and reflecting,
    refracting, and enlarging upon it enable others to
    profit by it also.
    Samuel Taylor Coleridge (1772–1834) British poet. Quoted in *The
    Jingle Bell Principle* (Miloslav Holub; 1992)

5   It is the genre that is produced by living and
    which lets the reader live, because a reader reads
    a book several times not to learn anything, but to
    keep living, to live more.
    Ramón Gómez de la Serna (1888–1963) Spanish novelist. Referring to
    the novel. *Ismos* (1931)

6   That ideal reader suffering from an ideal
    insomnia.
    James Joyce (1882–1941) Irish writer. *Finnegans Wake* (1939)

7   A good reader has imagination, memory, a
    dictionary, and some artistic sense.
    Vladimir Nabokov (1899–1977) Russian-born US novelist, poet, and critic.
    Attrib.

8   There was a time when the average reader read a
    novel simply for the moral he could get out of it,
    and however naïve that may have been, it was a
    good deal less naïve than some of the limited
    objectives he has now.
    Flannery O'Connor (1925–64) US novelist and short-story writer. Lecture,
    Wesleyan College, Macon, Georgia (1960), 'Some Aspects of
    the Grotesque in Southern Fiction'

9   The reader of the novel will doubt, even for a
    brief moment, his own physical reality and will
    believe himself to be, like us, no more than a
    character from a novel.
    Miguel de Unamuno y Jugo (1864–1936) Spanish writer and philosopher.
    Niebla (1914)

Reading

see also **Books**, **Readers**

1   Reading maketh a full man; conference a ready
    man; and writing an exact man.
    Francis Bacon (1561–1626) English philosopher, statesman, and lawyer.
    'Of Studies', *Essays* (1625)

2   Read not to contradict and confute, nor to
    believe and take for granted, nor to find talk and
    discourse, but to weigh and consider.
    Francis Bacon (1561–1626) English philosopher, statesman, and lawyer.
    'Of Studies', *Essays* (1625)

3   He has only half learned the art of reading who
    has not added to it the even more refined
    accomplishments of skipping and skimming.
    Arthur Balfour (1848–1930) British prime minister. Quoted in *Mr.
    Balfour* (E. T. Raymond; 1920)

4   When reading a novel, we often identify
    ourselves with a given character. In poetry we
    identify ourselves with language itself.
    John Berger (b. 1926) British novelist, essayist, and art critic. 'Ev'ry
    Time We Say Goodbye', *Keeping a Rendezvous* (1991)

5   When we read a story, we inhabit it. The covers
    of a book are like a roof and four walls.
    John Berger (b. 1926) British novelist, essayist, and art critic. 'Ev'ry
    Time We Say Goodbye', *Keeping a Rendezvous* (1991)

6   It takes me so long to read the 'paper
    said to me one day a novelist hot as a firecracker,
    because I have to identify myself with everyone
    in it,
    including the corpses, pal.
    John Berryman (1914–72) US poet. *The Dream Songs* (1968)

7   The possession of a book becomes a substitute
    for reading it.
    Anthony Burgess (1917–93) British writer and critic. *New York Times
    Book Review* (1966)

8   How clear, serene, and solid the best work still
    seems; it's as if there were a physical communion
    taking place among the fingers turning the page,
    the eyes taking in the words, the brain
    imaginatively recreating what the words stand for
    and, as Hemingway put it, 'making it part of
    your experience'.
    Raymond Carver (1938–88) US poet, short-story writer, and essayist.
    November 17, 1985. Referring to the work of Ernest
    Hemingway. 'Coming of Age, Going to Pieces', *No Heroics,
    Please* (1991)

9   The reading of all good books is like a conversation
    with the finest men of past centuries.
    René Descartes (1596–1650) French philosopher and mathematician.
    Discourse on Method (1637), pt. 1

10 When I want to read a novel I write one.
    Benjamin Disraeli (1804–81) British prime minister and writer. Quoted
    in *Life of Benjamin Disraeli* (W. Monypenny and G. Buckle;
    1920), vol. 6, ch. 17

11 I read, much of the night, and go south in the
    winter.
    T. S. Eliot (1888–1965) US-born British poet and playwright. 'The Burial
    of the Dead', *The Waste Land* (1922)

12 Read in order to live.
    Gustave Flaubert (1821–80) French novelist. Letter to Mme. de
    Chantepie (1857)

13 Reading is always a good way to define pleasure
    anew.
    Richard Ford (b. 1944) US writer. *The Granta Book of the Long
    Story* (Richard Ford, ed.; 1998), introduction

14 God forbid people should read our books to find
    the juicy passages.
    Graham Greene (1904–91) British novelist. *Observer* (October 14,
    1979), 'Sayings of the Week'

15 The art of reading is to skip judiciously.
    Philip Gilbert Hamerton (1834–94) British art critic. *The Intellectual
    Life* (1873), pt. 4, letter 4

16 There is no surer way to misread a document than to read it literally.
Learned Hand (1872–1961) US jurist. 'Giuseppi v. Walling' (1944)

17 Reading is sometimes an ingenious device for avoiding thought.
Arthur Helps (1813–75) British historian. 'Reading', *Friends in Council* (1859), vol. 2, ch. 1

18 A man ought to read just as inclination leads him; for what he reads as a task will do him little good.
Samuel Johnson (1709–84) British lexicographer and writer. July 14, 1763. Quoted in *Life of Samuel Johnson* (James Boswell; 1791)

19 Book reading is a solitary and sedentary pursuit, and those who do are cautioned that a book should be used as an integral part of a well-rounded life . . . *A book should not be used as a substitute or an excuse.*
Garrison Keillor (b. 1942) US writer and broadcaster. *The Book of Guys* (1993)

20 It is not easy to get a truly and constantly productive spirit to read. He is to a reader as a locomotive is to a tourist.
Karl Kraus (1874–1936) Austrian writer. 1909. Quoted in 'Sprüche und Widersprüche', *Karl Kraus* (Harry Zohn; 1971)

21 Where shall I find time to do all this non-reading?
Karl Kraus (1874–1936) Austrian writer. 1909. Quoted in 'Sprüche und Widersprüche', *Karl Kraus* (Harry Zohn; 1971)

22 I love to lose myself in other men's minds. When I am not walking, I am reading; I cannot sit and think. Books think for me.
Charles Lamb (1775–1834) British essayist. 'Detached Thoughts on Books and Reading', *Last Essays of Elia* (1833)

23 When I had read this story to the end, I was filled with awe. I could not remain in my room and went out of doors. I felt as if I were locked up in a ward too.
Vladimir Ilyich Lenin (1870–1924) Russian revolutionary leader. On reading 'Ward Number Six' by Anton Chekhov (1892). Quoted in *Anton Chekhov* (W. H. Bruford; 1957)

24 Reading—I discovered—comes before writing. A society can exist—many do exist—without writing, but no society can exist without reading.
Alberto Manguel (b. 1948) Argentinian writer. 'The Last Page', *A History of Reading* (1996)

25 To read too many books is harmful.
Mao Zedong (1893–1976) Chinese statesman. *New Yorker* (March 7, 1977)

26 I wish thee as much pleasure in the reading, as I had in the writing.
Francis Quarles (1592–1644) English poet. 'To the Reader', *Emblems* (1635)

27 There are two motives for reading a book: one, that you enjoy it, the other that you can boast about it.
Bertrand Russell (1872–1970) British philosopher and mathematician. *The Conquest of Happiness* (1930)

28 To expect a man to retain everything that he has ever read is like expecting him to carry about in his body everything that he has ever eaten.
Arthur Schopenhauer (1788–1860) German philosopher. *Parerga and Paralipomena* (1851)

29 Reading, to me, is simply the expansion of one's mind to include some people whom you just didn't get to meet before.
Ntozake Shange (b. 1948) US poet, novelist, essayist, and playwright. Quoted in *Black Women Writers at Work* (Claudia Tate, ed.; 1983)

30 People say that life is the thing, but I prefer reading.
Logan Pearsall Smith (1865–1946) US-born British writer. 'Myself', *Afterthoughts* (1931)

31 Their teacher had advised them not to read Tolstoy novels, because they were very long and would easily confuse the clear ideas which they had learned from reading critical studies of him.
Alexander Solzhenitsyn (b. 1918) Russian novelist. *The First Circle* (1968), ch. 40

32 Reading is to the mind what exercise is to the body.
Richard Steele (1672–1729) Irish-born English essayist, playwright, and politician. *The Tatler* (March 18, 1710), no. 147

33 Whatever sentence will bear to be read twice, we may be sure was thought twice.
Henry David Thoreau (1817–62) US writer. *The Writings of Henry David Thoreau* (1894)

34 As in the sexual experience, there are never more than two persons present in the act of reading— the writer who is the impregnator, and the reader who is the respondent.
E. B. White (1899–1985) US writer and humorist. *The Second Tree from the Corner* (1954)

35 Camerado, this is no book,
Who touches this touches a man,
(Is it night? are we together alone?)
It is I you hold and who holds you,
I spring from the pages into your arms—decease calls me forth.
Walt Whitman (1819–92) US poet. 1877. 'So Long!', *Leaves of Grass* (1892), ll. 53–57

36 No two people read the same book.
Edmund Wilson (1895–1972) US critic and writer. Quoted in *Sunday Times* (July 25, 1971)

37 Whenever I have time I now read James's 'Varieties of Religious Experience'. This book does me a *lot* of good . . . I think that it helps me get rid of the *Sorge*.
Ludwig Wittgenstein (1889–1951) Austrian philosopher. Referring to William James's work of 1902. *Sorge* approximates to melancholy. Letter to Bertrand Russell (June 22, 1912), quoted in *Ludwig Wittgenstein: Cambridge Letters* (B. McGuinness and G. H. von Wright, eds.; 1995)

38 Reading Proust is like bathing in someone else's dirty water.
Alexander Woollcott (1887–1943) US writer and critic. Attrib.

39 With this new interest I became painfully aware of my ignorance and even stupidity, and I feel enthused by the novelty and attraction of knowledge.
Yang Wenzhi (b. 1954) Chinese writer. 1978. Referring to reading. 'Ah, Books!', *The Wounded* (Geremie Barmé, tr.; 1979)

40 When I think of all the books I have read . . . and of the hopes that I have had, all life weighed in the scales of my own life seems to me preparation for something that never happens.
W. B. Yeats (1865–1939) Irish poet and playwright. *Autobiographies* (1926)

Realism

see also **Artistic Styles, Literary Style, Reality**

1 Mr. Lely, I desire you would use all your skill to paint my picture truly like me, and not flatter me at all; but remark all these roughnesses, pimples, warts, and everything as you see me, otherwise I will never pay a farthing for it.
Oliver Cromwell (1599–1658) English soldier and statesman. The origin of the expression 'warts and all'. Quoted in *Anecdotes of Painting in England* (Horace Walpole; 1763), vol. 3, ch. 1

2 A Realist is an Idealist who knows nothing of himself.

Novalis (1772–1801) German poet and novelist. *The Disciples at Sais* (1801)

3 In other words, apart from the known and the unknown, what else is there?

Harold Pinter (b. 1930) British playwright, theatre director, and screenwriter. *The Homecoming* (1965), Act 2

4 Whatever you touch and believe in and that seems real for you today, is going to be—like the reality of yesterday—an illusion tomorrow.

Luigi Pirandello (1867–1936) Italian dramatist, novelist, and short-story writer. *Six Characters in Search of an Author* (1921), Act 3

5 The mass of mankind is divided into two classes, the Sancho Panzas who have a sense for reality, but no ideals, and the Don Quixotes with a sense for ideals, but mad.

George Santayana (1863–1952) Spanish-born US philosopher, poet, and novelist. Referring to characters in *Don Quixote* (1605, 1615), by Miguel de Cervantes. Quoted in *Interpretations of Poetry and Religion* (William G. Holzberger and Herman J. Saatkaup, Jr.; 1989), preface

Reality

see also **Experience, Fantasy, Realism**

1 It would seem that we are condemned for some time always to speak *excessively* of reality.

Roland Barthes (1915–80) French philosopher and writer. *Mythologies* (1957)

2 There are no things, only processes.

David Bohm (1917–92) US physicist. Attrib.

3 The visible universe was an illusion or, more precisely, a sophism. Mirrors and fatherhood are abominable because they multiply it and extend it.

Jorge Luis Borges (1899–1986) Argentinian writer and poet. 'Tlön, Uqbar, Orbis Tertius', *Ficciones* (1945)

4 I have no respect for reality as soon as it is acknowledged as such. I am interested in what I can do with unacknowledged reality.

Elias Canetti (1905–94) Bulgarian-born writer. *The Agony of Flies* (1992)

5 It's as large as life, and twice as natural!

Lewis Carroll (1832–98) British writer and mathematician. *Through the Looking-Glass and What Alice Found There* (1871), ch. 7

6 In reality we apprehend nothing for certain, but only as it changes according to the condition of our body, and of the things that impinge or offer resistance to it.

Democritus (460?–370? BC) Greek philosopher. 5th–4th century BC. Attrib.

7 Reality is that which, when you stop believing in it, doesn't go away.

Philip K. Dick (1928–82) US science-fiction writer. 1972. 'How to Build a Universe That Doesn't Fall Apart Two Days Later', *I Hope I Shall Arrive Soon* (1986), introduction

8 Human kind
Cannot bear very much reality.

T. S. Eliot (1888–1965) US-born British poet and playwright. 'Burnt Norton', *Four Quartets* (1935)

9 Our doctrine here is therefore that all reality . . . is brought forth solely by the imagination.

Johann Fichte (1762–1814) German philosopher. 1794. *The Science of Knowledge* (P. Heath and J. Lachs, trs.; 1982)

10 There may always be another reality
To make fiction of the truth we think we've arrived at.

Christopher Fry (b. 1907) British playwright. *A Yard of Sun* (1970), Act 2

11 I exist, more than that, I'm alive. I'm breathing. The profound thing is the air. Reality invents me. I am its legend. Hail!

Jorge Guillén (1893–1984) Spanish poet. 'Beyond', *Cántico* (1950)

12 The real world calls for a predatory man's brand of thinking.

George Jackson (1941–71) US political activist and writer. February 1965. Letter to his mother, *Soledad Brother* (1970)

13 Everything real must be experienceable somewhere, and every kind of thing experienced must somewhere be real.

William James (1842–1910) US psychologist and philosopher. *Essays in Radical Empiricism* (1912)

14 How to reconcile this world of fact with the bright world of my imagining? My darkness has been filled with the light of intelligence, and behold, the outer daylight world was stumbling and groping in social blindness.

Helen Keller (1880–1968) US writer and lecturer. Quoted in *The Cry for Justice* (Upton Sinclair, ed.; 1915)

15 Einstein's space is no closer to reality than Van Gogh's sky.

Arthur Koestler (1905–83) Hungarian-born British writer and journalist. *The Act of Creation* (1964), pt. 2, ch. 10

16 Nothing lasts long enough to make any sense.

Dambudzo Marechera (1952–87) Zimbabwean writer and poet. 'The House of Hunger', *The House of Hunger* (1978)

17 Nobody can drown in the ocean of reality who voluntarily gives himself up to the experience.

Henry Miller (1891–1980) US novelist. *Big Sur and the Oranges of Hieronymos Bosch* (1957)

18 Reality is something you rise above.

Liza Minnelli (b. 1946) US singer, dancer, and actor. Attrib.

19 I didn't even believe in history, really. Real was what was happening to me right then. Real was a toothache and a man you trusted who did you the dirt.

Walter Mosley (b. 1952) US novelist. *A Red Death* (1991), ch. 35

20 We live in a fantasy world, a world of illusion. The great task in life is to find reality.

Iris Murdoch (1919–99) Irish-born British novelist and philosopher. *Times* (April 15, 1983)

21 There are Real things, whose characters are entirely independent of our opinions of them.

C. S. Peirce (1839–1914) US physicist and philosopher. Quoted in *Collected Papers* (Charles Hartshore and Paul Weiss, eds.; 1931–58), vol. 5

22 A robust sense of reality is very necessary in framing a correct analysis of propositions about unicorns, golden mountains, round squares, and other such pseudo-objects.

Bertrand Russell (1872–1970) British philosopher and mathematician. *Introduction to Mathematical Philosophy* (1919)

23 An object is the sum of its complications, seen
And unseen. This is everybody's world.
Here the total artifice reveals itself
As the total reality.

Wallace Stevens (1879–1955) US poet. 'Three Academic Pieces', *The Necessary Angel: Essays on Reality and the Imagination* (1951)

24 Where other poets use reality as a springboard
    into space, he uses it as a foothold when he
    returns from flight.
    Arthur Symons (1865–1945) British poet and literary critic. Referring to
    William Blake. *William Blake* (1907)

25 And even the most solid of things and the most
    real, the best-loved and the well-known, are only
    hand-shadows on the wall. Empty space and
    points of light.
    Jeanette Winterson (b. 1959) British novelist. *Sexing the Cherry*
    (1989)

Reason

see also **Rationalism, Secularism**

1   Reasoning draws a conclusion and makes us
    grant the conclusion, but does not make the
    conclusion certain, nor does it remove doubt.
    Roger Bacon (1220?–92) English monk, philosopher, and scientist. *Opus
    Majus* (1266–67)

2   No longer can we be satisfied with a life where
    the heart has its reasons which reason cannot
    know. Our hearts must know the world of
    reason, and reason must be guided by an
    informed heart.
    Bruno Bettelheim (1903–90) Austrian-born US psychoanalyst. *Guardian*
    (March 15, 1990)

3   Men have lost their reason in nothing so much as
    their religion, wherein stones and clouts make
    martyrs.
    Thomas Browne (1605–82) English physician and writer. *Urn Burial*
    (1658), ch. 4

4   Between craft and credulity, the voice of reason is
    stifled.
    Edmund Burke (1729–97) Irish-born British statesman and political
    philosopher. Letter to the Sheriffs of Bristol (1777)

5   What mazed confusion!
    It is a labyrinth wherein the reason
    Can find no clue.
    Pedro Calderón de la Barca (1600–81) Spanish playwright and poet. *Life
    is a Dream* (1635), Act 1

6   Man stands face to face with the irrational. He
    feels within him the longing for happiness and
    for reason. The absurd is born of the
    confrontation between the human need and the
    unreasonable silence of the world.
    Albert Camus (1913–60) Algerian-born French novelist, essayist, and
    playwright. *The Myth of Sisyphus* (1942)

7   Reason is itself a matter of faith. It is an act of
    faith to assert that our thoughts have any
    relation to reality at all.
    G. K. Chesterton (1874–1936) British writer and poet. *Orthodoxy*
    (1909), ch. 3

8   Cultivate a superiority to reason, and see how
    you pare the claws of all the sensible people
    when they try to scratch you for your own good!
    Wilkie Collins (1824–89) British novelist. *The Moonstone* (1868), ch.
    21

9   The man who is master of his passions is
    Reason's slave.
    Cyril Connolly (1903–74) British writer and journalist. Quoted in
    Turnstile One (V. S. Pritchett, ed.; 1948)

10 Reason cannot be forced into belief.
    Hasdai ben Abraham Crescas (1340–1410) Spanish philosopher and
    Talmudist. *Or Adonai* (1412)

11 And new Philosophy calls all in doubt,
    The Element of fire is quite put out;
    The Sun is lost, and th'earth, and no man's wit
    Can well direct him where to look for it.
    John Donne (1572?–1631) English metaphysical poet and divine. *An
    Anatomy of the World: The First Anniversary* (1611), ll. 205–
    208

12 A man is to be cheated into passion, but to be
    reasoned into truth.
    John Dryden (1631–1700) English poet, playwright, and literary critic.
    Religio Laici (1682), preface

13 Everything must justify its existence before the
    judgment seat of Reason, or give up existence.
    Friedrich Engels (1820–95) German socialist. *Anti-Dühring* (1878),
    pt. 3

14 In everything that is supposed to be scientific,
    Reason must be awake and reflection applied. To
    him who looks at the world rationally the world
    looks rationally back. The relation is mutual.
    G. W. F. Hegel (1770–1831) German philosopher. *Reason in History*
    (Robert S. Hartman, tr.; 1953)

15 The question of how Reason is determined in
    itself and what its relation is to the world
    coincides with the question *What is the ultimate
    purpose of the world?*
    G. W. F. Hegel (1770–1831) German philosopher. *Reason in History*
    (Robert S. Hartman, tr.; 1953)

16 Reason has ruled, and is still ruling the world,
    and consequently the world's history.
    G. W. F. Hegel (1770–1831) German philosopher. *The Philosophy of
    History* (1832)

17 The only Thought which Philosophy brings with
    it to the contemplation of History is the simple
    conception of Reason; that Reason is the
    Sovereign of the World; that the history of the
    world, therefore, presents us with a rational
    process.
    G. W. F. Hegel (1770–1831) German philosopher. *The Philosophy of
    History* (1832)

18 Reason has moons, but moons not hers
    Lie mirror'd on her sea,
    Confounding her astronomers,
    But, O! delighting me.
    Ralph Hodgson (1871–1962) British poet. 'Reason Has Moons',
    Poems (1917), st. 1

19 *Rationalization* may be defined as self-deception
    by reasoning.
    Karen Horney (1885–1952) German-born US psychoanalyst. *Our Inner
    Conflicts* (1945)

20 'Tis not contrary to reason to prefer the
    destruction of the whole world to the scratching
    of my finger . . . 'Tis not the passion, properly
    speaking, which is unreasonable, but the
    judgment.
    David Hume (1711–76) Scottish philosopher and historian. *A Treatise of
    Human Nature* (1739–40)

21 Our reason must be consider'd as a kind of
    cause, of which truth is the natural effect.
    David Hume (1711–76) Scottish philosopher and historian. *A Treatise of
    Human Nature* (1739–40)

22 Reason is nothing but a wonderful and
    unintelligible instinct in our souls, which carries
    us along a certain train of ideas, and endows
    them with particular qualities, according to their
    particular situations and relations.
    David Hume (1711–76) Scottish philosopher and historian. *A Treatise of
    Human Nature* (1739–40)

23 Reason is only one out of a thousand possibilities in the thinking of each of us. Who can count all the silly fancies, the grotesque suppositions, the utterly irrelevant reflections he makes in the course of a day?

William James (1842–1910) US psychologist and philosopher. *The Principles of Psychology* (1890), vol. 1

24 Come now, let us reason together.

Lyndon Baines Johnson (1908–73) US president. Often-used phrase. Attrib.

25 A man who does not lose his reason over certain things has none to lose.

Gotthold Ephraim Lessing (1729–81) German playwright and critic. *Emilia Galotti* (1772), Act 4, Scene 7

26 The heart has its reasons which reason knows nothing of.

Blaise Pascal (1623–62) French philosopher, mathematician, and physicist. *Pensées* (1669), sect. 4, no. 277

27 The weakness of human reason makes men prone, when they leave one extreme, to rush into the opposite . . . from ascribing active power to all things to conclude all things to be carried on by necessity.

Thomas Reid (1710–96) Scottish philosopher. *Inquiry into the Human Mind on the Principles of Common Sense* (1764)

28 Huddled in dirt the reasoning engine lies,
Who was so proud, so witty, and so wise.

2nd Earl of Rochester (1647–80) English courtier and poet. 'Homo Sapiens', *The New Oxford Book of English Verse* (Helen Gardner, ed.; 1972)

29 Reason must sit at the knee of instinct and learn reverence for the miraculous instinctual capacity for creation.

Jonathan Schell (b. 1943) US author. *The Fate of the Earth* (1982)

30 Once the people begin to reason, all is lost.

Voltaire (1694–1778) French writer and philosopher. Letter to Damilaville (April 1, 1766)

Rebellion

see also **Freedom, Radicalism, Revolution**

1 In this king's time there was nothing but disturbance and wickedness and robbery, for forthwith the powerful men who were traitors rose against him.

Anglo-Saxon Chronicle. Referring to the reign of Stephen, king of England (1135–54). *Anglo-Saxon Chronicle* (874–1154)

2 The spirit burning but unbent,
May writhe, rebel—the weak alone repent!

Lord Byron (1788–1824) British poet. *The Corsair* (1814), can. 2, st. 10

3 What is a rebel? A man who says no: but whose refusal does not imply a renunciation.

Albert Camus (1913–60) Algerian-born French novelist, essayist, and playwright. *The Rebel* (1951)

4 Though man may endure his ordeal like Sisyphus, the time must come for him to revolt like Prometheus before his powers are exhausted by the ordeal.

Milovan Djilas (1911–95) Montenegrin-born Yugoslavian politician, writer, and dissident. *The Unperfect Society* (1969)

5 A little rebellion now and then is a good thing.

Thomas Jefferson (1743–1826) US president. Letter to James Madison (January 30, 1787)

6 Every generation revolts against its fathers and makes friends with its grandfathers.

Lewis Mumford (1895–1990) US social philosopher and urban planner. *The Brown Decades* (1931)

7 Angry Young Man

Leslie Paul (1905–85) British writer. 1951. Book title. The phrase subsequently became associated with John Osborne's play *Look Back In Anger* (1956).

8 Outrageous Acts and Everyday Rebellions

Gloria Steinem (b. 1934) US writer and feminist. 1983. Book title.

Reconciliation

see **Agreement, Compromise, Diplomacy**

Regret

see also **Shame, Sorrow, Unhappiness**

1 The only thing I regret about my past life is the length of it. If I had my past life over again I'd make all the same mistakes—only sooner.

Tallulah Bankhead (1903–68) US actor. *Times* (July 28, 1981)

2 Remorse, the fatal egg by pleasure laid.

William Cowper (1731–1800) British poet. 'The Progress of Error' (1782), l. 239

3 If only I had known, I should have become a watchmaker.

Albert Einstein (1879–1955) German-born US physicist. Reflecting on his role in the development of the atom bomb. Attrib. *New Statesman* (April 16, 1965)

4 We might have been!—These are but common words,
And yet they make the sum of life's bewailing.

Letitia Elizabeth Landon (1802–38) British poet and novelist. 'We Might Have Been', ll. 1–2, quoted in *Life and Literary Remains of L. E. L.* (Laman Blanchard; 1841)

5 Make it a rule of life never to regret and never to look back. Regret is an appalling waste of energy; you can't build on it; it's only good for wallowing in.

Katherine Mansfield (1888–1923) New Zealand-born British short-story writer and poet. Attrib.

6 Remorse: beholding heaven and feeling hell.

G. E. Moore (1873–1958) British philosopher. Attrib.

7 When I consider how my life is spent,
I hardly ever repent.

Ogden Nash (1902–71) US humorist. 'Reminiscent Reflection' (1931)

8 How do you think it feels
when all you can say is if only.

Lou Reed (b. 1942) US rock singer and songwriter. Song lyric. 'How Do You Think It Feels' (1973)

9 Never feel remorse for what you have thought about your wife; she has thought much worse things about you.

Jean Rostand (1894–1977) French biologist and writer. *Marriage* (1927)

10 Remorse sleeps during a prosperous period, but wakes up in adversity.

Jean-Jacques Rousseau (1712–78) French philosopher and writer. 1765–70. *Confessions* (1782), bk. 2

11 But with the morning cool repentance came.

Sir Walter Scott (1771–1832) Scottish novelist. *Rob Roy* (1817), ch. 12

12   DUKE OF VENICE To mourn a mischief that is
     past and gone
     Is the next way to draw new mischief on.
     William Shakespeare (1564–1616) English poet and playwright. *Othello*
     (1602–04), Act 1, Scene 3

13   OTHELLO Then must you speak
     Of one that lov'd not wisely, but too well;
     Of one not easily jealous, but, being wrought,
     Perplexed in the extreme; of one whose hand,
     Like the base Indian, threw a pearl away
     Richer than all his tribe.
     William Shakespeare (1564–1616) English poet and playwright. *Othello*
     (1602–04), Act 5, Scene 2

14   SALISBURY O, call back yesterday, bid time return.
     William Shakespeare (1564–1616) English poet and playwright. *Richard
     II* (1595), Act 3, Scene 2

15   The bitterest tears shed over graves are for words
     left unsaid and deeds left undone.
     Harriet Beecher Stowe (1811–96) US writer and abolitionist. *Little Foxes*
     (1865), ch. 3

16   Once at supper, reflecting that he had done
     nothing for any that day, he broke out into that
     memorable and justly admired saying, 'My
     friends, I have lost a day!'
     Suetonius (69?–140?) Roman historian and biographer. Referring to the
     Emperor Titus (ruled 79–81). 'Titus', *Lives of the Caesars* (121?)

17   Spring wakens too; and my regret
     Becomes an April violet,
     And buds and blossoms like the rest.
     Alfred Tennyson (1809–92) British poet. 1833–49. 'A. H. H.' (Arthur
     Henry Hallam) was the fiancé of Tennyson's sister Emily and
     died suddenly in September 1833. *In Memoriam A. H. H.*
     (1850), can. 115, st. 5

18   No, I have no regrets.
     Michel Vaucaire (b. 1904) French songwriter. 1961. Song title. It was
     one of Edith Piaf's greatest hits. Music by Charles Dumont.

19   For of all sad words of tongue or pen,
     The saddest are these: 'It might have been!'
     John Greenleaf Whittier (1807–92) US poet. 'Maud Muller' (1856)

20   If this belief from heaven be sent,
     If such be Nature's holy plan,
     Have I not reason to lament
     What man has made of man?
     William Wordsworth (1770–1850) English poet. 'Lines Written in Early
     Spring', *Lyrical Ballads* (1798), ll. 21–24

Relationships

see also Lovers, Marriage

1   Two separate worlds:
     yours and mine
     collapsed at the bend of the road.
     Years lost in twisted ropes
     spread their wings like swans.
     Pranab Bandyopadhyay, Indian poet and writer. 'The Whistle', *The
     Voice of the Indian Poets* (Pranab Bandyopadhyay, ed.; 1975)

2   Between ourselves the best thing of all is a
     combination of the surprising and the beautiful.
     Ludwig van Beethoven (1770–1827) German composer. Letter, *The
     Letters of Beethoven* (E. Anderson, ed., tr.; July 16, 1823),
     no. 1209

3   It is probably true to say that the largest scope
     for change still lies in men's attitude to women,
     and in women's attitude to themselves.
     Vera Brittain (1893–1970) British writer and feminist. *Lady into
     Woman* (1953), ch. 15

4   Once a woman has forgiven her man, she must
     not reheat his sins for breakfast.
     Marlene Dietrich (1901–92) German-born US actor and singer. *Marlene
     Dietrich's ABC* (1962)

5   A different taste in jokes is a great strain on the
     affections.
     George Eliot (1819–80) British novelist. *Daniel Deronda* (1876), ch. 15

6   You must leave breathing-space in the
     architecture of your love.
     Nuruddin Farah (b. 1945) Somali novelist, playwright, and teacher.
     Sardines (1981)

7   Personal relations are the important thing for
     ever and ever, and not this outer life of telegrams
     and anger.
     E. M. Forster (1879–1970) British novelist. *Howards End* (1910), ch. 19

8   No human relation gives one possession in
     another—every two souls are absolutely different.
     In friendship or in love, the two side by side raise
     hands together to find what one cannot reach
     alone.
     Kahlil Gibran (1883–1931) Lebanese-born US mystic, painter, and poet.
     Quoted in *Beloved Prophet* (Virginia Hilu, ed.; 1972)

9   A hidden connection is stronger than an obvious
     one.
     Heraclitus (*fl.* 500 BC) Greek philosopher. 480? BC. Quoted in *The
     Presocratic Philosophers* (G. S. Kirk, J. E. Raven, and
     M. Schofield; 1983)

10   Each thing needs other things—once called 'the
     sympathy of all things'. Attachment is embedded
     in the soul of things, like an animal magnetism.
     James Hillman (b. 1926) US author. Paper for symposium, *Cosmos,
     Life, Religion: Beyond Humanism* (1988)

11   Male domination has not destroyed the longing
     men and women have to love one another, even
     though it makes fulfilling that longing almost
     impossible to realize.
     bell hooks (b. 1952) US feminist writer, poet, and educator. 'feminist
     focus on men: a comment', *Talking Back* (1989)

12   The difficult part of love
     Is being selfish enough,
     Is having the blind persistence
     To upset an existence
     Just for your own sake.
     Philip Larkin (1922–85) British poet. 'Love' (1966), quoted in *Philip
     Larkin Collected Poems* (Anthony Thwaite, ed.; 1988)

13   Despite your warning that nobody ever changes
     for a woman, I think we shall both change a
     little. What's the use of falling in love if you both
     remain inertly as-you-were?
     Mary McCarthy (1912–89) US writer. Referring to her relationship
     with James West, who became her fourth husband in 1961.
     Letter to Hannah Arendt (May 25, 1960), quoted in *Between
     Friends: The Correspondence of Hannah Arendt and Mary
     McCarthy, 1949–75* (Carol Brightman, ed.; 1995)

14   Imparadised in one another's arms.
     John Milton (1608–74) English writer. Referring to Adam and Eve.
     Paradise Lost (1667), bk. 4, l. 506

15   What thou art is mine;
     Our state cannot be severed, we are one,
     One flesh; to lose thee were to lose my self.
     John Milton (1608–74) English writer. Adam to Eve. *Paradise Lost*
     (1667), bk. 9, ll. 957–959

16   To love you was pleasant enough,
     And, oh! 'tis delicious to hate you!
     Thomas Moore (1779–1852) Irish poet. 'When I Lov'd You', *Juvenile
     Poems* (1812)

17 This eagerness to seek hidden but necessary connections, connections that revealed a close relationship between the world where I was born in the flesh and the other worlds where I was reborn, has been the enterprise of my whole life.

Victoria Ocampo (1891–1979) Argentinian writer and publisher. Speech, American Academy of Arts and Letters, New York (1973)

18 We pass
And lit briefly by one another's light
Think the way we go is right.

Brian Patten (b. 1946) British poet and playwright. *Love Poems* (1982)

19 OSCAR Everything you do irritates me. And when you're not here, the things I know you're gonna do when you come back in irritate me.

Neil Simon (b. 1927) US playwright. Said to Felix. *The Odd Couple* (1965)

20 We are so fond of one another because our ailments are the same.

Jonathan Swift (1667–1745) Irish writer and clergyman. Stella was Swift's private name for Esther Johnson; they may have been secretly married. *Journal to Stella* (February 1, 1711)

Relatives

see Family

Relief

see Comfort

Religion

see also Belief, Buddhism, Christianity, God, Islam, Judaism

1 As far as Religion, I'm a Baptist *and* a good friend of the Pope, and I always wear a Jewish Star for luck.

Louis Armstrong (1901–71) US jazz trumpeter. Quoted in *Louis* (Max Jones and John Chilton; 1975)

2 The true meaning of religion is thus not simply morality, but morality touched by emotion.

Matthew Arnold (1822–88) British poet and critic. *Literature and Dogma* (1873), ch. 1

3 The greatest vicissitude of things amongst men is the vicissitude of sects and religions.

Francis Bacon (1561–1626) English philosopher, statesman, and lawyer. 'Of Vicissitude of Things', *Essays* (1625)

4 And what is religion, you might ask. It's a technology of living.

Toni Cade Bambara (1939–95) US novelist, short-story writer, and educator. *The Salt Eaters* (1980)

5 If there were no religious reality, if God were only a fiction, it would be mankind's duty to demolish it.

Martin Buber (1878–1965) Austrian-born Israeli philosopher of religion and Zionist. 1923. Quoted in *On Judaism* (N. Glazer, ed., Eva Jose et al., trs.; 1967)

6 One religion is as true as another.

Robert Burton (1577–1640) English scholar and churchman. *The Anatomy of Melancholy* (1621), pt. 3, sect. 4

7 Religion is by no means a proper subject of conversation in a mixed company.

Lord Chesterfield (1694–1773) English statesman and writer. 1766? *Letters to His Godson* (1890)

8 Men will wrangle for religion; write for it; fight for it; anything but—live for it.

Charles Colton (1780–1832) British cleric and writer. *Lacon* (1820), vol. 1

9 Love and compassion are the essence of all religion.

Dalai Lama (b. 1935) Tibetan spiritual leader. *Ocean of Wisdom: Guidelines for Living* (1989)

10 Religion is a support that in the end always ruins the edifice.

Denis Diderot (1713–84) French encyclopedist and philosopher. Quoted in *Encyclopedia of Philosophy* (P. Edwards, ed.; 1967)

11 One lesson of history is that religion has many lives, and a habit of resurrection.

Will Durant (1885–1981) US historian. *The Lessons of History* (co-written with Ariel Durant; 1968)

12 If something is in me which can be called religious then it is the unbounded admiration for the structure of the world so far as our science can reveal it.

Albert Einstein (1879–1955) German-born US physicist. Letter (March 24, 1954), quoted in *Albert Einstein, The Human Side* (Helen Dukas and Banesh Hoffman; 1979)

13 The religions we call false were once true.

Ralph Waldo Emerson (1803–82) US poet and essayist. 'Character', *Essays, Second Series* (1844)

14 Religion is the dream of the human mind.

Ludwig Andreas Feuerbach (1804–72) German philosopher. *The Essence of Christianity* (G. Eliot, tr.; 1841)

15 Religious ideas have sprung from the same need as all the other achievements of culture: from the necessity for defending itself against the crushing supremacy of nature.

Sigmund Freud (1856–1939) Austrian psychoanalyst. 1928. *The Future of an Illusion* (1927), ch. 3

16 Religion
Has made an honest woman of the supernatural,
And we won't have it kicking over the traces again.

Christopher Fry (b. 1907) British playwright. *The Lady's Not for Burning* (1949), Act 2

17 Things divine are believed in
But by those who themselves are so.

Friedrich Hölderlin (1770–1843) German poet. 'Applause of Men' (1796–97), quoted in *Selected Poems* (J. B. Leishman, ed., tr.; 1944)

18 Nobody can have the consolations of religion or philosophy unless he has first experienced their desolations.

Aldous Huxley (1894–1963) British novelist and essayist. *Collected Essays* (1958)

19 To become a popular religion, it is only necessary for a superstition to enslave a philosophy.

William Ralph Inge (1860–1954) British churchman. 'The Idea of Progress', Romanes lecture, Oxford (May 27, 1920)

20 Many people think they have religion when they are troubled with dyspepsia.

Robert G. Ingersoll (1833–99) US lawyer. *Liberty of Man, Woman, and Child* (1903), pt. 3

21 A religion true to its natures must also be concerned about man's social conditions.

Martin Luther King, Jr. (1929–68) US civil rights leader. *Stride Toward Freedom* (1964)

22 In the county there are thirty-seven churches and no butcher shop. This could be taken as a matter of all form and no content.

Maxine Kumin (b. 1925) US poet and writer. 'Living Alone with Jesus' (1975), ll. 10–12

23 But I suppose even God was born
    too late to trust the old religion—
    all those settings out
    that never left the ground,
    beginning in wisdom, dying in doubt.
    Robert Lowell (1917–77) US poet. 'For the Union Dead', *For the Union Dead* (1964)

24 So much wrong could religion induce.
    Lucretius (99?–55? BC) Roman philosopher and poet. *De Rerum Natura* (1st century BC), pt. 1, l. 101

25 I count religion but a childish toy,
    And hold there is no sin but ignorance.
    Christopher Marlowe (1564–93) English playwright and poet. *The Jew of Malta* (1590?), prologue

26 Religion is the soul of soulless conditions, the heart of a heartless world, the opium of the people.
    Karl Marx (1818–83) German philosopher. *Critique of the Hegelian Philosophy of Right* (1844), Introduction

27 Things have come to a pretty pass when religion is allowed to invade the sphere of private life.
    Lord Melbourne (1779–1848) British prime minister. On hearing an evangelical sermon. Quoted in *Collections and Recollections* (G. W. E. Russell; 1898), ch. 6

28 There's no reason to bring religion into it. I think we ought to have as great a regard for religion as we can, so as to keep it out of as many things as possible.
    Sean O'Casey (1880–1964) Irish playwright. *The Plough and the Stars* (1926)

29 Men never do evil so completely and cheerfully as when they do it from religious conviction.
    Blaise Pascal (1623–62) French philosopher, mathematician, and physicist. *Pensées* (1669), no. 894

30 Religion has always been the wound, not the bandage.
    Dennis Potter (1935–94) British playwright. *Observer* (April 10, 1994), 'Sayings of the Week'

31 For a religion like Hinduism, which emphasizes Divine Immanence, the chosen people embraces all mankind. If we have something to teach our neighbours we also have something to learn from them.
    Sarvepalli Radhakrishnan (1888–1975) Indian philosopher and statesman. *Eastern Religions and Western Thought* (1939), ch. 5

32 Religion is not a popular error; it is a great instinctive truth, sensed by the people, expressed by the people.
    Ernest Renan (1823–92) French philosopher, philologist, and historian. *Les Apôtres* (1866)

33 We must reject a privatization of religion which results in its reduction to being simply a matter of personal salvation.
    Robert Runcie (1921–2000) British archbishop. *Observer* (April 17, 1988), 'Sayings of the Week'

34 Religions, which condemn the pleasures of sense, drive men to seek the pleasures of power. Throughout history power has been the vice of the ascetic.
    Bertrand Russell (1872–1970) British philosopher and mathematician. *New York Herald-Tribune Magazine* (May 6, 1938)

35 Religious law is like the grammar of a language. Any language is governed by such rules; otherwise it ceases to be a language. But within them, you can say many different sentences and write many different books.
    Jonathan Sacks (b. 1948) British chief rabbi. *Independent* (June 30, 1994)

36 I am a sort of collector of religions: and the curious thing is that I find I can believe in them all.
    George Bernard Shaw (1856–1950) Irish playwright. *Major Barbara* (1907), Act 2

37 The mystical and the ethical . . . There is no holiness and therefore no living religion without both elements.
    Paul Tillich (1886–1965) German-born US theologian and philosopher. *Christianity and the Encounter of the World Religions* (1961), ch. 3

38 Hinduism, if I have read it right, initially seeks to save the absoluteness of God at the cost of His goodness. The Judaic religions intuitively try to save His goodness at the cost of His absoluteness. And neither solution has been a true solution.
    Arnold Toynbee (1889–1975) British historian. 'What are the Criteria for Comparisons Between Religions?', *Christianity Among the Religions of the World* (1958), pt. 1

39 If we are to say that religion cannot be concerned with politics then we are really saying that there is a substantial part of human life in which God's writ does not run. If it is not God's, then whose is it? Who is in charge if not the God and Father of our Lord Jesus Christ?
    Desmond Tutu (b. 1931) South African clergyman and civil rights activist. Quoted in *The Words of Desmond Tutu* (Naomi Tutu, ed.; 1989)

40 The foundation of religion lies in that difference between the acts of men, which distinguishes them into good, evil, indifferent.
    William Wollaston (1659–1724) English philosopher. *The Religion of Nature Delineated* (1724)

Remedies

see also **Health and Healthy Living**, **Illness**, **Medicine**

1 He that will not apply new remedies must expect new evils: for time is the greatest innovator.
   Francis Bacon (1561–1626) English philosopher, statesman, and lawyer. 'Of Innovations', *Essays* (1625)

2 The remedy is worse than the disease.
   Francis Bacon (1561–1626) English philosopher, statesman, and lawyer. 'Of Seditions and Troubles', *Essays* (1625)

3 There are no such things as incurable, there are only things for which man has not found a cure.
   Bernard Mannes Baruch (1870–1965) US financier, statesman, and philanthropist. Speech, President's Committee on Employment of the Physically Handicapped (April 30, 1954)

4 Well, now, there's a remedy for everything except death.
   Miguel de Cervantes (1547–1616) Spanish novelist and playwright. *Don Quixote* (1605–15), pt. 2, ch. 10

5 When a lot of remedies are suggested for a disease, that means it can't be cured.
   Anton Chekhov (1860–1904) Russian playwright and short-story writer. *The Cherry Orchard* (1904), Act 1

6 If you are too fond of new remedies, first you will not cure your patients; secondly, you will have no patients to cure.
   Astley Cooper (1768–1841) British surgeon. Attrib.

7 What destroys one man preserves another.
   Corneille (1606–84) French playwright. *Cinna* (1641), Act 2, Scene 1

8 Every day, in every way, I am getting better and better.

Émile Coué (1857–1926) French psychotherapist and hypnotist. Formula for a cure by autosuggestion. *De la Suggestion et de ses Applications* (1915)

9 Time is the great physician.

Benjamin Disraeli (1804–81) British prime minister and writer. *Henrietta Temple* (1837), bk. 6, ch. 9

10 The poisons are our principal medicines, which kill the disease and save the life.

Ralph Waldo Emerson (1803–82) US poet and essayist. *The Conduct of Life* (1860)

11 Confidence and hope do be more good than physic.

Galen (129–199?) Greek physician and scholar. Attrib.

12 Like cures like.

Samuel Hahnemann (1755–1843) German physician. Motto for homeopathy. Attrib.

13 The most rational cure after all for the inordinate fear of death is to set a just value on life.

William Hazlitt (1778–1830) British essayist and critic. 'On the Fear of Death', *Table Talk* (1821–22)

14 Extreme remedies are most appropriate for extreme diseases.

Hippocrates (460?–377? BC) Greek physician. *Aphorisms* (415? BC), sect. 1

15 A calming influence on the nervous system, they say, can be obtained from travel on the Volga.

Robert Lindner (1915–56) US psychoanalyst. 1954. Quoting a remark by a Russian psychiatrist. *The Fifty-Minute Hour* (1986), ch. 2

16 It seems to me that whether or not our patients are hooked on the drugs, the doctors are certainly hooked on the diagnoses.

Marshall Marinker (b. 1930) British physician. July 2, 1972. 'The Medical Use of Psychotropic Drugs' (1997), quoted in *The Antidepressant Web* (Charles Medawar; 1997)

17 Most men die of their remedies, and not of their illnesses.

Molière (1622–73) French playwright. *Le Malade Imaginaire* (1673), Act 3, Scene 3

18 Two minutes with Venus, two years with mercury.

J. Earle Moore (1892–1957) US physician. Alluding to the former use of mercury compounds in the treatment of syphilis. Attrib.

19 The cure of many diseases is unknown to the physicians of Hellas, because they are ignorant of the whole, which ought to be studied also; for the part can never be well unless the whole is well.

Plato (428?–347? BC) Greek philosopher. *Charmides* (4th century? BC)

20 The body must be repaired and supported, if we would preserve the mind in all its vigour.

Pliny the Younger (62–113) Roman politician and writer. *Epistles* (3rd–2nd century BC), bk. 1

21 We can pray over the cholera victim, or we can give her 500 milligrams of tetracycline every 12 hours.

Carl Sagan (1934–96) US astronomer and writer. *The Demon-Haunted World: Science as a Candle in the Dark* (1995)

22 There is no cure for birth and death save to enjoy the interval.

George Santayana (1863–1952) Spanish-born US philosopher, poet, and novelist. 'War Shrines', *Soliloquies in England* (1922)

23 The physician's best remedy is *Tincture of Time*.

Béla Schick (1877–1967) Hungarian-born US physician. Quoted in *Aphorisms and Facetiae of Béla Schick* (Israel J. Wolf; 1965)

24 It is part of the cure to wish to be cured.

Seneca, 'the Younger' (4? BC–AD 65) Roman writer, philosopher, and statesman. *Phaedra* (63?), l. 249

25 HELENA Our remedies oft in ourselves do lie, Which we ascribe to heaven.

William Shakespeare (1564–1616) English poet and playwright. *All's Well That Ends Well* (1603), Act 1, Scene 1

26 Like a bridge over troubled water, I will ease your mind.

Paul Simon (b. 1942) US singer and songwriter. Song lyric. 'Bridge Over Troubled Water' (1970)

27 I watched what method Nature might take, with intention of subduing the symptom by treading in her footsteps.

Thomas Sydenham (1624–89) English physician. *Observationes Medicae* (1676), ch. 2

Republicanism

see also **Democracy, Government, Monarchy**

1 Complete liberty and absolute democracy are but reefs upon which all republican hopes have foundered.

Simón Bolívar (1783–1830) Venezuelan soldier and statesman. Speech, Angostura (February 15, 1819)

2 In a Republic in which some are overstuffed with riches and others lack the very necessities, neither peace nor happiness is possible.

Juan de Mariana, Spanish historian. *De Rege et Regis Institutione* (1599)

3 The most obvious defect which one finds in the body of this republic is that there does not exist in any one of its parts any love or regard for the conservation of the whole; for every man thinks solely of present utility and not at all of the future.

Don Martínez de la Mata (fl. 17th century) Spanish economist. *Discursos* (1659)

4 The Republican form of Government is the highest form of government; but because of this it requires the highest type of human nature—a type nowhere at present existing.

Herbert Spencer (1820–1903) British philosopher. 'The Americans', *Essays* (1891)

5 As there was no form of government common to the peoples thus segregated, nor tie of language, history, habit, or belief, they were called a Republic.

Evelyn Waugh (1903–66) British novelist. *Scoop* (1938), bk. 2, ch. 1

Reputation

see also **Celebrity, Fame, Identity, Posterity**

1 The greatest mistake I ever made was not to die in office.

Dean Acheson (1893–1971) US lawyer and statesman. March 27, 1959. Said on hearing the funeral eulogies for John Foster Dulles, US secretary of state (1953–59). Dean Acheson had also been secretary of state (1947–53). Attrib.

2 You lived aloof, maintaining to the end
your magnificent disdain.

Anna Akhmatova (1888–1966) Russian poet. Referring to Mikhail
Bulgakov. 'In Memory of M. B.' (Stanley Kunitz and Max
Hayward, trs.; 1940), quoted in *Anna Akhmatova: Selected
Poems* (Stanley Kunitz and Max Hayward, trs.; 1973)

3 When I appear in public people expect me to
neigh, grind my teeth, paw the ground and swish
my tail—none of which is easy.

Princess Anne (b. 1950) British princess. *Observer* (May 22, 1977),
'Sayings of the Week'

4 For my name and memory, I leave it to men's
charitable speeches, and to foreign nations, and
the next ages.

Francis Bacon (1561–1626) English philosopher, statesman, and lawyer.
Final will and testament (December 19, 1625), quoted in *The
Letters and Life of Francis Bacon* (J. Spedding, ed.; 1874),
vol. 7

5 Just as it is always said of slander that
something always sticks when people boldly
slander, so it might be said of self-praise (if it is
not entirely shameful and ridiculous) that if we
praise ourselves fearlessly, something will always
stick.

Francis Bacon (1561–1626) English philosopher, statesman, and lawyer.
The Advancement of Learning (1605)

6 All your better deeds
Shall be in water writ, but this in marble.

Francis Beaumont (1584–1616) English playwright. *The Nice Valour*
(1616?), Act 5, Scene 5

7 With the publication of his Private Papers in
1952, he committed suicide 25 years after his
death.

Max Aitken Beaverbrook, Lord (1879–1964) Canadian-born British
newspaper owner and politician. Referring to Earl Haig. *Men and
Power* (1956)

8 I hold it as certain, that no man was ever written
out of reputation but by himself.

Richard Bentley (1662–1742) English classical scholar. Referring to
Alexander Pope. Quoted in *The Works of Alexander Pope*
(W. Warburton; 1751), vol. 4

9 It takes 20 years to build a reputation and five
minutes to ruin it.

Warren Buffett (b. 1930) US financier. Attrib.

10 The Doctor fared even better. The fame of his
new case spread far and wide. People seemed to
think that if he could cure an elephant he could
cure anything.

Henry Cuyler Bunner (1855–96) US writer. 'The Infidelity of Zenobia',
Short Sixes (1891)

11 A good name is better than riches.

Miguel de Cervantes (1547–1616) Spanish novelist and playwright. *Don
Quixote* (1605–15), pt. 2, ch. 33

12 I would rather be a brilliant memory than a
curiosity.

Emma Eames (1865–1949) US opera singer. 1926. Referring to her
retirement at the age of 47. Quoted in *The Elephant that
Swallowed a Nightingale* (Charles Neilson Gattey; 1981)

13 'Abroad', that large home of ruined reputations.

George Eliot (1819–80) British novelist. *Felix Holt* (1866), Epilogue

14 Worldly wisdom teaches that it is better for the
reputation to fail conventionally than to succeed
unconventionally.

John Maynard Keynes (1883–1946) British economist. *General Theory
of Employment, Interest and Money* (1936), ch. 12

15 The king of France is called the most Christian
King, but this does him injustice, for he never did
a Christian thing. I am called the most Invincible
King, but I have been overcome. The Pope is
called his Holiness, but he is the biggest
scoundrel on earth. You are called the richest
king, and this is true.

Maximilian I (1459–1519) Austrian-born monarch. Said to Henry VIII.
Attrib.

16 Until you've lost your reputation, you never
realize what a burden it was or what freedom
really is.

Margaret Mitchell (1900–49) US novelist. Said by Rhett Butler. *Gone
with the Wind* (1936), ch. 9

17 A good reputation is more valuable than money.

Publilius Syrus (fl. 1st century BC) Roman writer. 1st century BC.
Maxims (Darius Lyman, tr.), 108

18 CASSIO Reputation, reputation, reputation! O, I
have lost my reputation! I have lost the immortal
part of myself, and what remains is bestial.

William Shakespeare (1564–1616) English poet and playwright. *Othello*
(1602–04), Act 2, Scene 3

19 MOWBRAY The purest treasure mortal times
afford
Is spotless reputation; that away,
Men are but gilded loam or painted clay.

William Shakespeare (1564–1616) English poet and playwright. *Richard
II* (1595), Act 1, Scene 1

20 My reputation grew with every failure.

George Bernard Shaw (1856–1950) Irish playwright. Referring to his
unsuccessful early novels. Quoted in *Bernard Shaw* (Hesketh
Pearson; 1975)

Research

see also **Experiments, Learning, Libraries, University**

1 We vivisect the nightingale
To probe the secret of his note.

Thomas Bailey Aldrich (1836–1907) US writer and editor. 'Realism', *The
Poems of Thomas Bailey Aldrich* (1907)

2 Man can learn nothing except by going from the
known to the unknown.

Claude Bernard (1813–78) French physiologist. *An Introduction to the
Study of Experimental Medicine* (1865), ch. 2

3 Research is formalized curiosity. It is poking and
prying with a purpose.

Zora Neale Hurston (1891?–1960) US writer and folklorist. *Dust Tracks
on a Road* (1942)

4 The aim of research is the discovery of the
equations which subsist between the elements of
phenomena.

Ernst Mach (1838–1916) Austrian physicist and philosopher. *Popular
Scientific Lectures* (Thomas J. McCormack, tr.; 1910, 4th ed.)

5 In research the horizon recedes as we advance,
and is no nearer at sixty than it was at twenty.
As the power of endurance weakens with age, the
urgency of the pursuit grows more intense.

Mark Pattison (1813–84) British rector and author. *Isaac Casaubon*
(1875), ch. 10

6 Aristotle maintained that women have fewer
teeth than men; although he was twice married, it
never occurred to him to verify this statement by
examining his wives' mouths.

Bertrand Russell (1872–1970) British philosopher and mathematician. *The
Impact of Science on Society* (1952)

7 It is too bad that we cannot cut the patient in half in order to compare two regimens of treatment.

Béla Schick (1877–1967) Hungarian-born US physician. Quoted in 'Early Years', *Aphorisms and Facetiae of Béla Schick* (Israel J. Wolf; 1965)

8 Research is fundamentally a state of mind involving continual reexamination of the doctrines and axioms upon which current thought and action are based. It is, therefore, critical of existing practices.

Theobald Smith (1859–1934) US pathologist. *American Journal of Medical Science* (1929), no. 178

9 The outcome of any serious research can only be to make two questions grow where only one grew before.

Thorstein Bunde Veblen (1857–1929) US social scientist and economist. *The Place of Science in Modern Civilization* (1919)

10 It requires a very unusual mind to undertake the analysis of the obvious.

A. N. Whitehead (1861–1947) British philosopher and mathematician. *Science and the Modern World* (1925)

Respect

see also **Self-Respect**

1 There exist only three beings worthy of respect: the priest, the soldier, the poet. To know, to kill, to create.

Charles Baudelaire (1821–67) French poet. 'Mon Coeur Mis à Nu', *Journaux Intimes* (1887)

2 Not to be sneezed at.

George Colman (1762–1836) British playwright and theatre owner. *The Heir at Law* (1797), Act 2, Scene 2

3 The respect that is only bought by gold is not worth much.

Frances E. W. Harper (1825–1911) US writer and social reformer. 'Our Greatest Want', *Anglo-African* (May 1859)

4 Kill reverence and you've killed the hero in man.

Ayn Rand (1905–82) Russian-born US writer and philosopher. *The Fountainhead* (1943)

5 I'm sick of just liking people. I wish to God I could meet somebody I could respect.

J. D. Salinger (b. 1919) US novelist. Said by Franny. 'Franny', *Franny and Zooey* (1961)

6 When people do not respect us we are sharply offended; yet deep down in his heart no man much respects himself.

Mark Twain (1835–1910) US writer and humorist. *Following the Equator* (1897), ch. 29

7 We owe respect to the living; to the dead we owe only truth.

Voltaire (1694–1778) French writer and philosopher. 'Première lettre sur Oedipe', *Oeuvres* (1785), vol. 1

8 His indolence was qualified with enough basic bad temper to ensure the respect of those about him.

Evelyn Waugh (1903–66) British novelist. *Put Out More Flags* (1942)

Respectability

see also **Conformity**, **Reputation**

1 The devil's most devilish when respectable.

Elizabeth Barrett Browning (1806–61) British poet. *Aurora Leigh* (1856), bk. 7

2 Let them cant about decorum
Who have characters to lose.

Robert Burns (1759–96) Scottish poet and songwriter. Also known as 'Love and Liberty—a Cantata'. 'The Jolly Beggars' (1799)

3 I wanted to spit. Respectable! Show me any artist who wants to be respectable.

Martha Graham (1893–1991) US dancer and choreographer. 1980. Reflecting on a fundraiser who complimented her on her respectability. *Blood Memory* (1991)

4 Politicians, ugly buildings, and whores all get respectable if they last long enough.

John Huston (1906–87) US film director and actor. Said as Noah Cross. *Chinatown* (Robert Towne; 1974)

5 So live that you wouldn't be ashamed to sell the family parrot to the town gossip.

Will Rogers (1879–1935) US actor, writer, and humorist. Attrib.

Responsibility

see also **Morality**, **Power**

1 The ancient Romans had a tradition: whenever one of their engineers constructed an arch, as the capstone was hoisted into place, the engineer assumed accountability for his work in the most profound way possible: he stood under the arch.

Michael Armstrong, US business executive. Speech (May 9, 1995)

2 Perhaps it is better to be irresponsible and right than to be responsible and wrong.

Winston Churchill (1874–1965) British prime minister and writer. Party political broadcast in London (August 26, 1950)

3 At moments when our attention is painfully acute, we notice peripheral things . . . as if to reaffirm to ourselves our basic irresponsibility.

E. L. Doctorow (b. 1931) US novelist. *The Waterworks* (1994)

4 Perhaps the biggest responsibility of any corporation is to own up when it makes a mistake.

Lee Iacocca (b. 1924) US business executive. *Talking Straight* (1988)

5 The most dangerous aspect of present-day life is the dissolution of the feeling of individual responsibility. Mass solitude has done away with any difference between the internal and external, between the intellectual and the physical.

Eugenio Montale (1896–1981) Italian poet. *Poet in Our Time* (1972)

6 You become responsible, forever, for what you have tamed. You are responsible for your rose.

Antoine de Saint-Exupéry (1900–44) French writer and aviator. *The Little Prince* (1943), ch. 21

7 In dreams begins responsibility.

W. B. Yeats (1865–1939) Irish poet and playwright. *Responsibilities* (1914), Epigraph

Retribution

see also **Revenge**

1 No one provokes me with impunity.

Anonymous. Motto of the Scottish Crown, and all Scottish regiments.

2 For they have sown the wind, and they shall reap the whirlwind: it hath no stalk: the bud shall yield no meal: if so be it yield, the strangers shall swallow it up.

Bible. Hosea, *King James Bible* (1611), 8:7

3 But the children of the kingdom shall be cast out into outer darkness: there shall be weeping and gnashing of teeth.
Bible. Matthew, *King James Bible* (1611), 8:12

4 Then said Jesus unto him, Put up again thy sword into his place: for all they that take the sword shall perish with the sword.
Bible. Matthew, *King James Bible* (1611), 26:52

5 The gods
Visit the sins of the fathers upon the children.
Euripides (480?–406? BC) Greek playwright. *Phrixus* (5th century BC), fragment 970

Revenge

see also **Retribution**

1 A man that studieth revenge keeps his own wounds green.
Francis Bacon (1561–1626) English philosopher, statesman, and lawyer. 'Of Revenge', *Essays* (1625)

2 Revenge is a kind of wild justice; which the more man's nature runs to, the more ought law to weed it out.
Francis Bacon (1561–1626) English philosopher, statesman, and lawyer. 'Of Revenge', *Essays* (1625)

3 And if any mischief follow, then thou shalt give life for life,
Eye for eye, tooth for tooth, hand for hand, foot for foot,
Burning for burning, wound for wound, stripe for stripe.
Bible. Exodus, *King James Bible* (1611), 21:23–25

4 I make war on the living, not on the dead.
Charles V (1500–58) Belgian-born Spanish monarch. 1546. After the death of Martin Luther, when it was suggested that he hang the corpse on a gallows. Attrib.

5 Decapitating the spring onions,
She made this mental note:
You can tell it's love, the real thing,
When you dream of slitting his throat.
Wendy Cope (b. 1945) British poet. 'From June to December, 5: Some People', *Making Cocoa for Kingsley Amis* (1986)

6 Perish the Universe, provided I have my revenge.
Savinien Cyrano de Bergerac (1619–55) French poet, playwright, and soldier. *La Mort d'Agrippine* (1654), Act 4

7 Don't get mad, get even.
Joseph Kennedy (1888–1969) US business executive and government official. Quoted in *Conversations with Kennedy* (B. Bradlee; 1976)

8 If an injury has to be done to a man it should be so severe that his vengeance need not be feared.
Niccolò Machiavelli (1469–1527) Italian historian, statesman, and political philosopher. *The Prince* (1513)

9 No more tears now; I will think upon revenge.
Mary, Queen of Scots (1542–87) Scottish monarch. Said after the murder of her secretary, David Rizzio, by an opposing faction led by her husband, Lord Darnley, on March 9, 1566. Lord Darnley was murdered the following year. Remark (1566), attrib.

10 It is the revenge of Dreyfus.
Charles Maurras (1868–1952) French poet, journalist, and political thinker. Referring to his life sentence for his support of the Vichy regime in France, which collaborated with the Germans during World War II. The French Jew Alfred Dreyfus was accused of treason (1893) for allegedly intending to pass French military documents on to the German embassy in Paris, for which he was sentenced to life imprisonment. In 1899 Dreyfus was pardoned. Remark (1945)

11 Revenge, at first though sweet,
Bitter ere long back on itself recoils.
John Milton (1608–74) English writer. *Paradise Lost* (1667), bk. 9, ll. 171–172

12 TAMORA I am Revenge, sent from th'infernal kingdom
To ease the gnawing vulture of thy mind
By working wreakful vengeance on thy foes.
Come down and welcome me to this world's light;
Confer with me of murder and of death;
There's not a hollow cave or lurking-place,
No vast obscurity or misty vale,
Where bloody murder or detested rape
Can couch for fear but I will find them out;
And in their ears tell them my dreadful name—
Revenge, which makes the foul offender quake.
William Shakespeare (1564–1616) English poet and playwright. *Titus Andronicus* (1590), Act 5, Scene 2

13 CLOWN And thus the whirligig of time brings in his revenges.
William Shakespeare (1564–1616) English poet and playwright. *Twelfth Night* (1601), Act 5, Scene 1

14 MALVOLIO I'll be reveng'd on the whole pack of you.
William Shakespeare (1564–1616) English poet and playwright. *Twelfth Night* (1601), Act 5, Scene 1

15 I am Toussaint L'Ouverture, my name is perhaps known to you. I have undertaken vengeance.
Toussaint L'Ouverture (1743–1803) Haitian revolutionary leader and general. August 29, 1793. Quoted in *The Black Jacobins* (C. L. R. James; 1938)

16 You have undertaken to cheat me. I won't sue you, for the law is too slow. I'll ruin you.
Cornelius Vanderbilt (1794–1877) US industrialist. Letter to former business associates (1853)

Revolution

see also **Anarchy**, **Change**, **French Revolution**, **Rebellion**, **Russian Revolution**

1 Inferiors revolt in order that they may be equal and equals that they may be superior. Such is the state of mind which creates revolutions.
Aristotle (384–322 BC) Greek philosopher. *Politics* (335–322? BC), bk. 5

2 Ground for a revolution is always fertile in the presence of absolute destitution.
Stephen Biko (1946–77) South African political leader. 1970. 'We Blacks', *Steve Biko: I Write What I Like* (Aelred Stubbs, ed.; 1978)

3 The reactionaries of 1815 hid their faces at the very name of revolution; those of 1940 used it to camouflage their seizure of power.
Marc Bloch (1886–1944) French historian. Referring to France. In 1815, the French monarchy was restored after the defeat of Napoleon at Waterloo. In 1940, after the defeat of France by Germany, the collaborationist Vichy government was formed, with many French politicians taking high office. *Apologie pour l'Histoire, ou Métier d'Historien* (1949)

4 The revolution is like Saturn, it devours its own children.
Georg Büchner (1813–37) German dramatist. Referring to the French Revolution (1789–99). *Danton's Death* (1835), Act 1, Scene 5, quoted in *Complete Plays, Lenz and Other Writings* (John Reddick, tr.; 1993)

5 The only hope of the masses now is in social revolution. It alone can save Spain from Fascism.

Francisco Largo Caballero (1869–1946) Spanish politician. February 1934. In response to Republican unwillingness to take agrarian reform seriously. Remark, quoted in *The Spanish Labyrinth* (Gerald Brenan; 1943)

6 All modern revolutions have ended in a reinforcement of the power of the State.

Albert Camus (1913–60) Algerian-born French novelist, essayist, and playwright. *The Rebel* (1951)

7 A revolution is not a bed of roses. A revolution is a struggle to the death between the future and the past.

Fidel Castro (b. 1927) Cuban leader. Second anniversary of the Cuban revolution. Speech, Havana (January 1961)

8 There are seasons . . . of inward and outward revolution, when new depths seem to be broken up in the soul, when new wants are unfolded in the multitudes, and a new and undefined good is thirsted for. These are periods when . . . to *dare* is the highest wisdom.

William Ellery Channing (1780–1842) US clergyman. 'The Union' (1829)

9 The scrupulous and the just, the noble, humane, and devoted natures; the unselfish and the intelligent may begin a movement—but it passes away from them. They are not the leaders of a revolution. They are its victims.

Joseph Conrad (1857–1924) Polish-born British novelist. *Under Western Eyes* (1911), pt. 2

10 'I've seen all sorts of revolutions', he remarks, 'and I've come to the conclusion that people are idiots. It doesn't make a darn bit of difference what the government is'.

e. e. cummings (1894–1962) US poet and painter. Referring to a man encountered on a train to Russia. *Eimi* (1933)

11 Revolution takes place on the basis of the needed material benefit. It would be idealism to emphasize the spirit of sacrifice to the neglect of material benefit.

Deng Xiaoping (1904–97) Chinese statesman. 'Emancipate the Mind, Seek Truth from Facts and Unite as One in Looking to the Future' (December 13, 1978), quoted in *Deng Xiaoping: Speeches and Writings* (Robert Maxwell, ed.; 1987)

12 The right to revolt has sources deep in our history.

William Orville Douglas (1898–1980) US jurist. *An Almanac of Liberty* (1954)

13 I am not a do-gooder. I am a revolutionary. A revolutionary woman.

Jane Fonda (b. 1937) US actor and political activist. Comment, *Los Angeles Weekly* (1971)

14 What is wrong with a revolution is that it is natural. It is as natural as natural selection, as devastating as natural selection, and as horrible.

William Golding (1911–93) British novelist. *Observer* (1974), 'Sayings of the Year'

15 Everywhere revolutions are painful yet fruitful gestations of a people: they shed blood but create light, they eliminate men but elaborate ideas.

Manuel González Prada (1844–1918) Peruvian politician and writer. *Horas de Lucha* (1908)

16 You cannot go to sleep with one form of economic system and wake up the next morning with another.

Mikhail Gorbachev (b. 1931) Russian statesman. Quoted in *Guardian* (December 14, 1990)

17 I believe in the armed struggle as the only solution for those people who fight to free themselves, and I am consistent with my beliefs.

Che Guevara (1928–67) Argentinian-born revolutionary. Written on leaving Cuba to resume an active role as a guerrilla leader, initially in the Congo and then Bolivia. Last letter to his parents (1965)

18 In a revolution (if it's real) either you win or you die.

Che Guevara (1928–67) Argentinian-born revolutionary. Letter to Fidel Castro (1967)

19 In the laborious work of revolutionaries, death is a frequent accident.

Che Guevara (1928–67) Argentinian-born revolutionary. Quoted in *We Say No* (Eduardo Galeano; 1992)

20 The spirit of revolution, the spirit of insurrection is a spirit radically opposed to liberty.

François Guizot (1787–1874) French statesman and historian. Speech, Paris (December 29, 1830)

21 'Liberty Mr. Gumboil?' he said, 'you don't suppose any serious minded person imagines a revolution is going to bring liberty do you?'

Aldous Huxley (1894–1963) British novelist and essayist. *Antic Hay* (1923)

22 Revolution has become the intellectually acceptable form of modern war. To call any large-scale conflict revolution and identify one side as the revolutionaries is enough to win the sympathy and support of well-meaning people . . . And, of course, the combination of 'left-wing' and 'revolution' is a double pedigree.

Kenneth David Kaunda (b. 1924) Zambian president. Quoted in *Kaunda on Violence* (Colin M. Morris, ed.; 1980)

23 If you feed people just with revolutionary slogans they will listen today, they will listen tomorrow, they will listen the day after tomorrow, but on the fourth day they will say 'To hell with you!'

Nikita Khrushchev (1894–1971) Soviet statesman. Attrib.

24 Neither can you expect a revolution, because there is no new baby in the womb of our society. Russia is a collapse, not a revolution.

D. H. Lawrence (1885–1930) British writer. 'The Good Man', *Phoenix* (1929)

25 The whole cause of world revolution hinges on the revolutionary struggles of the Asian, African, and Latin American people who make up the overwhelming majority of the world's population.

Lin Biao (1907–71) Chinese revolutionary and politician. 'Long Live the Victory of People's War' (1965), quoted in *Occidentalism* (Liu Xiaomei; 1995)

26 The question tonight, as I understand it, is 'The Negro Revolt, and Where Do We Go From Here?' or 'What Next?' In my little humble way of understanding it, it points toward either the ballot or the bullet.

Malcolm X (1925–65) US Black activist. Comment (April 3, 1964)

27 The German's revolutions are the puppet shows of world history.

Thomas Mann (1875–1955) German writer. 1947. *Doctor Faustus* (H. T. Lowe-Porter, tr.; 1949), ch. 14

28 A revolution is not a dinner party . . . or doing embroidery; it cannot be so refined, so leisurely.

Mao Zedong (1893–1976) Chinese statesman. Remark (1927)

29 Revolution is the ecstasy of history.

Mottos and Slogans. May 1968. Paris Students' Revolt slogan.

30   We now live in two revolutions: one demanding
     that we should unite together, love one another
     and strain every nerve to reach our goal; the
     other forces us . . . to disperse and give way to
     hatred, everyone thinking of himself.
     Gamal Abdel Nasser (1918–70) Egyptian statesman. *The Philosophy of
     the Revolution* (1952)

31   Take a Clear-Cut Stand against Unrest.
     Newspapers. In response to pro-democracy demonstrations.
     People's Daily (China; April 26, 1989), editorial, quoted in
     June Four: A Chronicle of the Chinese Democratic Uprising
     (photographers and reporters of the Ming Pao News; Zi Jin
     and Qin Zhou, trs.; 1989)

32   Cradle a soft black woman and burn fingers as
     you trace revolution beneath her woolly hair.
     Grace Nichols (b. 1950) Guyanese journalist, poet, and novelist. "Of
     Course When They Ask for Poems About the 'Realities' of
     Black Women", *Lazy Thoughts of a Lazy Woman and Other
     Poems* (1989)

33   Circumstances can be changed by revolution and
     revolutions are brought about by men, by men
     who think as men of action and act as men of
     thought.
     Kwame Nkrumah (1909–72) Ghanaian president. *Consciencism:
     Philosophy and Ideology for Decolonisation and Development*
     (1964)

34   Revolution is not the uprising against pre-existing
     order, but the setting-up of a new order
     contradictory to the traditional one.
     José Ortega y Gasset (1883–1955) Spanish writer and philosopher. *The
     Revolt of the Masses* (1930)

35   The uprising of the masses implies a fabulous
     increase of vital possibilities; quite the contrary of
     what we hear so often about the decadence of
     Europe.
     José Ortega y Gasset (1883–1955) Spanish writer and philosopher. *The
     Revolt of the Masses* (1930), ch. 2

36   There's no such thing as an orderly revolution.
     John Osborne (1929–94) British playwright and screenwriter. *Luther*
     (1961), Act 3, Scene 2

37   Nothing is so like a rising of Spanish
     revolutionaries, as a rising of Spanish
     reactionaries.
     Benito Pérez Galdós (1843–1920) Spanish novelist and playwright.
     Quoted in *The Spanish Labyrinth* (Gerald Brenan; 1943)

38   Revolutions are like a water wheel, for in the end
     they always bring the worst mistakes of human
     nature to the top.
     Johann Heinrich Pestalozzi (1746–1827) Swiss educational reformer.
     Quoted in *The Education of Man: Aphorisms* (Heinz and
     Ruth Norden, trs.; 1951)

39   Revolutions are not made; they come.
     Wendell Phillips (1811–84) US reformer. Speech (January 28, 1852)

40   Revolution . . . is the idea of justice . . . It divides
     power quantitatively, not qualitatively as our
     constitutionalists do . . . It is atheist in religion
     and anarchist in politics: anarchist in the sense
     that it considers power as a very passing
     necessity: atheist in that it recognizes no religion,
     because it recognizes them all.
     Francisco Pi y Margall (1824–1901) Spanish politician and author. *La
     Reacción y La Revolución* (1854)

41   Great conflagrations are born of tiny sparks.
     Cardinal Richelieu (1585–1642) French churchman and statesman.
     Testament Politique (1688), ch. 8

42   Remember this, Griffin. The revolution eats its
     own. Capitalism re-creates itself.
     Mordecai Richler (b. 1931) Canadian novelist. *Cocksure* (1968), ch. 22

43   Revolutionary spirits of my father's generation
     waited for Lefty. Existentialist heroes of my
     youth waited for Godot. Neither showed up.
     Theodore Roszak (b. 1933) US writer and editor. *Unfinished Animal*
     (1975)

44   We are dancing on a volcano.
     Comte de Salvandy (1795–1856) French nobleman. Remark made
     before the July Revolution (Paris, July 1830).

45   The revolution and women's liberation go
     together. We do not talk of women's
     emancipation as an act of charity or because of a
     surge of human compassion. It is a basic
     necessity for the triumph of the revolution.
     Women hold up the other half of the sky.
     Thomas Sankara (1950–87) Burkina Fasoan soldier and president.
     October 2, 1983. *Thomas Sankara Speaks* (1988)

46   You can jail a revolutionary, but you cannot jail
     the revolution.
     Bobby Seale (b. 1936) US civil rights activist. 1969. Attrib.

47   To attempt to export revolution is nonsense.
     Joseph Stalin (1879–1953) Soviet dictator. Message sent to Roy
     Howard, US newspaper owner (March 1, 1936)

48   The odd thing about revolution is that the
     further left you go politically the more bourgeois
     they like their art.
     Tom Stoppard (b. 1937) Czech-born British playwright and screenwriter.
     Travesties (1974), Act 1

49   Revolutions are always verbose.
     Leon Trotsky (1879–1940) Russian revolutionary leader. *History of the
     Russian Revolution* (1933), vol. 2, ch. 12

50   The word 'revolution' is a word for which you
     kill, for which you die, for which you send the
     labouring masses to their death, but which does
     not possess any content.
     Simone Weil (1909–43) French philosopher, mystic, and political activist.
     'Reflections Concerning the Causes of Liberty and Social
     Oppression', *Oppression and Liberty* (1958)

51   We invented the Revolution
     but we don't know how to run it.
     Peter Weiss (1916–82) German-born Swedish novelist and playwright. *The
     Persecution and Assassination of Marat as Performed by the
     Inmates of the Asylum of Charenton Under the Direction of
     the Marquis de Sade* (1964), Act 1, Scene 15

52   I want a revolution, and I want it to start in
     Crotonville.
     Jack Welch (b. 1935) US electronics executive. The headquarters of
     General Electric Company are in Crotonville, New York.
     Quoted in *Jack Welch Speaks* (Janet C. Lowe; 1998)

53   Beginning reform is beginning revolution.
     Duke of Wellington (1769–1852) Irish-born British general and prime
     minister. Remark (November 7, 1830)

54   You noble Diggers all, stand up now,
     The waste land to maintain, seeing Cavaliers by
     name
     Your digging do disdain and persons all defame.
     Gerrard Winstanley (1609?–60?) English reformer. The Diggers were a
     radical group that believed in land reform and practised an
     agrarian communism. Important in 1649, they were dispersed
     by the Commonwealth government in 1650. 'The Diggers'
     Song' (1649)

55   Every revolutionary movement also liberates
     language.
     Christa Wolf (b. 1929) German writer. Speech, Berlin (November 4,
     1989), quoted in *When the Wall Came Down* (Harold James
     and Marla Stone, eds.; 1992)

56 Revolutions aren't made by gadgets and technology. They're made by a shift in power, which is taking place all over the world. Today, intellectual capital is at least as important as money capital and probably more so.

Walter B. Wriston (b. 1919) US banker. Quoted in *Opening Digital Markets* (Walid Mougayar; 1997)

57 Women and Revolution! What tragic, unsung epics of courage lie silent in the world's history!

Yang Ping (b. 1908) Chinese writer, political activist, and journalist. *Fragments from a Lost Diary* (1973)

Rhetoric

see also **Language, Literary Style, Propaganda, Speech**

1 For rhetoric he could not ope
His mouth, but out there flew a trope.

Samuel Butler (1612–80) English satirist. *Hudibras* (1663), pt. 1, can. 1, ll. 81–2

2 That passage is what I call the sublime dashed to pieces by cutting too close with the fiery four-in-hand round the corner of nonsense.

Samuel Taylor Coleridge (1772–1834) British poet. January 20, 1834. On lines cut from his poem 'Limbo' (1817). *Table Talk* (1835)

3 Rhetorical oratory is the foundation upon which all the humbug in our political system rests.

James Weldon Johnson (1871–1938) US writer, lawyer, and diplomat. *Along This Way* (1933)

4 My dear friend, clear your *mind* of cant . . .
You may *talk* in this manner; it is a mode of talking in Society: but don't *think* foolishly.

Samuel Johnson (1709–84) British lexicographer and writer. May 15, 1783. Quoted in *Life of Samuel Johnson* (James Boswell; 1791)

5 In our time, political speech and writing are largely the defence of the indefensible.

George Orwell (1903–50) British writer. 'Politics and the English Language', *Shooting an Elephant* (1950)

6 HORATIO These are but wild and whirling words, my lord.

William Shakespeare (1564–1616) English poet and playwright. *Hamlet* (1601), Act 1, Scene 5

Ridicule

see also **Foolishness, Humour, Insults, Stupidity**

1 Look for the ridiculous in everything and you will find it.

Jules Renard (1864–1910) French writer. February 1890. *Journal* (1877–1910)

2 Ridicule often checks what is absurd, and fully as often smothers that which is noble.

Sir Walter Scott (1771–1832) Scottish novelist. *Quentin Durward* (1823)

Right

see also **Good, Morality, Righteousness**

1 The humblest citizen of all the land, when clad in the armor of a righteous cause, is stronger than all the hosts of error.

William Jennings Bryan (1860–1925) US politician and lawyer. *The First Battle: A Story of the Campaign of 1896* (1896), vol. 1, ch. 10

2 The need to be right—the sign of a vulgar mind.

Albert Camus (1913–60) Algerian-born French novelist, essayist, and playwright. *Notebooks* (1935–42)

3 When everyone is wrong, everyone is right.

Nivelle de La Chaussée (1692–1754) French playwright. *La Gouvernante* (1747), Act 1, Scene 2

4 The right people are rude. They can afford to be.

Somerset Maugham (1874–1965) British writer. *Our Betters* (1917), Act 2

5 An insignificant right becomes important when it is assailed.

William Pickens (1881–1954) US educator. 'The Ultimate Effects of Segregation', *The New Negro: His Political, Civil and Mental Status and Related Essays* (1916)

6 Always do right. This will gratify some people, and astonish the rest.

Mark Twain (1835–1910) US writer and humorist. Card to Greenpoint Presbyterian Church, Brooklyn, United States (February 16, 1901)

Righteousness

see also **Certainty, Right, Virtue**

1 The eternal *not ourselves* that makes for righteousness.

Matthew Arnold (1822–88) British poet and critic. *Literature and Dogma* (1873), ch. 8

2 The humble and meek are thirsting for blood.

Joe Orton (1933–67) British playwright. *Funeral Games* (1970)

3 If God be for us who can be against us?

Desmond Tutu (b. 1931) South African clergyman and civil rights activist. Nobel Peace Prize speech of acceptance, *African Forum* (December 10, 1984), vol. 2, no 1

Rivers

see also **The Environment, Landscapes, The Sea**

1 I have seen the Mississippi. That is muddy water. I have seen the St Lawrence. That is crystal water. But the Thames is liquid history.

John Elliot Burns (1858–1943) British engineer, politician and trade union leader. *Daily Mail* (January 12, 1943)

2 Ol' man river, dat ol' man river,
He must know sumpin', but don't say nothin',
He just keeps rollin', he keeps on rollin' along.

Oscar Hammerstein II (1895–1960) US lyricist and librettist. Song lyric. 'Ol' Man River', *Show Boat* (music by Jerome Kern; 1927)

3 riverrun, past Eve and Adam's, from swerve of shore to bend of bay, brings us by a commodius vicus of recirculation back to Howth Castle and Environs.

James Joyce (1882–1941) Irish writer. Opening words of novel. *Finnegans Wake* (1939)

4 Sweet Thames! run softly, till I end my Song.

Edmund Spenser (1552?–99) English poet. 'Prothalamion' (1596), refrain

5 Eastwards goes the great river,
its waves have swept away
a thousand years of gallant men.

Su Dongpo (1036–1101) Chinese poet and writer. 'The Charms of Nian-nu: Meditation on the Past at Red Cliff' (1082?), quoted in *An Anthology of Chinese Literature* (Stephen Lawson, tr.; 1996)

6 The Spirit of the River laughed for joy that all the beauty of the earth was gathered to himself. Down with the stream he journeyed east, until he reached the ocean. There, looking eastwards and seeing no limit to its waves, his countenance changed.

Zhuangzi (369?–286 BC) Chinese philosopher and teacher. 'Autumn Floods', quoted in *Chuang Tzu* (Herbert A. Giles, tr.; 1980), ch. 17

Romanticism

see also **Idealism**, **Nature**, **Philosophy**

1 When I behold, upon the night's starr'd face,
Huge cloudy symbols of a high romance,
. . . then on the shore
Of the wide world I stand alone, and think
Till love and fame to nothingness do sink.

John Keats (1795–1821) English poet. 'When I Have Fears' (1818), quoted in *Life, Letters, and Literary Remains of John Keats* (R. M. Milnes, ed.; 1848)

2 The sickness of our times for me has been just this damn thing that everything has been getting smaller and smaller and less and less important, that the romantic spirit has dried up.

Norman Mailer (b. 1923) US novelist and journalist. 'Hip, Hell, and the Navigator', *Western Review* (Winter 1959)

3 Let us set down as an incontestable maxim that the first movements of nature are always right. There is no original perversity in the human heart. There is not a single vice in it of which it cannot be said how and whence it entered.

Jean-Jacques Rousseau (1712–78) French philosopher and writer. *Émile, or On Education* (1762)

4 Romanticism is the art of presenting people with the literary works which are capable of affording them the greatest possible pleasure, in the present state of their customs and beliefs. Classicism, on the other hand, presents them with the literature that gave the greatest possible pleasure to their great-grandfathers.

Stendhal (1783–1842) French writer. *Racine and Shakespeare* (1825), ch. 3

5 A sense sublime
Of something far more deeply interfused,
Whose dwelling is the light of setting suns,
And the round ocean and the living air,
And the blue sky, and in the mind of man:
A motion and a spirit, that impels
All thinking things, all objects of all thought,
And rolls through all things.

William Wordsworth (1770–1850) English poet. July 13, 1798. Subtitled: 'On Revisiting the Banks of the Wye During a Tour, July 13, 1798'. 'Lines Composed a Few Miles Above Tintern Abbey', *Lyrical Ballads* (1798), ll. 95–102

Rome

see **European Cities**

Royalty

see **Monarchy**

Rules

see also **Law**, **Order**

1 Rules and models destroy genius and art.

William Hazlitt (1778–1830) British essayist and critic. 'On Taste', *Sketches and Essays* (William Carew Hazlitt, ed.; 1839)

2 Systems governed by only one set of rules are more vulnerable than those with variety.

Geoff Mulgan (b. 1961) British author and political analyst. *Connexity* (1997)

3 In their rules there was only one clause: Do what you will.

François Rabelais (1494?–1553?) French humanist and satirist. Referring to the fictional Abbey of Thélème. *Gargantua* (1534), bk. 1, ch. 57

4 The golden rule is that there are no golden rules.

George Bernard Shaw (1856–1950) Irish playwright. 'Maxims for Revolutionists', *Man and Superman* (1903)

5 Rules serve no purpose; they can only do harm . . . Not only must the artist's mind be clear, it should not be hindered and weighed down by a mechanical servility to such rules.

Federico Zuccaro (1542–1609) Italian painter and theorist. *The Idea of Painters, Sculptors and Architects* (1607)

Rumour

see also **Conversation**, **Gossip**, **Myths**

1 Plot me no plots.

Francis Beaumont (1584–1616) English playwright. *The Knight of the Burning Pestle* (1607), Act 2, Scene 5

2 You k'n hide de fier, but w'at you gwine do wid de smoke?

Joel Chandler Harris (1848–1908) US writer. 'Plantation Proverbs', *Uncle Remus: His Songs and His Sayings* (1880)

Russia

see also **Cold War**, **Europe**, **Russian Revolution**

1 Russian communism is the illegitimate child of Karl Marx and Catherine the Great.

Clement Attlee (1883–1967) British politician. Speech at Aarhus University (April 11, 1956), quoted in *Times* (April 12, 1956)

2 The future belongs to Russia, which grows and grows, looming above us as an increasingly terrifying nightmare.

Theobald von Bethmann Hollweg (1856–1921) German chancellor. Referring to Bethmann Hollweg's fear of the increasing threat posed by Russia, Serbia's ally, on the eve of World War I. Remark to his personal assistant (July 8, 1914), quoted in *Europe: A History* (Norman Davies; 1996), ch. 10

3 The Russians do not possess the kind of self-restraint that would make it possible for us to live alone with them and France on the continent.

Prince Otto von Bismarck (1815–98) German chancellor. Letter to his son, Herbert (October 1886), quoted in *Germany, 1866–1945* (Gordon A. Craig; 1978)

4 Russia is a sphinx. Grieving, jubilant, and covering herself with blood she looks, she looks, she looks at you—her slant eyes lit with hatred and with love.

Aleksandr Blok (1880–1921) Russian poet. 'The Scythians' (January 30, 1918), sect. 1, quoted in *Selected Poems: Alexander Blok* (Jon Stallworthy and Peter France, trs.; 1974)

5   Whether he wants it or not, a Soviet citizen is in a state of permanent inner dialogue with the official propaganda.

Vladimir Bukovsky (b. 1942) Russian writer and scientist. Attrib.

6   ANY SATIRIST IN THE SOVIET UNION MUST QUESTION THE SOVIET SYSTEM.
Am I conceivable in the USSR?

Mikhail Bulgakov (1891–1940) Russian novelist and playwright. Letter to the USSR government (March 28, 1930), quoted in *The KGB's Literary Archive* (John Crowfoot, ed., tr.; 1993), ch. 3

7   I must rule after my own fashion.

Catherine the Great (1729–96) German-born Russian empress. Said soon after her accession, following the deposition of her husband, Tsar Peter III. Speech to the Russian Senate, St. Petersburg (June 1762)

8   I cannot forecast to you the action of Russia. It is a riddle wrapped in a mystery inside an enigma.

Winston Churchill (1874–1965) British prime minister and writer. October 1, 1939. Radio broadcast.

9   The churches are drowning with stars, everywhere stars blossom, frank and gold and keen . . . Now (touched by a resonance of sexually celestial forms) the little murdered adventure called Humanity becomes a selfless symbol.

e. e. cummings (1894–1962) US poet and painter. Said after attending a Russian Orthodox Church service in Kiev. *Eimi* (1933)

10 I would rather live in Russia on black bread and vodka than in the United States at the best hotels. America knows nothing of food, love, or art.

Isadora Duncan (1877–1927) US dancer. Interview (1922)

11 There is a discussion in my country about a new name for the USSR . . . Philip Morris is sending us billions of cigarettes. So some people suggest our new name should be Marlboro Country.

Gennadi Gerasimov (b. 1930) Russian journalist. *Sunday Times* (October 29, 1990)

12 May God be my witness that there will not be a poor man in my Tsardom! And even to my last shirt I will share with all.

Boris Godunov (1551?–1605) Russian monarch. Coronation address, Moscow (September 1, 1598)

13 Ivan Yakovlevich, like any honest Russian working man, was a terrible drunkard.

Nikolay Gogol (1809–52) Russian novelist and playwright. 'The Nose' (1836), quoted in *Diary of a Madman and Other Stories* (Ronald Wilks, tr.; 1972)

14 Russia is such an amazing country, that if you pass any remark about *one* collegiate assessor, every assessor from Riga to Kamchatka will take it personally.

Nikolay Gogol (1809–52) Russian novelist and playwright. 'The Nose' (1836), quoted in *Diary of a Madman and Other Stories* (Ronald Wilks, tr.; 1972)

15 The Soviet people want full-blooded and unconditional democracy.

Mikhail Gorbachev (b. 1931) Russian statesman. Speech (July 1988)

16 And if the Russian word 'perestroika' has easily entered the international lexicon, this is due to more than just interest in what is going on in the Soviet Union. Now the whole world needs restructuring, i.e. progressive development, a fundamental change.

Mikhail Gorbachev (b. 1931) Russian statesman. *Perestroika: New Thinking for Our Country and the World* (1987)

17 What hope is there for Russia if Lenin, who transformed her most, did not destroy but strengthened the tie between Russian progress and Russian slavery?

Vasily Grossman (1905–64) Russian writer. Referring to Vladimir Ilyich Lenin. *Forever Flowing* (Thomas P. Whitney, tr.; 1970), ch. 22

18 Russia is our Africa, and the Russians are our Negroes.

Adolf Hitler (1889–1945) Austrian-born German dictator. Referring to the imperial and military ambition of Germany, compared with that of other European imperial powers in relation to Africa. Quoted in *Germany, 1866–1945* (Gordon A. Craig; 1978), ch. 20

19 The Communist Party, the KGB, and the army— the three ugly sisters—are the instruments of control in the Soviet Union.

Douglas Hurd (b. 1930) British politician. Referring to an abortive coup in the Soviet Union. *Observer* (August 25, 1991)

20 It is one thing if a small poodle tries to walk through these gates but quite another matter when an elephant like Russia tries to do the same thing.

Andrey Vladimirovich Kozyrev (b. 1951) Russian politician. Referring to the NATO Partnership for Peace agreement. *Observer* (June 26, 1994), 'Sayings of the Week'

21 Russia will certainly inherit the future. What we already call the greatness of Russia is only her pre-natal struggling.

D. H. Lawrence (1885–1930) British writer. Preface to *All Things are Possible* by Leo Shostov, *Phoenix* (1929)

22 My animal, my age, who will ever be able to look into your eyes?
Who will ever glue back together the vertebrae of two centuries with his blood?

Osip Mandelstam (1891–1938) Russian poet, writer, and translator. 1923. 'The Age', *Poems* (1928), ll. 1–4, quoted in *Osip Mandelstam: Selected Poems* (Clarence Brown and W. S. Merwin, tr.; 1973)

23 Absolutism tempered by assassination.

Ernst Friedrich Herbert Münster (1766–1839) Hanovarian statesman. Referring to the Russian Constitution. Letter, *Political Sketches of the State of Europe 1814–67* (1868)

24 My fear of losing or corrupting, through alien influence, the only thing I had salvaged from Russia—her language—became positively morbid.

Vladimir Nabokov (1899–1977) Russian-born US novelist, poet, and critic. *Speak, Memory* (1967)

25 What the Tsars had never been able to achieve, namely the complete curbing of minds to the government's will, was achieved by the Bolsheviks after the main contingent of the intellectuals had escaped abroad or been destroyed.

Vladimir Nabokov (1899–1977) Russian-born US novelist, poet, and critic. *Speak, Memory* (1967), ch. 14, sect. 2

26 Russia has two generals in whom she can confide—Generals Janvier and Février.

Nicholas I (1796–1855) Russian monarch. March 10, 1855. Referring to the Russian winter. Nicholas himself succumbed to a February cold in 1855, the subject of the famous Punch Cartoon, 'General Février turned traitor'. Attrib.

27 This is a historic moment. Russia has entered the family of civilized nations.

Gavril Popov (b. 1936) Russian economist and politician. Remark on his election as the first elected mayor of Moscow. *Observer* (June 16, 1991)

28 Yeltsin got where he is by slogans. He is an old party communist and has the old mentality. He is good at leading from the top of a tank.

Zianon Pozniak, Belarusian politician. Referring to Boris Yeltsin. *Times* (February 4, 1995)

29 This universal, obligatory force-feeding with lies is now the most agonizing aspect of existence in our country—worse than all our material miseries, worse than any lack of civil liberties.

Alexander Solzhenitsyn (b. 1918) Russian novelist. Letter to the Soviet leaders (1974), ch. 6

30 The people are not masters in their own house and therefore there is no democracy in Russia.

Alexander Solzhenitsyn (b. 1918) Russian novelist. *Independent* (July 22, 1994)

31 The difference between our decadence and the Russians' is that while theirs is brutal, ours is apathetic.

James Thurber (1894–1961) US writer, cartoonist, and humorist. *Observer* (February 5, 1961), 'Sayings of the Week'

32 I separate myself from the position and policies of Gorbachev, and I call for his immediate resignation. He has brought the country to dictatorship in the name of presidential rule.

Boris Yeltsin (b. 1931) Russian president. Referring to Mikhail Gorbachev. Speech (February 1991)

33 A historic document which will allow us to continue our course towards entering Europe without the discrimination which took place in the past. We move forward as equal partners towards our mutual interests.

Boris Yeltsin (b. 1931) Russian president. Signing a partnership and cooperation agreement with the European Union. *Guardian* (June 24, 1994)

34 I ask you to forgive me for not fulfilling some hopes of those people who believed that we would be able to jump from the totalitarian past into a bright, rich and civilized future in one go.

Boris Yeltsin (b. 1931) Russian president. Said on his retirement as Russian president. *Observer* (January 2, 2000)

35 People in our country don't like it when foreigners take too active a hand in our affairs.

Boris Yeltsin (b. 1931) Russian president. *The View from the Kremlin* (Catherine A. Fitzpatrick, tr.; 1994)

36 We are still too dependent upon dachas, cars, special government telephone lines, and armoured doors—the prerequisites of power.

Boris Yeltsin (b. 1931) Russian president. *The View from the Kremlin* (Catherine A. Fitzpatrick, tr.; 1994)

37 There, I've signed it.

Boris Yeltsin (b. 1931) Russian president. 1991. Yeltsin signed the agreement to end the USSR in December 1991. In response to the question, 'For a little light relief, how about halting the work of the Communist Party?' Quoted in *Times* (August 24, 1994)

38 No Jewish blood runs among my blood, but I am as bitterly and hardly hated by every anti-Semite as if I were a Jew. By this I am a Russian.

Yevgeny Yevtushenko (b. 1933) Russian poet. *Babi Yar* (1961)

39 The problem of civilization is a bitch of a problem . . . Things that are good in the bourgeois countries have a way of turning sour in our land.

Mikhail Zoshchenko (1895–1958) Russian satirist. 'The Charms of Civilization', *A Man is Not a Flea* (Serge Shishkoff, tr.; 1989)

Russian Revolution

see also **Revolution, Russia**

1 You cannot stand upright for the wind: the wind scouring God's world.

Aleksandr Blok (1880–1921) Russian poet. Referring to the Russian Revolution (1917). 'The Twelve' (January 1918), sect. 1, quoted in *Selected Poems: Alexander Blok* (Jon Stallworthy and Peter France, trs.; 1974)

2 The wind plays up; snow flutters down. Twelve men are marching through the town.

Aleksandr Blok (1880–1921) Russian poet. Referring to the Red Army. 'The Twelve' (January 1918), sect. 2, quoted in *Selected Poems: Alexander Blok* (Jon Stallworthy and Peter France, trs.; 1974)

3 Great and terrible was the year of Our Lord 1918, of the Revolution the second.

Mikhail Bulgakov (1891–1940) Russian novelist and playwright. The opening sentence of the novel. *The White Guard* (Michael Glenny, tr.; 1925)

4 Of all tyrannies in history the Bolshevik tyranny is the worst, the most destructive, the most degrading.

Winston Churchill (1874–1965) British prime minister and writer. Speech, London (April 11, 1919)

5 The Germans turned upon Russia the most grisly of all weapons. They transported Lenin in a sealed truck like a plague bacillus from Switzerland to Russia.

Winston Churchill (1874–1965) British prime minister and writer. *The World Crisis* (1923–29)

6 A foolish world is more foolish than royalty can suppose. And what has been miscalled the Russian revolution is a more foolish than supposable world's attempt . . . to substitute for the royal incognito of humility the ignoble affectation of equality.

e. e. cummings (1894–1962) US poet and painter. *Eimi* (1933)

7 The revolution of 1917 has defined the shape of the contemporary world, and we are only now emerging from its shadow.

Orlando Figes (b. 1959) British historian. Referring to the Russian Revolution. *A People's Tragedy: The Russian Revolution 1891–1924* (1996), preface

8 Do everything so that the people will see, tremble, and groan for miles and miles around . . . P.S. Search out hard people.

Vladimir Ilyich Lenin (1870–1924) Russian revolutionary leader. Directive sent to Bolshevik forces at Penza (August 11, 1918), quoted in *Corriere della Sera* (February 13, 1992)

9 Dear comrades, soldiers, sailors and workers! I am happy to greet in you the victorious Russian Revolution!

Vladimir Ilyich Lenin (1870–1924) Russian revolutionary leader. Speech at the Finland Station, Petrograd (April 1917)

10 Any day, if not today or tomorrow, the crash of the whole of European imperialism may come . . . Hail the worldwide socialist revolution.

Vladimir Ilyich Lenin (1870–1924) Russian revolutionary leader. Speech to the crowd on his arrival at the Finland Station, Petrograd (April 3, 1917), quoted in *Europe Since 1870* (James Joll; 1973), ch. 8

11   The substitution of the proletarian for the
bourgeois state is impossible without a violent
revolution.

Vladimir Ilyich Lenin (1870–1924) Russian revolutionary leader. *The State
and Revolution* (1919), ch. 1

12   Ten Days that Shook the World

John Reed (1887–1920) US journalist. 1919. Book title, referring to
the Bolshevik revolution in Russia.

13   Our hand will not tremble.

Joseph Stalin (1879–1953) Soviet dictator. Reply to a telegraph from
Lenin at the start of the Red Terror (1918), urging him to be
merciless against the Bolsheviks' enemies. (1918)

14   The revolution does not choose its paths: it made
its first steps towards victory under the belly of a
Cossack's horse.

Leon Trotsky (1879–1940) Russian revolutionary leader. *History of the
Russian Revolution* (1931), vol. 1, ch. 7

S

Sacrifice

see also **Martyrdom**

1 In any country there must be people who have to die. They are the sacrifices any nation has to make to achieve law and order.

Idi Amin (b. 1925) Ugandan dictator. 1976. Quoted in *The Cynic's Lexicon* (Jonathon Green, ed.; 1984)

2 And Abraham lifted up his eyes, and looked, and behold behind him a ram caught in a thicket by his horns: and Abraham went and took the ram, and offered him up for a burnt offering in the stead of his son.

Bible. Genesis, *King James Bible* (1611), 22:13

3 For God so loved the world, that he gave his only begotten Son, that whosoever believeth in him should not perish, but have everlasting life.

Bible. John, *King James Bible* (1611), 3:16

4 It is fair to judge people by the rights they will sacrifice the most for.

Clarence Shepard Day (1874–1935) US writer. *This Simian World* (1920)

5 A man who won't die for something is not fit to live.

Martin Luther King, Jr. (1929–68) US civil rights leader. *The Words of Martin Luther King Jr.* (Coretta Scott King, ed.; 1983)

6 Blood alone moves the wheels of history.

Benito Mussolini (1883–1945) Italian dictator. Attrib.

7 Not for all the universe contains would I, in the struggle for what I conceive my country's cause, consent to the effusion of a single drop of human blood, except my own.

Daniel O'Connell (1775–1847) Irish politician. Speech (February 28, 1843)

8 There are in every generation those who shrink from the ultimate sacrifice, but there are in every generation those who make it with joy and laughter and these are the salt of the generations.

Patrick Pearse (1879–1916) Irish poet and nationalist. Robert Emmet Commemoration Address, New York (March 2, 1914), quoted in *A Book of Irish Quotations* (Sean McMahon, ed.; 1984)

9 The universe is so vast and so ageless that the life of one man can only be justified by the measure of his sacrifice.

V. A. Rosewarne (1916–40) British pilot. 1940. Inscribed on the portrait of the 'Young Airman' in the RAF Museum. Last letter to his mother, quoted in *Times* (June 18, 1940)

10 I am . . . ready to risk my life against his in single combat to decide whether the kingdom of England should be his or mine.

William the Conqueror (1027–87) Norman-born English monarch. Referring to Harold II of England, shortly before the Battle of Hastings. Remark (October 14, 1066)

11 Too long a sacrifice
Can make a stone of the heart.

W. B. Yeats (1865–1939) Irish poet and playwright. September 25, 1916. 'Easter 1916', *Michael Robartes and the Dancer* (1921), st. 4

Sadness

see **Bereavement**, **Regret**, **Sorrow**

San Francisco

see **American Cities**

Sanity

see also **Mind**, **Normality**, **Reason**

1 Sanity is an unknown room: a known room is always smaller than an unknown.

Djuna Barnes (1892–1982) US writer and illustrator. *Nightwood* (1936)

2 Too much sanity may be madness. And maddest of all, to see life as it is and not as it should be!

Miguel de Cervantes (1547–1616) Spanish novelist and playwright. *Don Quixote* (1605–15)

3 Sanity is very rare: every man almost, and every woman, has a dash of madness.

Ralph Waldo Emerson (1803–82) US poet and essayist. 1866. *Journals* (1860–66)

4 It is the fully sane person who feels isolated in the insane society—and he may suffer so much from the incapacity to communicate that it is he who may become psychotic.

Erich Fromm (1900–80) German-born US psychoanalyst and philosopher. *The Anatomy of Human Destructiveness* (1973)

5 Show me a sane man and I will cure him for you.

Carl Gustav Jung (1875–1961) Swiss psychoanalyst. Quoted in *Observer* (July 19, 1975)

6   If you can keep your head when all about you
    Are losing theirs and blaming it on you,
    If you can trust yourself when all men doubt
    you,
    But make allowance for their doubting too.
    Rudyard Kipling (1865–1936) Indian-born British writer and poet. 'If',
    Rewards and Fairies (1910)

7   I am quite sure that a good number of 'cures' of
    psychotics consist in the fact that the patient has
    decided, for one reason or other, once more to
    play at being sane.
    R. D. Laing (1927–89) Scottish psychiatrist. *The Divided Self* (1965),
    ch. 7

8   The 'sane' man is not the one who has eliminated
    all contradictions from himself so much as the
    one who uses these contradictions and involves
    them in his work.
    Maurice Merleau-Ponty (1908–61) French existentialist philosopher. *Signes*
    (1960)

9   Sanity is not truth. Sanity is conformity to what
    is socially expected. Truth is sometimes in
    conformity, sometimes not.
    Robert T. Pirsig (b. 1928) US writer. *Lila: an Inquiry into Morals*
    (1991)

10 Sanity is madness put to good uses; waking life is
    a dream controlled.
    George Santayana (1863–1952) Spanish-born US philosopher, poet, and
    novelist. Attrib.

11 An asylum for the sane would be empty in
    America.
    George Bernard Shaw (1856–1950) Irish playwright. Attrib.

12 Sanity is a cozy lie.
    Susan Sontag (b. 1933) US writer. 'Notes on Camp', *Against
    Interpretation* (1966)

13 Every man has a sane spot somewhere.
    Robert Louis Stevenson (1850–94) Scottish novelist, essayist, and poet.
    Attrib.

Sarcasm

see also Irony, Wit

1   Sarcasm I now see to be, in general, the language
    of the devil.
    Thomas Carlyle (1795–1881) Scottish historian and essayist. *Sartor
    Resartus* (1833–34), bk. 2, ch. 4

Satire

see also Comedy, Humour

1   It's hard not to write satire.
    Juvenal (65?–128?) Roman poet. *Satires* (98?–128?), no. 1, l. 30

2   Through my satire I make little people so big
    that afterwards they are worthy objects of my
    satire and no one can reproach me any longer.
    Karl Kraus (1874–1936) Austrian writer. 1918. Quoted in *Karl Kraus*
    (Harry Zohn; 1971)

3   Satire died the day they gave Henry Kissinger the
    Nobel Peace Prize. There were no jokes left after
    that.
    Tom Lehrer (b. 1928) US mathematician and songwriter. *Daily
    Telegraph* (April 28, 1998)

4   Satire should, like a polished razor keen,
    Wound with a touch that's scarcely felt or seen.
    Mary Wortley Montagu (1689–1762) British writer. *Verses Addressed to
    the Imitator of the First Satire of the Second Book of Horace*
    (1733), bk. 2

5   My way of joking is to tell the truth. It's the
    funniest joke in the world.
    George Bernard Shaw (1856–1950) Irish playwright. *John Bull's Other
    Island* (1907)

6   Mark Twain and I are in the same position. We
    have to put things in such a way as to make
    people, who would otherwise hang us, believe
    that we are joking.
    George Bernard Shaw (1856–1950) Irish playwright. Attrib.

7   Raillery gives no Offence,
    Where Truth has not the least Pretense.
    Jonathan Swift (1667–1745) Irish writer and clergyman. 'Stella at
    Wood-Park' (1723)

8   Satire is a sort of glass, wherein beholders do
    generally discover everybody's face but their
    own.
    Jonathan Swift (1667–1745) Irish writer and clergyman. *The Battle of
    the Books* (1704), Preface

9   Satire picks a one-sided fight, and the more its
    intended target reacts, the more the practitioner
    gains the advantage.
    Garry Trudeau (b. 1948) US cartoonist. *Wall Street Journal* (January
    20, 1993)

10 Satire is alive and well and living in the White
    House.
    Robin Williams (b. 1951) US actor and comedian. Referring to
    Ronald Reagan's administration. *Rolling Stone* (February 25,
    1985)

Satisfaction

see Comfort, Happiness, Pleasure

Scepticism

see Belief, Cynicism, Doubt

Science

see also Astronomy, Experiments, Genetics, Knowledge,
Mathematics, Physics, Psychology, Research, Scientists,
Technology

1   Science will be the master of man. The engines
    he will have invented will be beyond his strength
    to control. Some day science shall have the
    existence of mankind in its power, and the
    human race commit suicide by blowing up the
    world.
    Henry Adams (1838–1918) US historian. Letter to his brother (April
    11, 1862)

2   Every great scientific truth goes through three
    stages. First, people say it conflicts with the Bible.
    Next they say it had been discovered before.
    Lastly, they say they always believed it.
    Louis Rodolphe Agassiz (1807–73) Swiss-born US naturalist. Quoted in
    Science-Week (January 9, 1998)

3 Science is the great instrument of social change . . . the most vital of all revolutions which have marked the development of modern civilization.

Arthur Balfour (1848–1930) British prime minister. Speech, London (1908)

4 There are more microbes *per person* than the entire population of the world. Imagine that. Per person. This means that if the time scale is diminished in proportion to that of space it would be quite possible for the whole story of Greece and Rome to be played out between farts.

Alan Bennett (b. 1934) British playwright, actor, and director. *The Old Country* (1978), Act 2

5 Science is some kind of cosmic apple juice from the Garden of Eden. Those of it are doomed to carry the burden of original sin.

Lew Branscomb (b. 1926?) US physicist and executive. *News Summaries* (April 9, 1971)

6 That is the essence of science: ask an impertinent question, and you are on the way to the pertinent answer.

Jacob Bronowski (1908–74) Polish-born British mathematician, poet, and humanist. *The Ascent of Man* (1973), ch. 4

7 Science . . . has opened our eyes to the vastness of the universe and given us light, truth, and freedom from fear where once was darkness, ignorance, and superstition.

Luther Burbank (1849–1926) US botanist. *The Harvest of the Years* (co-written with Wilbur Hale; 1927)

8 Science has a simple faith, which transcends utility. Nearly all men of science, all men of learning for that matter, and men of simple ways too, have it in some form and in some degree. It is the faith that it is the privilege of man to understand, and that this is his mission.

Vannevar Bush (1890–1974) US engineer and government official. 'The Search for Understanding', *Science Is Not Enough* (1967)

9 Science is a system of statements based on direct experience, and controlled by experimental verification. Verification in science is not, however, of single statements but of the entire system or a sub-system of such statements.

Rudolf Carnap (1891–1970) German philosopher. *The Unity of Science* (M. Black, tr.; 1934)

10 The goal of science is to seek naturalistic explanations for phenomena . . . within the framework of natural laws and principles and the operational rule of testability.

Committee on Science and Creationism, National Academy of Sciences, US academic body. *Science and Creationism: A View from the National Academy of Sciences* (1984), conclusion

11 It is always observable that the physical and exact sciences are the last to suffer under despotisms.

Richard Henry Dana (1815–82) US sailor, writer, and lawyer. *To Cuba and Back* (1859)

12 It would be quite extraordinary if a major new development in science was *not* applied in warfare, and there is probably little that we can do to prevent it.

Malcolm Dando, British author. *Biological Warfare in the 21st Century* (1994)

13 Every atom is offered billions of trajectories by the quantum randomization, and in the many-worlds theory it accepts them all, so every conceivable atomic arrangement will come about somewhere.

Paul Davies (b. 1946) British-born Australian physicist. *Other Worlds: Space, Superspace and the Quantum Universe* (1980)

14 Every great advance in science has issued from a new audacity of imagination.

John Dewey (1859–1952) US philosopher and educator. *The Quest for Certainty* (1929), ch. 11

15 The history of science is not a mere record of isolated discoveries; it is a narrative of the conflict of two contending powers, the expansive force of the human intellect on one side, and the compression arising from the traditionary faith and human interest on the other.

John Draper (1811–82) British-born US chemist. 1875. *History of the Conflict Between Religion and Science* (1874), preface

16 Every science begins as philosophy and ends as art.

Will Durant (1885–1981) US historian. *Story of Philosophy* (1926)

17 Science is a conspiracy of brains against ignorance . . . a revenge of victims against oppressors . . . a territory of freedom and friendship in the midst of tyranny and hatred.

Freeman Dyson (b. 1923) British-born US physicist. The credo of the science club he founded to escape bullying at his preparatory school. Quoted in *The Faber Book of Science* (John Carey, ed.; 1995)

18 Man is slightly nearer to the atom than the stars. From his central position he can survey the grandest works of Nature with the astronomer, or the minutest works with the physicist.

Arthur Eddington (1882–1944) British astronomer and physicist. *Stars and Atoms* (1928)

19 Thus will the fondest dream of Phallic science be realized: a pristine new planet populated entirely by little boy clones of great scientific entrepreneurs . . . free to smash atoms, accelerate particles, or, if they are so moved, build pyramids—without any social relevance or human responsibility at all.

Barbara Ehrenreich (b. 1941) US sociologist, feminist, and writer. 1988. 'Phallic Science', *The Worst Years of Our Lives* (1991)

20 Science is the attempt to make the chaotic diversity of our sense-experience correspond to a logically uniform system of thought.

Albert Einstein (1879–1955) German-born US physicist. *Out of My Later Years* (1950)

21 Concern for man himself and his fate must always form the chief interest of all technical endeavors . . . Never forget this in the midst of your diagrams and equations.

Albert Einstein (1879–1955) German-born US physicist. Quoted in *Knowledge for What?* (Robert S. Lynd; 1939)

22 To every man is given the key to the gate of heaven; the same key opens the gates of hell.

Richard Phillips Feynman (1918–88) US physicist. *What Do You Care What Other People Think?* (1988)

23 The pace of science forces the pace of technique. Theoretical physics forces atomic energy on us; the successful production of the fission bomb forces upon us the manufacture of the hydrogen bomb. We do not choose our problems, we do not choose our products; we are pushed, we are forced—by what? By a system which has no purpose.
Erich Fromm (1900–80) German-born US psychoanalyst and philosopher. 'Nineteenth Century Capitalism', *The Sane Society* (1955), ch. 5

24 Science has radically changed the condition of human life on earth. It has expanded our knowledge and our power but not our capacity to use them with wisdom.
J. William Fulbright (1905–95) US educator and politician. *Old Myths and New Realities* (1964)

25 The real accomplishment of modern science and technology consists in taking ordinary men, informing them narrowly and deeply and then, through appropriate organization, arranging to have their knowledge combined with that of other specialized but equally ordinary men. This dispenses with the need for genius.
J. K. Galbraith (b. 1908) Canadian-born US economist. *The New Industrial State* (1967), ch. 6

26 Thus I saw that most men only care for science so far as they get a living by it, and that they worship even error when it affords them a subsistence.
Johann Wolfgang von Goethe (1749–1832) German poet, playwright, and scientist. Quoted in *Conversations with Goethe* (Johann Peter Eckermann; 1836–48)

27 Science is an integral part of culture. It's not this foreign thing, done by an arcane priesthood. It's one of the glories of human intellectual tradition.
Stephen Jay Gould (1941–2002) US geologist and writer. *Independent* (January 24, 1990)

28 A science is said to be useful if its development tends to accentuate the existing inequalities of wealth, or more directly promotes the destruction of human life.
Godfrey Harold Hardy (1877–1947) British mathematician. *A Mathematician's Apology* (1941)

29 Even if there is only one possible unified theory, it is just a set of rules and equations. What is it that breathes fire into the equations and makes a universe for them to describe?
Stephen Hawking (b. 1942) British physicist. *A Brief History of Time* (1988)

30 Natural science does not simply describe and explain nature, it is part of the interplay between nature and ourselves.
Werner Heisenberg (1901–76) German physicist. *Physics and Philosophy* (1958)

31 Science has 'explained' nothing; the more we know the more fantastic the world becomes and the profounder the surrounding darkness.
Aldous Huxley (1894–1963) British novelist and essayist. 'Places: Views of Holland', *Along the Road: Notes and Essays of a Tourist* (1925)

32 The great tragedy of Science—the slaying of a beautiful hypothesis by an ugly fact.
T. H. Huxley (1825–95) British biologist. 'Biogenesis and Abiogenesis', *Collected Essays* (1893–94)

33 Reason, Observation, and Experience—the Holy Trinity of Science.
Robert G. Ingersoll (1833–99) US lawyer. *The Gods* (1876)

34 Many persons nowadays seem to think that any conclusion must be very scientific if the arguments in favor of it are derived from twitching of frogs' legs—especially if the frogs are decapitated—and that—on the other hand—any doctrine chiefly vouched for by the feelings of human beings—with heads on their shoulders—must be benighted and superstitious.
William James (1842–1910) US psychologist and philosopher. *Pragmatism: A New Name for Old Ways of Thinking* (1907)

35 If science produces no better fruits than tyranny, murder, rapine, and destitution of national morality, I would rather wish our country to be ignorant, honest, and estimable, as our neighboring savages are.
Thomas Jefferson (1743–1826) US president. Letter to John Adams (January 21, 1812)

36 We have genuflected before the god of science only to find that it has given us the atomic bomb, producing fears and anxieties that science can never mitigate.
Martin Luther King, Jr. (1929–68) US civil rights leader. *Strength To Love* (1963)

37 Science is all metaphor.
Timothy Leary (1920–96) US psychologist and guru. Remark (September 24, 1980)

38 It is not science that has destroyed the world, despite all the gloomy forebodings of the earlier prophets. It is man who has destroyed man.
Max Lerner (1902–92) Russian-born US editor and social scientist. 'The Human Heart and the Human Will', *Actions and Passions* (1949)

39 Science has proof without any certainty. Creationists have certainty without any proof.
Ashley Montagu (b. 1905) British-born US anthropologist. Attrib.

40 Do you really believe that the sciences would ever have originated and grown if the way had not been prepared by magicians, alchemists, astrologers, and witches whose promises and pretensions first had to create a thirst, a hunger, a taste for hidden and forbidden.
Friedrich Wilhelm Nietzsche (1844–1900) German philosopher and poet. *The Gay Science* (1882)

41 Traditional scientific method has always been at the very *best*, 20–20 hindsight. It's good for seeing where you've been.
Robert T. Pirsig (b. 1928) US writer. *Zen and the Art of Motorcycle Maintenance* (1974), pt. 3, ch. 24

42 A new scientific truth does not triumph by convincing its opponents and making them see the light, but rather because its opponents eventually die, and a new generation grows up that is familiar with it.
Max Planck (1858–1947) German physicist. *Scientific Autobiography and Other Papers* (1949)

43 Science is built up of facts, as a house is built of stones; but an accumulation of facts is no more a science than a heap of stones is a house.
Jules Henri Poincaré (1854–1912) French mathematician and scientist. *La Science et l'Hypothèse* (1903), ch. 9

44 Science may be described as the art of systematic over-simplification.

Karl Popper (1902–94) Austrian-born British philosopher. Remark, *Observer* (August 1982), quoted in *Sayings of the Eighties* (Jeffrey Care, ed.; 1989)

45 Physics investigates the essential nature of the world, and biology describes a local bump. Psychology, human psychology, describes a bump on the bump.

Willard V. Quine (1908–2000) US philosopher. *Theories and Things* (1981)

46 Science without conscience is the death of the soul.

François Rabelais (1494?–1553?) French humanist and satirist. *Gargantua and Pantagruel* (1546), bk. 2, ch. 8

47 Science is the Differential Calculus of the mind. Art the Integral Calculus; they may be beautiful when apart, but are greatest only when combined.

Ronald Ross (1857–1932) British physician and entomologist. Quoted in *The Complete Poems of Hugh MacDiarmid, 1920–76* (Michael Grieve and W. R. Aitken, eds.; 1978)

48 What science can measure is only a portion of what man can know. Our knowing reaches out to embrace the sacred; what bars its way, though it promises us dominion, condemns us to be prisoners of the empirical lie.

Theodore Roszak (b. 1933) US writer and editor. *Where the Wasteland Ends* (1972), ch. 2

49 Pseudoscience is embraced, it might be argued, in exact proportion as real science is misunderstood.

Carl Sagan (1934–96) US astronomer and writer. *The Demon-Haunted World: Science as a Candle in the Dark* (1995)

50 If all the arts aspire to the condition of music, all the sciences aspire to the condition of mathematics.

George Santayana (1863–1952) Spanish-born US philosopher, poet, and novelist. *Observer* (March 4, 1928), 'Sayings of the Week'

51 People must understand that science is inherently neither a potential for good nor for evil. It is a potential to be harnessed by man to do his bidding.

Glenn Seaborg (b. 1912) US chemist. Interview, Associated Press (September 29, 1964)

52 Science is always wrong. It never solves a problem without creating ten more.

George Bernard Shaw (1856–1950) Irish playwright. Attrib.

53 Science is the great antidote to the poison of enthusiasm and superstition.

Adam Smith (1723–90) Scottish economist and philosopher. *Wealth of Nations* (1776), bk. 5, ch. 1

54 Science robs men of wisdom and usually converts them into phantom beings loaded up with facts.

Miguel de Unamuno y Jugo (1864–1936) Spanish writer and philosopher. *Essays and Soliloquies* (1924)

55 Science says: 'We must live', and seeks the means of prolonging, increasing, facilitating and amplifying life, of making it tolerable and acceptable; wisdom says: 'We must die', and seeks how to make us die well.

Miguel de Unamuno y Jugo (1864–1936) Spanish writer and philosopher. 'Arbitrary Reflections', *Essays and Soliloquies* (1924)

56 As long as vitalism and spiritualism are open questions so long will the gateway of science be open to mysticism.

Rudolf Virchow (1821–1902) German politician, pathologist, archaeologist, and anthropologist. Quoted in *Bulletin of the New York Academy of Medicine* (F. H. Garrison; 1928), 4:994

Scientists

see also **Science**

1 When I find myself in the company of scientists, I feel like a shabby curate who has strayed by mistake into a drawing-room full of dukes.

W. H. Auden (1907–73) British poet. 'The Poet and the City', *The Dyer's Hand* (1963)

2 Touch a scientist and you touch a child.

Ray Bradbury (b. 1920) US science-fiction writer. *Los Angeles Times* (August 9, 1976)

3 The scientist is a lover of truth for the very love of truth itself, wherever it may lead.

Luther Burbank (1849–1926) US botanist. *The Harvest of the Years* (co-written with Wilbur Hale; 1927)

4 When a distinguished but elderly scientist states that something is possible, he is almost certainly right. When he states that something is impossible, he is very probably wrong.

Arthur C. Clarke (b. 1917) British writer and scientist. *Profiles of the Future* (1962)

5 He had in fact most of the qualities that make a great scientist: an innate curiosity and perceptiveness regarding natural phenomena, insight into the heart of a problem, technical ingenuity, persistence in seeing a job through and that physical and mental toughness that is essential to the top-class investigator.

Leonard Colebrook (1883–1967) British medical researcher. Referring to Alexander Fleming. *Journal of Pathology and Bacteriology* (1956)

6 The stumbling way in which even the ablest of scientists in every generation have had to fight through thickets of erroneous observations, misleading generalizations, inadequate formulations, and unconscious prejudice is rarely appreciated by those who obtain their scientific knowledge from textbooks.

James Bryant Conant (1893–1978) US chemist and diplomat. *Science and Common Sense* (1951)

7 But in science the credit goes to the man who convinces the world, not to the man to whom the idea first occurs.

Francis Darwin (1848–1925) British scientist. First Galton Lecture before the Eugenics Society, *Eugenics Review* (April 1914), 6: 1

8 One began to hear it said that World War I was the chemists' war, World War II was the physicists' war, World War III (may it never come) will be the mathematicians' war.

Philip J. Davis (b. 1923) US mathematician. *The Mathematical Experience* (co-written with Reuben Hersh; 1981)

9 If my theory of relativity is proven correct, Germany will claim me as a German and France will declare that I am a citizen of the world. Should my theory prove untrue, France will say that I am a German and Germany will declare that I am a Jew.

Albert Einstein (1879–1955) German-born US physicist. Address, Sorbonne, Paris (1929), quoted in *Einstein for Beginners* (J. Schwartz; 1979)

10 It is in this triple blow that the infallibility, the infused science of instinct, appear in all their magnificence . . . We find what the Sphex knew long before the anatomist, three nerve centres far apart. Thence the fine logic of three stabs. Proud Science! humble thyself.

Jean Henri Fabre (1823–1915) French entomologist. Referring to the method used by the Sphex wasp for paralysing the host for its eggs. *Souvenirs Entomologiques* (1879–1907)

11 He lived the life of a solitary, and like all men who are occupied with profound meditation, he acted strangely. Sometimes, in getting out of bed, an idea would come to him, and he would sit on the edge of the bed, half dressed, for hours at a time.

Louis Figuier (1819–94) French writer. 1879. Referring to Isaac Newton. *Vies de Savants* (B. H. Clark, tr.; 1897)

12 Scientists who falsify their results are regarded by their peers as committing an inexcusable crime. Yet the sad fact is that the history of science swarms with cases of outright fakery and instances of scientists who unconsciously distorted their work by seeing it through lenses of passionately held beliefs.

Martin Gardner (b. 1914) US philosopher, mathematician, and writer. *Science: Good, Bad and Bogus* (1981)

13 Immunologists are the function of a culture in which jumping to conclusions means endangering the survival of men, women, and infants.

Miroslav Holub (1923–98) Czech poet and immunologist. 'Zen and the Thymus', *Shedding Life* (1997)

14 Scientists are treated like gods handing down new commandments. People tend to assume that religion has been disproved by science. But the scientist may tell us how the world works, not why it works, not how we should live our lives, not how we face death or make moral decisions.

Susan Howatch (b. 1940) British writer. *Observer* (May 8, 1994)

15 As a man he was a failure; as a monster he was superb.

Aldous Huxley (1894–1963) British novelist and essayist. Referring to Isaac Newton. Quoted in *Contemporary Mind* (John William Navin Sullivan; 1934)

16 Had he not been an untidy man and apt to leave his cultures exposed on the laboratory table the spore of hyssop mould, the *penicillin notatum*, might never have floated in from Praed Street and settled on his dish of staphylococci.

André Maurois (1885–1967) French writer. Referring to Alexander Fleming. *Life of Alexander Fleming* (1961)

17 Yet had Fleming not possessed immense knowledge and an unremitting gift of observation he might not have observed the effect of the hyssop mould. 'Fortune', remarked Pasteur, 'favours the prepared mind'.

André Maurois (1885–1967) French writer. Referring to Alexander Fleming and Louis Pasteur. *Life of Alexander Fleming* (1961)

18 The scientist who yields anything to theology, however slight, is yielding to ignorance and false pretenses, and as certainly as if he granted that a horse-hair put into a bottle of water will turn into a snake.

H. L. Mencken (1880–1956) US journalist, critic, and editor. 'Minority Report', *Notebooks* (1956)

19 The wallpaper with which the men of science have covered the world of reality is falling to tatters.

Henry Miller (1891–1980) US novelist. *Tropic of Cancer* (1934)

20 If I have seen further it is by standing on the shoulders of giants.

Isaac Newton (1642–1727) English mathematician and physicist. Letter to Robert Hooke (February 5, 1676), quoted in *Correspondence of Isaac Newton* (H. W. Turnbull, ed.; 1959), vol. 1

21 Both the man of science and the man of art live always at the edge of mystery, surrounded by it. Both, as the measure of their creation, have always had to do with the harmonization of what is new with what is familiar.

J. Robert Oppenheimer (1904–67) US nuclear physicist. 1954? Quoted in *Brighter than a Thousand Suns* (Robert Jungk; 1956)

22 One has to be wary of engineers—they begin with sewing machines and end up with the atomic bomb.

Marcel Pagnol (1895–1974) French dramatist, filmmaker, and scriptwriter. *Critique des Critiques* (1949)

23 Nature, and Nature's laws lay hid in night: God said, *Let Newton be!* and all was light.

Alexander Pope (1688–1744) English poet. 'Intended for Sir Isaac Newton', *Epitaphs* (1730)

24 What Galileo and Newton were to the seventeenth century, Darwin was to the nineteenth.

Bertrand Russell (1872–1970) British philosopher and mathematician. *A History of Western Philosophy* (1945)

25 I have learned to have more faith in the scientist than he does in himself.

David Sarnoff (1891–1971) Russian-born US broadcasting executive. Quoted in *Newsweek* (December 27, 1971), obituary

26 A good scientist is a person in whom the childlike quality of perennial curiosity lingers on. Once he gets an answer, he has other questions.

Frederick Seitz (b. 1911) US physicist. *Fortune* (April 1976)

27 The true scientist never loses the faculty of amazement. It is the essence of his being.

Hans Selye (1907–82) Austrian-born Canadian physician and endocrinologist. *Newsweek* (March 31, 1958)

28 He has something demoniacal about him who can discern a law or couple two facts.

Henry David Thoreau (1817–62) US writer. *Excursions* (1863)

29 The degradation of the position of the scientist as independent worker and thinker to that of a morally irresponsible stooge in a science-factory has proceeded even more rapidly and devastatingly than I had expected.

Norbert Wiener (1894–1964) US mathematician. *Bulletin of the Atomic Scientists* (November 4, 1948)

30 The great scientists have been occupied with values—it is only their vulgar followers who think they are not . . . They have imaginations as powerful as any poet's.

Edmund Wilson (1895–1972) US critic and writer. Letter to Allen Tate (July 20, 1931)

Scotland

see also **Britain, Europe**

1 O Scotia! my dear, my native soil!
For whom my warmest wish to Heaven is sent!
Long may thy hardy sons of rustic toil
Be blest with health, and peace and sweet content!
And O! may heaven their simple lives prevent
From Luxury's contagion, weak and vile!

Robert Burns (1759–96) Scottish poet and songwriter. 1785. 'The Cotter's Saturday Night', *Poems and Songs of Robert Burns* (J. Barke, ed.; 1955), st. 20

2 The eighteenth century is rightly hailed as the age when Scotland became one of the most important centres of intellectual culture in the western world.

Michael Lynch (b. 1946) Scottish historian. *Scotland: a New History* (1991)

3 Bannockburn has been called one of the few decisive battles in Scottish history. Edward lost his shield, privy seal, court poet (who was obliged to compose victory verses for the Scots), and much of his credibility.

Michael Lynch (b. 1946) Scottish historian. Referring to the Battle of Bannockburn (June 24, 1314), which is considered the victory by which Scottish independence was won, and to Edward II of England. The English army lost an estimated 10,000 men. *Scotland: a New History* (1991)

4 The history of the Picts can be likened to a mystery with few clues and no satisfactory ending.

Michael Lynch (b. 1946) Scottish historian. The Picts were the ancient inhabitants of Scotland and Northern Ireland. They were believed to have arrived in Scotland from continental Europe about 1000 BC. *Scotland: a New History* (1991)

5 Scotland will never secure a measure of independence worth having without being forced to adopt means similar to those taken by the Irish.

Hugh MacDiarmid (1892–1978) Scottish poet and writer. 1930. 'Clan Albainn', *Selected Prose* (Alan Riach, ed.; 1992)

6 I know what civilization is here in the islands. But I never heard you had that kind of civilization down in England.

Compton Mackenzie (1883–1972) British writer. *Rockets Galore* (1957), ch. 6

7 Scotland must again have independence, but not to be ruled by traitor kings or chiefs, lawyers and politicians. The communism of the clans must be re-established on a modern basis.

John MacLean (1879–1923) Scottish socialist politician. 1920. 'The Scottish Workers' Republic', *In the Rapids of Revolution* (Nan Milton, ed.; 1978)

8 These unfortunate outbursts but gave the English the excuse and the chance to subdue the Highland chiefs and then corrupt them with an English education.

John MacLean (1879–1923) Scottish socialist politician. 1920. Referring to the Jacobite Risings of 1715 and 1745. 'The Scottish Workers' Republic', *In the Rapids of Revolution* (Nan Milton, ed.; 1978)

9 Scotland, I rush towards you
into my future that,
every minute,
grows smaller and smaller.

Norman McCaig (1910–96) Scottish poet. 'London to Edinburgh' (1988)

10 An old pot seething with dissatisfactions which fortunately can be relied on never to come to the boil—might be the English politician's view of Scotland.

Edwin Morgan (b. 1920) Scottish poet. 1972. 'The Resources of Scotland', *Crossing the Border* (1990)

11 The Scots still find it very difficult to unite against what has become their common enemy, the British State.

Tom Nairn (b. 1932) Scottish sociologist and author. *Common Cause* (1992)

12 Stands Scotland where it did? Well yes—drowning, in the alien stream of Anglo-British politics.

Tom Nairn (b. 1932) Scottish sociologist and author. The opening words are from William Shakespeare's *Macbeth* (Act 4, Scene 3). *Common Cause* (1992)

13 Modern patriotism has no natural persona in Scotland. Our old clothes are romantic rags, yet—embarrassingly, inexplicably—none of the new uniforms seems to fit either.

Tom Nairn (b. 1932) Scottish sociologist and author. *Faces of Nationalism* (1997)

14 Every single barrel of North Sea oil will go on being used to get the Crown Jewels back from the pawn-shop.

Tom Nairn (b. 1932) Scottish sociologist and author. Referring to the use of North Sea oil revenues to redeem the British economy. *The Break-Up of Britain* (1977)

Sculpture

see also **Aesthetics, Art, Artistic Styles**

1 You do not make sculpture because you like wood. That is absurd. You make sculpture because the wood allows you to express something that another material does not allow you to do.

Louise Bourgeois (b. 1911) French-born US sculptor. Quoted in *Bourgeois* (Donald Kuspit; 1988)

2 Nothing grows well in the shade of a big tree.

Constantin Brancusi (1876–1957) Romanian-born French sculptor. Refusing Rodin's invitation to work in his studio. Quoted in *Compton's Encyclopedia* (1992)

3 You can't make a sculpture, in my opinion, without involving your body. You move and you feel and you breathe and you touch . . . One is physically involved and this is sculpture. It's not architecture. It's rhythm and dance and everything.

Barbara Hepworth (1903–75) British sculptor. 1970. Quoted in *Art Talk: Conversations with 15 Women Artists* (Cindy Nemser; 1975)

4 I was a sculptor. But that's really a drawing—a drawing you fall over in the dark, a three-dimensional drawing.

Al Hirschfeld (b. 1903) US caricaturist. *New York Times* (June 21, 1988)

5 Sculpture: Your humble genealogy should make you silent. Painting: Well, yours is not astonishing either. Sculpture: You began in shadow. Painting: And you, in idolatry.

Juan de Jáuregui (1583–1641) Spanish poet. 'Diálogo entre la naturaleza y las dos artes pintura y escultura, de cuya preeminencia se disputa y juzga', *Rimas* (1618)

6 Sculpture to me is like poetry, and architecture like prose.

Maya Lin (b. 1959) US architect and sculptor. *Observer* (May 14, 1994), 'Sayings of the Week'

7 There is a right physical size for every idea.

Henry Moore (1898–1986) British sculptor. Attrib.

The Sea

see also **The Environment, Nature, Rivers**

1 The sea always ebbs after high tide.

Anonymous. Philippine proverb.

2 The sea is calm to-night,
The tide is full, the moon lies fair
Upon the Straits.

Matthew Arnold (1822–88) British poet and critic. 'Dover Beach' (1867)

3 And I have loved thee, Ocean! and my joy
Of youthful sports was on thy breast to be
Borne, like thy bubbles, onward; from a boy.
I wantoned with thy breakers, . . .
And trusted to thy billows far and near,
And laid my hand upon thy mane—as I do here.

Lord Byron (1788–1824) British poet. *Childe Harold's Pilgrimage* (1812–18), can. 4, st. 184

4 The voice of the sea speaks to the soul.

Kate Chopin (1850–1904) US novelist, short-story writer, and poet. *The Awakening* (1899), ch. 6

5 It is an ancient Mariner,
And he stoppeth one of three.
'By thy long grey beard and glittering eye,
Now wherefore stopp'st thou me?'

Samuel Taylor Coleridge (1772–1834) British poet. 'The Rime of the Ancient Mariner', *Lyrical Ballads* (1798), pt. 1

6 The fair breeze blew, the white foam flew,
The furrow followed free;
We were the first that ever burst
Into that silent sea.

Samuel Taylor Coleridge (1772–1834) British poet. 'The Rime of the Ancient Mariner', *Lyrical Ballads* (1798), pt. 2

7 Water, water, every where,
And all the boards did shrink;
Water, water, every where,
Nor any drop to drink.

Samuel Taylor Coleridge (1772–1834) British poet. 'The Rime of the Ancient Mariner', *Lyrical Ballads* (1798), pt. 2

8 I have known the sea too long to believe in its respect for decency.

Joseph Conrad (1857–1924) Polish-born British novelist. 'Falk: A Reminiscence' (1903)

9 A singular disadvantage of the sea lies in the fact that after successfully surmounting one wave you discover that there is another behind it just as important and just as nervously anxious to do something effective in the way of swamping boats.

Stephen Crane (1871–1900) US writer and journalist. 1897. 'The Open Boat', *The Open Boat and Other Stories* (1898)

10 West of these out to seas colder than the Hebrides I must go
Where the fleet of stars is anchored and the young star-captains glow
The dragon-green, the luminous, the dark, the serpent-haunted sea.

James Elroy Flecker (1884–1915) British poet. 'The Gates of Damascus' (1913)

11 With lack of sleep and too much understanding I grow a little crazy, I think, like all men at sea who live too close to each other and too close thereby to all that is monstrous under the sun and moon.

William Golding (1911–93) British novelist. 'Closing Words', *Rites of Passage* (1980)

12 White clouds surge angrily in the sky,
Ah, what a breathtaking view of the Arctic on a sunny day!
The unlimited Pacific tries to overthrow the earth with all its strength.
Ah, the rolling billows rush toward me!

Guo Moruo (1892–1978) Chinese writer. Quoted in *Twentieth Century Chinese Poetry* (Hsu Kai-yu, ed.; 1963)

13 How like
Is a journey by sea
To death,
To eternal life!

Juan Ramón Jiménez (1881–1958) Spanish poet. 'Dream Nocturne', *Roots and Wings: Poetry from Spain, 1900–75* (Hardie St. Martin, ed.; 1976), ll. 17–20

14 When men come to like a sea-life, they are not fit to live on land.

Samuel Johnson (1709–84) British lexicographer and writer. March 19, 1776. Quoted in *Life of Samuel Johnson* (James Boswell; 1791)

15 The snotgreen sea. The scrotumtightening sea.

James Joyce (1882–1941) Irish writer. *Ulysses* (1922)

16 It keeps eternal whisperings around
Desolate shores, and with its mighty swell
Gluts twice ten thousand Caverns.

John Keats (1795–1821) English poet. 'On the Sea' (April 17, 1817), quoted in *Life, Letters and Literary Remains of John Keats* (Richard Monckton Milnes, ed.; 1848)

17 Ocean people are different from land people. The ocean never stops saying and asking into ears, which don't sleep like eyes.

Maxine Hong Kingston (b. 1940) US writer. *China Men* (1980)

18 'Wouldst thou'—so the helmsman answered—
'Learn the secret of the sea?
Only those who brave its dangers
Comprehend its mystery!'

Henry Wadsworth Longfellow (1807–82) US poet. 'The Secret of the Sea' (1904)

19 I often sigh still
for the dark downward and vegetating kingdom
of the fish and reptile.

Robert Lowell (1917–77) US poet. 'For the Union Dead', *For the Union Dead* (1964)

20 This is the end of the whaleroad and the whale
Who spewed Nantucket bones on the thrashed swell
And stirred the troubled waters to whirlpools
To send the Pequod packing off to hell.

Robert Lowell (1917–77) US poet. Nantucket is an island in southeastern Massachusetts, in the Atlantic Ocean. *Pequod* was the name of the whaling ship led by Captain Ahab in Herman Melville's novel *Moby Dick* (1851). 'The Quaker Graveyard in Nantucket', *Poems 1938–49* (1950)

21 Do you realize Beethoven composed all his music without ever having looked upon the sea?

Anne Michaels (b. 1958) Canadian poet and novelist. *Fugitive Pieces* (1997)

22 And then went down to the ship,
Set keel to the breakers, forth on the godly sea.

Ezra Pound (1885–1972) US poet, translator, and critic. 1925. *The Cantos* (1976), can. 1

23 Smooth seas do not make skillful sailors.

African (Swahili) proverb.

24 The sea voyage is more than an adventure; it is a rite of passage, as decisive as a wedding. It marks the end of the old self and the birth of the new.

Jonathan Raban (b. 1942) British author. 'Sea-Room', *Granta Book of Travel* (Bill Buford, ed.; 1991)

25 The sea, trembling with a long line of radiance, and showing in the clear distance the sails of vessels stealing in every direction along its surface.

Ann Radcliffe (1764–1823) British novelist. *The Italian* (1797)

26 I have bathed in the Poem
Of the Sea, immersed in stars, and milky,
Devouring the green azures.

Arthur Rimbaud (1854–91) French poet. *Le Bateau Ivre* (1871)

27 A life on the ocean wave,
A home on the rolling deep.

Epes Sargent (1813–80) US writer and playwright. Song lyric. 'A Life on the Ocean Wave' (1838)

28 The sea! the sea!

Xenophon (430?–355? BC) Greek historian and soldier. Shouted by the Greeks when they reached the safety of the coast following their military retreat across Armenia. *Anabasis* (355? BC), bk. 4, ch. 7, l. 24

29 That dolphin-torn, that gong-tormented sea.

W. B. Yeats (1865–1939) Irish poet and playwright. September 1930. 'Byzantium', *The Winding Stair and Other Poems* (1933), st. 5

Seasons

see also **Autumn**, **Spring**, **Summer**, **Winter**

1 To every thing there is a season, and a time to every purpose under the heaven:
A time to be born, and a time to die; a time to plant, and a time to pluck up that which is planted;
A time to kill, and a time to heal; a time to break down, and a time to build up;
A time to weep, and a time to laugh; a time to mourn, and a time to dance.

Bible. Ecclesiastes, *King James Bible* (1611), 3:1–3

2 In seed time learn, in harvest teach, in winter enjoy.

William Blake (1757–1827) British poet, painter, engraver, and mystic. 'Proverbs of Hell', *The Marriage of Heaven and Hell* (1790–93), l. 1

3 People who don't even notice whether it's summer or winter are lucky!

Anton Chekhov (1860–1904) Russian playwright and short-story writer. *Three Sisters* (1901), Act 2

4 Leave me alone with the seasons
you animals, you caves.
But what is it that calls me
in the wake of waters and after the trees?

Fazil Hüsnü Dag larca (b. 1914) Turkish poet. 'The Single Leaf', *Modern Turkish Poetry* (Feyyaz Kayacan Fergar, ed.; 1992), ll. 1–4

5 Four seasons fill the measure of the year;
There are four seasons in the mind of man.

John Keats (1795–1821) English poet. 'The Human Seasons' (1819)

6 For ADORATION seasons change,
And order, truth, and beauty range,
Adjust, attract, and fill:
The grass the polyanthus cheques;
And polished porphyry reflects,
By the descending rill.

Christopher Smart (1722–71) British poet. 'A Song to David' (1763), quoted in *The New Oxford Book of English Verse* (Helen Gardner, ed.; 1972)

7 Through winter-time we call on spring,
And through the spring on summer call,
And when abounding hedges ring
Declare that winter's best of all.

W. B. Yeats (1865–1939) Irish poet and playwright. 'The Wheel', *The Tower* (1928), ll. 1–4

Secrecy

see also **Privacy**

1 A man who drinks only water has a secret to hide from his fellows.

Charles Baudelaire (1821–67) French poet. *Du Vin et du Haschisch* (1851)

2 I shall be as secret as the grave.

Miguel de Cervantes (1547–1616) Spanish novelist and playwright. *Don Quixote* (1605–15), pt. 2, ch. 62

3 Mum's the word.

George Colman (1762–1836) British playwright and theatre owner. *The Battle of Hexham* (1789), Act 2, Scene 1

4 I know that's a secret, for it's whispered every where.

William Congreve (1670–1729) English playwright and poet. *Love for Love* (1695), Act 3, Scene 3

5 Secrets with girls, like loaded guns with boys,
Are never valued till they make a noise.

George Crabbe (1754–1832) British poet and clergyman. *Tales of the Hall* (1819), bk. 11, 'The Maid's Story', ll. 84–85

6 Men with secrets tend to be drawn to each other, not because they want to share what they know but because they need the company of the like-minded, the fellow-afflicted.

Don DeLillo (b. 1936) US novelist. Said by Walter Everett, Jr. *Libra* (1988)

7 For secrets are edged tools,
And must be kept from children and from fools.

John Dryden (1631–1700) English poet, playwright, and literary critic. *Sir Martin Mar-All* (1667), Act 2, Scene 2

8 Three may keep a secret, if two of them are dead.

Benjamin Franklin (1706–90) US statesman and scientist. *Poor Richard's Almanack* (1735), July

9 It is a secret in the Oxford sense: you may tell it to only one person at a time.

Oliver Franks (1905–92) British administrator. *Sunday Telegraph* (January 30, 1977)

10 Closed like confessionals, they thread
Loud noons of cities, giving back
None of the glances they absorb.

Philip Larkin (1922–85) British poet. 'Ambulances' (1961)

11 The most difficult secret for a man to keep is his own opinion of himself.

Marcel Pagnol (1895–1974) French dramatist, filmmaker, and scriptwriter. Remark (March 15, 1954)

12 Each of us when he appears before his fellows is clothed in a certain dignity. But every man knows what unconfessable things pass within the secrecy of his own heart.

Luigi Pirandello (1867–1936) Italian dramatist, novelist, and short-story writer. *Six Characters in Search of an Author* (Edward Storer, tr.; 1921)

13 Secrecy is the first essential in affairs of the State.

Cardinal Richelieu (1585–1642) French churchman and statesman. *Testament Politique* (1688), maxims

14 The concept of the 'official secret' is bureaucracy's specific invention.

Max Weber (1864–1920) German economist and social historian. *Politik als Beruf* (1919)

Secularism

see also **Philosophy, Reason**

1 I do not believe in immortality of the individual, and I consider ethics to be an exclusively human concern with no superhuman authority behind it.

Albert Einstein (1879–1955) German-born US physicist. Draft response to Baptist pastor (1953), quoted in *Albert Einstein, The Human Side* (Helen Dukas and Banesh Hoffman; 1979)

2 I hold the Koran, the Vedas, the Bible, and all such religious texts determining the lives of their followers, as out of place and out of time . . . We have to move beyond these ancient texts if we want progress.

Taslima Nasreen (b. 1958) Bangladeshi writer. Remark (1994)

3 An important element in modernism is the secularization of culture, our achievement of independence as artists from the Church and the monarchy.

Antoni Tàpies (b. 1923) Spanish painter. Quoted in *Conversations with Antoni Tàpies* (Barbara Catoir; 1991)

Seduction

see also **Love, Lust, Sex**

1 Maidens, like moths, are ever caught by glare,
And Mammon wins his way where Seraphs might despair.

Lord Byron (1788–1824) British poet. *Childe Harold's Pilgrimage* (1812–18), can. 1, st. 9

2 Come live with me, and be my love,
And we will some new pleasures prove
Of golden sands, and crystal brooks,
With silken lines, and silver hooks.

John Donne (1572?–1631) English metaphysical poet and divine. 'The Bait' (1635), ll. 1–4

3 Mrs. Robinson, if you don't mind me saying so, this conversation is getting a little strange.

Dustin Hoffman (b. 1937) US actor. As Benjamin, reacting to Mrs. Robinson's attempts to seduce him. *The Graduate* (Calder Willingham and Buck Henry; 1967)

4 Square in your ship's path are Seirênês, crying beauty
to bewitch men coasting by; woe to the innocent who hears that sound!

Homer (*fl.* 8th century BC) Greek poet. Late 8th century BC. *Odyssey* (Robert Fitzgerald, tr.; late 8th century BC), bk. 12, ll. 41–42

5 Come, my Celia, let us prove,
While we can, the sports of love,
Time will not be ours for ever,
He, at length, our good will sever.

Ben Jonson (1572–1637) English playwright and poet. *Volpone* (1606), Act 3, Scene 5

6 And I thought well as well him as another and then I asked him with my eyes to ask again yes and then he asked me would I yes to say yes my mountain flower and first I put my arms around him yes and drew him down to me so he could feel my breasts all perfume yes and his heart was going like mad and yes I said yes I will Yes.

James Joyce (1882–1941) Irish writer. The closing words of Molly Bloom's soliloquy, and the closing words of the novel. *Ulysses* (1922)

7 Had we but world enough, and time,
This coyness, lady, were no crime.

Andrew Marvell (1621–78) English poet and government official. 'To His Coy Mistress' (1650?), ll. 1–2

8 'Do you come here often?'
'Only in the mating season'.

Spike Milligan (1918–2002) Indian-born British humorist, writer, and actor. BBC radio series. *The Goon Show* (1951–59)

9 Come on baby, light my fire.

Jim Morrison (1943–71) US rock singer and songwriter. Song lyric. 'Light My Fire' (1967)

10 I tried to resist his overtures, but he plied me with symphonies, quartettes, chamber music, and cantatas.

S. J. Perelman (1904–79) US humorist. 'The Love Decoy', *Crazy Like a Fox* (1944)

11 Let's do it; let's fall in love.

Cole Porter (1893–1964) US songwriter and composer. Song lyric. 'Let's Do It', *Paris* (1928)

12 With womankind, the less we love them,
the easier they become to charm.

Alexander Pushkin (1799–1837) Russian poet and writer. 1831. *Eugene Onegin* (Charles Johnstone, tr.; 1977), ch. 4, st. 7

The Self

see also **Character, Identity, Individuality, Selfishness, Selflessness**

1 It is not the world that confines you, you yourself are the World, which holds you so fast a prisoner with yourself in yourself.

Angelus Silesius (1624–77) Silesian poet and mystic. 'You Are Your Own Prison' (1657?), quoted in *The Penguin Book of German Verse* (Leonard Foster, ed.; 1957)

2 No, when the fight begins within himself,
A man's worth something.

Robert Browning (1812–89) British poet. 'Bishop Blougram's Apology', *Men and Women* (1855), ll. 693–4

3 What is sometimes called an act of self-expression might better be termed one of self-exposure; it discloses character—or lack of character—to others. In itself, it is only a spewing forth.

John Dewey (1859–1952) US philosopher and educator. *Art as Experience* (1934)

4 The unity of the self is the will. The will is the man, psychologically speaking.

John Dewey (1859–1952) US philosopher and educator. *Psychology* (1887)

5 Every man contemplates an angel in his future self.

Ralph Waldo Emerson (1803–82) US poet and essayist. 1866. *Journals* (1860–66)

6 No man is himself, he is the sum of his past. There is no such thing as was because the past is. It is part of every man, every woman, and every moment. All of his and her ancestry, background, is all a part of himself and herself at any moment.

William Faulkner (1897–1962) US novelist. Quoted in *Faulkner in the University: Class Conferences at the University of Virginia 1957–58* (Frederic L. Gwynn and Joseph L. Blotner, eds.; 1959)

7 *The self posits self*, and by virtue of this self-assertion it *exists*; and conversely, the self *exists* and *posits* its own existence by virtue of merely existing.

Johann Fichte (1762–1814) German philosopher. 1794. *The Science of Knowledge* (P. Heath and J. Lachs, trs.; 1982)

8 The ego represents what we call reason and sanity, in contrast to the id which contains the passions.

Sigmund Freud (1856–1939) Austrian psychoanalyst. *The Ego and the Id* (1923)

9 There is no humanity before that which starts with yourself.

Marcus Garvey (1887–1940) Jamaican-born black nationalist leader and publisher. 'African Fundamentalism, A Racial Hierarchy and Empire for Negroes' (1923)

10 It is by losing himself in the objective, in inquiry, creation, and craft, that a man becomes something.

Paul Goodman (1911–72) US writer, teacher, and psychotherapist. *The Community of Scholars* (1962)

11 Less and less are we able to locate our lives meaningfully in the pageant of history. More and more do we find ourselves retreating to the sanctuary of an insulated individualism, sealed off in our private concerns from the larger events which surround us.

Robert Heilbroner (b. 1919) US economist and author. *The Future as History* (1960)

12 My selfbeing, my consciousness and feelings of myself, that taste of myself, of *I* and *me* above and in all things . . . is incommunicable by any means to another man.

Gerard Manley Hopkins (1844–89) British poet, priest, and classicist. Quoted in *The Poems and Prose of Gerard Manley Hopkins* (W. H. Gardner, ed.; 1953)

13 The greatest hazard of all, losing one's self, can occur very quietly in the world, as if it were nothing at all. No other loss can occur so quietly; any other loss—an arm, a leg, five dollars, a wife, etc.—is sure to be noticed.

Søren Kierkegaard (1813–55) Danish philosopher. *The Sickness unto Death* (1849)

14 A man is always resident in the castle of his skin. If the castle is deserted, then we know the Devil has been at work.

George Lamming (b. 1927) Barbadian writer. *The Pleasures of Exile* (1960)

15 In order to be yourself you first have to be somebody.

Stanislaw Lec (1909–66) Polish writer. 1964. Quoted in *The Jingle Bell Principle* (Miroslav Holub; 1992)

16 Nature forms us for ourselves, not for others; to be, not to seem.

Michel de Montaigne (1533–92) French essayist. *Essays* (1580–88), bk.2, ch. 1

17 Too many lives are needed just to make one.

Eugenio Montale (1896–1981) Italian poet. *Le Occasioni* (1939)

18 I am myself plus my circumstance and if I do not save it, I cannot save myself.

José Ortega y Gasset (1883–1955) Spanish writer and philosopher. *Meditations on Quixote* (1914)

19 Almost always it is the fear of being ourselves that brings us to the mirror.

Antonio Porchia (1886–1968) Italian-born Argentinian writer. *Voces* (W. S. Merwin, tr.; 1968)

20 I is somebody else.

Arthur Rimbaud (1854–91) French poet. Letters to Georges Izambard and Paul Demeny (May 1871), quoted in *Lettres du Voyant: 13 et 15 Mai 1871* (Gérald Schaeffer, ed.; 1975)

21 Self-sacrifice enables us to sacrifice Other people without blushing.

George Bernard Shaw (1856–1950) Irish playwright. 'Maxims for Revolutionists', *Man and Superman* (1903)

22 None but himself can be his parallel.

Lewis Theobald (1688–1744) English playwright and critic. *The Double Falsehood* was claimed by Theobald to be a 'lost' play by William Shakespeare. *The Double Falsehood* (1728)

23 Would you hurt a man keenest, strike at his self-love.

Lew Wallace (1827–1905) US soldier and writer. *Ben Hur: A Tale of the Christ* (1880), bk. 6, ch. 2

24 I have said that the soul is not more than the body, And I have said that the body is not more than the soul, And nothing, but God, is greater to one than one's self is.

Walt Whitman (1819–92) US poet. 1855. 'Song of Myself', *Leaves of Grass* (1881), pt. 48

25 The self, what a brute it is. It wants, wants.

Reed Whittemore (b. 1919) US poet. 'Clamming', *Poems* (1967), quoted in *The Penguin Book of American Verse* (Geoffrey Moore, ed.; 1977)

Self-Confidence

see also **Arrogance, Courage, Pride, Talent**

1 The advantage of doing one's praising for oneself is that one can lay it on so thick and exactly in the right places.

Samuel Butler (1835–1902) British writer and composer. *The Way of All Flesh* (1903), ch. 34

2 I am my own foundation.

Frantz Fanon (1925–61) Martiniquan social scientist, physician, and psychiatrist. *Black Skin, White Masks* (1952)

3 Those who believe that they are exclusively in the right are generally those who achieve something.

Aldous Huxley (1894–1963) British novelist and essayist. *Proper Studies* (1927)

4 The bullet that is to kill me has not yet been moulded.

Napoleon I (1769–1821) French emperor. Replying to his brother Joseph, King of Spain, who had asked whether he had ever been hit by a cannonball. Remark (February 2, 1814)

5 MACBETH Hang out our banners on the outward walls;
The cry is still, 'They come'; our castle's strength
Will laugh a siege to scorn.

William Shakespeare (1564–1616) English poet and playwright. *Macbeth* (1606), Act 5, Scene 5

6 I am greater than the stars for I know that they are up there and they do not know that I am down here.

William Temple (1881–1944) British clergyman. Attrib.

7 These success encourages: they can because they think they can.

Virgil (70–19 BC) Roman poet. *Aeneid* (29–19 BC), bk. 5, l. 231

Self-Delusion

see also **Delusion, Vanity**

1 For what a man would like to be true, that he more readily believes.

Francis Bacon (1561–1626) English philosopher, statesman, and lawyer. *Novum Organum* (1620), aphorism 49

2 I think it's one of the scars in our culture that we have too high opinion of ourselves. We align ourselves with the angels instead of the higher primates.

Angela Carter (1940–92) British novelist, essayist, and short-story writer. Attrib.

3 You see, I always divide people into two groups. Those who live by what they know to be a lie, and those who live by what they believe, falsely, to be the truth.

Christopher Hampton (b. 1946) British playwright. *The Philanthropist* (1970), Scene 6

4 I have a certain hesitation in starting my biography too soon for fear of something important having not yet happened. Suppose I should end my days as President of Mexico; the biography would seem incomplete if it did not mention this fact.

Bertrand Russell (1872–1970) British philosopher and mathematician. Letter to Stanley Unwin (November 1930)

Self-Interest

see also **Egotism, The Self, Selfishness**

1 I have never yet met with anything that was dearer to anyone than his own self. Since to others, to each one for himself, the self is dear, therefore let him who desires his own advantage not harm another.

Buddha (563?–483? BC) Nepalese-born founder of Buddhism. Quoted in *Buddhism* (Edward Conze; 1951)

2 A fig for those by law protected!
Liberty's a glorious feast!
Courts for cowards were erected,
Churches built to please the priest.

Robert Burns (1759–96) Scottish poet and songwriter. Also known as 'Love and Liberty—a Cantata'. 'The Jolly Beggars' (1799)

3 Let them eat the lie and swallow it with their bread. Whether the two were lovers or no, they'll have accounted to God for it by now. I have my own fish to fry.

Miguel de Cervantes (1547–1616) Spanish novelist and playwright. *Don Quixote* (1605–15), pt. 1, ch. 25

4 Powerful people never teach powerless people how to take their power away from them.

John Henrik Clarke (1915–98) US historian and educator. *Essence* (September 1989)

5 Anyone informed that the universe is expanding and contracting in pulsations of eighty billion years has a right to ask, 'What's in it for me?'

Peter De Vries (1910–93) US novelist. *The Glory of the Hummingbird* (1974), ch. 1

6 The least pain in our little finger gives us more concern and uneasiness than the destruction of millions of our fellow-beings.

William Hazlitt (1778–1830) British essayist and critic. 'American Literature—Dr. Channing', *Edinburgh Review* (October 1829)

7 It is difficult to love mankind unless one has a reasonable private income and when one has a reasonable private income one has better things to do than loving mankind.

Hugh Kingsmill (1889–1949) British writer, critic, and anthologist. Quoted in *God's Apology* (R. Ingrams; 1977)

8 Self-interest speaks all sorts of tongues, and plays all sorts of roles, even that of disinterestedness.

François La Rochefoucauld (1613–80) French epigrammatist and moralist. *Reflections, or Sentences and Moral Maxims* (1665), no. 39

9 One had rather malign oneself than not speak of oneself at all.

François La Rochefoucauld (1613–80) French epigrammatist and moralist. *Reflections, or Sentences and Moral Maxims* (1665), no. 138

10 A prince who desires to maintain his position must learn to be not always good, but to be so or not as needs may require.

Niccolò Machiavelli (1469–1527) Italian historian, statesman, and political philosopher. 1513–17. *Discourses on the First Ten Books of Titus Livy* (1531)

11 Be lowly wise:
Think only what concerns thee and thy being.

John Milton (1608–74) English writer. Raphael to Adam. *Paradise Lost* (1667), bk. 8, ll. 173–174

12 'Tis a wise saying, Drive on your own track.

Plutarch (46?–120?) Greek biographer and philosopher. 'Of the Training of Children' (1st–2nd century)

13 Avoid having your ego so close to your position that when your position falls, your ego goes with it.

Colin Powell (b. 1937) US military leader and politician. 'Colin Powell's Rules', *Parade* (August 1989)

14 IAGO In the following him, I follow but myself.

William Shakespeare (1564–1616) English poet and playwright. *Othello* (1602–04), Act 1, Scene 1

Selfishness

see also **Desire, Egotism, The Self, Self-Interest**

1 I have been a selfish being all my life, in practice, though not in principle.

Jane Austen (1775–1817) British novelist. *Pride and Prejudice* (1813), ch. 58

2 SELFISH, adj. Devoid of consideration for the selfishness of others.

Ambrose Bierce (1842–1914?) US writer and journalist. *The Devil's Dictionary* (1911)

3 All sensible people are selfish, and nature is tugging at every contract to make the terms of it fair.

Ralph Waldo Emerson (1803–82) US poet and essayist. 'Considerations by the Way', *The Conduct of Life* (1860)

4 A system of isolation: *Look out for number one.* Your neighbor is neither your brother nor your lover. Your neighbor is a competitor, an enemy, an obstacle to clear or an object to use.

Eduardo Galeano (b. 1940) Uruguayan writer. *The Book of Embraces* (1989)

5 This fellow did not see further than his own nose.

Jean de La Fontaine (1621–95) French writer and poet. 'Le Renard et la Boue', *Fables* (1668), bk. 3

6 At bottom, Nationalism and Communism are variations of the same perverse theme: man's self-centred worship of himself.

Arnold Toynbee (1889–1975) British historian. 'What are the Criteria for Comparisons between Religions?', *Christianity Among the Religions of the World* (1958), pt. 1

Self-Knowledge

see also **The Self**, **Understanding**

1 Resolve to be thyself: and know, that he Who finds himself, loses his misery.

Matthew Arnold (1822–88) British poet and critic. 'Self-Dependence' (1852), ll. 31–32

2 Be so true to thyself, as thou be not false to others.

Francis Bacon (1561–1626) English philosopher, statesman, and lawyer. 'Of Wisdom for a Man's Self', *Essays* (1625)

3 There's a period of life when we swallow a knowledge of ourselves, and it becomes either good or sour inside.

Pearl Bailey (1918–90) US singer and actor. *The Raw Pearl* (1968)

4 I think knowing what you *cannot* do is more important than knowing what you can do. In fact, that's good taste.

Lucille Ball (1911–89) US film and television actor and comedian. Quoted in *The Real Story of Lucille Ball* (Eleanor Harris; 1954)

5 We wander but in the end there is always a certain peace in being what one is, in being that completely. The condemned man has that joy.

Ugo Betti (1892–1953) Italian playwright and poet. *Goat Island* (1946)

6 Between two worlds life hovers like a star, 'Twixt night and morn, upon the horizon's verge How little do we know that which we are! How less what we may be!

Lord Byron (1788–1824) British poet. *Don Juan* (1819–24), can. 15, st. 99

7 Self-contemplation is infallibly the symptom of disease.

Thomas Carlyle (1795–1881) Scottish historian and essayist. *Characteristics* (1877)

8 When you have faults, do not fear to abandon them.

Confucius (551–479 BC) Chinese philosopher, administrator, and moralist. *Analects* (5th century BC)

9 I have always disliked myself at any given moment; the total of such moments is my life.

Cyril Connolly (1903–74) British writer and journalist. *Enemies of Promise* (1938), ch. 18

10 The one thing that all religions recognize as separating us from our creator—our very self-consciousness—is also the one thing that divides us from our fellow creatures. It was a bitter birthday present from evolution, cutting us off at both ends.

Annie Dillard (b. 1945) US writer. *Pilgrim at Tinker's Creek* (1974), ch. 6

11 When I discover who I am, I'll be free.

Ralph Ellison (1914–94) US writer, jazz musician, and photographer. *Invisible Man* (1953)

12 'I know myself', he cried, 'but that is all'.

F. Scott Fitzgerald (1896–1940) US writer. *This Side of Paradise* (1920), bk. 2, ch. 5

13 The man who in himself can read, That man, I say, is wise indeed.

Freidank (*fl.* 1230) German poet. 13th century. Quoted in *A German Treasury* (Stanley Mason, tr.; 1993)

14 Let no voice but your own speak to you from the depths.

Marcus Garvey (1887–1940) Jamaican-born black nationalist leader and publisher. 'African Fundamentalism, A Racial Hierarchy and Empire for Negroes' (1923)

15 I do not know myself, and God forbid that I should.

Johann Wolfgang von Goethe (1749–1832) German poet, playwright, and scientist. April 10, 1829. Quoted in *Conversations with Goethe* (Johann Peter Eckermann; 1836–48)

16 I am always with myself, and it is I who am my tormentor.

Nikolay Gogol (1809–52) Russian novelist and playwright. 'Diary of a Madman' (1835)

17 Never know what you made of if you ain't arguing with the world about something.

Marita Golden (b. 1950) US writer and teacher. *Long Distance Life* (1989)

18 Self-reflection is the school of wisdom.

Baltasar Gracián (1601–58) Spanish writer and Jesuit. *The Art of Worldly Wisdom* (1647)

19 For most people, the chief obstacle in the way of acquiring self-consciousness consists in the fact that they think they possess it . . . a man will not be interested if you tell him that he can acquire by long and difficult work something which, in his opinion, he already has.

G. I. Gurdjieff (1865?–1949) Armenian-born French philosopher and writer. Quoted in *In Search of the Miraculous* (P. D. Ouspensky; 1950)

20 I am neither internee nor informer; An inner émigré, grown long-haired And thoughtful; a wood-kerne Escaped from the massacre, Taking protective colouring From bole and bark.

Seamus Heaney (b. 1939) Irish poet. 'Exposure', *North* (1975), ll. 34–39

21 I have no *knowledge* of myself as I am, but merely as I appear to myself.

Immanuel Kant (1724–1804) German philosopher. *Critique of Pure Reason* (1781), B 158

22 You have to start knowing yourself so well that you begin to know other people. A piece of us is in every person we can ever meet.
Stephen King (b. 1947) US novelist. *Night Shift* (1978)

23 There is no need to go to India or anywhere else to find peace. You will find that deep place of silence right in your room, your garden, or even your bathtub.
Elisabeth Kübler-Ross (b. 1926) Swiss-born US psychiatrist and author. Speech (1976)

24 It is no good casting out devils. They belong to us, we must accept them and be at peace with them.
D. H. Lawrence (1885–1930) British writer. 'The Reality of Peace', *Phoenix* (1929)

25 My body is that part of the world which can be altered by my thoughts. Even imaginary illnesses can become real. In the rest of the world my hypotheses cannot disturb the order of things.
Georg Christoph Lichtenberg (1742–99) German physicist and writer. *Aphorisms* (1764–99)

26 One of the greatest reasons why so few people understand themselves, is, that most writers are always teaching men what they should be, and hardly ever trouble their heads with telling them what they really are.
Bernard Mandeville (1670–1733) English physician and satirist. *An Enquiry into the Origin of Moral Virtue* (1725)

27 Open your eyes and look within.
Are you satisfied with the life you're living?
Bob Marley (1945–81) Jamaican musician, singer, and songwriter. Song lyric. 'Exodus', *Exodus* (1977)

28 A man can't help his feelings sometime. He don't even understand his damn self half the time and there the trouble starts.
Paule Marshall (b. 1929) US novelist, teacher, and journalist. *The Chosen Place, The Timeless People* (1969)

29 Self under self, a pile of selves I stand
Threaded on time, and with a metaphysic hand
Lift the farm like a lid and see
Farm within farm, and in the centre, me.
Norman McCaig (1910–96) Scottish poet. 'Summer Farm' (1955)

30 One should examine oneself for a very long time before thinking of condemning others.
Molière (1622–73) French playwright. *Le Misanthrope* (1666), Act 3, Scene 4

31 In seeing ourselves from outside we find it difficult to take our lives seriously. This loss of conviction, and the attempt to regain it, is the problem of the meaning of life.
Thomas Nagel (b. 1937) Yugoslavian-born US philosopher and educator. *The View from Nowhere* (1986)

32 The apprehension that one is someone else is all that one needs to believe that the world has changed from top to bottom.
Orhan Pamuk (b. 1952) Turkish novelist. *The Black Book* (Guneli Gun, tr.; 1990)

33 Know then thyself, presume not God to scan,
The proper study of Mankind is Man.
Alexander Pope (1688–1744) English poet. *An Essay on Man* (1733), Epistle 2, ll. 1–2

34 A man goes far to find out what he is—
Death of the self in a long, tearless night,
All natural shapes blazing unnatural light.
Theodore Roethke (1908–63) US poet. 'In a Dark Time', *The Far Field* (1964), ll. 16–18

35 GERTRUDE Speak no more;
Thou turn'st mine eyes into my very soul.
William Shakespeare (1564–1616) English poet and playwright. *Hamlet* (1601), Act 3, Scene 4

36 Self-knowledge is a dangerous thing, tending to make man shallow or insane.
Karl Shapiro (b. 1913) US poet, critic, and editor. *The Bourgeois Poet* (1964)

37 The unexamined life is not worth living.
Socrates (470?–399? BC) Greek philosopher. 399? BC. Quoted in *Apology* (Plato), 38a

38 Knowledge and love, the things that the great men of wisdom preach, can be found only by the individual, through introspection, which requires tremendous effort.
Antoni Tàpies (b. 1923) Spanish painter. Quoted in *Conversations with Antoni Tàpies* (Barbara Catoir; 1991)

39 Explore thyself. Herein are demanded the eye and the nerve.
Henry David Thoreau (1817–62) US writer. 'Conclusion', *Walden, or, Life in the Woods* (1854)

40 I know everything except myself.
François Villon (1431?–63?) French poet. 'Ballade of Small Talk' (1460?), refrain

41 Do I contradict myself?
Very well then I contradict myself,
I am large, I contain multitudes.
Walt Whitman (1819–92) US poet. 1855. 'Song of Myself', *Leaves of Grass* (1881), pt. 51

42 I am the only person in the world I should like to know thoroughly.
Oscar Wilde (1854–1900) Irish poet, playwright, and wit. *Lady Windermere's Fan* (1892), Act 2

43 Each has his past shut in him like the leaves of a book known to him by heart and his friends can only read the title.
Virginia Woolf (1882–1941) British novelist and critic. *Jacob's Room* (1922), ch. 5

Selflessness

see also **Humility**, **Modesty**, **The Self**

1 Greater love hath no man than this, that a man lay down his life for his friends.
Bible. John, *King James Bible* (1611), 15:13

2 I was speaking of compassion . . . Sometimes it creeps in through the narrowest cracks. That is why I suggested using rags to block them up.
Mikhail Bulgakov (1891–1940) Russian novelist and playwright. 1929–40. *The Master and Margarita* (Michael Glenny, tr.; 1966), ch. 24

3 Do we not find that we often desire the Happiness of others without any . . . selfish intention? How few have thought upon this part of our Constitution which we call a Publick Sense?
Francis Hutcheson (1694–1746) Irish-born English philosopher. *An Essay on the Nature and Conduct of the Passions and Affections* (1728)

4 The way to get things done is not to mind who gets the credit of doing them.
Benjamin Jowett (1817–93) British scholar. Attrib.

5 She's the sort of woman who lives for others—you can always tell the others by their hunted expression.
C. S. Lewis (1898–1963) Irish-born British novelist. *The Screwtape Letters* (1942), no. 26

6 How selfish soever man may be supposed, there are evidently some principles in his nature, which interest him in the fortune of others, and render their happiness necessary to him, though he derives nothing from it except the pleasure of seeing it.

Adam Smith (1723–90) Scottish economist and philosopher. *The Theory of Moral Sentiments* (1759)

7 And all for love, and nothing for reward.

Edmund Spenser (1552?–99) English poet. *The Faerie Queene* (1596), bk. 1, can. 8, st. 2

Self-Respect

see also **Respect**, **The Self**

1 To be a great man and a saint to oneself, that is the one important thing.

Charles Baudelaire (1821–67) French poet. 'Mon Coeur Mis à Nu', *Journaux Intimes* (1887)

2 It is better to die on your feet than to live on your knees.

Dolores Ibárruri (1895–1989) Spanish politician and journalist. Referring to the Spanish Civil War (1936–39). Speech in Paris, *L'Humanité* (September 4, 1936)

3 Self-respect—the secure feeling that no one, as yet, is suspicious.

H. L. Mencken (1880–1956) US journalist, critic, and editor. 'Sententiae: The Mind of Men', *A Mencken Chrestomathy* (1949)

4 Whoever despises himself still respects himself as one who despises.

Friedrich Wilhelm Nietzsche (1844–1900) German philosopher and poet. *Beyond Good and Evil* (1886)

5 Great God, I ask thee for no meaner pelf
Than that I may not disappoint myself.

Henry David Thoreau (1817–62) US writer. 'Pelf' is an archaic word for money, wealth. 'Great God, I Ask Thee for No Meaner Pelf', *The Penguin Book of American Verse* (Geoffrey Moore, ed.; 1977)

6 The worth of a man is certain only if he is prepared to sacrifice his own life for his convictions.

Henning von Tresckow (1901–44) German general. 1945. Henning von Tresckow plotted against Adolf Hitler. These words are from his suicide note. Attrib.

7 I celebrate myself, and sing myself,
And what I assume you shall assume.

Walt Whitman (1819–92) US poet. 1855. 'Song of Myself', *Leaves of Grass* (1881), pt. 1

Senses

see also **Consciousness**, **Perception**

1 Our sight is the most perfect and most delightful of all our senses. It fills the mind with the largest variety of ideas, converses with its objects at the greatest distance, and continues the longest in action without being tired or satiated with its proper enjoyments.

Joseph Addison (1672–1719) English essayist, poet, and statesman. *Spectator* (June 21, 1712), no. 411

2 Any nose
May ravage with impunity a rose.

Robert Browning (1812–89) British poet. *Sordello* (1840), bk. 6, l. 881

3 But perhaps it is this distrust of our senses that prevents us from feeling comfortable in the universe.

Italo Calvino (1923–85) Cuban-born Italian novelist and short-story writer. *Mr. Palomar* (William Weaver, tr.; 1983)

4 now the ears of my ears awake and
now the eyes of my eyes are opened.

e. e. cummings (1894–1962) US poet and painter. 'i thank You God for most this amazing', *XAIPE* (1950), quoted in *The Penguin Book of American Verse* (Geoffrey Moore, ed.; 1977)

5 Feeling . . . signifies not a special class of psychical facts, like memory or conception, but *one side of all mental phenomena*.

John Dewey (1859–1952) US philosopher and educator. *Psychology* (1887)

6 'Yes I have a pair of eyes', replied Sam, 'and that's just it. If they was a pair o' patent double million magnifyin' gas microscopes of hextra power, p'raps I might be able to see through a flight o' stairs and a deal door; but bein' only eyes, you see, my vision's limited'.

Charles Dickens (1812–70) British novelist. *The Pickwick Papers* (1837), ch. 34

7 If you fight against all your sensations, you will have no standard to which to refer, and thus no means of judging even those judgements which you pronounce false.

Epicurus (341–270 BC) Greek philosopher. *The Principal Doctrines* (4th century BC)

8 It is therefore correct to say that the senses do not err—not because they always judge rightly, but because they do not judge at all.

Immanuel Kant (1724–1804) German philosopher. *Critique of Pure Reason* (1781), A 293, B 350

9 O for a Life of Sensations rather than of Thoughts!

John Keats (1795–1821) English poet. Letter to Benjamin Bailey (November 22, 1817), quoted in *Letters of John Keats* (H. E. Rollins, ed.; 1958), vol. 1

10 The five colours make a man's eyes blind;
The five notes make his ears deaf;
The five tastes injure his palate;
Riding and hunting make his mind go wild with excitement.

Laozi (570?–490? BC) Chinese philosopher. The *Daode Jing* is an early Chinese Taoist text. While attributed to Laozi, it probably dates from the 3rd century BC *Daode Jing*, quoted in *Tao Te Ching* (D. C. Lau, tr.; 1963), bk. 1, pt. 12

11 We are more sensible of one little touch of a surgeon's lancet than of twenty wounds with a sword in the heat of fight.

Michel de Montaigne (1533–92) French essayist. Attrib.

12 The five senses are as spies. Each one of them has been entrusted with making one of the arts, so the eye has been entrusted with the world of colours, hearing with the world of voices, and so on.

Muhammad (570?–632?) Arab religious leader and prophet. Reported as spoken by Muhammad by Abu Dharr al-Ghifari. Quoted in *The Complete Forty Hadith* (Muhyid-Din al-Nawawi; 13th century), 6th Hadith

13 Fine pictures, fine statues, beautiful music; pleasure for the senses, and let the devil take the soul!

Benito Pérez Galdós (1843–1920) Spanish novelist and playwright. *Doña Perfecta* (1876)

14 They never taste who always drink;
    They always talk who never think.
    Matthew Prior (1664–1721) English diplomat and poet. 'Upon a Passage
    in the Scaligerana' (1740)

Sentimentality

see also Emotion, Nostalgia

1 Sentimentality is a superstructure covering
   brutality.
   Carl Gustav Jung (1875–1961) Swiss psychoanalyst. Quoted in
   Psychological Reflections: an Anthology of the Writings of C.
   G. Jung (Jolande Jacobi, ed.; 1953)

2 Sentimentality is the emotional promiscuity of
   those who have no sentiment.
   Norman Mailer (b. 1923) US novelist and journalist. 'My Hope for
   America', Cannibals and Christians (1966)

3 Sentimentality is only sentiment that rubs you up
   the wrong way.
   Somerset Maugham (1874–1965) British writer. A Writer's Notebook
   (1949)

Separation

see also Divorce, Parting, Unity

1 Absence from whom we love is worse than death.
   William Cowper (1731–1800) British poet. 'Hope' (1782), quoted in
   Cowper: Poetical Works (H. S. Milford, ed.; 1934)

2 Let's Call the Whole Thing Off!
   Ira Gershwin (1896–1983) US lyricist. Song title. Shall We Dance
   (1937)

3 Part of My Soul Went With Him
   Winnie Mandela (b. 1934) South African social worker and political
   activist. 1985. Book title. Referring to Nelson Mandela's
   imprisonment.

4 Most people are on the world, not in it—having
   no conscious sympathy or relationship to
   anything about them—undiffused, separate, and
   rigidly alone like marbles of polished stone,
   touching but separate.
   John Muir (1838–1914) US naturalist and explorer. Quoted in John of
   the Mountains (Linnie Marsh Wolfe, ed.; 1938)

5 Fortnight after I married her . . . I took the lid
   off a saucepan, you know what was in it? A pile
   of her underclothing, unwashed . . . That's when
   I left her and I haven't seen her since.
   Harold Pinter (b. 1930) British playwright, theatre director, and
   screenwriter. The Caretaker (1960), Act 1

6 As it will be the right of all, so it will be the duty
   of some, definitely to prepare for a separation,
   amicably if they can, violently if they must.
   Josiah Quincy (1772–1864) US politician. Part of a speech given on a
   state's constitutional rights of self-determination. Abridgement
   of Debates of Congress (January 14, 1811), vol. 4

Seriousness

1 They call me Battling Bella, Mother Courage, and a
   Jewish mother with more complaints than
   Portnoy . . . But whatever I am—and this ought to
   be made very clear—I am a very serious woman.
   Bella Abzug (1920–98) US lawyer, politician, and campaigner. Abzug
   was a member of the US House of Representatives when she
   said this. Bella! (1972)

2 The more serious the face, the more beautiful the
   smile.
   René Chateaubriand (1768–1848) French writer and statesman.
   Mémoires d'Outre-tombe (1849–50), bk. 14, ch. 10

3 Now for a change I am going to be serious—
   though only temporarily.
   Flann O'Brien (1911–66) Irish novelist and journalist. 'Politics', Further
   Cuttings from Cruiskeen Lawn (1989)

4 Everything must be taken seriously, nothing
   tragically.
   Adolphe Thiers (1797–1877) French statesman and historian. Speech to
   the French National Assembly (May 24, 1873)

Sex

see also Desire, Homosexuality, Love, Lust, Passion, Sexuality

1 It was the most fun I ever had without laughing.
   Woody Allen (b. 1935) US film actor and director. Referring to sex.
   Annie Hall (1977)

2 Sex between a man and a woman can be
   wonderful—provided you get between the right
   man and the right woman.
   Woody Allen (b. 1935) US film actor and director. Attrib.

3 Know that the appetite for sexual intercourse is
   one which the prophets and people of right
   action love . . . for it softens the heart.
   Muhyid-Din Abu Zakariyya ibn Sharaf al-Nawawi (1233–77) Syrian Islamic
   scholar. 13th century. The Complete Forty Hadith
   (Abdassamad Clarke, tr.; 1988), 25th Hadith

4 The sexual can only be the final inescapable
   release of enormous stored spiritual vital
   tensions.
   Peter Altenberg (1859–1919) Austrian writer. Prodomos (Andrew
   Barker, tr.; 1905)

5 The surest guarantee of sexual success is sexual
   success (you can't have one without the other
   and you can't have the other without the one).
   Martin Amis (b. 1949) British writer. Success (1978)

6 It was a spring day, a day for a lay, when the air
   Smelled like a locker-room, a day to blow or get
   blown.
   W. H. Auden (1907–73) British poet. 'The Platonic Blow', A History
   of Gay Literature (Gregory Woods; 1998)

7 The Seven Year Itch
   George Axelrod (b. 1922) US screenwriter. 1955. Play and film title.

8 I'll come and make love to you at five o'clock. If
   I'm late start without me.
   Tallulah Bankhead (1903–68) US actor. Quoted in Somerset
   Maugham (E. Morgan; 1980)

9 Erotic practices have been diversified. Sex used to
   be a single-crop farming, like cotton or wheat,
   now people raise all sorts of things.
   Saul Bellow (b. 1915) Canadian-born US writer. More Die of
   Heartbreak (1987)

10 The sexual thrust to reproduce and to fill the
    future is a thrust against the current of time
    which is flowing ceaselessly towards the past.
    John Berger (b. 1926) British novelist, essayist, and art critic. And Our
    Faces, My Heart, Brief as Photos (1984)

11 My beloved put in his hand by the hole of the
    door, and my bowels were moved for him.
    Bible. Song of Solomon, King James Bible (1611), 5:4

12 If God had meant us to have group sex, I guess he'd have given us all more organs.

Malcolm Bradbury (1932–2000) British academic, novelist, and critic. 'A Very Hospitable Person', *Who Do You Think You Are?* (1987)

13 I could be content that we might procreate like trees, without conjunction, or that there were any way to perpetuate the World without this trivial and vulgar way of coition: it is the foolishest act a wise man commits in all his life.

Thomas Browne (1605–82) English physician and writer. *Religio Medici* (1642), pt. 2, sect. 9

14 He said it was artificial respiration but now I find I'm to have his child.

Anthony Burgess (1917–93) British writer and critic. *Inside Mr. Enderby* (1963)

15 It doesn't matter what you do in the bedroom as long as you don't do it in the street and frighten the horses.

Mrs. Patrick Campbell (1865–1940) British actor. 1910? Quoted in *The Duchess of Jermyn Street* (Daphne Fielding; 1964), ch. 2

16 The pleasure is momentary, the position ridiculous and the expense damnable.

Lord Chesterfield (1694–1773) English statesman and writer. Attrib.

17 Sex is to women's history as color is to black history: a prime basis of differentiation and therefore a source of conflict.

Carl N. Degler (b. 1921) US historian. 'Remaking American History', *Journal of American History* (June 1980)

18 You think intercourse is a private act; it's not, it's a social act. Men are sexually predatory in life; and women are sexually manipulative.

Andrea Dworkin (b. 1946) US writer and feminist. *Intercourse* (1987)

19 If you know that your body is your enemy, and the enemy of God's glory, why do you treat it so gently?

José María Escriva de Balaguer y Albas, Spanish priest. Quoted in *The Spaniards* (John Hooper; 1986)

20 Personally I know nothing about sex because I've always been married.

Zsa Zsa Gabor (b. 1918) Hungarian-born US film actor. *Observer* (August 16, 1987), 'Sayings of the Week'

21 Despite a lifetime of service to the cause of sexual liberation I have never caught a venereal disease, which makes me feel rather like an arctic explorer who has never had frostbite.

Germaine Greer (b. 1939) Australian-born British writer and academic. *Observer* (March 4, 1973), 'Sayings of the Week'

22 For all the pseudo-sophistication of twentieth-century sex theory, it is still assumed that a man should make love as if his principal intention was to people the wilderness.

Germaine Greer (b. 1939) Australian-born British writer and academic. Attrib.

23 No sex is better than bad sex.

Germaine Greer (b. 1939) Australian-born British writer and academic. Attrib.

24 But did thee feel the earth move?

Ernest Hemingway (1899–1961) US writer. *For Whom the Bell Tolls* (1940), ch. 13

25 'Bed', as the Italian proverb succinctly puts it, 'is the poor man's opera'.

Aldous Huxley (1894–1963) British novelist and essayist. *Heaven and Hell* (1956)

26 Have you not as yet observed that pleasure, which is undeniably the sole motive force behind the union of the sexes, is nevertheless not enough to form a bond between them? And that, if it is preceded by desire which impels, it is succeeded by disgust which repels? That is a law of nature which love alone can alter.

Pierre Choderlos de Laclos (1741–1803) French novelist and politician. *Les Liaisons Dangereuses* (1782), Letter 131

27 Sexual intercourse began
In nineteen sixty-three
(Which was rather late for me)—
Between the end of the *Chatterley* ban
And the Beatles' first LP.

Philip Larkin (1922–85) British poet. 'Annus Mirabilis', *High Windows* (1974)

28 John Thomas says good-night to Lady Jane, a little droopingly, but with a hopeful heart.

D. H. Lawrence (1885–1930) British writer. The closing words of the book. *Lady Chatterley's Lover* (1928), ch. 19

29 You know the worst thing about oral sex? The view.

Maureen Lipman (b. 1946) British actor and comedian. Remark (1990)

30 The reproduction of mankind is a great marvel and mystery. Had God consulted me in the matter, I should have advised him to continue the generation of the species by fashioning them of clay.

Martin Luther (1483–1546) German theologian and religious reformer. Attrib.

31 If sex is such a natural phenomenon, how come there are so many books on how to?

Bette Midler (b. 1945) US singer and actor. Attrib.

32 Sex is one of the nine reasons for reincarnation . . . The other eight are unimportant.

Henry Miller (1891–1980) US novelist. *Sexus* (1949)

33 The orgasm has replaced the Cross as the focus of longing and the image of fulfilment.

Malcolm Muggeridge (1903–90) British journalist. 'Down With Sex', *The Most of Malcolm Muggeridge* (1966)

34 Sexual pleasure seems to consist in a sudden discharge of nervous energy. Aesthetic enjoyment is a sudden discharge of allusive emotions. Similarly, philosophy is like a sudden discharge of intellectual activity.

José Ortega y Gasset (1883–1955) Spanish writer and philosopher. *Meditations on Quixote* (1914)

35 One orgasm in the bush is worth two in the hand.

Robert Reisner (1921–74) US writer and humorist. 'Masturbation', *Graffiti: Two Thousand Years of Wall Writing* (1974)

36 The Christian view of sex is that it is, indeed, a form of holy communion.

John Robinson (1919–83) British clergyman and theologian. Giving evidence as a defence witness in the prosecution of Penguin Books for publishing *Lady Chatterley's Lover* by D. H. Lawrence. *Times* (October 28, 1960)

37 Sex is something I really don't understand too hot. You never know *where* the hell you are. I keep making up these sex rules for myself, and then I break them right away.

J. D. Salinger (b. 1919) US novelist. *The Catcher in the Rye* (1951), ch. 9

38 HELENA The hind that would be mated with the lion
Must die for love.
William Shakespeare (1564–1616) English poet and playwright. *All's Well That Ends Well* (1603), Act 1, Scene 1

39 In a culture where the aesthetic experience is
denied and atrophied, genuine religious ecstasy
rare, intellectual pleasure scorned—it is only
natural that sex should become the only personal
epiphany of most people.
Gary Snyder (b. 1930) US poet, essayist, and translator. August 9, 1953. 'Lookout's Journal: Sourdough', *Earth House Hold* (1969)

40 Someone asked Sophocles, 'How is your sex-life
now? Are you still able to have a woman?' He
replied, 'Hush, man; most gladly indeed am I rid
of it all, as though I had escaped from a mad
and savage master'.
Sophocles (496?–406? BC) Greek playwright. 5th century BC. Quoted in *Republic* (Plato), bk. 1, 329b

41 'Sex', she says, 'is a subject like any other
subject. Every bit as interesting as agriculture'.
Muriel Spark (b. 1918) British novelist. *The Hothouse by the East River* (1973), ch. 4

42 The variables are surprisingly few . . . One can
whip or be whipped; one can eat excrement or
quaff urine; mouth and private part can be met
in this or that commerce. After which there is the
grey area of morning and the sour knowledge
that things have remained fairly generally the
same since man first met goat and woman.
George Steiner (b. 1929) US scholar and critic. Referring to the possibilities of physical relations. 'Nightworks', *Language and Silence* (1967)

43 Once: a philosopher; twice: a pervert!
Voltaire (1694–1778) French writer and philosopher. Turning down an invitation to an orgy, having attended one the previous night for the first time. Attrib.

44 All this fuss about sleeping together. For physical
pleasure I'd sooner go to my dentist any day.
Evelyn Waugh (1903–66) British novelist. *Vile Bodies* (1930), ch. 6

The Sexes

see also Men, Relationships, Sexuality, Women

1 Mr. Darwin . . . has failed to hold definitely
before his mind the principle that the difference
of sex, whatever it may consist in, must itself be
subject to natural selection and to evolution.
Antoinette Louisa Blackwell (1825–1921) US Unitarian minister, feminist, and abolitionist. *The Sexes Throughout Nature* (1875)

2 However much a man might think ill of women,
there is no woman who does not think greater ill
of him.
Nicolas Chamfort (1741–94) French writer. *Maximes et Pensées* (1795)

3 There is more difference within the sexes than
between them.
Ivy Compton-Burnett (1884–1969) British novelist. *Mother and Son* (1955)

4 In company with several other old ladies of both
sexes.
Charles Dickens (1812–70) British novelist. Said by Mr. Meagles. *Little Dorrit* (1857), bk. 1, ch. 17

5 Right is of no sex.
Frederick Douglass (1817–95) US abolitionist, writer, and orator. 1847. Slogan on masthead of *The North Star*. *The Life and Writings of Frederick Douglass* (Philip S. Foner, ed.; 1950), vol. 1

6 A man's idea in a card game is war—cool,
devastating, and pitiless. A lady's idea of it is a
combination of larceny, embezzlement, and
burglary.
Finley Peter Dunne (1867–1936) US humorist and journalist. 'On the Game of Cards', *Mr. Dooley on Making a Will* (1919)

7 Men don't understand anything about women
and women understand nothing about men. And
it's better that way.
Vittorio Gassman (b. 1922) Italian actor. Attrib.

8 There are good women and good men but they
seldom join their lives together.
Bessie Head (1937–86) South African writer. 'Life', *The Collector of Treasures* (1977)

9 The only really happy people are married women
and single men.
H. L. Mencken (1880–1956) US journalist, critic, and editor. Attrib.

10 The opinion in favour of the present system
which entirely subordinates the weaker sex to the
stronger, rests upon theory only; for there was
never trial made of any other.
John Stuart Mill (1806–73) British philosopher and social reformer. *The Subjection of Women* (1869)

11 Y chromosomes of history, apologise to your
Xes!
Les Murray (b. 1938) Australian poet. 'Sound Bites', *Conscious and Verbal* (1999)

12 His mother said, 'What a man wants is a mate
and what a woman wants is infinite security',
and, 'What a man is is an arrow into the future
and what a woman is is the place he shoots off
from', until it made me tired.
Sylvia Plath (1932–63) US poet and novelist. *The Bell Jar* (1963), ch. 6

13 Man endures pain as an undeserved punishment;
woman accepts it as a natural heritage.
Proverb.

14 The male is a biological accident: the y (male)
gene is an incomplete x (female) gene, that is, has
an incomplete set of chromosomes. In other
words, the male is an incomplete female, a
walking abortion, aborted at the gene stage.
Valerie Solanas (b. 1940) US writer. 1968. From the manifesto for 'SCUM' (the 'Society for Cutting Up Men'). Quoted in *Feminist Experiences: The Woman's Movement in Four Cultures* (Susan Bassnett; 1986)

15 The false division of human nature into
'feminine' and 'masculine' is the root of all other
divisions into subject and object, active and
passive; the beginning of hierarchy.
Gloria Steinem (b. 1934) US writer and feminist. *Observer Life Magazine* (May 15, 1994)

16 You need not tell me what the proposal was, said
she, laying her hand upon both mine, as she
interrupted me. A man, my good Sir, has seldom an
offer of kindness to make to a woman, but she has
a presentiment of it some moments before.
Laurence Sterne (1713–68) Irish-born British writer and clergyman. 'The Remise, Calais', *A Sentimental Journey Through France and Italy* (1768)

17 Man is a creature who lives not upon bread
alone, but principally by catchwords; and the
little rift between the sexes is astonishingly
widened by simply teaching one set of
catchwords to the girls and another to the boys.
Robert Louis Stevenson (1850–94) Scottish novelist, essayist, and poet. *Virginibus Puerisque* (1881), pt. 2

18 There is no essential sexuality. Maleness and
    femaleness are something we are dressed in.
    Naomi Wallace (b. 1960) US writer. *Times* (August 2, 1994)

19 Instead of this absurd division into sexes they
    ought to class people as static and dynamic.
    Evelyn Waugh (1903–66) British novelist. *Decline and Fall* (1928),
    pt. 3, ch. 7

20 A man is designed to walk three miles in the rain
    to phone for help when the car breaks down—
    and a woman is designed to say, 'You took your
    time', when he comes back dripping wet.
    Victoria Wood (b. 1953) British writer and comedian. Attrib.

21 Why are women . . . so much more interesting to
    men than men are to women?
    Virginia Woolf (1882–1941) British novelist and critic. *A Room of
    One's Own* (1929)

Sexism

see also **Misogyny, Prejudice, Women's Rights**

1 It is annoying and impossible to suffer proud
   women, because in general Nature has given men
   proud and high spirits, while it has made women
   humble in character and submissive, more apt for
   delicate things than for ruling.
   Giovanni Boccaccio (1313–75) Italian writer and humanist. 'Niobe',
   Concerning Famous Women (1360–74)

2 In this country a wife is regarded as a chattel,
   just as a thoroughbred mare or cow.
   G. N. Butler. Addressing a Dublin jury. *Observer* (June 25,
   1972), 'Sayings of the Week'

3 The most popular image of the female despite the
   exigencies of the clothing trade is all boobs and
   buttocks, a hallucinating sequence of parabolas
   and bulges.
   Germaine Greer (b. 1939) Australian-born British writer and academic.
   The Female Eunuch (1970)

4 These are rare attainments for a damsel, but pray
   tell me, can she spin?
   James I (1566–1625) English monarch. On being introduced to a
   young girl proficient in Latin, Greek, and Hebrew. Attrib.

5 A man is in general better pleased when he has a
   good dinner upon his table, than when his wife
   talks Greek.
   Samuel Johnson (1709–84) British lexicographer and writer. Quoted in
   Johnsonian Miscellanies (G. B. Hill, ed.; 1897), vol. 2

6 A woman's preaching is like a dog's walking on
   his hinder legs. It is not done well; but you are
   surprised to find it done at all.
   Samuel Johnson (1709–84) British lexicographer and writer. July 30,
   1763. Quoted in *Life of Samuel Johnson* (James Boswell;
   1791)

7 To promote a Woman to bear rule, superiority,
   dominion or empire, above any Realm, Nation,
   or City, is repugnant to Nature; contumely to
   God, a thing most contrarious to his revealed
   will and approved ordinance, and finally it is the
   subversion of good Order, of all equity and
   justice.
   John Knox (1513?–72) Scottish religious reformer. The opening words
   of the pamphlet *The First Blast of the Trumpet Against the
   Monstrous Regiment of Women* (1558)

8 The usual masculine disillusionment is
   discovering that a woman has a brain.
   Margaret Mitchell (1900–49) US novelist. *Gone with the Wind*
   (1936), pt. 4, ch. 36

9 Women exist in the main solely for the
   propagation of the species.
   Arthur Schopenhauer (1788–1860) German philosopher. Attrib.

10 Women are but the toys which amuse our lighter
    hours; ambition is the serious business of life.
    Sir Walter Scott (1771–1832) Scottish novelist. *Ivanhoe* (1820)

11 It is a man's place to rule, and a woman's to
    yield. He must be held up as the head of the
    house, and it is her duty to bend so
    unmurmuringly to his wishes, that the rest of the
    household will follow her example, and treat him
    with the due respect his sex demands.
    Sarah Ann Sewell (*fl.* 1870s) British writer and social critic. *Women
    and Times We Live In* (1869)

12 Man is the hunter; woman is his game:
    The sleek and shining creatures of the chase,
    We hunt them for the beauty of their skins.
    Alfred Tennyson (1809–92) British poet. *The Princess* (1847), pt. 5,
    ll. 147–149

Sexuality

see also **Homosexuality, Love, Relationships, Seduction, Sex**

1 Sexuality is the lyricism of the masses.
   Charles Baudelaire (1821–67) French poet. *Journaux Intimes* (1887)

2 My sexuality struck me like a clap of thunder,
   incomprehensible, hostile, and tormenting.
   Ingmar Bergman (b. 1918) Swedish film and stage director. *The Magic
   Lantern* (Joan Tate, tr.; 1988)

3 It's true—I am bisexual. But I can't deny I've
   used the fact very well. I suppose it's the best
   thing that ever happened to me.
   David Bowie (b. 1947) British pop singer. Quoted in *Rock 'n' Roll
   Babylon* (Gary Herman; 1994)

4 When Eve ate this particular apple, she became
   aware of her own womanhood, mentally. And
   mentally she began to experiment with it. She has
   been experimenting ever since. So has man. To
   the rage and horror of both of them.
   D. H. Lawrence (1885–1930) British writer. *Fantasia of the
   Unconscious* (1922), ch. 7

5 If *Tales of the City* is radical, it's because . . . the
   gay characters are on exactly the same footing as
   the straight characters.
   Armistead Maupin (b. 1944) US novelist. *Sunday Times* (February 4,
   1990)

6 There's nothing I'd like better than to live in a
   world where my sexuality was utterly irrelevant.
   Armistead Maupin (b. 1944) US novelist. *Sunday Times* (February 4,
   1990)

7 The degree and kind of a man's sexuality reach
   up into the ultimate pinnacle of his spirit.
   Friedrich Wilhelm Nietzsche (1844–1900) German philosopher and poet.
   Beyond Good and Evil (1886)

8 I had a patent on masturbation when I was 12. I
   thought I invented it.
   Roman Polanski (b. 1933) French-born Polish filmmaker. Interview,
   Playboy (December 1971)

9 My sexuality has never been a problem to me
   but I think it has for some people.
   Dusty Springfield (1939–99) British singer. Referring to her
   lesbianism. Quoted in *Dusty* (Lucy O'Brien; 1989)

10   Eroticism has its own moral justification because it says that pleasure is enough for me; it is a statement of the individual's sovereignty.

Mario Vargas Llosa (b. 1936) Peruvian writer. *International Herald Tribune*, (Paris; October 23, 1990)

11   The artificial categories 'heterosexual' and 'homosexual' have been laid on us by a sexist society.

Allen Young (b. 1941) US journalist. 1992. Quoted in *Out of the Closets: Voices of Gay Liberation* (Karla Jay and Allen Young, eds.; 1994)

Shame

see also **Guilt, Regret**

1   A country in which the people go around stark naked and only cover their ears. In that land all shame resides in the ears.

Elias Canetti (1905–94) Bulgarian-born writer. *The Agony of Flies* (1992)

2   We who have grown up on a diet of honour and shame can still grasp what must seem unthinkable to people living in the aftermath of the death of God and of tragedy: that men will sacrifice their dearest love on the implacable altars of their pride.

Salman Rushdie (b. 1947) Indian-born British novelist. *Shame* (1983), pt. 3, ch. 7

3   JESSICA What! Must I hold a candle to my shames?

William Shakespeare (1564–1616) English poet and playwright. *The Merchant of Venice* (1596–98), Act 2, Scene 6

4   I never wonder to see men wicked, but I often wonder to see them not ashamed.

Jonathan Swift (1667–1745) Irish writer and clergyman. *Thoughts on Various Subjects* (1711)

5   It was enough to make a body ashamed of the human race.

Mark Twain (1835–1910) US writer and humorist. Referring to the fraudulent display of grief put on by the 'King' and the 'Duke' on hearing the news of Peter Wilks' death. *The Adventures of Huckleberry Finn* (1884), ch. 24

Sight

see **Senses**

Silence

1   An idiot's eloquence is silence.

Anonymous. Japanese proverb.

2   It will be silence, where I am, I don't know, I'll never know, in the silence you don't know, you must go on, I can't go on, I'll go on.

Samuel Beckett (1906–89) Irish playwright, novelist, and poet. *The Unnamable* (1958)

3   Silences have a climax, when you have got to speak.

Elizabeth Bowen (1899–1973) Irish novelist and short-story writer. *The Heat of the Day* (1949)

4   Try as we may to make a silence, we cannot.

John Cage (1912–92) US composer. *Silence* (1961)

5   A closed mouth catches no flies.

Miguel de Cervantes (1547–1616) Spanish novelist and playwright. *Don Quixote* (1605–15), pt. 1, bk. 3, ch. 11

6   No voice; but oh! the silence sank
Like music on my heart.

Samuel Taylor Coleridge (1772–1834) British poet. 'The Rime of the Ancient Mariner', *Lyrical Ballads* (1798), pt. 6

7   When you have nothing to say, say nothing.

Christopher Columbus (1451–1506) Italian explorer and colonialist. Attrib.

8   Dumb as a drum with a hole in it, sir.

Charles Dickens (1812–70) British novelist. Said by Sam Weller. *Pickwick Papers* (1837), ch. 25

9   One of the lessons of history is that nothing is often a good thing to do and always a clever thing to say.

Will Durant (1885–1981) US historian. Attrib. *Reader's Digest* (November 1972)

10   Silence is become his mother tongue.

Oliver Goldsmith (1730–74) Irish-born British novelist, playwright, and poet. *The Good-Natur'd Man* (1768), Act 2

11   I met the great little man, the man who can be silent in several languages.

James Guthrie Harbord (1866–1947) US general and business executive. Referring to Colonel House. Quoted in *Mr. Wilson's War* (John Dos Passos; 1962), ch. 3

12   That man's silence is wonderful to listen to.

Thomas Hardy (1840–1928) British novelist and poet. *Under the Greenwood Tree* (1872), ch. 14

13   Of the 'wee six' I sing
Where to be saved you only must save face
And whatever you say, you say nothing.

Seamus Heaney (b. 1939) Irish poet. 'Whatever You Say Say Nothing', *North* (1975), ll. 62–64

14   Silence is as full of potential wisdom and wit as the unhewn marble of great sculpture.

Aldous Huxley (1894–1963) British novelist and essayist. *Point Counter Point* (1928)

15   And then there crept
A little noiseless noise among the leaves,
Born of the very sigh that silence heaves.

John Keats (1795–1821) English poet. 'I Stood Tip-toe upon a Little Hill' (1820)

16   Silence is the best tactic for him who distrusts himself.

François La Rochefoucauld (1613–80) French epigrammatist and moralist. *Reflections, or Sentences and Moral Maxims* (1665), no. 79

17   And suddenly she craved again for the more absolute silence of America. English stillness was so soft, like an inaudible murmur of voices, of presences.

D. H. Lawrence (1885–1930) British writer. *St. Mawr* (1925)

18   Silence is a slow cauldron
that snuffs out dwellings, one by one,
with its dress of saffroning linen.

Antonio Martínez-Sarrión (b. 1939) Spanish poet, critic, and translator. 'Umma Gumma', *A Bilingual Anthology of Contemporary Spanish Poetry* (Luis A. Ramos-García; 1997)

19   But that which matters, that which insists, that which will last,
that! o my people, where shall you find it, how, where, where shall you listen
when all is become billboards, when, all, even silence, is spray-gunned?

Charles Olson (1910–70) US poet. 'I, Maximus of Gloucester, to You', *The Maximus Poems 1–10* (1953)

20 There are two silences. One where no word is spoken. The other where perhaps a torrent of language is being employed.

Harold Pinter (b. 1930) British playwright, theatre director, and screenwriter. Speech addressed to the National Student Drama Festival, Bristol (1962)

21 Stars open among the lilies.
Are you not blinded by such expressionless sirens?
This is the silence of astounded souls.

Sylvia Plath (1932–63) US poet and novelist. April 1962. 'Crossing the Water', *Crossing the Water* (1971)

22 A prating barber asked Archelaus how he would be trimmed. He answered, 'In silence'.

Plutarch (46?–120?) Greek biographer and philosopher. 'Archelaus' (1st–2nd century)

23 If silence be good for the wise, how much better for fools.

Proverb.

24 You get the impression that their normal condition is silence and that speech is a slight fever which attacks them now and then.

Jean-Paul Sartre (1905–80) French philosopher, playwright, and novelist. *Nausea* (1938)

25 O, learn to read what silent love hath writ!
To hear with eyes belongs to love's fine wit.

William Shakespeare (1564–1616) English poet and playwright. Sonnet 23 (1609)

26 CLAUDIO Silence is the perfectest herald of joy: I were but little happy if I could say how much.

William Shakespeare (1564–1616) English poet and playwright. *Much Ado About Nothing* (1598–99), Act 2, Scene 1

27 Silence is the most perfect expression of scorn.

George Bernard Shaw (1856–1950) Irish playwright. *Back to Methuselah* (1921), pt. 2

28 People talking without speaking,
People listening without hearing,
People writing songs that voices never shared.

Paul Simon (b. 1942) US singer and songwriter. Song lyric. 'The Sound of Silence' (1964)

29 The camps had taught him that people who say nothing carry something within themselves.

Alexander Solzhenitsyn (b. 1918) Russian novelist. *Cancer Ward* (1968), pt. 2, ch. 10

30 The most wise speech is not as holy as silence.

Lope de Vega (1562–1635) Spanish playwright and poet. *The Stupid Lady* (1613), Act 3, Scene 4

31 Silence alone is great; all else is weakness.

Alfred de Vigny (1797–1863) French poet, novelist, and playwright. 'La Mort du Loup' (1843)

32 Whereof one cannot speak, thereof one must remain silent.

Ludwig Wittgenstein (1889–1951) Austrian philosopher. *Tractatus Logico-Philosophicus* (1921), ch. 7

33 Like a long-legged fly upon the stream
His mind moves upon silence.

W. B. Yeats (1865–1939) Irish poet and playwright. 'Long-Legged Fly', *Last Poems* (1936–39), ll. 9–10

Similarity

see also **Imitation**, **Plagiarism**

1 Everything must be like something, so what is this like?

E. M. Forster (1879–1970) British novelist. 'Our Diversions', *Abinger Harvest* (1936)

2 As lyke as one pease is to another.

John Lyly (1554?–1606) English writer. *Euphues: An Anatomy of Wit* (1578)

3 Shall I compare thee to a summer's day?
Thou art more lovely and more temperate.
Rough winds do shake the darling buds of May,
And summer's lease hath all too short a date.

William Shakespeare (1564–1616) English poet and playwright. Sonnet 18 (1609)

Simplicity

see also **Brevity**, **Clarity**

1 Everything should be made as simple as possible, but not simpler.

Albert Einstein (1879–1955) German-born US physicist. Attrib.

2 In diagnosis think of the easy first.

Martin H. Fischer (1879–1962) German-born US physician and author. Quoted in *Fischerisms* (Howard Fabing and Ray Marr, eds.; 1944)

3 Simplicity is the soul of efficiency.

Richard Austin Freeman (1862–1943) British physician and writer. *The Eye of Osiris* (1911)

4 The ability to simplify means to eliminate the unnecessary so that the necessary may speak.

Hans Hofmann (1880–1966) German-born US painter and teacher. *Search for the Real* (1967)

5 I hate American simplicity. I glory in the piling up of complications of every sort.

Henry James (1843–1916) US-born British writer and critic. Quoted in *The Letters of Henry James* (Leon Edel, ed.; 1953–72), vol. 4, introduction

6 I have revered always not crude verbosity, but holy simplicity.

Saint Jerome (347?–419 or 420) Roman monk and scholar. 'Ad Pammachium', *Patrologia Latina* (1864), vol. 22, col. 579

7 Men are often led into error by the love of simplicity, which disposes us to reduce things to few principles, and to conceive a greater simplicity in nature than there really is.

Thomas Reid (1710–96) Scottish philosopher. *Inquiry into the Human Mind on the Principles of Common Sense* (1764)

8 Seek simplicity, and distrust it.

A. N. Whitehead (1861–1947) British philosopher and mathematician. Attrib.

Sincerity

see also **Frankness**, **Honesty**, **Truth**

1 He who is sincere hits what is right, and apprehends without the exercise of thought.

Confucius (551–479 BC) Chinese philosopher, administrator, and moralist. Quoted in *The Sayings of Confucius* (Lionel Giles, ed.; 1993)

2 Sincerity is all that counts. It's a wide-spread modern heresy. Think again. Bolsheviks are sincere. Fascists are sincere. Lunatics are sincere. People who believe the earth is flat are sincere. They can't all be right.

Tom Driberg (1905–76) British politician and journalist. *Daily Express* (1937)

3 Some of the worst men in the world are sincere and the more sincere they are the worse they are.

Lord Hailsham (1907–2001) British statesman. *Observer* (January 7, 1968), 'Sayings of the Week'

4 We are in the presence of the contradiction of a style of living which cultivates sincerity and is at the same time a fraud. There is truth only in an existence which feels its acts as irrevocably necessary.

José Ortega y Gasset (1883–1955) Spanish writer and philosopher. *The Revolt of the Masses* (1930)

5 I am not sincere even when I am saying that I am not sincere.

Jules Renard (1864–1910) French writer. 1910. *Journal* (1877–1910)

6 It is dangerous to be sincere unless you are also stupid.

George Bernard Shaw (1856–1950) Irish playwright. *Man and Superman* (1903)

7 A little sincerity is a dangerous thing, and a great deal of it is absolutely fatal.

Oscar Wilde (1854–1900) Irish poet, playwright, and wit. 'The Critic as Artist', *Intentions* (1891), pt. 2

8 He is *absolutely* sincere. That is what makes him dangerous.

Woodrow Wilson (1856–1924) US president. Quoted in *Defender of the Faith: William Jennings Bryan, the Last Decade, 1915–25* (L. W. Levine; 1965)

Singers and Singing

see also **Music, Popular Music, Songs, The Voice**

1 I liked to do the songs just the way they were written, getting the words out clearly and putting in the meaning the songwriters intended—no less . . . you don't want to change a Gershwin song around. It's too good.

Fred Astaire (1899–1987) US dancer and actor. Quoted in *Fascinating Rhythm* (Deena Rosenberg; 1991)

2 In this job, you tell of who you are . . . me, I work for myself . . . if you sing to please someone other than yourself, you cannot . . . but feel that you are prostituting yourself.

Jacques Brel (1929–78) Belgian singer and songwriter. Interview, *Le Parisien libre* (1963), quoted in *Jacques Brel* (Alan Clayson; 1996), prologue

3 I'd like to think that when I sing a song, I can let you know all about the heartbreak, struggle, lies and kicks in the ass I've gotten over the years for being black and everything else, without actually saying a word about it.

Ray Charles (b. 1932) US pianist and singer. Interview, *Playboy* (1970)

4 One discovers not one Aretha Franklin but a cast of hundreds of women: some sweet, some mad, some cool, some sad, some angry, and a good many playful and sexy.

Nelson George, US journalist. Referring to the diverse nature of Aretha Franklin's performance on songs like 'Dr. Feelgood', 'Say a Little Prayer', and 'Think'. *The Death of Rhythm and Blues* (1988)

5 Looks like whatever you try to do, somebody jumps up and hollers and raises cain—then the feller next to him jumps up and hollers how much he likes it.

Woody Guthrie (1912–67) US folksinger and songwriter. Quoted in *Music on My Beat: An Intimate Volume of Shop Talk* (Howard Taubman; 1943)

6 I can't stand to sing the same song the same way two nights in succession, let alone two years or ten years. If you can, then it ain't music, it's close-order drill, or exercise or yodeling or something, not music.

Billie Holiday (1915–59) US jazz singer. *Lady Sings the Blues* (co-written with William Duffy; 1956)

7 Being a blues singer is like being black two times.

B. B. King (b. 1925) US blues singer and guitarist. Quoted in *The Wit and Wisdom of Rock and Roll* (Maxim Jabukowski, ed.; 1983)

8 I learned very early in life that: 'Without a song, the day would never end; without a song, a man ain't got a friend; without a song, the road would never bend—without a song'. So I keep singing a song. Goodnight. Thank you.

Elvis Presley (1935–77) US pop singer. Acceptance speech, Ten Outstanding Young Men of the Year Awards (January 16, 1971)

9 His vocal chords were kissed by God.

Harold Schoenberg (b. 1915) US music critic. Referring to Luciano Pavarotti. *Times* (June 30, 1981)

10 You got to have smelt a lot of mule manure before you can sing like a hillbilly.

Hank Williams (1923–53) US country singer and songwriter. 1940? Quoted in *Look* (July 13, 1971)

Skills

see **Ability**

Slavery

see also **Civil Rights, Human Rights, Imperialism, Racism**

1 It is better to begin to abolish serfdom from above than to wait for it to abolish itself from below.

Alexander II (1818–81) Russian monarch. Remark (March 30, 1856)

2 He freed a thousand slaves with his own money in his desire to seek the face of God and to escape the fire of Hell, money which he had laboured for with his own hands and for which his own brow had sweated.

Abu Abdullah Muhammad al-Harithi al-Baghdadi al-Mufid (fl. 10th century) Iraqi scholar and jurist. Referring to Husain, grandson of Muhammad and younger son of Ali ibn Abi Talib. 'The Lives of the Other Imams: Imam Ali ben al-Husayn', *The Book of Guidance Into the Lives of the Twelve Imams* (I. K. A. Howard, tr.; 1981)

3 The history of anti-slavery begins with the first slave; similarly the history of anti-racism begins with the original object of scorn, derision, and insult.

Herbert Aptheker (b. 1915) US historian. 'The History of Anti-Racism in the United States', *Black Scholar* (January–February 1975)

4 It is thus clear that, just as some are by nature free, others are by nature slaves, and for these latter the condition of slavery is both beneficial and just.

Aristotle (384–322 BC) Greek philosopher. *Politics* (335–322? BC), 1255a

5 Perhaps the master who had coupled with his slave saw his guilt in his wife's pale eyes in the morning. And the wife saw his children in the slave quarters.

James Baldwin (1924–87) US writer and civil rights activist. *Nobody Knows My Name* (1961)

6 From the beginning all were created equal by nature, slavery was introduced through the unjust oppression of worthless men, against the will of God; for, if God had wanted to create slaves, he would surely have decided at the beginning of the world who was to be slave and who master.

John Ball (1338?–81) English priest and rebel. Sermon, Blackheath (1381)

7 Plantations didn't have any wire. Plantations were big open whitewashed places like heaven, and everybody on 'em was grooved to be there. Just strummin' and hummin' all day. And that's how the blues was born.

Imamu Amiri Baraka (b. 1934) US author, editor, playwright, and political activist. *The Dutchman* (1964), Scene 2

8 Slavery has been abandoned, with much beating of religious breasts, but it is mostly the name that has gone.

Learie Constantine (1901–71) Trinidadian cricketer, barrister, and politician. *Colour Bar* (1954)

9 Neither slavery nor involuntary servitude, except as a punishment for crime whereof the party shall have been duly convicted, shall exist within the United States, or any place subject to their jurisdiction.

Constitution of the United States, US system of fundamental laws. Section 1 of the thirteenth amendment of the Constitution of the United States. *Amendments to the Constitution* (1865), Article 13

10 If any man should buy another man without his consent, and compel him to his service and slavery without any agreement of that man to serve him, the enslaver is a robber, and a defrauder of that man every day.

Ottobah Cugoano (1757?–1803?) Ghanaian freed slave and abolitionist. *Thoughts and Sentiments on the Evil and Wicked Traffic of the Slavery and Commerce of the Human Species, Humbly Submitted to the Inhabitants of Great-Britain* (1787)

11 Heathenism and Liberty, before Christianity and Slavery.

Martin Robinson Delany (1812–85) US physician, abolitionist, and newspaper editor. Letter to William Garrison (May 14, 1852), quoted in *The Mind of the Negro As Reflected In Letters Written During the Crisis, 1800–60* (Carter G. Woodson, ed.; 1926)

12 Slavery cannot exist a day or an hour anywhere unless it is supported by local police regulations.

Stephen A. Douglas (1813–61) US senator. Speech (August 27, 1858)

13 This Fourth of July is *yours*, not *mine*. *You* may rejoice, *I* must mourn. To drag a man in fetters into the grand illuminated temple of liberty, and call upon him to join you in joyous anthems, were inhuman mockery and sacrilegious irony.

Frederick Douglass (1817–95) US abolitionist, writer, and orator. Address, Rochester, New York (July 1852), quoted in *The Life and Writings of Frederick Douglass* (Philip S. Foner, ed.; 1950), vol. 2

14 From my earliest recollection, I date the entertainment of a deep conviction that slavery would not always be able to hold me within its foul embrace; and in the darkest hours of my career in slavery, this living word of faith and spirit of hope departed not from me, but remained like ministering angels to cheer me through the gloom.

Frederick Douglass (1817–95) US abolitionist, writer, and orator. *Narrative of the Life of Frederick Douglass, an American Slave* (1845)

15 Fellow-citizens! . . . The existence of slavery in this country brands your republicanism as a sham, your humanity as a base pretence, and your Christianity as a lie. It destroys your moral power abroad; it corrupts your politicians at home.

Frederick Douglass (1817–95) US abolitionist, writer, and orator. *What to the Slave is the Fourth of July?* (1852), appendix, quoted in *The Heath Anthology of American Literature* (Paul Lauter, ed.; 1998), vol. 1

16 When the history of the emancipation movement shall have been fairly written, it will be found that the abolitionists of the nineteenth century were the only men who dared to defend the Bible from the blasphemous charge of sanctioning and sanctifying negro slavery.

Frederick Douglass (1817–95) US abolitionist, writer, and orator. Attrib.

17 When you make men slaves you deprive them of half their virtue, you set them in your own conduct an example of fraud, rapine, and cruelty, and compel them to live with you in a state of war; and yet you complain that they are not honest or faithful!

Olaudah Equiano (1745?–97) African-born British former slave. *The Interesting Narrative of the Life of Olaudah Equiano, or Gustavus Vassa* (1789)

18 I am not the slave of the Slavery that dehumanized my ancestors.

Frantz Fanon (1925–61) Martiniquan social scientist, physician, and psychiatrist. *Black Skin, White Masks* (1952)

19 Millions have come from eternity into time, and have returned again to the world of spirits, cursed and ruined by American slavery.

Henry Highland Garnet (1815–82) US clergyman and abolitionist. 1843. 'An address to the Slaves of the United States of America', *A Documentary History of the Negro People in the United States* (Herbert Aptheker; 1951), vol. 1

20 I am in earnest—I will not equivocate—I will not excuse—I will not retreat a single inch; and I will be heard!

William Lloyd Garrison (1805–79) US abolitionist. 'Salutory Address', *The Liberator* (January 1, 1831), vol. 1, no. 1

21 His headstone said
FREE AT LAST, FREE AT LAST
But death is a slave's freedom.

Nikki Giovanni (b. 1943) US writer, activist, and educator. 'The Funeral of Martin Luther King, Jr.', *Black Feeling, Black Talk, Black Judgement* (1968)

22 Hands that picked cotton in 1864 will pick a president in 1984.

Jesse Jackson (b. 1941) US clergyman, civil rights leader, and politician. Address at the Lincoln Memorial (August 27, 1983), quoted in *Jesse Jackson* (Robert E. Jakoubek; 1991)

23 Bondage and torture, scourges and chains Placed on our backs indelible stains.

Mattie J. Jackson (fl. 19th century) US writer. *The Story of Mattie J. Jackson* (1866), quoted in *Six Women's Slave Narratives* (William L. Andrews, ed.; 1988)

24 The whole commerce between master and slave is a perpetual exercise of the most boisterous passions, the most unremitting despotism on the one part, and degrading submissions on the other.

Thomas Jefferson (1743–1826) US president. *Notes on the State of Virginia* (1785)

25 Stolen from Africa,
brought to America,
Fighting on arrival,
fighting for survival.

Bob Marley (1945–81) Jamaican musician, singer, and songwriter. Song lyric. 'Buffalo Soldier' (1983)

26 Emancipate yourselves from mental slavery. None but ourselves can free our minds.

Bob Marley (1945–81) Jamaican musician, singer, and songwriter. 'Redemption Song', *Uprising* (1980)

27 I have not failed to give Uncle Sam due credit for his 2,000,000 slaves; nor to expose the cruel prejudices of the Americans to our colored race . . . And is this, they say, republican liberty? God deliver us from it.

Nathaniel Paul (1775–1839) US cleric and abolitionist. Letter to William Lloyd Garrison (April 10, 1833), quoted in *A Documentary History of the Negro People in the United States* (Herbert Aptheker; 1951), vol. 1

28 Slavery is trembling, prejudice is falling, and I hope will soon be buried—buried beyond resurrection; and we will write over its grave as over Babylon—'Prejudice, the mother of abominations, the liar, the coward, the tyrant, the waster of the poor, the brand of the white man, the bane of the black man, is fallen! is fallen!'

Charles Lenox Remond (1810–73) US abolitionist. Letter to Thomas Cole (July 3, 1838), quoted in *The Mind of the Negro As Reflected in Letters Written During the Crisis, 1800–60* (Carter G. Woodson, ed.; 1926)

29 It isn't those who are taken by force, put in chains and sold as slaves who are the real slaves: it is those who will accept it, morally and physically.

Ousmane Sembène (b. 1923) Senegalese writer, film director, and trade union leader. *God's Bits of Wood* (1960)

30 My children, France comes to make us slaves. God gave us liberty; France has no right to take it away. Burn the cities, destroy the harvests, tear up the roads with cannon, poison the wells, show the white man the hell he comes to make!

Toussaint L'Ouverture (1743–1803) Haitian revolutionary leader and general. Quoted in *This Gilded African* (Wenda Parkinson; 1978)

31 They think because they hold us in their infernal chains of slavery, that we wish to be white, or of their colour—but they are dreadfully deceived—we wish to be just as it pleased our Creator to have made us.

David Walker (1785–1830) US abolitionist and writer. *Walker's Appeal, in Four Articles* (September 1829), quoted in *A Documentary History of the Negro People in the United States* (Herbert Aptheker; 1951)

32 When freedom came, the slaves were almost as well fitted to begin life anew as the master, except in the matter of book learning and ownership of property. The slave owner and his sons had mastered no special industry.

Booker T. Washington (1856–1915) US educator and political activist. *Up from Slavery* (1901)

Sleep

see also **Night**

1 Sweet are the slumbers of the virtuous man.

Joseph Addison (1672–1719) English essayist, poet, and statesman. *Cato* (1713), Act 5, Scene 4

2 Half our days we pass in the shadow of the earth; and the brother of death exacteth a third part of our lives.

Thomas Browne (1605–82) English physician and writer. The opening sentence of this posthumously published essay. 'On Dreams' (1716), quoted in *Sir Thomas Browne's Works* (S. Wilkin, ed.; 1836), vol. 4

3 Sleep is a death;—O make me try
By sleeping, what it is to die!
And as gently lay my head
On my grave, as now my bed.

Thomas Browne (1605–82) English physician and writer. *Religio Medici* (1642), pt. 2, sect. 12

4 Laugh and the world laughs with you; snore and you sleep alone.

Anthony Burgess (1917–93) British writer and critic. *Inside Mr. Enderby* (1963)

5 Blessings on him who invented sleep, the mantle that covers all human thoughts, the food that satisfies hunger, the drink that slakes thirst, the fire that warms cold.

Miguel de Cervantes (1547–1616) Spanish novelist and playwright. *Don Quixote* (1605–15), pt. 2, ch. 68

6 Living is an illness to which sleep provides relief every sixteen hours. It's a palliative. The remedy is death.

Nicolas Chamfort (1741–94) French writer. *Maximes et Pensées* (1795), ch. 2

7 Golden slumbers kiss your eyes,
Smiles awake you when you rise.

Thomas Dekker (1572?–1632?) English playwright. *Patient Grissil* (1603), Act 4, Scene 2

8 Sleep is that golden chaine that ties health and our bodies together.

Thomas Dekker (1572?–1632?) English playwright. *The Guls Horn-Booke* (1609), ch. 2

9 He used to sleep like a glass of water held up in the hand of a very young girl.

Rita Dove (b. 1952) US poet. 'Straw Hat' (1986), ll. 8–9

10 Health is the first muse, and sleep is the condition to produce it.

Ralph Waldo Emerson (1803–82) US poet and essayist. 'Resources', *Uncollected Lectures* (1932)

11 Sleep is when all the unsorted stuff comes flying out as from a dustbin upset in a high wind.

William Golding (1911–93) British novelist. *Pincher Martin* (1956), ch. 6

12 Sleep is gross, a form of abandonment, and it is impossible for anyone to awake and observe its sordid consequences save with a faint sense of recent dissipation, of minute personal disquiet and remorse.

Patrick Hamilton (1904–62) British playwright and novelist. *The Slaves of Solitude* (1947)

13 For in sleep, when the channels of perception are shut, our mind is sundered from its kinship with its surrounding . . . casts off its former power of memory. But in the waking state it again peeps out through the channels of perception as though through a kind of window, and . . . puts on its power of reason.

Heraclitus (*fl.* 500 BC) Greek philosopher. Attrib.

14 Now deep in my bed I turn
and the world turns on the other side.

Elizabeth Jennings (b. 1926) British poet and writer. 1955. 'In the Night', *Collected Poems 1953–85* (1986)

15 As though a rose should shut, and be a bud again.

John Keats (1795–1821) English poet. 'The Eve of Saint Agnes' (1820), st. 27

16 Sleep, my body, sleep, my ghost,
Sleep, my parents and grand-parents,
And all those I have loved most:
One man's coffin is another's cradle.

Louis MacNeice (1907–63) Irish-born British poet. 1938. 'Autumn Journal', *The Collected Poems of Louis MacNeice* (E. R. Dodds, ed.; 1966)

17 What hath night to do with sleep?
John Milton (1608–74) English writer. *Comus* (1637), l. 122

18 I did not sleep. I never do when I am over-
happy, over-unhappy, or in bed with a strange
man.
Edna O'Brien (b. 1932) Irish novelist. *The Love Object* (1968)

19 Slepe is the nouryshment and food of a sucking
child.
Thomas Phaer (1510?–60) English lawyer, physician, and translator. *The Boke of Chyldren* (1553)

20 In bed my real love has always been the sleep
that rescued me by allowing me to dream.
Luigi Pirandello (1867–1936) Italian dramatist, novelist, and short-story writer. *The Rules of the Game* (William Murray, tr.; 1918)

21 The amount of sleep required by the average
person is just five minutes more.
Proverb.

22 KING HENRY IV O sleep, O gentle sleep,
Nature's soft nurse, how have I frighted thee,
That thou no more wilt weigh my eyelids down,
And steep my senses in forgetfulness?
William Shakespeare (1564–1616) English poet and playwright. *Henry IV, Part 2* (1597), Act 3, Scene 1

23 DOCTOR Our foster nurse of nature is repose.
William Shakespeare (1564–1616) English poet and playwright. *King Lear* (1605–06), Act 4, Scene 1

24 Come, Sleep! O Sleep, the certain knot of peace,
The bathing-place of wit, the balm of woe,
The poor man's wealth, the prisoner's release,
The indifferent judge between the high and low.
Philip Sidney (1554–86) English poet, courtier, and soldier. *Astrophel and Stella* (1591), Sonnet 39

25 Sleep's the only medicine that gives ease.
Sophocles (496?–406? BC) Greek playwright. *Philoctetes* (409? BC), l. 766

26 It is a common experience that a problem
difficult at night is resolved in the morning after
the committee of sleep has worked on it.
John Steinbeck (1902–68) US novelist. Attrib.

27 Of all the soft, delicious functions of nature this
is the chiefest; what a happiness it is to man,
when the anxieties and passions of the day are
over.
Laurence Sterne (1713–68) Irish-born British writer and clergyman. Attrib.

28 If sleeping and dreaming do not perform vital
biological functions, then they must represent
nature's most stupid blunder and most colossal
waste of time.
Anthony Stevens (b. 1933) British psychiatrist. *Evolutionary Psychiatry* (1996), ch. 17

29 I have come to the borders of sleep,
The unfathomable deep
Forest where all must lose
Their way, however straight,
Or winding, soon or late;
They cannot choose.
Edward Thomas (1878–1917) British poet, biographer, and critic. Originally published under the pseudonym Edward Eastaway. 'Lights Out', *Poems* (1917)

30 That sweet, deep sleep, so close to tranquil death.
Virgil (70–19 BC) Roman poet. *Aeneid* (29–19 BC), bk. 6

Smell

see **Senses**

Smoking

see also **Addiction, Drugs**

1 The Elizabethan age might be better named the
beginning of the smoking era.
J. M. Barrie (1860–1937) British playwright and novelist. *My Lady Nicotine* (1890)

2 Certainly not—if you don't object if I'm sick.
Thomas Beecham (1879–1961) British conductor and impresario. When asked whether he minded if someone smoked in a non-smoking compartment. Attrib.

3 If alcohol is Queen, then tobacco is her consort.
It's a fond companion for all occasions, a loyal
friend through fair weather and foul.
Luis Buñuel (1900–83) Spanish film director. *My Last Breath* (1983)

4 Divine in hookas, glorious in a pipe
When tipped with amber, mellow, rich, and ripe;
Like other charmers, wooing the caress
More dazzlingly when daring in full dress;
Yet thy true lovers more admire by far
Thy naked beauties—Give me a cigar!
Lord Byron (1788–1824) British poet. 'The Island, or Christian and his Comrades' (1823)

5 Smokers, male and female, inject and excuse idleness
in their lives every time they light a cigarette.
Colette (1873–1954) French novelist. 'Freedom', *Earthly Paradise: An Autobiography* (1966)

6 It is quite a three-pipe problem.
Arthur Conan Doyle (1859–1930) Scottish-born British writer and physician. 'The Red-Headed League', *The Adventures of Sherlock Holmes* (1892)

7 I have seen many a man turn his gold into
smoke, but you are the first who has turned
smoke into gold.
Elizabeth I (1533–1603) English monarch. Speaking to Sir Walter Raleigh. Quoted in *Sayings of Queen Elizabeth* (F. Chamberlin; 1923)

8 Tobacco surely was designed
To poison, and destroy mankind.
Philip Freneau (1752–1832) US poet. 'Tobacco', *Poems* (1795)

9 Sometimes a cigar is just a cigar.
Sigmund Freud (1856–1939) Austrian psychoanalyst. When asked by one of his students whether there was any symbolism in the large cigars that Freud smoked. Attrib.

10 But when I don't smoke I scarcely feel as if I'm
living. I don't feel as if I'm living unless I'm
killing myself.
Russell Hoban (b. 1925) US-born British novelist, children's writer, and illustrator. *Turtle Diary* (1975), ch. 7

11 A custom loathsome to the eye, hateful to the
nose, harmful to the brain, dangerous to the
lungs, and in the black, stinking fume thereof,
nearest resembling the horrible Stygian smoke of
the pit that is bottomless.
James I (1566–1625) English monarch. *A Counterblast to Tobacco* (1604)

12 Ods me, I marvel what pleasure or felicity they
have in taking their roguish tobacco. It is good
for nothing but to choke a man, and fill him full
of smoke and embers.
Ben Jonson (1572–1637) English playwright and poet. *Every Man Out of His Humour* (1599), Act 3, Scene 5

13 May my last breath be drawn through a pipe and exhaled in a pun.

Charles Lamb (1775–1834) British essayist. *Diary* (January 9, 1834)

14 This vice brings in one hundred million francs in taxes every year. I will certainly forbid it at once—as soon as you can name a virtue that brings in as much revenue.

Napoleon III (1808–73) French emperor. Reply when asked to ban smoking. Attrib.

15 To cease smoking is the easiest thing I ever did. I ought to know because I've done it a thousand times.

Mark Twain (1835–1910) US writer and humorist. Referring to giving up smoking. Attrib.

16 A cigarette is the perfect type of a perfect pleasure. It is exquisite, and it leaves one unsatisfied. What more can one want?

Oscar Wilde (1854–1900) Irish poet, playwright, and wit. *The Picture of Dorian Gray* (1891), ch. 6

Socialism

see also **Communism, Equality, Society**

1 Socialism in the context of modern society means the conquest of the commanding heights of the economy.

Aneurin Bevan (1897–1960) Welsh-born British politician. Speech at the Labour Party Conference (November 1959)

2 Socialism is a diminution, a narrowing, a finitizing of the Messianic ideal.

Martin Buber (1878–1965) Austrian-born Israeli philosopher of religion and Zionist. 1923. Quoted in *On Judaism* (N. Glazer, ed., Eva Jose et al., trs.; 1967)

3 Socialism with a human face must function again for a new generation. We have lived in the darkness for long enough.

Alexander Dubček (1921–92) Czech statesman. Speech, Wenceslas Square, Prague (November 4, 1989)

4 Real socialism is inside man. It wasn't born with Marx. It was in the communes of Italy in the Middle Ages. You can't say it's over.

Dario Fo (b. 1926) Italian playwright and actor. Referring to Karl Marx. *Times* (April 6, 1992)

5 The essence of perestroika lies in the fact that *it unites socialism with democracy* and revives the feminist concept of socialist construction both in theory and in practice.

Mikhail Gorbachev (b. 1931) Russian statesman. *Perestroika: New Thinking for Our Country and the World* (1987)

6 It is the duty of every one of you not to miss any opportunity to show that you belong to that international socialist party which, at this hour when the storm is breaking, represents the sole prospect of maintaining peace or of restoring peace.

Jean Jaurès (1859–1914) French politician and philosopher. Referring to his attempts to create an international socialist alliance, the possibility of which vanished when he was assassinated in July 1914. As a member of the French Chamber of Deputies he warned against the threat of world war. Speech, Vaise, France (July 24, 1914)

7 Under socialism *all* will govern in turn and will soon become accustomed to no one governing.

Vladimir Ilyich Lenin (1870–1924) Russian revolutionary leader. *The State and Revolution* (1919), ch. 6

8 In so far as socialism means anything, it must be about the wider distribution of smoked salmon and caviar.

Richard Marsh (b. 1928) British civil servant and politician. Remark (October 1976)

9 From each according to his abilities, to each according to his needs.

Karl Marx (1818–83) German philosopher. *Criticism of the Gotha Programme* (1875)

10 As with the Christian religion, the worst advertisement for Socialism is its adherents.

George Orwell (1903–50) British writer. *The Road to Wigan Pier* (1937), ch. 11

11 Socialism can only arrive by bicycle.

José Antonio Viera Gallo (b. 1943) Chilean politician. Said while assistant secretary of justice in the Chilean government. Quoted in *Energy and Equity* (Ivan Illich; 1974), Epigraph

12 Many people consider the things which government does for them to be social progress, but they consider the things government does for others as socialism.

Earl Warren (1891–1974) US jurist. Attrib.

Society

see also **Class, Culture, Politics**

1 A complete victory of society will always produce some sort of 'communistic fiction', whose outstanding characteristic is that it is indeed ruled by an 'invisible hand', namely, by nobody.

Hannah Arendt (1906–75) German-born US philosopher and historian. *The Human Condition* (1958)

2 For man seeketh in society comfort, use, and protection.

Francis Bacon (1561–1626) English philosopher, statesman, and lawyer. *The Advancement of Learning* (1605), bk. 2

3 Man was formed for society.

William Blackstone (1723–80) British jurist. *Commentaries on the Laws of England* (1765–69), Introduction, pt. 2

4 Social intercourse—a very limited thing in a half civilized country—becomes in our centers of civilization a great power.

Elizabeth Blackwell (1821–1910) British-born US physician. *Medicine as a Profession for Women* (co-written with Emily Blackwell; 1860), quoted in *The New Quotable Woman* (Elaine Partnow, ed.; 1993)

5 In every era, society must strike the right balance between the freedom businesses need to compete for a market share and to make profits and the preservation of family and community values.

Hillary Clinton (b. 1947) US lawyer and first lady. Speech at Sydney Opera House (November 21, 1996)

6 My ideal is a society full of responsible men and women who show solidarity to those who can't keep up.

Jacques Delors (b. 1925) French statesman. *Independent* (June 22, 1994)

7 Like art and politics, gangsterism is a very important avenue into mainstream society.

E. L. Doctorow (b. 1931) US novelist. Quoted in *International Herald Tribune* (October 1, 1990)

8 Willing submission to social restraint for the sake of the well-being of the whole of society enriches both the individual and the society of which he is a member.

Mahatma Gandhi (1869–1948) Indian national leader. Quoted in *Questions in the Philosophy of Restraint* (Indira Rothermund; 1963)

9 Society is an organism, not a machine.
Henry George (1839–97) US economist. *Progress and Poverty* (1877–79)

10 Man has become to so great a degree merely a cog in an intricate social system that alienation from the self is almost universal, and human values themselves have declined.
Karen Horney (1885–1952) German-born US psychoanalyst. *Our Inner Conflicts* (1945)

11 Nothing is so hard to understand as that there are human beings in this world besides one's self and one's own set.
William Dean Howells (1837–1920) US writer and critic. *Their Wedding Journey* (1872)

12 If a free society cannot help the many who are poor, it cannot save the few who are rich.
John Fitzgerald Kennedy (1917–63) US president. Speech (January 20, 1961)

13 A society which is clamoring for choice . . . will give each new generation no peace until all have chosen or gone under, unable to bear the conditions of choice.
Margaret Mead (1901–78) US anthropologist. *Coming of Age in Samoa* (1928)

14 For too long Society has resembled a pyramid which has been turned upside down and made to rest on its summit. I have replaced it on its base.
Napoleon III (1808–73) French emperor. Remark (March 29, 1852)

15 Get on with it, keep moving, keep in speed, the nerves, their speed, the perceptions, theirs, the acts, the split second acts, the whole business, keep it moving as fast as you can, citizen . . . fast, there's the dogma.
Charles Olson (1910–70) US poet. 'Projective Verse' (1950)

16 Our civilization . . . has not yet fully recovered from the shock of its birth—the transition from the tribal or 'closed society', with its submission to magical forces, to the 'open society' which sets free the critical powers of man.
Karl Popper (1902–94) Austrian-born British philosopher. *The Open Society and Its Enemies* (1945)

17 The general will rules in society as the private will governs each separate individual.
Maximilien Robespierre (1758–94) French lawyer and revolutionary. *Lettres à ses Commettants* (January 5, 1793), series 2

18 Every society to which you remain bound robs you of a part of your essence, and replaces it with a speck of the gigantic personality which is its own.
José Rodó (1871–1917) Uruguayan essayist. *Motivos de Proteo* (1941)

19 The body politic, like the human body, begins to die from the moment of its birth, and bears in itself the causes of its destruction.
Jean-Jacques Rousseau (1712–78) French philosopher and writer. *The Social Contract* (1762)

20 Man is not a solitary animal, and so long as social life survives, self-realization cannot be the supreme principle of ethics.
Bertrand Russell (1872–1970) British philosopher and mathematician. 'Romanticism', *A History of Western Philosophy* (1945)

21 There can be hope only for a society which acts as one big family, and not as many separate ones.
Anwar al-Sadat (1918–81) Egyptian statesman. *In Search of Identity* (1978)

22 IMOGEN Society is no comfort
To one not sociable.
William Shakespeare (1564–1616) English poet and playwright. *Cymbeline* (1609–10), Act 4, Scene 2

23 FALSTAFF Company, villainous company, hath been the spoil of me.
William Shakespeare (1564–1616) English poet and playwright. *Henry IV, Part 1* (1597), Act 3, Scene 3

24 Physically there is nothing to distinguish human society from the farm-yard except that children are more troublesome and costly than chickens and women are not so completely enslaved as farm stock.
George Bernard Shaw (1856–1950) Irish playwright. *Getting Married* (1911), Preface

25 There is no such thing as Society. There are individual men and women, and there are families.
Margaret Thatcher (b. 1925) British prime minister. *Woman's Own* (October 31, 1987)

Solidarity

see also **Faith, Friendship, Loyalty**

1 Two are better than one; because they have a good reward for their labour.
For if they fall, the one will lift up his fellow: but woe to him that is alone when he falleth; for he hath not another to help him up.
Bible. Ecclesiastes, *King James Bible* (1611), 4:9–10

2 And if one prevail against him, two shall withstand him; and a threefold cord is not quickly broken.
Bible. Ecclesiastes, *King James Bible* (1611), 4:12

3 Then join hand in hand, brave Americans all! By uniting we stand, by dividing we fall.
John Dickinson (1732–1808) US politician and writer. 'The Liberty Song' (1768)

4 All for one, and one for all.
Alexandre Dumas (1802–70) French novelist and playwright. *The Three Musketeers* (1844)

5 There are a million Negroes in Mississippi. I think they'll take care of me.
James Meredith (b. 1933) US civil rights advocate. June 7, 1966. Said after he had been shot by white supremacists at the start of a civil rights march. He rejoined the march on June 25. Attrib.

Solitude

see also **Loneliness, The Self**

1 The worst solitude is to be destitute of sincere friendship.
Francis Bacon (1561–1626) English philosopher, statesman, and lawyer. *De Dignitate et Augmentis Scientiarum* (Gilbert Watts, tr.; 1640), Antitheta, 37; bk. 1, ch. 7, sect. 81

2 Whosoever is delighted in solitude is either a wild beast or a god.
Francis Bacon (1561–1626) English philosopher, statesman, and lawyer. 'Of Friendship', *Essays* (1625)

3 Alone, practicality becomes dangerous; spirituality, alone, becomes feeble and pointless. Alone, either becomes dull. Each is the other's discipline, in a sense, and in good work the two are joined.
Wendell Berry (b. 1934) US poet, novelist, and essayist. 1985. 'Preserving Wildness', *The Landscape of Harmony* (1987)

4   When is man strong until he feels alone?
    Robert Browning (1812–89) British poet. *Colombe's Birthday* (1889),
    Act 3

5   I am monarch of all I survey,
    My right there is none to dispute;
    From the centre all round to the sea
    I am lord of the foul and the brute.
    Oh, solitude! where are the charms
    That sages have seen in thy face?
    Better dwell in the midst of alarms,
    Than reign in this horrible place.
    William Cowper (1731–1800) British poet. 'Verses Supposed to be
    Written by Alexander Selkirk' (1782), st. 1, quoted in *The
    Works of William Cowper* (Robert Southey, ed.; 1835–37)

6   In the tumult of great events, solitude was what I
    hoped for. Now it is what I love. How is it
    possible to be contented with anything else when
    one has come face to face with History?
    Charles de Gaulle (1890–1970) French president. *Mémoires de guerre*
    (1954–59), vol. 3

7   Anythin' for a quiet life, as the man said wen he
    took the sitivation at the lighthouse.
    Charles Dickens (1812–70) British novelist. *The Pickwick Papers*
    (1837), ch. 43

8   The soul selects her own Society—
    Then—shuts the Door.
    Emily Dickinson (1830–86) US poet. 1862? 'The Soul Selects Her
    Own Society', *Poems by Emily Dickinson* (1890), quoted in
    The Penguin Book of American Verse (Geoffrey Moore, ed.;
    1977)

9   No man is an Island, entire of itself; every man is
    a piece of the Continent, a part of the main; if a
    clod be washed away by the sea, Europe is the
    less, as well as if a promontory were, as well as
    if a manor of thy friends or of thine own were;
    any man's death diminishes me, because I am
    involved in Mankind; And therefore never send
    to know for whom the bell tolls; It tolls for thee.
    John Donne (1572?–1631) English metaphysical poet and divine.
    'Meditation XVII', *Devotions upon Emergent Occasions*
    (1624)

10 As *sickness* is the greatest misery so the greatest
    misery of sickness is *solitude*. *Solitude* is a
    torment which is not threatened in *hell* itself.
    John Donne (1572?–1631) English metaphysical poet and divine. Quoted
    in *Awakenings* (Oliver W. Sacks; 1973)

11 I want to be alone.
    Greta Garbo (1905–90) Swedish-born US film actor. Words spoken by
    Garbo in the film *Grand Hotel*, and associated with her for
    the rest of her career. *Grand Hotel* (1932)

12 I was never less alone than when by myself.
    Edward Gibbon (1737–94) British historian. *Memoirs of My Life* (1796)

13 One of the pleasantest things in the world is
    going on a journey; but I like to go by myself.
    William Hazlitt (1778–1830) British essayist and critic. 'On Going a
    Journey', *Table Talk* (1821–22)

14 You find in solitude only what you take to it.
    Juan Ramón Jiménez (1881–1958) Spanish poet. *Selected Writings*
    (1957)

15 It is a fine thing to be out on the hills alone. A
    man can hardly be a beast or a fool alone on a
    great mountain.
    Francis Kilvert (1840–79) British diarist and cleric. May 29, 1871. On
    the Black Mountain in Wales. *Diary* (W. Plomer, ed.; 1938)

16 The world is a prison in which solitary
    confinement is preferable.
    Karl Kraus (1874–1936) Austrian writer. 1909. Quoted in 'Sprüche
    und Widersprüche', *Karl Kraus* (Harry Zohn; 1971)

17 You know, I used to live like Robinson Crusoe,
    shipwrecked among eight million people. Then
    one day I saw a footprint in the sand and there
    you were.
    Jack Lemmon (b. 1925) US film actor. As C. C. Baxter, owner of the
    apartment of the film title, to Miss Kubelik (Shirley
    MacLaine). *The Apartment* (Billy Wilder and I. A. L.
    Diamond; 1960)

18 I want to be a movement
    But there's no one on my side.
    Adrian Mitchell (b. 1932) British poet and playwright. 'Loose Leaf
    Poem' (1971)

19 Man knows in the end that he is alone in the
    indifferent immensity of the Universe from
    which he has emerged by chance. Neither
    his destiny nor his duty is written down
    anywhere.
    Jacques Lucien Monod (1910–76) French biochemist. *Le Hasard et la
    Nécessité* (1970)

20 A man should keep for himself a little back shop,
    all his own, quite unadulterated, in which he
    establishes his true freedom and chief place of
    seclusion and solitude.
    Michel de Montaigne (1533–92) French essayist. *Essays* (1580–88),
    bk. 1, ch. 39

21 Life is for each man a solitary cell whose walls
    are mirrors.
    Eugene O'Neill (1888–1953) US playwright. *Lazarus Laughed* (1928)

22 I must plough my furrow alone.
    Lord Rosebery (1847–1929) British prime minister and biographer. July
    19, 1901. On remaining outside the Liberal Party leadership.
    Speech to the City of London Liberal Club, *Times* (July 20,
    1901)

23 Solitude, for the Torah, is not humanity's highest
    state, nor is it the condition in which we come
    most fully into the presence of God. The
    individual must share his life with others.
    Jonathan Sacks (b. 1948) British chief rabbi. *Community of Faith*
    (1995)

24 To be alone is the fate of all great minds—a fate
    deplored at times, but still always chosen as the
    less grievous of two evils.
    Arthur Schopenhauer (1788–1860) German philosopher. *Aphorismen zur
    Lebensweisheit* (1919)

25 One can acquire everything in solitude—except
    character.
    Stendhal (1783–1842) French writer. 'Miscellaneous Fragments', *De
    l'Amour* (1822)

26 I never found the companion that was so
    companionable as solitude.
    Henry David Thoreau (1817–62) US writer. 'Solitude', *Walden, or,
    Life in the Woods* (1854)

27 I wandered lonely as a cloud
    That floats on high o'er vales and hills,
    When all at once I saw a crowd,
    A host, of golden daffodils.
    William Wordsworth (1770–1850) English poet. 1804. 'I Wandered
    Lonely as a Cloud', *Poems in Two Volumes* (1807), vol. 2,
    ll. 1–4

28 For oft, when on my couch I lie
    In vacant or in pensive mood,
    They flash upon that inward eye
    Which is the bliss of solitude.
    William Wordsworth (1770–1850) English poet. 1804. 'I Wandered
    Lonely as a Cloud', *Poems in Two Volumes* (1807), vol. 2,
    ll. 19–22

Songs

see also **Music, Popular Music, Singers and Singing**

1   The only two things that matter to me, the only
motivation points for me writing all these songs
are revenge and guilt.
Elvis Costello (b. 1955) British singer and songwriter. Interview, *New
Musical Express* (August 27, 1977)

2   The songs of the slave represent the sorrows of
his heart; and he is relieved by them, only as an
aching heart is relieved by its tears.
Frederick Douglass (1817–95) US abolitionist, writer, and orator.
*Narrative of the Life of Frederick Douglass, an American
Slave* (1845)

3   A song belongs to no man, said Joey The Lips.
The Lord holds copyright on all songs.
Me arse, said Outspan.
Roddy Doyle (b. 1958) Irish novelist and playwright. *The Commitments*
(1987)

4   I've made my statement and I don't think I could
make it any better than in some of those songs.
Once I've said what I need to say in a song,
that's it. I don't want to repeat myself.
Bob Dylan (b. 1941) US singer and songwriter. 1980. Quoted in *Bob
Dylan Performing Artist, 1974–86 The Middle Years* (Paul
Williams; 1992)

5   The hills are alive with the sound of music
With the songs they have sung
For a thousand years.
Oscar Hammerstein II (1895–1960) US lyricist and librettist. Song lyric.
'The Sound of Music', *The Sound of Music* (music by Richard
Rodgers; 1959)

6   Blues are the songs of despair, but gospel songs
are the songs of hope.
Mahalia Jackson (1911–72) US gospel singer. *Movin' On Up*
(Mahalia Jackson and Evan McLeod Wylie; 1966)

7   Music, Maestro, Please
Herbert Magidson (1906–86) US songwriter. 1938. Song title.

8   I do not play the guitar for applause. I sing the
difference between what is true and what is false;
otherwise I do not sing.
Violeta Parra (1917–67) Chilean songwriter and political activist. Attrib.

9   What will a child learn sooner than a song?
Alexander Pope (1688–1744) English poet. *Imitations of Horace*
(1738), Epistle 2

10 Our sweetest songs are those that tell of saddest
thought.
Percy Bysshe Shelley (1792–1822) English poet. 'To a Skylark' (1819),
l. 90

11 Short swallow-flights of song, that dip
Their wings in tears, and skim away.
Alfred Tennyson (1809–92) British poet. 1833–49. 'A. H. H.' (Arthur
Henry Hallam) was the fiancé of Tennyson's sister Emily and
died suddenly in September 1833. *In Memoriam A. H. H.*
(1850), can. 48, st. 4

12 Now is this song both sung and past:
My lute, be still, for I have done.
Thomas Wyatt (1503–42) English poet. 'My Lute Awake!' (1542?),
quoted in *Silver Poets of the Sixteenth Century* (Gerald
Bullett, ed.; 1947)

Sorrow

see also **Bereavement, Regret**

1   My eye cried and woke me.
The night was pain.
al-Khansa (575–646) Arab poet. 'The Night' (7th century)

2   Life will suit
Itself to Sorrow's most detested fruit,
Like to the apples on the Dead Sea's shore,
All ashes to the taste.
Lord Byron (1788–1824) British poet. *Childe Harold's Pilgrimage*
(1812–18), can. 3, st. 34

3   The path of sorrow, and that path alone,
Leads to the land where sorrow is unknown.
William Cowper (1731–1800) British poet. 1781. 'An Epistle to a
Protestant Lady in France' (1789), ll. 9–10, quoted in
Cowper: Poetical Works (H. S. Milford, ed.; 1934)

4   Tears were to me what glass beads are to African
traders.
Quentin Crisp (1908–99) British writer. *The Naked Civil Servant*
(1968)

5   Miss Bolo rose from the table considerably
agitated, and went straight home, in a flood of
tears and a Sedan chair.
Charles Dickens (1812–70) British novelist. *The Pickwick Papers*
(1837), ch. 35

6   Farewell sadness
Good day sadness
You are written in the lines of the ceiling.
Paul Éluard (1895–1952) French surrealist poet. 'À Peine Défigurée'
(1932)

7   Yes, he thought, *between grief and nothing I will
take grief.*
William Faulkner (1897–1962) US novelist. Said by Wilborne. 'Wild
Palms', *The Wild Palms* (1939)

8   Sadness is almost never anything but a form of
fatigue.
André Gide (1869–1951) French novelist and critic. 1922. *Journal*
(1939–51)

9   My peace is gone,
My heart is heavy.
Johann Wolfgang von Goethe (1749–1832) German poet, playwright, and
scientist. 'Gretchens Stube', *Faust* (1808), pt. 1

10 All moanday, tearsday, wailsday, thumpsday,
frightday, shatterday.
James Joyce (1882–1941) Irish writer. *Finnegans Wake* (1939)

11 To sorrow
I bade good-morrow,
And thought to leave her far away behind;
But cheerly, cheerly,
She loves me dearly;
She is so constant to me, and so kind.
John Keats (1795–1821) English poet. *Endymion* (1818), bk. 4,
ll. 173–178

12 Into each life some rain must fall.
Henry Wadsworth Longfellow (1807–82) US poet. 'The Rainy Day',
Ballads and Other Poems (1842), st. 3

13 But the sorrowing are nomads, on a plain with
few landmarks and no boundaries; sorrow's
horizons are vague and its demands are few.
Larry McMurtry (b. 1936) US writer. *Some Can Whistle* (1989), pt. 4,
ch. 9

14 Thrice he essayed, and thrice in spite of scorn,
Tears such as angels weep, burst forth.
John Milton (1608–74) English writer. Satan weeps before addressing
the fallen angels. *Paradise Lost* (1667), bk. 1, ll. 620–621

15 Earth hath no sorrow that heaven cannot heal.
Thomas Moore (1779–1852) Irish poet. Attrib.

16 The world is a vale of tears, but, that said, well irrigated.
Paul Morand (1888–1976) French writer and diplomat. 'La Nuit de Babylone', *Fermé la Nuit* (1923)

17 Sorrow is tranquillity remembered in emotion.
Dorothy Parker (1893–1967) US writer and wit. Alluding to Wordsworth's phrase in the preface to *Lyrical Ballads* (1798) that poetry 'takes its origin from emotion recollected in tranquillity'. 'Sentiment', *Here Lies* (1939)

18 Line after line my gushing eyes o'erflow,
led through a sad variety of woe.
Alexander Pope (1688–1744) English poet. *Eloisa to Abelard* (1717), ll. 35–36

19 Not louder shrieks to pitying heav'n are cast,
When husbands, or when lap-dogs breathe their last.
Alexander Pope (1688–1744) English poet. *The Rape of the Lock* (1712), can. 3, ll. 157–158

20 I often want to cry. That is the only advantage women have over men—at least they can cry.
Jean Rhys (1894–1979) Dominican-born British novelist. *Good Morning, Midnight* (1939), pt. 2

21 It is such a secret place, the land of tears.
Antoine de Saint-Exupéry (1900–44) French writer and aviator. *The Little Prince* (1943), ch. 7

22 HAMLET But I have that within which passes show—
these but the trappings and the suits of woe.
William Shakespeare (1564–1616) English poet and playwright. *Hamlet* (1601), Act 1, Scene 2

23 ANTONY If you have tears, prepare to shed them now.
William Shakespeare (1564–1616) English poet and playwright. *Julius Caesar* (1599), Act 3, Scene 2

24 LEAR Down, thou climbing sorrow,
Thy element's below.
William Shakespeare (1564–1616) English poet and playwright. *King Lear* (1605–06), Act 2, Scene 4

25 OTHELLO This sorrow's heavenly,
It strikes where it doth love.
William Shakespeare (1564–1616) English poet and playwright. *Othello* (1602–04), Act 5, Scene 2

26 I am gone into the fields
To take what this sweet hour yields;—
Reflection, you may come to-morrow,
Sit by the fireside with Sorrow.
Percy Bysshe Shelley (1792–1822) English poet. 'Jane: the Invitation' (1822)

27 O Sorrow, wilt thou live with me
No casual mistress, but a wife.
Alfred Tennyson (1809–92) British poet. 1833–49. 'A. H. H.' (Arthur Henry Hallam) was the fiancé of Tennyson's sister Emily and died suddenly in September 1833. *In Memoriam A. H. H.* (1850), can. 59, st. 1

28 Comfort? comfort scorn'd of devils! this is truth the poet sings,
That a sorrow's crown of sorrow is remembering happier things.
Alfred Tennyson (1809–92) British poet. 1837–38. 'Locksley Hall', *Poems* (1842), ll. 75–76

29 Pure and complete sorrow is as impossible as pure and complete joy.
Leo Tolstoy (1828–1910) Russian writer. *War and Peace* (1865–69), bk. 15, ch. 1

30 Tears fall in my heart
As rain falls on the city.
Paul Verlaine (1844–96) French poet. 'Ariette Oubliée', *Songs Without Words* (1874), no. 3

31 A grief too much to be told, O queen, you bid me renew.
Virgil (70–19 BC) Roman poet. The opening words of Aeneas's account to Dido of the fall of Troy. *Aeneid* (29–19 BC), bk. 2, l. 3

32 When one grief afflicts us we choose a sharper grief
in hope that enormity will ease affliction.
Derek Walcott (b. 1930) St. Lucian poet and playwright. *Omeros* (1990)

33 Tears left unshed
turn to poison
in the ducts.
Alice Walker (b. 1944) US novelist and poet. 'S M', *Her Blue Body Everything We Know* (1991)

34 When lilacs last in the dooryard bloom'd,
And the great star early dropp'd in the western sky in the night,
I mourn'd, and yet shall mourn with ever-returning spring.
Walt Whitman (1819–92) US poet. 1865. Composed after the assassination of Abraham Lincoln (April 14, 1865). 'When Lilacs Last in the Dooryard Bloom'd', *Sequel to Drum-Taps* (1866)

35 Come away, O human child!
To the waters and the wild
With a faery, hand in hand,
For the world's more full of weeping than you can understand.
W. B. Yeats (1865–1939) Irish poet and playwright. 'The Stolen Child', *Crossways* (1889), ll. 9–12

The Soul

see also Character, Mind, Spirituality

1 The soul is characterized by these capacities: self-nutrition, sensation, thinking, and movement.
Aristotle (384–322 BC) Greek philosopher. *De Anima* (4th century BC), 413b

2 We cannot kindle when we will
The fire which in the heart resides,
The spirit bloweth and is still,
In mystery our soul abides.
Matthew Arnold (1822–88) British poet and critic. 'Morality' (1852)

3 For what shall it profit a man, if he shall gain the whole world, and lose his own soul? Or what shall a man give in exchange for his soul?
Bible. Mark, *King James Bible* (1611), 8:36–37

4 The soul fortunately, has an interpreter—often an unconscious, but still a truthful interpreter—in the eye.
Charlotte Brontë (1816–55) British novelist. *Jane Eyre* (1847), ch. 28

5 'Tis an awkward thing to play with souls,
And matter enough to save one's own.
Robert Browning (1812–89) British poet. 'A Light Woman', *Men and Women* (1855), st. 12

6 I count life just a stuff
To try the soul's strength on.
Robert Browning (1812–89) British poet. 'In a Balcony', *Men and Women* (1855), ll. 651–652

7 My soul is not by the side of my people; my people *is* my soul.

Martin Buber (1878–1965) Austrian-born Israeli philosopher of religion and Zionist. 1923. Quoted in *On Judaism* (N. Glazer, ed., Eva Jose et al., trs.; 1967)

8 I believe the souls of five hundred Sir Isaac Newtons would go to the making up of a Shakespeare or a Milton.

Samuel Taylor Coleridge (1772–1834) British poet. Letter to Thomas Poole (March 23, 1801)

9 Of consciousness, her awful Mate The Soul cannot be rid.

Emily Dickinson (1830–86) US poet. 1864? 'Of Consciousness Her Awful Mate', *Bolts of Melody* (1945), ll. 1–2, quoted in *A Choice of Emily Dickinson's Verse* (Ted Hughes, ed.; 1977)

10 For the sake of living on and on People have invented souls Have invented free and unhampered sails That do not suffer the torture of ropes And can sail on dry land.

Gu Cheng (1956–96) Chinese poet. 'The Flag' (1980), quoted in *The Red Azalea* (Edward Morin, ed.; 1990)

11 I cannot compare the soul more properly to any thing than to a republic or commonwealth, in which the several members are united by the reciprocal ties of government and subordination.

David Hume (1711–76) Scottish philosopher and historian. *A Treatise of Human Nature* (1739–40)

12 One great use of the Soul has always been to account for, and at the same time to guarantee, the closed individuality of each personal consciousness.

William James (1842–1910) US psychologist and philosopher. *The Principles of Psychology* (1890), vol. 1

13 The soul follows its own laws, and the body its own likewise, and they accord by virtue of the *harmony pre-established* among all substances, since they are all representations of one and the same universe.

Gottfried Wilhelm Leibniz (1646–1716) German philosopher and mathematician. *Monadology* (1714)

14 The soul does not like to be without its body because without the body it cannot feel or do anything.

Leonardo da Vinci (1452–1519) Italian artist, engineer, and inventor. Quoted in *The Stanislavski Method* (Sonia Moore; 1960)

15 Oh, empty spirit and full soul facing the smoky bonfire, the crackle of flames through roots, the watchfire on the border lighting up deep scars!

Antonio Machado (1875–1939) Spanish poet and playwright. 'The Death of Abel Martin', *Selected Poems* (Alan S. Trueblood, tr.; 1982), ll. 8–12

16 The soul . . . remains as much *outside* the *I* which you are, as the landscape remains outside the body.

José Ortega y Gasset (1883–1955) Spanish writer and philosopher. 'In Search of Goethe from Within', *Partisan Review* (December 1949)

17 The living voice is that which sways the soul.

Pliny the Younger (62–113) Roman politician and writer. Quoted in *The Letters of Pliny the Consul* (W. Melmoth, tr.; 1747), bk. 2, letter 3

18 Go, Soul, the body's guest, Upon a thankless warrant: Fear not to touch the best; The truth shall be thy errand: Go, since I needs must die, And give the world the lie.

Walter Raleigh (1554–1618) British explorer, courtier, and writer. Printed in *Poetical Rhapsody* (Francis Davison, 1608); manuscript copy traced to 1595. 'The Lie' (1595), st. 1

19 So transparent your soul so open I could find no way in.

Pedro Salinas (1891–1951) Spanish poet. 'So Transparent Your Soul', *Roots and Wings: Poetry from Spain (1900–75)* (Hardie St. Martin, ed.; 1976)

20 For echo is the soul of the voice exciting itself in hollow places.

Christopher Smart (1722–71) British poet. Quoted in *The English Patient* (Michael Ondaatje; 1991)

21 There is only one home to the life of a tortoise; there is only one shell to the soul of man: there is only one world to the spirit of our race. If that world leaves its course and smashes on the boulder of the great void, whose world will give us shelter?

Wole Soyinka (b. 1934) Nigerian novelist, playwright, poet, and lecturer. *Death and the King's Horseman* (1975), Act 1

22 I am positive I have a soul; nor can all the books with which materialists have pestered the world ever convince me of the contrary.

Laurence Sterne (1713–68) Irish-born British writer and clergyman. 'Maria, Moulines', *A Sentimental Journey Through France and Italy* (1768)

23 The soul descends once more in bitter love To accept the waking body.

Richard Wilbur (b. 1921) US poet. 1956. 'Love Calls Us to the Things of This World', *New and Collected Poems* (1988)

24 The human body is the best picture of the human soul.

Ludwig Wittgenstein (1889–1951) Austrian philosopher. *Philosophical Investigations* (1953)

25 We are laid asleep In body, and become a living soul: While with an eye made quiet by the power Of harmony, and the deep power of joy, We see into the life of things.

William Wordsworth (1770–1850) English poet. July 13, 1798. Subtitled: 'On Revisiting the Banks of the Wye During a Tour, July 13, 1798'. 'Lines Composed a Few Miles Above Tintern Abbey', *Lyrical Ballads* (1798), ll. 45–49

26 The gods approve The depth, and not the tumult, of the soul.

William Wordsworth (1770–1850) English poet. 1814. 'Laodamia', *Poems* (1815), ll. 74–75

Soundbites

see also Journalism, Quotations

1 A quotation is what a speaker wants to say— unlike a soundbite which is all that an interviewer allows you to say.

Tony Benn (b. 1925) British politician and author. Letter to Antony Jay (August 1996)

2 This is not the time for soundbites. I can feel the hand of history on our shoulders.

Tony Blair (b. 1953) British prime minister. Referring to the constitutional talks in Northern Ireland. *Daily Telegraph* (April 8, 1998)

South Africa

see African Countries, Apartheid

South America

see also The Caribbean, Central America

1 We want a Chile where the rights of man will be fully respected. Our message is not fear but hope, not hate, but joy. It is not the past, but the future, that we will build together.

Hortensia Bussi de Allende (b. 1915) Chilean politician. Speech, Santiago, Chile (September 24, 1988)

2 I am certain that the seed we planted in the worthy consciousness of thousands and thousands of Chileans cannot be definitively uprooted.

Salvador Allende (1908–73) Chilean president. Quoted in *A Nation of Enemies* (Pamela Constable and Arturo Valenzuela; 1991)

3 Colombia is not France, and I am not Napoleon.

Simón Bolívar (1783–1830) Venezuelan soldier and statesman. Referring to a suggestion that he could imitate the intellectual and political leaders of the Enlightenment. Letter to José Antonio Páez (March 6, 1826)

4 The vestiges of Spanish domination will long be with us . . . the contagion of despotism infects the atmosphere about us.

Simón Bolívar (1783–1830) Venezuelan soldier and statesman. Speech, Angostura (February 15, 1819)

5 Latins are tenderly enthusiastic. In Brazil they throw flowers at you. In Argentina they throw themselves.

Marlene Dietrich (1901–92) German-born US actor and singer. *Newsweek* (August 24, 1959)

6 We had believed the government was eternal, giving us time to work out the future peacefully, and now the fascists wanted to cut out our tongues; they were getting their public back, talking about the highest patriotic values, and as for us, well, we would be screwed.

Ariel Dorfman (b. 1942) Chilean playwright and novelist. Referring to the military coup in 1973 led by General Augusto Pinochet. *Hard Rain* (1973)

7 Military dictatorship, fear of listening, fear of speaking, made us deaf and dumb. Now democracy, with its fear of remembering, infects us with amnesia.

Eduardo Galeano (b. 1940) Uruguayan writer. *The Book of Embraces* (1989)

8 For us European earth-dwellers, the adventure played out in the . . . New World signifies in the first place that it was not our world and that we bear responsibility for the crime of its destruction.

Claude Lévi-Strauss (b. 1908) French anthropologist. *Tristes Tropiques* (1955), ch. 38

9 Whereas in North America colonization planted the seed of the spirit and economy then growing in Europe and representing the future, the Spaniard brought to America the effects and methods of an already declining spirit and economy that belonged to the past.

José Carlos Mariátegui (1895–1930) Peruvian political leader and essayist. *Seven Interpretive Essays on Peruvian Reality* (1928)

10 Latin America is very fond of the word 'hope'. We like to be called the 'continent of hope' . . . This hope is really something like a promise of heaven, an IOU whose payment is always being put off.

Pablo Neruda (1904–73) Chilean poet and diplomat. *Memoirs* (1974), ch. 11

11 The vision of an America de-Latinized of its own will, without threat of conquest, and reconstituted in the image and likeness of the North, now looms in the nightmares of many who are genuinely concerned about our future . . . We have our *USA-mania*. It must be limited by the boundaries our reason and sentiment jointly dictate.

José Rodó (1871–1917) Uruguayan essayist. *Ariel* (1900)

12 Since it is impossible to know what's really happening, we Peruvians lie, invent, dream . . . Because of these strange circumstances, Peruvian life, a life in which so few actually do read, has become literary.

Mario Vargas Llosa (b. 1936) Peruvian writer. *The Real Life of Alejandro Mayta* (1984)

Soviet Union

see Russia

Space

see also Astronomy, The Universe

1 Space . . . is big. Really big. You just won't believe how vastly hugely mindbogglingly big it is. I mean you may think it's a long way down the road to the chemist, but that's just peanuts to space.

Douglas Adams (1952–2001) British writer. *The Hitch Hiker's Guide to the Galaxy* (1979), ch. 8

2 At two-tenths the speed of light, dust and atoms might not do significant damage . . . but the faster you go, the worse it is . . . So 60,000 kilometers per second may be the *practical* speed limit for space travel.

Isaac Asimov (1920–92) Russian-born US writer. *The Relativity of Wrong* (1996)

3 Oh, it's mysterious lamplit evenings, here in the galaxy . . . Terror and a beauty insoluble are a ribband of blue woven into the fringes of garments of things both great and small.

Annie Dillard (b. 1945) US writer. *Pilgrim at Tinker's Creek* (1974), ch. 3

4 Space isn't remote at all. It's only an hour's drive away if your car could go straight upwards.

Fred Hoyle (1915–2001) British astronomer, mathematician, and writer. September 1979. *Observer* (September 9, 1979)

5 OK, Houston, we have had a problem here . . . Houston, we have a problem.

James Lovell (b. 1928) US astronaut. April 11, 1970. His message to mission control after an explosion on Apollo 13.

6 A broad and ample road, whose dust is gold
And pavement stars, as stars to thee appear,
Seen in the galaxy, that Milky Way
Which nightly as a circling zone thou seest
Powdered with stars.

John Milton (1608–74) English writer. *Paradise Lost* (1667), bk. 8, ll. 577–581

7 Space is out of this world.
Helen Sharman (b. 1963) British astronaut. Remark (May 1991)

8 Space—the final frontier . . . These are the voyages of the starship *Enterprise*. Its five-year mission . . . to boldly go where no man has gone before.
Star Trek, US television series. *Star Trek* (1966–69), opening titles

9 And all this science, I don't understand.
It's just my job, five days a week,
A rocket man.
Bernie Taupin (b. 1950) British songwriter. Song lyric. 'Rocket Man' (music by Elton John; 1972)

10 Everything in space obeys the laws of physics. If you know these laws and obey them, space will treat you kindly. And don't tell me that man doesn't belong out there. Man belongs wherever he wants to go; and he'll do plenty well when he gets there.
Wernher von Braun (1912–77) German-born US engineer. *Time* (February 17, 1958)

Spain

see **Europe, European Countries**

Speech

see also **Conversation, Language, Speeches, The Voice**

1 Speech was not given to man: he took it.
Louis Aragon (1897–1982) French writer. *Le Libertinage* (1924)

2 In me the need to talk is a primary impulse, and I can't help saying right off what comes to my tongue.
Miguel de Cervantes (1547–1616) Spanish novelist and playwright. *Don Quixote* (1605–15), pt. 1, ch. 30

3 I pass, like night, from land to land;
I have strange power of speech.
Samuel Taylor Coleridge (1772–1834) British poet. 'The Rime of the Ancient MarIner', *Lyrical Ballads* (1798), pt. 7

4 She lays it on with a trowel.
William Congreve (1670–1729) English playwright and poet. *The Double Dealer* (1694), Act 3, Scene 10

5 No, Sir, because I have time to think before I speak, and don't ask impertinent questions.
Erasmus Darwin (1731–1802) British physician, biologist, and poet. Reply when asked whether he found his stammer inconvenient. Quoted in 'Reminiscences of My Father's Everyday Life', *Autobiography, Charles Darwin* (Sir Francis Darwin, ed.; 1877), Appendix 1

6 The true use of speech is not so much to express our wants as to conceal them.
Oliver Goldsmith (1730–74) Irish-born British novelist, playwright, and poet. 'The Use of Language', *Essays* (1765)

7 Most men make little use of their speech than to give evidence against their own understanding.
George Savile Halifax (1633–95) English statesman. 'Of Folly and Fools', *Political, Moral and Miscellaneous Thoughts and Reflections* (1750)

8 True and False are attributes of speech, not of things. And where speech is not, there is neither Truth nor Falsehood.
Thomas Hobbes (1588–1679) English philosopher and political thinker. *Leviathan* (1651), pt. 1, ch. 4

9 It's as we speak that we find our ideas, our words, ourselves too, in our words, and the city, the gardens, perhaps everything comes back and we're not orphans any more.
Eugène Ionesco (1909–94) Romanian-born French playwright. *The Chairs* (1951)

10 It was an oddity of Mrs. Lowder's that her face in speech was like a lighted window at night, but that silence immediately drew the curtain.
Henry James (1843–1916) US-born British writer and critic. *The Wings of the Dove* (1902), bk. 11, ch. 2

11 The truth is that large tracts of human speech are nothing but *signs of direction* in thought.
William James (1842–1910) US psychologist and philosopher. *The Principles of Psychology* (1890), vol. 1

12 Talking and eloquence are not the same: to speak, and to speak well, are two things.
Ben Jonson (1572–1637) English playwright and poet. *Timber, or, Discoveries Made upon Men and Matter* (1640)

13 Speech is civilization itself. The word, even the most contradictory word, preserves contact—it is silence which isolates.
Thomas Mann (1875–1955) German writer. *The Magic Mountain* (1924), ch. 6

14 Speech is the small change of Silence.
George Meredith (1828–1909) British novelist and poet. *The Ordeal of Richard Feverel* (1859), ch. 34

15 Good heavens! I have been talking prose for over forty years without realizing it.
Molière (1622–73) French playwright. *Le Bourgeois Gentilhomme* (1670), Act 2, Scene 4

16 Simonides said 'that he never repented that he held his tongue, but often that he had spoken'.
Plutarch (46?–120?) Greek biographer and philosopher. 'Rules for the Preservation of Health' (1st–2nd century)

17 Themistocles said speech was like to tapestry; and like it, when it was spread it showed its figures, but when it was folded up, hid and spoiled them.
Plutarch (46?–120?) Greek biographer and philosopher. 'Themistocles', *Apophthegms of Kings and Great Commanders* (1st–2nd century)

18 The most precious things in speech are pauses.
Ralph Richardson (1902–83) British actor. Attrib.

19 Speech was given to man to disguise his thoughts.
Charles Maurice de Talleyrand (1754–1838) French statesman and diplomat. Attrib.

Speeches

see also **Quotations, Rhetoric, Soundbites**

1 Begin low, speak slow; take fire, rise higher; when most impressed be self-possessed; at the end wax warm, and sit down in a storm.
Anonymous. Advice to public speakers.

2 A monologue is not a decision.
Clement Attlee (1883–1967) British politician. Said to Winston Churchill, who complained that a matter had already been raised several times in Cabinet. Quoted in *A Prime Minister Remembers* (Francis Williams; 1961), ch. 7

3 I take the view, and always have done, that if you cannot say what you have to say in twenty minutes, you should go away and write a book about it.
Derek Brabazon (1910–64) British business executive. 1955. Attrib.

4 He is one of those orators of whom it was well said, 'Before they get up they do not know what they are going to say; when they are speaking, they do not know what they are saying; and when they sit down, they do not know what they have said'.

Winston Churchill (1874–1965) British prime minister and writer. Referring to Lord Charles Beresford. Speech to Parliament (December 20, 1912)

5 The art of making deep sounds from the stomach sound like important messages from the brain.

Winston Churchill (1874–1965) British prime minister and writer. Referring to the art of speechmaking.

6 Haven't you learned yet that I put something more than whisky into my speeches?

Winston Churchill (1874–1965) British prime minister and writer. Said to his son Randolph. Attrib.

7 In private conversation he tries on speeches like a man trying on ties in his bedroom to see how he would look in them.

Lionel Curtis (1872–1955) British writer and administrator. Referring to Winston Churchill. Letter to Nancy Astor (1912)

8 A good indignation makes an excellent speech.

Ralph Waldo Emerson (1803–82) US poet and essayist. Attrib.

9 Many have been the wise speeches of fools, though not so many as the foolish speeches of wise men.

Thomas Fuller (1608–61) English historian. *The Holy State and the Profane State* (1642)

10 I absorb the vapour and return it as a flood.

William Ewart Gladstone (1809–98) British statesman. Referring to public speaking. Quoted in *Some Things That Matter* (Lord Riddell, ed.; 1927)

11 What orators lack in depth they make up to you in length.

Montesquieu (1689–1755) French writer and jurist. Attrib.

12 Speak when you are angry—and you'll make the best speech you'll ever regret.

Laurence J. Peter (1919–90) Canadian writer. *Peter's Quotations* (1977)

13 ANTONY For I have neither wit, nor words, nor worth,
Action, nor utterance, nor the power of speech,
To stir men's blood; I only speak right on.

William Shakespeare (1564–1616) English poet and playwright. *Julius Caesar* (1599), Act 3, Scene 2

14 It usually takes more than three weeks to prepare a good impromptu speech.

Mark Twain (1835–1910) US writer and humorist. Attrib.

Spirituality

see also **Religion, The Soul, Vitality**

1 If one man gains spiritually, the whole world gains with him, and if one man fails, the whole world fails to that extent.

Mahatma Gandhi (1869–1948) Indian national leader. Quoted in *Questions in the Philosophy of Restraint* (Indira Rothermund; 1963)

2 The nature of Spirit may be understood by a glance at its direct opposite—Matter. As the essence of Matter is Gravity, so . . . we may affirm that the substance, the essence of Spirit is Freedom.

G. W. F. Hegel (1770–1831) German philosopher. *Reason in History* (Robert S. Hartman, tr.; 1953)

3 Pure spirituality . . . is the soil of science, is thinking, and can be only in mind.

G. W. F. Hegel (1770–1831) German philosopher. 1807. *The Phenomenology of Mind* (J. B. Baillie, tr.; 1910)

4 The spirit within nourishes, and mind instilled throughout the living parts activates the whole mass and mingles with the vast frame.

Virgil (70–19 BC) Roman poet. *Aeneid* (29–19 BC), bk. 6, l. 726

Spontaneity

see also **Creativity, Novelty, Originality**

1 Spontaneity is only a term for man's ignorance of the gods.

Samuel Butler (1835–1902) British writer and composer. *Erewhon* (1872), ch. 25

2 The quest for spontaneity is fundamental in art and football expresses it best.

Eric Cantona (b. 1966) French football player. *Independent* (January 27, 1995)

3 Away with all ideals. Let each individual act spontaneously from the for ever incalculable prompting of the creative wellhead within him. There is no universal law.

D. H. Lawrence (1885–1930) British writer. *All Things Are Possible* (Leon Shestov; 1929), Preface

4 The one and only basis of the moral life must be spontaneity, that is, the immediate, the unreflective.

Jean-Paul Sartre (1905–80) French philosopher, playwright, and novelist. *Notebooks for an Ethics* (1983)

5 Mistrust first impulses; they are nearly always good.

Charles Maurice de Talleyrand (1754–1838) French statesman and diplomat. Sometimes attributed to Count Montrond. Attrib.

Sports and Games

see also **Entertainment, Exercise, Health and Healthy Living**

1 I don't think sportsmen can use 'sports and politics don't mix' as an excuse. I didn't want to represent 50 million English people touring a country where the regime was abhorrent.

Stuart Barnes (b. 1962) British rugby player. Referring to his refusal to tour South Africa in 1984. *Independent* (May 11, 1994)

2 It's not in support of cricket but as an earnest protest against golf.

Max Beerbohm (1872–1956) British essayist, critic, and caricaturist. Said when giving a shilling towards W. G. Grace's testimonial. Quoted in *Carr's Dictionary of Extraordinary English Cricketers* (J. L. Carr)

3 The great fallacy is that the game is first and last about winning. It's nothing of the kind. The game is about glory. It's about doing things in style, with a flourish, about going out and beating the other lot, not waiting for them to die of boredom.

Danny Blanchflower (1926–93) Northern Irish footballer. Quoted in *The Glory Game* (Hunter Davies; 1985)

4 There has never been a great athlete who died not knowing what pain is.

Bill Bradley (b. 1943) US senator and basketball player. Quoted in *A Sense of Where You Are* (John McPhee; 1965)

5 This isn't no time for playin'
   the fool nor makin' no sport; this is cricket!
   Edward Kamau Brathwaite (b. 1930) Barbadian poet, playwright, and
   historian. 'Rites', *The Arrivants* (1973)

6 The most important thing in the Olympic Games
   is not winning but taking part . . . The essential
   thing in life is not conquering but fighting well.
   Pierre de Coubertin (1863–1937) French educator and thinker. Speech at
   a banquet for officials of the Olympic Games, London (July
   24, 1908)

7 Play the game, but don't believe in it.
   Ralph Ellison (1914–94) US writer, jazz musician, and photographer.
   Invisible Man (1953)

8 Wherein is nothing but beastly fury and extreme
   violence, whereof proceedeth hurt; and
   consequently rancour and malice do remain with
   them that be wounded.
   Thomas Elyot (1490?–1546) English diplomat and writer. Referring to
   football. *The Boke Called the Governour* (1531)

9 They came to see me bat, not to see you bowl.
   W. G. Grace (1848–1915) British cricketer. Refusing to leave the
   crease after being bowled out first ball in front of a large
   crowd. Attrib.

10 It's more than a game. It's an institution.
   Thomas Hughes (1822–96) British writer. Referring to cricket. *Tom
   Brown's Schooldays* (1857), pt. 2, ch. 7

11 What do they know of cricket who only cricket
   know? West Indians crowding to Tests bring
   with them the whole past history and future
   hopes of the islands.
   C. L. R. James (1901–89) Trinidadian writer, political theorist, and
   educator. *Beyond a Boundary* (1963)

12 Body-line was not an incident, it was not an
   accident, it was not a temporary aberration. It
   was the violence and ferocity of our age
   expressing itself in cricket.
   C. L. R. James (1901–89) Trinidadian writer, political theorist, and
   educator. 'Body-line' is the style of bowling first employed by
   English cricketer Harold Larwood in 1932, in which the
   bowler aims the ball hard and fast towards the body of the
   batsman. *Beyond a Boundary* (1963)

13 The goal was scored a little bit by the hand of
   God and a little bit by the head of Maradona.
   Diego Maradona (b. 1960) Argentinian football player. Referring to a
   goal he scored against England in the 1986 World Cup
   quarter-final; although it was scored illegally with his hand,
   the referee allowed it to stand. Interview, *Observer* (December
   28, 1986), 'Sayings of the Week'

14 In England, soccer is a grey game played by grey
   people on grey days.
   Rodney Marsh (b. 1944) British footballer. Describing football to an
   audience on Florida television. Remark (1979)

15 Football, it seemed to me, is not really played for
   the pleasure of kicking a ball about, but is a
   species of fighting.
   George Orwell (1903–50) British writer. 'Such, Such Were the Joys'
   (1946)

16 Serious sport has nothing to do with fair play. It
   is bound up with hatred, jealousy, boastfulness,
   disregard of all rules and sadistic pleasure in
   witnessing violence; in other words it is war
   minus the shooting.
   George Orwell (1903–50) British writer. 'The Sporting Spirit',
   Shooting an Elephant (1950)

17 I let my feet spend as little time on the ground as
   possible. From the air, fast down, and from the
   ground, fast up.
   Jesse Owens (1913–80) US athlete. Attrib.

18 Football? It's the beautiful game.
   Pelé (b. 1940) Brazilian footballer. Quoted in *The Beautiful Game*
   (Elizabeth Knowles; 2001)

19 Some people think football is a matter of life
   and death—I can assure them it is much more
   important than that.
   Bill Shankly (1913–81) Scottish football manager. *Sunday Times*
   (October 4, 1981)

20 In my sport the quick are too often listed among
   the dead.
   Jackie Stewart (b. 1939) British motor-racing driver. Attrib.

21 Football . . . causeth fighting, brawling,
   contention, quarrel picking, murder, homicide
   and great effusion of bloode, as daily experience
   teacheth.
   Philip Stubbes (1555?–1610?) English puritan pamphleteer. *Anatomy of
   Abuses* (1583)

22 Most sorts of diversion in men, children, and
   other animals, are an imitation of fighting.
   Jonathan Swift (1667–1745) Irish writer and clergyman. *Thoughts on
   Various Subjects* (1711)

23 The battle of Waterloo was won on the playing
   fields of Eton.
   Duke of Wellington (1769–1852) Irish-born British general and prime
   minister. Quoted in *Words on Wellington* (Sir William Fraser;
   1889)

24 I will not permit thirty men to travel four
   hundred miles to agitate a bag of wind.
   Andrew Dickson White (1832–1918) US educator and diplomat.
   Refusing to allow the Cornell American football team to
   visit Michigan to play a match. Quoted in *The People's
   Almanac* (D. Wallechinsky; 1978)

25 It requires one to assume such indecent postures.
   Oscar Wilde (1854–1900) Irish poet, playwright, and wit. Explaining
   why he did not play cricket. Attrib.

26 In the 1950s we went to learn, now we go to
   teach.
   Eric Williams (1911–81) Trinidadian prime minister. 1962. Referring to
   an upcoming tour of England by West Indian cricketers.
   Quoted in *Viv Richards: The Authorised Biography* (Trevor
   McDonald; 1984)

27 Golf is one of the few sports where a white
   man can dress like a black pimp and not look
   bad.
   Robin Williams (b. 1951) US actor and comedian. Attrib.

Spring

see also **Seasons**

1 Over increasingly large areas of the United States,
   spring now comes unheralded by the return of
   the birds, and the early mornings are strangely
   silent where once they were filled with the beauty
   of bird song.
   Rachel Carson (1907–64) US ecologist. *Silent Spring* (1962)

2 Whan that Aprill with his shoures soote
   The droghte of March hath perced to the roote.
   Geoffrey Chaucer (1343?–1400) English poet. 'The General
   Prologue', *The Canterbury Tales* (1390?), ll. 1–2, quoted in
   The Works of Geoffrey Chaucer (F. N. Robinson, ed.;
   1957)

3 I'll see you again,
Whenever spring breaks through again.
Noël Coward (1899–1973) British playwright, actor, and songwriter. *Bitter Sweet* (1929), Act 1, Scene 2

4 There is a parrot imitating spring
in the palace, its feathers parsley green.
Rita Dove (b. 1952) US poet. 'Parsley' (1983), ll. 1–2

5 It Might As Well Be Spring
Oscar Hammerstein II (1895–1960) US lyricist and librettist. Song title. *State Fair* (music by Richard Rodgers; 1945)

6 Sweet spring, full of sweet days and roses,
A box where sweets compacted lie.
George Herbert (1593–1633) English poet and cleric. 'Virtue', *The Temple: Sacred Poems and Private Ejaculations* (1633), st. 3, ll. 1–2

7 Spring is not on the willow tips nor in the grassy pond.
Li Jinfa (1900–76) US poet and diplomat. 'Thou Mayest Come Naked' (1922), quoted in *Anthology of Modern Chinese Poetry* (Michelle Yeh, ed., tr.; 1992)

8 The month of May was come, when every lusty heart beginneth to blossom, and to bring forth fruit; for like as herbs and trees bring forth fruit and flourish in May, in likewise every lusty heart that is in any manner a lover, springeth and flourisheth in lusty deeds.
Thomas Malory (d. 1471?) English writer. *Le Morte d'Arthur* (1470), bk. 18, ch. 25

9 A bad-cinema spring, full of paper leaves and cotton-wool blossoms and phony lighting.
Thomas Pynchon (b. 1937) US novelist. *Gravity's Rainbow* (1973)

10 Spring has returned. The earth is like a child that knows poems.
Rainer Maria Rilke (1875–1926) Austrian poet and novelist. *Sonnets to Orpheus* (1923), Sonnet 1, l. 21

11 The country habit has me by the heart,
For he's bewitched for ever who has seen,
Not with his eyes but with his vision, Spring
Flow down the woods and stipple leaves with sun.
Vita Sackville-West (1892–1962) British poet and novelist. 'Winter', *The Land* (1926)

12 When the hounds of spring are on winter's traces,
The mother of months in meadow or plain
Fills the shadows and windy places
With lisp of leaves and ripple of rain.
Algernon Charles Swinburne (1837–1909) British poet. 'When the Hounds of Spring', *Atlanta in Calydon* (1865), chorus, st. 1

13 I dreamed there would be Spring no more,
That Nature's ancient power was lost.
Alfred Tennyson (1809–92) British poet. 1833–49. 'A. H. H.' (Arthur Henry Hallam) was the fiancé of Tennyson's sister Emily and died suddenly in September 1833. *In Memoriam A. H. H.* (1850), can. 69, st. 1

14 In the Spring a young man's fancy lightly turns to thoughts of love.
Alfred Tennyson (1809–92) British poet. 1837–38. 'Locksley Hall', *Poems* (1842), l. 20

15 Spring is come home with her world-wandering feet.
And all things are made young with young desires.
Francis Thompson (1859–1907) British poet and critic. 'Ode to Easter', *Works* (Wilfred Meynell, ed.; 1913)

16 Sweet April showers
Do spring May flowers.
Thomas Tusser (1524–80) English farmer and writer. 'April's Husbandry', *Hundredth Good Pointes of Husbandrie* (1557)

17 Thrice welcome, darling of the Spring!
Even yet thou art to me
No bird, but an invisible thing,
A voice, a mystery.
William Wordsworth (1770–1850) English poet. 1802. 'To the Cuckoo', *Poems in Two Volumes* (1807), vol. 2, ll. 13–16

Statistics

see also **Facts, Information, Mathematics**

1 Medical statistics are like a bikini. What they reveal is interesting but what they conceal is vital.
Anonymous

2 One to mislead the public, another to mislead the Cabinet, and the third to mislead itself.
Herbert Henry Asquith (1852–1928) British prime minister. Explaining why the War Office kept three sets of figures. Quoted in *The Price of Glory* (Alastair Horne; 1962), ch. 2

3 I could prove God statistically.
George Gallup (1901–84) US statistician and public opinion analyst. Attrib.

4 We are just statistics, born to consume resources.
Horace (65–8 BC) Roman poet. *Epistles* (20? BC), bk. 1, no. 2, l. 27

5 Statistics: the mathematical theory of ignorance.
Morris Kline (1908–92) US mathematician. Quoted in *Mathematical Maxims and Minims* (N. Rose; 1988)

6 Politicians use statistics in the same way that a drunken man uses lamp-posts—for support rather than illumination.
Andrew Lang (1844–1912) Scottish writer and scholar. Speech (1910), quoted in *The Harvest of a Quiet Eye* (Alan L. Mackay; 1977)

7 Statistics will prove anything, even the truth.
Noël Moynihan (1916–94) British doctor and writer. Attrib.

8 I am one of the unpraised, unrewarded millions without whom Statistics would be a bankrupt science. It is we who are born, who marry, who die, in constant ratios.
Logan Pearsall Smith (1865–1946) US-born British writer. *Trivia* (1902)

9 There are two kinds of statistics, the kind you look up and the kind you make up.
Rex Stout (1886–1975) US writer. *Death of a Doxy* (1966), ch. 9

Storytelling

see also **Creativity, Fiction, Inspiration, Literature, Writing**

1 Death is the sanction of everything that the storyteller can tell. He has borrowed his authority from death.
Walter Benjamin (1892–1940) German writer and critic. Attrib.

2 Sometimes to refute a single sentence it is necessary to tell a life story.
John Berger (b. 1926) British novelist, essayist, and art critic. *Once in Europa* (1987)

3 Fairy tales unconsciously understand . . . offer examples of both temporary and permanent solutions to pressing difficulties.
Bruno Bettelheim (1903–90) Austrian-born US psychoanalyst. *The Uses of Enchantment* (1976)

4 A child's pleasure in listening to stories lies partly in waiting for things he expects to be repeated: situations, phrases, formulas.

Italo Calvino (1923–85) Cuban-born Italian novelist and short-story writer. 1985. 'Quickness', *Six Memos for the Next Millennium* (Patrick Creagh, tr.; 1992)

5 A good storyteller is a person who has a good memory and hopes other people haven't.

Irvin S. Cobb (1876–1944) US humorist and journalist. Attrib.

6 We tell ourselves stories in order to live . . . We look for the sermon in the suicide, for the social or moral lesson in the murder of five.

Joan Didion (b. 1934) US journalist and writer. 1978. *The White Album* (1979), pt. 1

7 Every storyteller is a child of Scheherazade, in a hurry to tell the tale so that death may be postponed one more time.

Carlos Fuentes (b. 1928) Mexican writer. 'The Storyteller', *The Picador Book of Latin American Stories* (1998)

8 Cynics have claimed there are only six basic plots. *Frankenstein* and *My Fair Lady* are really the same story.

Leslie Halliwell (1929–89) British film critic. *Filmgoer's Book of Quotes* (1973)

9 There is no agony like bearing an untold story inside you.

Zora Neale Hurston (1891?–1960) US writer and folklorist. *Dust Tracks on a Road* (1942)

10 I am prepared with the confession that the 'ghost story', as we for convenience call it, has ever been for me the most possible form of the fairy tale.

Henry James (1843–1916) US-born British writer and critic. 'The Altar of the Dead', *Prefaces* (1909)

11 Are you sitting comfortably? Then I'll begin.

Julia S. Lang (b. 1921) British broadcaster. Introduction to the story in *Listen with Mother*, a BBC radio programme for children. *Listen with Mother* (BBC Radio; 1950–82)

12 Three years he had spent between fear and hope, death and expectation; three years spent in the telling of stories . . . Yet like everything, the stories had come to an end, had ended yesterday.

Naguib Mahfouz (b. 1911) Egyptian writer. Referring to the Arabian Nights, in which after one thousand and one nights of storytelling by Scheherazade in order to suspend her death sentence, the sultan Schahriar sets her free. The end to her storytelling is the premise of Mahfouz's novel. *Arabian Nights and Days* (1982)

13 In its earlier phases storytelling, like poetry and drama, was a public art . . . But the short story, like the novel, is a modern art form; that is to say, it represents, better than poetry or drama, our own attitude to life.

Frank O'Connor (1903–66) Irish writer. *The Lonely Voice: A Study of the Short Story* (1962), Introduction

14 In storytelling there is always transgression, and in all art. Without transgression, without the red boundary, there is no danger, no risk, no *frisson*, no experiment, no discovery, and no creativity.

Ben Okri (b. 1959) Nigerian novelist, short-story writer, and poet. *A Way of Being Free* (1997)

15 Storytellers are reorganisers of accepted reality, dreamers of alternative histories, disturbers of deceitful sleep.

Ben Okri (b. 1959) Nigerian novelist, short-story writer, and poet. *A Way of Being Free* (1997)

16 If the story is to live up to its ideal duty, it must go back at least all the way to the Big Bang, that cosmic orgasm with which, presumably, all smaller bangs began.

Amos Oz (b. 1939) Israeli writer. 1996. *The Story Begins* (Maggie Bar-Tura, tr.; 2000)

17 The seaman tells stories of winds, the ploughman of bulls; the soldier details his wounds, the shepherd his sheep.

Sextus Propertius (50?–15? BC) Roman poet. *Elegies* (1st century BC), bk. 2, no. 1, l. 43

18 'What are all these stories? Life is not a storybook or a joke shop. All this fun will come to no good. What's the use of stories that aren't even true?'

Salman Rushdie (b. 1947) Indian-born British novelist. Said by Mr. Sengupta to Soraya, the wife of the storyteller Rashid Khalifa. *Haroun and the Sea of Stories* (1990)

19 QUEEN ELIZABETH An honest tale speeds best being plainly told.

William Shakespeare (1564–1616) English poet and playwright. *Richard III* (1591), Act 4, Scene 4

20 'The story is like the wind', the Bushman prisoner said. 'It comes from a far off place, and we feel it'.

Laurens Van der Post (1906–96) South African novelist and anthropologist. *A Story like the Wind* (1972)

21 That ability to take leave of everything around me, to live in a world of fantasy, to recreate through imagination the make-believe stories that held me spellbound.

Mario Vargas Llosa (b. 1936) Peruvian writer. Quoted in *A Fish in the Water* (Helen Lane, tr.; 1994)

22 A story is a formula for extracting meaning from chaos, a handful of water we scoop up to recall an ocean.

John Edgar Wideman (b. 1941) US writer. *Breaking Ice: An Anthology of Contemporary African-American Fiction* (Terry McMillan, ed.; 1992)

St. Petersburg

see **European Cities**

Strangers

see also **Xenophobia**

1 Let brotherly love continue.
Be not forgetful to entertain strangers: for thereby some have entertained angels unawares.

Bible. Hebrews, *King James Bible* (1611), 13:1–2

2 She was always alone, always wearing the same toque, followed by the white pomeranian. No one knew who she was, and she became known simply as the lady with the lapdog.

Anton Chekhov (1860–1904) Russian playwright and short-story writer. 'Lady with Lapdog' (1899), sect. 1

3 Never fight fair with a stranger, boy. You'll never get out of the jungle that way.

Arthur Miller (b. 1915) US playwright. *Death of a Salesman* (1949), Act 1

4 I have always depended on the kindness of strangers.

Tennessee Williams (1911–83) US playwright. *A Streetcar Named Desire* (1947), Act 2, Scene 3

Stress

see also **Despair**, **Work**, **World-Weariness**

1 A well adjusted executive is one whose intake of pep pills overbalances his consumption of tranquillizers just enough to leave him sufficient energy for the weekly visit to the psychiatrist.

Arthur Motley (1900–84) US business executive. Quoted in *The Pyramid Builders* (Vance Packard; 1962)

2 Art thou weary, art thou languid,
Art thou sore distressed?

John Mason Neale (1818–66) English clergyman and hymnwriter. 'Art Thou Weary?' (1912?)

3 Stop the World, I Want to Get Off

Anthony Newley (1931–99) British actor, composer, and comedian. Musical title, co-written with Leslie Bricusse. (1961)

Stupidity

see also **Foolishness**, **Gullibility**, **Nonsense**

1 A silly remark can be made in Latin as well as in Spanish.

Miguel de Cervantes (1547–1616) Spanish novelist and playwright. *The Dialogue of the Dogs* (1613)

2 That fellow seems to me to possess but one idea, and that is a wrong one.

Samuel Johnson (1709–84) British lexicographer and writer. 1770. Referring to 'a dull tiresome fellow, whom he chanced to meet'. Quoted in *Life of Samuel Johnson* (James Boswell; 1791)

3 Even stupidity is the product of highly organized matter.

Milan Kundera (b. 1929) Czech novelist. Quoted in *Shedding Life* (Miroslav Holub; 1997)

4 Just as the meanest and most vicious deeds require spirit and talent, so even the greatest deeds require a certain insensitiveness which on other occasions is called stupidity.

Georg Christoph Lichtenberg (1742–99) German physicist and writer. *Aphorisms* (1764–99)

5 You've got the brain of a four-year-old boy, and I bet he was glad to get rid of it.

Groucho Marx (1895–1977) US comedian and film actor. *Horse Feathers* (Bert Kalmar, Harry Ruby, S. J. Perelman, and Will B. Johnstone; 1932)

6 It is a stupidity second to none, to busy oneself with the correction of the world.

Molière (1622–73) French playwright. *Le Misanthrope* (1666), Act 1, Scene 1

7 Stupidity does not consist in being without ideas. Such stupidity would be the sweet, blissful stupidity of animals, molluscs, and the gods. Human Stupidity consists in having lots of ideas, but stupid ones.

Henri de Montherlant (1896–1972) French novelist and playwright. *Notebooks* (1930–44)

8 I've examined your son's head, Mr Glum, and there's nothing there.

Frank Muir (1920–98) British writer and broadcaster. *Take It from Here* (with Dennis Norden; 1957)

9 It is only one step from the sublime to the ridiculous.

Napoleon I (1769–1821) French emperor. Following the retreat from Moscow. Remark to the Abbé de Pradt, the Polish ambassador (1812), quoted in *Histoire de l'Ambassade dans le Grand-duché de Varsovie en 1812* (D. G. de Pradt; 1815)

10 As soon as he ceased to be mad he became merely stupid. There are maladies we must not seek to cure because they alone protect us from others that are more serious.

Marcel Proust (1871–1922) French novelist. 1921. Le Côté de Guermantes, *À la Recherche du Temps Perdu* (1913–27)

11 The trouble with the world is that the stupid are cocksure and the intelligent full of doubt.

Bertrand Russell (1872–1970) British philosopher and mathematician. *The Autobiography of Bertrand Russell* (1967–69)

12 Against stupidity the gods themselves struggle in vain.

Friedrich von Schiller (1759–1805) German poet, playwright, and historian. *The Maid of Orleans* (1801), Act 3, Scene 6

13 No man can be a pure specialist without being in the strict sense an idiot.

George Bernard Shaw (1856–1950) Irish playwright. Attrib.

Style

see also **Artistic Styles**, **Design**, **Literary Style**

1 Style is the man himself.

Comte de Buffon (1707–88) French naturalist. Speech given on his reception to the French Academy. 'Discourse on Style' (August 25, 1753)

2 It is the beginning of the end when you discover you have style.

Dashiell Hammett (1894–1961) US detective-story writer. Quoted in *Smithsonian* (May 1994)

3 Style in architecture is the peculiar form that expression takes under the influence of climate and materials at command.

Owen Jones (1809–74) British architect. *The Grammar of Ornament* (1856)

4 Hip is the sophistication of the wise primitive in a giant jungle.

Norman Mailer (b. 1923) US novelist and journalist. 'The White Negro', *Voices of Dissent* (1959)

5 My lapels were crimson, my shoes yellow suede. I had a light buzz on and my new Chrysler floated down the side streets like a yacht down some inland canals.

Walter Mosley (b. 1952) US novelist. *White Butterfly* (1992), ch. 8

6 Style is beginning something in the manner which will make it necessary for things that happen later to happen.

Mike Nichols (b. 1931) German-born US stage and film director. *Film Comment* (May 1991)

7 What a great many people still don't realize is that the Look isn't just the garments you wear. It's the way you put your make-up on, the way you do your hair, the sort of stockings you choose, the way you walk and stand; even the way you smoke your fag.

Mary Quant (b. 1934) British fashion designer. *Quant by Quant* (1966)

8 Camp is a vision of the world in terms of style— but a particular style. It is the love of the exaggerated.

Susan Sontag (b. 1933) US writer. 'Notes on Camp', *Against Interpretation* (1966)

9 All styles are good except the tiresome sort.

Voltaire (1694–1778) French writer and philosopher. *L'Enfant Prodigue* (1738), Preface

10 In matters of grave importance, style, not
sincerity, is the vital thing.
Oscar Wilde (1854–1900) Irish poet, playwright, and wit. *The Importance of Being Earnest* (1895), Act 3

Subjectivity

see also **Individuality**, **The Self**

1 Subjectivity and objectivity commit a series of
assaults on each other during a human life out of
which the first one suffers the worse beating.
André Breton (1896–1966) French writer. *Nadja* (1928), Preface

2 Feeling is the subjective side of consciousness,
knowledge its objective side. Will is the relation
between the subjective and the objective.
John Dewey (1859–1952) US philosopher and educator. *Psychology* (1887)

3 Every man takes the limits of his own field of
vision for the limits of the world.
Arthur Schopenhauer (1788–1860) German philosopher. 'Psychological Observations', *Studies in Pessimism* (1851)

Success

see also **Achievement**, **Glory**, **Victory**

1 Success is man's god.
Aeschylus (525?–456 BC) Greek tragedian and dramatist. *The Libation Bearers* (458 BC)

2 I'm short enough and ugly enough to succeed on
my own.
Woody Allen (b. 1935) US film actor and director. *Play It Again, Sam* (1972)

3 A minute's success pays the failure of years.
Robert Browning (1812–89) British poet. 'Apollo and the Fates' (1886), st. 42

4 Success is counted sweetest
By those who ne'er succeed.
Emily Dickinson (1830–86) US poet. No. 67 (1859?), st. 1, ll. 1–2, quoted in *The Complete Works of Emily Dickinson* (Thomas H. Johnson, ed.; 1970)

5 Success is relative. It is what we can make of the
mess we have made of things.
T. S. Eliot (1888–1965) US-born British poet and playwright. *The Family Reunion* (1939), Act 2, Scene 3

6 Success never satisfies me. Success is almost
always a momentary stroke of luck that has
nothing to do with a given work's intrinsic value.
Federico García Lorca (1899–1936) Spanish poet and playwright. Quoted in *A Dream of Life* (Leslie Stainton; 1998)

7 Most success comes from ignoring the obvious.
Trevor Holdsworth (b. 1927) British business executive. Quoted in *The New Elite* (Berry Ritchie and Walter Goldsmith; 1987)

8 The shortest and best way to make your fortune
is to let people see clearly that it is in their
interests to promote yours.
Jean de La Bruyère (1645–96) French essayist and moralist. *Characters, or the Manners of the Age* (1688)

9 To succeed in the world, we do everything we
can to appear successful.
François La Rochefoucauld (1613–80) French epigrammatist and moralist. *Reflections, or Sentences and Moral Maxims* (1665), no. 50

10 The Sweet Smell of Success
Ernest Lehman (b. 1915) US screenwriter. 1957. Novel and film title.

11 Often, the outward and visible material signs and
symbols of happiness and success only show
themselves when the process of decline has
already set in.
Thomas Mann (1875–1955) German writer. 1901. *Buddenbrooks: The Decline of a Family* (H. T. Lowe-Porter, tr.; 1924), pt. 7, ch. 6

12 Nothing fails like success; nothing is so defeated
as yesterday's triumphant Cause.
Phyllis McGinley (1905–78) US poet. 'How to Get Along with Men', *The Province of the Heart* (1959)

13 Keep looking tanned, live in an elegant building
(even if you're in the cellar), be seen in smart
restaurants (even if you nurse one drink), and if
you borrow, borrow big.
Aristotle Onassis (1900?–75) Turkish-born Greek shipping magnate. Referring to the secret of success. Quoted in *Times* (August 15, 1986)

14 Nothing is harder on your laurels than resting on
them.
Proverb.

15 To succeed you have to believe in something with
such a passion that it becomes a reality.
Anita Roddick (b. 1942) British business executive. *Body and Soul* (1991)

16 The only place where success comes before work
is a dictionary.
Vidal Sassoon (b. 1928) British hair stylist. Quoting one of his teachers in a BBC radio broadcast.

17 The winner is simply someone who gets up one
more time than they fall over.
Robin Sieger, British business executive. *Natural Born Winners* (1999)

18 Success to me is having ten honeydew melons
and eating only the top half of each one.
Barbra Streisand (b. 1942) US singer, film actor, director, and producer. *Life* (September 20, 1963)

19 It is not enough to succeed. Others must fail.
Gore Vidal (b. 1925) US novelist and essayist. *Antipanegyric for Tom Driberg* (G. Irvine; 1976)

20 The only way to succeed is to make people hate
you. That way, they remember you.
Josef Von Sternberg (1894–1969) Austrian-born US film director. *Fun in a Chinese Laundry* (1965)

21 I have learned that success is to be measured not
so much by the position that one has reached in
life as by the obstacles which he has had to
overcome while trying to succeed.
Booker T. Washington (1856–1915) US educator and political activist. *Up from Slavery* (1901)

22 I started at the top and worked my way down.
Orson Welles (1915–85) US actor, director, producer, and writer. Attrib.

Suffering

see also **Illness**, **Pain**

1 It is infinitely easier to suffer in obedience to a
human command than to accept suffering as free,
responsible men.
Dietrich Bonhoeffer (1906–45) German theologian. 1943–44. *Letters and Papers from Prison* (Eberhard Bethge, ed.; 1981)

2 There is no point in being overwhelmed by the
appalling total of human suffering; such a total
does not exist. Neither poverty nor pain is
accumulable.
Jorge Luis Borges (1899–1986) Argentinian writer and poet. 'A New Refutation of Time', *Other Inquisitions, 1937–52* (1952)

3 What deep wounds ever closed without a scar?

Lord Byron (1788–1824) British poet. *Childe Harold's Pilgrimage* (1812–18), can. 3, l. 787

4 In trouble to be troubled
Is to have your trouble doubled.

Daniel Defoe (1660–1731) English novelist and journalist. 1719. *The Farther Adventures of Robinson Crusoe* (G. Aitkin, ed.; 1895)

5 Well may I say my life has been
One scene of sorrow and of pain;
From early days I griefs have known,
And as I grew my griefs have grown.

Olaudah Equiano (1745?–97) African-born British former slave. *The Interesting Narrative of the Life of Olaudah Equiano, or Gustavus Vassa* (1789)

6 If suffer we must, let's suffer on the heights.

Victor Hugo (1802–85) French poet, novelist, and playwright. 'Les Malheureux', *Contemplations* (1856), bk. 5, no. 26

7 Pity is the feeling which arrests the mind in the presence of whatsoever is grave and constant in human sufferings and unites it with the human sufferer. Terror is the feeling which arrests the mind in the presence of whatsoever is grave and constant in human sufferings and unites it with the secret cause.

James Joyce (1882–1941) Irish writer. *A Portrait of the Artist as a Young Man* (1916), ch. 5

8 *The Two Ways.* One is to suffer, the other is to become a professor of the fact that another suffered.

Søren Kierkegaard (1813–55) Danish philosopher. Journal, *The Journals of Søren Kierkegaard* (Alexander Dru, tr.; 1938)

9 Rather suffer than die is man's motto.

Jean de La Fontaine (1621–95) French writer and poet. 'La Mort et le Bûcheron', *Fables* (1668), bk. 1

10 I am only half there when I am ill, and so there is only half a man to suffer. To suffer in one's whole self is so great a violation, that it is not to be endured.

D. H. Lawrence (1885–1930) British writer. Letter to Catherine Carswell (April 16, 1916)

11 He preferred suffering in freedom to all the happiness of a comfortable servility. He did not care to serve God. He cared to serve nothing. He was no figure-head. He stood on his own legs. He was an individual.

Jack London (1876–1916) US writer. Referring to Wolf Larsen. *The Sea-Wolf* (1904)

12 Know how sublime a thing it is
To suffer and be strong.

Henry Wadsworth Longfellow (1807–82) US poet. 'The Light of Stars in Knickerbocker' (1839)

13 Purgatory is not to be confused with hell, which is an eternal shipwreck. Purgatory is a pawnshop which lends out against all virtues on short terms and at high interest.

Joaquim Maria Machado de Assis (1839–1908) Brazilian novelist and short-story writer. *Dom Casmurro* (1899)

14 I knew that suffering did not ennoble; it degraded. It made men selfish, mean, petty and suspicious. It absorbed them in small things . . . it made them less than men.

Somerset Maugham (1874–1965) British writer. *The Summing Up* (1938)

15 Our torments also may in length of time
Become our elements.

John Milton (1608–74) English writer. Said by Mammon. *Paradise Lost* (1667), bk. 2, ll. 274–275

16 A man who fears suffering is already suffering from what he fears.

Michel de Montaigne (1533–92) French essayist. *Essays* (1580–88), bk. 3

17 The mind grows sicker than the body in contemplation of its suffering.

Ovid (43 BC–AD 17?) Roman poet. *Tristia* (AD 9), bk. 4

18 And taste
The melancholy joy of evils past:
For he who much has suffer'd, much will know.

Alexander Pope (1688–1744) English poet. *The Odyssey of Homer* (1725), bk. 15, ll. 434–436

19 Who breathes must suffer, and who thinks must mourn;
And he alone is bless'd who ne'er was born.

Matthew Prior (1664–1721) English diplomat and poet. 'Solomon on the Vanity of the World' (1718), bk. 2, ll. 240–241

20 It is certain that we cannot overcome anguish, for we are anguish.

Jean-Paul Sartre (1905–80) French philosopher, playwright, and novelist. *Being and Nothingness* (1943)

21 If the immediate and direct purpose of our life is not suffering then our existence is the most ill-adapted to its purpose in the world.

Arthur Schopenhauer (1788–1860) German philosopher. *Parerga and Paralipomena* (1851)

22 LEAR Take physic, pomp;
Expose thyself to feel what wretches feel.

William Shakespeare (1564–1616) English poet and playwright. *King Lear* (1605–06), Act 3, Scene 4

23 GLOUCESTER O ruin'd piece of nature! This great world
Should so wear out to nought.

William Shakespeare (1564–1616) English poet and playwright. *King Lear* (1605–06), Act 4, Scene 6

24 LEAR Thou art a soul in bliss; but I am bound
Upon a wheel of fire, that mine own tears
Do scald like molten lead.

William Shakespeare (1564–1616) English poet and playwright. On waking to find Cordelia at his bedside. *King Lear* (1605–06), Act 4, Scene 7

25 Oh! When I have the gout, I feel as if I was walking on my eyeballs.

Sydney Smith (1771–1845) British clergyman, essayist, and wit. Quoted in *A Memoir of the Rev. Sydney Smith* (Lady Holland; 1855), ch. 11

26 Suffering is, in effect, the barrier which unconsciousness, matter, sets up against consciousness, spirit; it is the resistance to will, the limit which the visible universe imposes upon God.

Miguel de Unamuno y Jugo (1864–1936) Spanish writer and philosopher. Quoted in *Keeping a Rendezvous* (John Berger; 1991)

27 I love the majesty of human suffering.

Alfred de Vigny (1797–1863) French poet, novelist, and playwright. *La Maison du Berger* (1844)

Suicide

see also Death and Dying

1 If I had the use of my body I would throw it out of the window.

Samuel Beckett (1906–89) Irish playwright, novelist, and poet. *Malone Dies* (1951)

2 If you must commit suicide . . . always contrive to do it as decorously as possible; the decencies, whether of life or of death, should never be lost sight of.
George Henry Borrow (1803–81) British writer and traveller. *Lavengro* (1851), ch. 23

3 As soon as one does not kill oneself, one must keep silent about life.
Albert Camus (1913–60) Algerian-born French novelist, essayist, and playwright. *Notebooks* (1935–42)

4 There is but one truly serious philosophical problem, and that is suicide. Judging whether life is, or is not worth living amounts to answering the fundamental question of philosophy.
Albert Camus (1913–60) Algerian-born French novelist, essayist, and playwright. *The Myth of Sisyphus* (1942)

5 The strangest whim has seized me . . . After all I think I will not hang myself today.
G. K. Chesterton (1874–1936) British writer and poet. 'A Ballade of Suicide' (1915)

6 There are many who dare not kill themselves for fear of what the neighbours might say.
Cyril Connolly (1903–74) British writer and journalist. *The Unquiet Grave* (1944)

7 The prevalence of suicide is a test of height in civilization; it means that the population is winding up its nervous and intellectual system to the utmost point of tension and that sometimes it snaps.
Havelock Ellis (1859–1939) British psychologist. *The Dance of Life* (1923)

8 However great a man's fear of life . . . suicide remains the courageous act, the clear-headed act of a mathematician. The suicide has judged by the laws of chance—so many odds against one, that to live will be more miserable than to die. His sense of mathematics is greater than his sense of survival.
Graham Greene (1904–91) British novelist. Said by Dr. Magiot. *The Comedians* (1966), pt. 1, ch. 4, sect. 1

9 Done because we are too menny.
Thomas Hardy (1840–1928) British novelist and poet. Suicide note of Jude's son. *Jude the Obscure* (1895), pt. 6, ch. 2

10 I take it that no man is educated who has never dallied with the thought of suicide.
William James (1842–1910) US psychologist and philosopher. Attrib.

11 Except for World War II, nothing ever interfered with the celebration of National Suicide Day.
Toni Morrison (b. 1931) US novelist. *Sula* (1973)

12 The thought of suicide is a great source of comfort: with it a calm passage is to be made across many a bad night.
Friedrich Wilhelm Nietzsche (1844–1900) German philosopher and poet. *Beyond Good and Evil* (1886)

13 You fellows, in your business, you have a way of handling problems like this. Somebody leaves a pistol in the drawer. I don't have a pistol.
Richard Nixon (1913–94) US president. August 7, 1974. Said to General Alexander Haig. Nixon resigned two days later. Quoted in *Final Days* (Bob Woodward and Carl Bernstein; 1976)

14 No one ever lacks a good reason for suicide.
Cesare Pavese (1908–50) Italian novelist and poet. Quoted in *The Savage God* (A. Alvarez; 1971)

15 Amid the miseries of our life on earth, suicide is God's best gift to man.
Pliny the Elder (23?–79) Roman scholar. *Natural History* (77), bk. 2

16 When you're between any sort of devil and the deep blue sea, the deep blue sea sometimes looks very inviting.
Terence Rattigan (1911–77) British playwright. *The Deep Blue Sea* (1952)

17 How many people have wanted to kill themselves, and have been contented with tearing up their photograph!
Jules Renard (1864–1910) French writer. December 29, 1888. *Journal* (1877–1910)

18 CAESAR She hath pursu'd conclusions infinite Of easy ways to die.
William Shakespeare (1564–1616) English poet and playwright. *Antony and Cleopatra* (1606–07), Act 5, Scene 2

19 HAMLET To be, or not to be—that is the question;
Whether 'tis nobler in the mind to suffer
The slings and arrows of outrageous fortune,
Or to take arms against a sea of troubles,
And by opposing end them? To die, to sleep—
No more; and by a sleep to say we end
The heart-ache and the thousand natural shocks
That flesh is heir to, 'tis a consummation
Devoutly to be wish'd. To die, to sleep;
To sleep, perchance to dream. Ay, there's the rub;
For in that sleep of death what dreams may come,
When we have shuffled off this mortal coil,
Must give us pause.
William Shakespeare (1564–1616) English poet and playwright. *Hamlet* (1601), Act 3, Scene 1

20 I find I am but a bad anatomist.
Wolfe Tone (1763–98) Irish nationalist. November 12, 1798. Whispered to his doctor after slashing his windpipe instead of jugular. Attrib.

21 If nothing else, suicide really *validates*, to use lit-crit's ultimate verb, the life if not the poetry . . . Death and then—triumphant transfiguration as A Cautionary Tale.
Gore Vidal (b. 1925) US novelist and essayist. 'Tennessee Williams: Someone to Laugh at the Squares With', *Armageddon* (1987)

22 There is no refuge from confession but suicide; and suicide is confession.
Daniel Webster (1782–1852) US lawyer, politician, and orator. April 6, 1830. Said at the trial of John Francis Knapp for the murder of Captain Joseph White. Quoted in *The Writings and Speeches of Daniel Webster* (J. W. McIntyre, ed.; 1903), vol. 11

23 Dearest, I feel certain that I am going mad again: I feel we can't go through another of those terrible times. And I shan't recover this time. I begin to hear voices, and can't concentrate. So I am doing what seems the best thing to do . . . If anybody could have saved me it would have been you.
Virginia Woolf (1882–1941) British novelist and critic. She was subject to bouts of severe depression that culminated in her suicide by drowning after completing *Between the Acts*. Suicide note addressed to her husband, Leonard Woolf (March 28, 1941)

Summer

see also **Seasons**

1 All the live murmur of a summer's day.
Matthew Arnold (1822–88) British poet and critic. 'The Scholar-Gipsy' (1853), l. 20

2 Summer has set in with its usual severity.

Samuel Taylor Coleridge (1772–1834) British poet. Letter to Vincent Novello (May 9, 1826), quoted in *Letters of Charles Lamb* (Alfred Ainger, ed.; 1888), vol. 2

3 Sumer is icumen in,
Lhude sing cuccu!
Groweth sed, and bloweth med,
And springth the wude nu.

Folk Verse. 'Cuckoo Song' (1250?)

4 Summertime
And the livin' is easy.

Ira Gershwin (1896–1983) US lyricist. Song lyric. 'Summertime', *Porgy and Bess* (1935)

5 Summer afternoon—summer afternoon; to me those have always been the two most beautiful words in the English language.

Henry James (1843–1916) US-born British writer and critic. Quoted in *A Backward Glance* (Edith Wharton; 1934)

6 In a somer seson, whan softe was the sonne.

William Langland (1330?–1400?) English poet. Opening line. *The Vision of Piers Plowman* (1365–86), Prologue, l. 1

7 One swallowe prouveth not that summer is neare.

John Northbrooke (fl. 1570) English preacher. *Treatise Against Dancing* (1577)

8 The way to ensure summer in England is to have it framed and glazed in a comfortable room.

Horace Walpole (1717–97) British writer. Letter to Rev. William Cole (May 28, 1774), quoted in *Correspondence* (Yale edn.), vol. 1

The Sun

see also **Astronomy, The Universe**

1 The sun shone, having no alternative, on the nothing new.

Samuel Beckett (1906–89) Irish playwright, novelist, and poet. *Murphy* (1938), ch. 1

2 When the Sun shrinks to a dull red dwarf, it will not be dying. It will just be starting to live—and everything that has gone before will be merely a fleeting prelude to its real history.

Arthur C. Clarke (b. 1917) British writer and scientist. *By Space Possessed* (1993)

3 Mother, give me the sun.

Henrik Ibsen (1828–1906) Norwegian playwright. *Ghosts* (1881), Act 3

4 In the sky, red as the Marseillaise,
shuddering in its death throes, the sunset died.

Vladimir Mayakovsky (1893–1930) Russian poet and playwright. *A Cloud in Trousers* (1914–15), sect. 3, quoted in *Mayakovsky* (Herbert Marshall, ed., tr.; 1965)

5 The sun has only memory of flame
and for centuries has watched
the earth dance like a clown
upon one foot,
someday it will drop and die,
laughing laughing madly.

Anna Sujartha Modayil (b. 1934) Indian poet. 'On the Beach at Baga', *The Voice of the Indian Poets* (Pranab Bandyopadhyay, ed.; 1975)

6 If sunbeams were weapons of war, we would have had solar energy long ago.

George Porter (b. 1920) British chemist. *Observer* (August 26, 1973), 'Sayings of the Week'

7 There is a project for the sun. The sun
Must bear no name, gold flourisher, but be,
In the difficulty of what it is to be.

Wallace Stevens (1879–1955) US poet. 'Notes Toward a Supreme Fiction', *Selected Poems* (1955)

8 Flaunt of the sunshine I need not your bask—lie over!

Walt Whitman (1819–92) US poet. *Leaves of Grass* (1855), st. 40

9 A boy I loved the sun, . . .
Not for his bounty to so many worlds—
But for this cause, that I had seen him lay
His beauty on the morning hills, had seen
The western mountain touch his setting orb.

William Wordsworth (1770–1850) English poet. *The Prelude* (1850), bk. 2

The Supernatural

see also **Horror, Magic, Myths, Wonder**

1 The idea of walking through walls frankly revolted him. It was something he had been trying strenuously to avoid all night.

Douglas Adams (1952–2001) British writer. *Dirk Gently's Holistic Detective Agency* (1993), ch. 15

2 In the same hour came forth fingers of a man's hand, and wrote over against the candlestick upon the plaister of the wall of the king's palace: and the king saw the part of the hand that wrote.

Bible. Daniel, *King James Bible* (1611), 5:5

3 Those apparitions and ghosts of departed persons are not the wandering souls of men, but the unquiet walks of Devils, prompting and suggesting unto mischief, blood, and villainy.

Thomas Browne (1605–82) English physician and writer. *Religio Medici* (1643)

4 'Man of the worldly mind!' replied the Ghost, 'do you believe in me or not?' 'I do', said Scrooge. 'I must'.

Charles Dickens (1812–70) British novelist. *A Christmas Carol* (1843)

5 One need not be a Chamber—to be Haunted—
One need not be a House—
The Brain has Corridors-surpassing
Material Place—
Far safer, of a Midnight Meeting
External Ghost
Than its interior Confronting—
That Cooler Host.

Emily Dickinson (1830–86) US poet. 'One Need Not Be a Chamber'

6 Death, the best of all mysteries.

Douglas Dunn (b. 1942) British poet and critic. 'Supreme Death' (1972)

7 "I never see'd a ghost myself, but then I says to myself, 'Very like I haven't got the smell for 'em'."

George Eliot (1819–80) British novelist. Landlord's comment. *Silas Marner* (1861)

8 One mode of the divine teaching is the incarnation of the spirit in a form—in forms, like my own.

Ralph Waldo Emerson (1803–82) US poet and essayist. Referring to divine inspiration. 'The Over-Soul', *Essays* (1841)

9   From ghoulies and ghosties and long-leggety
    beasties
    And things that go bump in the night,
    Good Lord, deliver us!

    Folk Verse. Cornish prayer

10 Where evidence takes a supernatural character,
    there is no disproving it.

    Elizabeth Gaskell (1810–65) British novelist. The story is set in Salem,
    Massachusetts, in 1692. 'Lois the Witch' (1859)

11 In this hamlet a man, or rather the devil in
    human form, often made his appearance. Why he
    came, and whence, no one knew. He prowled
    about, got drunk, and suddenly disappeared as if
    into the air, leaving no trace of his existence.

    Nikolay Gogol (1809–52) Russian novelist and playwright. St. John's Eve
    (C. J. Hogarth, tr.; 1830)

12 'I hear the piano playing—
    Just as a ghost might play'.
    —'O, but what are you saying?
    There's no piano today;
    The old one was sold and broken;
    Years past it went amiss'.
    —'I heard it, or shouldn't have spoken;
    A strange house, this!'

    Thomas Hardy (1840–1928) British novelist and poet. 'The Strange
    House' (1914)

13 How loathe were we to give up our pious belief
    in ghosts and witches, because we liked to
    persecute one and frighten ourselves to death
    with the other.

    William Hazlitt (1778–1830) British essayist and critic. 'On the
    Pleasure of Hating', The Plain Speaker (1826)

14 To end up in a draughty lamplit station
    After the trains have gone, the wet track
    Bared and tense as I am, all attention
    For your step following and damned if I look back.

    Seamus Heaney (b. 1939) Irish poet. The step following is that of
    James Joyce's ghost. 'The Underground', Station Island (1984)

15 If after our death they want to transform us into
    a tiny withered flame that walks along the paths
    of winds—we have to rebel.

    Zbigniew Herbert (b. 1924) Polish poet and essayist. 'Anything Rather
    than an Angel' (Czeslaw Milosz, tr.; 1961)

16 Not as we are but as we must appear,
    Contractual ghosts of pity; not as we
    Desire life but as they would have us live,
    Set apart in timeless colloquy.

    Geoffrey Hill (b. 1932) British poet. 'Funeral Music' is a sequence
    about the Wars of the Roses (1455–85). 'Funeral Music',
    King Log (1968), sonnet B

17 It was like fighting with a demon for a human soul.

    Henry James (1843–1916) US-born British writer and critic. Said by the
    governess, upon confronting the ghost of Peter Quint. The
    Turn of the Screw (1898)

18 A horrible, an intensely horrible face of crumpled
    linen.

    M. R. James (1862–1936) British writer and scholar. 1904. Description
    of an apparition. 'Oh, Whistle and I'll Come to You, My
    Lad', Collected Ghost Stories (1992)

19 It is wonderful that five thousand years have now
    elapsed since the creation of the world, and still
    it is undecided whether or not there has ever
    been an instance of the spirit of any person
    appearing after death. All argument is against it,
    but all belief is for it.

    Samuel Johnson (1709–84) British lexicographer and writer. March 31,
    1778. Quoted in Life of Samuel Johnson (James Boswell; 1791)

20 You've obviously never spoken to a ghost. You'll
    never get a straight answer out of one of them.

    Franz Kafka (1883–1924) Czech writer. 'Unhappiness'
    (J. A. Underwood, tr.; 1913)

21 We were afraid of the dead because we never
    could tell when they might show up again.

    Jamaica Kincaid (b. 1949) Antiguan-born US novelist, short-story writer,
    and journalist. Annie John (1986)

22 I believe there is an unseen world all around us.

    Stephen King (b. 1947) US novelist. Nightmares and Dreamscapes
    (1993), Introduction

23 There are terrible spirits, ghosts, in the air of
    America.

    D. H. Lawrence (1885–1930) British writer. Edgar Allan Poe (1924)

24 All houses wherein men have lived and died
    Are haunted houses. Through the open doors
    The harmless phantoms on their errands glide,
    With feet that make no sound upon the floors.

    Henry Wadsworth Longfellow (1807–82) US poet. 'Haunted Houses' (1858)

25 Many devils are in woods, in waters, in
    wildernesses, and in dark pooly places . . . some
    are also in the thick black clouds . . . the
    philosophers and physicians say, it is natural,
    ascribing it to the planets, and showing I know
    not what reasons for such misfortunes and
    plagues as ensue.

    Martin Luther (1483–1546) German theologian and religious reformer.
    Quoted in Table Talk (William Hazlitt, tr.; 1821–22)

26 The wind was a torrent of darkness among the
    gusty trees,
    The moon was a ghostly galleon tossed upon
    cloudy seas,
    The road was a ribbon of moonlight over the
    purple moor,
    And the highwayman came riding—
    Riding—riding—
    The highwayman came riding, up to the old inn-
    door.

    Alfred Noyes (1880–1958) British poet. 'The Highwayman' (1907)

27 I am the ghost of Shadwell Stair.
    Along the wharves by the water-house,
    And through the dripping slaughter-house,
    I am the shadow that walks there.

    Wilfred Owen (1893–1918) British poet. 'Shadwell Stair' (1918)

28 From hazy progs and flesh-pots half afloat, from
    bowls as big as baths, there rises and drifts like a
    miasmic tide the all but palpable odour of the
    day's belly-timber.

    Mervyn Peake (1911–68) British novelist, poet, and artist. Referring to
    Swelter's ghost. Gormenghast (1950), ch. 1

29 Phantoms in general are nothing more than
    trifling disorders of the spirit: images we cannot
    contain within the bounds of sleep.

    Luigi Pirandello (1867–1936) Italian dramatist, novelist, and short-story
    writer. Henry IV (Edward Storer, tr.; 1922)

30 In an instant I seemed to rise from the ground.
    But I had no bodily, no visible, audible, or
    palpable presence.

    Edgar Allan Poe (1809–49) US poet and writer. 'Tale of the Ragged
    Mountains', Tales of Mystery and Imagination (1839)

31 In a dark wood I saw
    I saw my several selves
    Come running from the leaves,
    Lewd, tiny, careless lives
    That scuttled under stones,
    Or broke, but would not go.

    Theodore Roethke (1908–63) US poet. 'The Exorcism' (1958)

32 If there is in the world one attested story it is that of the Vampires.

Jean-Jacques Rousseau (1712–78) French philosopher and writer. Letter to Christophe de Beaumont, Archbishop of Paris (1763)

33 There is nothing impossible in the existence of the supernatural: its existence seems to me to be decidedly probable.

George Santayana (1863–1952) Spanish-born US philosopher, poet, and novelist. *The Genteel Tradition at Bay* (1931)

34 BRUTUS Speak to me what thou art.
GHOST Thy evil spirit, Brutus.
BRUTUS Why com'st thou?
GHOST To tell thee thou shalt see me at Philippi.

William Shakespeare (1564–1616) English poet and playwright. Caesar's ghost appears to Brutus. Brutus later commits suicide at Philippi, having been defeated in battle by Mark Antony and Gaius Octavius, who became Emperor Augustus. *Julius Caesar* (1599), Act 4, Scene 3

35 His eyes flamed red with devilish passion; the great nostrils of the white aquiline nose opened wide and quivered at the edges; and the white sharp teeth, behind the full lips of the blood-dripping mouth; champed together like those of a wild beast . . . Further and further back he cowered, as we, lifting our crucifixes, advanced.

Bram Stoker (1845–1912) Irish-born British writer. *Dracula* (1897), ch. 21

36 I read the other day in a book by a fashionable essayist that ghosts went out when the electric light came in. What nonsense!

Edith Wharton (1862–1937) US novelist. *All Souls* (1937)

37 I saw battle-corpses, myriads of them,
And the white skeletons of young men, I saw them.

Walt Whitman (1819–92) US poet. 1865. Composed after the assassination of Abraham Lincoln (April 14, 1865). 'When Lilacs Last in the Dooryard Bloom'd', *Sequel to Drum-Taps* (1866)

38 Some element of the supernatural is so constant in poetry that one has come to look upon it as part of the normal fabric of the art, but in poetry, being etherealized, it scarcely evokes any emotion as gross as fear.

Virginia Woolf (1882–1941) British novelist and critic. Referring to Dorothy Scarborough's *The Supernatural in Modern English Fiction* (1917). Review, *The Supernatural in Fiction* (1918)

39 Fifteen apparitions have I seen;
The worst a coat upon a coat-hanger.

W. B. Yeats (1865–1939) Irish poet and playwright. 'The Apparitions', *Last Poems* (1936–39)

Survival

see also **Evolution, Extinction**

1 People are inexterminable—like flies and bed-bugs. There will always be some that survive in cracks and crevices—that's us.

Robert Frost (1874–1963) US poet. *Observer* (March 29, 1959)

2 The perpetual struggle for room and food.

Thomas Malthus (1766–1834) British clergyman and economist. *Essay on the Principle of Population* (1798), ch. 3

3 I feel like a fugitive from th' law of averages.

Bill Mauldin (b. 1921) US cartoonist. Cartoon caption. *Up Front* (1944)

4 When you get to the end of your rope, tie a knot and hang on.

Franklin D. Roosevelt (1882–1945) US president. Attrib.

5 Our loyalties are to the species and the planet. We speak for Earth. Our obligation to survive is owed not just to ourselves but also to that cosmos, ancient and vast, from which we spring.

Carl Sagan (1934–96) US astronomer and writer. *Cosmos* (1980)

6 If it is 'utopian' to want to survive, then it is 'realistic' to want to be dead.

Jonathan Schell (b. 1943) US author. *The Fate of the Earth* (1982)

7 The thing-in-itself, the will-to-live, exists whole and undivided in every being, even in the tiniest; it is present as completely as in all that ever were, are, and will be, taken together.

Arthur Schopenhauer (1788–1860) German philosopher. *Parerga and Paralipomena* (1851)

8 To preserve a man alive in the midst of so many chances and hostilities, is as great a miracle as to create him.

Jeremy Taylor (1613–67) English theologian. *The Rules and Exercises of Holy Dying* (1651)

9 Rejected by mankind, the condemned do not go so far as to reject it in turn. Their faith in history remains unshaken . . . They do not despair. The proof: they persist in surviving not only to survive, but to testify . . . The victims elect to become witnesses.

Elie Wiesel (b. 1928) Romanian-born US writer. Referring to the Holocaust. *One Generation After* (B. M. Mooyart, tr.; 1970)

10 One can survive everything nowadays, except death.

Oscar Wilde (1854–1900) Irish poet, playwright, and wit. *A Woman of No Importance* (1893), Act 1

Suspicion

see also **Doubt, Guilt**

1 The lion and the calf shall lie down together but the calf won't get much sleep.

Woody Allen (b. 1935) US film actor and director. 'The Scrolls', *Without Feathers* (1976)

2 Suspicions amongst thoughts are like bats amongst birds, they ever fly by twilight.

Francis Bacon (1561–1626) English philosopher, statesman, and lawyer. 'Of Suspicion', *Essays* (1625)

3 OTHELLO By heaven, he echoes me,
As if there were some monster in his thought
Too hideous to be shown.

William Shakespeare (1564–1616) English poet and playwright. *Othello* (1602–04), Act 3, Scene 3

4 An ally has to be watched just like an enemy.

Leon Trotsky (1879–1940) Russian revolutionary leader. Attrib. *Expansion and Coexistence* (A. Ulam; 1941)

5 The great suspicion:
without exaggeration there is no landscape;
without labyrinth there is no rigor; without luxury there is no writing.

José-Miguel Ullán (b. 1944) Spanish artist and writer. Untitled, *A Bilingual Anthology of Contemporary Spanish Poetry* (Luis A. Ramos-García, ed.; 1997)

6 Distrust that man who tells you to distrust.

Ella Wheeler Wilcox (1850–1919) US poet. Attrib.

Sweden

see **Europe, European Countries**

Switzerland

see **Europe, European Countries**

Sycophancy

see also **Flattery, Praise**

1   A rich man's joke is always funny.

    Thomas Edward Brown (1830–97) British schoolteacher and poet. 'The Doctor' (1887)

2   I am always of the opinion with the learned, if they speak first.

    William Congreve (1670–1729) English playwright and poet. *Incognita* (1692)

3   King of the perennial holly-groves, the riven sandstone: overlord of the M5: architect of the historic rampart and ditch, the citadel at Tamworth . . . guardian of the Welsh Bridge and the Iron Bridge: contractor to the desirable new estates: saltmaster . . . the friend of Charlemagne. 'I liked that', said Offa, 'sing it again'.

    Geoffrey Hill (b. 1932) British poet. 'The Naming of Offa', *Mercian Hymns* (1971), no. 1

Sympathy

see also **Friendship, Understanding**

1   Can I see another's woe,
    And not be in sorrow too?
    Can I see another's grief,
    And not seek for kind relief?

    William Blake (1757–1827) British poet, painter, engraver, and mystic. 'On Another's Sorrow', *Songs of Innocence* (1789), ll. 1–4

2   When the head aches, all the members partake of the pain.

    Miguel de Cervantes (1547–1616) Spanish novelist and playwright. *Don Quixote* (1605–15), pt. 2, ch. 2

3   One cannot live with sighted eyes and feeling heart and not know and react to the miseries which afflict this world.

    Lorraine Hansberry (1930–65) US writer. *To Be Young, Gifted and Black: An Informal Autobiography* (Robert Nemiroff, ed.; 1970)

4   If you wish me to weep, you yourself must first feel grief.

    Horace (65–8 BC) Roman poet. *Ars Poetica* (19–8 BC), l. 102

5   She was a machine-gun riddling her hostess with sympathy.

    Aldous Huxley (1894–1963) British novelist and essayist. 'The Gioconda Smile', *Mortal Coils* (1922)

6   Sympathy for the Devil

    Mick Jagger (b. 1943) British rock musician and songwriter. 1968. Song title. The song was co-written with Keith Richard.

7   One would have to have a heart of stone to read the death of Little Nell without laughing.

    Oscar Wilde (1854–1900) Irish poet, playwright, and wit. Lecture on Dickens, quoted in *Lives of the Wits* (Hesketh Pearson; 1962)

8   I can sympathize with everything, except suffering.

    Oscar Wilde (1854–1900) Irish poet, playwright, and wit. *The Picture of Dorian Gray* (1891), ch. 3

T

Talent

see also **Ability, Genius**

1 Mediocrity knows nothing higher than itself, but talent instantly recognizes genius.
Arthur Conan Doyle (1859–1930) Scottish-born British writer and physician. *The Valley of Fear* (1915), ch. 1

2 Talent develops in quiet places, character in the full current of human life.
Johann Wolfgang von Goethe (1749–1832) German poet, playwright, and scientist. *Torquato Tasso* (1790), Act 1

3 There is no substitute for talent. Industry and all the virtues are of no avail.
Aldous Huxley (1894–1963) British novelist and essayist. *Point Counter Point* (1928)

4 At school I was quite sure I was a talentless bastard, but at 15 I got my first part in a school play and learnt the art of upstaging.
Eddie Izzard (b. 1962) British comedian. *Independent* (June 14, 1994)

5 Talent wins games, but teamwork wins championships.
Michael Jordan (b. 1963) US basketball player. Attrib.

6 And never let a goblet of gold
face the bright moon empty.
Heaven bred in me talents,
and they must be put to use.
Li Bai (701–762) Chinese poet. 'Bring in the Wine' (8th century), quoted in *An Anthology of Chinese Literature* (Stephen Owen, tr.; 1996)

7 A career is born in public—talent in privacy.
Marilyn Monroe (1926–62) US film actor. Attrib.

8 Whatever talents I possess may suddenly diminish or suddenly increase. I can with ease become an ordinary fool. I may be one now. But it doesn't do to upset one's own vanity.
Dylan Thomas (1914–53) Welsh poet, playwright, and short-story writer. Quoted in *Notebooks* (Robert Maud, ed.; 1968)

9 Talent is hereditary; it may be the common possession of a whole family (e.g., the Bach family); genius is not transmitted; it is never diffused, but is strictly individual.
Otto Weininger (1880–1903) Austrian philosopher. *Sex and Character* (1903), pt. 2, ch. 4

10 If a man has talent and cannot use it, he has failed. If he has a talent and uses only half of it, he has partly failed. If he has a talent and learns somehow to use the whole of it, he has . . . won a satisfaction and a triumph few men ever know.
Thomas Wolfe (1900–38) US novelist. *The Web and the Rock* (1939), ch. 13

Taste

see also **Aesthetics, Design, Fashion, Senses**

1 She was one of the people who say, 'I don't know anything about music really, but I know what I like'.
Max Beerbohm (1872–1956) British essayist, critic, and caricaturist. *Zuleika Dobson* (1911), ch. 16

2 Good taste is better than bad taste, but bad taste is better than no taste.
Arnold Bennett (1867–1931) British writer. *Observer* (August 24, 1930), 'Sayings of the Week'

3 Taste is the best judge. It is rare. Art addresses itself only to an excessively limited number of individuals.
Paul Cézanne (1839–1906) French painter. Letter to Emile Bernard (1904), quoted in *Letters of Paul Cézanne* (John Rewald, ed.; 1976)

4 To satisfy taste while we satisfy the demands of utility: the problem, stated in these apparently simple terms is . . . the whole mystery of decorative art.
Ernest Chesneau (1833–90) French art critic. *The Education of the Artist* (1886)

5 To achieve harmony in bad taste is the height of elegance.
Jean Genet (1910–86) French writer. *The Thief's Journal* (1949)

6 I don't care anything about reasons but I know what I like.
Henry James (1843–1916) US-born British writer and critic. *The Portrait of a Lady* (1881), ch. 24

7 Matters of taste must be felt, not dogmatized about. A large crayfish or lobster rearing itself menacingly on its tail seems quite at home on the sideboard of a Brighton hotel-de-luxe, but will intimidate a shy guest at a small dinner party.
Lady Jekyll (1861–1937) British writer. *Kitchen Essays* (1922)

8 The *sublime* is what pleases immediately through its opposition to the interest of sense.
Immanuel Kant (1724–1804) German philosopher. *Critique of Judgment* (1790)

9 It is disgusting to pick your teeth. What is vulgar is to use a gold toothpick.
Louis Kronenberger (1904–80) US writer and critic. *The Cart and the Horse* (1964)

10 I wish you all sorts of prosperity with a little more taste.
Alain René Lesage (1668–1747) French writer. *Gil Blas* (1715–35), bk. 7, ch. 4

11 People who like this sort of thing will find this is the sort of thing they like.
Abraham Lincoln (1809–65) US president. A comment on a book. Quoted in *Collections and Recollections* (G. W. E. Russell; 1898), ch. 30

12 What is food to one man is bitter poison to others.

Lucretius (99?–55? BC) Roman philosopher and poet. *De Rerum Natura* (1st century BC), pt. 4, l. 637

13 The kind of people who always go on about whether a thing is in good taste invariably have very bad taste.

Joe Orton (1933–67) British playwright. Attrib.

14 Could we teach taste or genius by rules, they would be no longer taste and genius.

Sir Joshua Reynolds (1723–92) British painter and writer. Discourse to the students of the Royal Academy (December 14, 1770), quoted in *Discourses on Art* (R. Wark, ed.; 1975)

15 Taste does not come by chance: it is a long and laborious task to acquire it.

Sir Joshua Reynolds (1723–92) British painter and writer. *Memoirs of Sir Joshua Reynolds* (1813–15), vol. 1

16 There is not a taste, a mannerism, or a human act which is not revealing.

Jean-Paul Sartre (1905–80) French philosopher, playwright, and novelist. *Being and Nothingness* (1943)

17 Do not do unto others as you would they should do unto you. Their tastes may not be the same.

George Bernard Shaw (1856–1950) Irish playwright. 'Maxims for Revolutionists', *Man and Superman* (1903)

18 Taste has no systems and no proofs.

Susan Sontag (b. 1933) US writer. 'Notes on Camp', *Against Interpretation* (1966)

Teachers

see also **Education, Learning**

1 A schoolmaster should have an atmosphere of awe, and walk wonderingly, as if he was amazed at being himself.

Walter Bagehot (1826–77) British economist and journalist. Quoted in *Literary Studies* (Hartley Coleridge; 1878), vol. 1

2 It is the supreme art of the teacher to awaken joy in creative expression and knowledge.

Albert Einstein (1879–1955) German-born US physicist. Motto for the astronomy building of Junior College, Pasadena, California. Attrib.

3 And still they gazed, and still the wonder grew, That one small head could carry all he knew.

Oliver Goldsmith (1730–74) Irish-born British novelist, playwright, and poet. The villagers' perception of the schoolmaster. *The Deserted Village* (1770)

4 He who wishes to teach us a truth should not tell it to us, but simply suggest it with a brief gesture, a gesture which starts an ideal trajectory in the air along which we glide until we find ourselves at the feet of the new truth.

José Ortega y Gasset (1883–1955) Spanish writer and philosopher. *Meditations on Quixote* (1914)

5 The schoolteacher is certainly underpaid as a childminder, but ludicrously overpaid as an educator.

John Osborne (1929–94) British playwright and screenwriter. *Observer* (July 21, 1985), 'Sayings of the Week'

6 The successful teacher is no longer on a height, pumping knowledge at high pressure into passive receptacles . . . He is a senior student anxious to help his juniors.

William Osler (1849–1919) Canadian physician. *The Student Life* (1905)

7 There is no class of men whose rewards are so disproportionate to their usefulness to the community.

Lord Russell (1792–1878) British prime minister. Referring to the low pay of British schoolteachers. Attrib.

8 For every person wishing to teach there are approximately thirty who don't want to learn much.

W. C. Sellar (1898–1951) British humorous writer. *And Now All This* (1932), Introduction

9 He who can, does. He who cannot, teaches.

George Bernard Shaw (1856–1950) Irish playwright. 'Maxims for Revolutionists', *Man and Superman* (1903)

10 Give me a girl at an impressionable age, and she is mine for life.

Muriel Spark (b. 1918) British novelist. *The Prime of Miss Jean Brodie* (1961), ch. 1

11 A teacher should have maximal authority and minimal power.

Thomas Szasz (b. 1920) Hungarian-born US psychiatrist. 'Education', *The Second Sin* (1973)

12 We schoolmasters must temper discretion with deceit.

Evelyn Waugh (1903–66) British novelist. *Decline and Fall* (1928), pt. 1, ch. 1

Technology

see also **Inventions, Machines, Science**

1 God made a mistake in his calculations at the Tower of Babel: nowadays everybody speaks the same technology.

Elias Canetti (1905–94) Bulgarian-born writer. *The Agony of Flies* (1992)

2 Any sufficiently advanced technology is indistinguishable from magic.

Arthur C. Clarke (b. 1917) British writer and scientist. *The Lost Worlds of 2001* (1972)

3 For a successful technology, reality must take precedence over public relations.

Richard Phillips Feynman (1918–88) US physicist. Criticizing the response of the National Aeronautics and Space Administration (NASA) to the Challenger disaster. The space shuttle exploded on January 28, 1986, 73 seconds after take off, causing the death of the seven crew members. *Presidential Commission Report on the Challenger Explosion* (1986), Appendix

4 Technology is the knack of so arranging the world that we don't have to experience it.

Max Frisch (1911–91) Swiss playwright and novelist. *Homo Faber* (1957), pt. 2

5 They don't burn their dead in the West. They're not an ignorant people. They're advanced, they have science, they have guns and tanks and bombs.

Amitav Ghosh (b. 1956) Indian writer. 'The Imam and the Indian', *Granta Book of Travel* (Bill Buford, ed.; 1991)

6 A new organization of matter is building up: the technosphere or world of material goods and technological devices: or the surrogate world.

Edward Goldsmith (b. 1928) British business executive and ecologist. 'De-Industrializing Society', *The Great U-Turn* (1988)

7 Our rockets can find Halley's comet and fly to Venus with amazing accuracy, but side by side with these scientific and technical triumphs is an obvious lack of efficiency in using scientific achievements for economic needs, and many Soviet household appliances are of poor quality.
Mikhail Gorbachev (b. 1931) Russian statesman. *Perestroika: New Thinking for Our Country and the World* (1987)

8 Is it fact, or have I dreamt it—that by means of electricity, the world of matter has become a great nerve, vibrating thousands of miles in a breathless point of time?
Nathaniel Hawthorne (1804–64) US novelist and short-story writer. *The House of Seven Gables* (1851)

9 Death invented the phone
It looks like the altar of death
Do not worship the telephone
It drags its worshippers into actual graves
With a variety of devices, through a variety of disguised voices.
Ted Hughes (1930–98) British writer and poet. 'Do Not Pick Up the Telephone' (1979)

10 We are at risk of producing more technology than the world can adapt to.
Dan Hutcheson, US business executive. *New York Times* (September 17, 1997)

11 A neo-biological technology is far more rewarding than a world of clocks, gears, and predictable simplicity.
Kevin Kelly (b. 1952) US author and editor. *Out of Control* (1994)

12 The development of technology will leave only one problem: the infirmity of human nature.
Karl Kraus (1874–1936) Austrian writer. 1918. Quoted in *Karl Kraus* (Harry Zohn; 1971)

13 In the current fashionable denigration of technology, it is easy to forget that nuclear fission is a natural process. If something as intricate as life can assemble by accident, we need not marvel at the fission reactor, a relatively simple contraption, doing likewise.
James Lovelock (b. 1919) British scientist. *Gaia: A New Look at Life on Earth* (1979)

14 By his very success in inventing labor-saving devices modern man has manufactured an abyss of boredom that only the privileged classes in earlier civilizations have ever fathomed.
Lewis Mumford (1895–1990) US social philosopher and urban planner. *The Conduct of Life* (1951)

15 Computing corduroy, memory muslin, and solar silk might be the literal fabric of tomorrow's digital dress. Instead of carrying your laptop, wear it.
Nicholas Negroponte, US business executive and writer. *Being Digital* (1995)

16 The cost of the electronics in a modern car now exceeds the cost of its steel.
Nicholas Negroponte, US business executive and writer. *Being Digital* (1995)

17 As we push our technologies to exploit more and more resources, we now recognize that both the direct devastation and the unforeseen consequences are becoming increasingly global in nature.
Richard Norgaard (b. 1943) US author. Quoted in 'Co-evolution of Economy, Society and Environment', *Real-Life Economics* (Paul Ekins and Manfred Max-Neef, eds.; 1992)

18 Yesterday's lifesaving, fireproof building material is today's carcinogen.
Dean O'Hare (b. 1942) US insurance broker. Speech (October 1995)

19 The hard-pressed weavers of Northern England who rallied around the mythical General Ludd appear to have had no grudge against technology in and of itself; their grievance was with those who used machines to lower wages or eliminate jobs.
Theodore Roszak (b. 1933) US writer and editor. *The Cult of Information* (1986)

20 We turned the switch, saw the flashes, watched for ten minutes, then switched everything off and went home. That night I knew the world was headed for sorrow.
Leo Szilard (1898–1964) Hungarian-born US nuclear physicist. May 30, 1964. Referring to the first atomic fission (1939). Attrib.

21 Technology feeds on itself. Technology makes more technology possible.
Alvin Toffler (b. 1928) US writer. *Future Shock* (1970)

22 My poor fellow, why not carry a watch?
Herbert Beerbohm Tree (1853–1917) British actor and theatrical impresario. Remark to a man carrying a grandfather clock. Attrib. *Beerbohm Tree* (Hesketh Pearson; 1956)

23 Biotechnology has an ancient lineage. It is as old as the first fermented drink, the first bowl of yoghurt or the first piece of cheese.
Edward Yoxen, British author and academic. *The Gene Business* (1983)

24 No Winter Palace has been seized, no Bastille stormed, no monarchy abolished . . . (but) a technological assault is being prepared that will transform the economies of the developed and developing nations.
Edward Yoxen, British author and academic. Referring to advances in biotechnology. *The Gene Business* (1983)

Television

see also **Entertainment**, **Media**

1 TV . . . is our latest medium—we call it a medium because nothing's well done.
Goodman Ace (1899–1982) US radio and TV writer and comedian. Letter to Groucho Marx (1954), quoted in *The Groucho Letters* (Groucho Marx; 1967)

2 There is a bias in television journalism. It is not against any particular party or point of view—it is a bias against *understanding*.
John Birt (b. 1944) British broadcasting executive. This launched a series of articles written jointly with Peter Jay. *Times* (February 28, 1975)

3 Nothing is real unless it happens on television.
Daniel J. Boorstin (b. 1914) US historian and librarian. *New York Times* (February 19, 1978)

4 Some television programs are so much chewing gum for the eyes.
John Mason Brown (1900–69) US journalist. Interview (July 28, 1955)

5 Television—the drug of the nation
Breeding ignorance and feeding radiation.
Disposable Heroes of HipHoprisy, US rap group. 'Television: The Drug of the Nation' (1992)

6 Television is an invention that permits you to be entertained in your living room by people you wouldn't have in your home.

David Frost (b. 1939) British television personality. CBS television (1971)

7 Why should people go out and pay money to see bad movies when they can stay at home and see bad television for nothing?

Samuel Goldwyn (1882–1974) Polish-born US film producer. *Observer* (September 9, 1956), 'Sayings of the Week'

8 Television was the ultimate evidence of cultural anaemia.

Roy A. K. Heath (b. 1926) Guyanese novelist and teacher. *Kwaku* (1982)

9 I made a remark a long time ago. I said I was very pleased that television was now showing murder stories, because it's bringing murder back into its rightful setting—in the home.

Alfred Hitchcock (1899–1980) British-born US film director. *Observer* (August 17, 1969), 'Sayings of the Week'

10 If God had not meant everyone to be in bed by ten-thirty, He would never have provided the ten o'clock newscast.

Garrison Keillor (b. 1942) US writer and broadcaster. 'News', *Lake Wobegon Days* (1985)

11 For the love of God, folks, don't do this at home.

David Letterman (b. 1947) US entertainer. Demonstrating the Donut-o-pult. *Late Show* (CBS television; 1995)

12 I have had my aerials removed—it's the moral equivalent of a prostate operation.

Malcolm Muggeridge (1903–90) British journalist. *Radio Times* (April 1981)

13 William Shakespeare wrote for the masses. If he were alive today, he'd probably be the chief scriptwriter on *All in the Family* or *Dallas*.

Rupert Murdoch (b. 1931) Australian-born US media entrepreneur. *Sunday Express* (December 20, 1984), 'Quotes of the Year'

14 Mental reflection is so much more interesting than T.V., it's a shame more people don't switch over to it. They probably think that what they hear is unimportant but it never is.

Robert T. Pirsig (b. 1928) US writer. *Zen and the Art of Motorcycle Maintenance* (1974)

15 Television? No good will come of this device. The word is half Greek and half Latin.

C. P. Scott (1846–1932) British journalist. Attrib.

16 I've finally figured out why soap operas are, and logically should be, so popular with generations of housebound women. They are the only place in our culture where grown-up men take seriously all the things that grown-up women have to deal with all day long.

Gloria Steinem (b. 1934) US writer and feminist. 'Night Thoughts of a Media Watcher', *Outrageous Acts and Everyday Rebellions* (1983)

17 I'm always amazed that people will actually choose to sit in front of the television and just be savaged by stuff that belittles their intelligence.

Alice Walker (b. 1944) US novelist and poet. *I Dream a World: Portraits of Black Women Who Changed America* (Brian Lanker; 1989)

18 I hate television. I hate it as much as peanuts. But I can't stop eating peanuts.

Orson Welles (1915–85) US actor, director, producer, and writer. *New York Herald Tribune* (October 12, 1956)

Temptation

see also **Desire, Seduction**

1 Saintliness is also a temptation.

Jean Anouilh (1910–87) French playwright. *Becket* (1959)

2 One shouldn't believe that the Devil only tempts men of genius.

Charles Baudelaire (1821–67) French poet. 'Mon Coeur Mis à Nu', *Journaux Intimes* (1887)

3 Watch and pray, that ye enter not into temptation: the spirit indeed is willing, but the flesh is weak.

Bible. Matthew, *King James Bible* (1611), 26:41

4 The best way to get the better of temptation is just to yield to it.

Clementina Stirling Graham (1782–1877) Scottish writer. 'Soirée at Mrs. Russel's', *Mystifications* (1859)

5 To great evils we submit, we resent little provocations.

William Hazlitt (1778–1830) British essayist and critic. 'On the Great and the Little Things', *Table Talk* (1821–22)

6 'You oughtn't to yield to temptation'. 'Well, somebody must, or the thing becomes absurd'.

Anthony Hope (1863–1933) British novelist and playwright. *The Dolly Dialogues* (1894), no. 14

7 Honest bread is very well—it's the butter that makes the temptation.

Douglas Jerrold (1803–57) British playwright. *The Catspaw* (1850), Act 3

8 I never resist temptation because I have found that things that are bad for me never tempt me.

George Bernard Shaw (1856–1950) Irish playwright. *The Apple Cart* (1930)

9 There are several good protections against temptations, but the surest is cowardice.

Mark Twain (1835–1910) US writer and humorist. *Following the Equator* (1897), ch. 36

10 I can resist everything except temptation.

Oscar Wilde (1854–1900) Irish poet, playwright, and wit. *Lady Windermere's Fan* (1892), Act 1

Terrorism

see also **Crime, Fear, War**

1 Today we were unlucky. But remember, we have only to be lucky once. You will have to be lucky always.

Anonymous. Issued by the Provisional IRA after their bombing of the Grand Hotel, Brighton, failed to kill Margaret Thatcher. Statement (Irish Republican Army; October 1984)

2 What happened on 11 September was without parallel in the bloody history of terrorism. Within a few hours, up to 7,000 people were annihilated, the commercial centre of New York was reduced to rubble and in Washington and Pennsylvania further death and horror on an unimaginable scale.

Tony Blair (b. 1953) British prime minister. Speech, Labour Party Conference (October 2, 2001)

3 Terrorist attacks can shake the foundations of our biggest buildings, but they cannot touch the foundation of America. These acts shattered steel, but they cannot dent the steel of American resolve.

George W. Bush (b. 1948) US president. Referring to the terrorist attacks in the United States earlier in the day. Address to the Nation (September 11, 2001)

4 This crusade, this war on terrorism is going to take a while. And the American people must be patient.

George W. Bush (b. 1948) US president. Remark (September 16, 2001)

5 All terrorists, at the invitation of the Government, end up with drinks at the Dorchester.

Dora Gaitskell (1901–89) Russian-born British politician. Letter, *Guardian* (August 23, 1977)

6 What really alarms me about President Bush's 'War on Terrorism' is the grammar. How do you wage war on an abstract noun? It's rather like bombing Murder.

Terry Jones (b. 1942) British writer and film director. 'The Grammar of the War on Terrorism', *Voices for Peace* (Anna Kiernan, ed.; 2001)

7 No one can terrorize a whole nation, unless we are all his accomplices.

Ed Murrow (1908–65) US journalist and broadcaster. Closing words of his investigation into Senator Joseph McCarthy's campaign against 'Un-American Activities'. *See It Now* (CBS television; March 7, 1954)

8 There is a statistical terrorism inflicted on society by crime figures.

Lady Runciman of Doxford (b. 1936) British social reformer. *Times* (January 20, 1995)

9 Ten hostages is terrorism;
A million and it's strategy.

Vikram Seth (b. 1952) Indian novelist and poet. *The Golden Gate* (1986), ch. 7, st. 31

10 The greatest work of art by Lucifer.

Karlheinz Stockhausen (b. 1928) German composer. Referring to the terrorist attacks on the World Trade Center, New York City, on September 11, 2001. Remark (September 2001)

11 We must try to find ways to starve the terrorist and the hijacker of the oxygen of publicity on which they depend.

Margaret Thatcher (b. 1925) British prime minister. Speech to the American Bar Association, London (July 15, 1985)

Theatre

see also **Acting and Actors, The Arts, Performance**

1 The reason why Absurdist plays take place in No Man's Land with only two characters is primarily financial.

Arthur Adamov (1908–70) Russian-born French playwright. Speech to the Edinburgh International Drama Conference (September 13, 1963)

2 Theatre is the first serum to be invented by mankind against that malady, anguish.

Jean-Louis Barrault (1910–94) French actor, director, and producer. 1959. 'Comment le Théâtre Naît en Nous', *Nouvelles Réflexions sur le Théâtre* (Joseph Chiari, tr.; 1961)

3 Let a single completed action, all in one place, all in one day, keep the theatre packed to the end of your play.

Nicolas Boileau (1636–1711) French poet and critic. *L'Art Poétique* (1674), pt. 1

4 Drama is the need to be human even when we are buried inside social madness: to search for every remnant of life to use to recreate the world.

Edward Bond (b. 1934) British playwright. *The Hidden Plot* (2000)

5 My greatest fear for a vision of the theatre in the year 2000 would be a sort of elongated panto season, followed by two or three shows featuring stars of sitcoms in the classics of their choice.

Richard Eyre (b. 1943) British theatre, film, and television director. *Observer* (February 26, 1994), 'Sayings of the Week'

6 The world's a theatre, the earth a stage,
Which God and Nature do with actors fill.

Thomas Heywood (1574–1641) English playwright and writer. *Apology for Actors* (1612)

7 The seasoning of a play, is the applause.

Ben Jonson (1572–1637) English playwright and poet. *Volpone* (1606), Act 5, Scene 8

8 A farce or a comedy is best played; a tragedy is best read at home.

Abraham Lincoln (1809–65) US president. Said to John Hay after seeing *The Merchant of Venice*. Remark (1863), quoted in *The Guinness Dictionary of Theatrical Quotations* (Michele Brown; 1993)

9 We respond to a drama to that extent to which it corresponds to our dreamlife.

David Mamet (b. 1947) US writer and film director. 'A National Dream-Life', *Writing in Restaurants* (1986)

10 The structure of a play is always the story of how the birds came home to roost.

Arthur Miller (b. 1915) US playwright. 'Shadows of the Gods', *Harper's Magazine* (August 1958)

11 Shakespeare absolutely belongs to everyone: the Japanese student struggling with the hieroglyphics, the muttering commuter, the professional, the club bore, everybody who quotes him without realising it every day.

Michael Pennington (b. 1943) British actor and theatre director. *The English Shakespeare Company* (1990)

12 The weasel under the cocktail cabinet.

Harold Pinter (b. 1930) British playwright, theatre director, and screenwriter. Reply when asked what his plays were about. Quoted in *Anger and After* (J. Russell Taylor; 1962)

13 What do you expect me to do if nobody writes good plays any more and we're reduced to putting on plays by Pirandello?

Luigi Pirandello (1867–1936) Italian dramatist, novelist, and short-story writer. *Six Characters in Search of an Author* (1921), Act 1

14 Stage plays are sinfull, heathenish, lewde, ungodly Spectacles, and most pernicious Corruptions, condemned in all ages, as intolerable Mischiefs to Churches, to Republickes, to the manners, mindes and soules of men.

William Prynne (1600–69) English pamphleteer. *Histrio-Mastix* (1633)

15 Rehearsing a play is making the word flesh. Publishing a play is reversing the process.

Peter Shaffer (b. 1926) British playwright. Note (1973)

16 CHORUS Can this cockpit hold
The vasty fields of France? or may we cram
Within this wooden O the very casques
That did affright the air at Agincourt?

William Shakespeare (1564–1616) English poet and playwright. Probably referring to the Globe Theatre. *Henry V* (1599), Prologue

17 FABIAN If this were play'd upon a stage now, I could condemn it as an improbable fiction.

William Shakespeare (1564–1616) English poet and playwright. *Twelfth Night* (1601), Act 3, Scene 4

18 If drama shows people dealing nobly with their misery, it disenfranchises those watching who cannot cope like that.
Juliet Stevenson (b. 1956) British actor. *Observer* (May 22, 1994), 'Sayings of the Week'

19 The theatre has for a long time seemed to me a Biblia Pauperum, a picture Bible for those who cannot read, and the playwright merely a lay preacher who hawks the latest ideas in popular form, so . . . the middle classes . . . can grasp them without racking their brains too much.
August Strindberg (1849–1912) Swedish dramatist. *Miss Julie* (1889), Preface

20 In a good play every speech should be as fully flavoured as a nut or apple, and such speeches cannot be written by any one who works among people who have shut their lips on poetry.
J. M. Synge (1871–1909) Irish playwright. *The Playboy of the Western World* (1907), Preface

21 A novel is a static thing that one moves through; a play is a dynamic thing that moves past one.
Kenneth Tynan (1927–80) British theatre critic. *Curtains* (1961)

22 Musical theater is the highest, the most expressive and the most imaginative form of theater . . . a composer who has a talent and a passion for the theater can express himself completely in this branch of musical creativeness.
Kurt Weill (1900–50) German-born US composer. Quoted in *American Composers* (David Ewen; 1982)

23 The whole history of the world must be reduced to wallpaper in front of which the characters must speak and pose.
W. B. Yeats (1865–1939) Irish poet and playwright. Letter to Sean O'Casey, rejecting *The Silver Tassie* (1928). Quoted in *Sean O'Casey and His World* (David Krause; 1928)

Theft

see also **Crime**

1 What's breaking into a bank compared with founding a bank?
Bertolt Brecht (1898–1956) German playwright and poet. *The Threepenny Opera* (1929)

2 Thieves respect property; they merely wish the property to become their property that they may more perfectly respect it.
G. K. Chesterton (1874–1936) British writer and poet. *The Man Who Was Thursday* (1908), ch. 4

3 Thou shalt not steal; an empty feat,
When it's so lucrative to cheat.
Arthur Hugh Clough (1819–61) British poet. 'The Latest Decalogue' (1862)

4 He that first cries out stop thief, is often he that has stolen the treasure.
William Congreve (1670–1729) English playwright and poet. *Love for Love* (1695), Act 3, Scene 14

5 The law doth punish man or woman
That steals a goose from off the common,
But lets the greater felon loose
That steals the common from the goose.
Folk Verse. 1821. Referring to the General Enclosure Act (1801), in which common land was fenced and placed under private ownership. Quoted in *Tickler Magazine* (February 1, 1821)

6 What is a man if he is not a thief who openly charges as much as he can for the goods he sells?
Mahatma Gandhi (1869–1948) Indian national leader. *Non-Violence in Peace and War* (1948)

7 Stolen sweets are always sweeter,
Stolen kisses much completer,
Stolen looks are nice in chapels,
Stolen, stolen, be your apples.
Leigh Hunt (1784–1859) British poet and essayist. 'Song of Fairies Robbing an Orchard' (1830)

8 For de little stealin' dey gits you in jail soon or late. For de big stealin' dey makes you emperor and put you in de Hall o' Fame when you croaks.
Eugene O'Neill (1888–1953) US playwright. *The Emperor Jones* (1920)

9 Property is theft.
Pierre Joseph Proudhon (1809–65) French writer and political theorist. *Qu'est-ce que la Propriété* (1840), ch. 1

10 A man who will steal *for* me will steal *from* me.
Theodore Roosevelt (1858–1919) US president. Firing a cowboy who had applied Roosevelt's brand to a steer belonging to a neighbouring ranch. Quoted in *Roosevelt in the Bad Lands* (Herman Hagedorn; 1921)

11 To steal from the rich is a sacred and religious act.
Jerry Rubin (1938–94) US activist and author. *Do It* (1969)

12 If you give to a thief he cannot steal from you, and he is then no longer a thief.
William Saroyan (1908–81) US novelist. *The Human Comedy* (1943), ch. 4

13 When people come and talk to you of their aspirations, before they leave you had better count your spoons.
Logan Pearsall Smith (1865–1946) US-born British writer. 'Other People', *Afterthoughts* (1931)

14 A clever theft was praiseworthy amongst the Spartans; and it is equally so amongst Christians, provided it be on a sufficiently large scale.
Herbert Spencer (1820–1903) British philosopher. *Social Statics* (1850), pt. 2, ch. 16, sect. 3

Theory

see also **Ideas**, **Philosophy**

1 There is a theory which states that if ever anyone discovers exactly what the Universe is for and why it is here, it will instantly disappear and be replaced by something even more bizarre and inexplicable.
Douglas Adams (1952–2001) British writer. *The Restaurant at the End of the Universe* (1980), First Epigraph

2 To try to deduce the history of a people from the general laws of humanity would be like a European geometrician trying, with the sole aid of Euclid's theorems, to draw a map of Chile from his study.
Andrés Bello (1781–1865) Chilean politician and writer. 'The Craft of History' (1848)

3 A system is nothing more than the subordination of all aspects of the universe to any one such aspect.
Jorge Luis Borges (1899–1986) Argentinian writer and poet. 'Tlön, Uqbar, Orbis Tertius', *Labyrinths* (1962)

4 A thing may look specious in theory, and yet be ruinous in practice; a thing may look evil in theory, and yet be in practice excellent.

Edmund Burke (1729–97) Irish-born British statesman and political philosopher. Speech for the prosecution at the impeachment of Warren Hastings, former governor-general of India (February 19, 1788)

5 All generalizations are dangerous, even this one.

Alexandre Dumas (1802–70) French novelist and playwright. Attrib.

6 Don't confuse *hypothesis* and *theory*. The former is a possible explanation; the latter, the correct one. The establishment of theory is the very purpose of science.

Martin H. Fischer (1879–1962) German-born US physician and author. *Fischerisms* (Howard Fabing and Ray Marr, eds.; 1944)

7 Factual evidence can never 'prove' a hypothesis; it can only fail to disprove it, which is what we generally mean when we say, somewhat inexactly, that the hypothesis is 'confirmed' by experience.

Milton Friedman (b. 1912) US economist. *Essays in Positive Economics* (1953)

8 You know very well that unless you're a scientist, it's much more important for a theory to be shapely, than for it to be true.

Christopher Hampton (b. 1946) British playwright. *The Philanthropist* (1970), Scene 1

9 Those who are enamoured of practice without science are like a pilot who goes into a ship without rudder or compass and never has any certainty where he is going.
Practice should always be based upon a sound knowledge of theory.

Leonardo da Vinci (1452–1519) Italian artist, engineer, and inventor. *Notebooks* (1508–18)

10 Nothing is so practical as a good theory.

Kurt Levin, German social psychologist. Quoted in *The Age of Heretics* (Art Kleiner; 1996)

11 When a person or a group turns out well no one wants to know about the models, only the work; it is the work that counts.

Joaquim Maria Machado de Assis (1839–1908) Brazilian novelist and short-story writer. *Dom Casmurro* (1899)

12 In making theories always keep a window open so that you can throw one out if necessary.

Béla Schick (1877–1967) Hungarian-born US physician. Quoted in *Aphorisms and Facetiae of Béla Schick* (Israel J. Wolf; 1965)

Therapy

see also Neurosis, Psychoanalysis

1 A man should not strive to eliminate his complexes, but to get into accord with them: they are legitimately what directs his conduct in the world.

Sigmund Freud (1856–1939) Austrian psychoanalyst. Attrib.

2 Writing is a form of therapy; sometimes I wonder how all those who do not write, compose or paint can manage to escape the madness, the melancholia, the panic fear which is inherent in the human situation.

Graham Greene (1904–91) British novelist. *Ways of Escape* (1981)

3 Fortunately, analysis is not the only way to resolve inner conflicts. Life itself remains a very effective therapist.

Karen Horney (1885–1952) German-born US psychoanalyst. *Our Inner Conflicts* (1945)

4 Then something bent down and took hold of me and shook me like the end of the world. Whee-ee-ee-ee-ee, it shrilled, through an air crackling with blue light, and with each flash a great jolt drubbed me.

Sylvia Plath (1932–63) US poet and novelist. Referring to electro-convulsive therapy. *The Bell Jar* (1963), ch. 12

5 It is the attainment of a new kind of relationship with others and with himself which ultimately heals the patient.

Anthony Storr (b. 1920) British writer and psychiatrist. *The Integrated Personality* (1960)

Thinking

see also Consciousness, Ideas, Intelligence, Mind

1 True thoughts are those alone which do not understand themselves.

Theodor Adorno (1903–69) German philosopher, sociologist, and musicologist. *Minima Moralia* (E. F. N. Jephcott, tr.; 1951), pt. 2

2 He can't think without his hat.

Samuel Beckett (1906–89) Irish playwright, novelist, and poet. *Waiting for Godot* (1954), Act 1

3 His mind is open; yes, it is so open that nothing is retained; ideas simply pass through him.

F. H. Bradley (1846–1924) British philosopher. Attrib.

4 My thoughts ran a wool-gathering; and I did like the countryman who looked for his ass while he was mounted on his back.

Miguel de Cervantes (1547–1616) Spanish novelist and playwright. *Don Quixote* (1605–15), pt. 2, ch. 58

5 Mirrors should think longer before they reflect.

Jean Cocteau (1889–1963) French film director, novelist, and playwright. *Sunday Times* (October 20, 1963)

6 Learning without thought is labour lost; thought without learning is perilous.

Confucius (551–479 BC) Chinese philosopher, administrator, and moralist. *Analects* (5th century BC)

7 The Master said, 'If one learns from others but does not think, one will be bewildered. If, on the other hand, one thinks but does not learn from others, one will be in peril'.

Confucius (551–479 BC) Chinese philosopher, administrator, and moralist. *Analects* (5th century BC)

8 There is nothing
but what thinking makes
it less tangible.

Robert Creeley (b. 1926) US poet. 'I Keep to Myself Such Measures . . . ', *Words* (1967), quoted in *The Penguin Book of American Verse* (Geoffrey Moore, ed.; 1977)

9 The most important thing is transforming our minds, so that we have a new way of thinking and a new outlook. We should make an effort to develop a new inner world.

Dalai Lama (b. 1935) Tibetan spiritual leader. Referring to his hopes for the new millennium. *Observer* (January 2, 2000)

10 To think is to differ.

Clarence Darrow (1857–1938) US lawyer. Speech at the trial of John Scopes for teaching evolution in Tennessee (July 13, 1925)

11 Lateral thinking is a way of using information in order to bring about creativity.

Edward de Bono (b. 1933) Maltese-born British psychologist and writer. *Lateral Thinking for Management* (1971)

12 What was once thought can never be unthought.
Friedrich Dürrenmatt (1921–90) Swiss writer. *The Physicists* (1962)

13 He never is alone that is accompanied with noble thoughts.
John Fletcher (1579–1625) English playwright. 'Love's Cure', *The Lover's Progress* (1623)

14 We must dare to think about 'unthinkable things' because when things become unthinkable, thinking stops and action becomes mindless.
J. William Fulbright (1905–95) US educator and politician. Speech to the US Senate (March 27, 1964)

15 Thinking does not overcome metaphysics by climbing . . . surmounting it, transcending it somehow or other; thinking overcomes metaphysics by climbing . . . down into the nearness of the nearest.
Martin Heidegger (1889–1976) German philosopher. *Letter on Humanism* (1947)

16 The man who says what he thinks is finished, and the man who thinks what he says is an idiot.
Rolf Hochhuth (b. 1931) German playwright. *The Representative* (1963)

17 Thought is the labour of the intellect, reverie is its pleasure.
Victor Hugo (1802–85) French poet, novelist, and playwright. 'Saint Denis', *Les Misérables* (1862), bk. 1, ch. 4

18 What we think and feel and are is to a great extent determined by the state of our ductless glands and our viscera.
Aldous Huxley (1894–1963) British novelist and essayist. 'Meditation on El Greco', *Music at Night and Other Essays* (1949)

19 The transition between one thought and another is no more a break in the *thought* than a joint in a bamboo is a break in the wood. It is a part of the *consciousness* as much as the joint is a part of the *bamboo*.
William James (1842–1910) US psychologist and philosopher. *The Principles of Psychology* (1890), vol. 1

20 Thoughts without content are empty, intuitions without concepts are blind . . . The understanding can intuit nothing, the senses can think nothing. Only through their union can knowledge arise.
Immanuel Kant (1724–1804) German philosopher. *Critique of Pure Reason* (1781), A 51, B 75

21 The supreme paradox of all thought is the attempt to discover something that thought cannot think.
Søren Kierkegaard (1813–55) Danish philosopher. *Philosophical Fragments* (1844)

22 To take time to think is to gain time to live.
Nancy Kline, US author. *Time to Think* (1999)

23 We know of nothing but the existence of our impressions, feelings and thoughts. It thinks, we ought really to say; just as we now say, it thunders. To say *cogito* is too much, if you translate this into 'I think'. Still, to assume or postulate this 'I' is a practical necessity.
Georg Christoph Lichtenberg (1742–99) German physicist and writer. Quoted in *The Reflections of Lichtenberg* (Norman Alliston, tr.; 1908)

24 What generally passes for 'thought' among the majority of mankind is the time one takes out to rearrange one's prejudices.
Clare Boothe Luce (1903–87) US playwright, journalist, and public official. *Today's Woman* (April 1946)

25 Under all that we think, lives all we believe, like the ultimate veil of our spirits.
Antonio Machado (1875–1939) Spanish poet and playwright. *Juan de Mairena* (1943)

26 if you make people think they're thinking, they'll love you: but if you really make them think, they'll hate you.
Don Marquis (1878–1937) US journalist and writer. 'archy and mehitabel' (1927)

27 Today we no longer seek . . . Our thinking is a thought in retreat or in reply.
Maurice Merleau-Ponty (1908–61) French existentialist philosopher. Quoted in *The Essential Writings of Merleau-Ponty* (A. L. Fisher, ed.; 1969)

28 His thoughts, few that they were, lay silent in the privacy of his head.
Spike Milligan (1918–2002) Indian-born British humorist, writer, and actor. *Puckoon* (1963)

29 Pooh began to feel a little more comfortable, because when you are a Bear of Very Little Brain, and you Think of Things, you find sometimes that a Thing which seemed very Thingish inside you is quite different when it gets out into the open and has quite other people looking at it.
A. A. Milne (1882–1956) British writer. *The House at Pooh Corner* (1928)

30 Thought is not a gift to man but a laborious, precarious, and volatile acquisition.
José Ortega y Gasset (1883–1955) Spanish writer and philosopher. 'In Search of Goethe from Within', *Partisan Review* (December 1949)

31 We do not live to think, but, on the contrary, we think in order that we may succeed in surviving.
José Ortega y Gasset (1883–1955) Spanish writer and philosopher. 'In Search of Goethe from Within', *Partisan Review* (December 1949)

32 Thinking is the desire to gain reality by means of ideas.
José Ortega y Gasset (1883–1955) Spanish writer and philosopher. *The Dehumanization of Art* (1925)

33 Thought is only a flash between two long nights, but this flash is everything.
Jules Henri Poincaré (1854–1912) French mathematician and scientist. Quoted in *The World of Mathematics* (J. R. Newman; 1956)

34 The way not to vary is not to think.
Ernest Renan (1823–92) French philosopher, philologist, and historian. *L'Avenir de la Science: Pensées de 1848* (1890), Preface

35 One of the worst diseases to which the human creature is liable is its disease of thinking.
John Ruskin (1819–1900) British art critic, writer, and reformer. 'A Joy for Ever', *Lectures on the Political Economy of Art* (1858)

36 Many people would sooner die than think. In fact they do.
Bertrand Russell (1872–1970) British philosopher and mathematician. Quoted as an epigraph in *Thinking About Thinking* (Anthony Flew; 1975)

37 My thought is *me*: that is why I can't stop. I exist by what I think . . . and I can't prevent myself from thinking.
Jean-Paul Sartre (1905–80) French philosopher, playwright, and novelist. *Nausea* (1938)

38 HAMLET There is nothing either good or bad, but thinking makes it so.
William Shakespeare (1564–1616) English poet and playwright. *Hamlet* (1601), Act 2, Scene 2

39 Thinking is the most unhealthy thing in the world, and people die of it just as they die of any other disease.

Oscar Wilde (1854–1900) Irish poet, playwright, and wit. 'The Decay of Lying', *Intentions* (1891)

40 In order to draw a limit to thinking, we should have to be able to think both sides of this limit.

Ludwig Wittgenstein (1889–1951) Austrian philosopher. *Tractatus Logico-Philosophicus* (1921), Preface

41 Wound in mind's pondering
As mummies in the mummy-cloth are wound.

W. B. Yeats (1865–1939) Irish poet and playwright. 'All Souls' Night', *The Tower* (1928), ll. 13–14

Threats

see also **Danger, Warning**

1 And he said, Thou canst not see my face: for there shall no man see me, and live.

Bible. Exodus, *King James Bible* (1611), 33:20

2 Go ahead, make my day.

Clint Eastwood (b. 1930) US film actor and director. As the police detective 'Dirty Harry' Callahan. *Sudden Impact* (Joseph C. Stinson; 1983)

3 I will make you shorter by a head.

Elizabeth I (1533–1603) English monarch. Said to the leaders of her council, who were opposing her course towards Mary Queen of Scots. *Sayings of Queen Elizabeth* (F. Chamberlin; 1923)

4 If you start throwing hedgehogs under me, I shall throw two porcupines under you.

Nikita Khrushchev (1894–1971) Soviet statesman. *Observer* (November 10, 1963), 'Sayings of the Week'

5 We shall raze Bilbao to the ground and its bare desolate site will remove the British desire to support Basque Bolsheviks against our will.

Emilio Mola (1887–1937) Spanish general. Referring to the Nationalist-supported German bombing of the Basque town Guérnica. Remark (1937), quoted in *Franco* (Paul Preston; 1993)

6 I'll be back.

Arnold Schwarzenegger (b. 1947) Austrian-born US bodybuilder and film actor. As the android star of the film. *Terminator* (James Cameron and Gale Anne Hurd; 1984)

Tibet

see **Asian Countries**

Time

see also **The Future, The Past, The Present, Transience**

1 Will Time say nothing but I told you so?
If I could tell you I would let you know.

W. H. Auden (1907–73) British poet. 1940. 'If I Could Tell You', *W. H. Auden: Collected Poems* (Edward Mendelson, ed.; 1991)

2 But what is time? Who can explain it easily and briefly, or even, when he wants to speak of it, comprehend it in his thought? . . . If no one asks me, I know; if they ask and I try to explain, I do not know.

Saint Augustine of Hippo (354–430) Numidian Christian theologian and Doctor of the Church. *Confessions* (397–398), bk. 11, ch. 14, no. 17

3 HAMM What time is it?
CLOV The same as usual.

Samuel Beckett (1906–89) Irish playwright, novelist, and poet. 1957. *Endgame* (1958)

4 VLADIMIR That passed the time.
ESTRAGON It would have passed in any case.
VLADIMIR Yes, but not so rapidly.

Samuel Beckett (1906–89) Irish playwright, novelist, and poet. *Waiting for Godot* (1954), Act 1

5 Time is a great teacher, but unfortunately it kills all its pupils.

Hector Berlioz (1803–69) French composer. Attrib.

6 Men talk of killing time, while time quietly kills them.

Dion Boucicault (1820–90) Irish-born US actor and playwright. *London Assurance* (1841), Act 2, Scene 1

7 How you'd exult if I could put you back
Six hundred years, blot out cosmogony,
Geology, ethnology, what not.
. . . And set you square with Genesis again.

Robert Browning (1812–89) British poet. 'Bishop Blougram's Apology', *Men and Women* (1855), from l. 678

8 Nae man can tether time or tide.

Robert Burns (1759–96) Scottish poet and songwriter. 'Tam o' Shanter' (1791)

9 I recommend you to take care of the minutes: for hours will take care of themselves.

Lord Chesterfield (1694–1773) English statesman and writer. November 6, 1747. *Letters to His Son* (1774)

10 It is not that there isn't time, it is that we lose it.

Paul Claudel (1868–1955) French writer and diplomat. *Partage de Midi* (1906), Act 1

11 Time is a physician that heals every grief.

Diphilus (*fl.* 4th century BC) Greek poet. 300 BC. Attrib.

12 Time goes, you say? Ah no!
Alas, Time stays, *we* go.

Austin Dobson (1840–1921) British poet. 1877. A variation on Ronsard: 'Le temps s'en va, le temps s'en va, ma dame!/ Las! le temps non: mais *nous* nous en allons!' 'The Paradox of Time', *Collected Poems* (1913 (9th edition))

13 When you are courting a nice girl an hour seems like a second. When you sit on a red-hot cinder a second seems like an hour. That's relativity.

Albert Einstein (1879–1955) German-born US physicist. *News Chronicle* (March 14, 1949)

14 Time present and time past
Are both perhaps present in time future,
And time future contained in time past.

T. S. Eliot (1888–1965) US-born British poet and playwright. 'Burnt Norton', *Four Quartets* (1935)

15 Alcohol, hashish, prussic acid, strychnine are weak dilutions. The surest poison is time.

Ralph Waldo Emerson (1803–82) US poet and essayist. *Society and Solitude* (1870)

16 Time is dead as long as it is being clicked off little wheels; only when the clock stops does time come to life.

William Faulkner (1897–1962) US novelist. 'June Second 1910', *The Sound and the Fury* (1929)

17 Ah, my Belovéd, fill the Cup that clears
TO-DAY of past Regrets and future Fears:
To-morrow?—Why, To-morrow I may be
Myself with Yesterday's Sev'n thousand Years.

Edward FitzGerald (1809–83) British poet and translator. *The Rubáiyát of Omar Khayyám* (1859), st. 20

18 Time waste differs from material waste in that there can be no salvage.
Henry Ford (1863–1947) US car manufacturer. Quoted in *Key Management Ideas* (Stuart Crainer; 1996)

19 Dost thou love life? Then do not squander time, for that's the stuff life is made of.
Benjamin Franklin (1706–90) US statesman and scientist. *Poor Richard's Almanack* (1746)

20 Time goes by: reputation increases, ability declines.
Dag Hammarskjöld (1905–61) Swedish statesman and diplomat. *Markings* (Leif Sjöberg and W. H. Auden, trs.; 1964)

21 You must remember this;
A kiss is still a kiss,
A sigh is just a sigh—
The fundamental things apply
As time goes by.
Herman Hupfeld (1894–1951) US songwriter. Song from the film *Casablanca* (1942). 'As Time Goes By' (1931)

22 No hour is ever eternity, but it has its right to weep.
Zora Neale Hurston (1891?–1960) US writer and folklorist. *Their Eyes Were Watching God* (1937)

23 We haven't the time to take our time.
Eugène Ionesco (1909–94) Romanian-born French playwright. *Exit the King* (1962)

24 Time is but the shadow of the world upon the background of Eternity.
Jerome K. Jerome (1859–1927) British novelist and playwright. *Three Men in a Boat* (1889)

25 That old bald cheater, Time.
Ben Jonson (1572–1637) English playwright and poet. *The Poetaster* (1601), Act 1, Scene 1

26 Would to God that we might spend a single day really well!
Thomas à Kempis (1379?–1471) German monk and religious writer. *The Imitation of Christ* (1415–24?), bk. 1, ch. 23, sect. 2

27 Redeem thy mis-spent time that's past;
Live this day, as if 'twere thy last.
Thomas Ken (1637–1711) English bishop. Song lyric. 'A Morning Hymn' (1709), verse 2

28 We must use time as a tool, not as a couch.
John Fitzgerald Kennedy (1917–63) US president. *Observer* (December 10, 1961), 'Sayings of the Week'

29 O Time! arrest your flight, and you, propitious hours!
Stay your course.
Alphonse de Lamartine (1790–1869) French poet and politician. 'Le Lac', *Méditations Poétiques* (1820), st. 6

30 What is time? The Swiss manufacture it. Italians want it. The Americans say it is money. Hindus say it does not exist. I say time is a crook.
Peter Lorre (1904–64) Hungarian-born US film actor. As O'Hara. *Beat the Devil* (Truman Capote and John Huston; 1953)

31 Oh Time, oh Still and Now,
pregnant with things impending.
You travel the cold path with me,
arousing restlessness and hope.
Antonio Machado (1875–1939) Spanish poet and playwright. 'Last Lamentations of Abel Martin', *Selected Poems* (Alan S. Trueblood, tr.; 1982), ll. 22–25

32 We kill time; time buries us.
Joaquim Maria Machado de Assis (1839–1908) Brazilian novelist and short-story writer. *Epitaph of a Small Winner* (1880)

33 A watched clock never moves, they said?
Leave it alone and you'll grow up.
Nor will the sulking holiday train
Start sooner if you stamp your feet.
Louis MacNeice (1907–63) Irish-born British poet. 'The Slow Starter', *Solstices* (1961)

34 My desire is not to speak about myself but to track down the age, the noise and germination of time.
Osip Mandelstam (1891–1938) Russian poet, writer, and translator. *The Noise of Time* (Clarence Brown, tr.; 1923), ch. 13

35 Time is like a river made up of the events which happen, and its current is strong; no sooner does anything appear than it is swept away, and another comes in its place, and will be swept away too.
Marcus Aurelius (121–180) Roman emperor and philosopher. *Meditations* (170–180), bk. 4, sect. 35

36 Time is a traitor, millimeter by millimeter it betrays
the hope of uniting discontinuity,
of securing the incomplete,
all time is treachery.
Antonio Martínez-Sarrión (b. 1939) Spanish poet, critic, and translator. 'Umma Gumma', *A Bilingual Anthology of Contemporary Spanish Poetry* (Luis A. Ramos-García; 1997)

37 But at my back I always hear
Time's wingèd chariot hurrying near
And yonder all before us lie
Deserts of vast eternity
Thy beauty shall no more be found;
Nor, in thy marble vault, shall sound
My echoing song: then worms shall try
That long preserved virginity:
And your quaint honour turn to dust;
And into ashes all my lust.
Andrew Marvell (1621–78) English poet and government official. 'To His Coy Mistress' (1650?), ll. 21–30

38 Time wounds all heels.
Groucho Marx (1895–1977) US comedian and film actor. Remark (1950?), attrib.

39 A molecule of hydrogen . . . whether in Sirius or in Arcturus, executes its vibrations in precisely the same time. Each molecule therefore throughout the universe bears impressed upon it the stamp of a metric system as distinctly as does the metre of the Archives at Paris, or the double royal cubit of the temple of Karnac.
James Clerk Maxwell (1831–79) British physicist. *Discourse on Molecules* (1873)

40 I sit with my back to the future, watching time pouring away into the past.
Norman McCaig (1910–96) Scottish poet. 'Crossing the Border' (1968)

41 For tribal man space was the uncontrollable mystery. For technological man it is time that occupies the same role.
Marshall McLuhan (1911–80) Canadian sociologist. 'Magic that Changes Mood', *The Mechanical Bride* (1951)

42 Time presupposes a view of time. It is, therefore, not like a river, not a flowing substance.
Maurice Merleau-Ponty (1908–61) French existentialist philosopher. *Phenomenology of Perception* (1945)

43 Fly, envious Time, till thou run out thy race, Call on the lazy leaden-stepping hours.
John Milton (1608–74) English writer. 'On Time' (1645), ll. 1–2

44 Time the devourer of everything.
Ovid (43 BC–AD 17?) Roman poet. *Metamorphoses* (AD 8?), bk. 15

45 A physician can sometimes parry the scythe of
death, but has no power over the sand in the
hourglass.
Hester Lynch Piozzi (1741–1821) Welsh writer. Letter to Fanny Burney
(November 22, 1781)

46 It is only time that weighs upon our hands.
It is only time, and that is not material.
Sylvia Plath (1932–63) US poet and novelist. March 1962. 'Three
Women', *Winter Trees* (1971)

47 Be ruled by time, the wisest counsellor of all.
Plutarch (46?–120?) Greek biographer and philosopher. 'Life of
Pericles', *Parallel Lives* (1st–2nd century)

48 In theory one is aware that the earth revolves but
in practice one does not perceive it, the ground
on which one treads seems not to move, and one
can live undisturbed. So it is with Time in one's
life.
Marcel Proust (1871–1922) French novelist. 1918. À l'Ombre des
Jeunes Filles en Fleurs, *À la Recherche du Temps Perdu*
(1913–27)

49 And the snail
with the ticking luggage of God's time.
Nelly Sachs (1891–1970) German-Swedish poet. 'White Serpent'
(1959), quoted in *German Poetry 1910–75* (Michael
Hamburger, ed., tr.; 1977)

50 Three o'clock is always too late or too early for
anything you want to do.
Jean-Paul Sartre (1905–80) French philosopher, playwright, and novelist.
Nausea (1938)

51 Time is man's angel.
Friedrich von Schiller (1759–1805) German poet, playwright, and historian.
The Robbers and Wallenstein (1799), Act 5, Scene 11

52 Time heals what reason cannot.
Seneca, 'the Younger' (4? BC–AD 65) Roman writer, philosopher, and
statesman. *Agamemnon* (45?), l. 130

53 Time's thievish progress to eternity.
William Shakespeare (1564–1616) English poet and playwright. Sonnet
77 (1609)

54 KING Th' inaudible and noiseless foot of Time.
William Shakespeare (1564–1616) English poet and playwright. *All's
Well That Ends Well* (1603), Act 5, Scene 3

55 HOTSPUR But thoughts, the slaves of life, and life,
time's fool,
And time, that takes survey of all the world,
Must have a stop.
William Shakespeare (1564–1616) English poet and playwright. *Henry
IV, Part 1* (1597), Act 5, Scene 4

56 Time's glory is to calm contending kings,
To unmask falsehood, and bring truth to light.
William Shakespeare (1564–1616) English poet and playwright. *The
Rape of Lucrece* (1594)

57 ULYSSES Time hath, my lord, a wallet at his back,
Wherein he puts alms for oblivion,
A great-siz'd monster of ingratitudes.
William Shakespeare (1564–1616) English poet and playwright. *Troilus
and Cressida* (1602), Act 3, Scene 3

58 As if you could kill time without injuring
eternity.
Henry David Thoreau (1817–62) US writer. 'Economy', *Walden, or,
Life in the Woods* (1854)

59 Time carries all things, even our wits, away.
Virgil (70–19 BC) Roman poet. *Eclogues* (37 BC), no. 9, l. 51

60 But meanwhile it is flying, irretrievable time is
flying.
Virgil (70–19 BC) Roman poet. *Georgics* (29 BC), no. 3, l. 284

61 Time is the metre, memory the only plot.
Derek Walcott (b. 1930) St. Lucian poet and playwright. *Omeros*
(1990), bk. 2, ch. 24, sect. 2

62 Time is what prevents everything from happening
at once.
John Archibald Wheeler (b. 1911) US theoretical physicist. 1978. Attrib.

63 Antiquity doesn't matter. In but a decade
An empty house can gain centuries.
Reed Whittemore (b. 1919) US poet. 'Our Ruins', *The Fascination of
Abomination* (1939), quoted in *The Penguin Book of
American Verse* (Geoffrey Moore, ed.; 1977)

64 I didn't go to the moon, I went much further—
for time is the longest distance between two
places.
Tennessee Williams (1911–83) US playwright. *The Glass Menagerie*
(1945), Scene 7

65 The Hopi, an Indian tribe, have a language as
sophisticated as ours, but no tenses for past,
present and future. The division does not exist.
What does this say about time?
Jeanette Winterson (b. 1959) British novelist. *Sexing the Cherry*
(1989)

66 Time drops in decay,
Like a candle burnt out.
W. B. Yeats (1865–1939) Irish poet and playwright. 'The Moods', *The
Wind Among the Reeds* (1899), ll. 1–2

67 Time flies, death urges, knells call, heaven invites,
Hell threatens.
Edward Young (1683–1765) English poet. *The Complaint, or Night
Thoughts on Life, Death, and Immortality* (1742–45)

Tiredness

see **Stress, World-Weariness**

Tolerance

see also **Freedom, Liberalism, Liberty**

1 The various modes of worship, which prevailed
in the Roman world, were all considered by the
people as equally true; by the philosopher, as
equally false; and by the magistrate, as equally
useful. And thus toleration produced not only
mutual indulgence, but even religious concord.
Edward Gibbon (1737–94) British historian. *The Decline and Fall of
the Roman Empire* (1776–88), ch. 2

2 If we cannot now end our differences, at least we
can help make the world safe for diversity.
John Fitzgerald Kennedy (1917–63) US president. Address, American
University, Washington DC (June 10, 1963)

3 The old law of an eye for an eye leaves
everybody blind.
Martin Luther King, Jr. (1929–68) US civil rights leader. 1955. Attrib.

4 They're not in prison with their fingernails pulled
out.
Kuan Yew Lee (b. 1923) Singaporean statesman. Replying to an
interviewer's suggestion that he was too tough on his political
opponents in Singapore. Interview, *Newsweek* (December 10,
1990)

5 So long as a man rides his *Hobby-Horse* peaceably and quietly along the king's highway, and neither compels you or me to get up behind him,—pray, Sir, what have either you or I to do with it?
Laurence Sterne (1713–68) Irish-born British writer and clergyman. *Tristram Shandy* (1759–67), bk. 1, ch. 7

6 A tolerant scepticism, an ability to doubt one's own ideas as well as those of other people, is a good test of maturity: fanaticism, insanity, and an infantile attitude to others are closely related.
Anthony Storr (b. 1920) British writer and psychiatrist. *The Integrated Personality* (1960)

Torture

see also **Cruelty, Human Rights, Pain, Persecution, Suffering**

1 We have ways of making men talk.
Anonymous. Film catch phrase, often repeated as 'We have ways of making you talk'. *Lives of a Bengal Lancer* (co-writers Waldemar Young, John L. Balderston, Achmed Abdullah, Grover Jones, and William Slavens McNutt; 1934)

2 Under torture you are as if under the dominion of those grasses that produce visions. Everything you have heard told, everything that you have read returns to your mind, as if you were being transported, not toward heaven, but toward hell.
Umberto Eco (b. 1932) Italian writer and literary scholar. *The Name of the Rose* (William Weaver, tr.; 1980), First Day: Sext

3 CORNWALL Out vile jelly!
Where is thy lustre now?
William Shakespeare (1564–1616) English poet and playwright. Spoken before putting out Gloucester's remaining eye. *King Lear* (1605–06), Act 3, Scene 7

4 Whipping and abuse are like laudanum: You have to double the dose as the sensibilities decline.
Harriet Beecher Stowe (1811–96) US writer and abolitionist. *Uncle Tom's Cabin* (1852), ch. 20

Totalitarianism

see also **Authoritarianism, Dictators, Oppression, Tyranny**

1 Totalitarianism cannot renounce violence. If it does it perishes . . . Man does not renounce freedom voluntarily. This conclusion holds out hope for our time, hope for the future.
Vasily Grossman (1905–64) Russian writer. 1960. *Life and Fate* (Robert Chandler, tr.; 1980), pt. 1, ch. 50

2 It is a common failing of totalitarian regimes that they cannot really understand the nature of our democracy. They mistake dissent for disloyalty. They mistake restlessness for a rejection of policy . . . They mistake individual speeches for public policy.
Lyndon Baines Johnson (1908–73) US president. Speech, San Antonio, Texas (September 29, 1967)

3 Totalitarianism is not so good at industrial innovation and adaptation to consumer demand.
William Keegan (b. 1938) British author and journalist. *The Spectre of Capitalism* (1992)

4 The totalitarian state is not unleashed force, it is truth in chains.
Bernard Henri Lévy (b. 1949) Algerian-born French philosopher. *La Barbarie à Visage Humain* (1977)

5 The members of the exterminating profession had a little saying: 'Give us the man, and we'll make a case'.
Nadezhda Mandelstam (1899–1980) Russian writer. Referring to the Russian secret police. *Hope Against Hope* (Max Hayward, tr.; 1970), ch. 3

6 Our fierce totalitarian will.
Benito Mussolini (1883–1945) Italian dictator. Quoted in *Europe Since 1870* (James Joll; 1973), ch. 9

7 Big Brother is watching you.
George Orwell (1903–50) British writer. *Nineteen Eighty-Four* (1949)

8 Thoughtcrime was not a thing that could be concealed forever. You might dodge successfully for a while, even for years, but sooner or later they were bound to get you.
George Orwell (1903–50) British writer. *Nineteen Eighty-Four* (1949)

9 The more you are in the right the more natural that everyone else should be bullied into thinking likewise.
George Orwell (1903–50) British writer. *The Road to Wigan Pier* (1937)

10 People got so used to staying indoors that curfews were declared illegal.
Can Yücel (b. 1926) Turkish poet. 'The Latest Situation in Chile', *Modern Turkish Poetry* (Feyyaz Kayacan Fergar, ed.; 1992)

11 It is hereby proclaimed to all the members of The One State:
Everyone who feels able to do so is obligated to compose treatises, poems, odes and/or other pieces on the beauty and grandeur of The One State.
Yevgeny Zamyatin (1884–1937) Russian writer. *We* (Bernard Guilbert Guerney, tr.; 1920)

Touch

see **Senses**

Tourism

see **Travel**

Traditions

see also **Artistic Styles, Culture, History, Religion**

1 With the loss of tradition we have lost the thread which safely guided us through the vast realms of the past, but this thread was also the chain fettering each successive generation to a predetermined aspect of the past.
Hannah Arendt (1906–75) German-born US philosopher and historian. Quoted in *New York Review of Books* (1971)

2 No man can cause more grief than that one clinging blindly to the vices of his ancestors.
William Faulkner (1897–1962) US novelist. *Intruder in the Dust* (1948)

3 There are few things in life more agreeable than the hour dedicated to the ceremony known as afternoon tea.
Henry James (1843–1916) US-born British writer and critic. *The Portrait of a Lady* (1881), ch. 1

4   It is a tradition in our country that the public
    authorities should not attempt to act so as to
    enforce the law, to secure justice, to further
    culture, to increase prosperity, or to direct the life
    of the people towards the destinies that its
    peculiar genius and vocation point to.
    Antonio Maura (1853–1925) Spanish politician. Quoted in *The
    Spanish Labyrinth* (Gerald Brenan; 1943)

5   Traditionalists are pessimists about the future
    and optimists about the past.
    Lewis Mumford (1895–1990) US social philosopher and urban planner.
    Attrib.

Tragedy

see also **Comedy, Disaster, Suffering**

1   Real tragedy is never resolved. It goes on
    hopelessly for ever.
    Chinua Achebe (b. 1930) Nigerian novelist, poet, and essayist. *No
    Longer at Ease* (1960)

2   Tragedy represents the life of princes; comedy
    serves to depict the actions of the people.
    François Aubignac (1604–76) French playwright and critic. *La Pratique
    du Théâtre* (1657)

3   Tragedy is if I cut my finger. Comedy is if I walk
    into an open sewer and die.
    Mel Brooks (b. 1926) US film actor and director. *New Yorker*
    (October 30, 1978)

4   All tragedies are finish'd by a death,
    All comedies are ended by a marriage.
    The future states of both are left to faith.
    Lord Byron (1788–1824) British poet. *Don Juan* (1819–24), can. 3,
    st. 9

5   We participate in a tragedy; at a comedy we only
    look.
    Aldous Huxley (1894–1963) British novelist and essayist. *The Devils of
    Loudon* (1952), ch. 11

6   Men play at tragedy because they do not believe
    in the reality of the tragedy which is actually
    being staged in the civilized world.
    José Ortega y Gasset (1883–1955) Spanish writer and philosopher. *The
    Revolt of the Masses* (1930)

7   The secret of our tragedy is
    that our screams are louder than our voices
    and our swords taller than ourselves.
    Nizar Qabbani (b. 1923) Syrian poet. 'Marginal Notes on the Book
    of Defeat' (1967), pt. 6, quoted in *When the Words Burn*
    (John Mikhail Asfour, ed., tr.; 1988)

8   Live on the abnormal and unheard of . . . sing
    the anguish of ultimate grief and discover the
    calvaries of the earth, arrive at the tragic by way
    of what is mysterious.
    Santiago Rusiñol (1861–1931) Spanish painter and critic. Quoted in
    Success and Failure of Picasso (John Berger; 1965)

9   PRINCE For never was a story of more woe
    Than this of Juliet and her Romeo.
    William Shakespeare (1564–1616) English poet and playwright. *Romeo
    and Juliet* (1595), Act 5, Scene 3

10 The bad end unhappily, the good unluckily. That
    is what tragedy means.
    Tom Stoppard (b. 1937) Czech-born British playwright and screenwriter.
    Imitating Miss Prism in Oscar Wilde's *The Importance of
    Being Earnest* (1895). *Rosencrantz and Guildenstern Are
    Dead* (1966), Act 2

11 My tragedy *The Father* was recently criticized for
    being too sad—as if one wants cheerful tragedies!
    Everybody is clamouring for this supposed 'joy of
    life' . . . I myself find the joy of life in its strong
    and cruel struggles, and my pleasure in learning,
    in adding to my knowledge.
    August Strindberg (1849–1912) Swedish dramatist. 1898. *Miss Julie*
    (Elizabeth Sprigge, tr.; 1955), Foreword

12 We begin to live when we have conceived life as
    a tragedy.
    W. B. Yeats (1865–1939) Irish poet and playwright. *Autobiographies*
    (1926)

Trains

see also **Travel**

1   This is the night mail crossing the border,
    Bringing the cheque and the postal order,
    Letters for the rich, letters for the poor,
    The shop at the corner and the girl next door.
    W. H. Auden (1907–73) British poet. 1935. 'Night Mail', *The
    English Auden: Poems, Essays and Dramatic Writings, 1927–
    39* (Edward Mendelson, ed.; 1977)

2   The only way to be sure of catching a train is to
    miss the one before it.
    G. K. Chesterton (1874–1936) British writer and poet. Attrib.

3   When a train pulls into a great city I am
    reminded of the closing moments of an overture.
    Graham Greene (1904–91) British novelist. *Travels with My Aunt*
    (1969)

4   Mr Stephenson having taken me on the bench of
    the engine with him, we started at about ten
    miles an hour. You cannot imagine how strange
    it seemed to be journeying on thus, without any
    visible cause of progressing other than that
    magical machine.
    Fanny Kemble (1809–93) British actor and writer. Referring to George
    Stephenson, inventor of the railway train the *Rocket*. *Record
    of a Girlhood* (1879)

5   There are some lines where it would be cheaper
    to give every one a Bentley and ask them to drive
    to work.
    Richard Marsh (b. 1928) British civil servant and politician. Referring to
    the British railway system. *Liverpool Daily Post* (April 7,
    1971)

6   Ever since childhood, when I lived within earshot
    of the Boston and Maine, I have seldom heard a
    train go by and not wished I was on it.
    Paul Theroux (b. 1941) US writer. *The Great Railway Bazaar* (1975)

7   For some, this was the train to Sullivan Square,
    or Milk Street, or at the very most Orient
    Heights; for me, it was the train to Patagonia.
    Paul Theroux (b. 1941) US writer. *The Old Patagonian Express: By
    Train Through the Americas* (1979)

Transience

see also **Mortality, Time**

1   All lovely things will have an ending
    All lovely things will fade and die
    And youth that's now so bravely spending,
    Will beg a penny by and by.
    Conrad Aiken (1889–1973) US poet and novelist. 'All Lovely Things'
    (1916)

2 So passes the glory of the world.

Anonymous. Referring to the large number of ruined castles in England, Normandy, and Anjou, that had been demolished after the rebellion (1173–74) against Henry II. *Histoire de Guillaume le Maréchal* (Paul Meyer, ed.; 1891–1901)

3 Outside the huge negations pass
Like whirlwinds writing on the grass
Inscriptions teaching us that all
The lessons are ephemeral.

George Barker (1913–91) British poet. 'Verses for the Sixtieth Birthday of T. S. Eliot' (1948)

4 It was a dream of perfect bliss,
Too beautiful to last.

Thomas Haynes Bayly (1797–1839) British writer. 'It Was a Dream', *Songs, Ballads, and Other Poems* (1844), st. 1, ll. 1–2

5 Faith, Sir, we are here to-day, and gone tomorrow.

Aphra Behn (1640?–89) English novelist and playwright. *The Lucky Chance* (1686)

6 If after the manner of men I have fought with beasts at Ephesus, what advantageth it me, if the dead rise not? Let us eat and drink; for tomorrow we die.

Bible. I Corinthians, *King James Bible* (1611), 15:32–33

7 Being born again, not of corruptible seed, but of incorruptible, by the word of God, which liveth and abideth for ever.
For all flesh is as grass, and all the glory of man as the flower of grass. The grass withereth, and the flower thereof falleth away.

Bible. I Peter, *King James Bible* (1611), 1:23–24

8 Suddenly, as rare things will, it vanished.

Robert Browning (1812–89) British poet. 'One Word More', *Men and Women* (1855), st. 4

9 Now the peak of summer's past, the sky is overcast
And the love we swore would last for an age seems deceit.

Cecil Day-Lewis (1904–72) Irish-born British writer. *Hornpipe* (1943)

10 Come, fill the Cup, and in the Fire of Spring
The Winter Garment of Repentance fling:
The Bird of Time has but a little way
To fly—and Lo! the Bird is on the Wing.

Edward FitzGerald (1809–83) British poet and translator. *The Rubáiyát of Omar Khayyám* (1859), st. 7

11 The Worldly Hope men set their Hearts upon
Turns Ashes—or it prospers; and anon,
Like Snow upon the Desert's dusty Face,
Lighting a little Hour or two—is gone.

Edward FitzGerald (1809–83) British poet and translator. *The Rubáiyát of Omar Khayyám* (1859), st. 14

12 One thing is certain, that Life flies;
One thing is certain, and the Rest is Lies;
The Flower that once has blown for ever dies.

Edward FitzGerald (1809–83) British poet and translator. *The Rubáiyát of Omar Khayyám* (1859), st. 26

13 Ah, fill the Cup:—what boots it to repeat
How Time is slipping underneath our Feet:
Unborn TO-MORROW, and dead YESTERDAY,
Why fret about them if TO-DAY be sweet!

Edward FitzGerald (1809–83) British poet and translator. *The Rubáiyát of Omar Khayyám* (1859), st. 37

14 What is fame? an empty bubble;
Gold? a transient, shining trouble.

James Grainger (1721?–66) British physician and poet. 'Solitude' (1755), ll. 96–97

15 Nothing stays firm forever;
As the seasons turn, everything vanishes like morning dew.

He Qifang (1912–77) Chinese writer and editor. 'I'd Like to Talk to You About All Kinds of Pure Things' (1942), quoted in *Anthology of Modern Chinese Poetry* (Michelle Yeh, ed., tr.; 1992)

16 Gather ye rosebuds while ye may,
Old time is still a-flying:
And this same flower that smiles today
Tomorrow will be dying.

Robert Herrick (1591–1674) English poet. 'To the Virgins, To Make Much of Time', *Hesperides* (1648), st. 1

17 Life's short span forbids us to enter on far-reaching hopes.

Horace (65–8 BC) Roman poet. *Odes* (23 BC), bk. 1, no. 4, l. 15

18 Not to hope for things to last for ever, is what the year teaches and even the hour which snatches a nice day away.

Horace (65–8 BC) Roman poet. *Odes* (13? BC), bk. 4, no. 7, l. 7

19 Where's the cheek that doth not fade,
Too much gaz'd at? Where's the maid
Whose lip mature is ever new?

John Keats (1795–1821) English poet. 'Fancy' (1820), ll. 69–71

20 But she was of the world where the fairest things have the worst fate. Like a rose, she has lived as long as roses live, the space of one morning.

François de Malherbe (1555–1628) French poet. 'Consolation à Monsieur du Périer', *Stances Spirituelles* (1599)

21 Everything is only for a day, both that which remembers and that which is remembered.

Marcus Aurelius (121–180) Roman emperor and philosopher. *Meditations* (170–180), bk. 4, sect. 35

22 How fading are the joys we dote upon!
Like apparitions seen and gone.
But those which soonest take their flight
Are the most exquisite and strong,
Like angels' visits, short and bright;
Mortality's too weak to bear them long.

John Norris (1657–1711) English philosopher. 'The Parting', *The Miscellanies* (1687)

23 Like as the waves make towards the pebbled shore,
So do our minutes hasten to their end.

William Shakespeare (1564–1616) English poet and playwright. Sonnet 60 (1609)

24 JAQUES And so, from hour to hour, we ripe and ripe,
And then, from hour to hour, we rot and rot;
And thereby hangs a tale.

William Shakespeare (1564–1616) English poet and playwright. *As You Like It* (1599), Act 2, Scene 7

25 AGAMEMNON What's past, and what's to come is strew'd with husks
And formless ruin of oblivion.

William Shakespeare (1564–1616) English poet and playwright. *Troilus and Cressida* (1602), Act 4, Scene 5

26 Though nothing can bring back the hour
Of splendour in the grass, of glory in the flower;
We will grieve not, rather find
Strength in what remains behind.

William Wordsworth (1770–1850) English poet. 1802?–06. 'Ode: Intimations of Immortality from Recollections of Early Childhood', *Poems in Two Volumes* (1807), vol. 2, st. 10, ll. 181–184

Translation

see also **European Languages, Language, World Literature**

1 The original is unfaithful to the translation.

Jorge Luis Borges (1899–1986) Argentinian writer and poet. Referring to Henley's translation of *Vathek: An Arabian Tale* (1786) by the British writer William Beckford. "Sobre el 'Vathek' de William Beckford" (1943)

2 A translator is to be like his author, it is not his business to excel him.

Samuel Johnson (1709–84) British lexicographer and writer. Quoted in *A History of Reading* (Alberto Manguel; 1996)

3 A linguistic work translated into another language is like someone going across the border without his skin and putting on the local garb on the other side.

Karl Kraus (1874–1936) Austrian writer. 1912. Quoted in 'Pro domo et mundo', *Karl Kraus* (Harry Zohn; 1971)

4 Translating is the ultimate act of comprehending.

Alberto Manguel (b. 1948) Argentinian writer. *A History of Reading* (1996)

5 An idea does not pass from one language to another without change.

Miguel de Unamuno y Jugo (1864–1936) Spanish writer and philosopher. *The Tragic Sense of Life in Men and Peoples* (1913)

Travel

see also **Boats, Cars, Exploration, Flying, Places, Trains**

1 The world is a book, and those who do not travel, read only a page.

Saint Augustine of Hippo (354–430) Numidian Christian theologian and Doctor of the Church. Attrib.

2 Travel, in the younger sort, is a part of education; in the elder, a part of experience. He that travelleth into a country before he hath some entrance into the language, goeth to school, and not to travel.

Francis Bacon (1561–1626) English philosopher, statesman, and lawyer. 'Of Travel', *Essays* (1625)

3 Time was when you could go on an outing to a town barely thirty miles distant from your own and it was like visiting another country.

Beryl Bainbridge (b. 1934) British author and journalist. *Forever England North and South* (1987)

4 I have recently been all round the world and have formed a very poor opinion of it.

Thomas Beecham (1879–1961) British conductor and impresario. Speech at the Savoy, *News Review* (August 22, 1946)

5 We must travel in the direction of our fear.

John Berryman (1914–72) US poet. 'A Point of Age', *Poems* (1942)

6 When you halt in the desert make an arrow from pebbles, so, if suddenly woken up, you'll grasp which way to go.

Joseph Brodsky (1940–96) Russian-born US poet and writer. 'Advice to a Traveller', *Worst Journeys* (Keath Fraser, ed.; 1991)

7 The destination of all journeys is their beginning.

Angela Carter (1940–92) British novelist, essayist, and short-story writer. *The Passion of New Eve* (1977), ch. 11

8 Journey all over the universe in a map, without the expense and fatigue of travelling, without suffering the inconveniences of heat, cold, hunger, and thirst.

Miguel de Cervantes (1547–1616) Spanish novelist and playwright. *Don Quixote* (1605–15), pt. 3, ch. 6

9 Only a toothbrush is really indispensable: starting from the top this will neaten the hair, remove scurf from the collar, clean the teeth, then the fingernails—and then, if needs are dire, ream out between the toes and the welts of the shoes.

George Courtauld (b. 1938) British civil servant and author. The lesson of travelling light, learned as a Queen's Messenger. *The Travels of a Fat Bulldog* (1996)

10 Tourism is the march of stupidity.

Don DeLillo (b. 1936) US novelist. Said by James Axton. *The Names* (1982)

11 Happy he who like Ulysses has made a glorious journey.

Joachim du Bellay (1522?–60) French poet. Sonnet 31, *Les Regrets* (1558)

12 The weird mixture of smells which together compose the anthology of a Greek holiday under the pines—petrol, garlic, wine and goat.

Lawrence Durrell (1912–90) British novelist and poet. *Reflections on a Marine Venus* (1953)

13 A great traveller is a kind of introspective who, as she covers the ground outwardly, so she advances inwardly.

Lawrence Durrell (1912–90) British novelist and poet. Referring to travel writer Freya Stark. Quoted in *Virago Book of Women Travellers* (Mary Morris, ed.; 1996), Introduction

14 A cold coming we had of it,
Just the worst time of the year
For a journey, and such a long journey:
The ways deep and the weather sharp,
The very dead of winter.

T. S. Eliot (1888–1965) US-born British poet and playwright. 1927. 'Journey of the Magi', *Collected Poems 1909–35* (1936)

15 The woods are lovely, dark, and deep,
But I have promises to keep,
And miles to go before I sleep,
And miles to go before I sleep.

Robert Frost (1874–1963) US poet. 'Stopping by Woods on a Snowy Evening', *New Hampshire* (1923), st. 4

16 The only aspect of our travels that is guaranteed to hold an audience is disaster.

Martha Gellhorn (1908–98) US journalist and author. *Travels with Myself and Another* (1978)

17 Eighty per cent of the people of Britain want more money spent on public transport—in order that other people will travel on the buses so that there is more room for them to drive their cars.

John Selwyn Gummer (b. 1939) British politician. *Independent* (October 14, 1994)

18 Foreign places help your mind to float free
And reduce you to such simplicity
You only know the words for Good night and Good day
And Please.
You don't know how to say
'My life is torn between immutable existential uncertainties'.

Garrison Keillor (b. 1942) US writer and broadcaster. *Leaving Home* (1987)

19 No other form of transport in the rest of my life has ever come up to the bliss of my pram.

Osbert Lancaster (1908–86) English cartoonist and writer. *Observer* (January 25, 1976), 'Sayings of the Week'

20 A man travels the world in search of what he needs and returns home to find it.

George Moore (1852–1933) Irish writer. *The Brook Kerith* (1916), ch. 11

21 For forty years I have made a professional
speciality of the happy journey. When things have
gone wrong, I have resolutely forgotten them.
Jan Morris (b. 1926) British travel writer. 'My Worst Journey', *Worst
Journeys* (Keath Fraser, ed.; 1991)

22 The British travel book . . . grew out of a
particular set of historical circumstances. It was
an inevitable by-product of that lust for empire
which was the driving force behind the English
Renaissance.
Jonathan Raban (b. 1942) British author. 1991. Quoted in *Writers
Abroad* (The British Council; 1992)

23 In the Middle Ages people were tourists because of
their religion, whereas now they are tourists
because tourism is their religion.
Robert Runcie (1921–2000) British archbishop. *Observer* (December
11, 1988), 'Sayings of the Week'

24 Travel is the most private of pleasures. There is
no greater bore than the travel bore. We do not
in the least want to hear what he has seen in
Hong-Kong.
Vita Sackville-West (1892–1962) British poet and novelist. *Passenger to
Tehran* (1926), ch. 1

25 To travel
is to return
to strangers.
Dennis Scott (1939–91) Jamaican editor, actor, and poet. Quoted in
Breaklight: An Anthology of Caribbean Poetry (Andrew
Salkey, ed.; 1971)

26 That is my home of love: if I have rang'd,
Like him that travels, I return again.
William Shakespeare (1564–1616) English poet and playwright. Sonnet
109 (1609)

27 Once a journey is designed, equipped, and put in
process a new factor enters and takes over . . . it
has personality, temperament, individuality,
uniqueness. A journey is a person in itself, no
two are alike.
John Steinbeck (1902–68) US novelist. *Travels with Charley: In
Search of America* (1962)

28 We find after years of struggle that we do not
take a trip; a trip takes us.
John Steinbeck (1902–68) US novelist. *Travels with Charley: In
Search of America* (1962)

29 A journey is like a marriage. The certain way to
be wrong is to think you can control it.
John Steinbeck (1902–68) US novelist. *Travels with Charley: In
Search of America* (1962), pt. 1

30 For my part, I travel not to go anywhere, but to go.
I travel for travel's sake. The great affair is to move.
Robert Louis Stevenson (1850–94) Scottish novelist, essayist, and poet.
'Cheylard and Luc', *Travels with a Donkey in the Cévennes*
(1879)

31 To travel hopefully is a better thing than to
arrive, and the true success is to labour.
Robert Louis Stevenson (1850–94) Scottish novelist, essayist, and poet. 'El
Dorado', *Virginibus Puerisque* (1881)

32 I always love to begin a journey on Sundays,
because I shall have the prayers of the church, to
preserve all that travel by land, or by water.
Jonathan Swift (1667–1745) Irish writer and clergyman. *Polite
Conversation* (1738), Dialogue 2

33 Extensive travelling includes a feeling of
encapsulation, and travel, so broadening at first,
contracts the mind.
Paul Theroux (b. 1941) US writer. *The Great Railway Bazaar*
(1975), ch. 2

34 Travel is a vanishing act, a solitary trip down a
pinched line of geography to oblivion.
Paul Theroux (b. 1941) US writer. *The Old Patagonian Express: By
Train Through the Americas* (1979)

35 Journeys rarely begin where we think they do.
Mine, perhaps, started in that classroom, where
the green-tinted mystery hypnotized me during
maths lessons.
Colin Thubron (b. 1939) British travel writer and novelist. Referring to a
map of the world on the classroom wall. *Among the Russians*
(1983), ch. 1

36 The longest part of the journey is said to be the
passing of the gate.
Marcus Terentius Varro (116–27 BC) Roman scholar. *On Agriculture*
(37? BC), bk. 1

37 But from the final orders given him by his master
when he left the *Mongolia* Passepartout realized
that the same thing would happen in Bombay as
had happened in Paris. And he began to wonder
if that bet of Mr. Fogg's was not a serious
business after all and if fate would not drag him
round the world in eighty days in spite of his
desire for a quiet life.
Jules Verne (1828–1905) French writer. *Around the World in Eighty
Days* (1873)

Treason

see also **Betrayal**, **Blasphemy**, **Heresy**

1 It was not, as our enemies say, our intention to
kill the king and his sons, but to make him the
duke of Lancaster, which is what he ought to be.
Anonymous. Referring to Henry IV. Said by one of the
Franciscans condemned for plotting (1402) to overthrow him.
Eulogium Historiarum

2 But treason is not own'd when 'tis descried;
Successful crimes alone are justified.
John Dryden (1631–1700) English poet, playwright, and literary critic. *The
Medal* (1682), ll. 207–208

3 The last temptation is the greatest treason:
To do the right deed for the wrong reason.
T. S. Eliot (1888–1965) US-born British poet and playwright. *Murder in
the Cathedral* (1935), Act 1

4 A desperate disease requires a dangerous remedy.
Guy Fawkes (1570–1606) English conspirator. November 5, 1605.
Justifying the Gunpowder Plot, on being questioned by the
king and council immediately after his arrest. Quoted in
Dictionary of National Biography (1917)

5 Please to remember the Fifth of November,
Gunpowder Treason and Plot.
We know no reason why gunpowder treason
Should ever be forgot.
Folk Verse. Traditional rhyme referring to the plot by Guy
Fawkes and others to blow up the Houses of Parliament as a
protest against the anti-Roman Catholic laws (November 5,
1605).

6 Any service rendered to the temporal king to the
prejudice of the eternal king is, without doubt, an
act of treachery.
Stephen Langton (1150?–1228) English clergyman. Letter to the barons
of England (1207)

7 KING There's such divinity doth hedge a king
That treason can but peep to what it would.
William Shakespeare (1564–1616) English poet and playwright. *Hamlet*
(1601), Act 4, Scene 5

8 KING RICHARD II Mine eyes are full of tears, I
cannot see:
And yet salt water blinds them not so much
But they can see a sort of traitors here.
Nay, if I turn my eyes upon myself,
I find myself a traitor with the rest.
William Shakespeare (1564–1616) English poet and playwright. *Richard II* (1595), Act 4, Scene 1

9 If words spoken to friends, in familiar discourse,
spoken in one's chamber, spoken at one's table,
spoken in one's sick-bed . . . if these things shall
be brought against a man as treason . . . it will
be a silent world . . . and no man shall dare to
impart his solitary thoughts or opinions to his
friend and neighbour.
Thomas Wentworth (1593–1641) English statesman. Remark at his trial (April 5, 1641)

Trees

see also **The Environment, Nature**

1 Trees are poems that the earth writes upon the
sky. We fell them down and turn them into
paper that we may record our emptiness.
Kahlil Gibran (1883–1931) Lebanese-born US mystic, painter, and poet. *Sand and Foam* (1926)

2 I'm replacing some of the timber used up by my
books. Books are just trees with squiggles on
them.
Hammond Innes (b. 1913) British novelist. *Radio Times* (August 18, 1984)

3 I think that I shall never see
A poem lovely as a tree.
Joyce Kilmer (1886–1918) US poet. 'Trees', *Trees and Other Poems* (1914)

4 The difference between a gun and a tree is a
difference of tempo. The tree explodes every
spring.
Ezra Pound (1885–1972) US poet, translator, and critic. *Criterion* (July 1937)

5 Tree surgeons are taught to wear safety belts so
they won't fall out of patients.
Proverb.

Triviality

1 All is gas and gaiters.
Charles Dickens (1812–70) British novelist. *Nicholas Nickleby* (1839), ch. 49

2 What dire offence from am'rous causes springs,
What mighty contests rise from trivial things.
Alexander Pope (1688–1744) English poet. *The Rape of the Lock* (1712), can. 1, ll. 1–2

3 IAGO To suckle fools and chronicle small beer.
William Shakespeare (1564–1616) English poet and playwright. *Othello* (1602–04), Act 2, Scene 1

Trust

see also **Faith, Faithfulness, Friendship, Loyalty**

1 We are inclined to believe those whom we do not
know because they have never deceived us.
Samuel Johnson (1709–84) British lexicographer and writer. *The Idler* (1758)

2 A man who doesn't trust himself can never really
trust anyone else.
Cardinal de Retz (1613–79) French ecclesiastic and politician. *Mémoires* (1717)

3 The most distrustful are often the greatest dupes.
Cardinal de Retz (1613–79) French ecclesiastic and politician. *Mémoires* (1717)

4 Would you buy a second-hand car from this
man?
Mort Sahl (b. 1926) US political comedian. Referring to Richard Nixon. Attrib.

5 Trust the man who hesitates in his speech and is
quick and steady in action, but beware of long
arguments and long beards.
George Santayana (1863–1952) Spanish-born US philosopher, poet, and novelist. 'The British Character', *Soliloquies in England* (1922)

6 The more they trusted me, the less I could afford
to make a mistake.
Zhang Yimou (b. 1950) Chinese film director. Referring to the Chinese authorities. Quoted in 'Turandot in the Forbidden City', *China Review* (Yu Peng; Autumn/Winter 1998)

Truth

see also **Frankness, Honesty, Knowledge, Sincerity**

1 The truth which makes men free is for the most
part the truth which men prefer not to hear.
Herbert Agar (1897–1980) US writer and journalist. *A Time for Greatness* (1942)

2 Nothing is true except what is not said.
Jean Anouilh (1910–87) French playwright. *Antigone* (1942)

3 The truth of a proposition should be sought only
in the proposition itself.
Saint Anselm (1033–1109) Italian-born philosopher and prelate. *De Veritate* (1080)

4 Unless I am mistaken therefore, we can define
'truth' as 'rightness' perceptible by the mind
alone.
Saint Anselm (1033–1109) Italian-born philosopher and prelate. *De Veritate* (1080)

5 Piety requires us to honour truth over our
friends.
Aristotle (384–322 BC) Greek philosopher. *Nicomachean Ethics* (4th century BC), 1096a

6 Truth sits upon the lips of dying men.
Matthew Arnold (1822–88) British poet and critic. 'Sohrab and Rustum' (1853), l. 656

7 The inquiry of truth, which is the love-making,
or wooing of it, the knowledge of truth, which is
the presence of it, and the belief of truth, which
is the enjoying of it, is the sovereign good of
human nature.
Francis Bacon (1561–1626) English philosopher, statesman, and lawyer. 'Of Truth', *Essays* (1625)

8 I tore myself away from the safe comfort of
certainties through my love for truth; and truth
rewarded me.
Simone de Beauvoir (1908–86) French writer and feminist theorist. *All Said and Done* (1974)

9 Truth is true only as it brings down more
disgrace and dreariness upon human beings, so
that if it shows anything except evil it is illusion,
and not truth.
Saul Bellow (b. 1915) Canadian-born US writer. *Herzog* (1964)

10 Between truth and the search for truth, I opt for the second.

Bernard Berenson (1865–1959) Lithuanian-born US art historian. *Essays in Appreciation* (1958)

11 And ye shall know the truth, and the truth shall make you free.

Bible. John, *King James Bible* (1611), 8:32

12 Pilate saith unto him, What is truth? And when he had said this, he went out again unto the Jews, and saith unto them, I find in him no fault at all.

Bible. John, *King James Bible* (1611), 18:38

13 When I tell any Truth it is not for the sake of convincing those who do not know it, but for the sake of defending those who do.

William Blake (1757–1827) British poet, painter, engraver, and mystic. Public Address (1810?), quoted in *Complete Writings* (Geoffrey Keynes, ed.; 1957)

14 Truths of the past become lies of the present, and the effort to believe them is greater than the effort that would discover the truth.

Edward Bond (b. 1934) British playwright. *The Hidden Plot* (2000)

15 Truth exists; only lies are invented.

Georges Braque (1882–1963) French painter and sculptor. *Le Jour et la Nuit: Cahiers 1917–52* (1952)

16 A man may be in as just possession of truth as of a city, and yet be forced to surrender.

Thomas Browne (1605–82) English physician and writer. *Religio Medici* (1642), pt. 1, sect. 6

17 The most casual student of history knows that, as a matter of fact, truth does *not* necessarily vanquish . . . The cause of truth must be championed, and it must be championed dynamically.

William F. Buckley, Jr. (b. 1925) US writer. *God and Man at Yale* (1951)

18 There is nothing as boring as the truth.

Charles Bukowski (1920–94) German-born US writer. *Notes of a Dirty Old Man* (1969)

19 Some men love truth so much that they seem to be in continual fear lest she should catch a cold on overexposure.

Samuel Butler (1835–1902) British writer and composer. Quoted in *Note Books* (H. Festing Jones, ed.; 1912)

20 'Tis strange—but true; for truth is always strange;
Stranger than fiction: if it could be told,
How much would novels gain by the exchange!

Lord Byron (1788–1824) British poet. *Don Juan* (1819–24), can. 14, st. 101

21 It serves no purpose to tell oneself the truth and nothing but the truth. The only truth that does not transform itself into nothing is horror and annihilation.

Elias Canetti (1905–94) Bulgarian-born writer. *The Agony of Flies* (1992)

22 What I tell you three times is true.

Lewis Carroll (1832–98) British writer and mathematician. *The Hunting of the Snark* (1876)

23 Truth is a never-ending agony. The truth of this world is death. One must choose—die or lie. I've never been able to kill myself.

Louis-Ferdinand Céline (1894–1961) French novelist and physician. *Voyage au Bout de la Nuit* (1932)

24 Trouthe is the hyeste thyng that man may kepe.

Geoffrey Chaucer (1343?–1400) English poet. 'The Franklin's Tale', *The Canterbury Tales* (1390?), l. 1479, quoted in *The Works of Geoffrey Chaucer* (F. N. Robinson, ed.; 1957)

25 In wartime, truth is so precious that she should always be attended by a bodyguard of lies.

Winston Churchill (1874–1965) British prime minister and writer. Said to Stalin. *The Second World War* (1948–53)

26 If the truth were self-evident, eloquence would be unnecessary.

Cicero (106–43 BC) Roman orator and statesman. *De Oratore* (55 BC)

27 It is an old maxim of mine that when you have excluded the impossible, whatever remains, however improbable, must be the truth.

Arthur Conan Doyle (1859–1930) Scottish-born British writer and physician. *The Sign of Four* (1889), ch. 6

28 Ethical axioms are found and tested not very differently from the axioms of science. Truth is what stands the test of experience.

Albert Einstein (1879–1955) German-born US physicist. *Out of My Later Years* (1950)

29 Truth never turns tail like a disinterested cat: it purrs, it winks its feline eyes, it sees, it envisions; truth is the breath in the air, the breath that someone somewhere in the world will inhale, and then speak, in the end.

Nuruddin Farah (b. 1945) Somali novelist, playwright, and teacher. 'Why I Write', *Third World Quarterly* (July 1988), vol. 10, no. 4

30 Truth is only falsehood well disguised.

George Farquhar (1678–1707) Irish playwright. *The Constant Couple* (1699), Act 3, Scene 4

31 Truth made you a traitor as it often does in a time of scoundrels.

Lillian Hellman (1905–84) US playwright. Referring to the McCarthy era. *Scoundrel Time* (1976)

32 A man that seeketh precise truth had need to remember what every name he uses stands for, and to place it accordingly, or else he will find himself entangled in words, as a bird in lime twigs, the more he struggles, the more belimed.

Thomas Hobbes (1588–1679) English philosopher and political thinker. *Leviathan* (1651)

33 Truth is the breath of life to human society. It is the food of the immortal spirit. Yet a single word of it may kill a man as suddenly as a drop of prussic acid.

Oliver Wendell Holmes (1841–1935) US judge. Address at Harvard Commencement (March 10, 1858)

34 And seek for truth in the groves of Academe.

Horace (65–8 BC) Roman poet. Origin of the phrase 'the groves of Academe'. *Epistles* (20? BC), bk. 2, no. 2, l. 45

35 It's easy to make a man confess the lies he tells to himself; it's far harder to make him confess the truth.

Geoffrey Household (1900–88) British novelist. *Rogue Male* (1939)

36 If some great Power would agree to make me always think what is true and do what is right, on condition of being turned into a sort of clock and wound up every morning before I got out of bed, I should instantly close with the offer.

T. H. Huxley (1825–95) British biologist. 'On Descartes' Discourse on Method', *Method and Results* (1870)

37 Men will fight for superstition quite as quickly as for a living truth—often more so, since a superstition is so intangible you cannot get at it to refute it, but truth is a point of view, and so is interchangeable.

Hypatia (370?–415) Greek philosopher, mathematician, and astronomer. Quoted in 'Hypatia', *Little Journeys to the Homes of Great Teachers* (Elbert Hubbard; 1908)

38 The terrible *fluidity of self-revelation*.

Henry James (1843–1916) US-born British writer and critic. *The Ambassadors* (1903), Preface

39 The first casualty when war comes is truth.

Hiram W. Johnson (1866–1945) US politician and reformer. Speech, US Senate (1917)

40 Truth is a clumsy servant that breaks the dishes while cleaning them.

Karl Kraus (1874–1936) Austrian writer. 1909. Quoted in 'Sprüche und Widersprüche', *Karl Kraus* (Harry Zohn; 1971)

41 It is an indication of truth's jealousy that it has not made for anyone a path to it.

Naguib Mahfouz (b. 1911) Egyptian writer. *Arabian Nights and Days* (1982)

42 A great truth is a truth whose opposite is also a great truth.

Thomas Mann (1875–1955) German writer. *Essay on Freud* (1937)

43 There are no new truths, but only truths that have not been recognized by those who have perceived them without noticing.

Mary McCarthy (1912–89) US writer. 'Vita Activa', *On the Contrary* (1961)

44 No one wants the truth if it is inconvenient.

Arthur Miller (b. 1915) US playwright. *Observer* (January 8, 1989), 'Sayings of the Week'

45 Even if everything I say is wrong, is prejudiced, spiteful, malevolent, even if I am a liar and a poisoner, it is nevertheless the truth and it will have to be swallowed.

Henry Miller (1891–1980) US novelist. *Tropic of Capricorn* (1939)

46 Truth . . . never comes into the world but like a bastard, to the ignominy of him that brought her forth.

John Milton (1608–74) English writer. Introduction, *The Doctrine and Discipline of Divorce* (1643)

47 Truths are illusions about which one has forgotten that this is what they are; metaphors which are worn out and without sensuous power; coins which have lost their pictures and now matter only as metal, no longer as coins.

Friedrich Wilhelm Nietzsche (1844–1900) German philosopher and poet. 'On Truth and Lie in an Extra-Moral Sense', *The Portable Nietzsche* (Walter Kaufmann, ed., tr.; 1954)

48 I preach there are all kinds of truth, your truth and somebody else's. But behind all of them there is only one truth and that is that there's no truth.

Flannery O'Connor (1925–64) US novelist and short-story writer. Said by Hazel Motes. *Wise Blood* (1952), ch. 10

49 Your explanation had the ring of truth. Naturally I disbelieved it.

Joe Orton (1933–67) British playwright. *Loot* (1966)

50 We know the truth, not only by the reason, but also by the heart.

Blaise Pascal (1623–62) French philosopher, mathematician, and physicist. *Pensées* (1669), sect. 10, no. 1

51 He who does not bellow the truth when he knows the truth makes himself the accomplice of liars and forgers.

Charles Pierre Péguy (1873–1914) French writer and poet. 'Provincial Letter' (December 21, 1899), quoted in *Basic Verities* (A. and J. Green, trs.; 1943)

52 Truth often suffers more by the heat of its defenders than from the arguments of its opposers.

William Penn (1644–1718) English preacher and colonialist. *Some Fruits of Solitude* (1693)

53 The man of reflection discovers Truth; but the one who enjoys it and makes use of its heavenly gifts is the man of action.

Benito Pérez Galdós (1843–1920) Spanish novelist and playwright. *El Amigo Manso* (1882), ch. 39

54 Speak the truth and shame the Devil.

François Rabelais (1494?–1553?) French humanist and satirist. *Gargantua and Pantagruel* (1546), Prologue

55 Truth is no road to fortune.

Jean-Jacques Rousseau (1712–78) French philosopher and writer. *The Social Contract* (1762)

56 If you seek authenticity for authenticity's sake, you are no longer authentic.

Jean-Paul Sartre (1905–80) French philosopher, playwright, and novelist. *Notebooks for an Ethics* (1983)

57 He who never ventures beyond actuality will never win the prize of truth.

Friedrich von Schiller (1759–1805) German poet, playwright, and historian. Tenth letter (1793), quoted in *On the Aesthetic Education of Man* (E. M. Wilkinson and C. A. Willoughby, eds., trs.; 1967)

58 Truth has no special time of its own. Its hour is now—always.

Albert Schweitzer (1875–1965) German theologian, philosopher, physician, and musicologist. *Out of My Life and Thought* (1949)

59 LAUNCELOT Truth will come to light; murder cannot be hid long.

William Shakespeare (1564–1616) English poet and playwright. *The Merchant of Venice* (1596–98), Act 2, Scene 2

60 Truth telling is not compatible with the defence of the realm.

George Bernard Shaw (1856–1950) Irish playwright. *Heartbreak House* (1919)

61 When truth is discovered by someone else, it loses something of its attractiveness.

Alexander Solzhenitsyn (b. 1918) Russian novelist. *Candle in the Wind* (1972), Act 3

62 It takes two to speak the truth—one to speak, and another to hear.

Henry David Thoreau (1817–62) US writer. 'Wednesday', *A Week on the Concord and Merrimack Rivers* (1849)

63 Truth is the most valuable thing we have. Let us economize it.

Mark Twain (1835–1910) US writer and humorist. *Following the Equator* (1897), ch. 7

64 It is a terrible thing for a man to find out suddenly that all his life he has been speaking nothing but the truth.

Oscar Wilde (1854–1900) Irish poet, playwright, and wit. *The Importance of Being Earnest* (1895), Act 3

65 THE TRUTH IS OUT THERE.

The X Files, US television series. The creed of Fox Mulder, an FBI agent in the television series. *The X Files* (1990s)

Turkey

see **Europe**, **European Countries**

Twentieth Century

see also **Cold War**, **Modernity**, **World War I**, **World War II**

1   The marriage of reason and nightmare that has
    dominated the 20th century has given birth to an
    ever more ambiguous world . . . thermo-nuclear
    weapons systems and soft-drink commercials
    coexist in an overlit realm ruled by advertising
    and pseudo-events, science and pornography.

    J. G. Ballard (b. 1930) Chinese-born British writer. *Crash* (1995
    edition), Introduction

2   The horror of the twentieth century was the size
    of each event, and the paucity of the
    reverberation.

    Norman Mailer (b. 1923) US novelist and journalist. *Of a Fire on the
    Moon* (1970), ch. 2

3   If the nineteenth century was the age of the
    editorial chair, ours is the century of the
    psychiatrist's couch.

    Marshall McLuhan (1911–80) Canadian sociologist. *Understanding
    Media* (1964), Introduction

4   We are living a million lives in the space of a
    generation.

    Henry Miller (1891–1980) US novelist. *Tropic of Cancer* (1934)

5   Here we are, busily preparing ourselves for a war
    already described as 'unthinkable' . . . spying on
    each other, rewarding people on quiz programs
    with $100,000 for knowing how to spell 'cat',
    and Zwicky wants to make a hundred *new*
    worlds.

    E. B. White (1899–1985) US writer and humorist. June 14, 1956.
    Referring to astrophysicist Fritz Zwicky's proposal that 100
    new planets could be created. 'Coon Tree', *Essays of E. B.
    White* (1977)

Twenty-first Century

see also **The Future**, **Globalization**, **Modernity**

1   In retrospect, the Millennium marked only a
    moment in time. It was the events of September
    11 that marked a turning point in history, where
    we confront the dangers of the future and assess
    the choices facing humankind.

    Tony Blair (b. 1953) British prime minister. Referring to the terrorist
    attacks in the United States on September 11, 2001. Speech,
    Labour Party Conference, Brighton (October 2, 2001)

2   The 1970s for me was the beginning of the 21st
    century—it was the beginning of a true pluralism
    of social attitudes.

    David Bowie (b. 1947) British pop singer. Attrib.

3   High on the agenda for the 21st century will be
    the need to restore some kind of tragic
    consciousness.

    Carlos Fuentes (b. 1928) Mexican writer. Quoted in *An Agenda for
    the 21st Century* (Rushworth M. Kidder; 1987)

4   The American century—and the European half
    millennium—is coming to an end. The world
    century is beginning.

    Rosabeth Moss Kanter (b. 1943) US management educator, consultant, and
    writer. *World Class* (1995)

5   My fervent hope is for a Copernican shift: from a
    money-centred world to a human-centred world.
    For the subordination of money values to human
    and environmental values.

    Ann Pettifor, British activist. Referring to her hopes for the new
    millennium. As director of the organisation Jubilee 2000, she
    has campaigned for the elimination of debt of poorer nations
    to wealthy ones. *Observer* (January 2, 2000)

6   The 19th Century was the century of the UK.
    The 20th Century was the century of the US. The
    21st Century will be the century of China. Not
    Japan—China.

    Jim Rogers, US investor. *The Charlie Rose Show* (US Public
    Broadcasting Service; December 18, 1995)

Tyranny

see also **Authoritarianism**, **Fascism**, **Oppression**, **Persecution**

1   Under conditions of tyranny it is easier to act
    than think.

    Hannah Arendt (1906–75) German-born US philosopher and historian.
    Quoted in *A Certain World* (W. H. Auden; 1970)

2   Despotism accomplishes great things illegally;
    liberty doesn't even go to the trouble of
    accomplishing small things legally.

    Honoré de Balzac (1799–1850) French writer. *La Peau de Chagrin*
    (1831), ch. 3

3   If we take to dreaming once more . . . of a world
    where signs are certain, of a strong 'symbolic
    order', let's be under no illusions. For this order has
    existed, and it was a brutal hierarchy, since the
    sign's transparency is indissociably also its cruelty.

    Jean Baudrillard, French cultural critic. Quoted in *Symbolic
    Exchange and Death* (Iain Hamilton Grant, tr.; 1993)

4   He is an ordinary human being after all! . . .
    now he will put himself above everyone else and
    become a tyrant.

    Ludwig van Beethoven (1770–1827) German composer. Referring to
    Napoleon, on hearing that he had declared himself emperor.
    Attributed to him by a pupil (1804)

5   You cannot subjugate a man and recognize his
    humanity, his history, and his personality; so
    systematically, you must take this away from
    him. You begin by telling lies about this man's
    role in history.

    John Henrik Clarke (1915–98) US historian and educator. Address to
    Jewish Currents conference, New York (February 15, 1969)

6   Nature has left this tincture in the blood,
    That all men would be tyrants if they could.

    Daniel Defoe (1660–1731) English novelist and journalist. *The History
    of the Kentish Petition* (1712–13), Addenda, l. 11

7   Our system is one of detachment: to keep
    silenced people from asking questions, to keep
    the judged from judging, to keep solitary people
    from joining together, and the soul from putting
    together its pieces.

    Eduardo Galeano (b. 1940) Uruguayan writer. *The Book of Embraces*
    (1989)

8   So long as men worship the Caesars and
    Napoleons, Caesars and Napoleons will arise to
    make them miserable.

    Aldous Huxley (1894–1963) British novelist and essayist. *Ends and
    Means* (1937)

9   It is better that a man should tyrannize over his
    bank balance than over his fellow citizens.

    John Maynard Keynes (1883–1946) British economist. *General Theory
    of Employment, Interest and Money* (1936), ch. 24

10 Hold their noses to the grindstone.

Thomas Middleton (1580?–1627) English playwright. *Blurt, Master-Constable* (1602), Act 3, Scene 3

11 Which way? I'm like an animal trapped.
Somewhere: people, freedom, light
Behind me, the howls of the hunt,
but the exit eludes me.

Boris Pasternak (1890–1960) Russian poet and novelist. Pasternak was awarded the Nobel Prize for literature in 1958, which he initially accepted. However, he was later forced by the Soviet authorities to rescind his acceptance. 'The Nobel Prize' (1959), quoted in *Boris Pasternak: The Tragic Years 1930–60* (Ann Pasternak Slater and Craig Raine, eds., trs.; 1990)

12 Tyranny is always better organized than freedom.

Charles Pierre Péguy (1873–1914) French writer and poet. 'War and Peace', *Basic Verities* (A. and J. Green, trs.; 1943)

13 Necessity is the plea for every infringement of human freedom. It is the argument of tyrants; it is the creed of slaves.

William Pitt the Younger (1759–1806) British prime minister. Speech to Parliament (November 18, 1783)

14 Every man who has power over another is a tyrant.

Francisco Pi y Margall (1824–1901) Spanish politician and author. *La Reacción y La Revolución* (1854)

15 The people always have some champion whom they set over them and nurse into greatness . . . This and no other is the root from which tyranny springs.

Plato (428?–347? BC) Greek philosopher. *The Republic* (370? BC)

16 One should as a rule respect public opinion insofar as is necessary to avoid starvation and keep out of prison, but anything that goes beyond this is voluntary submission to an unnecessary tyranny.

Bertrand Russell (1872–1970) British philosopher and mathematician. *The Conquest of Happiness* (1930), ch. 9

17 The man dies in all who keep silent in the face of tyranny.

Wole Soyinka (b. 1934) Nigerian novelist, playwright, poet, and lecturer. *The Man Died* (1975)

U

Uncertainty

see also **Doubt**, **Indecision**, **Procrastination**

1 I have known uncertainty: a state unknown to the Greeks.

Jorge Luis Borges (1899–1986) Argentinian writer and poet. 'The Babylonian Lottery', *Ficciones* (1945)

2 Without measureless and perpetual uncertainty the drama of human life would be destroyed.

Winston Churchill (1874–1965) British prime minister and writer. *The Gathering Storm* (1948)

3 Not only does God play dice. He does not tell us where they fall.

Stephen Hawking (b. 1942) British physicist. Commenting on Albert Einstein's remark about quantum theory: 'God does not play dice'. *Nature* (1975), vol. 257

4 Such is irresolution that nothing is more uncertain than its conclusion.

Cardinal de Retz (1613–79) French ecclesiastic and politician. *Mémoires* (1717)

Understanding

see also **Intelligence**, **Knowledge**

1 You never understand everything. When one understands everything, one has gone crazy.

P. W. Anderson (1923–95) US physicist. Attrib.

2 I do not seek to understand so that I may believe, but I believe so that I may understand.

Saint Anselm (1033–1109) Italian-born philosopher and prelate. *Proslogion* (1078)

3 Should I refuse a good dinner simply because I do not understand the process of digestion?

Oliver Heaviside (1850–1925) British physicist. Referring to being criticized for using formal mathematical manipulations without understanding how they worked. Attrib.

4 Being misunderstood by someone is vexation. Being misunderstood by everyone is tragedy.

Liu Shahe (b. 1931) Chinese writer and editor. 1957. Quoted in *The Red Azalea* (Edward Morin, ed.; 1990)

5 It is one thing to show a man that he is in an error, and another to put him in possession of truth.

John Locke (1632–1704) English philosopher. *An Essay Concerning Human Understanding* (1690), bk. 4

6 LOHR The mind of man is less perturbed by a mystery he cannot explain than by an explanation he cannot understand.

David Mamet (b. 1947) US writer and film director. *The Water Engine* (1977)

7 You don't destroy the mystery of a rainbow by understanding the light processes that form it.

Anne McLaren (b. 1927) British geneticist. *Independent* (September 5, 1994)

8 When men understand what each other means, they see, for the most part, that controversy is either superfluous or hopeless.

John Henry Newman (1801–90) English clergyman and theologian. 1839. 'Faith and Reason, Contrasted as Habits of the Mind', *Oxford University Sermons* (1843), no. 10

9 I have striven not to laugh at human actions, not to weep at them, nor to hate them, but to understand them.

Baruch Spinoza (1632–77) Dutch philosopher and theologian. *Tractatus Theologico-Politicus* (1670), ch. 1, sect. 4

10 To be totally understanding makes one very indulgent.

Madame de Staël (1766–1817) French writer and intellectual. *Corinna, or Italy* (1807)

11 When dealing with an assortment of facts or observations, the natural tendency of the human mind is to dichotomise.

Anthony Stevens (b. 1933) British psychiatrist. *Evolutionary Psychiatry* (1996), ch. 10

12 All, everything that I understand, I understand only because I love.

Leo Tolstoy (1828–1910) Russian writer. *War and Peace* (1865–69), bk. 7, ch. 16

13 Lucky is he who could understand the causes of things.

Virgil (70–19 BC) Roman poet. *Georgics* (29 BC), no. 2, l. 490

14 From his close observation of life and his fathoming of life's laws, Chonkin had understood that it is usually warm in the summer and cold in winter.

Vladimir Voinovich (b. 1932) Russian novelist. *The Life and Extraordinary Adventures of Private Ivan Chonkin* (Richard Lourie, tr.; 1969), pt. 1, ch. 4

Unhappiness

see also **Bereavement**, **Sorrow**

1 And sigh that one thing only has been lent
To youth and age in common—discontent.

Matthew Arnold (1822–88) British poet and critic. 'Youth's Agitations' (1852)

2 Follow thy fair sun, unhappy shadow.

Thomas Campion (1567–1620) English poet, composer, and physician. *Follow Thy Fair Sun* (1614)

3 MEDVEDENKO Why do you wear black all the time?
MASHA I'm in mourning for my life, I'm unhappy.

Anton Chekhov (1860–1904) Russian playwright and short-story writer. *The Seagull* (1896), Act 1

4 Unhappiness is best defined as the difference between our talents and our expectations.

Edward de Bono (b. 1933) Maltese-born British psychologist and writer. *Observer* (June 12, 1977), 'Sayings of the Week'

5 The reason for the sadness of this modern age
   and the men that live in it is that it looks for the
   truth in everything and finds it.
   Edmond de Goncourt (1822–96) French novelist and diarist. October 23,
   1864. *Le Journal des Goncourts* (co-written with Jules de
   Goncourt; 1887–96)

6 It's not what isn't, it's what you wish *was* that
   makes unhappiness.
   Janis Joplin (1943–70) US rock singer. Quoted in *Rock 'n' Roll
   Babylon* (Gary Herman; 1994)

7 I have the true feeling of myself only when I am
   unbearably unhappy.
   Franz Kafka (1883–1924) Czech writer. *Diary* (1913)

8 The majority of men devote the greater part of
   their lives to making their remaining years
   unhappy.
   Jean de La Bruyère (1645–96) French essayist and moralist. *Characters,
   or the Manners of the Age* (1688)

9 It is better to be a human being dissatisfied than
   a pig satisfied; better to be Socrates dissatisfied
   than a fool satisfied.
   John Stuart Mill (1806–73) British philosopher and social reformer.
   Utilitarianism (1863)

10 I don't like this game.
   Spike Milligan (1918–2002) Indian-born British humorist, writer, and actor.
   BBC radio series. *The Goon Show* (1951–59)

11 As soon as one is unhappy one becomes moral.
   Marcel Proust (1871–1922) French novelist. 1918. À l'Ombre des
   Jeunes Filles en Fleurs, *À la Recherche du Temps Perdu*
   (1913–27)

12 He's simply got the instinct for being unhappy
   highly developed.
   Saki (1870–1916) British short-story writer. 'The Match-Maker', *The
   Chronicles of Clovis* (1911)

13 GLOUCESTER Now is the winter of our discontent
   Made glorious summer by this sun of York.
   William Shakespeare (1564–1616) English poet and playwright. *Richard
   III* (1591), Act 1, Scene 1

14 TRINCULO Misery acquaints a man with strange
   bedfellows.
   William Shakespeare (1564–1616) English poet and playwright. *The
   Tempest* (1611), Act 2, Scene 2

15 The secret of being miserable is to have leisure to
   bother about whether you are happy or not.
   George Bernard Shaw (1856–1950) Irish playwright. *Misalliance* (1914),
   Preface

16 Where does discontent start? You are warm
   enough, but you shiver. You are fed, yet hunger
   gnaws you. You have been loved, but your
   yearning wanders in new fields. And to prod all
   these there's time, the Bastard Time.
   John Steinbeck (1902–68) US novelist. *Sweet Thursday* (1954)

17 Half the misery in the world is caused by
   ignorance. The other half is caused by
   knowledge.
   Bonar Thompson (1888–1963) British orator. Attrib.

18 I was told I am a true cosmopolitan. I am
   unhappy everywhere.
   Stephen Vizinczey (b. 1933) Hungarian-born British writer, editor, and
   broadcaster. *Guardian* (March 7, 1968)

19 He spoke with a certain what-is-it in his voice,
   and I could see that, if not actually disgruntled,
   he was far from being gruntled.
   P. G. Wodehouse (1881–1975) British-born US humorous writer. *The
   Code of the Woosters* (1938), ch. 1

United States

see also **American Cities, American Imperialism, American
Literature, Americans, American War of Independence**

1 American society is a sort of flat, freshwater
   pond which absorbs silently, without reaction,
   anything which is thrown into it.
   Henry Adams (1838–1918) US historian. Letter to Royal Cortissoz
   (September 20, 1911)

2 To be black and conscious in America is to be in
   a constant state of rage.
   James Baldwin (1924–87) US writer and civil rights activist. Quoted in
   The White Album (Joan Didion; 1979)

3 America is the ultimate denial of the theory of
   man's continuous evolution.
   H. Rap Brown (b. 1943) US civil rights campaigner. *Die Nigger Die!*
   (1969)

4 When will Americans learn, that if they would
   encourage liberty in other countries, they must
   practice it at home?
   William Wells Brown (1814?–84) US writer and abolitionist. Quoted in
   Here I Stand (Paul Robeson; 1958)

5 This nation openly endorses, tolerates, and
   legalizes the very abuses against which she
   originally waged a bloody revolution.
   Nannie Helen Burroughs (1883–1961) US journalist. Referring to
   rioting in Harlem, New York City. *The Afro-American* (April
   13, 1935)

6 America is not a young land: it is old and dirty
   and evil before the settlers, before the Indians.
   The evil is there waiting.
   William S. Burroughs (1914–97) US writer. *The Naked Lunch* (1959)

7 When America is stronger, the world is safer.
   George Bush (b. 1924) US president. Address to Congress (February
   9, 1989)

8 I would hope our country would get beyond
   group thought and we'd herald each individual,
   regardless of their heritage and regardless of their
   background.
   George W. Bush (b. 1948) US president. January 26, 2000.
   Republican debate in New Hampshire, *New York Times*
   (January 27, 2000)

9 We are not a nation, but a union, a confederacy
   of equal and sovereign states.
   John C. Calhoun (1782–1850) US statesman. Letter to Oliver Dyer
   (January 1, 1849)

10 I called the New World into existence to redress
   the balance of the Old.
   George Canning (1770–1827) British prime minister. *The King's
   Message* (December 12, 1826)

11 America is the only nation in history which
   miraculously has gone directly from barbarism to
   degeneration without the usual interval of
   civilization.
   Georges Clemenceau (1841–1929) French prime minister and journalist.
   Attrib. *Saturday Review of Literature (New York)* (December
   1, 1945)

12 There is nothing wrong with America that cannot
   be cured by what is right with America.
   Bill Clinton (b. 1946) US president. Attrib.

13 Here individuals of all nations are melted into a
   new race of men, whose labors and posterity will
   one day cause great changes in the world.
   Jean de Crèvecoeur (1735–1813) French-born US writer and farmer.
   Letters from an American Farmer (1782)

14 The Indian's subtlest enemy was, and probably still is, humanitarianism bred of Enlightenment hope for reason in all things and universal *bon ton*.

Guy Davenport (b. 1927) US writer, translator, and educator. *Bon ton* is French for sophisticated manners. 'The Indian and His Image', *The Geography of the Imagination* (1984)

15 American history is perceived by most people as a luxury, an entertainment at best, and at worst, an escape from the present.

Carl N. Degler (b. 1921) US historian. 'Remaking American History', *Journal of American History* (June 1980)

16 The Nation is a body without a head; and the arms and legs are occupied in quarrelling with the trunk and each other, and exchanging bruises at random.

Charles Dickens (1812–70) British novelist. Referring to the United States. Letter from the United States (1842), quoted in *Dickens on America and the Americans* (Michael Slater, ed.; 1979)

17 America is false to the past, false to the present, and solemnly binds herself to be false to the future.

Frederick Douglass (1817–95) US abolitionist, writer, and orator. Comment (July 1852)

18 A great silence has fallen on the real soul of this nation.

W. E. B. Du Bois (1868–1963) US sociologist, poet, and novelist. *On McCarthyism* (1951)

19 There is a constant in the average American imagination and taste, for which the past must be preserved and celebrated in full-scale authentic copy; a philosophy of immortality as duplication.

Umberto Eco (b. 1932) Italian writer and literary scholar. 'The Fortresses of Solitude', *Travels in Hyperreality* (William Weaver, tr.; 1986)

20 Without God, there could be no American form of government, nor American way of life.

Dwight D. Eisenhower (1890–1969) US general and president. 1955. Quoted in *American Chronicle* (Lois and Alan Gordon; 1987)

21 America is woven of many strands; I would recognize them and let it so remain . . . Our fate is to become one, and yet many—This is not prophecy, but description.

Ralph Ellison (1914–94) US writer, jazz musician, and photographer. *Invisible Man* (1953)

22 I am ashamed to see what a shallow village tale our so-called history is.

Ralph Waldo Emerson (1803–82) US poet and essayist. Referring to the history of the United States. 'History', *Essays* (1841)

23 We should not want to think of America as a 'melting pot', but as a great inter-racial laboratory where Americans can really begin to build the thing which the rest of the world feels that they stand for today, and that is real democracy.

Crystal Bird Fauset, US feminist activist. Speech, Woman's Centennial Congress (November 26, 1940)

24 Far brighter scenes a future age,
The muse predicts, these states will hail,
Whose genius may the world engage,
Whose deeds may over death prevail,
And happier systems bring to view,
Than all the eastern sages knew.

Philip Freneau (1752–1832) US poet. 'On the Emigration to America and Peopling the Western Country' (1785)

25 Those who find America an especially violent and oppressive country have apparently never read the history of England or France, Germany or Russia, Indonesia or Burundi, Turkey or Uganda.

Eugene D. Genovese (b. 1930) US historian. Quoted in *New York Times* (June 18, 1978)

26 In America, with all of its evils and faults, you can still reach through the frost and see the sun. But we don't know yet whether that sun is rising or setting for our country.

Dick Gregory (b. 1932) US comedian and civil rights activist. 'One Less Door', *Nigger* (1964)

27 I wish for an America no less alert in guarding against dangers from within than it is watchful against enemies from without.

Warren G. Harding (1865–1923) US president. *New York Times* (March 5, 1921)

28 The United States, I believe, are under the impression that they are twenty years in advance of this country; whilst, as a matter of actual verifiable fact, of course, they are just about six hours behind it.

Harold Hobson (1904–92) British theatre critic and writer. *The Devil in Woodford Wells* (1946), ch. 8

29 We in America are nearer to the final triumph over poverty than ever before in the history of any land.

Herbert Hoover (1874–1964) US president. One year from this statement the stock market crashed, losing $40 billion. Speech (November 3, 1928), quoted in *Guide to Political Quotations* (Caroline Rathbone and Michael Stephenson; 1985)

30 America the beautiful,
Let me sing of thee;
Burger King and Dairy Queen
From sea to shining sea.

Ada Louise Huxtable (b. 1921?) US architecture critic. 'Goodbye History, Hello Hamburger', *New York Times* (March 21, 1971)

31 America is not a blanket woven from one thread, one color, one cloth.

Jesse Jackson (b. 1941) US clergyman, civil rights leader, and politician. Speech to the US Democratic National Convention, Atlanta (July 1988)

32 The American dream is not dead. True, it is gasping for breath but it is not dead.

Barbara Jordan (1936–96) US congresswoman, lawyer, and educator. Keynote address to the US Democratic National Convention (July 13, 1992)

33 We, the people . . . a very eloquent beginning. But when the document was completed on the 17th of September in 1787 I was not included in that 'We, the people' . . . But through . . . amendment, interpretation, and court decision I have finally been included in 'We, the people'.

Barbara Jordan (1936–96) US congresswoman, lawyer, and educator. Referring to the US Constitution, and the Equal Rights Amendment of 1972 and other legal developments facilitating equality of the sexes. Speech to the House of Representatives (July 24, 1974)

34 And so, my fellow Americans: ask not what your country can do for you—ask what you can do for your country. My fellow citizens of the world: ask not what America will do for you, but what together we can do for the freedom of man.

John Fitzgerald Kennedy (1917–63) US president. Inaugural address as president of the United States (January 20, 1961)

35 The American Way is so restlessly creative as to be essentially destructive; the American Way is to carry common sense itself almost to the point of madness.
Louis Kronenberger (1904–80) US writer and critic. 'Last Thoughts', *Company Matters* (1954)

36 A nation of one hundred fine, mob-hearted, lynching, relenting, repenting millions.
Vachel Lindsay (1879–1931) US poet. Referring to the United States. 'Bryan, Bryan, Bryan, Bryan', *Collected Poems* (1923)

37 America is a hurricane, and the only people who do not hear the sound are those fortunate if incredibly stupid and smug White Protestants who live in the center, in the serene eye of the big wind.
Norman Mailer (b. 1923) US novelist and journalist. "Advertisements for 'Games and Ends'", *Advertisements for Myself* (1959)

38 We kill the spirit here, we are the experts at that. We use psychic bullets and kill each other cell by cell.
Norman Mailer (b. 1923) US novelist and journalist. Contrasting the United States with Cuba, where Norman Mailer claims hatred runs over into the love of blood. 'The Fourth Presidential Paper—Foreign Affairs: Letter to Castro', *The Presidential Papers* (1963)

39 The true religion of America has always been America.
Norman Mailer (b. 1923) US novelist and journalist. Interview, *Time* (September 27, 1984)

40 I see America through the eyes of a victim. I don't see any American dream. I see an American nightmare.
Malcolm X (1925–65) US Black activist. Comment (April 3, 1964)

41 The United States has been called the melting pot of the world. But it seems to me that the colored man either missed getting into the pot or he got melted down.
Thurgood Marshall (1908–93) US civil rights lawyer and jurist. *The Encyclopaedia of Black Folklore and Humor* (Henry D. Spalding; 1972)

42 McCarthyism is Americanism with its sleeves rolled.
Joseph McCarthy (1909–57) US politician. McCarthy gave his name to the anticommunist movement in the 1940s and 1950s, which was institutionalized as the House Un-American Activities Committee. Speech, Wisconsin (1952), quoted in *Senator Joe McCarthy* (Richard Rovere; 1973), ch. 1

43 I have never been able to look upon America as young and vital, but rather as prematurely old, as a fruit which rotted before it had a chance to ripen.
Henry Miller (1891–1980) US novelist. *The Air-Conditioned Nightmare* (1945)

44 It isn't the oceans which cut us off from the rest of the world—it's the American way of looking at things.
Henry Miller (1891–1980) US novelist. 'Letter to Lafayette', *The Air-Conditioned Nightmare* (1945)

45 In the 18th century, Voltaire said that every man had two countries: his own and France. In the 20th century, that has come to be true of the United States.
Rupert Murdoch (b. 1931) Australian-born US media entrepreneur. Speech, New York City (November 9, 1989)

46 I have long believed there was a divine plan that placed this land here to be found by people of a special kind, that we have a rendezvous with destiny.
Ronald Reagan (b. 1911) US president and actor. Campaign letter (1976), quoted in *Sincerely, Ronald Reagan* (Helene von Damm; 1976)

47 If we ever pass out as a great nation, we ought to put on our tombstone, 'America died of the delusion she had moral leadership'.
Will Rogers (1879–1935) US actor, writer, and humorist. *The Autobiography of Will Rogers* (1949)

48 America . . . where law and customs alike are based on the dreams of spinsters.
Bertrand Russell (1872–1970) British philosopher and mathematician. *Marriage and Morals* (1929)

49 this country might have
been a pio
neer land
once.
but. there ain't
no mo
indians blowing
custer's mind
with a different
image of america.
Sonia Sanchez (b. 1934) US poet and writer. 'Right on: White America', *WE A baddDDD PEOPLE* (1973), quoted in *The Penguin Book of American Verse* (Geoffrey Moore, ed.; 1977)

50 America is the greatest of opportunities and the worst of influences.
George Santayana (1863–1952) Spanish-born US philosopher, poet, and novelist. *The Last Puritan* (1935)

51 Myths and legends die hard in America. We love them for the extra dimension they provide, the illusion of near-infinite possibility to erase the narrow confines of most men's reality.
Hunter S. Thompson (b. 1939) US writer and journalist. 1969. 'Those Daring Young Men in Their Flying Machines . . . Ain't What They Used to Be!', *The Great Shark Hunt* (1979), pt. 3, quoted in *Pageant* (September 1969)

52 America is a large, friendly dog in a very small room. Every time it wags its tail it knocks over a chair.
Arnold Toynbee (1889–1975) British historian. Broadcast news summary (July 14, 1954)

53 America is a vast conspiracy to make you happy.
John Updike (b. 1932) US writer. 'How to Love America and Leave It at the Same Time', *Problems* (1980)

54 Unless drastic reforms are made, we must accept the fact that every four years the United States will be up for sale, and the richest man or family will buy it.
Gore Vidal (b. 1925) US novelist and essayist. *Reflections upon a Sinking Ship* (1969), Postscript: The Holy Family

55 The American dream turned belly up, turned green, bobbed to the scummy surface of cupidity unlimited, filled with gas, went *bang* in the noonday sun.
Kurt Vonnegut (b. 1922) US novelist. *God Bless You, Mr. Rosewater* (1965), ch. 1

56 It is our true policy to steer clear of permanent alliance with any portion of the foreign world.
George Washington (1732–99) US president. Farewell Address, Washington, DC (September 17, 1796)

57 The United States are destined either to surmount the gorgeous history of feudalism, or else prove the most tremendous failure of all time.
Walt Whitman (1819–92) US poet. *Democratic Vistas* (1871)

58 America cannot be an ostrich with its head in the sand.
Woodrow Wilson (1856–1924) US president. Speech, Des Moines, Iowa (February 1, 1916)

Unity

see also **Order**, **Solidarity**

1   Now a whole is that which has a beginning, a
    middle, and an end.
    Aristotle (384–322 BC) Greek philosopher. Referring specifically to the
    dramatic form of tragedy. *Poetics* (335–322? BC), ch. 7

2   I sometimes think the gods have united human
    beings by some mysterious principle, like the
    according notes of music. Or is it as Plato has
    supposed, that souls originally one have been
    divided, and each seeks the half it lost.
    Lydia Maria Child (1802–80) US abolitionist, suffrage campaigner, and
    writer. *Philothea: A Romance* (1836), ch. 1

3   The unities, sir, are a completeness—a kind of a
    universal dovetailedness with regard to place and
    time.
    Charles Dickens (1812–70) British novelist. Said by Mr. Curdle.
    Nicholas Nickleby (1839), ch. 24

4   Wholeness is the unique mediation of spirit
    between partial images.
    Wilson Harris (b. 1921) Guyanese-born writer. Said by Masters.
    Carnival (1985)

5   Listening not to me but to the Logos it is wise to
    agree that all things are one.
    Heraclitus (*fl.* 500 BC) Greek philosopher. 480? BC. 'Logos' refers to
    the divine wisdom of the word of God. Quoted in *The
    Presocratic Philosophers* (G. S. Kirk, J. E. Raven, and M.
    Schofield; 1983)

6   Unity in a movement situation is overrated. If
    you were the Establishment, which would you
    rather see coming in the door, five hundred mice
    or one lion?
    Florynce R. Kennedy (1916–2000) US lawyer and activist. Quoted in
    Outrageous Acts & Everyday Rebellions (Gloria Steinem;
    1983)

7   Nothing unites the English like war. Nothing
    divides them like Picasso.
    Hugh Mills (1913–71) British screenwriter. *Prudence and the Pill*
    (1968)

8   Catholic and Episcopalian,
    Lutheran, Baptist, Methodist,
    Jew, Muslim, Buddhist, atheist,
    We are all here; no one is alien
    Now radiation's common laws
    Impel us into common cause.
    Vikram Seth (b. 1952) Indian novelist and poet. *The Golden Gate*
    (1986), ch. 7, st. 20

The Universe

see also **Astronomy**, **The Earth**, **The Moon**, **The Sun**

1   The universe is a machine for creating gods.
    Henri-Louis Bergson (1859–1941) French philosopher. *Two Sources for
    Morality and Religion* (1932)

2   In this unbelievable universe in which we live
    there are no absolutes. Even parallel lines,
    reaching into infinity, meet somewhere yonder.
    Pearl Buck (1892–1973) US novelist. *A Bridge for Passing* (1962)

3   It is a mathematical fact that the casting of this
    pebble from my hand alters the centre of gravity
    of the universe.
    Thomas Carlyle (1795–1881) Scottish historian and essayist. *Sartor
    Resartus* (1833–34)

4   I don't pretend to understand the Universe—it's a
    great deal bigger than I am . . . People ought to
    be modester.
    Thomas Carlyle (1795–1881) Scottish historian and essayist. Attrib.

5   The cosmos is about the smallest hole that a man
    can hide his head in.
    G. K. Chesterton (1874–1936) British writer and poet. *Orthodoxy*
    (1909), ch. 1

6   There is no reason to assume that the universe
    has the slightest interest in intelligence—or even
    in life. Both may be random accidental by-
    products of its operations like the beautiful
    patterns on a butterfly's wings. The insect would
    fly just as well without them.
    Arthur C. Clarke (b. 1917) British writer and scientist. *The Lost
    Worlds of 2001* (1972)

7   I am very interested in the Universe—I am
    specializing in the universe and all that surrounds
    it.
    Peter Cook (1937–95) British writer, actor, and comedian. *Beyond the
    Fringe* (1959)

8   listen: there's
    a hell of a good universe next door; let's go.
    e. e. cummings (1894–1962) US poet and painter. *1 x 1* (1944),
    no. 14

9   I look for what needs to be done . . . After all,
    that's how the universe designs itself.
    R. Buckminster Fuller (1895–1983) US architect, designer, and inventor.
    Christian Science Monitor (November 3, 1964)

10 My own suspicion is that the universe is not only
    queerer than we suppose, but queerer than we
    can suppose.
    J. B. S. Haldane (1892–1964) British geneticist. 'On Being the Right
    Size', *Possible Worlds* (1927)

11 Why does the universe go to all the bother of
    existing? Is the unified theory so compelling that
    it brings about its own existence? Or does it need
    a creator, and, if so, does he have any other
    effect on the universe? And who created him?
    Stephen Hawking (b. 1942) British physicist. *A Brief History of Time*
    (1988), ch. 11

12 The universe is not hostile, nor yet is it friendly.
    It is simply indifferent.
    John Haynes Holmes (1879–1964) US clergyman. *A Sensible Man's
    View of Religion* (1933), ch. 4

13 Look round this universe . . . The whole presents
    nothing but the idea of blind nature, impregnated
    by a great vivifying principle, and pouring forth
    from her lap, without discernment or parental
    care, her maimed and abortive children.
    David Hume (1711–76) Scottish philosopher and historian. *Dialogues
    Concerning Natural Religion* (1779)

14 The universe begins to look more like a great
    thought than like a great machine.
    James Jeans (1877–1946) British mathematician, physicist, and
    astronomer. *The Mysterious Universe* (1930), ch. 5

15 In my youth I regarded the universe as an open
    book, printed in the language of physical
    equations, whereas now it appears to me as a
    text written in invisible ink, of which in our rare
    moments of grace we are able to decipher a small
    fragment.
    Arthur Koestler (1905–83) Hungarian-born British writer and journalist.
    Bricks to Babel (1980), Epilogue

16 There is nothing waste, nothing sterile, nothing dead in the universe; no chaos, no confusions, save in appearance.
Gottfried Wilhelm Leibniz (1646–1716) German philosopher and mathematician. *Monadology* (1714)

17 My theology, briefly, is that the universe was dictated but not signed.
Christopher Darlington Morley (1890–1957) US writer and journalist. Attrib.

18 The universe ought to be presumed too vast to have any character.
C. S. Peirce (1839–1914) US physicist and philosopher. *Collected Papers* (1934), vol. 6

19 A universe in which everything is known would be static and dull, as boring as the heaven of some weak-minded theologians . . . The ideal universe for us is one very much like the universe we inhabit . . . not really much of a coincidence.
Carl Sagan (1934–96) US astronomer and writer. *Broca's Brain: The Romance of Science* (1979)

20 To make an apple pie from scratch, you must first invent the universe.
Carl Sagan (1934–96) US astronomer and writer. *Cosmos* (1980)

21 I am not fond of expecting catastrophes, but there are cracks in the universe.
Sydney Smith (1771–1845) British clergyman, essayist, and wit. Attrib.

22 Fifty-five crystal spheres geared to God's crankshaft is my idea of a satisfying universe. I can't think of anything more trivial than quarks, quasars, big bangs and black holes.
Tom Stoppard (b. 1937) Czech-born British playwright and screenwriter. *Observer* (May 22, 1994), 'Sayings of the Week'

23 The effort to understand the universe is one of the very few things that lifts human life a little above the level of farce and gives it some of the grace of tragedy.
Steven Weinberg (b. 1933) US physicist. *The First Three Minutes* (1977), ch. 8

24 The more the universe seems comprehensible, the more it also seems pointless.
Steven Weinberg (b. 1933) US physicist. *The First Three Minutes* (1977), Epilogue

University

see also Education, Learning, Libraries, Research

1 Universities incline wits to sophistry and affectation.
Francis Bacon (1561–1626) English philosopher, statesman, and lawyer. 1603. *Valerius Terminus*, quoted in *Letters and Remains of the Lord Chancellor Bacon* (Robert Stephens, ed.; 1734), ch. 26

2 The university's characteristic state may be summarized by the words of the lady who said, 'I have enough money to last me the rest of my life, unless I buy something'.
Hanna Gray (b. 1930) German-born US educator. *Christian Science Monitor* (November 26, 1986)

3 In American society, the university is traditionally considered to be a psychosocial moratorium, an ivory tower where you withdraw from the problems of society and the world around you to work on important things like your career and your marriage.
Abbie Hoffman (1936–89) US political activist. Speech, University of South Carolina (September 16, 1987)

4 Any attempt to reform the university without attending to the system of which it is an integral part is like trying to do urban renewal in New York City from the twelfth storey up.
Ivan Illich (b. 1926) Austrian-born US educator and researcher. *Deschooling Society* (1971), ch. 3

5 Universities hire professors the way some men choose wives—they want the ones the others will admire.
Morris Kline (1908–92) US mathematician. *Why the Professor Can't Teach* (1977)

6 Universities are the cathedrals of the modern age. They shouldn't have to justify their existence by utilitarian criteria.
David Lodge (b. 1935) British novelist and critic. *Nice Work* (1988), ch. 4

7 Like so many ageing college people, Pnin had long ceased to notice the existence of students on the campus.
Vladimir Nabokov (1899–1977) Russian-born US novelist, poet, and critic. *Pnin* (1957), ch. 3

8 So far as the mere imparting of information is concerned, no university has had any justification for existence since the popularization of printing in the fifteenth century.
A. N. Whitehead (1861–1947) British philosopher and mathematician. *Aims of Education* (1928)

9 The ivory tower is 'going plastic'; it is becoming a think-tank for major corporations, which have exclusive access to it, rather than remaining a general social resource.
Edward Yoxen, British author and academic. *The Gene Business* (1983)

Utopia

see Heaven, Idealism

V

Value

see also **Money, Morality**

1 PRICE, n. Value, plus a reasonable sum for the wear and tear of conscience in demanding it.
Ambrose Bierce (1842–1914?) US writer and journalist. *The Devil's Dictionary* (1911)

2 That which costs little is less valued.
Miguel de Cervantes (1547–1616) Spanish novelist and playwright. *Don Quixote* (1605–15)

3 What we must decide is perhaps how we are valuable, rather than how valuable we are.
F. Scott Fitzgerald (1896–1940) US writer. 1936. *The Crack-Up: with Other Uncollected Pieces, Note-Books and Unpublished Letters* (Edmund Wilson, ed.; 1945)

4 The value of a thing is the amount of laboring or work that its possession will save the possessor.
Henry George (1839–97) US economist. *The Science of Political Economy* (1897)

5 One person's price is another person's income.
Walter W. Heller (1915–87) US economist and writer. 'What's Right with Economics?', *American Economic Review* (March 1975)

6 The value of a whole must not be assumed to be the same as the sum of the values of its parts.
G. E. Moore (1873–1958) British philosopher. *Principia Ethica* (1903)

7 'The cost of a thing', says he, 'is the amount of what I will call life which is required to be exchanged for it, immediately or in the long run'.
Robert Louis Stevenson (1850–94) Scottish novelist, essayist, and poet. 'Henry David Thoreau', *Familiar Studies of Men and Books* (1882)

Vanity

see also **Boasts, Conceit, Pride**

1 Vanity plays lurid tricks with our memory.
Joseph Conrad (1857–1924) Polish-born British novelist. *Lord Jim* (1900)

2 It's a fallacy that women are attracted by power and money. No one has fallen in love with me for ages.
Terence Conran (b. 1931) British designer and entrepreneur. *Daily Express* (April 21, 1986)

3 Vanity, like murder, will out.
Hannah Cowley (1743–1809) British poet and playwright. *The Belle's Stratagem* (1780), Act 1, Scene 4

4 I know he is, and he adores his maker.
Benjamin Disraeli (1804–81) British prime minister and writer. Replying to a remark made in defence of the reformer John Bright (1818–89) that he was a self-made man. Attrib. *The Fine Art of Political Wit* (Leon A. Harris; 1965)

5 We are so vain that we even care for the opinion of those we don't care for.
Marie von Ebner-Eschenbach (1830–1916) Austrian novelist and poet. *Aphorism* (1905)

6 Self-love is the greatest of all flatterers.
François La Rochefoucauld (1613–80) French epigrammatist and moralist. *Reflections, or Sentences and Moral Maxims* (1665), no. 2

7 Mirrors are ices which do not melt: what melts are those who admire themselves in them.
Paul Morand (1888–1976) French writer and diplomat. 'La Nuit Écossaise . . .', *Ouvert la Nuit* (1922)

8 The phone: 'How will I recognize you?' 'I'm beautiful'.
Ned Rorem (b. 1923) US composer and writer. *The Paris Diary of Ned Rorem* (1966), quoted in *A Queer Reader* (Patrick Higgins, ed.; 1993)

9 You're so vain, you probably think this song is about you.
Carly Simon (b. 1945) US singer and songwriter. Popular conjecture has it that the song is about film actor Warren Beatty. 'You're So Vain' (1972)

10 Vanity dies hard; in some obstinate cases it outlives the man.
Robert Louis Stevenson (1850–94) Scottish novelist, essayist, and poet. *Prince Otto* (1885)

11 A man may hide his vanity beneath a veneer of humility . . . but at odd moments—in the supreme anonymity and isolation of a public bus or in the folds of a wispy day-dream—he will need assurance that somehow he is one of the chosen.
Varindra Tarzie Vittachi (b. 1921) Sri Lankan-born writer. *The Brown Sahib* (1962)

12 I cannot tell you that, madam. Heaven has granted me no offspring.
James Abbott McNeill Whistler (1834–1903) US painter and etcher. Replying to a lady who had inquired whether he thought genius was hereditary. Quoted in *Whistler Stories* (D. C. Seitz; 1913)

13 The Bonfire of the Vanities
Tom Wolfe (b. 1930) US journalist and novelist. 1987. Novel title, deriving from political preacher Girolamo Savonarola's 'burning of the vanities' in Florence, 1497.

Venice

see **European Cities**

Vice

see also **Corruption, Crime, Evil, Morality, Virtue**

1 We make ourselves a ladder out of our vices if we trample the vices themselves underfoot.
Saint Augustine of Hippo (354–430) Numidian Christian theologian and Doctor of the Church. 'De Ascensione', *Sermons* (400?), bk. 3

2 A man, indeed, is not genteel when he gets drunk; but most vices may be committed very genteelly: a man may debauch his friend's wife genteelly: he may cheat at cards genteelly.
James Boswell (1740–95) Scottish lawyer and biographer. 1775. *The Life of Samuel Johnson* (1791)

3 It is the function of vice to keep virtue within reasonable bounds.
Samuel Butler (1835–1902) British writer and composer. Quoted in *Note Books* (H. Festing Jones, ed.; 1912)

4 So for a good old gentlemanly vice,
I think I must take up with avarice.
Lord Byron (1788–1824) British poet. *Don Juan* (1819–24), can. 1, st. 216

5 Vice is its own reward.
Quentin Crisp (1908–99) British writer. *The Naked Civil Servant* (1968)

6 The greatest minds are capable of the greatest vices as well as of the greatest virtues.
René Descartes (1596–1650) French philosopher and mathematician. *Discourse on Method* (1637)

7 It is the restrictions placed on vice by our social code which makes its pursuit so peculiarly agreeable.
Kenneth Grahame (1859–1932) British banker and children's writer. *Pagan Papers* (1893)

8 No one ever suddenly became depraved.
Juvenal (65?–128?) Roman poet. *Satires* (98?–128?), no. 2, l. 83

9 If we had no faults of our own, we would not take so much pleasure in noticing those of others.
François La Rochefoucauld (1613–80) French epigrammatist and moralist. *Reflections, or Sentences and Moral Maxims* (1665), no. 31

10 Vice is waste of life. Poverty, obedience and celibacy are the canonical vices.
George Bernard Shaw (1856–1950) Irish playwright. *Man and Superman* (1903)

Victory

see also **Awards, Glory, Success**

1 In good politics or in good ethics, can we throw away the chance for an honorable peace, for the hope of a victory, no matter how brilliant?
Andrés Bello (1781–1865) Chilean politician and writer. 'On Relations with Spain' (1835–44)

2 David put his hand in his bag, and took thence a stone, and slang it, and smote the Philistine in his forehead; and he fell upon his face to the earth.
Bible. The young David's defeat of the Philistine champion, Goliath. I Samuel, *King James Bible* (1611), 17:49

3 This is *your* victory.
Winston Churchill (1874–1965) British prime minister and writer. Speech, London (May 8, 1945)

4 Victory at all costs, victory in spite of all terror, victory however long and hard the road may be; for without victory there is no survival.
Winston Churchill (1874–1965) British prime minister and writer. Speech to Parliament (May 13, 1940)

5 We triumph without glory when we conquer without danger.
Corneille (1606–84) French playwright. *Le Cid* (1636–37), Act 2, Scene 2

6 You must be master and win, or serve and lose, grieve or triumph, be the anvil or the hammer.
Johann Wolfgang von Goethe (1749–1832) German poet, playwright, and scientist. *Der Gross-Cophta* (1791), Act 2

7 The happy state of getting the victor's palm without the dust of racing.
Horace (65–8 BC) Roman poet. *Epistles* (20? BC), bk. 1, no. 1, l. 51

8 Victory has a thousand fathers but defeat is an orphan.
John Fitzgerald Kennedy (1917–63) US president. Attrib.

9 The conventional army loses if it does not win. The guerrilla wins if he does not lose.
Henry Kissinger (b. 1923) German-born US politician and diplomat. 'The Vietnam Negotiations', *Foreign Affairs* (January 1969), ch. 13

10 See, the conquering hero comes!
Sound the trumpets, beat the drums!
Thomas Morell (1703–84) British classicist. 1747. The libretto for Handel's oratorio. 'A Chorus of Youths', *Judas Maccabaeus* (1746), pt. 3

11 When you win, nothing hurts.
Joe Namath (b. 1943) US American football quarterback. Attrib.

12 The moment of victory is much too short to live for that and nothing else.
Martina Navratilova (b. 1956) Czech-born US tennis player. *Guardian* (June 21, 1989)

13 You can give the hope of victory and happiness to your unfortunate brethren only by waging war against the enemy inside.
Orhan Pamuk (b. 1952) Turkish novelist. *The Black Book* (Guneli Gun, tr.; 1990)

Vietnam

see **American Imperialism, Asian Countries**

Violence

see also **Aggression, Fighting, War**

1 Keep violence in the mind where it belongs.
Brian Aldiss (b. 1925) British science-fiction writer. 'Charteris', *Barefoot in the Head* (1969)

2 Violence is like money in the bank; it's only helpful if you don't have to use it.
Nikki Giovanni (b. 1943) US writer, activist, and educator. 'About a Poem', *Sacred Cows . . . and Other Edibles* (1988)

3 In an accident-prone, suicidal and conflict-ridden age, violence is a savage masquerade, is it not? It feeds on a void of sacrament and on the infliction of humiliation and shadow.
Wilson Harris (b. 1921) Guyanese-born writer. *Carnival* (1985)

4 Today the choice is no longer between violence and nonviolence. It is either nonviolence or nonexistence.
Martin Luther King, Jr. (1929–68) US civil rights leader. *Stride Toward Freedom* (1964)

5 We are effectively destroying ourselves by violence masquerading as love.
R. D. Laing (1927–89) Scottish psychiatrist. *The Politics of Experience* (1967), ch. 13

6 I'm sure he had a fork in the other.
Ada Leverson (1862–1933) British writer and journalist. Reply when told by Oscar Wilde of a devoted apache (Parisian gangster) who used to follow him with a knife in one hand. Attrib.

7 I'm nonviolent with those who are nonviolent with me.
Malcolm X (1925–65) US Black activist. 1965. Attrib.

8 There is a violence that liberates, and a violence that enslaves; there is a violence that is moral and a violence that is immoral.
Benito Mussolini (1883–1945) Italian dictator. Attrib.

9 The gains of violence are transient, the fruits of patience are imperishable.
Kwame Nkrumah (1909–72) Ghanaian president. 1955. *I Speak of Freedom* (1961)

10 Remove your pants before resorting to violence.
Yoko Ono (b. 1933) Japanese-born US musician, writer, campaigner, and artist. Attrib.

11 Black power does not mean violence, but it does not mean total nonviolence. It does not mean that you walk with a chip on your shoulder, but you walk letting the chips fly where they may.
Adam Clayton Powell, Jr. (1908–72) US clergyman and civil rights leader. *Adam by Adam* (1971)

12 Before I felt passion for any woman, I gambled my heart and lost it to violence.
José Eustasio Rivera (1888–1928) Colombian poet and novelist. *The Vortex* (1924)

13 I can hurt anybody. The question is, can I hurt him enough?
Sugar Ray Robinson (1921–89) US boxer. *The Black Lights: Inside the World of Professional Boxing* (Thomas Hauser; 1987)

14 OTHELLO Every puny whipster gets my sword.
William Shakespeare (1564–1616) English poet and playwright. *Othello* (1602–04), Act 5, Scene 2

15 The need for us to take up arms will never transform us into prisoners of the idea of violence.
Oliver Tambo (1917–93) South African nationalist leader. 1987. *Independent on Sunday* (April 25, 1993)

16 Violence in real life is terrible; violence in the movies can be cool. It's just another colour to work with.
Quentin Tarantino (b. 1963) US film director, screenwriter, and actor. *Observer* (October 16, 1994), 'Sayings of the Week'

17 To me, violence is a totally aesthetic subject. Saying you don't like violence in movies is like saying you don't like dance sequences in movies. I do like dance sequences in movies, but if I didn't, it doesn't mean I should stop dance sequences being made.
Quentin Tarantino (b. 1963) US film director, screenwriter, and actor. *True Romance* (1995), Introduction

Virtue

see also **Good, Hypocrisy, Purity, Righteousness**

1 Curious, but we have come to a place, a time, when virtue is no longer considered a virtue. The mention of virtue is ridiculed, and even the word itself has fallen out of favor.
Maya Angelou (b. 1928) US writer. 'When Virtue Becomes Redundant', *Wouldn't Take Nothing for My Journey Now* (1993)

2 Virtue is like precious odours—most fragrant when they are incensed or crushed.
Francis Bacon (1561–1626) English philosopher, statesman, and lawyer. 'Of Adversity', *Essays* (1625)

3 Righteous people terrify me . . . Virtue is its own punishment.
Aneurin Bevan (1897–1960) Welsh-born British politician. Quoted in *Aneurin Bevan* (Michael Foot; 1973)

4 Let your light so shine before men, that they may see your good works, and glorify your Father which is in heaven.
Bible. Matthew, *King James Bible* (1611), 5:16

5 Whenever there are tremendous virtues it's a sure sign something's wrong.
Bertolt Brecht (1898–1956) German playwright and poet. *Mother Courage and Her Children* (1941), Scene 2

6 There is no road or ready way to virtue.
Thomas Browne (1605–82) English physician and writer. *Religio Medici* (1642), pt. 1, sect. 55

7 We must soften into a credulity below the milkiness of infancy to think all men virtuous. We must be tainted with a malignity truly diabolical, to believe all the world to be equally wicked and corrupt.
Edmund Burke (1729–97) Irish-born British statesman and political philosopher. *Thoughts on the Cause of the Present Discontents* (1770)

8 Virtue consisted in avoiding scandal and venereal disease.
Robert Cecil (1864–1958) British statesman. *Life in Edwardian England* (1969)

9 My virtue's still far too small, I don't trot it out and about yet.
Colette (1873–1954) French novelist. *Claudine at School* (1900)

10 To be able to practise five things everywhere under heaven constitutes perfect virtue . . . gravity, generosity of soul, sincerity, earnestness, and kindness.
Confucius (551–479 BC) Chinese philosopher, administrator, and moralist. *Analects* (5th century BC)

11 And virtue, though in rags, will keep me warm.
John Dryden (1631–1700) English poet, playwright, and literary critic. *Imitation of Horace* (1685), bk. 3, ode 29, l. 87

12 How next to impossible is the exercise of virtue! It requires a constant watchfulness, constant guard.
William Golding (1911–93) British novelist. 'Colley's Letter', *Rites of Passage* (1980)

13 Our virtues and vices couple with one another, and get children that resemble both their parents.
George Savile Halifax (1633–95) English statesman. 'Of the World', *Political, Moral and Miscellaneous Thoughts and Reflections* (1750)

14 The greatest offence against virtue is to speak ill of it.
William Hazlitt (1778–1830) British essayist and critic. 'On Cant and Hypocrisy', *Sketches and Essays* (William Carew Hazlitt, ed.; 1839)

15 Of all the pleasures I know, I know of none comparable to that of feeling capable of virtue.
Eugenio María de Hostos (1839–1903) Puerto Rican educator, social reformer, and journalist. 'Hombres e Ideas', *Obras* (1939–54)

16 'Tis one thing to know virtue, and another to conform the will to it.
David Hume (1711–76) Scottish philosopher and historian. *A Treatise of Human Nature* (1739–40)

17 To be discontented with the divine discontent,
and to be ashamed with the noble shame, is the
very germ and first upgrowth of all virtue.
Charles Kingsley (1819–75) British novelist and cleric. *Health and
Education* (1874)

18 Most usually our virtues are only vices in
disguise.
François La Rochefoucauld (1613–80) French epigrammatist and moralist.
Reflections, or Sentences and Moral Maxims (1665), Epigraph

19 As the continual dropping of water has a
tendency to wear away the hardest and most
flinty substance, so likewise shall we, abounding
in good works, and causing our examples to
shine forth as the sun at noon day, melt their
callous hearts, and render sinewless the arm of
sore oppression.
George Lawrence (*fl.* 19th century) US abolitionist. 'An Oration on the
Abolition of the Slave Trade' (January 1, 1813)

20 Virtue is the habit of acting according to
wisdom. It is necessary that practice accompany
knowledge.
Gottfried Wilhelm Leibniz (1646–1716) German philosopher and
mathematician. 'Felicity', *Leibniz: Political Writings* (Patrick
Riley, ed., tr.; 1988)

21 Virtue may be assailed, but never hurt,
Surprised by unjust force, but not enthralled.
John Milton (1608–74) English writer. *Comus* (1637), ll. 589–590

22 Mortals that would follow me,
Love virtue, she alone is free.
John Milton (1608–74) English writer. The Attendant Spirit. *Comus*
(1637), ll. 1017–18

23 Virtue is to herself the best reward.
Henry More (1614–87) English philosopher and poet. *Cupid's Conflict*
(1646)

24 Let them recognize virtue and rot for having lost
it.
Persius (34–62) Roman satirist. 1st century. *Satires* (Niall Rudd,
tr.; 1973), no. 3, l. 138

25 Virtue is its own reward.
Matthew Prior (1664–1721) English diplomat and poet. *Ode in
Imitation of Horace* (1692)

26 Come what may, I am the friend of virtue and
not of fortune.
Scanderbeg (1405–68) Albanian patriot. Letter to Ferdinand I, King
of Naples (1460)

27 POLONIUS 'Tis too much proved, that with
devotion's visage
And pious action we do sugar o'er
The devil himself.
William Shakespeare (1564–1616) English poet and playwright. *Hamlet*
(1601), Act 3, Scene 1

28 GRIFFITH Men's evil manners live in brass: their
virtues
We write in water.
William Shakespeare (1564–1616) English poet and playwright. *Henry
VIII* (1613), Act 4, Scene 2

29 IAGO Virtue! a fig! 'tis in ourselves that we are
thus, or thus. Our bodies are our gardens, to the
which our wills are gardeners.
William Shakespeare (1564–1616) English poet and playwright. *Othello*
(1602–04), Act 1, Scene 3

30 SIR TOBY BELCH Is it a world to hide virtues in?
William Shakespeare (1564–1616) English poet and playwright. *Twelfth
Night* (1601), Act 1, Scene 3

31 Virtue herself is her own fairest reward.
Silius Italicus (25/26?–101) Roman poet and politician. *Punica* (1st
century), bk. 13, l. 663

Vitality

see also **Desire, Life, Passion**

1 Energy is Eternal Delight.
William Blake (1757–1827) British poet, painter, engraver, and mystic.
'The Voice of the Devil', *The Marriage of Heaven and Hell*
(1790–93), plate 4

2 To animate, in the precise sense of the word: to
give life to.
Federico García Lorca (1899–1936) Spanish poet and playwright. 1928.
Inaugural lecture for the Granada Athenæum Theatre's
season, *A Dream of Life* (Leslie Stainton; 1998)

3 The love of life is necessary to the vigorous
prosecution of any undertaking.
Samuel Johnson (1709–84) British lexicographer and writer. *The
Rambler* (1750–52)

4 Although none of the rules for becoming more
alive is valid it is healthy to keep formulating
them.
Susan Sontag (b. 1933) US writer. 'Debriefing', *American Review*
(September 1973)

5 The force that through the green fuse drives the
flower
Drives my green age.
Dylan Thomas (1914–53) Welsh poet, playwright, and short-story writer.
'The Force That Through the Green Fuse Drives the Flower',
18 Poems (1934), ll. 1–2

6 If we didn't live venturously, plucking the wild
goat by the beard, and trembling over precipices,
we should never be depressed, I've no doubt; but
already should be faded, fatalistic and aged.
Virginia Woolf (1882–1941) British novelist and critic. May 26, 1924.
A Writer's Diary (1953)

The Voice

see also **Conversation, Singers and Singing, Speech**

1 Her voice is full of money.
F. Scott Fitzgerald (1896–1940) US writer. *The Great Gatsby* (1925),
ch. 7

2 When it is genuine, when it is born of the need
to speak, no one can stop the human voice.
When denied a mouth, it speaks with the hands
or the eyes, or the pores, or anything at all.
Because every single one of us has something to
say to the others, something that deserves to be
celebrated or forgiven by others.
Eduardo Galeano (b. 1940) Uruguayan writer. *The Book of Embraces*
(1989)

3 The melting voice through mazes running;
Untwisting all the chains that tie
The hidden soul of harmony.
John Milton (1608–74) English writer. 'L'Allegro', *Poems of Mr.
John Milton* (1645), ll. 142–144

4 Words sweet as honey from his lips distill'd.
Alexander Pope (1688–1744) English poet. *The Iliad of Homer*
(1715–20), bk. 1, l. 332

W

Wales

see also **Britain, Europe**

1 The Welsh are all actors. It's only the bad ones who become professionals.

Richard Burton (1925–84) British actor. Quoted in *Listener* (January 9, 1986), 'Langham Diary'

2 Sewn on, so to speak, like a patch of different material to England's robe of state, Wales nevertheless has succeeded in retaining its own texture and colour.

Rhys Davies (1903–78) Welsh novelist and short-story writer. *The Story of Wales* (1943)

3 At Holly Well they speake Welsh, the inhabitants go barefoote and bare leg'd a nasty sort of people, their meate is very small here, the mutton is noe bigger than little lamb, and what of it is very sweet.

Celia Fiennes (1662–1741) English travel writer. 1698. Quoted in *The Journeys of Celia Fiennes* (Christopher Morris, ed.; 1947), pt. 3, ch. 5

4 The English are striving for power, the Welsh for freedom; the English are fighting for national gain, the Welsh to avoid a disaster.

Gerald of Wales (1146?–1223?) Welsh topographer, archdeacon, and writer. 1194? 'The Description of Wales', *The Journey Through Wales; and, the Description of Wales* (T. D. Lewis and W. Thorpe, trs.; 1978), bk. 1, ch. 10

5 Wales, which I have never seen,
Is gloomy, mountainous, and green,
And, as I judge from reading Borrow,
The people there rejoice in sorrow.

Rolfe Humphries (1894–1969) US poet. 'For My Ancestors', *Collected Poems* (1965)

6 The devotion of the Welsh to their land is proverbial, and homesickness is much the best-publicized of their national emotions—*hiraeth*, that sense of longing which has been sentimentalized in so many treacly songs.

Jan Morris (b. 1926) British travel writer. *The Matter of Wales* (1984), ch. 1

7 The Welsh people possess that surest of all retreats from the outsider, their own language.

H. V. Morton (1892–1979) British travel writer. *In Search of Wales* (1932), ch. 1

8 It was so dismal and gloomy on these mountains, and so were my spirits. I felt as though we were wandering under the sea, and ought to climb over these basalt blocks and porphyry rocks to the surface and light of day.

Julius Rodenberg (1831–1914) German poet and writer. 1856. Referring to his only experience of mountain-walking in North Wales, which took place in dense mist. 'Caernarvon and Llanberis', *An Autumn in Wales* (William Linnard, tr.; 1985)

9 This *Caru-ar-y-gwely*, called courting on the bed, is customary throughout Wales—the girl sits on the bed chatting with her beloved until morning.

Julius Rodenberg (1831–1914) German poet and writer. 1856. 'The Schoolmaster of Llanfairfechan', *An Autumn in Wales* (William Linnard, tr.; 1985)

10 MORTIMER This is the deadly spite that angers me, My wife can speak no English, I no Welsh.

William Shakespeare (1564–1616) English poet and playwright. *Henry IV, Part 1* (1597), Act 3, Scene 1

11 The land of my fathers. My fathers can have it.

Dylan Thomas (1914–53) Welsh poet, playwright, and short-story writer. Referring to Wales. 'Of Wales', *Adam* (1953)

War

see also **Aggression, Conflict, Imperialism, Terrorism, Violence**

1 I found myself
Suddenly, and too early in life,
Like the inner wall of a house
Which has become an outside wall after wars
and devastations.

Yehuda Amichai (b. 1924) German-born Israeli poet. 'Like the Inner Wall of a House', *Amen* (1978), ll. 1–4

2 It takes twenty years or more of peace to make a man, it takes only twenty seconds of war to destroy him.

Baudouin I (1930–93) Belgian monarch. Address to US Congress (May 12, 1959)

3 If we justify war, it is because all peoples always justify the traits of which they find themselves possessed, not because war will bear an objective examination of its merits.

Ruth Benedict (1887–1948) US anthropologist. *Patterns of Culture* (1934), ch. 1

4 I have never understood this liking for war. It panders to instincts already catered for within the scope of any respectable domestic establishment.

Alan Bennett (b. 1934) British playwright, actor, and director. *Forty Years On* (1969)

5 The inevitableness, the idealism, and the blessings of war, as an indispensable and stimulating law of development, must be repeatedly emphasized.

Friedrich von Bernhardi (1849–1930) Russian-born German soldier and writer. 1913. *Germany and the Next War* (Allan H. Powles, tr.; 1914), ch. 1

6 What this country needs—what every country needs occasionally—is a good hard bloody war to revive the vice of patriotism on which its existence as a nation depends.

Ambrose Bierce (1842–1914?) US writer and journalist. Referring to the United States. Letter (February 15, 1911)

7   Anyone who has ever looked into the glazed eyes of a soldier will think hard before starting a war.
Prince Otto von Bismarck (1815–98) German chancellor. Speech, Reichstag, Berlin (August 1867)

8   The wrong war, at the wrong place, at the wrong time, and with the wrong enemy.
Omar Bradley (1893–1981) US general. Concerning a proposal by Douglas MacArthur, commander of United Nations forces in Korea, that the Korean War should be extended into China. Said in evidence to a US Senate inquiry (May 1951)

9   What they could do with round here is a good war.
Bertolt Brecht (1898–1956) German playwright and poet. *Mother Courage and Her Children* (1941), Scene 1

10   I wanted the experience of war. I thought there would be no more wars.
Joyce Cary (1888–1957) Irish-born British novelist. Reason for going to the Balkan War in 1912. Attrib.

11   We should seek by all means in our power to avoid war . . . even if it does mean the establishment of personal contact with the dictators.
Neville Chamberlain (1869–1940) British prime minister. Speech to Parliament (October 6, 1938)

12   Wars, conflict, it's all business. One murder makes a villain. Millions a hero. Numbers sanctify.
Charlie Chaplin (1889–1977) British actor and director. *Monsieur Verdoux* (1947)

13   Those who can win a war well can rarely make a good peace and those who could make a good peace would never have won the war.
Winston Churchill (1874–1965) British prime minister and writer. *My Early Life* (1930), ch. 26

14   War is nothing but a continuation of politics with the admixture of other means.
Karl Marie von Clausewitz (1780–1831) Prussian general. Often misquoted as 'War is nothing but a continuation of politics by other means'. *On War* (1833)

15   All the gods are dead except the god of war.
Eldridge Cleaver (b. 1935) US writer and civil rights activist. 'Four Vignettes', *Soul on Ice* (1968)

16   My home policy? I wage war. My foreign policy? I wage war. Always, everywhere, I wage war . . . And I shall continue to wage war until the last quarter of an hour.
Georges Clemenceau (1841–1929) French prime minister and journalist. Speech to the French Chamber of Deputies (March 8, 1918)

17   But war's a game which were their subjects wise Kings would not play at.
William Cowper (1731–1800) British poet. 'The Winter Morning Walk', *The Task* (1785), bk. 5, ll. 187–188

18   War is one of the constants of history, and has not diminished with civilization or democracy.
Will Durant (1885–1981) US historian. *The Lessons of History* (co-written with Ariel Durant; 1968)

19   There is nothing that war has ever achieved that we could not better achieve without it.
Havelock Ellis (1859–1939) British psychologist. *The Philosophy of Conflict* (1919), Second series

20   The fact is that in guerilla warfare the struggle no longer concerns the place where you are, but the place where you are going. Each fighter carries his warring country between his bare toes.
Frantz Fanon (1925–61) Martiniquan social scientist, physician, and psychiatrist. 'Spontaneity: Its Strength and Weakness', *The Wretched of the Earth* (1961)

21   In civil war, a systematic occupation of territory accompanied by the necessary purge is preferable to a rapid rout of the enemy armies which leaves the country still infested with enemies.
Francisco Franco (1892–1975) Spanish general and dictator. Remark (1937), quoted in *Franco* (Paul Preston; 1993)

22   Our war is a religious war. We who fight, whether Christians or Muslims, are soldiers of God and we are not fighting against men but against atheism and materialism.
Francisco Franco (1892–1975) Spanish general and dictator. Referring to the Nationalist campaign in the Spanish Civil War. Remark (November 16, 1937), quoted in *Franco* (Paul Preston; 1993)

23   There never was a good war or a bad peace.
Benjamin Franklin (1706–90) US statesman and scientist. Letter to Josiah Quincy (September 11, 1783), quoted in *Works of Benjamin Franklin* (1882), vol. 10

24   My argument is that War makes rattling good history; but Peace is poor reading.
Thomas Hardy (1840–1928) British novelist and poet. 'Spirit Sinister', *The Dynasts* (1904), pt. 1, Act 2, Scene 5

25   I'd like to see the government get out of war altogether and leave the whole feud to private industry.
Joseph Heller (1923–99) US novelist. Said by Milo Minderbinder. *Catch-22* (1961), ch. 24

26   In starting and waging a war it is not right that matters, but victory.
Adolf Hitler (1889–1945) Austrian-born German dictator. Quoted in *The Rise and Fall of the Third Reich* (W. L. Shirer; 1960), ch. 16

27   War should belong to the tragic past, to history: it should find no place on humanity's agenda for the future.
John Paul II (b. 1920) Polish pope. Speech in Coventry (1982)

28   A war regarded as inevitable or even probable, and therefore much prepared for, has a very good chance of being fought.
George F. Kennan (b. 1904) US diplomat and scholar. *The Cloud of Danger* (1977), ch. 11

29   No man who witnessed the tragedies of the last war, no man who can imagine the unimaginable possibilities of the next war can advocate war out of irritability or frustration or impatience.
John Fitzgerald Kennedy (1917–63) US president. Veterans' Day Address, Arlington National Cemetery, Virginia (November 11, 1961)

30   Everything, everything in war is barbaric . . . But the worst barbarity of war is that it forces men collectively to commit acts against which individually they would revolt with their whole being.
Ellen Key (1849–1926) Swedish reformer and educationalist. *War, Peace, and the Future* (1916), ch. 6

31   The most persistent sound which reverberates through men's history is the beating of war drums.
Arthur Koestler (1905–83) Hungarian-born British writer and journalist. *Janus: A Summing Up* (1978), Prologue

32   War is, at first, the hope that one will be better off; then, the expectation that the other fellow will be worse off; then, the satisfaction that he isn't any better off; and finally, the surprise at everyone's being worse off.
Karl Kraus (1874–1936) Austrian writer. 1918. Quoted in *Karl Kraus* (Harry Zohn; 1971)

33 It is well that war is so terrible; else we would grow too fond of it.

Robert E. Lee (1807–70) US general. Speaking to another general during the battle of Fredericksburg. *The Reader's Digest Treasury of American Humor* (Clifton Fadiman; 1972)

34 A mighty accelerator of events.

Vladimir Ilyich Lenin (1870–1924) Russian revolutionary leader. Referring to war. *Letters from Afar* (1917), quoted in *Collected Works of V. I. Lenin* (Alexander Trachtenberg, ed.; 1930)

35 Suppose those
who made
wars
had to fight them?

Haki R. Madhubuti (b. 1942) US writer, publisher, and lecturer. Quoted in 'Nigerian Unity, or, Little Niggers Killing Little Niggers', *You Better Believe It* (Paul Breman, ed.; 1973)

36 A certain degree of preparation for war ... affords also the best security for the continuance of peace.

James Madison (1751–1836) US president. Quoted in *Smithsonian* (September 1987)

37 Nations have always managed to find some rational necessity, some ideological reasons for murdering each other.

Golo Mann (1909–94) German historian. *The History of Germany Since 1789* (1958), pt. 1

38 We are advocates of the abolition of war, we do not want war; but war can only be abolished through war, and in order to get rid of the gun it is necessary to take up the gun.

Mao Zedong (1893–1976) Chinese statesman. 'Problems of War and Strategy' (November 6, 1938)

39 War is the highest form of struggle, existing ever since the emergence of private property and social classes, for settling contradictions between classes, between nations, between states, or between political groups at five stages of their development.

Mao Zedong (1893–1976) Chinese statesman. *How to Study War* (1935), quoted in *Mao Tsetung: An Anthology of His Writings* (Anne Fremantle, ed.; 1962)

40 Make no mistake. We will abolish war or war will abolish mankind.

Benjamin E. Mays (1894–1984) US baptist minister and educator. 1968. *Born to Rebel—An Autobiography* (1971)

41 War will never cease until babies begin to come into the world with larger cerebrums and smaller adrenal glands.

H. L. Mencken (1880–1956) US journalist, critic, and editor. 'Minority Report', *Notebooks* (1956)

42 For what can war, but endless war still breed.

John Milton (1608–74) English writer. 'On the Lord General Fairfax at the Siege of Colchester' (1648), Sonnet XV, l. 10

43 War is an extreme of political action, which tends to bring about social change more rapidly than any other instrument.

Eduardo Chivambo Mondlane (1920–69) Mozambiquan politician and activist. *The Struggle for Mozambique* (1969)

44 War hath no fury like a non-combatant.

C. E. Montague (1867–1928) British novelist and essayist. *Disenchantment* (1922), ch. 16

45 War alone brings up to their highest tension all human energies and imposes the stamp of nobility upon the peoples who have the courage to make it.

Benito Mussolini (1883–1945) Italian dictator. 1930? Quoted in *Mussolini's Roman Empire* (Dennis Mark-Smith; 1976)

46 I don't care for war, there's far too much luck in it for my liking.

Napoleon III (1808–73) French emperor. Said after the narrow but bloody French victory at the Battle of Solferino (June 24, 1859). Quoted in *The Fall of the House of Habsburg* (Edward Crankshaw; 1963)

47 In trench warfare five things are important: firewood, food, tobacco, candles, and the enemy.

George Orwell (1903–50) British writer. *Homage to Catalonia* (1938)

48 The quickest way of ending a war is to lose it.

George Orwell (1903–50) British writer. 'Second Thoughts on James Burnham', *Polemic* (1946)

49 War to the knife.

José Palafox (1780–1847) Spanish general. Replying to the demand that he surrender at the siege of Saragossa. Remark (1808)

50 We prepare for war like ferocious giants, and for peace like retarded pygmies.

Lester Pearson (1897–1972) Canadian prime minister. Nobel Prize, acceptance speech (December 11, 1957)

51 History is littered with all the wars which everybody knew would never happen.

Enoch Powell (1912–98) British politician. Speech to the Conservative Party Conference (October 19, 1967)

52 War is, after all, the universal perversion. We are all tainted: if we cannot experience our perversion at first hand we spend our time reading war stories, the pornography of war; or seeing war films, the blue films of war; or titillating our senses with the imagination of great deeds, the masturbation of war.

John Rae (b. 1931) British school teacher and writer. *The Custard Boys* (1960), ch. 13

53 You no more win a war than you can win an earthquake.

Jeannette Rankin (1880–1973) US legislator. Quoted in *Jeannette Rankin: First Lady in Congress* (Hannah Josephson; 1974)

54 More than an end of war, we want an end to the beginnings of all wars.

Franklin D. Roosevelt (1882–1945) US president. Address written for Jefferson Day, broadcast on the day after his death. (April 13, 1945)

55 A just war is in the long run far better for a nation's soul than the most prosperous peace obtained by acquiescence in wrong or injustice.

Theodore Roosevelt (1858–1919) US president. Message to Congress (December 4, 1906)

56 War is not an adventure. It is a disease. It is like typhus.

Antoine de Saint-Exupéry (1900–44) French writer and aviator. *Flight to Arras* (1942)

57 Sometime they'll give a war and nobody will come.

Carl Sandburg (1878–1967) US poet and biographer. *The People, Yes* (1936)

58 All wars are popular for the first thirty days.

Arthur Schlesinger, Jr. (b. 1917) US historian. Attrib.

59 This is to make an end of all wars, to conclude an eternal and perpetual peace.

Edward Seymour (1506?–52) English soldier and statesman. Referring to the invasion of September 1547 and the English victory at the Battle of Pinkie. Open letter to the people of Scotland (January 1548)

60 FIRST SERVANT Let me have war, say I; it exceeds peace as far as day does night; it's spritely, waking, audible, and full of vent.

William Shakespeare (1564–1616) English poet and playwright. *Coriolanus* (1608), Act 4, Scene 5

61 KING HENRY V But when the blast of war blows in our ears,
Then imitate the action of the tiger;
Stiffen the sinews, summon up the blood,
Disguise fair nature with hard-favoured rage;
Then lend the eye a terrible aspect.
William Shakespeare (1564–1616) English poet and playwright. *Henry V* (1599), Act 3, Scene 1

62 A war, with its attendant human suffering, must, when that evil is unavoidable, be made to fragment more than buildings: it must shatter the foundations of thought and re-create. Only in this way does every individual share in the cataclysm and understand the purpose of sacrifice.
Wole Soyinka (b. 1934) Nigerian novelist, playwright, poet, and lecturer. *The Man Died* (1975)

63 War is capitalism with the gloves off.
Tom Stoppard (b. 1937) Czech-born British playwright and screenwriter. *Travesties* (1974), Act 1

64 War is much too serious a thing to be left to military men.
Charles Maurice de Talleyrand (1754–1838) French statesman and diplomat. Quoted by French Prime Minister Aristide Briand to his British counterpart, David Lloyd George, during World War I. Also attributed to Georges Clemenceau. Attrib.

65 I see wars, horrible wars, and the Tiber foaming with much blood.
Virgil (70–19 BC) Roman poet. Part of the Sibyl's prophecy to Aeneas, foretelling his difficulties in winning a home in Italy. *Aeneid* (29–19 BC), bk. 6, l. 86

66 World wars have been fought and lost; for every war is against the world and every war against the world is lost.
Alice Walker (b. 1944) US novelist and poet. *Possessing the Secret of Joy* (1992)

67 Like German opera, too long and too loud.
Evelyn Waugh (1903–66) British novelist. 1941. Giving his opinions on warfare after the Battle of Crete (1941). Attrib.

68 You can tell when a war starts, but when does the prewar start?
Christa Wolf (b. 1929) German writer. 1983. *Cassandra. A Novel and Four Essays* (Jan van Heurck, tr.; 1984)

Warning

see also **Danger**, **Threats**

1 Beware that you do not lose the substance by grasping at the shadow.
Aesop (620?–560 BC) Greek writer. 'The Dog and the Shadow', *Aesop's Fables* (6th century BC)

2 Beware of women with beards and men without beards.
Anonymous. Basque proverb.

3 And the Lord God took the man, and put him into the garden of Eden . . .
And the Lord God commanded the man, saying,
Of every tree of the garden thou mayest freely eat:
But of the tree of the knowledge of good and evil, thou shalt not eat of it: for in the day that thou eatest thereof thou shalt surely die.
Bible. Genesis, *King James Bible* (1611), 2:15–17

4 And all should cry, Beware! Beware!
His flashing eyes, his floating hair!
Weave a circle round him thrice,
And close your eyes with holy dread,
For he on honey-dew hath fed,
And drunk the milk of Paradise.
Samuel Taylor Coleridge (1772–1834) British poet. 'Kubla Khan' (1797), ll. 49–54, quoted in *The Portable Coleridge* (I. A. Richards, ed.; 1950)

5 Beware of the artist who's an intellectual also. The artist who doesn't fit.
F. Scott Fitzgerald (1896–1940) US writer. *This Side of Paradise* (1920), bk. 2, ch. 5

6 A huge dog, tied by a chain, was painted on the wall and over it was written in capital letters 'Beware of the dog'.
Petronius Arbiter (d. 66) Roman writer. *Satyricon* (1st century)

7 SOOTHSAYER Beware the ides of March.
William Shakespeare (1564–1616) English poet and playwright. Said as a warning to Caesar, foreshadowing his murder. *Julius Caesar* (1599), Act 1, Scene 2

Washington, DC

see **American Cities**

Weakness

see also **Failure**, **Mediocrity**

1 The concessions of the weak are the concessions of fear.
Edmund Burke (1729–97) Irish-born British statesman and political philosopher. Referring to 'Conciliation with America'. Speech to the British Parliament (March 22, 1775)

2 Like all weak men he laid an exaggerated stress on not changing one's mind.
Somerset Maugham (1874–1965) British writer. *Of Human Bondage* (1915), ch. 39

3 SURFACE It was an amiable weakness.
Richard Brinsley Sheridan (1751–1816) Irish-born British playwright and politician. Claiming excessive generosity towards his extravagant brother. *School for Scandal* (1777), Act 5, Scene 1

4 Never support two weaknesses at the same time. It's your combination sinners—your lecherous liars and your miserly drunkards—who dishonor the vices and bring them into bad repute.
Thornton Wilder (1897–1975) US novelist and playwright. *The Matchmaker* (1954), Act 3

Wealth

see also **Capitalism**, **Extravagance**, **Money**, **Poverty**

1 If you're so smart, why aren't you rich?
Anonymous. 'The American Question', *Intellectual Capital* (Thomas A. Stewart; 1997)

2 Rich men's houses are seldom beautiful, rarely comfortable, and never original. It is a constant source of surprise to people of moderate means to observe how little a big fortune contributes to Beauty.
Margot Asquith (1865–1945) British political hostess and writer. *As I Remember* (1922), ch. 17

3 Prosperity doth best discover vice; but adversity doth best discover virtue.

Francis Bacon (1561–1626) English philosopher, statesman, and lawyer. 'Of Adversity', *Essays* (1625)

4 It is easier for a camel to go through the eye of a needle, than for a rich man to enter into the kingdom of God.

Bible. Said by Jesus. Matthew, *King James Bible* (1611), 19:23–24

5 What you do is begin as a billionaire. Then you go into the airline business.

Richard Branson (b. 1950) British entrepreneur and publicist. Advice on becoming a millionaire. Speech to the Institute of Directors, London (May 1993)

6 Is not artificial wealth a masterpiece of human achievement?

Fernand Braudel (1902–85) French historian. Quoted in *Intellectual Capital* (Thomas A. Stewart; 1997)

7 To be clever enough to get all that money, one must be stupid enough to want it.

G. K. Chesterton (1874–1936) British writer and poet. *The Innocence of Father Brown* (1911)

8 Prosperity is only an instrument to be used, not a deity to be worshipped.

Calvin Coolidge (1872–1933) US president. Speech, Boston, Massachusetts (June 11, 1928)

9 Riches have wings, and grandeur is a dream.

William Cowper (1731–1800) British poet. 'The Garden', *The Task* (1785), bk. 3, l. 263

10 FITZGERALD The rich are different from us.
HEMINGWAY Yes, they have more money.

F. Scott Fitzgerald (1896–1940) US writer. 1936. 'Notebook E', *The Crack-Up: with Other Uncollected Pieces, Note-Books and Unpublished Letters* (Edmund Wilson, ed.; 1945)

11 Wealth has never been a sufficient source of honour in itself. It must be advertised, and the normal medium is obtrusively expensive goods.

J. K. Galbraith (b. 1908) Canadian-born US economist. *The Affluent Society* (1958), ch. 7

12 Increase of material comforts, it may be generally laid down, does not in any way whatsoever conduce to moral growth.

Mahatma Gandhi (1869–1948) Indian national leader. Quoted in his obituary. *News Chronicle* (1948)

13 I would prefer to be honestly wealthy, than miserably poor.

Marcus Garvey (1887–1940) Jamaican-born black nationalist leader and publisher. *The Philosophy and Opinions of Marcus Garvey* (Amy Jacques Garvey, ed.; 1923)

14 If you can actually count your money you are not really a rich man.

J. Paul Getty (1892–1976) US oil magnate. 'Gossip', *Observer* (Quoted by A. Barrow; November 3, 1957)

15 Good morning to the day: and, next, my gold!— Open the shrine, that I may see my saint.

Ben Jonson (1572–1637) English playwright and poet. *Volpone* (1606), Act 1, Scene 1

16 It is not right to seem richer than one really is.

Gotthold Ephraim Lessing (1729–81) German playwright and critic. *Minna von Barnhelm* (1763), Act 3, Scene 7, quoted in *Laocoon, Nathan the Wise and Minna von Barnhelm* (W. A. Steel, ed.; 1930)

17 Nothing happens to the very rich; that seems to be the definition of their state of being, which is close to burial alive.

Mary McCarthy (1912–89) US writer. Written during her six-week stay in Tripoli as the guest of Countess Anna Maria Cicogna. Letter to Hannah Arendt (November 11, 1959), quoted in *Between Friends: The Correspondence of Hannah Arendt and Mary McCarthy, 1949–75* (Carol Brightman, ed.; 1995)

18 He must have killed a lot of men to have made so much money.

Molière (1622–73) French playwright. *Le Malade Imaginaire* (1673), Act 1, Scene 5

19 I am rich beyond the dreams of avarice.

Edward Moore (1712–57) English playwright. *The Gamester* (1753), Act 2

20 Remoteness and isolation were once the condition of the poor. Today it is only the extremely rich who can easily escape other people.

Geoff Mulgan (b. 1961) British author and political analyst. *Connexity* (1997)

21 They will cheerfully speak of a bad man as happy and load him with honours and social esteem, provided he be rich and otherwise powerful.

Plato (428?–347? BC) Greek philosopher. *The Republic* (370? BC), bk. 2

22 We may see the small value God has for riches, by the people he gives them to.

Alexander Pope (1688–1744) English poet. *Thoughts on Various Subjects* (1727)

23 Who Wants To Be a Millionaire?

Cole Porter (1893–1964) US songwriter and composer. 1956. Song title.

24 A man's respect for law and order exists in precise relationship to the size of his paycheck.

Adam Clayton Powell, Jr. (1908–72) US clergyman and civil rights leader. 'Black Power: A Form of Godly Power', *Keep the Faith, Baby* (1967)

25 There are men who gain from their wealth only the fear of losing it.

Antoine de Rivarol (1753–1801) French journalist. *L'Esprit de Rivarol* (1802)

26 As long as there are rich people in the world, they will be desirous of distinguishing themselves from the poor.

Jean-Jacques Rousseau (1712–78) French philosopher and writer. *Discours sur l'Économie Politique* (1758)

27 Wealth is like seawater; the more we drink, the thirstier we become; and the same is true of fame.

Arthur Schopenhauer (1788–1860) German philosopher. *Parerga and Paralipomena* (1851)

28 ANNE O, what a world of vile ill-favour'd faults Looks handsome in three hundred pounds a year!

William Shakespeare (1564–1616) English poet and playwright. *The Merry Wives of Windsor* (1597), Act 3, Scene 4

29 One can never be too thin or too rich.

Wallis Simpson (1896–1986) US-born British aristocrat. Attrib.

30 Superfluous wealth can buy superfluities only.

Henry David Thoreau (1817–62) US writer. 'Conclusion', *Walden, or, Life in the Woods* (1854)

31 Prosperity or egalitarianism—you have to choose. I favour freedom—you never achieve real equality anyway: you simply sacrifice prosperity for an illusion.

Mario Vargas Llosa (b. 1936) Peruvian writer. *Independent on Sunday* (May 5, 1991)

Weapons

see also **Crime**, **Killing**, **Nuclear Weapons**, **War**

1 The weak have one weapon: the errors of those who think they are strong.
Georges Bidault (1899–1983) French statesman. 1962. *Observer* (15 July, 1962)

2 You can do everything with bayonets except sit on them.
Prince Otto von Bismarck (1815–98) German chancellor. Attrib. *Europe: A History* (Norman Davies; 1996), ch. 10

3 Bomb you are as cruel as man makes you and you're no crueller than cancer.
Gregory Corso (b. 1930) US poet. 'Bomb', *Minefield* (1989)

4 The evolution from happiness to habit is one of death's best weapons.
Julio Cortázar (1914–84) Argentinian writer. *The Winners* (1960), ch. 14

5 Being as this is a .44 Magnum, the most powerful handgun in the world, and would blow your head clean off, you've got to ask yourself one question: 'Do I feel lucky?' Well, do ya, punk?
Clint Eastwood (b. 1930) US film actor and director. As the police detective 'Dirty Harry' Callahan. *Dirty Harry* (Harry Julian Fink; 1976)

6 Every gun that is made, every warship launched, every rocket fired signifies, in the final sense, a theft from those who hunger and are not fed, those who are cold and are not clothed.
Dwight D. Eisenhower (1890–1969) US general and president. Speech, American Society of Newspaper Editors (April 16, 1953)

7 Like opium production, the world manufacture of armaments needs to be restricted. The sword is probably responsible for more misery in the world than opium.
Mahatma Gandhi (1869–1948) Indian national leader. *Young India* (November 19, 1925)

8 Our scientific power has outrun our spiritual power. We have guided missiles and misguided men.
Martin Luther King, Jr. (1929–68) US civil rights leader. *Strength To Love* (1963), ch. 7

9 Nonviolence is a powerful and just weapon. It is a weapon unique in history, which cuts without wounding and ennobles the man who wields it. It is a sword that heals.
Martin Luther King, Jr. (1929–68) US civil rights leader. *Why We Can't Wait* (1964)

10 To tell the range of the English longbows
At Agincourt, or Crécy,
We need look no further than the yews
That, even in Irish graveyards,
Are bent on Fitzwilliams, and de Courcys.
Paul Muldoon (b. 1951) Irish poet. 'Palm Sunday' (1982), ll. 1–5, quoted in *The Penguin Book of Contemporary British Poetry* (Blake Morrison and Andrew Motion, eds.; 1982)

11 Today industrial design has put murder on a mass-production basis.
Victor Papanek (b. 1925) Austrian-born US designer, teacher, and writer. *Design for the Real World: Human Ecology and Social Change* (1984)

12 Weapons speak to the wise; but in general they need interpreters.
Pindar (518–438 BC) Greek poet. *Olympian Odes* (5th century BC), bk. 2, l. 83

13 But bombs *are* unbelievable until they actually fall.
Patrick White (1912–90) British-born Australian novelist. *Riders in the Chariot* (1961), Act 1, Scene 4

Weather

see also **Nature**, **Seasons**

1 What dreadful hot weather we have! It keeps me in a continual state of inelegance.
Jane Austen (1775–1817) British novelist. Letter (September 18, 1796), quoted in *Jane Austen's Letters* (R. W. Chapman, ed.; 1952)

2 I like the weather, when it is not rainy,
That is, I like two months of every year.
Lord Byron (1788–1824) British poet. *Beppo* (1818)

3 Cyclones are colorblind. They overturn the possessions of whites and mulattos, they skin life and, for several days, redistribute the parts.
Patrick Chamoiseau (b. 1953) Martiniquan writer. *Childhood* (1993)

4 Rain, rain, go away, come another day.
Children's Verse

5 There are seven or eight categories of phenomena in the world that are worth talking about, and one of them is the weather.
Annie Dillard (b. 1945) US writer. *Pilgrim at Tinker's Creek* (1974), ch. 3

6 It ain't a fit night out for man or beast.
W. C. Fields (1879–1946) US entertainer. *W. C. Fields by Himself* (1974), pt. 2

7 A woman rang to say she heard there was a hurricane on the way. Well don't worry, there isn't.
Michael Fish (b. 1944) British meteorologist. Television announcement just before a major hurricane. Weather Forecast, *BBC TV* (October 15, 1987)

8 St. Swithin's Day, if thou dost rain, for forty days it will remain; St. Swithin's Day, if thou be fair, for forty days 'twill rain no more.
Folk Verse. Proverb.

9 I'm singin' in the rain, just singin' in the rain;
What a glorious feeling, I'm happy again.
Arthur Freed (1894–1973) US film producer and songwriter. Song. 'Singin' in the Rain', *Hollywood Review* (1929)

10 The first fall of snow is not only an event, it is a magical event. You go to bed in one kind of world and wake up in another quite different, and if this is not enchantment then where is it to be found?
J. B. Priestley (1894–1984) British writer. *Apes and Angels* (1928)

11 Who has seen the wind?
Neither you nor I:
But when the trees bow down their heads,
The wind is passing by.
Christina Rossetti (1830–94) British poet. 'Who Has Seen the Wind?' (1872)

12 LEAR Blow, winds, and crack your cheeks; rage, blow.
You cataracts and hurricanoes, spout
Till you have drench'd our steeples, drown'd the cocks.
William Shakespeare (1564–1616) English poet and playwright. *King Lear* (1605–06), Act 3, Scene 2

13 MACBETH So foul and fair a day I have not seen.

William Shakespeare (1564–1616) English poet and playwright. *Macbeth* (1606), Act 1, Scene 3

14 Rain is grace; rain is the sky condescending to the earth; without rain there would be no life.

John Updike (b. 1932) US writer. *Self-Consciousness: Memoirs* (1989), ch. 1

Wine

see also **Alcohol, Drinks and Drinking**

1 Others mocking said, These men are full of new wine.

Bible. Referring to the 'gift of tongues'. Acts, *King James Bible* (1611), 2:13

2 Yet wine is mightier than the king. For great and true . . . though the king may be, yet when he drinks the wine rules over him.

Micha Joseph Bin Gorion (1865–1921) Russian writer and collector of Jewish folktales. Referring to Nebuchadnezzar. Quoted in *Mimekor Yisrael* (Emanuel bin Gorion, ed.; I. M. Lask, tr.; 1976), vol. 1

3 'It wasn't the wine', murmured Mr. Snodgrass, in a broken voice, 'It was the salmon'.

Charles Dickens (1812–70) British novelist. Referring to his hangover. *Pickwick Papers* (1837), ch. 8

4 Bacchus, that first from out the purple grape Crushed the sweet poison of misused wine.

John Milton (1608–74) English writer. *Comus* (1637), ll. 46–47

5 Truth comes out in wine.

Pliny the Elder (23?–79) Roman scholar. *Natural History* (77), bk. 14

6 And wine can of their wits the wise beguile, Make the sage frolic, and the serious smile.

Alexander Pope (1688–1744) English poet. *The Odyssey of Homer* (1725), bk. 14, ll. 520–521

7 IAGO Come, come; good wine is a good familiar creature if it be well used; exclaim no more against it.

William Shakespeare (1564–1616) English poet and playwright. *Othello* (1602–04), Act 2, Scene 3

8 Wine is wont to show the mind of man.

Theognis of Megara (570?–490? BC) Greek elegiac poet. *Maxims* (6th century BC), l. 500

Winning

see **Glory, Success, Victory**

Winter

see also **Seasons**

1 'Tis the year's midnight, and it is the day's.

John Donne (1572?–1631) English metaphysical poet and divine. Saint Lucy's Day (December 13) is the day of the winter solstice. 'A Nocturnal upon St. Lucy's Day, Being the Shortest Day', *Songs and Sonnets* (1635), l. 1

2 The land's sharp features seemed to be The Century's corpse outleant, His crypt the cloudy canopy, The wind his death-lament.

Thomas Hardy (1840–1928) British novelist and poet. 'The Darkling Thrush' (1900), ll. 9–12

3 St. Agnes' Eve—Ah, bitter chill it was! The owl, for all his feathers, was a-cold; The hare limp'd trembling through the frozen grass, And silent was the flock in woolly fold.

John Keats (1795–1821) English poet. The poem takes the old superstition that virgins who observe the ritual of Eve of Saint Agnes, January 20, the coldest winter night, will see a vision of their husband-to-be, and dramatizes it. 'The Eve of Saint Agnes' (1820), st. 1, ll. 1–4

4 No one thinks of winter when the grass is green!

Rudyard Kipling (1865–1936) Indian-born British writer and poet. 'A St. Helena Lullaby', *Rewards and Fairies* (1910)

5 Winter is icummen in, Lhude sing Goddamm, Raineth drop and staineth slop And how the wind doth ramm! Sing: Goddamm.

Ezra Pound (1885–1972) US poet, translator, and critic. A parody of the Middle English lyric 'Sumer is icumen in' (1250?). 'Ancient Music', *Lustra* (1917)

6 In the bleak mid-winter Frosty wind made moan, Earth stood hard as iron, Water like a stone; Snow had fallen, snow on snow, Snow on snow, In the bleak mid-winter, Long ago.

Christina Rossetti (1830–94) British poet. 'Mid-Winter' (1875)

7 WINTER When icicles hang by the wall, And Dick the shepherd blows his nail, And Tom bears logs into the hall, And milk comes frozen home in pail, When blood is nipp'd, and ways be foul, Then nightly sings the staring owl: 'Tu-who; Tu-whit, Tu-who'—A merry note. While greasy Joan doth keel the pot.

William Shakespeare (1564–1616) English poet and playwright. *Love's Labour's Lost* (1595), Act 5, Scene 2

8 MAMILLIUS A sad tale's best for winter. I have one Of sprites and goblins.

William Shakespeare (1564–1616) English poet and playwright. *The Winter's Tale* (1610–11), Act 2, Scene 1

9 If Winter comes, can Spring be far behind?

Percy Bysshe Shelley (1792–1822) English poet. 'Ode to the West Wind' (1819), l. 70

10 It is a winter's tale That the snow blind twilight ferries over the lakes And floating fields from the farm in the cup of the vales.

Dylan Thomas (1914–53) Welsh poet, playwright, and short-story writer. 'A Winter's Tale', *In Country Sleep* (1952), ll. 1–3

Wisdom

see also **Knowledge, Self-Knowledge, Understanding**

1 A wise man will make more opportunities than he finds.

Francis Bacon (1561–1626) English philosopher, statesman, and lawyer. 'Of Ceremonies and Respects', *Essays* (1625)

2 The words of wise men are heard in quiet more than the cry of him that ruleth among fools.

Bible. Ecclesiastes, *King James Bible* (1611), 9:17

3 No mention shall be made of coral, or of pearls: for the price of wisdom is above rubies.
Bible. Job, *King James Bible* (1611), 28:18

4 Wisdom hath builded her house, she hath hewn out her seven pillars.
Bible. Proverbs, *King James Bible* (1611), 9:1

5 To know how to say what others only know how to think is what makes men poets or sages; and to dare to say what others only dare to think makes men martyrs or reformers—or both.
Elizabeth Charles (1828–96) British writer. *Chronicle of the Schönberg-Cotta Family* (1863)

6 Knowledge dwells
In heads replete with thoughts of other men;
Wisdom in minds attentive to their own.
William Cowper (1731–1800) British poet. 'The Winter Walk at Noon', *The Task* (1785), bk. 6, ll. 89–91

7 Knowledge is proud that he has learn'd so much;
Wisdom is humble that he knows no more.
William Cowper (1731–1800) British poet. 'The Winter Walk at Noon', *The Task* (1785), bk. 6, ll. 96–97

8 Our age has robbed millions of the simplicity of ignorance, and has so far failed to lift them to simplicity of wisdom.
Robertson Davies (1913–95) Canadian novelist and critic. *A Voice from the Attic* (1960)

9 Wisdom denotes the pursuing of the best ends by the best means.
Francis Hutcheson (1694–1746) Irish-born English philosopher. *Inquiry into the Original of our Ideas of Beauty and Virtue* (1725), pt. 1, sect. 5

10 The sage keeps to the deed that consists in taking no action and practises the teaching that uses no words.
Laozi (570?–490? BC) Chinese philosopher. The *Daode Jing* is an early Chinese Taoist text. While attributed to Laozi, it probably dates from the 3rd century BC *Daode Jing* (Unknown), quoted in *Tao Te Ching* (D. C. Lau, tr.; 1963), bk. 1, pt. 2

11 From the earliest times the old have rubbed it into the young that they are wiser than they, and before the young had discovered what nonsense this was they were old too, and it profited them to carry on the imposture.
Somerset Maugham (1874–1965) British writer. *Cakes and Ale* (1930), ch. 11

12 There is more wisdom in your body than in your deepest philosophy.
Friedrich Wilhelm Nietzsche (1844–1900) German philosopher and poet. *Human, All Too Human* (1878–80), pt. 2

13 If you are wise, be wise; keep what goods the gods provide you.
Plautus (254?–184 BC) Roman comic playwright. *Rudens* (3rd–2nd century BC), Act 4, Scene 7

14 Not by years but by disposition is wisdom acquired.
Plautus (254?–184 BC) Roman comic playwright. *Trinummus* (3rd–2nd century BC), Act 2, Scene 2

15 Consider the little mouse, how sagacious an animal it is which never entrusts its life to one hole only.
Plautus (254?–184 BC) Roman comic playwright. *Truculentus* (3rd–2nd century BC), Act 4, Scene 4

16 It is a point of wisdom to be silent when occasion requires, and better than to speak, though never so well.
Plutarch (46?–120?) Greek biographer and philosopher. 'Of the Training of Children' (1st–2nd century)

17 VIOLA This fellow is wise enough to play the fool;
And to do that well craves a kind of wit.
William Shakespeare (1564–1616) English poet and playwright. *Twelfth Night* (1601), Act 3, Scene 1

18 The highest wisdom has but one science—the science of the whole—the science explaining the whole creation and man's place in it.
Leo Tolstoy (1828–1910) Russian writer. *War and Peace* (1865–69), bk. 5, ch. 2

19 It is never wise to try to appear to be more clever than you are. It is sometimes wise to appear slightly less so.
William Whitelaw (1918–99) British politician. *Observer* (1975), 'Sayings of the Year'

20 And yet the wiser mind
Mourns less for what age takes away
Than what it leaves behind.
William Wordsworth (1770–1850) English poet. 1798. Subtitled 'A Conversation'. 'The Fountain', *Lyrical Ballads* (2nd ed.; 1800), ll. 34–36

21 Though leaves are many, the root is one;
Through all the lying days of my youth
I swayed my leaves and flowers in the sun;
Now I may wither into the truth.
W. B. Yeats (1865–1939) Irish poet and playwright. March 1909. Complete poem. 'The Coming of Wisdom with Time', *The Green Helmet and Other Poems* (1910)

Wit

see also **Humour, Knowledge, Wordplay**

1 Don't put too fine a point to your wit for fear it should get blunted.
Miguel de Cervantes (1547–1616) Spanish novelist and playwright. *The Little Gypsy* (1605)

2 Who wit with jealous eye surveys,
And sickens at another's praise.
Charles Churchill (1731–64) British poet. *The Ghost* (1763), bk. 2, ll. 663–664

3 It has been said that love robs those who have it of their wit, and gives it to those who have none.
Denis Diderot (1713–84) French encyclopedist and philosopher. *Paradoxe sur le Comédien* (1830)

4 A thing well said will be wit in all languages.
John Dryden (1631–1700) English poet, playwright, and literary critic. 'Of Dramatick Poesy' (1688)

5 Wit will shine
Through the harsh cadence of a rugged line.
John Dryden (1631–1700) English poet, playwright, and literary critic. 'To the Memory of Mr. Oldham' (1684), ll. 15–16, quoted in *The Poems and Fables of John Dryden* (James Kinsley, ed.; 1962)

6 Great Wits are sure to Madness near alli'd
And thin Partitions do their Bounds divide.
John Dryden (1631–1700) English poet, playwright, and literary critic. *Absalom and Achitophel* (1681), pt. 1

7 His foe was folly and his weapon wit.
Anthony Hope (1863–1933) British novelist and playwright. Written for the inscription on the memorial to W. S. Gilbert, Victoria Embankment, London. 'Epitaph for W. S. Gilbert' (1915)

8 Every man has, some time in his life, an ambition to be a wag.

Samuel Johnson (1709–84) British lexicographer and writer. Quoted in *Diary and Letters of Madame d'Arblay* (Charlotte Barrett, ed.; 1842–46), vol. 3, ch. 46

9 The greatest fault of a penetrating wit is to go beyond the mark.

François La Rochefoucauld (1613–80) French epigrammatist and moralist. *Reflections, or Sentences and Moral Maxims* (1665), no. 377

10 Impropriety is the soul of wit.

Somerset Maugham (1874–1965) British writer. *The Moon and Sixpence* (1919), ch. 4

11 The well of true wit is truth itself.

George Meredith (1828–1909) British novelist and poet. *Diana of the Crossways* (1885), ch. 1

12 Have you summoned your wits from wool-gathering?

Thomas Middleton (1580?–1627) English playwright. *The Family of Love* (1602), Act 5, Scene 3

13 Improvisation is the touchstone of wit.

Molière (1622–73) French playwright. *Les Précieuses Ridicules* (1659), Scene 10

14 Wit in women is apt to have bad consequences; like a sword without a scabbard, it wounds the weaker and provokes assailants. I am sorry to say the generality of women who have excelled in wit have failed in chastity.

Elizabeth Montagu (1720–1800) English writer and literary hostess. 1750. Quoted in *Reconstructing Aphra* (Angeline Goreau; 1980)

15 True wit is nature to advantage dress'd;
What oft was thought, but ne'er so well express'd.

Alexander Pope (1688–1744) English poet. *An Essay on Criticism* (1711), ll. 297–298

16 You beat your pate, and fancy wit will come;
Knock as you please, there's nobody at home.

Alexander Pope (1688–1744) English poet. *Epigram* (1732)

17 A wit with dunces, and a dunce with wits.

Alexander Pope (1688–1744) English poet. *The Dunciad* (1742), bk. 4, l. 90

18 With a sharp epigram it's pleasant
to infuriate a clumsy foe.

Alexander Pushkin (1799–1837) Russian poet and writer. 1831. *Eugene Onegin* (Charles Johnstone, tr.; 1977), ch. 6, st. 33

19 A proverb is one man's wit and all men's wisdom.

Lord Russell (1792–1878) British prime minister. Quoted in *Sir James Mackintosh* (R. J. Mackintosh; 1835), vol. 2, ch. 7

20 FALSTAFF I am not only witty in myself, but the cause that wit is in other men. I do here walk before thee like a sow that hath overwhelm'd all her litter but one.

William Shakespeare (1564–1616) English poet and playwright. *Henry IV, Part 2* (1597), Act 1, Scene 2

21 An ounce of a man's own wit is worth a ton of other people's.

Laurence Sterne (1713–68) Irish-born British writer and clergyman. *Tristram Shandy* (1759–67)

Women

see also **The Sexes**, **Sexuality**, **Women's Rights**

1 Women are really much nicer than men:
No wonder we like them.

Kingsley Amis (1922–95) British novelist. 'A Bookshop Idyll' (1956)

2 A woman, especially if she have the misfortune of knowing anything, should conceal it as well as she can.

Jane Austen (1775–1817) British novelist. *Northanger Abbey* (1818), ch. 14

3 Between women love is contemplative. There is no struggle, no victory, no defeat; in exact reciprocity each is at once subject and object, sovereign and slave; duality becomes mutuality.

Simone de Beauvoir (1908–86) French writer and feminist theorist. *The Second Sex* (1949)

4 One is not born a woman, one becomes one.

Simone de Beauvoir (1908–86) French writer and feminist theorist. *The Second Sex* (1949)

5 Who is't that to women's beauty would submit,
And yet refuse the fetters of their wit?

Aphra Behn (1640?–89) English novelist and playwright. *The Forced Marriage* (1670), Prologue

6 And what is better than wisedoom? Womman.
And what is better than a good womman? Nothyng.

Geoffrey Chaucer (1343?–1400) English poet. 'The Tale of Melibee', *The Canterbury Tales* (1390?), l. 1107, quoted in *The Works of Geoffrey Chaucer* (F. N. Robinson, ed.; 1957)

7 Wommen desiren to have sovereynetee
As wel over hir housbond as hir love.

Geoffrey Chaucer (1343?–1400) English poet. 'The Wife of Bath's Tale', *The Canterbury Tales* (1390?), quoted in *The Works of Geoffrey Chaucer* (F. N. Robinson, ed.; 1957)

8 She may be a woman but she isn't a sister; she may be a sister but she isn't a comrade.

Caryl Churchill (b. 1938) British playwright. Referring to Margaret Thatcher. Quoted in *Interviews with Contemporary Women Playwrights* (Karen Betsko and Rachel Koenig; 1987)

9 Women are like tricks by slight of hand,
Which, to admire, we should not understand.

William Congreve (1670–1729) English playwright and poet. *Love for Love* (1695), Act 4, Scene 21

10 I am a woman meant for a man, but I never found a man who could compete.

Bette Davis (1908–89) US actor. Attrib.

11 Ever since the myth of Eve giving Adam the apple was created, women have been presented as devils or angels, but definitely not as human beings.

Raya Dunayevskaya (1910–87) Ukrainian-born US author and philosopher. *Notes on Women's Liberation* (1970)

12 She has the smile of a woman who has just dined off her husband.

Lawrence Durrell (1912–90) British novelist and poet. Referring to the Mona Lisa. Attrib.

13 Women rule the world . . . no man has ever done anything that a woman either hasn't allowed him to do or encouraged him to do.

Bob Dylan (b. 1941) US singer and songwriter. *Rolling Stone* (June 21, 1984)

14 I'm not denyin' the women are foolish: God Almighty made 'em to match the men.

George Eliot (1819–80) British novelist. *Adam Bede* (1854), ch. 53

15 Woman is woman's natural ally.

Euripides (480?–406? BC) Greek playwright. *Alope* (5th century BC), fragment 109

16 She is abstract femininity . . . the prototype of a galactic New Woman.

Federico Fellini (1920–93) Italian film director. Referring to the US film actor Kim Basinger. Attrib.

17 A woman should be an illusion.

Ian Fleming (1908–64) British writer. *Life of Ian Fleming* (John Pearson; 1966)

18 The great question . . . which I have not been able to answer, despite my thirty years of research into the feminine soul, is 'What does a woman want?'

Sigmund Freud (1856–1939) Austrian psychoanalyst. Letter to Maria Bonaparte, quoted in *Sigmund Freud: Life and Work* (3 vols.) (Ernest Jones; 1953–55), vol. 3, ch. 16

19 The especial genius of Woman I believe to be electrical in movement, intuitive in function, spiritual in tendency. She excels not so easily in classification, or recreation, as in an instinctive seizure of causes.

Margaret Fuller (1810–50) US writer and reformer. *Woman in the Nineteenth Century* (1845), Preface, quoted in *The Heath Anthology of American Literature* (Paul Lauter, ed.; 1998), vol. 1

20 As though femininity is something you can lose the way you lose your pocketbook: hmm, where in the world did I put my femininity?

Françoise Giroud (b. 1916) Swiss-born French politician, journalist, and editor. *I Give You My Word* (1974)

21 Eternal Woman draws us upward.

Johann Wolfgang von Goethe (1749–1832) German poet, playwright, and scientist. Last line. 'Hochgebirg', *Faust* (1832), pt. 2

22 You can now see the Female Eunuch the world over . . . Wherever you see nail varnish, lipstick, brassieres, and high heels, the Eunuch has set up her camp.

Germaine Greer (b. 1939) Australian-born British writer and academic. *The Female Eunuch* (1991), Foreword (20th anniversary edition)

23 Women fail to understand how much men hate them.

Germaine Greer (b. 1939) Australian-born British writer and academic. 'Loathing and Disgust', *The Female Eunuch* (1970)

24 My mother said it was simple to keep a man, you must be a maid in the living room, a cook in the kitchen and a whore in the bedroom. I said I'd hire the other two and take care of the bedroom bit.

Jerry Hall (b. 1956) US model. *Observer* (October 1985), quoted in *Sayings of the Eighties* (Jeffrey Care, ed.; 1989)

25 A woman would rather visit her own grave than the place where she had been young and beautiful after she is aged and ugly.

Corra May Harris (1869–1935) US writer. *Eve's Second Husband* (1910), ch. 14

26 It makes me feel masculine to tell you that I do not answer questions like this without being paid for answering them.

Lillian Hellman (1905–84) US playwright. When asked by *Harper's Magazine* when she felt most masculine; this question had already been asked of several famous men. Quoted in *Reader's Digest* (July 1977)

27 Within patriarchal society, women who are victimized by male violence have had to pay a price for breaking the silence and naming the problem. They have had to be seen as fallen women, who have failed in their 'feminine' role to sensitize and civilize the beast in the man.

bell hooks (b. 1952) US feminist writer, poet, and educator. 'violence in intimate relationships: a feminist perspective', *Talking Back* (1989)

28 A new type of woman arises. She is called a career woman. A man is never a career man. That is his right and privilege. But the woman is called career woman because her 'career' in modern society demands she place herself in a subordinate position or even renounce normal life.

C. L. R. James (1901–89) Trinidadian writer, political theorist, and educator. Letter to Constance Webb (1943), quoted in *The C. L. R. James Reader* (Anna Grimshaw, ed.; 1992)

29 In Britain, an attractive woman is somehow suspect. If there is talent as well it is overshadowed. Beauty and brains just can't be entertained; someone has been too extravagant.

Vivien Leigh (1913–67) Indian-born British actor. *Light of a Star* (1967)

30 Any world which did not have a place for me loving women was not a world in which I wanted to live, nor one which I could fight for.

Audre Lorde (1934–92) US poet, novelist, and feminist. *Zami: A New Spelling of My Name* (1982)

31 When a man can't explain a woman's actions, the first thing he thinks about is the condition of her uterus.

Clare Boothe Luce (1903–87) US playwright, journalist, and public official. *Slam the Door Softly* (1970)

32 I think life is one long introductory course in tolerance, and in order for a woman to get her Ph.D. she's gotta pass Men 101.

Terry McMillan (b. 1951) US novelist and teacher. *Waiting to Exhale* (1992)

33 Women want mediocre men, and men are working to be as mediocre as possible.

Margaret Mead (1901–78) US anthropologist. *Quote Magazine* (May 15, 1958)

34 It's good, you know, when you got a woman who is a friend of your mind.

Toni Morrison (b. 1931) US novelist. *Beloved* (1987)

35 A man thanks God for not making him a woman and the woman simply thanks God for making her as she is.

Julia Neuberger (b. 1950) British rabbi, author, and broadcaster. Referring to part of the liturgy of Orthodox Judaism. *On Being Jewish* (1995)

36 It's all right for a woman to be, above all, human. I am a woman first of all.

Anaïs Nin (1903–77) French writer. June 1933. *The Diary of Anaïs Nin* (1966), vol. 1

37 As women, our historical role has been to clean up the mess. Whether it's the mess left by war or death or children or sickness . . . we know that life is messy.

Marsha Norman (b. 1947) US playwright. Quoted in 'Marsha Norman', *Interviews with Contemporary Women Playwrights* (Kathleen Betsko and Rachel Koenig; 1987)

38 There is no masculine power or privilege I did not covet. But slowly, step by step, decade by decade, I was forced to acknowledge that even a woman of abnormal will cannot escape her hormonal identity.

Camille Paglia (b. 1947) US academic and author. *Sex, Art, and American Culture* (1992)

39 Most good women are hidden treasures who are only safe because nobody looks for them.

Dorothy Parker (1893–1967) US writer and wit. *New York Times* (June 8, 1967)

40 Woman's at best a contradiction still.

Alexander Pope (1688–1744) English poet. Addressed to Mrs. M. Blount. 'To a Lady', *Moral Essays* (1735), Epistle 2, l. 270

41 Woman puts us back into communication with the eternal spring in which God looks at his reflection.

Ernest Renan (1823–92) French philosopher, philologist, and historian. *Souvenirs d'Enfance et de Jeunesse* (1883)

42 In the greater part of the world woman is a slave and a beast of burden.

Käthe Schirmacher (1865–1930) German author and feminist. *The Modern Woman's Rights Movement* (1905)

43 Any woman who has a great deal to offer the world is in trouble.

Hazel Scott (1920–81) US jazz musician, actor, and feminist. *Ms* (1974)

44 Where there is a woman there is magic.

Ntozake Shange (b. 1948) US poet, novelist, essayist, and playwright. *Sassafrass, Cypress & Indigo* (1977)

45 A woman without a man is like a fish without a bicycle.

Gloria Steinem (b. 1934) US writer and feminist. Attrib.

46 Women are the real architects of society.

Harriet Beecher Stowe (1811–96) US writer and abolitionist. 'Dress, or Who Makes the Fashions', *Atlantic Monthly* (19th century)

47 Nor do they trust their tongue alone,
But speak a language of their own;
Can read a nod, a shrug, a look,
Far better than a printed book;
Convey a libel in a frown,
And wink a reputation down.

Jonathan Swift (1667–1745) Irish writer and clergyman. 'The Journal of a Modern Lady' (1729)

48 Wonderful women! Have you ever thought how much we all, and women especially, owe to Shakespeare for his vindication of women in these fearless, high-spirited, resolute, and intelligent heroines?

Ellen Terry (1847–1928) British actor. 'Four Lectures on Shakespeare', *The Triumphant Women* (1911)

49 In politics, if you want anything said, ask a man; if you want anything done, ask a woman.

Margaret Thatcher (b. 1925) British prime minister. Quoted in *The Changing Anatomy of Britain* (Anthony Sampson; 1982)

50 A bad woman always has something she regards as a curse—a real bit of goodness hidden away somewhere.

Laura Troubridge (d. 1946) British writer. *The Millionaire* (1907)

51 Women, we need you to give us back our faith in humanity.

Desmond Tutu (b. 1931) South African clergyman and civil rights activist. *The Words of Desmond Tutu* (Naomi Tutu, ed.; 1989)

52 Women who live by the goodwill of men have no control over their lives, and that's the truth of it.

Fay Weldon (b. 1933) British writer. *The Heart of the Country* (1989)

53 Whatever women do they must do twice as well as men to be thought half as good. Luckily, this is not difficult.

Charlotte Whitton (1896–1975) Canadian politician and writer. *Canada Month* (June 1963)

54 Every woman is a rebel, and usually in wild revolt against herself.

Oscar Wilde (1854–1900) Irish poet, playwright, and wit. *A Woman of No Importance* (1893)

55 For women, writing is a medium which they place between themselves and the world of men.

Christa Wolf (b. 1929) German writer. 1983. 'A Work Diary', *Cassandra. A Novel and Four Essays* (Jan van Heurck, tr.; 1984)

56 Women have always been the guardians of wisdom and humanity which makes them natural, but usually secret, rulers. The time has come for them to rule openly, but together with and not against men.

Charlotte Wolff (b. 1904) German-born British psychiatrist and writer. *Bisexuality: A Study* (1977), ch. 2

57 If women be educated to dependence; that is, to act according to the will of another fallible being, and submit, right or wrong, to power, where are we to stop?

Mary Wollstonecraft (1759–97) British writer and feminist. *A Vindication of the Rights of Women* (1792), ch. 3

58 Women have served all these centuries as looking-glasses possessing the magic and delicious power of reflecting the figure of man at twice its natural size.

Virginia Woolf (1882–1941) British novelist and critic. *A Room of One's Own* (1929)

Women's Rights

see also **Civil Rights, Equality, Women**

1 Whilst you are proclaiming peace and good will to men, emancipating all nations, you insist upon retaining absolute power over your wives. But you must remember that arbitrary power is most like other things which are very hard, very liable to be broken.

Abigail Adams (1744–1818) US feminist. Written less than two months before the Declaration of Independence. Letter to John Adams (May 7, 1776)

2 The Prophet Mohammad wanted equality for women. But when Islam went from the desert to the palaces, men put in certain loopholes.

Zeenat Ali, Arab historian. *Independent* (September 16, 1993)

3 And I shall earnestly and persistently continue to urge all women to the practical recognition of the old Revolutionary maxim, 'Resistance to tyranny is obedience to God'.

Susan B. Anthony (1820–1906) US social reformer. Speech made in court (June 18, 1873)

4 Superiority we've always had; all we ask is equality.

Nancy Astor (1879–1964) US-born British politician. Referring to women. Attrib.

5 Society, being codified by man, decrees that woman is inferior; she can do away with this inferiority only by destroying the male's superiority.

Simone de Beauvoir (1908–86) French writer and feminist theorist. *The Second Sex* (1949)

6 I am obnoxious to each carping tongue,
Who sayes my hand a needle better fits,
A Poet's Pen, all scorne, I should thus wrong:
For such despight they cast on female wits:
If what I doe prove well, it won't advance,
They'll say it's stolne, or else, it was by chance.

Anne Bradstreet (1612–72) British-born US poet. 'The Prologue', *The Tenth Muse Lately Sprung up in America* (1650)

7 Feminism is an entire world view or gestalt, not just a laundry list of 'women's issues'.
Charlotte Bunch (b. 1944) US editor. *New Directions for Women* (September 1981)

8 While quacks of State must each produce his plan,
And even children lisp the Rights of Man;
Amid this mighty fuss just let me mention,
The Rights of Woman merit some attention.
Robert Burns (1759–96) Scottish poet and songwriter. 'Address on the Rights of Woman' (November 26, 1792)

9 When a just cause reaches its flood-tide, as ours has done in that country, whatever stands in the way must fall before its overwhelming power.
Carrie Chapman Catt (1859–1947) US women's rights campaigner and pacifist. Referring to the Woman Suffrage movement. Speech, Stockholm, Sweden (1911)

10 Nothing would induce me to vote for giving women the franchise. I am not going to be henpecked into a question of such importance.
Winston Churchill (1874–1965) British prime minister and writer. Attrib.

11 The liberation of language is rooted in the liberation of ourselves.
Mary Daly (b. 1928) US feminist and theologian. *Beyond God the Father, Toward a Philosophy of Women's Liberation* (1973)

12 The extension of women's rights is the basic principle of all social progress.
Charles Fourier (1772–1837) French social scientist. *Theory of Four Movements* (1808), vol. 2, ch. 4

13 Merely external emancipation has made of the modern woman an artificial being . . . Now, woman is confronted with the necessity of emancipating herself from emancipation, if she really desires to be free.
Emma Goldman (1869–1940) Lithuanian-born US anarchist. *Anarchism and Other Essays* (1917)

14 Liberation is an evershifting horizon, a total ideology that can never fulfill its promises.
Arianna Huffington (b. 1950) Greek-born US socialite and writer. *The Female Woman* (1973)

15 I am not even quite sure what women's rights really are. To me it has been a question of human rights . . . Of course it is incidentally desirable to solve the problem of women; but that has not been my whole object. My task has been the portrayal of human beings.
Henrik Ibsen (1828–1906) Norwegian playwright. Speech, the Norwegian Society for Women's Rights (May 26, 1898)

16 I am a warrior in the time of women warriors; the longing for justice is the sword I carry, the love of womankind my shield.
Sonia Johnson (b. 1936) US feminist and writer. *From Housewife to Heretic* (1981)

17 Just as Western feminists dress in 'un-feminine' ways to reject the stereotype of femininity, so . . . Muslim women taking on Islamic dress are saying: No, we are not sex symbols, and this is our way of expressing it.
Rana Kabbani (b. 1958) Syrian cultural historian. *Women in Muslim Society* (1992)

18 Women's Liberation is the liberation of the feminine in the man and the masculine in the woman.
Corita Kent (1918–86) US graphic artist. *Los Angeles Times* (July 11, 1974)

19 The emancipation of women is practically the greatest egoistic movement of the nineteenth century, and the most intense affirmation of the right of the self that history has yet seen.
Ellen Key (1849–1926) Swedish reformer and educationalist. *The Century of the Child* (1900), ch. 2

20 Women's history is the primary tool for women's emancipation.
Gerda Lerner (b. 1920) Austrian-born US educator and historian. *On the Future of Our Past* (1981)

21 What an extraordinary mixture of idealism and lunacy. Hasn't she the sense to see that the very worst method of campaigning for the franchise is to try and intimidate or blackmail a man into giving her what he would gladly give her otherwise.
David Lloyd George (1863–1945) British prime minister. Quoted in *Lloyd George* (Richard Lloyd George; 1960)

22 I'm furious about the Women's Liberationists. They keep getting up on soapboxes and proclaiming that women are brighter than men. That's true, but it should be kept very quiet or it ruins the whole racket.
Anita Loos (1888–1981) US writer. *Observer* (December 30, 1973), 'Sayings of the Year'

23 Is it to be understood that the principles of the Declaration of Independence bear no relation to half of the human race?
Harriet Martineau (1802–76) British writer and economist. 'Marriage', *Society in America* (1837), vol. 3

24 Women are no longer cooped up in harems, nor are they veiled and silent. They have massively infiltrated forbidden territory.
Fatima Mernissi (b. 1941) Moroccan writer. *Islam and Democracy* (1992)

25 The principle which regulates the existing social relations between the two sexes—the legal subordination of one sex to the other—is wrong in itself, and now one of the chief hindrances to human improvement.
John Stuart Mill (1806–73) British philosopher and social reformer. *The Subjection of Women* (1869)

26 In both fiction and non-fiction, women are making their voices heard. My interpretation of women's rights in Islam, like that of countless other Muslim-born feminists, clashes strongly with the conservative, official interpretation.
Taslima Nasreen (b. 1958) Bangladeshi writer. *Times* (June 18, 1994)

27 The vote, I thought, means nothing to women. We should be armed.
Edna O'Brien (b. 1932) Irish novelist. Quoted in *Fear of Flying* (Erica Jong; 1973), epigraph to ch. 16

28 We are here to claim our rights as women, not only to be free, but to fight for freedom. It is our privilege, as well as our pride and our joy, to take some part in this militant movement, which, as we believe, means the regeneration of all humanity.
Christabel Pankhurst (1880–1958) British suffragette. Speech, 'Votes for Women' (March 31, 1911)

29 Women have always fought for men, and for their children. Now they were ready to fight for their own human rights. Our militant movement was established.
Emmeline Pankhurst (1858–1928) British suffragette. Referring to the suffragette movement in the United Kingdom. *My Own Story* (1914)

30 There is a reaction from the ideal of an intellectual and emancipated womanhood, for which the pioneers toiled and suffered, to be seen in painted lips and nails, and the return of trailing skirts . . . which betoken the slave-woman's intelligent companionship.

Sylvia Pankhurst (1882–1960) British suffragette. *News of the World* (April 1928)

31 Women's chains have been forged by men, not by anatomy.

Estelle Ramey (b. 1917) US endocrinologist. *Men's Monthly Cycles* (1972)

32 They invent a legend to put the blame for the existence of humanity on women and, if she wants to stop it, they talk about the wonders of civilizations and the sacred responsibilities of motherhood. They can't have it both ways.

Dorothy M. Richardson (1873–1957) British writer. 'The Tunnel Interim', *Pilgrimage* (1919), vol. 2, ch. 24

33 Women have been emancipated on condition that they don't upset men, or interfere too much with men's way of life.

Constance Rover (b. 1910) British sociologist and feminist. Quoted in *There's Always Been a Women's Movement this Century* (Dale Spender; 1983), ch. 5, 'Constance Rover'

34 The Arab feminist movement will . . . rise from the soil of Arab lands, rather than become another copy of feminist movements in the West.

Nawal el-Saadawi (b. 1931) Egyptian novelist. 'Arab Women and Politics', *The Nawal el-Saadawi Reader* (1997)

35 No woman can call herself free who cannot choose the time to be a mother or not as she sees fit.

Margaret Sanger (1879–1966) US social reformer and leader of birth control movement. *The Case for Birth Control* (1917)

36 Give women the vote, and in five years there will be a crushing tax on bachelors.

George Bernard Shaw (1856–1950) Irish playwright. 'Preface', *Man and Superman* (1903)

37 The Bible and Church have been the greatest stumbling block in the way of woman's emancipation.

Elizabeth Cady Stanton (1815–1902) US suffragette. *Free Thought Magazine* (September 1896)

38 We still wonder at the stolid incapacity of all men to understand that woman feels the invidious distinctions of sex exactly as the black man does those of color, or the white man the more transient distinctions of wealth, family, position, place, and power; that she feels as keenly as man the injustice of disfranchisement.

Elizabeth Cady Stanton (1815–1902) US suffragette. *History of Woman Suffrage* (co-written with Susan B. Anthony and Matilda Gage; 1881), vol. 1

39 The Queen is most anxious to enlist every one who can speak or write to join in checking this mad, wicked folly of 'Woman's Rights', with all its attendant horrors, on which her poor feeble sex is bent, forgetting every sense of womanly feeling and propriety.

Victoria (1819–1901) British monarch. Letter to Sir Theodore Martin (May 29, 1870)

40 If we had left it to the men *toilets* would have been the greatest obstacle to human progress. *Toilets* was always the reason women couldn't become engineers, or pilots . . . They didn't have women's toilets.

Rebecca West (1892–1983) Irish-born British novelist, critic, and journalist. Quoted in *There's Always been a Women's Movement this Century* (Dale Spender; 1983)

41 We are in the midst of a violent backlash against feminism that uses images of female beauty as a political weapon against women's advancement: the beauty myth.

Naomi Wolf (b. 1962) US writer. *The Beauty Myth: How Images of Beauty are Used Against Women* (1990)

42 The *divine right* of husbands, like the divine right of kings, may, it is hoped, in this enlightened age, be contested without danger.

Mary Wollstonecraft (1759–97) British writer and feminist. *A Vindication of the Rights of Women* (1792), ch. 3

Wonder

see also Euphoria, Magic

1 Wonder, as the outgoing activity of mind, necessarily requires a surrender of all purely subjective and selfish interests, and the devotion of one's self to the object wholly for the sake of the latter. It is love of knowledge.

John Dewey (1859–1952) US philosopher and educator. *Psychology* (1887)

2 The fairest thing we can experience is the mysterious. It is the fundamental emotion which stands at the cradle of true art and true science. He who knows it not and can no longer wonder, no longer feel amazement, is as good as dead, a snuffed-out candle.

Albert Einstein (1879–1955) German-born US physicist. *Ideas and Opinions* (1954)

3 Men love to wonder, and that is the seed of our science, and such is the mechanical determination of our age, and so recent are our best contrivances, that use has not dulled our joy and pride in them.

Ralph Waldo Emerson (1803–82) US poet and essayist. 'Works and Days', *Society and Solitude* (1870)

4 How extraordinary ordinary
things are, like the nature of the mind
and the process of observing.

Norman McCaig (1910–96) Scottish poet. 'An Ordinary Day', *An Ordinary Day* (1966)

5 Miracles are instantaneous, they cannot be summoned, but come of themselves, usually at unlikely moments and to those who least expect them.

Katherine Anne Porter (1890–1980) US writer. *Ship of Fools* (1962), pt. 3

6 Wonders are many, and none is more wonderful than man.

Sophocles (496?–406? BC) Greek playwright. *Antigone* (after 441 BC), l. 332

Wordplay

see also Humour, Language, Wit, Words

1 No. The 't' is silent—as in 'Harlow'.

Margot Asquith (1865–1945) British political hostess and writer. When Jean Harlow asked whether the 't' was pronounced in 'Margot'. Quoted in *Great Tom* (T. S. Matthews; 1973), ch. 7

2 A man who could make so vile a pun would not scruple to pick a pocket.

John Dennis (1657–1734) English critic and playwright. *The Gentleman's Magazine* (1781), vol. 51, pt. 1, l. 1

3 Where in this small-talking world can I find
A longitude with no platitude?

Christopher Fry (b. 1907) British playwright. *The Lady's Not for Burning* (1949), Act 3

4 I'm glad you like adverbs—I adore them; they are the only qualifications I really much respect.

Henry James (1843–1916) US-born British writer and critic. Letter to Miss M. Bentham Edwards (January 5, 1912), quoted in *The Letters of Henry James* (Percy Lubbock, ed.; 1920)

5 A pun is a pistol let off at the ear; not a feather to tickle the intellect.

Charles Lamb (1775–1834) British essayist. 'Popular Fallacies', *Last Essays of Elia* (1833)

6 Many of us can still remember the social nuisance of the inveterate punster. This man followed conversation as a shark follows a ship.

Stephen Leacock (1869–1944) British-born Canadian writer and economist. *The Boy I Left Behind Me* (1947)

7 The conclusion of your syllogism, I said lightly, is fallacious, being based upon licensed premises.

Flann O'Brien (1911–66) Irish novelist and journalist. *At Swim-Two-Birds* (1939)

8 Meretricious and a Happy New Year.

Gore Vidal (b. 1925) US novelist and essayist. Said in reply to author Richard Adams who accused him of being meretricious. Attrib.

Words

see also **Grammar, Language, Meaning, Wordplay**

1 Words are the physicians of a mind diseased.

Aeschylus (525?–456 BC) Greek tragedian and dramatist. *Prometheus Bound* (5th century BC), l. 378

2 Words are the tokens current and accepted for conceits, as moneys are for values.

Francis Bacon (1561–1626) English philosopher, statesman, and lawyer. *The Advancement of Learning* (1605), bk. 2

3 Today the discredit of words is very great. Most of the time the media transmit lies. In the face of an intolerable world, words appear to be able to change very little. State power has become congenitally deaf.

John Berger (b. 1926) British novelist, essayist, and art critic. 'Lost off Cape Wrath', *Keeping a Rendezvous* (1991)

4 And I always thought: the very simplest words
Must be enough. When I say what things are like
Everyone's heart must be torn to shreds.

Bertolt Brecht (1898–1956) German playwright and poet. 'And I Always Thought' (Michael Hamburger, tr.; 1953–56)

5 But words are things, and a small drop of ink,
Falling like dew upon a thought, produces
That which makes thousands, perhaps millions,
think.

Lord Byron (1788–1824) British poet. *Don Juan* (1819–24), can. 3, st. 88

6 The word connects the visible trace with the invisible thing, the absent thing, the thing that is desired or feared, like a frail emergency bridge flung over an abyss.

Italo Calvino (1923–85) Cuban-born Italian novelist and short-story writer. 1985. 'Exactitude', *Six Memos for the Next Millennium* (Patrick Creagh, tr.; 1992)

7 Be not the slave of Words.

Thomas Carlyle (1795–1881) Scottish historian and essayist. *Sartor Resartus* (1833–34), bk. 1, ch. 8

8 'When *I* use a word', Humpty Dumpty said in rather a scornful tone, 'it means just what I choose it to mean—neither more nor less'.

Lewis Carroll (1832–98) British writer and mathematician. *Through the Looking-Glass and What Alice Found There* (1871), ch. 6

9 Words, as is well known, are great foes of reality.

Joseph Conrad (1857–1924) Polish-born British novelist. *Under Western Eyes* (1911), Prologue

10 A dictionary is a vocabulary restricted by the concept of diction.

Guy Davenport (b. 1927) US writer, translator, and educator. 'Dictionary', *The Geography of the Imagination* (1984)

11 The basic tool for the manipulation of reality is the manipulation of words. If you can control the meaning of words, you can control the people who must use the words.

Philip K. Dick (1928–82) US science-fiction writer. 'How to Build a Universe That Doesn't Fall Apart Two Days Later', *I Hope I Shall Arrive Soon* (1986), Introduction

12 It was a common saying of Myson that men ought not to investigate things from words, but words from things; for that things are not made for the sake of words, but words for things.

Diogenes Laërtius (*fl.* 3rd century) Greek historian and biographer. 'Myson', *Lives of the Philosophers* (3rd century?)

13 Words provide the battlefield in which the confirmation of his own art and any doubts with respect to it, in which suspicion and cooperation face each other off.

Ariel Dorfman (b. 1942) Chilean playwright and novelist. Referring to a novel within the novel, *Con-centrations*, by Arístides Ulloa. *Hard Rain* (1973)

14 Whenever ideas fail, men invent words.

Martin H. Fischer (1879–1962) German-born US physician and author. *Fischerisms* (Howard Fabing and Ray Marr, eds.; 1944)

15 A spade is never so merely a spade as the word Spade would imply.

Christopher Fry (b. 1907) British playwright. *Venus Observed* (1950), Act 2, Scene 1

16 Our words are dead
like the tyrant's conscience
They've never bathed in the fountain of life,
never known birth pangs or wounds,
the miracle of walking on spear points.

Ghazi al-Gosaibi (b. 1940) Saudi Arabian poet. 'Silence', *Modern Arabic Poetry* (Salma Khadra Jayyusi, ed.; 1987), ll. 1–5

17 The arrow belongs not to the archer when it has once left the bow; the word no longer belongs to the speaker when it has once passed his lips.

Heinrich Heine (1797–1856) German poet. *Religion and Philosophy* (1840), Preface

18 Thanks to words, we have been able to rise above the brutes; and thanks to words, we have often sunk to the level of the demons.

Aldous Huxley (1894–1963) British novelist and essayist. *Adonis and the Alphabet* (1956)

19 I am not yet so lost in lexicography, as to forget that words are the daughters of earth, and that things are the sons of heaven. Language is only the instrument of science, and words are but the signs of ideas.

Samuel Johnson (1709–84) British lexicographer and writer. *A Dictionary of the English Language* (1755), Preface

20 Words are, of course, the most powerful drug used by mankind.

Rudyard Kipling (1865–1936) Indian-born British writer and poet. Speech (1923)

21 Words can destroy. What we call each other ultimately becomes what we think of each other, and it matters.

Jeane Jordan Kirkpatrick (b. 1926) US political scientist and diplomat. Speech, Anti-Defamation League (February 11, 1982), 'Israel as Scapegoat'

22 The use . . . of words is to be sensible marks of ideas, and the ideas they stand for are their proper and immediate signification.

John Locke (1632–1704) English philosopher. An Essay Concerning Human Understanding (1690)

23 When we were children words were coloured
Harlot and murder were dark purple
And language was a prism.

Louis MacNeice (1907–63) Irish-born British poet. 'When We Were Children', Holes in the Sky (1948), ll. 1–3

24 She had always wanted words, she loved them, grew up on them. Words gave her clarity, brought reason, shape. Whereas I thought words bent emotions like sticks in water.

Michael Ondaatje (b. 1943) Sri Lankan-born Canadian novelist and poet. The English Patient (1992)

25 Everyone knew very well back then that words and what they described were so close that on mornings when fog descended on the phantom villages in the mountains, the words and what they described were intermingled.

Orhan Pamuk (b. 1952) Turkish novelist. The Black Book (Guneli Gun, tr.; 1990)

26 A word is not the same with one writer as with another. One tears it from his guts. The other pulls it out of his overcoat pocket.

Charles Pierre Péguy (1873–1914) French writer and poet. 'The Honest People', Basic Verities (A. and J. Green, trs.; 1943)

27 Isn't everyone consoled when faced with a trouble or fact he does not understand, by a word, some simple word, which tells us nothing and yet calms us?

Luigi Pirandello (1867–1936) Italian dramatist, novelist, and short-story writer. Six Characters in Search of an Author (Edward Storer, tr.; 1921)

28 Democritus said, words are but the shadows of actions.

Plutarch (46?–120?) Greek biographer and philosopher. 'Of the Training of Children' (1st–2nd century)

29 Words are like leaves; and where they most abound,
Much fruit of sense beneath is rarely found.

Alexander Pope (1688–1744) English poet. An Essay on Criticism (1711), ll. 109–110

30 As pine trees
hold the wind's imprint
after the wind has gone, is no longer there,
so words
retain a man's imprint
after the man has gone, is no longer there.

George Seferis (1900–71) Greek poet and diplomat. 1966. 'On Stage', Complete Poems (Edmund Keeley and Philip Sherrard, trs.; 1995)

31 Words may be false and full of art,
Sighs are the natural language of the heart.

Thomas Shadwell (1642?–92) English playwright and poet. Psyche (1675), Act 3

32 HAMLET Suit the action to the word, the word to the action; with this special observance, that you o'erstep not the modesty of nature.

William Shakespeare (1564–1616) English poet and playwright. Hamlet (1601), Act 3, Scene 2

33 KING My words fly up, my thoughts remain below:
Words without thoughts never to heaven go.

William Shakespeare (1564–1616) English poet and playwright. Hamlet (1601), Act 3, Scene 3

34 Words that are saturated with lies or atrocity, do not easily resume life.

George Steiner (b. 1929) US scholar and critic. 'K', Language and Silence (1967)

35 For words, like Nature, half reveal
And half conceal the Soul within.

Alfred Tennyson (1809–92) British poet. 1833–49. 'A. H. H.' (Arthur Henry Hallam) was the fiancé of Tennyson's sister Emily and died suddenly in September 1833. In Memoriam A. H. H. (1850), can. 5, st. 1

36 But we live like our names and you would have to be colonial to know the difference,
to know the pain of history words contain.

Derek Walcott (b. 1930) St. Lucian poet and playwright. 'The Schooner Flight', The Star-Apple Kingdom (1980)

Work

see also **Effort, Occupations**

1 Every man's work, whether it be literature or music or pictures or architecture or anything else, is always a portrait of himself.

Samuel Butler (1835–1902) British writer and composer. The Way of All Flesh (1903), ch. 14

2 There is dignity in work only when it is work freely accepted.

Albert Camus (1913–60) Algerian-born French novelist, essayist, and playwright. Notebooks (1935–42)

3 Work is the grand cure of all the maladies and miseries that ever beset mankind.

Thomas Carlyle (1795–1881) Scottish historian and essayist. Speech, Edinburgh (April 2, 1876)

4 They can expect nothing but their labour for their pains.

Miguel de Cervantes (1547–1616) Spanish novelist and playwright. From the old proverb 'Nothing is gotten without pains (labour)'. Don Quixote (1605–15), Author's Preface

5 Anyone, when he has brought his work to a state of statistical control, whether he trained well or badly, is in a rut. He has completed his learning in a particular job.

W. Edwards Deming (1900–93) US management expert. Out of the Crisis (1982)

6 I ain't gonna work on Maggie's farm no more.

Bob Dylan (b. 1941) US singer and songwriter. Song lyric. 'Maggie's Farm' (1965)

7 If the building of a bridge does not enrich the awareness of those who work on it, then that bridge ought not to be built and the citizens can go on swimming across the river or going by boat.

Frantz Fanon (1925–61) Martiniquan social scientist, physician, and psychiatrist. 'The Pitfalls of National Consciousness', The Wretched of the Earth (1961)

8 Man is so made that he can only find relaxation from one kind of labour by taking up another.

Anatole France (1844–1924) French novelist, poet, and critic. The Crime of Sylvestre Bonnard (1881), pt. 2, ch. 4

9 Capital is a result of labor, and is used by labor to assist it in further production. Labor is the active and initial force, and labor is therefore the employer of capital.

Henry George (1839–97) US economist. Progress and Poverty (1877–79)

10 Nice Work If You Can Get It

Ira Gershwin (1896–1983) US lyricist. Song title. *A Damsel in Distress* (1937)

11 When work is a pleasure, life is a joy! When work is a duty, life is slavery.

Maksim Gorky (1868–1936) Russian novelist, playwright, and short-story writer. *The Lower Depths* (1903)

12 If you want work well done, select a busy man: the other kind has no time.

Elbert Hubbard (1856–1915) US writer, printer, and editor. *The Note Book* (1927)

13 The best preparation for good work tomorrow is to do good work today.

Elbert Hubbard (1856–1915) US writer, printer, and editor. *The Note Book* (1927)

14 If hard work were such a wonderful thing, surely the rich would have kept it all to themselves.

Lane Kirkland (b. 1922) US trade union leader. Quoted in *Fortune* (October 31, 1983)

15 Why should I let the toad *work*
Squat on my life?
Can't I use my wit as a pitchfork
And drive the brute off?

Philip Larkin (1922–85) British poet. 'Toads', *The Less Deceived* (1955)

16 It's Been a Hard Day's Night

Lennon & McCartney, British rock musicians. Song title. Originally said by Ringo Starr, during filming of the then untitled Beatles film, *A Hard Day's Night*. (1964)

17 As soon as labour is distributed, each man has a particular, exclusive sphere of activity which is forced upon him and from which he cannot escape. He is a hunter, a fisherman, a shepherd, or a critic, and must remain so if he does not want to lose his means of livelihood.

Karl Marx (1818–83) German philosopher. *The German Ideology* (1846)

18 Nothing should be made by man's labour which is not worth making or which must be made by labour degrading to the makers.

William Morris (1834–96) British designer, socialist reformer, and poet. Quoted in *The Arts and Crafts Movement* (Thomas Sanderson; 1905)

19 Work expands so as to fill the time available for its completion.

Cyril Northcote Parkinson (1909–93) British political scientist, historian, and writer. *Parkinson's Law* (1958), ch. 1

20 They say hard work never hurt anybody, but I figure why take the chance?

Ronald Reagan (b. 1911) US president and actor. Attrib.

21 Work banishes those three great evils, boredom, vice, and poverty.

Voltaire (1694–1778) French writer and philosopher. *Candide* (1759), ch. 30

22 Work is the curse of the drinking classes.

Oscar Wilde (1854–1900) Irish poet, playwright, and wit. Attrib.

The World

see also **The Earth**

1 For the world, I count it not an inn, but an hospital, and a place, not to live, but to die in.

Thomas Browne (1605–82) English physician and writer. *Religio Medici* (1642), pt. 2

2 The world is out of order!

Georg Büchner (1813–37) German dramatist. 1836. *Woyzeck* (1879), Scene 12

3 The World with its smells hints its follies hatreds laughter mistakes whispers its sins . . . through doubtful certainties remembering each contradiction surely and beyond hideous victory all beautiful disasters.

e. e. cummings (1894–1962) US poet and painter. *Eimi* (1933)

4 The world's a stage where God's omnipotence,
His justice, knowledge, love, and providence
Do act the parts.

Guillaume du Bartas (1544–90) French poet. 'First Week, First Day', *Divine Weekes and Workes* (1578)

5 This world is so sad that the rainbows come out in black and white and so ugly that the vultures fly upside down after the dying.

Eduardo Galeano (b. 1940) Uruguayan writer. 'Salgado, 17 Times', *An Uncertain Grace* (Sebastião Salgado; 1990)

6 The world, that gray-bearded and wrinkled profligate, decrepit, without being venerable.

Nathaniel Hawthorne (1804–64) US novelist and short-story writer. *The House of Seven Gables* (1851), ch. 12

7 Man knows that the world is not made on a human scale; and he wishes that it were.

André Malraux (1901–76) French writer and statesman. *Les Noyers de l'Altenburg* (1945), pt. 2, ch. 3

8 We should not ask ourselves if we perceive the world truly; on the contrary: the world is that which we perceive.

Maurice Merleau-Ponty (1908–61) French existentialist philosopher. *Phenomenology of Perception* (1945)

9 The world is but a school of inquiry.

Michel de Montaigne (1533–92) French essayist. *Essays* (1580–88), bk. 3

10 Socrates said he was not an Athenian or a Greek, but a citizen of the world.

Plutarch (46?–120?) Greek biographer and philosopher. 'Of Banishment' (1st–2nd century)

11 The world only gives itself to Man in the form of food and warmth if Man gives himself to the world in the form of labour.

Simone Weil (1909–43) French philosopher, mystic, and political activist. *The Need for Roots* (A. F. Wills, tr.; 1952)

World English

see also **Language, World Literature**

1 I feel that English will be able to carry the weight of my African experience. But it will have to be a new English, still in communion with its ancestral home but altered to suit its new African surroundings.

Chinua Achebe (b. 1930) Nigerian novelist, poet, and essayist. *Morning Yet on Creation Day* (1964)

2 The price a world language must be prepared to pay is submission to many different kinds of use.

Chinua Achebe (b. 1930) Nigerian novelist, poet, and essayist. *Morning Yet on Creation Day* (1964)

3 English is destined to be in the next and succeeding centuries more generally the language of the world than Latin was in the last or French is in the present age.

John Adams (1735–1826) US president. 1780. Quoted in *Speaking Freely* (Stuart Berg Flexner and Anne H. Soukhanov; 1997)

4 Today there are more Chinese studying English than there are Americans.

Michael Armstrong, US business executive. Speech (February 11, 1997)

5 The English language ceased to be the sole possession of the English some time ago.

Salman Rushdie (b. 1947) Indian-born British novelist. 'Commonwealth Literature Does Not Exist', *Imaginary Homelands* (1991)

6 What seems to me to be happening is that those peoples who were once colonized by the language are now rapidly remaking it, domesticating it, becoming more and more relaxed about the way they use it. Assisted by the English language's flexibility and size, they are carving out large territories for themselves within its frontier.

Salman Rushdie (b. 1947) Indian-born British novelist. 'Commonwealth Literature Does Not Exist', *Imaginary Homelands* (1991)

7 England and America are two countries separated by the same language.

George Bernard Shaw (1856–1950) Irish playwright. Attributed in this and other forms, but not found in Shaw's published writings.

8 The English language is nobody's special property. It is the property of the imagination; it is the property of language itself.

Derek Walcott (b. 1930) St. Lucian poet and playwright. Interview, *Writers at Work* (George Plimpton, ed.; 1988)

World Literature

see also **American Literature, European Literature, Literature, Writers**

1 Divine Poetry,
   you who live in solitude
   and are taught to learn your songs
   in the silence of the shady forest;
   you whose company was the mountain's echo;
   it is time that you now abandon Europe,
   that cultivated land that no longer appreciates
   your native rusticity;
   and direct your flight to a place
   where the world of Columbus opens its great
   stage to you.

Andrés Bello (1781–1865) Chilean politician and writer. 'Alocución a la Poesía' (1823), ll. 1–10

2 The Caribbean writer today is a creature balanced between limbo and nothingness, exile abroad and homelessness at home.

Jan Carew (b. 1922) Guyanese-born novelist, actor, and newspaper editor. *Fulcrums of Change* (1988)

3 We writers cannot speak of taking up the challenge of a new century for African literature unless writing in African languages becomes the major component of the continent's literature.

Nadine Gordimer (b. 1923) South African novelist. *Living in Hope and History* (1999)

4 The new literature, whose life blood is realism, has become a national artery, a national nerve, and serves as a spiritual weapon of the people.

Hu Feng (b. 1903) Chinese writer and critic. *Realism Today* (1943), quoted in *Literature of the People's Republic of China* (Kai-yu Hsu, ed.; 1980)

5 My motive is to expose the illness in order to induce people to pay attention to its cure.

Lu Xun (1881–1936) Chinese writer. 'How I Came to Write Fiction', *Literature of the People's Republic of China* (Kai-yu Hsu, ed.; 1980)

6 Write and risk damnation. Avoid damnation and cease to be a writer. That is the lot of the writer in a neocolonial state.

Ngugi wa Thiongo (b. 1938) Kenyan writer. *Writing Against Neocolonialism* (1986)

7 If this realm of dreams that we call the world is a house into which we enter disorientated as a somnambulist, then the various literatures are like clocks hung up on the walls of the rooms.

Orhan Pamuk (b. 1952) Turkish novelist. *The Black Book* (Guneli Gun, tr.; 1990)

8 It may be that writers in my position, exiles or emigrants or expatriates, are haunted by some sense of loss, some urge to reclaim, to look back, even at the risk of being mutated into pillars of salt.

Salman Rushdie (b. 1947) Indian-born British novelist. According to Genesis (19:26), Lot was warned by angels to flee the city of Sodom, taking care not to look back. Lot's wife did look back and was changed into a pillar of salt. *Imaginary Homelands* (1991), pt. 1, ch. 1

9 Foreign Publishers hovered like benevolent vultures over the still-born foetus of the African Muse.

Wole Soyinka (b. 1934) Nigerian novelist, playwright, poet, and lecturer. 'The Writer in a Modern African State', *The Writer in Modern Africa* (Per Wästburg, ed.; 1968)

10 Well, good luck to you, kid! I'm going to write the Great Australian Novel.

Patrick White (1912–90) British-born Australian novelist. *The Vivisector* (1970)

11 New Wave literature is nothing more than canned soft drink, fashionable but not yet affordable for the majority of the Chinese people.

Henry Y. H. Zhao (b. 1943) Chinese critic, fiction writer, and poet. *Sensing the Shift—New Wave Literature and Chinese Culture* (1991)

12 Since very early times, Chinese culture has predominantly been a culture that values literature highly. Oral and other non-literate texts (music, for instance) did not have sufficient meaning.

Henry Y. H. Zhao (b. 1943) Chinese critic, fiction writer, and poet. *Sensing the Shift—New Wave Literature and Chinese Culture* (1991)

World War I

see also **Twentieth Century, War**

1 It is thanks to the armies of the Republic that France, yesterday the soldier of God and today the soldier of Humanity, will be forever the soldier of the Ideal.

Georges Clemenceau (1841–1929) French prime minister and journalist. Referring to the signing of the armistice ending World War I. Speech to the French Chamber of Deputies (November 11, 1918)

2 The purpose of the Allies is exactly the purpose of the Central Powers, and that is the conquest and spoliation of the weaker nations that have always been the purpose of war.

Eugene Victor Debs (1855–1926) US trade union leader, socialist, and pacifist. Speech, Canton, Ohio (June 16, 1918)

3 This is not peace: it is an armistice for twenty years.

Ferdinand Foch (1851–1929) French general. 1919. Remark at the signing of the Treaty of Versailles. *Mémoires* (Paul Reynaud; 1963), vol. 2

4 Madam, I am the civilization they are fighting to
   defend.
   Heathcote William Garrod (1878–1960) British classical scholar and literary
   critic. Replying to criticism during World War I (1914–18)
   that he was not fighting to defend civilization. Quoted in
   Oxford Now and Then (D. Balsdon; 1970)

5 The Germans, if this Government is returned, are
   going to pay every penny; they are going to be
   squeezed, as a lemon is squeezed—until the pips
   squeak. My only doubt is not whether we can
   squeeze hard enough, but whether there is
   enough juice.
   Eric Geddes (1875–1937) British politician. Referring to German
   reparations after World War I (1914–18). Speech at
   Cambridge Guildhall, *Cambridge Daily News* (December 10,
   1918)

6 I have many times asked myself whether there
   can be more potent advocates of peace upon
   earth through the years to come than this massed
   multitude of silent witnesses to the desolation of
   war.
   George V (1865–1936) British monarch. May 13, 1922. Message
   read at the Terlincthun Cemetery, Boulogne, referring to the
   massed World War I graves in Flanders. *Times* (May 15,
   1922)

7 When the days of rejoicing are over,
   When the flags are stowed safely away,
   They will dream of another wild 'War to End
   Wars'
   And another wild Armistice day.
   Robert Graves (1895–1985) British poet and novelist. 1918. 'Armistice
   Day, 1918', *Beyond Giving* (1969), st. 7

8 The lamps are going out over all Europe; we
   shall not see them lit again in our lifetime.
   Edward Grey (1862–1933) British statesman. August 3, 1914. From a
   speech made on the eve of Britain's declaration of war against
   Germany, at the beginning of World War I. *Twenty-five
   Years, 1892–1916* (1925), vol. 2, ch. 18

9 Please God—let there be victory, before the
   Americans arrive.
   Douglas Haig (1861–1928) British field marshal. *Diary* (1917)

10 'Peace upon earth!' was said. We sing it,
   And pay a million priests to bring it.
   After two thousand years of mass
   We've got as far as poison-gas.
   Thomas Hardy (1840–1928) British novelist and poet. 'Christmas:
   1924', *Winter Words* (1928), complete poem

11 LUDENDORFF The English soldiers fight like lions.
   HOFFMANN True. But don't we know that they
   are lions led by donkeys.
   Max Hoffmann (1869–1927) German general. 1915. Referring to the
   performance of the British Army in World War I. Quoted in
   The Donkeys (Alan Clark; 1961), Epigraph

12 Rotary steel hail split and lashed in sharp spasms
   along the vibrating line; great solemn guns
   leisurely manipulated their expensive discharges
   at rare intervals, bringing weight and full
   recession to the rising orchestration.
   David Jones (1895–1974) British poet and graphic artist. Describing an
   artillery bombardment in World War I. 'Starlight Order', *In
   Parenthesis* (1937), pt. 3

13 This all depriving darkness split now by crazy
   flashing; marking hugely clear the spilled bowels
   of trees, splinter-spike, leper-ashen, sprawling
   receding, unknowable, wall of night.
   David Jones (1895–1974) British poet and graphic artist. Describing an
   artillery bombardment in World War I. 'Starlight Order', *In
   Parenthesis* (1937), pt. 3

14 If any question why we died,
   Tell them because our fathers lied.
   Rudyard Kipling (1865–1936) Indian-born British writer and poet.
   'Common Form', *Epitaphs of the War* (1914–18)

15 If, therefore, war should ever come between these
   two countries, which Heaven forbid! it will not, I
   think, be due to irresistible natural laws, it will
   be due to the want of human wisdom.
   Bonar Law (1858–1923) Canadian-born British prime minister. Referring
   to Britain and Germany. Speech to Parliament (November 27,
   1911)

16 I cannot get any sense of an enemy—only of a
   disaster.
   D. H. Lawrence (1885–1930) British writer. Referring to World War
   I. Letter to Edward Marsh (October 1914)

17 We have all lost the war. All Europe.
   D. H. Lawrence (1885–1930) British writer. 'The Ladybird', *The
   Ladybird* (1923)

18 This war, like the next war, is a war to end war.
   David Lloyd George (1863–1945) British prime minister. Referring to
   the popular opinion that World War I would be the last
   major war. Attrib.

19 In Flanders fields the poppies blow
   Between the crosses, row on row,
   That mark our place.
   John McCrae (1872–1918) Canadian poet and physician. 'In Flanders
   Fields' (May 3, 1915)

20 Some of the places we passed were liquid mud up
   to our knees. The town we passed through was
   an absolute ruin, not a house that is not blown
   to bits . . . what devastation—a day of judgement
   more like.
   Peter McGregor (1871–1916) British soldier. Letter to his wife (June
   21, 1916)

21 Six million young men lie in premature graves,
   and four old men sit in Paris partitioning the
   earth.
   Newspapers. *New York Nation* (1919)

22 We are going into war on the command of gold.
   We are going to run the risk of sacrificing
   millions of our countrymen's lives in order that
   other countrymen may coin their lifeblood into
   money. We are about to do the bidding of
   wealth's terrible mandate.
   George W. Norris (1861–1944) US politician. Referring to US entry
   into World War I. Speech to US Congress (April 4, 1917)

23 Above all I am not concerned with Poetry. My
   subject is War, and the pity of War. The Poetry
   is in the pity.
   Wilfred Owen (1893–1918) British poet. 1918. 'Preface', *Poems*
   (1920)

24 I could not give my name to aid the slaughter in
   this war, fought on both sides for grossly
   material ends, which did not justify the sacrifice
   of a single mother's son. Clearly I must continue
   to oppose it, and expose it, to all whom I could
   reach with voice or pen.
   Sylvia Pankhurst (1882–1960) British suffragette. Referring to World
   War I. *The Home Front* (1932), ch. 25

25 We mutually agreed to call it *The First World
   War* in order to prevent the millennium folk
   from forgetting that the history of the world was
   the history of war.
   Charles à Court Repington (1858–1925) British soldier and journalist.
   September 10, 1918. Attrib.

26 We are fighting in the quarrel of civilization against barbarism, of liberty against tyranny. Germany has become a menace to the whole world. She is the most dangerous enemy of liberty now existing.

Theodore Roosevelt (1858–1919) US president. Speech, Oyster Bay, Long Island, New York City (April 1917)

27 That's what you are. That's what you all are. All of you young people who served in the war. You are all a lost generation.

Gertrude Stein (1874–1946) US writer. Referring to World War I. Stein heard the phrase 'lost generation' being used by a French mechanic abusing an apprentice. Epigraph in *The Sun Also Rises* (Ernest Hemingway; 1926)

28 It's no good asking 'What factors caused the outbreak of war?' The question is rather 'Why did the factors that had long preserved the peace of Europe fail to do so in 1914?'

A. J. P. Taylor (1906–90) British historian. Referring to secret diplomacy, the balance of power, and the standing armies. *The Struggle for Mastery in Europe* (1954), ch. 22

29 Now all roads lead to France
And heavy is the tread
Of the living; but the dead
Returning lightly dance.

Edward Thomas (1878–1917) British poet, biographer, and critic. Originally published under the pseudonym Edward Eastaway. 'Roads', *Poems* (1917)

30 It was said in the First World War that the French fought for their country, the British fought for freedom of the seas, and the Americans fought for souvenirs.

Harry S. Truman (1884–1972) US president. Quoted in *Harry S. Truman* (Margaret Truman; 1973)

31 In Europe people have thought a lot about the War. The English thought about it before, the French during the War, and the Germans after the War.

Kurt Tucholsky (1890–1935) German philosopher. Referring to World War I (1914–18). Quoted in 'Selected Aphorisms', *Kurt Tucholsky. The Ironic Sentimentalist* (Bryan P. Grenville; 1981)

32 We draw the sword with a clear conscience and with clean hands.

William II (1859–1941) German monarch. Remark, Berlin (August 4, 1914)

World War II

see also **The Holocaust, Twentieth Century, War**

1 Time is now writing the twenty-fourth drama
Of Shakespeare with a passionless hand.

Anna Akhmatova (1888–1966) Russian poet. Addressed to Londoners during the Blitz. 'To Londoners' (Peter Norman, tr.; 1940), quoted in *The Akhmatova Journals: 1938–41* (Lydia Chukovskaya, ed.; 1989), no. 51

2 This morning the British Ambassador in Berlin handed the German Government a final note stating that, unless we heard from them by eleven o'clock that they were prepared at once to withdraw their troops from Poland, a state of war would exist between us. I have to tell you that no such undertaking has been received, and that consequently this country is at war with Germany.

Neville Chamberlain (1869–1940) British prime minister. Speech, London (September 3, 1939)

3 How horrible, fantastic, incredible, it is that we should be digging trenches and trying on gas-masks here because of a quarrel in a far-away country between people of whom we know nothing.

Neville Chamberlain (1869–1940) British prime minister. September 27, 1938. Referring to Germany's annexation of the Sudetenland. *Times* (September 28, 1938)

4 This morning I had another talk with . . . Herr Hitler, and here is the paper which bears his name upon it as well as mine . . . 'We regard the agreement signed last night . . . as symbolic of the desire of our two peoples never to go to war with one another again.'

Neville Chamberlain (1869–1940) British prime minister. 1938. Said at Heston airport on returning from signing the Munich Pact.

5 Do not let us speak of darker days; let us rather speak of sterner days. These are not dark days: these are great days—the greatest days our country has ever lived.

Winston Churchill (1874–1965) British prime minister and writer. Address to Harrow School (October 29, 1941)

6 If we can stand up to Hitler, all Europe may be free and the life of the world may move forward into broad, sunlit uplands.

Winston Churchill (1874–1965) British prime minister and writer. Speech to Parliament (June 18, 1940)

7 We shall fight in France, we shall fight on the seas and oceans, we shall fight . . . in the air, we shall defend our island, whatever the cost may be, we shall fight on the beaches, we shall fight on the landing grounds, we shall fight in the fields and in the streets, we shall fight in the hills; we shall never surrender.

Winston Churchill (1874–1965) British prime minister and writer. Speech to Parliament (June 4, 1940)

8 This was their finest hour.

Winston Churchill (1874–1965) British prime minister and writer. Referring to the Dunkirk evacuation. Speech to Parliament (July 1, 1940)

9 Never in the field of human conflict was so much owed by so many to so few.

Winston Churchill (1874–1965) British prime minister and writer. Referring to the pilots who took part in the Battle of Britain. Speech to Parliament (August 20, 1940)

10 I have only one purpose, the destruction of Hitler, and my life is much simplified thereby. If Hitler invaded Hell I would make at least a favourable reference to the Devil in the House of Commons.

Winston Churchill (1874–1965) British prime minister and writer. *The Grand Alliance* (1950)

11 It is a phoney war.

Édouard Daladier (1884–1970) French prime minister. The early period of World War II before the evacuation of British troops at Dunkirk (1940) was known in Europe as 'the phoney war'. Speech to Chamber of Deputies, Paris (December 22, 1939)

12 To all Frenchmen: France has lost a battle but France has not lost the war.

Charles de Gaulle (1890–1970) French president. Radio broadcast, London (June 18, 1940), quoted in 'Proclamation', *Discours, Messages et Déclarations du Général de Gaulle* (1941)

13 They entered the war to prevent us from going into the East, not to have the East come to the Atlantic.

Hermann Goering (1893–1946) German Nazi leader. Referring to the war aims of the British in World War II. Quoted in *Nuremberg Diary* (G. M. Gilbert; 1948)

14 A historical revision on a unique scale has been imposed on us by the Creator.

Adolf Hitler (1889–1945) Austrian-born German dictator. Announcing Germany's declaration of war on the United States. Speech, Berlin (December 11, 1941)

15 Before us stands the last problem that must be solved and will be solved. It is the last territorial claim which I have to make in Europe, but it is the claim from which I will not recede.

Adolf Hitler (1889–1945) Austrian-born German dictator. Referring to negotiations with Britain, France, and Italy which led to the Munich Pact (September 29, 1938), allowing Germany to annexe the Sudetenland, the German-speaking part of Czechoslovakia. Speech, Sportpalast, Berlin (September 26, 1938), quoted in *Hitler: Reden und Proklamationen 1932–45* (Max Domarus, ed.; 1962)

16 Before we launched the attack on D-Day I was frightened but I fought . . . The first time I fought a German hand-to-hand I screamed for help the whole time I was killing him.

Walter Mosley (b. 1952) US novelist. *Devil in a Blue Dress* (1990), ch. 7

17 We are having one hell of a war.

George S. Patton (1885–1945) US general. Letter to A. D. Surles (December 15, 1944)

18 To make a union with Great Britain would be fusion with a corpse.

Henri Philippe Pétain (1856–1951) French political and military leader. 1940. Referring to Winston Churchill's suggestion for an Anglo-French union. Quoted in *Their Finest Hour* (Winston S. Churchill; 1949), ch. 10

19 The hand that held the dagger has struck it into the back of its neighbour . . . Neither those who sprang from that ancient stock nor those who have come hither in later years can be indifferent to the destruction of freedom in their ancestral lands across the seas.

Franklin D. Roosevelt (1882–1945) US president. Said on the day that Italy declared war on France and Britain. Speech, Charlottesville, Virginia (June 10, 1940)

20 If we see that Germany is winning the war we ought to help Russia, and if Russia is winning we ought to help Germany, and in that way let them kill as many as possible.

Harry S. Truman (1884–1972) US president. On the invasion of Russia by Germany during World War II. *New York Times* (July 24, 1941)

21 Their only English-speaking guard told them to memorize their simple address, in case they got lost in the city. Their address was this: 'Schlachthof-fünf'. *Schlachthof* meant *slaughterhouse. Fünf* was good old *five.*

Kurt Vonnegut (b. 1922) US novelist. *Slaughterhouse-Five* (1969), ch. 6

World-Weariness

see also **Age, Cynicism, Stress**

1 All my life I've been sick and tired. Now I'm sick and tired of being sick and tired.

Fannie Lou Hamer (1917–77) US civil rights activist. *The Nation* (June 1, 1964)

2 Sleep is good, death is better; but of course, the best thing would be never to have been born at all.

Heinrich Heine (1797–1856) German poet. 'Morphine'

3 The flesh, alas, is wearied; and I have read all the books there are.

Stéphane Mallarmé (1842–98) French poet. 'Brise Marine', *Poésies* (1887)

4 If it be a short and violent death, we have no leisure to fear it; if otherwise, I perceive that according as I engage myself in sickness, I do naturally fall into some disdain and contempt of life.

Michel de Montaigne (1533–92) French essayist. *Essays* (1580–88)

5 'What a long time life takes!' said Clarice at last. 'Sometimes I think it's hardly worth encroaching on'.

Mervyn Peake (1911–68) British novelist, poet, and artist. *Gormenghast* (1950), ch. 8

6 MACBETH I gin to be aweary of the sun, And wish th' estate o' th' world were now undone.

William Shakespeare (1564–1616) English poet and playwright. *Macbeth* (1606), Act 5, Scene 5

Worry

see also **Fear**

1 Worrying about the past is like trying to make birth control pills retroactive.

Joey Adams (b. 1911) US actor. Attrib.

2 When I look back on all these worries I remember the story of the old man who said on his deathbed that he had had a lot of trouble in his life, most of which had never happened.

Winston Churchill (1874–1965) British prime minister and writer. *Their Finest Hour* (1949)

3 The secret of not having worries, for me at least, is to have ideas.

Eugène Delacroix (1798–1863) French painter. July 14, 1850. *Journal* (1893–95)

Writers

see also **Books, Literature, Writing**

1 Writers don't give prescriptions. They give headaches!

Chinua Achebe (b. 1930) Nigerian novelist, poet, and essayist. *Anthills of the Savannah* (1987)

2 No poet or novelist wishes he were the only one who ever lived, but most of them wish they were the only one alive, and quite a number fondly believe their wish has been granted.

W. H. Auden (1907–73) British poet. 'Writing', *The Dyer's Hand* (1963)

3 Writers, like teeth, are divided into incisors and grinders.

Walter Bagehot (1826–77) British economist and journalist. 'The First Edinburgh Reviewers', *Estimates of Some Englishmen and Scotchmen* (1858)

4 The writer knows nothing any longer. He has no moral stance. He offers the reader the contents of his own head, a set of options and imaginative alternatives.

J. G. Ballard (b. 1930) Chinese-born British writer. 1995. *Crash* (1995 edition), Introduction

5 There are things that get whispered about that writers are there to overhear.

Ann Beattie (b. 1947) US writer and art critic. Referring to *Best American Short Stories. New York Times* (November 1, 1987)

6 Except for Shakespeare, all writers are made to look like schoolboys by history and nature.

Georg Büchner (1813–37) German dramatist. February 21,1835. Quoted in *Complete Plays, Lenz and Other Writings* (John Reddick, tr.; 1993)

7 Writers live the sad truth just like everyone else. The only difference is, they file reports.

William S. Burroughs (1914–97) US writer. *The Naked Lunch* (1959)

8 The great aphorists read as if they had all known each other well.

Elias Canetti (1905–94) Bulgarian-born writer. *The Human Province* (1973)

9 Stevenson seemed to pick the right word up on the point of his pen, like a man playing spillikins.

G. K. Chesterton (1874–1936) British writer and poet. Referring to Robert Louis Stevenson. Spillikins was a Victorian parlour game played with thin pointed sticks. *The Victorian Age in Literature* (1913)

10 Until you understand a writer's ignorance, presume yourself ignorant of his understanding.

Samuel Taylor Coleridge (1772–1834) British poet. *Biographia Literaria* (1817), ch. 12

11 Our myriad-minded Shakespeare.

Samuel Taylor Coleridge (1772–1834) British poet. Coleridge says he borrowed this phrase from a Greek monk who applied it to a patriarch of Constantinople. *Biographia Literaria* (1817), ch. 15

12 A great writer creates a world of his own and his readers are proud to live in it. A lesser writer may entice them in for a moment, but soon he will watch them filing out.

Cyril Connolly (1903–74) British writer and journalist. *Enemies of Promise* (1938), ch. 1

13 The writer writes *in* a language and *in* a logic whose proper system, laws, and life his discourse by definition cannot dominate absolutely.

Jacques Derrida (b. 1930) Algerian-born French philosopher. *Of Grammatology* (1967)

14 But who shall be master? The writer or the reader?

Denis Diderot (1713–84) French encyclopedist and philosopher. *Jacques le Fataliste et son Maître* (1796)

15 The writer isn't made in a vacuum. Writers are witnesses. The reason we need writers is because we need witnesses to this terrifying century.

E. L. Doctorow (b. 1931) US novelist. Quoted in *Writers at Work* (George Plimpton, ed.; 1988)

16 Shakespeare is the very Janus of poets; he wears almost everywhere two faces; and you have scarce begun to admire the one, ere you despise the other.

John Dryden (1631–1700) English poet, playwright, and literary critic. 'Essay on the Dramatic Poetry of the Last Age' (1672)

17 I hold that the novelist is the historian of the present, just as the historian is the novelist of the past.

Georges Duhamel (1884–1966) French writer and physician. *Chronique: La Nuit de Saint-Jean* (1937), Preface

18 Webster was much possessed by death And saw the skull beneath the skin.

T. S. Eliot (1888–1965) US-born British poet and playwright. 'Whispers of Immortality', *Poems, 1920* (1920)

19 Talent alone cannot make a writer. There must be a man behind the book.

Ralph Waldo Emerson (1803–82) US poet and essayist. 'Goethe; or, the writer', *Representative Men* (1850)

20 Alas! a woman that attempts the pen, Such an intruder on the rights of men, Such a presumptuous creature, is esteemed, The fault can by no virtue be redeemed.

Anne Finch (1661–1720) English poet. 'Written by a Lady', *Miscellany Poems on Several Occasions* (1713)

21 Creative writers are always greater than the causes that they represent.

E. M. Forster (1879–1970) British novelist. 1943. 'Gide and George', *Two Cheers for Democracy* (1951)

22 The coming into being of the notion of 'author' constitutes the privileged moment of individualization in the history of ideas.

Michel Foucault (1926–84) French philosopher. 'What Is an Author?', *The Foucault Reader* (1984)

23 The best way to become a successful writer is to read good writing, remember it, and then forget where you remember it from.

Gene Fowler (1890–1960) US author. Attrib.

24 There are many reasons why novelists write, but they all have one thing in common—a need to create an alternative world.

John Fowles (b. 1926) British novelist. *Sunday Times Magazine* (October 2, 1977)

25 If a story is a declaration against death, its author is nothing but a perpetual convalescent.

Carlos Fuentes (b. 1928) Mexican writer. 'The Storyteller', *The Picador Book of Latin American Stories* (1998)

26 Singular as he or she may seem, the novelist is a team of painters, city planners, gossip columnists, fashion experts, architects and set designers; a justice of the peace, a real estate agent, midwife, undertaker; a witch and a high priest all in one.

Carlos Fuentes (b. 1928) Mexican writer. 'The Storyteller', *The Picador Book of Latin American Stories* (1998)

27 Sooner or later, every writer gets hamburgerized.

Eduardo Galeano (b. 1940) Uruguayan writer. Quoting a friend. In Spanish, a play on the words *hamburguesa* (hamburger) and *burgués* (bourgeois). *The Book of Embraces* (1989)

28 Rage is to writers what water is to fish. A laid-back writer is like an orgasmic prostitute—an anomaly—something that doesn't quite fit.

Nikki Giovanni (b. 1943) US writer, activist, and educator. 'In Sympathy with Another Motherless Child', *Sacred Cows . . . and Other Edibles* (1988)

29 The remarkable thing about Shakespeare is that he is really very good—in spite of all the people who say he is very good.

Robert Graves (1895–1985) British poet and novelist. *Observer* (December 6, 1964), 'Sayings of the Week'

30 Oscar Wilde did not dive very deeply below the surface of human nature, but found, to a certain extent rightly, that there is more on the surface of life than is seen by the eyes of most people.

Jack Grein (1862–1935) Dutch-born British drama critic. *Sunday Special* (December 9, 1900)

31 No author is a man of genius to his publisher.

Heinrich Heine (1797–1856) German poet. Attrib.

32 The most essential gift for any writer is a built-in, shock-proof, shit detector. This is the writer's radar and all great writers have had it.
Ernest Hemingway (1899–1961) US writer. Interview, *Paris Review* (Spring 1958)

33 I do not believe that she wrote one word of fiction which does not put out boundaries a little way; one book which does not break new ground and form part of the total experiment.
Susan Hill (b. 1942) British novelist and playwright. Referring to Virginia Woolf. *Daily Telegraph* (May 5, 1974)

34 For Lawrence, existence was one continuous convalescence; it was as though he was newly reborn from a mortal illness every day of his life. What these convalescent eyes saw, his most casual speech would reveal.
Aldous Huxley (1894–1963) British novelist and essayist. Referring to D. H. Lawrence. 'D. H. Lawrence', *The Olive Tree and Other Essays* (1936)

35 'It's like the question of the authorship of the *Iliad*', said Mr Cardan. 'The author of that poem is either Homer or, if not Homer, somebody else of the same name'.
Aldous Huxley (1894–1963) British novelist and essayist. *Those Barren Leaves* (1925), pt. 5, ch. 4

36 I am a camera with its shutter open, quite passive, recording, not thinking.
Christopher Isherwood (1904–86) British-born US writer. Autumn 1930. 'Berlin Diary', *Goodbye to Berlin* (1939)

37 No man was more foolish when he had not a pen in his hand, or more wise when he had.
Samuel Johnson (1709–84) British lexicographer and writer. Referring to Oliver Goldsmith. Quoted in *Life of Samuel Johnson* (James Boswell; 1791)

38 He delivered Ireland from plunder and oppression; and showed that wit, confederated with truth, had such force as authority was unable to resist.
Samuel Johnson (1709–84) British lexicographer and writer. Referring to Jonathan Swift. Attrib.

39 Authors are easy to get on with—if you're fond of children.
Michael Joseph (1897–1958) British publisher. *Observer* (1949)

40 We have met too late. You are too old for me to have any effect on you.
James Joyce (1882–1941) Irish writer. On meeting W. B. Yeats. Quoted in *James Joyce* (Richard Ellmann; 1959)

41 I'd rather be a lightning rod than a seismograph.
Ken Kesey (b. 1935) US writer. Referring to writing. Quoted in *The Electric Kool-aid Acid Test* (Tom Wolfe; 1968)

42 Clear writers, like clear fountains, do not seem so deep as they are; the turbid look the most profound.
Walter Savage Landor (1775–1864) British poet and writer. 'Southey and Porson', *Imaginary Conversations of Literary Men and Statesmen* (1824)

43 I am a man, and alive . . . For this reason I am a novelist. And being a novelist, I consider myself superior to the saint, the scientist, the philosopher, and the poet, who are all great masters of different bits of man alive, but never get the whole hog.
D. H. Lawrence (1885–1930) British writer. 'Why the Novel Matters', *Phoenix* (1929)

44 In other countries, art and literature are left to a lot of shabby bums living in attics and feeding on booze and spaghetti, but in America the successful writer or picture-painter is indistinguishable from any other decent business man.
Sinclair Lewis (1885–1951) US novelist. *Babbitt* (1922), ch. 14

45 I am a deceased writer not in the sense of one who has written and is now deceased, but in the sense of one who has died and is now writing.
Joaquim Maria Machado de Assis (1839–1908) Brazilian novelist and short-story writer. *Epitaph of a Small Winner* (1880)

46 But remember the dismal, ridiculous condemnation of Oscar Wilde. Intellectual Europe will never forgive you for it.
Filippo Tommaso Marinetti (1876–1944) Italian writer, poet, and political activist. Referring to the persecution of writer and wit Oscar Wilde, who in 1895 was convicted for sodomy, served two years' hard labour, and was subsequently driven to exile in Paris. Speech to the Lyceum Club, London (1910), quoted in *Marinetti: Selected Writings* (R. W. Flint, ed., tr., A. Coppotelli, tr.; 1972)

47 The trouble with our younger authors is that they are all in their sixties.
Somerset Maugham (1874–1965) British writer. *Observer* (October 17, 1951), 'Sayings of the Week'

48 The sweet witty soul of Ovid lives in mellifluous honey-tongued Shakespeare.
Francis Meres (1565–1647) English clergyman and writer. 1594–1616? Attrib.

49 I think of Mr. Stevenson as a consumptive youth weaving garlands of sad flowers with pale, weak hands.
George Moore (1852–1933) Irish writer. 1870. Referring to Robert Louis Stevenson. *Confessions of a Young Man* (1888)

50 The shelf life of the modern hardback writer is somewhere between the milk and the yoghurt.
John Mortimer (b. 1923) British lawyer, novelist, and playwright. *Observer* (June 28, 1987)

51 A novelist is, like all mortals, more fully at home on the surface of the present than in the ooze of the past.
Vladimir Nabokov (1899–1977) Russian-born US novelist, poet, and critic. *Strong Opinions* (1951), ch. 20

52 I am the kind of writer that people think other people are reading.
V. S. Naipaul (b. 1932) Trinidadian-born British novelist. Attrib.

53 Like a piece of litmus paper he has always been quick to take the colour of his times.
Newspapers. Referring to Aldous Huxley. *Observer* (February 27, 1949), 'Author Profile'

54 Writers are the dream mechanisms of the human race.
Ben Okri (b. 1959) Nigerian novelist, short-story writer, and poet. *A Way of Being Free* (1997)

55 Shakespeare—the nearest thing in incarnation to the eye of God.
Laurence Olivier (1907–89) British actor and director. Quoted in 'Sir Laurence Olivier', *Kenneth Harris Talking To . . .* (Kenneth Harris; 1971)

56 I myself would be hard pressed if I had to decide who had written what I write. I accept no responsibility for the writing process; but I can vouch for the accuracy of what is depicted.
Benito Pérez Galdós (1843–1920) Spanish novelist and playwright. *Nazarín* (Jo Labanyi, tr.; 1895)

57 I'm not a theorist. I'm not an authoritative or reliable commentator on the dramatic scene, the social scene, any scene. I write plays, when I can manage it, and that's all.
Harold Pinter (b. 1930) British playwright, theatre director, and screenwriter. Speech addressed to the National Student Drama Festival, Bristol (1962)

58 Virgil's great judgement appears in putting things together, and in his picking gold out of the dunghills of old Roman writers.
Alexander Pope (1688–1744) English poet. Quoted in *Observations, Anecdotes and Characters of Books and Men* (Rev. Joseph Spence; 1820)

59 Detestable person but needs watching. I think he learned the proper treatment of modern subjects before I did.
Ezra Pound (1885–1972) US poet, translator, and critic. Referring to D. H. Lawrence. Remark (March 1913)

60 There are plenty of clever young writers. But there is too much genius, not enough talent.
J. B. Priestley (1894–1984) British writer. *Observer* (September 29, 1968), 'Sayings of the Week'

61 He was a kind of saint, and in that character, more likely in politics to chastise his own side than the enemy.
V. S. Pritchett (1900–97) British writer. Referring to George Orwell. *New Statesman* (1950)

62 The true writer has nothing to say, just a way of saying it.
Alain Robbe-Grillet (b. 1922) French novelist and screenwriter. *Pour un Nouveau Roman* (1963)

63 He was not only the greatest literary stylist of his time. He was also the only living representative of the European tradition of the artist who carries on with his creative work unaffected by the storm which breaks around him in the world outside his study.
Stephen Spender (1909–95) British poet and critic. Referring to James Joyce. *Listener* (January 23, 1941)

64 A novelist is not in the world to do good but to try to know and submit what is known; or is it to invent and transmit what is intuited?
Luisa Valenzuela (b. 1938) Argentinian writer. *The Lizard's Tail* (Gregory Rabassa, tr.; 1983)

65 That night I slept badly. I dreamed of a white saucepan for milk . . . and I tried to answer the question: Could it be considered a writer? For some reason I decided that although it probably couldn't be considered a writer, it could be admitted into the Writers' Union.
Vladimir Voinovich (b. 1932) Russian novelist. *The Life and Extraordinary Adventures of Private Ivan Chonkin* (Richard Lourie, tr.; 1969), pt. 1

66 Who am I to tamper with a masterpiece?
Oscar Wilde (1854–1900) Irish poet, playwright, and wit. Refusing to make alterations to one of his own plays. Attrib.

67 I think it's good for a writer to think he's dying; he works harder.
Tennessee Williams (1911–83) US playwright. *Observer* (October 31, 1976), 'Sayings of the Week'

68 There's nothing worse than the writer who learns to do something and then goes on doing it because it's comfortable and safe. It is a gift of wings, and you learn to trust yourself, that you will not fall—or if you do, that you will just swoop up again.
Jeanette Winterson (b. 1959) British novelist. *Guardian* (June 18, 1994)

69 The poet gives us his essence, but prose takes the mould of the body and mind entire.
Virginia Woolf (1882–1941) British novelist and critic. 'Reading', *The Captain's Death Bed* (1950)

70 Every great and original writer, in proportion as he is great and original, must himself create the taste by which he is to be relished.
William Wordsworth (1770–1850) English poet. *Lyrical Ballads* (2nd ed.; 1800), Preface

Writing

see also **Books, Creativity, Literary Style, Literature, Storytelling, Writers**

1 To write a story in just five minutes you need— as well as the customary pen and blank paper, of course—a small hourglass, which will provide accurate information both on the passing of time and on the vanity and worthlessness of the things of this life.
Bernardo Atxaga (b. 1951) Basque writer. *Obabakoak* (Margaret Jull Costa, tr.; 1989)

2 Speech conquers thought, but writing commands it.
Walter Benjamin (1892–1940) German writer and critic. 'One-Way Street', *Reflections* (Peter Demetz, ed.; 1986)

3 No writing anywhere can begin to be credible unless it is informed by political awareness and principles. Writers who have neither produce utopian trash.
John Berger (b. 1926) British novelist, essayist, and art critic. 'Lost off Cape Wrath', *Keeping a Rendezvous* (1991)

4 I have that continuous uncomfortable feeling of 'things' in the head, like icebergs or rocks or awkwardly placed pieces of furniture. It's as if all the nouns were there but the verbs were lacking.
Elizabeth Bishop (1911–79) US poet. Referring to difficulties in writing. Letter to Marianne Moore (September 11, 1940), quoted in *One Art: The Selected Letters of Elizabeth Bishop* (Robert Giroux, ed.; 1994)

5 No one who cannot limit himself has ever been able to write.
Nicolas Boileau (1636–1711) French poet and critic. *L'Art Poétique* (1674), pt. 1

6 Writing always means hiding something in such a way that it is then discovered.
Italo Calvino (1923–85) Cuban-born Italian novelist and short-story writer. *If on a Winter's Night a Traveller* (William Weaver, tr.; 1979), ch. 8

7 The pen is the tongue of the mind.
Miguel de Cervantes (1547–1616) Spanish novelist and playwright. *Don Quixote* (1605–15), pt. 2, ch. 16

8 My voice will be the voice of those who suffer and have no voice. My voice, the freedom of those weakened in the dungeon of despair.
Aimé Césaire (b. 1913) Martiniquan poet, teacher, and political leader. *Cahier d'un retour au pays natal* (1939)

9 To write is to take the conch out of the sea to shout: here's the conch! The word replies: where's the sea?
Patrick Chamoiseau (b. 1953) Martiniquan writer. *Solibo Magnificent* (1998)

10 When in doubt have a man come through a door with a gun in his hand.
Raymond Chandler (1888–1959) US novelist. *The Simple Art of Murder* (1950)

11 Men will forgive a man anything except bad prose.
Winston Churchill (1874–1965) British prime minister and writer. Election speech, Manchester (1906)

12 To write is an act of love. If it isn't it's just writing.
Jean Cocteau (1889–1963) French film director, novelist, and playwright. 'Des Moeurs', *La Difficulté d'Être* (1947)

13 Better to write for yourself and have no public, than write for the public and have no self.
Cyril Connolly (1903–74) British writer and journalist. *Turnstile One* (V. S. Pritchett, ed.; 1948)

14 The narrative impulse is always with us; we couldn't imagine ourselves through the day.
Robert Coover (b. 1932) British journalist. *Time Out* (May 7, 1986)

15 Writing is turning one's worst moments into money.
J. P. Donleavy (b. 1926) US novelist. Quoted in *Playboy* (May 1979)

16 Each venture
Is a new beginning, a raid on the inarticulate,
With shabby equipment always deteriorating
In the general mess of imprecision of feeling.
T. S. Eliot (1888–1965) US-born British poet and playwright. 'East Coker', *Four Quartets* (1940)

17 Good writing is like a bomb: it explodes in the face of the reader.
Nuruddin Farah (b. 1945) Somali novelist, playwright, and teacher. *Sardines* (1981)

18 All good writing is *swimming under water* and holding your breath.
F. Scott Fitzgerald (1896–1940) US writer. Letter to his daughter, Frances Scott Fitzgerald, *The Crack-Up: with Other Uncollected Pieces, Note-Books and Unpublished Letters* (Edmund Wilson, ed.; 1945)

19 Only connect! That was the whole of her sermon. Only connect the prose and the passion, and both will be exalted, and human love will be seen at its height.
E. M. Forster (1879–1970) British novelist. 'Only Connect!' is famous as the epigraph to *Howards End*. It also appears in the text of the novel. *Howards End* (1910), ch. 22

20 Writing free verse is like playing tennis with the net down.
Robert Frost (1874–1963) US poet. Speech at the Milton Academy (May 17, 1935)

21 Why does one write, if not to put one's pieces together? From the moment we enter school or church, education chops us into pieces: it teaches us to divorce soul from body and mind from heart.
Eduardo Galeano (b. 1940) Uruguayan writer. *The Book of Embraces* (1989)

22 My English text is chaste, and all licentious passages are left in the decent obscurity of a learned language.
Edward Gibbon (1737–94) British historian. *Memoirs of My Life* (1796), ch. 8

23 The method must be purest meat,
and no symbolic dressing,
actual visions & actual prisons
as seen then and now.
Allen Ginsberg (1926–97) US poet. 1954. Referring to William S. Burroughs. 'On Burroughs' Work', *The Green Automobile* (1961), quoted in *The Penguin Book of American Verse* (Geoffrey Moore, ed.; 1977)

24 Today it is necessary to use two images every five seconds of writing so that tomorrow we can use three in the same five seconds.
Ramón Gómez de la Serna (1888–1963) Spanish novelist. *Ismos* (1931)

25 When one says one writes for 'anyone who reads me' one must be aware that 'anyone' excludes a vast number of readers who cannot 'read' you or me because of givens they do not share with us in unequal societies.
Nadine Gordimer (b. 1923) South African novelist. *Living in Hope and History* (1999)

26 The secret equation lying behind your twofold deviation: unproductive (onanistic) manipulation of the written word, self-sufficient (poetic) enjoyment of illicit pleasure.
Juan Goytisolo (b. 1931) Spanish novelist and essayist. Referring to Juan Sin Tierra ('Juan the Landless'), the novel's hero. *Juan the Landless* (1975)

27 Between my finger and my thumb
The squat pen rests; snug as a gun . . .
I'll dig with it.
Seamus Heaney (b. 1939) Irish poet. 'Digging', *Death of a Naturalist* (1966), ll. 1–2, l. 31

28 I think technique is different from craft. Craft is what you can learn from other verse . . . Technique . . . involves the discovery of ways to go out of . . . normal cognitive bounds and raid in the inarticulate.
Seamus Heaney (b. 1939) Irish poet. October 1974. 'Feeling into Words', *Preoccupations: Selected Prose 1968–78* (1980)

29 You will have written exceptionally well if, by skilful arrangement of your words, you have made an ordinary one seem original.
Horace (65–8 BC) Roman poet. *Ars Poetica* (19–8 BC), l. 47

30 I imagine this midnight moment's forest:
Something else is alive
Beside the clock's loneliness
And this blank page where my fingers move.
Ted Hughes (1930–98) British writer and poet. 'The Thought Fox', *The Hawk in the Rain* (1957)

31 Read over your compositions, and where ever you meet with a passage which you think is particularly fine, strike it out.
Samuel Johnson (1709–84) British lexicographer and writer. April 30, 1773. Recalling the advice of a college tutor. Quoted in *Life of Samuel Johnson* (James Boswell; 1791)

32 It was the ecstasy of striking matches in the dark.
Erica Jong (b. 1942) US writer. Referring to writing poetry. *What Do Women Want?* (1998), Preface

33 Many suffer from the incurable disease of writing, and it becomes chronic in their sick minds.
Juvenal (65?–128?) Roman poet. *Satires* (98?–128?), no. 7, l. 51

34 One reason for writing, of course, is that no-one's written what you want to read.
Philip Larkin (1922–85) British poet. Interview, *Paris Review* (1982)

35 I like to write when I feel spiteful: it's like having a good sneeze.
D. H. Lawrence (1885–1930) British writer. Letter to Lady Cynthia Asquith (November 1913)

36 Beneath the rule of men entirely great,
The pen is mightier than the sword.
Bulwer Lytton (1803–73) British novelist and politician. *Richelieu* (1839), Act 2, Scene 2

37 Writing books is the closest men ever come to childbearing.
Norman Mailer (b. 1923) US novelist and journalist. Quoted in *Conversations with Norman Mailer* (J. Michael Lennon; 1988)

38 Writing is like getting married. One should never commit oneself until one is amazed at one's luck.

Iris Murdoch (1919–99) Irish-born British novelist and philosopher. 'Bradley Pearson's Foreword', *The Black Prince* (1974)

39 Don't make observations on cats and dogs, concern yourself with the problems of your homeland.

Orhan Pamuk (b. 1952) Turkish novelist. Advice to columnists. *The Black Book* (Guneli Gun, tr.; 1990)

40 The last thing one knows in constructing a work is what to put first.

Blaise Pascal (1623–62) French philosopher, mathematician, and physicist. *Pensées* (1669), sect. 1, no. 976

41 When the characters are really alive before their author, the latter does nothing but follow them in their action, in their words, in the situations which they suggest to him.

Luigi Pirandello (1867–1936) Italian dramatist, novelist, and short-story writer. *Six Characters in Search of an Author* (Edward Storer, tr.; 1921)

42 If you get the landscape right, the characters will step out of it, and they'll be in the right place.

E. Annie Proulx (b. 1935) US writer. *Time* (November 29, 1993)

43 Writing is a way of talking without being interrupted.

Jules Renard (1864–1910) French writer. April 10, 1895. *Journal* (1877–1910)

44 Writing is the only profession where no one considers you ridiculous if you earn no money.

Jules Renard (1864–1910) French writer. 1906. *Journal* (1877–1910)

45 The road to hell is paved with works-in-progress.

Philip Roth (b. 1933) US novelist. *New York Times Book Review* (July 15, 1979)

46 The most important thing for me is that I've used my talents as a writer to enable the Ogoni people to confront their tormentors. I was not able to do it as a politician or a businessman. My writing did it. And it sure makes me feel good! I'm mentally prepared for the worst, but hopeful for the best. I think I have the moral victory.

Ken Saro-Wiwa (1941–95) Nigerian writer and political and human rights activist. Letter to William Boyd, *A Month and a Day: A Detention Diary* (1995)

47 I'll make thee famous by my pen,
And glorious by my sword.

Sir Walter Scott (1771–1832) Scottish novelist. *The Legend of Montrose* (1819), ch. 15

48 A little like a quiet explosion in your head.

Maurice Sendak (b. 1928) US writer and illustrator. Referring to writing. Radio interview, Station WAMU, Washington (December 24, 1991)

49 Learn to write well, or not to write at all.

John Sheffield (1648–1721) English poet and statesman. *Essay on Satire* (1680?)

50 Writing is not a profession but a vocation of unhappiness.

Georges Simenon (1903–89) Belgian-born French writer. Interview, *Paris Review* (Summer 1955)

51 The great struggle of a writer is to learn to write as he would talk.

Lincoln Steffens (1866–1936) US journalist. 1933. Attrib. *Lincoln Steffens: A Biography* (Justin Kaplan; 1974)

52 When it comes right down to it, nothing has changed. The English sentence is just as difficult to write as it ever was.

John Steinbeck (1902–68) US novelist. 1962. In a letter to his editor a week after accepting a Nobel Prize for literature. Quoted in *John Steinbeck* (Jay Parini; 1995)

53 Writing, when properly managed (as you may be sure I think mine is), is but a different name for conversation.

Laurence Sterne (1713–68) Irish-born British writer and clergyman. *Tristram Shandy* (1759–67), bk. 2, ch. 11

54 A metaphor I am now turning into reality, because that's how the pendulum of history wants it as it goes from fact to symbol to fact in the blink of an eye, with a flip of the fingers—of the Finger.

Luisa Valenzuela (b. 1938) Argentinian writer. *The Lizard's Tail* (Gregory Rabassa, tr.; 1983)

55 People who, like me, hold power—and there are so few!—are the only ones who can allow themselves this incomparable luxury: turning dreams into reality, passing from word to deed with complete impunity.

Luisa Valenzuela (b. 1938) Argentinian writer. *The Lizard's Tail* (Gregory Rabassa, tr.; 1983)

56 It is healthier, in any case, to write for the adults one's children will become than for the children one's 'mature' critics often are.

Alice Walker (b. 1944) US novelist and poet. 'A Writer, Because of, Not in Spite of, Her Children', *Ms* (January 1976)

57 Writing saved me from the sin and inconvenience of violence.

Alice Walker (b. 1944) US novelist and poet. 'One Child of One's Own', *Ms* (August 1979)

58 I wouldn't give up writing about God at this stage, if I was you. It would be like P. G. Wodehouse dropping Jeeves half-way through the Wooster series.

Evelyn Waugh (1903–66) British novelist. Said to Graham Greene, who proposed to write a political novel. Quoted in *Evelyn Waugh* (Christopher Sykes; 1975)

59 What is writing a novel like? The beginning: A ride through a spring wood. The middle: The Gobi desert. The end: Going down the cresta run . . . I am now (p. 166 of 'The Buccaneers') in the middle of the Gobi desert.

Edith Wharton (1862–1937) US novelist. Quoting from her diary of 1934. Letter to Bernard Berenson (January 12, 1937), quoted in *The Letters of Edith Wharton* (R. W. B. Lewis and Nancy Lewis, eds.; 1988)

60 Drop 30 per cent of your Latinisms . . . mow down every old cliché, uproot all the dragging circumlocutions, compress, diversify, clarify, vivify, & you'll make a book that will be read and talked of.

Edith Wharton (1862–1937) US novelist. Letter to W. Morton Fullerton (March 24, 1910), quoted in *The Letters of Edith Wharton* (R. W. B. Lewis and Nancy Lewis, eds.; 1988)

61 Phew! How tough it is to write literature. You sweat buckets while trying to hack your way through impenetrable jungle.
And for what?

Mikhail Zoshchenko (1895–1958) Russian satirist. 'What the Nightingale Sang About', *A Man is Not a Flea* (Serge Shishkoff, tr.; 1989)

X

Xenophobia

see also **Hate**, **Prejudice**, **Racism**

1 'Most Welshmen are worthless,
an inferior breed, doctor'.
He did not know I was Welsh.
Then he praised the architects
of the German death-camps—
did not know I was a Jew.
Dannie Abse (b. 1923) Welsh poet and physician. *White Coat,
Purple Coat: Collected Poems, 1948–88* (1989), quoted in
Twentieth-Century Anglo-Welsh Poetry (Dannie Abse, ed.;
1997)

2 That kind of patriotism which consists in hating
all other nations.
Elizabeth Gaskell (1810–65) British novelist. *Sylvia's Lovers*
(1863), ch. 1

3 As I look ahead, I am filled with foreboding.
Like the Roman, I seem to see 'the River Tiber
foaming with much blood'.
Enoch Powell (1912–98) British politician. Talking about immigration
at the annual meeting of the West Midlands Area Conservative
Political Association. Speech, Birmingham (April 20, 1968)

4 The comfortable people in tight houses felt pity
at first, and then distaste, and finally hatred for
the migrant people.
John Steinbeck (1902–68) US novelist. *The Grapes of Wrath* (1939),
ch. 29

5 We cannot bring ourselves to believe it possible
that a foreigner should in any respect be wiser
than ourselves. If any such point out to us our
follies, we at once claim those follies as the
special evidences of our wisdom.
Anthony Trollope (1815–82) British novelist. *Orley Farm* (1862), ch. 18

Y

Youth

see also **Age**, **Childhood**, **Children**

1 A stage between infancy and adultery.
Anonymous. On youth.

2 A man that is young in years may be old in hours, if he have lost no time.
Francis Bacon (1561–1626) English philosopher, statesman, and lawyer. 'Of Youth and Age', *Essays* (1625)

3 The secret of staying young is to live honestly, eat slowly, and lie about your age.
Lucille Ball (1911–89) US film and television actor and comedian. Quoted in *Esquire* (February 1993)

4 It is good for a man that he bear the yoke in his youth.
Bible. Lamentations, *King James Bible* (1611), 3:27

5 Let age approve of youth, and death complete the same!
Robert Browning (1812–89) British poet. 'Rabbi Ben Ezra', *Dramatis Personae* (1864), st. 32, ll. 693–4

6 The arrogance of age must submit to be taught by youth.
Edmund Burke (1729–97) Irish-born British statesman and political philosopher. Letter to Fanny Burney (July 29, 1782)

7 Youth is something very new: twenty years ago no one mentioned it.
Coco Chanel (1883–1971) French fashion designer. *Coco Chanel, Her Life, Her Secrets* (Marcel Haedrich; 1987)

8 He was as fresh as is the month of May.
Geoffrey Chaucer (1343?–1400) English poet. Referring to the squire. 'The General Prologue', *The Canterbury Tales* (1390?), l. 92, quoted in *The Works of Geoffrey Chaucer* (F. N. Robinson, ed.; 1957)

9 The young always have the same problem—how to rebel and conform at the same time. They have now solved this by defying their parents and copying one another.
Quentin Crisp (1908–99) British writer. *The Naked Civil Servant* (1968)

10 You can stay young as long as you can learn, acquire new habits and suffer contradictions.
Marie von Ebner-Eschenbach (1830–1916) Austrian novelist and poet. Quoted in *The New Quotable Woman* (Elaine Partnow; 1993)

11 I never dared be radical when young, for fear it would make me conservative when old.
Robert Frost (1874–1963) US poet. 'Precaution', *A Further Range* (1936)

12 No young man believes he shall ever die.
William Hazlitt (1778–1830) British essayist and critic. 'On the Feeling of Immortality in Youth', *Monthly Magazine* (1827)

13 Now that the April of your youth adorns
The garden of your face.
Edward Herbert (1583–1648) English philosopher, historian, and diplomat. 'Ditty in Imitation of the Spanish: Entre tanto que L'Avril', *Occasional Verses* (1665), st. 1, ll. 1–2

14 When I was one-and-twenty
I heard a wise man say,
'Give crowns and pounds and guineas
But not your heart away;
Give pearls away and rubies,
But keep your fancy free'.
But I was one-and-twenty,
No use to talk to me.
A. E. Housman (1859–1936) British poet and classicist. *A Shropshire Lad* (1896), no. 13, quoted in *The Collected Poems of A. E. Housman* (John Carter, ed.; 1967)

15 A majority of young people seem to develop mental arteriosclerosis forty years before they get the physical kind.
Aldous Huxley (1894–1963) British novelist and essayist. Interview, quoted in *Writers at Work: Second Series* (George Plimpton, ed.; 1977)

16 Youth will come here and beat on my door, and force its way in.
Henrik Ibsen (1828–1906) Norwegian playwright. *The Master Builder* (1892), Act 1

17 In the lexicon of youth, which Fate reserves
For a bright manhood, there is no such word
As fail?
Bulwer Lytton (1803–73) British novelist and politician. *Richelieu* (1839), Act 2, Scene 3

18 Youth in the ultimate sense has nothing to do with political history, nothing to do with history at all. It is a metaphysical endowment, an essential factor, a structure, a conditioning.
Thomas Mann (1875–1955) German writer. 1947. *Doctor Faustus* (H. T. Lowe-Porter, tr.; 1949), ch. 14

19 Youth is a malady of which one becomes cured a little every day.
Benito Mussolini (1883–1945) Italian dictator. 1933. Said on his 50th birthday. Attrib.

20 One starts to get young at the age of sixty and then it is too late.
Pablo Picasso (1881–1973) Spanish painter and sculptor. *Sunday Times* (October 20, 1963)

21 Youth is the season of credulity.
William Pitt the Elder (1708–78) British prime minister. Speech to Parliament (January 14, 1766)

22 He whom the gods love dies young, while he has his strength and senses and wits.
Plautus (254?–184 BC) Roman comic playwright. *Bacchides* (3rd–2nd century BC), Act 4, Scene 8

23 Inexperience is what makes a young man do what an older man says is impossible.
Herbert V. Prochnow (b. 1897) US writer. *Saturday Evening Post* (December 4, 1948)

24 The May of life blooms once, and not again.
Friedrich von Schiller (1759–1805) German poet, playwright, and historian. 'Resignation' (1788)

25 Youth is in itself so amiable, that were the soul as perfect as the body, we could not forbear adoring it.
Madame de Sévigné (1626–96) French writer. Letter to her daughter (17th century)

26 CLEOPATRA My salad days,
When I was green in judgment, cold in blood,
To say as I said then!
William Shakespeare (1564–1616) English poet and playwright. *Antony and Cleopatra* (1606–07), Act 1, Scene 5

27 Far too good to waste on children.
George Bernard Shaw (1856–1950) Irish playwright. Reflecting upon youth. Quoted in *10,000 Jokes, Toasts, and Stories* (Lewis Copeland; 1940)

28 Live as long as you may, the first twenty years are the longest half of your life.
Robert Southey (1774–1843) English poet and writer. *The Doctor* (1812), ch. 130

29 It was remarked to me by the late Mr Charles Roupell . . . that to play billiards well was a sign of an ill-spent youth.
Herbert Spencer (1820–1903) British philosopher. *Life and Letters of Spencer* (Duncan; 1908), ch. 20

30 Here about the beach I wander'd nourishing a youth sublime
With the fairy tales of science, and the long result of Time.
Alfred Tennyson (1809–92) British poet. 1837–38. 'Locksley Hall', *Poems* (1842), ll. 11–12

31 The old-fashioned respect for the young is fast dying out.
Oscar Wilde (1854–1900) Irish poet, playwright, and wit. *The Importance of Being Earnest* (1895), Act 1

32 Fair seed-time had my soul, and I grew up Fostered alike by beauty and by fear.
William Wordsworth (1770–1850) English poet. 1799. 'Childhood and School-Time', *The Prelude* (1850), bk. 1, ll. 301–302

KEYWORD INDEX

adolescence a man suffering from petrified a.
POLITICAL INSULTS, 14
adoration For A. seasons change SEASONS, 6
adores he a. his maker VANITY, 4
adult An a. . . . has ceased to grow vertically ADULTHOOD, 5
adultery A. . . . the application of democracy to love
ADULTERY, 13
Do not a. commit ADULTERY, 6
first breath of a. is the freest ADULTERY, 19
rather . . . taken in a. than . . . provincialism ADULTERY, 10
adults A. are obsolete children ADULTHOOD, 6
advance Every great a. in science SCIENCE, 14
advanced closed operational universe of a. industrial
civilization MODERNITY, 8
advantage The a. of doing one's praising SELF-CONFIDENCE, 1
you have the a. of me ARGUMENTS, 13
advent a. of a new age of communication and
information COMMUNICATION, 20
adventurer Many will call me an a. COURAGE, 4
adverbs I'm glad you like a.—I adore them WORDPLAY, 4
advertisement The a. . . . careens at us out of a film screen
ADVERTISING, 1
the worst a. for Socialism SOCIALISM, 10
advertising A. . . . arresting human intelligence long
enough ADVERTISING, 10
A. . . . legitimizes the idealized, stereotyped roles of
women ADVERTISING, 8
a. industry thus encourages the pseudo-emancipation
of women ADVERTISING, 9
A. is an environmental striptease ADVERTISING, 12
A. isn't a science ADVERTISING, 2
A. is the most fun ADVERTISING, 6
advocaat a., a drink made from lawyers ALCOHOL, 1
aerials had my a. removed TELEVISION, 12
aeroplane a. . . . destroys men and women EQUALITY, 3
thanks to the a., England has become as much a part
of Europe EUROPEAN COUNTRIES, 52
aesthetic a. experience is denied and atrophied SEX, 39
a. purity of absolute moral indifference INDIFFERENCE, 8
affair An a. wants to spill PRIVACY, 7
affections a. must be confined . . . to a single country
PATRIOTISM, 13
affluence a. through domination of other races IMPERIALISM, 8
afraid be not a. to do thine office EXECUTION, 14
not . . . a. to die . . . don't want to be there
DEATH AND DYING, 1
We must no longer be a. of . . . opinions FREE SPEECH, 11
We were a. of the dead THE SUPERNATURAL, 21
Africa A. must refuse to be humiliated, exploited, and
pushed around AFRICA, 9
A. to me: Copper sun or scarlet sea AFRICA, 3
How can I turn from A. and live AFRICA, 15
more familiar with A. than my own body CHILDHOOD, 11
only thing A. has left . . . the future AFRICA, 6
something new out of A. AFRICA, 11
Stolen from A., /brought to America SLAVERY, 25
The 'scramble for A.' AFRICA, 4
the hour of A.'s Redemption cometh AFRICA, 5
underpopulated countries in A. are vastly
underpolluted POLLUTION, 10
We believe in the freedom of A. DECOLONIZATION, 4
African On the liberation of the A. depends the liberation
of the whole world AFRICA, 13
The A. is conditioned . . . freedom of which Europe
has little conception AFRICA, 7
the still-born foetus of the A. Muse WORLD LITERATURE, 9
African history final interpretation of A. AFRICA, 2
African literature a new century for A. WORLD LITERATURE, 3
Africans A. have lived so long on promises AFRICA, 10
after you who come a. me POSTERITY, 5

afterlife the a. will be . . . less exasperating AFTERLIFE, 6
To emphasize the a. is to deny life AFTERLIFE, 16
against A. whom? EGOTISM, 1
age a. appears . . . best in four things AGE, 1
A. became middle MIDDLE AGE, 8
A. doesn't protect you from love AGE, 21
a. does not make more wrinkles AGE, 20
A. is deformed, youth unkind OLD AGE, 6
A. is our reconciliation with dullness AGE, 15
A. will bring all things AGE, 19
A. will not be defied AGE, 2
A green old a. OLD AGE, 33
an a. in which useless knowledge was . . . important
KNOWLEDGE, 20
At twenty years of a. AGE, 10
characteristic of the present a. . . . credulity GULLIBILITY, 3
Just at the a. 'twixt boy and youth GROWING UP, 10
one spirit of the a. . . . discernible in a poet's work
POETS, 34
Our a. . . . nationalization of intellect INTELLECT, 2
We do not necessarily improve with a. AGE, 11
what a. takes away WISDOM, 20
agenda Our a. is now exhausted AGREEMENT, 9
agents a. of the unification of the planet's history MEDIA, 7
aggression the forces of a. against lawlessness
AMERICAN IMPERIALISM, 28
aggressor whole world . . . against an a. DIPLOMACY, 1
agitate I will not permit thirty men . . . to a.
SPORTS AND GAMES, 24
agit-prop fed up to the teeth with a. CENSORSHIP, 20
agony no a. like bearing an untold story inside you
STORYTELLING, 9
The daily a. of Third World peoples GLOBALIZATION, 5
agree a. to a thing in principle AGREEMENT, 2
All colours will a. in the dark AGREEMENT, 1
don't say you a. with me AGREEMENT, 10
agreeable an a. person . . . person who agrees with me
AGREEMENT, 4
agreements our a. with Poland . . . purely temporary
significance EUROPEAN COUNTRIES, 32
AIDS A. is a perfect illness AIDS, 1
A. obliges people to think of sex AIDS, 10
ignorance has increased the spread of A. AIDS, 2
ailments our a. are the same RELATIONSHIPS, 20
aim So a. above morality MORALITY, 43
The a. of life is to live LIFE, 33
aims the unsearchable and secret a. /Of nature BEAUTY, 5
air Get your room full of good a. LONGEVITY, 8
air-conditioned in the a. train /I kissed her KISSING, 11
Alaska those who have undergone life in A. ACCIDENTS, 8
Albion perfidious A. ENGLAND, 33
alcohol A. . . . enables Parliament to do things at eleven
ALCOHOL, 20
A. is like love ALCOHOL, 4
If a. is Queen . . . tobacco is her consort SMOKING, 3
my Uncle George . . . discovered that a. was a food
ALCOHOL, 27
The sway of a. over mankind ALCOHOL, 9
alcoholic An a. . . . drinks as much as you ALCOHOL, 26
Alexander A. wept when he heard . . . infinite number of
worlds IMPERIALISM, 18
If I were not A. BOASTS, 1
algebra a. . . . those three-cornered things MATHEMATICS, 4
algebraically To speak a., Mr. M. is execrable
LITERARY INSULTS, 45
alike among so many million of faces, . . . none a.
INDIVIDUALITY, 2
alimony eight hundred dollars behind in a. GAMBLING, 2
alive Not while I'm a., he ain't ENEMIES, 1
all A. for one, and one for a. SOLIDARITY, 4

ancestors when his half-civilized a. were hunting   RACISM, 4
ancestral A. voices prophesying war   PROPHECY, 4
ancient move beyond these a. texts   SECULARISM, 2
   the a. glory of your Rome   EUROPEAN COUNTRIES, 24
Andes To live is to climb the A.   LIFE, 22
angel a. . . . gazing at the violent abyss   ANGELS, 11
   contemplates an a. in his future self   THE SELF, 5
   O lyric Love, half-a. and half-bird   LOVE, 17
angels A. can fly   ANGELS, 4
   ne'er like a. till our passion dies   ANGELS, 5
   on the side of the a.   EVOLUTION, 11
   walk the a. on . . . walls of heaven   ANGELS, 6
   We align ourselves with the a.   SELF-DELUSION, 2
anger A. is a momentary madness   ANGER, 10
   A. is an emotion that has some hope in it   ANGER, 14
   A. is never without an argument   ANGER, 16
   A. is one of the sinews of the soul   ANGER, 8
   he that is slow to a. is better than the mighty   ANGER, 5
   peculiar . . . a. women my age . . . feel   POPULAR MUSIC, 35
   The a. that breaks the soul   ANGER, 18
   There is a sense of being in a.   ANGER, 15
   Why such great a. in those heavenly minds   ANGER, 19
angry An a. man is always a stupid man   ANGER, 1
   A. Young Man   REBELLION, 7
   cannot be a. at God   ATHEISM, 1
   gets a. at the right things   ANGER, 3
   Speak when you are a.   SPEECHES, 12
   when very a., swear   ANGER, 17
anguish we are a.   SUFFERING, 20
animal Any a. . . . would . . . acquire a moral sense   EVOLUTION, 8
   I'm like an a. trapped   TYRANNY, 11
   My a., my age   RUSSIA, 22
   true to your a. instincts   HUMAN NATURE, 21
animals All a. are equal   EQUALITY, 21
   A. are such agreeable friends   ANIMALS, 16
   capturing a. and writing poems   POETRY, 28
   Never work with a. or children   ACTING AND ACTORS, 17
   The a. of the planet are in desperate peril   ANIMALS, 38
   There are two things for which a. are . . . envied   ANIMALS, 37
animate To a., in the precise sense   VITALITY, 2
Ankara A. might be able . . . drain the sea   EUROPEAN COUNTRIES, 37
annihilating A. all that's made   GARDENS, 3
annihilation I undertake to face the possibility of a.   MARTYRDOM, 4
anon A. . . . was often a woman   POETS, 66
answer a. a fool according to his folly   FOOLISHNESS, 4
   But a. came there none   ANSWERS, 2
   I can a. but for three things   AMERICAN WAR OF INDEPENDENCE, 9
   There ain't no a.   ANSWERS, 5
answered They only a. 'Little Liar!'   LYING, 10
antagonism A. is a . . . struggle within a contradiction   CONFLICT, 2
anthem national a. belongs to the eighteenth century   BRITISH IMPERIALISM, 20
anthology a. . . . a complete dispensary of medicine   BOOKS, 17
   a. is like all the plums and orange peel picked out of a cake   BOOKS, 43
anticipate What we a. seldom occurs   ANTICIPATION, 2
anti-communism The psychological impact of a.   COMMUNISM, 3
antidote the a. to desire   INDIFFERENCE, 4
antipodal Her full a. eyes   ANIMALS, 23
anti-Semitism A. . . . a movement among civilized nations   RACISM, 13
anti-slavery The history of a. begins   SLAVERY, 3
anti-white not a., but anti-wrong   RACISM, 17
anxiety the Age of A., the age of the neurosis   NEUROSIS, 11

anxious a. to do the wrong thing correctly   MANNERS, 6
   I am a. . . . for the survival of Israel   MIDDLE EAST, 36
anyone a. here whom I have not insulted   INSULTS, 5
apartheid closed the book on a.   APARTHEID, 4
   We don't want a. liberalized   APARTHEID, 13
apathy where the a. is   EFFORT, 1
ape having an a. for his grandfather   EVOLUTION, 18
   How like us is . . . the a.   EVOLUTION, 12
   not the a. . . . in man that I fear   HUMAN NATURE, 34
   the a. from which he is descended   EVOLUTION, 27
apéritif a. is the evensong of the French   DRINKS AND DRINKING, 5
aphorism An a. . . . spares the writer an essay   QUOTATIONS, 1
aphorists The great a.   WRITERS, 8
Apollo A. . . . god of physic . . . sender of disease   DOCTORS, 14
apologies A. . . . do not alter   APOLOGIES, 3
apologize a good rule in life never to a.   APOLOGIES, 5
apostle the a. of class-hatred   POLITICAL INSULTS, 31
apparitions a. and ghosts . . . unquiet walks of Devils   THE SUPERNATURAL, 3
   Fifteen a. . . . worst a coat upon a coat-hanger   THE SUPERNATURAL, 39
appear Not as we are but as we must a.   THE SUPERNATURAL, 16
   not wish to a. the best   AMBITION, 1
appearances A. are not . . . a clue to the truth   APPEARANCE, 4
   Keep up a.   APPEARANCE, 3
appeaser An a. is one who feeds a crocodile   DIPLOMACY, 10
appetite A. comes with eating   APPETITE, 4
appetites Subdue your a. my dears   APPETITE, 1
applause A. is a receipt   AUDIENCES, 13
   I want to thank you for stopping the a.   PRIDE, 4
   seasoning of a play . . . the a.   THEATRE, 7
   win the a. but lose the fight   GOVERNMENT, 41
appreciate never a. anything if you . . . hurry   HASTE, 3
apprehend In reality we a. nothing for certain   REALITY, 6
apprehension The a. that one is someone else   SELF-KNOWLEDGE, 32
approaching we are a. the limits of something   ECOLOGY, 10
approved I never a. . . . the errors of his book   FREE SPEECH, 13
approves He who a. evil   EVIL, 29
April A. of your youth   YOUTH, 13
   Sweet A. showers /Do spring May flowers   SPRING, 16
Aprill Whan that A. with his shoures soote   SPRING, 2
Arab like an A. stallion I smelled . . . rain   DECLARATIONS OF LOVE, 9
Arabs A. and the Jews . . . cousins in race   MIDDLE EAST, 12
   A. today . . . see a travesty of modernism   MIDDLE EAST, 18
   can a Westerner believe . . . A. have culture   MIDDLE EAST, 33
archaeologist An a. is the best husband   OLD AGE, 14
   An a. of morning   POETS, 44
archangel Less than a. ruined   THE DEVIL, 10
Archelaus A prating barber asked A.   SILENCE, 22
arches a. in Rome . . . prototype of the billboard   ARCHITECTURE, 26
Archimedes rather have the fame of A.   FAME, 12
   truths . . . A. would have sacrificed his life   PROGRESS, 22
architect an a. . . . should be not only correct, but entertaining   ARCHITECTURE, 20
   An a.'s most useful tools   ARCHITECTURE, 32
   An a. should live as little in cities   ARCHITECTURE, 21
   a. of his own fate   FATE, 4
architects Good a. nurture . . . psychological, mental, and spiritual needs   ARCHITECTURE, 12
architecture A. . . . art of how to waste space   ARCHITECTURE, 13
   A. . . . play of masses brought together in light   ARCHITECTURE, 15
   A. . . . thing of art   ARCHITECTURE, 14
   A. begins where engineering ends   ARCHITECTURE, 9

Being an a. means ceasing	ARTISTS, 31
Being an a. now . . . question the nature of art	ARTISTS, 20
believe only what an a. does	ARTISTS, 18
Beware of the a. who's an intellectual	WARNING, 5
Every a. writes his own autobiography	AUTOBIOGRAPHY, 3
I do not believe any a. works in . . . fever	ARTISTS, 15
Like any a. with no art form she became dangerous	ARTISTS, 28
Never trust the a.	CRITICS, 20
No a. is ahead of his time	ARTISTS, 16
Remember I'm an a.	ARTISTS, 9
Show me any a. who wants to be respectable	RESPECTABILITY, 3
The aim of every a.	ARTISTS, 14
The a. . . . is always an anarchist	ANARCHY, 7
The a. . . . needs a vocabulary	ARTISTIC STYLES, 8
The a.'s hand is more powerful	ARTISTS, 32
the a. is forgotten	ARTISTS, 17
The a. is like the hand that holds and moves the mirror	ART, 42
The a., like the God of the creation	AESTHETICS, 1
The great a. . . . conquers the romantic	ARTISTS, 24
What is an a.	ARTISTS, 45
artistic There never was an a. period	PHILISTINISM, 4
artists A common vice among a. . . . mental cowardice	ARTISTS, 23
A. . . . live mainly in the red	ARTISTS, 34
A. . . . monks of the bourgeois state	ARTISTS, 33
a. dream . . . silence	ARTISTS, 29
A. go through periodic crises	ARTISTS, 46
A. often depend on the manipulation of symbols	ARTISTS, 43
Great a. have no country	ARTISTS, 30
I don't believe any real a.	ARTISTS, 27
arts a. . . . attempts of the mind	MIND, 12
If all the a. aspire to the condition of music	SCIENCE, 50
secret of the a. is to correct nature	THE ARTS, 6
The a. cannot thrive	THE ARTS, 4
ashamed a. of confessing . . . I have nothing to confess	GUILT, 3
Be a. to die	AMBITION, 20
make a body a. of . . . human race	SHAME, 5
ashes a. where once I was fire	FIRE, 3
Asia There is too much A. . . . she is too old	ASIA, 2
Asiatic an A. planet held to its orbit	PHILOSOPHY, 4
ask a., and it shall be given	FAITH, 4
A. me no questions	QUESTIONS, 3
A. no one's view but your own	OPINIONS, 15
a. not what your country can do for you	UNITED STATES, 34
Don't ever a. where the Empire's gone	BRITISH IMPERIALISM, 21
asp wicked a. of Twickenham	POLITICAL INSULTS, 43
aspires a., however humbly, to the condition of art	LITERATURE, 17
assassin The greatest a. of life	HASTE, 4
assassinate You may a. us . . . you won't intimidate us	ASSASSINATION, 4
assassinating I thought of a. many	ASSASSINATION, 6
assassination A. . . . the extreme form of censorship	ASSASSINATION, 9
assembly proper office of a representative a.	PARLIAMENTS AND ASSEMBLIES, 9
asshole You really are an a.	INSULTS, 36
assume A. a virtue, if you have it not	HYPOCRISY, 20
asylum An a. for the sane . . . empty in America	SANITY, 11
ate I a. his liver with some . . . beans	FOOD, 12
atheism the rock of a.	ATHEISM, 2
atheist I am an a. . . . thank God	ATHEISM, 3
atheists a. . . . citizens, nor . . . patriots	ATHEISM, 4

Athens A. arose	EUROPEAN CITIES, 25
A. holds sway over all Greece	POWER, 42
athlete great a. who died not knowing . . . pain	SPORTS AND GAMES, 4
athletics a. as inferior forms of fox-hunting	CLASS, 36
Atlantic cheaper to lower the A.	EXTRAVAGANCE, 2
atom bomb The a. is a paper tiger	NUCLEAR WEAPONS, 10
atomic every conceivable a. arrangement will come about	SCIENCE, 13
The a. threat . . . brought us to the brink	NUCLEAR WAR, 18
The way to win an a. war	NUCLEAR WAR, 2
atomic age I was ten . . . when 'the a.'	NUCLEAR WEAPONS, 2
atomic bomb a. . . . made . . . future war unendurable	NUCLEAR WEAPONS, 13
atomic war dangers of a. are underrated	NUCLEAR WAR, 11
atone a. for the sins of your fathers	INJUSTICE, 10
attachment A. is embedded in the soul . . . animal magnetism	RELATIONSHIPS, 10
attainments rare a. . . . but . . . can she spin?	SEXISM, 4
attention It's easy to get people's a., what counts is getting their *interest*	COMMUNICATION, 16
attested one a. story . . . of the Vampires	THE SUPERNATURAL, 32
Attila A. the Hen	POLITICAL INSULTS, 24
attraction a. of the virtuoso for the public	MUSICIANS, 5
audacity I had . . . shameful a. very much needed	CHARACTER, 3
audience Always make the a. suffer	AUDIENCES, 5
An a. is never wrong	AUDIENCES, 18
a. was a disaster	AUDIENCES, 17
I'm draggin' the a. to hell	HELL, 9
I know two kinds of a.	AUDIENCES, 12
The a. is a huge mirror	AUDIENCES, 16
the a. want to be surprised	AUDIENCES, 3
think of the a. when I'm directing	AUDIENCES, 15
audiences A.? No, the plural is impossible	AUDIENCES, 2
aunt If my a. had bollocks she'd be me uncle	FAMILY, 3
Auschwitz a man can read Goethe . . . work at A.	THE HOLOCAUST, 6
A. was the modern industrial application of . . . extermination	THE HOLOCAUST, 4
Austen A.'s novels . . . seem . . . vulgar	LITERARY INSULTS, 18
Australia Being lost in A.	AUSTRALIA, 1
the fern-dark indifference of . . . A.	AUSTRALIA, 7
Australian I'm going to write the Great A. Novel	WORLD LITERATURE, 10
Waiting for the A. republic	AUSTRALIA, 8
Austria A. is Switzerland . . . with history	EUROPEAN COUNTRIES, 48
authenticity If you seek a. for authenticity's sake	TRUTH, 56
author go to the a. to get at his meaning	CRITICISM, 20
No a. is . . . genius to his publisher	WRITERS, 31
notion of 'a.' constitutes . . . individualization	WRITERS, 22
you wish the a. . . . was a terrific friend	BOOKS, 49
authority a. be a stubborn bear	BRIBERY, 11
A. compels . . . obedience . . . reason persuades	OBEDIENCE, 5
authorize to a. what you have yourself forbidden	LAW, 29
authors A. are easy to get on with	WRITERS, 39
The trouble with our younger a. is	WRITERS, 47
autobiography a. is an obituary	AUTOBIOGRAPHY, 2
A. is the poor man's history	AUTOBIOGRAPHY, 1
autocracy a. . . . glory of the citizen, the state	AUTHORITARIANISM, 1
maintain the principle of a.	MONARCHY, 28
autocrat be an a.: that's my trade	AUTHORITARIANISM, 2
automobile A. . . . runs up hills and down pedestrians	CARS, 2
Money differs from an a., a mistress	MONEY, 18
autonomy We offer you . . . a., self-government	INDEPENDENCE, 7

must be a b. of any great matter — PERSISTENCE, 1
begins exception of the equator, everything b. somewhere — BEGINNING, 7
begun Everything has already b. before — FIRST LINES, 2
To have b. is half the job — BEGINNING, 9
behavior b. . . . controlled by our genetic inheritance — GENETICS, 9
Beijing I . . . lived in B. too long — ASIAN CITIES, 3
being A B., erect upon two legs — APPEARANCE, 7
Always at the Edge of B. — BEING, 10
B.'s poem . . . is man — BEING, 4
The truth of B. and of Nothing — BEING, 2
Beirut B. will be the Hanoi and Stalingrad — MIDDLE EAST, 4
Belfast I was born in B. — BIRTH, 11
belief Our b. in . . . natural law — BELIEF, 26
our pious b. in ghosts and witches — THE SUPERNATURAL, 13
believe b. . . . what . . . the hierarchical Church so
defines — BELIEF, 19
B. me now, my Christian friends — CHRISTIANITY, 8
How can I b. in God — BELIEF, 1
I b. because it is impossible — BELIEF, 30
I b. so that I may understand — UNDERSTANDING, 2
I don't b. in an afterlife — AFTERLIFE, 1
I don't b. in fairies — FAIRIES, 1
I don't b. in God — BELIEF, 14
I do not b. in moral issues — PACIFISM, 6
If you'll b. in me — BELIEF, 10
inclined to b. those whom we do not know — TRUST, 1
It is hard to b. that a man is telling the truth — LYING, 25
I wish to b. in immortality — IMMORTALITY, 13
I would as soon b. /in paradise — BELIEF, 2
only make b. that I love you — DELUSIONS OF LOVE, 4
The temerity to b. in nothing — BELIEF, 32
To b. and to understand . . . not diverse things — BELIEF, 12
what we b. is not necessarily true — LIBERTY, 3
when you cease to b. you may cease to behave — BELIEF, 16
believed I've b. . . . six impossible things — BELIEF, 9
two things . . . be b. of any man — ALCOHOL, 25
bell B., book, and candle — DETERMINATION, 4
bellow He who does not b. the truth — TRUTH, 51
belly Every man with a b. full of the classics — LITERATURE, 37
benefactors Our gratitude to most b. is the same as . . .
for dentists — GRATITUDE, 4
benevolence Is b. really far away — KINDNESS, 2
Bentley give every one a B. — TRAINS, 5
besiege When forty winters shall b. thy brow — OLD AGE, 39
best b. men are moulded out of faults — MEN, 28
letting the b. be the enemy of the good — DANGER, 6
The b. is the enemy of the good — ENEMIES, 5
the b. of all possible worlds — OPTIMISM, 12
the b. of all possible worlds — PERFECTION, 11
the b. of times . . . worst of times — FIRST LINES, 3
The b. thing others can do — LYING, 34
best-seller A b. is the gilded tomb of a mediocre talent — BOOKS, 50
bet b. you . . . he ain't in here — FUNERALS, 4
Bethlehem O little town of B. — CHRISTMAS, 4
betray All a man can b. is his conscience — CONSCIENCE, 4
b., you must first belong — BETRAYAL, 14
betraying if I had to choose between b. my country and
my friend — PATRIOTISM, 12
better B. the occasional faults of a government — GOVERNMENT, 50
b. to be at the right place — OPPORTUNITY, 14
b. to deal by speech than . . . letter — COMMUNICATION, 3
Give me b. wood . . . a b. cabinet — GOVERNMENT, 34
I am getting b. and b. — REMEDIES, 8
It is b. to be an artist — ARTISTS, 35
It is b. to be beautiful — BEAUTY, 42
no b. than you should be — CHARACTER, 7

We have seen b. days — NOSTALGIA, 16
what is b. than a good womman — WOMEN, 6
beware 'B. of the dog' — WARNING, 6
all should cry, B. — WARNING, 4
B. of the man who does not return your blow — FORGIVENESS, 12
B. of the scribes — HYPOCRISY, 2
B. of those who are homeless by choice — PLACES, 6
B. the ides of March — WARNING, 7
B. the Jabberwock — NONSENSE, 5
bias Commodity, the b. of the world — GREED, 10
There is a b. in television journalism — TELEVISION, 2
big B. Brother is watching you — TOTALITARIANISM, 7
b. emotions come from b. words — LITERARY STYLE, 6
The b. print giveth and the fine print taketh away — LAW, 32
bigamy B. . . . one wife too many — MARRIAGE, 2
Bilbao We shall raze B. — THREATS, 5
bile likes . . . the b. when it is black — LITERARY INSULTS, 24
bill give me your b. of company — FRIENDSHIP, 43
billboard A b. lovely as a tree — ADVERTISING, 13
When a man throws a b. across a view — ADVERTISING, 4
billiards to play b. well . . . sign of an ill-spent youth — YOUTH, 29
billionaire begin as a b. — WEALTH, 5
bill of rights b. is what the people are entitled to — HUMAN RIGHTS, 6
biography all b. is ultimately fiction — BIOGRAPHY, 12
hesitation in starting my b. too soon — SELF-DELUSION, 4
how difficult it is to write b. — BIOGRAPHY, 19
Read . . . nothing but b. — BIOGRAPHY, 7
biology B. . . . at least 50 more interesting years — GENETICS, 11
b. and culture interpenetrate in an inextricable manner — HUMAN NATURE, 17
biotechnology B. has an ancient lineage — TECHNOLOGY, 23
birch I'm all for bringing back the b. — PUNISHMENT, 13
bird A b. of brilliant plumage — MUSICIANS, 2
b. . . . instrument . . . according to a mathematical
law — BIRDS, 7
The b. seeks the tree — BIRDS, 2
The early b. who catches the worm — CAPITALISM, 29
birds b. of this year — CHANGE, 3
where . . . b. fly after the last sky — ENDING, 3
birth b. of the Universe — CREATION, 17
Our b. is but a sleep — BIRTH, 19
The memory of b. — INDIVIDUALITY, 5
To hinder a b. is . . . speedier man-killing — ABORTION, 8
birthday is it my b. or am I dying — LAST WORDS, 1
birthdays they don't understand about b. — GROWING UP, 1
birthright I cannot sell my b. — PRINCIPLES, 7
bisexual I am b. . . . it's the best thing — SEXUALITY, 7
bishop symbol of a b. is a crook — CORRUPTION, 3
bites when a man b. a dog that is news — JOURNALISM, 4
bitterness B. is like cancer — ANGER, 2
black A lady asked me why . . . I wore b. — BEREAVEMENT, 10
B. A, white E, red I . . . vowels — LANGUAGE, 33
B. is beautiful when . . . a slum kid . . . enter college — CIVIL RIGHTS, 16
B. tulips in my heart — ANGER, 6
have it . . . in b. and white — ACTION, 9
People think we do not understand our b. . . .
countrymen — APARTHEID, 3
Take that b. box away — FILMS, 48
That old b. magic — MAGIC, 4
There is a b. which is old — COLOUR, 6
The world said you spelled b. with a capital nothing — RACISM, 25
To be b. and conscious in America — UNITED STATES, 2
When what is b. is mixed with . . . the sun — COLOUR, 2
Who art as b. as hell, as dark as night — DECEPTION, 27

B. are made . . . like pyramids — BOOKS, 15
b. are only words — BOOKS, 63
B. create eras and nations — BOOKS, 2
B. think for me — READING, 22
Give me b., fruit, French wine and fine weather — PLEASURE, 19
He felt about b. as doctors . . . cynical but hopeful — BOOKS, 27
If my b. had been any worse — HOLLYWOOD, 4
I had to do the b. I did — BOOKS, 38
I keep my b. at the British Museum — LIBRARIES, 1
No furniture so charming as b. — BOOKS, 51
read . . . b. to find the juicy passages — READING, 14
secrets of companionship inherent in b. — BOOKS, 54
Some b. are to be tasted — BOOKS, 4
Some b. are undeservedly forgotten — BOOKS, 3
The Beckett Bowel B. — BOOKS, 5
think of all the b. I have read — READING, 40
To read too many b. — READING, 25
two classes of b. are of universal appeal — BOOKS, 16
We all know that b. burn — BOOKS, 47
bore A healthy male adult b. — PATIENCE, 14
B. . . . person who talks — BORES AND BOREDOM, 3
thou shalt not b. — FILMS, 53
you are . . . the club B.: I am the club Liar — PRIORITIES, 4
bored b. as enthusiasm would permit — BORES AND BOREDOM, 4
I wanted to be b. to death — BORES AND BOREDOM, 6
so b. with it all — BORES AND BOREDOM, 5
boredom B. is . . . a vital problem for the moralist — BORES AND BOREDOM, 13
The effect of b. on a large scale — BORES AND BOREDOM, 8
bores he b. for England — POLITICAL INSULTS, 45
boring Somebody's b. me, I think it's me — BORES AND BOREDOM, 18
There is nothing as b. as the truth — TRUTH, 18
born Better mankind b. without mouths — MONEY, 34
b. again, not of corruptible seed — TRANSIENCE, 7
b. in a duckyard — CLASS, 2
B. in the USA — AMERICANS, 24
B. of the sun — FAME, 24
I am not yet b. — BIRTH, 10
I was b. in a cellar — BIRTH, 5
I was b. intoxicated — DRUNKENNESS, 1
I was b. on a day — BIRTH, 18
I was b. when she kissed me — LOVERS, 3
We all are b. mad — MADNESS, 2
borrow if you b. a million — DEBT, 2
if you b., b. big — SUCCESS, 13
Boston In B. they ask, How much — AMERICAN CITIES, 41
We say the cows laid out B. — AMERICAN CITIES, 14
bottom I'm the b. you're the top — DECLARATIONS OF LOVE, 5
bouillabaisse B. . . . good because cooked by the French — FOOD, 8
bound There is no one so b. — THE FACE, 10
boundary right to fix the b. of . . . a nation — IRELAND, 30
bounty My b. is as boundless as the sea — DECLARATIONS OF LOVE, 16
Your b. threatens me, Mandela — AFRICA, 14
bourgeois B. . . . is an epithet — CLASS, 16
The b. prefers comfort to pleasure — CLASS, 15
bowels a good reliable set of b. is worth more . . . than . . . brains — THE BODY, 5
my b. were moved for him — SEX, 11
bower-bird I'm a bit of a b. — LITERATURE, 53
bowers to the b. of bliss conveyed — PRAISE, 10
boy a nicens little b. named baby tuckoo — CHILDHOOD, 7
every b. and every gal /That's born into the world alive — BABIES, 6
sit next to the b. you fancy — HOMOSEXUALITY, 6
When I was a b. of 14 — FATHERS, 11
boys wild b. innocent as strawberries — INNOCENCE, 14

bra pulled herself up by her b. straps — AMBITION, 22
bracelet diamond and sapphire b. lasts forever — MATERIALISM, 6
Brahms B. . . . an extraordinary musician — MUSICIANS, 9
brain b. . . . seat of, all our joys — MIND, 16
B. . . . with which we think that we think — MIND, 6
b. is the means by which we think — MIND, 44
b. the size of a planet — COMPLAINTS, 1
It is good to rub and polish our b. — INTELLECT, 14
keep his little b. attic stocked — MEMORY, 16
our b. is a mystery — MIND, 39
the b. . . . more than a telephone-exchange — MIND, 41
The b. has muscles for thinking — MIND, 23
the human b. is a device to keep the ears from grating — MIND, 11
You've got the b. of a four-year-old boy — STUPIDITY, 5
brains b. enough to make a fool of himself — INTELLIGENCE, 12
sometimes his b. go to his head — INTELLECTUALS, 2
brave Any fool can be b. on a battle field — COURAGE, 11
I'm very b. generally — COWARDICE, 1
It is hard to be b. — COURAGE, 9
Many b. men . . . before Agamemnon's time — POETS, 35
The b. man thinks of himself . . . last — COURAGE, 14
the b. poet is afraid to die — POETS, 29
We should look for . . . b. men in prisons — POLITICIANS, 51
Brazil In B. they throw flowers — SOUTH AMERICA, 5
bread b. and circuses — MATERIALISM, 5
I am the b. of life — CHRISTIANITY, 2
The Royal slice of b. — FOOD, 24
break I'll b. my staff — MAGIC, 13
Let's b. away from rationality — RATIONALISM, 6
breath last b. be drawn through a pipe and exhaled in a pun — SMOKING, 13
breathes Who b. must suffer — SUFFERING, 19
breathing Keep b. — LONGEVITY, 11
breathing-space b. in the architecture of your love — RELATIONSHIPS, 6
breeding Good b. . . . concealing how much we think — MANNERS, 7
breeze The fair b. blew — THE SEA, 6
brevity B. is the soul of lingerie — CLOTHES, 12
B. is the soul of wit — BREVITY, 8
brews As he b., so shall he drink — JUSTICE, 18
bribe a b. gives away . . . his own importance — BRIBERY, 5
The taking of a B. or Gratuity — BRIBERY, 8
brick found it b. and left it marble — EUROPEAN CITIES, 26
bridge Like a b. over troubled water — REMEDIES, 26
briefly lit b. by one another's light — RELATIONSHIPS, 18
brighter Far b. scenes a future age — UNITED STATES, 24
Had I been b. — BIOGRAPHY, 14
brink scared to go to the b. — DIPLOMACY, 13
Britain B. . . . where the ruling class does not rule — CLASS, 25
B. has lived . . . on borrowed time — BRITAIN, 8
B. is not . . . easily rocked by revolution — BRITAIN, 17
In B., an attractive woman is somehow suspect — WOMEN, 29
British B. . . . cowering on the very island — BRITAIN, 2
B. Cinema hasn't developed . . . ideas in films — FILMS, 25
but we are B.—thank God — HOMOSEXUALITY, 15
I would rather be B. than just — NORTHERN IRELAND, 13
last B. Prime Minister with jurisdiction in Ireland — IRELAND, 1
no spectacle so ridiculous as the B. public — BRITAIN, 22
the B. have more heritage than is good for them — BRITAIN, 6
We're B. and loyal /And love every royal — BRITAIN, 14
Yes, it is wonderful to be B.—until one comes to Britain — BRITAIN, 5
British Empire the liquidation of the B. — BRITISH IMPERIALISM, 8
British Isles This little speck, the B. — BRITAIN, 19
broadcasting B. . . . too important to be left to the broadcasters — MEDIA, 1

thirty-seven c. /and no butcher shop — RELIGION, 22
Cicero C. /And many-minded Homer — MADNESS, 51
cigar Sometimes a c. — SMOKING, 9
cigarette c. . . . perfect pleasure — SMOKING, 16
cinema c. . . . experience without danger all the excitement — FILMS, 19
C.'s . . . what's in the frame — FILMS, 41
c. is not a slice of life — FILMS, 15
two kinds of c. — FILMS, 52
circle wheel is come full c. — FATE, 27
circumlocution the C. Office — BUREAUCRACY, 5
circumstantial evidence Some c. is very strong — FACTS, 16
circus run away from the c. to become an accountant — POLITICAL INSULTS, 7
cissies Some kids are c. by nature — COWARDICE, 7
cities c. . . . built by the sound of music — CITIES, 4
C. belong to human nature — CITIES, 6
citizen humblest c. . . . stronger than all the hosts of error — RIGHT, 1
I wished . . . c. of the world — EUROPEAN CITIES, 10
Socrates . . . a c. of the world — THE WORLD, 10
city A c. . . . no need to wait — CITIES, 11
A c. must be a place . . . seeking and developing — CITIES, 10
A c. where everyone mutinies — AMERICAN CITIES, 17
c. is . . . a human zoo — CITIES, 12
c. is arrayed in squares just like a chess-board — ASIAN CITIES, 4
C. of Magnificent Distances . . . of Magnificent Intentions — AMERICAN CITIES, 12
C. of my birth . . . of my dreams — MIDDLE EAST, 22
c. where you can see a sparrow fall — EUROPEAN CITIES, 22
great c. . . . has the greatest men and women — CITIES, 17
The C. is of Night — NIGHT, 13
the c. of perspiring dreams — BRITISH CITIES, 18
This is a c. of water — AMERICAN CITIES, 32
What is the c. but the people — CITIES, 14
civilisation c. . . . imprisoned in a linguistic contour — LANGUAGE, 15
civilisations All great c. . . . based on success in war — CIVILIZATION, 6
civilization A c. that proves incapable — CIVILIZATION, 3
C. . . . not in man's heart — CIVILIZATION, 7
C. . . . progress toward a society of privacy — CIVILIZATION, 23
c. . . . something to learn from the primitive — CIVILIZATION, 27
c. /always results in deserts — CIVILIZATION, 20
c. is a bitch of a problem — RUSSIA, 39
C. is a method of living — CIVILIZATION, 1
C. is a movement, not a condition — CIVILIZATION, 29
C. is an architecture of responses — CIVILIZATION, 16
c. is here in the islands — SCOTLAND, 6
c. is marked by . . . disregard — CIVILIZATION, 21
fighting in the quarrel of c. against barbarism — WORLD WAR I, 26
I am the c. they are fighting to defend — WORLD WAR I, 4
little in c. to appeal to . . . Yeti — CIVILIZATION, 14
Our boasted c. is but a thin veneer — CIVILIZATION, 5
So does c. question itself — CIVILIZATION, 13
You can't say c. don't advance — CIVILIZATION, 24
civilizations c. decay quite leisurely — CIVILIZATION, 8
civilized c. man becomes again almost a savage — BRITISH CITIES, 21
civil rights c. . . . 172 years late — CIVIL RIGHTS, 5
civil service British c. . . . effective braking mechanism — BUREAUCRACY, 9
civil war In a c., a general must know — BETRAYAL, 15
claim not c. the discovery as your own — PLAGIARISM, 11
claims no c. against fidelity to truth — HONESTY, 4

clap Don't c. too hard — AUDIENCES, 10
claret C. is the liquor for boys — ALCOHOL, 12
clarity C. . . . politeness of the man of letters — CLARITY, 6
class Without c. differences, England would cease to be . . . theatre — CLASS, 7
classes three c. which need sanctuary — POLITICIANS, 2
classic c. attempt /at beauty — BEAUTY, 44
classical c. Canon and the multicultural cause — LITERATURE, 20
classics The c. are only primitive literature — LITERATURE, 32
class struggles history of c. — CLASS, 24
clean air we can continue to enjoy c. — GLOBALIZATION, 23
cleanliness secret of resistance to disease is c. — HEALTH AND HEALTHY LIVING, 16
clear c. . . . as the nose in a man's face — CLARITY, 1
If I turn out to be particularly c. — CLARITY, 4
Cleopatra Had C.'s nose been shorter — THE FACE, 12
clerk The best c. I ever fired — POLITICAL INSULTS, 41
clever never wise to try to appear . . . more c. — WISDOM, 19
To be c. enough to get . . . money, one must be stupid — WEALTH, 7
cleverness height of c. is . . . to conceal it — INTELLECT, 12
cliché poised between a c. and an indiscretion — DIPLOMACY, 25
climbed c. to the top of the greasy pole — ACHIEVEMENT, 7
climbing c. is performed . . . same position with creeping — AMBITION, 32
Clinton C. . . . philandering, pot-smoking draft dodger — POLITICAL INSULTS, 42
cloathing c. . . . a covering for shame — CLOTHES, 6
clock He turned and saw the accusing c. — MORTALITY, 6
clocks Stop all the c., cut off the telephone — FUNERALS, 1
the c. were striking thirteen — FIRST LINES, 7
closed A c. mouth catches no flies — SILENCE, 5
C. like confessionals, they thread — SECRECY, 10
cloth make . . . c. give expression to the body — CLOTHES, 19
clothes In c. there are no new fashions — LANDSCAPES, 8
pay more for my c. . . . you probably don't sleep in yours — CLOTHES, 4
club I don't want to belong to any c. — HUMOUR, 12
coat His c. resembles the snow — ANIMALS, 40
cocaine c. . . . separates you from your soul — DRUGS, 16
C.—such a perfunctory, unintelligent drug — DRUGS, 24
C. is God's way of saying . . . too much money — DRUGS, 25
C. isn't habit-forming — ADDICTION, 1
still remains the c. bottle — DRUGS, 8
cock c. has great influence on his own dunghill — INFLUENCE, 6
we owe a c. to Aesculapius — DEBT, 18
cockpit Can this c. hold — THEATRE, 16
cockroach c. world of compromise — COMPROMISE, 2
to choose between him and a c. as a companion — INSULTS, 46
cocktail parties c. of the geriatric set — FUNERALS, 7
Cocteau C. thinks me a bad thief — EUROPEAN LITERATURE, 8
cod serve both c. and salmon — FOOD, 20
coffee c., chocolate, cocoa . . . not good for man — DRINKS AND DRINKING, 11
C. for all — EUROPEAN COUNTRIES, 49
Instant c. is just old beans — DRINKS AND DRINKING, 10
coffee-house folly . . . echo of a London c. — GOSSIP, 9
coffin c. after c. /Seemed to float — FUNERALS, 9
coke Happiness is like c. — HAPPINESS, 21
cold I could no longer stand . . . c. mutton — EMIGRATION, 6
It leapt straight past the common c. — MEDICINE, 3
cold war we are . . . in the midst of a c. — COLD WAR, 3
Coliseum While stands the C., Rome shall stand — EUROPEAN CITIES, 6
collaboration C.—that's the word producers use — FILMS, 43
collector I am a sort of c. of religions — RELIGION, 36
Colombia C. is not France . . . I am not Napoleon — SOUTH AMERICA, 3

conceptual art C. . . . another kind of artistic style
ARTISTIC STYLES, 12
  In C. the idea   ARTISTIC STYLES, 13
concern C. for man himself . . . chief interest of all
  technical endeavors   SCIENCE, 21
concessions c. of the weak . . . concessions of fear
WEAKNESS, 1
conciliation Draw back the rifles . . . trust in c.   PEACE, 11
conclusion c. of your syllogism   WORDPLAY, 7
condemnation the dismal, ridiculous c. of Oscar Wilde
WRITERS, 46
condemned Man is c. to be free   FREEDOM, 48
  the c. . . . persist in surviving   SURVIVAL, 9
condition c. upon which God hath given liberty . . .
  eternal vigilance   LIBERTY, 10
  the c. of our sex is so deplorable   PROTEST, 14
  thinks about . . . c. of her uterus   WOMEN, 31
conditions no c. of life . . . cannot get accustomed
HUMAN CONDITION, 21
conducive anything c. to our national stability
ASIAN COUNTRIES, 15
confess easy to make a man c. . . . lies   TRUTH, 35
  only c. our little faults   FRANKNESS, 3
  We c. our bad qualities . . . out of fear   FEAR, 6
confession no refuge from c. but suicide   SUICIDE, 22
confidence C. and hope . . . more good than physic
REMEDIES, 11
conflagrations Great c. . . . born of tiny sparks   REVOLUTION, 41
conformist c. is not born. He is made   CONFORMITY, 6
confronted c. primarily with a moral issue   EQUALITY, 13
confuse c. the minds of others   DECEPTION, 11
confused Anyone who isn't c. . . . doesn't really
  understand   CONFUSION, 1
confusion C. is a word we have invented   CONFUSION, 6
  c. is the sign of the times   CONFUSION, 2
  nothing . . . except my own c.   CONFUSION, 5
  What mazed c.   REASON, 5
conked John Le Mesurier . . . c. out on November 15th
OBITUARIES, 3
connect I can c. /Nothing with nothing   NOTHINGNESS, 5
  Only c.   WRITING, 19
connected Everything is c.   INTERNET, 3
connection c. between history and nature   IMMORTALITY, 2
  hidden c. . . . stronger than an obvious one
RELATIONSHIPS, 9
conquer easier to c. it   ASIA, 5
  when we c. without danger   VICTORY, 5
conquering See, the c. hero comes   VICTORY, 10
conquest c. and spoliation of the weaker nations
WORLD WAR I, 2
conscience A bad c. creates malignant behaviour
CONSCIENCE, 16
  a good digestion depends upon a good c.   DIGESTION, 4
  A man has less c. when in love   CONSCIENCE, 17
  A still and quiet c.   CONSCIENCE, 20
  c. . . . other people inside you   CONSCIENCE, 15
  c. . . . weakest when he needs it most   CONSCIENCE, 8
  C. and self-love . . . lead us the same way   CONSCIENCE, 2
  c. hath a thousand several tongues   CONSCIENCE, 21
  C. is . . . rejection of a particular wish   CONSCIENCE, 7
  C. is a coward   CONSCIENCE, 10
  C. is the inner voice   CONSCIENCE, 13
  cruelty with a good c.   CRUELTY, 6
  I cannot . . . cut my c. to fit   CONSCIENCE, 11
  Never do anything against c.   CONSCIENCE, 5
  our own c. is asleep   CONSCIENCE, 14
  should not C. have *Vacation*   CONSCIENCE, 3
  The disease of an evil c.   CONSCIENCE, 9
  Thus c. does make cowards of us all   CONSCIENCE, 19
conscious To be c. is an illness   ILLNESS, 7

consciousness All c. is c. *of* something   CONSCIOUSNESS, 14
  C. . . . is nothing jointed; it flows   CONSCIOUSNESS, 10
  C. . . . teeming multiplicity of objects and relations
CONSCIOUSNESS, 11
  C. can neither be described nor defined   CONSCIOUSNESS, 2
  c. constructs . . . that linguistic mechanism
CONSCIOUSNESS, 12
  c., her awful Mate   THE SOUL, 9
  c. is . . . a state of nerves   CONSCIOUSNESS, 13
  c. is . . . consciousness of the object   CONSCIOUSNESS, 8
  C. is thoroughgoing dialectical restlessness
CONSCIOUSNESS, 7
  delusion imprisons the c. that projects it   DELUSION, 5
  effort of c. to raise matter   EVOLUTION, 2
consequences do anything . . . take the c.   ACHIEVEMENT, 1
conservation C. is a state of harmony   THE ENVIRONMENT, 6
conservatism c. is based upon the idea   CONSERVATISM, 3
  The c. of to-morrow   RADICALISM, 1
  What is c.?   CONSERVATISM, 8
conservative c., n. A statesman . . . enamored of existing
  evils   CONSERVATISM, 1
  the most c. thing is to be a revolutionary   CONSERVATISM, 2
  which makes a man more c.   CONSERVATISM, 7
considerable to appear c. in his native place   AMBITION, 13
consideration Devoid of c. for the selfishness   SELFISHNESS, 2
consistency c. is the hobgoblin of little minds   CHARACTER, 20
conspicuous consumption C. . . . is a means of reputability
MATERIALISM, 11
conspiracy a vast, amorphous, unwitting, unconscious c.
BUREAUCRACY, 2
  Science . . . c. of brains against ignorance   SCIENCE, 17
constellations Those who first invented . . . the c.
ASTRONOMY, 1
constitution c. or national army is totally out
EUROPEAN COUNTRIES, 5
constraint arbitrariness of the c.   CREATIVITY, 21
consumer In a c. society there are . . . two kinds of slaves
CAPITALISM, 17
consummatum c. est   LAST WORDS, 2
consumption The c. explosion in the West   MATERIALISM, 1
  this c. of the purse   DEBT, 14
consumptive c. youth weaving garlands of sad flowers
WRITERS, 49
contemporary C. man has rationalized the myths   MYTHS, 9
  No, I was no one's c.   EUROPEAN LITERATURE, 12
contempt C. mates well with pity   CONTEMPT, 2
contend Let's c. no more, Love   ARGUMENTS, 2
contented quite c. to have become an adjective   NAMES, 9
contentment C. and fulfilment don't make . . . good
  fiction   FICTION, 7
continence sexual perversion known as c.   PERVERSITY, 3
continuous C. change is comfortable change   CHANGE, 14
contradict Do I c. myself?   SELF-KNOWLEDGE, 41
contradictions C. . . . can spark off the fires of invention
CREATIVITY, 1
  c. that are pushing our society forward   ASIAN COUNTRIES, 20
contradicts One often c. an opinion   ARGUMENTS, 14
control 'c. of nature' . . . phrase conceived in arrogance
ECOLOGY, 2
  impulse to c. . . . essential element in obsessional
  neurosis   NEUROSIS, 10
controversies The most savage c.   ARGUMENTS, 18
controversy c. is either superfluous   UNDERSTANDING, 8
conventionality C. is not morality   HYPOCRISY, 5
conversation C. has a kind of charm   CONVERSATION, 20
  c. must be an exchange of thought   CONVERSATION, 19
  happiest c. where there is no competition   CONVERSATION, 18
  many thousand subjects for elegant c.   CONVERSATION, 7
  never-ending worldwide c.   INTERNET, 9
  no such thing as c.   CONVERSATION, 21

reasonable c. . . . frightens us in a madman
    CONVERSATION, 9
spin c. . . . out of thy own bowels   HYPOCHONDRIA, 5
this c. is getting a little strange   SEDUCTION, 3
conversationalist the c. who adds 'in other words'
    CONVERSATION, 18
converted not c. a man because you have silenced him
    OPPRESSION, 9
conviction loss of c. . . . meaning of life   SELF-KNOWLEDGE, 31
convictions encompassed by a cloud of comforting c.
    COMFORT, 3
convicts C. are the best audience   AUDIENCES, 4
cook A good c. is like a sorceress   COOKING, 9
c. that cannot lick his own fingers   COOKING, 10
cookery C. . . . pandering which corresponds to medicine
    COOKING, 7
cooks c. . . . spoiled by going into the arts   COOKING, 3
Too many c. spoil the broth . . . one to burn it
    COOKING, 1
cool once c. but Mr. Gravity's been very unkind   AGE, 25
co-operative C. capitalism does not spontaneously emerge
    CAPITALISM, 13
copier A . . . c. of nature can never produce anything
great   ARTISTIC STYLES, 22
cops c. in LA looked like handsome gigolos   HOLLYWOOD, 9
copyright there's no c. on your own life   PRIVACY, 4
cork Lighter than a c. I danced   BOATS, 8
corn The c. is as high   OPTIMISM, 8
Whoever could make two ears of c.   POLITICIANS, 48
cornered-animal A sound of c. fear   FEAR, 17
coronets Kind hearts are more than c.   KINDNESS, 12
corporation c. . . . device for securing individual profit
    BUSINESS, 1
corporations US c. are run like . . . Soviet economy
    BUSINESS, 17
corpse buried the putrid c. of liberty   FASCISM, 8
He'd make a lovely c.   DEATH AND DYING, 16
One can't carry one's father's c.   ARTISTIC STYLES, 1
corpses battle-c. . . . white skeletons of young men
    THE SUPERNATURAL, 37
does not eat c.   FOOD, 29
corridor Life is a dusty c.   LIFE, 11
corrupt All things . . . c. perverted minds   CORRUPTION, 10
corrupted They had been c. by money   CORRUPTION, 6
corruption C., the most infallible symptom of
constitutional liberty   CORRUPTION, 5
cosmetics c.' names seemed obscenely obvious   MARKETING, 2
cosmopolitan I was told I am a true c.   UNHAPPINESS, 18
cosmos c. is about the smallest hole   THE UNIVERSE, 5
cost The c. of a thing   VALUE, 1
costs That which c. little is less valued   VALUE, 2
cotton Hands that picked c. . . . will pick a president
    SLAVERY, 22
couch when on my c. I lie   SOLITUDE, 28
cough C. A convulsion of the lungs   ILLNESS, 13
count I c. the votes   CORRUPTION, 16
counted the faster we c. our spoons   HYPOCRISY, 11
countries every man had two c.   UNITED STATES, 45
No two c. that . . . have a McDonald's   GLOBALIZATION, 6
country Every c. has the government it deserves
    GOVERNMENT, 37
Every c. should realize   IMPERIALISM, 11
good c. for all of us   EQUALITY, 20
How soon c. people forget   CITIES, 13
if a man takes away the character of the people
of my c.   FORGIVENESS, 8
love a c. that brings . . . people happiness   PATRIOTISM, 8
my c. /has known a thousand conquerors   IMPERIALISM, 24
My c. right or wrong   PATRIOTISM, 10
suck'd on c. pleasures, childishly   LOVERS, 6

The c. was on the slide   ASIAN COUNTRIES, 24
The undiscover'd c.   AFTERLIFE, 18
very fine c. to be acutely ill   BRITAIN, 20
We have a c. full of words   NATIONS, 8
What this c. needs . . . 5-cent cigar   LUXURY, 3
What this c. needs . . . hard bloody war   WAR, 6
Who dare to love their c., and be poor   PATRIOTISM, 22
Why did my c. . . . gateway /to hell   MIDDLE EAST, 34
your c. . . . on the soles of your shoes   EMIGRATION, 2
countryman the c. who looked for his ass while . . .
mounted on his back   THINKING, 4
countryside known our c. . . . roads were too dangerous
    POLLUTION, 7
couple Splendid c.—slept with both of them   ADULTERY, 4
courage C. consists of staying at home   COURAGE, 10
C. is the price . . . for granting peace   COURAGE, 2
C. mounteth with occasion   COURAGE, 15
c. to love . . . courage to suffer   COURAGE, 16
Let your c. rise with danger   COURAGE, 8
The Red Badge of C.   COURAGE, 1
two o'clock in the morning c.   COURAGE, 12
courting c. on the bed . . . customary throughout Wales
    WALES, 9
When . . . c. . . . an hour seems like a second   TIME, 13
covenant age-old c. between man and dog   AGREEMENT, 7
covenanted And they c. with him for thirty pieces of silver
    BETRAYAL, 4
cover Never judge a c. by its book   BOOKS, 24
coward None but a c. . . . has never known fear   COWARDICE, 3
cowards C. die many times   COWARDICE, 4
C. in scarlet   COWARDICE, 10
cows Sacred c. make the tastiest hamburger   HERESY, 4
coxcomb to hear a c. ask two hundred guineas   ARTISTS, 40
crack Blow, winds, and c. your cheeks   WEATHER, 12
cracks c. in the universe   THE UNIVERSE, 21
cradle c. rocks above an abyss   LIFE, 37
craft Between c. and credulity . . . reason is stifled
    REASON, 4
C. . . . what you can learn from other verse   WRITING, 28
crafty She's too c. . . . to invent a new lie   LYING, 24
crash-proof No c. system can be built   COMPUTERS, 23
crazy a little c. . . . like all men at sea   THE SEA, 11
I was c. and . . . he was drunk   LOYALTY, 10
created Nothing can be c. out of nothing   NOTHINGNESS, 9
We c. man from dry clay   CREATION, 11
creation c. comes out more beautiful   CREATIVITY, 11
c. of a world . . . governed by justice   PEACE, 3
c. of the juridical entity of the citizen   FRENCH REVOLUTION, 15
whole of C. /To produce my foot   CREATION, 6
creative All men are c. . . . few are artists   CREATIVITY, 12
c. act is not performed by the artist alone   CREATIVITY, 4
C. imagination awakens early   CREATIVITY, 4
no c. activity is possible   CENSORSHIP, 30
creativeness C. . . . turning up what is already there
    CREATIVITY, 10
creativity C. is a highfalutin word   CREATIVITY, 15
c. is mastery of simplicity   CREATIVITY, 23
creator If one can call . . . C. to account   CREATION, 13
Man . . . hasn't been a c., only a destroyer
    THE ENVIRONMENT, 1
the c. . . . is apt to create *anything*   CREATION, 4
creators When c. do not compromise   COMPROMISE, 1
creature No c. smarts . . . as a fool   FOOLISHNESS, 19
creatures Like following life through c. you dissect   LIFE, 44
credit not to mind who gets the c.   SELFLESSNESS, 4
credulity c. . . . to think all men virtuous   VIRTUE, 7
C. is . . . the child's strength   BELIEF, 18
credulous Thus c. fools are caught   GULLIBILITY, 7
creeds other c. and different nationalities . . . live
amongst us   MIDDLE EAST, 15

crème All my pupils are the c. de la c. ELITISM, 3
cricket This isn't no time for playin' / . . . this is c.
SPORTS AND GAMES, 5
What do they know of c. SPORTS AND GAMES, 11
cried I had never c. for my father's death BEREAVEMENT, 8
crime c. . . . not to avoid failure CRIME, 23
c. . . . repressed desire for aesthetic expression CRIME, 22
C. always seems impossible in retrospect CRIME, 14
c. and the criminal . . . perplexity of radical evil CRIME, 3
C. has its heroes JUDGMENT, 25
C., like virtue, has its degrees CRIME, 19
c. pays. The hours are good CRIME, 1
c. to examine the laws of heat HERESY, 9
C. which is prosperous . . . is called virtue CRIME, 20
duty to worship the sun . . . c. to examine . . . heat
BLASPHEMY, 4
Every c. destroys more Edens CRIME, 10
From the one c. recognize them all as culprits CRIME, 21
He who secretly meditates c. . . . guilty CRIME, 12
hour of their c. HISTORY, 19
Street c. begins psychologically in a walkless world
CRIME, 11
study of c. . . . knowledge of oneself CRIME, 16
The worst c. is to leave a man's hands empty
CREATIVITY, 22
worst c. is faking it DECEPTION, 8
crimes C. of which a people is ashamed CRIME, 9
Successful c. alone are justified TREASON, 2
The c. of extreme civilization CIVILIZATION, 2
criminals more c. out of jail than in jail CRIME, 8
crisis To create such a c. . . . foster such a tension
PROTEST, 7
critic A c. is a man who CRITICS, 33
A c. should be a conduit CRITICS, 22
A good c. . . . narrates the adventures of his mind
CRITICS, 11
c. . . . historian who records CRITICS, 13
C. and whippersnapper, in a rage CRITICS, 6
c. is . . . the younger brother of genius CRITICS, 14
c. is a bunch of biases CRITICS, 2
c. is a legless man CRITICS, 24
drama c. . . . surprises the playwright CRITICS, 21
ever seen a dramatic c. in the daytime CRITICS, 35
Intellectual currents can generate . . . the c. CRITICS, 4
Nor in the c. let the man be lost CRITICS, 25
the function of the c. CRITICS, 3
critical c. judgement is so exquisite CRITICS, 12
nothing if not c. JUDGMENT, 24
criticism A great deal of contemporary c. CRITICISM, 5
c. is a letter to the public CRITICISM, 19
my own definition of c. CRITICISM, 1
People ask you for c. CRITICISM, 14
Writing c. is . . . hugging the shore CRITICISM, 26
criticize don't c. /What you can't understand CRITICISM, 7
criticizing The pleasure of c. CRITICISM, 10
critics c. . . . desire our blood CRITICS, 23
C.! . . . Those cut-throat bandits CRITICS, 7
I had listened to the c. CRITICS, 10
The greater part of c. are parasites CRITICS, 26
crocodile How doth the little c. ANIMALS, 13
crocodiles c. . . . shed tears when they would devour
HYPOCRISY, 1
crooked the c. timber of humanity HUMANKIND, 28
cross We can't always c. a bridge ANTICIPATION, 1
cross-bow With my c. /I shot the Albatross DESPAIR, 3
crow I'd rather c. /And be a rooster INDECISION, 3
crowd Far from the madding c. HUMILITY, 8
The c. are on the pitch ENDING, 10
crowds C. without company BRITISH CITIES, 10
Crown influence of the C. has increased MONARCHY, 12

Crown Jewels get the C. . . . from the pawn-shop SCOTLAND, 14
crucify Do you want to c. the boy BIGOTRY, 1
cruel A c. story runs on wheels GOSSIP, 7
be c. only to be kind CRUELTY, 8
c. and deadly enemy—society IDEALISM, 4
cruelties The c. of property and privilege CLASS, 17
cruelty C. has a Human Heart HUMAN NATURE, 6
C. is contagious in uncivilized communities CRUELTY, 4
inflict c. . . . immediately before slaughter CRUELTY, 2
The c. . . . is lack of imagination CRUELTY, 9
cruising C. . . . was a lot like hitchhiking HOMOSEXUALITY, 12
crusade This c., this war on terrorism TERRORISM, 4
crush I've Got a C. on You DECLARATIONS OF LOVE, 3
cry I c. all the way to the bank CRITICISM, 11
I often want to c. SORROW, 20
the c. of him that ruleth among fools WISDOM, 2
cubic foot One c. less . . . would have constituted adultery
ADULTERY, 3
cuckoo C.-echoing, bell-swarmèd, lark-charmèd
BRITISH CITIES, 11
cucumber A c. should be well sliced FOOD, 15
cucumbers project for extracting sun-beams out of c.
EXPERIMENTS, 9
they are but c. after all LITERARY INSULTS, 30
Cuernavaca in C. I learned more about the mind MIND, 26
cuisine Every c. tells a story FOOD, 28
cult a c. . . . not enough . . . to make a minority
POPULARITY, 1
cultural c. health . . . is political POLITICS, 40
c. transmission is geared to learning CULTURE, 3
Cultural Revolution the C., an earthshaking disaster
ASIAN COUNTRIES, 1
culture 'C.' is simply how one lives CULTURE, 2
C. . . . abhors all simplification CULTURE, 4
C. . . . an instrument wielded by professors CULTURE, 9
c. . . . gives itself its own self-consciousness CULTURE, 5
C. . . . perishing in overproduction CULTURE, 8
C. is the passion for sweetness and light CULTURE, 1
c. that . . . subscribes to the piratical ethic ANARCHY, 5
c. that worships aggression FILMS, 46
serious c. is being engulfed ASIAN COUNTRIES, 28
cultures apt to leave his c. exposed SCIENTISTS, 16
cunning Be as c. as a serpent and as harmless as a dove
LIFE, 18
C. and deceit will every time serve a man better
DECEPTION, 22
In saying . . . never choose c. COMMUNICATION, 13
cup Ah, fill the C. TRANSIENCE, 13
between the c. and the lip CHANCE, 4
Come, fill the C., and in the Fire of Spring
TRANSIENCE, 10
curbing c. of minds to the government's will RUSSIA, 25
cure a c. that destroys the depression DEPRESSION, 12
It is part of the c. to wish to be cured REMEDIES, 24
most rational . . . for . . . fear of death REMEDIES, 13
no c. for birth and death REMEDIES, 22
We all labour against our own c. DEATH AND DYING, 9
curfew The C. tolls the knell of parting day EVENING, 2
curfews c. were declared illegal TOTALITARIANISM, 10
curiosity C. will conquer fear CURIOSITY, 6
My c. was aroused to fever-pitch CURIOSITY, 7
curious I am c. to see . . . the next world LAST WORDS, 12
curiouser C. and c. CURIOSITY, 2
currencies system of national c. GLOBALIZATION, 24
current we must take the c. when it serves OPPORTUNITY, 1
curse c. of all the human race POLITICAL INSULTS, 3
make a c. sound like a caress POLITICAL INSULTS, 23
the c. of every evil deed EVIL, 30
The c. of literacy LITERACY, 5
The great c. of our modern society POVERTY, 9

I stare at d. in a mirror AIDS, 5

Life is . . . d. /in small daily doses LIFE, 34

man fears . . . only the stroke of d. FEAR, 3

Man has given a false importance to d. MORTALITY, 8

Many men on the point of an edifying d.
DEATH AND DYING, 51

Men fear d., as children fear . . . dark FEAR, 2

My name is d.; the last best friend DEATH AND DYING, 60

nothing can be said to be certain but d. and taxes
DEATH AND DYING, 28

O D., thou comest DEATH AND DYING, 23

one way to be prepared for d. DEATH AND DYING, 46

report of my d. was an exaggeration OBITUARIES, 5

so natural . . . so universal as d. DEATH AND DYING, 63

the brother of d. exacteth a third part SLEEP, 2

the idea of d. as an individual EXTINCTION, 6

the struggle against d. DEATH AND DYING, 33

We fear our d. FEAR, 11

world's an inn . . . d. the journey's end DEATH AND DYING, 19

deaths it is chiefly our own d. that we mourn FUNERALS, 2

debauch d. the currency ECONOMICS, 17

debt A d. may get mouldy DEBT, 1

d. makes a man your debtor DEBT, 12

d. which cancels all others DEATH AND DYING, 14

I can pay some of my d. DEBT, 6

debts When d. are not paid DEBT, 4

decadence The difference between our d. and the
Russians' RUSSIA, 31

decay Bodily d. is gloomy in prospect MIND, 20

D. and disease are often beautiful ILLNESS, 34

deceased I am a d. writer WRITERS, 45

deceive D. boys with toys DECEPTION, 21

deceived The world is still d. with ornament DECEPTION, 31

decent D. without Indecent within CORRUPTION, 2

decision Persuade the d. makers DECISION, 3

decisions At a thousand feet we make quick d. FLYING, 3

d. should be made as low as possible DECISION, 4

declaiming when you are d., declaim COMPLAINTS, 6

Declaration of Independence the principles of the D.
WOMEN'S RIGHTS, 23

decomposing d. in the eternity of print LITERARY INSULTS, 59

decompression the d. of the Western imagination THE MOON, 16

dedicated You must all grow up to be d. women
COMMITMENT, 5

deed a good d. in a naughty world GOOD, 27

a good d. to forget a poor joke FORGETTING, 2

right d. for the wrong reason TREASON, 3

The d. is all, and not the glory ACTION, 6

worth of a kind d. KINDNESS, 11

deeds better d. /Shall be in water writ REPUTATION, 6

Our d. still travel with us CHARACTER, 19

deep That sweet, d. sleep SLEEP, 30

defeat we are not interested in the possibilities of d.
DEFEAT, 5

We are out to d. injustice INJUSTICE, 13

defect Chief D. of Henry King ADDICTION, 2

The most obvious d. REPUBLICANISM, 3

defects When the d. of others are perceived IMPERFECTION, 4

defence Never make a d. or apology APOLOGIES, 1

Preparing for suicide is not a . . . means of d.
NUCLEAR WEAPONS, 6

defend d. to . . . death your right to agree LIBERALISM, 5

Defender of Faith my title as D. MONARCHY, 6

defiance The d. of established authority PROTEST, 2

deficit The d. is big enough DEBT, 9

defined We have since d. Gaia THE EARTH, 10

degenerates world d. and grows worse every day PESSIMISM, 9

degree Observe d., priority, and place ORDER, 8

Take but d. away CHAOS, 5

deities the d. so kindly FATE, 20

Delacroix The recipe for making a man like D. ARTISTS, 37

delay D. . . . breeds danger PROCRASTINATION, 3

D. is the deadliest form of denial PROCRASTINATION, 7

deleted D. by French censor NEWSPAPERS, 5

deliberation D. is the work of many men ACTION, 3

delight All for your d. /We are not here ABSENCE, 10

She discovered with great d. CHILDREN, 13

sweet airs, that give d., and hurt not MAGIC, 12

delightful d., it's delicious, it's de-lovely PLEASURE, 28

delude we d. ourselves if we think that humanity is
becoming ever more civilised PROGRESS, 8

deluge After us the d. PROPHECY, 10

delusions D. . . . only things which render life tolerable
DELUSION, 11

demagogues the vilest specimens of human nature . . .
found among d. DICTATORS, 7

demand Be realistic, d. the impossible PROTEST, 11

democracies D. . . . short in their lives DEMOCRACY, 30

d. . . . think that a stupid man is more likely to be
honest POLITICIANS, 44

democracy A modern d. is a tyranny DEMOCRACY, 31

D. . . . difficult kind of government DEMOCRACY, 24

d. . . . infects us with amnesia SOUTH AMERICA, 7

d. . . . may unwittingly lead us into hell DEMOCRACY, 18

d. . . . recognizes the subjecting of the minority
DEMOCRACY, 26

D. . . . superior form of government DEMOCRACY, 25

D. . . . worship of jackals by jackasses DEMOCRACY, 35

D. . . . written into law DEMOCRACY, 11

D.! Bah! ELITISM, 1

d. can be cured by more d. DEMOCRACY, 45

D. gives every man a right DEMOCRACY, 29

D. is a charming form of government DEMOCRACY, 39

D. is the theory that the common people know what
they want DEMOCRACY, 34

D. is the wholesome and pure air DEMOCRACY, 17

D. means choosing your dictators DEMOCRACY, 10

D. means government by discussion DEMOCRACY, 4

D. passes into despotism DEMOCRACY, 40

D. sometimes seems to be an end DEMOCRACY, 33

extreme d. or absolute oligarchy INEQUALITY, 1

heroic example of d.'s solidarity DEMOCRACY, 20

I still can't see /Why D. means /Everybody but me
DEMOCRACY, 19

supporters of D. . . . obliged to attack Confucianism
PROTEST, 3

there has never been a true d. DEMOCRACY, 42

Western d. . . . the seeds of death MIDDLE EAST, 21

democratic A d. nation of persons . . . is an impossibility
DEMOCRACY, 23

the ideal of a d. and free society IDEALISM, 10

thoroughly d. and patronise everybody DEMOCRACY, 44

demon fighting with a d. THE SUPERNATURAL, 17

demoniacal something d. . . . discern a law SCIENTISTS, 28

denature easier to d. plutonium than . . . evil spirit of
man EVIL, 13

Denmark rotten in the state of D. CORRUPTION, 13

Denver D. . . . like the Promised Land AMERICAN CITIES, 22

deny d. or delay, right or justice JUSTICE, 24

dependent too d. upon dachas RUSSIA, 36

depraved suddenly became d. VICE, 5

depression best cures for d. DEPRESSION, 10

d. takes on . . . quality of physical pain DEPRESSION, 11

deprivation D. is for me what daffodils were INSPIRATION, 7

derived we d. . . . in a bolt of lightning CREATION, 18

descend Never d. to the ways of those above you CLASS, 22

descended D. from the apes EVOLUTION, 1

we are d. from barbarians EVOLUTION, 7

desert The d., the abode of enforced sterility LANDSCAPES, 2

When you halt in the d. TRAVEL, 6

dignity man added to his d. by standing on it	PRIDE, 3
there is no d. without freedom	FREEDOM, 52
Without d. there is no liberty	LIBERTY, 25
digressions D. . . . the soul of reading	BOOKS, 55
dikes our d., . . . are ten feet deep	BOASTS, 15
dined More d. against than dining	EATING, 3
you have d. in every house in London	POPULARITY, 10
diner a strange d. in the South	PARANOIA, 1
dinner a good d. and feasting reconciles everybody	EATING, 16
a good d. upon his table	SEXISM, 5
dinner party best number for a d. is two	EATING, 9
dinosaur The d. didn't know it was extinct either	EXTINCTION, 8
Diogenes D. lighted a candle in the daytime	CYNICISM, 3
diplomacy D. . . . game of chess	DIPLOMACY, 22
diplomat A d. . . . always remembers a woman's birthday	DIPLOMACY, 18
A real d. . . . can cut his neighbour's throat	DIPLOMACY, 23
d. these days is nothing but a head-waiter	DIPLOMACY, 32
diplomatic d. nuanced circles	DIPLOMACY, 7
diplomats aged d. to be bored	DIPLOMACY, 2
direct can't d. a Laughton picture	ACTING AND ACTORS, 12
I always d. the same film	FILMS, 9
To be d. and honest is not safe	HONESTY, 11
directing d. . . . coming out of your individual loneliness	FILMS, 17
director d. makes only one film in his life	FILMS, 35
working for a good d., you become . . . submissive	ACTING AND ACTORS, 26
directors two kinds of d.—allies and judges	FILMS, 16
dirt Huddled in d. the reasoning engine lies	REASON, 28
dirty You d. double-crossing rat	BETRAYAL, 6
disadvantage I saw it at a d.	CRITICISM, 29
disagree possible to d. . . . about . . . non-violence	PACIFISM, 4
disappoint I may not d. myself	SELF-RESPECT, 5
disarmament Vertical d. makes a catastrophe	NUCLEAR WEAPONS, 17
disasters d. come at the same time	DISASTER, 3
disbelief willing suspension of d.	FAITH, 6
discandy do d., melt their sweets /On blossoming Caesar	BETRAYAL, 17
discipline Without d. true freedom cannot survive	FREEDOM, 43
discommendeth He who d. others obliquely	CRITICS, 5
discontent lent /To youth and age . . . —d.	UNHAPPINESS, 1
Where does d. start	UNHAPPINESS, 16
discourse d. . . . cannot dominate absolutely	WRITERS, 13
discover not d. new lands	DISCOVERY, 6
When I d. who I am, I'll be free	SELF-KNOWLEDGE, 11
discovered d. something that he will die for	IDEALISM, 6
We have d. the secret of life	DISCOVERY, 5
discoverers ill d. that think there is no land	EXPLORATION, 1
discovery d. is mathematical in form	MATHEMATICS, 8
discretion D. is the better part of reading	JUDGMENT, 5
temper d. with deceit	TEACHERS, 12
discrimination d. based simply on race . . . barbarous	APARTHEID, 5
discussion D. in class, which means	EDUCATION, 12
If we had had more time for d.	MISTAKES, 20
disease Cure the d. . . . kill the patient	MEDICINE, 4
desperate d. requires a dangerous remedy	TREASON, 4
D. . . . social as well as physical . . . causes	ILLNESS, 31
d. . . . whole and entire within itself	ILLNESS, 10
d. in the family	IRELAND, 3
d. is connected only with immediate causes	ILLNESS, 33
D. is very old	ILLNESS, 4
D. makes men more physical	ILLNESS, 18
favourite d.	DOCTORS, 7

Have a chronic d. and take care	LONGEVITY, 6
he does not die from the d. alone	DEATH AND DYING, 52
Nip d. in the bud	ILLNESS, 25
remedy is worse than the d.	REMEDIES, 2
strange d. of modern life	MODERNITY, 1
That d. is called Incubus	ILLNESS, 1
The d. which must be cured	DEMOCRACY, 36
when the cause of d. is discovered	DOCTORS, 4
diseases d. . . . no less natural than the instincts which preserve	ILLNESS, 29
D. are the tax on pleasures	ILLNESS, 27
D. crucify the soul of man	ILLNESS, 2
D. of the soul are more dangerous	ILLNESS, 5
The cure of many d. is unknown	REMEDIES, 19
disenchanting Is there anything . . . so d. as attainment?	ACHIEVEMENT, 21
disgusting A crawling and d. parasite	LITERARY INSULTS, 13
disinterested D. intellectual curiosity . . . real civilisation	INTELLECT, 16
dismal so d. and gloomy on these mountains	WALES, 8
the D. Science	ECONOMICS, 7
disobedience Acts of d. . . . postal service of disbelief	OBEDIENCE, 2
dispepsia d. is the apparatus of illusions	DIGESTION, 6
displacement The d. of a little sand	CHANGE, 11
dispute Many a long d. among divines	ARGUMENTS, 7
dissatisfied better . . . d. than a pig satisfied	UNHAPPINESS, 9
dissimulate how to d. is the knowledge of kings	MONARCHY, 37
dissociation a d. of sensibility	HUMAN CONDITION, 9
dissolution d. of the feeling of individual responsibility	RESPONSIBILITY, 5
dissolve d. the political bonds	AMERICAN WAR OF INDEPENDENCE, 7
distance D. sometimes endears friendship	FRIENDSHIP, 19
The d. doesn't matter	BEGINNING, 3
The shortest d. between two points	MATHEMATICS, 24
distinguish no longer d. direct experience from . . . television	MEDIA, 2
distinguishing d. fragrant flowers from poisonous weeds	CENSORSHIP, 16
distrust d. of our senses	SENSES, 3
D. that man who tells you to d.	SUSPICION, 6
distrustful most d. . . . the greatest dupes	TRUST, 3
diversion d. . . . an imitation of fighting	SPORTS AND GAMES, 22
diversity biological and cultural d. are now severely threatened	ECOLOGY, 4
divide I shall d. and subdivide power	POWER, 35
You cannot d. peace in Europe	EUROPE, 2
divine cannot d. . . . conditions that will make happiness	HAPPINESS, 8
D. in hookas, glorious in a pipe	SMOKING, 4
D. Poetry, /you who live in solitude	WORLD LITERATURE, 1
domain where the d. is visible . . . art	ART, 33
I will make d. magnetic lands	FRIENDSHIP, 48
Things d. are believed in	RELIGION, 17
To be discontented with the d. discontent	VIRTUE, 17
divine right d. of husbands	WOMEN'S RIGHTS, 42
divinity a d. . . . shapes our ends	FATE, 25
There's such d. doth hedge a king	TREASON, 7
there is d. in odd numbers	CHANCE, 10
division false d. . . . 'feminine' and 'masculine'	THE SEXES, 15
divorce d. . . . Blame our obsolete sex roles	DIVORCE, 4
d. between the producer of the text	LITERATURE, 4
D.? Never. But murder often	DIVORCE, 9
Everyone should have a d. once	DIVORCE, 8
Suffer the women whom ye d.	DIVORCE, 5
divorced d. from his wife	DIVORCE, 7
divorces three d. and four wives to decide	MISOGYNY, 2
DNA If all the D. . . . were stretched out	GENETICS, 5
do d. what the mob d.	PRUDENCE, 2
doctor A d. . . . is a patient half-cured	OCCUPATIONS, 5

duty of a d. to prolong life — DOCTORS, 9
Give me a d. partridge-plump — DOCTORS, 2
I am like a d. — DIPLOMACY, 28
no point in calling a d. — FATE, 3
The D. fared even better — REPUTATION, 10
When a d. does go wrong — CRIME, 5
doctors d. are certainly hooked on the diagnoses — REMEDIES, 16
D. are just the same as lawyers — DOCTORS, 3
D. bury their mistakes — OCCUPATIONS, 6
doctrines makes all d. plain and clear — BRIBERY, 1
document historic d. . . . towards entering Europe — RUSSIA, 33
dodo The D. never had a chance — EXTINCTION, 2
dog A d. starv'd at his Master's Gate — HUNGER, 3
as though my d. has just died — POLITICAL INSULTS, 52
a truly faithful d. — FAITH, 10
cat will mew . . . d. will have his day — FATE, 24
ever d. that praised his fleas — LITERARY INSULTS, 61
The d. barks but the caravan passes — CRITICS, 1
The great pleasure of a d. — ANIMALS, 11
dogma D. is credulous — BELIEF, 22
You can't teach an old d. — BIGOTRY, 3
dogs d. delight to bark and bite — AGGRESSION, 5
D. show us their tongues — ANIMALS, 17
doing Anything worth d. is worth d. poorly — ACHIEVEMENT, 8
dolmens Like d. round my childhood, the old people — OLD AGE, 28
dolphin That d.-torn, that gong-tormented sea — THE SEA, 29
domestic D. happiness, thou only bliss — HAPPINESS, 11
Donald Duck D. . . . and the bourgeoisie can sleep peacefully — AMERICAN IMPERIALISM, 6
done D. because we are too menny — SUICIDE, 9
If it were d. when 'tis d. — HASTE, 8
dong The D. with a luminous Nose — NONSENSE, 11
donkey The d. . . . is still a d. — ANIMALS, 1
door keep ajar the d. that leads to madness — POETS, 43
the d. . . . opens like a wound — MIDDLE EAST, 27
doors Men shut their d. against a setting sun — BETRAYAL, 18
the d. of perception were cleansed — PERCEPTION, 3
doublethink D. means . . . holding two contradictory beliefs — BELIEF, 23
doubt Attempt the end, and never . . . d. — DETERMINATION, 4
d. . . . an art . . . acquired with difficulty — DOUBT, 10
D. . . . necessary precondition to meaningful action — DOUBT, 3
never d. /What nobody is sure — DOUBT, 4
To d. everything or . . . believe everything — DOUBT, 11
When a man is in d. about . . . his writing — POSTERITY, 3
doubting d. in order to philosophize — DOUBT, 9
Everyone who observes himself d. — DOUBT, 1
The game of d. itself presupposes certainty — DOUBT, 15
doughty The d. knight of the stuffed cravat — POLITICAL INSULTS, 2
down He that is d. — HUMILITY, 3
drama d. . . . people dealing nobly with . . . misery — THEATRE, 18
D. is the need to be human — THEATRE, 4
d. is when the audience cries — ACTING AND ACTORS, 5
d. of people struggling — HISTORY, 5
We respond to a d. — THEATRE, 9
drama critic d. . . . perceives what is not happening — CRITICS, 34
draught O, for a d. of vintage — INSPIRATION, 6
draw I d. what I feel in my body — ART, 25
drawing D. is the true test — ART, 27
drawing board back to the old d. — FAILURE, 1
drawing rooms d. . . . spoiled more poets — LUXURY, 1
dream A d. can be the highest point of a life — DREAMS, 16
A d. is a scripture — DREAMS, 6
a d. of perfect bliss — TRANSIENCE, 4
All men d.: but not equally — DREAMS, 13

All that we see . . . Is but a d. — DREAMS, 17
awakened from the d. of life — POETS, 56
d. . . . reality eludes altogether the consciousness — DREAMS, 20
God pity a one-d. man — DREAMS, 8
his d. . . . turn the age to gold — DREAMS, 9
I d. things that never were — POSSIBILITY, 3
I d. when I am awake — DREAMS, 2
I have a d. — DREAMS, 12
I have had a d., past the wit of man — DREAMS, 22
in a d. she had come to him after her death — AFTERLIFE, 11
In a d. you are never eighty — OLD AGE, 38
one must d. one's revolution — ARTISTS, 9
The d. is real, my friends — DREAMS, 1
the fondest d. of Phallic science — SCIENCE, 19
What is a d.? /What is reality — DREAMS, 32
dreamed I d. of a white saucepan — WRITERS, 65
dreaming a man d. I was a butterfly — DREAMS, 34
dreams do we not live in d. — DREAMS, 28
d. . . . imagination informs the understanding — DREAMS, 21
D. /are cages — DREAMS, 31
D. are necessary to life — DREAMS, 15
D. are the most powerful motivators — MOTIVE, 5
D. release the soul's love urge — DREAMS, 5
Gregory Samsa woke from uneasy d. — METAMORPHOSIS, 2
I arise from d. of thee — DREAMS, 26
I like the d. of the future — THE FUTURE, 11
In d. begins responsibility — RESPONSIBILITY, 7
My d. were all my own — DREAMS, 25
Our d. are our real life — DREAMS, 7
People . . . turning d. into reality — WRITING, 55
power of d. . . . multiformity of animals — DREAMS, 4
We are such stuff /As d. are made on — DREAMS, 24
dress A d. has no life of its own — CLOTHES, 16
A d. that is not worn — CLOTHES, 1
Englishman's d. is like a traitor's body — CLOTHES, 5
Those who make their d. . . . themselves — CLOTHES, 8
dress'd man /D. in a little brief authority — PRIDE, 11
dressed All d. up, with nowhere to go — PURPOSE, 6
Dreyfus It is the revenge of D. — REVENGE, 10
drink D. to-day, and drown all sorrow — DRINKS AND DRINKING, 4
First you take a d. . . . then the d. takes you — ALCOHOL, 7
I d. no more than a sponge — DRINKS AND DRINKING, 8
I shall d. water. It's a mixer — DRINKS AND DRINKING, 6
never . . . d. by daylight — ALCOHOL, 13
One more d. and I'd be under the host — DRUNKENNESS, 17
We d. one another's health — ALCOHOL, 10
you shall d. twice while I d. once — FATHERS, 12
drinking I have been d. it for sixty-five years and I am not dead yet — DRINKS AND DRINKING, 13
I was out of work, d. . . . crazy — MADNESS, 9
much d., little thinking — ALCOHOL, 24
two reasons for d. — DRINKS AND DRINKING, 6
drive D. on your own track — SELF-INTEREST, 12
driven d. /Into a desperate strait — EXTREMES, 2
driving busy d. cabs and cutting hair — GOVERNMENT, 12
d. alone . . . exhilarates some people — AMERICAN CITIES, 13
drollery fatal d. . . . representative government — GOVERNMENT, 16
drop a single d. of human blood — SACRIFICE, 7
D. 30 per cent of your Latinisms — WRITING, 60
drown Nobody can d. in the ocean of reality — REALITY, 17
drowning If I rescued a child from d. — NEWSPAPERS, 4
drug A d. . . . when injected into a rat, will produce a scientific report — DRUGS, 21
A miracle d. — DRUGS, 12
D. misuse is not a disease — DRUGS, 7
No d. . . . causes the . . . ills of society — DRUGS, 20
drugs D. are the greatest threat — DRUGS, 15
drum major say that I was a d. for justice — JUSTICE, 20

drummer d. . . . kicking his drums to the cellar   JAZZ, 10
drunk D. in charge of a narrative   DRUNKENNESS, 8
   I was very d.   ACCIDENTS, 4
   Lord George Brown d. is a better man   POLITICAL INSULTS, 5
   Man, being reasonable, must get d.   DRUNKENNESS, 7
   not so think as you d.   DRUNKENNESS, 21
drunken What shall we do with the d. sailor   DRUNKENNESS, 11
drunkenness D. . . . spoils health   DRUNKENNESS, 18
   d. . . . the supremely valid human experience
     DRUNKENNESS, 13
   d. an expression identical with ruin   DRUNKENNESS, 9
   D. is never anything but a substitute for happiness
     DRUNKENNESS, 12
   D. is simply voluntary insanity   DRUNKENNESS, 20
   D. is temporary suicide;   DRUNKENNESS, 19
   D., the ruin of reason   DRUNKENNESS, 3
Dublin D. . . . not so bad as Iceland   EUROPEAN CITIES, 16
   first day in D. . . . your worst   EUROPEAN CITIES, 4
   When I die, D. will be written on my heart
     EUROPEAN CITIES, 17
duck I forgot to d.   ASSASSINATION, 8
   looks like a d.   COMMUNISM, 18
dues Many d. imposed by law are hostile   LAW, 1
dull as d. as ditch water   CHARACTER, 16
   He was d. in a new way   LITERARY INSULTS, 29
   Like a d. actor now   FAILURE, 12
   not only d. in himself   INSULTS, 14
dullard The d.'s envy of brilliant men   ENVY, 2
dumb D. as a drum vith a hole in it   SILENCE, 8
   so d. that he can't fart and chew   POLITICAL INSULTS, 34
dungeon What other d. . . . dark as one's own heart
     THE HEART, 4
dupe d. of friendship . . . the fool of love   HATE, 9
duration D. . . . the continuous progress of the past
     THE PAST, 9
dust like d., I'll rise   ENDURANCE, 1
   not worth the d.   INSULTS, 40
duty the d. of being happy   HAPPINESS, 53
dwarf d. sees farther than the giant   KNOWLEDGE, 12
dying 'Tis not the d. for a faith   FAITH, 16
   D. for an idea   MARTYRDOM, 7
   d. for their country   KILLING, 10
   D. /is an art   DEATH AND DYING, 53
   D. is a very dull, dreary affair   DEATH AND DYING, 42
   d. is more the survivors' affair   DEATH AND DYING, 39
   If this is d.   LAST WORDS, 16
   We're d. from not knowing . . . our past   THE PAST, 5
eagerness e. to seek hidden but necessary connections
     RELATIONSHIPS, 17
ear more is meant than meets the e.   MEANING, 10
early E. to rise and e. to bed   MODERATION, 8
   you have to get up e. if you want to get out of bed
     MORNING, 10
earnest I am in e.—I will not equivocate   SLAVERY, 20
earnings gap between men's and women's e.   INEQUALITY, 6
earrings e. for the price of a . . . sandwich   FRANKNESS, 5
ears now the e. of my e. awake   SENSES, 4
earth As the e. darkens when . . . sun departs   MONARCHY, 36
   But did thee feel the e. move   SEX, 24
   e. . . . blue like an orange   THE EARTH, 4
   E. . . . too small and fragile a basket   THE EARTH, 7
   E. has not anything to show more fair: BRITISH CITIES, 23
   E. hath no sorrow . . . heaven cannot heal   SORROW, 15
   E. is here so kind   AUSTRALIA, 5
   e. is the mother of all people   EQUALITY, 11
   E. was bountiful . . . the Great Mystery   NATURE, 34
   Spaceship E.—an instruction book didn't come with it
     THE EARTH, 6
   The e. is as full of brutality   ILLNESS, 16
   the e. is barren as the moon   ECOLOGY, 6

   the E. is perfectly suitable for life   CREATION, 16
   the e. seems . . . a step-dame   THE EARTH, 3
   the e. was the road /Of the body   THE EARTH, 9
   this e. . . . a mote . . . in the abyss   INFINITY, 3
earthquake Not by the e. daunted   AMERICAN CITIES, 27
East Neither E. nor West   INDEPENDENCE, 3
   The E. is a career   BRITISH IMPERIALISM, 13
   The wind from the E. prevails   ASIA, 3
   to prevent us from going into the E.   WORLD WAR II, 13
Eastwards E. goes the great river   RIVERS, 5
easy E. is the way down to the Underworld   HELL, 20
   not e. to get a . . . productive spirit to read   READING, 20
eat E. . . . perform successively . . . the functions of
   mastication   EATING, 2
   e. moderately . . . and don't worry
     HEALTH AND HEALTHY LIVING, 9
   E. not to dullness   MODERATION, 4
   E. slowly: only men in rags   MANNERS, 5
   Let them e. the lie   SELF-INTEREST, 3
   men lived to e. . . . he ate to live   EATING, 7
   that must e. with the devil   THE DEVIL, 13
   they know I don't e. babies   POLITICIANS, 20
   To e. well in England . . . breakfast three times   EATING, 14
   what you e. . . . what you are   FOOD, 3
eaten e. me out of house and home   GREED, 9
eating E. cannot be a solitary affair   EATING, 13
   E. people is wrong   MORALITY, 10
eats The thing that e. the heart   THE HEART, 5
echo e. is the soul of the voice   THE SOUL, 20
ecologist I became an e.   ECOLOGY, 7
ecologists e. . . . the ultimate accountants   ECOLOGY, 11
ecology E. . . . compulsory subject for all economists
     ECOLOGY, 9
   That land is a community . . . basic concept of e.
     ECOLOGY, 5
economic cold metal of e. theory   MARXISM, 10
   E. activity should . . . be socially just   ECONOMICS, 1
   e. and military unification . . . not brought peace
     GLOBALIZATION, 1
   Modern e. thinking . . . consider the long term
     ECONOMICS, 34
   time . . . to build an e. force   ECONOMICS, 14
economical e. with the truth   LYING, 4
economics attempt to isolate e. from other disciplines
     ECONOMICS, 16
   E. . . . as much a study in fantasy   ECONOMICS, 29
   e. forecast may well affect the economy   ECONOMICS, 21
   E. without ethics   ECONOMICS, 37
   nobler e. . . . not afraid to discuss spirit   ECONOMICS, 30
   sense of history . . . divides good e. from bad
     ECONOMICS, 11
economic system A mature e.   ECONOMICS, 15
economies emerging e. . . . entire industrial revolution
     POLLUTION, 9
   successful e. . . . generating and disseminating
   knowledge   ECONOMICS, 5
economist An e. . . . expert who will know tomorrow
     ECONOMICS, 24
   e. . . . knows 100 ways of making love   ECONOMICS, 6
economists If all e. were laid end to end   ECONOMICS, 35
economy e. . . . description of the career of money
     ECONOMICS, 3
   E. . . . Purchasing the barrel of whiskey   ECONOMICS, 4
   understand the workings of the e.   ECONOMICS, 36
   world e. will shift to the Asia-Pacific   ASIA, 6
ecstasy e. of striking matches in the dark   WRITING, 32
Edison If Thomas E. had gone to business school
     BUSINESS, 16
editor E.: a person employed . . . to see that chaff is
   printed   JOURNALISM, 15

editorial the nineteenth century . . . age of the e. chair
                                                        TWENTIETH CENTURY, 3
education E. . . . an admirable thing   EDUCATION, 25
  E. . . . formation of character   CHARACTER, 34
  e. . . . makes a straight cut ditch   EDUCATION, 20
  e. . . . one who INSISTS on knowing   EDUCATION, 16
  e. . . . reverent joining of the past   EDUCATION, 15
  e. . . . teaches us to divorce soul from body   WRITING, 21
  E. is . . . the soul of a society   EDUCATION, 2
  e. is a leading out of what is . . . in the pupil's soul
                                                     EDUCATION, 19
  E. is that which remains   EDUCATION, 6
  E. made us what we are   EDUCATION, 11
  e. was an ornament in prosperity   EDUCATION, 4
  philosophic aim of e.   EDUCATION, 10
  Soap and e. . . . are more deadly   EDUCATION, 21
  Upon . . . e. . . . this country depends   EDUCATION, 5
  When a man's e. is finished   EDUCATION, 8
educational e. process . . . is its own end   EDUCATION, 3
efficiency lack of e. . . . scientific achievements for
  economic needs   TECHNOLOGY, 7
efforts Wherever man would not . . . spend his e.
                                                     BETRAYAL, 13
egalitarian For all its e. promise   INTERNET, 12
egalitarianism E. in Islam is more pronounced   ISLAM, 1
  The majestic e. of the law   EQUALITY, 1
egg Everything from an e.   BEGINNING, 8
  Only as an e. . . . are we all equal   EQUALITY, 6
eggs putting all my e. in one bastard   ABORTION, 6
ego Avoid having your e. so close to your position
                                                     SELF-INTEREST, 13
  e. locks the muse   INSPIRATION, 13
  e. represents what we call reason . . . sanity   THE SELF, 8
  male e. . . . is elephantine   MEN, 9
  The human e. is like an insatiable tick   EGOTISM, 10
egoist E. . . . more interested in himself than in me EGOTISM, 3
egos An aggregate of e. . . . a mob   EGOTISM, 5
egotism E. . . . dulls the pains of stupidity   EGOTISM, 9
Egyptians Ancient E. . . . contemporary man all have a
  kinship   HUMAN CONDITION, 13
  the E. worshipped an insect   POLITICAL INSULTS, 21
Eichmann They hanged E. yesterday   INDIFFERENCE, 7
Eiffel Tower E. . . . representing the world's age HUMANKIND, 51
Einstein E.'s space is no closer to reality than Van Gogh's
  sky   REALITY, 15
  E. was right. The world is crazy   PHYSICS, 7
  The genius of E. leads to Hiroshima   GENIUS, 13
elder the idea of e. wisdom   OLD AGE, 48
elderly distinguished but e. scientist states   SCIENTISTS, 4
elder statesman posing . . . as an e.   POLITICIANS, 16
electricity by means of e., the world of matter TECHNOLOGY, 8
  e. was dripping invisibly   FEAR, 33
electronic 'E. democracy' . . . open new doors for
  participation   DEMOCRACY, 43
  They are e. lice   POPULAR MUSIC, 2
electronics cost of the e. in a modern car   TECHNOLOGY, 16
elegance Has she e.   FLATTERY, 3
elegant If you can't be e. . . . be extravagant EXTRAVAGANCE, 4
elephant African e.'s ear / . . . the shape of Africa ANIMALS, 39
  I shot an e. in my pajamas   NONSENSE, 13
  rogue e. among British prime ministers POLITICAL INSULTS, 44
elimination work toward the e. of human rights
                                                     HUMAN RIGHTS, 13
Elizabethan E. age . . . beginning of the smoking era
                                                     SMOKING, 1
Elysian The immortals will send you . . . E. plain HEAVEN, 5
emancipate E. yourselves from mental slavery   SLAVERY, 26
  one of these days we'll e. *you!*   CIVIL RIGHTS, 15
emancipating woman is . . . e. herself from emancipation
                                                     WOMEN'S RIGHTS, 13

emancipation After e. . . . they needed the music more
                                                     JAZZ, 2
  All e. is from within   FREEDOM, 23
  greatest stumbling block in the way of woman's e.
                                                     WOMEN'S RIGHTS, 37
  The e. of women . . . the greatest egoistic movement
                                                     WOMEN'S RIGHTS, 19
  When the history of the e. movement   SLAVERY, 16
embalmed I am e. in a book   BOOKS, 62
embalmer A triumph of the e.'s art   POLITICAL INSULTS, 51
embraced e. the summer dawn   MORNING, 14
embroidered two blankets e. with smallpox
                                                     BRITISH IMPERIALISM, 16
embryo This e. capital, where Fancy sees   AMERICAN CITIES, 31
emerald A livelier e. twinkles in the grass   GLORY, 6
Emerson E. . . . lives . . . on ambrosia   LITERARY INSULTS, 42
  I could . . . see in E. a gaping flaw   ARROGANCE, 5
émigré An inner é., grown long-haired   SELF-KNOWLEDGE, 20
eminence E. engenders enemies   ENEMIES, 7
emotional seven constituents of e. make-up   EMOTION, 6
emotions E. are the lowest form of consciousness
                                                     EMOTION, 9
  e.! Don't leave them on the road   EMOTION, 5
  She ran . . . e. from A to B   INSULTS, 33
  Strong and e. and passions   EMOTION, 14
emperor For . . . big stealin' dey makes you e. THEFT, 8
  the E. has nothing on   NAKEDNESS, 1
empire a more powerful or a more united e.
                                                     BRITISH IMPERIALISM, 12
  An e. founded by war   IMPERIALISM, 15
  e. is . . . power in trust   IMPERIALISM, 6
  How is the E.   LAST WORDS, 5
  the downfall of the British E.   BRITISH IMPERIALISM, 10
  To found a great e. . . . for a nation of shopkeepers
                                                     BRITISH IMPERIALISM, 22
empires Old and entire e. have been dissolved
                                                     IMPERIALISM, 1
empiricist e. view . . . has the character of a superstition
                                                     RATIONALISM, 1
employer ideal of the e. . . . production without
  employees   BUSINESS, 25
empty An e. house can gain centuries   TIME, 63
  e. and awake . . . emptiness and awakedness of
  everything   BUDDHISM, 1
enamour'd Methought I was e. of an ass DELUSIONS OF LOVE, 10
enchanted e. by his own ugliness   NARCISSISM, 5
encomium e. in Greek has a marvellous effect   BOOKS, 36
end And now the e. is near   POPULAR MUSIC, 1
  an e. to the beginnings of all wars   WAR, 54
  beginning of the e. when you . . . have style   STYLE, 2
  e. is where we start from   BEGINNING, 4
  looks like the e. of the world   THE ENVIRONMENT, 16
  the e. begins to come into view   ENDING, 9
  The e. must justify the means   ACTION, 15
  the same thing at the e.   ENDING, 1
  This is . . . an e. of all wars   WAR, 59
  what e. the gods have in store   FATE, 15
endeavor Human e. . . . betrays /Humanity   HUMANKIND, 25
endeavour To e. to forget anyone   FORGETTING, 6
endings E. are elusive, middles are nowhere   BEGINNING, 1
ends the best e. by the best means   WISDOM, 9
endure e. my own despair   PESSIMISM, 14
endures only thing that e. is character   CHARACTER, 33
enemies my e. have a point   ENEMIES, 13
  Of the e. of the soul   ENEMIES, 11
  we have been mortal e. ever since   PEACE, 1
enemy despise your e. strategically . . . respect him
  tactically   ENEMIES, 10
  discover what your e. fears most   FEAR, 16
  e. of clear language is insincerity   LANGUAGE, 31

I cannot get any sense of an e.   WORLD WAR I, 16
It takes your e. and . . . friend   ENEMIES, 14
no more sombre e. of good art   BABIES, 3
the e. who can . . . teach us   ENEMIES, 3
We have met the e., and they are ours   ENEMIES, 12
energy E. is Eternal Delight   VITALITY, 1
engineer the e. assumed accountability for his work   RESPONSIBILITY, 1
engineers e. . . . . end up with the atomic bomb   SCIENTISTS, 22
England E. . . . . racist, homophobic, narrow-minded, authoritarian rat-hole   ENGLAND, 15
E.—a happy land we know   ENGLAND, 7
E. invented the phrase, 'Her Majesty's Opposition'   GOVERNMENT, 5
E. is a nation of shopkeepers   ENGLAND, 20
E. is an empire   EUROPEAN COUNTRIES, 46
E. is the paradise of individuality   ENGLAND, 25
Happy is E.! I could be content   ENGLAND, 14
Hating E. . . . . a form of self-defense   HUMAN RIGHTS, 8
In E., pop art and fine art   ARTISTIC STYLES, 14
no man in E. will take away my life   ASSASSINATION, 2
The only E. he had known was . . . passionate in incest with its past   ENGLAND, 16
You poison E. at her roots   ECOLOGY, 1
English Correct E. is the slang of prigs   GRAMMAR, 4
E. . . . . admire any man who has no talent   MEDIOCRITY, 1
E. . . . . have the most rigid code of immorality   ENGLAND, 4
E. . . . . the language of the world   WORLD ENGLISH, 3
E. character . . . iron force of the Latins   ENGLAND, 10
E. drunkard made the rolling E. road   ENGLAND, 6
E. expect . . . everything should be the same   ENGLAND, 24
E. is the language of the fox   EUROPEAN LANGUAGES, 7
E. language is nobody's special property   WORLD ENGLISH, 8
E. nation . . . successfully regulated the power of its kings   ENGLAND, 31
E. soldiers fight like lions   WORLD WAR I, 11
E. will . . . carry the weight of my African experience   WORLD ENGLISH, 1
E. winter—ending in July   ENGLAND, 5
learn E. . . . . in thirty hours   EUROPEAN LANGUAGES, 6
Nothing unites the E. like war   UNITY, 7
range of the E. longbows   WEAPONS, 10
The baby doesn't understand E.   LANGUAGE, 18
the E. seem, as it were, to have conquered and peopled half the world   BRITISH IMPERIALISM, 19
The E. sentence is just as difficult   WRITING, 52
the E. would manage to meet and dine   ENGLAND, 13
This is the sort of E.   GRAMMAR, 5
To Americans E. manners are . . . frightening   AMERICANS, 12
English language if I created the E.   ORIGINALITY, 1
If the E. had been properly organized   LANGUAGE, 25
The E. ceased to be the sole possession   WORLD ENGLISH, 5
Englishman An E. . . . . forms an orderly queue of one   MANNERS, 4
An E.'s way of speaking   ENGLAND, 17
An E. is never so natural   ENGLAND, 12
E. does not joke   ENGLAND, 30
E. thinks he is moral   ENGLAND, 27
every E. is an island   ENGLAND, 21
never find an E. among the underdogs   CLASS, 37
some other E. despise him   CLASS, 33
You may be the most liberal Liberal E.   CLASS, 18
Englishmen to see the absurd nature of E.   ENGLAND, 23
enjoyment E. is *not* a goal   PLEASURE, 12
enlarged condensed and e. in New York   AMERICAN CITIES, 5
enmity Walls of e. have fallen, borders . . . disappeared   GLOBALIZATION, 20
enough Why, then, have we not e.   FOOD, 14
entered I should never have e. the church on that day   MODESTY, 2

entertained have e. angels unawares   STRANGERS, 1
three unhappy women . . . e. within an inch of their lives   BORES AND BOREDOM, 16
entertainers people think that e. see the world   ENTERTAINMENT, 5
entrances story of my life is about back e. and side doors   PRIVACY, 2
entrapment e. in sterile, bureaucratic corporate slots   ECONOMICS, 26
envious An e. heart makes a treacherous ear   ENVY, 5
environment The e. is man's first right   THE ENVIRONMENT, 17
won't have a society . . . destroy the e.   THE ENVIRONMENT, 8
envy e. is a kind of praise   ENVY, 4
E. will merit as its shade pursue   ENVY, 7
ephemeral all /The lessons are e.   TRANSIENCE, 3
epic e. disappeared along with . . . heroism   HEROISM, 13
epidemic living this e. every minute   AIDS, 7
epidemics E. . . . . more influential than statesmen and soldiers   ILLNESS, 8
Epipsychidion understand *E.* best when you are in love   LITERATURE, 35
epoch a new e. in the history of the world   FRENCH REVOLUTION, 5
Every e. bears its own ending   ENDING, 5
Epstein If people . . . a thousand years hence . . . found E.'s statues   CIVILIZATION, 17
equal All men are e.   EQUALITY, 7
all men are e. is a proposition   EQUALITY, 9
all were created e. by nature   SLAVERY, 6
E. wealth and opportunities of culture   CLASS, 4
Everybody should have an e. chance   EQUALITY, 29
equality E. . . . . is the thing   EQUALITY, 23
e. . . . . with our superiors   EQUALITY, 4
e. is an ethical aspiration   EQUALITY, 22
e. of the white and black races   RACISM, 20
e. pulls everyone down   EQUALITY, 19
pushes for e. . . . . is declared 'PC'   EQUALITY, 1
eras When e. die . . . left to strange police   THE PAST, 15
Eros capitalist society has converted E. into an employee   CAPITALISM, 38
erotic E. practices have been diversified   SEX, 9
erotica E. is about sexuality   PORNOGRAPHY, 9
eroticism E. has its own moral justification   SEXUALITY, 10
err to e. in opinion . . . is at least human   MISTAKES, 13
To e. is human; to forgive, divine   FORGIVENESS, 10
error a political e. to practice deceit   DECEPTION, 15
show a man that he is in an e.   UNDERSTANDING, 5
errors e. do not count as failures in science   MISTAKES, 7
e. in religion are dangerous   MISTAKES, 8
escape There is only one way left to e.   MODERNITY, 2
estimate e. what we do . . . from instinct   HUMAN NATURE, 27
eternal of e. importance, like baseball   CLOTHES, 9
real, true, e. love   DELUSIONS OF LOVE, 3
The e. . . . . makes for righteousness   RIGHTEOUSNESS, 1
We feel . . . we are e.   IMMORTALITY, 19
eternally He who is e. without desire   DESIRE, 8
eternity A circular e. may seem atrocious   ETERNITY, 2
All things from e. . . . . come round in a circle   ETERNITY, 8
E.'s a terrible thought   ETERNITY, 9
E. was in that moment   ETERNITY, 5
I saw E. the other night   ETERNITY, 10
PRESENT, . . . part of e. dividing   THE PRESENT, 4
Who can speak of e. without a solecism   ETERNITY, 3
ethical e. behavior should be based . . . on sympathy   MORALITY, 9
I lost my e. compass   MORALITY, 2
ethics The condition of all human e.   MORALITY, 46
Eton the playing fields of E.   SPORTS AND GAMES, 23
eureka E.   DISCOVERY, 1
Europe any other E. than . . . Europe of states   EUROPE, 14

expenditure E. rises to meet income ECONOMICS, 23
expensive The most e. habit in the world is celluloid not
heroin FILMS, 44
experience all e. is an arch EXPERIENCE, 17
E. . . . name everyone gives to their mistakes
EXPERIENCE, 19
E. is a good teacher EXPERIENCE, 1
E. isn't interesting till it begins to repeat EXPERIENCE, 5
E. is never limited EXPERIENCE, 10
E. is the mother of science EXPERIENCE, 14
e. of life . . . drawn from life EXPERIENCE, 4
E. teaches slowly EXPERIENCE, 7
fairest thing we can e. . . . the mysterious WONDER, 2
To a great e. one thing is essential EXPERIENCE, 2
What e. and history teach HISTORY, 46
experiment E. alone crowns the efforts of medicine
EXPERIMENTS, 8
single e. can prove me wrong EXPERIMENTS, 3
explain If I could e. it to . . . average person ARROGANCE, 3
You e. nothing, O poet POETS, 14
explained A world that can be e. MYTHS, 3
explanation Your e. had the ring of truth TRUTH, 49
exploitation E. and manipulation produce boredom and
triviality EXPLOITATION, 4
explore E. thyself SELF-KNOWLEDGE, 39
exploring E. is delightful to look forward to EXPLORATION, 3
explosion a quiet e. in your head WRITING, 48
exposes A man who e. himself when . . . intoxicated
DRUNKENNESS, 15
express e. what I really am through light FILMS, 47
It is better not to e. what one means COMMUNICATION, 10
exterminate E. all the brutes IMPERIALISM, 4
exterminating members of the e. profession TOTALITARIANISM, 5
extinction threat of universal e. EXTINCTION, 1
extraordinary How e. ordinary /things are WONDER, 4
extravagance e. . . . thrift and adventure seldom go hand
in hand EXTRAVAGANCE, 1
extreme E. justice is e. injury EXTREMES, 6
E. justice is e. injustice INJUSTICE, 5
E. remedies . . . for e. diseases REMEDIES, 14
leave one e. . . . rush into the opposite REASON, 27
extremism e. . . . defence of liberty is no vice LIBERTY, 15
exuberance E. is Beauty BEAUTY, 4
exult How you'd e. if I could put you back TIME, 7
exultantly Walk not on the earth e. HUMILITY, 11
eye all looks yellow to the jaundiced e. CYNICISM, 8
an e. for an e. leaves everybody blind TOLERANCE, 3
e. for e. REVENGE, 3
He had but one e. THE FACE, 7
less in this than meets the e. CRITICISM, 3
My e. . . . woke me SORROW, 1
the sort of e. . . . open an oyster THE FACE, 19
eye-lids the opening e. of the morn MORNING, 11
eyes bein' only e. . . . my vision's limited SENSES, 6
His e. flamed red with devilish passion
THE SUPERNATURAL, 35
I gave her e. my own e. to take FLIRTATION, 1
Open your e. and look within SELF-KNOWLEDGE, 27
People who shut their e. to reality INNOCENCE, 2
The e. and the hand of Picasso ARTISTS, 1
The e. of a lover tell lies DELUSIONS OF LOVE, 1
The e. will see no evil colours BABIES, 1
Your e. shine like the pants FLATTERY, 8
fable The f. is the best storytelling device FANTASY, 4
fables Man is fed with f. through life DELUSION, 7
fabulous How f., in a bathtub, in Paris DEATH AND DYING, 54
fabulously man believes himself f. capable of creation
CREATIVITY, 20
face a f. like a benediction THE FACE, 5
a gross and repulsive f. LITERARY INSULTS, 25

At 50 . . . the f. he deserves MIDDLE AGE, 10
f. looks like a wedding cake THE FACE, 1
from whose f. the earth and the heaven fled JUDGMENT, 10
her f. in speech . . . a lighted window SPEECH, 10
his f. fell out of the mirror DESPAIR, 2
The f. of 'evil' . . . face of . . . need EVIL, 8
The f. the index of a feeling mind THE FACE, 6
The more serious the f. SERIOUSNESS, 2
Who has seen the f. of the God GOD, 46
faces he wears . . . two f. WRITERS, 16
facetious to be f. . . . not necessary to be indecent
INSULTS, 38
fact A f. is like a sack FACTS, 12
a physical f. denotes a state of consciousness ARTISTS, 42
factory In the f. we make cosmetics BUSINESS, 23
facts a good body of f. . . . not . . . a principle FACTS, 4
F. alone are wanted in life FACTS, 5
F. are not science FACTS, 6
F. are ventriloquists' dummies FACTS, 8
F. can't be recounted FACTS, 2
F. do not cease to exist FACTS, 7
F. do not make history FACTS, 1
f. must never get in the way of truth JOURNALISM, 5
F. speak louder than statistics FACTS, 14
F. to be dealt with, as the sea FACTS, 10
People who mistake f. for ideas . . . gossips FACTS, 11
The f. are to blame, my friend FACTS, 13
treat your f. with imagination FACTS, 3
fading How f. are the joys TRANSIENCE, 22
fail I would sooner f. than not be among the greatest
AMBITION, 14
to f. conventionally REPUTATION, 14
failing f. . . . greatest arts in the world FAILURE, 9
F. is good FAILURE, 5
failings even his f. leaned to virtue's side GOOD, 11
man's greatest f. . . . excuse in the misfortune
ALIBIS AND EXCUSES, 5
failure f. . . . only thing that worked predictably FAILURE, 8
F. is inevitable FAILURE, 13
F. is success's only launching pad FAILURE, 10
failures f. . . . an explosion of virulent cells FAILURE, 11
fainted He f. on his vengefulness FORGIVENESS, 7
fair all's f. in love and war DECEPTION, 13
He that builds a f. house HOUSES, 1
Who'd see the F. FESTIVALS, 1
fairest the f. things have the worst fate TRANSIENCE, 20
fairies There are f. at the bottom of our garden FAIRIES, 2
fairy tales F. . . . temporary and permanent solutions
STORYTELLING, 3
faith But F., fanatic F. FAITH, 12
F. . . . a charisma not granted to all FAITH, 8
F. . . . an illogical belief FAITH, 11
F. . . . believing . . . beyond the power of reason
FAITH, 17
F. is necessary to victory FAITH, 7
f. is the substance of things hoped for FAITH, 3
f. today . . . struggle for liberation CHRISTIANITY, 16
If ye have f. as a grain of mustard seed FAITH, 5
Nothing in life is more wonderful than f. FAITH, 13
To believe only possibilities, is not f. BELIEF, 6
Without f. nothing is possible FAITH, 2
faithful if you had been f. FAITHFULNESS, 3
falcon Soaring f., noble Poet, come to my aid POETS, 30
Falklands F. . . . a fight between two bald men BRITISH
IMPERIALISM, 3
fall Whenever you f., pick up something ACCIDENTS, 2
fallacy great f. is that the game is . . . about winning
SPORTS AND GAMES, 3
falling I have a feeling I'm f. PARANOIA, 2
We were f. women LOVE, 3

false beware of f. prophets — PROPHECY, 1
　By the glare of f. science betray'd — BETRAYAL, 2
　F. face must hide what the f. heart — DECEPTION, 28
　In a f. quarrel there is no true valour — ARGUMENTS, 19
falsehood unmask f., and bring truth to light — TIME, 56
fame F. . . . the quintessence of all the misunderstandings — FAME, 23
　F. and tranquility can never be bedfellows — FAME, 16
　F. creates its own standard — FAME, 8
　F. is a constant effort — FAME, 22
　F. is a food — FAME, 9
　F. is a powerful aphrodisiac — FAME, 11
　F. is like a river — FAME, 1
　F. is sometimes like unto a . . . mushroom — FAME, 10
　F. is the spur — FAME, 15
　I handle f. by not being famous — FAME, 14
　I owe my f. only to myself — FAME, 7
　Love of f. is the last thing — FAME, 27
　What is f. — TRANSIENCE, 14
　What is the end of f. — FAME, 4
families All happy f. resemble one another — FAMILY, 24
　F. ain't just born — FAMILY, 10
　Good f. are generally worse — FAMILY, 8
　There are only two f. in the world — INEQUALITY, 4
family A f. with the wrong members in control — ENGLAND, 22
　f. . . . most ridiculous and least respectable — FAMILY, 4
　f. always creeps back — FAMILY, 17
　F. is a mixed blessing — FAMILY, 19
　I am the f. face — FAMILY, 6
　preservation of f. and community values — SOCIETY, 5
　the f. . . . source of all our discontents — FAMILY, 12
　The f. is strongest where objective reality — FAMILY, 5
　The f., that . . . octopus . . . we never quite escape — FAMILY, 22
family tree It is hazardous to shake a f. — FAMILY, 23
famine They . . . die by f. die by inches — HUNGER, 12
　you look as if there were f. in the land — HUNGER, 19
famous awoke one morning . . . found myself f. — FAME, 5
　everyone will be f. for 15 minutes — FAME, 30
　f. men have the whole earth — FAME, 21
　I'll make thee f. by my pen — WRITING, 47
　so f., that it would permit me . . . to break wind — FAME, 2
　To f. men all the earth . . . sepulchre — FAME, 28
　What are you f. *for* — FAME, 18
　Why am I so f. — FAME, 25
fanatic f. . . . does what he thinks — FANATICISM, 2
　f. . . . over-compensates a secret doubt — FANATICISM, 5
fanatical F. enthusiasm . . . mark of the real man — FANATICISM, 11
fanaticism They charge me with f. — FANATICISM, 13
fanatics F. have their dreams — FANATICISM, 8
fancy F. is . . . a mode of memory — IMAGINATION, 5
fantasies A thousand f. . . . throng into my memory — FANTASY, 11
fantasy A f. can be equivalent — FANTASY, 7
　a solitary f. can totally transform — FANTASY, 1
　live in a f. world — REALITY, 20
far As f. as we can see — EMIGRATION, 8
farce f. or a comedy is best played — THEATRE, 8
　longest-running f. in the West End — PARLIAMENTS AND ASSEMBLIES, 13
　There is no greater f. than . . . democracy — DEMOCRACY, 5
farmer good f. is . . . a handy man — OCCUPATIONS, 8
farthing burning a f. candle at Dover — LITERARY INSULTS, 28
fascism F. is . . . the future refusing to be born — FASCISM, 3
　F. is a religion — FASCISM, 2
　F. is not an article for export — FASCISM, 7
　F. is the open, terrorist dictatorship — FASCISM, 1
　F. means war — FASCISM, 12
　F. was a fairly popular political philosophy — FASCISM, 14

For F. the State is absolute — FASCISM, 9
fashion a dedicated follower of f. — FASHION, 4
　f. . . . creating authority through provocation — FASHION, 7
　F. . . . image of an age — FASHION, 3
　F. . . . sub-art and . . . not intellectual — FASHION, 6
　f. . . . wear what suits you — CLOTHES, 13
　F.'s job . . . combat the tedium of routine — FASHION, 5
　F.—a word which knaves and fools may use — FASHION, 2
　F. is about profit and expansion — FASHION, 17
　F. is made to become unfashionable — FASHION, 1
　God, f. moves fast — FASHION, 10
　love of f. makes the economy go — FASHION, 18
　One cannot f. a credible deterrent — NUCLEAR WEAPONS, 4
fashionable an idea . . . to be f. is ominous — FASHION, 14
fashions Every man f. and stays with the gods — GOD, 52
　F., . . . are only induced epidemics — FASHION, 16
faster F. than a speeding bullet — HEROISM, 18
　f. you go, the worse it is — SPACE, 2
　Will you walk a little f.? — NONSENSE, 3
fat till the f. lady sings — OPERA, 4
fatal f. question . . . the meaning of their lives — MEANING, 8
　Yes, I am a f. man — PASSION, 14
fate f. and character are the same conception — CHARACTER, 22
　F. chooses your relations — FRIENDSHIP, 3
　it is . . . our f. . . . to lose innocence — INNOCENCE, 4
　It is F. that draws the plan — FATE, 10
　We may become the makers of our f. — FATE, 19
fated We have been f. to live together — MIDDLE EAST, 29
father a wise f. that knows his own child — FATHERS, 4
　f. whose son raises . . . hand against him — FATHERS, 6
　I wish either my f. or . . . mother — PARENTS, 12
　my f. moved through dooms of love — FATHERS, 2
　My f. was a slave — PATRIOTISM, 23
　No man is responsible for his f. — FATHERS, 10
fatherland One F., One State, One Leader — FASCISM, 5
　the filth of my f. — HOME, 8
Faulkner F.'s hallucinatory tendencies — AMERICAN LITERATURE, 4
fault never commit a f. — HUMAN NATURE, 29
　only f. is that he has no f. — PERFECTION, 10
faultless F. to a fault — PERFECTION, 3
faults If we had no f. of our own — VICE, 9
　When you have f. — SELF-KNOWLEDGE, 8
favorite These are a few of my f. things — PLEASURE, 13
fear f. and deny the reality of death — DEATH AND DYING, 36
　f. clawed at my mind and body — FEAR, 13
　F. has many eyes — FEAR, 8
　f. in a handful of dust — FEAR, 12
　f. in passing judgment — JUDGMENT, 7
　F. is of being in the world — FEAR, 28
　F. is the parent of cruelty — CRUELTY, 1
　F. is very exciting — FEAR, 22
　F. lent wings to his feet — FEAR, 34
　f. of one evil leads us into a worse — EVIL, 4
　F. prophets . . . and those prepared to die — FANATICISM, 3
　f. weakens judgment most — FEAR, 25
　greatest f. for . . . the theatre — THEATRE, 5
　I f. God . . . and I have no other f. — FEAR, 24
　I learned not to f. infinity — INFINITY, 6
　It was the f. of himself — FATHERS, 1
　only thing we have to f. is f. itself — FEAR, 26
　the f. of being ourselves — THE SELF, 19
　Three years . . . spent between f. and hope — STORYTELLING, 12
fearful Nothing gives a f. man more courage — COURAGE, 3
fears A man who f. suffering — SUFFERING, 16
　f. that I may cease to be — MORTALITY, 4
feathers not only fine f. . . . make fine birds — CHARACTER, 1
feedeth he f. among the lilies — LOVERS, 2
feel how you really f. about someone — EMOTION, 11
feeling A man gets tired of f. too much — EMOTION, 13

F. . . . not a special class of psychical facts   SENSES, 5
F. is the subjective side of consciousness   SUBJECTIVITY, 2
feelings f. time cannot benumb   EMOTION, 1
feet my f. . . . little time on the ground   SPORTS AND GAMES, 17
My f., so deep in the earth   POETS, 36
those f. in ancient time   ENGLAND, 2
felicity f. consists not in the outward and visible   HAPPINESS, 38
Fellini I can understand F.   FILMS, 21
female a f. goes over the boundary from childhood   GROWING UP, 4
image of the f. . . . all boobs and buttocks   SEXISM, 3
Our great poet-teacher, has given us 126 . . . f. characters   CHARACTER, 12
see the F. Eunuch the world over   WOMEN, 22
femininity where in the world did I put my f.   WOMEN, 20
feminism F. is an entire world view   WOMEN'S RIGHTS, 7
violent backlash against f.   WOMEN'S RIGHTS, 41
feminist f. movement will . . . rise from . . . Arab lands   WOMEN'S RIGHTS, 34
fervor F. is the weapon of choice of the impotent   FANATICISM, 4
fetus A f. is a benign tumor   PREGNANCY, 4
fever F. the eternal reproach   ILLNESS, 20
few f. historians . . . diligent enough   HISTORIANS, 13
fiber Every f. of me is thrilling   EUPHORIA, 5
fiction F. is indispensable for mankind   FICTION, 9
f. is made of that which is real   FICTION, 3
f. which . . . put out boundaries   WRITERS, 33
If f. is the suprareal spirit   FICTION, 8
no longer any such thing as f.   FICTION, 2
She regarded me as a piece of f.   MOTHERS, 13
fictions We live in a world ruled by f.   FICTION, 1
field What though the f. be lost   DETERMINATION, 6
fiend forgive the f. for becoming a torrent   POLITICAL INSULTS, 36
fier You k'n hide de f.   RUMOUR, 2
fifteen At f. I set my heart on learning   AGE, 6
F. men on the dead man's chest   DRUNKENNESS, 22
we might more reasonably expect f. years of peace   EUROPE, 30
fifth One f. of the people are against everything   CYNICISM, 5
fifty You'll see, when you're f.   AGE, 24
fig A f. for those by law protected   SELF-INTEREST, 2
fight don't want to f., but, by jingo   BRITISH IMPERIALISM, 15
easier to f. for one's principles   PRINCIPLES, 1
f. in your own cause . . . committed to winning   COMMITMENT, 4
f. like hell for the living   LOYALTY, 5
f. to save wild beauty . . . democracy   PROTEST, 18
If you f. against all your sensations   SENSES, 7
Never f. fair with a stranger   STRANGERS, 3
The only time . . . ever put up a f.   INSULTS, 10
We f. . . . to set a country free   AMERICAN WAR OF INDEPENDENCE, 8
we shall f. on the beaches   WORLD WAR II, 7
Why f. against the flesh   POETS, 26
fighting f. in the street   FIGHTING, 3
F. is like champagne   FIGHTING, 7
not fifty ways of f. . . . only one   FIGHTING, 5
figure f. that out   CLARITY, 2
figures don't have to be good with f.   EXPLOITATION, 3
file my f. . . . lost . . . means my disappearance   IDENTITY, 6
filling F. her compact & delicious body   FOOD, 2
film A f. must be alive   FILMS, 34
F. . . . dust and heat and noise   FILMS, 29
f. . . . petrified fountain of thought   FILMS, 4
f. has to be close to music   FILMS, 23
f. has to be preceded by . . . dream   FILMS, 51
I like a f. to have a beginning   FILMS, 13
No matter if the f. is banned   CENSORSHIP, 29

To make a f. . . . improve on life   FILMS, 49
you want to make the greatest f.   FILMS, 6
films All f. are subversive   FILMS, 7
all f. are surrealist   FILMS, 31
good European f. . . . turning . . . into very bad American   HOLLYWOOD, 6
modern f. . . . close-ups of people's feet   FILMS, 10
film script A good f. . . . without dialogue   FILMS, 27
filths F. savour but themselves   GOOD, 26
final solution The f. of the Jewish problem   THE HOLOCAUST, 3
fine art F. can only be . . . exclusive   ARTISTIC STYLES, 20
F. has its own . . . tradition   ARTISTIC STYLES, 21
finest their f. hour   WORLD WAR II, 8
finger a f. in every pie   GREED, 3
fingers f. of a man's hand, and wrote   THE SUPERNATURAL, 2
Just as my f. . . . Make music   MUSIC, 30
finite All f. things reveal infinitude   INFINITY, 5
We are f. beings   KNOWLEDGE, 29
fire bound /Upon a wheel of f.   SUFFERING, 24
falsely shouting 'F.!' in a theater   FREE SPEECH, 3
f. in his eye . . . fever in his blood   POETS, 33
f. near Fish Street in London   FIRE, 4
F., /O enemy and image of ourselves   FIRE, 6
I live between . . . f. and the plague   POETRY, 1
Look not for f. in Hell   HELL, 7
The beauty of f. from . . . embers   MEMORY, 30
fires Big f. flare up   FIRE, 5
burning f. . . . threatening to consume   DETERMINATION, 10
fireside Sit by the f. with Sorrow   SORROW, 26
firm not a family; we're a f.   MONARCHY, 17
Nothing stays f. forever . . . everything vanishes   TRANSIENCE, 15
first what to put f.   WRITING, 40
First World War We mutually agreed to call it *The F.*   WORLD WAR I, 25
fish neither f. nor beast is the otter   ANIMALS, 19
The f. in the water is silent   HUMANKIND, 49
fishes f. live in the sea   OPPRESSION, 12
fit a pleasing f. of melancholy   MELANCHOLY, 9
Fitzgerald F. was an alcoholic   AMERICAN LITERATURE, 7
Fitzgeralds The F. . . . were the sights   AMERICAN LITERATURE, 27
fixed God deliver you . . . from a f. idea   IDEAS, 13
flag the f. to which you have pledged allegiance   PATRIOTISM, 3
flame a tiny withered f. . . . we have to rebel   THE SUPERNATURAL, 15
Flanders In F. fields   WORLD WAR I, 19
flatter F. the mountain-tops with sovereign eye   MORNING, 15
not f. me   REALISM, 1
flattered He that loves to be f. is worthy o' the flatterer   FLATTERY, 10
flatterers f. live at the expense of those who listen   FLATTERY, 7
flattering f. some men to endure them   FLATTERY, 5
talent of f. with delicacy   FLATTERY, 1
flattery A little f. will support a man   FLATTERY, 9
consider whether . . . your f. is worth his having   FLATTERY, 6
Everyone likes f.   MONARCHY, 10
f.'s the food of fools   FLATTERY, 15
f. hurts no one . . . if he doesn't inhale   FLATTERY, 12
Imitation is the sincerest form of f.   IMITATION, 3
None are more taken in with f. than the proud, who wish to be the first and are not   FLATTERY, 11
The f. of posterity   FLATTERY, 2
flaunt if you've got it, f. it   BEAUTY, 7
fled I f. Him, down the nights   GOD, 58
Fleming had F. not possessed immense knowledge   SCIENTISTS, 17
flesh 'Tis the way of all f.   HUMAN NATURE, 30

frames The finest collection of f.   INSULTS, 12
France all roads lead to F.   WORLD WAR I, 29
   For us, sons of F.   POLITICS, 32
   F. . . . eternal resort of Germany   EUROPEAN COUNTRIES, 54
   F. . . . forever the soldier of the Ideal   WORLD WAR I, 1
   F. before everything   PATRIOTISM, 17
   F. has lost a battle   WORLD WAR II, 12
   F. has more need of me   BOASTS, 13
   F. has neither winter nor summer nor morals   EUROPEAN COUNTRIES, 58
   F. is revolutionary or . . . nothing at all   EUROPEAN COUNTRIES, 42
   F., mother of arts   EUROPEAN COUNTRIES, 21
   F. was a long despotism   EUROPEAN COUNTRIES, 15
   I am bored with F.   EUROPEAN COUNTRIES, 7
   I have chased . . . English out of F.   EUROPEAN COUNTRIES, 43
Franco I picked F. out   DICTATORS, 1
Franklin not one Aretha F. . . . hundreds of women   SINGERS AND SINGING, 4
fraud one f., the other fornication   CITIES, 9
freakish The f. is no longer a private zone   EXTREMES, 4
free All human beings are born f. and equal   HUMAN RIGHTS, 16
   all men are by nature equally f.   HUMAN RIGHTS, 10
   ask to be f. . . . butterflies are f.   FREEDOM, 12
   In a f. society the state . . . administers justice among men   GOVERNMENT, 32
   Man was born f.   FREEDOM, 47
   O f., strong people . . . brave race   EUROPEAN COUNTRIES, 16
   order you to hold a f. election   MONARCHY, 21
   So f. we seem   FREEDOM, 5
   there are . . . no f. beings   FREEDOM, 13
   We are not f., separate, and independent entities   HUMAN CONDITION, 14
   We must be f. or die   ENGLAND, 32
   We must f. ourselves from . . . nation states   NATIONS, 1
freed He f. a thousand slaves   SLAVERY, 2
freedom cannot defend f. abroad by deserting   FREEDOM, 41
   fit to use their f.   FREEDOM, 33
   F. . . . never voluntarily given up   FREEDOM, 30
   F. . . . the disciplined overcoming of self   FREEDOM, 40
   f.'s battle   FREEDOM, 6
   F. and Whisky gang tegither   ALCOHOL, 3
   F. brings responsibilities   COLONIALISM, 8
   F. does not consist . . . dream of independence   FREEDOM, 19
   F.! Equality! Brotherhood   FRENCH REVOLUTION, 10
   f. flame . . . never be put down   FREEDOM, 35
   F. has a thousand charms   FREEDOM, 11
   F. has many flaws   COLD WAR, 7
   F. has never been free   FREEDOM, 20
   F. in economic arrangements   FREEDOM, 22
   F. is . . . the f. for the one who thinks differently   FREEDOM, 32
   F. is always somewhere else   FREEDOM, 1
   F. is a more complex . . . thing than force   FREEDOM, 37
   F. is an indivisible word   FREEDOM, 53
   f. is f. from poverty   FREEDOM, 51
   f. is something people take   FREEDOM, 3
   F. is the most-used word   FREEDOM, 28
   F. is the right to be wrong   FREEDOM, 14
   F. is the right to tell people   FREE SPEECH, 8
   F. lives only in . . . dreams   FREEDOM, 49
   F. of men under government   LAW, 24
   f. of person   FREEDOM, 29
   f. of speech, f. of conscience   CIVIL RIGHTS, 13
   F. of the press in Britain   FREE SPEECH, 7
   f. without discipline is anarchy; discipline without f. is tyranny   FREEDOM, 44
   He who believes in f. of the will   FREEDOM, 16
   How good can f. be   POVERTY, 33

I am free, deliver me from f.   FREEDOM, 8
If f. were not so economically efficient   ECONOMICS, 10
None can love f. heartily, but good men   FREEDOM, 39
our f. to determine our own future   AFRICAN COUNTRIES, 14
right to be let alone . . . beginning of all f.   FREEDOM, 15
So greatly did she care for f. that she died for it   MARTYRDOM, 8
The f. of the press   FREE SPEECH, 7
the idea of F.   DEMOCRACY, 38
The price of f. can never be too high   FREEDOM, 42
There is no easy walk to f. anywhere   FREEDOM, 34
This f., this liberty, this beautiful / . . . thing   FREEDOM, 26
Those who deny f. to others   OPPRESSION, 6
to reap the blessings of f.   FREEDOM, 45
what is F.   FREEDOM, 10
When f. came   SLAVERY, 32
Who ever walked behind anyone to f.?   EQUALITY, 25
yearning for f. . . . suppressed but never destroyed   FREEDOM, 25
You only get your f. by sweating   ART, 38
Your f. and mine cannot be separated   FREEDOM, 36
freedoms few remaining f. . . . the blank page   FREE SPEECH, 6
   four essential human f.   FREEDOM, 46
free lunch no such thing as a f.   MONEY, 2
free market f. . . . legitimate through democratic institutions   CAPITALISM, 10
free-market our f. system was not nature   ECONOMICS, 13
free speech f. will be extinguished   AMERICAN IMPERIALISM, 23
free thought a horrible example of f.   INDIVIDUALITY, 8
free will We have to believe in f. We've got no choice   FREEDOM, 50
French Food isolates the F.   EUROPEAN COUNTRIES, 62
   F. . . . big in the culture business   INTELLECTUALS, 6
   F. rhetorical models are too narrow   PHILOSOPHY, 30
   F. want no one to be their *superior*   PRIDE, 12
   Imagine the Lord talking F.   GOD, 23
   The F. . . . united under the threat of danger   EUROPEAN COUNTRIES, 20
   The F., for all their slogans, are becoming modern   EUROPEAN COUNTRIES, 61
   The F. took three years of struggle   EUROPEAN COUNTRIES, 4
   to the F. the empire of the land   IMPERIALISM, 19
   What is not clear is not F.   EUROPEAN LANGUAGES, 3
French Revolution too early . . . judgement on the F.   FRENCH REVOLUTION, 17
Freud F. . . . never had to play the old Glasgow Empire   HUMOUR, 5
   F. . . . propound a new myth   MYTHS, 14
   F. is all nonsense   NEUROSIS, 15
   F. is midwife to the soul   PSYCHOANALYSIS, 13
Freudian importance of . . . F. concept of the Unconscious   CONSCIOUSNESS, 6
friend A F. . . . the masterpiece of Nature   FRIENDSHIP, 14
   a f. in need   FRIENDSHIP, 33
   A f. should bear his friend's infirmities   FRIENDSHIP, 37
   being a f. . . . mastering the art of timing   FRIENDSHIP, 30
   Each f. represents a world in us   FRIENDSHIP, 31
   f. . . . enough to tell him disagreeable truths   FRIENDSHIP, 28
   f. is another self   FRIENDSHIP, 1
   f. of virtue and not of fortune   VIRTUE, 26
   good f. that she will throw   FRIENDSHIP, 44
   He makes no f.   FRIENDSHIP, 45
   the f. of all humanity is not my f.   MISANTHROPY, 7
   What trusty treasure . . . can countervail a f.   FRIENDSHIP, 18
   Whenever a f. succeeds   ENVY, 11
friends Don't tell your f. their social faults   FRIENDSHIP, 40
   F. are God's apology for relations   FRIENDSHIP, 23
   F., carve a monument /out of dream stone   POETS, 42
   Have no f. not equal   FRIENDSHIP, 12

You shouldn't say it is not g.   AESTHETICS, 5
goodbye science of saying g.   PARTING, 6
goodbyes never any good dwelling on g.   PARTING, 1
good example if the lower orders don't set us a g.   CLASS, 38
good man You was a g.   GOOD, 13
goodness G. does not . . . make men happy   GOOD, 18
goodnight G., my darlings   LAST WORDS, 3
goods All social primary g. . . . distributed equally   EQUALITY, 24
good will A g. is . . . good in itself   GOOD, 16
goose Lone g. . . . yearns for the flock   LONELINESS, 3
gordian She was a g. shape of dazzling hue   FAIRIES, 3
gorilla these g. damnifications of humanity   EVOLUTION, 4
gospel Either this is not the g.   CHRISTIANITY, 13
The g. is meant to . . . afflict the comfortable   CHRISTIANITY, 11
gossip Men . . . detested women's g.   GOSSIP, 4
gossips No one g. about . . . secret virtues   GOSSIP, 8
gothic G. cathedral . . . a blossoming in stone   ARCHITECTURE, 6
gout When I have the g. . . . I was walking on my eyeballs   SUFFERING, 25
govern I will g. according to the common weal   GOVERNMENT, 25
Let the people think they g.   GOVERNMENT, 45
No man is good enough to g. another man   DEMOCRACY, 28
government a g. organization could do it that quickly   BUREAUCRACY, 4
art of g. is to deal with threats   GOVERNMENT, 29
Do not adopt the best system of g.   GOVERNMENT, 9
Every g. degenerates   GOVERNMENT, 26
function of a g. . . . to calm   GOVERNMENT, 44
function of g. . . . easy for us to do good   GOVERNMENT, 14
good g. . . . less, not more, democracy   GOVERNMENT, 36
g. . . . big enough to give you all you want   GOVERNMENT, 19
g. . . . built upon the rights of the people   GOVERNMENT, 51
G. . . . instituted for the common benefit   GOVERNMENT, 38
G., . . . is but a necessary evil   GOVERNMENT, 43
G. . . . organized benevolence or organized madness   GOVERNMENT, 54
G.'s purposes are beneficent   LIBERTY, 4
G. gives me a count of corpses   ASSASSINATION, 10
g. gives us is charity at election time   CENTRAL AMERICA, 3
G. intervention . . . benefit of economic progress   GOVERNMENT, 8
G. is a contrivance of human wisdom   GOVERNMENT, 11
g. is best in which every man   GOVERNMENT, 2
g. is best which governs not at all   GOVERNMENT, 53
G. is not the solution . . . government is the problem   GOVERNMENT, 47
G. is the common enemy   GOVERNMENT, 6
No G. . . . long secure without . . . Opposition   GOVERNMENT, 15
no necessary evils in g.   GOVERNMENT, 24
people's g.   DEMOCRACY, 48
the g. and the governed in opposition   GOVERNMENT, 27
The g. burns down whole cities   OPPRESSION, 8
The g. must always be in advance of the public opinion   GOVERNMENT, 3
The g. of the absolute majority   GOVERNMENT, 13
The important thing for G.   GOVERNMENT, 28
The object of g. . . . is not the glory of rulers   GOVERNMENT, 7
there was no form of g. common to the peoples   REPUBLICANISM, 5
the things which g. does . . . social progress   SOCIALISM, 12
The worst g. is the most moral   GOVERNMENT, 39
We had believed the g. was eternal   SOUTH AMERICA, 6

governments G. need . . . both shepherds and butchers   GOVERNMENT, 55
g. to choose only *between* evils   GOVERNMENT, 42
grace G. under pressure   COURAGE, 5
gracehoper G. was always jigging ajog   HAPPINESS, 25
Graces the G. do not seem . . . natives of Great Britain   BRITAIN, 10
grammar G., which can govern even kings   GRAMMAR, 11
I am . . . above g.   GRAMMAR, 13
grammatical refine our language to g. purity   GRAMMAR, 9
grammere G., that grounde is of al   GRAMMAR, 10
grand G. Inquisitor came into the room   FEAR, 14
Grand Canyon coming across him at the G.   LITERARY INSULTS, 47
Grand Central Station By G. I Sat Down and Wept   AMERICAN CITIES, 38
grandeur beauty and g. of The One State   TOTALITARIANISM, 11
g. of the dooms   GREATNESS, 11
grapes I am sure the g. are sour   ENVY, 1
grasshoppers G. . . . are exceptionally nutritious food   FOOD, 9
gratitude g. . . . a secret hope for greater favours   GRATITUDE, 7
G., like love, is never . . . dependable   GRATITUDE, 1
The still small voice of g.   GRATITUDE, 6
gratuities g. rather than any direct bribe   BRIBERY, 4
grave G., . . . place in which the dead are laid   DEATH AND DYING, 6
one foot already in the g.   OLD AGE, 32
They give birth astride of a g.   MORTALITY, 1
graveyard A g. for pleasure   PAINTING, 1
gravity alters the . . . g. of the universe   THE UNIVERSE, 3
great Almost everything that is g.   ACHIEVEMENT, 6
g., ere fortune made him   GREATNESS, 7
G. men are but life-sized   GREATNESS, 1
No g. man lives in vain   GREATNESS, 5
The g. man . . . walks across his century   GREATNESS, 12
those who were truly g.   GREATNESS, 18
To be g. is to be misunderstood   GREATNESS, 8
great-aunt A person may be indebted . . . a g.   FAMILY, 7
Great Britain G. has lost an Empire   BRITISH IMPERIALISM, 1
greater g. love hath no man   SELFLESSNESS, 1
g. than the *Iliad*   LITERATURE, 46
Something . . . which nothing g. can be thought   EXISTENCE, 1
The g. the power   POWER, 4
greatest g., nor the worst of men   DICTATORS, 3
greatness g. in goodness   GOOD, 3
measure g. . . . from the manger up   GREATNESS, 10
Men who have g. . . . don't go in for politics   POLITICIANS, 7
some have g. thrust upon 'em   GREATNESS, 16
Greece G.! sad relic   EUROPEAN COUNTRIES, 12
greed G. . . . bottomless pit which exhausts   GREED, 6
G. is essential to the proper functioning   GREED, 5
Greek it was G. to me   CONFUSION, 7
mixture of smells . . . anthology of a G. holiday   TRAVEL, 12
Greeks G. . . . practical and open-minded   EUROPEAN COUNTRIES, 19
greetings perhaps the g. are intended for me   CELEBRITY, 2
grey hair There is only one cure for g. . . . the guillotine   EXECUTION, 20
grief A g. too much to be told   SORROW, 31
between g. and nothing I will take g.   SORROW, 7
calms one's g. by recounting it   BEREAVEMENT, 4
G. and disappointment give rise to anger   EMOTION, 7
G. has turned her fair   BEREAVEMENT, 12
G. tears his heart . . . In all the raging impotence of woe   BEREAVEMENT, 9
My g. and my smile   MOTHERS, 9
No man can cause more g.   TRADITIONS, 2

When one g. afflicts us we choose a sharper g.
SORROW, 32

you . . . must first feel g. SYMPATHY, 4

grievance a g. is . . . a purpose in life INJUSTICE, 9

grin ending with the g., which remained some time
ANIMALS, 14

groaning hear the g. of oppressed people OPPRESSION, 10

Groucho No, G. is not my real name NAMES, 13

group A g. of closely related persons FAMILY, 14

groupies We don't get g. POPULAR MUSIC, 34

growing up I wasn't good /At g. GROWING UP, 5

So much of g. is an unbearable waiting GROWING UP, 9

growl a fellow . . . who does nothing . . . but . . . g.
COWARDICE, 5

grown-ups g. . . . have forgotten what it is like to be a
child ADULTHOOD, 4

grows Nothing g. in our garden BABIES, 11

Nothing g. well in the shade SCULPTURE, 2

growth G. is a greater mystery than death GROWING UP, 7

grub First comes the g., then . . . morals MORALITY, 4

grudges I don't hold . . . g. more'n five years FORGIVENESS, 6

grumbler I have always been a g. COMPLAINTS, 8

gruntled he was far from being g. UNHAPPINESS, 19

guerilla in g. warfare WAR, 20

guided missiles We have g. and misguided men PROGRESS, 18

guilt g. to make you turn pale GUILT, 4

guilty are you not as g. . . . as I GUILT, 8

better that ten g. persons escape JUSTICE, 5

It is quite gratifying to feel g. GUILT, 1

Let g. men remember their black deeds GUILT, 21

guinea pigs Laboratory g. say to themselves ANIMALS, 18

We're all of us g. in the laboratory of God
HUMAN CONDITION, 23

guitar I do not play the g. for applause SONGS, 8

Gulf War G. . . . surprised to find yourself singing PEACE, 21

gun Every g. . . . theft from those who hunger WEAPONS, 6

have a man come through a door with a g. in his
hand WRITING, 10

hear the word 'culture' . . . reach for my g. CULTURE, 6

The difference between a g. and a tree TREES, 4

gunpowder G., Printing, and the Protestant Religion
MODERNITY, 5

gutter We are all in the g. HUMAN CONDITION, 22

gymnasium I was sitting in the g. writing PSYCHIATRY, 13

habit A h. the pleasure of which increases COMMUNICATION, 1

habitation to airy nothing /A local h. POETS, 53

had you h. it in you BIRTH, 13

Hadrian's Wall pace /the H. /of her shoulder LOVERS, 9

Hagia Sophia H. EUROPEAN CITIES, 19

hail H. fellow, well met GREETINGS, 6

hair He may have h. upon his chest MEN, 24

like a h. across your cheek RACISM, 2

half I am only h. there when I am ill SUFFERING, 10

halo What, after all, /Is a h. GOOD, 10

Hamlet H. was just a badly conditioned rat PSYCHIATRY, 11

hammer h. your iron when it is . . . hot OPPORTUNITY, 9

hand a little bit by the h. of God SPORTS AND GAMES, 13

Our h. will not tremble RUSSIAN REVOLUTION, 2

The h. that held the dagger WORLD WAR II, 19

This was the h. that wrote it PUNISHMENT, 5

hands h. of science must ever be at work KNOWLEDGE, 15

He hath shook h. with time DEATH AND DYING, 26

I want a pair of h. BUSINESS, 3

With my own h. I had done BOATS, 3

You cannot shake h. with a clenched fist AGREEMENT, 6

hang Here they h. a man first EXECUTION, 13

I am worth inconceivably more to h. MARTYRDOM, 2

We must indeed all h. together
AMERICAN WAR OF INDEPENDENCE, 3

hanged being h. in all innocence EXECUTION, 18

h. in a fortnight . . . concentrates his mind EXECUTION, 7

H. privily by night INJUSTICE, 1

live to be h. . . . cutting a purse EXECUTION, 8

to be h. for nonsense NONSENSE, 8

hanging H. . . . makes murderers EXECUTION, 3

H. is too good for him PUNISHMENT, 4

h. prevents a bad marriage MARRIAGE, 45

hapless H. are the favorites of heaven MIDDLE EAST, 20

happens Nothing h. BORES AND BOREDOM, 2

happiest He is h. of whom the world says least HAPPINESS, 22

happiness A lifetime of h. . . . hell on earth HAPPINESS, 50

H.: a good bank account, a good cook, a good
digestion HAPPINESS, 43

H. is a mystery like religion HAPPINESS, 9

H. is an imaginary condition HAPPINESS, 54

H. is beneficial for the body HAPPINESS, 39

h. is born of a trifle HAPPINESS, 1

h. is despised nowadays HAPPINESS, 4

H. is like a butterfly HAPPINESS, 36

H. is no laughing matter HAPPINESS, 56

h. is no longer a possibility HAPPINESS, 45

H. is not an ideal of reason HAPPINESS, 26

H. is not best achieved HAPPINESS, 44

h. is produced . . . by a good tavern HAPPINESS, 24

H. is the only sanction of life HAPPINESS, 47

H. occurs when people can give . . . themselves
HAPPINESS, 6

h. of man that he be mentally faithful BELIEF, 24

h. of the wicked HAPPINESS, 42

h. through another man's eyes HAPPINESS, 49

Let no one trust the h. of the moment HAPPINESS, 30

not the h. of all men HAPPINESS, 55

supreme h. of life . . . we are loved HAPPINESS, 19

the greatest h. for the greatest numbers ACTION, 7

the outward . . . signs . . . of h. and success SUCCESS, 11

Were . . . h. . . . apprehended . . . it were a
martyrdom to live AFTERLIFE, 3

happy Ask . . . whether you are h. HAPPINESS, 32

Few people can be h. unless they hate HATE, 18

H. beings . . . carry their happiness cautiously
HAPPINESS, 3

H. he who like Ulysses TRAVEL, 11

H. that Nation, fortunate that age HISTORY, 38

h. who does not think himself so HAPPINESS, 40

His h. good-night air /Some blessed Hope HOPE, 12

If one only wished to be h. HAPPINESS, 34

Made h. by compulsion HAPPINESS, 10

never so h. nor so unhappy HAPPINESS, 28

Oh, this *is* a h. day HAPPINESS, 5

only really h. people THE SEXES, 9

utterly h. . . . refrain from comparing this moment
HAPPINESS, 16

harbor Being thus arrived in a good h. EMIGRATION, 1

hard better for h. words to be on paper DIARIES, 2

It's Been a H. Day's Night WORK, 16

hardboiled I've met a lot of h. eggs CHARACTER, 35

hardest h. to confess . . . ridiculous and shameful GUILT, 12

hardware the h. could stand up by itself HOUSES, 2

hare Take your h. when it is cased COOKING, 4

Harlem H. was Seventh Heaven AMERICAN CITIES, 28

harm I didn't want to h. the man MURDER, 4

No people do . . . h. GOOD, 9

harmless Mostly h. THE EARTH, 1

harmony h. in bad taste . . . height of elegance TASTE, 5

Inner h. is attained . . . with the environment
THE ENVIRONMENT, 2

harpoon exploding h. in the guts PASSION, 1

Harry God for H.! England and Saint George PATRIOTISM, 24

haste always in h. . . . never in a hurry HASTE, 10

Make h. slowly HASTE, 1

hat a h. that lets the rain in	MONARCHY, 15
hate H. is also creative	HATE, 6
h. that which we often fear	FEAR, 29
If you h. a person, you hate . . . yourself	HATE, 10
men h. one another so damnably	HATE, 14
hated I never h. a man enough	HATE, 8
to be h. is to achieve distinction	HATE, 1
hates Everybody h. me	POPULARITY, 4
It does not matter . . . what a man h.	HATE, 2
hating The price of h. other human beings is loving	
oneself less	HATE, 4
hatred An intellectual h. is the worst	INTELLECT, 19
H. is a feeling	HATE, 16
h. is by far the longest pleasure	HATE, 3
hats H. divide . . . into three classes	CLOTHES, 20
Hawthorne H. is grounded in Puritanism	AMERICAN LITERATURE, 3
hay make h. while the sun shines	OPPORTUNITY, 2
hazard The greatest h. . . . losing one's self	THE SELF, 13
head shorter by a h.	THREATS, 3
show my h. to the people	LAST WORDS, 4
Uneasy lies the h. that wears a crown	MONARCHY, 38
When the h. aches	SYMPATHY, 2
headmasters H. have powers	POWER, 7
headmistress a h. . . . wearing calico knickers	
	POLITICAL INSULTS, 32
heads H. I win	GULLIBILITY, 2
headstone His h. said /FREE AT LAST, FREE AT LAST	
	SLAVERY, 21
health A person . . . returns to h. much disappointed	
	HEALTH AND HEALTHY LIVING, 4
Attention to h. is the greatest hindrance to life	
	HEALTH AND HEALTHY LIVING, 14
H. indeed is a precious thing	HEALTH AND HEALTHY LIVING, 3
H. is a precious thing	HEALTH AND HEALTHY LIVING, 13
H. is the first muse	SLEEP, 10
H. is the first of all liberties	HEALTH AND HEALTHY LIVING, 1
h.! the blessing of the rich	HEALTH AND HEALTHY LIVING, 11
He destroys his h. by labouring to preserve it	
	HEALTH AND HEALTHY LIVING, 22
I'd make h. catching instead of disease	
	HEALTH AND HEALTHY LIVING, 10
preservation of h. is a duty	HEALTH AND HEALTHY LIVING, 19
The h. of the people	HEALTH AND HEALTHY LIVING, 5
Too much h., the cause of illness	HEALTH AND HEALTHY LIVING, 7
To preserve one's h.	HEALTH AND HEALTHY LIVING, 12
to signalize the inauguration of the National H.	
service	POLITICAL INSULTS, 18
Use your h.	HEALTH AND HEALTHY LIVING, 8
What have I gained by h.	MODERATION, 6
Without h. life is not life	HEALTH AND HEALTHY LIVING, 17
healthy 'Tis h. to be sick sometimes	HEALTH AND HEALTHY LIVING, 21
heart A gen'rous h. repairs a sland'rous tongue	
	GENEROSITY, 4
h. of man is the place the Devil's in	HELL, 4
I Left My H. in San Francisco	AMERICAN CITIES, 11
I love thee for a h. that's kind	KINDNESS, 3
In a full h. . . . room for everything	THE HEART, 7
My h. aches, and a drowsy numbness pains	
	MELANCHOLY, 7
My h. is a lonely hunter	LONELINESS, 16
My h. shall be thy garden	GARDENS, 5
My h. sings, full of sadness	EMOTION, 12
Out-worn h., in a time out-worn	THE HEART, 9
The h. has its reasons	REASON, 26
The h. is an organ of fire	THE HEART, 6
The h. is deceitful above all things	DECEPTION, 4
the motions and uses of the h.	THE HEART, 3
We had fed the h. on fantasies	FANTASY, 13
What comes from the h.	THE HEART, 2
when every lusty h. beginneth to blossom	SPRING, 8

heartbreak h., struggle . . . for being black	
	SINGERS AND SINGING, 3
hearts False h. and broken vows	COMMITMENT IN LOVE, 4
live in h. we leave . . . not to die	IMMORTALITY, 6
Our h. are surviving at the poverty level	POVERTY, 25
heathenism H. and Liberty	SLAVERY, 11
heaven for the unbelievers a gate in h.	HEAVEN, 7
H. . . . is a place so inane, so dull	HEAVEN, 18
H. affords /unlimited accommodation	HEAVEN, 20
h. and earth shall pass away	IMMORTALITY, 4
H. and hell /Are words	HEAVEN, 8
H. bred in me talents	TALENT, 6
H. has granted me no offspring	VANITY, 12
H. has its seasons . . . Man . . . government	
	HUMANKIND, 55
h. make me poor	POVERTY, 20
h. on earth	HEAVEN, 11
H. without being naturally qualified	HEAVEN, 17
If this belief from h. be sent	REGRET, 20
In h. an angel is nobody in particular	ANGELS, 9
key to the gate of h.	SCIENCE, 22
knockin' on H.'s door	HEAVEN, 3
more things in h. and earth	PHILOSOPHY, 39
no invention came more easily to man than H.	HEAVEN, 9
steep and thorny way to h.	HYPOCRISY, 19
trouble deaf h. with my bootless cries	DESPAIR, 12
We shall roll up . . . h. like a scroll	DOOMSDAY, 1
who has once strayed into H.	DISILLUSIONMENT, 1
heavenly Such h. touches ne'er touched earthly faces	
	BEAUTY, 34
heaventree The h. of stars	NIGHT, 4
Hebrew H. and Arabic . . . stones on the tongue	LANGUAGE, 1
hedgehogs If you start throwing h. under me	THREATS, 4
heights The h. by great men reached	ACHIEVEMENT, 15
hell all h. broke loose	DISORDER, 2
All place . . . be h. that is not heaven	DOOMSDAY, 2
H. . . . is to love no more	HELL, 2
h. . . . small chat to the babbling of Lethe	HELL, 1
H. has three gates	HELL, 3
h. is a beach-fire at night	HELL, 22
H. is a city much like London	HELL, 19
H. is full of musical amateurs	HELL, 18
H. is oneself; /H. is alone	HELL, 6
H. is other people	MISANTHROPY, 9
H. the Shadow of a Soul on fire	HEAVEN, 4
h. upon earth . . . a melancholy man's heart	
	MELANCHOLY, 4
H. was right now	HELL, 14
I believe I am in h.	HELL, 16
I shall move H.	HELL, 21
There is no other h. for man	HELL, 17
The road to h. . . . works-in-progress	WRITING, 45
Ugly h., gape not	CENSORSHIP, 7
Why this is h.	HELL, 12
hell-broth Like a h. boil and bubble	MAGIC, 11
help h. one . . . by trampling down a dozen	EXPLOITATION, 1
h. those we love to escape from us	HELP, 3
past my h. is past my care	HELP, 1
with a little h. from my friends	FRIENDSHIP, 24
you will find light and h. and human kindness	
	KINDNESS, 9
hen a broody h. sitting on a china egg	BUREAUCRACY, 6
A h. . . . an egg's way of making another egg	
	EVOLUTION, 3
Henry James The work of H. . . . seemed divisible	
	AMERICAN LITERATURE, 15
hereditary Talent is h.	TALENT, 9
heredity law of h. is that all undesirable traits	GENETICS, 8
heresy h. of one age becomes . . . orthodoxy	HERESY, 6
heretic h. that makes the fire	HERESY, 11

I shall never be a h.	HERESY, 8
heretics Modern h. . . . are relegated to backwaters	
	HERESY, 7
hero a h. . . . would argue with Gods	HEROISM, 10
a h. with coward's legs	COWARDICE, 6
Being a h.	HEROISM, 14
h. . . . one who does what he can	HEROISM, 15
h. and I will write you a tragedy	HEROISM, 7
h. appears . . . when the tiger is dead	HEROISM, 2
irrelevant . . . conception of the h. as a morally	
worthy man	MORALITY, 12
The H. can be Poet	HEROISM, 5
Today's h., the urban animal	HEROISM, 8
heroes fit country for h. to live in	GOVERNMENT, 33
if h. were never afraid	HEROISM, 6
setting up of h., mainly bogus	HEROISM, 12
There are few h. or villains	HEROISM, 17
heroic h. element in the soldier's work	HEROISM, 16
heterosexual artificial categories 'h.' and 'homosexual'	
	SEXUALITY, 11
heterosexuality failed to convert me to h.	HOMOSEXUALITY, 13
hibernated I h. in my past	THE PAST, 2
hidden wot's h. in each other's hearts	PRIVACY, 1
hide H. nothing from the masses of our people	HONESTY, 3
highlights h. and shadows of our history	EUROPEAN COUNTRIES, 25
highwayman The h. came riding	THE SUPERNATURAL, 26
hill H. and house should live together	ARCHITECTURE, 30
hills a fine thing to be out on the h. alone	SOLITUDE, 15
after climbing a great hill . . . many more h. to climb	
	ACHIEVEMENT, 16
The h. are alive . . . sound of music	SONGS, 5
those blue remembered h.	NOSTALGIA, 6
himself None but h. can be his parallel	THE SELF, 22
Therein the patient /Must minister to h.	GUILT, 19
hind The h. that would be mated	SEX, 38
hinder h. the reception of every work	CRITICS, 17
Hinduism H. . . . emphasizes Divine Immanence	RELIGION, 31
hip H. . . . sophistication of the wise primitive	STYLE, 4
Hippocleides H. doesn't care	INDIFFERENCE, 5
Hiroshima H., the flower, petalled off into extinction	
	EXTINCTION, 3
historian A h. is a prophet in reverse	HISTORIANS, 20
h. . . . performs an act of faith	HISTORIANS, 4
h. . . . trying to do in time	HISTORIANS, 7
h. is doomed . . . writing in the sand	HISTORIANS, 10
If an h. were to relate truthfully	HISTORY, 9
The h. is . . . detective who asks questions	HISTORIANS, 9
The h. must have . . . some conception of how men	
. . . behave	HISTORIANS, 15
The h. must not try to know what is truth	HISTORIANS, 1
The h. who attempts to interpret the past	HISTORIANS, 2
historians day is past when h. glory in war	HISTORIANS, 14
h. . . . creating a true ensemble	HISTORIANS, 19
H. are like deaf people	HISTORIANS, 23
h. left blanks in their writings	IGNORANCE, 15
h. must tell their tale convincingly	HISTORIANS, 11
H. of literature . . . regard a century	LITERATURE, 19
H. relate . . . what they would have believed	
	HISTORIANS, 16
H. repeat each other	HISTORIANS, 3
H. seek to be detached, impartial	HISTORIANS, 22
H. tell the story of the past	HISTORIANS, 17
When h. . . . have exhausted their resources	
	HISTORIANS, 12
historic Our h. imagination is . . . slightly developed	
	HISTORY, 25
historical A h. revision on a unique scale	WORLD WAR II, 14
histories H. make men wise	LEARNING, 5
there are two h.	HISTORY, 11
history 'facts' of h. do not exist	HISTORIANS, 6
'H.' . . . nightmare	HISTORY, 52
A h. without moral dimension	HISTORY, 27
All h. is the h. of thought	HISTORY, 23
all past h. . . . history of class struggles	CLASS, 13
ancient h. . . . is no more than accepted fiction	
	HISTORY, 65
And h.? What use is h.?	HISTORY, 57
end of a thousand years of h.	EUROPE, 20
feel the hand of h.	SOUNDBITES, 2
great deal of h. to produce a little literature	LITERATURE, 27
H. . . . account, mostly false, of events	HISTORY, 12
H. . . . a fragment of biology	HISTORY, 30
H. . . . a post-mortem examination	HISTORY, 29
h. . . . a record of man's cruel inhumanity	HISTORY, 24
H. . . . a vast early warning system	HISTORY, 22
h. . . . blink of the Earth Woman's eye	HISTORY, 61
H. . . . Cannot be unlived	HISTORY, 1
h. . . . huge libel on human nature	HISTORY, 50
h. . . . must be reduced to wallpaper	THEATRE, 23
H. . . . trash-bag of coincidences	HISTORY, 47
H. . . . working of the spirit of man	HISTORY, 67
H. . . . written by the winners	HISTORY, 44
h. cannot give us panaceas	HISTORY, 14
H. does not long entrust . . . freedom	FREEDOM, 18
H. does repeat itself, with variations	HISTORY, 4
H. employs evolution to structure . . . events in time	
	EVOLUTION, 16
H. has no 'meaning'	HISTORY, 37
H., I contend, is the present	HISTORY, 7
H., in illuminating the past	HISTORY, 18
h. is . . . production and reproduction of real life	
	HISTORY, 35
H. is a bath of blood	HISTORY, 51
H. is a cage, a conundrum we must escape or resolve	
	HISTORY, 66
H. is a clock	HISTORY, 20
H. is more or less bunk	HISTORY, 36
H. is philosophy teaching by examples	HISTORY, 28
h. is subversive because it always changes	POWER, 19
h. is the beating of war drums	WAR, 31
H. is the essence of . . . biographies	BIOGRAPHY, 5
H. is too serious	HISTORIANS, 18
H. is vanishing allegory	HISTORY, 34
H. never looks like h.	HISTORY, 40
H. never stops	HISTORY, 56
H. offers no comfort	HISTORY, 43
h. of man . . . nine months preceding his birth	BIRTH, 4
h. of the progress of human liberty	LIBERTY, 13
H. smiles at all attempts	HISTORY, 31
H. subverts the stereotype of science	HISTORY, 42
I like h. because my reading	HISTORY, 53
In the modern age h.	HISTORY, 3
lack of a sense of h. could have mortal consequences	
	NUCLEAR WAR, 7
minute hand of h.	JOURNALISM, 18
most interesting thing about h. . . . its invention	
HISTORIANS, 8	
no h.; only biography	BIOGRAPHY, 8
one of these is the h. of political power	HISTORY, 59
People are trapped in h. and h. is trapped in them	
	HISTORY, 6
real makers of h. are the ordinary men and women	
DEMOCRACY, 32	
riddle of h. is not in Reason but in Desire	HISTORY, 16
September 11 . . . marked a turning point in h.	
	TWENTY-FIRST CENTURY, 1
shallow village tale our so-called h. is	UNITED STATES, 22
That great dust-heap called 'h.'	HISTORY, 13
That is the triumph of h.	HISTORY, 8
The h. of the World is the World's court	HISTORY, 63

hypochondriac h. affection in men . . . hysteric in women
HYPOCHONDRIA, 2

hypochondriacs H. squander large sums of time
HYPOCHONDRIA, 6

hypocrisy H. is the most . . . nerve-racking vice   HYPOCRISY, 15
neither man nor angel can discern /H.   HYPOCRISY, 17

hypocrite No man is a h. in his pleasures   HYPOCRISY, 8
see . . . into a h.   HYPOCRISY, 9

hypotheses Questions, h., call them that   CURIOSITY, 1

hypothesis an h. . . . assimilates every thing to itself
IDEAS, 20
Factual evidence can never 'prove' a h.   THEORY, 7
I have no need of that h.   GOD, 41
slaying of a beautiful h.   SCIENCE, 32

hysteria h. . . . snake whose scales are tiny mirrors
MADNESS, 50

I I. am not what I. am   DECEPTION, 29
I. is somebody else   THE SELF, 20

ice A Shape of I.   DISASTER, 2
green i. /Of envy's mean gaze   ENVY, 8
his father took him to discover i.   FIRST LINES, 5
The i. was here, the i. was there   LANDSCAPES, 4

ice cream just enjoy your i. while it's on your plate
QUESTIONS, 10

icicles When i. hang by the wall   WINTER, 7

id the care of the i. by the odd   PSYCHIATRY, 15

idea An i. does not pass from one language   TRANSLATION, 5
An i. isn't responsible for the people   BELIEF, 21
do in the hope of an i.   IDEAS, 4
i.'s worth having once   IDEAS, 22
intensity of an i. depends . . . somatic excitation   IDEAS, 17
I think it would be a good i.   CIVILIZATION, 10
live in the shadow of an i. without grasping it   IDEAS, 2
Nothing is more dangerous than an i.   IDEAS, 1
to possess but one i.   STUPIDITY, 2

ideal my i. the life of Jesus   POLITICIANS, 37
The i. universe for us   THE UNIVERSE, 19

idealism What an extraordinary mixture of i. and lunacy
WOMEN'S RIGHTS, 21

idealist An i. . . . on noticing . . . a rose smells better
than a cabbage   IDEALISM, 11
true i. . . . true realist   IDEALISM, 2

ideals Away with all i.   SPONTANEITY, 3

ideas I. are born, they struggle   IDEAS, 7
i. are of more importance than values   INTELLECTUALS, 7
i. grow better when transplanted   IDEAS, 6
i. simply pass through him   THINKING, 3
I. that enter . . . mind under fire remain   IDEAS, 23
Keep on the lookout for novel i.   INVENTIONS, 2
Learn our i., or otherwise get out   COLONIALISM, 7
no i., no information   INFORMATION, 3
Old i. give way slowly   IDEAS, 3
We are constantly hatching . . . false i.   IDEAS, 16
Whenever i. fail, men invent words   WORDS, 14

identity The i. crisis . . . occurs in that period   IDENTITY, 2

idiocy between the i. of infancy and the folly of youth
CHILDHOOD, 4

idiot An i.'s eloquence is silence   SILENCE, 1
he is a sort of i. *savant* of language   LITERARY INSULTS, 27
I. memory repeats itself as tragic litany   MEMORY, 20

idleness i. and crime . . . deferring of our hopes   CRIME, 7

ignoramus I. . . . person unacquainted with . . .
knowledge familiar to yourself   IGNORANCE, 3

ignorance From i. our comfort flows   IGNORANCE, 16
he knew nothing, except . . . his i.   IGNORANCE, 6
His i. was an Empire State Building of i.   IGNORANCE, 13
I. . . . a delicate exotic fruit   IGNORANCE, 26
i. . . . the source of our anguish   IGNORANCE, 18
I., arrogance, and racism have bloomed as Superior
Knowledge in all too many universities   IGNORANCE, 25

I. is an evil weed   IGNORANCE, 1
I. is preferable to error   IGNORANCE, 8
knowledge increases . . . i. unfolds   KNOWLEDGE, 24
Let us all honestly own our i.   IGNORANCE, 4
man's i. of the gods   SPONTANEITY, 1
Our age has robbed millions of the simplicity of i.
WISDOM, 8
Somebody else's i. is bliss   IGNORANCE, 23

ignorant conscious that you are i. . . . step to knowledge
IGNORANCE, 7
Have the courage to be i.   IGNORANCE, 22
The i. man always adores   IGNORANCE, 12

ill being i. as one of the greatest pleasures of life   ILLNESS, 3
human i. does not dawn seem . . . an alternative
MORNING, 19
If . . . someone is speaking i. of you   HUMILITY, 6
means to do i. deeds   OPPORTUNITY, 11
One who is i. . . . duty to seek medical aid   ILLNESS, 17

illegitimate There are no i. children   CHILDREN, 37

illiteracy To deliver the nation from i.   LITERACY, 1

illiterate An i. king is a crowned ass   MONARCHY, 20

illiterates I. have to dictate   AUTHORITARIANISM, 4

ill-luck I. . . . seldom comes alone   MISFORTUNE, 3

illness A long i. . . . between life and death   ILLNESS, 14
Considering how common i. is   ILLNESS, 35
I. is in part what the world has done to a victim
ILLNESS, 19
In i. the physician is a father   DOCTORS, 12
in moments of i. . . . we live not alone   ILLNESS, 26

image an i. of the Cosmos   FLOWERS, 12
I made my own i.   POPULAR MUSIC, 16
i. is one thing . . . human being . . . another
APPEARANCE, 15
The painted i. delivers what it depicts   PAINTING, 6

images A heap of broken i.   DESPAIR, 5
maker of i. /Carves the human shape   HAPPINESS, 27

imaginary no other way to conceive an i. world
IMAGINATION, 24

imagination I. . . . defined as *that operation of the intellect*
IMAGINATION, 8
I. . . . is the irrepressible revolutionist   IMAGINATION, 19
I. . . . not an empirical . . . power of consciousness
IMAGINATION, 15
I. alone never did . . . produce works   IMAGINATION, 7
I. and fiction make up . . . our real life   IMAGINATION, 25
I. creates the real not the illusionary   IMAGINATION, 3
i. in a mathematician   MATHEMATICS, 1
i. is a necessary ingredient of perception   IMAGINATION, 10
I. is more important than knowledge   IMAGINATION, 9
lack of i. that makes us come   IMAGINATION, 1
no i., dying doesn't mean much   DEATH AND DYING, 11
the i. is a miracle of logic   IMAGINATION, 20
The i. is the only genius   IMAGINATION, 22
The primary i.   IMAGINATION, 6
Using one's i. avoids many misfortunes   MISFORTUNE, 9
where the i. . . . is rich and living   IMAGINATION, 23

imaginative I. consciousness represents . . . certain type of
thought   IMAGINATION, 16

imagine I. there's no heaven   IDEALISM, 9
Why . . . i. Others to be Fools   FOOLISHNESS, 1

imbecility i. . . . lowered the character of Great Britain
BRITAIN, 13

imitate Those who do not . . . i. . . . produce nothing
IMITATION, 4

imitation An i. rough diamond   INSULTS, 2
I. is not inspiration   INSPIRATION, 12
Man . . . is an i.   HUMANKIND, 39
pleasure of i. . . . most innate   IMITATION, 5

Immaculate Conception the I. was spontaneous combustion
HERESY, 10

immature i. man . . . wants to die nobly   AGE, 28
immediate I call for his i. resignation   RUSSIA, 32
   I distrust an i. morality   MORALITY, 38
immersed We all become so i. in the habits of American
   culture that . . . we mistake them for life itself
                                             PROPAGANDA, 3
immodesty towering i. . . . of his self love
                           AMERICAN LITERATURE, 1
immoral Call a thing i. or ugly   ECONOMICS, 33
   either i., illegal, or fattening   PLEASURE, 30
   worse than i.   AMERICAN IMPERIALISM, 1
immortal those i. dead who live   IMMORTALITY, 9
   though dead . . . the i. mind remains   IMMORTALITY, 16
immortality do not believe in i. of the individual SECULARISM, 1
   I . . . want to achieve i. . . . through not dying
                               IMMORTALITY, 1
   I believe in the i. of influence   INFLUENCE, 2
   I. . . . to labour at an eternal task   IMMORTALITY, 18
   I. is what nature possesses   IMMORTALITY, 3
immunologists I. are the function of a culture   SCIENTISTS, 13
imparadised I. in one another's arms   RELATIONSHIPS, 14
impeach i. him in the name of the people of India
                          BRITISH IMPERIALISM, 5
imperatives i. created by genetic history   GENETICS, 14
imperfection i. itself may have its . . . perfect state
                            IMPERFECTION, 2
imperialism I. . . . deep inside every material thing in
   America   IMPERIALISM, 5
   i. is the monopoly stage of capitalism IMPERIALISM, 12
   I. knows no law beyond its own interests IMPERIALISM, 17
   I., sane I.   IMPERIALISM, 20
impiety i., n. Your irreverence toward my deity   HERESY, 1
importance Everything i. has been said   ORIGINALITY, 10
important One doesn't recognize . . . the really i. moments
   . . . until it's too late   LIFE, 13
impossibilities I. . . . things of which we have not learned
                           IMPOSSIBILITY, 4
impossibility i. of obeying   OBEDIENCE, 3
impossible i. for one class to appreciate . . . wrongs
                             CLASS, 34
   nothing i. in the existence of the supernatural
                        THE SUPERNATURAL, 33
impostors sure that we are not i.   DECEPTION, 19
impress made his i. on eternity   INFLUENCE, 4
Impressionism We cannot use I.   ARTISTIC STYLES, 16
imprint set it in i.   PUBLISHING, 3
improbable could condemn it as an i. fiction   THEATRE, 17
   whatever remains, however i., must be the truth
                                  TRUTH, 27
impromptu three weeks to prepare . . . good i. speech
                             SPEECHES, 14
improper having i. thoughts about their neighbours
                             MORALITY, 3
impropriety I. is the soul of wit   WIT, 10
improve i. the international situation   DIPLOMACY, 19
improvisation I. is the touchstone of wit   WIT, 13
impulse i. to mar and to destroy   THE ENVIRONMENT, 5
inaccuracy i. sometimes saves . . . explanation   LYING, 37
inarticulate a raid on the i.   WRITING, 16
   speak for the i. and the submerged   FREE SPEECH, 1
in between If it wasn't for the 'ouses i.   BRITISH CITIES, 2
incarnation i. of the spirit in a form   THE SUPERNATURAL, 8
incense I. of death   GARDENS, 6
incest try everything . . . except i. and folk-dancing
                             EXPERIENCE, 3
income a good i.   MONEY, 42
incomes decent people live beyond their i.   DEBT, 10
incomprehensible The most i. talk   CONVERSATION, 16
incredibly I., . . . adorably beautiful   BEAUTY, 6
incurable no such things as i.   REMEDIES, 3

incurably Just like those who are i. ill   OLD AGE, 34
indebted Be still i. to somebody   DEBT, 7
indebtedness A man's i. . . . is not virtue   GRATITUDE, 2
indecent much more i. . . . than a good smack PUNISHMENT, 11
   such i. postures   SPORTS AND GAMES, 25
indecision Nothing is so exhausting as i.   INDECISION, 6
independence Complete i. through truth and non-violence
                            INDEPENDENCE, 2
indexes He writes i. to perfection   LITERARY INSULTS, 22
India Establish . . . sure English dominion in I.
                         BRITISH IMPERIALISM, 2
   If I. won her freedom through truth ASIAN COUNTRIES, 11
   I. . . . the strength and the greatness of England
                        BRITISH IMPERIALISM, 11
   I. is a geographical term   BRITISH IMPERIALISM, 9
   midnight hour, I. will awake to . . . freedom
                        ASIAN COUNTRIES, 25
   no need . . . to I. . . . to find peace SELF-KNOWLEDGE, 23
indians ain't /no mo /i. blowing /custer's mind
                        UNITED STATES, 49
indication an i. of truth's jealousy   TRUTH, 41
indifference and cold i. came   INDIFFERENCE, 9
   i. closely bordering on aversion   INDIFFERENCE, 10
indifferent An i. spectator like myself   INDIFFERENCE, 1
indigestion An i. is an excellent common-place
                        CONVERSATION, 12
   I. . . . A disease   DIGESTION, 1
   I. is charged by God   DIGESTION, 5
indignation i. makes an excellent speech   SPEECHES, 8
   i. makes me write verse   ANGER, 13
indirections By i. find directions out   DISCOVERY, 10
individual each i., regardless of their heritage UNITED STATES, 8
   i.'s desire to dominate his environment   DREAMS, 30
   Over himself . . . the i. is absolute   INDIVIDUALITY, 11
individuality i. lies in . . . universal element of mind
                        INDIVIDUALITY, 7
   Untalented i. is . . . useless   INDIVIDUALITY, 6
individuals I. pass like shadows   BRITISH IMPERIALISM, 4
   Since i. are by nature equal   NATIONS, 4
indolence i. . . . qualified with . . . bad temper RESPECT, 8
industrial design i. . . . on a mass-production basis
                        WEAPONS, 11
industrialization I. . . . happening to the biosphere
                      THE ENVIRONMENT, 3
industrialized i. nation consumes . . . energy and raw
   materials   THE ENVIRONMENT, 19
industry Every time the i. gets powerful POPULAR MUSIC, 32
   I. is . . . like the human body   BUSINESS, 11
   i. is . . . rife with jealousy   JOURNALISM, 20
inelegance a continual state of i.   WEATHER, 1
inequality I. . . . is about self-esteem   INEQUALITY, 5
   i. that has no special utility . . . injustice INEQUALITY, 3
inevitable Nothing is i. until it happens   FATE, 28
inexperience I. . . . makes a young man do . . . impossible
                             YOUTH, 23
infancy between i. and adultery   YOUTH, 1
   i., childhood, adolescence, and obsolescence AGE, 14
inferior greatest possible number of i. beings HUMAN RIGHTS, 1
inferiority i. complex . . . readily developed in Hollywood
                        HOLLYWOOD, 11
   i. of all . . . who were not white   RACISM, 6
inferiors I. revolt . . . that they may be equal REVOLUTION, 1
inferno the i. of his passions   EMOTION, 8
infinite i. number of possible universes   GOD, 43
infinity i. torments me   INFINITY, 4
inflammation i. of his weekly bills   DEBT, 3
influence i. . . . accumulation of a lifetime's thoughts
                            INFLUENCE, 9
   proper time to i. the character of a child CHILDREN, 19
influenced I am easily i.   INFLUENCE, 1

information computerized i. services . . . democratic society COMPUTERS, 15
I. and knowledge are . . . weapons INFORMATION, 4
I. is not knowledge MUSIC, 38
Withholding i. . . . act of intellectual imperialism INFORMATION, 2
infuriate pleasant /to i. a clumsy foe WIT, 18
infusion The i. of a China plant DRINKS AND DRINKING, 1
inhumanity Man's i. to man HUMANKIND, 7
injury An i. is much sooner forgotten INSULTS, 8
If an i. has to be done REVENGE, 8
injustice I. . . . a threat to justice INJUSTICE, 12
i. done to an individual INJUSTICE, 11
i. is always in the right hands INJUSTICE, 14
I., swift, erect, and unconfin'd INJUSTICE, 15
I. which lasts for three long centuries INJUSTICE, 21
mortgage his i. . . . for his fidelity INJUSTICE, 3
National i. . . . national downfall INJUSTICE, 8
No i. is done INJUSTICE, 20
threatened with a great i. INJUSTICE, 4
what you still have planned . . . shows the . . . i. in
your death AMBITION, 5
injustices thought only to justify their i. MEN, 32
ink he hath not drunk i. IGNORANCE, 20
i. of the scholar LEARNING, 21
in-laws i. was that they were outlaws FAMILY, 15
innocence I. is a kind of insanity INNOCENCE, 6
I. is no earthly weapon INNOCENCE, 7
i. that is full and experience . . . empty INNOCENCE, 9
my i. begins to weigh me down INNOCENCE, 11
Ralph wept for the end of i. INNOCENCE, 5
sensitive i. which Holden Caulfield retained
AMERICAN LITERATURE, 25
innocent An i. man is a sin before God INNOCENCE, 8
not . . . without distress . . . killed an i. animal
ANIMALS, 30
The i. . . . no enemy but time INNOCENCE, 15
innocuous There is nothing i. left INNOCENCE, 1
innovation i. occurs when . . . new idea is adopted
INNOVATION, 4
innovations i. . . . are the births of time INNOVATION, 2
insane i. person . . . running a private unapproved film
MADNESS, 36
Man is quite i. MADNESS, 31
Ordinarily he is i. POLITICAL INSULTS, 28
the i. take themselves . . . seriously CONCEIT, 2
insanities I've always been interested . . . i. of people
ART, 26
insanity a world of i. DESPAIR, 4
I. . . . logic of an accurate mind overtaxed MADNESS, 25
I. in individuals is something rare MADNESS, 33
insert i. . . . certain genes into subsequent generations
GENETICS, 16
insight moment's i. is . . . worth a life's experience
EXPERIENCE, 9
insignificant utterly i. little blue green planet THE EARTH, 2
insomnia every man's i. is as different from his neighbor's
INDIVIDUALITY, 4
inspiration He who . . . is waiting for . . . i. INSPIRATION, 10
inspired An i. idiot LITERARY INSULTS, 10
i. by the abusive hopelessness of everything FUTILITY, 5
instant considered an i. classic LITERARY INSULTS, 9
instinct triple blow . . . science of i. SCIENTISTS, 10
instincts Our i. are at war HUMAN NATURE, 22
instructions i. for being a pigeon BIRDS, 3
instrument i. to mould . . . minds of the young CENSORSHIP, 23
insult adding i. to injuries INSULTS, 29
i. the river god INSULTS, 34
integrity I. without knowledge is weak INTEGRITY, 2
intellect A towering i., grand in its achievements INTELLECT, 7

I. is invisible INTELLECT, 15
Our meddling i. INTELLECT, 18
take care not to make the i. our god INTELLECT, 3
The i. is always fooled by the heart INTELLECT, 11
The i. is part of life INTELLECT, 17
The i. of man . . . forced to choose CHOICE, 6
The voice of the i. is a soft one INTELLECT, 6
intellects highest i., like the tops of mountains INTELLECT, 13
intellectual An i. . . . says a simple thing INTELLECTUALS, 8
called many things, but never an i. INTELLECTUALS, 4
Every i. . . . ought to refuse to testify INTELLECTUALS, 11
I. . . . A man who's untrue to his wife INTELLECTUALS, 3
i. . . . doesn't know how to park a bike INTELLECTUALS, 1
i. community . . . stand up for freedom of the
imagination FREE SPEECH, 9
i. has been . . . an outsider, a servant INTELLECTUALS, 12
I. honesty . . . more than what's legislated HONESTY, 8
I. virtue owes . . . its growth to teaching INTELLECT, 1
The i. rigour of Marxism MARXISM, 2
intellectual capital I. is . . . competitive edge COMPETITION, 5
intellectuals i.' chief cause of anguish INTELLECTUALS, 5
vanishing race . . . the i. INTELLECTUALS, 14
intellectual slavery I. masquerading as sophistication
INTELLECTUALS, 13
intelligence i. . . . recognize it when we see it INTELLIGENCE, 10
I. becomes an asset INTELLIGENCE, 13
I. begins with the external INTELLIGENCE, 6
i. cannot be hidden; like a cough INTELLIGENCE, 5
I. is . . . a natural incomprehension of life INTELLIGENCE, 7
I. is almost useless INTELLIGENCE, 4
I. is quickness to apprehend INTELLIGENCE, 14
i. is the great polluter THE ENVIRONMENT, 18
i. of the American people INTELLIGENCE, 8
let the i. of . . . individuals unfold ASIAN COUNTRIES, 29
No tool is more beneficial than i. INTELLIGENCE, 1
The more i. one has ORIGINALITY, 6
intelligent i. man feels what other men . . . know
INTELLIGENCE, 9
Is an i. human being likely INTELLIGENCE, 11
intelligible aim at being i. CLARITY, 5
intention call the i. good GOOD, 1
i., ability, success, and correctness HAPPINESS, 20
slightest i. of honouring that Declaration HUMAN RIGHTS, 3
interaction the most direct i. with the earth EATING, 12
intercourse i. is . . . a social act SEX, 18
interested always been i. in people CURIOSITY, 5
i. in a woman who is i. in him MEN, 10
interests i. are eternal and perpetual DIPLOMACY, 27
Internet I. . . . technology in search of a strategy INTERNET, 2
I. is becoming the town square INTERNET, 4
interpretation i. . . . not to play what is written
PERFORMANCE, 1
I. . . . revenge of . . . intellect upon art CRITICISM, 23
interviewer gain . . . as an i. access to both sexes
JOURNALISM, 21
intimidation Years of i. and violence could not stop us
AFRICAN COUNTRIES, 8
intolerably I would grow i. conceited CONCEIT, 6
introduce let me i. you to that leg of mutton INTRODUCTIONS, 1
intrusions i. of the state into the private PRIVACY, 5
invasion One . . . cannot resist the i. of ideas IDEAS, 8
invent I just i., then wait INVENTIONS, 5
make an apple pie . . . i. the universe THE UNIVERSE, 20
invention i. . . . arises directly from idleness INVENTIONS, 1
I. is the mother of necessity INVENTIONS, 11
resorted to elaborate i. only after . . . simple falsehood
LYING, 22
inventions my i. go to the wrong hands INVENTIONS, 12
inventor i. is not just someone . . . with ideas INVENTIONS, 10
The i. of the Xerox machine MACHINES, 3

joking J. . . . third best method of hoodwinking people
DECEPTION, 16
My way of j. is to tell the truth SATIRE, 5
journalism J. . . . challenge of filling the space JOURNALISM, 32
J. . . . consists of saying 'Lord Jones is dead' JOURNALISM, 8
j. . . . in touch with the ignorance of the community
JOURNALISM, 33
J. is the only job that requires no degrees JOURNALISM, 6
The farmers of j. JOURNALISM, 34
journalist A j. is stimulated by a deadline JOURNALISM, 16
Good taste . . . dispensable part of . . . j.'s equipment
JOURNALISM, 14
j.: no ideas and the ability to express them JOURNALISM, 17
life of the j. is poor, nasty JOURNALISM, 11
the functions of the modern j. JOURNALISM, 9
journalists J. belong in the gutter JOURNALISM, 25
no j. is even better JOURNALISM, 2
journey A j. is a person in itself TRAVEL, 27
A j. is like a marriage TRAVEL, 29
A j. of a thousand miles BEGINNING, 10
begin a j. on Sundays TRAVEL, 32
dawn speeds a man on his j. MORNING, 6
How like /Is a j. by sea THE SEA, 13
J. . . . the universe in a map TRAVEL, 8
longest part of the j. TRAVEL, 36
pleasantest things . . . going on a j. SOLITUDE, 13
worst time of the year /For a j. TRAVEL, 14
journeys J. rarely begin where we think TRAVEL, 35
joy All the j. . . . solitude of childhood CHILDHOOD, 6
he who kisses the j. as it flies EUPHORIA, 1
One inch of j. surmounts of grief a span HAPPINESS, 41
The melancholy j. of evils past SUFFERING, 18
ther ys j. in hevene and peyne in helle AFTERLIFE, 5
Joyce J. . . . Nothing but . . . cabbage stumps of
quotations LITERARY INSULTS, 34
joys Great j., like griefs, are silent HAPPINESS, 31
Hence, vain deluding J. DELUSION, 10
present j. are more to flesh PLEASURE, 10
redoubleth j., and cutteth griefs FRIENDSHIP, 4
the j. of sense, /Lie in three words, health, peace, and
competence PLEASURE, 27
jubilation day of j., a day of remembrance
EUROPEAN COUNTRIES, 26
Judaism For J., God is not a Kantian idea JUDAISM, 7
J. . . . attempt to bring the Divine presence JUDAISM, 11
judge A j. is not supposed to know JUDGMENT, 17
Do not j. . . . never be mistaken JUDGMENT, 21
duty of a j. . . . administer justice JUSTICE, 21
It is fair to j. people SACRIFICE, 4
j. is a law student LAW, 26
j. not, that ye be not judged JUDGMENT, 3
others j. us by what we have . . . done JUDGMENT, 14
shallow people . . . do not j. by appearances
APPEARANCE, 19
judged j. on how much sex you've had AIDS, 3
judgement For j. I am come into this world JUDGMENT, 2
judging no way of j. the future but by the past THE FUTURE, 10
judgment I expect a j. JUDGMENT, 12
in my j., hindsight proves us wrong AMERICAN IMPERIALISM, 18
I was green in j. YOUTH, 26
j. . . . how to choose between two disadvantages
JUDGMENT, 20
J. is the typical act of intelligence JUDGMENT, 11
One cool j. . . . a thousand hasty councils JUDGMENT, 26
What j. shall I dread INNOCENCE, 4
judgments 'Tis with our j. as our watches JUDGMENT, 19
Value j. . . . founded on the study of literature
CRITICISM, 8
jump We'd j. the life to come CONSEQUENCES, 6
junk J. . . . the ultimate merchandise DRUGS, 3

Jupiter J. . . . turned into a satyr . . . for love LUST, 2
just In a j. cause the weak o'ercome the strong JUSTICE, 36
When a j. cause reaches its flood-tide WOMEN'S RIGHTS, 9
justice 'J.' was done FATE, 13
capacity for j. makes democracy possible DEMOCRACY, 37
I have loved j. . . . I die in exile JUSTICE, 14
J. . . . allowed to do whatever I like JUSTICE, 8
J. . . . limps along JUSTICE, 13
J. . . . will be pursued JUSTICE, 15
J.! Custodian of the world JUSTICE, 4
J. is a human illusion JUSTICE, 2
J. is not to be taken by storm JUSTICE, 10
J. is open to all JUSTICE, 26
J. is such a fine thing JUSTICE, 23
J. must . . . be seen to be believed JUSTICE, 27
j. must be . . . more or less done JUSTICE, 37
J. should . . . be seen to be done JUSTICE, 16
J. without force is impotent JUSTICE, 29
Let j. be done JUSTICE, 12
one must start from an absolute principle of j. JUSTICE, 7
Recompense injury with j. JUSTICE, 11
Revenge is a kind of wild j. REVENGE, 2
The j. of my quarrel ARGUMENTS, 12
The love of j. . . . is . . . the fear of . . . injustice
JUSTICE, 22
The place of j. is . . . hallowed JUSTICE, 1
There is a j. . . . behind injustice JUSTICE, 32
We have chosen to accept human j. JUSTICE, 9
we must do j. upon ourselves JUSTICE, 17
When . . . they close the doors of j. JUSTICE, 33
withers . . . like j. and truth . . . patriotic passion
HUMOUR, 13
You want j. . . . you want to pay JUSTICE, 6
justified life of one man can only be j. SACRIFICE, 9
justifies something that j. the end MORALITY, 45
justify Everything must j. its existence REASON, 13
If we j. war WAR, 3
Kansas This doesn't look like K., Toto PLACES, 2
KBO We must just K. DETERMINATION, 3
keep If you can k. your head SANITY, 6
k. on saying it . . . it will be true JOURNALISM, 1
keeping up K. with the Joneses was a full-time job
COMPETITION, 2
Kerouac Jack K. sat beside me AMERICAN LITERATURE, 14
kick I get no k. from champagne COMPLIMENTS, 3
K. is seeing things from a special angle DRUGS, 2
kid keep a k. at home CHILDREN, 11
kill As soon as one does not k. oneself SUICIDE, 3
How many people have wanted to k. themselves
SUICIDE, 17
K. a man, and you are a murderer KILLING, 9
k. a wife with kindness KINDNESS, 10
Next week . . . I'll k. myself PROCRASTINATION, 8
not . . . our intention to k. the king TREASON, 5
To k. a human being MURDER, 7
We k. time; time buries us TIME, 32
killed He must have k. a lot of men WEALTH, 18
ten to twenty million people k. NUCLEAR WAR, 15
killer the first trained k. to be a party leader
POLITICAL INSULTS, 8
killing K. is the lowest form of survival KILLING, 1
K. /Is the ultimate simplification of life KILLING, 6
K. myself to die upon a kiss MURDER, 11
medal for k. . . . a discharge for loving HOMOSEXUALITY, 9
no difference between . . . k. and making decisions
KILLING, 7
kills Who k. a man k. a reasonable creature BOOKS, 34
Yet each man k. the thing he loves KILLING, 12
kin more than k., and less than kind FAMILY, 20
kind a k. parent . . . or a merciless step-mother NATURE, 30

Do not ask me to be k.	KINDNESS, 8

kindle k. a light in the darkness of mere being — EXISTENCE, 11
kindness A man . . . has seldom an offer of k. — THE SEXES, 16

A word of k. is better than a fat pie	KINDNESS, 1
if your k. is rewarded with ingratitude	KINDNESS, 7
the k. of strangers	STRANGERS, 4
True k. . . . imagining as one's own the suffering . . . others	KINDNESS, 4

king A k. of shreds and patches — MEDIOCRITY, 11

better have one K. than five hundred	MONARCHY, 8
He played the K. as though . . . someone else was about to play the ace	PERFORMANCE, 2
k. of France . . . never did a Christian thing	REPUTATION, 15
lessened my esteem of a k.	MONARCHY, 30
Let a k. recall	MONARCHY, 13
the k. can do no wrong	MONARCHY, 4
The k. reigns . . . the people govern themselves	MONARCHY, 42
The k. shall be contented	MONARCHY, 40
What is a K.	MONARCHY, 34

kingdom I'm going to try for the the k. — DRUGS, 22

K. of God is within us	HEAVEN, 15
No k. has . . . had as many . . . wars as the k. of Christ	CHRISTIANITY, 14

kings K. . . . are made by artificial hallucination — MONARCHY, 41

K. are earth's gods	MONARCHY, 39
k. enough in England	MONARCHY, 16
k. of England . . . never had any superior but God	MONARCHY, 22
the K. of England, Diamonds, Hearts, Spades, and Clubs	MONARCHY, 14

kingship Whenever k. approaches tyranny — MONARCHY, 29
kiss 'Scuse me while I k. the sky — EUPHORIA, 2

A k. is but a k. now	KISSING, 6
K. me, Hardy	LAST WORDS, 9
K. till the cow comes home	KISSING, 1
waste his whole heart in one k.	KISSING, 10
Whenever you k. a man	KISSING, 8
you must not k. and tell	LOYALTY, 3
You must remember this; /A k. is still a k.	TIME, 21

kissed He k. me . . . I am someone else — KISSING, 7
kisses Dear as remember'd k. after death — NOSTALGIA, 5

more than k., letters mingle souls	COMMUNICATION, 6

kissing it was made /For k. — CONTEMPT, 4

when the k. had to stop	KISSING, 2

Kissinger K. brought peace to Vietnam — POLITICAL INSULTS, 29
knew k. I would never be so happy — HAPPINESS, 14
knitter a beautiful little k. — LITERARY INSULTS, 51
knocked we k. the bastard off — MOUNTAINS, 3
know don't k. anything about music . . . but I k. what I like — TASTE, 1

I don't k. everything, I just do everything	ACTION, 12
I do not k. myself	SELF-KNOWLEDGE, 15
I k. everything except myself	SELF-KNOWLEDGE, 40
I k. I am God	GOD, 13
I k. not where I am going	IGNORANCE, 17
I k. what I have given you	GIFTS, 6
K. then thyself, presume not God to scan	SELF-KNOWLEDGE, 33
Never k. what you made of	SELF-KNOWLEDGE, 17
No one can really k. the life	HISTORIANS, 5
Not many people k. that	KNOWLEDGE, 10
one thing to k. virtue	VIRTUE, 16
say 'I do not k.'.	HUMILITY, 14
To k. how to say what others only . . . think	WISDOM, 5
We k. more about . . . primitive peoples	CAPITALISM, 28
What do I k.?	KNOWLEDGE, 28
What we k. is not much	KNOWLEDGE, 25
What you don't k. . . . make a great book	BOOKS, 52

You k. I k. you k.	KNOWLEDGE, 16

knowing k. what you *cannot* do . . . good taste — SELF-KNOWLEDGE, 4

K. who you are	IDENTITY, 7

knowledge all k. to be my province — KNOWLEDGE, 4

civilizations . . . abandon the quest for k.	CIVILIZATION, 18
compelled to drive toward total k.	GENETICS, 15
deny *k*. . . . to make room for *faith*	KNOWLEDGE, 23
enthused by . . . attraction of k.	READING, 39
genuine k. originates in direct experience	KNOWLEDGE, 26
If a little k. is dangerous	KNOWLEDGE, 19
if a little k. was a dangerous thing	KNOWLEDGE, 34
I have no *k*. of myself	SELF-KNOWLEDGE, 21
k. . . . bounds of possible experience	KNOWLEDGE, 22
K. . . . is becoming dispensable	KNOWLEDGE, 36
k. . . . mine from melancholizing	MELANCHOLY, 3
k. . . . understood in human and political terms	KNOWLEDGE, 33
K. can be communicated but not wisdom	KNOWLEDGE, 17
K. dwells /In heads replete	WISDOM, 6
k. if out of proportion . . . is invalid	KNOWLEDGE, 1
K. is of two kinds	KNOWLEDGE, 21
K. is proportionate to being	KNOWLEDGE, 18
K. itself is power	KNOWLEDGE, 5
K., like Nature, feeds on ruins	KNOWLEDGE, 7
k. of the limits of human understanding	EUROPEAN LITERATURE, 3
k. of the other world can be obtained	AFTERLIFE, 12
k. passes . . . through three different theoretical states	PHILOSOPHY, 6
Our k. can only be finite	KNOWLEDGE, 32
Our k. forms an enormous system	KNOWLEDGE, 38
Real k. . . . one's ignorance	KNOWLEDGE, 13
Shall I teach you what k. is	KNOWLEDGE, 14
the k. of a lifetime	PAINTING, 41
the k. of causes	KNOWLEDGE, 6
The k. of the world	KNOWLEDGE, 11
true lover of k. . . . strives for truth	KNOWLEDGE, 31
we swallow a k. of ourselves	SELF-KNOWLEDGE, 3

known apart from the k. and the unknown — REALISM, 3

going from the k. to the unknown	RESEARCH, 2

knows he thinks he k. everything — POLITICIANS, 45

k. too much . . . hard not to lie	LYING, 47
who k. only his own . . . case k. little	JUDGMENT, 16

Koran verses of the K. . . . value of sunlight — ISLAM, 3
Kurdish Have the K. people committed such crimes — NATIONS, 3
Kurtz Mistah K.—he dead — DEATH AND DYING, 16
Kuwait If K. . . . sold bananas — AMERICAN IMPERIALISM, 24
LA L. . . . most brutal of American cities — AMERICAN CITIES, 24
L.A. there's so much smog in L. — AMERICAN CITIES, 8
label The only l. she wears is 'drip dry' — FASHION, 15
labor A man who will not l. to gain his rights — HUMAN RIGHTS, 2
laboratory All the world is a l. — EXPERIMENTS, 4
laborious In the l. work of revolutionaries — REVOLUTION, 19
labour Man . . . can only find relaxation from . . . l. — WORK, 8

nothing but their l. for their pains	WORK, 4

labyrinth without l. there is no rigor — SUSPICION, 4
lack l. of power corrupts absolutely — POWER, 40
lad A Grecian l. . . . that many loved — NARCISSISM, 6
ladder make . . . a l. out of our vices — VICE, 1
ladies several other old l. of both sexes — THE SEXES, 4
lady a l. says no . . . means perhaps — DIPLOMACY, 12

l. doth protest too much	COMPLAINTS, 10
the l. with the lapdog	STRANGERS, 2

Lambeth doin' the L. walk — BRITISH CITIES, 9
lame still a l. dog — HELP, 5
lament l. /our perforated words, like old shoes — LANGUAGE, 32

l. the past . . . conceive extravagant hopes of the future	COMPLAINTS, 2

the L. and the Idea are one — DICTATORS, 6

The most effective l. . . . satisfies . . . psychological
needs — LEADERSHIP, 15

leaders L. learn by leading — LEADERSHIP, 2

leadership L. . . . consists of telling the truth — LEADERSHIP, 17

l. is saying no — LEADERSHIP, 3

L. is the art of accomplishing more — LEADERSHIP, 16

L. is the priceless gift — LEADERSHIP, 9

Ninety percent of l. — LEADERSHIP, 8

The aim of l. — LEADERSHIP, 6

leaf The last red l. is whirl'd away — AUTUMN, 8

Turn over a new l. — BEGINNING, 4

lean grow l. /in loneliness — LONELINESS, 14

learn always ready to l. — LEARNING, 13

Beware . . . the man who works hard to l. — IGNORANCE, 24

In the 1950s we went to l., now we go to teach — SPORTS AND GAMES, 26

know enough who know how to l. — LEARNING, 2

l. about money — MONEY, 44

l. from mistakes, not from example — LEARNING, 20

l. the simplest things /last — LEARNING, 22

L. to write well — WRITING, 49

we l. by doing — LEARNING, 4

learned A l. fool is more foolish than an ignorant one — FOOLISHNESS, 14

A l. man is an idler — EDUCATION, 18

l. man who is not cleansed — PURITANISM, 3

the l. roast an egg — COOKING, 8

learning adds not to his l. — LEARNING, 29

A little l. is a dangerous thing — LEARNING, 24

He . . . overflowed with l. — POLITICAL INSULTS, 49

I thought that I was l. how to live — LIFE, 30

l. . . . grants the greatest enjoyment — LEARNING, 18

l. . . . the growth of cognitive structures — LEARNING, 12

L. had made us not more human — LEARNING, 10

L. hath gained most — LEARNING, 17

L. is a common journey — LEARNING, 30

L. is not worth a penny — LEARNING, 23

L., that cobweb of the brain — LEARNING, 9

L. without thought is labour lost — THINKING, 6

neglects l. in his youth — LEARNING, 16

not l. from our history — POLITICS, 13

Whence is thy l. — LEARNING, 19

learns one l. from others — THINKING, 7

leaves After the l. have fallen — IMAGINATION, 18

before the l. have fallen — OPTIMISM, 20

cool as . . . l. /of lily-of-the-valley — MORNING, 13

Though l. are many . . . root is one — WISDOM, 21

lectures l. or a little charity — COMMITMENT, 6

left the further l. . . . the more bourgeois — REVOLUTION, 48

legacy l. should be . . . you made it better — AMBITION, 11

legs the longest of l. to the smallest of ideas — IDEAS, 12

Lenin L.'s method leads to this — COMMUNISM, 27

transported L. . . . like a plague bacillus — RUSSIAN REVOLUTION, 5

Leningrad L. is like no other city — EUROPEAN CITIES, 27

Leonardo I could have been L. da Vinci — POSSIBILITY, 2

Leopold Bloom Mr L. ate with relish the inner organs of
beasts and fowls — FOOD, 16

less L. and l. are we able to locate our lives — THE SELF, 11

L. is a bore — ARCHITECTURE, 27

L. is more — ARCHITECTURE, 17

l. you do . . . better you do it — ACTING AND ACTORS, 15

lesson This taught me a l. — LOSS, 6

let L. there be light — LIGHT, 1

letter I have made this l. longer — COMMUNICATION, 14

I just got your beautiful l. — DECLARATIONS OF LOVE, 12

letters Don't you like writing l. — COMMUNICATION, 9

if you do not keep the l. — NOSTALGIA, 9

Levin When L. puzzled over what he was — MEANING, 14

liar A l. is always lavish of oaths — LYING, 12

A l. should have a good memory — LYING, 31

even if I am a l. and a poisoner — TRUTH, 45

libel worst l. is the truth — INSULTS, 35

liberal A l. is a conservative who has been arrested — LIBERALISM, 6

l. dreams of a better world — IDEALISM, 13

Modern l. political and economic institutions — GLOBALIZATION, 7

Of good natural parts . . . l. education — CHARACTER, 10

To be a l. you have to be white — RADICALISM, 2

When a l. is abused, he says — LIBERALISM, 4

liberality L. lies less in giving liberally — GENEROSITY, 2

liberals L. think that goats are just sheep — LIBERALISM, 1

liberate l. themselves from the fear of man — FEAR, 18

liberation L. is an evershifting horizon — WOMEN'S RIGHTS, 14

l. of women . . . time of freedom — FREEDOM, 21

L. will only arrive — LIBERTY, 32

The l. of language — WOMEN'S RIGHTS, 11

liberationists I'm furious about the Women's L. — WOMEN'S RIGHTS, 22

liberties Freedom, what l. are taken — FREEDOM, 24

people never give up their l. — LIBERTY, 5

protect all l. but one — LIBERTY, 11

liberty an hour, of virtuous l. — LIBERTY, 1

Climb ye the heights of l. — LIBERTY, 14

Complete l. and absolute democracy — REPUBLICANISM, 1

give me l. or give me death — AMERICAN WAR OF INDEPENDENCE, 5

It is true that l. is precious — LIBERTY, 2

l. . . . measured . . . by the paucity of restraints — LIBERTY, 36

L. . . . not . . . mere declarations of the rights of man — LIBERTY, 41

L. . . . right of any person to . . . say anything — LIBERTY, 37

L. . . . the absence of coercion — LIBERTY, 3

l. / . . . with right reason dwells — LIBERTY, 28

L.'s in every blow — LIBERTY, 8

l. connected with order — LIBERTY, 6

l. for one person is constrained only — LIBERTY, 20

L. is so much latitude as the powerful choose — LIBERTY, 18

L. is the hardest test — LIBERTY, 40

L. is the right to do everything — LIBERTY, 29

L. is to Science what air is — LIBERTY, 31

L. is won with the edge of the machete — LIBERTY, 26

L. means responsibility — LIBERTY, 34

L. of action, l. of movement — LIBERTY, 16

L. plucks justice by the nose — LIBERTY, 33

Loss of l. is a human disaster — LIBERTY, 35

love of l. . . . the love of others — LIBERTY, 19

Oh l.! . . . What crimes are committed in thy name — EXECUTION, 16

price of l. is . . . eternal dirt — LIBERTY, 30

price of L. is eternal vigilance — LIBERTY, 12

The L. of Man, in Society — LIBERTY, 24

The l. of the individual . . . limited — LIBERTY, 27

The tree of l. must be refreshed — LIBERTY, 21

When the People contend for their L. — LIBERTY, 17

library A l. is thought in cold storage — LIBRARIES, 4

half a l. to make one book — LIBRARIES, 3

lie A l. . . . very present help in trouble — LYING, 41

a l. plausible enough to believe — LYING, 46

a l. which is part a truth — LYING, 43

allowed to l. for the good of the State — LYING, 29

Father, I cannot tell a l. — GUILT, 20

He who does not . . . l. is proud — LYING, 28

if a l. may do thee grace — LYING, 38

l. that sinketh in . . . doth the hurt — LYING, 7

man . . . should never . . . l. — LYING, 26

mixture of a l. doth . . . add pleasure — LYING, 6

limits l. of . . . vision for the l. of the world   SUBJECTIVITY, 3
limousine One perfect l.   GIFTS, 5
line draw a l. in the sand   MIDDLE EAST, 8
   l. that fits the music   POPULAR MUSIC, 27
lines give me six l. . . . by the most honest man   GUILT, 11
lion Another l. gave a grievous roar   BORES AND BOREDOM, 12
lionized wasn't spoilt by being l. was Daniel   FAME, 29
lions two huge l. tearing at my flanks   ALIBIS AND EXCUSES, 4
lips All those l. that . . . kissed me   LOVE, 9
lipstick left l. on every pair of underpants   AMBITION, 6
liquor But l. /Is quicker   ALCOHOL, 14
listener good l. . . . good talker with a sore throat   CONVERSATION, 23
literacy l. is . . . surest . . . means to true education   LITERACY, 2
   The ratio of l. to illiteracy   LITERACY, 6
literary A l. movement   LITERATURE, 1
   l. life in this country begins in jail   CENSORSHIP, 28
   L. men are . . . a perpetual priesthood   LITERATURE, 13
   the greatest l. stylist of his time   WRITERS, 63
literature 'l.' is more pluralistic now   AMERICAN LITERATURE, 23
   difference between l. and life   LITERATURE, 25
   English l.'s performing flea   LITERARY INSULTS, 43
   Great works of l. . . . have been stories   LITERATURE, 38
   He knew . . . l. except how to enjoy it   LITERATURE, 24
   How tough it is to write l.   WRITING, 61
   L. . . . art of writing something . . . read twice   LITERATURE, 16
   L. . . . strewn with the wreckage of men   LITERATURE, 54
   L. and butterflies are the two sweetest passions   LITERATURE, 39
   L. flourishes best   LITERATURE, 26
   l. is . . . not a matter of courtesy   AMERICAN LITERATURE, 31
   l. is a drug   LITERATURE, 52
   l. is an old couch stuffed with fleas   LITERATURE, 52
   L. is a state of culture   LITERATURE, 28
   L. is a world . . . we try to build up   LITERATURE, 22
   L. is mostly about having sex   LITERATURE, 33
   L. is never the product of a single subject   LITERATURE, 9
   L. is news   LITERATURE, 44
   l. is nothing but carpentry   LITERATURE, 23
   L. is simply language charged with meaning   LITERATURE, 45
   L. is the honey of a nation's soul   LITERATURE, 40
   l. seeks to communicate power   BOOKS, 11
   l. wavers between nature and paradise   LITERATURE, 12
   l. which called itself 'realistic'   LITERARY STYLE, 5
   modern l. . . . was not taught in school   LITERATURE, 36
   new l., whose life blood is realism   WORLD LITERATURE, 4
   No l. can outdo the cynicism of real life   LITERATURE, 14
   Your true lover of l. is never fastidious   LITERATURE, 48
literatures the various l. are like clocks   WORLD LITERATURE, 7
litigation l. takes the place of sex   MIDDLE AGE, 13
little l. things are infinitely the most important   PRIORITIES, 2
live Do not try to l. forever   LONGEVITY, 9
   How may I l. without my name   NAMES, 15
   known I was gonna l. this long   LONGEVITY, 3
   l. dangerously   DANGER, 8
   l. for ever . . . die in the attempt   IMMORTALITY, 11
   l. in the cities . . . sick with unused self   CITIES, 5
   l. long enough . . . venerability factor creeps in   LONGEVITY, 10
   L. Now, Pay Later   DEBT, 19
   l. with me, and be my love   SEDUCTION, 2
   not fit to l. on land   THE SEA, 14
   One cannot l. with sighted eyes   SYMPATHY, 3
   They l. ill who expect . . . live always   IMMORTALITY, 17
   This is the urgency: L.   ACTION, 2
   Those who can't find anything to l. for   FANATICISM, 12
   Those who l. by . . . a lie   SELF-DELUSION, 3

To l. is like love   LIFE, 10
To l. is to be slowly born   LIFE, 46
We do not l. to think   THINKING, 31
We l. in our own world   CHILDHOOD, 15
We l. in stirring times   BORES AND BOREDOM, 9
We l. our lives, for ever taking leave   PARTING, 10
lived to have l. . . . unnecessary and unaccommodated   FUTILITY, 7
   You l. aloof, maintaining . . . your magnificent disdain   REPUTATION, 2
liver the positions of the l. and the heart   MEDICINE, 25
lives he who l. more l. than one   DEATH AND DYING, 66
   many l. are needed . . . to make one   THE SELF, 17
   our l. are free of danger   BIRTH, 6
   The l. of small men are like spiders' webs   GREATNESS, 13
   We spend our l. talking about . . . mystery   LIFE, 45
living L. is abnormal   NORMALITY, 2
   L. is an illness   SLEEP, 6
   L. is like . . . one long addition sum   LIFE, 42
   L. well and beautifully and justly   LIFE, 53
   start l. . . . first got to redeem our past   THE PRESENT, 5
   The l. . . . the dead on holiday   DEATH AND DYING, 38
   We, who are the l., possess the past   THE PAST, 16
Livingstone Dr. L., I presume   GREETINGS, 5
Lloyd George L. could not see a belt   POLITICAL INSULTS, 10
loathe I l. people who keep dogs   COWARDICE, 11
loathings My l. are simple   HATE, 15
Lolita L., light of my life   FIRST LINES, 6
London dominate a L. dinner-table   EATING, 17
   I would sell L.   BRITISH CITIES, 19
   L.: a nation, not a city   BRITISH CITIES, 6
   L. doesn't love the latent   BRITISH CITIES, 12
   L. is a modern Babylon   BRITISH CITIES, 1
   L. is a teenager   EUROPEAN CITIES, 3
   L., that great sea   BRITISH CITIES, 20
   L. was a city not to be visited   BRITISH CITIES, 13
   lowest and vilest alleys of L.   COUNTRYSIDE, 2
   MPs never see the L. . . . beyond the wine bars   POLITICIANS, 30
   tired of L. . . . tired of life   BRITISH CITIES, 14
loneliness a reflection of my own . . . l.   LONELINESS, 10
   Beside the clock's l.   WRITING, 30
   each of us must live with . . . l.   LONELINESS, 9
   L. . . . the great American disease   LONELINESS, 2
   l. may spur you into finding something   LONELINESS, 7
   l. of my country and my God   LONELINESS, 17
lonely All the l. people   LONELINESS, 12
   l. while eating spaghetti   EATING, 15
   So l. am I /My body is a floating weed   LONELINESS, 11
lonesome A l. man . . . who does not know how to read   LITERACY, 4
longevity L. is the revenge of talent   LONGEVITY, 5
   L., n. Uncommon extension   LONGEVITY, 2
Long Island L. represents the American's idea   AMERICANS, 8
look I love the l., austere, immaculate   LANDSCAPES, 11
   L., stranger, at this island now   DISCOVERY, 2
   The longer you l. . . . the more it transforms   METAMORPHOSIS, 4
   the L. isn't . . . garments you wear   STYLE, 7
looking The art of l. for trouble   POLITICS, 6
looking glass The cracked l. of a servant   IRELAND, 20
looks A man who l. a part   APPEARANCE, 13
   l. commercing with the skies   MYSTICISM, 5
   never had the l. to lose   APPEARANCE, 2
   No man ever l. . . . with pristine eyes   PERCEPTION, 1
loosed For l. till dawn are we   ANIMALS, 21
lord a L. among wits   POLITICAL INSULTS, 35
   l. of lycht and lamp of day   MORNING, 2
Lord the L. is a man of war   GOD, 15
   thy L. shall give thee a reward   AFTERLIFE, 14

lordlike what makes men walk l. . . . love of women *MEN, 25*

lords Great l. have their pleasures *PLEASURE, 24*

Los Angelean To qualify for a L. *AMERICAN CITIES, 7*

Los Angeles L. . . . you've got to be an actor *AMERICAN CITIES, 15*

To live sanely in L. *AMERICAN CITIES, 19*

lose A man who does not l. his reason *REASON, 25*

I hate to l. more than . . . win *LOSS, 2*

No man can l. *LOSS, 8*

nothing to l. but our aitches *CLASS, 28*

We are bound to l. Ireland *IRELAND, 15*

You l. *BREVITY, 2*

losing art of l. isn't hard to master *LOSS, 1*

loss better to incur l. than to make gain *LOSS, 7*

lost I can't say I was ever l. *EXPLORATION, 2*

My friends, I have l. a day *REGRET, 16*

loud l. and troublesome insects of the hour *OPINIONS, 1*

lov'd Of one that l. not wisely, but too well *REGRET, 13*

love 'L.', till its incantation *LONELINESS, 13*

all for l., and nothing for reward *SELFLESSNESS, 7*

all the world and l. were young *LOVE, 50*

All You Need Is L. *LOVE, 38*

A man in l. is incomplete until . . . married *MARRIAGE, 26*

a man in l. with a dimple *DELUSIONS OF LOVE, 5*

Any scientist who has ever been in l. *EXPERIENCE, 13*

breeze of l. blows for an hour *LOVE, 42*

Can one l. so fleetingly? *LOVE, 21*

Could we forbear dispute and practise l. *LOVE, 63*

For l. deceives the best of womankind *DELUSIONS OF LOVE, 7*

give . . . your l. but not your thoughts *CHILDREN, 14*

God is l. *LOVE, 12*

He that falls in l. with himself . . . no rivals *NARCISSISM, 3*

he told men to l. their neighbour *HUNGER, 4*

How alike are the groans of l. to those of the dying *LOVE, 40*

How do I l. thee *LOVE, 16*

I'm tired of L. *MONEY, 8*

I do l. nothing in the world so well as you *DECLARATIONS OF LOVE, 14*

I hate all that don't l. me *HATE, 7*

in l. with the whole world *IDEALISM, 3*

let's fall in l. *SEDUCTION, 11*

L. . . . delusion . . . one woman differs from another *DELUSIONS OF LOVE, 6*

L. . . . destroys the inbetween *LOVE, 2*

l. . . . has one arch-enemy . . . life *LOVE, 1*

L. . . . is . . . the exchange of two fantasies *LOVE, 20*

L. . . . known by him who hopelessly persists *LOVE, 54*

l. . . . looks more like hatred than like friendship *HATE, 12*

l. . . . pleasure in the perfection of another *LOVE, 37*

L. . . . rarer than genius *FRIENDSHIP, 32*

L. . . . sole and everlasting foundation *LOVE, 48*

L. . . . someone to call you darling after sex *LOVE, 7*

l. . . . the beauty of certain degradations *NATURE, 38*

l. . . . the dirty trick *LOVE, 43*

L.'s like the measles *LOVE, 33*

L. and compassion . . . essence of all religion *RELIGION, 9*

L. ceases to be a pleasure *LOVE, 10*

L. conquers all . . . except poverty and toothache *LOVE, 64*

L. conquers all things *LOVE, 61*

L. does not consist in gazing at each other *LOVE, 53*

L. I did the fairest boy *HOMOSEXUALITY, 1*

L., I find, is like singing *LOVE, 31*

l. is . . . not individual *LOVE, 14*

L. is above the laws *LOVE, 57*

L. is a growing . . . constant light *LOVE, 23*

L. is among the most pernicious . . . of diseases *LOVE, 27*

l. is blind *DELUSIONS OF LOVE, 13*

L. Is Here To Stay *LOVE, 28*

L. is like a motor that's going *LOVE, 15*

L. is like linen *LOVE, 26*

L. is moral even without . . . marriage *MARRIAGE, 34*

L. is my religion *LOVE, 35*

L. is not l. /Which alters *LOVE, 55*

L. is the difficult realization *LOVE, 44*

L. is the wisdom of the fool *LOVE, 34*

L. leaped out *LOVE, 18*

l. oneself . . . lifelong romance *EGOTISM, 11*

l. robs those who have it of their wit *WIT, 3*

L. seldom haunts the breast where learning lies *LEARNING, 26*

L. that dare not speak its name *HOMOSEXUALITY, 19*

L. that dare not speak its name *LOVE, 24*

l. that reassembles the fragments *LOVE, 62*

l. we give away . . . we keep *LOVE, 30*

Make l. not war *PROTEST, 10*

make l. to you at five o'clock *SEX, 8*

most wonderful kind of delirium is . . . l. *LOVE, 67*

Murmur, a little sadly, how L. fled *LOVE, 66*

my l. swears that she is made of truth *DELUSIONS OF LOVE, 9*

my real l. . . . sleep that rescued me *SLEEP, 20*

no such . . . l. since humanity was divided into classes *CLASS, 23*

Nothing is too much trouble for l. *LOVE, 60*

Oh mighty l. *LOVE, 29*

O tell me the truth about l. *LOVE, 4*

secure the l. of your neighbour *MORALITY, 33*

So true a fool is l. *DELUSIONS OF LOVE, 8*

Ten men l. what I hate *BELIEF, 7*

The difficult part of l. /Is being selfish *RELATIONSHIPS, 12*

the l. machine would appear a natural development *MACHINES, 8*

The l. of life is necessary to . . . any undertaking *VITALITY, 3*

They that l. beyond the world *LOVE, 46*

To fall in l. is to create a religion *LOVE, 13*

To fear l. is to fear life *LOVE, 52*

to l. and be loved *HAPPINESS, 46*

To l. a thing *LOVE, 22*

To l. you was pleasant enough *RELATIONSHIPS, 16*

True L. . . . differs from gold and clay *LOVE, 56*

weight of the world /is l. *HUMAN CONDITION, 11*

what a mischievous devil L. is *GOD, 20*

What is commonly called l. *LUST, 4*

when I l. thee not, /Chaos is come *DECLARATIONS OF LOVE, 15*

why should l. stop at the border *PATRIOTISM, 6*

loved I have l. thee, Ocean *THE SEA, 3*

I l. much, I never l. long *COMMITMENT IN LOVE, 1*

l. him too much to feel no hate *HATE, 17*

Only one who has l. knows *LOVE, 32*

lovely All l. things will have an ending *TRANSIENCE, 1*

love-quarrels L. oft in pleasing concord end *AGREEMENT, 8*

lover A l. without indiscretion is no l. *LOVERS, 8*

One l. is always more moved *LOVERS, 1*

satisfied with her l.'s mind *LOVERS, 18*

lovers l. run into strange capers *LOVERS, 13*

loves A woman must marry the man who l. her *MARRIAGE, 4*

He l. his bonds *MARRIAGE, 31*

He that l. not his wife and children *FATHERS, 9*

real l., real revolts, real desires *MOTIVE, 2*

very rarely that a man l. *LOVE, 41*

low Begin l., speak slow *SPEECHES, 1*

lowliness l. is young ambition's ladder *AMBITION, 28*

loyalty An ounce of l. *LOYALTY, 4*

l. . . . possible only when fidelity is emptied *LOYALTY, 1*

Party l. lowers the greatest of men *POLITICS, 31*

Lucifer L. legend is in no sense . . . absurd *THE DEVIL, 7*

m. think all . . . mortal, but themselves IMMORTALITY, 22
m. who think as m. of action and act as m. of
thought REVOLUTION, 33
M. will always be mad MADNESS, 48
M. will say (and accept) anything MEN, 16
M. with secrets SECRECY, 6
Nature has given m. proud and high spirits SEXISM, 1
The more I see of m., the more I admire dogs MEN, 26
The most positive m. are the most credulous GULLIBILITY, 5
the race of m. is almost extinct in Europe MEN, 18
those m. have their price POLITICIANS, 54
Unfortunately, most m. are deaf MEN, 20
until m. are prepared to kill each other MURDER, 12
We live under . . . m. and morning newspapers
GOVERNMENT, 46
when M. & Mountains meet GREATNESS, 2
menstrual period history of a missed m. PREGNANCY, 3
menstruation m. would become . . . masculine event MEN, 29
mental A m. stain can neither be blotted out PSYCHIATRY, 2
every 'm.' symptom . . . veiled cry of anguish
OPPRESSION, 14
Every m. act is conscious CONSCIOUSNESS, 1
how the m. apparatus is constructed MIND, 14
m. processes are . . . unconscious PSYCHOANALYSIS, 9
mental fight I will not cease from M. ENGLAND, 3
mental reflection M. . . . more interesting than T.V.
TELEVISION, 14
Mephistopheles The M. of politics POLITICAL INSULTS, 1
merit m. Heaven by making earth a Hell HEAVEN, 1
merry-go-round where to put us on the m. APARTHEID, 6
mesa The m. plain had an appearance of . . .
incompleteness LANDSCAPES, 3
Messiah M. will come . . . much less probable DELUSION, 6
Messianism M. is Judaism's . . . original idea JUDAISM, 5
met We have m. too late WRITERS, 40
metamorphosis In a m. . . . essential truth overruns the
external illusion METAMORPHOSIS, 5
metaphor A m. . . . turning into reality WRITING, 54
m. is . . . the most fertile power LANGUAGE, 29
Science is all m. SCIENCE, 37
Through m. to reconcile IDEAS, 25
metaphysics M. . . . an attempt to prove the incredible
METAPHYSICS, 7
M. . . . bad reasons for what we believe METAPHYSICS, 3
m. . . . speaks the language of Plato METAPHYSICS, 5
The unrest which keeps . . . m. going METAPHYSICS, 6
metaquizzical The great M. poet POETS, 9
method-acting term m. is so much nonsense
ACTING AND ACTORS, 25
methods By different m. different men excel EXCELLENCE, 1
Methuselah all the days of M. LONGEVITY, 1
metropolis steam-heated, air-conditioned m. THE ENVIRONMENT, 13
the m. of the empire BRITISH CITIES, 4
Mexico Poor M. . . . so near to the United States
CENTRAL AMERICA, 2
Michelangelo If M. had been straight HOMOSEXUALITY, 17
microbes There are more m. *per person* SCIENCE, 4
microscope It is only in the m. that our life looks so big
LIFE, 48
middle people who stay in the m. of the road INDECISION, 1
middle age M. . . . every new person . . . reminds you of
someone MIDDLE AGE, 9
M. . . . youth without its levity MIDDLE AGE, 3
m. is the best time MIDDLE AGE, 7
M. is when your age starts to show MIDDLE AGE, 5
M. snuffs out more talent MIDDLE AGE, 6
One of the pleasures of m. MIDDLE AGE, 11
the dead center of m. MIDDLE AGE, 1
Middle Ages In the M. they would have burned me
CENSORSHIP, 10

middle-class the healthy type that was essentially m. CLASS, 14
Middle East complex problems that face the M.
MIDDLE EAST, 35
not possible to create peace . . . M. MIDDLE EAST, 7
Our region is not the M. MIDDLE EAST, 37
middle years In a man's m. there is scarcely a part of the
body MIDDLE AGE, 14
midnight It came upon the m. clear CHRISTMAS, 10
M. brought on the dusky hour NIGHT, 8
mid-point The m. being passed MISTAKES, 11
midst In the m. of life we are in death DEATH AND DYING, 8
mid-stream best not to swap horses in m. LOYALTY, 7
midsummer this is very m. madness DISORDER, 1
mid-winter In the bleak m. WINTER, 6
might We m. have been REGRET, 4
mighty a m. man . . . the humblest of creatures HUMILITY, 2
migrating like two m. birds, male and female LOVERS, 4
militarism M. . . . is one of the chief bulwarks of
capitalism CAPITALISM, 22
milk between the m. and the yoghurt WRITERS, 50
too full o' th' m. of human kindness FEAR, 30
miller M. . . . a discerning though hardboiled person
AMERICAN LITERATURE, 24
Miller M. is . . . a non-stop talker LITERARY INSULTS, 6
million We are living a m. lives TWENTIETH CENTURY, 4
millionaire Who Wants To Be a M. WEALTH, 23
millions M. long for immortality IMMORTALITY, 10
Milton M.'s Devil . . . far superior to his God POETS, 54
M., Madam, was a genius POETS, 37
mind a m. of winter PERCEPTION, 12
a m. to kill KILLING, 3
a prodigious quantity of m. INDECISION, 8
clear your *m*. of cant RHETORIC, 4
force of m. is only as great MIND, 15
His m. moves upon silence SILENCE, 33
human m. . . . created celestial and terrestrial physics
METAPHYSICS, 4
human m. . . . device for survival and reproduction
MIND, 49
human m. *has* to ask . . . why am I MIND, 22
human m. invents its Puss-in-Boots FANTASY, 10
human m. treats a new idea IDEAS, 14
I call the . . . m. thinking substance MIND, 4
if anything . . . the matter with your m. MIND, 18
inability of the human m. to correlate MIND, 28
I took my m. a walk MIND, 31
Measure your m.'s height by the shade it casts MIND, 7
m. . . . an erogenous zone MIND, 48
M. . . . the great lever of all things MIND, 47
m. grows sicker than the body SUFFERING, 17
m. has added nothing to human nature MIND, 42
M. is ever the ruler of the universe MIND, 37
m. is properly conceived as an inner principle MIND, 3
m. is utterly indivisible MIND, 10
m., once expanded to . . . larger ideas MIND, 17
m. thinks, not with data, but . . . ideas IDEAS, 18
m. was that of Lord Beaverbrook POLITICAL INSULTS, 11
Murphy's m. . . . a large hollow sphere MIND, 5
My m. is . . . open and so is my mouth POLITICIANS, 3
my m. is clouded with a doubt AFTERLIFE, 21
My m. is not a bed MIND, 1
natural tendency of . . . m. is to dichotomise
UNDERSTANDING, 11
never to ransack any m. but his own ARTISTS, 38
No m. is thoroughly well organized MIND, 8
out of my m., it's all right FIRST LINES, 1
someone whose m. watches itself INTELLECTUALS, 10
suppose the M. . . . void of all Characters MIND, 27
that m. free which . . . guards its intellectual rights
FREEDOM, 7

we do not call m. an illness BEREAVEMENT, 5
mouse Consider the little m., how sagacious WISDOM, 15
mouse-trap make a better m. INVENTIONS, 3
mouth His m. has been used as a latrine DRUNKENNESS, 2
Sweet red splendid kissing m. KISSING, 9
movement I want to be a m. SOLITUDE, 18
moves Yet it m. ASTRONOMY, 6
movie don't like his m., you're dead HOLLYWOOD, 19
Making a m. . . . going down a mine FILMS, 36
This is a m., not a lifeboat CELEBRITY, 16
movie-making M. is . . . turning money into light FILMS, 3
movies Good m. make you care FILMS, 20
M. are an inherently stupid art form FILMS, 33
M. are the repository of myth FILMS, 2
M. for me are a heightened reality FILMS, 45
My own start in m. was . . . lucky one HOLLYWOOD, 20
What's history going to say about . . . m.? FILMS, 30
Why . . . pay money to see bad m. TELEVISION, 7
Mozart He was simply the M. of conversation CONVERSATION, 5
M. would have written . . . while awaiting a transplant ILLNESS, 11
when M. was my age AGE, 13
much so m. owed by so many to so few WORLD WAR II, 9
muchness Much of a m. MEDIOCRITY, 13
mud liquid m. up to our knees WORLD WAR I, 20
One sees the m., and one the stars PERCEPTION, 7
muddle-headed He's a m. fool FOOLISHNESS, 8
mule smelt a lot of m. manure SINGERS AND SINGING, 10
mules The m. that angels ride come slowly ANGELS, 12
multitude The m. of the sick HEALTH AND HEALTHY LIVING, 6
this massed m. of silent witnesses to . . . war WORLD WAR I, 6
mum M.'s the word SECRECY, 3
munch So m. on, crunch on . . . dinner, luncheon EATING, 5
murder M. . . . had a mask like Castlereagh MURDER, 13
m. . . . its rightful setting—in the home TELEVISION, 9
m. can be justified MURDER, 2
M., like talent, seems . . . to run in families FAMILY, 13
M. most foul MURDER, 9
m. shrieks out MURDER, 14
Sooner m. an infant in its cradle DESIRE, 3
murdered I m. my grandmother this morning MURDER, 8
The man who m. his parents HYPOCRISY, 14
murderer I have never yet heard of a m. MURDER, 6
murderers M. . . . are people who are consistent MURDER, 1
murmur live m. of a summer's day SUMMER, 1
muse the M. gave native wit EUROPEAN COUNTRIES, 35
mushroom a supramundane m. NUCLEAR WEAPONS, 2
music a m. with strong rhythmic foundations CIVILIZATION, 19
Can m. be something more than shadows MUSIC, 28
God tells me how . . . this m. played ARROGANCE, 6
hear m. in the heart of noise MUSIC, 16
If m. be the food of love MUSIC, 26
If one hears bad m. MUSIC, 37
I hear m., I fear no danger MUSIC, 35
M. . . . best means we have of digesting MUSIC, 5
M. . . . certain effect on the moral character MUSIC, 3
M. . . . confirm human loneliness MUSIC, 12
m. . . . People should die for it MUSIC, 25
M. . . . sets the soul in operation MUSIC, 6
M. . . . sum total of scattered forces MUSIC, 11
M. . . . the source of the mystery MUSIC, 22
M. . . . the speech of angels MUSIC, 7
M. . . . ways God has of beating MUSIC, 18
M. begins to atrophy MUSIC, 24
M. creates order out of chaos MUSIC, 21
m. in the air MUSIC, 13
M. is going to break the way MUSIC, 17
M. is not written in red, white and blue MUSIC, 20

M. is the crystallization of sound MUSIC, 34
M. is your own experience MUSIC, 23
M., Maestro, Please SONGS, 7
M., not sex, got me aroused POPULAR MUSIC, 11
M. revives the recollections MUSIC, 29
M. that gentlier on the spirit lies MUSIC, 33
M., the greatest good MUSIC, 1
Nothing is . . . well set to m. NONSENSE, 1
Talking about m. . . . like dancing about architecture CRITICISM, 12
The m. of what happens MUSIC, 15
Too many pieces of m. MUSIC, 32
where the speech of man stops . . . M.'s reign begins MUSIC, 36
Without m. we shall surely perish MUSIC, 27
musical Most m., most melancholy BIRDS, 9
musical instruments deliver all our m. to . . . Gestapo JAZZ, 27
musical theater M. . . . highest . . . form of theater THEATRE, 22
music critics m. . . . rodent-like with padlocked ears CRITICS, 32
musician A m., if he's a messenger, is like a child MUSICIANS, 7
musicians assumed that a lot of m. . . . underprivileged MUSICIANS, 3
Muslim M. women . . . we are not sex symbols WOMEN'S RIGHTS, 17
mustache a man outside with a big black m. THE FACE, 11
myself I am always with m. SELF-KNOWLEDGE, 16
I am m. plus my circumstance THE SELF, 18
I follow but m. SELF-INTEREST, 14
I have always disliked m. SELF-KNOWLEDGE, 9
I know m. SELF-KNOWLEDGE, 12
I m. am hell HELL, 10
mysteries Talk of m. THE ENVIRONMENT, 22
mystery don't destroy the m. of a rainbow UNDERSTANDING, 7
In m. our soul abides THE SOUL, 2
you would pluck out the heart of my m. MANIPULATION, 2
mystic The m. sees the ineffable MYSTICISM, 4
mystical The m. and the ethical . . . no living religion RELIGION, 37
mysticism I regard m. as a state of mind MYSTICISM, 6
M. . . . a direct and present religious experience MYSTICISM, 8
mystics M. always hope that science MYSTICISM, 7
myth 'm.' a form of expression MYTHS, 13
A m. is, of course, not a fairy story MYTHS, 11
At the centre of every m. is another MYTHS, 6
M. deals in false universals MYTHS, 5
The 1916 m. . . . is in my bloodstream IRELAND, 23
myths A people needs legends, heroes, m. CULTURE, 7
m. . . . products of the human mind MYTHS, 4
M. and legends die hard in America UNITED STATES, 51
old m. never die MYTHS, 1
nail Hit the n. on the head CLARITY, 3
naked I give you my n. soul NAKEDNESS, 5
To see you n. is to recall the Earth NAKEDNESS, 4
naked ape The exception is a n. HUMANKIND, 9
name A good n. is better than riches REPUTATION, 11
I don't like your Christian n. NAMES, 3
like putting a n. on the universe POETS, 65
my n. and memory, I leave REPUTATION, 4
So-and-so, whose other n. was so-and-so BIOGRAPHY, 10
that was the n. thereof ANIMALS, 6
To *n.* an object is to destroy POETRY, 34
What's in a n. NAMES, 17
With a n. like yours NAMES, 6
names All the n. that I gave NAMES, 11
N. should be charms NAMES, 18

Negritude N. is the sum total of the values of the
   civilization of the African world   AFRICA, 12
Negro Being a N. in America   RACISM, 18
   One of the things that makes a N. unpleasant RACISM, 24
Negroes N. . . . to have a little more democracy CIVIL RIGHTS, 4
   restricting N. to the bleachers and pavilion   APARTHEID, 11
   There are a million N. in Mississippi   SOLIDARITY, 5
neighbor Your n. is a competitor, an enemy   SELFISHNESS, 4
neighborhood n. . . . out of it, you get beat   PLACES, 1
neighbours fear of what the n. might say   SUICIDE, 6
neither better if n. of us had been born   FRENCH REVOLUTION, 11
neo-biological A n. technology   TECHNOLOGY, 11
nervous system you're being attacked by the n.   FEAR, 15
Net The N. still resembles a congested street   INTERNET, 8
nettle Tender-handed stroke a n.   COURAGE, 6
networks Our n. . . . cooperative communities COMPUTERS, 21
neurosis by accepting the universal n. he is spared . . . a
   personal n.   BELIEF, 13
   Modern n. began with the discoveries of Copernicus
      NEUROSIS, 12
   N. . . . always a substitute for legitimate suffering
      NEUROSIS, 9
   N. . . . avoiding non-being by avoiding being NEUROSIS, 18
   N. . . . battle between two tendencies   NEUROSIS, 5
   N. . . . spontaneous archaeology of the libido NEUROSIS, 3
   N. has an absolute genius for malingering   NEUROSIS, 17
neurotic All the pretenses to which . . . n. resorts NEUROSIS, 6
   n. . . . airplane directed by remote control   NEUROSIS, 7
   n. . . . dread of that grim certainty   NEUROSIS, 14
   N. . . . not as sensible as I am   NEUROSIS, 13
   n. individual is the typical killjoy   NEUROSIS, 1
   N. nuclei . . . in the minds of normal   NEUROSIS, 4
   The n. striving for power   NEUROSIS, 8
neurotics A mistake which is commonly made about n.
      NEUROSIS, 2
   Everything great in the world is done by n.   NEUROSIS, 16
neutrality 'positive n.' is a contradiction in terms
      DIPLOMACY, 26
   The cold n. of an impartial judge   JUDGMENT, 8
never Better n. than late   INSULTS, 42
new A n. type of woman . . . a career woman   WOMEN, 28
   doing something impossibly n. . . . an illusion
      ORIGINALITY, 8
   The n. always happens against . . . overwhelming
      odds   INNOVATION, 1
new-born What is the use of a n. child   INVENTIONS, 4
New England most serious charge . . . against N. . . .
   February   PLACES, 3
newmoon n. new in all /the ancient sky   THE MOON, 10
news Ill n. hath wings   MISFORTUNE, 4
   only n. until he's read it. After that it's dead
      NEWSPAPERS, 23
newspaper A n. is a court   NEWSPAPERS, 10
   good n. . . . is a nation talking to itself   NEWSPAPERS, 16
   good n. is never nearly good enough   NEWSPAPERS, 12
   Moses . . . n. rates for the Ten Commandments
      NEWSPAPERS, 22
   Once a n. touches a story, the facts are lost   FACTS, 9
   Reading someone else's n.   NEWSPAPERS, 7
   The n. . . . denies itself   NEWSPAPERS, 3
   yesterday's n. and today's garbage   JOURNALISM, 3
newspapers I read the n. avidly   NEWSPAPERS, 6
   n. . . . filled with good news   NEWSPAPERS, 18
   n.! . . . they are the most villainous   NEWSPAPERS, 21
   N. always excite curiosity   NEWSPAPERS, 14
New Testament the N. is a divinely inspired book
      CHRISTIANITY, 4
new wave N. literature is . . . fashionable WORLD LITERATURE, 11
New World N. . . . crime of its destruction   SOUTH AMERICA, 8
   we may rightly call a N.   EXPLORATION, 10

New Year Meretricious and a Happy N.   WORDPLAY, 8
New-year happiest time of all the glad N.   FESTIVALS, 2
New York N. . . . that unnatural city   AMERICAN CITIES, 16
   N. . . . the mad dream   AMERICAN CITIES, 25
   N. is a small place   AMERICAN CITIES, 44
   N. is the most fatally fascinating thing AMERICAN CITIES, 21
   N. makes one think . . . collapse of civilization
      AMERICAN CITIES, 4
   N., New York—a helluva town   AMERICAN CITIES, 10
   One belongs to N. instantly   AMERICAN CITIES, 45
   Outside of N. there's nothing   EMIGRATION, 7
   The present in N. is so powerful   AMERICAN CITIES, 9
   two million interesting people in N.   AMERICAN CITIES, 37
nice Be n. to people on your way up   PRUDENCE, 4
   very n. if there were a God   GOD, 28
nickname n. is the heaviest stone   NAMES, 10
nicknames N. . . . give away the whole drama of man
      NAMES, 2
night at n. things live   NIGHT, 2
   By n. . . . atheist half believes a God   ATHEISM, 9
   Come n., strike hour   ENDURANCE, 2
   eldest N. /And Chaos   CHAOS, 4
   How long a n. can last   DEPRESSION, 7
   In the n. reason disappears   NIGHT, 9
   It ain't a fit n. out   WEATHER, 6
   N. and day   DECLARATIONS OF LOVE, 7
   N. hath a thousand eyes   NIGHT, 6
   N. of the Long Knives   FASCISM, 6
   real dark n. of the soul   DEPRESSION, 3
   The n. roared like a lion   NIGHT, 5
   This is the n. mail crossing   TRAINS, 1
   What hath n. to do with sleep   SLEEP, 17
nightingale the n. is homesick   BIRDS, 1
nightmare The marriage of reason and n. TWENTIETH CENTURY, 1
nights I long for the n.   THE CARIBBEAN, 1
nihilism what is coming . . . the rise of n.   NIHILISM, 4
nihilist a part-time n.   NIHILISM, 2
nihilists The n. say it is the end   DEATH AND DYING, 24
Nile as well dam . . . the N. with bulrushes
      BRITISH IMPERIALISM, 7
ninepence I have but n. in ready money   CONVERSATION, 1
ninety n.-odd years is gradual enough   CIVIL RIGHTS, 10
Nineveh Quinquireme of N.   BOATS, 7
noble a n. nature, . . . a serious subject   POETRY, 3
   Our most n. byword: progress   PROGRESS, 16
   The n. living and the n. dead   GREATNESS, 19
   though thy tackle's torn, /Thou show'st a n. vessel
      APPEARANCE, 17
nobody a man is n. unless his biography   BIOGRAPHY, 18
   n. ever changes for a woman   RELATIONSHIPS, 13
   N. ever tells me anything   COMPLAINTS, 4
   What will we do /when there is n. left /to kill KILLING, 4
noise A little noiseless n. among the leaves   SILENCE, 15
   A loud n. at one end   BABIES, 7
   Those people . . . are making such a n.   AUDIENCES, 11
noisy A n. man is always in the right   ARGUMENTS, 4
nominate n. a spade a spade   FRANKNESS, 1
non-existent You're entering a n. universe   INTERNET, 11
nonsense little n. now and then is treasured   NONSENSE, 1
nonviolence N. is a powerful and just weapon   WEAPONS, 9
non-violence N. . . . law of our species   PACIFISM, 3
nonviolent I'm n. with those who are n.   VIOLENCE, 7
   N. direct action seeks to create   CIVIL RIGHTS, 6
Northern Ireland consent of a majority . . . of N.
      NORTHERN IRELAND, 2
   politics of N. . . . macho in style   NORTHERN IRELAND, 8
nose Any n. /May ravage . . . a rose   SENSES, 2
   could not blow his n. without moralising
      LITERARY INSULTS, 14
   My n. bleeds for you   INSULTS, 44

My n. is huge! THE FACE, 17
see further than his own n. SELFISHNESS, 5
noses Hold their n. to the grindstone TYRANNY, 10
nostalgia n. . . . a hypertrophied sense of lost childhood
NOSTALGIA, 11
N. isn't what it used to be NOSTALGIA, 1
not n. one . . . who left their land PATRIOTISM, 2
not guilty I am one hundred percent n. INNOCENCE, 13
nothin' You ain't heard n. yet BOASTS, 11
nothing Adapt the n. therein to the purpose NOTHINGNESS, 7
Certainly n. is unnatural NATURE, 32
from n. to a state of extreme poverty POVERTY, 23
having n. a-year, paid quarterly POVERTY, 31
I believe in n. . . . everything is absurd NIHILISM, 1
N. FRENCH REVOLUTION, 6
n. . . . except empty curved space ASTRONOMY, 9
N. . . . said that's not been said before ORIGINALITY, 7
N. begins and n. ends PAIN, 13
n. can be known KNOWLEDGE, 9
N. can be produced out of n. NOTHINGNESS, 4
n. can bring back the hour TRANSIENCE, 26
n. either good or bad THINKING, 38
N. happens to the very rich WEALTH, 17
N. in the world matters NIHILISM, 3
n. is often a good thing to do SILENCE, 9
N. lasts long enough to make any sense REALITY, 16
N., like something, happens anywhere NOTHINGNESS, 8
there is n. else here to enjoy PARTIES, 7
There is n. to be said in mitigation GUILT, 5
When you have n. to say, say n. SILENCE, 7
nothingness Those who . . . have a taste for n. NOTHINGNESS, 2
notice n. whether it's summer or winter SEASONS, 3
noticeboard planetary n. open to everyman INTERNET, 10
nought This . . . world /Should so wear out to n.
SUFFERING, 23
nourishment turn . . . n. . . . into a painful attack THE BODY, 8
Nouvelle Vague The dream of the N. FILMS, 11
novel A good n. tells us the truth LITERATURE, 15
a n. about this astonishing metropolis
AMERICAN LITERATURE, 32
A n. can be approached in two ways LITERATURE, 42
A n. is a mirror LITERATURE, 49
A n. is a river LITERATURE, 41
A n. is a static thing THEATRE, 4
In the n. as in literature LITERATURE, 3
no more beautiful mission than . . . the free n. FICTION, 4
No one says a n. has to be one thing BOOKS, 44
not a n. to be tossed aside lightly LITERARY INSULTS, 44
the n. . . . none of our culture's business
EUROPEAN LITERATURE, 14
The n. being dead LITERATURE, 51
The n. is a way of life LITERATURE, 2
the n. tells a story LITERATURE, 21
things that the n. does not say LITERATURE, 11
to read a n. I write one READING, 10
novelist a n. hot as a firecracker READING, 6
A n. is, like all mortals WRITERS, 51
A n. is not in the world WRITERS, 64
being a n., I consider myself superior to the saint, the
scientist WRITERS, 43
n. is the historian of the present WRITERS, 17
n. sits over his work like . . . god FILMS, 26
the n. is a team of painters WRITERS, 26
novelists There are many reasons why n. write WRITERS, 24
novels The lies of n. are never gratuitous BOOKS, 59
novelty N., n., n. NOVELTY, 1
nuclear discovery of n. chain reactions . . . destruction of
mankind NUCLEAR WAR, 6
Following a n. attack on . . . United States
NUCLEAR WAR, 16

n. sword of Damocles NUCLEAR WAR, 9
nuclear family Nobody has ever before asked the n.
FAMILY, 16
nuclear fission n. . . . natural process TECHNOLOGY, 13
nuclear weapons a market in . . . portable n. BUSINESS, 28
nude The trouble with n. dancing DANCING, 8
nuisance social n. of the inveterate punster WORDPLAY, 6
nuisances a change of n. is as good as a vacation
HAPPINESS, 29
number N. theorists are like lotus-eaters MATHEMATICS, 22
numbers N. . . . only universal language MATHEMATICS, 34
nuptial N. love maketh mankind LOVE, 5
Nuremberg Rally I know it's like a N. AUDIENCES, 9
nurse n. . . . one of the great blessings MEDICINE, 27
Our foster n. of nature is repose SLEEP, 23
nuttin' I got plenty o' n. POVERTY, 16
nymphomaniac n. of the heart EMOTION, 4
oath No o. too binding for a lover LOVERS, 16
obedience O. is the mother of success OBEDIENCE, 1
object don't o. if I'm sick SMOKING, 2
Every o. is the mirror PERCEPTION, 9
o. is the sum of its complications REALITY, 23
o. of . . . civil government is the improvement
GOVERNMENT, 1
she was only an o. of contempt CHARACTER, 4
objection The principal o. to old age OLD AGE, 1
objective by losing himself in the o. THE SELF, 10
O. knowing is alienated knowing ECOLOGY, 8
oblivion formless ruin of o. TRANSIENCE, 25
observation From his close o. of life UNDERSTANDING, 14
o. of nature . . . an artist's life ARTISTS, 26
observations Don't make o. on cats and dogs WRITING, 39
observe Whenever you o. an animal closely ANIMALS, 12
obsession O. of all the beds . . . pigeonhole bedrooms
OBSESSIONS, 1
obstacle chief o. in the way of . . . self-consciousness
SELF-KNOWLEDGE, 19
obstacles many o. and difficulties . . . of revolution
ASIAN COUNTRIES, 22
obvious the analysis of the o. RESEARCH, 10
occupied Although they are an o. nation NATIONS, 11
ocean A life on the o. wave THE SEA, 27
ocean people O. are different from land people THE SEA, 17
Odyssey O. and . . . Exodus . . . early travel books
LITERATURE, 47
Oedipus complex mother . . . the O. PSYCHOANALYSIS, 8
Oedipuses a tense and peculiar family, the O.
PSYCHOANALYSIS, 1
offence dire o. from am'rous causes springs TRIVIALITY, 2
greatest o. against virtue VIRTUE, 14
o. of the political prisoner . . . political boldness
HUMAN RIGHTS, 4
offensive o. letter follows POLITICAL INSULTS, 4
offer make him an o. he can't refuse BRIBERY, 9
office in o. but not in power GOVERNMENT, 30
tall modern o. building is the machine ARCHITECTURE, 33
official secret the 'o.' is bureaucracy's specific invention
SECRECY, 14
off-shore O., by islands hidden in the blood MAGIC, 6
often Do you come here o. SEDUCTION, 8
Ogoni O. people . . . confront their tormentors WRITING, 46
old being o. is having lighted rooms OLD AGE, 24
desire o. age . . . prolonged infirmity OLD AGE, 3
Forty is the o. age of youth MIDDLE AGE, 12
grew o. first . . . in other people's eyes OLD AGE, 4
Growing o. is . . . a bad habit OLD AGE, 27
If you want to be a dear o. lady at seventy OLD AGE, 35
nicest o. ladies I ever met LITERARY INSULTS, 19
No matter how o. a mother is MOTHERS, 12
O. age . . . an island surrounded by death OLD AGE, 30

pave we could p. the whole country   AMERICAN IMPERIALISM, 29
pay Can't P.! . . . Won't P.!   PROTEST, 5
    not my interest to p. the principal   DEBT, 17
pays He that dies p. all debts   DEBT, 15
peace a period of cold p.   COLD WAR, 10
    Arms alone are not enough to keep the p.   PEACE, 15
    forbidden . . . to make p. with a monarch   IMPERIALISM, 9
    Give P. a Chance   PEACE, 16
    He accepted p.   PEACE, 25
    I live in p. with men   PEACE, 19
    I want p. . . . I'm willing to fight   PEACE, 33
    Knowledge of p. /passes . . . like children's games   PEACE, 1
    Let him who desires p., prepare for war   PEACE, 34
    My p. is gone, /My heart is heavy   SORROW, 9
    never was a good war or a bad p.   WAR, 23
    no p. . . . unto the wicked   PEACE, 5
    Nothing is more conducive to p. of mind   OPINIONS, 10
    no way to p. P. is the way   PEACE, 24
    P. . . . is no original state   PEACE, 8
    P. . . . period of cheating   PEACE, 7
    P., commerce, and honest friendship   NATIONS, 14
    P. goes into the making of a poem   POETRY, 41
    p. has broken out   PEACE, 10
    P. hath her victories   PEACE, 22
    p. in being what one is   SELF-KNOWLEDGE, 5
    P. is indivisible   PEACE, 18
    P. is made with yesterday's enemies   PEACE, 26
    P. is much more precious than . . . land   PEACE, 29
    P. is not only better than war   PEACE, 30
    P. took them all prisoner   PEACE, 14
    p. with honour. I believe it is p. for our time   PEACE, 13
    Perpetual p. is a dream   PEACE, 23
    plant p. . . . I do not want discord   PEACE, 2
    seek the true meaning of p.   ASIAN COUNTRIES, 6
    the miasma of p. seems more suffocating   PEACE, 31
    There can be no p. of mind in love   LOVE, 49
    there is nothing . . . meaning of p.   PEACE, 4
    When p. has been broken anywhere   PEACE, 27
    You may either win your p. or buy it   PEACE, 28
peach dare to eat a p.   INDECISION, 2
    ripest p. is highest on the tree   AMBITION, 26
pearls P. before swine   INSULTS, 32
peas I eat my p. with honey   EATING, 8
pease As lyke as one p. is to another   SIMILARITY, 2
pedantic I acquired a certain p. presumption   CLASS, 29
peer A life p. is like a mule   POLITICAL INSULTS, 48
peerage When I want a p., I shall buy one   CORRUPTION, 9
Peking P.'s food . . . part of the city's life   ASIAN CITIES, 2
pen p. is mightier than the sword   WRITING, 36
    p. is the tongue   WRITING, 7
    The squat p. rests   WRITING, 27
pendulum The p. of the mind   MIND, 11
pennies P. from Heaven   OPTIMISM, 2
penny P. saved is a p. got   MONEY, 15
people all God's p. . . . like to play   PLEASURE, 25
    A p. not prepared to face its own history   HISTORY, 45
    Every p. should be left free   FREEDOM, 14
    For a p. to be without History   HISTORY, 21
    forget that . . . p. are human   PROPAGANDA, 2
    Hell of Too Many P.   HELL, 15
    I didn't think p. invented anymore   INVENTIONS, 9
    If p. behaved . . . the way nations do   NATIONS, 21
    make p. think they're thinking   THINKING, 26
    my p. *is* my soul   THE SOUL, 7
    not one . . . who think . . . the p. are never . . . wrong   DEMOCRACY, 8
    Once the p. begin to reason   REASON, 30
    p. . . . complained of the long voyage   EXPLORATION, 4
    P. . . . taking care of their health   HYPOCHONDRIA, 8

    p. . . . usually imitate each other   CONFORMITY, 7
    p. annoy me . . . talking about . . . dumb animals   BIRDS, 8
    P. are either charming or tedious   CHARM, 6
    P. are inexterminable   SURVIVAL, 1
    P. are not willing to be governed   DEMOCRACY, 47
    P. are worms   MISANTHROPY, 1
    P. don't want to like you   BEAUTY, 40
    P. have power when p. think they have   POWER, 18
    P. must help one another   HELP, 4
    p. on long-distance buses   AMERICANS, 3
    p. under suspicion are better moving   JUDGMENT, 13
    P. who can't talk . . . who can't read   JOURNALISM, 35
    P. who do things   ACHIEVEMENT, 18
    P. who like this sort of thing   TASTE, 11
    P. whose company is coveted   CELEBRITY, 10
    p. will see, tremble, and groan   RUSSIAN REVOLUTION, 8
    P. will swim through shit   GREED, 7
    suppose the p. good, and the magistrate corruptible   GOVERNMENT, 48
    talk of p. trying to convince themselves   PHILOSOPHY, 40
    the only p. who like to be told how bad things   BRITAIN, 12
    The p.—could you patent the sun?   DISCOVERY, 9
    The p. are unreal   HOLLYWOOD, 2
    The p. would be just as noisy   POPULARITY, 3
    Too many p. grow up   GROWING UP, 3
    two p. entitled to refer to themselves as 'we'   JOURNALISM, 24
    we are not a small p.   BRITAIN, 18
    We, the p. . . . a very eloquent beginning   UNITED STATES, 33
    When p. . . . talk . . . of their aspirations   THEFT, 13
perception Organized p. . . . what art is all about   ART, 30
perceptions All the p. of the human mind   PERCEPTION, 5
perestroika 'p.' has easily entered the international lexicon   RUSSIA, 16
    essence of p.   SOCIALISM, 5
perfect No one is p. in this imperfect world   PERFECTION, 6
    the most p. actual world which is possible   EXISTENCE, 12
    the p. and unique cause of all things   MYSTICISM, 1
perfection Only p. was good enough   PERFECTION, 8
    P. has one grave defect   PERFECTION, 7
    P. is the child of Time   PERFECTION, 5
    The pursuit of p.   PERFECTION, 1
    What's come to p. perishes   PERFECTION, 2
performance The only true p.   PERFORMANCE, 3
performances p. where the public is . . . without talent   AUDIENCES, 7
performing p. gives . . . a place where I hide   PERFORMANCE, 5
perfumes All the p. of Arabia will not sweeten   GUILT, 17
perhaps I am going in search of a great p.   AFTERLIFE, 15
perish P. the Universe   REVENGE, 6
perished If all else p., and he remained   DELUSIONS OF LOVE, 2
permanence love p. more than . . . beauty   BRITAIN, 3
permissive society The p. has . . . become a dirty phrase   LIBERALISM, 3
Perón If I had not been born P.   PRIDE, 8
perpendicular p. expression of a horizontal desire   DANCING, 15
perpetrate p. thirty bad novels   LITERARY INSULTS, 17
perpetuate To p. was the task of life   NATURE, 24
perpetuation Why should I consent to the p. of the image   THE FACE, 13
persecution P. is a bad . . . way to plant religion   PERSECUTION, 1
    P. produced its natural effect   PERSECUTION, 3
    Religious p. may shield itself   PERSECUTION, 2
perseverance p. in a good cause   PERSISTENCE, 3
person 'p.', . . . individual substance of a rational nature   INDIVIDUALITY, 1
    A p. can run for years   HOME, 11

I am not . . . the sort of p.   APPEARANCE, 1
only p. . . . I should like to know   SELF-KNOWLEDGE, 42
p. . . . most likely to kill you is yourself   MURDER, 15
the only thing that can exist is an uninterested p.
                                                     CURIOSITY, 3
We know what a p. thinks   ACTION, 17
personal don't have a warm p. enemy left   ENEMIES, 9
personality disturbance of the p. . . . psychic illness
                                                     PSYCHIATRY, 6
persons I am made up of several p.   IDENTITY, 5
Peruvians we P. lie, invent, dream   SOUTH AMERICA, 12
perverse the most p. and malevolent creature
                                              LITERARY INSULTS, 60
perversity no original p. in the human heart   ROMANTICISM, 3
P. is not very inventive   PERVERSITY, 5
P. is the muse of modern literature   PERVERSITY, 7
pessimism P. . . . as agreeable as optimism   PESSIMISM, 2
p. is a mark of superior intellect   PESSIMISM, 6
pessimist A p. . . . looks both ways   PESSIMISM, 11
p. . . . believes things couldn't possibly be worse
                                                     PESSIMISM, 3
Scratch a p.   PRIVILEGE, 2
pessimistic Nothing makes me more p.   PESSIMISM, 7
pessimists p. end up . . . desiring the things they fear
                                                     PESSIMISM, 10
Peter see Shock-headed P.   CHILDREN, 16
Petersburg live in P. . . . sleep in a grave   EUROPEAN CITIES, 18
P. burned in delirium   EUROPEAN CITIES, 29
petrifactions p. of a plodding brain   INSULTS, 6
petty P. intrigues and dramatic scenes among the relatives
                                                     FUNERALS, 8
phantoms P. . . . trifling disorders of the spirit
                                             THE SUPERNATURAL, 29
phenomena eight . . . p. . . . worth talking about   WEATHER, 5
phenomenology P. . . . a transcendental philosophy
                                                     PHILOSOPHY, 22
Philadelphia P. . . . City of Bleak November Afternoons
                                               AMERICAN CITIES, 34
Philippi thou shalt see me at P.   THE SUPERNATURAL, 34
Philippines People of the P.   ASIAN COUNTRIES, 18
Philistine smote the P. in his forehead   VICTORY, 2
philosopher Be a p. . . . be still a man   PHILOSOPHY, 14
Once: a p.; twice: a pervert   SEX, 43
p. . . . redefines his subject   PHILOSOPHY, 9
p.'s treatment of a question . . . illness   QUESTIONS, 11
p. no circumstance . . . is too minute   PHILOSOPHY, 10
p. /That could endure the toothache   ENDURANCE, 8
philosophers p. have only interpreted the world   CHANGE, 24
p. intent on forcing others   PHILOSOPHY, 28
The great p. are poets   POETS, 41
till p. become kings   POLITICIANS, 39
philosophic the p. anarchists of the North   ANARCHY, 15
philosophical European p. tradition . . . footnotes to Plato
                                                     PHILOSOPHY, 43
proof of p. mediocrity   PHILOSOPHY, 33
philosophizing two main requirements for p.   PHILOSOPHY, 38
philosophy a great advantage for . . . p. to be . . . true
                                                     PHILOSOPHY, 37
great p. is . . . a fearless one   PHILOSOPHY, 32
How charming is divine p.   PHILOSOPHY, 23
I've not got a first in p.   CONFUSION, 3
knowing its limits . . . p. consists   PHILOSOPHY, 16
mere touch of cold p.   CHARM, 3
modern p. holds passion in contempt   PASSION, 3
new P. calls all in doubt   REASON, 11
Not to care for p.   PHILOSOPHY, 31
P. . . . is a fight against . . . fascination   PHILOSOPHY, 44
P. . . . is metaphysics getting underway   PHILOSOPHY, 13
P. . . . living voluntarily among ice   PHILOSOPHY, 26
p. . . . the personal confession of its author   PHILOSOPHY, 25

P. does not exist   PHILOSOPHY, 18
P. has always gone astray   PHILOSOPHY, 29
P. is . . . like Russia   PHILOSOPHY, 27
P. is the childhood of the intellect   PHILOSOPHY, 24
P., like medicine, has plenty of drugs   PHILOSOPHY, 3
p. ought to . . . unravel people's mental blocks
                                                     PHILOSOPHY, 35
P. triumphs . . . over past evils   PHILOSOPHY, 19
The goal of p. . . . men to understand themselves
                                                     PHILOSOPHY, 1
The point of p. is to start with something . . . simple
                                                     PHILOSOPHY, 36
Phoebus And P. 'gins arise   MORNING, 16
phone E. T. p. home   COMMUNICATION, 7
phone call p. . . . a rude metal double-fart   COMMUNICATION, 15
the most historic p. ever made   COMMUNICATION, 12
phoney a p. war   WORLD WAR II, 11
photograph A p. is not an accident, it is a concept
                                                     PHOTOGRAPHY, 1
A p. is not only an image   PHOTOGRAPHY, 10
one criterion for a good p. . . . unforgettable
                                                     PHOTOGRAPHY, 3
p. guards the memory of a man   MEMORY, 9
things nobody would see . . . didn't p. them
                                                     PHOTOGRAPHY, 2
photographs burning the p. /of divided Jerusalem
                                                 MIDDLE EAST, 3
photography P. is truth   FILMS, 12
phrase I summed up all systems in a p.   QUOTATIONS, 9
physic the p. of the field   ANIMALS, 34
physical a right p. size for every idea   SCULPTURE, 7
man thinks about his p. or moral state   ILLNESS, 9
p. care . . . psychological care at these stages
                                                     CHILDREN, 35
physician A p. can . . . parry the scythe of death   TIME, 45
A p. is one who pours drugs   DOCTORS, 16
p.'s best remedy . . . *Tincture of Time*   REMEDIES, 23
The p. cannot prescribe by letter   DOCTORS, 1
the strength of the p.   DOCTORS, 15
physicians p. are the class of people who kill other men
                                                     DOCTORS, 10
P. must discover the weaknesses of the human mind
                                                     DOCTORS, 5
the help of too many p.   DOCTORS, 1
physicists The p. have known sin   PHYSICS, 11
physics Classical p. . . . superseded by quantum theory
                                                     PHYSICS, 13
P. . . . the greatest collective work of science   PHYSICS, 4
P. . . . too hard for physicists   PHYSICS, 9
The pope of P. has moved   PHYSICS, 10
There is no democracy in p.   PHYSICS, 1
piano I hear the p. playing . . . as a ghost might play
                                             THE SUPERNATURAL, 12
I hit the p. with my elbow   JAZZ, 20
notes lying around on that old p.   MUSICIANS, 4
Piccadilly Circus Crossing P.   EXPLORATION, 9
picnic p. is the Englishman's grand gesture   EATING, 1
Picts the P. can be likened to a mystery   SCOTLAND, 4
picture A well-painted p. gives us a pleasure   PAINTING, 29
Every time I make a p.   FILMS, 8
pie p. in the sky when you die   AFTERLIFE, 10
You don't want no p. in the sky   DESIRE, 1
piece A p. of us is in every person   SELF-KNOWLEDGE, 22
When a p. gets difficult make faces   PERFORMANCE, 7
piety P. . . . honour truth over our friends   TRUTH, 5
pigeon-liver'd But I am p., and lack gall   INDECISION, 7
pigmies P. . . . on the shoulders of giants   DISCOVERY, 8
pillar a p. of salt   PUNISHMENT, 2
pillars The four p. of government   GOVERNMENT, 4
pillow like a p. on a bed   LOVERS, 5

pills It is an age of p. — DRUGS, 19
pimples like p. on an angel's arse — HUMAN NATURE, 4
pin like a p., but without . . . head or . . . point — INSULTS, 18
pink The very p. of perfection — PERFECTION, 4
pint A P. OF PLAIN IS YOUR ONLY MAN — ALCOHOL, 15
pin-up p., the centerfold, the poster — PORNOGRAPHY, 5
pioneering The two p. forces of modern sensibility — THE ARTS, 5
pious A p. man . . . would be an atheist if the king were — BELIEF, 17
pipe p. for Fortune's finger — INTEGRITY, 3
Pirandello reduced to putting on plays by P. — THEATRE, 13
piss I can p. the old boy — BOASTS, 7
pistol Somebody leaves a p. in the drawer — SUICIDE, 13
pits You are the p. — INSULTS, 26
pity P. . . . arrests the mind — SUFFERING, 7
p. this busy monster, manunkind, /not — PROGRESS, 10
place A p. for everything — ORDER, 9
this is an awful p. — EXPLORATION, 8
plagiarism P. has many advantages — PLAGIARISM, 1
plague I watch the progress of the p. — AIDS, 4
plan This p. . . . reserve against more evil days — MIDDLE EAST, 14
plane only two emotions in a p.: boredom and terror — FLYING, 7
planet Our p. . . . consists . . . of lumps of fall-out — CREATION, 12
Pity the p., all joy gone — THE EARTH, 11
planets The p. in their station listening stood — CREATION, 15
plantations P. didn't have any wire — SLAVERY, 7
plastic No p. expression . . . residue of an experience — ART, 35
platonic I know nothing about p. love — FRIENDSHIP, 20
platonism P. provided Christianity with its unique Gospel — CHRISTIANITY, 20
play In a good p. every speech . . . fully flavoured — THEATRE, 20
Knowing how to p. . . . the barest superficiality — MUSICIANS, 1
p. is an expression of the highest seriousness — HUMAN NATURE, 16
structure of a p. . . . always the story — THEATRE, 10
The p.'s the thing — CONSCIENCE, 18
The p. is memory — MEMORY, 45
plays p. about rape, sodomy and drug addiction — ENTERTAINMENT, 2
p. are sinfull, heathenish . . . Spectacles — THEATRE, 14
playthings p. of blind chance — CHANCE, 2
pleasant If we do not find anything p. — NOVELTY, 2
p. to be urged to do something — ABILITY, 4
please Nothing can permanently p. — PLEASURE, 8
pleasing art of p. consists in being pleased — PLEASURE, 14
pleasure admit the Muse of sweet p. — PLEASURE, 26
as much p. in the reading — READING, 26
He that will do anything for . . . p. — PLEASURE, 17
p. . . . In being mad — MADNESS, 17
P. . . . knowledge or feeling of perfection — PLEASURE, 20
p. . . . the criterion of every good thing — PLEASURE, 11
P.'s a sin — PLEASURE, 4
P. after all is a safer guide — PLEASURE, 3
p. for the senses, and let the devil — SENSES, 13
P. is . . . seldom found where it is sought — PLEASURE, 18
P. is . . . the intermission of pain — PLEASURE, 29
P. is a lovely flame — PLEASURE, 6
P. is labour too — PLEASURE, 9
The p. is momentary — SEX, 16
pleasures Look not on p. — PLEASURE, 16
Mid p. and palaces though we may roam — HOME, 15
one of the p. of having a rout — PARTIES, 4
p. . . . of feeling capable of virtue — VIRTUE, 15

P. newly found are sweet — PLEASURE, 31
Pledge of Allegiance P. . . . Hail Satan — PATRIOTISM, 26
plot P. me no plots — RUMOUR, 1
Those blessed structures, p. and rhyme — POETRY, 32
plots there are only six basic p. — STORYTELLING, 8
plough I must p. my furrow alone — SOLITUDE, 22
plow man who pulls the p. gets . . . plunder — POLITICS, 34
plums p. /that were in /the icebox — APOLOGIES, 4
plural in the p. and they bounce — INSULTS, 24
pluralism true p. of social attitudes — TWENTY-FIRST CENTURY, 2
poem A p. is energy transferred — POETRY, 42
A p. is never finished — POETRY, 54
A p. lovely as a tree — TREES, 3
a p. shd happen to you like cold water or a kiss — POETRY, 51
A p. should be wordless /As the flight of birds — POETRY, 33
a pretty p., Mr. Pope — LITERARY INSULTS, 3
bathed in the P. /Of the Sea — THE SEA, 26
don't make a p. with thoughts — POETRY, 15
I do not think this p. will reach its destination — CRITICISM, 28
p. . . . not made up of these letters — POETRY, 14
The p. /feeds upon thought — POETRY, 19
the p. wants to glorify suffering — POETRY, 22
the visible p. of the world — GOD, 26
poems all the p. that ever were invented — CRITICS, 9
They're just people that write p. — POETS, 50
poet All the p. can do today is to warn — POETS, 46
A p. is . . . unpoetical — POETS, 38
A p., starving in a garret — POETS, 60
a p. who writes with a knife — MIDDLE EAST, 26
A true p. does not bother to be poetical — POETS, 15
But the p.'s job — POETS, 20
How does the p. speak — POETS, 13
like a p. woo the moon — POETS, 10
lunatic, the lover, and the p. — IMAGINATION, 17
No man was ever yet a great p. . . . profound
    philosopher — POETS, 16
No p. . . . has his complete meaning alone — POETS, 22
not possible for a p. . . . to protect — POETS, 6
p. . . . medium /of Nature — POETS, 27
p. . . . priest of the invisible — POETS, 59
p. can earn much more money . . . talking — POETS, 2
p. is like the prince of the clouds — POETS, 3
p. like an acrobat /climbs on rime — POETS, 24
p. may be used as the barometer — POETS, 63
p., prying locksmith of invisible things — POETS, 23
p. without love — POETS, 12
The p. begins where the man ends — POETS, 45
The p. gives us his essence — WRITERS, 69
The p. lives by exaggeration — POETS, 11
The P. of Immortal Youth — POETS, 64
the room of the p. in disgrace — POETS, 1
To be a p. is a condition — POETS, 31
You should have been a p. — POETS, 4
poetic p. effect . . . generate different readings — POETRY, 20
poetry can't ignore p. . . . into the Top Ten — POPULAR MUSIC, 36
complexities of p. . . . destroyed by the media — POETRY, 5
essential elements of our p. . . . courage, audacity — POETRY, 35
If P. comes not . . . as Leaves to a tree — POETRY, 29
In p. we identify ourselves with language — READING, 4
I would define . . . p. . . . as the rhythmical creation
    of Beauty — BEAUTY, 26
motive of p. — POETRY, 43
no man ever talked p. — POETRY, 18
not p., but prose run mad — POETRY, 46
P. . . . cat concert under the window — POETRY, 52
P. . . . is perfection's sweat — POETRY, 57
P. . . . man explores his own amazement — POETRY, 24

p. . . . religion represents the world as a man   MYTHS, 8
P. . . . spontaneous overflow of powerful feelings
                                                   POETRY, 61
p. . . . to me it's the oil of life   POETRY, 8
p. after Auschwitz is barbaric   POETRY, 2
P. and painting . . . same way you make love
                                                   PAINTING, 24
P. can speak of immortality   POETRY, 7
p. had the strength to rival . . . narcotics   POETRY, 6
p. is . . . excavation   POETRY, 59
P. is a comforting piece of fiction   POETRY, 37
P. is as much a part of the universe   POETRY, 9
P. is a weapon loaded with the future   POETRY, 12
P. is the revelation of a feeling   POETRY, 47
P. is the supreme fiction   POETRY, 53
P. is the voice of a poet   POETRY, 17
P. is to fall in love   POETRY, 58
P. is to prose   POETRY, 55
P. is what gets lost in translation   POETRY, 23
P., I will swear by /You   POETRY, 44
P. makes nothing happen   POETRY, 4
P. makes things happen   POETRY, 40
P. will steal death from me   POETRY, 13
The difference between genuine p.   LITERARY INSULTS, 2
The thing that makes p. different   POETRY, 38
Today's p. . . . poetry of strife   POETRY, 36
To search the heart is p.'s lifeblood   POETRY, 11
What is p.   POETRY, 49
poets For p., language is a maze   POETS, 58
Immature p. imitate   PLAGIARISM, 5
I must have wanton p., pleasant wits   MONARCHY, 26
Modern p. . . . more wonderful material than Homer
                                                   POETS, 5
P. and painters are outside the class system   POETS, 7
P. are . . . more concerned to conjure   GOVERNMENT, 21
P. are . . . the trumpets which sing   POETS, 55
p. being second-rate   MEDIOCRITY, 7
p. steal from Homer   PLAGIARISM, 3
Popular p. are the parish priests   POETS, 51
The p. and philosophers . . . have discovered the
  unconscious   CONSCIOUSNESS, 5
point of view A p. can be a dangerous luxury   OPINIONS, 13
poison a subtle p. from ordinary trifles   GOSSIP, 2
pellet with the p.'s in the vessel   KILLING, 5
P. more deadly than a mad dog's tooth   JEALOUSY, 14
the p. is in the sugar   DANGER, 7
The surest p. is time   TIME, 15
poisons p. are our principal medicines   REMEDIES, 10
poker I'm at a p. table with five guys   FILMS, 5
P. shouldn't be played . . . house with women
                                                 GAMBLING, 3
Poland P. is in the position . . . I wanted her
                                     EUROPEAN COUNTRIES, 33
pole One step beyond the p.   EXPLORATION, 6
polecat A semi-house-trained p.   POLITICAL INSULTS, 22
policy if the p. isn't hurting, it isn't working ECONOMICS, 19
My home p.? I wage war   WAR, 16
Our p. is directed . . . against hunger   EUROPE, 25
politeness P. is organized indifference   MANNERS, 8
political All p. lives . . . end in failure   POLITICIANS, 41
a man . . . enough to have discovered a p. theory
                                       CENTRAL AMERICA, 1
formation of the p. will   NATIONS, 12
Man is by nature a p. animal   POLITICS, 2
p. chaos . . . decay of language   LANGUAGE, 30
P. genius . . . identifying oneself with a principle
                                                 POLITICS, 25
p. speech . . . defence of the indefensible   RHETORIC, 5
Seek ye first the p. kingdom   POLITICS, 43
When p. ammunition runs low   POLITICAL INSULTS, 50

political correctness P. is a really inane concept ORTHODOXY, 4
political science new world demands a new p.   POLITICS, 50
political systems To model our p. upon speculations
                                               GOVERNMENT, 20
politician a bit of a murderer, to be a p.   POLITICIANS, 34
A p. . . . can give away . . . his soul   POLITICIANS, 33
a p. is an arse   POLITICIANS, 12
A p. rises on the backs   POLITICIANS, 23
career p. . . . bull elk in the rut   POLITICIANS, 50
carefully packaged persona of today's p.   POLITICIANS, 53
p. . . . approaches every question with . . . open
  mouth   POLITICIANS, 47
p. . . . with whose politics you did not agree   POLITICIANS, 31
p. is a man who understands government   POLITICIANS, 52
p. is the devil's quilted anvil   POLITICIANS, 56
p. ought to be born a foundling   POLITICIANS, 25
p. will . . . even become a patriot   POLITICIANS, 21
The p. is an acrobat   POLITICIANS, 4
the p. poses as the servant   POLITICIANS, 14
unfair to expect a p. to live in private   HYPOCRISY, 16
politicians All p. have selective memories   POLITICIANS, 49
All p. have vanity   POLITICIANS, 46
Old p. . . . revive in the limelight   POLITICIANS, 36
P. . . . get respectable if they last   RESPECTABILITY, 4
P. . . . order more tunnel   POLITICIANS, 42
P. are the same all over   POLITICIANS, 26
P. can forgive almost anything   POLITICIANS, 55
p. have promised the moon   THE MOON, 9
P. tend to live *in character*   POLITICIANS, 29
p. will always be there   POLITICIANS, 35
politics can't adopt p. . . . and remain honest   POLITICS, 26
don't play p. with people's jobs   POLITICS, 30
first rule of p. is not to lie   LYING, 21
first thing that one loses in p.   POLITICS, 35
I am not made for p.   POLITICS, 17
In p. . . . ask a woman   WOMEN, 49
Never judge a country by its p.   ENGLAND, 11
p. . . . art of staying /out of jail   POLITICS, 54
P. . . . between the disastrous and the unpalatable
                                                 POLITICS, 22
p. . . . makes men arrogant   POLITICS, 38
p. . . . of this country are frozen   POLITICS, 27
P. . . . only profession for which no preparation
                                                 POLITICS, 49
P. . . . reflex of the business and industrial POLITICS, 23
P. does work better when citizens   POLITICS, 48
p. is . . . undignified contest between groups   POLITICS, 37
P. is a blood sport   POLITICS, 8
p. is for the present   MATHEMATICS, 11
P. is just like show business   POLITICS, 46
P. is opposed to morality   POLITICS, 33
P. is the art of preventing people from taking part
                                                 POLITICS, 51
P. is the art of the possible   POLITICS, 11
p. is the bow of idealism   POLITICS, 42
P. is the clearing house of pressures   POLITICS, 29
Practical p. . . . ignoring facts   POLITICS, 1
We cannot safely leave p. to politicians   DEMOCRACY, 14
polling booth Now we can go to the p. without a bad
  conscience   AFRICAN COUNTRIES, 3
polyphiloprogenitive P.   LANGUAGE, 13
poodle small p. tries to walk through   RUSSIA, 20
Pooh P. began to feel a little more comfortable THINKING, 29
Supposing P. . . . a tree fell on us   POSSIBILITY, 4
poor being p. . . . takes up all your time   POVERTY, 10
how p. a thing is man   HUMANKIND, 7
I, being p., have only my dreams   DREAMS, 33
If a free society cannot help the . . . p.   SOCIETY, 12
If there were no p.   POVERTY, 18
not be a p. man . . . Tsardom   RUSSIA, 12

only the p. . . . are forbidden to beg — POVERTY, 13
Resolve not to be p. — POVERTY, 19
The p. are our brothers and sisters — POVERTY, 32
To be p. and independent . . . an impossibility — POVERTY, 7
pop P. is the perfect religious vehicle — POPULAR MUSIC, 8
P. music is . . . lots of drugs — POPULAR MUSIC, 20
P. was . . . the new Art — ARTISTIC STYLES, 26
Pope Anybody can be P. — ACHIEVEMENT, 13
popular a p. politics reconciling themes — POLITICS, 12
We're more p. than Jesus Christ — POPULARITY, 8
popularity P.? . . . glory's small change — POPULARITY, 6
P. is a crime — POPULARITY, 5
P. is exhausting — POPULARITY, 9
population starving p. . . . absentee aristocracy . . . alien
Church — IRELAND, 11
The purpose of p. . . . is to fill heaven — PURPOSE, 2
porcelain precious p. of human clay — THE HEART, 1
pornographers P. are the enemies of women — PORNOGRAPHY, 3
P. subvert this last, vital privacy — PORNOGRAPHY, 10
pornographic every p. and erotic possibility — PERVERSITY, 1
pornography p. . . . it is terribly, terribly boring
                                                                                — PORNOGRAPHY, 4
p. is really about . . . death — PORNOGRAPHY, 8
P. is the attempt to insult sex — PORNOGRAPHY, 6
show that gives p. a bad name — PORNOGRAPHY, 2
portion best p. of a good man's life — GOOD, 29
portrait daguerreotyped p. of a commonplace face
                                                                                — LITERARY INSULTS, 7
Every time I paint a p. I lose a friend — PAINTING, 36
I do not paint a p. to look like the subject — PAINTING, 13
p. . . . something wrong with the mouth — PAINTING, 37
two styles of p. painting — ARTISTIC STYLES, 7
portrayal My task . . . p. of human beings — WOMEN'S RIGHTS, 15
positive P., adj. Mistaken at the top of one's voice
                                                                                — CERTAINTY, 2
possess We p. nothing certainly except the past — CERTAINTY, 7
possessed Men are p. by the devil — THE DEVIL, 8
possession P. is eleven points in the law — LAW, 10
possessions Why grab p. like thieves — MATERIALISM, 2
possible all things are p. to him that believeth — BELIEF, 5
The only way of finding the limits of the p.
                                                                                — IMPOSSIBILITY, 5
Possum P.'s hommage to Milton — POETS, 40
posterity always doing something for p. — POSTERITY, 1
down to p. talking bad grammar — GRAMMAR, 7
P. . . . wrong as anybody else — POSTERITY, 2
What has p. done for us — POSTERITY, 8
posture things spoken by means of p. and gesture
                                                                                — DANCING, 13
pot The p. calls the kettle black — CRITICISM, 4
potent He is the most p. man — MONARCHY, 32
potter Who *is* the P. — CREATIVITY, 9
poverty For every talent that p. has stimulated — POVERTY, 15
P. . . . is confoundedly inconvenient — POVERTY, 30
p.'s catching — POVERTY, 3
p. and oysters always seem to go together — POVERTY, 11
P. is an anomaly to rich people — POVERTY, 1
P. of goods is easily cured — POVERTY, 26
We don't need a War on P. — POVERTY, 6
well governed p. is something to be ashamed of
                                                                                — POVERTY, 8
Where p. is mocked by extravagance — POVERTY, 22
why is there so much p. — POVERTY, 5
world p. . . . problem of two million villages — POVERTY, 28
power concentration of p. in the heart of Europe — EUROPE, 21
Every man who has p. — TYRANNY, 14
greatest p. available to man — POWER, 13
It is not in . . . p. of professors — ACADEMICS, 2
It lies not in our p. to love — FATE, 18
love of p. . . . apt to inflict pain — POWER, 36

Men of p. have not time to read — POWER, 16
P. . . . and Liberty . . . seldom upon good Terms
                                                                                — POWER, 21
P.? . . . like a dead sea fruit — POWER, 28
P. at its best is love . . . justice — POWER, 24
P. buries those who wield it — POWER, 41
P. concedes nothing without demand — POWER, 11
P. doesn't have to show off — POWER, 15
p. has been the vice of the ascetic — RELIGION, 34
p. is apt to corrupt — POWER, 34
P. is my mistress — POWER, 31
P. is not merely shouting aloud — POWER, 32
p. is the law of man — POWER, 14
P. is the only argument — POWER, 20
P. is the ultimate aphrodisiac — POWER, 26
P. must always be balanced by responsibility — POWER, 12
P. never takes a back step — POWER, 29
p. of the people . . . greater potential for violence
                                                                                — POWER, 23
p. of the spirit — POLITICIANS, 11
p. pressed too far . . . relaxed too much — POWER, 2
P. to the People — CIVIL RIGHTS, 11
p. without responsibility — NEWSPAPERS, 2
P. without responsibility — POWER, 25
The balance of p. — POWER, 44
The cold reality of p. — POWER, 39
the easier it is to wield p. — POWER, 6
the market value of all p. — CAPITALISM, 1
The p. of kings and magistrates — MONARCHY, 27
What makes p. hold good — POWER, 17
When p. narrows the areas of man's concern — POETRY, 30
You only have p. over people — POWER, 38
powerful P. people never teach powerless people
                                                                                — SELF-INTEREST, 4
Who is all-p. . . . fear all things — POWER, 8
power politics P. . . . the law of the jungle — POLITICS, 18
powers P. . . . of themselves our minds impress — MIND, 50
p. of a first-rate man — POLITICAL INSULTS, 12
power saw a p. can fell a tree — THE ENVIRONMENT, 20
practical Nothing . . . so p. as a good theory — THEORY, 10
practicality Alone, p. becomes dangerous — SOLITUDE, 3
practice P. should always be based upon a sound
knowledge of theory — THEORY, 9
prairies The wondrous, beautiful p. — LANDSCAPES, 6
praise how a man takes p. — PRAISE, 4
no such whetstone . . . as is p. — PRAISE, 1
P. and blame are much the same — CRITICISM, 30
p. any man that will p. me — PRAISE, 9
P. from a friend, or censure from a foe — PRAISE, 8
refuse p. reveals a desire to be praised — MODESTY, 7
The man worthy of p. — IMMORTALITY, 12
The moment you p. a book . . . awaken resistance
                                                                                — BOOKS, 32
we but p. ourselves in other men — PRAISE, 6
praises He who p. everybody — PRAISE, 3
pram the bliss of my p. — TRAVEL, 19
pray Do you p. for the senators — POLITICIANS, 18
We can p. over the cholera victim — REMEDIES, 21
precautions the necessary p. to avoid having parents
                                                                                — PARENTS, 4
precedency p. between a louse and a flea — LITERARY INSULTS, 31
predatory real world calls for a p. man's brand of
thinking — REALITY, 12
predict only p. things after they've happened — PROPHECY, 6
prediction seldom does p. fail, when evil — PROPHECY, 2
predictions cut back on p. — PROPHECY, 9
pregnant If men could get p. — ABORTION, 5
prehistoric find themselves . . . in p. fields — BIRTH, 14
prejudice I am free of all p. — PREJUDICE, 4
P. . . . , the brand of the white man — SLAVERY, 28

proper He never does a p. thing without . . . an improper
    reason   MORALITY, 39
    P. words in p. places   LITERARY STYLE, 12
property P. is theft   THEFT, 9
prophecy Among all forms of mistake, p.   PROPHECY, 5
prophet every P. knows the convulsion of truth LITERATURE, 29
    The p. who fails to present . . . alternative   PROPHECY, 7
    the sole qualification to be a p.   PROPHECY, 3
    What-you-may-call-it is his p.   IGNORANCE, 5
proportion p. . . . Musicke is measured by it   BEAUTY, 15
propositions resolve the p. of a lover   LOVERS, 14
prose a p. which knows no reason   LITERARY INSULTS, 53
    good p. is an affair of good manners   MANNERS, 2
    I have been talking p. for over forty years   SPEECH, 15
    P. . . . can bear a great deal of poetry   POETRY, 31
    p. = words in their best order   POETRY, 16
prospects p. of the world population   GLOBALIZATION, 22
prosperity In p. men friends may find   FRIENDSHIP, 16
    I wish you all sorts of p.   TASTE, 10
    P. doth best discover vice   WEALTH, 3
    P. is only an instrument   WEALTH, 8
    P. or egalitarianism—you have to choose   WEALTH, 31
protections several good p. against temptations TEMPTATION, 9
protest an earnest p. against golf   SPORTS AND GAMES, 2
    open, unorganized p. against empty stomachs PROTEST, 15
    voice of p. . . . is never more needed   PROTEST, 13
protons p. in the universe . . . same number of electrons
                                      PHYSICS, 6
proud Yes; I am p.   PRIDE, 10
Proust Where is the P. of Papua   LITERATURE, 6
proved What is now p. was . . . imagin'd   IMAGINATION, 2
    Which was to be p.   MATHEMATICS, 14
proverb p. is one man's wit . . . all men's wisdom WIT, 19
providence a kind of P. will . . . end . . . the acts of God
                                       FATE, 6
    I go the way that P. dictates   FATE, 14
provincial worse than p. . . . parochial LITERARY INSULTS, 26
provision make p. for . . . your return to God   AFTERLIFE, 2
provokes No one p. me with impunity   RETRIBUTION, 1
Prussia P. . . . only the kings who make revolution
                          EUROPEAN COUNTRIES, 9
    P.: freedom of movement with a muzzle
                        EUROPEAN COUNTRIES, 41
pseudoscience P. is embraced   SCIENCE, 49
psyche through lands, caves of the p., doctrines, creeds
                                   POETS, 8
psychedelic drugs Pursuing the religious life today . . .
    using p.   DRUGS, 17
psychedelics discovery of p.   DRUGS, 14
psychiatric P. treatment . . . the promulgation of a dogma
                            PSYCHIATRY, 14
psychiatrist p. . . . man who goes to the Folies-Bergères
                            PSYCHIATRY, 17
    p. . . . may not be a mental healer   PSYCHIATRY, 10
    p. has learned . . . first single phrases   PSYCHIATRY, 5
    p. now animalizes man   PSYCHIATRY, 19
    see a p. out of boredom   PSYCHIATRY, 16
psychiatrists P. classify a person as neurotic PSYCHIATRY, 21
    p. necessarily correspond . . . natures   PSYCHIATRY, 7
    The relation between p. and other kinds of lunatics
                            PSYCHIATRY, 8
psychic p. development of the individual   GROWING UP, 6
    the p. invalid throws away his crutches PSYCHIATRY, 12
    We use p. bullets . . . kill each other UNITED STATES, 38
psychoanalysis goal of p. . . . cultural achievement
                          PSYCHOANALYSIS, 10
    Like Communism and Christianity, p. . . . revered
    orthodoxy   PSYCHOANALYSIS, 18
    p. . . . an end product . . . like a dinosaur
                          PSYCHOANALYSIS, 20

P. . . . essentially a theory of unconscious strivings
                          PSYCHOANALYSIS, 11
p. . . . has returned our myths to us PSYCHOANALYSIS, 21
P. . . . in essence a cure through love PSYCHOANALYSIS, 7
P. . . . raised understanding to an art PSYCHOANALYSIS, 19
p. . . . regular supply of sustained, careful *attention*
                          PSYCHOANALYSIS, 12
P. cannot be considered a method of education
                          PSYCHOANALYSIS, 14
P. can provide a theory of 'progress', PSYCHOANALYSIS, 3
P. is a permanent fad   PSYCHOANALYSIS, 5
P. is confession   PSYCHOANALYSIS, 4
P. is the disease it purports to cure PSYCHOANALYSIS, 15
The aim of p. is very daring   PSYCHOANALYSIS, 22
psychoanalyst A p. . . . pretends he doesn't know
    everything   PSYCHOANALYSIS, 23
psychoanalysts P. . . . believe in . . . cerebral intestine
                          PSYCHOANALYSIS, 2
    P. are father confessors   PSYCHOANALYSIS, 16
psycho-linguistics the p. of racism   RACISM, 16
psychological p. observer ought to be more agile
                               PSYCHOLOGY, 7
    There is no such thing as p.   BIOGRAPHY, 15
psychologist animal p. . . . pulls habits out of rats
                             PSYCHOLOGY, 11
psychology Modern p. . . . does not like to see PSYCHOLOGY, 9
    My tyrant is p.   PSYCHOLOGY, 4
    p. . . . a sublimated spiritualism   PSYCHOLOGY, 12
    P. . . . describes a bump on the bump   SCIENCE, 45
    P. . . . skin on the surface of the ethical PSYCHOLOGY, 2
    P. as a science has its limitations   PSYCHOLOGY, 5
    P. can never tell . . . truth about madness PSYCHOLOGY, 3
    P. has a long past   PSYCHOLOGY, 1
    p. has the right to postulate   PSYCHOLOGY, 6
    P. is as unnecessary as . . . poison   PSYCHOLOGY, 8
    P. which explains everything   PSYCHOLOGY, 10
    The object of p. is to give us a totally different idea
                              PSYCHOLOGY, 13
    There is no p.   BIOGRAPHY, 17
psychopathologist The greatest p. has been Freud
                          PSYCHOANALYSIS, 17
psychosis All forms of p. . . . inability to be objective
                              MADNESS, 20
psychotic Freud . . . compared *p.* patients to crystals
                             PSYCHIATRY, 4
public p. buys its opinions as it buys its meat OPINIONS, 5
    P. participation . . . essence of democracy DEMOCRACY, 21
public bath great p. . . . *New York Times* NEWSPAPERS, 24
publicity no such thing as bad p.   OBITUARIES, 1
public opinion One should . . . respect p.   TYRANNY, 16
public property consider himself as p.   POLITICIANS, 24
public school p., where . . . learning was painfully beaten
    into him   EDUCATION, 13
public transport more money spent on p.   TRAVEL, 17
publish I'll p., right or wrong   PUBLISHING, 6
    p. and be sued   PUBLISHING, 5
publishing p. faster than you think   PUBLISHING, 7
pun A p. is a pistol let off at the ear   WORDPLAY, 5
    make so vile a p.   WORDPLAY, 2
punches P. did not often hurt   FIGHTING, 4
punctuality P. is the politeness of kings PUNCTUALITY, 1
    P. is the virtue of the bored   PUNCTUALITY, 4
punctuation The p. of anniversaries is terrible LOSS, 4
punishment All p. is mischief   PUNISHMENT, 1
    No p. has ever . . . power of deterrence   CRIME, 2
    power of p. is to silence   PUNISHMENT, 10
    P. . . . art of unsupportable sensations PUNISHMENT, 6
    P. is not for revenge   PUNISHMENT, 7
punishments In nature there are neither rewards nor p.
                                  NATURE, 21

punk P. . . . a musical movement without music POPULAR MUSIC, 24
puny Every p. whipster gets my sword VIOLENCE, 14
purchasers a pattern to encourage p. BUSINESS, 29
pure All those who are not racially p. RACISM, 14
No man can be a p. specialist STUPIDITY, 13
P. . . . to mount unto the stars PURITY, 3
p. as the driven slush PURITY, 1
purgatory And now that the p. is over DESPAIR, 15
P. is a pawnshop SUFFERING, 13
puritan A p.'s a person who pours righteous indignation PURITANISM, 2
To the P. all things are impure PURITANISM, 4
Puritanism P.—the haunting fear that someone . . . may
be happy PURITANISM, 5
Puritans P. . . . ceased to . . . find pleasure in ritual PURITANISM, 1
purpose My p. is, indeed, a horse PURPOSE, 5
P. is the central ingredient of power PURPOSE, 1
p. of our life is not suffering SUFFERING, 21
p. of our lives . . . is beyond all human wisdom PURPOSE, 3
The final p. of art ART, 32
The p. of studying economics ECONOMICS, 28
ultimate p. of the world REASON, 15
purse the longest p. finally wins LAW, 17
Pyrenees I see the P. MOUNTAINS, 4
qualities display q. which he does not possess PERFORMANCE, 4
quarrel a very pretty q. as it stands ARGUMENTS, 21
It takes . . . one to make a q. ARGUMENTS, 10
Out of the q. . . . we make rhetoric POETRY, 62
quarrels q. of lovers . . . the renewal of love LOVERS, 17
Q. would not last so long ARGUMENTS, 11
quart one cannot put a q. in a pint cup FUTILITY, 3
Queen Anne Q.'s dead INFORMATION, 1
Queen Mab Q. hath been with you DELUSIONS OF LOVE, 12
Queen Victoria a parlourmaid as ignorant as Q. IGNORANCE, 21
queer I'm putting my q. shoulder to the /wheel HOMOSEXUALITY, 4
question Every q. . . . the mask of another q. PHILOSOPHY, 7
If a q. can be framed . . . answer it ANSWERS, 6
man who sees both sides of a q. QUESTIONS, 9
On this q. of principle BRITISH IMPERIALISM, 23
q. . . . which I have not been able to answer WOMEN, 18
The q. of the ultimate meaning of life QUESTIONS, 8
the q. that we do not know QUESTIONS, 7
questioning Q. . . . not the mode of conversation QUESTIONS, 5
quick the q. . . . listed among the dead SPORTS AND GAMES, 20
quickly Desire to have things done q. HASTE, 2
quiet Anythin' for a q. life SOLITUDE, 7
quixotic One may be q. FANTASY, 2
quotation Every q. contributes something QUOTATIONS, 4
q. at the right moment QUOTATIONS, 7
q. covers the absence of original thought QUOTATIONS, 6
q. is a national vice QUOTATIONS, 8
quote can q. Shakespeare in an economic crisis ECONOMICS, 25
rabbits a tale of four little r. FIRST LINES, 8
Rabelais R. is the wondrous mask of ancient comedy EUROPEAN LITERATURE, 10
race A relay r., run with a Ming vase ASIAN COUNTRIES, 13
Nothing is more narrow-minded than . . . r. hatred PREJUDICE, 7
r. is not to the swift FATE, 2
Some view our sable r. with scornful eye RACISM, 30
racial R. oppression of black people in America RACISM, 26
racism modern r. . . . traced to . . . conquest IMPERIALISM, 3
R. . . . everyone . . . today is exposed RACISM, 3
R. . . . is a weapon used by the wealthy RACISM, 7
racist the r. who creates his inferior RACISM, 11

radiance Life . . . Stains the white r. of eternity LIFE, 52
There is r. in the darkness, if we could but see DARKNESS, 1
radiation r. . . . much in mind these days NUCLEAR WEAPONS, 9
r.'s . . . laws /Impel us into common cause UNITY, 8
radical A r. is a man with both feet . . . in the air POLITICIANS, 43
I never dared be r. when young YOUTH, 11
r. invents the views . . . the conservative adopts RADICALISM, 3
radicals Few r. have good digestions DIGESTION, 2
radio I had the r. on NAKEDNESS, 7
Simply a r. personality who outlived his prime POLITICAL INSULTS, 54
radio 4 What do we want? R. PROTEST, 12
rage If the winds r., doth not the sea wax mad DEPRESSION, 9
R. can only with difficulty ANGER, 4
R. is to writers what water is to fish WRITERS, 28
raillery R. gives no Offence SATIRE, 7
rain A Hard R.'s A-Gonna Fall NUCLEAR WAR, 5
R. is grace WEATHER, 14
R., r., go away WEATHER, 4
rainbow r. to the storms of life OPTIMISM, 3
Somewhere over the r. FANTASY, 5
the R. gave thee birth COLOUR, 3
raise If you do not r. your eyes AMBITION, 24
ram a r. caught in a thicket SACRIFICE, 2
randolph the only part of R. that was not malignant POLITICAL INSULTS, 53
rank O! my offence is r., it smells GUILT, 15
rap R. music is information POPULAR MUSIC, 6
Raphael When I was their age, I could draw like R. ARTISTIC STYLES, 19
rapists All men are r. MEN, 13
rapture There is a r. on the lonely shore NATURE, 5
rare as r. things will, it vanished TRANSIENCE, 8
rarer A r. spirit never /Did steer humanity HUMAN NATURE, 31
rat you can r., but you can't re-r. BETRAYAL, 7
rational could an entirely r. being speak of RATIONALISM, 5
there is that which is r. RATIONALISM, 2
What is r. is actual PHILOSOPHY, 11
yet to meet the famous R. Economic Man ECONOMICS, 32
rationality r. . . . factors governing human behaviour RATIONALISM, 4
rationalization R. . . . self-deception by reasoning REASON, 19
rats I see some r. have got in POLITICAL INSULTS, 38
R.! /They fought the dogs ANIMALS, 8
rattle r. the sabre at every diplomatic entanglement DIPLOMACY, 4
the rest of you . . . r. your jewellery AUDIENCES, 8
raznochinetz r. needs no memory ACADEMICS, 5
reach a man's r. should exceed his grasp AMBITION, 2
reactionaries r. are paper tigers CONSERVATISM, 10
r. of 1815 hid . . . name of revolution REVOLUTION, 3
reactors R. breed plutonium /bloodcells pay their dues POLLUTION, 5
read I've just r. that I am dead . . . OBITUARIES, 2
I have never r. it EUROPE, 13
never r. a book before reviewing it CRITICISM, 22
O, learn to r. what silent love hath writ SILENCE, 25
R. . . . to weigh and consider READING, 7
R. in order to live READING, 12
r. just as inclination leads him READING, 18
R., mark, learn and inwardly digest LEARNING, 8
Something that everybody wants to have r. LITERATURE, 50
The man who in himself can r. SELF-KNOWLEDGE, 18
When we r. a story READING, 5
Who r. to doubt, or . . . scorn CRITICS, 27
reader A good r. has imagination READERS, 7
A r. seldom peruses a book with pleasure READERS, 1

Hypocrite r. . . . my brother   READERS, 2
ideal r. . . . ideal insomnia   READERS, 6
r. read a novel . . . for the moral   READERS, 8
The r. of the novel   READERS, 9
readers r. and writers . . . bereft when criticism remains
    too polite   CRITICISM, 15
    R. may be divided into four classes   READERS, 4
reading art of r. is to skip judiciously   READING, 15
half learned the art of r.   READING, 3
no society can exist without r.   READING, 24
R. . . . good way to define pleasure   READING, 13
R. . . . ingenious device for avoiding thought   READING, 17
r. . . . is like a conversation   READING, 9
R. . . . is simply the expansion of one's mind   READING, 29
R. is to the mind   READING, 32
R. maketh a full man   READING, 1
There are two motives for r. a book   READING, 27
reaffirm to r. to ourselves our basic irresponsibility
    RESPONSIBILITY, 3
real abyss that separates . . . r. from the imaginary
    DESIRE, 11
Everything r. must be experienceable   REALITY, 13
Nothing . . . r. unless it happens on television   TELEVISION, 3
Nothing ever becomes r. till it is experienced
    EXPERIENCE, 11
R. . . . was happening to me right then   REALITY, 19
There are R. things   REALITY, 21
whether Zelda and I are r.   AMERICAN LITERATURE, 12
real estate act of r. rather than . . . God   AMERICAN CITIES, 18
realism necessity of r. in art   ARTISTIC STYLES, 6
realist R. . . . Idealist who knows nothing of himself
    REALISM, 2
reality Cannot bear very much r.   REALITY, 8
He had surrendered all r.   DOCTORS, 6
I have no respect for r.   REALITY, 4
may always be another r.   REALITY, 10
r. . . . brought forth solely by the imagination   REALITY, 9
R. . . . something you rise above   REALITY, 18
r. and his brain came into contact   ACCIDENTS, 7
r. as a springboard into space   REALITY, 24
R. invents me   REALITY, 11
R. is that which . . . doesn't go away   REALITY, 7
r. of yesterday . . . illusion tomorrow   REALISM, 4
robust sense of r. is very necessary   REALITY, 22
speak *excessively* of r.   REALITY, 1
realization There can be no . . . complete r. of utility
    without beauty   BEAUTY, 21
realm I came not into this r. as merchandise   DIVORCE, 1
reap sown the wind . . . r. the whirlwind   RETRIBUTION, 2
reason contrary to r. . . . that there is a vacuum
    NOTHINGNESS, 3
Cultivate a superiority to r.   REASON, 8
hearts must know the world of r.   REASON, 2
let us r. together   REASON, 24
R. . . . one out of a thousand possibilities   REASON, 23
R. cannot be forced into belief   REASON, 10
R. has moons   REASON, 18
R. has ruled . . . the world's history   REASON, 16
R. is itself a matter of faith   REASON, 7
R. is nothing but . . . unintelligible instinct   REASON, 22
R. is the Sovereign of the World   REASON, 17
R. must be awake and reflection applied   REASON, 14
r. must be consider'd . . . kind of cause   REASON, 21
R. must sit at . . . knee of instinct   REASON, 29
R., Observation, and Experience   SCIENCE, 33
R. to rule . . . mercy to forgive   FORGIVENESS, 4
wanted to be the r. for everything   EGOTISM, 2
reasoning R. draws a conclusion   REASON, 1
reasons greatest r. why so few people understand
    themselves   SELF-KNOWLEDGE, 26

man always has two r.   ALIBIS AND EXCUSES, 3
never give your r.   JUSTICE, 25
R. are not like garments   MOTIVE, 3
rebel go on being a r. too long   ANARCHY, 6
What is a r.   REBELLION, 3
rebellion A little r. now and then   REBELLION, 5
little r. . . . shirt undone   POPULAR MUSIC, 19
reborn If I must be r.   AFTERLIFE, 4
recall machinery of r. . . . machinery of association
    MEMORY, 26
receives r. a plum . . . return a peach   GIFTS, 1
recessions every government . . . promises . . . to cure r.
    GOVERNMENT, 17
reckoning No man gets away from his r.   FATE, 12
reconcile How to r. this world . . . with . . . my
    imagining   REALITY, 14
record companies All r. prefer third-rate talents
    POPULAR MUSIC, 33
recorded What is not r. is not remembered   FORGETTING, 1
recording When I'm r. I could have orgasm   POPULAR MUSIC, 29
red asking for . . . r. piece of green chalk   JAZZ, 7
good Tray grew very r.   CRUELTY, 3
So much depends /upon /a r. wheel /barrow   POETRY, 60
That man is a R. . . . a Communist   BIGOTRY, 2
Red Sea I will set thy bounds from the R.   JUDAISM, 3
reduce more we r. ourselves to machines   MACHINES, 1
reeling R. and Writhing   EDUCATION, 1
referendum R. . . . popular vote to learn the nonsensus
    POLITICS, 9
refined One of those r. people   CLASS, 10
reflection The man of r. discovers Truth   TRUTH, 53
The r. in my shaving mirror   THE FACE, 16
reform Beginning r. is beginning revolution   REVOLUTION, 53
R. never comes to a class or a people   CHANGE, 2
reforms point of all r. . . . human liberation   FREEDOM, 55
refusal r. to act, not of inability   ACTION, 11
refuse do not always r. to believe in others   BELIEF, 20
r. to cooperate with an evil system   EVIL, 20
r. to give the title of art   ART, 44
Should I r. a good dinner   UNDERSTANDING, 3
refute I r. it *thus*   ANSWERS, 4
regard r. and affection for a young man   HOMOSEXUALITY, 20
reggae r. music . . . carry earth force, people rhythm
    POPULAR MUSIC, 21
regime No r. has ever loved great writers   CENSORSHIP, 25
regimen R. is superior to medicine   HEALTH AND HEALTHY LIVING, 23
regret my r. /Becomes an April violet   REGRET, 17
R. is an appalling waste of energy   REGRET, 5
regrets No, I have no r.   REGRET, 18
rehearsing R. a play is making the word flesh   THEATRE, 15
reign Better to r. in hell, than serve in heaven   POWER, 30
we r. unchallenged in the realm /of . . . abstract
    notions   IMPERIALISM, 10
relate Anyone who attempts to r. his life   BIOGRAPHY, 2
relations Personal r. . . . important thing   RELATIONSHIPS, 7
The sum total of these r. of production   ECONOMICS, 20
relationship attainment of a new kind of r.   THERAPY, 5
religion And what is r.   RELIGION, 4
As far as R., I'm a Baptist   RELIGION, 1
consolations of r. or philosophy   RELIGION, 18
foundation of r. . . . acts of men   RELIGION, 40
just enough r. to make us hate   BIGOTRY, 5
Many people think they have r.   RELIGION, 20
Men will wrangle for r.   RELIGION, 8
missionary r. . . . experimental economic technique
    COMMUNISM, 10
no reason to bring r. into it   RELIGION, 28
Nothing is so fatal to r. as indifference   INDIFFERENCE, 2
One r. is as true as another   RELIGION, 6
R. . . . a great instinctive truth   RELIGION, 32

r. . . . must also be concerned about man's social
   conditions   RELIGION, 21
R. . . . the dream of the human mind   RELIGION, 14
R. . . . the wound, not the bandage   RELIGION, 30
r. cannot be concerned with politics   RELIGION, 39
R. /Has made an honest woman of the supernatural
                                                RELIGION, 16
r. has many lives, and a habit of resurrection   RELIGION, 11
R. is . . . the opium of the people   RELIGION, 26
R. is a support . . . ruins the edifice   RELIGION, 10
R. is by no means a proper subject   RELIGION, 7
The equation of r. with belief   BELIEF, 31
The true meaning of r.   RELIGION, 2
To become a popular r.   RELIGION, 19
To die for a r. is easier than to live it absolutely
                                               MARTYRDOM, 1
when r. is allowed to invade . . . private life RELIGION, 27
when r. was strong . . . men mistook magic for
   medicine   MEDICINE, 37
religions r. we call false were once true   RELIGION, 13
sixty different r., and only one sauce   FOOD, 4
religious If there were no r. reality   RELIGION, 5
My relationship with formal r. belief . . . chequered
                                                  BELIEF, 28
R. cultures produce poetry   FICTION, 8
R. ideas . . . sprung from the same need   RELIGION, 15
reluctant He who is r. to recognize me   ENEMIES, 5
remarks no one hears his own r. as prose   CONVERSATION, 2
said our r. before us   PLAGIARISM, 4
remedies If you are too fond of new r.   REMEDIES, 6
Most men die of their r. . . . not . . . illnesses
                                                REMEDIES, 17
Our r. oft in ourselves do lie   REMEDIES, 25
r. . . . suggested for a disease   REMEDIES, 5
remedy a r. for everything except death   REMEDIES, 4
I never think of finding a r.   ILLNESS, 23
remember I can never r. whether it snowed   FORGETTING, 11
I r., I r. /How my childhood   CHILDHOOD, 14
I r. the way we parted   PARTING, 3
Please to r. the Fifth of November   TREASON, 5
R. me when I am gone away,   MEMORY, 41
things I r. . . . may never have happened   MEMORY, 37
we shall be glad to r. even these hardships   ENDURANCE, 10
Who will r., . . . The unheroic dead   MEMORIALS, 1
remembrance R. . . . secret of reconciliation MEMORIALS, 2
remorse In other words, r. has become insane   GUILT, 6
R.: beholding heaven and feeling hell   REGRET, 6
r. for what you have thought about your wife   REGRET, 9
R. is nothing but the wry face   GUILT, 7
r. is the poison of life   GUILT, 2
R. sleeps during a prosperous period   REGRET, 10
R., the fatal egg by pleasure laid   REGRET, 2
remove R. the document . . . you r. the man BUREAUCRACY, 3
Renaissance R. . . . the green end of one of civilization's
   hardest winters   CIVILIZATION, 9
render r. to everyone his due   JUSTICE, 19
renegades Political r. always start their career of treachery
                                               POLITICIANS, 27
rent r. an MP just like . . . a . . . taxi   BRIBERY, 6
you can't r. a heart   PASSION, 4
repent I hardly ever r.   REGRET, 7
repentance with the morning cool r.   REGRET, 11
repented never r. that he held his tongue   SPEECH, 16
repetition constant r. will finally succeed MARKETING, 1
replace no one can r. him   HUMILITY, 9
reporter I am a r.   JOURNALISM, 13
r. . . . has renounced everything   JOURNALISM, 23
representative Your r. owes you . . . his judgement
                                               POLITICIANS, 6
reproach r. to religion and government   INEQUALITY, 7

reproduction The r. of mankind is a great marvel and
   mystery   SEX, 30
republic founding the R. of Equals   FRENCH REVOLUTION, 1
In a R. in which some   REPUBLICANISM, 2
make the . . . r. into a collective farm   COMMUNISM, 20
we are talking of a r., . . . yet Louis lives!
                                        FRENCH REVOLUTION, 13
republican r. liberty . . . God deliver us from it   SLAVERY, 27
The R. form of Government is the highest   REPUBLICANISM, 4
repulsive The most r. thing . . . inside of a camel's mouth
                                                EATING, 4
reputation 20 years to build a r.   REPUTATION, 9
good r. is more valuable than money   REPUTATION, 17
My r. grew with every failure   REPUTATION, 20
obtain the r. of popular authorship   MARKETING, 5
R., r., r.!   REPUTATION, 18
Until you've lost your r., you never realize   REPUTATION, 16
written out of r. but by himself   REPUTATION, 8
research In r. the horizon recedes   RESEARCH, 1
R. is formalized curiosity   RESEARCH, 3
R. is fundamentally a state of mind   RESEARCH, 8
steal from many, it's r.   PLAGIARISM, 8
The aim of r. is the discovery of . . . equations
                                               RESEARCH, 4
The outcome of any serious r.   RESEARCH, 9
resignation The r. to a language   LANGUAGE, 40
resist r. everything except temptation   TEMPTATION, 10
strength to r. . . . renders acting powerful
                                     ACTING AND ACTORS, 14
to r. . . . mortal passions   PASSION, 7
resistance 'R. to tyranny is obedience to God'.
                                         WOMEN'S RIGHTS, 3
resolve R. to be thyself   SELF-KNOWLEDGE, 1
resolves He that r. to deal with none but honest men
                                               BUSINESS, 6
respect I r. only those who resist me   ENEMIES, 4
now I don't have to r. *anybody*   OLD AGE, 10
only three beings worthy of r.   RESPECT, 1
r. that is only bought by gold   RESPECT, 3
R. the past   THE PAST, 22
We owe r. to the living   RESPECT, 7
When people do not r. us   RESPECT, 6
responsibility first r. of a leader . . . define reality
                                             LEADERSHIP, 7
Moral r. is what is lacking in a man   MORALITY, 23
the biggest r. of any corporation   RESPONSIBILITY, 4
responsible every man is r. for his face   THE FACE, 4
You become r., forever, for what you have tamed
                                         RESPONSIBILITY, 6
rest I have nothing; the r. I leave to the poor   DEBT, 8
restrictions two kinds of r. upon human liberty   LIBERTY, 9
retain To expect a man to r. everything . . . ever read
                                               READING, 28
reticence R. in three volumes   BIOGRAPHY, 2
retrace r. with certainty . . . footsteps of my soul MEMORY, 47
reveng'd r. on the whole pack of you   REVENGE, 14
revenge A man that studieth r.   REVENGE, 1
I am R., sent from th'infernal kingdom   REVENGE, 12
R., at first though sweet   REVENGE, 11
reverence Kill r. and you've killed the hero   RESPECT, 4
review We r. the past   THE PAST, 14
review copy In the beginning was the r.   LITERATURE, 30
reviewer Unless a r. has the courage . . . ignore the
   bastard   CRITICS, 29
reviewing Prolonged . . . r. of books   CRITICISM, 16
re-vision R. . . . is an act of survival   CRITICISM, 17
revolt r. into a style   POPULAR MUSIC, 14
right to r. . . . deep in our history   REVOLUTION, 12
revolution 'r.' is a word for which you kill   REVOLUTION, 50
A r. is not a dinner party   REVOLUTION, 28

don't suppose . . . r. is going to bring liberty

REVOLUTION, 21

Ground for a r. is always fertile — REVOLUTION, 2

In a r. . . . either you win or you die — REVOLUTION, 18

I want a r. . . . in Crotonville — REVOLUTION, 52

no such thing as an orderly r. — REVOLUTION, 36

r. . . . devours its own children — REVOLUTION, 4

R. . . . ecstasy of history — REVOLUTION, 29

R. . . . intellectually acceptable form of modern war

REVOLUTION, 22

R. . . . is the idea of justice — REVOLUTION, 40

R. . . . not a nursery of future revolutions

FRENCH REVOLUTION, 3

R. . . . on the basis of . . . material benefit — REVOLUTION, 11

R. is . . . the setting-up of a new order — REVOLUTION, 34

r. is a struggle to the death — REVOLUTION, 7

r. of 1917 . . . defined . . . the contemporary world

RUSSIAN REVOLUTION, 7

spirit of r. . . . radically opposed to liberty — REVOLUTION, 20

The history of our r. — AMERICAN WAR OF INDEPENDENCE, 1

The r. and women's liberation go together — REVOLUTION, 45

The r. does not choose its paths — RUSSIAN REVOLUTION, 14

The r. eats its own — REVOLUTION, 42

the r. made us — FRENCH REVOLUTION, 2

the R. may . . . devour each of her children

FRENCH REVOLUTION, 18

The whole cause of world r. — REVOLUTION, 25

They are not the leaders of a r. They are its victims

REVOLUTION, 9

to export r. is nonsense — REVOLUTION, 47

trace r. beneath her woolly hair — REVOLUTION, 32

We invented the R. — REVOLUTION, 51

What is wrong with a r. . . . natural — REVOLUTION, 14

revolutionary A r. woman — REVOLUTION, 13

Every r. movement also liberates language — REVOLUTION, 55

fierce and r. in a bathroom — AMERICANS, 15

R. spirits of my father's generation — REVOLUTION, 43

revolutions All modern r. have ended — REVOLUTION, 6

Everywhere r. are painful — REVOLUTION, 15

I've seen all sorts of r. — REVOLUTION, 10

R. . . . like a water wheel — REVOLUTION, 38

R. are always verbose — REVOLUTION, 49

R. aren't made by gadgets and technology — REVOLUTION, 56

R. are not made — REVOLUTION, 39

R. are not made for export — COLD WAR, 9

We now live in two r. — REVOLUTION, 30

reward r. of a thing well done — ACHIEVEMENT, 9

rewards r. . . . disproportionate to their usefulness to the

community — TEACHERS, 7

Reynolds When Sir Joshua R. died — ARTISTS, 7

rheumatism never have occurred to me to complain of r.

COMPLAINTS, 9

rhyme it was neither r. nor reason — POETRY, 39

rich a r. man cannot imagine poverty — POVERTY, 27

a r. man shall hardly enter into . . . heaven — WEALTH, 4

only the extremely r. . . . escape other people — WEALTH, 20

r. . . . distinguishing themselves from the poor — WEALTH, 26

r. are different from us — WEALTH, 10

r. beyond the dreams of avarice — WEALTH, 19

r. man's joys increase . . . poor's decay — POVERTY, 17

R. men's houses are seldom beautiful — WEALTH, 2

The r. have become richer — INEQUALITY, 8

whether to be r. in things — MATERIALISM, 4

why aren't you r. — WEALTH, 1

you are not really a r. man — WEALTH, 14

richer not right to seem r. than one really is — WEALTH, 16

riches R. have wings — WEALTH, 9

rich man A r.'s joke is always funny — SYCOPHANCY, 1

richness r. of life . . . memories we have forgotten

FORGETTING, 8

riddle a r. wrapped in a mystery inside an enigma — RUSSIA, 8

ride r. not a free horse to death — EXPLOITATION, 2

ridicule R. often checks what is absurd — RIDICULE, 2

ridiculous Look for the r. . . . you will find it — RIDICULE, 1

sense of the r. — HUMOUR, 2

right Always do r. — RIGHT, 6

An insignificant r. becomes important when it is

assailed — RIGHT, 5

a r. to utter . . . truth — FREE SPEECH, 5

believe that they are . . . in the r. — SELF-CONFIDENCE, 3

have a r. to censure, that . . . help — JUDGMENT, 18

R. is of no sex — THE SEXES, 5

r. of all, . . . duty of some — SEPARATION, 6

r. of the people . . . ownership of Ireland — IRELAND, 35

The more you are in the r. — TOTALITARIANISM, 9

The R. Divine of Kings to govern wrong — MONARCHY, 33

The r. of a man to stand upright — HUMAN RIGHTS, 12

the r. to be plainly dressed — CLOTHES, 11

the r. to blaspheme — FREE SPEECH, 4

the r. to criticize Shakespeare — CRITICISM, 21

the r. wing of the middle of the road — POLITICIANS, 5

To know what is r. — COWARDICE, 2

To see what is r., and not do it — PRINCIPLES, 3

righteous r. people who anger slowly — ANGER, 12

right hand this r. shall work it all off — DEBT, 11

rights interpretation of women's r. in Islam

WOMEN'S RIGHTS, 26

men their r. and nothing more — EQUALITY, 2

R. that depend on the sufferance — CIVIL RIGHTS, 7

Stand up for your r. — HUMAN RIGHTS, 9

rights of woman The R. merit some attention — WOMEN'S RIGHTS, 8

riot A r. is . . . the language of the unheard — PROTEST, 9

riots Urban r. . . . a durable social phenomenon — PROTEST, 8

ripeness R. is all — ENDURANCE, 7

rise able to r. above the brutes — WORDS, 18

risk r. of producing more technology — TECHNOLOGY, 10

rites where do r. and justice spring from — HUMAN NATURE, 37

rivals r. for resources . . . no methods for conserving

GLOBALIZATION, 11

river Ol' man r. — RIVERS, 2

riverrun r., past Eve and Adam's — RIVERS, 3

roach Timid r., why be so shy — HUNGER, 16

road A broad and ample r., whose dust is gold — SPACE, 6

There is a r. from the eye to the heart — EMOTION, 2

wrong r., if it is your own — INDIVIDUALITY, 14

roads How many r. must a man walk down — ADULTHOOD, 3

Two r. diverged in a wood — CHOICE, 5

rob R. Peter, and pay Paul — MONEY, 10

robbed Terrible place to be r. or murdered — EUROPEAN CITIES, 20

We wuz r. — DEFEAT, 3

Robbins President R. . . . adjusted to his environment

POLITICAL INSULTS, 33

Robinson Crusoe live like R., shipwrecked — SOLITUDE, 17

rock r. concert . . . inside my head — CREATIVITY, 18

rocket A r. man — SPACE, 9

rocking r. the cradle . . . rocked the system — IRELAND, 37

rocking horse They sway'd about upon a r. — LITERARY INSULTS, 32

rock 'n' roll 'r. . . . jazz *before* getting this name

POPULAR MUSIC, 26

rod spoils the r. . . . never spares the child — PUNISHMENT, 9

role saw his r. as being that of Moses — LEADERSHIP, 10

rolling stone Like a r. — IDENTITY, 1

Romans Friends, R., countrymen — MEMORIALS, 3

The ancient R. built their greatest masterpieces

ARCHITECTURE, 28

Romantic In the R. age, history . . . was more real

HISTORY, 17

Romanticism R. is . . . the greatest possible pleasure

ROMANTICISM, 4

Rome at R., do as they do at R. — EUROPEAN CITIES, 8

In R. you long for the country — EUROPEAN CITIES, 14
R.'s just a city like anywhere else — EUROPEAN CITIES, 5
The R. . . . of the 20th century — AMERICAN CITIES, 46
When in R., live as the Romans — CONFORMITY, 1
Romeo R.! wherefore art thou R. — LOVERS, 15
room r. for me and a mountain lion — ANIMALS, 24
roots What good is r. if you can't go back to 'em? — NOSTALGIA, 10
rope the end of your r., tie a knot — SURVIVAL, 4
the r. stood straight up in the air — MAGIC, 7
rose a r. should shut, and be a bud again — SLEEP, 15
not the r. for me — CHOICE, 1
R. is a r. — FLOWERS, 11
the last r. of summer — ENDING, 6
The r. is fairest — FLOWERS, 10
Through what wild centuries /Roves back the r. — FLOWERS, 1
rosemary There's r., that's for remembrance — MEMORY, 42
roses It was r., r., all the way — HAPPINESS, 7
I will make thee beds of r. — FLOWERS, 7
R. at first were white — FLOWERS, 2
Send two dozen r. to Room 424 — DECLARATIONS OF LOVE, 3
When r. are fresh — FLOWERS, 6
rots It r. a writer's brain — JOURNALISM, 31
round At the r. earth's imagin'd corners — DEATH AND DYING, 18
Royal Family Loss of the R.'s symbolism — MONARCHY, 9
rude The right people are r. — RIGHT, 4
ruin With hideous r. and combustion down — DAMNATION, 4
ruined r. on the side of their natural propensities — FAILURE, 2
rule few men are wise enough to r. — ANARCHY, 16
I must r. after my own fashion — RUSSIA, 7
I was born to r. — MONARCHY, 23
r. by fettering the mind — GOVERNMENT, 23
R. yon Isle and be a Slave — IRELAND, 41
That's not a regular r. — LAW, 7
the greatest r. of all . . . to give pleasure — PLEASURE, 23
rules R. and models destroy genius and art — RULES, 1
r. for becoming more alive — VITALITY, 4
R. freeze companies inside a glacier — INNOVATION, 5
R. serve no purpose — RULES, 5
Systems governed by . . . one set of r. — RULES, 2
run Gwine to r. all night — GAMBLING, 1
r. scared and never think — ACHIEVEMENT, 25
running you been r. through my mind *all* day — FLIRTATION, 5
rush hour R. . . . traffic . . . at a standstill — CARS, 6
Russell R.'s beautiful mathematical mind — MIND, 30
Russia For us in R. communism is a dead dog — COMMUNISM, 22
I have signed legislation which outlaws R. — NUCLEAR WAR, 13
R. has entered the family of civilized nations — RUSSIA, 27
R. has two generals — RUSSIA, 26
R. is a sphinx — RUSSIA, 4
R. is no longer our enemy — COLD WAR, 4
R. is our Africa — RUSSIA, 18
R. is such an amazing country — RUSSIA, 14
R. will certainly inherit the future — RUSSIA, 21
salvaged from R.—her language — RUSSIA, 24
there is no democracy in R. — RUSSIA, 30
What hope is there for R. — RUSSIA, 17
Russian hated /by every anti-Semite / . . . I am a R. — RUSSIA, 38
like any honest R. . . . a terrible drunkard — RUSSIA, 13
Russians R. do not possess . . . self-restraint — RUSSIA, 3
test the R., not the bombs — COLD WAR, 6
sack Enter and s. the decadent civilization — ANARCHY, 14
sacred s. hunger of ambitious minds — AMBITION, 29
s. land . . . land of the godhead — GOD, 4
The idea of the s. . . . most conservative notions — CONSERVATISM, 11
sacrifice Too long a s. — SACRIFICE, 11

sacrifices s. . . . to achieve law and order — SACRIFICE, 1
sad A s. tale's best for winter — WINTER, 8
How s. and bad and mad it was — NOSTALGIA, 4
sadist s. . . . exploitation becomes a kind of passion — EXPLOITATION, 5
sadists repressed s. are supposed to become policemen or butchers — PUBLISHING, 4
sadness Farewell s. — SORROW, 6
S. is . . . but a form of fatigue — SORROW, 8
s. of this modern age — UNHAPPINESS, 5
safari I want you to accompany me on the s. — NONSENSE, 14
sage The s. . . . practises . . . teaching that uses no words — WISDOM, 10
said 'Tis s. . . . some have died for love — LOVE, 65
When a thing has been s. and s. well — QUOTATIONS, 3
sailors like s. who must rebuild their ship — HUMAN CONDITION, 18
saint seem a s. when most I play the devil — DECEPTION, 30
saintliness S. is also a temptation — TEMPTATION, 1
sales Today's s. should be better than yesterday's — BUSINESS, 22
Salinger S. was the perfect *New Yorker* — AMERICAN LITERATURE, 6
salt the s. of the earth — VIRTUE, 4
salvation The s. of mankind — HUMANKIND, 47
Sam Play it, S. — NOSTALGIA, 3
same The s. as usual — TIME, 3
sanctions S. are now the only . . . way of ending apartheid — APARTHEID, 8
San Domingo you have cut down in S. . . . the tree of liberty — LIBERTY, 39
sane 's.' man . . . not the one who has eliminated all contradictions — SANITY, 8
s. person . . . feels isolated in the insane society — SANITY, 4
Show me a s. man — SANITY, 5
to *play at being* s. — SANITY, 7
San Francisco S. . . . most European of all American cities — AMERICAN CITIES, 2
S. supplemented . . . anti-Chinese state laws — RACISM, 19
sanity pursuit of s. . . . a form of madness — MADNESS, 3
S. is a cozy lie — SANITY, 12
S. is an unknown room — SANITY, 1
S. is madness put to good uses — SANITY, 10
S. is not truth. S. is conformity — SANITY, 9
S. is very rare — SANITY, 3
Too much s. may be madness — SANITY, 2
San Narciso S. lay further south, near L.A. — AMERICAN CITIES, 35
sans S. teeth, s. eyes, s. taste, s. everything — OLD AGE, 40
Sappho S. survives . . . we sing her songs — IMMORTALITY, 5
sarcasm S. . . . the language of the devil — SARCASM, 1
sat The . . . gentleman has s. so long on the fence — INDECISION, 5
Satan Incensed with indignatio S. stood — THE DEVIL, 11
S. comes as a man of peace — THE DEVIL, 5
S. had come around with sweet corn — FOOD, 17
Satanic Verses The author of the S. . . . against Islam, the Prophet and the Koran — CENSORSHIP, 14
satire hard not to write s. — SATIRE, 1
S. . . . like a polished razor keen — SATIRE, 4
S. died . . . Kissinger the Nobel Peace Prize — SATIRE, 3
S. is alive and well — SATIRE, 10
S. is a sort of glass — SATIRE, 8
S. picks a one-sided fight — SATIRE, 9
Through my s. I make little people so big — SATIRE, 2
satisfaction I can't get no s. — COMPLAINTS, 5
satisfied Don't be s. . . . just selling a song — POPULAR MUSIC, 7
savage The young man who has not wept is a s. — EMOTION, 10
savaged s. by a dead sheep — POLITICAL INSULTS, 26
Savannah S. is a living tomb — AMERICAN CITIES, 30
save s. a man's life against his will — BETRAYAL, 9
saw I s. it, but I did not realize it — PERCEPTION, 10
say and you s. 'Oh, nothing' — NOTHINGNESS, 10

cannot s. what you have to s. in twenty minutes
     SPEECHES, 3
I have nothing to s., I am saying it   POETRY, 10
people who s. nothing   SILENCE, 29
The great consolation . . . is to s. what one thinks
     FRANKNESS, 6
they do not know what they are going to s.   SPEECHES, 4
whatever you s., you s. nothing   SILENCE, 13
saying something is not worth s. . . . sing it   OPERA, 3
scandal It is a public s. that gives offence   GOSSIP, 6
Praise undeserv'd is s. in disguise   PRAISE, 7
There is no s. like rags   POVERTY, 12
scarecrow a s. of the law   LAW, 31
scarecrows s. of fools . . . beacons of wise men
     CONSEQUENCES, 4
scared What difference . . . if the thing you s. of is real
     or not?   FEAR, 23
scent s. of bitter almonds . . . unrequited love   MEMORY, 21
scepticism tolerant s. . . . a good test of maturity
     TOLERANCE, 6
sceptred this s. isle   ENGLAND, 26
schizophrenia S. . . . the price . . . for language   PSYCHIATRY, 3
S. will continue to be a mystery   PSYCHIATRY, 18
schizophrenic S. behaviour is a special strategy   PSYCHIATRY, 9
school never gone to s. may steal from a freight car
     EDUCATION, 17
schoolboy I see a s. . . . face . . . pressed to a sweetshop
     window   LITERARY INSULTS, 62
schoolboys s. . . . educate my son   EDUCATION, 7
schoolgirl a priggish s., captain of the hockey team
     MONARCHY, 18
schooling s. interfere with my education   EDUCATION, 22
schoolmaster s. should have . . . awe   TEACHERS, 1
schoolteacher s. . . . underpaid as a childminder   TEACHERS, 5
science A s. is said to be useful   SCIENCE, 28
do not need s. and philosophy   MORALITY, 20
drawback that s. was invented after I left school
     MODESTY, 1
Experimental s. is the mistress of . . . sciences
     EXPERIMENTS, 1
extraordinary if . . . s. was *not* applied in warfare
     SCIENCE, 12
goal of s. . . . seek naturalistic explanations for
     phenomena   SCIENCE, 10
history of s. . . . conflict of two contending powers
     SCIENCE, 15
If s. produces no better fruits than tyranny   SCIENCE, 35
In everything that relates to s.   MODESTY, 6
man of s. and the man of art   SCIENTISTS, 21
men only care for s. . . . get a living   SCIENCE, 26
not s. . . . who has destroyed man   SCIENCE, 38
One s. only will one genius fit   GENIUS, 15
pace of s. forces . . . pace of technique   SCIENCE, 23
real accomplishment of modern s. and technology
     SCIENCE, 25
s. . . . achieved its most spectacular triumphs
     MODERNITY, 10
S. . . . attempt to make the chaotic diversity   SCIENCE, 20
S. . . . changed the condition of human life   SCIENCE, 24
S. . . . given us light, truth   SCIENCE, 7
S. . . . kind of cosmic apple juice   SCIENCE, 5
S. . . . system of statements based on . . . experience
     SCIENCE, 9
S. . . . the art of systematic over-simplification SCIENCE, 44
S. . . . the Differential Calculus of the mind   SCIENCE, 47
S. . . . the great instrument of social change   SCIENCE, 3
S. . . . the interplay between nature and ourselves
     SCIENCE, 30
s. begins as philosophy . . . ends as art   SCIENCE, 16
S. has 'explained' nothing   SCIENCE, 31

S. has a simple faith . . . transcends utility   SCIENCE, 8
s. is . . . neither a potential for good nor for evil
     SCIENCE, 51
S. is always wrong   SCIENCE, 52
S. is an integral part of culture   SCIENCE, 27
S. is built up of facts   SCIENCE, 43
s. is either physics or stamp collecting   PHYSICS, 12
S. is the great antidote   SCIENCE, 53
S. robs men of wisdom   SCIENCE, 54
S. says: 'We must live',   SCIENCE, 55
s. swarms with . . . outright fakery   SCIENTISTS, 12
S. will be the master of man   SCIENCE, 1
S. without conscience   SCIENCE, 46
the essence of s.: ask an impertinent question   SCIENCE, 6
the god of s. . . . has given us the atomic bomb
     SCIENCE, 36
What s. can measure . . . man can know   SCIENCE, 48
sciences exact s. . . . last to suffer under despotisms
     SCIENCE, 11
s. . . . prepared by magicians, alchemists, astrologers,
     and witches   SCIENCE, 40
scientific A new s. truth does not triumph   SCIENCE, 42
s. truth goes through three stages   SCIENCE, 2
very s. if . . . derived from twitching of frogs' legs
     SCIENCE, 34
where we do our s. work . . . place of prayer
     EXPERIMENTS, 6
scientific method Traditional s. . . . 20–20 hindsight
     SCIENCE, 41
scientist degradation of the position of the s.   SCIENTISTS, 29
good s. . . . perennial curiosity lingers on   SCIENTISTS, 26
have more faith in the s.   SCIENTISTS, 25
He had . . . qualities that make a great s.   SCIENTISTS, 5
s. is a lover of truth   SCIENTISTS, 3
s. never loses the faculty of amazement   SCIENTISTS, 27
s. who yields anything to theology   SCIENTISTS, 18
Touch a s. . . . touch a child   SCIENTISTS, 2
scientists great s. have been occupied with values
     SCIENTISTS, 30
in the company of s., I feel like a . . . curate SCIENTISTS, 1
S. are treated like gods   SCIENTISTS, 14
scissor The great, long, red-legged s.-man   CHILDREN, 17
scorched maybe we might have s. the moon   JAZZ, 6
scorn s. ride sparkling in her eyes   CONTEMPT, 3
Scotia O S.! my dear, my native soil   SCOTLAND, 1
Scotland patriotism has no . . . persona in S.   SCOTLAND, 13
S. . . . drowning, in the alien stream   SCOTLAND, 12
S. . . . most important centres of intellectual culture
     SCOTLAND, 2
S. . . . never secure a measure of independence
     SCOTLAND, 5
S., I rush towards you   SCOTLAND, 9
the English politician's view of S.   SCOTLAND, 10
Scots S. . . . find it very difficult to unite   SCOTLAND, 11
Scottish few decisive battles in S. history   SCOTLAND, 3
scream I have to s. a spring s.   EUPHORIA, 4
screech-owls when s. cry, and ban-dogs howl   NIGHT, 10
screenplays S. are not works of art   FILMS, 37
Scrooge 'I do', said S. 'I must'.   THE SUPERNATURAL, 4
sculpture S. museums are places where parents   CHILDREN, 15
S. to me is like poetry   SCULPTURE, 4
S.: You began in shadow   SCULPTURE, 5
You can't make a s. . . . without involving your body
     SCULPTURE, 3
You make s. because . . . wood allows you to express
     something   SCULPTURE, 1
sea A singular disadvantage of the s.   THE SEA, 9
forth on the godly s.   THE SEA, 22
I have known the s. too long   THE SEA, 8
Learn the secret of the s.   THE SEA, 18

s., trembling with a long line of radiance   THE SEA, 25
The s. always ebbs   THE SEA, 1
The s. is calm to-night   THE SEA, 2
The s. is the universal sewer   POLLUTION, 6
The s.! the s.!   THE SEA, 28
The voice of the s. speaks to the soul   THE SEA, 4
seagulls s. are following a trawler   JOURNALISM, 7
search I must s. *for being*   BEING, 5
seas West of these out to s. . . . I must go   THE SEA, 10
season always the s. for . . . old to learn   LEARNING, 3
to every thing there is a s.   SEASONS, 1
seasons a man for all s.   COMPLIMENTS, 5
second I'm a s. eleven sort of chap   MEDIOCRITY, 3
second-hand Would you buy a s. car   TRUST, 4
second-rate an infallible sign of the s.   MEDIOCRITY, 8
secrecy S. is the first essential   SECRECY, 13
secret a s. in the Oxford sense   SECRECY, 9
At last the s. is out   GOSSIP, 1
I know that's a s.   SECRECY, 4
most difficult s. for a man   SECRECY, 11
s. as the grave   SECRECY, 2
s. hidden since the world began   MEDICINE, 21
s. of a successful life   DESTINY, 4
Three may keep a s.   SECRECY, 8
secrets s. are edged tools   SECRECY, 7
sects no s. in geometry   MATHEMATICS, 32
secular a kind of s. priest   POLITICIANS, 1
security s. we . . . seek in foreign adventures   AMERICAN IMPERIALISM, 12
seducer Thou strong s., opportunity   OPPORTUNITY, 5
see I s. the steady gain of man   PROGRESS, 27
Something I cannot s. . . . libidinous prongs   PERCEPTION, 15
there shall no man s. me, and live   THREATS, 1
We s. only the appearances . . . of things   PERCEPTION, 2
seed he spills his s. on the ground   NAMES, 16
I am certain that the s. we planted   SOUTH AMERICA, 2
seed time In s. learn, in harvest teach   SEASONS, 2
seed-time Fair s. had my soul   YOUTH, 32
seeming beguile /The thing I am by s.   DELUSIONS OF LOVE, 11
seen they that have not s., and yet have believed   BELIEF, 4
seer one must be a s.   POETS, 49
segregation s. now, s. tomorrow, s. forever   APARTHEID, 14
seize S. the day   OPPORTUNITY, 6
selection Natural S.   EVOLUTION, 6
self dearer to anyone than his own s.   SELF-INTEREST, 1
perhaps within a few days I should dissent my s.   AGREEMENT, 3
S. under s., a pile of selves   SELF-KNOWLEDGE, 29
The s. posits s.   THE SELF, 7
The s., what a brute it is   THE SELF, 25
where the s. that was no self made its home   DESPAIR, 9
selfbeing My s., my consciousness   THE SELF, 12
self-censorship serious game of s.   CENSORSHIP, 19
self-consciousness s. . . . divides us from our fellow creatures   SELF-KNOWLEDGE, 10
self-contemplation S. is . . . the symptom of disease   SELF-KNOWLEDGE, 7
self-delusion Nothing causes s. . . . so readily as power   POWER, 27
self-denial S. is not a virtue   PRUDENCE, 5
self-determination S. is not a mere phrase   INDEPENDENCE, 9
self-disgust I asked for s.   HATE, 20
self-government s. and self-determination . . . no turning back   INDEPENDENCE, 4
We prefer s. with danger to servitude in tranquility   AFRICAN COUNTRIES, 13
self-interest S. speaks all sorts of tongues   SELF-INTEREST, 8
selfish been a s. being all my life   SELFISHNESS, 1
How s. soever man may be supposed   SELFLESSNESS, 6
the s. propriety of civilized man   CIVILIZATION, 22

self-knowledge S. is a dangerous thing   SELF-KNOWLEDGE, 36
self-love S. is the greatest of all flatterers   VANITY, 6
self-made man A s. . . . believes in luck   PRIVILEGE, 5
s. . . . owed his lack of success   FAILURE, 7
self-parody S. . . . the first portent of age   AGE, 18
self-reflection S. is the school of wisdom   SELF-KNOWLEDGE, 18
self-respect S.—the secure feeling that no one . . . is suspicious   SELF-RESPECT, 3
self-revelation terrible *fluidity of s.*   TRUTH, 38
self-rule Never . . . has an alien ruler granted s.   IMPERIALISM, 16
self-sacrifice S. enables us to sacrifice   THE SELF, 21
sell Everything we s., we s. on image   ADVERTISING, 7
I s. . . . what all the world desires   POWER, 3
selling Every one lives by s. something   BUSINESS, 27
semantic S. inflation   MEANING, 13
semiology s. postulates . . . a signifier and a signified   LANGUAGE, 4
senator S., you're no Jack Kennedy   POLITICAL INSULTS, 13
sensations S. rather than of Thoughts   SENSES, 9
sense Take care of the s.   MEANING, 4
sense of humour God withheld the s. from women   MEN, 8
senses The five s. are as spies   SENSES, 12
the s. do not err   SENSES, 8
sensible s. people are selfish   SELFISHNESS, 3
sensitivity You must have . . . s.—a cutting edge   ACTING AND ACTORS, 18
sensual the average s. man impassioned   EUROPEAN LITERATURE, 1
sentence simple declarative s. with seven grammatical errors   GRAMMAR, 6
Whatever s. . . . bear to be read twice   READING, 33
sentences Backward ran s.   JOURNALISM, 12
sentimental s. cheats of the movie screen   LYING, 23
sentimentality S. is . . . emotional promiscuity   SENTIMENTALITY, 2
S. is a superstructure   SENTIMENTALITY, 1
S. is only sentiment   SENTIMENTALITY, 3
sentiments s. that no legislature can manufacture   MONARCHY, 1
sepulchres whited s.   HYPOCRISY, 4
serf No man should be a s.   CIVIL RIGHTS, 14
serfdom better to . . . abolish s. from above   SLAVERY, 1
seriously Everything must be taken s., nothing tragically   SERIOUSNESS, 4
serpent sharper than a s.'s tooth   CHILDREN, 31
The s. subtlest beast of all the field   ANIMALS, 28
servant good s. does not all commands   OBEDIENCE, 6
servants he wouldn't have white s.   RACISM, 27
serve s. his time to every trade   CRITICS, 8
settled Thank God, that's s.   DEBT, 16
seventy Being over s. is like being engaged in a war   OLD AGE, 44
Oh, to be s. again   OLD AGE, 22
several I see s. Africas   AFRICA, 1
sewage piped growing volumes of s. into the sea   POLLUTION, 3
sewer A trip through a s.   HOLLYWOOD, 14
sex Being the inventor of s.   INVENTIONS, 7
His excessive emphasis on s.   LITERARY INSULTS, 48
If God . . . meant us to have group s.   SEX, 12
If s. is such a natural phenomenon   SEX, 31
it's s. with someone you love   MASTURBATION, 1
No s. is better than bad s.   SEX, 23
Personally I know nothing about s.   SEX, 20
pseudo-sophistication of twentieth-century s. theory   SEX, 22
S. . . . Every bit as interesting as agriculture   SEX, 41
s. . . . must itself be subject . . . to evolution   THE SEXES, 1
S. between a man and a woman   SEX, 2
s. is . . . a form of holy communion   SEX, 36
S. is one of the nine reasons for reincarnation   SEX, 32
S. is something I really don't understand   SEX, 37

Man was formed for s.   SOCIETY, 3
no such thing as S.   SOCIETY, 25
open s. . . . unrestricted access to knowledge
    KNOWLEDGE, 30
S. . . . prepares crimes   CRIME, 18
s. can crave lethal weapons   ADDICTION, 3
S. has resembled a pyramid . . . turned upside down
    SOCIETY, 14
S. is an organism, not a machine   SOCIETY, 9
S. is no comfort /To one not sociable   SOCIETY, 22
S. is now one polish'd horde   BORES AND BOREDOM, 4
S. needs to condemn a little   IGNORANCE, 12
s. which acts as one big family   SOCIETY, 21
There are two classes in good s.   CLASS, 32
the vanilla of s.   INFLUENCE, 8
socks His s. compelled one's attention   CLOTHES, 15
Socrates S. was the first to call philosophy down
    PHILOSOPHY, 5
soft the s., delicious functions of nature   SLEEP, 27
soil Untilled s. . . . thistles and thorns   MIND, 43
solar s. and stellar systems could only kill you once
    DISASTER, 1
soldier glazed eyes of a s. will think . . . before starting a
war   WAR, 7
s. who hated war   MIDDLE EAST, 31
The summer's. and the sunshine patriot   PATRIOTISM, 21
soldiers S. in peace are like   OCCUPATIONS, 2
solemn great s. guns leisurely manipulated   WORLD WAR I, 12
solid How . . . s. the best work still seems   READING, 8
solitary He lived the life of a s.   SCIENTISTS, 11
Only s. men know the full joys of friendship
    FRIENDSHIP, 10
solitude One can acquire everything in s.   SOLITUDE, 25
so companionable as s.   SOLITUDE, 26
s. . . . a wild beast or a god   SOLITUDE, 2
S. . . . is not humanity's highest state   SOLITUDE, 23
s. of his own originality   INDIVIDUALITY, 13
s. was what I hoped for   SOLITUDE, 6
worst s. . . . destitute of sincere friendship   SOLITUDE, 1
You find in s.   SOLITUDE, 14
solo sweet, fairy-tale s. on an alto   JAZZ, 11
solution If you're not a part of the s.   PROGRESS, 19
solve We do not s. them   QUESTIONS, 2
someone Getting s. to do something for you   POLITICS, 47
somer In a s. seson   SUMMER, 6
something gentlemen, let us do s. today   ACHIEVEMENT, 4
I too hoped to become 's.'.   AMBITION, 9
son examined your s.'s head . . . there's nothing there
    STUPIDITY, 8
I'm the s. of a painter   INFLUENCE, 7
song mighty orb of s., the divine Milton   POETS, 67
said what I need . . . in a s.   SONGS, 4
without a s. . . . road would never bend
    SINGERS AND SINGING, 8
songs I liked to do the s.   SINGERS AND SINGING, 1
Our sweetest s. are those that tell of saddest thought
    SONGS, 10
Simple s., one-line lyrics, gimmicks   POPULAR MUSIC, 3
The Lord holds copyright on all s.   SONGS, 3
The s. of the slave   SONGS, 2
sonnet make my life as slick as a s.   FEAR, 4
s. is a moment's monument   POETRY, 48
sons of bitches Now we are all s.   NUCLEAR WAR, 1
sorrow Down, thou climbing s.   SORROW, 24
One scene of s. and of pain   SUFFERING, 5
O S., wilt thou live with me   SORROW, 27
Pure and complete s. is as impossible   SORROW, 29
S.'s most detested fruit   SORROW, 2
S. and silence are strong   ENDURANCE, 4
s. is remembering happier things   SORROW, 28

S. is tranquillity remembered in emotion   SORROW, 17
the land where s. is unknown   SORROW, 3
To s. /I bade good-morrow   SORROW, 11
sorrowing the s. are nomads   SORROW, 13
sorrows When s. come, they come not single spies
    MISFORTUNE, 10
soufflé can't make a s. rise twice   POLITICAL INSULTS, 40
soul become a living s.   THE SOUL, 25
dim Windows of the S.   DECEPTION, 5
gods approve /The depth . . . of the s.   THE SOUL, 26
Go, S., the body's guest   THE SOUL, 18
Hang there like fruit, my s.   FAITH, 15
Heaven take my s., and England my bones   AFTERLIFE, 19
I am positive I have a s.   THE SOUL, 22
I have too great a s.   ASSASSINATION, 1
I must place a motor in my s.   DANCING, 5
life . . . in which the s. is in a ferment   INDECISION, 4
Never mind about my s. . . . get my tie right   PAINTING, 19
Part of My S. Went With Him   SEPARATION, 3
S. . . . individuality of each personal consciousness
    THE SOUL, 12
s. descends . . . To accept the waking body   THE SOUL, 23
s. follows its own laws   THE SOUL, 13
s. of Ovid lives in . . . Shakespeare   WRITERS, 48
the . . . essence of a human s.   BOOKS, 8
the s. . . . a republic or commonwealth   THE SOUL, 11
The s. . . . has an interpreter . . . in the eye   THE SOUL, 4
The s. . . . remains as much *outside*   THE SOUL, 16
The s. . . . without its body   THE SOUL, 14
The s. is characterized by these capacities   THE SOUL, 1
the s. is not more than the body   THE SELF, 24
The s. selects her own Society   SOLITUDE, 8
turn'st mine eyes into my very s.   SELF-KNOWLEDGE, 35
souls a follower of hounds to become a shepherd of s.
    MARTYRDOM, 5
every two s. are absolutely different   RELATIONSHIPS, 8
Most people sell their s.   HYPOCRISY, 23
Our s. have sight of . . . immortal sea   IMMORTALITY, 21
People have invented s.   THE SOUL, 10
s. originally one . . . seeks the half it lost   UNITY, 2
the s. of five hundred . . . Newtons   THE SOUL, 8
Tis an awkward thing to play with s.   THE SOUL, 5
Two s. with but a single thought   LOVE, 39
sound The last s. on the worthless earth   ENDING, 4
soundbite s. . . . all that an interviewer allows you to say
    SOUNDBITES, 1
sounds deep s. from the stomach   SPEECHES, 5
When it s. good   MUSIC, 14
soup I live on good s., not fine words   FOOD, 25
south go s. in the winter   READING, 11
The S. creates the civilizations   IMPERIALISM, 7
South Africa racial policy of the Union of S.   APARTHEID, 10
S., renowned both far and wide   AFRICAN COUNTRIES, 4
victory for all the people of S.   AFRICAN COUNTRIES, 10
you have mandated us to change S.   AFRICAN COUNTRIES, 9
South African I was ashamed of being S.   AFRICAN COUNTRIES, 1
The S. Police would leave no stone unturned
    AFRICAN COUNTRIES, 15
sovereign That s. of insufferables   LITERARY INSULTS, 4
two s. masters, *pain* and *pleasure*   MORALITY, 1
Soviet S. citizen . . . state of permanent inner dialogue
    RUSSIA, 5
S. people want full-blooded . . . democracy   RUSSIA, 15
Soviet Union the three ugly sisters . . . in the S.   RUSSIA, 19
soweth whatsoever a man s., that shall he also reap
    CONSEQUENCES, 2
space annihilate but s. and time   LOVERS, 12
Empty s. and points of light   REALITY, 25
Outer s. is no place   CLASS, 5
S. . . . is big. Really big   SPACE, 1

S. will prove anything — STATISTICS, 7
There are two kinds of s. — STATISTICS, 9
unrewarded millions without whom S. . . . a bankrupt science — STATISTICS, 8
We are just s., born to consume — STATISTICS, 4
statue No s. . . . put up to a critic — CRITICS, 28
steak he wanted s. and they offered spam — DISAPPOINTMENT, 4
steal A man who will s. *for* me — THEFT, 10
if we're smart . . . s. from great directors — PLAGIARISM, 7
Thou shalt not s.; an empty feat — THEFT, 3
To s. from the rich is . . . sacred — THEFT, 11
stealing s. an office and s. a purse — CIVILIZATION, 25
steals s. the common from the goose — THEFT, 5
stealth greatest pleasure I know, is to do a good action by s. — KINDNESS, 6
Stein Gertrude S. . . . unreadable at times — AMERICAN LITERATURE, 5
step For your s. following and damned if I look back — THE SUPERNATURAL, 14
one small s. for man — THE MOON, 2
One s. forward, two steps back — PROGRESS, 20
stereotype The resort to s. . . . chief strategy of the bigot — BIGOTRY, 4
stew It's like s. . . . cook it properly — NORTHERN IRELAND, 1
stigma Any s. . . . to beat a dogma — OPINIONS, 8
still s. point of the turning world — MYSTICISM, 2
stirring s. times we live in — CHANGE, 15
stocking a glimpse of s. /Was . . . something shocking — FASHION, 12
stolen S. sweets are always sweeter — THEFT, 7
stomach a s., gentlemen, a s. — THE BODY, 10
my s. must just digest in its waistcoat — ALCOHOL, 22
The s. is a bottomless pit — HUNGER, 2
The way to a man's heart is through his s. — FOOD, 10
stop s. everyone from doing it — CENSORSHIP, 12
S. the World, I Want to Get Off — STRESS, 3
The way to s. the spread of HIV — AIDS, 2
stories If we change the s. we live by — FICTION, 6
tell ourselves s. in order to live — STORYTELLING, 6
The seaman tells s. of winds — STORYTELLING, 17
story 'The s. is like the wind — STORYTELLING, 20
A s. is a formula for extracting meaning from chaos — STORYTELLING, 22
Beginning to tell a s. — BEGINNING, 11
For never was a s. of more woe — TRAGEDY, 9
From the great S. Sea — INSPIRATION, 11
If a s. is a declaration against death — WRITERS, 25
If the s. is to live — STORYTELLING, 16
it is necessary to tell a life s. — STORYTELLING, 2
That's the s. of our life — LYING, 44
To write a s. in just five minutes — WRITING, 1
your life is a s. — LIFE, 32
storybook Life is not a s. — STORYTELLING, 18
storyteller Every s. is a child of Scheherazade — STORYTELLING, 7
good s. . . . has a good memory — STORYTELLING, 5
storytellers S. are reorganisers of accepted reality — STORYTELLING, 15
storytelling In s. there is always transgression — STORYTELLING, 14
s. . . . a public art — STORYTELLING, 13
strangers among s. . . . preserve appearances — APPEARANCE, 8
strawberry I'm not a s. — ACCIDENTS, 2
Like s. wives — DECEPTION, 2
street don't do it in the s. — SEX, 15
streets s. are paved with gold — BRITISH CITIES, 5
S. full of water — EUROPEAN CITIES, 2
strength My s. . . . as the s. of ten — PURITY, 4
stress an exaggerated s. on not changing one's mind — WEAKNESS, 2
strikes s. where it doth love — SORROW, 25
strings I had two s. to my bow — MODESTY, 5
There are s. . . . in the human heart — EMOTION, 3

strive Always s. to excel — EFFORT, 2
I s. to be brief — BREVITY, 4
striven s. not to laugh at human actions — UNDERSTANDING, 9
strives s. to touch the stars — AMBITION, 30
striving what are we actually s. for — ACHIEVEMENT, 5
strivings parcel of vain s. — MODESTY, 11
strong disarm the s. and arm the weak — INJUSTICE, 7
s. enough to bear the misfortunes of others — MISFORTUNE, 7
strongest The s. and the fiercest spirit — AGGRESSION, 4
struck s. all of a heap — DISORDER, 4
structure A s. becomes architecture — ARCHITECTURE, 1
struggle after years of s. . . . a trip takes us — TRAVEL, 28
I believe in the armed s. — REVOLUTION, 17
no s. . . . no progress — PROGRESS, 12
s. between capitalism and socialism is . . . progress — PROGRESS, 2
s. for peace and . . . human rights . . . inseparable — PEACE, 9
The perpetual s. for room and food — SURVIVAL, 2
The s. is my life — CIVIL RIGHTS, 9
The s. of any nation — NATIONS, 19
The s. with the past — THE PAST, 27
student a s. to the end of my days — LEARNING, 11
students ceased to notice the existence of s. — UNIVERSITY, 7
study S. more and criticize less — LEARNING, 14
studying By s. the masters — LEARNING, 1
stuff ordinary-sized s. which is our lives — PROPHECY, 12
to s. a mushroom — COOKING, 2
stupid s. are cocksure and . . . intelligent full of doubt — STUPIDITY, 11
The s. neither forgive nor forget — FORGIVENESS, 13
stupidity Against s. the gods . . . struggle in vain — STUPIDITY, 12
Human S. consists in having lots of ideas — STUPIDITY, 7
Nothing . . . is more dangerous . . . conscientious s. — IGNORANCE, 10
s. . . . product of highly organized matter — STUPIDITY, 3
s. . . . to busy oneself with . . . correction — STUPIDITY, 6
style can you say one s. is better than another — ARTISTIC STYLES, 25
Poor s. reflects imperfect thought — LITERARY STYLE, 9
S. is beginning something — STYLE, 6
S. is the man himself — STYLE, 1
s., not sincerity, is the vital thing — STYLE, 10
there is no beautiful s. — BEAUTY, 29
styles All s. are good except the tiresome sort — STYLE, 9
stylist A good s. should have a narcissistic enjoyment — LITERARY STYLE, 8
subdue chance to s. the Highland chiefs — SCOTLAND, 8
would I could s. the flesh — LUST, 1
subjectivity S. and objectivity . . . assaults on each other — SUBJECTIVITY, 1
subjugate You cannot s. a man — TYRANNY, 5
sublime A sense s. /Of something . . . deeply interfused — ROMANTICISM, 5
from the s. to the ridiculous — STUPIDITY, 9
how s. . . . To suffer and be strong — SUFFERING, 12
more s. and intense than . . . revolution — EUROPEAN COUNTRIES, 6
s. . . . pleases immediately — TASTE, 8
s. dashed to pieces . . . round the corner of nonsense — RHETORIC, 1
S. moments, heroic acts — INTELLIGENCE, 2
submission Willing s. to social restraint — SOCIETY, 8
subordination the legal s. of one sex to the other — WOMEN'S RIGHTS, 25
substance A s. that makes you ill — HEALTH AND HEALTHY LIVING, 20
lose the s. by grasping at the shadow — WARNING, 1
substitute s. for a real experience — PORNOGRAPHY, 1
subtlety one-dimensional s. of a comic-strip — POLITICAL INSULTS, 25

suburbs Nineteen s. in search of a metropolis
AMERICAN CITIES, 29

succeed don't s., try, try again. Then quit FAILURE, 6
It is not enough to s. SUCCESS, 19
Never having been able to s. in the world FAILURE, 14
To s. you have to believe SUCCESS, 15
way to s. . . . make people hate you SUCCESS, 20

success A minute's s. pays the failure of years SUCCESS, 3
Man owes his s. to his creativity CREATIVITY, 6
Never let s. hide its emptiness ACHIEVEMENT, 10
no s. like failure FAILURE, 4
Nothing fails like s. SUCCESS, 12
only place where s. comes before work SUCCESS, 16
S. . . . is having ten honeydew melons SUCCESS, 18
s. . . . nothing like we had anticipated ANTICIPATION, 4
s. comes from ignoring the obvious SUCCESS, 7
S. Four flights Thursday morning FLYING, 9
s. in ad writing is the product ADVERTISING, 3
s. in journalism . . . rat-like cunning JOURNALISM, 30
S. is counted sweetest SUCCESS, 4
S. is man's god SUCCESS, 1
s. is relative SUCCESS, 5
s. is to be measured . . . by the obstacles SUCCESS, 21
S. never satisfies me SUCCESS, 6
The Sweet Smell of S. SUCCESS, 10

successful we do everything we can to appear s. SUCCESS, 9

sucker s. an even break GULLIBILITY, 4
There's a s. born every minute GULLIBILITY, 1

sudden you shouldn't make a s. move AMERICAN CITIES, 26

sue I won't s. you . . . I'll ruin you REVENGE, 16

Suez Canal S. . . . flowing through my drawing room
DIPLOMACY, 16

suffer Can they s. ANIMALS, 5
easier to s. in obedience to a human command
SUFFERING, 1
let's s. on the heights SUFFERING, 6
Rather s. than die SUFFERING, 9
s. fools gladly FOOLISHNESS, 3

sufferance s. is the badge of all our tribe ENDURANCE, 9

suffering He preferred s. in freedom SUFFERING, 11
I love the majesty of human s. SUFFERING, 27
S. . . . is the resistance to will SUFFERING, 26
s. did not ennoble SUFFERING, 14
the appalling total of human s. SUFFERING, 2

suicide committed s. 25 years after his death REPUTATION, 7
dallied with the thought of s. SUICIDE, 10
If you must commit s. SUICIDE, 2
No one ever lacks a good reason for s. SUICIDE, 14
nothing ever interfered with . . . National S. Day
SUICIDE, 11
one truly serious philosophical problem . . . s. SUICIDE, 4
s. is a test of height in civilization SUICIDE, 7
s. is God's best gift to man SUICIDE, 15
s. really *validates* . . . the life SUICIDE, 21
s. remains the courageous act SUICIDE, 8
thought of s. is a . . . comfort SUICIDE, 12

sumer S. is icumen SUMMER, 3

summer Now the peak of s.'s past TRANSIENCE, 9
S. afternoon . . . two most beautiful words SUMMER, 5
S. has set in with its usual severity SUMMER, 2
way to ensure s. in England SUMMER, 8

summertime S. /And the livin' is easy SUMMER, 4

sun before you let the s. in OBSESSIONS, 5
Busy old fool, unruly S. LOVERS, 7
Follow thy fair s. UNHAPPINESS, 2
I loved the s. THE SUN, 9
Lovely day: s. . . . weed-killer DISILLUSIONMENT, 4
Mother, give me the s. THE SUN, 3
on which the s. never sets BRITISH IMPERIALISM, 17
s. had risen to hear him crow CONCEIT, 3

S. remains fixed in the centre ASTRONOMY, 4
S. shrinks to a dull red dwarf THE SUN, 2
Thank heavens the s. has gone in PERVERSITY, 6
the rising s. has first breathed on us with his panting horses MORNING, 18
The s. has only memory of flame THE SUN, 5
The s. in my dominion never sets IMPERIALISM, 22
The s. /Must bear no name THE SUN, 7
The s. shone, having no alternative THE SUN, 1

sunburn S. is very becoming APPEARANCE, 5

sunny side Keep your s. up OPTIMISM, 1

suns The mass starts into a million s. CREATION, 3

sunshine Flaunt of the s. THE SUN, 8

superfluity S. of Good Things EXCESS, 1

superior s. . . . because one sees the world in an odious light CYNICISM, 2
What the s. man seeks HUMANKIND, 10

superiority S. we've always had . . . ask is equality
WOMEN'S RIGHTS, 4

superiors In America everybody . . . has no . . . s.
AMERICANS, 20

Superman I teach you the S. HUMANKIND, 37
S. comics . . . deep cry for help HEROISM, 11

supernatural Some element of the s. . . . poetry
THE SUPERNATURAL, 38

superstition Men will fight for s. TRUTH, 37

support s. of . . . the decent opinion of mankind
AMERICAN IMPERIALISM, 17

suppress No, don't s. CENSORSHIP, 21

supreme Our s. governors, the mob POWER, 43

sure nothing is s., everything is possible CERTAINTY, 4

surge a probing s. against the world NIGHT, 3

surgeon one little touch of a s.'s lancet SENSES, 11
s. . . . tempted to supplant . . . Nature MEDICINE, 22

surgeons Tree s. . . . wear safety belts TREES, 1

surly I have slipped the s. bonds of earth FLYING, 5

surpasses s. or subdues mankind ENVY, 3

surprised it is *I* who am s.; you are merely astonished
ADULTERY, 20

surprising a combination of the s. and the beautiful
RELATIONSHIPS, 2
s. . . . a man who could write it would ACADEMICS, 4

surrender if you s. your personality CHARACTER, 9
we will never s. our heritage NORTHERN IRELAND, 11

survival s. of the European order in jeopardy EUROPE, 5
S. of the fittest EVOLUTION, 26
We are s. machines GENETICS, 2

survive as fitted to s. . . . as a tapeworm EVOLUTION, 13
obligation to s. is owed . . . to that cosmos SURVIVAL, 5
One can s. everything . . . except death SURVIVAL, 10
What will s. of us is love LOVE, 36

suspense This s. is terrible ENDURANCE, 11

suspicion S. always haunts the guilty mind GUILT, 16

sustainable development policy challenge of s. ECONOMICS, 22
S. challenges . . . industrial and commercial system
ECONOMICS, 2

swallowe One s. prouveth not that summer SUMMER, 7

swallow-flights Short s. of song SONGS, 11

swallows I hate a man who s. it FOOD, 18

swamp That Indian s. in the wilderness AMERICAN CITIES, 20

Sweden S. should be . . . the people's home
EUROPEAN COUNTRIES, 30

sweet How s. the moonlight sleeps THE MOON, 15

swine a s. to show you where the truffles are NECESSITY, 1

swines Curse the blasted, jelly-boned s. PUBLISHING, 6

swing s. low sweet chariot HOPE, 8

Swiss if the S. had designed these mountains MOUNTAINS, 8
The S. . . . are not a people so much as a . . . business
EUROPEAN COUNTRIES, 22

Swithin St. S.'s Day, if thou dost rain WEATHER, 8

Switzerland S. . . . five hundred years of democracy and
  . . . The cuckoo clock   EUROPEAN COUNTRIES, 60
  S. only seems small   EUROPEAN COUNTRIES, 38
sword draw the s. with a clear conscience   WORLD WAR I, 32
  s. . . . responsible for more misery . . . than opium
        WEAPONS, 7
  they that take the s. shall perish with the s.   RETRIBUTION, 4
swords Keep up your bright s.   FIGHTING, 8
  s. shall play the orators for us   FIGHTING, 6
  s. taller than ourselves   TRAGEDY, 7
  They shall beat their s. into plowshares   PEACE, 6
sworn I am s. brother, sweet, /To grim Necessity
        NECESSITY, 17
Sydney There was the vast town of S.   AUSTRALIA, 6
symbols night's starr'd face, /Huge cloudy s. of a high
  romance   ROMANTICISM, 1
sympathize s. with everything, except suffering   SYMPATHY, 8
sympathy S. for the Devil   SYMPATHY, 6
symphony s. means slavery in any jazzman's dictionary
        JAZZ, 16
system A s. is . . . subordination of all aspects   THEORY, 3
  present s. . . . subordinates the weaker sex   THE SEXES, 10
systematic enormous s. buildings   PHILOSOPHY, 17
  s. occupation of territory   WAR, 21
t The 't.' is silent   WORDPLAY, 1
table put them at a t. together   FEAR, 9
  The t. I write on . . . exists   EXISTENCE, 3
tables t. of stone, and a law   JUDAISM, 4
tainted the supply is not t.   JOURNALISM, 26
tale t. to tell of the hardihood . . . of my companions
        EXPLORATION, 7
talent man has t. and cannot use it   TALENT, 10
  no . . . great t. without great will-power   DETERMINATION, 1
  no substitute for t.   TALENT, 3
  T. alone cannot make a writer   WRITERS, 19
  T. develops in quiet places   TALENT, 2
  t. instantly recognizes genius   TALENT, 1
  t. of our English nation   ENGLAND, 9
  T. wins games . . . teamwork wins championships
        TALENT, 5
talk first t. is of the weather   CONVERSATION, 13
  I t. it best through an interpreter   EUROPEAN LANGUAGES, 5
  I want to t. like a lady   GRAMMAR, 12
  T. had feet . . . gossip had wings   GOSSIP, 10
  the need to t. is a primary impulse   SPEECH, 1
  the t. slid north . . . the t. slid south   CONVERSATION, 15
  They . . . t. who never think   SENSES, 14
  Two may t. . . . yet never really meet   FRIENDSHIP, 11
  we never t. about anything except me   CONVERSATION, 22
talk'd So much they t.   CONVERSATION, 8
talked one thing . . . worse than being t. about   FAME, 31
talker good t.—learn to listen   CONVERSATION, 17
talking if you ain't t. about him, ain't listening
        ACTING AND ACTORS, 1
  I wouldn't be . . . t. to someone like you   CLASS, 9
  People t. without speaking   SILENCE, 28
  T.'s something you can't do judiciously   CONVERSATION, 11
  T. and eloquence are not the same   SPEECH, 12
  Therefore people ought to be prohibited from t.
        LANGUAGE, 20
Tam T.! thou'll get thy fairin'   HELL, 5
tambourine Hey! Mr T. Man   DRUGS, 9
tangerine t. trees and marmalade skies   FANTASY, 8
tank leading from the top of a t.   RUSSIA, 28
tap Some people t. their feet   POPULAR MUSIC, 28
task The real t. of the historian   HISTORIANS, 21
  the t. . . . one dare not start   PROCRASTINATION, 1
Tasmanians the T., who never committed adultery, are
  now extinct   ADULTERY, 12
taste bad t. is better than no t.   TASTE, 2

go on about . . . good t.   TASTE, 13
great common sense and good t.   MEDIOCRITY, 12
If you want to see bad t.   DESIGN, 5
Matters of t. must be felt   TASTE, 7
satisfy t. . . . satisfy the demands of utility   TASTE, 4
T. all . . . hand the knowledge down   KNOWLEDGE, 35
T. does not come by chance   TASTE, 15
T. has no systems and no proofs   TASTE, 18
T. is the best judge   TASTE, 3
The t. was that of the little crumb of madeleine
        MEMORY, 39
Things sweet to t. prove in digestion sour   DIGESTION, 9
willing to t. any drink once   DRINKS AND DRINKING, 3
tastes cater to . . . pubescent t. of the public
        POPULAR MUSIC, 37
  t. may not be the same   TASTE, 17
tatter'd Through t. clothes small vices do appear CLOTHES, 17
taught You t. me language   LANGUAGE, 35
tavern A t. chair is the throne   ALCOHOL, 11
tavernes knew the t. wel in every toun   ALCOHOL, 5
tea Take some more t.   MEANING, 3
  T. for two, and two for t.   EATING, 10
  When I makes t. I makes t.   FRANKNESS, 6
teach For every person wishing to t.   TEACHERS, 8
  He who wishes to t.   TEACHERS, 4
  He who would t. men to die   DEATH AND DYING, 45
  t. taste or genius by rules   TASTE, 14
  t. them in the city   CITIES, 16
  t. you how to make strawberry jam   BOOKS, 35
  To t. how to live without certainty   DOUBT, 12
teacher art of the t. to awaken joy   TEACHERS, 2
  t. . . . have maximal authority and minimal power
        TEACHERS, 11
  t. . . . is a senior student   TEACHERS, 6
teaches He who cannot, t.   TEACHERS, 9
teaching T. has ruined more American novelists EDUCATION, 24
tears If you have t., prepare to shed them   SORROW, 23
  in a flood of t. and a Sedan chair   SORROW, 5
  No more t. now   REVENGE, 9
  T. fall in my heart /As rain falls   SORROW, 30
  T. left unshed /turn to poison /in the ducts   SORROW, 33
  T. such as angels weep   SORROW, 14
  T. were to me   SORROW, 4
  The bitterest t. shed over graves   REGRET, 15
  the land of t.   SORROW, 21
technical prowess t. of nations such as India GLOBALIZATION, 8
technique perfect t. . . . not noticed at all   ABILITY, 2
technological a t. assault is being prepared   TECHNOLOGY, 24
  t. equivalent of unsafe sex   COMPUTERS, 2
technologies As we push our t.   TECHNOLOGY, 17
technology For a successful t., reality must take
  precedence   TECHNOLOGY, 3
  t. . . . important to modern man   COMMUNICATION, 5
  t. . . . indistinguishable from magic   TECHNOLOGY, 2
  T. feeds on itself   TECHNOLOGY, 21
  T. is the knack   TECHNOLOGY, 4
  The development of t. will leave only one problem
        TECHNOLOGY, 12
teeming city of t. millions and multi-millionaires
        ASIAN CITIES, 1
teetotaller a beer t., not a champagne t.   ALCOHOL, 19
television amazed that people will actually choose to sit in
  front of the t.   TELEVISION, 17
  I hate t. . . . as much as peanuts   TELEVISION, 18
  T. . . . half Greek and half Latin   TELEVISION, 15
  T. . . . permits you to be entertained in your living
  room   TELEVISION, 6
  T.—the drug of the nation   TELEVISION, 5
  t. programs are . . . chewing gum for the eyes
        TELEVISION, 4

T. was the ultimate evidence of cultural anaemia
                                                                                              TELEVISION, 8
tell I t. for precisely what it is   LITERARY STYLE, 13
tells man never t. you anything   ARGUMENTS, 20
temper A tart t. never mellows with age   ANGER, 11
   Never lose your t. with the Press   MEDIA, 10
temperance T. is the love of health   MODERATION, 7
   T. is the nurse of chastity   MODERATION, 9
tempt T. me no more   POETS, 5
temptation best way to get the better of t.   TEMPTATION, 4
   he resisted every t. to magical thought   AFTERLIFE, 8
   I never resist t.   TEMPTATION, 8
   The great t. in these difficult days   MORALITY, 17
tempts Not all that t. . . . is lawful prize   DECEPTION, 17
ten T. Days that Shook the World   RUSSIAN REVOLUTION, 12
tenderness its t., its joys and fears   THE HEART, 8
terrible t. thing for a man to find out   TRUTH, 64
terrifying In a world we find t.   FEAR, 19
terrorism t. inflicted on society by crime figures   TERRORISM, 8
   without parallel in the bloody history of t.   TERRORISM, 2
terrorist T. attacks can shake . . . our biggest buildings
                                                                                              TERRORISM, 3
terrorists All t. . . . end up with drinks at the Dorchester
                                                                                              TERRORISM, 1
terrorize No one can t. a whole nation   TERRORISM, 7
tether Nae man can t. time or tide   TIME, 8
Thames Sweet T.! run softly   RIVERS, 4
   the T. is liquid history   RIVERS, 1
thank not going to t. anybody   AWARDS, 4
   T. me no thankings   GRATITUDE, 8
   T. you for not killing me   AMERICAN CITIES, 6
Thatcherism T. . . . reversion to the idea of nature   POVERTY, 2
theatre nobody goes to the t. unless he . . . has bronchitis
                                                                                              AUDIENCES, 1
t. . . . picture Bible for those who cannot read
                                                                                              THEATRE, 19
   t. . . . school of the moral   MORALITY, 26
   T. is the first serum   THEATRE, 2
theft A clever t. . . . praiseworthy . . . amongst Christians
                                                                                              THEFT, 14
theories In making t. . . . keep a window open   THEORY, 12
theorist I'm not a t.   WRITERS, 57
theory Don't confuse *hypothesis* and *t.*   THEORY, 6
   more important . . . t. to be shapely   THEORY, 8
   physical t. is not an explanation   PHYSICS, 5
theory of relativity If my t. is proven correct   SCIENTISTS, 9
thief He that first cries out stop t.   THEFT, 4
   If you give to a t. he cannot steal   THEFT, 12
   What is a man if he is not a t.   THEFT, 6
thieves T. respect property   THEFT, 2
thin One can never be too t.   WEALTH, 29
   Outside every t. girl   LUST, 12
thing If a t. is worth doing   MEDIOCRITY, 5
   something between a t. and a thought   PAINTING, 28
   when the t. itself is missing   ABSENCE, 7
things all t. are one   UNITY, 5
   There are no t., only processes   REALITY, 2
   T. . . . are what they are   DELUSION, 2
   T. are always best seen   ORDER, 2
   T. are entirely what they appear to be   APPEARANCE, 16
   T. are seldom what they seem   APPEARANCE, 9
   Two t. are certain   CERTAINTY, 3
   uncomfortable feeling of 't.' in the head   WRITING, 4
think can't t. without his hat   THINKING, 2
   I t., therefore I am   BEING, 1
   I t. with my hands   EXPERIMENTS, 5
   let us t. that we build for ever   ARCHITECTURE, 22
   T. nothing done while aught remains to do
                                                                                              ACHIEVEMENT, 20
time to t. before I speak   SPEECH, 5

To t. is to differ   THINKING, 10
Under all that we t.   THINKING, 25
where I do not t. to t.   BEING, 7
thinking action of the t. power called an idea   IDEAS, 9
I am t., therefore I exist   EXISTENCE, 6
In order to draw a limit to t.   THINKING, 40
   its disease of t.   THINKING, 35
   T. . . . most unhealthy thing in the world   THINKING, 39
   t. . . . thought in retreat or in reply   THINKING, 27
   T. is the desire to gain reality   THINKING, 32
   t. makes /it less tangible   THINKING, 8
   t. overcomes metaphysics   THINKING, 15
   We are t. beings   INTELLECT, 9
   when things become unthinkable, t. stops   THINKING, 14
thinks A thing that t.   EXISTENCE, 8
   It t., we ought really to say   THINKING, 23
   man who says what he t. is finished   THINKING, 16
Third Estate the T. contains . . . a nation   FRENCH REVOLUTION, 1
third sex if there was a t.   MEN, 31
thirst the t. to come   DRINKS AND DRINKING, 7
Thomas first time I saw Dylan T.   POETS, 57
thought a t. came like a full-blown rose   FLOWERS, 3
   conscious utterance of t. . . . is Art   ART, 19
   formal t. . . . direct consequence of puberty   GROWING UP, 8
   My t. is *me*   THINKING, 37
   the slow, assiduous, corrosive worm of t.   CREATIVITY, 17
   T. . . . labour of the intellect   THINKING, 17
   t. . . . to know that you know not   DECEPTION, 3
   T. is not a gift   THINKING, 30
   T. is only a flash   THINKING, 33
   To give a . . . perfect form to . . . t.   ARTISTS, 12
   transition between one t. and another   THINKING, 19
   What was once t.   THINKING, 12
thoughtcrime T. was not a thing . . . concealed
                                                                                              TOTALITARIANISM, 8
thoughts His t. . . . borne on the gusts of genius
                                                                                              INSPIRATION, 4
   His t. . . . lay silent   THINKING, 28
   my t. remain below   WORDS, 33
   Suspicions amongst t.   SUSPICION, 2
   t. . . . value for him who thinks them   IDEAS, 19
   T. without content are empty   THINKING, 20
   True t. . . . do not understand themselves   THINKING, 1
three There are only t. events in a man's life   LIFE, 28
   t. men who have ever understood it   POLITICS, 45
   t. of us in this marriage   ADULTERY, 7
   t. species: first, the servile American   AMERICANS, 9
three-dimensional a t. drawing   SCULPTURE, 4
threefold a t. cord is not quickly broken   SOLIDARITY, 2
three o'clock T. is always too late or too early   TIME, 50
three-pipe problem a t.   SMOKING, 6
thunder T. is the cracking of his joints   GOD, 3
thunder-cloud big bossy, well-charged t.   MOUNTAINS, 5
thyself Be so true to t.   SELF-KNOWLEDGE, 2
Tiber the River T. foaming with much blood   XENOPHOBIA, 3
Tibet Any relationship between T. and China
                                                                                              ASIAN COUNTRIES, 4
Tibetans T. . . . the list of endangered peoples
                                                                                              ASIAN COUNTRIES, 7
tide there is a t. in the affairs of men   FATE, 16
   T. and wind stay no man's pleasure   OPPORTUNITY, 13
   t. is eventually coming in   CHANGE, 22
tied I am t. to the stake   ENDURANCE, 6
tiger catch t. cubs . . . entering the tiger's lair   ACHIEVEMENT, 1
   the t. sniffs the rose   POETS, 52
   This t. has other ideas   COLD WAR, 5
   T. well repays the trouble   ANIMALS, 3
tight T. boots are one of the greatest goods   PLEASURE, 21
tightrope You may reasonably expect a man to walk a t.
                                                                                              NUCLEAR WAR, 14

t. is an experience of hyperinvolvement COMEDY, 8
T. is if I cut my finger TRAGEDY, 3
T. represents the life of princes TRAGEDY, 2
we have conceived life as a t. TRAGEDY, 12
We participate in a t. TRAGEDY, 5
tragic 21st century . . . some kind of t. consciousness
TWENTY-FIRST CENTURY, 3
train a t. pulls into a great city TRAINS, 3
If you board the wrong t. MISTAKES, 1
I have seldom heard a t. go by TRAINS, 6
The only way . . . of catching a t. TRAINS, 2
train set the biggest electric t. FILMS, 50
traitor I find myself a t. with the rest TREASON, 8
traitors t. rose against him REBELLION, 1
tram Oh the after-t.-ride quiet NOSTALGIA, 2
tramp It's hard to call a lousy t. your brother HYPOCRISY, 24
tranquillisers lot of t. and my mother AWARDS, 5
tranquillizers t. . . . bought as easily . . . as aspirin DRUGS, 13
transcendent t. capacity of taking trouble GENIUS, 3
transform t. society . . . transform business BUSINESS, 20
transformation the t. of former European colonies
DECOLONIZATION, 5
t. . . . imagination and memory work together MEMORY, 14
We are living through a t. GLOBALIZATION, 21
transformed man can be t. . . . by will ACHIEVEMENT, 12
transforming most important thing is t. our minds THINKING, 9
transition A permanent state of t. CHANGE, 19
translated A linguistic work t. into another language
TRANSLATION, 3
translating T. is the ultimate act of comprehending
TRANSLATION, 4
translator A t. is to be like his author TRANSLATION, 2
transparent So t. your /soul THE SOUL, 19
transsexual small talk to a t. bird cage POLITICS, 4
trap the t. you set for yourself DANGER, 1
travaille Myn be the t. GLORY, 3
travel men t. first class . . . literature goes as freight
PRIORITIES, 3
those who do not t. TRAVEL, 1
tired with labour of far t. HOME, 1
To t. hopefully . . . a better thing than to arrive
TRAVEL, 31
To t. /is to return /to strangers TRAVEL, 25
T. . . . is a part of education TRAVEL, 2
t. in the direction of our fear TRAVEL, 5
T. is a vanishing act TRAVEL, 34
T. is the most private of pleasures TRAVEL, 24
t. not to go anywhere, but . . . go TRAVEL, 30
travel book A t. . . . the simplest sort of narrative BOOKS, 57
traveller A great t. is a kind of introspective TRAVEL, 13
travelling Extensive t. includes a feeling of encapsulation
TRAVEL, 33
t. post from Tiflis EUROPEAN LITERATURE, 11
travels A man t. the world TRAVEL, 20
aspect of our t. . . . disaster TRAVEL, 16
Like him that t., I return again TRAVEL, 26
treachery service rendered to the temporal king . . .
act of t. TREASON, 6
treated didn't want to be t. alphabetically PRIDE, 5
treaties T. are like roses and young girls DIPLOMACY, 11
trees do not . . . t. . . . furnish us with models
ARCHITECTURE, 11
T. are poems . . . earth writes upon the sky TREES, 1
trenches digging t. and trying on gas-masks WORLD WAR II, 3
trench warfare In t. five things are important WAR, 47
trends Extreme t. are breeding grounds EXTREMES, 3
triangles if t. invented a god GOD, 51
trick t. is to love somebody LOVE, 6
trip don't t. over the furniture ACTING AND ACTORS, 6
t. . . . the light fantastic toe DANCING, 10

trivial pursuit of the t. and . . . the third rate MEDIOCRITY, 2
trod t. upon eggs DIPLOMACY, 6
trouble a lot of t. in his life WORRY, 2
saves me the t. of liking them MISANTHROPY, 2
to have your t. doubled SUFFERING, 4
trousers bottoms of my t. rolled OLD AGE, 17
trout t. that must be caught with tickling ANTICIPATION, 6
trouthe T. is the hyeste thyng TRUTH, 24
trowel laid on with a t. EXCESS, 5
true A thing is not necessarily t. MARTYRDOM, 11
He said t. things ALIBIS AND EXCUSES, 1
I am as t. as truth's simplicity FAITHFULNESS, 4
Nothing is t. except what . . . not said TRUTH, 2
think what is t. . . . do what is right TRUTH, 36
T. and False are attributes of speech SPEECH, 8
T. as the needle to the pole LOYALTY, 2
t. sons /Of great and mighty resolutions GREATNESS, 3
t. to you, darlin', in my fashion FAITHFULNESS, 2
What I tell you three times is t. TRUTH, 22
trust I don't t. him. We're friends FRIENDSHIP, 7
T. one who has gone through it EXPERIENCE, 18
trusted more they t. me, the less . . . mistake TRUST, 6
truth 't.' . . . 'rightness' perceptible by the mind alone
TRUTH, 4
Absolute t. . . . rare and dangerous commodity
JOURNALISM, 29
A man that seeketh precise t. TRUTH, 32
a t. universally acknowledged MARRIAGE, 3
Between t. and the search TRUTH, 10
It takes two to speak the t. TRUTH, 62
just possession of t. as of a city TRUTH, 16
Much t. . . . may be concealed DECEPTION, 9
No one wants the t. if it is inconvenient TRUTH, 44
only one t. . . . that there's no t. TRUTH, 48
Severe t. is expressed with some bitterness CRITICISM, 25
Speak the t. and shame the Devil TRUTH, 54
The cause of t. must be championed TRUTH, 17
The only t. . . . horror and annihilation TRUTH, 21
The seeming t. which cunning times put on ARTIFICE, 4
the t. has got its boots on LYING, 11
the t. hears him and hides HONESTY, 1
the t. is out there TRUTH, 65
the t. shall make you free TRUTH, 11
The worst enemy of t. and freedom MAJORITY, 4
to make it laugh LAUGHTER, 7
T. . . . brings down more disgrace TRUTH, 9
t. . . . catch a cold on overexposure TRUTH, 19
T. . . . falsehood well disguised TRUTH, 30
t. . . . is the sovereign good of human nature TRUTH, 7
T. . . . Let us economize it TRUTH, 63
T. . . . never comes into the world TRUTH, 46
T. . . . no road to fortune TRUTH, 55
T. . . . not compatible with the defence of the realm
TRUTH, 60
T. comes out in wine WINE, 3
T. exists; only lies are invented TRUTH, 15
T. has no special time of its own TRUTH, 58
t. in the groves of Academe TRUTH, 34
t. in the pleasant disguise of illusion AMERICAN LITERATURE, 30
T. is . . . the test of experience TRUTH, 28
T. is a clumsy servant TRUTH, 40
t. is always strange TRUTH, 20
T. is a never-ending agony TRUTH, 23
t. is so precious TRUTH, 25
T. is the breath of life to . . . society TRUTH, 33
t., justice, and the American way HEROISM, 1
T. made you a traitor TRUTH, 31
T. never turns tail TRUTH, 29
t. of a proposition TRUTH, 3
T. often suffers . . . by the heat of its defenders TRUTH, 52

true U. . . . collection of books — LIBRARIES, 2
u. is traditionally . . . a psychosocial moratorium — UNIVERSITY, 3
unjust nothing can be u. — ANARCHY, 9
unknown the U. Prime Minister — POLITICAL INSULTS, 9
unlucky person born /who is so u. — ACCIDENTS, 9
unmoral It is by becoming u. that history serves — HISTORY, 10
unnatural nothing so u. as the commonplace — NORMALITY, 1
unnecessary u. for me to bend . . . my reason — COMPROMISE, 5
unparticular A nice u. man — CHARACTER, 23
unreliability The felt u. of human experience — EXPERIENCE, 15
unrest Take a Clear-Cut Stand against U. — REVOLUTION, 31
unscrupulous It is an u. intellect — INTELLECT, 4
unseen an u. world — THE SUPERNATURAL, 22
unspellables u. killing the unpronounceables — AMERICAN IMPERIALISM, 25
unstable u. pact to commit . . . total mutual suicide — NUCLEAR WAR, 3
untrue he never was u. — ADULTERY, 16
unusual The u. . . . is exactly what makes literature — LITERATURE, 18
unwashed The great U. — CLASS, 6
uproar u.'s your only music — ANARCHY, 10
uranium u. . . . new and important source of energy — NUCLEAR WEAPONS, 3
urban The u. man is an uprooted tree — CITIES, 7
urine nose-painting, sleep, and u. — ALCOHOL, 17
US U. foreign policy . . . is to bring Canada — AMERICAN IMPERIALISM, 13
U. is a truly monstrous force — AMERICAN IMPERIALISM, 27
used words . . . already been u. by Barbara Cartland — LOVE, 25
useful nothing . . . you do not know to be u. — HOUSES, 6
useless A u. life is an early death — FUTILITY, 4
no man is u. while . . . a friend — FRIENDSHIP, 42
USSR Am I conceivable in the U. — RUSSIA, 6
usual Business as u. — BRITAIN, 11
Utopia this U. is far less attractive — IDEALISM, 5
utopian it is 'u.' to want to survive — SURVIVAL, 6
vaccination V. . . . corresponding to baptism — MEDICINE, 8
vacuum A v. can only exist, . . . by the things which enclose it — NOTHINGNESS, 6
v. is a hell of a lot better — ABSENCE, 12
vain You're so v. — VANITY, 9
valuable decide . . . how we are v. — VALUE, 3
value I have never believed . . . intrinsic v. of art — ART, 54
the small v. God has for riches — WEALTH, 22
The v. of a whole — VALUE, 6
v. of a thing is the . . . work — VALUE, 4
what v. is anything . . . except the imagination — IMAGINATION, 21
valued never v. till they make a noise — SECRECY, 5
values V. are determined by systems — MORALITY, 7
yield to . . . v. . . . prescribed by the State — MORALITY, 8
Van Gogh V.'s ear for music — INSULTS, 45
vanity man may hide his v. beneath . . . humility — VANITY, 11
V. dies hard — VANITY, 10
V., like murder, will out — VANITY, 3
V. plays lurid tricks — VANITY, 1
variety a sad v. of woe — SORROW, 18
V.'s the source of joy below — CHANGE, 10
V. is the soul of pleasure — PLEASURE, 2
V. of opinion . . . necessary for objective knowledge — AGREEMENT, 5
vary not to v. is not to think — THINKING, 34
Vegas V. is like stumbling into a Time Warp — AMERICAN CITIES, 40
veil v. has been abolished . . . by the women — MIDDLE EAST, 2
venerate I . . . v. a petticoat — LUST, 3
venereal disease Despite a lifetime of service . . . v. — SEX, 21

vengeance I have undertaken v. — REVENGE, 15
Venice V. is like eating . . . chocolate liqueurs — EUROPEAN CITIES, 7
V., the eldest Child of Liberty — EUROPEAN CITIES, 28
Venus She is V. when she smiles — PRAISE, 4
Two minutes with V., two years with mercury — REMEDIES, 18
V. entire latched onto her prey — PASSION, 10
verb a v. meaning 'to believe falsely' — BELIEF, 33
verbosity not crude v., but holy simplicity — SIMPLICITY, 6
Versailles treaty That bastard of the V. — EUROPEAN COUNTRIES, 47
verse Writing free v. — WRITING, 20
vertue To maken v. of necessitee — NECESSITY, 8
vice Above, V. smiles and revels — CLASS, 21
restrictions placed on v. by our social code — VICE, 7
the function of v. to keep virtue — VICE, 3
This v. brings in one hundred million francs — SMOKING, 14
V. is its own reward — VICE, 5
V. is waste of life — VICE, 10
v. pays homage to virtue — HYPOCRISY, 6
vices v. . . . require moderate use rather than total abstinence — MODERATION, 2
vicissitude v. of sects and religions — RELIGION, 3
victim v. . . . killed by . . . man from another book — BOOKS, 56
victor happy state of getting the v.'s palm — VICTORY, 7
victory declare v. and leave — AMERICAN IMPERIALISM, 2
every v. turns into a defeat — DISILLUSIONMENT, 2
let there be v., before the Americans — WORLD WAR I, 4
moment of v. is much too short — VICTORY, 12
Such another v. and we are ruined — FUTILITY, 9
This is *your* v. — VICTORY, 3
V. at all costs — VICTORY, 4
v. finds a hundred fathers — DEFEAT, 1
V. has a thousand fathers — VICTORY, 8
Viet Cong no quarrel with the V. — PROTEST, 1
Vietnam To win in V., we will have to exterminate a nation — AMERICAN IMPERIALISM, 30
war in V. destroyed three ancient civilizations — AMERICAN IMPERIALISM, 8
vile make v. things precious — NECESSITY, 15
villain v. of the earth — GUILT, 13
violence a v. that is moral — VIOLENCE, 8
Keep v. in the mind — VIOLENCE, 1
prisoners of the idea of v. — VIOLENCE, 15
remake the v. of reality itself — PAINTING, 4
The gains of v. are transient — VIOLENCE, 9
through v. that one must achieve liberty — FRENCH REVOLUTION, 7
v. can only breed more v. — ASIAN COUNTRIES, 5
v. in the movies can be cool — VIOLENCE, 16
v. is a totally aesthetic subject — VIOLENCE, 17
V. is like money in the bank — VIOLENCE, 2
v. masquerading as love — VIOLENCE, 5
violent better to be v. . . . to cover impotence — PROTEST, 6
violet V. is red withdrawn from humanity — COLOUR, 8
violets Good God, I forgot the v. — FLOWERS, 5
virtual Sometimes v. crimes lie dormant — CRIME, 15
This is a v. world — INTERNET, 13
virtue A minimum of comfort is necessary for . . . v. — COMFORT, 2
kindled his fire but extinguished his v. — LUST, 5
Let them recognize v. and rot for having lost it — VIRTUE, 24
Love v., she alone is free — VIRTUE, 22
Make a v. of necessity — NECESSITY, 6
much v. in 'If' — COMPROMISE, 7
My v.'s still far too small — VIRTUE, 9
next to impossible is the exercise of v. — VIRTUE, 12
no distinction between v. and vice — MORALITY, 18
no road or ready way to v. — VIRTUE, 6

no v. like necessity — NECESSITY, 16
to practise five things . . . constitutes perfect v. — VIRTUE, 10
V. . . . habit of acting according to wisdom — VIRTUE, 20
V. . . . own fairest reward — VIRTUE, 31
v. . . . will keep me warm — VIRTUE, 11
V.! a fig! 'tis in ourselves — VIRTUE, 29
V. consisted in — VIRTUE, 8
V. is its own punishment — VIRTUE, 3
V. is its own reward — VIRTUE, 25
V. is like precious odours — VIRTUE, 2
v. is no longer considered a v. — VIRTUE, 1
V. is to herself the best reward — VIRTUE, 23
V. may be assailed, but never hurt — VIRTUE, 21
virtues a world to hide v. in — VIRTUE, 30
few v. . . . the Poles do not possess — EUROPEAN COUNTRIES, 17
v. and vices couple with one another — VIRTUE, 13
v. are . . . vices in disguise — VIRTUE, 18
v. /We write in water — VIRTUE, 28
Whenever there are tremendous v. — VIRTUE, 5
vision Five per cent v. is better than no v. — EVOLUTION, 10
V. is the art of seeing things invisible — PERCEPTION, 14
Was it a v., or a waking dream — DREAMS, 10
visionary Whither is fled the v. gleam — MYSTICISM, 9
visions actual v. & actual prisons — WRITING, 23
visiting like v. another country — TRAVEL, 3
vitalism As long as v. and spiritualism are open questions — SCIENCE, 56
vivisect We v. the nightingale — RESEARCH, 1
vixen strong-footed, but sore-eyed v. — PREJUDICE, 5
vocal His v. chords were kissed by God — SINGERS AND SINGING, 9
voice A still small v. spake unto me — DESPAIR, 16
Her v. is full of money — THE VOICE, 1
If you'll be my v. today — COMMITMENT, 1
Let no v. but your own speak to you — SELF-KNOWLEDGE, 14
My v., the freedom of those weakened — WRITING, 8
no one can stop the human v. — THE VOICE, 2
The melting v. through mazes running — THE VOICE, 3
the v. of the lobster — NONSENSE, 4
v. . . . sways the soul — THE SOUL, 17
v. of the people is the v. of God — DEMOCRACY, 2
Your v. of white fire — LIGHT, 3
voices Two v. . . . sea . . . mountains — LIBERTY, 42
void Keys to the V. of civilization — CIVILIZATION, 12
voluntary v. act . . . guided by idea, perception — ACTION, 8
vote Nothing would induce me to v. for . . . women — WOMEN'S RIGHTS, 10
One man shall have one v. — DEMOCRACY, 9
right of citizens of the United States to v. — CIVIL RIGHTS, 2
v. . . . means nothing to women — WOMEN'S RIGHTS, 27
v. is the most powerful instrument — DEMOCRACY, 22
voting not the v. that's democracy — DEMOCRACY, 46
voyage sea v. is more than an adventure — THE SEA, 24
vulgar It's v. to be famous — FAME, 20
the most v.-minded genius — LITERARY INSULTS, 15
the sign of a v. mind — RIGHT, 2
v. . . . a gold toothpick — TASTE, 9
vulture a v. can't stand . . . a glass eye — FOOD, 13
I eat like a v. — APPETITE, 3
vultures the v. fly upside down after the dying — THE WORLD, 5
wager w. that he does exist — BELIEF, 25
Wagner I can't listen to that much W. — MUSIC, 2
wait ability to w. . . . requisite of practical policy — PATIENCE, 4
told you to w. in the car — ABSENCE, 1
waiting w. for the cock to crow — BETRAYAL, 11
We've been w. 700 years — PATIENCE, 5
wake I w. to sleep — FATE, 21
waking w. from a troubled dream — AFTERLIFE, 9
Wales different material to England's robe of state, W. — WALES, 2

W., which I have never seen — WALES, 5
walk If you w. hard enough — EXERCISE, 1
walking idea of w. through walls — THE SUPERNATURAL, 1
walks She w. the waters — BOATS, 3
wall an outside w. after wars and devastations — WAR, 1
Something . . . doesn't love a w. — NATURE, 13
wallflower call me a w. — DANCING, 1
wallpaper Either that w. goes, or I do — LAST WORDS, 18
w. with which the men of science — SCIENTISTS, 19
walls w. . . . covered with gold and silver — EXTRAVAGANCE, 5
wandered I w. lonely as a cloud — SOLITUDE, 27
wandering W. between two worlds — EXILE, 2
want If there's anything that you w. — GENEROSITY, 3
The w. of a thing is perplexing enough — MATERIALISM, 10
wanting Always leave them w. less — EXCESS, 7
war abolish w. or w. will abolish mankind — WAR, 40
advocate w. out of irritability — WAR, 29
A w. . . . must shatter the foundations of thought and re-create — WAR, 62
Before the w. . . . it was summer all . . . year — NOSTALGIA, 12
better to have a w. for justice — JUSTICE, 30
desire of our two peoples never to go to w. — WORLD WAR II, 4
every w. is against the world and . . . is lost — WAR, 66
first casualty when w. comes is truth — TRUTH, 39
glorify w.—the world's only hygiene — ANARCHY, 13
How do you wage w. on an abstract noun? — TERRORISM, 6
I'd like . . . government get out of w. — WAR, 25
I make w. on the living — REVENGE, 4
In starting and waging a w. — WAR, 26
into w. on the command of gold — WORLD WAR I, 22
It is well that w. is so terrible — WAR, 33
I wanted the experience of w. — WAR, 10
just w. . . . better for a nation's soul — WAR, 55
Let me have w., say I; it exceeds peace — WAR, 60
no more win a w. than . . . an earthquake — WAR, 53
nothing that w. has ever achieved — WAR, 19
Our w. is a religious w. — WAR, 22
quickest way of ending a w. — WAR, 48
seek by all means . . . to avoid w. — WAR, 11
subject is W. . . . the pity — WORLD WAR I, 23
the second rule of w. — AMERICAN IMPERIALISM, 20
the W. is being deliberately prolonged — PROTEST, 16
The wrong w., at the wrong place — WAR, 8
they'll give a w. and nobody will come — WAR, 57
This w. . . . is a w. to end w. — WORLD WAR I, 18
this w. . . . which did not justify the sacrifice — WORLD WAR I, 24
Those who can win a w. well — WAR, 13
twenty seconds of w. to destroy — WAR, 2
W. . . . a continuation of politics — WAR, 14
w. . . . forces men collectively to commit acts — WAR, 30
W. . . . imposes the stamp of nobility — WAR, 45
W. . . . one of the constants of history — WAR, 18
W. . . . the hope that one will be better off — WAR, 32
W. . . . too serious . . . to be left to military men — WAR, 64
w.'s a game — WAR, 17
w. can only be abolished through w. — WAR, 38
W. hath no fury like a non-combatant — WAR, 44
W. is, after all, the universal perversion — WAR, 52
W. is an extreme of political action — WAR, 43
W. is capitalism with the gloves off — WAR, 63
W. is not an adventure — WAR, 56
W. is the highest form of struggle — WAR, 39
W. is the trade of kings — MONARCHY, 11
W. makes rattling good history — WAR, 24
w. regarded as inevitable . . . even probable — WAR, 28
W. should belong to the tragic past — WAR, 27

AUTHOR INDEX

Abakanowicz, Magdalena ART, 1
Abel, Niels Henrik LEARNING, 1
Abelard, Peter GOOD, 1
Abrahams, Peter APARTHEID, 1; DELUSIONS OF LOVE, 1
Abse, Dannie XENOPHOBIA, 1
Abzug, Bella SERIOUSNESS, 1
Ace, Goodman TELEVISION, 1
Achebe, Chinua ANGER, 1; CREATIVITY, 1; DEBT, 1; FATHERS, 1; TRAGEDY, 1; WORLD ENGLISH, 1, 2; WRITERS, 1
Acheson, Dean AMERICAN IMPERIALISM, 1; BRITISH IMPERIALISM, 1; REPUTATION, 1
Acland, Richard PUBLISHING, 1
Acton, Lord DEMOCRACY, 1; POWER, 1
Adair, John LEADERSHIP, 1; MANIPULATION, 1
Adamov, Arthur THEATRE, 1
Adams, Abigail COMMUNICATION, 1; WOMEN'S RIGHTS, 1
Adams, Ansel PHOTOGRAPHY, 1
Adams, Douglas ANSWERS, 1; COMPLAINTS, 1; THE EARTH, 1, 2; FATE, 1; HUMOUR, 1; QUESTIONS, 1; SPACE, 1; THE SUPERNATURAL, 1; THEORY, 1
Adams, Franklin P. INFLUENCE, 1; MIDDLE AGE, 1
Adams, Gerry IRELAND, 1; NORTHERN IRELAND, 1
Adams, Henry HISTORIANS, 1; LEARNING, 2; POLITICAL INSULTS, 1; POLITICS, 1; SCIENCE, 1; UNITED STATES, 1
Adams, Joey WORRY, 1
Adams, John AMERICAN WAR OF INDEPENDENCE, 1; WORLD ENGLISH, 3
Adams, John Quincy GOVERNMENT, 1; POLITICAL INSULTS, 2
Adams, Samuel BRITAIN, 1
Adams, Samuel Hopkins MEDICINE, 1
Addams, Jane CIVILIZATION, 1
Addison, Joseph CHRISTMAS, 1; CONVERSATION, 1; DRINKS AND DRINKING, 1; LIBERTY, 1; MUSIC, 1; NONSENSE, 1; PATRIOTISM, 1; POSTERITY, 1; READERS, 1; SENSES, 1; SLEEP, 1
Adenauer, Konrad EUROPEAN COUNTRIES, 1; NATIONS, 1
Adler, Alfred EGOTISM, 1; NEUROSIS, 1; PRINCIPLES, 1
Adler, Viktor EUROPEAN COUNTRIES, 2
Adonis BOOKS, 1; CHILDHOOD, 1; POETRY, 1
Adorno, Theodor EUROPEAN COUNTRIES, 3; FEAR, 1; INNOCENCE, 1; KNOWLEDGE, 1; LYING, 1; POETRY, 2; THINKING, 1
Æ (George William Russell) DRUNKENNESS, 1; LITERATURE, 1
Aeschylus AMBITION, 1; JUDGMENT, 1; LEARNING, 3; OBEDIENCE, 1; SUCCESS, 1; WORDS, 1
Aesop CHARACTER, 1; DECEPTION, 1; ENVY, 1; GREED, 1; LYING, 2; MEN, 1; PATIENCE, 1; WARNING, 1
Aga Khan III, Sir ALCOHOL, 1
Agar, Herbert TRUTH, 1
Agassiz, Louis Rodolphe PRIORITIES, 1; SCIENCE, 2
Agate, James AUDIENCES, 1; MEDIOCRITY, 1; MIND, 1
Agathon CHANCE, 1; THE PAST, 1
Aggrey, James Emman Kwegyir PREJUDICE, 1; RACISM, 1
Agnew, Spiro T. INTELLECTUALS, 1
Agre, Philip A. COMPUTERS, 1
Ahmed, Akbar ISLAM, 1, 2; MIDDLE EAST, 1
Ahrends, Martin FREEDOM, 1
Aidoo, Ama Ata FOOLISHNESS, 1; HOPE, 1; MARRIAGE, 1; MISANTHROPY, 1
Aiken, Conrad TRANSIENCE, 1
Aiken, George AMERICAN IMPERIALISM, 2
Ai Qing HOPE, 2

Akhmatova, Anna ADULTERY, 1; PATRIOTISM, 2; POETS, 1; REPUTATION, 2; WORLD WAR II, 1
Akhter, Farida MATERIALISM, 1
Alain IDEAS, 1
Alain-Fournier DISILLUSIONMENT, 1
Albee, Edward HUMOUR, 2; NECESSITY, 1; PARTIES, 1; PORNOGRAPHY, 1
Alberti, Rafael ANGELS, 1; ARTISTS, 1; PAINTING, 1
Albo, Joseph GOD, 1
Alcala Galiano, Juan Valera EUROPEAN COUNTRIES, 4
Alcuin DEMOCRACY, 2
Aldiss, Brian VIOLENCE, 1
Aldrich, Thomas Bailey RESEARCH, 1
Aldrin, Buzz THE MOON, 1
Alembert, Jean le Rond d' MATHEMATICS, 1
Alexander I POLITICAL INSULTS, 3
Alexander II EUROPEAN COUNTRIES, 5; SLAVERY, 1
Alexander the Great BOASTS, 1; DOCTORS, 1
al-Fayed, Mohamed CRITICS, 1
Alfonso X CREATION, 1
Alfonso XIII CLASS, 1; DICTATORS, 1
al-Ghazali GOD, 2; ISLAM, 3
Algren, Nelson AMERICAN CITIES, 1
Alhegelan, Nouha MIDDLE EAST, 2
Ali, Muhammad BOASTS, 2; DESIRE, 1; HUMILITY, 1; ISLAM, 4; LIFE, 1; PROTEST, 1
Ali, Zeenat WOMEN'S RIGHTS, 2
Alibhai-Brown, Yasmin EQUALITY, 1
al-Khansa SORROW, 1
Allainval, Abbé d' EXCESS, 1
Allen, Fred CELEBRITY, 1; HOLLYWOOD, 1; MEN, 2
Allen, Woody AFTERLIFE, 1; BELIEF, 1; CRIME, 1; DEATH AND DYING, 1; IMMORTALITY, 1; MASTURBATION, 1; MONEY, 1; MUSIC, 2; PARENTS, 1; PESSIMISM, 1; SEX, 1, 2; SUCCESS, 2; SUSPICION, 1
Allende, Hortensia Bussi de SOUTH AMERICA, 1
Allende, Salvador SOUTH AMERICA, 2
al-Mufid, Abu Abdullah Muhammad al-Harithi al-Baghdadi AFTERLIFE, 2; DEATH AND DYING, 2; HUMILITY, 2; INTELLIGENCE, 2; SLAVERY, 2
al-Nawawi, Muhyid-Din Abu Zakariyya ibn Sharaf THE BODY, 1; OBEDIENCE, 2; SEX, 3
Al-Razi MEDICINE, 2
Alsop, Joseph GRATITUDE, 1
Altenberg, Peter MELANCHOLY, 1; QUOTATIONS, 1; SEX, 4
Altgeld, John Peter DEMOCRACY, 3
Alther, Lisa ADULTHOOD, 1
Altman, Robert POPULARITY, 1
Alvarez, Luis PHYSICS, 1
Ambrose, Saint CONFORMITY, 1
Amichai, Yehuda LANGUAGE, 1; MEMORY, 1; MIDDLE EAST, 3; PACIFISM, 1; PEACE, 1; WAR, 1
Amiel, Henri Frédéric HEALTH AND HEALTHY LIVING, 1
Amin, Idi SACRIFICE, 1
Amis, Kingsley CHILDREN, 1; DRUNKENNESS, 2; WOMEN, 1
Amis, Martin AMERICAN LITERATURE, 1; FLYING, 1; SEX, 5
Ammons, A. R. BELIEF, 2
Ampère, Jean-Jaques BOOKS, 2; THE FUTURE, 1
Anaxagoras MIND, 2
Andersen, Hans Christian CLASS, 2; NAKEDNESS, 1
Anderson, Eric MEDIOCRITY, 2

Anderson, John ACCIDENTS, 1
Anderson, Marian RACISM, 2
Anderson, Maxwell GLORY, 1
Anderson, P. W. UNDERSTANDING, 1
Angelou, Maya ANGER, 2; CHILDREN, 2; CYNICISM, 1; ENDURANCE, 1; FANTASY, 1;
    HISTORY, 1; HUMAN NATURE, 1; JEALOUSY, 1; PEACE, 2; VIRTUE, 1
Angelus Silesius THE SELF, 1
Anglo-Saxon Chronicle REBELLION, 1
Anka, Paul POPULAR MUSIC, 1
Anne, Princess REPUTATION, 3
Anonymous AFRICAN COUNTRIES, 1; ANIMALS, 1; BABIES, 1; BIRDS, 1, 2; BOATS, 1;
    BRITISH IMPERIALISM, 2; CENSORSHIP, 1; CLOTHES, 1; CONFUSION, 1; DEBT, 2;
    EVOLUTION, 1; FASCISM, 1, 2; FIRE, 1; GIFTS, 1; GOD, 3, 4; GREETINGS, 1;
    HEROISM, 1, 2; HUNGER, 1; IMPERFECTION, 1; INJUSTICE, 1; INSULTS, 1;
    INTEGRITY, 1; KINDNESS, 1; KNOWLEDGE, 2; LITERARY INSULTS, 1; LYING, 3;
    MARRIAGE, 2; MONEY, 2; NAMES, 1; NORTHERN IRELAND, 2; NOSTALGIA, 1;
    OLD AGE, 1; PLACES, 1; POLITICAL INSULTS, 4–7; POLITICIANS, 1; POLLUTION, 1;
    RETRIBUTION, 1; THE SEA, 1; SILENCE, 1; SPEECHES, 1; STATISTICS, 1;
    TERRORISM, 1; TORTURE, 1; TRANSIENCE, 2; TREASON, 1; WARNING, 2;
    WEALTH, 1; YOUTH, 1
Anouilh, Jean ART, 2; GOD, 5; LOVE, 1; NEWSPAPERS, 1; TEMPTATION, 1; TRUTH, 2
Anselm, Saint EXISTENCE, 1; TRUTH, 3, 4; UNDERSTANDING, 2
Ant, Adam POPULARITY, 2
Antall, Jozsef COLD WAR, 1
Anthony, Susan B. EQUALITY, 2; WOMEN'S RIGHTS, 3
Antiphon LAW, 1
Antrim, Minna EXPERIENCE, 1; FOOLISHNESS, 2; HATE, 1; JEALOUSY, 2
Apollinaire, Guillaume ARCHITECTURE, 1; ARTISTIC STYLES, 1; ENDURANCE, 2;
    MEMORY, 2; THE PAST, 2
Appel, Karel PAINTING, 2, 3
Appelfield, Aharon JUDAISM, 1
Appleton, Edward Victor OPERA, 1
Aptheker, Herbert HISTORY, 2; SLAVERY, 3
Aquinas, Thomas EVIL, 1; GOD, 6; LAW, 2; NECESSITY, 2
Arabian Nights, The MAGIC, 1
Arafat, Yasir MIDDLE EAST, 4
Aragon, Louis GENIUS, 1; SPEECH, 1
Arbus, Diane PHOTOGRAPHY, 2
Arbuthnot, John CITIES, 1; MATHEMATICS, 2
Archer, Gilbert POLITICAL INSULTS, 8
Archilochus KNOWLEDGE, 3
Archimedes DISCOVERY, 1; PHYSICS, 2
Arenas, Reinaldo AIDS, 1; EXILE, 1
Arendt, Hannah CRIME, 2, 3; DEATH AND DYING, 3; EVIL, 2; FORGIVENESS, 1;
    FREEDOM, 2; GUILT, 1; HISTORY, 3; THE HOLOCAUST, 1; HUMAN CONDITION, 1;
    IMMORTALITY, 2, 3; INNOVATION, 1; LOVE, 2; LOYALTY, 1; NECESSITY, 3, 4;
    THE PAST, 3; PROMISES, 1; PROTEST, 2; SOCIETY, 1; TRADITIONS, 1; TYRANNY, 1
Ariosto, Ludovico CHARACTER, 2
Aristophanes OLD AGE, 2
Aristotle ACTION, 1; ANGER, 1; COLOUR, 1, 2; ETERNITY, 1; FRIENDSHIP, 1;
    GOOD, 2; GOVERNMENT, 2; HUMAN CONDITION, 2; HUMANKIND, 1, 2;
    IMPOSSIBILITY, 1; INEQUALITY, 1; INTELLECT, 1; LEARNING, 4; MUSIC, 3;
    NECESSITY, 5; OPINIONS, 1; POLITICS, 2; REVOLUTION, 1; SLAVERY, 4;
    THE SOUL, 1; TRUTH, 5; UNITY, 1
Armah, Ayi Kwei EUROPE, 1; MEMORY, 3
Armstrong, D. M. MIND, 3
Armstrong, Louis IMITATION, 1; MUSIC, 4; RELIGION, 1
Armstrong, Michael RESPONSIBILITY, 1; WORLD ENGLISH, 4
Armstrong, Neil THE MOON, 2
Armstrong, Robert LYING, 4
Arnauld, Antoine MIND, 4
Arnim-Boytzenburg, Adolf Heinrich von GOVERNMENT, 3
Arno, Peter FAILURE, 1
Arnold, Matthew BRITISH CITIES, 1; CLASS, 3; CRITICISM, 1, 2; CULTURE, 1;
    EUROPEAN LITERATURE, 1; EXILE, 2; LITERARY INSULTS, 2; MIDDLE AGE, 2;
    MODERNITY, 1; PERFECTION, 1; PHILISTINISM, 1; POETRY, 3; RELIGION, 2;
    RIGHTEOUSNESS, 1; THE SEA, 2; SELF-KNOWLEDGE, 1; THE SOUL, 2; SUMMER, 1;
    TRUTH, 6; UNHAPPINESS, 1
Aron, Raymond THE PAST, 4
Arp, Jean ART, 3; ARTISTIC STYLES, 2

Artaud, Antonin CONFUSION, 2; PSYCHIATRY, 1
Ascham, Roger PRAISE, 1
Asher, Richard LAUGHTER, 1
Ashrawi, Hanan MIDDLE EAST, 5
Asimov, Isaac SPACE, 2
Asquith, Herbert Henry POLITICAL INSULTS, 9; STATISTICS, 2
Asquith, Margot INSULTS, 2; INTELLECTUALS, 2; LYING, 5; POLITICAL INSULTS, 10;
    WEALTH, 2; WORDPLAY, 1
Astaire, Fred DANCING, 1; SINGERS AND SINGING, 1
Astor, Nancy CHARACTER, 3; LAST WORDS, 1; MEN, 3; WOMEN'S RIGHTS, 4
Ataturk, Kemal EUROPEAN COUNTRIES, 6; INEQUALITY, 2; LANGUAGE, 2;
    LITERACY, 1
Athenaeus GOOD, 3
Athenagoras GOD, 7
Atkins, P. W. PHYSICS, 3
Attlee, Clement BETRAYAL, 1; DEMOCRACY, 4; DIPLOMACY, 1; EUROPE, 2;
    PARLIAMENTS AND ASSEMBLIES, 1; PEACE, 3; POLITICAL INSULTS, 11; RUSSIA, 1;
    SPEECHES, 2
Atwood, Margaret LOVE, 3
Atxaga, Bernardo LANGUAGE, 3; PLAGIARISM, 1; WRITING, 1
Aubignac, François TRAGEDY, 2
Auden, W. H. ACADEMICS, 1; ART, 4; BIOGRAPHY, 1; BOOKS, 3; CHILDHOOD, 2;
    CONFORMITY, 2; CONVERSATION, 2; DESPAIR, 1; DISCOVERY, 2; DOCTORS, 2;
    EVIL, 3; THE FACE, 1; FUNERALS, 1; GOD, 8; GOSSIP, 1; HUMAN CONDITION, 3, 4;
    INTELLECTUALS, 3; LOVE, 4; MUSIC, 5; NARCISSISM, 1; OPERA, 2; POETRY, 4;
    POETS, 2; SCIENTISTS, 1; SEX, 6; TIME, 1; TRAINS, 1; WRITERS, 2
Augustine of Hippo, Saint ARGUMENTS, 1; DANCING, 2; DOUBT, 1; OLD AGE, 3;
    PAIN, 1; TIME, 2; TRAVEL, 1; VICE, 1
Augustus HASTE, 1
Austen, Jane CHARACTER, 4, 5; CONVERSATION, 3; FLATTERY, 1; MARRIAGE, 3;
    MISANTHROPY, 2; PARTIES, 2; PLEASURE, 1; SELFISHNESS, 1; WEATHER, 1;
    WOMEN, 2
Auster, Paul BLASPHEMY, 1; EUROPEAN CITIES, 1; HUNGER, 2; MEMORY, 4;
    MONEY, 3
Austin, Alfred GRAMMAR, 1
Austin, Mary PURITANISM, 1
Austin, Warren Robinson DIPLOMACY, 2
Avedon, Richard BEAUTY, 1
Avery, Oswald Theodore ACCIDENTS, 2
Avicenna ILLNESS, 1
Awolowo, Obafemi DARKNESS, 1; LITERACY, 2
Axelrod, George SEX, 7
Ayala, Francisco FILMS, 1
Ayckbourn, Alan ADULTERY, 2
Ayer, A. J. CONSEQUENCES, 1
Ayres, Pam MEDICINE, 3
Azikiwe, Nnamdi CREATIVITY, 2
Bâ, Mariama FRIENDSHIP, 2; HAPPINESS, 1; HUMANKIND, 3; MARRIAGE, 4
Babeuf, François Noël FRENCH REVOLUTION, 1
Bacall, Lauren THE FACE, 2
Bacon, Francis AGE, 1, 2; AGREEMENT, 1; BEAUTY, 2; THE BODY, 2; BOOKS, 4;
    COMMUNICATION, 2, 3; CONCEIT, 1; DANCING, 3; DECEPTION, 2, 3; DESIRE, 2;
    DOUBT, 2; EXPLORATION, 1; FAME, 1; FEAR, 2, 3; FRIENDSHIP, 3, 4; GARDENS, 1;
    GOVERNMENT, 4; HEALTH AND HEALTHY LIVING, 2; HOPE, 3; HOUSES, 1;
    HUMAN CONDITION, 5; HUMAN NATURE, 2, 3; HYPOCRISY, 1; INNOVATION, 2;
    JUSTICE, 1; KNOWLEDGE, 4–6; LEARNING, 5, 6; LOVE, 5; LYING, 6, 7;
    MARRIAGE, 5; MEDICINE, 4, 5; METAPHYSICS, 1; MONEY, 4; NATIONS, 2;
    NATURE, 1, 2; PAINTING, 4; PARENTS, 2; POWER, 2; READING, 1, 2; RELIGION, 3;
    REMEDIES, 1, 2; REPUTATION, 4, 5; REVENGE, 1, 2; SELF-DELUSION, 1;
    SELF-KNOWLEDGE, 2; SOCIETY, 2; SOLITUDE, 1, 2; SUSPICION, 2; TRAVEL, 2;
    TRUTH, 7; UNIVERSITY, 1; VIRTUE, 2; WEALTH, 3; WISDOM, 1; WORDS, 2; YOUTH, 2
Bacon, Roger EXPERIMENTS, 1; MATHEMATICS, 3; REASON, 1
Bagehot, Walter DIPLOMACY, 3; EXPERIENCE, 2; GOVERNMENT, 5;
    MONARCHY, 1, 2; POLITICAL INSULTS, 12; POVERTY, 1; TEACHERS, 1; WRITERS, 3
Bai Juyi ARROGANCE, 1
Bailey, Pearl SELF-KNOWLEDGE, 3
Bailey, Thomas A. HISTORIANS, 2; HISTORY, 4; MYTHS, 1
Bailyn, Bernard HISTORY, 5
Bainbridge, Beryl FAMILY, 1; HAPPINESS, 2; NARCISSISM, 2; PREJUDICE, 2;
    TRAVEL, 3

Bainbridge, Kenneth T. NUCLEAR WAR, 1
Bainville, Jacques BORES AND BOREDOM, 1; THE PAST, 5
Bakunin, Mikhail ANARCHY, 1, 2; GOD, 9; PRIVILEGE, 1
Baldwin, James ANGER, 4; ART, 5; CHILDREN, 3; CIVIL RIGHTS, 1; DANGER, 1;
    EXTINCTION, 1; FREEDOM, 3; THE FUTURE, 2, 3; GOD, 10; HISTORY, 6, 7;
    INNOCENCE, 1; LOVE, 6; MONEY, 5; OCCUPATIONS, 1; THE PAST, 6;
    PATRIOTISM, 3; PURITY, 1; SLAVERY, 5; UNITED STATES, 2
Baldwin, Stanley NEWSPAPERS, 2; OPPORTUNITY, 1; POLITICIANS, 2; POLITICS, 3
Balfour, Arthur CHRISTIANITY, 1; HISTORIANS, 3; MIDDLE EAST, 6; READING, 3;
    SCIENCE, 3
Ball, John SLAVERY, 6
Ball, Lucille SELF-KNOWLEDGE, 4; YOUTH, 3
Balladur, Édouard BRITAIN, 2
Ballard, J. G. FICTION, 1; MADNESS, 1; PERVERSITY, 1; TWENTIETH CENTURY, 1;
    WRITERS, 4
Balliett, Whitney CRITICS, 2
Balzac, Honoré de DETERMINATION, 1; FAME, 2; HUMANKIND, 4; IRONY, 1;
    MARRIAGE, 6; TYRANNY, 2
Bambara, Toni Cade CONVERSATION, 4; DREAMS, 1; LITERATURE, 2; RELIGION, 4
Banchao ACHIEVEMENT, 1
Bandyopadhyay, Pranab RELATIONSHIPS, 1
Banerjee, Sudhansu Mohan ASIAN CITIES, 1
Banham, John CONFUSION, 3
Banham, Reyner HOUSES, 2
Bankhead, Tallulah ABSENCE, 1; ADDICTION, 1; CRITICISM, 3; DIARIES, 1;
    FEAR, 4; INTELLECTUALS, 4; PURITY, 2; REGRET, 1; SEX, 8
Banks, Russell FACTS, 1; PAIN, 2
Banks, Tony POLITICIANS, 3
Banks-Smith, Nancy ARCHITECTURE, 2
Baraka, Imamu Amiri CULTURE, 2; FREEDOM, 4; GOD, 11, 12;
    INDEPENDENCE, 1; JAZZ, 1; LYING, 8; MUSICIANS, 1; SLAVERY, 7
Barbey d'Aurevilly, Jules-Amédée CIVILIZATION, 2; HAPPINESS, 3
Bardot, Brigitte ANIMALS, 2
Baring, Maurice MONEY, 6
Barker, George TRANSIENCE, 3
Barker, Howard ARTISTS, 2; POETRY, 5; POVERTY, 2
Barnes, Clive PORNOGRAPHY, 2
Barnes, Djuna EGOTISM, 2; HUMAN CONDITION, 6; LIFE, 2; NAMES, 2; SANITY, 1
Barnes, Ernest William EQUALITY, 3
Barnes, Julian CERTAINTY, 1; FAITH, 1; HAPPINESS, 4; LOVE, 7; OLD AGE, 4
Barnes, Peter GOD, 13
Barnes, Stuart SPORTS AND GAMES, 1
Barney, Natalie Clifford MATERIALISM, 2
Barnfield, Richard HOMOSEXUALITY, 1
Barnum, P. T. GULLIBILITY, 1
Baroja, Pío FANTASY, 2; INDIFFERENCE, 1; INTELLIGENCE, 2; JUSTICE, 2;
    LITERATURE, 3
Barrault, Jean-Louis THEATRE, 2
Barrès, Maurice POLITICIANS, 4
Barrie, J. M. CHARACTER, 6; DEATH AND DYING, 4; FAIRIES, 1; MATHEMATICS, 4;
    MEDIOCRITY, 3; MEMORY, 5; MOTIVE, 1; SMOKING, 1
Barry, Dave AMERICANS, 1; FAMILY, 2
Barrymore, Ethel ACTING AND ACTORS, 1; HOLLYWOOD, 2
Barrymore, John AUDIENCES, 2
Barth, John HUMAN NATURE, 4
Barth, Karl GOOD, 4
Barthelme, Donald BEGINNING, 1; CHILDREN, 4; DOUBT, 3
Barthes, Roland CARS, 1; THE FACE, 3; LANGUAGE, 4; LITERATURE, 4, 5;
    MODERNITY, 2; REALITY, 1
Bartholomaeus Anglicus MELANCHOLY, 2
Barton, Bruce CHANGE, 1; COLD WAR, 2
Baruch, Bernard Mannes ANTICIPATION, 1; COLD WAR, 3; OLD AGE, 5;
    REMEDIES, 3
Barzani, Mustafa NATIONS, 3
Barzun, Jacques HISTORY, 8; INTELLECTUALS, 5
Basil the Great, Saint DRUNKENNESS, 3
Bastard, Thomas OLD AGE, 6
Bastos, Augusto Roa BIOGRAPHY, 2; FACTS, 2; IMITATION, 2; MEMORY, 6
Bateman, Edgar BRITISH CITIES, 2
Bateson, Gregory CULTURE, 3

Battiscombe, Georgina EATING, 1
Baudelaire, Charles AMERICAN LITERATURE, 2; BEAUTY, 3; THE DEVIL, 1;
    EUROPEAN COUNTRIES, 7; EVENING, 1; GOD, 14; MEMORY, 7; MUSICIANS, 2;
    POETS, 3; PROCRASTINATION, 1; READERS, 2; RESPECT, 1; SECRECY, 1;
    SELF-RESPECT, 1; SEXUALITY, 1; TEMPTATION, 2
Baudouin I WAR, 2
Baudrillard, Jean TYRANNY, 3
Baum, L. Frank FANTASY, 3; MAGIC, 2; PLACES, 2
Bax, Arnold EXPERIENCE, 3
Bayle, Pierre HISTORY, 9
Bayly, Thomas Haynes CHOICE, 1; TRANSIENCE, 4
Beale, Betty ABORTION, 1
Beard, Charles HISTORIANS, 4; HISTORY, 10
Beard, James FOOD, 1
Beaton, Cecil AMERICAN CITIES, 2
Beattie, Ann WRITERS, 5
Beattie, James BETRAYAL, 2; OLD AGE, 7
Beaumarchais, Pierre-Augustin Caron de INSULTS, 3; LAUGHTER, 2; OPERA, 3
Beaumont, Francis REPUTATION, 6; RUMOUR, 1
Beaumont & Fletcher CHARACTER, 7; CHOICE, 2; DETERMINATION, 2; HELP, 1;
    KISSING, 1; LOVE, 8; MISFORTUNE, 1
Beauvoir, Simone de ABORTION, 2; ADULTHOOD, 2; ATHEISM, 1;
    DISILLUSIONMENT, 2; MEN, 4–6; MOTIVE, 2; TRUTH, 8; WOMEN, 3, 4;
    WOMEN'S RIGHTS, 5
Beaverbrook, Max Aitken, Lord FREE SPEECH, 1; REPUTATION, 7
Bechet, Sidney JAZZ, 2
Beck, Earl R. HISTORIANS, 5
Becker, Carl HISTORIANS, 6; HISTORY, 11; MEANING, 1; THE PAST, 7, 8
Beckett, Samuel BOOKS, 5; BORES AND BOREDOM, 2; CHILDREN, 5;
    CURIOSITY, 1; DEATH AND DYING, 5; DEPRESSION, 1; EXISTENCE, 2;
    FORGIVENESS, 2; HAPPINESS, 5; HELL, 1; IRELAND, 2; LOVE, 9; MADNESS, 2;
    MIND, 5; MORTALITY, 1; PATIENCE, 2; POETS, 4; SILENCE, 2; SUICIDE, 1;
    THE SUN, 1; THINKING, 2; TIME, 3, 4
Becon, Thomas DRUNKENNESS, 4
Becque, Henry EQUALITY, 4
Bede ENGLAND, 1
Beecham, Thomas NAMES, 3; SMOKING, 2; TRAVEL, 4
Beecher, Henry Ward LAW, 3, 4
Beefheart, Captain GENIUS, 2
Beer, Thomas LUXURY, 1
Beerbohm, Max AMERICANS, 2; ANARCHY, 3; CONCEIT, 2; CONFORMITY, 3;
    ENVY, 2; EXPERIENCE, 4; GREATNESS, 1; MEDIOCRITY, 4; PSYCHOANALYSIS, 1;
    SPORTS AND GAMES, 2; TASTE, 1
Beethoven, Ludwig van CELEBRITY, 2; INSPIRATION, 1; RELATIONSHIPS, 2;
    TYRANNY, 4
Behan, Brendan BELIEF, 3; COMMUNISM, 1; FAMILY, 3; JUSTICE, 3; OBITUARIES, 1
Behn, Aphra LOVE, 10; MONEY, 7; PLEASURE, 2; POVERTY, 3; TRANSIENCE, 5;
    WOMEN, 5
Bell, Clive CRITICS, 3; LIBERTY, 2
Bell, Eric Temple MATHEMATICS, 5
Bell, Martin POLITICS, 4
Bell, Ronald POLITICS, 5
Bellamy, Edward CLASS, 4
Bello, Andrés IMPERIALISM, 1; KNOWLEDGE, 7; NATIONS, 4; THEORY, 2;
    VICTORY, 1; WORLD LITERATURE, 1
Belloc, Hilaire ADDICTION, 2; ANIMALS, 3; BUREAUCRACY, 1; DOUBT, 4; DRINKS
    AND DRINKING, 2; LYING, 9, 10; MONEY, 8
Bellori, Giovanni Pietro ARTISTS, 3
Bellow, Saul AMERICAN CITIES, 3–5; BIOGRAPHY, 3; CENSORSHIP, 2;
    CONVERSATION, 5; FIRST LINES, 1; HONESTY, 1; INNOCENCE, 3;
    INTELLECTUALS, 6; LITERATURE, 6; LOVERS, 1; MADNESS, 3; POETRY, 6;
    POETS, 5; THE PRESENT, 1; SEX, 9; TRUTH, 9
Benchley, Robert ADULTERY, 3; ALCOHOL, 2; EUROPEAN CITIES, 2
Benda, Julien INTELLECT, 2
Benedetti, Mario DOUBT, 5
Benedict, Ruth GRATITUDE, 2; PERCEPTION, 1; RACISM, 3; WAR, 3
Benét, Stephen Vincent NAMES, 4
Benjamin, Judah RACISM, 4
Benjamin, Walter ADVERTISING, 1; BOOKS, 6; CAPITALISM, 1; CRITICS, 4;
    NEWSPAPERS, 3; STORYTELLING, 1; WRITING, 2

Burgess, Anthony AMERICAN LITERATURE, 7; CLASS, 7; DEATH AND DYING, 10;
  EUROPE, 10; EUROPEAN CITIES, 5; POPULAR MUSIC, 2; READING, 7; SEX, 14;
  SLEEP, 4
Burke, Billie HOLLYWOOD, 3
Burke, Edmund AMBITION, 3; BEAUTY, 8; BRITISH IMPERIALISM, 4, 5;
  COMPLAINTS, 2; DANGER, 2; DEMOCRACY, 6–8; EUROPE, 11; EVIL, 6, 7;
  FAILURE, 2; FRENCH REVOLUTION, 3; GOVERNMENT, 11; INDIFFERENCE, 2;
  INJUSTICE, 2, 3; JUDGMENT, 8; LAW, 6; LIBERTY, 5–7; MODERATION, 1;
  OPINIONS, 2; OPPRESSION, 3; ORDER, 1; PARLIAMENTS AND ASSEMBLIES, 4;
  PERSECUTION, 2; POLITICIANS, 6; POLITICS, 15, 16; POWER, 4; PROGRESS, 6;
  REASON, 4; THEORY, 4; VIRTUE, 7; WEAKNESS, 1; YOUTH, 6
Burke, Johnny OPTIMISM, 2
Burke, Thomas PRAISE, 2
Burnet, Gilbert GRAMMAR, 2
Burney, Fanny GUILT, 3
Burns, George ACTING AND ACTORS, 3; GOVERNMENT, 12; OLD AGE, 10
Burns, John Elliot RIVERS, 1
Burns, Robert ALCOHOL, 3; ANIMALS, 10; CRITICS, 7; DELUSION, 1;
  DRUNKENNESS, 6; FRIENDSHIP, 8; HELL, 5; HUMANKIND, 7; HUMAN NATURE, 9;
  LIBERTY, 8; LOVE, 19; RESPECTABILITY, 2; SCOTLAND, 1; SELF-INTEREST, 2;
  TIME, 8; WOMEN'S RIGHTS, 8
Burroughs, John FACTS, 3
Burroughs, Nannie Helen UNITED STATES, 5
Burroughs, William S. ACCIDENTS, 4; DRUGS, 2, 3; EVIL, 8; INTELLECTUALS, 9;
  ISLAM, 5; MEANING, 2; UNITED STATES, 6; WRITERS, 7
Burton, Richard ACTING AND ACTORS, 4; WALES, 1
Burton, Robert CHANCE, 4; CLARITY, 1; THE DEVIL, 4; DIPLOMACY, 6; HEALTH AND
  HEALTHY LIVING, 3; ILLNESS, 2; LUST, 2; MELANCHOLY, 3–5; MONEY, 10;
  NECESSITY, 6; PLAGIARISM, 2, 3; RELIGION, 6
Bush, George AMERICAN IMPERIALISM, 3; ATHEISM, 4; CLARITY, 2; MIDDLE
  EAST, 8; OPINIONS, 3; POLITICAL INSULTS, 17; UNITED STATES, 7
Bush, George W. COLD WAR, 4; DIPLOMACY, 7; EVIL, 9; GENETICS, 1;
  TERRORISM, 3, 4; UNITED STATES, 8
Bush, Vannevar SCIENCE, 8
Bussy-Rabutin ABSENCE, 2
Butler, G. N. SEXISM, 2
Butler, Joseph CONSCIENCE, 2; DELUSION, 2
Butler, Samuel ANIMALS, 11; BRIBERY, 1; CONFORMITY, 4; CONSCIENCE, 3;
  DIGESTION, 2; EVOLUTION, 3; EXPLORATION, 8; GOD, 20; GRATITUDE, 3;
  GREATNESS, 3; HATE, 2; HYPOCRISY, 6, 7; ILLNESS, 3; JUSTICE, 8; LANGUAGE, 7;
  LEARNING, 9; LIBRARIES, 1; LIFE, 9, 10; MARRIAGE, 10; MATHEMATICS, 7;
  MEDICINE, 8; MODERATION, 2; MONEY, 11; OPINIONS, 4, 5; PARENTS, 3;
  PLEASURE, 3; POSTERITY, 3; PROGRESS, 7; PRUDENCE, 1; RHETORIC, 1; SELF-
  CONFIDENCE, 1; SPONTANEITY, 1; TRUTH, 19; VICE, 3; WORK, 1
Byatt, A. S. MOTHERS, 1
Byng, George LITERARY INSULTS, 10
Byrne, David MUSICIANS, 3
Byron, Lord BEAUTY, 9; BEREAVEMENT, 2; BOATS, 3; BORES AND BOREDOM, 4; BRITISH
  IMPERIALISM, 6; COMMITMENT IN LOVE, 3; CRITICS, 8; DEBT, 3; DICTATORS, 3;
  DRUNKENNESS, 7; EATING, 6; EMOTION, 1; ENGLAND, 5; ENVY, 3; EUROPEAN
  CITIES, 6; EUROPEAN COUNTRIES, 12–14; FAME, 3–5; FANATICISM, 1; FIRE, 3;
  FLIRTATION, 2; FREEDOM, 6; FRIENDSHIP, 9; GREATNESS, 4; HATE, 3; THE HEART, 1;
  HEAVEN, 1; HEROISM, 4; INSULTS, 6; KNOWLEDGE, 9; LITERARY INSULTS, 11; LUST, 3;
  MADNESS, 7; MARRIAGE, 11; NATURE, 5; NIGHT, 1; NOSTALGIA, 5; OLD AGE, 11;
  OPTIMISM, 3; PEACE, 12; PLEASURE, 4, 5; POETS, 9; PUBLISHING, 2; REBELLION, 2;
  THE SEA, 3; SEDUCTION, 1; SELF-KNOWLEDGE, 6; SMOKING, 4; SORROW, 2;
  SUFFERING, 3; TRAGEDY, 4; TRUTH, 20; VICE, 4; WEATHER, 2; WORDS, 5
Cabell, James Branch DRINKS AND DRINKING, 3; PATRIOTISM, 5; PESSIMISM, 4
Caballero, Francisco Largo REVOLUTION, 5
Cabral, Amilcar HONESTY, 3
Caesar, Julius BETRAYAL, 5; BOASTS, 6
Cage, John ANARCHY, 4; MUSIC, 6; POETRY, 10; SILENCE, 4
Cage, Nicolas INDIVIDUALITY, 3
Cagney, James BETRAYAL, 6
Caine, Michael AMERICAN CITIES, 7; KNOWLEDGE, 10
Cai Qijiao POETRY, 11
Calasso, Roberto LITERATURE, 9, 10
Calder, Nigel CREATION, 2
Calderón de la Barca, Pedro BIRTH, 3; DREAMS, 2, 3; PLEASURE, 6;
  PROPHECY, 2; REASON, 5

Calhoun, John C. GOVERNMENT, 13; UNITED STATES, 9
Callaghan, Jim BRITAIN, 8; LYING, 11
Callcott, George H. HISTORY, 17
Calment, Jeanne LONGEVITY, 4
Calvino, Italo BOOKS, 7; EUROPEAN LITERATURE, 2; FIRST LINES, 2;
  IMAGINATION, 4; LITERATURE, 11; MEDIA, 2; SENSES, 3; STORYTELLING, 4;
  WORDS, 6; WRITING, 6
Câmara, Dom Helder POVERTY, 5
Cambó, Francisco CONSERVATISM, 2
Cameron, James JOURNALISM, 5
Campbell, Glen AMERICAN CITIES, 8
Campbell, James JAZZ, 4
Campbell, Joseph PLEASURE, 7
Campbell, Mrs. Patrick MARRIAGE, 12; MEN, 8; SEX, 15
Campbell, Patrick JOURNALISM, 6
Campbell, Roy AFRICAN COUNTRIES, 4; LIFE, 11; POETS, 10
Campbell, Thomas AMBITION, 4; IMMORTALITY, 6
Campion, Thomas UNHAPPINESS, 2
Camus, Albert AMERICAN LITERATURE, 8, 9; CRIME, 4; THE FACE, 4; THE
  FUTURE, 5; GOD, 21; HYPOCRISY, 8; INTELLECTUALS, 10; JUDGMENT, 9;
  JUSTICE, 9; LITERARY STYLE, 1; MODERNITY, 4; MYTHS, 5; NIHILISM, 1, 2;
  POLITICIANS, 7; POLITICS, 17; POWER, 5; REASON, 6; REBELLION, 3;
  REVOLUTION, 6; RIGHT, 2; SUICIDE, 3, 4; WORK, 2
Canetti, Elias AMBITION, 5; ANIMALS, 12; DREAMS, 4; HEALTH AND HEALTHY
  LIVING, 4; HISTORIANS, 8; KILLING, 1; LITERATURE, 12; NAMES, 5; POETS, 11;
  REALITY, 4; SHAME, 1; TECHNOLOGY, 1; TRUTH, 21; WRITERS, 8
Canning, George NATIONS, 7; UNITED STATES, 10
Cánovas del Castillo, Antonio POLITICIANS, 8
Cantona, Eric JOURNALISM, 7; SPONTANEITY, 2
Capone, Al MURDER, 3
Capote, Truman EUROPEAN CITIES, 7; LITERARY INSULTS, 12; MURDER, 4
Capra, Frank ACTING AND ACTORS, 5
Caracciolo, Francesco FOOD, 4
Cardozo, Benjamin HISTORY, 18; JUSTICE, 10
Carducho, Vicente ARTISTIC STYLES, 5
Carew, Jan LEARNING, 10; WORLD LITERATURE, 2
Carey, George MIDDLE EAST, 9
Carkesse, James MADNESS, 8
Carlyle, Jane APPEARANCE, 1; INJUSTICE, 4
Carlyle, Thomas ACHIEVEMENT, 3; BIOGRAPHY, 5, 6; BOOKS, 8; BRIBERY, 2;
  CLOTHES, 3; DISASTER, 1; ECONOMICS, 7; EUROPEAN COUNTRIES, 15;
  EVOLUTION, 4; GENIUS, 5; GREATNESS, 5; HEROISM, 5; LANGUAGE, 8;
  LAUGHTER, 3; LIBRARIES, 2; LITERATURE, 13; MEDIA, 3; MODERNITY, 5;
  MUSIC, 7; NATURE, 6; ORTHODOXY, 1; POETS, 12, 13; SARCASM, 1; SELF-
  KNOWLEDGE, 7; THE UNIVERSE, 3, 4; WORDS, 7; WORK, 3
Carnap, Rudolf SCIENCE, 9
Carnegie, Andrew LEADERSHIP, 4
Carnegie, Dale ARGUMENTS, 3; INFLUENCE, 3
Carrel, Alexis INTELLIGENCE, 4
Carrington, Lord COLD WAR, 5; MODESTY, 1
Carroll, Lewis ANIMALS, 13, 14; ANSWERS, 2; BEGINNING, 2; BELIEF, 9, 10;
  BOOKS, 9; COWARDICE, 1; CRITICS, 9; CURIOSITY, 2; EDUCATION, 1; EUROPEAN
  LANGUAGES, 1; FIGHTING, 1; INTRODUCTIONS, 1; LAW, 7; MEANING, 3–5;
  MORALITY, 5; NAMES, 6; NONSENSE, 2–6; REALITY, 5; TRUTH, 22; WORDS, 8
Carson, Johnny INSULTS, 7
Carson, Rachel ECOLOGY, 2; POLLUTION, 2; SPRING, 1
Carter, Angela AMBITION, 6; APPEARANCE, 2; THE BODY, 7; CHILDREN, 7;
  CLASS, 8; COMEDY, 1; COMPROMISE, 2; DRUNKENNESS, 8; LANDSCAPES, 2;
  MARRIAGE, 13; MYTHS, 4, 5; THE PAST, 11; PESSIMISM, 5; PORNOGRAPHY, 3;
  SELF-DELUSION, 2; TRAVEL, 7
Carter, Jimmy AMERICANS, 4; BUREAUCRACY, 4; GOVERNMENT, 14
Cartier-Bresson, Henri PHOTOGRAPHY, 4–6
Cartland, Barbara CLASS, 9; FOOD, 5
Cartwright, John DEMOCRACY, 9
Carver, George Washington ABILITY, 1
Carver, Raymond AUTOBIOGRAPHY, 1; CERTAINTY, 3; MADNESS, 9; READING, 8
Cary, Joyce ARTISTS, 9; OLD AGE, 12; WAR, 10
Casals, Pablo ABILITY, 2; MUSIC, 8; PATRIOTISM, 6; PERFORMANCE, 1
Casely-Hayford, Joseph Ephraim CHANGE, 2
Casement, Roger EXECUTION, 2; IRELAND, 4; PATRIOTISM, 7

Cohn, Hans W. DESPAIR, 2
Cohn, Nik POPULAR MUSIC, 3
Cohn, Roy LAW, 13
Coker, Cheo Hodari POPULAR MUSIC, 4
Cole, Nat King MUSICIANS, 4
Colebrook, Leonard SCIENTISTS, 5
Coleridge, Hartley FREEDOM, 10
Coleridge, Mary BEREAVEMENT, 3
Coleridge, Samuel Taylor BELIEF, 12; BIRTH, 4; CHRISTIANITY, 7; DESPAIR, 3;
    FAITH, 6; HAPPINESS, 10; THE HEART, 2; IMAGINATION, 5, 6; KNOWLEDGE, 12;
    LANDSCAPES, 4; LONELINESS, 1; MARRIAGE, 15; MIND, 8; MOTHERS, 2;
    PLEASURE, 8; POETRY, 16; POETS, 16; PROPHECY, 4; READERS, 4; RHETORIC, 2;
    THE SEA, 5–7; SILENCE, 6; THE SOUL, 8; SPEECH, 3; SUMMER, 2; WARNING, 4;
    WRITERS, 10, 11
Colette CLASS, 10; SMOKING, 5; VIRTUE, 9
Collingwood, Cuthbert ACHIEVEMENT, 4
Collingwood, R. G. ART, 12; ARTISTS, 11
Collins, Michael IRELAND, 6; PATIENCE, 5
Collins, Wilkie REASON, 8
Colman, George BRITISH CITIES, 5; INFORMATION, 1; MODESTY, 4; RESPECT, 2;
    SECRECY, 3
Colton, Charles DEATH AND DYING, 14; DOCTORS, 5; IMITATION, 3; RELIGION, 8
Coltrane, John MUSIC, 9
Columbus, Christopher COLONIALISM, 2; DISCOVERY, 3; EXPLORATION, 4;
    SILENCE, 7
Comden, Betty AMERICAN CITIES, 10
Commager, Henry Steele HISTORY, 21
Committee on Science and Creationism, National Academy of
    Sciences SCIENCE, 10
Compton, Arthur Holly DISCOVERY, 4
Compton-Burnett, Ivy APPEARANCE, 4; THE SEXES, 3
Comte, Auguste METAPHYSICS, 4; PHILOSOPHY, 6
Conant, James Bryant SCIENTISTS, 6
Confucius ABILITY, 4; AGE, 10; BEAUTY, 10; CHANGE, 5, 6; CHARM, 1;
    COWARDICE, 2; FRIENDSHIP, 12; GLORY, 4; HASTE, 2; HUMANKIND, 10; HUMAN
    NATURE, 11; JUSTICE, 11; KINDNESS, 2; KNOWLEDGE, 13, 14; LOVE, 22;
    MISTAKES, 2, 3; ORDER, 3; THE PAST, 13; POVERTY, 8; PRINCIPLES, 3; SELF-
    KNOWLEDGE, 8; SINCERITY, 1; THINKING, 6, 7; VIRTUE, 10
Congreve, William BEAUTY, 11; BETRAYAL, 8; BIRTH, 5; ETERNITY, 5; HATE, 5;
    INDIFFERENCE, 4; LAUGHTER, 5; LOYALTY, 3; MARRIAGE, 16;
    PROCRASTINATION, 4; SECRECY, 4; SPEECH, 4; SYCOPHANCY, 2; THEFT, 4;
    WOMEN, 9
Connolly, Billy MARRIAGE, 17
Connolly, Cyril AMERICAN LITERATURE, 10; BABIES, 3; CHARM, 2; ENDING, 2;
    LIFE, 14; LITERARY INSULTS, 14; LITERARY STYLE, 3; LITERATURE, 16;
    LONGEVITY, 5; NEUROSIS, 2; PUBLISHING, 4; REASON, 9; SELF-KNOWLEDGE, 9;
    SUICIDE, 6; WRITERS, 12; WRITING, 13
Connors, Jimmy LOSS, 2
Conrad, Joseph ASIA, 1; CONSCIENCE, 4; DEATH AND DYING, 15; EVIL, 11;
    HORROR, 1; IMPERIALISM, 4; JUDGMENT, 10; LITERATURE, 17; REVOLUTION, 9;
    THE SEA, 8; VANITY, 1; WORDS, 9
Conran, Shirley COOKING, 2
Conran, Terence DESIGN, 1; VANITY, 2
Constable, John IMAGINATION, 7
Constantine, Learie HUMAN RIGHTS, 3; SLAVERY, 8
Constitution of the United States CIVIL RIGHTS, 2; SLAVERY, 9
Cook, Daniel John OPERA, 4
Cook, Peter ENTERTAINMENT, 2; THE UNIVERSE, 7
Coolidge, Calvin BREVITY, 2; MAJORITY, 2; THE PAST, 14; WEALTH, 8
Cooper, Astley REMEDIES, 6
Cooper, James Fenimore BRITAIN, 13; RACISM, 6
Coover, Robert WRITING, 14
Cope, Wendy BRITAIN, 14; REVENGE, 5
Copland, Aaron MUSIC, 10
Coppola, Francis Ford COMMUNICATION, 5; FILMS, 5, 6
Coren, Alan ALCOHOL, 6; DEMOCRACY, 10; EUROPEAN COUNTRIES, 18
Corneille BEREAVEMENT, 4; EVIL, 12; FAME, 7; GIFTS, 2; LYING, 12, 13; POWER, 8;
    REMEDIES, 7; VICTORY, 5
Cornford, F. M. PROPAGANDA, 1
Cornford, Frances POETS, 17

Cornish, Samuel Eli NEWSPAPERS, 9
Corry, John LONELINESS, 2
Corso, Gregory WEAPONS, 3
Cortázar, Julio LITERATURE, 18; WEAPONS, 4
Cortez, Jayne POLLUTION, 5
Corvisart des Marets, Jean Nicolas MEDICINE, 10
Cosby, Bill CHILDREN, 8
Costello, Elvis POPULAR MUSIC, 5; SONGS, 1
Coubertin, Pierre de SPORTS AND GAMES, 6
Coué, Émile REMEDIES, 8
Courtauld, George TRAVEL, 9
Cousin, Victor ART, 13
Cousins, Norman HISTORY, 22
Cousteau, Jacques POLLUTION, 6
Covey, Stephen R. MISTAKES, 4
Coward, Noël ACTING AND ACTORS, 6, 7; AFTERLIFE, 6; APPEARANCE, 5;
    CRITICISM, 6; INSULTS, 11; LAST WORDS, 3; OPERA, 5; PORNOGRAPHY, 4;
    SPRING, 3
Cowley, Abraham GARDENS, 2
Cowley, Hannah VANITY, 3
Cowper, William ARGUMENTS, 4; BRITAIN, 15; FREEDOM, 11; HAPPINESS, 11;
    HOPE, 5; HYPOCRISY, 10; LIFE, 15; LYING, 14; MANNERS, 1; MOUNTAINS, 1;
    NATURE, 7, 8; PLEASURE, 9; REGRET, 2; SEPARATION, 1; SOLITUDE, 5;
    SORROW, 3; WAR, 17; WEALTH, 9; WISDOM, 6, 7
Crabbe, George THE FACE, 6; GOOD, 8; SECRECY, 5
Crane, Stephen COURAGE, 1; NATURE, 9; NEWSPAPERS, 10; THE SEA, 9
Cranmer, Thomas PUNISHMENT, 5
Craven, Avery O. HISTORIANS, 10
Creeley, Robert THINKING, 8
Creighton, Mandell GOOD, 9; PARADOX, 2
Crescas, Hasdai ben Abraham REASON, 10
Crèvecoeur, Jean de AMERICANS, 7; CHARACTER, 13; UNITED STATES, 13
Crick, Francis DISCOVERY, 5
Cripps, Stafford POLITICIANS, 11
Crisp, Quentin AUTOBIOGRAPHY, 2; COMPETITION, 2; HOMOSEXUALITY, 3; LAW, 14;
    LIFE, 16; PARENTS, 4; SORROW, 4; VICE, 5; YOUTH, 9
Crittenden, John PATRIOTISM, 10
Croce, Benedetto ART, 14; HISTORY, 23; POETS, 18
Croker, John Wilson GULLIBILITY, 2
Cromwell, Oliver MISTAKES, 5; NATURE, 10; POPULARITY, 3; REALISM, 1
Cronenberg, David FILMS, 7
Cronin, Mary J. INTERNET, 2
Crosby, Philip B. MONEY, 12
Cross, Douglas AMERICAN CITIES, 11
Crouse, Russell M. NUCLEAR WAR, 4
Crow, Tim J. PSYCHIATRY, 3
Crowther, Geoffrey MONEY, 13
Crummell, Alexander POWER, 9
Cugoano, Ottobah SLAVERY, 10
Culbertson, Ely POLITICS, 18
Cullen, Countee AFRICA, 3
cummings, e. e. FATHERS, 2; GRAMMAR, 6; HUMANKIND, 11; THE MOON, 4;
    NAKEDNESS, 2; POLITICIANS, 12; PROGRESS, 10; REVOLUTION, 10; RUSSIA, 9;
    RUSSIAN REVOLUTION, 6; SENSES, 4; THE UNIVERSE, 8; THE WORLD, 3
Cunningham, J. V. GROWING UP, 2
Cuomo, Mario POLITICS, 19
Cuppy, Will EXTINCTION, 2
Curran, John Philpot LIBERTY, 10; MURDER, 6
Currie, James EUROPEAN LITERATURE, 3
Curtis, Lionel SPEECHES, 7
Curzon, George Nathaniel BRITISH IMPERIALISM, 11, 12; JOURNALISM, 9
Cyrano de Bergerac, Savinien REVENGE, 6
D, Chuck POPULAR MUSIC, 6, 7
Dacre, Harry MARRIAGE, 18
Dagerman, Stig CREATIVITY, 4
Dai Wangshu MEMORY, 13
Daladier, Édouard WORLD WAR II, 11
Dalai Lama ASIAN COUNTRIES, 4–7; ENEMIES, 3; RELIGION, 9; THINKING, 9
Dalí, Salvador BEAUTY, 12; IMITATION, 4; PAINTING, 13, 14
Daly, Mary WOMEN'S RIGHTS, 11

Dana, Richard Henry SCIENCE, 11
Dando, Malcolm SCIENCE, 12
Daniel, Samuel HUMANKIND, 12
Dante Alighieri EUROPEAN LITERATURE, 4; PURITY, 3
Danton, Georges Jacques LAST WORDS, 4
Darío, Rubén LITERARY STYLE, 4
Darling, Charles John DECEPTION, 9; LAW, 15
Darrow, Clarence CLOTHES, 4; EXECUTION, 3; FUTILITY, 1; HISTORY, 24;
     POLITICIANS, 13; THINKING, 10
Darwin, Charles EVOLUTION, 5–8; FACTS, 4; HUMANKIND, 13, 14; MATHEMATICS, 8
Darwin, Charles Galton EVOLUTION, 9
Darwin, Erasmus CREATION, 3; SPEECH, 5
Darwin, Francis SCIENTISTS, 7
Darwish, Mahmoud ANGER, 6; ENDING, 3; MARTYRDOM, 3; NATIONS, 8
Daudet, Alphonse HEROISM, 6; NIGHT, 2
Davenport, Guy POETRY, 17; UNITED STATES, 14; WORDS, 10
David, Jacques-Louis ARTISTS, 12
David, Larry MASTURBATION, 2
Davies, John IRELAND, 7
Davies, Norman AFRICA, 4; EUROPEAN COUNTRIES, 19; HISTORIANS, 11;
     MARXISM, 2
Davies, Paul SCIENCE, 13
Davies, Ray FASHION, 4
Davies, Rhys WALES, 2
Davies, Robertson INTELLIGENCE, 5; WISDOM, 8
Davies, Scrope MIND, 9
Davies, W. H. COLOUR, 3; KINDNESS, 3
Davis, Angela COMMUNISM, 3; HUMAN RIGHTS, 4; RACISM, 7
Davis, Bette MEN, 9; WOMEN, 10
Davis, Bob PROGRESS, 11
Davis, Philip J. SCIENTISTS, 8
Davis, Sammy, Jr. FAME, 8; RACISM, 8
Davis, Thomas IRELAND, 8
Davy, Humphry INSULTS, 12
Dawkins, Richard EVOLUTION, 10; GENETICS, 2
Dawson, Christopher POVERTY, 9
Day, Clarence Shepard CREATIVITY, 5; GOD, 23; THE PAST, 15; POWER, 10;
     SACRIFICE, 4
Day, Robin POLITICAL INSULTS, 20
Day-Lewis, Cecil POETS, 19; TRANSIENCE, 9
Dean, John CORRUPTION, 1
Deane, Seamus RATIONALISM, 2
de Blank, Joost AFRICAN COUNTRIES, 5; COLOUR, 4
de Bono, Edward CREATIVITY, 6; MORALITY, 7; THINKING, 11; UNHAPPINESS, 4
de Botton, Alain QUOTATIONS, 2
Debs, Eugene Victor INJUSTICE, 6; MAJORITY, 3; WORLD WAR I, 2
Debussy, Claude BEAUTY, 13; MUSIC, 11; MUSICIANS, 5
De Chirico, Giorgio ARCHITECTURE, 5
Deffand, Marie du BEGINNING, 3
Defoe, Daniel ENGLAND, 8; FATE, 5; MIDDLE AGE, 3; MOUNTAINS, 2; NECESSITY, 9;
     SUFFERING, 4; TYRANNY, 6
Degas, Edgar MEMORY, 14
de Gaulle, Charles ACTION, 3; ASSASSINATION, 3; DIPLOMACY, 11; ENEMIES, 4;
     EUROPE, 14; EUROPEAN COUNTRIES, 20; EUROPEAN LITERATURE, 5; OLD
     AGE, 15; POLITICIANS, 14; SOLITUDE, 4; WORLD WAR II, 12
Degler, Carl N. HISTORIANS, 12; NATIONS, 9; SEX, 17; UNITED STATES, 15
de Jouvenel, Bertrand ACHIEVEMENT, 5
Dekker, Thomas ANGELS, 5; BEGINNING, 4; CLOTHES, 5; SLEEP, 7, 8
de Klerk, F. W. AFRICAN COUNTRIES, 6, 7; APARTHEID, 4
de Kooning, Willem POVERTY, 10
Delacroix, Eugène BOOKS, 10; PAINTING, 15, 16; WORRY, 3
de la Mare, Walter DIGESTION, 3; FLOWERS, 1; ILLNESS, 6; LANGUAGE, 10
Delaney, Shelagh DARKNESS, 3
Delany, Martin Robinson DESTINY, 2; SLAVERY, 11
Delille, Jacques FRIENDSHIP, 13
DeLillo, Don EUROPE, 15; FAMILY, 5; INTERNET, 3; MADNESS, 13; NUCLEAR
     WEAPONS, 1; SECRECY, 6; TRAVEL, 10
Delors, Jacques EUROPE, 16–18; IDEALISM, 2; SOCIETY, 6
De Mille, Cecil B. FILMS, 8
Deming, W. Edwards LEADERSHIP, 6; WORK, 5

Democritus REALITY, 6
Deng To IGNORANCE, 4; LEARNING, 14
Deng Xiaoping ASIAN COUNTRIES, 8–10; DEMOCRACY, 11; PROTEST, 4;
     REVOLUTION, 11
Denisova, Galina BRIBERY, 3
Denning, Lord DIPLOMACY, 12
Dennis, John WORDPLAY, 2
Depew, Chauncey EXERCISE, 2
de Pree, Max LEADERSHIP, 7
De Quincey, Thomas BOOKS, 11; DRUGS, 5, 6; IMPERFECTION, 2
Derrida, Jacques LANGUAGE, 11; WRITERS, 13
Descartes, René BEING, 1; EXISTENCE, 6–8; MIND, 10; NOTHINGNESS, 3;
     RATIONALISM, 3; READING, 9; VICE, 6
des Rieux, Virginie MARRIAGE, 19
Dessalines, Jean Jacques DECOLONIZATION, 2
Destouches, Philippe ABSENCE, 3
Deutsch, Babette POETS, 20
de Valera, Eamon IRELAND, 9, 10; NORTHERN IRELAND, 3
Devereux, Robert MOTIVE, 3
Devlin, Denis BEAUTY, 14
DeVoto, Bernard ART, 15
De Vries, Peter BORES AND BOREDOM, 6; CHILDREN, 9; FATE, 6; GOD, 24;
     GREED, 4; MIND, 11; PARENTS, 5; POPULARITY, 4; PSYCHOANALYSIS, 5; SELF-
     INTEREST, 5
Dewey, John CHARACTER, 14; CONSCIOUSNESS, 2, 3; EDUCATION, 3; THE
     ENVIRONMENT, 2; HISTORY, 25; HUNGER, 6; IDEAS, 3; IMAGINATION, 8;
     INTELLIGENCE, 6; JUDGMENT, 11; LANGUAGE, 12; MIND, 12; QUESTIONS, 2;
     SCIENCE, 14; THE SELF, 3, 4; SENSES, 5; SUBJECTIVITY, 2; WONDER, 1
de Wyzewa, Téodor ARTISTIC STYLES, 6
Diana, Princess ADULTERY, 7; AIDS, 2; BABIES, 4; THE BODY, 8
Díaz, Porfirio CENTRAL AMERICA, 2
Díaz Ordaz, Gustavo LIBERTY, 11
Dibdin, Charles BRITAIN, 16
Dick, Philip K. DRUGS, 7; REALITY, 7; WORDS, 11
Dickens, Charles ACCIDENTS, 5; AMERICAN CITIES, 12; APPEARANCE, 6, 7;
     APPETITE, 1; ARTISTIC STYLES, 7; BABIES, 5; BUREAUCRACY, 5;
     CHARACTER, 15, 16; COMFORT, 1; DEATH AND DYING, 16; DECEPTION, 10;
     EMOTION, 3; THE FACE, 7; FACTS, 5; FEAR, 10; FIRST LINES, 4; FOOD, 7;
     FREEDOM, 12; GREETINGS, 2; HUMANKIND, 15; HUMILITY, 4; HUNGER, 7;
     IGNORANCE, 5; INSULTS, 13; JUDGMENT, 12; LAW, 16; LITERACY, 3;
     NEWSPAPERS, 11; POETRY, 18; POVERTY, 11; PRIVACY, 1; PRUDENCE, 2;
     SENSES, 6; THE SEXES, 4; SILENCE, 8; SOLITUDE, 7; SORROW, 5; THE
     SUPERNATURAL, 4; TRIVIALITY, 1; UNITED STATES, 16; UNITY, 3; WINE, 3
Dickinson, Emily DEPRESSION, 2; ENDURANCE, 3; HOPE, 6; MADNESS, 14;
     PAIN, 3; SOLITUDE, 8; THE SOUL, 9; SUCCESS, 4; THE SUPERNATURAL, 5
Dickinson, John SOLIDARITY, 3
Diddley, Bo EXPLOITATION, 3
Diderot, Denis ART, 16; COMEDY, 3; FREEDOM, 13; HISTORY, 26; MADNESS, 15;
     RELIGION, 10; WIT, 3; WRITERS, 14
Didion, Joan AMERICAN CITIES, 13; MARXISM, 3; NUCLEAR WEAPONS, 2;
     STORYTELLING, 6
Diefenbaker, John FREEDOM, 14
Dietrich, Marlene MEN, 10; RELATIONSHIPS, 4; SOUTH AMERICA, 5
Diggins, John P. HISTORY, 27
Dillard, Annie CREATION, 4; HAPPINESS, 12; THE PRESENT, 6; SELF-
     KNOWLEDGE, 10; SPACE, 3; WEATHER, 5
Diller, Phyllis ARGUMENTS, 5
Dillingham, Charles Bancroft FUNERALS, 4
Dimma, William GREED, 5
Dinesen, Isak HUMANKIND, 16
Diogenes HUNGER, 8; MADNESS, 16
Diogenes Läertius CYNICISM, 3; DRUNKENNESS, 9; EATING, 7; EDUCATION, 4;
     HUMANKIND, 17; IGNORANCE, 6; MEMORY, 15; MODERATION, 3; NOTHINGNESS, 4;
     WORDS, 12
Dionysius of Halicarnassus HISTORY, 28
Dionysius the Areopagite ETERNITY, 6; MYSTICISM, 1
Diphilus TIME, 11
Dipoko, Mbella Sonne CORRUPTION, 2
Dirac, Paul GOD, 25
Disney, Walt FANTASY, 4; GROWING UP, 3

Forbes, Miss C. F. CLOTHES, 7
Forché, Carolyn ENDING, 5; POETS, 25
Ford, Ford Madox BOOKS, 16
Ford, Harrison AMERICAN CITIES, 15
Ford, Henry ABILITY, 5; BUSINESS, 3, 4; CHOICE, 4; DESTINY, 4; HISTORY, 36; MONEY, 17; TIME, 18
Ford, John ACTING AND ACTORS, 9; DEATH AND DYING, 26; FATE, 8; MELANCHOLY, 6
Ford, Richard MARRIAGE, 25; READING, 13
Foreman, George HEALTH AND HEALTHY LIVING, 8
Forrest, Nathan Bedford DECEPTION, 13
Forster, E. M. AFTERLIFE, 7; DEATH AND DYING, 27; EDUCATION, 9; EQUALITY, 7; HISTORIANS, 15; INDIVIDUALITY, 5; LITERATURE, 21; PATRIOTISM, 12; POLLUTION, 7; RELATIONSHIPS, 7; SIMILARITY, 1; WRITERS, 21; WRITING, 19
Fortune, Timothy Thomas NECESSITY, 10
Forty, Adrian HOME, 3
Foster, Stephen GAMBLING, 1
Foucault, Michel DELUSION, 5; HISTORY, 37; MADNESS, 19; NEUROSIS, 3; POWER, 17; PSYCHOLOGY, 2, 3; PUNISHMENT, 6; WRITERS, 22
Fourier, Charles WOMEN'S RIGHTS, 12
Fowler, Gene WRITERS, 23
Fowler, William Wyche POWER, 18
Fowles, John CIVILIZATION, 9; WRITERS, 24
Fox, Harrison W., Jr. BRIBERY, 4
France, Anatole ASTRONOMY, 3; CHANGE, 8; CONVERSATION, 9; CRITICS, 11; EQUALITY, 8; IDEAS, 5; INJUSTICE, 7; LYING, 16; POVERTY, 13; QUOTATIONS, 3; WORK, 8
Francis I DEFEAT, 2
Francis de Sales, Saint FIRE, 5
Franck, Sebastian DECEPTION, 14
Franco, Francisco EUROPEAN COUNTRIES, 23; FASCISM, 5; WAR, 21, 22
Frank, Anne DIARIES, 2; FEAR, 13
Franklin, Benjamin AGE, 10; AMERICAN WAR OF INDEPENDENCE, 3; ARGUMENTS, 7; DEATH AND DYING, 28; DISAPPOINTMENT, 2; HISTORIANS, 16; HISTORY, 38; HOPE, 9; INVENTIONS, 4; LITERACY, 4; MODERATION, 4; NARCISSISM, 3; PROCRASTINATION, 5; SECRECY, 8; TIME, 19; WAR, 23
Franks, Oliver SECRECY, 9
Fraser, Antonia FREEDOM, 21
Fraser, Keith IRELAND, 13
Frayn, Michael LIBERALISM, 2; NAKEDNESS, 3
Frederick I EUROPEAN COUNTRIES, 24
Frederick II DECEPTION, 15; HUMAN NATURE, 15; MONARCHY, 15
Freed, Arthur WEATHER, 9
Freeman, Richard Austin SIMPLICITY, 3
Freidank SELF-KNOWLEDGE, 13
French, Marilyn MEN, 13
Freneau, Philip EMIGRATION, 3; SMOKING, 8; UNITED STATES, 24
Freud, Anna NEUROSIS, 4; PSYCHIATRY, 4, 5; PSYCHOANALYSIS, 6
Freud, Clement POLITICAL INSULTS, 24
Freud, Sigmund AFTERLIFE, 8; BELIEF, 13; CENSORSHIP, 10; CONSCIENCE, 7; CONSCIOUSNESS, 4, 5; DELUSION, 6; DESTINY, 5; EXPERIENCE, 6; GOD, 28; GROWING UP, 6; HAPPINESS, 15; INTELLECT, 6; MIND, 13, 14; PHILOSOPHY, 8; PSYCHOANALYSIS, 7–10; PSYCHOLOGY, 4; RELIGION, 15; THE SELF, 8; SMOKING, 9; THERAPY, 1; WOMEN, 18
Friedan, Betty DIVORCE, 4
Friedman, Milton CAPITALISM, 6; DECISION, 2; ECONOMICS, 10; FREEDOM, 22; THEORY, 7
Friedman, Thomas L. GLOBALIZATION, 6
Friel, Brian HISTORY, 39; LANGUAGE, 15
Frisch, Max CHANGE, 9; DECEPTION, 16; TECHNOLOGY, 4
Fromm, Erich BIRTH, 7, 8; BUSINESS, 5; CONSCIENCE, 8; EXPLOITATION, 4; GREED, 6; HUMAN CONDITION, 10; LONELINESS, 4, 5; MADNESS, 20; MOTHERS, 3; NARCISSISM, 4; NEUROSIS, 5; OPTIMISM, 7; PSYCHOANALYSIS, 11; PSYCHOLOGY, 5; SANITY, 4; SCIENCE, 23
Frost, David TELEVISION, 6
Frost, Robert BOASTS, 7; CHOICE, 5; DIPLOMACY, 18; GOD, 29; HOME, 4; INFINITY, 2; NATURE, 13; POETRY, 23; SURVIVAL, 1; TRAVEL, 15; WRITING, 20; YOUTH, 11
Froude, J. A. CRUELTY, 1; EXPERIENCE, 7

Fry, Christopher CRITICS, 12; EXILE, 3; GOOD, 10; INSULTS, 15; MADNESS, 21; THE MOON, 6; POETRY, 24; REALITY, 10; RELIGION, 16; WORDPLAY, 3; WORDS, 15
Fry, Elizabeth EXECUTION, 4; PUNISHMENT, 7
Frye, Northrop AMERICAN LITERATURE, 13; CRITICISM, 8; EGOTISM, 5; LITERATURE, 22; NATIONS, 10
Fuentes, Carlos STORYTELLING, 7; TWENTY-FIRST CENTURY, 3; WRITERS, 25, 26
Fukuyama, Francis GLOBALIZATION, 7
Fulbright, J. William SCIENCE, 24; THINKING, 14
Fuller, Margaret AMERICANS, 9; CRITICS, 13, 14; ENGLAND, 10; WOMEN, 19
Fuller, R. Buckminster THE EARTH, 5, 6; INVENTIONS, 5; THE UNIVERSE, 9
Fuller, Thomas ANGER, 8; ARCHITECTURE, 7; BUSINESS, 6; FAME, 10; LEARNING, 17; SPEECHES, 9
Furber, Douglas BRITISH CITIES, 9
Fyleman, Rose FAIRIES, 2
Gable, Clark CELEBRITY, 7
Gabor, Zsa Zsa HATE, 8; MARRIAGE, 26; SEX, 20
Gadamer, Hans-Georg HUMAN NATURE, 16
Gaitskell, Dora TERRORISM, 5
Gaitskell, Hugh COLD WAR, 6; EUROPE, 20
Galbraith, J. K. CONSERVATISM, 5; ECONOMICS, 11; MONEY, 18; PATRIOTISM, 13; PESSIMISM, 6; POLITICS, 22; SCIENCE, 25; WEALTH, 11
Galeano, Eduardo EXECUTION, 5; GOD, 30; HUNGER, 9; LOVE, 27; MEMORY, 20; OBSESSIONS, 2; POWER, 19; SELFISHNESS, 4; SOUTH AMERICA, 7; TYRANNY, 7; THE VOICE, 2; THE WORLD, 5; WRITERS, 27; WRITING, 21
Galen REMEDIES, 11
Galileo ACADEMICS, 2; ASTRONOMY, 4–7; THE MOON, 7
Gallagher, Noel POPULAR MUSIC, 10
Gallup, George STATISTICS, 3
Galsworthy, John COMPLAINTS, 4; EUROPEAN LITERATURE, 6; LITERARY INSULTS, 21
Gambetta, Léon COLONIALISM, 5
Games, Abram DESIGN, 3
Gandhi, Indira AGREEMENT, 6; IMPERIALISM, 8
Gandhi, Mahatma ASIAN COUNTRIES, 11; CAPITALISM, 7; CIVILIZATION, 10; DECOLONIZATION, 3; GOD, 31; INDEPENDENCE, 2; LAW, 17; PACIFISM, 3; POVERTY, 14; PROTEST, 6; SOCIETY, 8; SPIRITUALITY, 1; THEFT, 6; WEALTH, 12; WEAPONS, 7
Garbo, Greta PRIVACY, 2; SOLITUDE, 11
Garcia, Jerry DRUGS, 10
García Lorca, Federico ANARCHY, 7; ARTISTS, 15; HOPE, 10; IDEALISM, 4; NAKEDNESS, 4; POETS, 26, 27; SUCCESS, 6; VITALITY, 2
García Márquez, Gabriel BELIEF, 14; CHILDHOOD, 6; CHILDREN, 13; DEATH AND DYING, 29; EMOTION, 4; FIRST LINES, 5; GOD, 32; JUSTICE, 13; LITERATURE, 23; MARRIAGE, 27; MEMORY, 21; NECESSITY, 11; OLD AGE, 19, 20; POETS, 28; PRIORITIES, 3
Gardner, Ed OPERA, 6
Gardner, John W. FATE, 9; HISTORY, 40; POVERTY, 15
Gardner, Martin SCIENTISTS, 12
Garfield, James A. HISTORY, 41
Garfield, Leon THE FACE, 8
Garner, Alan PARENTS, 6
Garnet, Henry Highland SLAVERY, 19
Garrison, William Lloyd SLAVERY, 20
Garrod, Heathcote William WORLD WAR I, 4
Garvey, Marcus AFRICA, 5; CRIME, 8; DECOLONIZATION, 4; FREEDOM, 23; LIBERTY, 14; POWER, 20; THE SELF, 9; SELF-KNOWLEDGE, 14; WEALTH, 13
Gaskell, Elizabeth THE SUPERNATURAL, 10; XENOPHOBIA, 2
Gassman, Vittorio THE SEXES, 7
Gates, Bill COMPUTERS, 5; GLOBALIZATION, 8; INTERNET, 4
Gauguin, Paul COOKING, 3
Gauss, Carl Friedrich LEARNING, 18; MATHEMATICS, 16
Gautier, Théophile CREATIVITY, 11
Gay, John ARGUMENTS, 8; CHANGE, 10; ENVY, 4; FAITHFULNESS, 1; FLIRTATION, 3; HOPE, 11; LEARNING, 19
Gaye, Marvin COMPETITION, 3; POPULAR MUSIC, 11, 12
Geddes, Eric WORLD WAR I, 5
Geldof, Bob HUNGER, 10
Gellhorn, Martha AMERICAN IMPERIALISM, 8; TRAVEL, 16
Gell-Mann, Murray ECOLOGY, 4; RATIONALISM, 4

Gellner, Ernest CONSCIOUSNESS, 6; EUROPEAN LITERATURE, 7; ISLAM, 6; PHILOSOPHY, 9; PSYCHOANALYSIS, 12
Genet, Jean CRIME, 9; EUROPEAN LITERATURE, 8; TASTE, 5
Genghis Khan IMPERIALISM, 9
Genovese, Eugene D. UNITED STATES, 25
Genscher, Hans-Dietrich EUROPEAN COUNTRIES, 25, 26
George, Daniel FREEDOM, 24
George, Henry DEMOCRACY, 14; SOCIETY, 9; VALUE, 4; WORK, 9
George, Nelson POPULAR MUSIC, 13; SINGERS AND SINGING, 4
George II ADULTERY, 8; MONARCHY, 16
George III AMERICAN WAR OF INDEPENDENCE, 4
George V FATHERS, 3; LAST WORDS, 5, 6; WORLD WAR I, 6
George VI MONARCHY, 17
Gerald of Wales LUST, 5; WALES, 4
Gerasimov, Gennadi RUSSIA, 11
Gershwin, George DOUBT, 7; MUSIC, 16
Gershwin, Ira DECLARATIONS OF LOVE, 1; LOVE, 28; POVERTY, 16; SEPARATION, 2; SUMMER, 4; WORK, 10
Getty, J. Paul BUSINESS, 7; CONFORMITY, 6; HUMILITY, 7; WEALTH, 14
Ghosh, Amitav TECHNOLOGY, 5
Gibbon, Edward BRITISH CITIES, 10; CORRUPTION, 5; PROGRESS, 14; SOLITUDE, 12; TOLERANCE, 1; WRITING, 22
Gibbons, Orlando BEAUTY, 15
Gibbons, Stella JOURNALISM, 11; MEN, 14; NATURE, 14
Gibbs, Wolcott JOURNALISM, 12
Gibran, Kahlil CHILDREN, 14; PAIN, 5; RELATIONSHIPS, 8; TREES, 1
Giddens, Anthony GLOBALIZATION, 9
Gide, André DISCOVERY, 6; DRUNKENNESS, 12; HAPPINESS, 16; KINDNESS, 4; SORROW, 8
Gilbert, W. S. APPEARANCE, 9; BABIES, 6; BOASTS, 8; EXECUTION, 6; HELP, 2
Gillespie, Dizzy EXPERIENCE, 8
Gilman, Charlotte Perkins AMERICAN CITIES, 16; FUTILITY, 3
Ginsberg, Allen AMERICAN LITERATURE, 14; ELITISM, 1; HOLLYWOOD, 7; HOMOSEXUALITY, 4; HUMAN CONDITION, 11; MADNESS, 22; WRITING, 23
Giovanni, Nikki SLAVERY, 21; VIOLENCE, 2; WRITERS, 28
Giraudoux, Jean HUMANKIND, 22; LAW, 18
Giroud, Françoise WOMEN, 20
Gish, Lillian FILMS, 10; HOLLYWOOD, 8
Gladstone, William Ewart BIOGRAPHY, 9; BRITISH IMPERIALISM, 14; CONSCIENCE, 9; DEMOCRACY, 15; INJUSTICE, 8; IRELAND, 14, 15; SPEECHES, 10
Glancey, Jonathan ARCHITECTURE, 8
Glaser, Milton FASHION, 7
Glasse, Hannah COOKING, 4
Gleick, James CHAOS, 2
Godard, Jean-Luc AMERICAN IMPERIALISM, 9; FILMS, 11–13
Goddard, Robert DREAMS, 8
Godunov, Boris RUSSIA, 12
Goering, Hermann EUROPEAN COUNTRIES, 27; THE HOLOCAUST, 2; WORLD WAR II, 13
Goethe, Johann Wolfgang von ACTION, 6; ART, 22; COLOUR, 5; THE DEVIL, 9; DOCTORS, 8; FATE, 10; FRENCH REVOLUTION, 5; FUTILITY, 4; ILLNESS, 9; MADNESS, 23; PAINTING, 17; SCIENCE, 26; SELF-KNOWLEDGE, 15; SORROW, 9; TALENT, 2; VICTORY, 6; WOMEN, 21
Gogol, Nikolay EMOTION, 5; FEAR, 14; GOVERNMENT, 18; LOSS, 3; MEMORY, 22; RUSSIA, 13, 14; SELF-KNOWLEDGE, 16; THE SUPERNATURAL, 11
Goizueta, Roberto ADVERTISING, 7; BUSINESS, 8
Goldblum, Jeff GENETICS, 3
Golden, Marita AFRICA, 6; LONELINESS, 6; SELF-KNOWLEDGE, 17
Golding, William EVOLUTION, 13; INNOCENCE, 5; LAUGHTER, 8; REVOLUTION, 14; THE SEA, 3; SLEEP, 11; VIRTUE, 12
Goldman, Emma POLITICS, 23; WOMEN'S RIGHTS, 13
Goldsmith, Edward THE ENVIRONMENT, 3; PROGRESS, 15; TECHNOLOGY, 6
Goldsmith, James ADULTERY, 9; IDENTITY, 3
Goldsmith, Oliver ARGUMENTS, 9; CONSCIENCE, 10; EVIL, 14; FRIENDSHIP, 17; GENIUS, 9; GOOD, 11; LAW, 19; LITERARY INSULTS, 22; PERFECTION, 4; PHILOSOPHY, 10; POVERTY, 17; QUESTIONS, 3; SILENCE, 10; SPEECH, 6; TEACHERS, 3
Goldwater, Barry AMERICAN IMPERIALISM, 10; GOVERNMENT, 19; LIBERTY, 15
Goldwyn, Samuel FILMS, 14; INSULTS, 16; TELEVISION, 7
Gombrich, E. H. ARTISTIC STYLES, 8

Gómez de la Serna, Ramón ANIMALS, 17, 18; CHILDREN, 15; FICTION, 4; INVENTIONS, 6; LANGUAGE, 16; READERS, 5; WRITING, 24
Goncharova, Natalia INDIVIDUALITY, 6
Goncourt, Edmond de BUSINESS, 9; CONVERSATION, 10; HISTORIANS, 17; UNHAPPINESS, 5
González Prada, Manuel CHANGE, 11; REVOLUTION, 15
Goodison, Nicholas MACHINES, 3
Goodman, Paul AMERICANS, 10; CENSORSHIP, 11; CREATIVITY, 12; EDUCATION, 10; PLEASURE, 12; THE SELF, 10
Gorbachev, Mikhail CAPITALISM, 8; COMMUNISM, 7; DEMOCRACY, 16, 17; DIPLOMACY, 19; POLITICS, 24; REVOLUTION, 16; RUSSIA, 15, 16; SOCIALISM, 5; TECHNOLOGY, 7
Gordimer, Nadine CHANGE, 12; FICTION, 5; WORLD LITERATURE, 3; WRITING, 25
Gorky, Maksim GOOD, 12; WORK, 11
Gosaibi, Ghazi al- POETS, 29; WORDS, 16
Gosse, Edmund BORES AND BOREDOM, 7
Gould, Stephen Jay EVOLUTION, 14–16; HISTORY, 42; HUMAN NATURE, 17; MISTAKES, 7; NATURE, 15; SCIENCE, 27
Gourmont, Rémy de MEDICINE, 13
Gournay, Jean-Claude-Marie-Vincent de LIBERTY, 16
Goytisolo, Juan CITIES, 2; EXILE, 4; HEROISM, 8; POETS, 30; PROGRESS, 16; WRITING, 26
Grace, W. G. SPORTS AND GAMES, 9
Gracián, Baltasar BREVITY, 3; SELF-KNOWLEDGE, 18
Grade, Lew BIGOTRY, 1; EXTRAVAGANCE, 2
Graham, Clementina Stirling TEMPTATION, 4
Graham, Martha ARTISTS, 16; RESPECTABILITY, 3
Grahame, Kenneth BOASTS, 9; VICE, 7
Grainger, James TRANSIENCE, 14
Grandma Moses MEMORY, 23
Grant, Ulysses S. LAW, 20
Granville, George COWARDICE, 4
Grass, Günter EUROPE, 21; EUROPEAN COUNTRIES, 28, 29; HISTORY, 43
Graves, Robert BOOKS, 17; FLYING, 2; MARRIAGE, 28; POETS, 31; WORLD WAR I, 7; WRITERS, 29
Gray, Hanna UNIVERSITY, 2
Gray, John AMERICAN IMPERIALISM, 11; ANARCHY, 8; CAPITALISM, 9, 10; DECOLONIZATION, 5; ECONOMICS, 12; GLOBALIZATION, 10, 11
Gray, Thomas DECEPTION, 17; DESIRE, 6; EVENING, 2; GRATITUDE, 6; HUMILITY, 8
Greenberger, Daniel PHYSICS, 7
Greene, Graham BRIBERY, 5; COMMITMENT, 3; CONTEMPT, 1; CORRUPTION, 6; FAME, 11; INNOCENCE, 6; JOURNALISM, 13; MARRIAGE, 29; MEDIA, 5; READING, 14; SUICIDE, 8; THERAPY, 2; TRAINS, 3
Greene, Robert FATE, 11
Greenspan, Alan CLARITY, 4; ECONOMICS, 13
Greer, Germaine MEN, 15; MOTHERS, 4; SEX, 21–23; SEXISM, 3; WOMEN, 22, 23
Greer, Ian BRIBERY, 6
Gregory, Dick APARTHEID, 6; CIVILIZATION, 11; RACISM, 12; UNITED STATES, 26
Gregory VII, Saint JUSTICE, 14
Grein, Jack WRITERS, 30
Greville, Fulke ABSENCE, 4; HUMAN CONDITION, 12
Grey, Edward EUROPE, 22; WORLD WAR I, 8
Griffith, Arthur ASSASSINATION, 4; IRELAND, 16
Griffiths, Trevor COMEDY, 4
Grigg, John MONARCHY, 18
Grimald, Nicholas FRIENDSHIP, 18
Gropius, Walter ARCHITECTURE, 9, 10
Grossart, Angus AMBITION, 8
Grossman, Vasily FREEDOM, 25; LITERARY STYLE, 5; RUSSIA, 17; TOTALITARIANISM, 1
Grossmith, George HOME, 5
Grove, Andrew S. BUSINESS, 10
Guare, John ENTERTAINMENT, 3; FORGETTING, 3
Gu Cheng THE SOUL, 10
Guedalla, Philip AMERICAN LITERATURE, 15; OPINIONS, 8
Guest, Edgar A. HOME, 6
Guevara, Che COURAGE, 4; REVOLUTION, 17–19
Guillén, Jorge REALITY, 11
Guimard, Hector Germain ARCHITECTURE, 11
Guitry, Sacha MARRIAGE, 30

Lowry, Malcolm LOVE, 40
Loyola, Ignatius of BELIEF, 19; HATE, 13
Lucan DISCOVERY, 8
Luce, Clare Boothe ENEMIES, 9; THINKING, 24; WOMEN, 31
Lucretius EVOLUTION, 21; LUST, 7; MIND, 29; MORTALITY, 5; NOTHINGNESS, 9; RELIGION, 24; TASTE, 12
Lumumba, Patrice COMFORT, 2; LIBERTY, 25; PERFECTION, 6
Luther, Martin THE DEVIL, 8, 9; HERESY. 8; PESSIMISM, 9; SEX, 30; THE SUPERNATURAL, 25
Luthuli, Albert COURAGE, 8
Lutyens, Edwin Landseer FOOD, 23; INSULTS, 24
Luxemburg, Rosa FREEDOM, 32
Lu Xun ASIAN CITIES, 3; BIOGRAPHY, 10; CREATION, 13; EXECUTION, 12; HOPE, 14; WORLD LITERATURE, 5
Lydgate, John APPEARANCE, 12; JEALOUSY, 6
Lyell, Charles EXTINCTION, 7; NATURE, 25
Lyly, John CERTAINTY, 5; NIGHT, 6; SIMILARITY, 2
Lynch, Jack NORTHERN IRELAND, 6
Lynch, Michael SCOTLAND, 2–4
Lyndhurst, John Singleton Copley BIOGRAPHY, 11
Lysander DECEPTION, 21
Lyttelton, Humphrey CIVILIZATION, 19; JAZZ, 13
Lytton, Bulwer CLASS, 21; FRIENDSHIP, 28; WRITING, 36; YOUTH, 17
MacArthur, Douglas ASIAN COUNTRIES, 18; POLITICAL INSULTS, 41
Macaulay, Rose BOOKS, 27, 28; FAMILY, 14; MIDDLE EAST, 19
Macaulay, Thomas Babington BRITAIN, 22; CHANGE, 22; DICTATORS, 7; FREEDOM, 33; INTELLECT, 13; LITERARY INSULTS, 37; MONARCHY, 25; NEWSPAPERS, 15; PERSECUTION, 3; PRIVACY, 2
MacCarthy, Desmond ART, 31; CELEBRITY, 10; JOURNALISM, 18; LITERATURE, 35
MacDiarmid, Hugh KILLING, 6; LOVE, 41; SCOTLAND, 5
MacDonagh, Donagh PRIDE, 5
Macdonald, John A. GOVERNMENT, 34
MacDonald, George ANIMALS, 26
MacDonald, John D. CAPITALISM, 29
Maceo, Antonio LIBERTY, 26
Mach, Ernst RESEARCH, 4
Machado, Antonio BLASPHEMY, 3; DARKNESS, 5; THE FACE, 10; GOD, 46, 47; LANGUAGE, 22; PEACE, 19; POETS, 41, 42; THE SOUL, 15; THINKING, 25; TIME, 31
Machado de Assis, Joaquim Maria BELIEF, 20; CLOTHES, 10; CRIME, 15; EXPLORATION, 5; FLOWERS, 6; GUILT, 7; HAPPINESS, 30; HUMANKIND, 32; HUNGER, 15; IDEAS, 12, 13; INDIVIDUALITY, 10; KINDNESS, 7; LIFE, 31; LYING, 22; MEMORY, 29; NOSTALGIA, 9; PLEASURE, 21; POLITICS, 35; SUFFERING, 13; THEORY, 11; TIME, 32; WRITERS, 45
Machiavelli, Niccolò CHANGE, 23; DECEPTION, 22, 23; POLITICIANS, 32; REVENGE, 8; SELF-INTEREST, 10
MacInnes, Colin ARTISTIC STYLES, 14
Mackenzie, Compton SCOTLAND, 6
Mackie, J. L. CREATION, 14
Mackintosh, James OPINIONS, 12; PARLIAMENTS AND ASSEMBLIES, 8
Mackintosh, Margaret Macdonald DESIGN, 7
MacLean, John SCOTLAND, 7, 8
MacLeish, Archibald POETRY, 33; QUESTIONS, 7
Macleod, Iain EQUALITY, 18; GOVERNMENT, 35; HISTORIANS, 18
Macmillan, Harold DIPLOMACY, 25; ECONOMICS, 18; FUNERALS, 7; MARXISM, 6; POWER, 28
MacNeice, Louis ABSENCE, 5; BIRTH, 10, 11; FIRE, 6; MIDDLE AGE, 8; MORTALITY, 6; SLEEP, 16; TIME, 33; WORDS, 1
Madariaga y Rogo, Salvador de POLITICS, 36
Madhubuti, Haki R. WAR, 35
Madison, James DEMOCRACY, 30; MONEY, 26; WAR, 36
Maeterlinck, Maurice DEATH AND DYING, 38
Magee, John Gillespie FLYING, 5
Magidson, Herbert SONGS, 7
Magna Carta JUSTICE, 24
Magruder, Jeb MORALITY, 27
Mahbubani, Kishore GOVERNMENT, 36
Mahfouz, Naguib DECEPTION, 24; DISASTER, 3; EVIL, 23; FANTASY, 9; HUMAN RIGHTS, 8; LOVE, 42; STORYTELLING, 12; TRUTH, 41

Mailer, Norman AMERICAN IMPERIALISM, 15, 16; ART, 32; BOOKS, 29; DEMOCRACY, 31; EXISTENCE, 15; FACTS, 9; FANATICISM, 9; FIGHTING, 4; FILMS, 26; GROWING UP, 7; HEROISM, 10; LYING, 23; MISANTHROPY, 6; MISOGYNY, 2; POLITICIANS, 33; ROMANTICISM, 2; SENTIMENTALITY, 2; STYLE, 4; TWENTIETH CENTURY, 2; UNITED STATES, 37–39; WRITING, 37
Maimonides HUMILITY, 14; ILLNESS, 17; MEDICINE, 20
Maistre, Joseph Marie de GOVERNMENT, 37; PARADOX, 6
Major, John CONSERVATISM, 9; ECONOMICS, 19; IGNORANCE, 12; NORTHERN IRELAND, 7
Makarios III OBITUARIES, 4
Makeba, Miriam AGE, 16
Malamud, Bernard BIOGRAPHY, 12; DISAPPOINTMENT, 4
Malcolm X AMERICAN CITIES, 28; CAPITALISM, 30; FAMILY, 15; POWER, 29; RACISM, 21; REVOLUTION, 26; UNITED STATES, 40; VIOLENCE, 7
Malesherbes, Chrétien de MISTAKES, 9
Malherbe, François de TRANSIENCE, 20
Mallaby, George CLASS, 22
Mallarmé, Stéphane OPTIMISM, 13; POETRY, 34; WORLD-WEARINESS, 3
Mallet, Robert PESSIMISM, 10
Mallory, George AMBITION, 18
Malory, Thomas SPRING, 8
Malraux, André ART, 33, 34; FANTASY, 10; FIGHTING, 5; HELL, 11; THE WORLD, 7
Malthus, Thomas SURVIVAL, 2
Mama Cass POPULAR MUSIC, 20
Mamet, David ACTING AND ACTORS, 14; ARTISTS, 22; CENSORSHIP, 15; FEAR, 19; FILMS, 27; HEROISM, 11; HOLLYWOOD, 13; HUMAN NATURE, 23; PRINCIPLES, 6; THEATRE, 9; UNDERSTANDING, 6
Mandela, Nelson ACHIEVEMENT, 16; AFRICAN COUNTRIES, 8–11; APARTHEID, 9; CIVIL RIGHTS, 9; DEMOCRACY, 32; FREEDOM, 34–36; GOOD, 19; IDEALISM, 10; OPPRESSION, 7; THE PAST, 24; PRINCIPLES, 7
Mandela, Winnie FEAR, 20; SEPARATION, 3
Mandelstam, Nadezhda FORGETTING, 7; TOTALITARIANISM, 5
Mandelstam, Osip ACADEMICS, 5; AMBITION, 19; AMERICAN LITERATURE, 20, 21; BORES AND BOREDOM, 10; EUROPEAN CITIES, 18, 19; EUROPEAN LITERATURE, 12; IMMORTALITY, 15; PARTING, 5, 6; RUSSIA, 22; TIME, 34
Mandeville, Bernard SELF-KNOWLEDGE, 26
Manguel, Alberto READING, 24; TRANSLATION, 4
Mankiewicz, Herman J. GOD, 48
Manley, Michael POLITICS, 37; POVERTY, 22; PROPAGANDA, 3
Mann, Golo WAR, 37
Mann, Horace AMBITION, 20; LOSS, 5
Mann, Thomas DEATH AND DYING, 39; EUROPEAN COUNTRIES, 44, 45; FREEDOM, 37; HUMAN CONDITION, 14, 15; ILLNESS, 18; POLITICS, 38; REVOLUTION, 27; SPEECH, 13; SUCCESS, 11; TRUTH, 42; YOUTH, 18
Mannin, Ethel MIND, 30
Man Ray ART, 35; EXTREMES, 1
Mansfield, Katherine MONEY, 27; REGRET, 5
Mansfield, William Murray JUSTICE, 25
Manson, Charles DEATH AND DYING, 40
Manzoni, Piero ARTISTS, 23
Mao Zedong ASIA, 3; ASIAN COUNTRIES, 19–22; CENSORSHIP, 16; CLASS, 23; COMMUNISM, 14, 15; CONFLICT, 2; CONSERVATISM, 10; DEMOCRACY, 33; ENEMIES, 10; IMPERIALISM, 13; KNOWLEDGE, 26; NUCLEAR WEAPONS, 10; OPPRESSION, 8; READING, 25; REVOLUTION, 28; WAR, 38, 39
Mapanje, Jack HOPE, 15
Maradona, Diego SPORTS AND GAMES, 13
Maragall, Joan MOUNTAINS, 4
Marat, Jean Paul FRENCH REVOLUTION, 7, 8
Marcos, Subcomandante CENTRAL AMERICA, 3
Marcus Aurelius BEING, 8; ETERNITY, 8; METAMORPHOSIS, 3; TIME, 35; TRANSIENCE, 21
Marcuse, Herbert CAPITALISM, 31; MODERNITY, 8
Marechera, Dambudzo GREATNESS, 13; REALITY, 16
Mariana, Juan de REPUBLICANISM, 2
Marías, Javier KISSING, 3; MISFORTUNE, 9
Mariátegui, José Carlos SOUTH AMERICA, 9
Marie-Antoinette INDIFFERENCE, 6
Marinetti, Filippo Tommaso ANARCHY, 12, 13; POETRY, 35; RATIONALISM, 6; WRITERS, 46
Marinker, Marshall REMEDIES, 16

Marley, Bob FAME, 14; HUMAN RIGHTS, 9; OPTIMISM, 14; POPULAR MUSIC, 21; SELF-KNOWLEDGE, 27; SLAVERY, 25, 26

Marlowe, Christopher ANGELS, 6; ARGUMENTS, 12; CENSORSHIP, 17; DAMNATION, 2, 3; DOOMSDAY, 2; FATE, 17, 18; FIGHTING, 6; FLOWERS, 7; GREED, 7; HELL, 12; MONARCHY, 26; RELIGION, 25

Marmion, Shackerley HAPPINESS, 31

Marquis, Don ACCIDENTS, 9; BELIEF, 21; CENSORSHIP, 18; CHANCE, 6; CIVILIZATION, 20; ECOLOGY, 6; OPTIMISM, 15; PROCRASTINATION, 6; THINKING, 26

Marsalis, Wynton JAZZ, 14

Marsh, Richard POPULAR MUSIC, 22; SOCIALISM, 8; TRAINS, 5

Marsh, Rodney SPORTS AND GAMES, 14

Marshall, George EUROPE, 25; PEACE, 20

Marshall, Paule ATHEISM, 5; DEPRESSION, 6; HOME, 11; MOTHERS, 7; SELF-KNOWLEDGE, 28

Marshall, Thomas R. LUXURY, 3

Marshall, Thurgood CIVIL RIGHTS, 10; UNITED STATES, 41

Martí, José CHARM, 5; FREEDOM, 38

Martin, Graham Dunstan BELIEF, 22

Martin, Steve CRITICISM, 12

Martineau, Harriet WOMEN'S RIGHTS, 23

Martínez de la Mata, Don REPUBLICANISM, 3

Martínez-Sarrión, Antonio SILENCE, 18; TIME, 36

Marvell, Andrew GARDENS, 3, 4; GLORY, 5; SEDUCTION, 7; TIME, 37

Marx, Chico INFIDELITY, 1

Marx, Groucho AGE, 17; APPETITE, 3; ARGUMENTS, 13; CHILDREN, 23; COMPLAINTS, 7; CRITICISM, 13; DANCING, 9; DEATH AND DYING, 41; DECLARATIONS OF LOVE, 3; THE FACE, 11; FLATTERY, 8; HUMOUR, 12; IDENTITY, 4; INSULTS, 25; INTRODUCTIONS, 2; KISSING, 4; LEADERSHIP, 13; LITERARY INSULTS, 38; MARRIAGE, 37; MORNING, 14; NAMES, 13; NONSENSE, 13; POVERTY, 23; PREJUDICE, 9; STUPIDITY, 5; TIME, 38

Marx, Karl CAPITALISM, 32; CHANGE, 24; CLASS, 24; COMMUNISM, 16, 17; ECONOMICS, 20; HISTORY, 54; MARXISM, 7, 8; MATERIALISM, 7; MONEY, 28; PHILOSOPHY, 21; RELIGION, 26; SOCIALISM, 9; WORK, 17

Mary, Queen of Scots REVENGE, 9

Masefield, John BIRTH, 12; BOATS, 7; MEDICINE, 21; MEMORY, 30

Maslow, Abraham PERCEPTION, 8

Mason, George FREE SPEECH, 7; GOVERNMENT, 38; HUMAN RIGHTS, 10

Mason, John ECONOMICS, 21

Massinger, Philip AMBITION, 21; EXTREMES, 2

Mastroianni, Marcello ACTING AND ACTORS, 15

Matalin, Mary POLITICAL INSULTS, 42

Mathew, James JUSTICE, 26

Matisse, Henri ART, 36; ARTISTIC STYLES, 15; PAINTING, 22

Matlovich, Leonard HOMOSEXUALITY, 9

Mattos e Guerra, Gregório CITIES, 9

Maudsley, Henry MEDICINE, 22

Maugham, Somerset ACHIEVEMENT, 17; ACTION, 10; ADULTERY, 12; AMERICANS, 16; BABIES, 8; BOOKS, 30, 31; CIVILIZATION, 21; COMPLIMENTS, 2; CRITICISM, 14; CURIOSITY, 6; DEATH AND DYING, 42; DIVORCE, 6; EATING, 14; THE FUTURE, 17; HYPOCRISY, 15, 16; IDENTITY, 5; LOVE, 43; LYING, 24; MANNERS, 3; MONEY, 29; MYSTICISM, 4; NIGHT, 7; OLD AGE, 26; PERFECTION, 7; PRINCIPLES, 8; RIGHT, 4; SENTIMENTALITY, 3; SUFFERING, 14; WEAKNESS, 2; WISDOM, 11; WIT, 10; WRITERS, 47

Mauldin, Bill SURVIVAL, 3

Maupassant, Guy de APPEARANCE, 13

Maupin, Armistead CENSORSHIP, 19; HOMOSEXUALITY, 10–12; SEXUALITY, 5, 6

Maura, Antonio TRADITIONS, 4

Maurois, André AMERICANS, 17; OLD AGE, 27; SCIENTISTS, 16, 17

Maurras, Charles REVENGE, 10

Mauthner, Fritz LANGUAGE, 23

Maximilian I REPUTATION, 15

Maxwell, James Clerk TIME, 39

May, Brian AUDIENCES, 9

Mayakovsky, Vladimir ART, 37; CENSORSHIP, 20, 21; POETRY, 36; THE SUN, 4

Mayo, William James KNOWLEDGE, 27; MEDICINE, 23

Mays, Benjamin E. WAR, 40

Mazarin, Jules DEBT, 6

Mazzini, Giuseppe NATIONS, 18

Mboya, Tom POVERTY, 24; PREJUDICE, 10

McCaig, Norman GOD, 49; LITERACY, 5; LONELINESS, 13; MEANING, 9; MIND, 31; SCOTLAND, 9; SELF-KNOWLEDGE, 29; TIME, 40; WONDER, 4

McCarthy, Eugene J. AMERICAN IMPERIALISM, 17

McCarthy, Joseph COMMUNISM, 18; UNITED STATES, 42

McCarthy, Mary FILMS, 28; INDIFFERENCE, 7; LITERATURE, 36; NEUROSIS, 12; RELATIONSHIPS, 13; TRUTH, 43; WEALTH, 17

McCormack, Mark BUSINESS, 16; JUDGMENT, 15; PASSION, 4

McCormick, Robert Rutherford NUCLEAR WAR, 10

McCrae, John WORLD WAR I, 19

McDaniel, Hattie ACTING AND ACTORS, 16

McEnroe, John INSULTS, 26; LOSS, 6

McEwan, Ian FILMS, 29

McGinley, Phyllis SUCCESS, 12

McGregor, Peter WORLD WAR I, 20

McInerney, Jay FASHION, 9

McKay, Claude RACISM, 22

McKellen, Ian AIDS, 8; HOMOSEXUALITY, 13, 14

McKinney, Joyce DECLARATIONS OF LOVE, 4

McLaren, Anne UNDERSTANDING, 7

McLuhan, Marshall ADVERTISING, 12; CARS, 5; COMMUNICATION, 11; EXTINCTION, 8; GLOBALIZATION, 14; MACHINES, 8; MONEY, 30; OPINIONS, 13; TIME, 41; TWENTIETH CENTURY, 3

McMillan, Terry MARRIAGE, 38, 39; MEN, 20; NOSTALGIA, 10; POVERTY, 25; RACISM, 23; WOMEN, 32

McMurtry, Larry AGE, 18; SORROW, 13

McNamara, Robert AMERICAN IMPERIALISM, 18; NUCLEAR WEAPONS, 11

McQueen, Alexander FASHION, 10

McWilliams, Monica NORTHERN IRELAND, 8

Mead, Margaret CITIES, 10, 11; THE ENVIRONMENT, 8; FAMILY, 16, 17; HUMAN NATURE, 24; PROPHECY, 7; SOCIETY, 13; WOMEN, 33

Medawar, Peter IDEAS, 14; PSYCHOANALYSIS, 20

Meir, Golda KILLING, 7; LEADERSHIP, 14

Melba, Nellie MUSIC, 20

Melbourne, Lord HATE, 14; PRINCIPLES, 9; RELIGION, 27

Melly, George JAZZ, 15

Melville, Herman ARROGANCE, 5; THE BODY, 13; COOKING, 6; EUROPEAN CITIES, 20; HEAVEN, 10; MIDDLE EAST, 20; NAMES, 14

Ménage, Gilles MEDICINE, 24

Menander DEATH AND DYING, 43; LAW, 25

Mencius ACTION, 11

Mencken, H. L. ADULTERY, 13; ALCOHOL, 13; AMERICAN CITIES, 29; CONSCIENCE, 13; CYNICISM, 6; DELUSIONS OF LOVE, 6; DEMOCRACY, 34, 35; FAITH, 11; GOVERNMENT, 39; HEROISM, 12; HUMOUR, 13; IDEALISM, 11; INTELLIGENCE, 8; KISSING, 5; LAW, 26; LYING, 25; METAPHYSICS, 7; OPERA, 7; POETRY, 37; PURITANISM, 5; RACISM, 24; SCIENTISTS, 18; SELF-RESPECT, 3; THE SEXES, 9; WAR, 41

Mendes, Chico ECOLOGY, 7

Menninger, Karl ILLNESS, 19; NEUROSIS, 13

Menon, V. K. Krishna DIPLOMACY, 26

Menuhin, Yehudi MUSIC, 21

Mercer, Johnny INSULTS, 27; MAGIC, 4

Meredith, George DIGESTION, 6; FORGIVENESS, 7; KISSING, 6; MAGIC, 5; THE MOON, 8; SPEECH, 14; WIT, 11

Meredith, James SOLIDARITY, 5

Meres, Francis WRITERS, 48

Merleau-Ponty, Maurice CONSCIOUSNESS, 12; EXISTENCE, 16, 17; IDEAS, 15; PERCEPTION, 9; PHILOSOPHY, 22; PSYCHOANALYSIS, 21; SANITY, 8; THINKING, 27; TIME, 42; THE WORLD, 8

Mernissi, Fatima GLOBALIZATION, 15; MIDDLE EAST, 21; PEACE, 21; WOMEN'S RIGHTS, 24

Merwin, W. S. POETRY, 38

Metternich DEMOCRACY, 36; EUROPE, 26

Meynell, Alice GARDENS, 5

Mezzrow, Mezz JAZZ, 16–18

Michaels, Anne LANGUAGE, 24; LIFE, 32; MEMORY, 31; METAMORPHOSIS, 4; PAINTING, 23; THE SEA, 3

Michelet, Jules EUROPEAN COUNTRIES, 46; HISTORY, 55; PRAISE, 5

Michitsuna no Haha DEPRESSION, 7

Middleton, Thomas GUILT, 8; TYRANNY, 10; WIT, 12

Midgley, Mary MORALITY, 28

Oakeley, Frederick CHRISTMAS, 9

Oates, Joyce Carol CYNICISM, 7; THE PRESENT, 13

Oates, Lawrence LAST WORDS, 10

O'Brien, Conor Cruise EUROPEAN CITIES, 22; PROPHECY, 9

O'Brien, Edna SLEEP, 18; WOMEN'S RIGHTS, 27

O'Brien, Flann ALCOHOL, 15; IRELAND, 24, 25; LANGUAGE, 28; MOTHERS, 10; POLITICIANS, 38; SERIOUSNESS, 3; WORDPLAY, 7

O'Brien, Tim INDIFFERENCE, 8

Ocampo, Victoria MORALITY, 31; RELATIONSHIPS, 17

O'Casey, Sean IRELAND, 26; LITERARY INSULTS, 43; RELIGION, 28

O'Connell, Daniel IRELAND, 27; SACRIFICE, 7

O'Connor, Edwin ENDING, 7

O'Connor, Flannery IDENTITY, 7; READERS, 8; TRUTH, 48

O'Connor, Frank COWARDICE, 7; STORYTELLING, 13

O'Connor, Joseph IRELAND, 28

O'Connor, Sandra Day INEQUALITY, 6

O'Donoghue, Bernard MISTAKES, 11

Ogilvy, David ADVERTISING, 14; LEADERSHIP, 15

O'Hare, Dean TECHNOLOGY, 18

Ohmae, Kenichi BUSINESS, 17; GLOBALIZATION, 18

Okri, Ben DREAMS, 16; FICTION, 6; HOPE, 18; HUNGER, 17; LITERATURE, 41; METAMORPHOSIS, 5; STORYTELLING, 14, 15; WRITERS, 54

O'Leary, John IRELAND, 29

Olitski, Jules PAINTING, 26

Olivier, Laurence ACTING AND ACTORS, 18; WRITERS, 55

Olmedo, José Juaquín AMBITION, 23

Olmsted, Frederick Law AMERICAN CITIES, 33; PLACES, 5

Olsen, Tillie MONEY, 34

Olson, Charles AESTHETICS, 2; FACTS, 10; LEARNING, 22; MAGIC, 6; MEMORY, 35; THE MOON, 10, 11; POETRY, 42; POETS, 44; SILENCE, 19; SOCIETY, 15

O'Malley, Austin FATHERS, 4

Onassis, Aristotle SUCCESS, 13

Ondaatje, Michael DEATH AND DYING, 49; THE HEART, 6; WORDS, 24

O'Neill, Eugene GUILT, 9; LIFE, 38; SOLITUDE, 21; THEFT, 8

O'Neill, Hugh BETRAYAL, 13

Ono, Yoko VIOLENCE, 10

Opie, John PAINTING, 27

Oppen, George INDIVIDUALITY, 12; POETRY, 43

Oppenheimer, J. Robert CHANGE, 26; KNOWLEDGE, 30; MATHEMATICS, 25; NUCLEAR WAR, 12; NUCLEAR WEAPONS, 12, 13; PHYSICS, 11; SCIENTISTS, 21

O'Rourke, P. J. AMERICAN IMPERIALISM, 25; DRUGS, 20; MEDIA, 9

Ortega y Gasset, José ARTISTS, 31; BIOGRAPHY, 13; CLASS, 27; CREATIVITY, 20; DANGER, 9; DESIRE, 9; EUROPE, 29; GOOD, 22; HAPPINESS, 35; HATE, 16; HISTORY, 58; LANGUAGE, 29; LIFE, 39–41; THE PAST, 25–27; PHILOSOPHY, 29; POETS, 45; REVOLUTION, 34, 35; THE SELF, 18; SEX, 34; SINCERITY, 4; THE SOUL, 16; TEACHERS, 4; THINKING, 30–32; TRAGEDY, 6

Orton, Joe CHILDHOOD, 11; FATHERS, 5; LUXURY, 5; RIGHTEOUSNESS, 2; TASTE, 13; TRUTH, 49

Orwell, George AGE, 22; AMERICAN LITERATURE, 24; ANARCHY, 14; ANIMALS, 32; BELIEF, 23; BOOKS, 39, 40; CAPITALISM, 35; CLASS, 28; CRITICISM, 16; ENGLAND, 22; EQUALITY, 21; FIRST LINES, 7; FREE SPEECH, 8; THE FUTURE, 19; HUMAN NATURE, 25; LANGUAGE, 30, 31; LIBERTY, 30; LITERACY, 7; MIDDLE AGE, 10; NOSTALGIA, 12; OCCUPATIONS, 4; PERFECTION, 9; POWER, 33; RHETORIC, 5; SOCIALISM, 10; SPORTS AND GAMES, 15, 16; TOTALITARIANISM, 7–9; WAR, 47, 48

Osborne, John AUDIENCES, 10; NEWSPAPERS, 19; NOSTALGIA, 13; REVOLUTION, 36; TEACHERS, 5

Osler, William FAITH, 13; MEDICINE, 27; TEACHERS, 6

Ossietzky, Carl von CONSCIENCE, 14; EUROPEAN COUNTRIES, 50, 51; EUROPEAN LITERATURE, 11

O'Sullivan, John L. ALCOHOL, 16; AMERICAN IMPERIALISM, 26

Ouida GOSSIP, 7

Ousby, Ian AMERICAN LITERATURE, 25

Ouspensky, Peter HUMANKIND, 39; HYPOCHONDRIA, 6; OLD AGE, 31

Ovid CORRUPTION, 10; MEDICINE, 28; METAMORPHOSIS, 6; MIND, 35; SUFFERING, 17; TIME, 44

Owen, Meredith GENIUS, 12

Owen, Wilfred PATRIOTISM, 20; POETS, 46; THE SUPERNATURAL, 27; WORLD WAR I, 23

Owens, Jesse SPORTS AND GAMES, 17

Oz, Amos BEGINNING, 11; THE HOLOCAUST, 5; MIDDLE EAST, 22–25; OPPRESSION, 10; STORYTELLING, 16

Ozick, Cynthia COMMUNICATION, 13; EMIGRATION, 5; EXILE, 6; FACTS, 11

Padmore, George AFRICA, 10; EUROPEAN COUNTRIES, 52; INDEPENDENCE, 4

Paglia, Camille ANIMALS, 33; BEAUTY, 25; CAPITALISM, 36; HUMAN NATURE, 26; MEN, 23; NATURE, 29; PHILOSOPHY, 30; PREGNANCY, 4; PRIVACY, 5; WOMEN, 38

Pagnol, Marcel SCIENTISTS, 22; SECRECY, 11

Paine, Thomas AMERICAN WAR OF INDEPENDENCE, 8; BELIEF, 24; COURAGE, 13; FREEDOM, 45; GOVERNMENT, 43; PATRIOTISM, 21; POLITICS, 44

Paisley, Ian NORTHERN IRELAND, 10–13

Palafox, José WAR, 49

Palmer, Samuel PAINTING, 28

Palmerston, Lord DIPLOMACY, 27; GOVERNMENT, 44; LAST WORDS, 11; PHILISTINISM, 2; POLITICS, 45

Pamuk, Orhan BOOKS, 41; EUROPEAN LITERATURE, 14; MARXISM, 9; MEMORY, 36; SELF-KNOWLEDGE, 32; VICTORY, 13; WORDS, 25; WORLD LITERATURE, 7; WRITING, 39

Panassie, Hugues JAZZ, 22, 23; POPULAR MUSIC, 26

Pankhurst, Christabel MARTYRDOM, 8; MEDIA, 10; PRIDE, 7; WOMEN'S RIGHTS, 28

Pankhurst, Emmeline ARGUMENTS, 15; PROTEST, 14; WOMEN'S RIGHTS, 29

Pankhurst, Sylvia CAPITALISM, 37; WOMEN'S RIGHTS, 30; WORLD WAR I, 24

Papanek, Victor DESIGN, 8; WEAPONS, 11

Paracelsus MEDICINE, 29

Parker, Charlie MUSIC, 23

Parker, Dorothy ABORTION, 6; ADULTERY, 16; BIGOTRY, 3; BIRTH, 13; CLOTHES, 12; DRUNKENNESS, 17; GIFTS, 5; HERESY, 10; IGNORANCE, 13; INSULTS, 31–33; LITERARY INSULTS, 44; NAMES, 16; PRIVACY, 6; QUOTATIONS, 5; RACISM, 27; SORROW, 17; WOMEN, 39

Parker, Henry Taylor AUDIENCES, 11

Parker, Hubert Lister JUDGMENT, 17

Parker, Sir Peter BUSINESS, 18

Parker, Theodore DEMOCRACY, 38

Parkinson, Cyril Northcote ECONOMICS, 23; PROCRASTINATION, 7; WORK, 19

Parks, Rosa APARTHEID, 12

Parmenter, Ross THE ENVIRONMENT, 13

Parnell, Charles Stewart IRELAND, 30–32

Parra, Violeta SONGS, 8

Parris, Matthew PERSECUTION, 5

Parton, James ABILITY, 7

Pascal, Blaise BELIEF, 25; COMMUNICATION, 14; THE FACE, 12; FRANKNESS, 4; JUSTICE, 29; MADNESS, 34; MORALITY, 32; ORIGINALITY, 6; PHILOSOPHY, 31; REASON, 26; RELIGION, 29; TRUTH, 50; WRITING, 40

Pasolini, Pier Paolo BIRTH, 14; DEATH AND DYING, 50; MOTHERS, 11

Pasternak, Boris ARTISTS, 32; BIRTH, 15; FAME, 20; THE MOON, 12; POETRY, 44; POETS, 47; TYRANNY, 11

Pasteur, Louis EXPERIMENTS, 7; ILLNESS, 23

Pater, Walter ART, 43

Patmore, Coventry PARTING, 8

Paton, Alan Stewart PURPOSE, 3

Patten, Brian POETRY, 45; RELATIONSHIPS, 18

Pattison, Mark RESEARCH, 5

Patton, George S. WORLD WAR II, 17

Paul, Leslie REBELLION, 7

Paul, Nathaniel SLAVERY, 27

Pauli, Wolfgang PUBLISHING, 7

Pauling, Linus GENETICS, 7

Pavese, Cesare ARTISTS, 33; CHILDREN, 26; DEATH AND DYING, 51; THE ENVIRONMENT, 14; FORGETTING, 8; LIFE, 42; SUICIDE, 14

Pavlov, Ivan Petrovich EXPERIMENTS, 8

Pavlova, Anna HAPPINESS, 36

Payne, Frank MEDICINE, 30

Payne, John Howard HOME, 15

Paz, Octavio ADVERTISING, 15; CAPITALISM, 38; EQUALITY, 22; MYTHS, 9

Peabody, Elizabeth PERCEPTION, 10

Peacock, Thomas Love DRINKS AND DRINKING, 6; EDUCATION, 13; LAUGHTER, 12

Peake, Mervyn CAPITALISM, 39; EQUALITY, 23; HOME, 16; THE SUPERNATURAL, 28; WORLD-WEARINESS, 5

Pearce, Lord ARTISTS, 34

Richler, Mordecai BOOKS, 45; REVOLUTION, 42

Richter, Gerhard ART, 47

Richter, Jean Paul IMPERIALISM, 19

Ridge, William Pett CHANCE, 8

Riley, James Whitcomb AMBITION, 26

Rilke, Rainer Maria CRITICISM, 19; FAME, 23; LOVE, 51; PARTING, 10; SPRING, 10

Rimbaud, Arthur BOATS, 8; HELL, 16; LANGUAGE, 33; LITERARY STYLE, 10; MORNING, 14; POETS, 49; THE SEA, 26; THE SELF, 20

Rivarol, Antoine de DEMOCRACY, 41; EUROPEAN LANGUAGES, 3; WEALTH, 25

Rivera, José Eustasio VIOLENCE, 12

Roach, Stephen S. EXTREMES, 3

Robbe-Grillet, Alain ART, 48; WRITERS, 62

Robbins, Tom AFTERLIFE, 16; HUMANKIND, 42

Robens, Alfred LEADERSHIP, 17

Robeson, Paul PATRIOTISM, 23

Robespierre, Maximilien FRENCH REVOLUTION, 13, 14; GOVERNMENT, 48; SOCIETY, 17

Robin, Leo LUXURY, 6; MEMORY, 40

Robinson, Joan ECONOMICS, 28

Robinson, John SEX, 36

Robinson, Mary IRELAND, 37

Robinson, Sugar Ray VIOLENCE, 13

Roche, Boyle POSTERITY, 8

Rochester, 2nd Earl of COMMITMENT IN LOVE, 4; REASON, 28

Roddick, Anita BUSINESS, 24; SUCCESS, 15

Roden, Claudia FOOD, 28

Rodenberg, Julius WALES, 8, 9

Rodin, Auguste AESTHETICS, 4; BEAUTY, 29

Rodó, José SOCIETY, 18; SOUTH AMERICA, 11

Roepke Bahamonde, Gabriela THE FACE, 16; LYING, 34

Roethke, Theodore ENVY, 8; FATE, 21; INFINITY, 5, 6; MADNESS, 38; PERCEPTION, 11; SELF-KNOWLEDGE, 34; THE SUPERNATURAL, 31

Rogers, Everett INNOVATION, 4

Rogers, Jim TWENTY-FIRST CENTURY, 6

Rogers, Samuel ACHIEVEMENT, 20; BOOKS, 46; GOOD, 25; MARRIAGE, 42; NOSTALGIA, 14

Rogers, Thorold INSULTS, 38

Rogers, Will CIVILIZATION, 24; COMEDY, 7; COMMUNISM, 21; GOVERNMENT, 49; HEROISM, 14; HUMOUR, 16; IRELAND, 38; RESPECTABILITY, 5; UNITED STATES, 47

Roland, Madame EXECUTION, 16

Rolland, Romain CHARACTER, 30; EUROPEAN COUNTRIES, 54; HEROISM, 15; PASSION, 12

Romains, Jules FRIENDSHIP, 34; ILLNESS, 28

Romero, Oscar LIBERTY, 32; MARTYRDOM, 9; OPPRESSION, 11

Rooke, Sir Denis BRIBERY, 10

Rooney, Mickey BIOGRAPHY, 14

Roosevelt, Franklin D. THE ARTS, 4; BOOKS, 47; DESTINY, 7; EDUCATION, 17; FEAR, 26; FREEDOM, 46; GOVERNMENT, 50; MURDER, 8; PEACE, 27; POLITICIANS, 43; SURVIVAL, 4; WAR, 54; WORLD WAR II, 19

Roosevelt, Theodore CIVILIZATION, 25; DIPLOMACY, 29; FANATICISM, 10; THEFT, 10; WAR, 55; WORLD WAR I, 26

Rorem, Ned MEDIOCRITY, 10; VANITY, 8

Rorty, Richard EFFORT, 2

Rose, Frank COMPUTERS, 12–14

Rosebery, Lord BRITISH IMPERIALISM, 18; IMPERIALISM, 20; SOLITUDE, 22

Rosenberg, Harold ARTISTS, 39

Rosewarne, V. A. SACRIFICE, 9

Ross, Ronald SCIENCE, 47

Rossetti, Christina DREAMS, 18; MEMORY, 41; WEATHER, 11; WINTER, 6

Rossetti, Dante Gabriel POETRY, 48

Rostand, Edmond DREAMS, 19; THE FACE, 17

Rostand, Jean KILLING, 9; MARRIAGE, 43; REGRET, 9

Roszak, Theodore COMPUTERS, 15; ECOLOGY, 8; ECONOMICS, 29, 30; IDEAS, 18; INFORMATION, 3; REVOLUTION, 43; SCIENCE, 48; TECHNOLOGY, 19

Roth, David Lee POPULAR MUSIC, 30

Roth, Philip INTELLIGENCE, 11; LYING, 35; OLD AGE, 34; WRITING, 45

Rothko, Mark PAINTING, 35

Rotten, Johnny EXPLOITATION, 6

Rousseau, Jean-Jacques CIVILIZATION, 26; CORRUPTION, 11; DEMOCRACY, 42; FEAR, 27; FREEDOM, 47; GUILT, 12; HAPPINESS, 43; JUDGMENT, 21, 22; LAW, 30; MONEY, 37; REGRET, 10; ROMANTICISM, 3; SOCIETY, 19; THE SUPERNATURAL, 32; TRUTH, 55; WEALTH, 26

Routsong, Alma MEN, 25

Rover, Constance WOMEN'S RIGHTS, 33

Rowe, Nicholas INDIFFERENCE, 9

Rowland, Helen ADULTERY, 17; FOOLISHNESS, 20, 21

Rowland, Sherwood THE ENVIRONMENT, 16

Roy, Arundhati CLASS, 31; HISTORY, 61, 62

Royden, Maud OLD AGE, 35

Rubin, Jerry THEFT, 11

Rubinstein, Arthur MUSICIANS, 8

Rule, Jane MORALITY, 35

Rumi, Jalal al-Din Muhammad DANCING, 14

Runcie, Robert RELIGION, 33; TRAVEL, 23

Runciman of Doxford, Lady TERRORISM, 8

Rushdie, Salman ABSENCE, 8; ATHEISM, 7; BELIEF, 28; BLASPHEMY, 5; CONSERVATISM, 11; ENEMIES, 13; FREE SPEECH, 9; INSPIRATION, 11; ISLAM, 11; MODERNITY, 9; SHAME, 2; STORYTELLING, 18; WORLD ENGLISH, 5, 6; WORLD LITERATURE, 8

Rusiñol, Santiago TRAGEDY, 8

Rusk, Dean DIPLOMACY, 30

Ruskin, John ARCHITECTURE, 20–22; ARTISTIC STYLES, 23; ARTISTS, 40, 41; BEAUTY, 30; BOOKS, 48; CRITICISM, 20; HEROISM, 16; MOUNTAINS, 7; PEACE, 28; POETRY, 49; THINKING, 35

Russell, Bertrand AMERICANS, 20; ARGUMENTS, 18; ATHEISM, 8; BELIEF, 29; BORES AND BOREDOM, 13; CHRISTIANITY, 17; COMFORT, 3; CRUELTY, 5, 6; DOUBT, 12; DRUNKENNESS, 19; EXTINCTION, 9; GOSSIP, 8; HAPPINESS, 44, 45; HATE, 18; HUMANKIND, 43; HYPOCRISY, 18; INDECISION, 6; KILLING, 10; LANGUAGE, 34; LITERARY INSULTS, 48; LOVE, 52; LYING, 36; MATHEMATICS, 28–31; MODERNITY, 10; NUCLEAR WAR, 14; OPINIONS, 16, 17; PHILOSOPHY, 36; POLITICIANS, 44; POWER, 36; PROGRESS, 23; READING, 27; REALITY, 12; RELIGION, 34; RESEARCH, 6; SCIENTISTS, 24; SELF-DELUSION, 4; SOCIETY, 20; STUPIDITY, 11; THINKING, 36; TYRANNY, 16; UNITED STATES, 48

Russell, Lord TEACHERS, 7; WIT, 19

Rustin, Bayard BIGOTRY, 4

Rutherford, Ernest PHYSICS, 12

Ryder, Albert Pinkham INSPIRATION, 12

Ryle, Gilbert MIND, 40; MYTHS, 11

Saadawi, Nawal el- ISLAM, 12; WOMEN'S RIGHTS, 34

Sachs, Nelly TIME, 49

Sacks, Jonathan JUDAISM, 11, 12; MIDDLE EAST, 30, 31; RELIGION, 35; SOLITUDE, 23

Sackville-West, Vita ENGLAND, 24; HEAVEN, 16; SPRING, 11; TRAVEL, 24

Sadat, Anwar al- MATERIALISM, 9; PEACE, 29; SOCIETY, 21

Sade, Marquis de HELL, 17; MORALITY, 36

Sagan, Carl CREATION, 16; EVOLUTION, 24; GENETICS, 9; IGNORANCE, 19; REMEDIES, 21; SCIENCE, 49; SURVIVAL, 5; THE UNIVERSE, 19, 20

Sagan, Françoise ART, 49; JEALOUSY, 7

Sagasta, Práxedes JUSTICE, 33

Sahl, Mort TRUST, 4

Said, Edward W. AMERICANS, 21; ASIA, 4; IMPERIALISM, 21; KNOWLEDGE, 33; MIDDLE EAST, 32

Saint-Exupéry, Antoine de LIFE, 46; LOVE, 53; NIGHT, 9; PROGRESS, 24; RESPONSIBILITY, 6; SORROW, 21; WAR, 56

Saint Laurent, Yves CLOTHES, 14

Saki AGE, 23; ASIAN COUNTRIES, 26; CLOTHES, 15; COMMUNICATION, 17; COMPLAINTS, 9; DEBT, 10; FASHION, 13; INFIDELITY, 3; LITERARY INSULTS, 49, 50; LYING, 37; MANNERS, 6; PRIORITIES, 4; UNHAPPINESS, 12

Salinas, Pedro THE SOUL, 19

Salinger, J. D. BOOKS, 49; CELEBRITY, 14; CHILDREN, 29; DECLARATIONS OF LOVE, 12; FIRST LINES, 9; POETS, 50; RESPECT, 5; SEX, 37

Salk, Jonas E. DISCOVERY, 9

Sallust FRIENDSHIP, 35

Salvandy, Comte de REVOLUTION, 44

Samuel, Herbert LIBRARIES, 4; MARRIAGE, 44; MORALITY, 37; PARLIAMENTS AND ASSEMBLIES, 12

Samuelson, P. A. ECONOMICS, 31

Southwell, Robert CHANCE, 11; OPPORTUNITY, 13

Soyinka, Wole AFRICA, 14; AMERICANS, 23; BORES AND BOREDOM, 17; EMOTION, 13; HATE, 20; HISTORY, 64; POWER, 39; THE PRESENT, 14; THE SOUL, 21; TYRANNY, 17; WAR, 62; WORLD LITERATURE, 9

Spaak, Paul Henri AGREEMENT, 9

Spark, Muriel AGE, 27; COMMITMENT, 5; EDUCATION, 19; ELITISM, 3; EXTREMES, 5; OLD AGE, 44; PARENTS, 11; PSYCHIATRY, 16; SEX, 41; TEACHERS, 10

Speicher, Eugene PAINTING, 37

Speight, Johnny INSULTS, 43

Spencer, Herbert CHARACTER, 34; EVOLUTION, 26; FOOLISHNESS, 27; HEALTH AND HEALTHY LIVING, 19; LIBERTY, 36; PAIN, 12; REPUBLICANISM, 4; THEFT, 14; YOUTH, 29

Spender, Stephen ANIMALS, 35; BEING, 10; FAME, 24; GREATNESS, 18; WRITERS, 63

Spenser, Edmund AMBITION, 29, 30; EVIL, 34; RIVERS, 4; SELFLESSNESS, 7

Spielberg, Steven AUDIENCES, 15; FAILURE, 13; FILMS, 44, 45

Spinoza, Baruch DESIRE, 14; FLATTERY, 11; IMMORTALITY, 19; UNDERSTANDING, 9

Spivak, Gayatri FREEDOM, 51

Spock, Benjamin AMERICAN IMPERIALISM, 30; CHILDREN, 33

Springfield, Dusty SEXUALITY, 9

Springsteen, Bruce AMERICANS, 24

Spyri, Johanna DISAPPOINTMENT, 6

Squire, J. C. DRUNKENNESS, 21

Staël, Madame de LOVE, 57; MUSIC, 29; NATIONS, 20; UNDERSTANDING, 10

Stalin, Joseph COMMUNISM, 23; DEATH AND DYING, 61; MARXISM, 11; PARANOIA, 6; REVOLUTION, 47; RUSSIAN REVOLUTION, 13

Standing Bear, Luther NATURE, 34

Stanislavsky, Constantin ACTING AND ACTORS, 22, 23; AUDIENCES, 16

Stanley, Henry Morton GREETINGS, 5

Stanshall, Vivian ALCOHOL, 23

Stanton, Elizabeth Cady CLASS, 34; EQUALITY, 27; WOMEN'S RIGHTS, 37, 38

Stapledon, Olaf AMERICANS, 25

Star Trek SPACE, 8

Star Wars FIRST LINES, 10

Stead, Christina PRIVILEGE, 5

Steel, David POLITICIANS, 46

Steele, Richard READING, 32

Steffens, Lincoln COMMUNISM, 24; LIBERTY, 37; WRITING, 51

Steiger, Rod ACTING AND ACTORS, 24

Stein, Gertrude ANSWERS, 5; BOASTS, 14; FLOWERS, 11; GENIUS, 19; WORLD WAR I, 27

Steinbeck, John AMERICAN CITIES, 39; AMERICANS, 26; BOOKS, 53; CRITICS, 29, 30; HUMANKIND, 48; PHILOSOPHY, 41; SLEEP, 26; TRAVEL, 27–29; UNHAPPINESS, 16; WRITING, 52; XENOPHOBIA, 4

Steinem, Gloria LANGUAGE, 37; MEN, 29; PORNOGRAPHY, 9; REBELLION, 8; THE SEXES, 15; TELEVISION, 16; WOMEN, 49

Steiner, George BOOKS, 54; THE HOLOCAUST, 6; INTERNET, 10; LANGUAGE, 38; THE MOON, 16; PEACE, 31; PORNOGRAPHY, 10; SEX, 42; WORDS, 34

Steiner, Rudolf ILLNESS, 33

Stekel, Wilhelm AGE, 28

Stendhal LITERATURE, 49; ROMANTICISM, 4; SOLITUDE, 25

Stephen, James Kenneth LITERARY INSULTS, 52, 53

Stephen, Leslie BIOGRAPHY, 16

Stephens, James ADULTHOOD, 7; CURIOSITY, 6

Sterne, Laurence BOOKS, 55; DETERMINATION, 9; FIRST LINES, 11; HUMOUR, 19; HYPOCHONDRIA, 8; IDEAS, 20; PARENTS, 12; PERSISTENCE, 3; THE SEXES, 16; SLEEP, 27; THE SOUL, 22; TOLERANCE, 5; WIT, 21; WRITING, 53

Stevens, Alfred ARTISTS, 44

Stevens, Anthony SLEEP, 28; UNDERSTANDING, 11

Stevens, Wallace ANGELS, 10–12; ANIMALS, 36; BEAUTY, 39; DEATH AND DYING, 62; HEAVEN, 19; HUMAN NATURE, 33; IDEAS, 21; IMAGINATION, 18–22; MIND, 42; MUSIC, 30; ORDER, 10; PERCEPTION, 12, 13; POETRY, 53; POETS, 59; REALITY, 23; THE SUN, 7

Stevenson, Adlai COMMUNISM, 25; COMPLIMENTS, 4; FLATTERY, 12; HUMILITY, 19; LYING, 41; NUCLEAR WEAPONS, 18; POLITICAL INSULTS, 50; POLITICIANS, 47; POWER, 40

Stevenson, Juliet THEATRE, 18

Stevenson, Robert Louis ACHIEVEMENT, 21; AMBITION, 31; BUSINESS, 27; DREAMS, 27; DRUNKENNESS, 22; EXECUTION, 18; EXPERIENCE, 16; FORGETTING, 9; FRIENDSHIP, 42; HAPPINESS, 53; HASTE, 9; INDIFFERENCE, 10; INTELLIGENCE, 12; LYING, 42; MARRIAGE, 48; MORALITY, 42; NORMALITY, 3; PLAGIARISM, 10; POLITICS, 49; SANITY, 13; THE SEXES, 17; TRAVEL, 30, 31; VALUE, 7; VANITY, 10

Stewart, Jackie SPORTS AND GAMES, 20

Stewart, Thomas A. COMPETITION, 5; COMPUTERS, 19; INFORMATION, 4; INTELLIGENCE, 13

Stipe, Michael POPULAR MUSIC, 34

Stockhausen, Karlheinz HUMAN CONDITION, 20; MUSIC, 31; TERRORISM, 10

Stockwood, Mervyn PSYCHIATRY, 17

Stoddard, Elizabeth HATE, 21

Stoker, Bram THE SUPERNATURAL, 35

Stoll, Clifford COMPUTERS, 20, 21; INTERNET, 11, 12

Stone, I. F. LONGEVITY, 10

Stone, Oliver FILMS, 46

Stoppard, Tom ARTISTS, 45; CRITICISM, 24; CRITICS, 31; DEMOCRACY, 46; ETERNITY, 9; FREE SPEECH, 10; IDEAS, 22; JOURNALISM, 27; JUSTICE, 37; LIFE, 54; MEDIA, 12; PARLIAMENTS AND ASSEMBLIES, 14; PROPHECY, 12; REVOLUTION, 48; TRAGEDY, 10; THE UNIVERSE, 22; WAR, 63

Storaro, Vittorio FILMS, 47

Storr, Anthony DELUSION, 11; PSYCHIATRY, 18; THERAPY, 5; TOLERANCE, 6

Story, Jack Trevor DEBT, 19

Stout, Rex STATISTICS, 9

Stowe, Harriet Beecher REGRET, 15; TORTURE, 4; WOMEN, 46

Strachey, John St. Loe FASCISM, 12

Strachey, Lytton LAST WORDS, 16

Strasberg, Susan ACTING AND ACTORS, 25

Stravinsky, Igor CREATIVITY, 21; CRITICS, 32; MUSIC, 32

Streatfield, Geoffrey FACTS, 14

Streisand, Barbra FAME, 25; SUCCESS, 18

Strindberg, August COWARDICE, 11; FLOWERS, 12; THEATRE, 19; TRAGEDY, 11

Strong, Maurice F. THE ENVIRONMENT, 19

Stubbes, Philip SPORTS AND GAMES, 21

Styron, William DEPRESSION, 11

Suckling, John THE DEVIL, 15

Su Dongpo RIVERS, 5

Suetonius EUROPEAN CITIES, 26; REGRET, 16

Sugar, Alan BUSINESS, 28; MARKETING, 4

Suharto FREE SPEECH, 11

Sullivan, Anne LANGUAGE, 39

Sulzberger, Arthur Hays JOURNALISM, 28

Summers, Lawrence H. POLLUTION, 10, 11

Sun, Madame EQUALITY, 28

Sun Yat-sen GOVERNMENT, 51; LIBERTY, 38

Surtees, Robert S. POVERTY, 31

Susruta EMOTION, 14

Sutherland, Donald ACTING AND ACTORS, 26

Svevo, Italo FORGETTING, 10

Swaffer, Hannen FREE SPEECH, 12

Swartley, Ariel POPULAR MUSIC, 35

Swift, Jonathan ACTION, 18; AGE, 29; ALCOHOL, 24; AMBITION, 32; BIGOTRY, 5; BUSINESS, 29; CLOTHES, 18; DEATH AND DYING, 63; DOCTORS, 14; EXPERIMENTS, 4; FAME, 26; FLATTERY, 13; FOOD, 30, 31; FRIENDSHIP, 43; GENEROSITY, 7; GENIUS, 20; GOSSIP, 9; GREETINGS, 6; IRELAND, 41; LAW, 34; LITERARY STYLE, 12; MONEY, 43; OLD AGE, 45; PERCEPTION, 14; POETS, 60; POLITICIANS, 48; PROMISES, 3; RELATIONSHIPS, 20; SATIRE, 7, 8; SHAME, 4; SPORTS AND GAMES, 22; TRAVEL, 32; WOMEN, 47

Swinburne, Algernon Charles AFTERLIFE, 20; KISSING, 9; PARTING, 13; POETS, 61; SPRING, 12

Sydenham, Thomas AGE, 30; REMEDIES, 27

Sylvester, Robert BOOKS, 56

Symons, Arthur POETS, 62; REALITY, 24

Synge, J. M. IMAGINATION, 23; THEATRE, 20

Szasz, Thomas BIOGRAPHY, 17; FORGIVENESS, 13; GROWING UP, 11; HAPPINESS, 54; MASTURBATION, 4; MEANING, 13; MEDICINE, 37; OPPRESSION, 14; PSYCHIATRY, 19–22; TEACHERS, 11

Szent-Györgyi, Albert HEALTH AND HEALTHY LIVING, 20

Szilard, Leo TECHNOLOGY, 20